Metaphors
Dictionary

Metaphors
Dictionary

Elyse Sommer with Dorrie Weiss

DETROIT
NEW YORK
TORONTO
WASHINGTON, D.C.

Metaphors Dictionary

Copyright © 1996 by Visible Ink Press™

This publication is a creative work fully protected by all applicable copyright laws, as well as by misappropriation, trade secret, unfair competition, and other applicable laws. The authors and editors of this work have added value to the underlying factual material herein through one or more of the following: unique and original selection, coordination, expression, arrangement, and classification of the information.

Published by Visible Ink Press™
a division of Gale Research
835 Penobscot Building
645 Griswold St.
Detroit, MI 48226-4094

Visible Ink Press is a trademark of Gale Research

Most Visible Ink Press™ books are available at special quantity discounts when purchased in bulk by corporations, organizations, or groups. Customized printings, special imprints, messages, and excerpts can be produced to meet your needs. For more information, contact Special Markets Manager, Visible Ink Press, 835 Penobscot Bldg., Detroit, MI 48226. Or call 1-800-776-6265.

Art Director: Pamela A. E. Galbreath
Developmental Editors: Rebecca Nelson and Christa Brelin

Library of Congress Cataloging-in-Publication Data

Elyse Sommer, executive editor; Dorrie Weiss, associate editor. — 1st ed.
    p.   cm.
Includes bibliographical references and index.

    1. English language—Terms and phrases.   2. Metaphor—Dictionaries. I. Sommer, Elyse. II. Weiss, Dorrie.
PE1689.M47 1994
081—dc2094-36728

    CIP

Printed in the United States of America

All rights reserved

10 9 8 7 6 5 4 3 2 1

Contents

Introduction

■ Many people view metaphor as an esoteric literary device beyond their use or understanding. However, while few qualify as "master of metaphor," most people use metaphors regularly without realizing they do. For a quick overview of garden-variety (a metaphor!) metaphors heard in everyday speech, turn to the alphabetically arranged list of Common Metaphors (beginning on page 471) that follows the A–Z main entries.

Whether poetic or colloquial, simple or complex, a metaphor compares two unlike objects or ideas and illuminates the similarities between them. It accomplishes in a word or phrase what could otherwise be expressed only in many words, if at all. If we say "don't let her rough manner scare you, she's a pussycat," we condense into a single word the characteristics associated with an affectionate, gentle, non-intimidating personality. Since the word or phrase used to set up the comparison evokes a mental picture, you might say that metaphor embodies the phrase "a picture is worth a thousand words."

While poetry would be impoverished without metaphor, so indeed would all language. Great writers and orators use metaphors to peel away layers of camouflaged meaning. The metaphor's usefulness for presenting technical information to laymen is typified by syndicated health columnist Jane E. Brody's description of an aneurysm as "an abdominal time bomb lurking in the aorta which is the body's super-highway."

Anyone—even someone without a special perception for hidden likeness—can learn to look beyond the obvious to create a pungent metaphor or bring freshness to an old one. To raise one's metaphoric consciousness requires no more than a willingness to smell the linguistic flowers.

Dorrie Weiss and I have compiled this dictionary with three basic aims:

The greatest thing by far is to be a master of metaphor. It is the one thing that cannot be learned from others; it is also a sign of genius, since a good metaphor implies an eye for resemblance.

—Aristotle, De Poetica, *322 B.C.*

1. To create a useful and enjoyable source for examples of metaphor in all its permutations
2. To heighten the reader's appreciation and understanding of metaphor
3. To provide inspiration for writers and speakers.

The more than 6,500 metaphors in these pages illustrate more than 2,500 images applied to 600 subjects. The Subject Index (beginning on page 576) provides an overview of the images most often used. The Table of Thematic Categories (beginning on page xvii) with its many *See/See also* cross-references works as a subject finder.

For utmost comprehensiveness, entries span the entire timeline of history and illustrate origination and use by poets, novelists, prose writers, speech writers journalists, scientists, philosophers, business people, actors, students, and "just plain folks." Simple and obvious images rub shoulders—metaphorically—with the subtle and complex, as do the beautiful with the more coarsely spun, the derivative with the original, the humorous with the sad, and the light-footed with the ponderous.

To enhance the dictionary's usefulness, authors have been cited for all entries except proverbial metaphors and those by the ubiquitous "Anon." This attribution means that the author is the originator, the author is the popularizer, or the author's work is an example of the metaphor. Attribution is often clarified in a comment following an entry.

To achieve our goal of comprehensive coverage we also addressed the following:

Mixed Metaphor. When a metaphor draws its comparison from two illogical and opposite sources, it becomes what the late Theodore M. Bernstein (author and *New York Times* editor) aptly dubbed a "mixaphor." These failed metaphors often result in unintended humor, as when former *Washington Week in Review* host Paul Duke put his metaphoric foot in his mouth with "Clinton stepped up to the plate and grabbed the bull by the horn." The most frequently quoted example is from that unimpeachable source, Shakespeare, when his melancholy dane, Hamlet, ponders whether "it is nobler to suffer the slings and arrows of outrageous fortune or to take arms against a sea of troubles." According to poet Babette Deutsch (in *Poetry Handbook*), Shakespeare's metaphor is a valid one. She believes that Shakespeare's passage alludes to the Celtic warriors' custom of fighting waves with their swords drawn. This interpretation makes for a logical connection to the second image, which implies that Hamlet's troubles are as threatening as the sea and as persistent as its waves. Even those who disagree with this interesting defense of the metaphor will concede that, right or wrong, the Bard's phrases always resonate more than they jar.

Extended Metaphor. Professor Max Black (author of *Models and Metaphor*) defined a simple metaphor as one with a principal subject and a subsidiary subject. Based on this definition, the extended metaphor is one that sets up a principal subject with several subsidiary subjects or comparisons. President Lyndon B. Johnson's inaugural address successfully pictured America as "the uncrossed desert and the unclimbed ridge . . . the star that is not reached and the harvest that's sleeping in the unplowed ground." In *The Bubba Stories* Lee Smith writes "I was ill at ease among them: a thistle in the rose garden, a mule at the racetrack, Cinderella at the fancy dress ball." Such multiple or extended images are fine as long as they stay logically connected to the principal subject.

Some metaphors draw out a simple comparison into almost untenable shape. Such violent exaggerations are known as conceits. A famous conceit by John Donne tells of lovers who "if they be two, they are two so / As stiff twin compasses are two. . . ." Then Donne compares the lovers' movements to a compass drawing a circle, so that the moving foot has no choice but to circle the fixed foot. (What a way to tell your spouse that you can never stray far!)

Similes. Like metaphors, similes compare two unlike objects or ideas. However, metaphors and similes are not interchangeable figures of speech. Think of them instead as the salt and pepper on your linguistic spice shelf, each with its own distinct flavor. The simile compares explicitly and uses "as," "like," or "as if" to announce the comparison. For example, the phrase "she fought like a tiger for her position" is a simile. Metaphor implies the comparison by substituting something or the attributes of something with another. Thus when you say "she became a tiger in her own cause," you picture a woman who has metamorphosed into the image, and so, this phrase is a metaphor.

This dictionary includes many examples of metaphors and similes effectively paired in one sentence or paragraph, or metaphors clarified by or dependent upon similes. For example, in a review of a dance performance, *New York Times* critic Jack Anderson wrote, "Ballet, like language, is capable of extraordinary richness—at least, in theory. In actual practice, ballet is often tongue-tied." He thus set out a comparison with a simile ("ballet . . . [is] like language") and enhanced it with a metaphor ("ballet is often tongue-tied"). Shakespeare begins "Sonnet 68" with a metaphor, "Thus is his cheek the map of days outworn." In the next line, he explains it with this simile: "When beauty lived and died as flowers do now."

Personification/Allusion/Metonymy/Antonomasia. Metaphor can take the form of a variety of related figurative devices. Metaphors of personification are particularly common. These imbue abstract ideas or inanimate things with human qualities. "Death, an unseen stranger" and "age is gray, a toothless hag, / Stumbling in the dark" are metaphors of personification. In his Pulitzer prize-winning book *Lenin's Tomb,* David Remnick humanized Russia as "an old tyrant slouched in the corner with cataracts and gallstones, his muscles gone slack. He wore plastic shoes and a shiny suit that stank of sweat. He hogged all the food and fouled his pants. Mornings, his tongue was coated with the ash-taste of age."

Metaphors of allusion are also used fairly often. These link the comparison to a well-known character or situation from literature, history, or popular culture, or to a proverb or topical saying. "He has met his Waterloo" is a common metaphor of allusion. A more recent example, again from *Lenin's Tomb,* pictures the mechanisms of daily life in Russia after Stalin's death as "a vast Rube Goldberg machine that somehow, if just barely, kept moving."

Metonymy, which substitutes the name or attribute of one thing for the name of another, is occasionally used as metaphor. The figurative phrase "And I am come down to deliver them . . . unto a land flowing with milk and honey," from the *Old Testament,* illustrates a food metaphor in this form. Another figure of substitution, antonomasia, uses the name of a person noted for certain characteristics as a substitute for a literal name. Metaphoric nicknames like The Iron Lady exemplify antonomasia.

* * *

The vast storehouse from which to gather metaphors precluded an all-inclusive collection of metaphors. We therefore did not attempt the impossible but determined instead to reap the most diverse and comprehensive harvest possible. For historic comprehensiveness, we revisited most of the great and respected names in the annals of cultural literacy. To make the collection timely we dipped into current literature and the sources that we use in our daily lives. This strategy drew on our very active interest in music and the theater, the periodicals we read regularly, and Dorrie's involvement with the United Nations in New York and her two trips to the Far East. We targeted the end of the 1993 calendar year as the cutoff date for our collecting effort. Thus the bulk of our work coincided with the launching of the 1992 presidential campaign and the first year of the new administration. Not surprisingly our net caught the collapse of the Bush presidency under an avalanche of voter discontent, Bill Clinton's struggle to prevent the hangnail problem of public acceptance from turning into a fatal chest wound, and the cactus-tongued third party candidate Ross Perot's promises to get under the hood to fix America's problems.

Though our collecting for this book has come to a halt, the flow of metaphoric usage continues unabated:

A piece by Alan Brinkly about President Clinton's first State of the Union address reminded us of an overlooked metaphor by another president, Theodore Roosevelt: "A good political speech is a poster, not an etching." The metaphor was illustrated with a cartoon of the president, dressed in an artist's smock and holding a brush and paint palette. If you check the Author/Speaker Index, you'll see that we did catch many good presidential metaphors, including some by T. R.

The fiftieth anniversary of D-Day brought to mind another overlooked metaphor by journalist John Mason Brown, who observed the landing on Omaha Beach from the cruiser *Augusta* and wrote "Seen through binoculars, the shore is an anthill in turmoil. The fateful dent has been made in Hitler's armor."

There was also a burst of metaphoric comments on President and Mrs. Clinton's ties to an Arkansas real estate development. In addition to twists on the familiar, such as the accusations that the president was "skating along the slippery edges of the truth" and "cheap-skating on ethical thin ice," the First Lady was pictured as being "in the bell jar of Little Rock, where everyone who was anyone knew everyone else," a situation that entangled her "in a cat's cradle of conflicts." By mid-April 1994 the waning public interest in the Whitewater drama was resuscitated by the First Lady's brief fling in the commodities market and reporters were asking themselves if all this was "just egg beater journalism—froth whipped up by prize-hungry sensationalists?"

The information superhighway, a vogue metaphor when we began, became a super-vogue metaphor before we finished.

The superhighway seeded such succinct variants as "I-way" and "Infobahn." To extend the metaphor, there's been talk of routing and traffic problems. Call it what you will, tolls and bridges notwithstanding, perhaps we can all log onto one of the highway's meeting places and continue to exchange metaphors on an interactive basis.

The Bibliography (beginning on page 509) cites the sources consulted for the main text. There the reader will find a list of the works from which we culled the metaphors found in these pages. What follows this Introduction is a list of books on and studies of metaphors that we've found interesting and helpful. These are the works we suggest consulting for further study of metaphoric language.

—Elyse Sommer
Forest Hills, N.Y./Lee, Mass.

Further Reading on Metaphors

Black, Max. *Models and Metaphor.* Cornell University Press, 1962.

Brimfiels, Renee M. *Metaphor and Curriculum Discourse.* Dissertation for Doctor of Philosophy degree, d. u.

On Metaphor. Edited by Sheldon Sacks. The University of Chicago Press, 1978–79.

Deutsch, Babette. *Poetry Handbook.* Funk & Wagnalls, 1957, 1962.

Garfield, Eugene. "Current Comments," Institute for Scientific Information, October 20, 1986.

Gilbert, Scott. "The Metaphorical Structuring of Social Perceptions." In *Soundings.* Summer, 1979.

Lakoff, George, and Mark Johnson. *Metaphors We Live By.* The University of Chicago Press, 1980.

Ricoeur, Paul. *The Rule of Metaphor.* Translated by Robert Czerny. University of Toronto Press, 1977.

Spurgeon, Caroline. *Shakespeare's Imagery.* Cambridge University Press, 1935.

How to Use This Book

■ *Metaphors Dictionary* is designed for the browser's enjoyment and as a source of inspiration for writers and speakers. Because many metaphors work as independent quotations, aphorisms, and proverbs, the book also serves as a quotation finder.

To make *Metaphors Dictionary* as useful and accessible as possible, the more than 6,500 entries have been grouped into 600 thematic categories, with more than 500 synonyms to ease and enhance ready reference. The Table of Thematic Categories (beginning on page xvii) is an alphabetical list of all the thematic categories, synonyms, and *See/See also* cross references. All synonyms and cross references are also included throughout the text.

Entries within each thematic category are arranged (and numbered) alphabetically by author. (Where proverbs have been quoted, the author has been cited as "Anon.")

To Find Metaphors through the Thematic Headings. Since the metaphor's meaning is the guiding principle underlying this dictionary's organization, readers will probably want to begin their search by turning to the Table of Thematic Categories (page xvii). If you look for a metaphor under ABANDONMENT, you will find it listed as a main heading with cross references (*See also*) to thematically related entries under the headings DESTRUCTION/DESTRUCTIVENESS and PEOPLE, INTERACTION, which are listed as cross references. If you look for a metaphor for ADAPTABILITY, you will find it listed as a synonym with a cross reference (*See*) to the main heading FLEXIBILITY/INFLEXIBILITY.

To Find Metaphors by Browsing. Begin perusing at the first entry and let the thematic categories and cross references serve as your guides.

To Find Metaphors by Author/Speaker. Turn to the Author/Speaker Index (beginning on page 526) if you want to identify the metaphors used by a particular author. For deceased authors, birth and death dates are listed in parentheses after the person's name. When dates could not be found, a century or dynasty has been given or the dates have been given as unknown (d.u.). If no dates appear, the author/speaker is contemporary.

A *"-c"* following an entry number indicates that the author's or speaker's metaphor is in the comment of another metaphor.

To Find Familiar Metaphors. To look up the exact form of a commonly used metaphor, turn to page 471 where you'll find a list of Common Metaphors, arranged alphabetically by key word. These phrases can also be found under their appropriate thematic headings, often with more detailed information about the metaphor's origins. Many common metaphors are proverbs. The Author/Speaker Index includes a listing of all proverbs found in the main text (the A-Z thematic listings).

To Find Metaphors by Shakespeare. Sir Walter Raleigh said that Shakespeare seemed to literally think in metaphor. The main text includes more than 800 Shakespearean metaphors, many with background comments. For quick reference to the Bard's use of metaphor, more than 600 are alphabetized by key word or phrase in a special section that begins on page 479.

About the Bibliography. The Bibliography, beginning on page 509, cites the books from which the metaphors were culled. Since the editors did not always work with the same edition, in some instances (for example, with Shakespeare's works) several citations appear. Since text may vary from one edition to another or from one translation to another, we have chosen to list all the sources we used. For a bibliography of studies of and books on metaphors, turn to the end of the Introduction (page xiii).

About the Subject Index. The Subject Index (beginning on page 576) serves as a guide to the many images represented in this collection. Not every entry lent itself to this type of indexing. But whenever an image was evident in the metaphor, we have indexed it. For example, the entry DEVOTION 3 refers to a spaniel and so has been indexed under ANIMAL/MARINE LIFE, under the metaphoric sub-category DOGS.

Notes About the Entries

1. Every entry includes the metaphor, the name of the author or speaker, and the name of the work from which the metaphor was culled.

2. To enhance browsing and usefulness, many entries include the editors' comments, which provide information about the metaphor's origins, include additional text from the same source, or cite related metaphors by another author/speaker.

3. Text in parentheses ( ) is part of the metaphor as found. Text in brackets [ ] was added by the editors for clarification.

4. Unless otherwise indicated, ellipses indicate that some of the author's or speaker's text was eliminated.

5. All entries begin in upper case as a matter of style. The reader should note that since most of these metaphors are extracts, the metaphor may have been picked up in the middle of a line or sentence.

6. For poetry or plays in verse, line breaks are indicated by oblique strokes (solidi), / .

Table of Thematic Categories

A

ABANDONMENT
See also: DESTRUCTION/
DESTRUCTIVENESS; PEO-
PLE, INTERACTION

ABILITY
See also: ACHIEVEMENT;
GROWTH; SELF-
CONFIDENCE

ABSENCE
See also: SEPARATION

ABUNDANCE
See also: EXCESS; MANY;
RICHES

ACCEPTANCE
See: ADMIRATION

ACCUSATIONS
See also: BELIEFS; INSULTS

ACHIEVEMENT
See also: ABILITY; PRIDE;
SELF-ACTUALIZATION

ACTING/ACTORS

ACTION/INACTION
See also: MOBILITY/
IMMOBILITY

ACTIONS
See also: DESCRIPTIONS,
MISC.; PROBLEMS AND
SOLUTIONS

**ACTIVENESS/
INACTIVENESS**
See also: APATHY;
DESCRIPTIONS, MISC.;
POLITICS/POLITICIANS;
WINNING/LOSING

ADAPTABILITY
See: FLEXIBILITY/
INFLEXIBILITY

ADMIRATION
See also: MEN AND
WOMEN

ADORATION
See: LOVE

ADULTERY
See: MARRIAGE;
TEMPTATION

ADVANTAGEOUSNESS
See also:
CHARACTERIZATIONS

ADVERSITY
See also: DIFFICULTIES;
ILLNESS

ADVERTISING
See: BUSINESS
DESCRIPTIONS

*In the following table, catego-
ries used throughout the book
and synonyms that are cross-
referenced to categories are
combined in one alphabetically ordered list.*

ADVICE
See also: WISDOM

AERIAL VIEWS
See also: CITIES;
COUNTRIES, MISC.;
NATURE SCENES; PLACES,
MISC.; SKY/SKYSCAPES;
STARS

AFFECTION
See also: FEELINGS; LOVE;
MEN AND WOMEN

AFFLICTION
See also: ADVERSITY; PAIN
AND SUFFERING

AFTERLIFE
See: IMMORTALITY

AGE/AGING
See also: DEATH; MIDDLE
AGE; OLD AGE; YOUTH
AND AGE

AGGRAVATION
See: IRRITANTS

AGGRESSION
See also: STRENGTH/
WEAKNESS; WAR

AGITATION
See also: CALMNESS/VOLA-
TILITY; EXCITEMENT

**AGREEMENT/
DISAGREEMENT**
See also: CONFLICT;
DIPLOMACY;
FLEXIBILITY/
INFLEXIBILITY; PEOPLE,
INTERACTION;
PROBLEMS AND
SOLUTIONS; QUARRELS/
QUARRELSOMENESS

AGRICULTURAL SCENES
See: DESCRIPTIONS, MISC.

AID
See: ASSISTANCE

AIMLESSNESS

ALERTNESS
See also: AWARENESS/
UNAWARENESS

ALLIANCES
See also: CONNECTIONS

ALONENESS
See: ISOLATION

AMBIGUITY
See: CLARITY/AMBIGUITY

AMBITION
See also: DESIRE; DREAMS;
HOPE

AMBIVALENCE
See also: DOUBT;
UNCERTAINTY

AMERICA/AMERICANS
See also: COUNTRIES, MISC.

ANCESTRY/ANCESTORS
See also: FAMILIES/FAMI-
LY RELATIONSHIPS;
HISTORY

ANGER
See also: PERSONALITY
PROFILES; WORDS AS
WEAPONS

ANGER, DIVINE
See also: GOD; PAIN AND
SUFFERING

ANIMALS

ANIMATION
See also:
CHARACTERISTICS;
PERSONALITY PROFILES

ANNOYANCES
See: IRRITANTS

ANXIETY
See: WORRY

APATHY
See also: EXCITEMENT

APOCALYPSE
See: DESTRUCTION/
DESTRUCTIVENESS

APOLOGY

APPAREL
See: FASHION AND STYLE

APPEARANCE
See: PHYSICAL
APPEARANCE

APPEARANCE
See also: PHYSICAL
APPEARANCE

APPEASEMENT
See also: COMPROMISE

APPLAUSE
See also: APPROVAL/
DISAPPROVAL

APPRECIATION
See: GRATITUDE/
INGRATITUDE

**APPROVAL/
DISAPPROVAL**
See also: CRITICS/
CRITICISM

APTITUDE
See: ABILITY

ARCHITECTURE
See also: BUILDINGS AND
BRIDGES

ARGUMENTS
See also: AGREEMENT/
DISAGREEMENT; WORDS
AS WEAPONS

ARMS
See: BODIES/THE BODY

AROUSAL/ROUSERS

ARROGANCE/HUMILITY
See also: EGO/EGOTISM;
PRIDE

BETRAYAL
See: MARRIAGE; TREACH-ERY; TRUSTWORTHINESS/
UNTRUSTWORTHINESS

THE BIBLE
See: BOOKS

BIGNESS/SMALLNESS
See: BUSINESS
DESCRIPTIONS

BIGOTRY
See also:
ENCOURAGEMENT;
HATE; OPINION

**BIOGRAPHIES/
AUTOBIOGRAPHIES**
See also: BOOKS; WRITING/
WRITERS

BIRDS
See also: ANIMALS;
NATURE SCENES; SKY/
SKYSCAPES

BIRTH
See also: LIFE

BIRTHDAYS
See also: DESCRIPTIONS,
MISC.; LIFE; YOUTH AND
AGE

BITTERNESS
See: DESPAIR;
DISAPPOINTMENT

BLAME
See: ACCUSATIONS

BLINDNESS
See also: AWARENESS/
UNAWARENESS;
SENSITIVITY

BLISS
See: HAPPINESS/UNHAP-PINESS; JOY

BLUSHES
See also: FACIAL COLOR

**BOASTERS/
BOASTFULNESS**
See also:
CHARACTERISTICS;
INSULTS; NAME
CALLING; PERSONALITY
PROFILES; PRIDE

BOATS/BOATING
See also: DESCRIPTIONS,
MISC.; SEASCAPES

BODIES/THE BODY
See also: DESCRIPTIONS,
MISC.; FATNESS/
THINNESS; HAIR; MOVE-MENTS; PHYSICAL
APPEARANCE

BOLDNESS
See: COURAGE

BOOKS
See also: KNOWLEDGE;
READING/READERS;
THINKING/THOUGHT

BOREDOM
See: DULLNESS;
MONOTONY

BORROWING
See: DEBT

BOSTON
See: CITIES; STREET
SCENES

BOXING
See: SPORTS

BRAIN
See also: MIND; THINKING/
THOUGHT

BRAVERY
See: COURAGE

BREASTS/BOSOMS
See also: MEN AND WOM-EN; PHYSICAL
APPEARANCE; SEX/
SEXUALITY

BREATH
See also: DESCRIPTIONS,
MISC.; PEOPLE,
INTERACTION

BREEZES
See: WIND

BRIGHTNESS
See also: ANIMALS;
DESCRIPTIONS, MISC.; FA-CIAL EXPRESSIONS; PER-SONALITY PROFILES

BROADWAY
See: STREET SCENES

BUDGETING/BUDGETS
See: ECONOMICS

BUGS
See: INSECTS

**BUILDINGS AND
BRIDGES**
See also: DESCRIPTIONS,
MISC.; HOUSES

BUSINESS DESCRIPTIONS
See also: DIFFICULTIES;
ECONOMICS; FAILURE;
IMPORTANCE /
UNIMPORTANCE; PLACES,
MISC.

BUSYNESS
See also: ACTIVENESS/
INACTIVENESS; BUSINESS
DESCRIPTIONS;
CHARACTERIZATIONS

BUYING/SELLING
See: PEOPLE,
INTERACTION

C

CALAMITY
See: ADVERSITY; DANGER

CALMNESS/VOLATILITY
See also: CHARACTERIZA-
TIONS; DANGER;
PERSONALITY PROFILES;
TRANQUILITY

CALUMNY
See: SLANDER

CANDOR
See also: PEOPLE,
INTERACTION

CAPABILITY
See: ABILITY

CAREFULNESS
See: CAUTION

CATS
See: ANIMALS

CAUSE AND EFFECT

CAUTION
See also: BUSINESS
DESCRIPTIONS

CELEBRITY
See: FAME

CENSURE
See: CRITICISM/CRITICS

CEREMONIES
See: POLITICS/
POLITICIANS

CESSATION
See: ENDINGS

CHANCE
See also: FATE

CHANGE
See also: CALMNESS/VOLA-
TILITY; DETERIORATION/
DIMINISHMENT; HABIT;
REFORM;
TRANSFORMATION

**CHANGEABLENESS/
UNCHANGEABLENESS**
See also: FLEXIBILITY/
INFLEXIBILITY; HABIT;
TOUGHNESS

CHAOS
See: ORDER/DISORDER

CHARACTER
See also: CHARACTERIZA-
TIONS; GOODNESS; PER-
SONALITY PROFILES

CHARACTERISTICS
See also: EGO/ID; PERSON-
ALITY PROFILES

CHARACTERIZATIONS
See also:
CHANGEABLENESS/
UNCHANGEABLENESS;
ENDURANCE;
EXCITEMENT; GOOD/
EVIL; HUMANITY/
HUMANKIND; NAME
CALLING; OCCUPATIONS;
PERSONALITY PROFILES;
TEMPERAMENT

CHARITY
See also: GENEROSITY;
KINDNESS

CHICAGO
See: CITIES

CHILDHOOD/CHILDREN
See also: FAMILIES/FAMI-
LY RELATIONSHIPS

CHINS
See: FACES

**CHOICES AND
DECISIONS**
See also: DIFFICULTIES;
LIFE

CHRONOLOGY
See: HISTORY

CHURCHES
See: BUILDINGS AND
BRIDGES

CIRCUMSTANCE
See: CHANCE; FATE

CITIES
See also: PLACES, MISC.;
STREET SCENES

CITY DWELLERS
See: CITIES

CITYSCAPES
See also: CITIES; STREET
SCENES

CIVILIZATION
See also: CHANGE;
HUMANITY/
HUMANKIND

CLARITY/AMBIGUITY
See also: LANGUAGE;
WORDS

CLERGY

CLEVERNESS
See: ALERTNESS; INTELLI-
GENCE; WIT

CLICHE
See: ORIGINALITY/
UNORIGINALITY

CLINGING
See also: PEOPLE,
INTERACTION

CLOTHING
See: FASHION AND STYLE

CLOUDS
See also: SKY/SKYSCAPES

COINCIDENCE
See: CHANCE

COLDNESS

COLLAPSE
See: DISINTEGRATION

COLLEGE
See: EDUCATION AND
LEARNING

COLOR

COMBATIVENESS
See: CHARACTERISTICS;
CONFRONTATION

COMEDY
See: HUMOR

**COMFORT/COMFORT-
GIVERS**

COMMITMENT
See also: LOVE

COMMONPLACE
See: ORDINARINESS/
EXTRAORDINARINESS

COMMON SENSE
See: PRUDENCE

**COMMUNICATION/
NON-COMMUNICATION**
See also: ARTICULATENESS/
INARTICULATENESS;
ATTENTIVENESS/
INATTENTIVENESS; PEO-
PLE, INTERACTION

COMPANIONSHIP
See: FRIENDSHIP/
FRIENDS

COMPARISONS

COMPASSION
See also: KINDNESS

COMPETENCE
See: ABILITY;
ACHIEVEMENTS

**COMPETITION/
COMPETITORS**
See also: POLITICS/
POLITICIANS

COMPLACENCY
See: CONTENTMENT

**COMPLETENESS/
INCOMPLETENESS**

COMPLEXION
See also: COLOR; FACES;
FACIAL COLOR;
PHYSICAL APPEARANCE

COMPLICATIONS
See: PROBLEMS AND
SOLUTIONS

COMPLIMENTS
See: FLATTERY; PRAISE

COMPREHENSION
See: UNDERSTANDING/
MISUNDERSTANDING

COMPROMISE
See also: CHOICES AND DE-
CISIONS; POLITICS/
POLITICIANS

CONCEALMENT
See: CRAFTINESS; DECEP-
TION; SECRECY

CONCEIT
See: BOASTERS/
BOASTFULNESS; VANITY

**CONCENTRATION/
DISTRACTION**
See also: LOYALTY; SELF-
CONTROL

CONCILIATION
See: APPEASEMENT

CONDEMNATION
See: APPROVAL/
DISAPPROVAL

CONDESCENSION
See: ARROGANCE/
HUMILITY

CONFIDENCE
See: SELF-CONFIDENCE

CONFINEMENT
See also: FREEDOM/
RESTRAINT

CONFLICT
See also: AGREEMENT/
DISAGREEMENT;
WINNING/LOSING

**CONFORMITY/
NONCONFORMITY**
See also: CUSTOM; INDI-
VIDUALITY; MONOTONY

CONFRONTATION
See also: AGGRESSION;
AGREEMENT/
DISAGREEMENT

CONFUSION
See also: ORDER/
DISORDER

CONNECTIONS
See also: ALLIANCES; FAMI-
LIES/FAMILY RELATION-
SHIPS; FRIENDSHIP/
FRIENDS

CONSCIENCE

CONSCIOUSNESS
See also: MIND

CONSEQUENCES
See: CAUSE AND EFFECT

**CONSISTENCY/
INCONSISTENCY**

**CONSTANCY/
INCONSTANCY**
See: LOYALTY;
TRUSTWORTHINESS/
UNTRUSTWORTHINESS

CONTEMPLATION
See: THINKING/
THOUGHT

CONTEMPT
See: ARROGANCE/
HUMILITY

CONTENTMENT
See also: HAPPINESS/
UNHAPPINESS

DEATH, DEFINED

DEBT
See also: ECONOMICS;
PROBLEMS AND
SOLUTIONS

DECADENCE
See: CORRUPTION

DECAY
See: AGE/AGING; DETE-
RIORATION/
DIMINISHMENT

DECENCY
See: GOODNESS

DECEPTION
See also: DANGER; GOOD/
EVIL; HYPOCRISY; LIES/
LIARS; MALICE; NAME
CALLING; TREACHERY;
TRUSTWORTHINESS/UN-
TRUSTWORTHINESS; VIL-
LAINY/VILLAINS

**DECISIVENESS/
INDECISIVENESS**
See also: CHOICES AND DE-
CISIONS; WORRY

DECLINE
See: DISINTEGRATION;
OLD AGE

DEDICATION
See: COMMITMENT;
PERSEVERANCE

DEEDS
See: ACTIONS

DEFEAT
See also: CAUSE AND EF-
FECT; ENTRAPMENT;
FAILURE; LIFE AND
DEATH; MASTERY/SUB-
ORDINATION; POLITICS/
POLITICIANS; WINNING/
LOSING

DEJECTION
See: DESPAIR; EMOTIONS

DELAY
See: ACTION/INACTION;
PATIENCE

DELIGHT
See: JOY

DELUSION
See: ILLUSION/REALITY

DEMANDS
See: ACCUSATIONS

DEMOCRACY
See also: FREEDOM/RE-
STRAINT; GOVERNMENT;
INTERNATIONAL
RELATIONS

DENIAL
See also: PROBLEMS AND
SOLUTIONS

DENUNCIATION
See: INSULTS

DEPENDENCY
See: CLINGING

DESCRIPTIONS, MISC.
See also:
CHARACTERIZATIONS

DESERTION
See: ABANDONMENT

DESIRE
See also: AFFECTION; LOV-
ERS' DECLARATIONS AND
EXCHANGES; MEN AND
WOMEN; PASSION; SEX/
SEXUALITY; YEARNING

DESPAIR
See also: DEATH;
EMOTIONS; ENDINGS;
GRIEF; HOPE;
ISOLATION; LAMENTS;
SUCCESS/FAILURE;
TEARS

DESTINY
See: FATE

**DESTRUCTION/
DESTRUCTIVENESS**
See also: DEFEAT; DETE-
RIORATION/
DIMINISHMENT;
ENDINGS; EVIL; FAILURE;
HELL AND DAMNATION;
REVENGE/VENGEANCE;
WARNINGS

DETACHMENT
See: COMMUNICATION/
NON-COMMUNICATION

**DETERIORATION/
DIMINISHMENT**
See also: DESTRUCTION/
DESTRUCTIVENESS;
FAILURE

DETROIT
See: CITIES

DEVELOPMENT
See: MATURATION

DEVOTION
See also: LOVE; LOVERS'
DECLARATIONS AND EX-
CHANGES; MASTERY/
SUBORDINATION

DIARIES
See: JOURNAL WRITING

DICTIONARIES
See: BOOKS

DIFFERENCE/SAMENESS
See also: CONSISTENCY/
INCONSISTENCY;
MONOTONY

DIFFICULTIES
See also: ADVERSITY; DAN-
GER; PROBLEMS AND
SOLUTIONS

DIGNITY
See also: HONOR

DIGRESSION
See: CONCENTRATION/
DISTRACTION

E

EARTH

ECOLOGY
See also: PROBLEMS AND SOLUTIONS

ECONOMICS
See also: BUSINESS DESCRIPTIONS; INTERNATIONAL RELATIONS; MONEY; POLITICS/ POLITICIANS

ECSTASY
See: PASSION

EDUCATION AND LEARNING
See also: KNOWLEDGE; WISDOM

EFFECTIVENESS/ INEFFECTIVENESS
See also: PROBLEMS AND SOLUTIONS; STRENGTH/ WEAKNESS

EFFICIENCY

EGO/EGOTISM
See also: BOASTERS/ BOASTFULNESS; VANITY

EGO/ID
See also: AWARENESS/ UNAWARENESS; CONSCIOUSNESS; DESIRE; PERSONALITY PROFILES; SELF-IMAGES

ELATION
See: JOY

ELOQUENCE
See also: PERSUASIVENESS/ PERSUADERS

EMBELLISHMENT
See: BEAUTY

EMBRACES
See also: AFFECTION; KISSES; PASSION

EMINENCE
See: FAME

EMOTIONS
See also: DESPAIR; FEELINGS; GRIEF; GUILT; JOY; PASSION; SORROW; WORRY

EMPATHY
See: KINDNESS/UNKINDNESS; PITY; SYMPATHY; UNDERSTANDING/ MISUNDERSTANDING

ENCOURAGEMENT
See also: CRITICISM/CRITICS; PROMISES

ENDINGS
See also: DEATH; ENTRANCES/EXITS

ENDURANCE
See also: PERMANENCE/ IMPERMANENCE

ENEMIES

ENERGY
See also: ANIMATION; POWER

ENGLAND
See: COUNTRIES, MISC.

ENJOYMENT
See: PLEASURE

ENNUI
See: DULLNESS

ENTANGLEMENTS
See also: PEOPLE, INTERACTION

ENTHUSIASM
See: ZEAL

ENTRANCES/EXITS
See also: ENDINGS; POLITICS/POLITICIANS

ENTRAPMENT
See also: MANIPULATION; MASTERY/ SUBORDINATION; PEOPLE, INTERACTION

ENVIRONMENT
See: ECOLOGY

ENVY
See also: JEALOUSY; COMPETITION/COMPETITORS

EPITAPHS

EPITHETS
See: BOASTERS/ BOASTFULNESS

EQUALITY
See: BARRIERS

EQUANIMITY
See: CALMNESS/ VOLATILITY

ERRORS
See: MISTAKES

ESCAPE
See also: EVASIVENESS; FREEDOM/RESTRAINT

ESSENCE

ETERNITY
See: IMMORTALITY

ETHICS
See also: CORRUPTION; VICE/VIRTUE

ETIQUETTE
See: MANNERS; TACT

EUPHEMISMS
See: LANGUAGE

EVASIVENESS
See also: ESCAPE

FASCINATION
See: ATTRACTION

FASHION AND STYLE

FATE
See also: CHANCE;
FORTUNE/MISFORTUNE

FATHERS
See: CHILDHOOD/CHILD-
REN; FAMILIES/FAMILY
RELATIONSHIPS

FATNESS/THINNESS
See also: BODIES/THE
BODY; PHYSICAL
APPEARANCE

FAULT FINDING
See: ACCUSATIONS; CRITI-
CISM/CRITICS

FAVORITES
See also: INFLUENCE;
POWER

FEAR
See also: WORRY

FEELINGS
See also: ANGER;
EMOTIONS; JOY; PAIN
AND SUFFERING

**FEMINISTS/FEMINIST
BEHAVIOR**
See: WOMEN

FENCES
See: BARRIERS

FERTILITY/INFERTILITY

FICTION
See: BOOKS; WRITING/
WRITERS

FIDELITY
See: LOYALTY

FIGHTING
See also: CONFLICT

FINGERS
See: BODIES/THE BODY

FIRMNESS
See: TOUGHNESS

FISH
See also: ANIMALS

FLATTERY

FLAWS

**FLEXIBILITY/
INFLEXIBILITY**
See also:
CHANGEABLENESS/
UNCHANGEABLENESS;
COMPROMISE

FLIES
See: INSECTS

FLOWERS
See also: NATURE; NATURE
SCENES; TREES

FOG
See also: NATURE SCENES

FOLLY
See: FOOLHARDINESS

FOOD AND DRINK

FOOLHARDINESS
See also: DANGER;
MISTAKES; STUPIDITY

FOOTBALL
See: SPORTS

FORBEARS
See: ANCESTRY/
ANCESTORS

FORCE
See: AGGRESSION; POW-
ER; STRENGTH/
WEAKNESS

FOREBODING
See also: FATE; FEAR;
WORRY

FOREIGN RELATIONS
See: INTERNATIONAL
RELATIONS

FORESIGHT
See: ALERTNESS

FORGETFULNESS
See: MEMORY/MEMORIES

FORGETTING
See: MEMORY/MEMORIES

FORGIVENESS
See also: SIN/REDEMPTION

FORTUNE/MISFORTUNE
See also: FAILURE; FATE;
SUCCESS/FAILURE

FRAGILITY
See also: HELPLESSNESS

FRAGMENTATION
See: CONCENTRATION/
DISTRACTION

FRANKNESS
See: CANDOR

FRAUD
See: DECEPTION

FRECKLES
See also: FACES

FREE WILL
See: SELF-RELIANCE

**FREEDOM OF
EXPRESSION**
See also: JOURNALISM/
JOURNALISTS

FREEDOM/RESTRAINT
See also: CONTROL; EN-
TRAPMENT; LIBERTY;
MASTERY/
SUBORDINATION

FRESHNESS/STALENESS
See also: ORIGINALITY/
UNORIGINALITY

GUILT

H

HABIT
See also:
CHANGEABLENESS/
UNCHANGEABLENESS;
CONFORMITY/
NONCONFORMITY

HAIR
See also: PHYSICAL
APPEARANCE

HAIR COLOR
See also: AGE/AGING;
PHYSICAL APPEARANCE

HANDS
See: BODIES/THE BODY;
PHYSICAL APPEARANCE

**HAPPINESS/
UNHAPPINESS**
See also: CONTENTMENT;
DESPAIR; JOY

HARD-HEARTEDNESS
See also:
CHARACTERIZATIONS

**HARMONY/
DISHARMONY**
See also: AGREEMENT/
DISAGREEMENT;
ARGUMENTS;
CONTENTMENT;
DISSENT/DISSENTERS

HASTE
See: SLOWNESS; SPEED

HATE
See also: EMOTIONS; LOVE

HEART
See also: EMOTIONS; FEEL-
INGS; LOVE

HEAT
See also: SEASONS; SUM-
MER; SUN

HEAVEN
See also: GOD

HELL AND DAMNATION

HELP
See: ASSISTANCE

HELPLESSNESS
See also: SIGNIFICANCE/
INSIGNIFICANCE;
SUCCESS/FAILURE

HISTORY
See also: PAST

HONESTY
See: CANDOR; TRUTH/
FALSEHOOD

HONOR
See also: REPUTATION;
TRUSTWORTHINESS/
UNTRUSTWORTHINESS

HOPE
See also: DESPAIR; DREAMS;
OPTIMISM/PESSIMISM;
YEARNING

HOPELESSNESS
See: DESPAIR

HORSES
See: ANIMALS

HOUSES

**HUMANITY/
HUMANKIND**
See also: DIVERSITY; LIFE
AND DEATH;
SIGNIFICANCE/
INSIGNIFICANCE

HUMILIATION
See: DEFEAT; RIDICULE

HUMILITY
See: ARROGANCE/
HUMILITY

HUMOR
See also:
CHARACTERISTICS; WIT

HUNGER

HUSBANDS AND WIVES
See also: MARRIAGE; SEX/
SEXUALITY

HYPOCRISY
See also: CRAFTINESS; DE-
CEPTION; TREACHERY

HYSTERIA
See: MADNESS

I

IDEALISM
See: REFORM

IDEALS
See: ETHICS

IDEAS
See also: CREATIVITY; IM-
AGINATION; MIND;
THINKING/THOUGHT

IDENTITY
See also: SELF-
KNOWLEDGE

IDLENESS
See also: ACTIVENESS/
INACTIVENESS

IGNORANCE
See also: STUPIDITY

ILLNESS
See also: LIFE AND DEATH;
MORTALITY

ILLUSION/REALITY
See also: DECEPTION;
TRUTH

ILLUSTRIOUSNESS
See: FAME; REPUTATION

IMAGINATION
See also: CREATIVITY;
SELF-EXPRESSION;
THINKING/THOUGHT

IMMATURITY
See: EMOTIONS

IMMIGRATION
See: BIGOTRY; TRAVEL

IMMODESTY
See: BOASTERS/
BOASTFULNESS

IMMORALITY/MORALITY
See also: EVIL; SEX/SEXU-
ALITY; SIN

IMMORTALITY
See also: LIFE AND DEATH;
SOUL

IMPATIENCE
See also: CALMNESS/
VOLATILITY

IMPERMANENCE
See: PERMANENCE/
IMPERMANENCE

**IMPORTANCE/
UNIMPORTANCE**
See also: SELF-
EFFACEMENT;
SIGNIFICANCE/
INSIGNIFICANCE

IMPOSSIBILITY
See also: EFFECTIVENESS/
INEFFECTIVENESS;
FUTILITY

IMPOTENCE
See: FRUSTRATION;
HELPLESSNESS

IMPRECISION
See: CLARITY/AMBIGUITY

IMPRISONMENT
See also: CONFINEMENT;
ISOLATION

INACTION
See: ACTION/INACTION

INCAUTIOUSNESS
See: FOOLHARDINESS

INCOMPETENCE
See: STUPIDITY;
USELESSNESS

INCORRECTNESS
See: MISTAKES

INDECISION
See: DECISIVENESS/
INDECISIVENESS

INDEPENDENCE
See: FREEDOM/
RESTRAINT; LIBERTY

INDIFFERENCE
See: APATHY

INDIGNATION
See: ANGER

INDIVIDUALITY
See also: CONFORMITY/
NONCONFORMITY;
HUMANITY/
HUMANKIND;
ORIGINALITY/
UNORIGINALITY;
PERSONALITY PROFILES

INDOLENCE
See: ACTION/INACTION

INDUSTRIOUSNESS
See: WORK/WORKERS

INDUSTRY
See: ECONOMICS

INEQUALITY
See: BIGOTRY; FAIRNESS/
UNFAIRNESS

INERTIA
See: ACTIVENESS/
INACTIVENESS

INEXPERIENCE
See: YOUTH

INFIDELITY
See: MARRIAGE;
TREACHERY

INFLATION
See: ECONOMICS

INFLUENCE
See also: CHARACTERIZA-
TIONS; FAVORITES; MA-
NIPULATION;
PERSONALITY PROFILES;
POWER

INFORMATION
See also: BOOKS; COMMU-
NICATION/NON-COM-
MUNICATION;
EDUCATION AND LEARN-
ING; KNOWLEDGE

INGRATITUDE
See: GRATITUDE/
INGRATITUDE

**INHERITANCE/
INHERITORS**
See also: ANCESTRY/AN-
CESTORS; FAMILIES/
FAMILY RELATIONSHIPS

INHIBITION
See: SELF-CONTROL

INJURY
See also: PAIN AND
SUFFERING

INJUSTICE
See: JUSTICE/INJUSTICE

**INNOCENCE/
INEXPERIENCE**
See also: AWARENESS/
UNAWARENESS;
VULNERABILITY

INNOVATION
See: CHANGE;
FRESHNESS/STALENESS

INSANITY
See: MADNESS

INSECTS
See also: ANIMALS;
DESCRIPTIONS, MISC.

INSENSITIVITY
See: MISTAKES;
SENSITIVITY

INSIGHT
See: AWARENESS/
UNAWARENESS; SELF-
KNOWLEDGE;
UNDERSTANDING

INSIGNIFICANCE
See: SIGNIFICANCE/
INSIGNIFICANCE

INSINCERITY
See: HYPOCRISY

INSOLENCE
See: PRIDE

INSPIRATION
See also: AROUSAL/
ROUSERS; IMAGINATION;
POETRY/POETS; SPEECH-
ES; WRITING/WRITERS

INSTABILITY
See: TRANSIENCE

INSTITUTIONS

INSULTS
See also: NAME CALLING

INTEGRITY
See: CHARACTER;
LOYALTY

INTELLIGENCE
See also: EDUCATION AND
LEARNING;
KNOWLEDGE; MIND

INTENSITY

**INTERNATIONAL
RELATIONS**
See also: DIPLOMACY;
PEACE

INTOLERANCE
See: BIGOTRY

**INTOXICATION/
INTOXICANTS**
See also: COMFORT/COM-
FORT-GIVERS; FOOD
AND DRINK;
FOOLHARDINESS

INTRIGUE
See: MYSTERY/
MYSTERIOUSNESS

INTROSPECTION
See: SELF-KNOWLEDGE

IRONY

IRREVOCABILITY
See: ENTRANCES/EXITS

IRRITANTS
See also: AROUSAL/
ROUSERS; TROUBLE/
TROUBLEMAKERS

ISOLATION
See also: LONELINESS

J

JARGON
See: ARTICULATENESS/
INARTICULATENESS;
WORDS

JEALOUSY
See also: ENVY

JERUSALEM
See: CITIES

JESUS
See: GUIDANCE/GUIDES;
RESCUE/RESCUERS

JOBS
See: OCCUPATIONS

**JOURNALISM/
JOURNALISTS**
See also: WRITING/
WRITERS

JOURNAL WRITING
See also: WRITERS/
WRITING

JOY
See also: EMOTIONS; HAP-
PINESS/UNHAPPINESS;
PASSION; PLEASURE; SEX/
SEXUALITY

JOY/SORROW
See also: EMOTIONS;
GRIEF; HAPPINESS/UN-
HAPPINESS; PAIN AND
SUFFERING; SORROW

JUSTICE/INJUSTICE
See also: BIGOTRY; FAIR-
NESS/UNFAIRNESS; GOD;
LAW/LAWYERS

K

KINDNESS/UNKINDNESS
See also: CHARACTERIZA-
TIONS; GOODNESS;
HARD-HEARTEDNESS;
SYMPATHY

KISSES
See also: MEN AND WOM-
EN; PASSION; SEX/
SEXUALITY

KNOWLEDGE
See also: EDUCATION AND
LEARNING; IGNORANCE;
REVELATION

L

LAMENTS

LANDSCAPES
See also: DESCRIPTIONS, MISC.; NATURE SCENES; PLACES, MISC.; SEASONS

LANGUAGE
See also: GRAMMAR AND STYLE; POETRY/POETS; SPEECH; WORDS; WORDS AS WEAPONS; WRITING/ WRITERS

LANGUAGE EXPERTS
See also: WORDS AS WEAPONS

LAUGHTER

LAW/LAWYERS
See also: JUSTICE/INJUS-TICE; OCCUPATIONS

LEADERS/FOLLOWERS
See also: ALLIANCES; GUID-ANCE/GUIDES; POWER

LEADERSHIP
See also: BUSINESS DESCRIPTIONS; COMPETI-TION/COMPETITORS; GUIDANCE/GUIDES; REFORM

LETTERS
See also: WRITERS/ WRITING

LIBERTY
See also: FREEDOM/RE-STRAINT; FREEDOM OF EXPRESSION

LIES/LIARS
See also: TRUTH/ FALSEHOOD

LIFE
See also: ACHIEVEMENT; COURAGE; EXISTENCE;

FRAGILITY; HAPPINESS; HUMANITY/ HUMANKIND; PERMANENCE/ IMPERMANENCE; SELF-ACTUALIZATION; TRANSIENCE; VULNERABILITY

LIFE AND DEATH
See also: DEATH; ENDINGS; ESCAPE; JOY

LIFE, DEFINED

LONELINESS
See also: FRIENDSHIP/ FRIENDS; ISOLATION; LOVE

LOOKS
See also: FACIAL EXPRES-SIONS; PEOPLE, INTERACTION

LOVE
See also: DEVOTION; EMO-TIONS; ENDINGS; HATE; LUST; MEN AND WOMEN; PASSION; PERMANENCE/ IMPERMANENCE; SORROW; REVENGE/ VENGEANCE; VULNERABILITY

LOVE, DEFINED
See also: PASSION

LOVERS' DECLARATIONS AND EXCHANGES
See also: MEN AND WOM-EN; PRAISE; SUCCESS/ FAILURE

LOYALTY
See also: DEVOTION; FI-DELITY; MARRIAGE

LUST
See also: DESIRE; PASSION; SEX/SEXUALITY

M

MADNESS
See also: CHARACTERIZATIONS

MALICE
See also: ENTRAPMENT

MANHATTAN
See: CITIES; CITYSCAPES

MANIPULATION
See also: CRAFTINESS; DE-CEPTION; ENTRAPMENT; EXPLOITATION; MASTERY /SUBORDINA-TION; MEN AND WOMEN; PEOPLE, INTERACTION

MANKIND
See: HUMANITY/HUMAN-KIND; LIFE

MANNERS

MANY
See also: ABUNDANCE

MARRIAGE
See also: CHARACTERIZA-TIONS; COMMITMENT; DIVORCE; HUSBANDS AND WIVES; LOVE; LUST; MEN AND WOMEN; PER-MANENCE/ IMPERMANENCE; TREACHERY

MARTYRDOM
See: ENDINGS

MASCULINITY/ FEMININITY
See: MEN AND WOMEN

MASOCHISM
See: PAIN AND SUFFER-ING; SELF-DESTRUCTIVENESS

**MASTERY/
SUBORDINATION**
See also: CONTROL;
EXPLOITATION;
FAMILIES/FAMILY RELA-
TIONSHIPS; MARRIAGE;
MEN AND WOMEN; PEO-
PLE, INTERACTION; POLI-
TICS/POLICTICIANS;
POWER

MATERIALISM
See: PRUDENCE;
RELIGION

MATURATION
See also: BEING/BECOM-
ING; TRANSFORMATION

MEDIA
See: ARTS AND
ENTERTAINMENT; JOUR-
NALISM/JOURNALISTS

MEDIOCRITY

MEDITATION
See: THINKING/
THOUGHT

MELANCHOLY
See: DESPAIR; EMOTIONS;
GLOOM

MEMORY/MEMORIES
See also: ILLUSION/REALI-
TY; PAST

MEN AND WOMEN
See also: CONFLICT; DOMI-
NANCE; ENTRAPMENT;
LOVERS' DECLARATIONS
AND EXCHANGES; MAR-
RIAGE; MASTERY/SUBOR-
DINATION; PEOPLE, IN-
TERACTION;
PERSONALITY PROFILES;
CONFLICT

MERCY
See: FORGIVENESS

METAPHORS
See also: LANGUAGE

METAPHYSICS
See: PHILOSOPHY

MIAMI
See: CITYSCAPES

**MICROCOSM/
MACROCOSM**
See: HUMANITY/HUMAN-
KIND; THINKING/
THOUGHT

MIDDLE AGE
See also: AGE/AGING;
CHARACTERIZATIONS;
PERSONALITY PROFILES

MIGRATION
See: MOVEMENTS

MIND
See also: BRAIN; FEELINGS;
IMAGINATION;
INTELLIGENCE;
THINKING/THOUGHT

MIRACLES
See: RELIGION

MISANTHROPY
See: HATE

MISERY
See: PAIN AND SUFFERING

MISFORTUNE
See: FORTUNE/
MISFORTUNE

MISOGYNY
See: NAME CALLING

MISTAKES
See also: EVIL; FORGIVE-
NESS; SENSITIVITY; SIN/
REDEMPTION

MISTRUST
See also: DOUBT

MISUNDERSTANDINGS
See: QUARRELS/
QUARRELSOMENESS

MIXTURE
See also: DIVERSITY

MOBILITY/IMMOBILITY
See also: ACTION/INAC-
TION; GUIDANCE/
GUIDES

MODERATION
See: CAUTION; PRUDENCE

MODESTY
See: CHARACTERISTICS

MONEY
See also: CHARACTERIZA-
TIONS; ECONOMICS;
RICHES

MONOTONY
See also: DULLNESS; EN-
TRAPMENT; LIFE; WORK/
WORKERS

MOOD SWINGS
See: DARKNESS/LIGHT;
OPTIMISM/PESSIMISM

MOODS
See: EMOTIONS; FEELINGS

MOON
See also: DESCRIPTIONS,
MISC.; NATURE SCENES;
NIGHT AND DAY; SKY/
SKYSCAPES; SUN

MORALITY/IMMORALITY
See also: GOOD/EVIL; PO-
ETRY/POETS; SIN/
REDEMPTION

MORNING
See also: DAWN; EVENING;
NATURE SCENES; NIGHT
AND DAY

MORTALITY
See also: DEATH

MOSCOW
See: CITIES

OCCUPATIONS
See also: CHARACTERIZA-TIONS; MUSIC/MUSICIANS; POLITICS/POLITICIANS; SCIENCE; WARRIORS AND PEACEMAKERS

OCEAN
See: SEA

OLD AGE
See also: AGE/AGING; YOUTH AND AGE

OMNIPRESENCE
See: CHARACTERIZATIONS; POWER

OPEN-MINDEDNESS
See: CHANGEABLENESS/UNCHANGEABLENESS; FLEXIBILITY/INFLEXIBILITY

OPENNESS/PRIVACY
See also: CANDOR; LIFE; SECRECY

OPINION

OPPORTUNITY
See also: ACTION/INAC-TION; FAIRNESS/UNFAIR-NESS; FEAR; CHANCE; INSPIRATION

OPPOSITION
See: AGREEMENT/DISAGREEMENT

OPTIMISM/PESSIMISM
See also: GLOOM; HOPE; JOY; LIFE

ORATORY
See: ELOQUENCE; SPEECHES

ORDER/DISORDER
See also: CONFUSION; CROWDS; GOVERNMENT; LIBERTY

ORDINARINESS/EXTRAORDINARINESS
See also: DULLNESS; EX-CITEMENT; ILLUSION/REALITY; MEDIOCRITY; SELF IMAGES

ORIGINALITY/UNORIGINALITY
See also: CHANGE; CREA-TIVITY; INDIVIDUALITY; MUSIC/MUSICIANS; PEO-PLE, INTERACTION; PRAISE; WRITING/WRITERS

ORIGINS
See: DESCRIPTIONS, MISC.

OUT OF PLACE
See: BELONGING/OUTCAST

OUTSPOKENNESS
See: CANDOR

OVERREACHING
See: SUCCESS/FAILURE

P

PAIN AND SUFFERING
See also: DIFFICULTIES; FAMILIES/FAMILY RELA-TIONSHIPS; GRIEF; ILLNESS; SENSITIVITY; MEN AND WOMEN; SORROW

PALLOR
See: FACIAL COLOR

PARENTS/CHILDREN
See: CHILDHOOD/CHILD-REN; FAMILIES/FAMILY RELATIONSHIPS

PARIS
See: CITIES

PARTICIPATION
See: ENTRANCES/EXITS

PASSION
See also: CALMNESS/VOLA-TILITY; CHARACTERIZATIONS; DESIRE; DESPAIR; EMO-TIONS; ENDINGS; FEEL-INGS; HEART; LOVE; LOV-ER'S DECLARATIONS AND EXCHANGES; MEN AND WOMEN; SEX/SEXUALI-TY; TEMPTATION; ZEAL

PAST
See also: FUTURE; HISTO-RY; ILLUSION/REALITY; MEMORY/MEMORIES

PATIENCE

PATRIOTISM
See also: BIGOTRY

PEACE
See also: AGREEMENT/DISAGREEMENT; ENTAN-GLEMENTS; FRIENDSHIP/FRIENDS; INTERNATION-AL RELATIONS; WAR; WARRIORS AND PEACEMAKERS

PEACEFULNESS
See: STILLNESS

PEAK
See: ZENITH

PEDANTRY
See also: KNOWLEDGE

PEOPLE
See: HUMANITY/HUMANKIND

PEOPLE, INTERACTION
See also: ALLIANCES; CON-VERSATION; FRIENDSHIP/FRIENDS; GROUP SCENES; MANIPULATION; MEN AND WOMEN; POLITICS/

PRESS
See: JOURNALISM/
JOURNALISTS

PRESUMPTUOUSNESS
See: PRIDE

PRETTINESS
See: BEAUTY

PREVENTION
See: RESTRICTION

PRIDE
See also: AMBITION; ARRO-
GANCE/HUMILITY

PRINCIPLES
See: BELIEFS; ETHICS

**PROBLEMS AND
SOLUTIONS**
See also: ACTION/INAC-
TION; DESCRIPTIONS,
MISC.; DIFFICULTIES;
ECONOMICS; GRIEF; IN-
TERNATIONAL
RELATIONS; REFORM

PROCREATION

PROFESSIONS
See: OCCUPATIONS

PROFICIENCY
See: ABILITY

PROFILES
See: FACES

PROFUSION
See: ABUNDANCE

PROGRESS
See also: CIVILIZATION;
FREEDOM/RESTRAINT;
HUMANITY/
HUMANKIND; LIFE

**PROMINENCE/
PERIPHERY**
See also: VISIBILITY/
INVISIBILITY

PROMISES

PROPHECY
See: DEATH

PROS AND CONS
See: AGREEMENT/
DISAGREEMENT

PROSE
See: WRITING/WRITERS

**PROTECTION/
PROTECTORS**
See also: FAMILIES/FAMI-
LY RELATIONSHIPS; MAR-
RIAGE; MEN AND
WOMEN

PROTEST
See: DISSENT/DISSENTERS

PROTESTS
See: REVOLT

PROVOCATION
See: AROUSAL/ROUSERS

PRUDENCE
See also: CAUTION; CHAR-
ACTERISTICS; REASON;
STINGINESS

PSYCHOLOGY
See: OCCUPATIONS

PUBLIC OPINION
See also: OPINION

PUNISHMENT
See: RETRIBUTION

PURPOSE
See: RESOLVE

PURSUIT
See: MEN AND WOMEN

PUTDOWNS
See: ACTING/ACTORS

Q

**QUARRELS/
QUARRELSOMENESS**
See also: AGREEMENT/
DISAGREEMENT

QUICKNESS
See: SPEED

QUIET
See: STILLNESS

QUOTATIONS
See also: LANGUAGE; WIT

R

RACISM
See: BIGOTRY

RAGE
See: ANGER

RAIN
See also: SKY/SKYSCAPES;
STORMS

RAINBOWS
See: SKY/SKYSCAPES

READING/READERS
See also: POETRY/POETS

REALITY/UNREALITY
See also: DREAMS

REASON
See also: PRUDENCE

RECOLLECTION
See: MEMORY/MEMORIES

RECRIMINATION
See: CALMNESS/
VOLATILITY; INSULTS;
NAME CALLING

REFORM
See also: CHANGE; GOVERNMENT; POLITICS/POLITICIANS

REGENERATION
See: DEATH; RENEWAL

REGRETS
See: APOLOGY

REJECTION
See: ABANDONMENT; PEOPLE/INTERACTIONS

RELATIONSHIPS
See: FAMILIES/FAMILY RELATIONSHIPS; FRIENDSHIP/FRIENDS; MEN AND WOMEN; PEOPLE, INTERACTION

RELIEF
See: COMFORT/COMFORT-GIVERS

RELIGION
See also: BELIEFS; FAITH

REMEMBRANCE
See: PAST; REGRETS

REMORSE
See: EMOTIONS

RENEWAL
See also: CHANGE; REFORM; SEASONS

RENUNCIATIONS
See: LOVERS' DECLARATIONS AND EXCHANGES

REPENTANCE
See: SIN/REDEMPTION

REPETITION
See: TALKATIVENESS

REPOSE
See: STILLNESS

REPRESSION
See: ANGER; SELF; SOUL

REPROACH
See: ACCUSATIONS

REPUTATION
See also: CHARACTER; SLANDER

RESCUE/RESCUERS
See also: VILLAINY/VILLAINS; ESCAPE

RESENTMENTS
See: AROUSAL/ROUSERS

RESERVE
See: SELF-ACTUALIZATION

RESIGNATION
See: DESPAIR

RESOLVE

RESPONSIBILITY

RESTLESSNESS

RESTRICTION
See also: CONTROL; MASTERY/SUBORDINATION

RETIREMENT
See: ACTIVENESS/INACTIVENESS; ENDINGS

RETRIBUTION
See also: GOD; REVENGE/VENGEANCE

REVELATION
See also: CANDOR; COMMUNICATION/NON-COMMUNICATION; OPENNESS/PRIVACY; SECRECY

REVENGE/VENGEANCE
See also: RETRIBUTION

REVOLT
See also: ARGUMENTS; CONFRONTATION; DISINTEGRATION; DISSENT/DISSENTERS

REWARDS
See also: GRATITUDE/INGRATITUDE

RHETORIC
See: SPEECHES

RICHES
See also: ABUNDANCE; FORTUNE/MISFORTUNE; MONEY; POVERTY/PROSPERITY

RIDICULE
See also: INSULTS; NAME CALLING; MEN AND WOMEN

RISK-TAKING
See also: CAUTION; COURAGE; TIMIDITY

RIVALRY
See: COMPETITION/COMPETITORS

ROAD SCENES
See also: STREET SCENES

ROLE MODELS
See: GUIDANCE/GUIDES; INSPIRATION

ROMANCE
See: LOVE; MEN AND WOMEN

ROME
See: CITIES

ROOMS
See also: FURNITURE/FURNISHINGS

RUDENESS
See: CHARACTERISTICS

RUIN
See: FAILURE

RUMOR
See also: GOSSIP

RUTHLESSNESS
See: VILLAINS/VILLAINY

S

SACRIFICE
See also: DEATH; SORROW;
SUFFERING

SADNESS
See: DARKNESS / LIGHT;
DESPAIR; GRIEF

SAFETY
See also: CAUTION;
ECONOMICS; PROBLEMS
AND SOLUTIONS;
SURVIVAL

SANCTIMONIOUSNESS
See: EGO / EGOTISM

SARCASM
See also: ACCUSATIONS;
HUMOR; WORDS AS
WEAPONS

SATIRE
See also: REVELATION

SCAPEGOATING
See: ACCUSATIONS;
BIGOTRY

SCHOOLS
See: EDUCATION AND
LEARNING

SCIENCE
See also: CREATIVITY; EX-
PLOITATION;
IMAGINATION;
MANIPULATION;
RELIGION

SCRUTINY
See also: APPROVAL/DIS-
APPROVAL; AWARENESS/
UNAWARENESS;

CRAFTINESS; CRITICISM/
CRITICS; EYE
EXPRESSIONS;
EXACTNESS/
INEXACTNESS; LOOKS;
MISTAKES; PEOPLE,
INTERACTION

SEA
See also: COLOR; NATURE;
NATURE SCENES; SOUND

SEASCAPES
See also: FOG; NATURE
SCENES; SKY/SKYSCAPES;
STORMS

SEASONS
See also: FALL; NATURE
SCENES; PERMANENCE/
IMPERMANENCE; SPRING;
SUMMER; SUN;
TRANSIENCE; WIND

SECRECY
See also: CANDOR; INTER-
NATIONAL RELATIONS

SEDUCTION
See: MEN AND WOMEN

SEGREGATION
See: BIGOTRY

SELF
See also: EGO/ID; EMO-
TIONS; SELF-ACTUALIZA-
TION; SELF-CONTROL;
SELF-KNOWLEDGE;
THINKING/THOUGHT;
YEARNING

SELF-ABSORPTION
See: EGO/EGOTISM

SELF-ACTUALIZATION
See also: ACHIEVEMENT;
ADVICE; EMOTIONS;
HAPPINESS/
UNHAPPINESS; HUMANI-
TY/HUMANKIND;
OPPORTUNITY; SELF
IMAGES

SELF-CONFIDENCE
See also: ADVICE; AGE/AG-
ING; CHARACTERISTICS;
FATE; PRIDE

SELF-CONSCIOUSNESS
See also: DESCRIPTIONS,
MISC.

SELF-CONTROL
See also: CAUTION; CHAR-
ACTERIZATIONS;
CONCENTRATION/
DISTRACTION; CONTROL;
EMOTIONS; FEELINGS;
PERSONALITY PROFILES;
PASSION; REASON

SELF-DEFENSE
See: FUTURE

SELF-DELUSION
See: ILLUSION/REALITY

SELF-DESTRUCTIVENESS
See also: CHARACTERIZA-
TIONS; HUMANITY/HU-
MANKIND; PLACES, MISC.

SELF-DETERMINATION
See: SELF-RELIANCE

SELF-EFFACEMENT
See also: MASTERY/SUBOR-
DINATION; SACRIFICE

SELF-EXPRESSION
See also: WORDS

SELF IMAGES
See also: ALERTNESS;
CALMNESS/VOLATILITY;
DESCRIPTIONS, MISC.;
LONELINESS

SELF-IMPROVEMENT

SELFISHNESS
See: EGO/EGOTISM

SELF-KNOWLEDGE
See also: AWARENESS/
UNAWARENESS; EGO/ID;
HUMANITY/

HUMANKIND; ILLUSION/
REALITY; PEOPLE, INTER-
ACTION; SELF-CONTROL;
UNDERSTANDING

SELF-PITY

SELF-PRAISE
See: BOASTERS/
BOASTFULNESS

SELF-PROTECTIVENESS
See: DECEPTION

SELF-RELIANCE
See also: COURAGE; HU-
MANITY/HUMANKIND;
INDIVIDUALITY; SELF-
KNOWLEDGE

SELF-RIGHTEOUSNESS
See: COMMUNICATION/
NON-COMMUNICATION

SENSES
See also: FEELINGS; MIND;
SEX/SEXUALITY

SENSITIVITY
See also: CALMNESS/VOLA-
TILITY; FEELINGS; FRA-
GILITY; HUMANITY/
HUMANKIND

SENTIMENTALITY
See: WRITING/WRITERS

SEPARATION
See also: ACCUSATIONS;
DEATH; PEOPLE, INTER-
ACTION; POETRY/POETS

SEX/SEXUALITY
See also: ATTRACTION;
MASTERY/
SUBORDINATION; MEN
AND WOMEN; PASSION;
SENSES; WOMEN

SHALLOWNESS
See: SUPERFICIALITY

SHAME
See also: GUILT

SHELTER
See also: ASSISTANCE;
COMFORT/COMFORT-
GIVERS; PROTECTION/
PROTECTORS

SHOCK
See also: FEAR; WORDS AS
WEAPONS

SHREWDNESS
See: CRAFTINESS

SHYNESS
See: TIMIDITY

SIGHS
See also: GRIEF; TEARS

SIGHT
See: DESCRIPTIONS, MISC.

**SIGNIFICANCE/
INSIGNIFICANCE**
See also: HUMANITY/HU-
MANKIND; IMPORTANCE/
UNIMPORTANCE

SILENCE
See also: CHARACTERIZA-
TIONS;
COMMUNICATION/NON-
COMMUNICATION;
FAITH; PEOPLE, INTER-
ACTIONS; PLEAS AND
PRAYERS;
SPEECHLESSNESS;
TRANQUILITY

SILLINESS
See: FOOLHARDINESS

**SIMILARITY/
DISSIMILARITY**
See also: HUMANITY/HU-
MANKIND;
INDIVIDUALITY

**SIMPLICITY/
SIMPLIFICATION**
See also: FURNITURE/
FURNISHINGS

**SINGING/SONGS/
SINGERS**
See also: ARTS AND ENTER-
TAINMENT; CHARACTERI-
ZATIONS; DIVERSITY; MU-
SIC/MUSICIANS; VOICES

SIN/REDEMPTION
See also: BODIES/BODY;
EVIL; FORGIVENESS;
GOOD/EVIL

SKEPTICISM
See: DOUBT

SKILL
See: ABILITY

SKY/SKYSCAPES
See also: CITIES; CLOUDS;
DAWN; HEAVEN; MOON;
NATURE SCENES; NIGHT
AND DAY; SNOW;
STORMS; SUNSET

SLANDER
See also: GOSSIP; MALICE

SLAVERY
See: FREEDOM/
RESTRAINT

SLEEP
See also: DEATH; NIGHT
AND DAY; PLEAS AND
PRAYERS; SLEEPLESSNESS

SLEEPLESSNESS

SLOWNESS
See also: ARTS AND ENTER-
TAINMENT; TIME

SLYNESS
See: CRAFTINESS; SMILES

SMALLNESS
See also: CHILDREN/
CHILDHOOD; PHYSICAL
APPEARANCE

SMELLS
See also: CHARACTERIZA-
TIONS; INSULTS; SENSES

SMILES
See also: DECEPTION; FACIAL EXPRESSIONS; LOOKS

SMUGNESS
See: COMMUNICATION/NON-COMMUNICATION

SNOW
See also: DESCRIPTIONS, MISC.; LANDSCAPES; NATURE SCENES; SEASONS; SKY/SKYSCAPES; STORMS; WINTER

SOCIETY/SOCIAL SITUATIONS
See also: CHANGE; CHANGEABLENESS/UNCHANGEABLENESS; GROUP SCENES; HUMANITY/HUMANKIND; ISOLATION; MIXTURE; PEOPLE, INTERACTION; SEPARATION

SOLITUDE
See: ISOLATION; LONELINESS

SONS
See: FAMILIES/FAMILY RELATIONSHIPS

SORROW
See also: DESPAIR; GRIEF; JOY/SORROW; PAIN AND SUFFERING

SOUL
See also: CONTINUITY; DEATH; IMMORTALITY; HUMANITY/HUMANKIND; LAMENTS

SOUND
See also: ANIMALS

SPECIALISTS
See: WORDPLAY/WORDWATCHING

SPEECH
See also: ARTICULATENESS/INARTICULATENESS; LANGUAGE; PERSUASIVENESS/PERSUADERS; TALKATIVENESS; WORDS

SPEECHES
See also: ARTICULATENESS/INARTICULATENESS; GRAMMAR AND STYLE; POLITICS/POLITICIANS

SPEECHLESSNESS
See also: ARTICULATENESS/INARTICULATENESS; EFFECTIVENESS/INEFFECTIVENESS; SILENCE; VOICES

SPEED

SPIRIT

SPITE
See: CRIME AND PUNISHMENT; MALICE; SELF-DESTRUCTIVENESS

SPORTS
See also: COMPETITION/COMPETITORS; FAILURE; MISTAKES; POWER

SPRING
See also: CHANGE; LANDSCAPES; NATURE SCENES; SEASONS; TREES

STARS
See also: NATURE SCENES; SKY/SKYSCAPES

STEALTH
See: CRAFTINESS

STILLNESS
See also: NATURE SCENES; ROOMS; SILENCE

STINGINESS
See also: MONEY

STOPPING AND STARTING
See: ADVICE

STORMS
See also: NATURE SCENES; NIGHT AND DAY; RAIN; SOUND; STREET SCENES; THUNDER AND LIGHTNING; WIND; WINTER

STRATEGIES
See also: CRAFTINESS; MANIPULATION; POLITICS/POLITICIANS; PREPAREDNESS/UNPREPAREDNESS; REFORM; THINKING/THOUGHT

STREET SCENES
See also: CITIES; DESCRIPTIONS, MISC.; GROUP SCENES; HEAT; PLACES, MISC.; SNOW; SUMMER; WINTER

STRENGTH/WEAKNESS
See also: ABILITY; BUSINESS DESCRIPTIONS; EFFECTIVENESS/INEFFECTIVENESS; ENDURANCE; FRAGILITY; LEADERSHIP; POLITICS/POLITICIANS; POWER; SELF-RELIANCE; SMALLNESS

STUBBORNNESS
See: AGREEMENT/DISAGREEMENT; FLEXIBILITY/INFLEXIBILITY

STUDENTS AND TEACHERS
See: EDUCATION AND LEARNING

STUPIDITY
See also: IGNORANCE; INSULTS; INTELLIGENCE; MIND

SUBSERVIENCE
See: MASTERY/
SUBORDINATION

**SUBSTANTIALITY/
INSUBSTANTIALITY**

SUBTLETY
See: TACT

SUCCESS, DEFINED
See also: ACHIEVEMENT;
FAME; INDIVIDUALITY;
SELF-RELIANCE;
WINNING/LOSING

SUCCESS/FAILURE
See also: ARTS AND ENTER-
TAINMENT; FORTUNE/
MISFORTUNE; MISTAKES;
WINNING/LOSING

SUFFERING
See: ADVERSITY; PAIN
AND SUFFERING

SUMMER
See also: NATURE SCENES;
NIGHT AND DAY; SEA-
SONS; TIME

SUN
See also: NATURE SCENES;
ROOMS; SKY/SKYSCAPES;
STREET SCENES

SUNRISE
See also: DAWN; NATURE
SCENES; NIGHT AND DAY

SUNSET
See also: LANDSCAPES; NA-
TURE SCENES; NIGHT
AND DAY; SKY/
SKYSCAPES

SUPERFICIALITY
See also:
CHARACTERISTICS;
HUMANITY/
HUMANKIND

SUPERSTITION

SURFING
See: SPORTS

SURVIVAL
See also: CHARACTERIZA-
TIONS; ENDURANCE; IN-
HERITANCE/INHERITORS

SUSPICION
See also: DOUBT; LOVERS'
DECLARATIONS AND EX-
CHANGES; MISTRUST

SWEAT
See also: FACES; PHYSICAL
APPEARANCE

SYMBOLS
See also: CHARACTERIZA-
TIONS; RELIGION

SYMPATHY
See also: FEELINGS; PITY;
SENSITIVITY;
UNDERSTANDING

T

TACITURNITY
See: SILENCE

TACT
See also: DIPLOMACY

TACTICS
See: STRATEGIES

TACTLESSNESS
See: CHARACTERISTICS

TALKATIVENESS
See also: ANIMATION; EF-
FECTIVENESS/
INEFFECTIVENESS;
EXCITEMENT; FOOLHAR-
DINESS; GOSSIP; INSULTS

TASTE

TEACHERS/TEACHING
See: EDUCATION AND
LEARNING;
OCCUPATIONS

TEARS
See also: ACTING/ACTORS;
DECEPTION; GRIEF; LA-
MENTS; LOVERS' DECLA-
RATIONS AND
EXCHANGES; SELF-CON-
TROL; SORROW

TECHNOLOGY
See also: PROGRESS

TELEVISION
See: ARTS AND
ENTERTAINMENT

TEMPERAMENT

TEMPTATION
See also: LUST; SIN/
REDEMPTION

TENACITY
See: PERSEVERANCE

TENDERNESS
See: SENSITIVITY

**TENSION/TENSION
RELIEF**
See also: AGREEMENT/
DISAGREEMENT; ARTS
AND ENTERTAINMENT;
MEN AND WOMEN; POLI-
TICS/POLITICIANS

TENTATIVENESS
See: UNCERTAINTY

TERROR
See: FEAR

THANKFULNESS
See: GRATITUDE/
INGRATITUDE

THEATER
See: ACTORS/ACTING

THINKING/THOUGHT
See also:
COMMUNICATION/NON-
COMMUNICATION; EMO-
TIONS; IDEAS; IMAGINA-
TION; MIND; SOCIETY;
TALKING

THOUGHTLESSNESS
See: SELF-IMAGES

THREATS
See: WARNINGS

THRIFT
See: STINGINESS

**THUNDER AND
LIGHTNING**
See also: SKY/SKYSCAPES;
STORMS

TIME
See also: AGE/AGING; AN-
CESTRY/ANCESTORS;
DEATH; FOREBODING;
FRAGILITY;
INHERITANCE/
INHERITORS; LIFE AND
DEATH; MASTERY/SUB-
ORDINATION;
MATURATION; MEMORY/
MEMORIES; PAST;
PEOPLE, INTERACTION;
TRANSIENCE

**TIMELINESS/
UNTIMELINESS**
See also: ACTION/INAC-
TION; DEATH; FATE; IN-
SULTS; OBSOLESCENCE;
OPPORTUNITY

TIMIDITY
See also: CAUTION; COUR-
AGE; COWARDICE

**TOLERANCE/
INTOLERANCE**
See: BIGOTRY

TORONTO
See: CITIES

TOUGHNESS
See also:
CHARACTERISTICS;
CHARACTERIZATIONS;
COURAGE; ENDURANCE;
MASTERY/
SUBORDINATION;
STRENGTH/WEAKNESS

TRADITION
See also: CHANGE; REFORM

TRAFFIC
See: ROAD SCENES

TRANQUILITY
See also: CALMNESS/VOLA-
TILITY; NATURE SCENES;
SINGERS/SINGING/
SONGS

TRANSFORMATION
See also: CHANGE; CHAR-
ACTERIZATIONS;
STRENGTH/WEAKNESS

TRANSIENCE
See also: CHANGE; DEATH;
LAMENTS; LIFE; PERMA-
NENCE/IMPERMANENCE

TRAVEL

TREACHERY
See also: ACCUSATIONS;
DANGER; DECEPTION;
GOOD/EVIL; NAME
CALLING

TREES
See also: ANCESTORS/AN-
CESTRY; DESCRIPTIONS,
MISC.; FALL;
LANDSCAPES; NATURE
SCENES; SEASONS; SNOW;
STREET SCENES; WINTER

TRITENESS
See also: ORIGINALITY/
UNORIGINALITY

TRIVIA
See: ORDINARINESS/
EXTRAORDINARINESS

**TROUBLE/
TROUBLEMAKERS**
See also: CAUSE AND EF-
FECT;
CHARACTERIZATIONS;
PERSONALITY PROFILES

**TRUSTWORTHINESS/
UNTRUSTWORTHINESS**
See also: ADVICE; CHARAC-
TER; FEAR; PERSONALITY
PROFILES

TRUTH/FALSEHOOD
See also: DESTRUCTION/
DESTRUCTIVENESS; EVA-
SIVENESS; FACTS; LIES/
LIARS; MARRIAGE; PEO-
PLE, INTERACTION; PER-
SONALITY PROFILES

TWILIGHT
See: NIGHT AND DAY

U

UNATTRACTIVENESS
See: CHARACTERIZATIONS

UNAWARENESS
See: AWARENESS/
UNAWARENESS

UNCERTAINTY
See also: DANGER; END-
INGS; PAST; UNITY/
DISUNITY

UNCLEANLINESS
See: FASHION AND STYLE

UNDERSTANDING
See also: CHARACTERIZA-
TIONS;
COMMUNICATION/NON-
COMMUNICATION;
EDUCATION AND LEARN-
ING; GUIDANCE/GUIDES;
HUMANITY/
HUMANKIND;
KNOWLEDGE; PEOPLE,

WATER
See: SEA; SEASCAPES

WEAKNESS
See: STRENGTH/
WEAKNESS

WEALTH
See: RICHES

WEARINESS

WEATHER
See: CLOUDS; FOG; HEAT;
RAIN; SEASONS; SNOW;
STORMS; SUMMER; THUN-
DER AND LIGHTNING;
WINTER

WHISKERS
See: FACIAL HAIR

THE WHITE HOUSE
See: ISOLATION;
POLITICS/POLITICIANS

WICKEDNESS
See: EVIL

WILINESS
See: CRAFTINESS

WIND
See also: EVENING; FALL;
LANDSCAPES; NATURE
SCENES; NIGHT AND
DAY; STORMS; WINTER

WINNING/LOSING
See also: DEFEAT; FIGHT-
ING; LIFE AND DEATH;
POLITICS/POLITICIANS;
STRATEGIES; WARRIORS
AND PEACEMAKERS

WINTER
See also: NATURE SCENES;
SEASONS; STORMS;
TREES; WEATHER

WISDOM
See also: ADVICE; CHARAC-
TERIZATIONS;

EDUCATION AND LEARN-
ING; GUIDANCE/GUIDES;
KNOWLEDGE

WISHES
See: DESIRE; YEARNING

WIT
See also: CONVERSATION;
INTELLIGENCE; WORDS

WOE
See: GRIEF

WOMEN
See also: FAMILIES/FAMI-
LY RELATIONSHIPS; MEN
AND WOMEN

WORDINESS
See: LANGUAGE;
TALKATIVENESS

**WORDPLAY/WORD-
WATCHING**

WORDS

WORDS AS WEAPONS
See also: ABILITY; INSULTS;
INTENSITY; SATIRE;
SLANDER; SPEECHES;
WOMEN; WRITING/
WRITERS

WORK/WORKERS
See also: BUSINESS
DESCRIPTIONS; EXCESS;
MONOTONY

WORLD
See also: HISTORY;
HUMANITY/
HUMANKIND; ORDER/
DISORDER; PAST

WORRY
See also: FEAR; PERSONALI-
TY PROFILES

WRINKLES
See: FACES; PHYSICAL
APPEARANCE

WRITING ADVICE
See also: POETRY/POETS;
WRITING/WRITERS

WRITING/WRITERS
See also: ABILITY; BOOKS;
CHARACTERIZATIONS;
IMAGINATION; JOURNAL-
ISM/JOURNALISTS; MIS-
TAKES; POETRY/POETS

Y

YEARNING
See also: DESIRE; HOPES;
MEN AND WOMEN; SELF;
SELF-ACTUALIZATION

YOUTH
See also: AGE/AGING; EX-
PERIENCE/
INEXPERIENCE;
INNOCENCE/
INEXPERIENCE;
TRANSIENCE

YOUTH AND AGE
See also: AGE/AGING; HU-
MANITY/HUMANKIND;
LAMENTS; MIDDLE AGE;
OLD AGE

Z

ZEAL
See also: AMBITION; ANI-
MATION; CHARACTERIZA-
TIONS; ENERGY; PASSION

ZENITH
See also: SUCCESS

■ ABANDONMENT

See also: *DESTRUCTION/DESTRUCTIVE-
NESS; PEOPLE, INTERACTION*

1. Party leaders were ready to pull the plug on him [Democratic candidate Bill Clinton] —Elizabeth Drew, "Letter from Washington," *The New Yorker,* April 20, 1992

2. Rows'd by report of Fame, the Nations meet, / . . . No *Persian* Carpets spread th' imperial way, / But scatter'd Limbs of mangled Poets lay; / Martyrs of Pies and Reliques of the Bum —John Dryden, "MacFlecknoe, or a Satyr Upon the True— Blew Protestant Poet, T.S."
   The scattered limbs are the discarded poems of neglected poets, with the paper now being put to a second use, for pie-wrapping or—worse—chamber-pot tissue.

3. My old life was a discarded husk —L. P. Hartley, *The Go-Between*

4. Many women actually abandon ship before they reach the pinnacle of their success —Linda Liehter, Entertainment lawyer, quoted in *The New York Times,* January 17, 1993

5. One day you turned away / and left me here / to founder in the stillness of your wake —Mark Strand, "The Man in the Mirror," *Selected Poems*
   The despair of leave-taking is heightened by the fact that the "wake" of the boat is silent.

6. Sooner or later . . . Krzysinski is going to be opening the bays and dropping Jake without a parachute, golden or otherwise —Scott Turow, *Pleading Guilty*
   The golden parachute became a popular business metaphor for benefit-loaded employment contracts between 1980–85. No matter what happened to their jobs or their companies, executives with such contracts were able to bail out with their wealth intact.

■ ABILITY

See also: *ACHIEVEMENT; GROWTH; SELF-
CONFIDENCE*

1. With the development of technique and variety, more rich and colorful flowers of silk skill were out —Anon., Legend on exhibit in The Silk Museum, Hangzhou, China
   The English may be strange, but the metaphor loses nothing in the translation. The flowering of skill is obvious in the display of weavings.

2. Moving blindfold in this matter, you have added to the burden of anxiety which she has had to bear, by innocently threatening her secret with discovery, through your exertions —Wilkie Collins, *The Moonstone*

3. Skill and confidence are an unconquered army —George Herbert, *Outlandish Proverbs*

4. There were several experienced verbal stunt pilots in the Glass family —J. D. Salinger, *Franny and Zooey*

■ ABSENCE

See also: SEPARATION

1. Absence . . . the dark-room in which lovers develop negatives —Anon., d.u.

2. Absence . . . the pain without the peace of death —Thomas Campbell, "Absence"

3. Absence that common cure of love — Miguel de Cervantes, *Don Quixote*
   This contradicts the proverbial "absence makes the heart grow fond."

4. Absence is death, or worse, to them that love —Sir Philip Sidney, "A Country Song"

■ ABUNDANCE

See also: EXCESS; MANY; RICHES

1. My cup runneth over —The Bible, *O.T., Psalms 23:5*
   Émile Zola, charged with libel after he accused the press of anti-semitism in connection with the Dreyfus Affair, told the court, "And my condemnation . . . will be only a fresh seed of passion and disorder. The cup, I tell you, is full; do not make it run over!"

2. And I am come down to deliver them . . . unto a land flowing with milk and honey —The Bible, *O.T., Exodus 3:8*
   This is a food metaphor in the form of metonymy. A land that is fertile becomes a land "flowing with milk and honey" in a substitution of specific terms that are closely associated with the general term.

3. Daddy was a fountain of money [to his young son reminiscing about a childhood family trip] —Harold Brodkey, "Verona: A Young Woman Speaks," *Esquire*, 1977

4. Shower upon him every earthly blessing, drown him in a sea of happiness, so that nothing but bubbles of bliss can be seen on the surface . . . even then out of sheer ingratitude, sheer spite, man would play you some nasty trick —Fyodor Mikhailovich Dostoevsky, *Notes from Underground*

5. A perfect torrent of information burst on them [a group of tourists in Italy] —E. M. Forster, *A Room With a View*

6. The mutual recognition agreement between Israel and the Palestine Liberation Organization . . . unearths a mother lode of diplomatic opportunities for the United States, which will no longer have to choose between friendships with Israel or the Arab world —Thomas L. Friedman, *The New York Times*, September 10, 1993
   Friedman used a commonly used mining metaphor.

7. There is an ocean of things for us to talk about and arrange —Joseph Hergesheimer, "The Token"
   One of the things the speaker is trying to arrange is the defection of her seaman lover from the ocean he loves.

8. In the hailstorm of publicity that surround the film's opening, Ms.[Chambers] Lynch has been trying hard to leap past the lurid to the metaphorical —Janet Maslin, "Review/Film," *The New York Times*, September 3, 1993
   The director of the movie, Boxing Helena, wanted audiences to look beyond a doctor's mutilating surgery to the metaphorical theme of love and obsession.

9. We add his letter to the large delta of unanswered mail on our desk —Christopher Morley, "On Unanswering Letters"
   The letter will lie there until "it has been gently silted over by about twenty other pleasantly postponed manuscripts."

10. Cleopatra: I'll set thee in a shower of gold, and hail rich pearls upon thee —William Shakespeare, *Antony and Cleopatra*, Act 2, scene 5, line 47
    The man promised this shower of plenty must assure Cleopatra that Antony is safe.

11. He exploded entire barrages of comments, jokes, puns, witticisms across the river to F.P.A. [columnist Franklin P. Adams] as a reward —Howard Teichmann, *George S. Kaufman*

 > *George S. Kaufman was still an unknown from New Jersey for whom seeing his words in print did "what the switch does for the electric light bulb."*

■ ACCEPTANCE

See: ADMIRATION

■ ACCUSATIONS

See also: BELIEFS; INSULTS

1. Many women, especially those who work in offices, have taken up Professor Hill's 75-trombone accusation —Anon., Editorial, *The New York Times*, October 10, 1992

 > *The metaphor is a double allusion, to Professor Anita Hill who brought charges of sexual molestation against Supreme Court nominee Clarence Thomas—and the trombone-playing Professor Hill of* The Music Man.

2. Your religion resides in your vulva — Anon., "The Story of the Negro Dorerame," *The Perfumed Garden of the Shaykh Nefzawi.*

3. Thief, / Give back that cloak of mine you nabbed . . . Unglue / them from your talons instantly —Catullus, Poem 25

 > *In this accusation against a visitor who has stolen or borrowed things from his host, the visitor is pictured as a hawk. The "glue" makes the basic metaphor come unglued, turning it into a* mixaphor.

4. They [the Arabs] have their fanatics, of course, but before we throw stones of gross generalizations, we ought to check our own glass house —Richard Cohen, *Washington Post Writers Group*, July 27, 1992

 > *The writer turns a common metaphor into an arresting image. Benjamin Franklin, in* Poor Richard's Almanack, *wrote "Don't throw stones at your neighbors, if your own windows are glass."*

5. The press typically makes a mayor its target in a periodic game of pin the tail on the donkey —Leland T. Jones, New York Mayor David Dinkins' spokesman, quoted *The New York Times*, July 25, 1993

 > *The metaphoric allusion to the children's game was prompted by a rather negative report on the Mayor's management of the riots in the Crown Heights section of Brooklyn. The mayor himself defended himself with a metaphor borrowed from Martin Luther King: "Bend your back and they'll ride it."*

6. It is time for all sensible people to wake up and stop this witch hunt. It is time to focus on the real problem: the laws that make it so hard to find good and legal child care —Anthony Lewis, "Abroad at Home," *New York Times*, February, 8, 1993

 > *Lewis dusted off this metaphor of the scapegoat when non-payment of taxes for domestic employees hobbled the appointments of several female candidates for high office. While usually associated with Salem, witch hunting is Biblical in origin.*

7. Othello: I should make very forges of my cheeks, / That would to cinders burn up modesty, / Did I but speak thy deeds — William Shakespeare, *Othello*, Act 4, scene 2, line 76

 > *Othello thinks his wife unchaste. If he told the list of her imagined sins, he would speak fire from the furnace of his mouth.*

8. Mercutio: A plague a [on] both your houses. / They have made worms' meat of me —William Shakespeare, *Romeo and Juliet*, Act 3, scene 1, line 110

9. Westmoreland: Wherefore do you so ill translate yourself . . . / Turning your books to greaves, your ink to blood, / Your pens to lances, and your tongue divine / To a loud trumpet and a point of war? —William Shakespeare, *The Second Part of King Henry the Fourth*, Act 4, scene 1, line 42

 > *Five metaphors are packed into one line.*

10. Gaunt: Thy deathbed is no lesser than thy land, / Wherein thou liest in reputation sick; / And thou, too careless patient as

thou art, / Committ'st thy anointed body to the cure / Of those physicians that first wounded thee —William Shakespeare, *The Tragedy of King Richard the Second,* Act 2, scene 1, line 95

> *Gaunt, dying, says that England is Richard's deathbed. There are four metaphors here: England as a deathbed, Richard as the patient, failing reputation as an illness, and the court flatterers as false physicians.*

■ ACHIEVEMENT

See also: ABILITY; PRIDE; SELF-ACTUALIZATION

1. An achievement is a bondage. It obliges on to a higher achievement —Albert Camus, *Notebooks: 1942–51*

2. Time / flourished the whip that made them climb / frail Everests —Michael Hamburger, "A Song About Great Men"
   > *"Whether an empire or a book / was the rich bait upon the hook / that landed them" the poet continues in a later metaphor.*

3. We can make our lives sublime, / And, departing, leave behind us / Footprints in the sands of time —Henry Wadsworth Longfellow, "A Psalm of Life"

4. I don't feel so sinful this day as I did, because I have written something and the tide is still high —Katherine Mansfield, January 12, 1922 diary entry

5. My job as an indoor aviator at the St. George Hotel was about what Miss Fitzpatrick [the protagonist's teacher] had predicted for me —Gloria Naylor, *Bailey's Cafe*
   > *Here we have a metaphor used as a euphemism for an elevator attendant.*

6. Messenger: He hath borne himself beyond the promise of his age, doing in the figure of a lamb, the feats of a lion — William Shakespeare, *Much Ado About Nothing,* Act 1, scene 1, line 12

■ ACTING/ACTORS

1. An actor is a sculptor who carves in snow —Edwin Booth, also ascribed to Lawrence Barrett, who lived at the same time

2. She has made an acting style of postnasal drip —Pauline Kael, quoted in obituary for actress Sandy Dennis, *The New York Times,* March 5, 1992

3. Those two ladies [Natasha Richardson and Maggie Smith] have the home-run parts, but I brought the baseball —Rob Lowe, quoted, *The New York Times,* January 3, 1993
   > *The interview with Lowe coincided with his appearance as Dr. Sugar in a public television production of Tennessee Williams's* Suddenly Last Summer.

4. It's a Vesuvius of a performance, all right, full of sound and fury, signifying an actor [Ron Leibman in *Angels in America*] hard at work —David Richards, "Sunday View," *The New York Times,* May 16, 1993

5. Hamlet: [When speaking] in the very torrent, tempest, and (as I may say) whirlwind of your passion, you must acquire and beget a temperance that may give it smoothness —William Shakespeare, *Hamlet,* Act 3, scene 2, line 6
   > *Hamlet tells the players to aim for articulateness as well as passion when speaking.*

6. Hamlet: O it offends me to the soul to hear a robustious periwig-pated fellow tear a passion to tatters, to very rags —William Shakespeare, *Hamlet,* Act 3, scene 2, line 9
   > *This comes from Hamlet's advice to the players and constitutes a source book of bad acting.*

7. The actor is a metaphysician in the dark —Wallace Stevens, "Of Modern Poetry"
   > *And the new poet, according to Stevens has to "construct a new stage" for "an invisible audience" . . . "The poem of the act of the mind."*

■ ACTION/INACTION

See also: MOBILITY/IMMOBILITY

1. When you are an anvil, be patient; when you are a hammer, strike —Anon., Arabian Proverb

2. The unpleasant truth is that House Speaker Thomas Foley is still backpedaling on his pledge of swift action to clean up campaign financing —Anon., Editorial, *New York Times,* February, 8, 1993

   Any bicyclist will recognize the thrust of the motion.

3. But once again, the Mayor has seemed able to bestir himself only when licked by the flames of crisis —Anon., Editorial, "Danger for Mayor Dinkins," *The New York Times,* August 22, 1993

   The Mayor, unable to put out the flames, was defeated.

4. Let me out of here, my motor's running— Anon., Headline, *The New York Times,* August 30, 1993

   This headline illustrates the use of metaphor to condense similes. The article talked of the Mets willingness "to swing away at first and second pitches as if they had left their car motors running in a no-standing zone and they had better places to go before dark."

5. I meant to see more of her. But I saw nothing. She was in the warehouse of intentions —Saul Bellow, *The Bellarosa Connection*

6. Littlefield and Agoglia [chief executives at NBC] decided not to pull the trigger right away —Peter J. Boyer, "Jay Leno's Hard Bargain," *The New Yorker,* November 9, 1992

   While they were not excessively quick on the trigger, the men did not hang fire for long. When they did pull the trigger, the producer of The Tonight Show was out of a job.

7. He [the onlooker] does not bring in the grass as green fodder, as the observer does; he turns it over and lets the sun shine on it —Martin Buber, "Dialogue"

8. For months I had been living in a cave with my own small demons. Now I was ready to go out into the desert, which was my life —Laurie Colwin, "Saint Anthony of the Desert," *The Lone Pilgrim*

9. After more than six months of near silence about the baseball team that he owns, rules and cherishes, George Steinbrenner shed his muzzle today and challenged the Yankees to produce a pennant —Jack Curry, *The New York Times,* September 14, 1993

   "Steinbrenner Transforms His Muzzle Into a Prod," wrote the headline writer, mounting the horse metaphor with one of his own.

10. Yet as President Clinton has said, "Their [the Soviet's] struggle to build free societies . . . is one of the great human dramas of our day." . . . But I would add that we could miss the great promise of the future by passively "sleepwalking through history" if we choose to be onlookers rather than actors in this drama —James Goodby, "Building Confidence and Partnership Through the Safe and Secure Dismantlement of Nuclear Weapons," April 13–16, 1993, United Nations Conference on Regional Security, Kyoto, Japan

    Ambassador Goodby uses two discrete but closely related metaphors in this sentence. The sleepwalking image is acknowledged but not attributed. The acting metaphor harks back to the familiar Shakespearian "all the world's a stage."

11. To reach the port of heaven, we must sail sometimes with the wind and sometimes against it,—but we must sail, and not drift, nor lie at anchor —Oliver Wendell Holmes, *The Autocrat of the Breakfast-Table*

    Holmes compares early friendships to the way a seaman uses the log to mark his progress. He continues, "Every now and then we throw an old schoolmate over the stern with a string of thought tied to him . . . to see the rate at which the string reels off while we are dashing along with the white foam and bright sparkle at our bows."

12. We left Fort Churchill and run out into the Bay with a light pair o' heels; but I had been vexed to death with their red-tape

rigging at the company's office —Sarah Orne Jewett, *The Country of the Pointed Firs*

The sea captain uses a dancing metaphor to describe the ship's sailing, and a sailing metaphor to describe the office paperwork.

13. Those are not proper judges of his conduct who have slumbered away their time on the down of plenty —Samuel Johnson, *The Life of Mr. Richard Savage*

14. Two of the Whips took the plunge together and two edged back from the abyss — Clifford Krauss, "Whips' Honeyed Touch the Recipe for Success," *The New York Times*, August 7, 1993

The action involved support for President Clinton's budget package. According to William Safire the nickname for the Congressional leader is a hunting metaphor from "whipper-in" for the man assigned to keep the hounds from straying in a fox hunt.

15. To be sure, people have been predicting for a decade that Shanghai is finally waking from its slumber, only to find that it is simply rolling over in its sleep —Nicholas D. Kristof, "Shanghai Journal," *New York Times*, September 1, 1992

Mr. Kristof commented on the swiftness of free-market conversion in Shanghai.

16. The conqueror must arrange to commit all his cruelties at once . . . Whoever acts otherwise, either through timidity or bad counsel, is always obliged to stand with knife in hand —Niccolo Machiavelli, *The Prince*

17. [Future discords] being foreseen they can easily be remedied, but if one waits till they are at hand, the medicine is no longer in time as the malady has become incurable —Niccolo Machiavelli, *The Prince*

18. I believe it is a duty assigned to a Yedo man [a man from Tokyo] to cheer up a man in distress with a kind word or two. He, however, was not so ready to dance to the pipe —Natsume Soseki, *Botchan*

Botchan tries to cheer up a fellow teacher who has been forced out of his assignment.

19. Even if you're on the right track, you'll get run over if you just sit there —Will Rogers, s.u.

20. Those Americans who believed that we could live under the illusion of isolationism wanted the American eagle to imitate the tactics of the ostrich. Now, many of those same people, afraid that we may be sticking our necks out, want our national bird to be turned into a turtle —Franklin Delano Roosevelt, Radio Address, February 23, 1942

This World War II Fireside Chat was designed to fight defeatism after a series of setbacks. Roosevelt wound up the metaphor of the eagle-as-turtle with "I know I speak for the mass of the American people when I say that we reject the turtle policy . . . ."

21. I believe that we have been right in the course we have charted. To abandon our purpose of building a greater, a more stable, and a more tolerant America, would be to miss the tide and perhaps to miss the port —Franklin Delano Roosevelt, Fireside Chat, April 14, 1938

The familiar metaphor of the ship of state serves as a building block for this metaphor which brought the President's fireside chat to a close.

22. We cannot . . . be content to rot by inches in ignoble ease within our borders, taking no interest in what goes on beyond them; sunk in a scrambling commercialism — Theodore Roosevelt, "The Strenuous Life"

"Sunk" and "scrambling" do nothing to unscramble the mixaphor, *but Teddy's sea of commercialism still threatens to engulf us.*

23. Hamlet: I . . . unpack my heart with words —William Shakespeare, *Hamlet*, Act 2, scene 2, line 590

Hamlet despises himself as "a whore" for letting off his anger with words rather than action.

24. King: The sun shines hot, and if we use delay, / Cold biting winter mars our hop'd-for hay —William Shakespeare, *The Third Part of Henry the Sixth*, Act 4, scene 8, line 60.

This is a variant of the proverbial metaphor urging action, make hay while the sun shines.

25. Duchess: Thou showest the naked pathway to thy life, / Teaching stern murder how to butcher thee —William Shakespeare, *The Tragedy of King Richard the Second,* Act 1, scene 2, line 30
    The Duchess implores John of Gaunt to avenge his late brother's death, threatening that he will share the same fate if he does not stir.

26. Northumberland: But, lords, we hear this fearful tempest sing, / Yet seek no shelter to avoid the storm. / We see the wind sit sore upon our sails, / And yet we strike not —William Shakespeare, *The Tragedy of King Richard the Second,* Act 2, scene 1, line 263
    The storm is the coming battle, for which they are making no preparations.

27. Today is the day. This is the bullet — Representative Al Swift, quoted by journalist Richard L. Berk, *The New York Times,* May 28, 1993
    This was one of several twists on to bite the bullet *heard during the House of Representatives debate on President Clinton's economic plan. According to word maven, William Safire, the metaphor gained political popularity during Lyndon B. Johnson's administration.*

28. The cup had come within the reach of her fingers, but she had not grasped it — Anthony Trollope, *The Duke's Children,* Volume 3

29. Delio: If too immoderate sleep be truly said / To be an inward rust unto the soul, / It then doth follow want of action / Breeds all black malcontents —John Webster, *The Duchess of Malfi,* Act 1, scene 1
    Delia concludes his metaphor with a simile: "and their close rearing, / Like moths in cloth, do hurt for want of wearing."

■ ACTIONS

See also: DESCRIPTIONS, MISC.; PROBLEMS AND SOLUTIONS

1. Michael never could remember which one of them it was who had put in the first oar —Conrad Aiken, "Impulse"
   This is akin to such common expressions as to dip one's toes in the water *and* to get one's feet wet. *It probably stems from* to put one's oar in another's boat *in the sense of meddling or interfering.*

2. Action is only coarsened thought —H. F. Amiel, *Journal,* December 30, 1850

3. Our acts are an abridged edition of our possibilities —Anon.

4. Clinton deftly navigates shoals of racial issues —Anon., Headline, *The New York Times,* June 17, 1992
   Sailing metaphors are perennial favorites for describing political difficulties. In this case, the Democratic presidential candidate Bill Clinton had criticized a controversial rap singer.

5. And, facing toward the window's light, / you swallow the warm air in giant gulps —Joseph Brodsky, "Sonnet"

6. I put him all into my arms / and staggered banged with terror through / a million billion trillion stars —e. e. cummings, "A Man Who Had Fallen Among Thieves"
   In this version of the parable of the Good Samaritan, the poet finds a man by the roadside, brushes the "stiffened puke" from him, and, though revolted, picks him up and carries him off.

7. Behavior . . . a mirror in which everyone displays his own image —Johann Wolfgang von Goethe, *Elective Affinities*

8. Each act is an island in time, to be judged on its own —Alan Lightman, *Einstein's Dreams*
   Lightman writes about the mysteries of space and time in the sense that they affect human psychology.

9. She took off one glove, stroked the bed table, and consulted the face of her finger —Vladimir Nabokov, *King, Queen, Knave*

10. Long ago, at the end of the last century, my great-grandfather . . . was deported to Siberia for having "let out the red rooster"

in his landlord's house —Yevgeny Yevtushenko, *A Precocious Autobiography*
The poet explains that the peasant expression "letting out the red rooster" means setting a fire.

■ ACTIVENESS/INACTIVENESS

See also: APATHY; DESCRIPTIONS, MISC.; POLITICS/POLITICIANS; WINNING/LOSING

1. Business as usual in eclipse / goes down to the sea in ships —Robert Lowell, "Waking Early Sunday Morning"
   The seaport is at rest on Sunday.

2. But . . . I couldn't put the old white horse out to pasture, hock the tin armor, stand the lance in a corner of the barn —John O'Hara, *Free Fall In Crimson*
   O'Hara's Travis McGee ponders that one can only retreat from an active life for so long, that "you can't cut your life back like some kind of ornamental shrub."

3. The purpose of a holiday is not to become as near as possible to a vegetable, but to refresh mind and body by enjoying the meat and potatoes of postponed activity in a changed atmosphere —William Safire, "Essay," *The New York Times*, August 26, 1993
   People often go on a vacation to "become a vegetable." Had Safire left out the incriminating "near as possible," he would have given us a second metaphor. He decried the media's "lust for political beefcake" and suggested that public figures like the President should be allowed "to recharge their batteries without relentlessly exhibiting themselves at leisure."

4. There is a sort of dead-alive, hackneyed people about . . . and unless Necessity lays about them with a stick, they will ever stand still —Robert Louis Stevenson, "An Apology for Idlers"

5. The blood of the mind fell / to the floor. I slept —Wallace Stevens, "A Weak Mind in the Mountains"

6. Mr. Bush is the Timex President: having taken a licking he is still ticking, with no clear indication of stopping anytime soon —Michael Wines, *The New York Times*, January 1, 1993
   The "lame duck" president's final flurry of activity notwithstanding, the White House staff was rumored to be "on auto-pilot."

■ ADAPTABILITY

See: FLEXIBILITY/INFLEXIBILITY

■ ADMIRATION

See also: MEN AND WOMEN

1. She [Cousin Bette] . . . saw the Baron nailed to the spot with admiration —Honoré de Balzac, *Cousin Bette*
   Thus begins the Baron's passion for a young woman which proves to be his family's downfall.

2. She drank in admiration, frankly courted it —Alice Munro, "A Real Life," *The New Yorker*, February 10, 1992

3. My admiration still lies there somewhere, a fossil in my memory —Frank O'Connor, "The Man of the World," *The New Yorker*, 1950–60

4. The sultan silenced them all saying he would take Hoja's words as the earring for his ear —Orhan Pamuk, *The White Castle*
   The sultan was much impressed with what he heard.

■ ADORATION

See: LOVE

■ ADULTERY

See: MARRIAGE; TEMPTATION

■ ADVANTAGEOUSNESS

See also: CHARACTERIZATIONS

1. There were few of the Pynchons left to sun themselves in the glow of the Judge's prosperity —Nathaniel Hawthorne, *The House of Seven Gables*

2. She might change . . . and find . . . that his limitations should some day prove . . . a blessing in disguise—a clear and quiet harbor, inclosed by a fine granite break-water —Henry James, *Portrait of a Lady*

3. Mr. Mandela's buoyant mood reflects a new marriage of expediency with President F. W. de Klerk after repeated break-downs in negotiations and periods of re-crimination —Bill Keller, "Despite Critics Right and Left, Mandela Pushes Talks With de Klerk," *The New York Times*, January 18, 1993

   Ten months later Mandela and de Klerk were jointly awarded the Nobel Peace Prize.

5. Clown: there is no true cuckold but ca-lamity —William Shakespeare, *Twelfth Night*, Act 1, scene 5

   The clown uses the image of marital betrayal as a metaphor for life as a game of chance to which everyone is married.

6. Florizel: O! the thorns we stand upon —William Shakespeare, *The Winter's Tale*, Act 4, scene 4, line 599

7. Sickness and trouble; that's what Ethan's had his plate full up with, ever since the first helping —Edith Wharton, *Ethan Frome*

   The image of a full plate has become a favorite way to describe any excess of work or problems. To illustrate, a New York Times *article (March 26, 1993) quoted a newly appointed head of the justice department as saying: "with personnel problems piled on her plate, Ms. [Janet] Reno has promised to decide whether William S. Sessions will keep his job." [He didn't!]*

■ ADVERSITY

See also: DIFFICULTIES; ILLNESS

1. The sea has no bottom and Jewish troub-les have no shores —Anon., Yiddish Proverb

2. They choose to sit / on the sharp points / of needles and thorns —Tun-Yu Chu, "To the Tune of Chien Tzu Mu-lan Hua"

3. My fellow Americans, our long national nightmare is over —Gerald Ford, Inau-gural Speech, 1975

   Nixon, while not impeached, resigned after the Watergate Hearings. According to William Safire, Ford's aide, Robert Hartmann, was the author of this simple but effective metaphor.

4. Friar: I'll give thee armor to keep off that word, / Adversity's sweet milk, philoso-phy. / To comfort thee though thou art banished —William Shakespeare, *Romeo and Juliet*, Act 3, scene 3, line 54

   Romeo is not appeased by the Friar's double metaphor, telling him to "Hang up Philosophy" unless it can reverse his "doom."

■ ADVERTISING

See: BUSINESS DESCRIPTIONS

■ ADVICE

See also: WISDOM

1. Advice is a stranger; if welcome he stays for the night; if not welcome, he returns home the same day —Anon., Malagasia Proverb

2. I say these things now . . . not by way of sinking one who is tossed by the waves, but as instructing those who are sailing with a favorable breeze, so that they may not be —(Saint) John Chrysostom, Ser-mon, c. 387

   The speaker was known as "the golden-mouthed."

3. Hitch your wagon to a star —Ralph Waldo Emerson, "Civilization," *Society and Solitude*

   A more poetic alternative by William Blake is "No bird soars too high if he soars with his own wing."

4. I thought I would sit back . . . and stuff advice in the cracks of the walls of their lives, but no longer feel responsible for sustaining them —Michelle Gillett, "Mothers to Daughters," *The Berkshire Eagle*, July 5, 1993
   A mother of grown daughters reflected on her role.

5. String your blood to chord with this music —Amy Lowell, "Little Ivory Figures Pulled with String"
   Blood is compared to a stringed instrument that makes its own music.

6. In levying taxes and in shearing sheep, it is well to stop when you get down to the skin —Austin O'Malley

■ AERIAL VIEWS

See also: CITIES; COUNTRIES, MISC.; NATURE SCENES; PLACES, MISC.; SKY/ SKYSCAPES; STARS

1. If you fly across the nation . . . the bones of the land are still apparent from ten thousand feet up —John Keats, "The Call of the Open Road"

2. Santa Teresa was a colored air map on the mountains' knees, the sailboats in the harbor white soap chips in a tub of bluing — Ross MacDonald, *The Moving Target*

3. It was a little city made of sugar cubes. The cubes increased in size —Ross MacDonald, "Wild Goose Chase," *The Name Is Archer*
   The imagery of this aerial view continues: "Cars crawled like colored beetles between the buildings, and matchstick figures hustled jerkily along the white morning pavements."

4. Already Buenos Aires was dyeing the horizon with pink fires, soon to flaunt its diadem of jewels —Antoine de Saint-Exupery, *Night Flight*

5. For now the little towns of Argentina were stringing through the night their golden beads, beneath the paler gold of the star-cities —Antoine de Saint-Exupery, *Night Flight*

6. The mantle of a golden evening had fallen on South America —Antoine de Saint-Exupery, *Night Flight*

7. The villages were lighting up, constellations that greeted each other across the dusk —Antoine de Saint-Exupery, *Night Flight*
   The pilot of the early prop plane looks down at a world that seems to reflect the heavens at night.

■ AFFECTION

See also: FEELINGS; LOVE; MEN AND WOMEN

1. Affection seemed to have died under the bruise that had fallen on its keenest nerves —George Eliot, *Silas Marner*
   The protagonist is bruised from being falsely accused of theft.

2. How wearily Ethel regarded Jim sometimes, as if she wondered why she had trained the vines of her affection on such a wind-shaken poplar —F. Scott Fitzgerald, "Bernice Bobs Her Hair," *Flappers and Philosophers*

3. Enobarbus: The itch of his affection should not then / Have nick'd [made a fool of, diminished] his captainship —William Shakespeare, *Antony and Cleopatra*, Act 3, scene 2, line 7

4. Martius: your affections / Are a sick man's appetite —William Shakespeare, *Coriolanus*, Act 1, scene 1, line 183

5. Cressida: If I could temporize with my affection / Or brew it to a weak and colder palate, / The like allayment could I give my grief —William Shakespeare, *Troilus and Cressida*, Act 4, scene 4, line 5

6. Affection is a coal that must be cool'd / Else, suffered, it will set the heart on fire —William Shakespeare, *Venus and Adonis*, line 231

Coriolanus expresses his contempt for the angry citizens, disdaining their affections as "a sick man's appetite."

■ AFFLICTION

See also: ADVERSITY; PAIN AND SUFFERING

1. I have chosen thee in the furnace of affliction —The Bible, *O.T., Isaiah 47:9*

2. Feed him with bread of affliction and water of affliction. —The Bible, *O.T., 1 Kings 22:27; 2 Chronicles 18:26*

3. Anath: I thought he was a dust-storm we had shut outside. / Even now I sometimes bite on the grit —Christopher Fry, *The Firstborn,* Act 1, scene 1
   Pharaoh's sister speaks of Moses, her foster child, who has just returned from exile. He brings with him his stormy protestations, and Pharoah's sister has trouble protecting him.

4. He could not have said with certitude if he found this blurry lady attractive. Near-sightedness is chaste —Vladimir Nabokov, *King, Queen, Knave*

■ AFTERLIFE

See: IMMORTALITY

■ AGE/AGING

See also: DEATH; MIDDLE AGE; OLD AGE; YOUTH AND AGE

1. I have lived in this old and frail tenement a great many years; it is very much dilapidated; and, from all that I can learn, my landlord doesn't intend to repair it — John Adams, June 17, 1826
   This was the frail, 90-year-old ex-president's reply to Daniel Webster's inquiry after his health.

2. But I cannot help wondering where the aging bear I should then be would look for honey in the arid gardens of a postwar world —Louis Auchincloss, "The Epicurean," *Three Lives*

The middle-aged anti-hero has entered the fray of the second World War at a time it is not going too well.

3. My days are in the yellow leaf; / The flowers and fruits of love are gone —Lord George Gordon Byron, "On This Day I Complete My Thirty-Sixth Year"

4. It's slow to set in at this age, not the violent shaking grip of death, instead—a slow leak, nothing more. A bicycle tire: rimless, thready, worn treadless already and now losing its fatness. A war of attrition. The tall camels of the spirit steering for the desert —Ethan Canin, "We Are Nighttime Travelers"
   The author dishes up metaphors to match the array of symptoms that accompany the protagonist's physical deterioration.

5. Astrov: My sun has set, yes —Anton Chekhov, *Uncle Vanya,* Act 3

6. Every woman after forty is a wasting asset —Cyril Connolly, "Covetousness." *The Seven Deadly Sins*

7. Age, death's twilight —John Donne, "Satyres"

8. Ride ten thousand daies and nights, / Till age snow white haires on thee —John Donne, "Song"
   The image derives from winter as the metaphor for old age, as well as the whiteness that provides the obvious comparison.

9. The grass has long been green on the graves of Shepherd Fennel and his frugal wife; . . . the baby in whose honor they all had met is a matron in the sere and yellow leaf —Thomas Hardy, "The Three Strangers"
   Hardy here tips his hat to Shakespeare's Macbeth, who in act 4 (scene 2, line 4) says, "My way of life / has fall'n into the sere, the yellow leaf. . ." to sum up his misuse of time and opportunity.

10. All merely graceful attributes are usually the most evanescent; nor does Nature adorn the human ruin with blossoms of new beauty that have their roots and prop-

er nutriment only in the chinks and crevices of decay —Nathaniel Hawthorne, *The Scarlet Letter*

11. In his prime, / Ere the pruning-knife of Time / Cut him down, / Not a better man was found —Oliver Wendell Holmes, Sr., "The Last Leaf"

12. Slowly my years / go into dark —Chiang Lu, "Spring Lingering"

13. Be with me, Beauty, for the fire is dying — John Masefield, "On Growing Old"

14. Age is gray, a toothless hag, / Stumblin in the dark —Isaac Peretz, "Sewing the Wedding Gown
    Personification is used as a metaphor.

15. She thought also of time's fingerprints on her thighs —Yannis Ritsos, "Marpessa's Choice"

16. Our days of winter count for double. That is the compensation of the old —George Sand (Amandine Aurore Lucie Dudevant), Letter to Joseph Dessauer, July 5, 1868

17. King: But on us both did haggish age steal on —William Shakespeare, *All's Well That Ends Well*, Act 1, scene 2, line 29
    A double metaphor to depict age as a witch and a stealthy thief.

18. Adam: My age is a lusty Winter, / Frosty, but kindly —William Shakespeare, *As You Like It*, Act 2, scene 3, line 52

19. Hamlet: There's the respect / That makes calamity of so long a life; / For who would bear the whips and scorns of time? —William Shakespeare, *Hamlet*, Act 3, scene 1, line 70

20. Clown: age with his stealing steps, / Hath claw'd me in his clutch —William Shakespeare, *Hamlet*, Act 5, scene 1, line 73
    The clown uses personification for his metaphor of age as a thief.

21. Othello: I am declined into a vale of years —William Shakespeare, *Othello*, Act 3, scene 3, line 265

22. Young Clifford: Wast thou ordain'd, dear father, / . . . to achieve / The silver livery of advised age —William Shakespeare, *The Second Part of Henry the Sixth*, Act 5, scene 2, line 45

23. York: Of Salisbury, who can report of him, / That winter lion, who in rage forgets, / Aged contusions and all brush of time —William Shakespeare, *The Second Part of Henry the Sixth*, Act 5, scene 3, line 1

24. When forty winters shall besiege thy brow, / And dig deep trenches in thy beauty's field —William Shakespeare, "Sonnet 2," line 1
    The poet threatens his love with the ravages of age, the plowman.

25. Then let not winter's ragged hand deface / In thee thy summer ere thou be distilled —William Shakespeare, "Sonnet 6," line 1

26. [Devouring Time] O, carve not with thy hours my love's fair brow, / Nor draw no lines there with thine antique pen —William Shakespeare, "Sonnet 19," line 8

27. I now fortify / Against confounding Age's cruel knife, / That he shall never cut from memory / My sweet love's beauty — William Shakespeare, "Sonnet 63," line 9

28. Gaunt: My oil-dried lamp and time-bewasted light / Shall be extinct with age and endless night —William Shakespeare, *The Tragedy of King Richard the Second*, Act 1, scene 3, line 221

29. The blossoms snow down in my hair; / The trees and I will soon be bare — William DeWitt Snodgrass, "April Inventory"
    Continuing the blossom imagery in a later metaphor, Snodgrass writes, "The sleek, expensive girls I teach, / Younger and pinker every year, / Bloom gradually out of reach."

30. And what would it be to grow old? For, after a certain distance, every step we take in life we find the ice growing thinner

below our feet, and all around us and behind us we see our contemporaries going through —Robert Louis Stevenson, "Aes Triplex"

> *The author gave a fresh twist to skating on thin ice, a commonly used metaphor for anyone who risks danger.*

31. Captain: [When men grow old]. Those who crowed were no longer cocks, but capons, and the pullets answered their call, so that when we thought the sun was about to rise we found ourselves in the bright moonlight amid ruins —August Strindberg, *The Father*, Act 2

32. Living now in death's immediate neighborhood, he was developing a soldier's jaunty indifference. —John Updike, "Playing With Dynamite," *The New Yorker*, October 5, 1992

33. Age with stealing steps has clawed me — Thomas Vaux, "The Aged Lover Renounceth Love"

> *The metaphor uses personification to portray time as a predatory animal.*

34. behold / Yourself old! . . . A vine among oaks —William Carlos Williams, "Soothsay"

35. I was very frightened by time's appetite — Irvin D. Yalom, *When Nietzsche Wept*

> *A fictional Dr. Joseph Breuer sees the decline of age as a sentence to be served, and wishes desperately that he could begin again.*

36. These gray bristles were, he knew, the advance scouts of a relentless, wintry invasion. And there would be no stopping the march of the hours, the days, the years —Irvin D. Yalom, *When Nietzsche Wept*

> *The warlike metaphor illustrates Dr. Joseph Breuer's distress at the physical signs of aging. He further reflects on his graying beard and sideburns as "the gray tide."*

37. An aged man is but a paltry thing, / A tattered coat upon a stick, unless / Soul clap its hands and sing, and louder sing / For every tatter in its mortal dress —

William Butler Yeats, "Sailing to Byzantium"

> *In two successive lines, Yeats has given us two of the most celebrated metaphors in poetry. The image of an old man as a scarecrow crops up again in his poetry. In "Among School Children," he speaks of "Old clothes upon old sticks to scare a bird."*

■ AGGRAVATION

See: IRRITANTS

■ AGGRESSION

See also: STRENGTH/WEAKNESS; WAR

1. A man in armor is his armor's slave — Robert Browning, "Herakles"

2. Then, as if in slow motion, she tumbles forward, a thrashing avalanche of patriotism and motherhood, crushing three spectators and a table of apple tartlets — Cristina Garcia, *Dreaming in Cuban*

> *A young artist who's painted a mural for her mother's bakery, watches the mother she has regarded as an antagonist fiercely defend the people who mock the mural.*

3. You're a damned little wooly lamb yourself, I suppose —Dashiell Hammett, *Red Harvest*

> *Hammett gives the metaphor of the lamb as a symbol of meekness a twist of irony.*

4. The three with the medals were like hunting hawks; and I was not a hawk, although I might seem a hawk to those who had never hunted; they, the three, knew better and so we drifted apart —Ernest Hemingway, "In Another Country"

> *The three soldiers in the simile had earned their medals by killing men; the soldier in the metaphor—the narrator—had earned his simply by being wounded at the front.*

5. I may have felt a kind of friendship for the poor minotaur in his maze [Edmund Wilson], so sadly dependent on the yearly

sacrifice of maidens —Mary McCarthy, *Intellectual Memoirs*

> *The allusion is to the mythological Bull that wandered in the Cretan maze, to which Athenian maidens were sacrificed every year. Wilson, the sexually needy minotaur, must have known he risked being spitted on by McCarthy's pen when he married her.*

6. Every man who has in him any real power of joy in battle knows that he feels it when the wolf begins to rise in his heart — Theodore Roosevelt, c. 1880s–90s

7. Queen: Seems he a dove? His feathers are but borrowed, / For he's disposed as the hateful raven —William Shakespeare, *The Second Part of Henry the Sixth,* Act 3, scene 1, line 75

8. King: O bloody times! / While Lions war and battle for their dens, / Poor harmless lambs abide their enmity —William Shakespeare, *The Third Part of Henry the Sixth,* Act 2, scene 5, line 73

> *The image reappears as a simile (5, 6, 7), when Henry declares "He flies the reckless shepherd from the wolf; / So first the harmless sheep doth yield his fleece, / And next his throat unto the butcher's knife."*

9. Bolingbroke: Destruction straight shall dog them at the heels —William Shakespeare, *The Tragedy of King Richard the Second,* Act 5, scene 4, line 140

> *To dog at someone's heels has become a common metaphor.*

10. Her skill as an executive was sometimes overshadowed by a reputation for an abrasive, take-no-prisoners style —Bernard Weinraub, *The New York Times,* August 30, 1993

> *Hollywood executive Dawn Steel had turned author of an autobiography at the time of this interview. Her explanation for why male executives rapidly advanced her career was "One was that I was funny. I wasn't heavy furniture."*

11. I'm not talking about that pack of young wolves that has been convinced since '36 that the whole universe is a playground in which it can kick the globe around like a football —A. B. Yehoshua, *Mr. Mani*

> *The first of two metaphors leading to a final simile depicts fiery young Germans as "young wolves." The narrator is a thoughtful German soldier who sees what is happening to the aspirations of the Hitler Reich.*

■ AGITATION

See also: CALMNESS/VOLATILITY; EXCITEMENT

1. Poisonville [town where novel is set] was beginning to boil under the lid —Dashiell Hammett, *Red Harvest*

2. The blood seethes and boils in the veins, the brains are boiling in the skull, the heart in the breast is glowing and bursting, the bowels a redhot mass of burning pulp — James Joyce, *A Portrait of the Artist as a Young Man*

3. You are too excited—you are on fire!" — Samuel J. May, Speech, 1861

> *Slavery was a highly emotional issue when Reverend May thus tried to calm down his fellow abolitionist William Lloyd Garrison.*

4. Chorus: Now all the Youth of England are on fire, / And silken dalliance in the wardrobe lies —William Shakespeare, *The Life of Henry the Fifth,* Act 2, Introductory Chorus, line 1

> *The metaphor of the young people fired up to go to war is followed by the image of their playing clothes stored in the closet.*

5. Narrator: My pulse was a drum solo [after being hit with a bottle] —Scott Wentworth, *Gunmetal Blues*

> *The voice belongs to the character played by the author of a 1992 Off-Broadway musical mystery.*

■ AGREEMENT/DISAGREEMENT

See also: CONFLICT; DIPLOMACY; FLEXIBILITY/INFLEXIBILITY; PEOPLE, INTERACTION; PROBLEMS AND SOLU-

TIONS; QUARRELS/QUARRELSOME-NESS

1. I talk cellar and he talks attic —Anon., Yiddish Proverb

2. Mr. Candy, hitting back smartly, said that Mr. Franklin was groping in the dark after sleep. Mr. Franklin, keeping the ball up on his side, said he had often heard of the blind leading the blind —Wilkie Collins, *The Moonstone*

    The metaphorical ball game is a verbal dispute in which a doctor tries to convince Franklin to take medicine for his nerves.

3. You rise to the bait of what I refuse to stand for —John Hollander, "Disagreements'

    It takes two to quarrel, even when one party to contention doesn't really believe what he says.

4. And if a beachhead of co-operation may push back the jungle of suspicion, let both sides join in creating a new endeavor —John F. Kennedy, Inaugural address, January 20, 1961

5. I think everyone agrees that it is far more important to prevent disputes from escalating to conflicts than to try to put out fires after they have started —Tommy Koh, *The Singapore Symposium,* United Nations. 1992

    Regional conflicts are the fires that will have to be put out if preventive diplomacy is not successful.

6. Whenever he had patiently and tolerantly given his son some rope, the boy had dug his heels in and argued in an even more extreme fashion —Naguib Mahfouz, *Palace of Desire*

    Al-Sayyid Ahmad tries to convince Kamal to study for a profession that will be lucrative and prestigious. To give a man enough rope is cowboy lingo, but an inversion of the metaphor results in Give a man enough rope and he'll hang himself. *The second metaphor signifying stubbornness and a refusal to move away from a position, is also in common usage.*

7. Most coverage has taken the form of evidence Ping-Pong: one scientist serves up a potential peril and another expert lobs back a calming reassurance —Anthony Ramirez, "Market Place," *The New York Times,* February 3, 1993

    Ramirez discussed the possible medical threats of cellular phones.

8. On our banners will beat the dark clouds of opposition from those who have entrenched themselves behind the stormy bulwarks of custom and authority —Elizabeth Cady Stanton, Keynote address, First Woman's Rights Convention, July 19, 1848

9. She can go in a minute . . . if the agreement is to go overboard she ought to see it sink —Rex Stout, *Fer-de-Lance*

    Nero Wolfe's sidekick, Archie Goodwin, addresses a man who wants to end an arrangement his sister made with Wolfe.

10. I want to be sure we're singing from the same hymnal —Scott Turow, *Pleading Guilty*

11. The spectacle of taxpayers' money being spent on people who can at least technically be described as former soldiers of the enemy army, has provoked a thunderclap of opposition —Sam Howe Verhovek, "Iraqi Rebels Seek Refuge in U.S. and Find Themselves in Crossfire," *The New York Times,* September 7, 1993

    Note the headline's use of the metaphor.

12. My parents were, psychologically, at opposite poles from one another —Yevgeny Yevtushenko, *A Precocious Autobiography*

■ AGRICULTURAL SCENES
See: DESCRIPTIONS, MISC.

■ AID
See: ASSISTANCE

■ AIMLESSNESS

1. Peter: Here we are, we lean on our lives /
   Expecting purpose to keep her date —
   Christopher Fry, *A Sleep of Prisoners*
       *Peter is just marking time while he waits for
       something to happen to him.*

2. He had lost all sense of things; in the
   absence of air and space, of light and sky,
   he circled aimlessly in the dense core of a
   huge ball —Peter Matthiessen, *At Play in
   the Fields of The Lord*
       *Matthiessen gives a sense of what it is like to be lost
       in a jungle.*

3. A shrill altercation between Jake and a
   new fling . . . is the major attempt to inject
   sustained laughter into a rudderless second act —Frank Rich, "Review/Thea-
   ter," *The New York Times*, March 25, 1992
       *The luckless play singled out for one of the critic's
       biting reviews was Neil Simon's* Jake's Women.

4. He [Pete Sampras] seems to have gone
   through the demons of too-much, too-
   soon that kept Mats Wilander in Connecticut in his mid-20's, that are turning
   introspective Boris Becker into a modern
   Flying Dutchman, a haunted vessel —
   George Vecsey, "Sports of the Times,"
   The New York Times, September 13, 1993
       *According to Vecsey the 23-year-old Sampras,
       who had just won his second U.S. Open trophy
       was on a surer career path than Becker, the mythic
       ship that never found a port after a Wimbledon
       win at age 17.*

5. Ashley arrived at the Fonda at the moment when Mrs. Wickersham was losing
   control of her life's rudder —Thornton
   Wilder, *The Eighth Day*
       *Mrs. Wickersham's rudder had heretofore steered
       her through a life of good works.*

■ ALERTNESS

See also: AWARENESS/UNAWARENESS

1. She [Tina Brown] can put her ear to the
   tracks and hear the rumble long before the
   train appears —Steven T. Florio, quoted,
   The New York Times, July 2, 1992
       *This compliment opened Deidre Carmody's story
       about Ms. Brown's appointment as editor of* The
       New Yorker. *The railroad metaphor continued
       with "The greatest challenge facing Ms. Brown
       . . . will be to restore the knack for reporting the
       rumble on the tracks and to do so in* The New
       Yorker's *voice."*

2. What radar on that woman! —Philip
   Roth, *Portnoy's Complaint*
       *Portnoy relates that his mother had such foresight
       that she warned her neighbors to take their drying
       laundry off the line before even a drop of rain had
       fallen.*

■ ALLIANCES

See also: CONNECTIONS

1. "Very true," said the Duchess: "flamin-
   goes and mustard both bite. And the moral of that is—'Birds of a feather flock
   together'" —Lewis Carroll, *Alice's Adventures in Wonderland*
       *Alice is quick to notice the faulty syllogism that
       engenders the flawed metaphor, and to assure the
       Duchess that mustard isn't a bird.*

2. Mutual interest, the greatest of all purpos-
   es, was the cement of this alliance —
   Henry Fielding, *The Life of Mr. Jonathan
   Wild the Great*
       *Jonathan makes a friend who is almost as great a
       scoundrel as he is himself.*

3. One would rather swim than get in the
   same dinghy as the P.C. [politically cor-
   rect] folk —Robert Hughes, *Culture of
   Complaint*

4. While Mr. [Edward] Koch and Mr. [Ru-
   dolph] Giuliani draw similar pictures of a
   city needing firm leadership and a new
   emphasis on law and order, they would be
   strange   bedfellows   —Catharine   S.
   Manegold, *The New York Times*, August
   31, 1993
       *The former mayor of New York was rumored to be
       on the verge of endorsing the candidate who ended
       up winning. The now common metaphor for odd
       political alliances, had a more literal meaning in
       Shakespeare's day, as illustrated in* The Tem-

pest *when Caliban says that the best way to deal with a storm is "to creep under his gaberdine; there is no other shelter hereabout: misery acquaints a man with strange bedfellows."*

5. Agrippa: To knit your hearts / With an unslipping knot, take Antony / Octavia to his wife —William Shakespeare, *Antony and Cleopatra*, Act 1, scene 5, line 130

   Agrippa thus advises Antony to marry Caesar's widowed sister. In Act 5, scene 2, Cleopatra uses the knot as a metaphor for difficult-to-resolve problems when she asks Charmian to untie the "intrinsicate" knot of life.

6. March: For both of you are birds of the self-same feather —William Shakespeare, *The Third Part of Henry the Sixth*, Act 3, scene 3, line 161

   The commonly used variant of this metaphor for the attraction of like-minded people to one another is birds of a feather flock together.

7. Yusef: Take strength from me and become the arrow to my bow —August Strindberg, *Simoom*

   Yusef and his beloved, Biskra, pool their hatred against the Frank.

8. Neither can I, a believing Communist, equate the essence of my religion with the crooks who climb on its bandwagon — Yevgeny Yevtushenko, *A Precocious Autobiography*

   The poet uses a common metaphor to explain that you cannot judge a philosophy by the failings of its practitioners.

■ ALONENESS

See: ISOLATION

■ AMBIGUITY

See: CLARITY/AMBIGUITY

■ AMBITION

See also: DESIRE; DREAMS; HOPE

1. He who sacrifices his conscience to ambition burns a picture to obtain the ashes — Anon., Chinese Proverb

2. But he always yoked his ambition to the chariot of virtue —Louis Auchincloss, "The Stoic," *Three Lives*

3. The young lions roar after their prey — The Bible, O.T., *Psalms 104:21*

   Irwin Shaw's novel The Young Lions *pictures soldiers in World War II as those who do the roaring.*

4. And now let us discard all . . . hankerings after the gilded crumbs which fall from the table of power —Henry Clay, speech, 1850

   This metaphor illustrates the eloquence with which the senator managed to earn his nickname as "The Great Compromiser."

5. Ambition is the mind's immodesty —Sir William Davenant, *Gondibert*

6. I should like to bear leaves and flowers and fruit, I should like the whole world — Margaret Drabble, *A Summer Bird-Cage*

   The novel's protagonist wants the satisfactions of love and marriage, and a career.

7. Ambition and love are the wings of great actions —Johann Wolfgang von Goethe, *Iphigenie and Tauris*

8. "The moral flabbiness born of the exclusive worship of the bitch-goddess SUCCESS . . . is our national disease —Henry James, letter to H.G. Wells, 1906

9. Ambition is but avarice on stilts and masked —Walter Savage Landor, *Imaginary Conversations*

10. Too many people have gone in for this senseless chasing of rainbows —Frederick Loew, October 1, 1964, explanation of his retirement

    "How many rainbows does one need?" the composer asks. Rainbow chasing as a metaphor for wasteful or insubstantial ambition was popularized by political journalists during the 1890s. Dorothy's plaintive "Somewhere Over the Rainbow" in The Wizard of Oz *put a more idealistic cast on the metaphor.*

11. Ambition is a little creeper that creeps and creeps in your heart night and day, singing a little song, 'Come and find me, come and find me' —Carl Sandburg, "Three Boys with Jugs of Molasses and Secret Ambitions"

    The metaphor is introduced midway and as the story's closing image.

12. Prince Hal: Ill-weav'd ambition how much art though shrunk! —William Shakespeare, *The First Part of King Henry the Fourth*, Act 5, scene 3, line 88

    Where once Hotspur's ambition was unbounded "now two paces of the vilest earth / Is room enough."

13. Hamlet: O God, I could be bounded in a nutshell, and count myself a king of infinite space, were it not that I have bad dreams —William Shakespeare, *Hamlet*, Act 2, scene 2, line 256

    These dreams, says Guildenstern "indeed, are ambition, for the very substance of the ambitious is merely the shadow of a dream."

14. Brutus: lowliness is young ambition's ladder, / Whereto the climber-upward turns his face; / But when he once attains the upmost round, / He then unto the ladder turns his back —William Shakespeare, *Julius Caesar*, Act 2, scene 1, line 23

15. Brutus: Ambition's debt is paid —William Shakespeare, *Julius Caesar*, Act 3, scene 1, line 82

    Caesar is dead, slain by Brutus.

16. Macbeth: I have no spur / To prick the sides of my intent, but only / Vaulting ambition, which o'er-leaps itself / And falls on the' other —William Shakespeare, *Macbeth*, Act 1, scene 7, line 25

    Ambition is shown as a rider who jumps on his horse so over-eagerly that he misses the saddle, and falls down on the other side. In "Lycidas" (1637), John Milton wrote "Fame is the spur that the clear spirit doth raise."

17. Gloucester: And dogged York, that reaches at the moon, / whose overweening [presumptuous] arm I have cut back —

William Shakespeare, *The Second Part of Henry the Sixth*, Act 3, scene 1, line 158

18. King: the eagle-winged pride / Of sky-aspiring and ambitious thoughts / With rival-hating envy set on you / To wake our peace, which in our country's cradle / Draws the sweet infant breath of gentle sleep —William Shakespeare, *The Tragedy of King Richard the Second*, Act 1, scene 3, line 130

    Here we have two unrelated metaphors—the eagle as ambition and the country as a young infant in its cradle—strung together.

19. King Richard: Northumberland, thou ladder wherewithal / The mounting Bolingbroke ascends my throne —William Shakespeare, *The Tragedy of King Richard the Second*, Act 5, scene 1, line 55

20. King Richard: Thoughts tending to ambition, . . . / how these vain weak nails / May tear a passage through the flinty ribs / Of this hard world —William Shakespeare, *The Tragedy of King Richard the Second*, Act 5, scene 5, line 18

21. Antonio: Ambition, madam, is a great man's madness, / That is not kept in chains and close-pent rooms, / But in fair lightsome lodgings, and is girt / With the wild noise of prattling visitants, / Which makes it lunatic beyond all cure —John Webster, *The Duchess of Malfi*, Act 1, scene 2

■ AMBIVALENCE

See also: DOUBT; UNCERTAINTY

1. When I talk to my daughters about how they might achieve success, a dry crumb of ambivalence rises in my throat —Michelle Gillett, "Mothers to Daughters," *The Berkshire Eagle*, July 5, 1993

2. To / you I offer my hull and the tattered cordage / of my will —Frank O'Hara, "To the Harbormaster"

The poet writes that he is "always tying up and then deciding to depart."

■ AMERICA/AMERICANS

See also: COUNTRIES, MISC.

1. America! half brother of the world! — Philip James Bailey, "The Surface," *Festus*

2. Most Americans . . . have a sort of permanent intoxication from within, a sort of invisible champagne —G. K. Chesterton, *The New York Times,* June 28, 1931

3. It [America] is the uncrossed desert and the unclimbed ridge. It is the star that is not reached and the harvest that's sleeping in the unplowed ground —Lyndon B. Johnson, Inaugural address, January 20, 1965

4. America is a tune. It must be sung together —Gerald Stanley Lee, *Crowds*

5. America is a supremely wasteful civilization about to be swept away by a rising tide of plastic debris —Christopher Lehmann-Haupt, "Books of the Times," *The New York Times,* June 9, 1992
   The review was of Rubbish! The Archeology of Garbage by William Rathje and Cullen Murphy.

6. America . . . can she, poor giant, tormented girl, deliver a babe of a new world — Norman Mailer, *The Armies of the Night: History as a Novel, The Novel as History*

7. The surface of American society is covered with a layer of democratic paint, but from time to time one can see the old aristocratic colors breaking through — Alexis-Charles-Henri de Tocqueville, *Democracy in America, Vol. 1*

8. America is God's Crucible, the great Melting Pot where all races of Europe are merging and reforming —Israel Zangwill, *The Melting Pot,* Act One
   This has become a popular catch phrase for America's population. A salad bowl in which "the lettuce can still be distinguished from the chicory, the tomatoes from the cabbage" is a more multi-culturally attuned image suggested by Carl N. Degler in Out of Our Past: The Forces That Shaped Modern America, 1970. *Another popular variant is "a mosaic." Politically correct or not, Zangwill's metaphor lives. In a June 19, 1992 public television script* The First Universal Nation, *Ben Wattenberg wrote that "the melting pot is alive, flourishing and expanding." In a November 17, 1982 column about legalizing homosexuals in the military, Russell Baker recalled recruits of the 1940s being "tossed into the melting pot that was the typical military barracks." The following week he wrote about the shift from melting pot to "uneasy federation of hostile tribal cultures."*

■ ANCESTRY/ANCESTORS

See also: FAMILIES/FAMILY RELATIONSHIPS; HISTORY

1. To forget one's ancestors is to be a brook without a source, a tree without a root — Anon., Chinese Proverb

2. A good tree cannot bear bad fruit, or a poor tree good fruit. And when a tree does not yield good fruit it is cut down and burnt. That is why we say you will recognize them by their fruit —The Bible, *N. T., Matthew 7:20*
   Variations of this also appear in Matthew 11:33 *and* Luke 6:43. *A commonly used everyday version is* The apple doesn't fall far from the tree.

3. For all the Cowan family's warmth . . . our pasts had been amputated. We were orphans in history —Paul Cowan, *An Orphan in History: Retrieving a Jewish Legacy*

4. Giving an account of as many of our hero's ancestors as can be gathered out of the rubbish of antiquity, which hath been carefully sifted for that purpose —Henry Fielding, *The Life of Mr. Jonathan Wild the Great*
   This is the heading for Chapter 2, very much in the Victorian tradition.

5. I am the son of some man's wild oats, the son of chance and misfortune —Carlos Fuentes, *The Old Gringo*

    A wild oat is actually a translation of the Latin Avena fatua, for an actual grass weed. The figurative use of sowing one's wild oats dates back to the sixteenth century.

6. I had learned, too, the very remarkable fact that the stem of the Usher race, all time-honored as it was, had put forth, at no period, any enduring branch —Edgar Allan Poe, "The Fall of the House of Usher"

    The last two Ushers, brother and sister, end their line horribly in this story.

7. Henry: Thy mother felt more than a mother's pain, / And yet brought forth less than a mother's hope; / To wit an indigested and deformed lump / Not like the fruit of such a goodly tree —William Shakespeare, *The Third Part of Henry the Sixth*, Act 5, scene 6, line 49

    Henry uses the metaphor of a good tree bearing rotten fruit to tell the hunchbacked Richard what he thinks of him. Richard responds by stabbing him, asserting that he was born legs forward and "with teeth" which "plainly signified / That I should snarl and bite and play the dog" (line 76).

8. Richard: The royal tree has left us royal fruit, / Which, mellow'd by the stealing hours of time, / Will well become the seat of majesty —William Shakespeare, *The Tragedy of King Richard the Third*, Act 3, scene 7, line 166

    Here the cut-tree metaphor depicts a hypocritical refusal to accept the crown. The expression family tree *for all the members or descendants of a family group has been in common use since about 1800.*

9. Toby: Look where the youngest wren of mine comes —William Shakespeare, *Twelfth Night*, Act 3, scene 2, line 66

    "mine" is often printed as "nine" as an allusion to the fact that wrens lay from nine to ten eggs and that the last of the brood—like Toby's daughter Maria—is generally the smallest.

10. Mrs. Manford spoke of them [those with "old New York Blood"] with mingled contempt and pride, as if they were the last of the Capetians, exhausted by a thousand years of sovereignty. Her own red corpuscles were tinged with a more plebeian dye —Edith Wharton, *Twilight Sleep*

    The metaphor rests on the foundation on the simile about her "blue-blooded" first husband's family.

■ ANGER

See also: PERSONALITY PROFILES; WORDS AS WEAPONS

1. This thought cooled his boiling anger and brought a calm pride and satisfaction —Ryūnosuke Akutagawa, "Rashōmon"
    Anger is often associated with heat.

2. Anger is a thorn in the heart —Anon., Yiddish Proverb

3. Anger is a bow that will shoot sometimes when another feeling will not —Henry Ward Beecher, *Life Thoughts*

4. Anger repressed can poison a relationship as surely as the cruelest words —Joyce Brothers, When Your Husband's Affection Cools," *Good Housekeeping*, May 1972

5. Ben: She has been gathering foul weather in her mouth, and now it rains out at her eyes —William Congreve, *Love For Love*, Act 3, scene 3

6. He had been loading the gun to shoot the nameless fury which pursued him ten, twenty, a good many years before. All that had happened now was that the wraith had taken a name —Joan Didion, *Run River*

    The man whose figuratively loaded gun became a literal death weapon is the protagonist's husband. The wraith is her lover.

7. Anger broke the pane of glass between us —Nancy Friday, *My Mother, My Self*

8. Only three chairs and an empty table top separated him [Woody Allen] from Ms. Farrow, a still figure . . . a small, smolder-

ing volcano —William Grimes, *The New York Times,* March 25, 1993

> *The metaphoric portrait of the pixie actress concluded an article about the famous couple's acrimonious custody battle. A similar use of the metaphor can also be found in Act 4 of James M. Barrie's* The Admirable Chrichton *when Lord Loam gloomily refers to the title character with "We're sitting on a volcano."*

9. As I walked on, anger turned over in its sleep in me —John Hersey, "Mr. Quintillian," *The Yale Review,* Fall 1987

10. Anger is a brief lunacy —Horace, *Epistles, I*

11. Sometimes it seemed as if he, [Mark Twain], let loose all the artillery of Heaven against an intruding mouse —Helen Keller, *Our Mark Twain*

> *The metaphor is a gentle jab at Twain's tendency to get into a frenzy about minor as well as major injustices.*

12. [A voter revolution] sweeping all before it in a tsunami of voter rage —Michael Kelly, *The New York Times,* June 12, 1992

> *On October 7, 1993, another* Times *writer, Anna Quindlen, wrote that Senator Phill Gramm was "riding a tsunami of public opinion" when he urged U.S. withdrawal from Somalia.*

13. People feel bruised, they feel hurt . . . I think they were determined to give the Government a bloody nose —John Major, quoted in article headlined "British Leader Links Tories' Election Loss to Economic Slump," *New York Times,* May 9, 1993

> *The Prime Minister of England felt the economy made the people fighting mad.*

14. General Carreno followed him along the terrace and found him pissing his ammoniacal bitterness into the pots of geranium —Gabriel García Márquez, *The General in his Labyrinth*

15. She has a real gift for honing her anger to an epigrammatic edge —Michael Vincent Miller, "Books of the Times," *The New York Times,* May 17, 1992

> *Miller was reviewing Wendy Kaminer's* I'm Dysfunctional, You're Dysfunctional.

16. Vinegar he poured on me all his life; I am well marinated; how can I be honey now? —Tillie Olsen, *Tell Me a Riddle*

17. I am a burning bush. / My rage is a cloud of flame —Marge Piercy, "A just anger," *To Be of Use*

18. He became a hurricane of wrath —Katherine Anne Porter, *Noon Wine* in *Pale Horse, Pale Rider*

19. Angry men make themselves beds of nettles —Samuel Richardson, *Clarissa*

> *A bed of nettles is the metaphor for a thorny, difficult life—as a bed of roses would imply a delightful one.*

20. Volscian: Anger's my meat; I sup upon myself / And so shall starve with feeding —William Shakespeare, *Coriolanus,* Act 4, scene 2, line 50

21. King Richard: Let's purge this choler without letting blood —William Shakespeare, *The Tragedy of King Richard the Second,* Act 1, scene 1, line 153

> *Medieval medicine had the body controlled by four humors; blood, black bile, yellow bile, and phlegm. Anger, or choler, was cured by bloodletting.*

22. I let the night / and the thick woods of my anger enclose me —Charlie Smith, "Defiance," *The New Yorker,* March 22, 1993

> *Smith's poem about a man's remembrance of his defiance of his father began, "I go through periods, a grown man, still reluctant / to talk to my father."*

■ ANGER, DIVINE

See also: GOD; PAIN AND SUFFERING

1. The arrows of the Almighty are within me, the poison whereof drinketh up my spirit —The Bible, *Job 6:4*

2. And the angel . . . gathered the vine of the earth, and cast it into the great winepress

of the wrath of God —The Bible, *N.T.*, *Revelation 4:19*

> *This metaphor is the obvious source for Julia Ward Howe's line in "The Battle Hymn of the Republic," when she writes "He is trampling out the vintage where the grapes of wrath are stored."*

3. There are the black clouds of God's wrath now hanging directly over your heads, full of the dreadful storm, and big with thunder —Jonathan Edwards, "Sinners in the Hands of an Angry God"

> *"The bow of God's wrath is bent, and the arrow made ready on the string . . . " writes Edwards at another point.*

4. The floods of God's vengeance have been withheld; . . . if God should only withdraw his hand from the floodgate, it would immediately fly open, and the fiery floods . . . would rush forth —Jonathan Edwards, "Sinners in the Hands of an Angry God"

> *The name of Jonathan Edwards has been synonymous with "fire and brimstone" preaching since the eighteenth century.*

5. Consider the fearful danger you are in: 'tis a great furnace of wrath, a wide and bottomless pit, full of the fire of wrath — Jonathan Edwards, "Sinners in the Hands of an Angry God"

> *Edwards paints a scary picture of hell. Each sinner hangs "by a slender thread, with the flames of divine wrath flashing about it, and ready every moment to singe it, and burn it asunder." One can only attribute Edwards' great popularity to the masochism of his parishioners.*

■ ANIMALS

1. As the train stopped a soft pink tide of pigs rose out of the station-yard —Kay Boyle, "On the Run," *Wedding Day and Other Stories*

2. His sky-splashed mane / Hummed with the current of surcharged hoofs —Melvin Walker La Follette, "The Blue Horse"

3. See him [a pig] in the dish, his second cradle, how meek he lieth! —Charles Lamb, "A Dissertation Upon Roast Pig"

4. His [the pig's] memory is odoriferous— he hath a fair sepulchre in the grateful stomach of the judicious epicure—and for such a tomb might be content to die — Charles Lamb, "A Dissertation Upon Roast Pig"

> *This is obviously the view of the epicure. One wonders whether the pig would agree.*

5. Chariots / like a running stream / so many / The horses / curveting dragons —Li Yu, "To the Tune of Wang Chiang-nan"

> *A simile, picturing the smooth movement of the carriages, is completed with the dragon metaphor for the horses pulling them.*

6. [Kittens] bitten navel cords / barely dried, / already fierce / at the trough —John Montague, "Mother Cat"

> *The trough becomes a nursing metaphor (And how many mothers would equate the breast with the square box used for feeding animals?)*

7. [A reindeer's] candelabrum-headed ornament —Marianne Moore, "Rigorists"

8. I shall not forget him— / that Gilgamesh / among the hairy carnivora—that cat — Marianne Moore, "The Monkeys"

> *Moore places her cat among the mythical, epic heroes by alluding to the legendary Babylonian king.*

9. [The porcupine] in distressed— / pincushion thorn-fur coats, / everything is battle-dressed —Marianne Moore, "His Shield"

> *Moore might have said that the porcupine's fur was as thorny as a pincushion. She chooses the metaphoric form over the weaker simile, and makes it more unusual with her use of adjective. The thorns and pincushion do not describe the fur; they are the fur.*

10. Toto [Dorothy's dog in *The Wizard of Oz*]: that little yapping hairpiece of a creature, that meddlesome rug! —Salman Rushdie, [analysis of] *The Wizard of Oz*

The humor in Rushdie's lengthy analysis of the movie that greatly influenced his youth arises from the use of the slang term, "rug," for a hairpiece, or wig.

11. Horatio: The cock, that is the trumpet to the morn, / Doth with his lofty and shrill-sounding throat / Awake the god of day —William Shakespeare, *Hamlet*, Act 1, scene 1, line 148

12. At your approach the great horse stomps and paws / Bringing the hurricane of his heavy tail —Karl Shapiro, "Nostalgia"

13. A polar bear . . . his huge paws wearing short boots of mud —Jean Stafford, "In the Zoo," *The New Yorker*, 1950–60

14. "Magic itself, tact by wavelength," as his master described him —George Steiner, "Books," *The New Yorker*, August 24, 1992
    This description of the cat, Bebert gives almost magical properties to the feline. Steiner's review of Frederic Vitoux's biography of Celine shows that he likes the cat but not the cat's master, Celine.

15. In sheen-swept pastureland, the horse's neck / Clothed with its usual thunder and the stones / Beginning now to tug their shadows in / And track the air with glitter —Richard Wilbur, "Lying"
    This is one of a series of images to which, according to the poet, we are "merely bearing witness."

■ ANIMATION

See also: CHARACTERISTICS; PERSONALITY PROFILES

1. He whose face gives no light, shall never become a star —William Blake, "Proverbs of Hell"
   There is a double meaning to the word "star"—both in the physical sense, which becomes the metaphor and which is introduced by "light," and in the more general sense of being outstanding.

2. The pleasures of living did more than percolate his chunky person. They boiled over —John Mason Brown, Introduction, *The Portable Woollcott*

Compare this metaphoric description of Alexander Woollcott's ebullience with Ernest Longfellow's portrait of his father as a man who "was not a rushing river, boiling and tumbling over rocks, but the placid stream flowing through the quiet meadows."

3. [Jesse] Jackson's grandmother—a small, sprightly cricket of a lady, in her eighties —Marshall Fraidy, *The New Yorker*, April 15, 1992

4. He was a cork that could not be kept under water many moments at a time —Mark Twain, *The Gilded Age*
   The colorful Colonel Sellers is undaunted by floundering fortunes.

5. A charming woman . . . a touch of the bird about her, of the jay, blue-green, light, vivacious —Virginia Woolf, *Mrs. Dalloway*
   The metaphor describes the novel's title character.

■ ANNOYANCES

See: IRRITANTS

■ ANXIETY

See: WORRY

■ APATHY

See also: EXCITEMENT

1. I'm just not up to this, I'm really running on empty —Alice Adams, "Earthquake Damage," *The New Yorker*, 1990
   An earthquake in San Francisco had forced the narrator's plane to return to its departure point, Toronto.

2. President Buchanan . . . Our great iceberg melting away —Anon., *Vanity Fair*, 1861, cartoon headline
   This was the text accompanying a cartoon that depicted President Buchanan, "the president of icy indifference," melting away.

3. Mr. Cogito tears off / the bandages of polite indifference —Zbigniew Herbert, "Mr. Cogito—the Return"

4. The color of the voter's light is amber, not green —William Safire, "Essay," *The New York Times*, September 21, 1992
   The unenthusiastic voters he refers to were the French and the issue was their willingness to join a union of European currencies.

5. After Nora, my volcano seems more or less extinct —Scott Turow, *Pleading Guilty*
   Nora is the protagonist's ex-wife whose "coming out" as a lesbian left him feeling emotionally and sexually bereft.

6. She didn't believe he ever opened a book nowadays: he was living on the dwindling capital of his early enthusiasms —Edith Wharton, *Twilight Sleep*

■ APOCALYPSE

See: DESTRUCTION/DESTRUCTIVENESS

■ APOLOGY

1. Apology is only egotism wrong side out —Oliver Wendell Holmes, Sr., *The Professor at the Breakfast Table*

2. I was quite indifferent as to how my blunders in class would affect the students . . . I am timid at heart, but am not a man who will look back with his hands on the plough —Natsume Soseki, *Botchan*
   In the life of this new teacher, there is no room for regret. Natsume is here using a folk saying to indicate that Botchan intends to forge ahead.

3. He [Bill Clinton, during his democratic primary campaign] seemed to be doing a complicated minuet with his real self, the dance of the apologist for the person he once was —Anna Quindlen, "Public & Private," *The New York Times*, April 8, 1992
   Quindlen explained her wariness of candidate Clinton's pragmatism with a sentence containing personification and a metaphor associated with the world of finance: "Every four years idealism

seizes me by the throat and I wait for a white knight." She expressed hope that he would shake the voters' hands and look into their eyes "at least metaphorically."

4. Beatrice: Will you not eat your word? / Benedick: With no sauce that can be devised to it —William Shakespeare, *Much Ado About Nothing*, Act 4, scene 1, line 284
   This is a forerunner to the popular expression I'll make you eat those words.

■ APPAREL

See: FASHION AND STYLE

■ APPEARANCE

See: PHYSICAL APPEARANCE

■ APPEARANCE

See also: PHYSICAL APPEARANCE

1. The outward forms the inward man reveal— / We guess the pulp before we eat the peel —Oliver Wendell Holmes, Sr., "A Rhymed Lesson"

2. The paramount value of looking right is not something you walk away from . . . it is something you embrace, the broken plank you are left with after the ship has gone down —Jane Smiley, *A Thousand Acres*
   When life is in a shambles, only appearance matters, for, as Polonius says in Hamlet, "the apparel oft proclaims the man."

■ APPEASEMENT

See also: COMPROMISE

1. No man can tame a tiger into a kitten by stroking it —Franklin Delano Roosevelt, Radio Address, December 29, 1940
   By the time Roosevelt gave this famous talk, the metaphoric tigers, the Nazis, failed to respond to all attempts at appeasement.

2. Margaret: Why strew'st thou sugar on that bottled spider, / Whose deadly web ensnareth thee about? —William Shakespeare, *The Tragedy of King Richard the Third,* Act 1, scene 3, line 242
   Margaret feels Elizabeth should not be nice to the evil Richard.

■ APPLAUSE

See also: APPROVAL/DISAPPROVAL

1. The audience stormed with applause — Jefferson Davis, quoted in Carl Sandburg's Abraham Lincoln, The War Years. Vol. One

2. Volpone: The seasoning of a play, is the applause —Ben Johnson, *Volpone, or The Fox,* Act 5, scene 7
   This begins Volpone's exit line.

3. Messenger: the commons made / A shower and thunder with their caps and shouts —William Shakespeare, *Coriolanus,* Act 2, scene 1, line 284

■ APPRECIATION

See: GRATITUDE/INGRATITUDE

■ APPROVAL/DISAPPROVAL

See also: CRITICS/CRITICISM

1. The First Lady . . . can't be perceived by other people in the White House, the public or the press as interfering, because then she'd be fried in oil —Letitia Baldridge, quoted in *The New York Times* article on the role of the soon-to-be First Lady, Hillary Clinton, November 16, 1992.

2. Firm *Dorique* Pillars found Your solid Base: / The Fair *Corinthian* Crowns the her Space; / Thus all below is Strength, and all above is Grace —John Dryden, "To My Dear Friend Mr. Congreve, On His Comedy, Call'd, The Double-Dealer"

Dryden derides most of the writers of his day before praising Congreve in this architectural metaphor.

3. I follow Auden in his derision [of middle class ineptitude] . . . but when he also derides the other soft little harmless things which make my life comfortable, I feel a chill autumn wind —Sir Harold Nicolson, August 4, 1933 diary entry

4. Iago: She puts her tongue a little in her heart, / And chides with thinking — William Shakespeare, *Othello,* Act 2, scene 1, line 106

5. We do not expect our path will be strewn with the flowers of popular applause, but over the thorns of bigotry and prejudice will be our way —Elizabeth Cady Stanton, Keynote address, First Woman's Rights Convention, July 19, 1848

■ APTITUDE

See: ABILITY

■ ARCHITECTURE

See also: BUILDINGS AND BRIDGES

1. Architecture is petrified music —Johann Wolfgang von Goethe, Letter, c. 1829

2. Architecture is frozen music —Johann Wolfgang von Goethe, *Conversations with Eckemann*

■ ARGUMENTS

See also: AGREEMENT/DISAGREEMENT; WORDS AS WEAPONS

1. Strepsiades: Stay: how can I, forgetful, slow, old fool, / Learn the nice hairsplittings of subtle Logic? —Aristophanes, *The Clouds*
   To split hairs remains a popular metaphor.

2. Do not argue with a long-winded man, and so add fuel to his fire —The Bible, *Apocrypha, 1 Ecclesiasticus 8:3*

3. Any subject became a point of contention for them, and they would duel over it bitterly: Hugh armored and weaponed with his massive assurance, Raymond flicking away with a rapier, trying to find chinks in the armor —Stanley Elkin, "The Moment of Decision," *Mystery Stories*

4. He delivered his arguments with fine force, and they exploded torpedoes all over the hall —H. L. Mencken, June 29, 1920
    The orator under Mencken's scrutiny was Homer S. Cummings, Republican convention keynoter.

5. Argument being a cool field where the farmer could meet and match him, the young man got on the tramroad of passion and went ahead —George Meredith, *The Ordeal of Richard Feverel*

■ ARMS

See: BODIES/THE BODY

■ AROUSAL/ROUSERS

1. The juror offered wise and soothing counsel to a city whose citizens sometimes seem determined to keep throwing gas on the fires lit by the murder and subsequent acquittal —Anon., Editorial, *The New York Times*, November 23, 1992
    The inflammatory trial involved the murder of an Australian Jew during a mob riot in Crown Heights in 1990.

2. This does light a fuse under the Government which will require them to change course —Paddy Ashdown, a leader of the Liberal Democrats, quoted in the *New York Times*, May 9, 1993
    To light a fuse under something has become a common incendiary metaphor meaning, to get things started quickly.

3. Mrs. St. Maugham: If there's a fire to be lit—you've set a match to it! —Enid Bagnold, *The Chalk Garden*, Act 3
    The accusation is directed at the mysterious governess who has stirred up the problems in Mrs. St. Maugham's household.

4. We live in times of great challenge, hope and opportunity, times of transition and change . . . keep the drum beat of activism alive —Ronald H. Brown, "Commencements," *New York Times*, May, 9, 1993
    The Secretary of Commerce spoke to Howard University graduates.

5. When the cancer threatened my sexuality, my mind became immediately erect — Anatole Broyard, *Intoxicated By My Illness*

6. Ambitious men . . . sprang up with programs to kindle the embers of old resentments —John F. Burns, "The World," *The New York Times*, January 17, 1973

7. Amorwe whan that day bigan to springe / Up roos oure Host and was oure aller cok —Geoffrey Chaucer, "The Prologue," *The Canterbury Tales*
    In modern English: In the morning our host rose and was the rooster for us all.

8. He [Franklin D. Roosevelt] was a great tickler of sacred cows not bred in his own pastures —Alistair Cooke, *Talk About America*
    And Cooke here shows himself to be a great tickler of the familiar phrase.

9. The NPT [Nuclear Non-Proliferation Treaty] remains an indispensable core of our nonproliferation efforts but it is also, unfortunately, a lightning rod for controversy —Prvoslav Davinic, closing statement at UN conference, Kyoto, Japan, April 1993
    The director of the United Nations Office for Disarmament Affairs made this rueful comment on a beleaguered treaty due for extension in 1995.

10. It could not be said that Otoko was entirely responsible, but certainly she had fanned

the flames within her —Kawabata Yasunari, *Beauty and Sadness*

11. This is the reveille of the plains . . . the performer is the assistant wagonmaster . . . the musical instruments are his lungs and a detached ox-bow —T.S. Kenderdine, quoted in an exhibit of American history under the great silver arches of the museum in Saint Louis

12. The pianist Peter Serkin was moderately successful in his attempts to light a fire under the quartet —Allan Kozinn, *The New York Times,* Review/Music, April 12, 1993

    Kozinn was less enthusiastic about the Guinari String quartet than Mr. Serkin whose "colorful, textured playing was the glue that held the performance together."

13. If he [the student] has in him any ability beyond that of the common herd, his tutor, interested in his studies, will smoke at him until he kindles him into a flame — Stephen Leacock, "Oxford as I See It"

    It is the tutor's smoke that will fume the Oxford student into a scholar.

14. Squeezing the bellows of propaganda, he [Stalin] rewards some authors and exposes others who show "bourgeois tendencies" —Herbert Mitgang, "Books of the Times," *The New Yorker,* October 7, 1992

    In fanning the flames, to use a more common form of the metaphor, Stalin creates opinion by generating heated criticism.

15. They [the students] first sowed the seeds of evil, but after all you would reap the result of being looked upon as the real cause of the quarrel —Natsume Soseki, *Botchan*

    If a teacher tried revenge, the boys would "snarl at and bite" him.

16. Jaffeir: I could tell a story / Would rowse thy Lyon Heart out of its Den —Thomas Otway, *Venice Preserved,* Act 3, scene 2

17. My role is that of a grain of sand to the oyster. We've got to irritate Washington a little bit —Ross Perot, Conference call with reporters, March 19, 1993

    Perot thus explained the purpose of the referendum for which he had purchased time on network television.

18. I raised a Hornet's Nest about my Ears, that . . . may have stung to Death my Reputation Anath —Samuel Richardson, *Pamela*

    In Christopher Fry's 1945 play, The Firstborn, *Pharaoh's sister, expresses her defiance of the court with "I was ready to raise a hornet's nest to keep him [the baby Moses]; in fact / I raised one. All the court flew up and buzzed." To stir up a hornet's nest is the metaphor's most common form.*

19. Coriolanus: In soothing them we nourish . . . The cockles of rebellion . . . / Which we ourselves have plough'd for, sow'd and scatter'd —William Shakespeare, *Coriolanus,* Act 3, scene 1, line 68

20. Menenius: This is the way to kindle, not to quench —William Shakespeare, *Coriolanus,* Act 3, scene 1, line 196

21. King Edward: I need not add more fuel to your fire —William Shakespeare, *The Third Part of Henry the Sixth,* Act 5, scene 4, line 70

    This is biblical in origin: "Do not argue with a long-winded man, and so add fuel to his fire," can be found in Apocrypha, 1 Ecclesiasticus 8:3.

22. He was content to be the drama editor of the *Times,* but Bea [his wife] lit a fire under him that burned for the rest of his life — Howard Teichmann, *George S. Kaufman*

    Sometimes just a few additional words stir the embers of a metaphor whose flame is flickering from overuse.

23. My condemnation . . . will be only a fresh seed of passion and disorder. The cup, I tell you, is full; do not make it run over! — Émile Zola, Speech, February 22, 1898

    Zola, had been sued for libel because of his outcry of anti-semitism surrounding the Dreyfus affair. With the second metaphor he invoked a familiar image from the Bible (O.T., Psalms, 23:5).

■ ARROGANCE/HUMILITY

See also: EGO/EGOTISM; PRIDE

1. The State of New Jersey is a valley of humility between two peaks of conceit [New York City and Philadelphia] —Anon., *The New York Times*, May 3, 1992
   This is an updated use of a metaphor often attributed to Benjamin Franklin.

2. Contempt is egoism in ill humor —Samuel Taylor Coleridge, "Omniana"

3. One of the good things about this love affair," she said "is that it's shot my high horse right out from under me —Laurie Colwin, "A Mythological Subject," *The Lone Pilgrim*

4. I could feel the worm of condescension stirring when we talked —Norman Mailer, *Harlot's Ghost*

5. Ulysses: Shall the proud lord / That bastes his arrogance with his own seam [lard] / . . . shall he be worshipp'd / Of what we hold an idol more than he? —William Shakespeare, *Troilus and Cressida*, Act 2 scene 3, line 188
   Achilles needs no outside reassurance to feed his excessive ego—like a piece of meat basted with its own juices.

6. She didn't need to get on her high horse like that, though —Jane Smiley, *A Thousand Acres*
   Smiley uses a common metaphor as part of the everyday speech of one of her characters.

■ ART/ARTISTS

See also: CREATIVITY; SELF-EXPRESSION

1. That beggar to whom you gave no cent / Striped the night with his strange descant —John Ashbery, "The Picture of Little J.A. in a Prospect of Flowers"
   In a poem that hints here of an ancient Chinese poem, filtered through acres and pounds of poets, Ashbery compares the beggar with a painter.

2. If the artist does not throw himself into his work . . . then the work remains unfinished . . . and the artist is a looker-on at his talent's suicide —Honoré de Balzac, *Cousin Bette*

3. Modern art thus begins, and sometimes ends, as a confession of spiritual poverty. That is its greatness and its triumph, but also the needle it jabs into the Philistine's sore spot, for the last thing he wants to be reminded of is his spiritual poverty —William Barrett, "Modern Art"

4. Modern art dishes out unpalatable truths —William Barrett, "Modern Art"

5. Art is not a mirror held up to nature, the creation of an object according to the rules, say, of harmony or perspective, designed to give pleasure —Isaiah Berlin, "The Apotheosis of the Romantic Will"
   "It is, as Herder taught, a means of communication, of self-expression for the individual spirit," writes Berlin.

6. Frida Kahlo: A Ribbon Around a Bomb —André Breton, *The New York Times*, May 22, 1992
   The metaphor, used as the subtitle of a film on Kahlo's life, comes from Breton's description of the artist's work. For a writer, the pen may be mightier than the sword, but the artist hides his protests and explosions in visual metaphors.

7. Rafael made a century of sonnets —Robert Browning, "One Word More"
   Rafael's paintings were poems, making not books, not canvases, but "centuries."

8. Every art is a church without communicants —Hortense Calisher, *Herself*

9. Art is science—in the flesh —Jean Cocteau, "The Public and the Artist," *Vanity Fair*, 1992

10. An artist must make his way on foot. He is the cat that walks by itself —Jean Cocteau, "The Cat That Walks by Itself"
    Cocteau decries the speed that leaves the artist standing by the wayside while lesser beings rush by.

11. However hard the road, the artist must walk along the dark side, and keep to the edge of the great main roads, of the autostradas —Jean Cocteau, "The Cat That Walks by Itself"

12. These outstanding men [Vermeer, Renoir, Goya, Picasso] burn with a light which sometimes casts deep shadows —Jean Cocteau, "The Cat That Walks by Itself"

13. We have in our keeping an angel whom we are continually shocking. We must be that angel's guardian —Jean Cocteau, "The Public and the Artist," *Vanity Fair*, 1992

14. Art is the stored honey of the human soul, gathered on wings of misery and travail— Theodore Dreiser

15. A truth about art is the company it keeps with the slightly askew, the fly in that woodpile of symmetry —Stanley Elkin, "Some Overrated Masterpieces," *Art & Antiques*, 1991

16. Georgia O'Keeffe . . . Her desert subject matter is, in a way, the flip, parched, only apparently sunnier side of Turner's wet coin—blanched, bleached landscapes of polished, picked-clean death —Stanley Elkin, "Some Overrated Masterpieces," *Art & Antiques*, 1991

17. Art is a jealous mistress —Ralph Waldo Emerson, "Wealth," *Conduct of Life*
   A much earlier variant, "art is a jealous thing; it requires the whole and entire man" is attributed to Michelangelo (1474–1538).

18. Color eventually became the mortar of his [Henri Matisse's] art—but its building blocks were unidealized human forms — Adam Gopnik, "The Unnatural," *The New Yorker*, October 12, 1992

19. In truth your frozen art [sculpture] has nothing like the scope and freedom of Hilda's and mine [painting] —Nathaniel Hawthorne, *The Marble Faun*

20. Although repeatedly declared dead, the Dada virus nonetheless remains viably buried in much of today's postmodernist art —Walter Hopps, Explanatory display, Museum of Modern Art, New York, 1993
   Mr. Hopps, the consulting curator of The Meni Collection in Houston, explains the Dada influence in an introduction to the works of Max Ernst.

21. Your book, wherever we look, is rife / with artists' antidotes: the verbs of life — Richard Howard, "Lives of the Painters: Artists' Antidotes," *The New Yorker*, August 3, 1992
   The poem derides a remaindered book on art, and counters that artists' antidotes are breathing, moving, and writing.

22. Art . . . It is the light by which human things can be mended —Iris Murdoch, *The Black Prince*

23. Art is only a prudent steward that lives on managing the riches of nature —Alexander Pope, from Preface to the translation of Homer's *Iliad*

24. Art is the contest of life with clay —John Ruskin, Lecture on art, 1872
   In another metaphoric lecture, he said art "gives Form to Knowledge and Grace to utility."

25. And art made tongue-tied by authority — William Shakespeare, "Sonnet 66," line 9

26. Art is the magic mirror you make to reflect your invisible pleasures —George Bernard Shaw, The She-Ancient, *Back to Methuselah*
   Shaw elaborates on the metaphor with "You use a glass mirror to see your face; you use works of art to see your soul."

27. Antillean art is this restoration of our shattered histories, our shards of vocabulary, our archipelago becoming a synonym for pieces broken off from the original continent —Derek Walcott, Nobel Prize acceptance speech, December 8, 1992

■ ARTICULATENESS/INARTICULATENESS

See also: CLARITY/AMBIGUITY; COMMU-NICATION/NON-COMMUNICATION; LANGUAGE; SPEECH; WORDS

1. In solitude, my thoughts hell-bent will flow / But speech, breakwater, checks them as they go —Catherine Davis, "Insights: 4"

2. At every painful step the reader sinks to the hip in jargon and generalizations, with never a patch of firm intellectual ground to rest on and only rarely, in that endless expanse of jelly, the blessed relief of a hard, concrete, particular fact —Aldous Huxley, "Mother"

3. With what a dexterity and skill the bubble of speech must be maneuvered if mind is to meet and mingle with mind —Christopher Morley, "What Men Live By"

4. Edith—always trying to confine things into the shape of a phrase, like pouring water into a ewer, but great gourds of meaning and implications invariably ran over and slopped about and were lost — Vita Sackville-West, *All Passion Spent*
   The metaphor contained in a simile, is occasioned by the gathering of a family of mourners whom Edith describes as "old, black ravens."

5. Words fluttered sideways and struck the object inches too low —Virginia Woolf, *To the Lighthouse*

■ ARTIFICIALITY

See: SUPERFICIALITY

■ ARTS AND ENTERTAINMENT

1. Ballet, like language, is capable of extraordinary richness—at least, in theory. In actual practice, ballet is often tongue-tied —Jack Anderson, "Dance View," *The New York Times*, August 26, 1992
   Mr. Anderson set out the comparison with a simile and enhanced it with a metaphor.

2. New plays opening on Broadway . . . have the life span of a mayfly —Anon., Editorial, *The New York Times*, February 19, 1992

3. [The audience] That big black giant — Oscar Hammerstein II, *Me and Juliet*

4. Television . . . the new gladiatorial arena —Josephine Hart, *Damage*
   The phrase pertains to a woman good looking enough to compete in this metaphoric arena.

5. The houselights / Obey some planetary rheostat / And bring a stillness on — Anthony Hecht, "Peripeteia"
   Hecht's "planetary rheostat" brings the theater out of the world and into the spheres, to the vastness of time and space and "soft Einsteinian tides."

6. If you tried to tie *The Piano* down as a costume picture, or as a love story, or as a gothic horror, it slips its moorings and drifts away —Anthony Lane, "Sheet Music," *The New Yorker*, November 29, 1993
   To underscore the hard-to-categorize quality of this much-praised film, readers could interpret the review's title as a metaphor for the music that is so important to its heroine, or the passionate affair it leads to—or both.

7. Summer visitors—many of them—see Tanglewood as a casino. Itzhak Perlman is the jackpot. An all-Mozart program is a royal flush. Contemporary music is a losing hand. And the bar never closes — Andrew L. Pincus, "Rambling About Tanglewood," *The Berkshire Eagle*, September 5, 1993
   In looking ahead somewhat wistfully to the sparser musical offerings available to Berkshire residents after the famous summer festival, Mr. Pincus takes a swipe at the very people without whom his "musical platter" would be filled with diet-sized portions all year.

8. Public television . . . the green vegetables of video viewing —Anna Quindlen, "Public & Private," *The New York Times*, November 30, 1991

9. The classics may be the mountains of the theater, but you don't climb them just because they're there —Frank Rich, "Review/Theater," *The New Yorker*, November 30, 1992

> *Rich ho-hummed over yet another production of Chekhov's* The Seagull.

10. From the outdoor balcony of Avery Fisher Hall it seemed as if the public were being offered circuses while nourishing bread was promised to those within . . . As it turned out, the bread inside seemed a bit stale —Edward Rothstein, "Review/Music," *The New York Times*, December 9, 1992

> *The New York Philharmonic's 150th birthday celebration at Lincoln Center included outdoor performances by a lion and a clown from the Big Apple Circus. Too bad that the reviewer was so unenthusiastic about the Philharmonic's performance.*

11. Broadway is pretty much of a specialty shop for pretested work, most of it musical —Alfred Uhry, Theater Development, *News Digest*, March, 1992

■ ASPIRATION

See: AMBITION

■ ASSISTANCE

1. Will you load my gun, leaving me only to pull the trigger and let fly the powder and ball? —Susan B. Anthony, letter to Elizabeth Cady Stanton, June, 1856

> *Anthony was asking Stanton to provide her with the text for a speech she was scheduled to give.*

2. Is not a Patron, my Lord, one who looks with unconcern on a man struggling for life in the water, and, when he has reached ground, encumbers him with help? — Samuel Johnson, Letter to The Earl of Chesterfield, February 7, 1755

> *The Earl, who had refused to see Johnson when he needed support for his dictionary, had recently written a "honeyed" essay in hopes of still having*

the work dedicated to him. This was Johnson's way of saying "Thanks, but no thanks."

3. Messer Nicia: But this fellow's stupidity has got this to be said for it—it's a handle for Callimaco —Niccolo Machiavelli, *Mandragola*, Act 1

> *Callimaco will use the "handle" as a primitive tool to cuckold his dull-witted opponent.*

4. Percy: My gracious lord, I tender you my service, / Such as it is, being tender, raw, and young; / Which elder days shall ripen and confirm / To more approved service and desert —William Shakespeare, *The Tragedy of King Richard the Second*, Act 2, scene 3, line 41

> *Young Percy offers his services to Bolingbroke, hoping that they will be worth more when he grows older and wiser.*

5. King: For every man that Bolingbroke hath press'd / . . . God for his Richard hath in heavenly pay / A glorious angel —William Shakespeare, *The Tragedy of King Richard the Second*, Act 3, scene 2, line 58

> *Bolingbroke has raised an army. God will raise an army of angels for Richard.*

■ ASSUAGERS

See: COMFORT/COMFORT-GIVERS

■ ASSURANCE

See: PROMISES; SELF-RELIANCE; UNCERTAINTY

■ ASTROLOGY

See: SCIENCE

■ ATTENTIVENESS/ INATTENTIVENESS

1. Lady Rosaline: Aged ears play truant at his tales —William Shakespeare, *Love's Labour's Lost*, Act 2, scene 1, line 74

The old are seduced from more important or serious matters by the merriment of youth.

2. Manford's attention, tugging at its moorings, had broken loose again and was off and away —Edith Wharton, *Twilight Sleep*

   Toward the novel's end, this lawyer in mid-life crisis does sail off for a brief fling, before returning to the safe anchor of his marriage.

■ ATTRACTION

See also: MEN AND WOMEN; PASSION; SEX/ SEXUALITY

1. This beautiful binding stood before her, wrapped in his lavish emotions without any text —Laurie Colwin, "The Smile Beneath the Smile"

   The metaphor of a beautifully bound book without a text worth reading, springs from the protagonist's work with rare books. Colwin likens this man's seductive power to the beauty appeal in product advertising, an appeal which "had never come across so receptive a public as Rachel Manheim."

2. Ah, she could feel the charm mounting over her again . . . could feel the snake biting her heart —D. H. Lawrence, *The Captain's Doll*

   The rekindling of sexual desire in a woman who thought herself out of love with the man she'd been having an affair with.

3. She was the sickle; I, poor I, the rake, / Coming behind her for her pretty sake — Theodore Roethke, "I Knew A Woman"

4. She was a lamp for every moth that flew —Wallace Stegner, *Angle of Repose*

   In his Pulitzer Prize–winning novel, Stegner thus describes how the heroine attracted interesting people and conversation even though her "salon" was a mining engineer's simple cabin.

■ ATTRACTIVENESS

See: BEAUTY

■ AUSTRALIA

See: COUNTRIES, MISC.

■ AUTHORITY

See also: MASTERY/SUBORDINATION; POWER

1. Authority intoxicates, / And makes me sots of magistrates; / The fumes of it invade the brain, / And make men giddy, proud and vain —Samuel Butler, *Miscellaneous Thoughts*

2. I cannot fight against the thunder of authority —Thomas Erskine, Speech in defense of Thomas Paine's "The Rights of Man," December 18, 1792

3. His authority [Abraham Lincoln's], worn often as a garment of thongs, was tied and knotted with responsibilities —Carl Sandburg, *Abraham Lincoln, The War Years, Vol. One*

4. Isabella: Authority, though it err like others, / Hath yet a kind of medicine in itself, / That skins the vice o' the top —William Shakespeare, *Measure for Measure*, Act 2, scene 2, line 135

5. Clown: though authority be a stubborn bear, yet he is oft led by the nose with gold —William Shakespeare, *The Winter's Tale*, Act 4, scene 4, line 835

   The idea of dominating someone by means of a ring through the nose appears in The Bible *(Isaiah 37:29): "Because thy rage against me, and thy tumult, is come up to mine ears, therefore I will put my hook in thy nose. . . ." The common usage form is to lead someone by the nose.*

■ AUTHORS

See: POETRY/POETS; WRITING/WRITERS

■ AUTOBIOGRAPHY

See: BIOGRAPHIES/AUTOBIOGRAPHIES

■ AUTOMOTIVE DESCRIPTIONS

See also: DESCRIPTIONS, MISC.

1. Meanwhile, another older truck grinds up / in a blue cloud of burning oil. It has / a syphilitic nose —Elizabeth Bishop, "Under the Window: Ouro Prêto"
   "Nevertheless, its gallant driver tells the passerby, not much money but it is amusing."

2. Hours before the show, there'd be a city of cars in the parking lot —Jane Shapiro, *The New Yorker*, April 15, 1992

3. Cars are whispering home from work — John Updike, *Rabbit, Run*

■ AUTONOMY

See: SELF-RELIANCE

■ AUTUMN

See: SEASONS; WIND

■ AVARICE

See: GREED

■ AWAKENINGS

See: AROUSAL/ROUSERS

■ AWARENESS/UNAWARENESS

See also: KNOWLEDGE; LIFE; MEN AND WOMEN; REALITY/UNREALITY; SCRUTINY; UNDERSTANDING/MISUNDERSTANDING

1. But if on the other hand he is one of those upon whose mental horizon the Sun of Letters and the Stars of Song have not yet shone, and who grope in darkness not by preference but merely because they do not know that the light is there, then I am sorry for him —John Kendrick Bangs, "My Silent Servants"
   Bangs comments on the difference between those who are content to know nothing, and those who do not know that they know nothing.

2. Voynitsky: We used to think of you as almost superhuman, but now the scales have fallen off my eyes and I see you as you are! —Anton Chekhov, *Uncle Vanya*, Act 3
   The metaphor brings to mind a lizard, whose scales seem to cover his eyes so he cannot see.

3. The secret of seeing is to sail on solar wind. Hone and spread your spirit till you yourself are a sail, whetted, translucent, broadside to the merest puff —Annie Dillard, *Pilgrim at Tinker Creek*

4. Existence is laid bare, and married / to a movement of caught perception / where the unknown will become the known —Donald Hall, "Munch's Scream"

5. We drink the cup of earthly life / With blinded eyes —Mikhail Lermontov, "The Cup of Life"
   This has also been translated as "The Chalice of Life."

6. For years she had her back against the stone wall of Rhett's love —Margaret Mitchell, *Gone With the Wind*

7. The bandage that had long been loosened fell completely from her eyes —George Sand, *Indiana*
   This caps the heroine's awakening to her true feelings.

8. As long as she had continued to be fond of her husband she had seen him incompletely and confusedly; but under the X-ray of her settled indifference every muscle and articulation had become visible — Edith Wharton, *Hudson River Bracketed*
   'X-ray vision' has become a common metaphor, but the technology was still new for Wharton.

9. A faint shadow brushed Pauline's cloudless horizon; but she resolutely turned her

eyes from it —Edith Wharton, *Twilight Sleep*

10. America can not be an ostrich with its head in the ground —Woodrow Wilson, speech, February 1, 1916

B

■ BABIES

See: CHILDHOOD/CHILDREN

■ BADNESS

See: GOOD/EVIL; EVIL; WICKEDNESS

■ BANALITY/TRITENESS

See: FRESHNESS/STALENESS

■ BARGAINING

See: PEOPLE, INTERACTION

■ BARRIERS

See also: BIGOTRY; DIFFICULTIES; PROBLEMS AND SOLUTIONS

1. The fence that makes good neighbors needs a gate to make good friends —Anon.

   In Robert Frost's famous poem, "The Mending Wall" one neighbor says "Something there is that doesn't love a wall" while another insists "Good fences make good neighbors."

2. I've told the Clinton team that anytime they find there may be sand thrown into the gears, that I want to know about it —Andrew H. Card, Jr., "Bush Aide Defends GOP Job," *The Record,* December 6, 1992

3. What might be called her genius in communicating with girls when and after they slip behind the glass curtain of pre-adolescence draws attention to some thorny issues —Susan Ferraro, "Girl Talk," *New York Times Magazine,* December 6, 1992

   Ferraro's profile of Ann Martin, author of the Baby-Sitters Club series for pre-teen girls, provides yet another variation of the metaphor of the glass ceiling as a barrier, especially as it affects women. Ferraro found Martin's prose "efficient and correct" but commented "there is little metaphor and few if any wonderful phrases."

4. We must break the glass ceiling that stretches across our Government and our economy, so that at last, all Americans will be equal in life as well as in law —Senator Edward M. Kennedy, Speech, Democratic National Convention, July 15, 1992

   The Senator is just one of many who have used the glass ceiling as a metaphor for an invisible prejudicial barrier. It is most frequently used in relation to women's equality in the work place.

5. The tension we are witnessing in race relations today can be explained in part by . . . the Negro's evaluation of himself and his determination to struggle and sacrifice until the walls of segregation have been fully crushed by the battering rams of justice —Martin Luther King, Quoted in editorial, *The New York Times,* January 18, 1993

6. Oedipus: So long as you are here, / you'll be a stumbling block and a vexation — Sophocles, *Oedipus the King*
   > *Oedipus wants Teiresias to leave, since the prophet's puzzling prophecies enrage him.*

7. Si Bero: Get out of the way, will you. Are you now the doorstop that I must step on you to get out of my own house? —Wole Soyinka, *Madmen and Specialists*, Part 1
   > *The mendicants with their practiced deformities lie in wait for Si Bero in order to get a handout.*

■ BASEBALL

See: SPORTS

■ BASHFULNESS

See: TIMIDITY

■ BASKETBALL

See: SPORTS

■ BEARDS

See: FACIAL HAIR

■ BEAUTY

See also: AGE/AGING; FACES; LOVERS' DEC-LARATIONS AND EXCHANGES; PHYSI-CAL APPEARANCE; PRAISE; TRAN-SIENCE

1. Your beauty is a thunder —Maya Angelou, "Black Ode," *Just Give Me a Cool Drink of Water 'fore I Diie*

2. Beauty without virtue is a flower without perfume —Anon., French Proverb

3. Beauty is a fading flower —The Bible, *O.T., Isaiah 18: 1*

> *The many variants of this include Thomas Nashe's "Beauty is but a flower, / Which wrinkles will devour" from* Summer's Last Will and Testament *and "For what is beauty but a fading Flower?" from the seventeenth century American poet Michael Wigglesworth's "Vanity of Vanities."*

4. Beauty is the melody of the features — Josh Billings
   > *At another time, Billings warned that "beauty alone won't wear well, and there is a great deal of it that won't wash at all and keep its color."*

5. The honey of her Infant lips, / The bread & wine of her sweet smile, / The wild game of her roving Eye —William Blake, "The Mental Traveller"

6. Gradus: Beauty is a talisman which works through miracles, and, without a fable, transforms mankind —Hannah Cowley, *Who's the Dupe?* Act 2, scene 1

7. Beauty—what is it? A perfume without name —Arthur Davison Ficke, "Epitaph for the Poet"

8. Beauty's a Flower, despis'd in decay — John Gay, *The Beggar's Opera*, Act 2, scene 4
   > *Flowers, because of their evanescence, are a common metaphor for beauty or youth.*

9. Beauty is eternity gazing at itself in the mirror. But you are eternity and you are the mirror —Kahlil Gibran, *The Prophet*

10. For so many years / I was good enough to eat: the world looked at me / And its mouth watered —Randall Jarrell, "Next Day"
    > *The speaker in the poem is a woman who has aged and becomes plain.*

11. Beauty is truth, truth beauty —John Keats, "Ode on a Grecian Urn"

12. She was a French New Year card angel-face, set in tinsel and blossoms —Rosamond Lehmann, *The Ballad and the Source*

13. She was managing her capital perfectly — Doris Lessing, "Notes for a Case History"

The capital being managed consists of a young girl's style and good looks.

14. She [Clare Booth Luce's mother] was tiny but perfectly formed—a pocket Venus — Ralph Martin, *Henry and Clare*

15. Beauty is a blind alley . . . a mountain peak which once reached leads nowhere —W. Somerset Maugham, *Cakes and Ale*

16. Beauty is Nature's coin, must not be hoarded, / . . . Beauty is Nature's brag, and must be shown —John Milton, "Comus"

17. She broke open the shell of her increasingly doubtful and expensive prettiness; and got out —Alice Munro, "Hold Me Past, Don't Let Me Pass," *Friend of Youth,*

18. Beauty is but a flower / Which wrinkles will devour —Thomas Nashe, "A Litany in Time of Plague"

19. Beauty . . . She is a visitor who leaves behind / The gift of grief, the souvenir of pain —Robert Nathan, "Beauty Is Ever"

20. A fair exterior is a silent recommendation —Publilius Syrus

21. For your heart / Beauty is a burned-out torch —Marjorie Allen Seiffert, "A Woman of Thirty"

    In another poem, ("Sorrow"), Seiffert describes beauty and joy as "petals blown."

22. Berowne: Beauty doth varnish age, as if new-born, / And gives the crutch the cradle's infancy —William Shakespeare, *Love's Labour's Lost,* Act 4, scene 3, line 244

23. Berowne: Beauty . . . O 'tis the sun that maketh all things shine! —William Shakespeare, *Love's Labour's Lost,* Act 4, scene 3, line 246

24. Morocco: Never so rich a gem / Was set in worse than gold —William Shakespeare, *The Merchant of Venice,* Act 2, scene 7, line 54

The gem is a metaphor for Portia.

25. Claudio: beauty is a witch / Against whose charms faith melteth into blood — William Shakespeare, *Much Ado About Nothing,* Act 2, scene 1, line 188

26. Beauty . . . / A brittle glass that's broken presently —William Shakespeare, *The Passionate Pilgrim,* Section 12, line 4

27. Romeo: What doth her beauty serve but as a note / Where I may read who pass'd that passing fair? —William Shakespeare, *Romeo and Juliet,* Act 1, scene 1, line 238

    Juliet's beauty is unsurpassable; therefore, none can surpass her.

28. Thou that art now the world's fresh ornament, / And only herald to the gaudy spring —William Shakespeare, "Sonnet 1," line 9

    Spring is not only the beauteous season, but also the one that metaphorically indicates youth.

29. For thou art so possessed with murd'rous hate, / That 'gainst thyself thou stick'st not to conspire, / Seeking that beauteous roof to ruinate, / Which to repair should be thy chief desire —William Shakespeare, "Sonnet 10," line 5

30. That beauty which you hold in lease — William Shakespeare, "Sonnet 13," line 5

    Beauty is simply a tenant housed in the body.

31. For all the beauty that doth cover thee / Is but the seemly raiment of my heart — William Shakespeare, "Sonnet 22," line 5

    The poet says he will not age while his love is young.

32. Thus is his cheek the map of days outworn, / When beauty lived and died as flowers do now —William Shakespeare, "Sonnet 68," line 1

    The simile that follows the metaphor explains it. The person being described has beauty that is natural, as flowers are natural, and not cosmetically enhanced.

33. The ornament of beauty is suspect / A crow that flies in heaven's sweetest air — William Shakespeare, "Sonnet 70," line 3

34. Clown: Beauty's a flower —William Shakespeare, *Twelfth Night*, Act 1, scene 5, line 52

    The Bard adapted this image from The Bible, and used it also in one of his sonnets as "Beauty is but a blossom." One of the most quoted versions is "Beauty is but a flower, / Which wrinkles will devour" from Thomas Nashe's Summer's Last Will and Testament.

35. Beauty within itself should not be wasted: / Fair flowers that are not gather'd in their prime / Rot and consume themselves in little time —William Shakespeare, *Venus and Adonis*, line 131

36. When thou saw'st, in nature's cabinet, / Stella —Sir Philip Sidney, "Sonnet 11," *Astrophel and Stella*

    The lady in nature's cabinet was Stella, the star. Sidney himself was Astrophel, the stargazer.

37. Beauties which do in excellence pass (surpass) / His who till death looked in a watery glass —Sir Philip Sidney, "Sonnet 82," *Astrophel and Stella*

    The metaphor is joined to an allusion to Narcissus, who gazed, entranced by his own beauty, into the looking glass of a lake.

38. Julien admired Madame de Rénal's looks, but hated her for her beauty; it . . . was the first reef on which his fortune had nearly foundered —Marie-Henri Beyle de Stendhal, *The Red and the Black*

    The young man fighting the attraction of the beautiful woman is Stendhal's hero, Julien Sorel.

39. On your head / No crown is simpler than the simplest hair —Wallace Stevens, "Sea Surface Full of Clouds"

40. Beauty is a mute deception —Theophrastus, *Apothegm*

41. Thy face is a sword, And behold, I am slain —Helen Waddell, "Love Song"

42. She regarded herself as afflicted with a Greek nose, masses of wavy amber hair, and a richly glowing dusky complexion, as other women might have borne the cross of a birthmark or a crooked spine —Edith Wharton, *Hudson River Bracketed*

    "Bearing a cross" has long meant carrying a burden, or affliction. Because of its heavy religious connotation it becomes humorous here, being used for a woman 'cursed' by her beauty.

43. It was one of her moments of beauty—that fitful beauty which is so much more enchanting and perilous than the kind that gets up and lies down every day with its wearer —Edith Wharton, *The Children*

    A bachelor watches a young woman who he realizes will never be more than a passing episode in his life.

44. She was a phantom of delight / When first she gleamed upon my sight; / A lovely apparition, sent / To be a moment's ornament —William Wordsworth, "She Was a Phantom of Delight"

■ BEGINNINGS

See also: ENDINGS; OPPORTUNITY

1. The honeymoon . . . was ended by the press before the groom had got to the church, before he'd bought the ring before he'd even made the proposal —Anon., "Comment," *The New Yorker*, November 23, 1992

    The honeymoon metaphor is especially popular in depicting relations between the Congress and the press and a new President. In this case, the metaphor was prompted by a spade of critical articles within a few weeks of Bill Clinton's election.

2. Always coming back / To the mooring of starting out, that day so long ago —John Ashbery, "Soonest Mended"

3. Work, it seemed to me even at the threshold of life, is an activity reserved for the dullard —Henry Miller, "The Creative Life"

    Again we see the common metaphor of the threshold, not as a precipitous crossing into life or death, but to indicate burgeoning youth.

■ BEHAVIOR

See: ACTIONS

■ BEING/BECOMING

See also: DISAPPEARANCE; GROWTH; LIFE AND DEATH

1. Only when all relations, uncurtailed, are taken into the one relation, do we set the ring of our life's world round the sun of our being —Martin Buber, "The Question to the Single One"

   Buber pictures "being" as the jewel in the world's setting, when the human spirit is open enough to accept all relationships.

2. At Gaya, at the time when I won enlightenment, I got rid of the causes of becoming, which are nothing but a gang of harmful vipers —Buddha

   This was reported by Buddha's followers near the time of his death.

3. The process of becoming is also called the chain of causation, the chain of dependent origination, or, more commonly, the wheel of life and death —Philip Kapleau, *The Wheel of Life and Death*

   Kapleau uses two Buddhist images here, the chain and the wheel; the latter is more common, especially in its tangible or physical representations.

4. As soon as she received the letter Manuela set out [but] she was a whole lifetime too late. The news erased her from the world. She sank into her own shadows —Gabriel García Márquez, *The General in his Labyrinth*

5. Perhaps the great sorrow . . . only makes the chrysalis break open a little sooner, hastens the metamorphosis and the appearance of a person whom we carry within us —Marcel Proust, *Cities of the Plain.*

6. Now the man who has his heart on his sleeve, and a good whirling weathercock of a brain . . . [he] may shoot up and become a constellation in the end —Robert Louis Stevenson, "Aes Triplex"

■ BELIEFS

See also: OPINION; POLITICS/POLITICIANS

1. Doctrine is nothing but the skin of truth set up and stuffed —Henry Ward Beecher, *Life Thoughts*

2. I can only say that those who rest on such comfortable beds of dogma are victims of forms of self-induced myopia, blinkers that may make for contentment, but not for understanding of what it is to be human. —Isaiah Berlin, "The Pursuit of the Ideal," *The Crooked Timber of Humanity*

   There is no single harmony, no unbreakable law: man is doomed to choose, according to Berlin. Even his metaphor puts man to bed with blinkers and myopia. One wonders if Man needs a cane to find the way (or a seeing-eye dogma.)

3. Heresy—false beliefs about the ends of men—is surely a poison more dangerous to the health of society than even hypocrisy or dissimulation, which at least do not openly attack the true doctrine —Isaiah Berlin, "The Apotheosis of the Romantic Will"

   Berlin uses the drug metaphor to contend that religious believers in the sixteenth century were not moved by the sincerity of heretics. On the contrary, they persecuted them the more for the strength of their dissenting beliefs.

4. A precedent embalms a principle —Benjamin Disraeli, Speech, February 22, 1848

5. We are all tattooed in our cradles with the beliefs of our tribe, the record may seem superficial, but it is indelible —Oliver Wendell Holmes, Sr., *The Poet of the Breakfast Table*

6. A creed is an ossified metaphor —Elbert Hubbard, *The Note Book*

7. It [communism] is a cancer in full metastasis on the body of the Western world —Norman Mailer, *Harlot's Ghost*

8. Belief . . . is the demi-cadence which closes a musical phrase in the symphony of our intellectual life —Charles S. Peirce,

"How to Make Our Ideas Clear," *Popular Science Monthly,* 1878

9. Even grandma Scrimser . . . somewhere in the big lumber room of her mind had found a point where otherworldliness and "pep" lay down together in amity — Edith Wharton, *Hudson River Bracketed*

   Grandma was the member of the family who was bigger on religious idealism than on making or keeping money. Of the two metaphors here, the latter is allusory, with "pep" being the lion and otherworldliness the lamb.

■ BELONGING/OUTCAST

See also: *CHARACTERIZATIONS; CONFORMITY/NONCONFORMITY; SELF-CONSCIOUSNESS*

1. I am a worm, and no man; a reproach of men, and despised of the people —The Bible, *O.T., Psalms, 22:6*

   The metaphor is commonly used for a sneaky or despicable person.

2. When you don't know something, it's hard to react. We were not in the loop — George Bush, Quoted, in "Shultz Describes Bush as Backing Iran Arms Sales," *The New York Times,* January 31, 1993

   The connotation of "loop" as a circle of power and inside information is very much in the loop of Washington jargon-speak.

3. They were . . . sunk in a ghetto —Cynthia Ozick, "Levitation"

   The ghetto is the social world of a couple on the periphery of publishing, with friends in mundane jobs, "not the glittering eagles."

4. Indeed, religious conservatives have spent the last decade with their noses against the glass of the culture —Ralph Reed, Jr., *The New York Times,* August 22, 1993

   The metaphor pictures religious conservatives as poor kids with their noses pressed against the window of a bakery store or toy store.

5. I was ill at ease among them: a thistle in the rose garden, a mule at the racetrack, Cinderella at the fancy dress ball —Lee Smith, "The Bubba Stories," *The Southern Review,* 1991

6. Here you are . . . back in the fold —Ivan Turgenev, *Fathers and Sons*

   Arcady's father welcomes his son back. The metaphor indicates a coming together as part of a community, as sheep stay together.

7. [Tom] Snyder always seemed too outsized and ungainly to suit the TV medium, a jumbo order trying to fit into an economy box —James Wolcott, *The New Yorker,* April 12, 1993

   This was from a profile on the late-night talk show hosts.

8. And for the first time in three days I felt that I wasn't going against the current anymore but flowing right along with it — A. B. Yehoshua, *Mr. Mani*

   A Jewish woman in a taxicab has traversed the Arab neighborhoods, and now finds herself back in the Jewish part of the city.

■ BENEVOLENCE

See: *CHARITY; KINDNESS/UNKINDNESS*

■ BEST-SELLERS

See: *BOOKS*

■ BETRAYAL

See: *MARRIAGE; TREACHERY; TRUSTWORTHINESS/UNTRUSTWORTHINESS*

■ THE BIBLE

See: *BOOKS*

■ BIGNESS/SMALLNESS

See: *BUSINESS DESCRIPTIONS*

■ BIGOTRY

See also: *ENCOURAGEMENT; HATE; OPINION*

1. Prejudice—a vagrant opinion without visible means of support —Ambrose Bierce, *The Devil's Dictionary*

2. Bigotry . . . is an opportunistic infection attacking most virulently when the body politic is in a weakened state —Henry Louis Gates, Jr., "Black Demagogues and Pseudo-Scholars, *The New York Times,* July 20, 1992

3. The word *nigger* is "a knife with a whetted edge" —Andrew Hacker, *Two Nations*

4. Prejudice is a raft onto which the shipwrecked mind clambers and paddles to safety —Ben Hecht, *A Guide for the Bedevilled*

5. My hostess was suffering from a malady become as common in the world as a head cold. She had picked up some anti-Semitism germs —Ben Hecht, *A Guide for the Bedevilled*
   This woman's challenge to the author to explain why Jews are so much disliked, motivated him to write this book which deals with anti-Semitism.

6. True tolerance does not consist in saying, "You may be right, but let us not make hard demands on ourselves: if you will put your critical intelligence to sleep, I'll put mine to bed, too" —Walter Kaufmann, "The Faith of a Heretic"

7. It would be tragic if "color blind," a figure of speech used by Justice John Marshall Harlan in an unsuccessful effort to break down de jure racial barriers in the late 19th century, was used successfully in the late 20th century to derail efforts to uproot de facto racial barriers —Randall Kennedy, Op-Ed, *The New York Times,* July 21, 1993
   Justice Harlan's metaphor has been extended to include "gender blindness."

8. The Republican Party watered this tree of racism; it's now grown to maturity and it's dropped this fellow David Duke from its branches —Bob Kerrey, Speech, by Senator from Nebraska, November 24, 1992

9. For too long have we been trampled under the iron feet of oppression, too long bound in the starless midnight of racism —Martin Luther King, Quoted in a profile on Jesse Jackson by Marshall Fraidy, *The New Yorker,* April 20, 1992
   Fraidy cited the above as typical of the "oratorical raptures" Jackson absorbed during his boyhood.

10. Segregation is the offspring of an illicit intercourse between injustice and immorality —Martin Luther King, Jr.

11. Father used to say that the beautiful lands had vomited us up here in blind hatred —Amos Oz, *The Hill of Evil Counsel*
    Anger is expressed at the European homelands from which Jewish exiles had fled during the Nazi era, coming to rest in unfamiliar Palestine.

12. Notoriously, the Jew was the bacillus whose resistant ubiquity infected, with miscegenation, the blood (weakened by war) of nobler breeds —George Steiner, "Books," *The New Yorker,* August 24, 1992
    Steiner details the virulently anti-Semitic views of Louis-Ferdinand Destouches, a "manic crank," who wrote under the name Celine—the subject of a biography by Frederic Vitoux.

13. Anti-semitism is the bitter fruit of a profound self-destructive impulse, nurtured on the vines of hopelessness —Cornel West, Quotation in Op-Ed by Henry Louis Gates, Jr., *The New York Times,* July 20, 1992

14. The Jews were the underlying reason for the whole enterprise, the bull's eye flickering behind every target in this war. —A. B. Yehoshua, *Mr. Mani*
    A German soldier looks for reasons for Hitler's wars.

15. It is with this poisoned bread that the unclean press has been nourishing our poor people for months —Émile Zola, Speech, February 22, 1898
    Zola's outcry against the anti-semitism surrounding the trial of Captain Alfred Dreyfus resulted in

a libel suit. The above is from his courtroom appearance which did not help his own case but did serve to free Dreyfus.

■ BIOGRAPHIES/ AUTOBIOGRAPHIES

See also: BOOKS; WRITING/WRITERS

1. At its most daring, and maybe even at its best, all autobiography is "authorized," a striptease with the pasties of G-string that covers the mind left on —Stanley Elkin, "Out of One's Tree," *Harper's,* January 1993

2. By its very nature, a perfectly true autobiography might cut against but must finally break its blade on the diamond-hard grain of the superego because, though scissors cuts paper, paper covers rock, and rock smashes scissors, decorum is, strictly speaking, life's ultimate weapon —Stanley Elkin, "Out of One's Tree," *Harper's,* January 1933

3. The writing of the old-fashioned biography was . . . to cast a bronze effigy from the clay mask —Lewis Mumford, "The Task of Modern Biography"
   According to Mumford, biographers of the past would often "gild the bronze head."

4. Biographies are but the clothes and buttons of the man—the biography of the man himself cannot be written —Mark Twain, *Autobiography*

■ BIRDS

See also: ANIMALS; NATURE SCENES; SKY/ SKYSCAPES

1. In the flickering evening the martins grow denser. / Rivers of wings surround us and vast tribulation —John Ashbery, "Glazunoviana"
   The poem is an impressionistic portrayal of Russia as seen through Glazunov's music.

2. [The birds] cluster at the feeding station, and rags of song / Greet the neighbors —John Ashbery, "The Orioles"

3. They [peacocks] carry a musical score in their bones, / which are so thin—toothpicks, really —Marvin Bell, "Three Propositions: Hooey, Dewey, and Loony," *The American Poetry Review,* 1990
   This double metaphor is from a poem within the story.

4. I offered him a crumb, / And he unrolled his feathers, / And rowed him softer home / Than oars divide the ocean —Emily Dickinson, Poem 328
   The metaphor of a bird rowing in the sky is followed by a simile that compares the oars that part the seas.

5. Moses: the hawk . . . a bright lash on the cheek of the wind —Christopher Fry, *The Firstborn,* Act 1, scene 2

6. They [birds] stayed and ate, inky spots on the nut-brown soil —Thomas Hardy, *Jude the Obscure*
   Young Jude has provided the birds with dinner, a kindness for which he is beaten and fired by the farmer he works for.

7. Have you ever observed a humming-bird . . . a living prismatic gem that changes its colour with every change of position . . . ? —William Henry Hudson, *Green Mansions*
   Rima, the bird-girl, has the same darting nature as the humming bird.

8. This bird is the sun's key-hole —Ted Hughes, "The Interrogator"
   Hughes pictures the vulture with "a dripping bagful of evidence under her humped robe" who briefly "ruffles the light that chills the startled eyeball" and then returns to the courts of the after-life.

9. I'll admit he's a beggar, a gangster, a bum, / But I take off my hat to the sparrow —Minna Irving, "The Sparrow"

10. Spiteful grackles with their clothespin legs, / Black-winged gossips rising out of mud —Howard Moss, "Einstein's Bathrobe"

11. Or how could thy notes flow in such a crystal stream? —Percy Bysshe Shelley, "To a Skylark"

Shelley's rhapsodic poem also compares the singing of the skylark to that of a sprite "that panted forth a flood of rapture."

12. The nightingale . . . / Sings out her woes, a thorn her song-book making —Sir Philip Sidney, "The Nightingale"

13. Everywhere the larks trilled in an endless rivulet of song —Ivan Turgenev, *Fathers and Sons*

14. Long now, / The last thrush is still, the last bat / Now cruises in his sharp hieroglyphics —Robert Penn Warren, "Evening Hawk"

15. His wing / Scythes down another day — Robert Penn Warren, "Evening Hawk"

As the hawk "scythes," the metaphor continues, "we hear the crashless fall of stalks of Time."

16. See how the sparrow burrows in the sky! —Richard Wilbur, "Praise in Summer"

By using a verb for concealment or excavation, Wilbur likens the bird to a small animal and the sky to the earth.

17. [The rooks] went up again, and the air was shoved aside by their black wings and cut into exquisite scimitar shapes —Virginia Woolf, *To the Lighthouse*

The image of a bird's wings as a pair of shears is reflected in the name of one bird, the shearwater, that flies so close to the waves that it seems to cut them.

18. Ethereal minstrel! pilgrim of the sky! — William Wordsworth, "To a Skylark"

■ BIRTH

See also: LIFE

1. In our Mothers wombs we are close prisoners all —John Donne, "Quis Homo?"

In "Let Me Wither," Donne once again uses a prison image for the end of life: "Let me wither and wear out mine age in a discomfortable, in an unwholesome, in a penurious prison, and so pay my debts with my bones."

2. Mourn rather for all / Who breathlessly issue from the bone gates, / The gates of horn, / For truly it is the best of all the fates / Not to be born —Anthony Hecht, "The Vow"

The poet mourns the miscarriage of a three-month fetus. The "gates of ivory, gates of horn" are, in Greek mythology, the doorsteads of the abode of Sleep. Dreams that issue from the gates of horn are true. Hecht substitutes bone for ivory because of the connotation here.

3. Our mothers' wombs the tiring houses be / Where we are dressed for this short comedy —Sir Walter Ralegh (also spelled Raleigh), "On the Life of Man"

A tiring house was a dressing room at the Elizabethan playhouse, the place where one put on one's 'attire.'

4. Lear: When we are born, we cry that we are come / To this great stage of fools — William Shakespeare, *King Lear*, Act 4, scene 6, line 178

5. Our birth is but a sleep and a forgetting: / The Soul that rises with us, our life's Star, / Hath had elsewhere its setting, and cometh from afar —William Wordsworth, "Ode: Intimations of Immortality from Recollections of Early Childhood"

■ BIRTHDAYS

See also: DESCRIPTIONS, MISC.; LIFE; YOUTH AND AGE

1. The bread of my twentieth birthday / I buttered with the sun —Charles Causley, "Cowboy Song"

2. At twenty man is a peacock, at thirty a lion, at forty a camel, at fifty a serpent, at sixty a dog, at seventy an ape, at eighty nothing at all —Baltasar Gracian, *Orácula Manual*

A metaphorical variation from Benjamin Franklin's Almanac: "At 20 years of age the will reigns; at 30 the wit; at 40 the judgment."

3. At thirty we are all trying to cut our names in big letters upon the walls of this tenement of life; twenty years later we have carved it, or shut up our jack-knives — Oliver Wendell Holmes, *The Autocrat of the Breakfast-Table*

According to Holmes, it is only at the later stage in life that "men, like peaches and pears, grow sweet."

■ BITTERNESS

See: DESPAIR; DISAPPOINTMENT

■ BLAME

See: ACCUSATIONS

■ BLINDNESS

See also: AWARENESS/UNAWARENESS; SENSITIVITY

1. The blind have eyes in their fingers — Anon., European Proverb

2. (The *Clouds* silently take their places.) Socrates: There, now you must see how resplendent they be, or your eyes must be pumpkins, I vow —Aristophanes, *The Clouds*

3. Edgar: My father with his bleeding rings, / Their precious stones new lost —William Shakespeare, *King Lear*, Act 5, scene 3, line 189

Gloucester is blinded by the loss of his eyes, the "precious stones."

■ BLISS

See: HAPPINESS/UNHAPPINESS; JOY

■ BLUSHES

See also: FACIAL COLOR

1. The flood of red has subsided under Perry Diss's skin —A. S. Byatt, "The Chinese Lobster," *The New Yorker*, October 26, 1992

2. [Love] clad in the arms wherein with me he fought, / Oft in my face he doth his banner rest —Henry Howard (Earl of Surrey), "Love, That doth Reign and Live Within my Thought"

The notion of the blush as Love's banner was common at this time, and was used also by Wyatt and by other poets.

3. Shepherd: Come quench your blushes — William Shakespeare, *The Winter's Tale*, Act 4, scene 4, line 67

A single verb evokes a picture of blushes to be put out like a fire.

4. The bashful blood her snowy cheekes did dye —Edmund Spenser, *The Faerie Queene*

5. Her paleness turned to a fugitive flush — Edith Wharton, *The Age of Innocence*

■ BOASTERS/BOASTFULNESS

See also: CHARACTERISTICS; INSULTS; NAME CALLING; PERSONALITY PROFILES; PRIDE

1. "Old windbag," he sputtered —Sherwood Anderson, "Sophistication," Winesburg, Ohio

George Willard is maturing and growing impatient with boastfulness.

2. He was not a youth to hide his light under a bushel —Samuel Butler, *The Way of All Flesh*

This still common metaphor for anyone free from false modesty dates back to The Bible (N.T., Matthew, 5:14): "A city that is set on a hill cannot be hid. Neither do men light a candle, and put it under a bushel, but on a candlestick." Another common variant is to toot one's own horn.

3. Bellmour: . . . the drum to his own praise —William Congreve, *The Old Bachelor*, Act 1, scene 1

   Bellmour adds that "being full of blustering noise and emptiness" the drum is "the only implement of a soldier" the man thus characterized resembles." A commonly used variation is to beat one's own drum.

4. The Badger [the principal of the school] has beaten his belly-drum too hard and his bowels are probably upside down — Natsume Soseki, *Botchan*

   The stomach is described in the same way elsewhere, when Natsume says "He gave a big beat upon his professional drum." A more common version, in English, is to beat your own drum.

5. Goneril: I have been worth the whistling —William Shakespeare, *King Lear*, Act 4, scene 2, line 28

   Goneril alludes to the proverbial "it is a poor dog that is not worth whistling for" to remind her husband that he once regarded her highly and worthy of his attention. Some editors render this line, "I have been worth the whistle."

■ BOATS/BOATING

See also: DESCRIPTIONS, MISC.; SEASCAPES

1. The air—for wind it could scarce be called—was still light, it is true, but it had increased a little in the course of the night, and as the canoes were mere feathers on the water, they had drifted twice the expected distance —James Fenimore Cooper, *The Deerslayer*

   Deerslayer finds that he has drifted perilously close to shore and to Indian perils.

2. His rowboat turned turtle on the Kingston reef —Robert Hughes, *The Fatal Shore*

   The metaphor depends upon the visual image of an upturned boat.

3. When the river and bay are smooth . . . and I run along ripping it up with my knife edged shell of a boat, the rent closing after me —Oliver Wendell Holmes, "Boating"

■ BODIES/THE BODY

See also: DESCRIPTIONS, MISC.; FATNESS/ THINNESS; HAIR; MOVEMENTS; PHYSICAL APPEARANCE

1. Strepsiades: So then the rump is trumpet to the gnats! —Aristophanes, *The Clouds*

   They argue that the gnat hums through his rear-end rather than its mouth. The humor lies in the fact that humming is just another form of passing wind.

2. The healthy body, the is a guest-chamber for the soul; a sick body is a prison —Sir Francis Bacon, *Advancement of Learning*, Book 1

3. Thy neck is a tower of ivory —The Bible, *O.T., Song of Solomon 7:4*

4. The body is truly the garment of the soul which has a living voice —Hildegarde von Bingen, Letter 1178

5. His back made the angle of a jack-knife three-quarters open —Willa Cather, "The Sculptor's Funeral," *Youth and the Bright Medusa*.

6. This house of clay not built with hands — Samuel Taylor Coleridge, *Youth and Age*

   The image of man as God's sculpture has been used since its origins in The Bible *(Isaiah 64:8).*

7. The body is our school, our lesson, our protagonist, our beloved enemy . . . the jumping off place into the higher realms —John P. Conger, Quoted in introduction to "Part 4 . . . The Disowned Body: Illness, Health, and Sexuality"

8. With his bird-of-prey hands, [he] hung up ten new suits —Jose Donoso, *The Obscene Bird of Night*

9. Phoebe Ann was thin and shapeless, a very umbrella of a woman —Theodore Dreiser, "The Lost Phoebe"

10. The body . . . a tenement of clay —John Dryden, *Absalom and Achitophel*, I

11. She was pale and fair . . . and [had] hands of alabaster —Alexandre Dumas, *The Three Musketeers*

12. His [man's] body is a jar in which the liquor of life is stored —Ralph Waldo Emerson, "Wealth," *Conduct of Life*

13. The human body is the magazine of inventions, the patent office where are the models from which every hint is taken —Ralph Waldo Emerson, *Society and Solitude*

14. It was the Jane [female] who had been sitting with the human octopus —Erle Stanley Gardner, "Dead Men's Letters"
    The octopus is a man with long, constantly moving "threshing" arms.

15. From the sleeves of his nightshirt projected two knobbed sticks, his arms with a pair of immense skeleton hands fastened to the ends of them, like rakes at the end of their slender hafts —Aldous Huxley, *Point Counter Point*
    The metaphor is explained with a simile.

16. The body of man is a machine that winds its own springs —Julien Offroy de La Mettrie, "L'Homme Machine"

17. Celia is looking at her hands. They are . . . more used to typing or sealing envelopes than they are to . . . raking the uneven landscape of Seth's chest —David Leavitt, "I See London, I See France," *A Place I've Never Been*

18. She . . . waved the tiny sausages of fingers up and down in the air —Sean O'Faolain, "Mother Matilda's Book"

19. The body is the tomb of the soul —Plato, *Cratylus*, XVII

20. He was standing there, his body furred with grey —V. S. Pritchett, "On the Edge of the Cliff"
    The furry body belongs to a 70-year-old man about to take a hazardous dive.

21. His fleshly clothes,— / The flying fabric stitched on bone, / The vesture of the skeleton —Theodore Roethke, "Epidermal Macabre"

22. I not only burn my candle from both ends: I send off pyrotechnical displays from my behind —Theodore Roethke, *Straw for the Fire, Notebooks of Theodore Roethke*
    This description of passing wind might be called a metaphoric euphemism.

23. He watched her dress for dinner, her body flashing by in parts, a machine programmed with strategies to achieve goals —Lynne Sharon Schwartz, "The Two Portraits of Rembrandt"
    The husband who thus views his wife, wants a less strenuously organized and success-oriented life style with more warmth and intimacy.

24. The body of a man is not a home but an inn—and that only briefly —Seneca, *Epistulae Morales and Lucilium*, CXX

25. Iago: Our bodies are gardens, to which our wills the gardeners; so that if we will plant nettles or some lettuce . . . either to have it sterile with idleness or manured with industry, why, the power and corrigible authority of this lies in our will —William Shakespeare, *Othello*, Act 1, scene 3, line 323

26. Titus: my heart, all mad with misery, / Beats in this hollow prison of my flesh —William Shakespeare, *Titus Andronicus*, Act 3, scene 2, line 9

27. Bolingbroke: had the king permitted us, / One of our souls had wand'red in the air, / Banish'd this frail sepulchre of our flesh / As now our flesh is banish'd from this land —William Shakespeare, *The Tragedy of King Richard the Second*, Act 1, scene 3, line 195
    Shakespeare's metaphors include many that point to man's transience and that he wends his way toward death from the moment of his birth.

28. And what, pathologically looked at, is the human body with all its organs, but a mere bagful of petards? —Robert Louis Stevenson, "Aes Triplex"
    And what is a petard for, but to be hoist with?

29. My body, which my dungeon is, / And yet my parks and palaces —Robert Louis Stevenson, "To a Gardener," *Underwoods*

30. Rabbit watches her back recede . . . the thick notched rope of her spine between the blue-brown pillows of muscle —John Updike, *Rabbit, Run*

31. That old stretched-leather feeling makes his whole body go taut, gives his arms wings —John Updike, *Rabbit, Run*

32. Bosola: What's this flesh? a little crudded [curdled] milk, fantastical puff-paste —John Webster, *The Duchess of Malfi*, Act 4, scene 2

    Bosola thus responds when the duchess asks "Who am I?" He goes on to compare the soul in the body to a lark in the cage.

33. The ugly legs of the young girls, pistons / Too powerful for delicacy! —William Carlos Williams, "Paterson—The Strike"

34. Dear Tenement of clay / Endure another day / As coffin sweetly fitted to my measure —Elinor Wylie, "This Corruptible"

    Implicit in the metaphor is the theory that we begin to die the very day that we are born.

■ BOLDNESS

See: COURAGE

■ BOOKS

See also: KNOWLEDGE; READING/READERS; THINKING/THOUGHT

1. A book is a garden carried in the pocket —Anon., Arabian Proverb

2. Food of the spirit —Anon., Inscription on the Berlin Royal Library, 1780

3. Literature is a candle lighted in the mind and left alight —Anon.

4. Some books are to be tasted, others to be swallowed, and some few to be chewed and digested —Sir Francis Bacon, "Of Studies," *Dedication to the Essay*

    A variation on this well-known metaphoric advice is "Every book must be chewed to get out the juice."

5. Whether used as anesthetic to soothe a distraught nerve, or as tonic to stir to action a sluggish circulation, . . . books serve the purpose, and justify the assertion of the already quoted Bovée that "the worth of a book is a matter of expressed juices" —John Kendrick Bangs, "My Silent Servants"

6. A book is good company . . . full of conversation without loquacity —Henry Ward Beecher, *Proverbs from Plymouth Pulpit*

7. Books are the compasses and telescopes and sextants and charts which other men have prepared to help us navigate the dangerous seas of human life —Jesse Lee Bennett

8. Fiction is a kind of halfway house between the temples of truth and Falsehood where the good and bad meet to lie a little —Josh Billings

9. "A good heavy book holds you down. It's an anchor that keeps you from getting up and having another gin and tonic" —Roy Blount, Quoted in "Books of the Times," *The New York Times,* November 29, 1992

10. Books are embalméd minds / . . . [but] *real books* are nothing of the sort —C. N. Bovée, Quoted by John Kendrick Bangs in essay "My Silent Servants"

    The essay also cites books as "medicine for the soul" (as inscribed over the door of the library in Thebes) and as "the medicine of the mind" (Diodorous). If that line of reasoning is pursued, writers will have to join the AMA.

11. Books—The monument of vanish'd minds —Sir William Davenant, "Gondibert"

12. A book of fiction was a bomb. It was a land mine you wanted to go off. You

wanted it to blow your whole day —
Annie Dillard, *An American Childhood*
Dillard thus explains her early caution regarding fiction.

13. In my room / Among cities of books /
Stacked in towers. / Each book is a room
—Gjertrud Schnackenberg, "Paper Cities"
"The cities spring up from your pencil point," the poet writes.

14. Each [book] was a crystal in which the
child dreamed that he saw life moving —
Graham Greene, "The Lost Childhood,"
Collected Essays

15. The Bible, that great medicine chest of
humanity —Heinrich Heine, *Ludwig Marcus*

16. Browsing in the *New Grove Dictionary of Opera* is like an unguided tour of Paris's
Père Lachaise cemetery, but with a differ-
ence: knock on Mr. Sadie's equally vast
collection of gravestones and their inhabitants will rise, briefly explain themselves
and then disappear forever —Bernard
Holland, "Critic's Notebook," *The New York Times*, January 2, 1993
This is a case of a simile evolving into metaphor.

17. The New Grove [*The New Grove Dictionary of Opera*], is really not a body of water to be
sailed across; from its point of departure,
"Aachen," to its final port of call, "Zylis-
Gara." It is one to be fished. Both the
professional trawler and the casual angler
are invited. Toss out your line and come
up with Buleslaw Wallek-Walewsky: He
wrote "Jontek's Revenge" in 1926 —Ber-
nard Holland, "Critic's Notebook," *The New York Times*, January 2, 1993

18. Books are sepulchers of thought —Henry
Wadsworth Longfellow, "The Wind Over
the Chimney"

19. All books are either dreams or swords —
Amy Lowell, "Sword Blades and Poppy
Seeds"

20. He fed his spirit with the bread of books, /
And slaked his thirst at the wells of thought
—Edwin Markham, "Young Lincoln,"
Lincoln and Other Poems

21. Books, the mind's food, not exercise! —
Hannah More, "Conversation"

22. It's a giddy soufflé of a novel —Joyce
Carol Oates, *The New York Times Book Review*, 1991
The light-hearted novel was Wise Children *by the late Angela Carter.*

23. Books are keys to wisdom's treasure; /
Books are gates to lands of pleasure —
Emilie Poulsson
These lines from Poulsson's poem appear as an inscription for the Children's Reading Room in Hopkington, Massachusetts.

24. A best-seller is the gilded tomb of a
mediocre talent —Logan Pearsall Smith,
Afterthoughts

25. Books, the children of the brain —Jonathan Swift, *The Tale of a Tub*

26. Novels are sweets. All people with healthy
literary appetites love them —William
Makepeace Thackeray, *Roundabout Papers*

27. This wintry tale is a steel etching on a
stark white ground —John Updike, "Critic
at Large," *The New Yorker*, October 4, 1993
To tie in with Edith Wharton's renewed populari-ty, Updike's article examined her novels, includ-ing Ethan Frome.

28. Books are lighthouses erected in the great
sea of time —Edward Percy Whipple

29. [Books:] The home-traveler's ship . . . the
opiate of idle weariness . . . the mind's
best garden . . . the seed-plot of immortality —Richard Whitlock, *Zootomia*
In modern usage, the "home-traveler" has evolved into the armchair traveler.

■ BOREDOM
See: DULLNESS; MONOTONY

■ BORROWING

See: DEBT

■ BOSTON

See: CITIES; STREET SCENES

■ BOXING

See: SPORTS

■ BRAIN

See also: MIND; THINKING/THOUGHT

1. The brain is a good stagehand. It gets on with its work while we're busy acting out our scenes —Diane Ackerman, *A Natural History of the Senses*

2. The brain . . . a grab bag of evolutionary tricks —Gerald M. Edelman, *Bright Air, Brilliant Fire*

3. Just get this settled in your think tank. I'm coming, and I'm going to be there with bells on —Erle Stanley Gardner, "Dead Men's Letters"

   The speaker, Ed Jenkins, is one of Gardner's earliest heroes. The use of think tank for one's mind precedes the current association with gatherings of people with special intelligence.

4. The brain becomes more efficient through a process he [Dr. Richard Haier] calls "neural pruning" . . . During this process, Dr. Haier says, the brain is weeding out unnecessary synaptic connections — Dr. Richard Haier, "Campus Journal," *New York Times*, August 26, 1992

5. Our brains are seventy-year clocks. The Angel of Life winds them up once for all, then closes the case and gives the key to the Angel of Resurrection —Oliver Wendell Holmes, *The Autocrat of the Breakfast-Table*

■ BRAVERY

See: COURAGE

■ BREASTS/BOSOMS

See also: MEN AND WOMEN; PHYSICAL APPEARANCE; SEX/SEXUALITY

1. If I had the nerve, I swear I'd buy me some bigger breasts instead of walking around . . . with these little sunny-side-ups on my chest —Terry McMillan, *Waiting to Exhale*

2. Beth: Mom and Aunt Sue had killer knockers. But mine, it turned out, were to be a winter harvest —Jordan Roberts, *At The Still Point*

3. Her thin light-blue blouse fitted so tightly that you saw her breasts as two big, firm hemispheres standing apart — Sigrid Undset, "The Loss and the Healing,"

4. The pearls on that shelf / of expensive bosom —Mona Van Duyn, "Views," *The New York Times*, 1992

   In this poem the Pulitzer prize winning U.S. poet laureate of 1992 writes about a woman assuaging her fear of flying by concentrating on the appearance of people around her.

5. He felt her hot breath on his face, the smothering flood of her breasts —Thomas Wolfe, *Look Homeward Angel*

■ BREATH

See also: DESCRIPTIONS, MISC.; PEOPLE, INTERACTION

1. Celia feels the warm breeze of his breath on her face —Cristina Garcia, *Dreaming in Cuban*

2. Breath's a ware that will not keep —A. E. Housman

3. Our breath was clouds, a stump / steamed quietly —Melvin Walker La Follette, "Hunt"

■ BREEZES

See: WIND

■ BRIGHTNESS

*See also: ANIMALS; DESCRIPTIONS, MISC.;
FACIAL EXPRESSIONS; PERSONALITY
PROFILES*

1. [A peacock:] So beauti-ful. A tail full of
    suns —Flannery O'Connor, "The Dis-
    placed Person"
    > *The beautiful peacock has "the grand self-confi-
    > dence of a mountain."*

2. His smile broadened; he was the gayest of
    Della Robbia angels —Aldous Huxley,
    Time Must Have a Stop
    > *This metaphoric angel is a handsome schoolboy.*

■ BROADWAY

See: STREET SCENES

■ BUDGETING/BUDGETS

See: ECONOMICS

■ BUGS

See: INSECTS

■ BUILDINGS AND BRIDGES

See also: DESCRIPTIONS, MISC.; HOUSES

1. Bridges are America's cathedrals —Anon.

2. Cathedrals, / Luxury liners laden with
    souls —W. H. Auden, "On This Island"

3. The Hotel du Nord—that tall prism . . .
    which brings together the hateful blank
    white walls of a hospital, the numbered
    chambers of a cell block, and the overall
    appearance of a brothel —Jorge Luis
    Borges, "Death and the Compass"
    > *The third term in the series is not a true metaphor.
    > If the metaphor were to hold, the hotel would be a
    > brothel, rather than just appearing to be one.*

4. Far astern of the pilgrim ship a screw-pile
    lighthouse, planted by unbelievers on a
    treacherous shoal, seemed to wink at her
    its eye of flame [at the ship *Patna*], as if in
    derision of her errand of faith —Joseph
    Conrad, *Lord Jim*
    > *The ship is carrying eight hundred Arab pilgrims
    > on their way to Mecca.*

5. Bridges . . . with heads tall as cities and
    skirts of cable strands —F. Scott Fitzger-
    ald, "The Sensible Thing," *All the Sad
    Young Men*
    > *An example of simile and metaphor linked to one
    > source.*

6. Here [in New York] the skyscraper is . . .
    not an element in city planning, but a
    banner in the sky, a fireworks rocket —Le
    Corbusier, "The Fairy Catastrophe"

7. The building . . . stood narrow and glass-
    eyed —Doris Lessing, "Dialogue"

8. It appeared to them . . . forlorn and de-
    feated, something the wind might take
    away—something that could rumble with
    footsteps and shriek with bells and hold
    them in its belly for six hours each day
    only in the wildest . . . of dreams —Alice
    McDermott, *At Weddings and Wakes*
    > *McDermott uses a metaphor of personification to
    > picture how a school appears to its students during
    > the summer.*

9. The Island Motel is a whitewashed shoebox
    —James Robison, "Between Seasons,"
    The New Yorker, June 14, 1993

10. The roof of the booking-hall / sails out
    into the air —Richard Wilbur, "For the
    New Railway Station in Rome"

■ BUSINESS DESCRIPTIONS

*See also: DIFFICULTIES; ECONOMICS; FAIL-
URE; IMPORTANCE / UNIMPORTANCE;
PLACES, MISC.*

1. Upstairs, last season's cottons . . . stuffed into sales racks . . . are overripe. Whereas the new stuff . . . is ready for harvest — Anon., "Topics of the Times," *New York Times,* August 26, 1992

    The shoppers who want to reap bargains, however, will stay with the old stuff. And the manufacturers will always complain that the season is only "sow sow."

2. Mr. Schwager's traders, plucked from the market grapevine, range from a woman who could play the Moonlight sonata on her piano, to a Vietnam veteran who had studied for the priesthood, to a first class mathematician completing his Ph.D. — Stanley W. Angrist, *The Wall Street Journal,* December 23, 1992

    The book review considered The New Market Wizards *by Jack Schwager. Since information passes along the grapevine, one may assume that the fruits of his recruitment were the result of friendly tips.*

3. Practicing law, particularly making rain for a big-time Washington law firm, was never on his list of dream jobs. —David Beck, *The New York Times,* May 7, 1993

    This jargon metaphor for bringing new business to law firms or advertising agencies was used by former vice-president Dan Quayle's erstwhile spokesperson in response to rumors that Mr. Quayle might join an Indianapolis law firm.

4. For Jerry Jones, a onetime Arkansas wildcatter, it proved to be a perfect time to roll the dice and buy the distressed property— the Dallas Cowboys football team —Thomas C. Hayes, *The New York Times,* January 24, 1993

    "But winning has made Mr. Jones chary of raising the ante too fast in contract talks," the writer continued, extending the poker image. With the phrase "advertisers joined the Cowboys bandwagon" he later added another common metaphor.

5. Businesses are poking their heads out, hoping to spy an end to the long winter — Herbert B. Herring, "Business Diary," *The New York Times,* November 15, 1992

    The cautious banks, however, acted as if being a groundhog simply means hogging the ground.

6. The drug Centoxin is not the only egg in Centocor's basket, but it is by far the biggest one —Herbert B. Herring, "Business Diary," *The New York Times,* January 24, 1993

    The metaphor builds on the proverbial advice not to put all your eggs in one basket.

7. "GM Takes Some Big Lumps" But as Chrysler cruises, General Motors keeps hitting potholes. First it swallowed, in one accounting gulp, future retiree health costs —Herbert B. Herring, "Business Diary," *The New York Times,* February 7, 1993

    In three short sentences, including the paragraph head, three unrelated metaphors constitute a kind of shorthand to tell a long story quickly.

8. Nor is . . . the Mall of America just a pumped-up Paramus-on-the-Prairie, one more cookie-cutter amalgam of stores, frozen-yogurt stands and packs of free-range adolescents in Guess jeans —Neal Karlen, "The Mall that Ate Minnesota" *The New York Times,* August 30, 1992

    In one line, Mr. Karlen took a swipe at New Jersey, mushed together his cookie batter, and compared kids to cattle.

9. It is also a 78-acre full-sensory smorgasbord of consumerism —Neal Karlen, "The Mall that Ate Minnesota," *The New York Times,* August 30, 1992

    This mall sounds like an immoveable feast.

10. A manufacturer, of course, would commit economic hara-kiri if he were to try to sell us a car on truthful grounds, for how could he ask anyone to pay $4,500 for a three-hundred-horsepower contraption on grounds that it would be used only two hours a day . . . ? —John Keats, "The Call of the Open Road"

    For the 1958 sticker price, most modern consumers would risk a degree of prevarication.

11. Eighty percent of everything ever built in America has been built in the last 50 years and most of it is depressing: . . . Potemkin village shopping plazas with their vast

parking lagoons —James Howard Kunstler, *The Geography of Nowhere*
> *There are also "Lego-block hotel complexes and jive-plastic commuter tract home wastelands."*

12. Intel and Advanced Micro officials, setting aside their animosities for a moment, agreed at Comdex to disparage the Cyrix chip as not a true 486 wolf but rather a 386SX sheep with some admittedly impressive clothing —Peter H. Lewis, "The Executive Computer," *The New York Times*, November 29, 1992
> *Many of us, confronted with computer jargon, feel rather sheepish ourselves.*

13. The premiere issue of *Reader's Digest* . . . introduced the master recipe that Wally [De Witt Wallace] and his editorial sous chefs would follow for the next 71 years —Richard Lingemann, *The New York Times Book Review*, August 22, 1993
> *The article was titled "Processed in Pleasantville" and illustrated with a plate of soup and soup cans bearing the* Reader's Digest *imprint—a case of the metaphor dominating the whole editorial mix.*

14. On Wall Street, IBM isn't just a company—it's a religion with at least two rival theologies —Steve Lohr, "Market Place," *The New York Times*, October 19, 1992
> *Lohr pointed out that one "theology" held that the company was trapped in a cycle of inevitable decline and another rested on its ability to come back.*

15. Timothy is my agent . . . I am the goose that lays his golden eggs —Ross MacDonald, *The Moving Target*
> *The metaphoric goose is a successful writer.*

16. Salomon's partners sat in a zoo of trading rooms, cheek by jowl with their clerks and each other, shouting —Martin Mayer, *Nightmare on Wall Street*
> *Two very common metaphors contrast Salomon's atmosphere with that of more spacious and elegant trading companies like Morgan Stanley. The second image can be traced to the sixteenth century as* cheek by cheek *and Demetrius's "I'll go with thee, cheek by jole," (Shakespeare's* A Midsummer Night's Dream, *3, 2, 338).*

17. This is a wonderful bull market. Technology stocks are hot and the speculative juices are flowing —Floyd Norris, *The New York Times*, January 24, 1993
> *There are three metaphors here. A bull market trends upwards, as a bull throws its head (and its prey) upward. Stocks are "hot" or in demand when they are as fresh and hot from the oven as mother's biscuits were before the era of frozen food—and the very thought of them makes the digestive juices flow.*

18. The transaction attests to changes that are starting to loosen the bonds of Japanese supplier networks, or keiretsu, that have been a hallmark of Japan's success — Andrew Pollack, *The New York Times* August 30, 1992
> *Both "network" and "hallmark" have become idiomatic. A hallmark is an official stamp on gold or silver to validate its purity, and is used here as an idiom. The writer freshened the first metaphor by making it concrete.*

19. We're in an industry of sequoias and acorns, and what we were doing was operating outside the radar screen of large houses, looking for things that they had overlooked and finding a way to make them work —Arthur H. Samuelson, Quoted in "Book Notes," *The New York Times*, June 23, 1993
> *The comment was occasioned by the news that the medium-sized publishing company of which Mr. Samuelson had been editor-in-chief was for sale.*

20. Advertising tries to be a pyromaniac igniting conflagrations of desires for instant gratification —George Will, "The Madison Legacy," *Washington Post Syndicate*, December 7, 1981
> *Will linked Madison Avenue's long ties to advertising with his analysis of the "Madisonian society."*

■ BUSYNESS

See also: ACTIVENESS/INACTIVENESS; BUSINESS DESCRIPTIONS; CHARACTERIZATIONS

1. The life of this stupendously energetic Earth Mother remained an amazing balancing act —Francine Du Plessix Gray, "A Critic At Large," *The New Yorker,* July 26, 1923

   The multi-faceted woman was George Sand, who juggled domesticity, romance and career long before the Women's Movement.

2. In five days they would be in the cyclone of examinations —Sinclair Lewis, *Main Street*

3. We have other fish to fry —François Rabelais, *Works,* Book 5

   This much-used metaphor also appeared in Cervantes' Don Quixote.

4. The sports industry is approaching full throttle; hockey playoffs are under way, pro basketball is rushing towards its dramatic conclusion, and pro football's annual draft is set for Sunday. And baseball's back —William C. Rhoden, "Sports of the Times," *The New York Times,* April 21, 1993

5. Look at one of your industrious fellows . . . He sows hurry and reaps indigestion —Robert Louis Stevenson, "An Apology for Idlers"

■ BUYING/SELLING

See: PEOPLE, INTERACTION

CALAMITY

See: ADVERSITY; DANGER

CALMNESS/VOLATILITY

See also: CHARACTERIZATIONS; DANGER;
PERSONALITY PROFILES; TRANQUILITY

1. Long before the first firebomb exploded in anti-refugee attacks in Rostock, economic and social trauma wrought by the transition from Communism to capitalism had made the city a powder keg —Anon., *The New York Times,* September 3, 1992
   The container for gunpowder has become a common metaphor for explosive, dangerous situations.

2. My desire to possess the voluptuous Alfreda threatened to make rubble of my long-cultivated equanimity —Louis Auchincloss, "The Epicurean," *Three Lives*

3. He was not a rushing river, boiling and tumbling over rocks, but the placid stream flowing through the quiet meadows — Ernest Longfellow, About his father, the poet, who died in 1882

4. Abbess: Thou say'st his meat was sauc'd with thy upraidings: / Unquiet meals make ill digestions —William Shakespeare, *The Comedy of Errors,* Act 5, scene 1, line 73
   Variations of the sauce metaphor appear in other Shakespeare plays.

5. His inner weather became less troubled — Thornton Wilder, *The Eighth Day*

CALUMNY

See: SLANDER

CANDOR

See also: PEOPLE, INTERACTION

1. Education Minister Shulamit Aloni . . . has plagued the [Israeli] Prime Minister with a tatoo of blunt remarks on just about everything from God to the future of the Golan Heights —Clyde Haberman, *The New York Times,* September 25, 1992
   The metaphor is a two-edged sword since Jewish tradition forbids anyone with a tatoo to be buried in consecrated ground.

2. Honesty . . . can become at times the moral equivalent of assault and battery. I don't think it hurts to cover hurts—the bandage principle of human intercourse —John Hersey, "Fling," *Grand Street*

3. But total candor can be the rape of hope —Martha Weinman Lear, "Should Doctors Tell the Truth?" *The New York Times Magazine,* January 24, 1993
   The author concluded that when it comes to "terminal candor" what we need is a middle ground with any changes coming from the de-

mands of a society which seems unsure what it wants.

4. Menenius: his heart's his mouth —William Shakespeare, *Coriolanus*, Act 3, scene 1, line 255

■ CAPABILITY

See: ABILITY

■ CAREFULNESS

See: CAUTION

■ CATS

See: ANIMALS

■ CAUSE AND EFFECT

1. If you sow turkeys you will reap fools — Anon., European Proverb

2. When the community gets a boil, the individual also gets a blister —Anon., Yiddish Proverb

3. I am going to let Paris stew in her own gravy —Otto von Bismarck, Quoted during the siege of Paris

   Bismarck's comment is said to have led to the now common, to stew in one's own juice, as a metaphor for self-induced suffering. In its literal beginnings fried in one's own grease referred to a person burned at the stake. In The Merry Wives of Windsor *Shakespeare changed "fried" to "melting Falstaff in his own grease."*

4. The thorns which I have reap'd are of the tree I planted —Lord George Gordon Byron, "Childe Harold"

5. The dust from those hearings is a long way from settling —Stephen L. Carter, Op-Ed, *The New York Times*, October 4, 1992

   Carter was referring to Judge Clarence Thomas's Supreme Court nomination.

6. The doctrine of karma teaches that what we reap accords with what we have sowed

—Philip Kapleau, *The Wheel of Life and Death*

   This is one of the cornerstones of Buddhist teaching.

7. The chickens of the past eight years are coming home to roost and you're in charge of the henhouse —Douglas (General) MacArthur, to John F. Kennedy, 1961

   The General's remark to President John F. Kennedy, an update of Robert Southey's The chickens come home to roost *(c. 1810), was prompted by the Bay of Pigs fiasco and the country's increasing involvement in Vietnam. It was requoted in a 1993* New York Times *article on the many foreign policy problems facing Bill Clinton on the eve of his election on a platform of domestic reforms.*

8. Callimaco: It's all too true that fortune and nature balance our accounts between them: nothing good happens but something bad is sure to follow —Niccolo Machiavelli, *Mandragola*, Act 4

9. Let's hope that the changing military doesn't dry up the heterodox talent pool from which he [Shalikashvili] and his predecessor [Colin Powell] came —James Pinkerton, *The Berkshire Eagle*, August 23, 1993

   Pinkerton takes the word "pool" meaning aggregate and twists it to mean a pool of water by using "dry up." It is a mixed metaphor using a homonym, but it is cleverly done.

10. The changes wrought by death are in themselves so sharp and final, . . . [that] when the business is done, there is sore havoc made in other people's lives, and a pin knocked out by which many subsidiary friendships hung together —Robert Louis Stevenson, "Aes Triplex"

■ CAUTION

See also: BUSINESS DESCRIPTIONS

1. We put a little toe in the water, but we didn't go all the way —Anon., *The New York Times*, August 26, 1992

A representative of the Islanders' front office thus described the early stages of a labor negotiation. Another water metaphor, getting one's feet wet, pictured a novice's action.

2. Or, as Assembly Minority leader C. D. (Rapp) Rappleyea said regarding a dead-of-night pay-raise voted in December 1984: "If you're going to walk the plank, you might as well do it in shallow water" —Anon., "Political Notes," *The New York Times,* November 15, 1992
   This apt metaphor for the Assembly's political maneuver originated with eighteenth century pirates who thus got rid of their prisoners.

3. Although a lion in the field, / A lamb in town thou shalt him find —attributed to Nicholas Breton, "A Cradle Song"

4. A wise man does not trust all his eggs to one basket —Miguel de Cervantes, *Don Quixote*
   This has become a common proverbial expression.

5. Richard Daenzer [a real estate manager] believes in the "Tarzan theory" of employment: You don't let go of one vine until you have the next one in hand — Richard Daenzer, Quoted in "Executives the Economy Left Behind," *The New York Times,* November 22, 1992

6. I have measured out my life with coffee spoons —T. S. Eliot, "The Love Song of J. Alfred Prufrock"

7. What was striking about Mr. Clinton's first week in office was the way he swung for the fences on the domestic front and laid down bunts in the foreign affairs field —Thomas L. Friedman, *The New York Times,* January 31, 1993

8. Moderation is the silken string running through the pearl—chain of all virtues — Thomas Fuller, *The Holy State and the Profane State,* III

9. She was so cautious . . . that with Jasper Gibbon she almost missed the bus —W. Somerset Maugham, *Cakes and Ale*

This woman is cautious about risking her reputation for launching literary reputations.

10. It is always well to moor your ship with two anchors —Publilius Syrus, *Sententiae*

11. One picked one's way among the mines and booby traps of the hospital, hoping only to avoid the hemorrhage and perforation of disgrace —Richard Selzer, "Imelda"
    Selzer reflects on the path of the third-year medical student.

■ CELEBRITY

See: FAME

■ CENSURE

See: CRITICISM/CRITICS

■ CEREMONIES

See: POLITICS/POLITICIANS

■ CESSATION

See: ENDINGS

■ CHANCE

See also: FATE

1. Luck never gives, it only lends —Anon., Swedish Proverb

2. I am the beneficiary of a lucky break in the genetic sweepstakes —Isaac Asimov, Quoted in his obituary, *The New York Times,* April 7, 1992
   This modest self-appraisal was an apt metaphor for the author of many science-based works.

3. [Alexander] Woollcott rejoiced in coincidence. He was never happier than when giving its long arm a tug —John Mason Brown, Introduction, *The Portable Woollcott*
   To underscore, Brown quotes Woollcott himself: "We love to catch life in the very act of rhyming."

4. Chance is the pseudonym of God when he did not want to sign —Thèophile Gautier, *La Croix de Berny*

> *From a book of letters composed by Gautier and three other writers, all of whom used pseudonyms.*

5. Under the bludgeoning of chance / My head is bloody but unbowed —William Ernest Henley, "Invictus"

6. All the affairs of men hang by a slender thread —Ovid, "Ex Ponto"

7. Chance makes a football of man's life — Seneca, *Letters to Lucillus*

8. That Rich fool, who by blind Fortune's lot, / The richest gem of love and life enjoys —Sir Philip Sidney, "Sonnet 24," *Astrophel and Stella*

> *Life is a game of chance, where the prize sometimes goes to the least qualified of players.*

9. I am . . . / A nosegay which Time clutched from out / Those fair Elysian fields . . . / a parcel of vain striving tied / By a chance bond together —Henry David Thoreau, "Sic Vita"

■ CHANGE

See also: CALMNESS/VOLATILITY; DETERIORATION/DIMINISHMENT; HABIT; REFORM; TRANSFORMATION

1. President Vaclav Havel, the playwright who led his country's "Velvet Revolution" against Communism, left office today —Anon., *The New York Times,* July 21, 1992

> *On the same day that this metaphor, born during the collapse of Communism in Eastern Europe appeared,* Times *columnist Russell Baker spoofed political handlers with "You've got to handle handlers with a velvet touch or they'll quit handling you." And by January 1, 1993, the "velvet revolution" had metamorphosed into "the velvet divorce."*

2. No man putteth a piece of new cloth unto an old garment . . . [nor] new wine into old bottles . . . put new wine into new bottles, and both are preserved —The Bible, *N.T., Matthew 9:16, 9:17; Mark 2:22; Luke 5:38*

> *The cloth and garment and the wine and bottles are metaphors for the new shape and practices needed to implement new ideas and organizations.*

3. Every Universal Form was become barren mountains of Moral / Virtue, and every Minute Particular harden'd into grains of sand —William Blake, "Jerusalem," Chapter 2

4. Our twentieth century had inverted the story of Mohammed and the mountain; nowadays the mountain came to the modern Mohammed —Jorge Luis Borges, "The Aleph"

> *In 1945 technology was much less advanced than it is today, yet Borges even then saw man in his "castle tower" waiting for information rather than going out to seek it.*

5. The lamps are lit for the night, against that death which is change —Hortense Calisher, "Time, Gentlemen!"

> *For a 20th-century family headed by a father strongly linked to the Victorian era, the break with the family's old-fashioned patterns is equated with death.*

6. Seti: You have fermented in your Midian bottle —Christopher Fry, *The Firstborn,* Act 1, scene 1

> *Seti, the Pharaoh, thinks the time Moses spent in Midian exile has made him lose his Egyptian rationality.*

7. If the time is long past when distinguished musicians and critics like Tchaikovsky and Ernest Newman could dismiss Mussorgsky's [sic] works as hopeless crude and amateurish, the pendulum more recently had swung to the other extreme — Donal Henahan, *The New York Times Book Review,* January 31, 1993

> *The review of* Musorgsky, *by Richard Taruskin used the common metaphor of the swinging pendulum as an indicator of reversal.*

8. I have seen Europe, for twenty-five hundred years the crown of the world, become

its beggar and cripple —Robinson Jeffers, "The World's Wonders"
> *One of the many strange things the poem's protagonist has seen in his sixty-odd years of life.*

9. Three months into the new [Trenton, NJ] legislative session, the ground may be shifting. It is by no means an earthquake, but there are tremors —Wayne King, *The New York Times,* April 26, 1992

10. He does not yet understand why with a little more, or a little louder, lying he should not be able permanently to break the chain of that law of cause and effect— the Justice without the Mercy—which he hates —Rudyard Kipling, "Independence"

11. Then his temper switched tracks and he smiled cordially again —John Knowles, *A Separate Peace.*
> *A father who sees military service as a lifelong badge of honor, is temporarily put off by two young men's unwillingness to enlist during the second World War.*

12. The problem for China is that while it has abandoned many of its Maoist policies and is now trying on pin-striped business suits, some of its former comrades-in-arms are still wearing camouflage gear — Nicholas D. Kristof, *The New York Times,* May 9, 1993
> *The clothing metaphor, used here to indicate political, radical change, depends on an implicit personification of China to make it work.*

13. I think all of us at this symposium are aware of the fact that we live in one of those grand moments in world history when we have an opportunity to redesign the architecture of the world political order —Tommy Koh, *The Singapore Symposium,* United Nations

14. I can't turn into a pillar of salt in five minutes just because you and I can't live together! It takes years for a woman like me to turn into a pillar of salt —D. H. Lawrence, "Two Blue Birds"
> *"After all, I've got to live," says the wife, without much regard for the fact that the metaphor carries an allusion to Lot's wife.*

15. The newly founded [monarchies] are either entirely new, or else they are new members grafted on to the hereditary possessions of the prince that annexes them —Niccolo Machiavelli, *The Prince*
> *The metaphor is borrowed from gardening.*

16. As our wars have been long, so must our healing be swift. Deep gaps call for lofty breezes —Shimon Peres, Statement at the signing of the Middle East Pact, September 13, 1993

17. Our epoch in history, which has produced one of the greatest achievements of the human race, may be passing into a twilight that does not precede the dawn —I. I. Rabi, "Scientist and Humanist"
> *Science, according to the Nobel Laureate, has been used for the destruction of life and the degradation of the human spirit.*

18. How different [are] these AIDS interviews now from the ones four years ago . . . when all was well and I was just a spectator to the train wreck, not riding in one of the cars —Jeffrey Schmaltz, *The New York Times,* December 20, 1992
> *The reporter reflected on the difference between covering the AIDS beat as a healthy gay man and as an AIDS sufferer.*

19. Here, / in the room of my life / the objects keep changing —Anne Sexton, "The Room of My Life"

20. Romeo: O sweet Juliet, / Thy beauty hath made me effeminate, / And in my temper soften'ed valor's steel —William Shakespeare, *Romeo and Juliet,* Act 3, scene 1, line 109

21. Cardinal Beaufort: Your lady is forthcoming [under arrest] yet in London. This news, I think, has turned your weapon's edge —William Shakespeare, *The Second Part of Henry the Sixth,* Act 2, scene 1, line 178

22. The director [Deborah Warner] is famous for sandblasting texts and leaving them hanging in the wind —Fiona Shaw, Introduction to Public Broadcasting production of *Hedda Gabler,* March 28, 1993

23. Toward the end of his days, the pattern of his life shifted to a lower gear —Howard Teichmann, *George S. Kaufman*
Playing on the automotive metaphor, Teichmann adds that though Kaufman traded his street shoes for slippers "his basic drive" did not change.

24. Once you have made up your mind to scythe, why, you must scythe your very feet from under you —Ivan Turgenev, *Fathers and Sons*
Bazarov, the anarchist, wants to rid Russia of the old order.

25. He had cut loose from the familiar shores of habit, and launched himself on uncharted seas of emotion; all the old tests and measures were left behind and his course was to be shaped by new stars —Edith Wharton, *The House of Mirth*
Unfortunately, Selden "sailed" too late to prevent the tragic death of Lily Barth.

26. His coming had broken in on the slumber of circumstance, widening the present till it became the encloser of remotest chance —Edith Wharton, "The Journey," *The Greater Inclination*
A sheltered schoolteacher's horizons are briefly broadened by marriage. When her husband becomes ill, life again becomes narrow. "Life had a grudge against her: she was never to be allowed to spread her wings," the young woman reflects.

27. The lobbyists are forming new business coalitions, and dusting off old ones to seek a quick repeal [of the recently passed tax legislation] on Capitol Hill —Michael Wines, *The New York Times,* August 26, 1993
The simple domestic metaphor is a popular figure for giving new life to old ideas and practices. During the 1993 summer season, the Williamstown Theater Festival's artistic director, Peter Hunt, told an interviewer "It's fun to dust off these plays and these writers who have sort of fallen out of fashion."

■ CHANGEABLENESS/UNCHANGEABLENESS

See also: FLEXIBILITY/INFLEXIBILITY; HABIT; TOUGHNESS

1. [Great food, beautiful women, God, promises of heaven or hell:] Not one of all these powers could induce him to transfer a single straw from one saucer of his scales into another —Honoré de Balzac, "The Commission in Lunacy"

2. Can the Ethiopian change his skin, or the leopard his spots? —The Bible, *O.T., Proverbs 26:11*
The second part of the metaphor has become a common expression for describing someone resistant to change. Tiger's stripes are also frequently used as a metaphor instead of the leopard's spots.

3. [Ross] Perot has become almost a Rorschach candidate . . . people can read into him anything they want —E. J. Dionne, *MacNeil-Lehrer News Hour,* May 22, 1992
The metaphor alludes to the ink blot test used to assess personality.

4. Of course you don't change a person's nature. You retouch it —André Maurois, "Home Port"
The metaphor concludes a story about a woman who marries a man very much like the lover she gave up because of a transformation supposedly wrought in her by a chance encounter.

5. I never intend to change more than my spots. But I want the outer semblance of the things I used to know, the utter boredom of respectability —Margaret Mitchell, *Gone With the Wind*
Rhett Butler, about to return to the roots he has scorned, draws on the common adage of the leopard's unerasable spots to explain his action to Scarlett.

6. There was no vacuum cleaner in the world that could instantly restore all the rooms of her brain to their former immaculate condition —Vladimir Nabokov, *King, Queen, Knave*

7. They were optimistic rationalists who imagined whole populations sliced free of their limiting past and present, then flipped over to fry in a new, clean future —John Ralston Saul, *Voltaire's Bastards*

    A simile describes these people as having all the passivity of a Big Mac. You might say the simile is the slice of pickle that tops off the food metaphor.

8. Old Man: Insistence on a floppy old coat, a rickety old chair, a moth-eaten hat which no certified lunatic would ever consider wearing, a car which breaks down twenty times in twenty minutes, an old idea riddled with the pellets of incidence —Wole Soyinka, *Madmen and Specialists*, Part 1

    The old man rails against the idea of freedom of choice. "Choice! Particularity! What redundant self-deceptive notions!"

■ CHAOS

See: ORDER/DISORDER

■ CHARACTER

See also: CHARACTERIZATIONS; GOODNESS; PERSONALITY PROFILES

1. Character is a kettle that, once mended, always needs repairs —Anon., Proverb

2. Here, God bless it, was the original English foundation of him showing through all the foreign varnish at last! —Wilkie Collins, *The Moonstone*

    Master Franklin had been educated abroad, which accounted for the "varnish" on his sound English construction.

3. Every true man is a cause, a country, and an age —Ralph Waldo Emerson, "Self Reliance"

    Character "takes place of the whole creation," says Emerson.

4. There are only two kinds of people in the world that really count. One kind's wheat and the other kind's emeralds —Edna Ferber, *So Big*

5. Though nature had given [Jonathan] the greatest and most shining endowments, she had not given them absolutely pure and without alloy —Henry Fielding, *The Life of Mr. Jonathan Wild the Great*

    Another form of this metaphor is the more common to see what metal a man is made of.

6. The current opinion of the Indian character, however, is too apt to be formed from the miserable hordes which infest the frontiers, and hang on the skirts of the settlements —Washington Irving, "Traits of Indian Character"

7. Freedom and nobility seemed to clothe him and stoic wildness. A young eagle with plumage ruffled by the storm . . . ! —Ludwig Lewisohn, *Up Stream: An American Chronicle*

    The title of Lewisohn's book about his immigrant experience is itself a metaphor.

■ CHARACTERISTICS

See also: EGO/ID; PERSONALITY PROFILES

1. All men are full of dogs. Temper is a snarly cur; destructiveness is a bull-dog; combativeness is a hound that runs and barks and bites —Henry Ward Beecher, Sermon, (1813–87)

2. Behind us we have an invisible bag, and the part of us our parents don't like, we, to keep our parents' love, put in the bag. —Robert Bly, "The Long Bag We Drag Behind Us"

    According to the author we "spend our life until we're twenty deciding what parts of ourself to put into the bag, and we spend the rest of our lives trying to get them out again."

3. Modesty is the only sure bait when you angle for praise —Earl of Chesterfield (Philip Dormer Stanhope), *Letters to His Son*, May 8, 1750

4. Beauty, strength, youth are flowers but fading seen; / Duty, faith, love are roots,

and ever green —George Peele, "His Golden Locks Time Hath to Silver Turned"

The poem here identified by its first line is also known by the title "A Farewell to Arms."

5. Menenius: [Coriolanus] is ill school'd / In bolted language; meal and bran together / He throws without distinction — William Shakespeare, *Coriolanus,* Act 3, scene 1, line 319

Trying to excuse Coriolanus' lack of diplomacy, Menenius compares his spontaneous speech to a baker's throwing together ingredients haphazardly.

6. Falstaff: If then the tree may be known by the fruit, as the fruit by the tree . . . there is virtue in that Falstaff —William Shakespeare, *The First Part of King Henry the Fourth,* Act 2, scene 4, line 433

This is Falstaff's argument against banishment.

7. Cassius: This rudeness is a sauce to his good wit, / Which gives men stomach to digest his words / With better appetite — William Shakespeare, *Julius Caesar,* Act 1, scene 2, line 305

In As You Like It, *(act 3, scene 5, line 69), Rosalind says "as fast as she answers thee with frowning looks, I'll sauce her with bitter words."*

■ CHARACTERIZATIONS

See also: CHANGEABLENESS/UNCHANGE-ABLENESS; ENDURANCE; EXCITE-MENT; GOOD/EVIL; HUMANITY/HU-MANKIND; NAME CALLING; OCCUPA-TIONS;PERSONALITYPROFILES;TEM-PERAMENT

1. The cactus-tongued Texan, Ross Perot — Anon., Editorial, *The New York Times,* January 18, 1993

2. Nevertheless, Moira was our fantasy . . . she was lava beneath the crust of everyday life —Margaret Atwood, *The Handmaid's Tale*

"Moira was like an elevator with open sides," writes Atwood of her flamboyant character.

3. My brother is a crocodile—he is impulsive and angry, he changes like the wind —Cecilia Bartoli, Quoted in *The New York Times Magazine,* March 14, 1993

In an interview with Linda Blandford, the diva thus described the brother in whose care she was frequently left during her childhood.

4. Her graph went beyond the chart and filled up a whole wall —Saul Bellow, *The Bellarosa Connection*

The woman compared to a line on a chart is literally and figuratively larger-than life, "off the continuum."

5. Although his horizons [Alexander Woollcott's] widened, the world through which he subsequently moved . . . continued to be lighted by a spotlight . . . He never touched life without rouging it —John Mason Brown, Introduction, *The Portable Woollcott*

Brown comments on the long-lasting influence of his life in the theater.

6. He was a mixture of bull-dog and gamecock, with a dash of the savage —Wilkie Collins, *The Moonstone*

This is a difficult transmogrification even to imagine, especially to describe a man called Honorable John.

7. How happy he was . . . out in the countryside with a divorced American woman . . . who had been through the fiery crucible and emerged on top of the mountain, a finer alloy —Laurie Colwin, "Sentimental Memory"

8. She brings everything to a grindstone and sharpens it, as she has sharpened her own face and figure these years past. She has worn herself away by constant sharpening. She is all edge —Charles Dickens, *David Copperfield*

Steerforth thus appraises Miss Rosa Dartle; David had more kindly called her "clever."

9. President Clinton has left Candidate Clinton in the dust, taking a hard left turn out of the mainstream and speeding onto the liberal autobahn, where there are no limits

on taxing and spending —Senator Robert Dole, Op-Ed, *The New York Times,* June 25, 1993

> *The Senator thus defended his negative stance toward the President's deficit reduction plan.*

10. Old Henry Reifsneider and his wife Phoebe were a loving couple . . . with simple natures that fasten themselves like lichens on the stones of circumstance and weather their days to a crumbling conclusion —Theodore Dreiser, "The Lost Phoebe"

> *The metaphor is founded on a simile.*

11. When Miss Emily Grierson died, our whole town went to her funeral: the men through a sort of respectful affection for a fallen monument —William Faulkner, "A Rose for Emily"

> *Miss Emily's forbidding presence had made her a remote entity.*

12. It never occurred to this gypsy of the unattainable that there was a certain resemblance in those who refused to love her —F. Scott Fitzgerald, "The Rich Boy," *All the Sad Young Men*

> *The "gypsy" is a debutante with a history of picking the wrong boys to fall in love with.*

13. Cecil, this afternoon, seemed such a twittering sparrow —E. M. Forster, *A Room With a View*

> *This suddenly unappealing image of Cecil marks the beginning of the end of the heroine's involvement with him.*

14. Peachum: Polly is Tinder, and a Spark will at once set her on a Flame —John Gay, *The Beggar's Opera,* Act 1, scene 4

> *Peachum, whose name suggests* informer *because he* peaches on *or impeaches people, thinks that allowing his daughter Polly to marry would be bad for his business.*

15. The rare perfection of his animal nature, the moderate proportion of intellect, and the very trifling admixture of moral and spiritual ingredients; these latter qualities, indeed, being in barely enough measure to keep the old gentleman from walking on all-fours —Nathaniel Hawthorne, *The Scarlet Letter*

> *The Darwinian view of man drives this metaphor.*

16. His sensibilities are not diffused over so wide a surface as those of the white man, but they run in steadier and deeper channels —Washington Irving, "Traits of Indian Character"

17. I could not help thinking that, with his queer head and length of thinness, he was made to hop along the road of life rather than to walk —Sarah Orne Jewett, *The Country of the Pointed Firs*

> *There are two metaphors here, one of life as a road, the other of the man as a toad.*

18. The soulcontracted son of the secret cell groped through life at the expense of the taxpayers, dejected into day and night with jesuit bark and bitter bite —James Joyce, *Finnegans Wake*

> *The small 'j' in Jesuit represents Joyce's condemnation of the church, as does the metaphor itself.*

19. He [Ross Perot] needs a pleasant, positive image, and he has found that his opponents are determined to paint him in darker hues —Michael Kelly, "Perot at a Turning Point," *The New York Times,* July 9, 1992

20. She was both doer and sufferer . . . and, at the same time, physician, for, as she was the weapon that dealt the wound, she was also the balm —Mary McCarthy, "Cruel and Barbarous Treatment"

> *This physician is a woman in a highly charged adulterous affair.*

21. Something, someone has made you realize that the unfortunate Mr. [Ashley] Wilkes is too large a mouthful of Dead Sea fruit for even you to chew —Margaret Mitchell, *Gone With the Wind*

> *Rhett Butler thus responds to Scarlett when she finally realizes that she loves him and not the elusive Ashley Wilkes.*

22. Bill Clinton . . . a male Southern Belle who charmed his way to the top . . . a

pinball moving back and forth to the pressures of external events without an internal gyroscope to guide him —James Pinkerton, former Bush administration analyst, quoted in *The New York Times*, June 6, 1993

23. [Judge Sol] Wachtler . . . was a mensch, not another lizard in a long black robe — Eric Poley, "Crazy for You," *New York Magazine*, December 14, 1992
    Poley was writing about the New York State Judge whose bizarre and criminal behavior shocked all who had respected and liked him.

24. Henry Cabot Lodge . . . Thin soil . . . highly cultivated —Thomas B. Reed
    Lodge, then senator of Massachusetts, was the epitome of the proper, well-educated, well-connected Bostonian.

25. He is a heart that strikes a whole octave; after him almost all songs are possible — Rainer Maria Rilke, *The Notebooks of Malte Laurids Brigge*
    In his only novel, Rilke writes about a young Danish nobleman who moves from deep misery to eternal bliss.

26. Cleopatra: He's speaking now, / . . . 'Where's my serpent of old Nile?' / (For so he calls me) —William Shakespeare, *Antony and Cleopatra*, Act 1, scene 5, line 24

27. King: O Westmoreland! thou art a summer bird, / Which ever in the haunch of winter sings / The lifting up of day — William Shakespeare, *The Second Part of King Henry the Fourth*, Act 4, scene 4, line 91
    The second metaphor, "haunch of winter," pictures the last of the cold as the rear part of an animal.

28. Queen: And what is Edward, but a ruthless sea? What Clarence but a quicksand of deceit? And Richard but a ragged fatal rock? —William Shakespeare, *The Third Part of Henry the Sixth*, Act 5, scene 4, line 25
    There are three metaphors here on which the Queen elaborates as follows: "Say you can swim; alas! 'tis but a while: / Tread on the sand; why,
    there you quickly sink: / Bestride the rock; the tide will wash you off / Or else you famish; that's a threefold death.

29. He is not a man, but a poorly cooked dumpling —Mikhail Sholokhov, "Prisoners of War"
    The "dumpling is a German prisoner of war who still clings to the super race theories on which he was raised.

30. Where are the bridges in the labyrinth of that soul? —George Steiner, "Books," *The New Yorker*, August 24, 1992
    Rebatet was "a true killer, a hunter-down of Jews, Resistance fighters, and Gaullists," writes Steiner in his review of Frederic Vitoux's biography of Celine. "What can possibly give us any intelligible grasp of the connections between the abject, twisted Rebatet and the wonders of his fiction?"

31. Scotty Briggs, in after days, achieved the distinction of becoming the only convert to religion that was ever fathered from the Virginia roughs; and it transpired that the man who had it in him to espouse the quarrel of the weak out of inborn nobility of spirit was no mean timber whereof to construct a Christian —Mark Twain, "Buck Fanshaw's Funeral," *Roughing It*

32. May's white bony face as she innocently, unchallengeably confesses her triumph becomes a monstrous hammer pounding Archer into his fate —John Updike, "Critic at Large," *The New Yorker*, October 4, 1993
    This review of the movie adaption of Edith Wharton's Age of Innocence *used the "hammer" metaphor for the scene where May reveals that she's scared off Ellen Olenska with a premature announcement of her pregnancy.*

33. The President . . . —played by Jim Curley, a Los Angeles high school principal, not a professional actor—has Richard Nixon's marionette movements and George Bush's vacuous syntax down pat —Tim Weiner, "Reviews/Film," *The New York Times*, July 25, 1993
    Weiner was reviewing the Summer 1993 hit movie, Line of Fire.

34. 'A fire that warms everything but itself,' she had once defined him; but he had snapped back: "I don't warm, I singe" — Edith Wharton, *Hudson River Bracketed*

    This man, while able to give out a "communicative glow" to others "had never lit up his own path."

35. Whenever Mrs. Spear emerged thus suddenly from the sea of her perplexities, her still lovely face wore a half-drowned look which made Halo feel as if one ought to give her breathing exercises and other first-aid remedies —Edith Wharton, *Hudson River Bracketed*

36. Mrs. Holman was off, thinking her [Mabel] the most dried-up, unsympathetic twig she had ever met —Virginia Woolf, "The New Dress"

37. Mrs. Webb . . . divines a little what one's natural proclivities are, & she irradiates them with her bright electric torch — Virginia Woolf, Diary entry, September 18, 1918

38. She [Dorothy Parker] is so odd a blend of Little Nell and Lady Macbeth. It is not so much the familiar phenomenon of a hand of steel in a velvet glove as a lacy glove with a bottle of vitriol concealed in its folds —Alexander Woollcott, "Some Neighbors," *While Rome Burns*

    Woollcott draws on familiar allusions and twists an old metaphor.

■ CHARITY

See also: GENEROSITY; KINDNESS

1. Lady Bountiful —George Farquhar, Name of character in *The Beaux' Stratagem*

2. He who deserves to drink from the ocean of life deserves to fill his cup from your little stream —Kahlil Gibran, *The Prophet*

3. Joseph Surface: The silver ore of pure charity is an expensive article in the catalogue of a man's good qualities, whereas the sentimental French plate I use instead of it, makes just as good a show and pays no tax —Richard Brinsley Sheridan, *The School for Scandal*, Act 5, scene 1

   The speaker wants to feign charity without paying its cost.

■ CHICAGO

See: CITIES

■ CHILDHOOD/CHILDREN

See also: FAMILIES/FAMILY RELATIONSHIPS

1. So this little worm is our daughter — Shmuel Yosef Agnon, *Shira*

   A new father knows he "was expected to say something."

2. Babies are bits of star-dust blown from the hand of God. Lucky the woman who knows the pangs of birth for she has held a star —Laurence Brevoort (Larry) Barretto, *The Indiscreet Years*

3. Children's children are the crown of old men —The Bible, *O.T., Proverbs 17:6*

4. A child running is a living globe of energy —Robert Bly, "The Long Bag We Drag Behind Us"

5. My earliest memory is of weaving my way through a forest of legs —Roger Burlingame, "The Analyst's Couch and the Creative Mind"

6. A happy childhood can't be cured. Mine'll hang around my neck . . . instead of a noose —Hortense Calisher, *Queenie*

7. Children are a bridge joining this earth to a heavenly paradise, filled with fresh springs and blooming gardens —Lydia M. Child, *Philothea, A Romance*

8. This speck of clay / And spirit shall begin to feed on hope —C. Day-Lewis, "The Newborn"

   This line ends the second stanza of a poem written by Day-Lewis to celebrate the birth of his son, the actor Daniel Day-Lewis and was also quoted in an interview.

9. All of us once dwelt, half lost in a forest of Legs and Don'ts —Clifton Fadiman, "It's a Small World—and a Better One"

10. These [children] are my jewels —Cornelia Gracchus, Conversational retort by a Roman matron to whom another had bragged about her wearable jewels

11. In childhood each night is a deep wide gulf between one day and the next —Thomas Mann, "Disorder and Early Sorrow"
    A man, looking at his little daughter sleeping, is happy that today's disappointment "will be a pale shadow, powerless to darken her little heart."

12. Childhood is the Kingdom Where Nobody Dies —Edna St. Vincent Millay, "Childhood Is the Kingdom Where Nobody Dies," *Wine from These Grapes*
    The "dead" according to the poet were the grown ups "who neither listen or speak.

13. Childhood is the sleep of reason —Jean-Jacques Rousseau, *Émile*

■ **CHINS**

See: FACES

■ **CHOICES AND DECISIONS**

See also: DIFFICULTIES; LIFE

1. Seated at Life's Dining Table, with the menu of Morals before you, your eye wonders a bit over the entrées, the hors d'oeuvres, and the things à la though you know that Roast Beef, Medium, is safe and sane, and sure —Edna Ferber, Foreword, *Roast Beef, Medium: The Adventures of Emma McChesney*

2. The family, who lived as one household, had sacrificed the plebeian daughter to the pretty one, the astringent fruit to the bril-

liant flower —Honoré de Balzac, *Cousin Bette*
    This choice sets in motion the leitmotif of bitterness and vengeance of the last novel in Balzac's Comedie Humaine.

3. I would rather be a bright leaf on the stream of a dying civilization than a fertile seed dropped in the oil of a new era —Lucius Beebe, *Nobody Said it Better!*

4. As a metaphor for a difficult decision, it ["between a rock and a hard place"] has wrestled "the horns of a dilemma" to the ground and inundated "the devil and the deep blue sea" —William Safire, *On Language*
    In addition to the three metaphors in quotation marks, Safire managed two more with the verbs "wrestled" and "inundated." Whew!

5. Each of us is free to embark on a large, four-masted vessel or on a fishing boat —George Sand, Letter to Gustave Flaubert, September 21, 1866

■ **CHRONOLOGY**

See: HISTORY

■ **CHURCHES**

See: BUILDINGS AND BRIDGES

■ **CIRCUMSTANCE**

See: CHANCE; FATE

■ **CITIES**

See also: PLACES, MISC.; STREET SCENES

1. The well-versed metropolitan knows the slums as a sort of house of detention for poor aliens, where they live on probation till they can show a certificate of good citizenship —Mary Antin, *The Promised Land*
    This is part of an immigrant's first impressions upon arriving in Boston at the turn of the century.

2. [Toronto neighborhood in the 1920s:] The sort of constipated, lower-middle-class white-bread ghetto he'd fled as soon as he could —Margaret Atwood, "Isis in Darkness," *Wilderness Tips*

    In coupling white-bread with constipation, Atwood underscores the every day ordinariness that has moved the term "white-bread" into common usage.

3. Culturally, Los Angeles has always been a humid jungle alive with seething L.A. projects that . . . people from other places can't see —Eve Babitz, *Eve's Hollywood*

4. A valley of crumbling stucco . . . a valley full of real suffering and often deceptive joys —Honoré de Balzac, *Old Goriot*

    This is the dreary Parisian setting occupied by the novel's main character and others of mediocre means.

5. Paris . . . A vast field of perpetual turmoil from a storm of interests from beneath which are whirled along a crop of human beings —Honoré de Balzac, "The Girl With the Golden Eyes"

6. Jerusalem is taken, / . . . London is a stone of her ruins, Oxford is the dust of her walls, / Sussex and Kent are her scatter'd garments —William Blake, "Jerusalem," Chapter 2

7. I saw a splintered labyrinth (it was London) —Jorge Luis Borges, "The Aleph"

8. Paris is a mighty schoolmaster —Mary Elizabeth Braddon, *The Cloven Foot*

9. It is a myth, the city . . . an idol-head with traffic-light eyes winking a tender green, a cynical red —Truman Capote, "New York"

    This is the metaphoric beginning of Capote's tale of New York.

10. Some cities are women and must be loved —Angela Carter, *The War of Dreams*

11. This great hive, the city —Abraham Cowley, "The Wish"

12. London, that great cesspool into which all the loungers of the Empire are irresistibly drained —Sir Arthur Conan Doyle, "A Study in Scarlet"

13. We say the cows laid out Boston. Well, there are worse surveyors —Ralph Waldo Emerson, "Wealth," *Conduct of Life*

14. There were many like him penduluming up and down the narrow tongue of land between the Hudson and the East River —Edna Ferber, "Hey! Taxi!" *They Brought Their Women*

15. If Brest ever seems more lighthearted, it is when a feeble sun gilds the facades which are as noble as those of Venice, or when its narrow streets teem with carefree sailors —Jean Genet, *Querelle*

    The metaphor lies in the verb, which makes the comparison of sunlight to gold leaf or gold paint.

16. This town of marionettes —O. Henry, "The Making of a New Yorker," *The Trimmed Lamp*

    The author builds on this metaphor by calling Manhattan "a pitiless city without a soul" and goes back to the manikin metaphor by calling its inhabitants "manikins moved by wires and strings.

17. Vienna . . . All masks and deception — Christopher Lehmann-Haupt, "Books of the Times," *The New York Times*, October 4, 1993

    In Henry James's Midnight Song by Carol De Chellis Hill, a fictional Arthur Schnitzler, one of the novel's many figures from cultural history, explains that "Vienna lies like a dream, singing songs to us of our daylight selves."

18. [Moscow:] You tossed salad / of wood, glass, milk —Osip Mandelstam, "Stanza 8"

19. It [New York] is the icing on the pie called Christian civilization —H. L. Mencken, *Here Is New York*

20. In 1939 he [Gianni Agnelli] made the obligatory trip to Detroit, the Lourdes of the automobile industry —William Murray, *The Last Italian*

    Murray's portrait of Italians includes a chapter on the family that owns Fiat.

21. New York was wine to Pat Lenihan — Sean O'Faolain, "A Born Genius"

22. Dublin . . . a stock exchange for gossip, a casino of scandal —Sean O'Faolain, "The Faithless Wife"

23. The city of Jerusalem was stricken with sea-longing. The stone and corrugated iron were burnished brass, and the forests of washing were flights of birds in the wind —Amos Oz, *The Hill of Evil Counsel*

24. Rome was a flea market of borrowed gods and conquered peoples, a bargain basement on two floors, earth and heaven — Boris Pasternak, *Doctor Zhivago*
    "The ancient world ended with Rome, because of overpopulation," writes Nikolai.

25. New York . . . Babylon piled on Imperial Rome —J. B. Priestley
    Foreigners like to outdo each other with putdowns for New York City. Here reference to Babylon and Imperial Rome metaphorically links New York with excess.

26. Hog Butcher for the World —Carl Sandburg, "Chicago"
    Sandburg also calls the city "Stormy, husky, brawling, / City of the Big Shoulders."

27. Manhattan: the Great American Desert —Jean-Paul Sartre, "Manhattan The Great American Desert"
    From an article about Sartre's first impressions of New York.

28. New York, home of the vivisectors of the mind, and of the mentally vivisected still to be reassembled —Muriel Spark, *The Hothouse of the East River*

29. Naples sitteth by the sea, the keystone of an arch of azure —Martin Farquhar Tupper, *Proverbial Philosophy*

30. There is the New York of the commuter— the city that is devoured by locusts each day and spat out each night —E. B. White, *Here Is New York*

31. That giant wink that blazes in the moon is the pendant lake that it [Chicago] is built upon . . . There's Boston, ringed with the bracelet of its shining little towns . . . The long chain of lights there is the necklace of Long Island and the Jersey shore . . . St. Louis, hot and humid in the cornfield belly of the land, and bedded on the mid-length coil and fringes of the snake [the Mississippi River] —Thomas Wolfe, "The Promise of America"

32. Charleston, fat weed that roots itself on Lethe wharf, lived in another time — Thomas Wolfe, *Look Homeward Angel*

33. [I was in Jerusalem.] And I got to know that stone womb that is the mother of us all —A. B. Yehoshua, *Mr. Mani*
    "It is a last stop of history, no less than that board in the train station—a blank wall with no open-sesames or hidden crypts," writes the author.

34. For I am not yet over my departure from your Jerusalem, madame, which is a most obdurate city—hard to swallow and hard to spew out —A. B. Yehoshua, *Mr. Mani*

35. Massachusetts has been the wheel within New England, and Boston the wheel within Massachusetts. Boston therefore is often called the "hub of the world," since it has been the source and fountain of the ideas that have reared and made America — Rev. E. B. Zingle, *Last Winter in the United States*

■ CITY DWELLERS

See: *CITIES*

■ CITYSCAPES

See also: *CITIES; STREET SCENES*

1. A quiet little eye in the Chinatown hurricane —Eric Asimov, "Restaurants," *The New York Times,* April 17, 1992

2. High ruins on the hills bend down and peer / into the mirror of the streetcar's

windows —Joseph Brodsky, "Einem alten Architekten in Rom"

3. The hot-blooded heartbeat of this passionate and mercurial city touches my soul . . . towering clouds under full sail, lightning that pirouettes across a limitless horizon —Edna Buchanan, *Never Let Them See You Cry*

> *Miami has proved a fertile mystery novel background for this former New Jersey journalist.*

4. The guts and innards of the weeping coughing car, the empty lonely tincans with their rusty tongues alack . . . . —Allen Ginsberg, "Sunflower Sutra"

> *Ginsberg and his friend are surveying a devastated urban landscape near a railroad yard, with a single sunflower growing in it.*

5. The great city of Baghdad-on-the-Subway is caliph-ridden. Its palaces, bazaars, khans and byways are thronged with Al Rashids in diverse disguises, seeking diversion and victims for their unbridled generosity —O. Henry, "A Night in New Arabia," *The Trimmed Lamp*

> *The colorful metaphor begins one of the author's many stories about the city of New York, with which he clearly had a love-hate relationship.*

6. Manhattan, the night-blooming cereus, was beginning to unfold its dead-white, heavy-odored petals. —O. Henry, "An Unfinished Story," *The Four Million*

7. The sun was low over the brownstones on the other side of the yard, and an ailanthus stood silhouetted against its golden rim, its budding branches forming a lace curtain through which a wind moved softly —Chaim Potok, *The Chosen*

8. black hairy roots,— / Those lewd monkey-tails hanging from drainholes —Theodore Roethke, "Weed Puller"

9. High on the roof of one of the skyscrapers was a tin brass goat looking . . . out across silver snakes of winding rivers —Carl Sandburg, "The Two Skyscrapers Who Decided to Have a Child," *Rootabaga Stories*

10. The city stretches from dollhouse rows at the base of the park through a broad blurred belly of flowerpot red patched with tar roofs and twinkling cars —John Updike, *Rabbit, Run*

11. On weekends in summer . . . the whole city is honeycombed with abandoned cells—a jail that has been effectively broken —E. B. White, *Here Is New York*

12. We drank wine instead of water and asked for tea when we were thirsty and let it cool while looking out at the sea that sent its long, lavishly bejeweled fingers into the city—fingers, mind you, that could easily have seized and swallowed us had the tide but risen a little . . . . —A. B. Yehoshua, *Mr. Mani*

13. And then, suddenly, there was Jerusalem: a wall with turrets and domes, a clear, austere verse written on the horizon —A. B. Yehoshua, *Mr. Mani*

■ CIVILIZATION

See also: CHANGE; HUMANITY/HUMANKIND

1. Civilization is the lamb's skin in which barbarism masquerades —Thomas Bailey Aldrich, *Ponkapog Papers*

2. Of course, if we did not have any values in common with these distant figures, each civilisation would be enclosed in its own impenetrable bubble —Isaiah Berlin, "The Pursuit of the Ideal"

> *Plato or medieval Japan may be remote, but it is possible for us to read and empathize because of the commonalities between us.*

3. Only so [by seeking to be themselves] can true cultures be generated, each unique, each making its own peculiar contribution to human civilisation, each pursuing its own values in its own way, not to be submerged in some general cosmopolitan ocean which robs all native cultures of their particular substance and colour, of

their national spirit and genius, which can only flourish on its own soil, from its own roots, stretching far back into a common past —Isaiah Berlin, "The Apotheosis of the Romantic Will"

> *This concept according to Berlin "is the beginning of nationalism."*

4. Civilisation is a garden made rich and beautiful by the variety of its flowers, delicate plants which great conquering empires—Rome, Vienna, London—trample and crush out of existence —Isaiah Berlin, "The Apotheosis of the Romantic Will"

5. No man is an island entire of itself —John Donne, "Devotions"

> *This is one of the best known metaphors of English literature. It continues as follows: "every man is a piece of the Continent, a part of the maine."*

6. All civilization has from time to time become a thin crust over a volcano of revolution —Havelock Ellis, *The Task of Social Hygiene*

7. Ulysses: . . . the universe knows that destiny wasn't preparing alternative ways for civilization to flower. It was contriving the dance of death, letting loose the brutality and human folly which is all that the gods are really contented by —Jean Giraudoux, *Tiger at the Gates*, Act 2

> *In Giraudoux's fable, the Trojan War is all war: the gods of war will always exploit brutality and folly.*

■ CLARITY/AMBIGUITY

See also: LANGUAGE; WORDS

1. For now we see through a glass, darkly; but then face to face —The Bible, *N.T., 1 Corinthians, 13:02*

2. So far the plot is as clear as bouillon. Before the film is over, it's become the sort of ragout that has to be cut with a knife — Vincent Canby, "Review/Film," *The New York Times*, August 26, 1992

> *In this review of the film* Storyville, *even the simile that preceded the metaphor was ironic. Canby's potage was simmered of "politics, lust, greed, oil leases, murder and closeted skeletons crying to get out."*

3. It [President Warren G. Harding's English] drags itself out of a dark abyss . . . of pish, and crawls insanely up the topmost pinnacle of posh. It is rumble and bumble. It is flap and doodle. It is balder and dash —H. L. Mencken

> *"It reminds me of a string of wet sponges; it reminds me of tattered washing on the line; it reminds me of stale bean soup, of college yells, of dogs barking idiotically through endless nights," wrote Mencken.*

4. Aelfrida: Thy speech is a thread full of knots —Edna St. Vincent Millay, *The King's Henchman*, Act 3

5. She cuts a wide swath through the thickets of self-help books published every year — Michael Vincent Miller, "Books of the Times," *The New York Times*, May 17, 1992

> *In his review of Wendy Kaminer's* I'm Dysfunctional, You're Dysfunctional, *Miller pictured the author as a scyther trimming.*

6. Everybody's . . . peering through the thick fog of dismal economic data —Sylvia Nasar, *The New York Times*, February 16, 1992

> *Fog is a favorite metaphor for inscrutability.*

7. A kind of fog always hangs over the talk of the dean —Natsume Soseki, *Botchan*

> *The dean talks vaguely, his words full of hints and innuendo, always protesting that "the time is not ripe" to make things known fully.*

8. Out of the slimy mud of words, out of the sleet and hail of verbal imprecision, come approximate thoughts and feelings, words that have taken the place of thoughts and feelings, and the beauty of incantation — William Trevor, "A School Story"

> *The schoolmaster in Trevor's story may have been influenced by Hermann Hesse who said "words are really a mask" and that they therefore tend to hide rather than express true meaning.*

■ CLERGY

1. Looking at clergymen in the street, I notice the same inward stitching of worry in their faces that was characteristic of the profession when I went to church as a boy —Edward Hoagland, "Other Lives," *Harper's,* 1973

2. If we are a priestridden race we ought to be proud of it. They are the apples of God's eye —James Joyce, *Portrait of the Artist as a Young Man*
   The common metaphor is included in the speech of a common man.

3. Scotty: " . . . you are the head clerk of the doxology-works next door" Minister: "I am the shepherd in charge of the flock whose fold is next door" —Mark Twain, "Buck Fanshaw's Funeral," *Roughing It*
   The minister and his petitioner are having trouble understanding each other's metaphors.

4. The fair young man with his throat manacled in white lets his car glide diagonally against the curb —John Updike, *Rabbit, Run*

■ CLEVERNESS

See: *ALERTNESS; INTELLIGENCE; WIT*

■ CLICHE

See: *ORIGINALITY/UNORIGINALITY*

■ CLINGING

See also: *PEOPLE, INTERACTION*

1. She glued herself to me all day —Elizabeth Barrett Browning, Diary entry, August 2, 1831

2. She clung to Mary as though she were sinking but sometimes of her own accord Iris let go the boat —Mavis Gallant, "Careless Talk"

The metaphor of the independently steered boat serves as an anchor for the simile about the drowning.

3. King: 'Tis seldom when the bee doth leave her comb / In the dead carrion —William Shakespeare, *The Second Part of King Henry the Fourth,* Act 4, scene 4, line 79
   The King is uncertain that his son will "cast off his followers" and so uses the metaphor of the bee stuck in the honeycomb.

4. Old Man: Is it sensible to cling so desperately to bits of the bitter end of a rundown personality? To the creak in an old chair, the crack in a cup, a crock of an old servant, the crick in the bottleneck of a man's declining years —Wole Soyinka, *Madmen and Specialists,* Part 1
   The old man protests that it is wrong to cling to faded ideas and customs.

■ CLOTHING

See: *FASHION AND STYLE*

■ CLOUDS

See also: *SKY/SKYSCAPES*

1. A day of dappled seaborne clouds —James Joyce, *Portrait of the Artist as a Young Man*

2. Through the hemless fields of heaven / Wander wide and tracelessly / Clouds, unshepherded —Mikhail Lermontov, "The Cup of Life"

3. Sky still blue / not a rag of cloud —Li Po, "Night Mooring at Cow's Creek—I think of the Old Days," T'ang Dynasty

4. When thunder was near I've seen sleepy clouds suddenly stand erect, casting their white bedclothes aside, then bulge into titanic genii to the bidding of the gale —Guy Murchie, *Song of the Sky*

5. Clouds are . . . the sheet music of the heavens, the architecture of moving air

... some are ragged coattails of storms that have passed. Some are stagnant blankets of warm air resting on cold. Some are mare's tails floating in the chill upper sky. Some are herringbones, sheets, cream puffs, ox-bends, veils, hammerheads, spangled mantillas, sponges, black shrouds —Guy Murchie, *Song of the Sky*

> *Refer to this, if you're ever tempted to play* who can invent the most metaphors about a single subject.

6. With something of a start I did remember: a windy autumn night, full moon obscured by dusty rags of clouds —Donna Tartt, *The Secret History*.

7. The sky was full of white windy white rags of cloud —Thomas Wolfe, *Look Homeward Angel*.

■ COINCIDENCE
See: CHANCE

■ COLDNESS

1. Drummle: She *was* an iceberg! . . . He had reckoned, poor wretch, that in the early days of marriage she would thaw. But . . . the thaw never set in! I believe she kept a thermometer in her stays and always registered ten degrees below zero —Arthur Wing Pinero, *The Second Mrs. Tanqueray*, Act 1

> *Aubrey has just told his friends that he is marrying a woman quite outside their social circle and is suggesting a clean break as preferable to the metaphorical hemorrhage.*

2. Miss Cooper: She looks exactly the way you described her. Carved in ice —Terence Rattigan, *Separate Tables*, Scene 1

3. How shall I free myself from this marble envelope which grips me round the knees —George Sand, *Lelia*

4. Still, she knew these two people by reputation, and was aware that they were not

icebergs when they were in their own waters —Mark Twain, *The Gilded Age*

> *The figurative icebergs are two very proper Washington ladies who cause a less conventional woman to observe, "I could always enjoy icebergs—as scenery—but not as company."*

■ COLLAPSE
See: DISINTEGRATION

■ COLLEGE
See: EDUCATION AND LEARNING

■ COLOR

1. Their [sparrows'] color is the elderly, moleskin gray / Of doggedness —Anthony Hecht, "House Sparrows"

2. Colors are the smiles of nature. When they are extremely smiling and break forth into other beauty besides, they are her laughs, as in the flowers —Leigh Hunt, "The Seer"

■ COMBATIVENESS
See: CHARACTERISTICS; CONFRONTATION

■ COMEDY
See: HUMOR

■ COMFORT/COMFORT-GIVERS

1. Is there no balm in Gilead? —The Bible, *O.T., Jeremiah 8:22*

> *There actually was a place called Gilead which had balsam trees that yielded healing herbs. The metaphor endures as a phrase synonymous with healing or comfort.*

2. Jesus: In my father's house are many mansions —The Bible, *N.T., John 14:2*

3. The lust for comfort . . . enters the house a guest, and then becomes a host, and then a master —Kahlil Gibran, *The Prophet*

4. Hetty was a Shoulder. Hers was a sharp, sinewy shoulder; but all her life people had laid their heads upon it, metaphorically or actually —O. Henry, "The Third Ingredient"

5. Two great European narcotics, alcohol and Christianity —Friedrich Wilhelm Nietzsche

6. Lucius: thy grandsire lov'd thee well: / Many a time he . . . / Sung thee asleep, his loving breast thy pillow —William Shakespeare, *Titus Andronicus*, Act 5, scene 3, line 161

7. He could feel them [the pints of beers consumed] thick and comforting—a moat against Roche —William Trevor, "The Introspections of J. P. Powers"

8. How well I feathered my nest —François Rabelais, *Works*, Book 1
   This has become a common, everyday metaphor.

9. Underneath this fatalistic feeling was the deep sense of relief that he had, after all, said and done nothing that could in the least degree affect the welfare of Sophy Viner. That fact took a millstone off his neck —Edith Wharton, *The Reef*
   Wharton used a common metaphor—the miller's weighing device—to picture a heavy burden or obligation. Jesus used it literally in Matthew 18:6 *when he said, "whoso shall offend one of these little ones which believe in me, it were better for them that a millstone were hanged about his neck, and that he were drowned in the depth of the sea."*

■ COMMITMENT

See also: LOVE

1. He had crossed over the gulf to her —D. H. Lawrence, "The Horse Dealer's Daughter"

A man has come to love a woman.

2. I love people who harness themselves, an ox to a heavy cart —Marge Piercy, "To be of use," *To Be of Use*
   The poem is an ode to worthy work and those willing to dedicate themselves to it, opening with the metaphor of the swimmer who dives right into the deep: "The people I love best / jump into work head first / without dallying in the shallows."

3. When Kevin Kline joined the rescue team at the New York Shakespeare Festival, taking the title associate producer, he was not just another celebrity blithely paying lip service to a worthy cause. Mr. Kline is putting his artistic capital where his mouth is, contributing a scintillating performance to *Measure for Measure* at the Delacorte Theater in Central Park —Frank Rich, *The New York Times*, 1993
   Rich used the images of a fire fighter and a financier to illustrate the actor's total commitment to the annual Shakespeare-in-the-Park performances.

4. Longaville: I am resolv'd; 'tis but a three years' fast; / The mind shall banquet, though the body pine: Fat paunches have lean pates, and dainty bits / Make rich the ribs but bankrupt quite the wits —William Shakespeare, *Love's Labour's Lost*, Act 1, scene 1, line 24
   Longaville pledges to renounce worldly pleasures for scholarship for a period of three years. He uses two metaphors to illustrate the advantages and disadvantages of such a regime.

5. Mrs. George: When you loved me I gave you the whole sun and stars to play with. I gave you eternity in a single moment, strength of the mountains in one clasp of your arms, and the volume of all the sea in one impulse of your soul —George Bernard Shaw, *Getting Married*
   Shaw's spokeswoman for feminism felt that what she offered should not include performing the duties of a housekeeper.

■ COMMONPLACE

See: ORDINARINESS/EXTRAORDINARINESS

COMMON SENSE

See: PRUDENCE

COMMUNICATION/NON-COMMUNICATION

See also: ARTICULATENESS/INARTICU-LATENESS; ATTENTIVENESS/INAT-TENTIVENESS; PEOPLE, INTERAC-TION

1. Possessing the body language of a frog — Nina Berberova, *The Italics Are Mine*
   This is one of several caustic comments about well-known Russian writers appearing in Berberova's memoirs, first published in 1969 and reissued a year before her death in 1993.

2. I lacked no words now; fluent I told my tale; it streamed on my tongue —Charlotte Brontë, *Villette*

3. "Was he always a good deal of an oyster?" —Willa Cather, "The Sculptor's Funeral," *Youth and the Bright Medusa*
   This draws an affirmative response: "Yes, he was an oyster . . . he always gave one the impression of being detached."

4. The network is poised to deliver vast intelligence in a digital stream, but these are dumb buckets at the end of the pipeline — James Gleick, *The New York Times Magazine,* May 16, 1993
   Some of us who have tried to hook into the advanced technology wonder if we, ourselves, aren't the dumb buckets at the other end.

5. As long as one is content to gloat over the silver lining of one's own religion, one bars any serious conversation and merely makes the first move in a game of skill — Walter Kaufmann, "The Faith of a Heretic"
   Unless the game were one of cloud-dodging, this smacks of mixed metaphor.

6. Mary: It was hard to communicate with you . . . the line was busy —Jean Kerr, *Mary, Mary,* Act 2
   A commonly used variant of this is to say that someone is out to lunch.

7. I knew I was now expected to reply in kind [by talking about myself], but I didn't feel like raiding my own meager cupboard —Norman Mailer, *Harlot's Ghost*

8. In reality they all lived in a kind of hieroglyphic world, where the real thing was never said or done or even thought, but only represented by a set of arbitrary signs —Edith Wharton, *The Age of Innocence*
   The metaphor suits Wharton's almost archeological examination of Old New York society's mores.

9. The Bush campaign like Bush himself, uses words not to convey meaning but as audible confetti —George Will, Syndicated column, July 19, 1992
   The confetti image came from the column in which Will suggested that the President should not run for office again.

COMPANIONSHIP

See: FRIENDSHIP/FRIENDS

COMPARISONS

1. By what latitude could we, abandoned thus to the fury of symbols, be occasionally a prey to the demon of analogy — André Breton, *Nadja*

2. Do not hunt here for the heaven of burnt oils / or the ice-skating Flemish brush-stroke —Osip Mandelstam, "On a board of raspberry," translated by W. S. Merwin and Clarence Brown
   The speaker is a painter who does not want to be compared with older craftsmen

COMPASSION

See also: KINDNESS

1. Refilling the well of compassion —Anon., Blurb, *The New York Times,* April 11, 1992
   The editorial blurb writer tapped into this metaphor for an article on the efforts of former President Jimmy Carter to overcome a problem his

colleague, Emery University president James F. Lancey, called "compassion fatigue."

2. We are members of mankind. If I am drowning you must assist to save me — Bernard Malamud, "Man in the Drawer"

   Against a Cold War background, a Russian writer contacts the protagonist and asks for help in getting his work published. When the protagonist protests that he might be unable to "swim in unknown waters" the writer replies, "If not, throw me a rope."

3. Lady Macbeth: Yet do I fear thy nature; / It is too full o' the milk of human kindness —William Shakespeare, *Macbeth,* Act 1, scene 5, line 16

   Lady Macbeth's metaphor is a nursing image and implies nurturing. The Lady, though she says, "I have given suck," seems never to have had a child. It is one of the eternal puzzles of the play.

■ COMPETENCE

See: ABILITY; ACHIEVEMENTS

■ COMPETITION/COMPETITORS

See also: POLITICS/POLITICIANS

1. The EC [European Community] leaders dismissed any talk of a small core of states racing ahead in a "two-speed Europe" — Anon., *China Daily,* October 19, 1992

2. As I was saying, old man, we are game-all now; let's play out the deciding game. You want to finish the rubber, don't you? —Honoré de Balzac, *Cousin Bette*

   Two men are vying for the same mistress and one challenges the other to complete the game

3. It's David versus Goliath, but that slingshot is getting pretty big and pretty heavy —Edmund G. (Jerry) Brown, Jr., quoted in *The New York Times,* March 25, 1992

   Brown used this allusionary metaphor when his campaign to become the "people's candidate" was gaining some strength. The headline writer tagged this with his own twist on a popular political metaphor: "Dark Horse or Not, Brown Enjoys Being Able to Strut."

4. What you see are these few tall-standing trees and a huge amount of smaller growth on the ground, but not a lot in the middle level. So the forest floor continues to be very fecund. The second level gets sort of shaded out by the leafy canopy on top — Esther Dyson, *The New York Times,* July 18, 1993

   Dyson, a computer newsletter publisher, thus commented on a possible "shakeout" in the computer industry in an interview with computer columnist, Peter Lewis. Lewis picked up on Dyson's extended metaphor with, "How long can the ferns stay green under this leafy canopy?" Dyson responded with, "The little guys? As long as they don't try to become big trees, they can do quite well by focusing on niches.

5. Other stores are not going to roll over and play dead forever like weak organizations in the Hinterlands where Wal-Mart just waltzed in and blew them out of town — Joe Grimes, Quote by Chicago retail consultant, *The New York Times,* September 23, 1992

   The article about the powerful retail organization was metaphorically headlined: "3 Discounters on a Collision Course."

6. In April, American Airlines had a brainstorm. With great fanfare, it slashed away at the jungle of air fares —Herbert B. Herring, "Business Diary," *The New York Times,* January 24, 1993

7. Right now, Digital isn't even a slice on the personal computer pie chart —Jack Karp, *The New York Times,* August 30, 1992

   The use of a pie as a metaphor is quite common, especially for indicating fractions. The whole pie simply stands for 100 percent or the 360 degrees of a circle.

8. Trapped between not one but two onrushing infernos, in the form of Lotus 1–2–3 and Microsoft Excel, Borland chose to light a fire under its own spreadsheet — Peter H. Lewis, "The Executive Computer," *The New York Times,* September 5, 1993

   Lewis built his metaphor around forest fire fighters' risky strategy of lighting a second fire parallel to the first in order to destroy the primary blaze's fuel. The big risk is that the fire fighters might be consumed by their own fire. In the Borland computer company's case, the second fire was set to its price.

9. Each book in the current wave [of books about the British Royals] is in danger of being washed up by the others —Sarah Lyall, *The New York Times,* June 21, 1993

10. Harpagon: What you rogue! You dare to hunt my game? / Cléante: It's you who are hunting mine; I was there first — Molière, *The Miser,* Act 4
    Father and son are quarreling about a woman both want to marry.

11. Mr. Abrams has never faced a pit bull like Mr. D'Amato, even one facing his first one-on-one Senate race and who is at the other end of a long leash held by a besieged Republican President —Sam Roberts, *The New York Times,* September 17, 1992
    Final score: pit bull 1; opposition 0; handler 0.

12. Here's my morning line on the Republican race [of 1996]: Jack Kemp was propelled out of the gate to take an early lead, wisely fell back to conservative strength before the first turn . . . Phil Gramm has fallen off the pace as a dove on Bosnia; Lamar Alexander, Dick Cheney, Pat Robertson, Pat Buchanan, Bill Bennett are bunched in back —William Safire, "Essay," *The New York Times,* May 6 1993
    The extended horse-racing metaphor began and ended with Safire's focus on Massachusetts Governor William F. Weld as a "long shot to win, a good bet to place."

13. We're going to the big dance —Gerard Tillman, Quoted in "Pittsfield 13s win N.E. title; nationals next," *The Berkshire Eagle,* June 6, 1993
    The dance the Pittsfield infielder referred to was the national playoff.

14. Let everybody struggle to get their bucket in the stream and then do what they will with the water they fish out —Scott Turow, *Pleading Guilty*

15. There are now three successors to DOS . . . each grabbing for the baton —H. Allan Wallach, "At the Computer," *The Berkshire Eagle,* August 29, 1993
    Musical images come naturally to a columnist whose home abuts the famous Tanglewood Music Festival.

■ COMPLACENCY
See: CONTENTMENT

■ COMPLETENESS/ INCOMPLETENESS

1. The Missouri crisis was a mere preamble—a title page to a great tragic volume —John Quincy Adams
    Adams expressed his concern about Missouri's request to be admitted into the Union as a slave state. Thomas Jefferson, also uncomfortable about this situation, likened it to "a firebell in the night."

2. There were a lot of beautiful men, but the others seemed blank, unwritten on, compared to him —Margaret Atwood, "Wilderness Tips"
    A one-man woman reflects on men whose minds don't keep pace with their physical development.

3. Forster's discursive but tart and schoolmarmish biography grazes the rich grass of the du Maurier meadow but fails to chew, let alone, digest, the cud —Sally Beauman, "Books," *The New Yorker,* November 8, 1993
    The biography being reviewed was Daphne du Maurier: The Secret Life of the Renowned Storyteller *by Margaret Forster.*

4. Jefferson [James Stewart]: You—you've got a first name, haven't you? / Saunders [Jean Arthur]: Look—I think we ought to skip it. / Jefferson: All right. Sure. Just curious. The picture popped into my mind all of a sudden of a pump without a handle —Sidney Buchman, *Mr. Smith Goes to Washington*

After a bit more bantering, Jean Arthur finally "puts the handle on the pump" by telling James Stewart that her name is Clarissa. The movie was based on a novel by Lewis R. Foster from which screenwriter Buchman may or may not have taken this line.

5. The Zionist movement without Zion is just soup without meat or vegetables — Rabbi Shlomo Goren, Op-Ed, *The New York Times,* October 29, 1991
   The Rabbi also called the disputed areas of Judea, Samaria, and the Gaza Strip the "heart and brains" of Israel.

6. When we speak of an individual we have likewise to speak of the age in which he lived. You disguise a portrait if you cut it out of its frame —Henry Wadsworth Longfellow, Lecture on Molière, c. 1832

7. Before, I thought everybody was one-armed, like me. Now I feel the surgery. The crunch of bone when it is sundered, the sliced flesh and the tubes of blood cut through, shocking the bloodrun and disturbing the nerves —Toni Morrison, *Jazz*
   The figurative missing arm is a hitherto unknown black father of a son raised by a white mother. By understanding what having "the missing arm" would have been like, the son can accept that it can not be recovered.

8. You do not, however, need to buy the whole cloth to see some merit in the fabric —Peter Passell, *The New York Times,* September 1992

9. The page is blank or a frame without a glass / Or a glass that is empty when he looks —Wallace Stevens, "Phosphor Reading by his Own Light"
   Stevens plays on the word "glass." He refers first to a glassed-in picture and then to a drinking glass.

10. To get as many of the bare facts of the book into a play as possible, Patrick Kennedy had to pack tight and then sit on the lid —Alexander Woollcott, "Plays: Pleasant and Unpleasant"
    Woollcott felt that the lead in American Tragedy telescoped his role and thus "transformed

Dreiser's puzzled, storm-tossed, inert bit of American driftwood into an intensive Lothario." His overall opinion was that the play was "a puppet show" contrived "from an overwhelming novel.

■ COMPLEXION

See also: COLOR; FACES; FACIAL COLOR; PHYSICAL APPEARANCE

1. Her skin was a shed snakeskin, ageless — T. Coraghessan Boyle, *Water Music*

2. His face is a grid of scratches —T. Coraghessan Boyle, *Water Music*
   The author sharpens the metaphor with a simile: "thin as cut hair."

3. There is a garden in her face / Where roses and white lilies grow —Thomas Campion, "There Is a Garden in Her Face"
   The poem is also known as "Cherry Ripe," based on the last lines of the first stanza: "There cherries grow, which none may buy / Till 'Cherry ripe!' themselves do cry."

4. His complexion is that of a corpse considerably advanced in corruption —Germaine de Staël, Letter, 1803.
   The subject of Madame de Staël's incisive description was the Abbey de Talleyrand.

5. Trost's face would go mahogany with choler —Edna Ferber, "Meadow Lake"

6. Brown skin . . . the skin of a russet apple —Alice Munro, "Hold Me Fast, Don't Let Me Pass"

7. [Deep lines in a man's face:] I could imagine him dragging these little dikes open when shaving —Sean O'Faolain, "Up the Bare Stairs"

8. Morachus: Mislike me not for my complexion, / The shadow'd livery of the burnish'd sun —William Shakespeare, *The Merchant of Venice,* Act 2, scene 1, line 1

9. Lysander: Why is your cheek so pale? / How chance the roses there do fade so fast? —William Shakespeare, *A Midsummer Night's Dream,* Act 3, scene 2, line 129

The rose has become an everyday metaphor to depict facial color.

10. The beautiful children—red flags in their cheeks —Eudora Welty, "The Bride of the Innisfallen"

■ COMPLICATIONS

See: PROBLEMS AND SOLUTIONS

■ COMPLIMENTS

See: FLATTERY; PRAISE

■ COMPREHENSION

See: UNDERSTANDING/ MISUNDERSTANDING

■ COMPROMISE

See also: CHOICES AND DECISIONS; POLITICS/POLITICIANS

1. So on practical grounds there is little choice but to take half a loaf —Anon., Editorial, *The New York Times,* July 20, 1993
   As the President compromised his position on full acceptance of gays in the Military to accommodate the conservatism of the Joint Chiefs of Staff, so time-pressured editorial writers often reach for a cliché metaphor.

2. What a writer writes measures his ability, or the compromise his ability must strike with that universal horse-trader, the world —Clifton Fadiman, "Some Day"

3. Most people hew the battlements of life from compromise, erecting their impregnable keeps from judicious submissions, fabricating their philosophical drawbridges from emotional retractions and scalding marauders in the boiling oil of sour grapes —Zelda Fitzgerald, *Save Me the Waltz*

4. The compromise our fathers made was a coffin of honor and the cradle of war —

Robert Green Ingersoll, Decoration Day address, 1870s
   Ingersoll led into this with his view of compromise as "a bargain in which each party defrauds the other and himself."

5. Compromise makes a good umbrella but a poor roof —James Russell Lowell, "Democracy"

6. In the end, Mr. Yeltsin got the referendum he demanded, but so embroidered with conditions that it could not resolve the power struggle —Serge Schmemann, *The New York Times,* March 30, 1993

7. If he paid for each day's comfort with the small change of illusion, he grew daily to value the comfort more and set less store upon the coin —Edith Wharton, *The Descent of Man*

■ CONCEALMENT

See: CRAFTINESS; DECEPTION; SECRECY

■ CONCEIT

See: BOASTERS/BOASTFULNESS; VANITY

■ CONCENTRATION/ DISTRACTION

See also: LOYALTY; SELF-CONTROL

1. I've been criticized for spreading myself too thin —Merrill Joan Gerber, Quoted from an interview with Lisa See, *Publishers Weekly,* November 8, 1993
   The author of popular magazine fiction as well as more "serious" work added that, "Cynthia Ozick has said of me that I have too many arrows in my quiver."

2. I am picked up and sorted to a pip —John Keats, Letter to Percy Bysshe Shelley, August, 1820
   Pips are the spots on playing cards or dice. Keats, who urges Shelley to be more self-disciplined,

admits that his own mind had once been "like a pack of scattered cards."

3. The thought of such discipline must fall like cold chains upon you, who perhaps never sat with your wings furled for six months together —John Keats, Letter to Percy Bysshe Shelley, August, 1820
   The metaphor-within-simile is tied to Keats' telling Shelley to focus all energies on his art and "load every rift of your subject with ore."

4. Foreign issues have inevitably pressed on him despite his efforts to stick to his domestic last —Anthony Lewis, "At Home Abroad," *The New York Times,* July 12, 1993
   The metaphoric cobbler was President Bill Clinton.

5. Still he is faithful to the stage, although his bi-weekly outings with her wicked stepsister, the radio, might be considered mild cheating —Dorothy Parker, "A Valentine for Mr. Woollcott," *Vanity Fair,* 1934
   Parker was writing about Alexander Woollcott as a New York drama critic.

6. Since leaving college . . . he [Edward Gorey] has cultivated the life of a vestal, the anchoritic handmaiden of his art — Stephen Schiff, "Edward Gorey and the Tao of Nonsense," *The New Yorker,* November 9, 1992

7. Arcady played the Sybarite, and Bazarov kept his nose to the grindstone —Ivan Turgenev, *Fathers and Sons*
   The metaphor for exacting hard labor from someone, dates back to the sixteenth century. Its current usage often refers to self-discipline.

8. Let us . . . before we float farther on the waves of this debate, refer to the point from which we departed, that we may at least be able to conjecture where we now are —Daniel Webster, Webster-Hayne debate, January 26–27, 1830

■ CONCILIATION

See: APPEASEMENT

■ CONDEMNATION

See: APPROVAL/DISAPPROVAL

■ CONDESCENSION

See: ARROGANCE/HUMILITY

■ CONFIDANTES

■ CONFIDENCE

See: SELF-CONFIDENCE

■ CONFINEMENT

See also: FREEDOM/RESTRAINT

1. A cat pent up becomes a lion —Anon., Italian Proverb

2. [President John F.] Kennedy was undoubtedly a cold warrior, but Mr. Reeves too often straitjackets him into this role, giving little heed to his intellect —Douglas Brinkley, *The New York Times Book Review,* October 24, 1993
   The book being reviewed was Profile of Power *by Richard Reeves.*

3. Meadows: Cage of the world / Holds your prowling. Howl, Cain, jackal afraid —Christopher Fry, *A Sleep of Prisoners*
   A prisoner dreams that one of his taunting fellow prisoners is Cain.

4. Valere: It's a good idea to hold her in with a tight rein —Molière, *The Miser,* Act 1
   The Miser is full of horsemanship metaphors.

5. We are all of us cramped and we put out our roots and branches where and how we can —George Sand, Letter to Gustave Flaubert, November 30, 1866
   The letter begins, "Nature, our sovereign" . . . has established a balance in our instincts that rapidly determines the limits of our appetites."

6. Prologue: within the girdle of these walls / Are now confin'd two mighty monar-

chies —William Shakespeare, *The Life of Henry the Fifth,* Prologue, line 19

7. Here I stand, hobbled in a sack of doom, determined to tear out of it —Kate Simon, *Bronx Primitive*

■ CONFLICT

See also: AGREEMENT/DISAGREEMENT; WINNING/LOSING

1. He that troubleth his own house shall inherit the wind —The Bible, *O.T., Proverbs 11:29*

2. The upheaval in the former Yugoslavia illustrates how the closing of the cold war opened a Pandora's box of causes and conflicts that had been kept down by the ideological struggle of that era —Boutros Boutros-Ghali, *Report on the Work of the Organization,* United Nations, 1992

   The allusion to the Greek myth has become a common metaphor. While most people use it to mean the loosing of pent-up plagues, they often forget that the last to leave the box was Hope.

3. Not betrayed by the black blood and not wilfully betrayed by his mother, but betrayed by her all the same, who had bequeathed him not only the blood of slaves but even a little of the very blood which had enslaved it; himself his own battleground, the scene of his own vanquishment and the mausoleum of his defeat —William Faulkner, "The Old People"

   The long sentence sets the scene for the three metaphors that end it, explaining how the character is torn asunder by conflicting genetic forces.

4. Lourdes sends her snapshots of pastries from her bakery in Brooklyn. Each glistening éclair is a grenade aimed at Celia's political beliefs —Cristina Garcia, *Dreaming in Cuban*

   Celia is a Cuban revolutionary and Lourdes is her antagonistic Americanized daughter.

5. Callimaco: I am a ship rocked by opposing winds, and the nearer she gets to the harbor, the more she has to fear —Niccolo Machiavelli, The Mandrake, Act 4, scene 1

6. Dole limps after he tries to put a dart through Moynihan —Senator Jay Rockefeller, Quoted in "Letter from Washington," *The New Yorker,* July 5, 1993

   Moynihan, head of the senate finance committee, summed up his own power in opposing Senator Bob Dole with this brief metaphor: "The heavy lifting comes in Finance."

7. We are watching bureaucratic elephants fighting under a huge tarpaulin. The pro-Israel elephant is part of the technology control establishment at the Pentagon... The pro-Arab elephant ... irritated at criticism of having ended the [Gulf] war prematurely, is out to seize control of mid-level policy planning —William Safire, "Essay," *The New York Times,* March 19, 1992

■ CONFORMITY/ NONCONFORMITY

See also: CUSTOM; INDIVIDUALITY; MONOTONY

1. Another thing that sets him apart is his unwillingness to join the priesthood of craft, that often flagellant order —Joan Acocella, "Books," *The New Yorker,* July 19, 1993

   Acocella was reviewing City Poet: The Life and Times of Frank O'Hara, *by Brad Gooch. She summarized O'Hara's "Personism" as follows: "Above all, with their craft so lightly worn, the poems constituted a clear refusal ... to kneel before the throne."*

2. Never try to swim against the current — The Bible, *Apocrypha, 1 Ecclesiasticus 4:26*

   Contrary to this advice, modern usage tends to equate the willingness to swim against the current with courage, as in he is not afraid to swim against the current *of popular opinion.*

3. He had gone headlong over all the social hedges —Stephen Crane, "The Bride Comes to Yellow Sky"

The metaphor pertains to the impulsive marriage of a small town marshall to a girl he'd met in San Antonio.

4. You're surrounded 24 hours a day. Either you become a herd animal or you dig a cave deep inside your head in which to hide —John Dulgan, *Flirting*

   This is how the lead character in an Australian film about life in a boarding school viewed the loss of privacy.

5. For nonconformity the world whips you with its displeasure —Ralph Waldo Emerson, "Self Reliance"

6. Meantime nature is not slow to equip us in the prison uniform of the party to which we adhere —Ralph Waldo Emerson, "Self Reliance"

7. A man must consider what a blindman's-buff is this game of conformity —Ralph Waldo Emerson, "Self Reliance"

   The conformist "is a retained attorney, and these airs of the bench are the emptiest affectation."

8. We are grown stiff with the ramrod of convention down our backs —O. Henry, "The Green Door"

   The story's hero happily recognizes that "in the big city the twin spirits of Romance and Adventure are always aboard seeking worthy wooers." He therefore accepts a card from a stranger and finds romance.

9. Billy . . . the city has gobbled you up. It has taken you and cut you to its pattern and stamped you with its brand —O. Henry, "The Lost Blend"

   Billy's accuser adds that he finds him so nearly like thousands of others that "you couldn't be picked out from them if it weren't for your laundry marks."

10. One flew over the cuckoo's nest —Ken Kesey, *One Flew Over the Cuckoo's Nest*

    Kesey's title is an implied metaphor for his view of America as an insane asylum run by a monster mother with only one—the rebellious McMurtry—actively seeking freedom or, to use another metaphorical expression, he flew the coop.

11. Much of private industry tends to follow the pack, seeking the surest returns and quickest profits —Jeff Madrick, *The New York Times*, January 19, 1993

    Public politicos, on the other hand, tend to follow the PACs.

12. Men are not horses to be herded together —Christopher Morley, "On Doors"

    This metaphor of what men are not *is a metaphor in the guise of a* negaphor.

13. There are those who will call you a recluse—but it is better to listen to your own different drummer than to go through life with a ringing in your ears —William Safire, *On Language*

    Safire, while thumbing his nose at the telephone, is tipping his hat to Thoreau, who wrote in 1854, "If a man does not keep pace with his companions, perhaps it is because he hears a different drummer."

14. His stubborn refusal to mount, in this era of artistic coup d'état and herd movement, any bandwagon but that of his own . . . sensibility —John Updike, *Bech: A Book*

    Updike here jumps on the bandwagon of the familiar, but with a distinctly "Updikian" twist.

15. They belonged to the vast group of human automata who go through life without neglecting to perform a single one of the gestures executed by the surrounding puppets —Edith Wharton, *The House of Mirth*

    The novel's title alludes to "the heart of fools is in the house of mirth," from Ecclesiastes *(O.T. 7:4).*

■ CONFRONTATION

See also: AGGRESSION; AGREEMENT/ DISAGREEMENT

1. The in-your-face lecturing of indecorous journalists works —Phil Donahue, "Infidelity is a Valid Campaign Issue," *New York Times*, August 26, 1992

   This is the sort of metaphor that catches on, runs rampant, and then either disappears or becomes idiomatic—disappearance seems the likeliest fate in this case.

2. Hector: Do you think this is a conversation between enemies we are having?— Ulysses: I should say a duet before the full orchestra —Jean Giraudoux, *Tiger at the Gates,* Act 2

   Ulysses knew that the conversational sparring was merely the prelude to all-out war between the Greeks and the Trojans.

3. Faced with a chance to radically change their sport's rules about fighting, the lords of the National Hockey League put up their dukes for debate today and then backed off from the essence of the confrontation —Joe Lapointe, *The New York Times,* August 26, 1992

   At one time fingers were referred to as forks. *Since fingers were used to make a fist, the expression* Dukes of Yorks, *and the shortened* dukes *became common in Cockney rhyming slang and in every day English.*

4. The organization [the UN] was liberated from the chains of ideological confrontation —Vladimir Petrovsky, UN conference, Kyoto, April, 1993

   the Under-Secretary-General, Director General of the United Nations Office at Geneva was speaking about a resolution that some commentators said "symbolized the end of the cold war."

5. Who better than [Germaine] Greer to deploy a fiery contrarian sword against society's contempt for older women — Kate Pollitt, "Books," *The New Yorker,* November 2, 1992

   The reviewer felt that Ms. Greer brandished the sword in The Change: Women Aging and Menopause *but without successfully making her case.*

6. Senator Howard Baker called President Carter's response to the Soviet combat brigade in Cuba "inadequate" and added: "In a toe-to-toe confrontation, we blinked" —William Safire, *On Language*

   Safire notes that toes do not blink. He also notes that the metaphor was "fixed in the lexicon by columnists Charles Bartlett and Stewart Alsop as,

   'We're eyeball to eyeball and the other fellow just blinked.'"

■ CONFUSION

See also: ORDER/DISORDER

1. "A pretty kettle of fish altogether!" said the magistrate —Thomas Hardy, "The Three Strangers"

   This common metaphor for any hopelessly mixed-up situation, stems from its literal role at old-time Scottish picnics. Other literary works in which it appears include Henry Fielding's 1742 novel, Joseph Andrews and W. S. Gilbert's Iolanthe.

2. His thoughts were a chaos . . . the confused orders of a routed army to rally itself before it was too late —Patricia Highsmith, "The Birds Poised to Fly"

3. The deceptiveness of beauty, so that all one's perceptions . . . were tangled in a golden mesh —Virginia Woolf, *To the Lighthouse*

■ CONNECTIONS

See also: ALLIANCES; FAMILIES/FAMILY RELATIONSHIPS; FRIENDSHIP/ FRIENDS

1. Given that the Wilm's gene is the toggle switch between rapid cell growth and cell maturation, scientists said, it is not surprising that under some circumstances a defect in the gene can result in cancer — Natalie Angier, "Gene Experiment Offers Insight Into the Basis Of a Childhood Cancer," *The New York Times,* August 31, 1993

2. It's good to connect yourself to the community handle —Anon., Yiddish Proverb

3. The cords that bind the States together are not only many, but various in character — John C. Calhoun, Speech on the question of slavery, delivered by James Madison, March 4, 1850

4. He [Steavens] would not help wondering what link there could have been between the porcelain vessel and so sooty a lump of potter's clay —Willa Cather, "The Sculptor's Funeral," *Youth and the Bright Medusa*
   The porcelain vessel was the exquisitely sensitive sculptor whose funeral Steavens was attending; the lump of clay was a hard-drinking lawyer who had been corrupted by the local mores.

5. I'm not suggesting that we do not anchor ourselves in our communities. But I think, to use a metaphor, the rope attached to that anchor should be large enough to allow us to move into other communities —Angela Davis, *The New York Times*, May 24, 1992
   "Race has become an increasingly obsolete way of constructing community . . . that we have to find ways of coming together in a different way," the African-American wrote.

6. She was the golden thread that united him to a Past beyond misery, and to a Present beyond his misery —Charles Dickens, *A Tale of Two Cities*
   The "she" of the golden thread is Lucy Manette, the one bright light in her father's tragic life.

7. He had created a private new science that brought past and future together in a starkly majestic tapestry —James Gleick, *Genius: The Life and Science of Richard Feynman*
   Feynman made a creative leap by showing particles of antimatter going backward in time.

8. A magic thread of fellow feeling united his life [Jude's] with theirs [the birds] —Thomas Hardy, *Jude the Obscure*
   Young Jude's happiness is rudely interrupted by his boss, who beats him for feeding the birds.

9. Isn't the worthless rooster the poet's bird brother? —Jim Harrison, "The Rooster"
   The rooster no longer has any part in the eggs, since "chickens have largely been denatured, you know," but he insists on mounting the hens anyway. Perhaps that is why he's the poet's blood brother, or "bird brother."

10. Making connections is something the music business suddenly can't do without. Friday night at Avery Fisher Hall it was Richard Strauss holding hands with Mozart in a *Mostly Mozart* concert —Bernard Holland, "Review/Music," *The New York Times*, July 19, 1993
    The only genuine shared link Holland saw between the composers was that in the works of both "beauty and seduction are inseparable."

11. These days [David] Durk runs a sort of underground railroad for the delivery of whistle-blowers and their information —James Lardner, "The Whistle-Blower—Part I," *The New Yorker*, July 5, 1993
    Allusion to the nineteenth century networks for runaway slaves was used as a metaphor for an ex-policeman's crusade to encourage and abet others in exposing police corruption.

12. New Jersey is on a threshold. Here you have two of the great historic areas of New Jersey—Hudson and Essex—on the verge of forging new transportation sinews. They're not just lines on the map. They are people in seats —John McGoldrick, *The Record*, April 28, 1993
    Any English teacher with a red pen would have a field day with this mixaphor in a story concerning the approval of new rail links into Newark International Airport.

13. Like most alliances, the cement has always been an external threat . . . The cement now is a general and alarming threat of global instability —David Reynolds, Quoted in, *The New York Times*, January 24, 1993
    A Cambridge University historian commented on the strategic goals of the U.S. and Britain.

14. Iago: I profess me thy friend, and I confess me knit to thy deserving, with cables of perdurable toughness —William Shakespeare, *Othello*, Act I, scene 3, line 338

15. The drug companies have every intention of keeping Tomlinson's marriage to his prescription pad intact —Elizabeth Stone, "Off the Couch," *The New York Times Magazine*, December 6, 1992
    The article about the new emphasis on drug therapy rather than talk therapy carries this blurb:

"On the front line of the psych wars, Freud is under siege."

■ CONSCIENCE

1. A quiet conscience sleeps in thunder — Anon., English Proverb

2. A good conscience is a continual feast — Robert Burton, *The Anatomy of Melancholy*

3. A good conscience is a continual Christmas —Benjamin Franklin, *Poor Richard's Almanack*

4. There is no sting to the worm of conscience —Thomas Lodge, *Rosalynde*
   In Richard III *Shakespeare turned this around to "The worm of conscience shall begnaw thy soul." Another variant appears in Act 5, scene 1 of Friedrich Schiller's play 1784 Kabale and Liebe: "The worm of conscience consorts [or watches] with the owl."*

5. And I, conscience, contain the orchestra of regimental brasses / on which the moustachioed ones blew for the Elevation —Czeslaw Milosz, "Consciousness"
   The poet remembers his devotions, though he sometimes believes, sometimes disbelieves in the "truth in the painted Jesus" He contains it all, as Walt Whitman contained "multitudes"

6. The worm of conscience keeps the same hours as the owl —Johann Christoph Friedrich von Schiller, *Kabala and Liebe*, V

7. Margaret: The worm of conscience shall begnaw thy soul —William Shakespeare, *The Tragedy of King Richard the Third*, Act 1, scene 3, line 221

8. Richard: My conscience hath a thousand several tongues —William Shakespeare, *The Tragedy of King Richard the Third*, Act 5, scene 3, line 192

9. My conscience is my crown —Robert Southwell, "Content and Rich"

10. Conscience and cowardice are really the same things . . . conscience is the trade name of the firm —Oscar Wilde, *The Picture of Dorian Gray*

■ CONSCIOUSNESS

See also: MIND

1. Descartes and Locke are evidently mistaken—the mind is not a wax tablet upon which nature imprints what she pleases, it is not an object, but a perpetual activity which shapes its world to respond to its ethical demands —Isaiah Berlin, "The Apotheosis of the Romantic Will"
   The author refers to John Locke's metaphor of a tabula rasa—a smooth tablet on which sense impressions are built up.

2. But yet I am firmly persuaded that a great deal of consciousness, every sort of consciousness, in fact, is a disease —Fyodor Mikhailovich Dostoevsky, *Notes from Underground*
   In another metaphor, the narrator writes "the more conscious I was of goodness . . . the more deeply I sank into my mire."

3. Consciousness is a poison when we apply it to ourselves —Boris Pasternak, *Doctor Zhivago*
   Yura is trying to console Anna Ivanovna, who worries about her soul after death.

4. Consciousness is a light directed outward, it lights up the way ahead of us so that we don't stumble —Boris Pasternak, *Doctor Zhivago*
   "It's like the headlights on a locomotive," says Yura.

■ CONSEQUENCES

See: CAUSE AND EFFECT

■ CONSISTENCY/ INCONSISTENCY

1. [Alexander] Woollcott was . . . a mountain of contradictions; a congress of op-

posing parties —John Mason Brown, Introduction, *The Portable Woollcott*

2. A foolish consistency is the hobgoblin of little minds, adored by little statesmen and philosophers and divines —Ralph Waldo Emerson, "Self Reliance"
   Watch those "littles" in this much-quoted example of Emerson wit and wisdom—the pejorative adjectives that damn the statesmen and philosophers and, even the divines.

3. Consistency is a paste jewel that only cheap men cherish —William Allen White, *Emporia Gazette,* November 17, 1923
   This was White's response to an item in a rival paper implying that the Gazette *never checked past files to see if current proposals were consistent with past statements.*

■ CONSTANCY/INCONSTANCY

See: LOYALTY; TRUSTWORTHINESS/ UNTRUSTWORTHINESS

■ CONTEMPLATION

See: THINKING/THOUGHT

■ CONTEMPT

See: ARROGANCE/HUMILITY

■ CONTENTMENT

See also: HAPPINESS/UNHAPPINESS

1. A mind content both crown and kingdom is —Robert Greene, "Farewell to Folly"

2. Content's a kingdom —Thomas Heywood, *A Woman Kill'd With Kindness,* Act 3, scene 1

3. Kublail: Contentment is a warm sty for the eaters and sleepers —Eugene O'Neill, *Marco's Millions,* Act 2, scene 2

4. He drew the feet of contentment under the skirt of security —Saadi (also known as Sadi), *The Rose Garden* (Gulistan)

5. King: My crown is in my heart, not in my head . . . / My crown is called content — William Shakespeare, *The Third Part of Henry the Sixth,* Act 3, scene 1, line 62

■ CONTINUITY

See also: PERMANENCE/IMPERMANENCE

1. All EC [European Community] states want the European train to keep rolling —Chancellor Helmut Kohl, Quoted in *China Daily,* October 19, 1992

2. The day that does not carry the seed of tomorrow in its womb is sterile —Lewis Mumford, *The Freeman*

■ CONTROL

See also: MANIPULATION; MASTERY/SUBORDINATION; PEOPLE, INTERACTION

1. The teacher flogs with a stick and the rich man with a wallet —Anon., Yiddish Proverb

2. Come up, and you shall see how I will throw the reins over their heads —Henry Clay, Quoted remark, while he was Speaker of the House of Representatives
   The invitation was issued to a friend who wondered how he could preside over the House after having spent most of the night at a party.

3. A mouth is not always a mouth, but a bit is always a bit, and it matters little what it bridles —Colette, "The Sick Child"

4. Under present circumstances, the one thing to be done was to clap the extinguisher upon Penelope's curiosity on the spot — Wilkie Collins, *The Moonstone*
   An extinguisher was meant to snuff out a candle and put out the flame of curiosity that burned in the narrator's daughter.

5. Mr. [André] Previn's puts them [his jazz pieces] on their best behavior . . . wild outgrowths gardened into a formal sub-

mission —Bernard Holland, "Review/ Music," *The New York Times,* July 13, 1993
The "gardened" pieces were "Honey and Rue," presented at an opening concert at the annual Tanglewood Music Festival and sung by soprano Kathleen Battle for whom they were composed.

6. Peterson keeps the narrative on a very short leash; a quick jerk and it's back on the straight narrow path of stop-the-killer suspense —Terrence Rafferty, "Current Cinema," *The New Yorker,* July 12, 1993
The man holding the metaphoric leash was director Wolfgang Peterson and the subject of his control, the movie In the Line of Fire.

7. To bring the world under a rule, / Who are but weasels / fighting in a hole — William Butler Yeats, "Nineteen Hundred and Nineteen"
Press Secretary Marlin Fitzwater alluded to this poem when he called Democrats who opposed President Bush's economic plans "weasels going into a hole." This slightly inaccurate use of the metaphor was quickly spotted and discussed in William Safire's "On Language" column.

■ CONTROVERSY

See: AGREEMENT/DISAGREEMENT; ARGUMENTS; QUARRELS/QUARRELSOMENESS

■ CONVERSATION

See also: COMMUNICATION/NON-COMMUNICATION; PEOPLE, INTERACTION

1. And as for conversation—that feast of reason, that flow of the soul—our house is silent as the bone yard —Ethan Canin, "We Are Nighttime Travelers"
The metaphor leads into simile.

2. Dr. McPhail: Everybody's conversation about everybody else is a diagnosis — John Colton and Clemence Randolph, *Rain,* Act 3, scene 1
The play was based on a short story of the same name by W. Somerset Maugham.

3. Sweet discourse, the banquet of the mind —John Dryden, "The Flower and The Leaf"
The metaphor also appears in Alexander Pope's translation of The Odyssey.

4. Much of our conversation is a series of dittos, often typed on fifth carbons — Clifton Fadiman, "In Praise of Quotation"
The modern office makes this an example of a dinosaur metaphor.

5. Mrs. Owens, trying hard to follow the strange rabbit paths of this dialogue, turned almost involuntarily —Mavis Gallant, "By the Sea"

6. They tossed the feathery ball of conversation —O. Henry, "Transients in Arcadia"

7. A good housewife, she knew how to hash up the conversational remains of last night's dinner to furnish out this morning's lunch. Monday's funeral baked meats did service for Tuesday's wedding —Aldous Huxley, *Point Counter Point*
The last part of the metaphor alludes to Hamlet's bitter reference to the "funeral baked meats" prepared for his father's burial and now served at his mother's wedding.

8. So often a conversation is shipwrecked by the very eagerness of one member to contribute —Christopher Morley, "What Men Live By"

9. How few, how few are those gifted for real talk! There are fine merry fellows . . . who will not abide by one topic, who must always be lashing out upon some new byroad, snatching at every bush they pass —Christopher Morley, "What Men Live By"

10. Several subjects started, and dropped down the abyss of Eliza's silence —Lore Segal, "The Talk in Eliza's Kitchen," *The New Yorker,* April 6, 1992

11. All day she [a nurse] will use her strong body . . . spinning threads of cheerful talk —Richard Selzer, "Semiprivate, Female"

12. Benedick: The body of your discourse is sometimes guarded [decorated] with fragments, and the guards [decorative additions] are but slightly basted on neither; ere you flout old ends any further, examine your conscience —William Shakespeare, *Much Ado About Nothing,* Act 1, scene 1, line 204
> Benedick advises Don Pedro not to clutter his conversation with antiquated phrases by using a sewing metaphor.

13. His Judgment is so good and unerring, and accompanied with so cheerful a Spirit, that his Conversation is a continual Feast —Richard Steele

14. Our conversation limped —D. M. Thomas, *Memories and Hallucinations*
> Limp *has become a common one-verb metaphor for slowdowns in all sorts of activities.*

15. When a conversation becomes a monologue, poked along with tiny cattle-prod questions, it isn't a conversation any more —Barbara Walters, *How to Talk with Practically Anybody About Practically Anything*

16. Conversation was their brightly lighted stage and their battlefield. There they knew their triumphs and their massacres —Thornton Wilder, *The Eighth Day*
> The conversationalists are a group of Chicago journalists at the turn of the century who know much more than they are allowed to print by their editors.

■ CORRESPONDENCE

See: LETTERS

■ CORRUPTION

See also: GOOD/EVIL

1. Thy silver has become dross, thy wine mixed with water —The Bible, *O.T., Isaiah 1:22*

2. All nations have drunk of the wine of the wrath of her fornication —The Bible, *N.T., Revelation 18:3*
> This image of Babylon as a fornicating woman became the source for the epithet "the whore of Babylon" that Puritans used to deride the Catholic Church. Babylon was regarded as the city of the Antichrist.

3. [Isaiah Berlin] swam too easily in rancid water —Marion Frankfurter, Quoted by Joseph W. Alsop in *I've Seen the Best of It*
> According to Alsop, the accusation was based on jealousy about Berlin's enormous and instantly-gained social success in Washington circles.

4. Ajax: Suppose I tell you what the people of Greece thinks of Troy, that Troy is a cess-pit of vice and stupidity? —Jean Giraudoux, *Tiger at the Gates,* Act 2

5. Hamlet: Mother / for love of grace, / Lay not that flattering unction to your soul, / . . . It will but skin and film the ulcerous place, / Whiles rank corruption, mining all within, / Infects unseen —William Shakespeare, *Hamlet,* Act 3, scene 4, line 148

6. King: Most subject is the fattest soil to weeds; / And he, the noblest image of my youth, / Is overspread with them — William Shakespeare, *The Second Part of King Henry the Fourth,* Act 4, scene 4, line 54
> The king uses the metaphor of an overgrown garden for the pervasive influence of his son's followers.

7. Duke: My business in this state / Made me a looker-on here in Vienna, / Where I have seen corruption boil and bubble / 'Till it o'er-run the stew —William Shakespeare, *Measure for Measure,* Act 5, scene 1, line 320
> In Act 3, scene 4, line 95, Hamlet tells the Queen that her marriage bed is "stew'd in corruption."

8. Servant: our sea-walled garden, the whole land / Is full of weeds; her fairest flowers choked up, / Her fruit-trees all unpruned, her hedges ruin'd, / and her knots disorder'd, / and her wholesome herbs / Swarming with caterpillars —William Shakespeare,

The Tragedy of King Richard the Second, Act 3, scene 4, line 44
The messy garden is the corruption laden land.

■ COUNSEL

See: ADVICE

■ COUNTENANCES

See: FACES

■ COUNTRIES, MISC.

See also: AMERICA/AMERICANS; PLACES, MISC.

1. Greece . . . an eternal blank page waiting for a note or a word —John Fowles, Quoted about the influence of the Greek landscape on his imagination, c. 1952

2. This land, the bright wrists / Of the world on which the centuries are bracelets — Christopher Fry, *The Firstborn,* Act 3, scene 2

3. An unexplored continent would become a jail —Robert Hughes, *The Fatal Shore*
". . . the very air and sea, the whole transparent labyrinth of the South Pacific, would become a wall 14,000 miles thick," writes Hughes, speaking of the shipping of convicts to Australia.

4. Australia was a cloaca, invisible, its contents filthy and unnameable —Robert Hughes, *The Fatal Shore*
During the late eighteenth century, the British thought it could get rid of its entire criminal population by shipping it to Australia to colonize the continent.

5. Yugoslavia, once a nation, now a scream of agony —A. M. Rosenthal, "On My Mind," *The New York Times,* May 22, 1992

6. Gaunt: [England] This precious stone set in a silver sea —William Shakespeare, *The Tragedy of King Richard the Second,* Act 2, scene 1, line 46
In the same speech, Gaunt also uses the metaphor of a caretaker and a mother's womb for the country: *"This nurse, this teeming womb of royal kings."*

■ COURAGE

See also: PERSONALITY PROFILES; RISK-TAKING; SELF-RELIANCE

1. He [baseball player Dennis Eckersley] has been the Zorro of his era, and is never dull —Roger Angell, "The Sporting Scene," *The New Yorker,* "Shades of Blue," December 7, 1992
Angell saw the pitcher as metaphorically filling the shoes of the comic book and movie serial masked defender of the weak. He "rides the edge out there, always imagining failure and prepared to fight it off, hand to hand, with his most dazzling effort yet."

2. O man-tiger —Anon., *The Bhagavad Gita, 17:4*

3. But he that dares not grasp the thorn / Should never crave the rose —Anne Brontë, "The Narrow Way"

4. Voynitsky: There's mermaid's blood flowing in your veins. So . . . let yourself go . . . dive head first into deep water and leave the learned professor and the rest of us gasping on the shore —Anton P. Chekhov, *Uncle Vanya,* Act 3, 1899
Helen recalls this advice some time later, but it's clear she's not going to heed it.

5. It was the nation and the race swelling all around the globe that had the lion's heart. I had the luck to be called upon to give the roar. I also hope that I sometimes suggested to the lion the right place to use his claws —Winston Churchill, Speech, November 30, 1954
The English statesman, much lionized for his leadership during the second World War, thus down-played his role.

6. The Red Badge of Courage —Stephen Crane, Title of novel, 1896
The author elaborates on the title's metaphor in chapter 9: "He wishes that he, too, had a wound, a red badge of courage."

7. For courage is the vegetable king, / The sprig of all ontologies, the weed / That beards the slag-heap with his hectoring — Donald Davie, "Remembering the 'Thirties, I'"

> *Anyone who has seen the miracle of a tree forcing its way through a rock, or the weed in a crack of a city sidewalk, will recognize this image of "vegetable" courage.*

8. O friend, never strike sail to a fear! Come into port greatly, or sail with God the seas —Ralph Waldo Emerson, "Heroism," *The First Series*

9. Osmer: I've got a screw of courage you can chew —Christopher Fry, *Thor, With Angels*

> *A screw is a small packet of tobacco. The metaphor works in the same way that* Dutch courage *or* English courage—*the artificial courage that comes from a bottle of liquor—works in a common drinking metaphor.*

10. Brave actions never want a trumpet — Thomas Fuller, *Gnomologia*

11. He took the great round world in his hand —O. Henry, "A Cosmopolite in a Café," *The Four Million*

> *The implied ballplayer is a man of the world, unafraid to discuss and disdain anything and everything.*

12. We no longer need to clip the wings of our humanity. It's time we flew again —John Le Carré, Speech to the Boston Bar Association, May 3, 1993

> *Le Carré's speech was a plea for the courage to make a commitment to humanitarianism in a world where "the rule of law is a far safer haven" than the clandestine maneuverers who peopled his espionage books.*

13. In the world's broad field of battle, / In the bivouac of Life, / . . . Be a hero in the strife! —Henry Wadsworth Longfellow, "A Psalm of Life"

> *The poet used the metaphor of life as a battleground to urge the reader not to act like "dumb, driven cattle."*

14. We ourselves must Pilgrims be, / Launch our Mayflower, and steer boldly / Through the desperate winter sea, / Nor attempt the Future's portal / With the Past's blood-rusted key —Wendell Phillips, Speech at Harvard College, June 30, 1881

> *The advocate of unpopular causes introduced this concluding verse with a simile that advised "Sit not, like the figure on our silver coin, looking ever backward.*

15. Talbot: How are we park'd and bounded in a pale, / A little herd of England's timorous deer, / Mazed with a yelping kennel of French curs! —William Shakespeare, *The First Part of Henry the Sixth*, Act 4, scene 2, line 46

> *General Talbot advises his overwhelmed soldiers to turn against the enemy like "moody-mad and desperate stags."*

16. Lady Macbeth: We fail? But screw your courage to the sticking-place, / And we'll not fail —William Shakespeare, *Macbeth*, Act 1, scene 7, line 60

> *In Shakespeare's day the sticking-place referred to the tightening of the screw of a crossbow to make it stick. While the crossbow has become a dead metaphor, everyone understands that* to screw up one's courage *means to force oneself to face up to something difficult.*

17. York: But in this kind to come, in braving arms, / Be his own carver and cut out his way / To find out right with wrong—it may not be —William Shakespeare, *The Tragedy of King Richard the Second*, Act 2, scene 3, line 142

> *York compares Bolingbroke to someone who carves his own meat at the table and serves himself what he wants.*

18. Richard: I have set my life upon a cast, / And I will stand the hazard of the die — William Shakespeare, *The Tragedy of King Richard the Third*, Act 5, scene 4, line 9

> *A much-used variation of the king's metaphor of life as a game of chance is* let the dice fall where they may *or to* accept the roll of the dice. *Other games of chance metaphors pervade literature and journalism; for example, Samuel Butler's* Note-Books *(1912) spoke of the world as "a gambling-*

table, so arranged that all who enter the casino must play and all must lose more or less heavily in the long run, though they win occasionally by the way.

19. A man should stop his ears against paralyzing terror, and run the race that is set before him with a single mind —Robert Louis Stevenson, "Aes Triplex"

    The image of life as a race and death as a goal is a common one.

20. The brave, serviceable men of every nation tread down the nettle danger, and pass flying over all the stumbling blocks of prudence —Robert Louis Stevenson, "Aes Triplex"

21. If you can't stand the heat, stay out of the kitchen —Harry S Truman

    This much quoted image made news soon after President Truman settled into the Presidency. When, shortly after his re-election he decided not to run again, he cited the kitchen metaphor as his reason.

22. He learned to walk the highwire, sailing along with gumption and a parasol — Scott Turow, *Pleading Guilty*

    A mixed metaphor.

■ COURTESY

See: MANNERS

■ COURTSHIP

See: MEN AND WOMEN

■ COWARDICE

See also: RISK-TAKING; TIMIDITY

1. Bialystock [Zero Mostel]: You miserable cowardly, wretched little caterpillar. Don't you ever want to become a butterfly? Don't you want to spread your wings and flap your way to glory? —Mel Brooks, *The Producers*

To make his point to the timid accountant he's addressing, Bialystock flaps his arms like a huge predatory bird.

2. Cowardice . . . The jaundice of the soul — John Dryden, *The Hind and the Panther*, VII

3. Edna: You gutless piece of boloney — Clifford Odets, *Waiting for Lefty*, Part 1

    Edna thus berates her husband Joe for not standing up to his boss.

4. But on each occasion it was Morel, the dangerous person, who turned tail and fled —Marcel Proust, *Cities of the Plain*

    Proust uses an old metaphor to show Morel's fright at the sight of some photographs that seemed to look accusingly at him.

5. Philip the Bastard: You are the hare of whom the proverb goes, / Whose valour plucks dead lions by the beard —William Shakespeare, *The Life and Death of King John*, Act 2, scene 1, line 137

    The proverb alluded to is A dead lion hares insult.

6. Chiron: Foul-spoken coward, that thunder'st with thy tongue —William Shakespeare, *Titus Andronicus*, Act 2, scene 2, line 58

■ CRAFTINESS

See also: PERSONALITY PROFILES; UNTRUSTWORTHINESS

1. At heart, he remains one of the shrewdest horse-traders in the world —Bennett Cerf, *Try And Stop Me*

    Cerf rebuts critics who say that George Bernard Shaw is approaching senility.

2. He resolved, therefore, to go immediately to the gaming-house, not so much with an intention of trusting to fortune as to play the surer card of attacking the winner in his way home —Henry Fielding, *The Life of Mr. Jonathan Wild the Great*

3. In them [in Hetty's eyes] he saw the Jolly Roger fly to the masthead and an able seaman with a dirk between his teeth

scurry up the ratlines and nail it there. But as yet he did not know that the cargo he carried was the thing that had caused him to be so nearly blown out of the water without even a parley —O. Henry, "The Third Ingredient"

The overblown metaphor is used to depict a wily woman trying to con an onion—his 'cargo'—from a passer-by. An onion! Using this image is swatting a fly with a baseball bat.

4. The disease [of Europe's monetary system] is renationalization—with a vengeance in the East and on cat's feet in the West —Josef Joffe, Op-Ed, *The New York Times,* September 20, 1992

    The author went on to remark that even without a threat of war, metaphors pertaining to the monetary system were increasingly military, with allusions to "Dunkirk" and the "Alamo."

5. If my husband is Byzantine on matters so minor as a dinner party, I assure you that he is Bach's harpsichordist when it comes to tweaking Company strings —Norman Mailer, *Harlot's Ghost*

    The Company referred to is the CIA.

6. He had the instincts and timing of a cornered snake —Ridley Pearson, *Hard Fall*

7. Buckingham: Attend. This holy fox, / Or wolf, or both—for he is equal ravenous as he is subtle, and as prone to mischief — William Shakespeare, *The Life of King Henry the Eighth,* Act 1, scene 1, line 159

    Shakespeare regularly used the sly fox and the avaricious wolf to paint his portraits.

8. That Anstey woman is a walking confidence trick —William Trevor, "Raymond Bamber and Mrs. Fitch"

    The narrator thinks Anstey is romantically involved with her husband. She reflects on his infidelity as follows: "Why shouldn't he want to graze where the grass grows greener, or appears to grow greener?"

9. You never felt that you saw all round him; you always suspected . . . some ingenuity in ambush, behind his lucid frankness — H. G. Wells, *The Time Machine*

■ CREATION

1. For Me great Brahman is a womb; / Therein I plant the germ —Anon., *The Bhagavad Gita, 14:3*

2. And the waves flourished at my prayer, / The rivers spawned their sand —Geoffrey Hill, "Genesis"

    The metaphor here resides in the verb, so that the river gives birth to sand the way a fish spawns.

3. To realize one's high conception / On the night's canvas with a dot, just one — Nikolai Morshen, "Two Poems"

■ CREATIVITY

See also: IDEAS; ORIGINALITY / UNORIGINALITY

1. Execution [of artistic inspiration] means creating, bringing to birth, laboriously rearing the child, putting it to bed every evening gorged with milk, kissing it every morning with a mother's never spent affection, licking it clean, clothing it over and over again in the prettiest garments, which it spoils again and again. —Honoré de Balzac, *Cousin Bette*

    The Polish artist in Balzac's novel lacked the wherewithal needed; the prolific Balzac did not.

2. The beings of the mind are not of clay; / Essentially immortal, they create —Lord George Gordon Byron, "Childe Harold"

    This metaphor establishes that literature, like Nature, is both worthy and permanent.

3. After she left me and I quit my job and wept for a year and / all my poems were born dead, I decided I would only fish and drink —Jim Harrison, "Drinking Song"

4. He is a tree that cannot produce good fruit; he only bears crabs [small, sour fruit] —Samuel Johnson, Quoted in *Short Saying of Great Men*

    The metaphoric insult pertained to a contemporary poet. Johnson tempered it with a compliment about the poet's productivity: "a tree that produc-

es a great many crabs is better than a tree which produces only a few."

5. Welcome, O Life! I go to encounter for the millionth time the reality of experience and to forge in the smithy of my soul the uncreated conscience of my race — James Joyce, *Portrait of the Artist as a Young Man*

    After a series of epiphanies, Joyce forsakes both home and church and leaves Ireland.

6. If there be nothing new, but that which is / Hath been before, how are our brains beguiled, / Which, laboring for invention, bear amiss / The second burden of a former child! —William Shakespeare, "Sonnet 59," line 1

    The poet mourns that in laboring to create something new, he merely gives birth to another version of the old.

7. I burn for my own lies. / The nights electrocute my fugitive, / My mind — James Wright, "At the Executed Murderer's Grave. 2"

    "I am not dead. / I croon my tears at fifty cents per line," writes the poet.

8. He [Nietzsche] says his head is pregnant with books, and he thinks that his cephalgia is cerebral labor pain —Irvin D. Yalom, *When Nietzsche Wept*

    The young Sigmund Freud with whom Dr. Joseph Breuer is discussing the philosopher's illness exclaims "what a metaphor! Like Minerva born from the brow of Zeus!" Actually, the phrase to be pregnant with ideas *has become a fairly common metaphor.*

■ CREEDS

See: BELIEFS

■ CRIME AND PUNISHMENT

See also: REVENGE/VENGEANCE

1. Your schemes [to obtain unjust gains] . . . will bring dishonour to your house . . .

and . . . the stone shall cry out of the wall, and the beam out of the timber shall answer it —The Bible, *O.T., Habakkuk 2:11*

2. Yea, I am one the Avenger God inspires; / He has marked my forehead with the breath of spite —Gerard de Nerval, "Antéros"

    de Nerval uses a mythological subject who rages against the gods, but incorporates a Biblical reference to God's marking of Cain for his brother's murder.

3. Crime and punishment grow out of one stem. Punishment is a fruit that unsuspected ripens within the flower of pleasure which concealed it —Ralph Waldo Emerson, "Compensation," *Essays: First Series*

4. Commit a crime and the earth is made of glass —Ralph Waldo Emerson, "Compensation," *Essays: First Series*

5. Price defended his "severities" . . . on the ground the prisoners were wild beasts who would rise and take the island if they got an inch of slack —Robert Hughes, *The Fatal Shore*

■ CRITICISM/CRITICS

See also: APPROVAL/DISAPPROVAL; ARTS AND ENTERTAINMENT; INSULTS; NAME CALLING

1. Precisely what I predicted. The knives are flashing —Truman Capote, Telephone remark to John Malcom Brinnon, recorded in the latter's journal, 1947

    The metaphoric knife referred to is The New York Times *whose critics according to Capote "are going to slice me paper thin."*

2. Those thugs that wait for people like me— that pack of wolves around the *Partisan*. What if they decide to gang up on me? — Truman Capote, Quoted in John Malcom Brinnon's journal, 1947

    Capote's worries were prompted by the forthcoming publication of Other Voices, Other Rooms.

3. In coterie / the arguments / all geese-gabble —Yi Chao, "Speaking of Poetry," Ch'ing Dynasty

   Judgement of poetry must be made by an individual, the poet feels, and not by a group.

4. [Critics:] Disinterested thieves of our good name —Samuel Taylor Coleridge, "Modern Critics"

5. Critics in general are venomous serpents that delight in hissing —W. B. Daniel, "Rural Sports"

6. Weak stomachs, with a long Disease opprest, / Cannot the Cordials of strong Wit digest; / Therefore thin Nourishment of Farce ye choose, / Decoctions of a Barly-water Muse: / A meal of Tragedy wou'd make ye Sick —John Dryden, "Prologue (for Nahum Tate's *The Loyal General*)"

   If Dryden decried the "barley water" theater in the seventeenth century, how would he respond to the thin-gruel diet of Broadway?

7. Those who write not, and yet all Writers nick, / Are Bankrupt Gamesters, for they damn on Tick —John Dryden, "Second Prologue to Secret Love; or The Maiden Queen"

   "Tick" is credit; talent is like money in the bank.

8. No Criticks verdict, should, of right, stand good, / They are excepted all as men of blood; / And the same Law should shield him from their fury / Which has exclud'd Butchers from a Jury —John Dryden, "Second Prologue to Secret Love; or The Maiden Queen"

   Not much has changed since this 17th-century poet's opinion of critics as butchers, although the passing of over three hundred years has lost them their jury exclusion.

9. Art is long, and critics are the insects of a day —Randall Jarrell, Quoted by Brad Leitthauser, *The New Yorker*, June 15, 1992

   The quote appeared in a review of Palgrave's Golden Treasury.

10. This was the drama critic he had met the day before, giving free rein to his pen —Kume Masao, "The Tiger"

    In a common metaphor for freedom, or for curtailment of freedom, things are reined in or one gives free rein.

11. All in all, they [critics] are a wretched race of hungry alligators —Henry Wadsworth Longfellow

    Another Longfellow metaphor on the same topic: "Critics are sentinels in the grand army of letters, stationed at the corners of newspapers and reviews, to challenge every author."

12. I felt it would be somehow unfair to your very important book, if I did not express the whirl of thought that its shimmering propeller produced —Vladimir Nabokov, Letter to Edmund Wilson, December 15, 1940

    Nabokov nicely wraps a few points of criticism in a generally complementary view of the editor/critic's book on Marx and Lenin.

13. I cannot possibly think of you / other than you are: the assassin / of my orchards —Frank O'Hara, "The Critic," quoted in "Books," *The New Yorker*, July 19, 1993

    O'Hara's poem begins with this double-barrelled metaphor depicting the critic as a killer of the fruits of his labors.

14. Criticism has positive popular attractions in its . . . gladiatorship —George Bernard Shaw

    Shaw used allusion as a metaphor for critics as ancient warriors.

15. Censure is the tax a man pays for being eminent —Jonathan Swift, *Thoughts on Various Subjects*

16. My bait will not tempt the rats, they are too well fed —Henry David Thoreau

    Thoreau's comment about the New York Newspaper editors he generally despised, was quoted in a review of a 1993 collection of his writings, "The Dispersion of Seeds and Other Late Natural History Writings."

17. He is one of the serpents of literature who feed on filth and venom; he is a scribbler —Voltaire, *Candide*

18. When the show received uniform, stake-in-the-heart critical pans it became one of the greatest calamities in Broadway history —Bruce Weber, *The New York Times,* December 30, 1993

    Adding a sewing metaphor, Weber explained that the ill-fated Broadway adaptation of the 1948 movie The Red Shoes *was "a stitched-together effort, its seams in embarrassing evidence."*

19. I see critics as bus drivers. They ferry the visitors round the City of Invention and stop the bus here or there, at whim, and act as guides —Fay Weldon, *Letters to Alice*

    The author extends the metaphor to the writer as the builder who listens to what the bus driver has to say with half an ear, but prefers "lurking in the edifice of his own conceit, to hear what the actual visitors have to say."

20. [The novels of Henry James:] A church lit but without a congregation . . . with every light and line focused on the high altar. And on the altar . . . is a dead kitten, an egg-shell, a bit of string —H. G. Wells, *Critique,* 1915

    This scathing critique also contained a metaphor aimed at James's syntax: He splits his infinitives and fills them up with adverbial stuffing.

■ CROWDS

See also: STREET SCENES

1. I love to dive into the bath of street life, the waves of the crowds flowing over me, to impregnate myself with the fluids of the people —Isabelle Eberhardt, Journal entry

2. Outside the mob shifts on its terrible / haunches —Donald Finkel, "Juan Belmonte, Torero"

    The mob is the beast in the stands, watching the bullfight in the ring.

3. The streets were filled with the rush hour flood of people —O. Henry, "An Unfinished Story," *The Four Million*

4. I used to love to get into the thick of crowds . . . The tussling beefiness of everybody poured into me like broth —Edward Hoagland, "Americana by the Acre," *Harper's,* October, 1970

    After the two food images, one a metaphor and the second a simile, Hoagland switches to a sea image with, "I liked swimming against the tide and with the tide."

5. At St. Patrick's Cathedral waves of [Easter] worshippers transformed aisles into flows and eddies of prayer —Catherine S. Manegold, *The New York Times,* April 19, 1992

6. Down the street people came pouring in a torrent—faces, faces, faces, quilted winter coats and sheepskin hats —Boris Pasternak, *Doctor Zhivago*

    The metaphor is followed by metonymy.

7. Chorus: How London doth pour out her citizens! —William Shakespeare, *The Second Part of King Henry the Fourth,* Act 5, line 24

    The people are crowding the streets to celebrate peace.

8. It was a whole bunch of people made into one big crawling beast —John Steinbeck, *The Red Pony*

    Steinbeck used the "beast" image for the process of American migration to the western part of the country.

9. The reign of King Mob seemed triumphant —Justice Joseph Story

    The reference is to the rowdy inaugural of President Andrew Jackson.

■ CRUELTY

See: PAIN AND SUFFERING

CRYING

See: TEARS

CULTURE

See also: ARTS AND ENTERTAINMENT; MU-SIC/MUSICIANS; SOCIETY/SOCIAL IN-STITUTIONS; SONGS/SINGING

1. When men die, they become History. When statues die, they become Art. This botany of death is what we refer to as culture —Anon., Description of short film, *Les Statues Meurent Aussi*, Bulletin: The Museum of Modern Art Department of Film, April 16–June 8, 1993

2. One culture is no mere step to another. Greece is not an antechamber to Rome —Isaiah Berlin, "The Apotheosis of the Romantic Will"
     Berlin argues that the values of one civilization may be different from, and incompatible with, those of another.

3. If we allow that culture by its nature imprisons perception, that for a poignant creative moment it may enlighten us but then, perversely, transforms itself into a jailhouse walling out reality, then songs comprise the cells of our imprisonment. Behind them rise the tiers and guard towers and electrified fences—sitcoms, sermons, movies, newspapers, presidential elections, art galleries, museums, therapies, plays, poems, novels and university curricula. But the bars we grasp are our songs —E. L. Doctorow, "Standards," *Harper's Magazine*, 1991
     This extended metaphor concludes Doctorow's essay on songs and songwriters.

4. For every culture is an island. It communicates with other islands but it is only familiar with itself —Arthur Koestler, "The Boredom of Fantasy"

5. He was a very good stick to beat the Philistines with —W. Somerset Maugham, *Cakes and Ale*

The "he" refers to an author taken up by the culturally elite of the time; the stick, a weapon of cultural correctness.

CURIOSITY

See also: EDUCATION AND LEARNING; THINKING/THOUGHT

1. Mister, sir—a humble M.R.C.S.... a picker up of shells on the shores of the great unknown ocean —Sir Arthur Conan Doyle, *The Hound of the Baskervilles*
     A man mistaken by Sherlock Holmes as a practicing physician, thus portrays his amateur interest in science.

2. A gust of curiosity stirred the assembled guests —Aldous Huxley, *Point Counter Point*

3. I keep six honest serving men / They taught me all they knew: / Their names were Where and What and When / And Why and How and Who —Rudyard Kipling, "The Elephant's Child," *Just-So Stories*

4. A mind forever / Voyaging through strange seas of thought alone —Henry Wadsworth Longfellow, Lines on Sir Isaac Newton's statue in Cambridge
     Newton himself likened the way he spent his life to a schoolboy playing on the seashore, seeking out pretty pebbles "whilst the great ocean of truth lay all undiscovered before me."

CURSES

See: ACCUSATIONS; NAME CALLING

CUSTOM

See also: HABIT

1. Custom is a tyrant. —Anon., Latin maxim
     The legal variant of this is "Common custom is common law."

2. Custom is the principal magistrate of man's life —Sir Francis Bacon, "Of Custom and Education"

3. Once more . . . lapsing from the passionate pain of change to the palsy of custom —Charlotte Brontë, *Villette*

■ CYNICISM
See: SARCASM

DANCE

See: ARTS AND ENTERTAINMENT

DANGER

See also: CALMNESS/VOLATILITY; DEATH;
PROBLEMS AND SOLUTIONS; SAFETY;
TROUBLE/TROUBLEMAKERS;
UNCERTAINTY

1. Lord Loam: While he is here we are sitting on a volcano —James M. Barrie, *The Admirable Chrichton*, Act 4
   The volcano, frequently used as a metaphor for explosive situations or potentially trouble-making people, here pertains to the butler of the play's title.

2. We are not yet out of the wood —Fanny Burney, *Diary and Letters of Madame D'Arblay*
   The more popular variant is not yet out of the woods.

3. In the jaws of death —Guillaume de Salluste, Seigneur Du Bartas, *Divine Weekes and Workes*, Part 4
   Many metaphors, used first by others, were popularized by Shakespeare; to illustrate, "out of the jaws of death," from Twelfth Night.

4. Saddam Hussein's defiance of U.N. inspection rights in Iraq has put George Bush out on the shakiest limb of his Presidency —Leslie H. Gelb, "Foreign Affairs," *The New York Times*, July 23, 1992

   Even the most over-used metaphor can be twisted into a serviceable image when the appropriate occasion presents itself, as it did here.

5. The expected appointees . . . know where the land mines are —Leslie H. Gelb, *The New York Times*, December 20, 1992
   In Washington politics, one treads very carefully.

6. In an era newly sensitive as well to power relationships, to sexual disequilibrium between parent and child . . . a 57-year-old father-figure, ought to see the quicksand of involvement with a 21-year-old — Ellen Goodman, "Woody Allen, We Hardly Know You," *The Boston Globe*, September 25, 1992
   "Instead, Woody Allen threw a cluster bomb into the extended Farrow-Allen family," Goodman writes.

7. In recent months, the Federal Reserve has walked a tightrope between wanting to keep interest rates low . . . and wanting to talk tough on inflation —Steven Greenhouse, *The New York Times*, July 21, 1993
   Greenhouse used two other familiar metaphors: "He [Alan Greenspan of the Federal Reserve] said that despite the first quarter's anemic growth, the economy seemed to be on track."

8. To all it stands on the razor's edge, either woeful ruin or life for the Acheans — Homer, *Iliad*
   The metaphor was used even earlier when Dionysius (495 B.C.) spoke of his army's cause as being "on the razor's edge of decision." It was borrowed by

Somerset Maugham as the title for a novel; and in The Skin of Our Teeth, *Thornton Wilder wrote* "Every good thing in the world stands on the razor-edge of danger."

9. Man is cruelly wasteful of life when his own safety is endangered, . . . when he feels the sting of the reptile and is conscious of the power to destroy —Washington Irving, "Traits of Indian Character"
In comparing the Indian to a reptile, Irving focused on naturalness rather than evil. "The rights of the savage have seldom been respected by the white man," he wrote.

10. While we are laughing, the seed of some trouble is put into the wide, arable land of events . . . While we are laughing, it sprouts, it grows and suddenly bears a poison fruit which we must pluck —John Keats, Unattributed letter, 1819, quoted in *The World's Great Letters*

11. There is an ambush everywhere from the army of accidents —Häfiz Keller, Poem, 14th Century
The 14th-century poet follows these war-related metaphors with a horsemanship image: "Therefore the rider of life runs with loosened reins."

12. She is a loose cannon, but some might prefer her inside, firing out —Bill Keller, "Winnie Mandela Free," *The New York Times,* June 6, 1993
"Others suggest the congress should take her [Winnie Mandela] back into the fold," Keller writes, in a second metaphor from sheep herding.

13. But it is impossible to shield an entire museum from terrorism, especially one knitted into the fabric of a crowded city —Michael Kimmelman, *The New York Times,* May 28, 1993
The Uffizi Gallery in Florence was partially destroyed by a terrorist bomb.

14. The ride became a steeplechase —D. H. Lawrence, "Tickets, Please"
During World War I trams were driven by men unfit for active service who had "the spirit of the devil in them."

15. Do you see that object on the pillow? It's a bomb to blow up smugness. If you Tories were wise, you wouldn't arrest anarchists, you'd arrest all these children while they're asleep in their cribs. —Sinclair Lewis, *Main Street*
Having a baby also marks Carol Kennicott's submission to the ways of the town.

16. Eadgar: 'Twix thee and the singing arrow with the darkened fang, / I stand with open breast! —Edna St. Vincent Millay, *The King's Henchman,* Act 1
The king swears his loyalty to his henchman.

17. The scary part is that everyone is flying blind —Peter Passell, "Economic Scene," *The New York Times,* November 19, 1992
The subject was the Russian economy.

18. There loomed an imperceptible, a terrifying border-line. One step and you would be hurled into an abyss —Boris Pasternak, *Doctor Zhivago*
The border line, which Lara will overstep, begins with dancing and ends in bed. An abyss is a common metaphor for any terrifying situation, with hell representing the final abyss.

19. A defeat in New York [Democratic primary] raises the possibility that Mr. Clinton's hangnail problem of public acceptance could turn into a sucking chest wound —Howell Raines, *The New York Times,* March 31, 1992
The paper's headline writer picked up on the hangnail metaphor with "Nail-Biting Time Nears for Democratic Party."

20. Here are a few examples of minefields . . . we will be watching our President try to walk his way through —A. M. Rosenthal, "On My Mind," *The New York Times,* October 20, 1992
The writer questioned the presidential candidates' concentration on domestic issues, without sufficient attention to problems pertaining to Russia, China and Cuba.

21. But the wireless operator was thinking: these storms had lodged themselves somewhere or other, as worms do in a fruit; . . .

and he loathed entering this shadow that was ripe to rottenness —Antoine de Saint-Exupery, *Night Flight*
The simile defines the storms as the worms; the metaphor defines the macrocosm, the shadowing of the clouds, as the fruit.

22. Hotspur: Out of this nettle, danger, we pluck this flower, safety —William Shakespeare, *The First Part of King Henry the Fourth* Act 2, scene 3, line 10
When writer Katherine Mansfield died in 1923, this metaphor became her epitaph.

23. Richard: my ki gdom stands on brittle glass —William Shakespeare, *The Tragedy of King Richard the Third*, Act 4, scene 2, line 61
The king feels the only way to make his kingdom more "shatterproof" is to marry his dead brother's daughter.

24. On the simplest narrative level, *Cleopatra's Sister* [by Penelope Lively] is the story of Howard Beamish and Lucy Falkner, beginning when they are children and continuing along a road riddled with hairpin turns and forks —Scott Spencer, *The New York Times Book Review*, April 25, 1993

25. Let the threatened thunders roll and the lightning flash through the sky —William Lowndes Yancey, Southern rights speech, 1860

■ DARKNESS/LIGHT

See also: NIGHT AND DAY

1. My yin and yang were my parents —Louis Auchincloss, "The Epicurean"
His father represented life's more rigorous traits, plus the darkness of death; while his mother represented the lighter side of life, plus "at least to a puritan, sin."

2. They plunged into the black cloister of woodlands, which ran by them in a dim tapestry of [tree] trunks —Gilbert Keith Chesterton, "The Sign of the Broken Sword"

3. Dead clods of sadness, or light squibs of mirth —John Donne, "Holy Sonnets: XV"
Sadness is of the earth, while mirth rises toward heaven in bursts of brightness.

4. The light of your room / Crept through my window-blinds, throwing ladders of light up / My ceiling in the dark —John Hollander, *Powers of Thirteen–3*

5. Darkness stalks the hunters —Joseph Langland, "Hunters in the Snow: Brueghel"
Langland inverts the usual sense, so that the hunters become the hunted.

6. The cave wandered on, roof lower and lower except / Where chambers of darkness rose and stalactites down-stabbed / To the heart of my light —Robert Penn Warren, "Speleology"
The speaker of the poem explores both the cave and the self, and asks, "Who am I?" The poet seems to have been influenced by Plato's parable, both here and elsewhere in his work.

■ DAUGHTERS

See: FAMILIES/FAMILY RELATIONSHIPS

■ DAWN

See also: MORNING; NATURE SCENES; NIGHT AND DAY

1. The first hour of the morning is the rudder of the day —Henry Ward Beecher, *Proverbs from Plymouth Pulpit*

2. And it is dawn / the world / goes forth to murder dreams —e. e. cummings, "the hours rise up"

3. In the false dawn when the chickens blink / And the east shakes a lazy baby toe at tomorrow —Carl Sandburg, "Blue Island Intersection"

4. Under the opening eyelids of the morn, / We drove afield —John Milton, *Paradise Lost*, Book 6

5. Prospero: the morning steals upon the night, / Melting the darkness —William Shakespeare, *The Tempest*, Act 5, scene 1, line 65

6. In the pleasant morning dawns . . . the trenches and craters . . . are now laced with gossamer . . . and every tiny thread sags and quivers gently, all embroidered with the tiny glittering tears of dew — Mikhail Sholokhov, "A Word In Our Country"

7. Through the window he saw the long grey fingers of the dawn clutching at the fading stars —Oscar Wilde, "The Young King"
   In another poem, "Humanitad," Wilde writes about "Autumn's gaudy livery."

■ DAYDREAMS

See also: MEMORY/MEMORIES

1. Her mother could go on scolding her for hours without even penetrating the wonderful foliage of reveries —Harold Brodkey, "Laura," *The New Yorker*, d.u.

2. When I am, long ago, / An island in dishonoured grass / Whom none but daisies know —Emily Dickinson, Poem 290
   Dickinson's switch of tenses here is startling.

3. They built castles in the air and thought to do great wonders —Thomas North
   This still popular metaphor can also be found in the writings of Thoreau, Emerson, Dickens and many others.

■ DEATH

See also: COURAGE; DISAPPEARANCE; ENDINGS; FAILURE; FATE; FOREBODING; ILLNESS; LAMENTS; LIFE AND DEATH; LOVERS' DECLARATIONS AND EXCHANGES; MURDER; OLD AGE; PLEAS AND PRAYERS; PREPAREDNESS/UNPREPAREDNESS; TIMELINESS/UNTIMELINESS; TRANQUILITY

1. I have a rendezvous with death —Achipoeta
   This is most commonly associated with the first line and title of a poem written during World War I by Alan Seeger. A variation by Countee Cullen (1903–1946) is "I Have a Rendezvous With Life."

2. Death the Healer, scorn thou not, I pray, / To come to me —Aeschylus, "Fragments"
   The same fragment calls Death "the one physician" and that "Pain lays not its touch / Upon a corpse." Another often encountered metaphoric healer is time.

3. All unready is my book of reckoning — Anon., *Everyman*
   In this medieval morality play the figure of Everyman stands for all men. Some morality plays referred to him as Christian. Like all morality plays, Everyman had a didactic, religious purpose. It personified traits like beauty and knowledge as well as the figure of Death. The story is told as an allegory and the form itself is an extended metaphor.

4. Therefore to the soul Good is a thief / For when thou art dead this is my guise (custom)— / Another to deceive in the same wise / As I have done thee —Anon., *Everyman*
   Everyman discovers that his worldly goods will not accompany him to the other world when he dies.

5. For into this cave must I creep / And turn to earth, and there to sleep —Anon., *Everyman*

6. As the doctor says, he's ripe for the scythe at any moment —Honoré de Balzac, *Cousin Bette*

7. Behold a pale horse: and his name that sat on him was Death, and Hell followed with him —The Bible, *N.T., Revelation 6:8*
   The "pale horse, pale rider" was one of a quartet: the four horsemen of the Apocalypse. One of the best-known literary references to this metaphoric personification appears in Milton's Paradise Lost *"Behind her Death / Close following pace for pace, not mounted yet on his pale horse."*

8. Death is swallowed up in victory —The Bible, *N.T., 1 Corinthians, 15:54*

9. The sting of death is sin —The Bible, *N.T., 1 Corinthians, 15:56*
   Elsewhere in Corinthians the metaphor is questioned joyfully in terms of the promised resurrection, and changes to "O death, where is thy sting? O grave, where is thy victory?"

10. Yea, though I walk through the valley of the shadow of death, I will fear no evil; for Thou art with me —The Bible, *O.T. Psalms, 23:4*

11. His sun is setting, and he shall rise no more —Black Hawk, Addressing General Street shortly after his surrender in 1833

12. If death do strike me with his lance, / Yet mayst thou me to him commend —Nicholas Breton, "A Cradle Song"
    Breton is the author to whom this song is usually attributed.

13. The angel of Death has been abroad throughout the land; you may almost hear the beating of his wings —John Bright, Speech against continuation of Crimean war, February 23, 1855

14. I would hate that death bandaged my eyes, and forebore, / And bade me creep past —Robert Browning, "Prospice"
    Shortly after his wife's death, Browning thus expressed his contempt for death and joy in living life fully.

15. Born in what was known as "the grippe year," I was frequently on the threshold of death —Roger Burlingame, "The Analyst's Couch and the Creative Mind"
    Death or birth are each pictured as a door to be passed through, either entering or leaving the corridor of life. The metaphor of the threshold is a logical extension of the image.

16. Blotted from life's page —Lord George Gordon Byron, "Childe Harold"
    Byron used this metaphor to describe the woe of losing a loved one and having to live one's old age alone.

17. Under the willow the willow / Death spreads her dripping wings —Charles Causley, "Recruiting Drive"

18. There is in the world a very aged rioter and demagogue who breaks into the most refined retreats with the dreadful information that all men are brothers, and wherever this leveller went on his pale horse it was Father Brown's trade to follow —Gilbert Keith Chesterton, "The Queer Feet"
    This is an extension of the biblical "And I looked, and behold, a pale horse" (N.T., Revelation 6:8).

19. The only balmless wound is the departed human life we had learned to need —Emily Dickinson, Letter, March 1879

20. The Dance of Death —Austen Dobson, Title for play, 1877
    The play also refers to death as "the most terrible of kings." The composer Saint-Saens' Danse Macabre inspired this variation: "This dance of death, which sounds so musically, / Was sure intended for the corpse de ballet."

21. From rest and sleepe, which but thy pictures bee, / Much pleasure, then from thee, much more must flow —John Donne, "Holy Sonnets: X"
    "Death be not proud," begins the sonnet. It goes on to explain that people should not fear death which is like sleep—and sleep is pleasurable.

22. I have seen the eternal Footman hold my coat, and snicker —T. S. Eliot, "The Love Song of J. Alfred Prufrock"

23. The long sleep that outlasts love, that conquers even the grimace of love, had cuckolded him —William Faulkner, "A Rose for Emily"
    As the lover had been false to Emily, so had death made a fool of him.

24. Giovanni: Death, thou'rt a guest long looked for —John Ford, *'Tis Pity She's a Whore*, Act 4, scene 6

25. Death takes no bribes —Benjamin Franklin, *Poor Richard's Almanack*

26. Adams: It's old hey-presto death: you learn the trick / And death's the rabbit out of the hat: / Rolling oblivion for someone —Christopher Fry, *A Sleep of Prisoners*

Indirect reference to the magician's trick of pulling a rabbit out of a hat is a common metaphor for surprising or amazing solutions.

27. Teusret: Doesn't their brightness come to you? Do they glimmer / Nowhere into the cupboards of your sleep? —Christopher Fry, *The Firstborn*, Act 3, scene 2
    Rameses, being the firstborn of the Pharaoh, has been scourged, and the dead quickly lose interest in jewels.

28. Moses: God will unfasten the hawk of death from his / Grave wrist, to let it rake our world —Christopher Fry, *The Firstborn*, Act 3, scene 1
    The image of God as a falconer takes on added weight from the double meaning of "grave" as both solemn, and a place of interment. "The hawk of death will scour the land and kill the firstborn in all of Egypt."

29. Mrs. Peachum: If an unlucky Session does not cut the Rope of thy Life, I pronounce, Boy, thou wilt be a Great Man in History —John Gay, *The Beggar's Opera*, Act 1, scene 5
    Cutting the "rope of life" alludes to the Fates who spun out the thread of life and ended it by cutting the thread. There is also a macabre humor since the rogues and robbers in the play often ended their lives at the dangling end of a rope.

30. Winter came too soon —Matthew Guerewitsch, *Stagebill*, October 1993
    In 1993, the opera world lost one of its leading divas to cancer. A brief tribute to Tatiana Troyanos closed with this metaphor.

31. In the blind, final precinct of the dead, / A wall takes aim —Jorge Guillen, "Death from a Distance"

32. At his decease there is only a vacancy and a momentary eddy— . . . and a bubble or two, ascending out of the black depth, and bursting at the surface —Nathaniel Hawthorne, *The House of Seven Gables*
    In the novel, this alludes to the death of Judge Pynchon. Hawthorne went on to say that death is a genuine fact that excludes falsehood—"a touchstone that proves the gold and dishonors the baser metal."

33. On Christmas Eve when Santa Claus had set / Death in the stocking —Anthony Hecht, "The Vow"
    The poem is a dirge for a miscarriage, for someone "neither girl nor boy . . . nearly my child."

34. The candelabra sobbed / as if he were still living . . . but the moon is the moon even without the sonata —Zbigniew Herbert, "Beethoven"
    The sonata referred to is Beethoven's.

35. Death tickled him in a gradual crescendo —Edward Hoagland, "The Threshold and the Jolt of Pain," *The Village Voice*, April 17, 1969

36. Death's boatman takes no bribe —Horace, *Odes*, Book 2

37. Spectral, gigantified, / Protozoic, bloodeating. / The carapace / of foreclosure —Ted Hughes, "The Summoner"

38. North, the night, the berg of death / Crowd me out of the ignorant darkness —Randall Jarrell, "90 North"
    The poet goes to bed "Like a bear to its floe."

39. Some . . . Shall face, / The knotted fabric of their lives / Woven in darkness and unseen till now, / And will be glad to die —Josephine W. Johnson, "Final Autumn"
    The poem's title pictures autumn as a metaphor for the last and taking-stock season of life.

40. Only one ship is seeking us, a black- / Sailed unfamiliar, towing at her back / A huge and birdless silence —Philip Larkin, "Next, Please"

41. He continued with a psaltery of bitter laments, remnants of a ruined glory that the wind of death was carrying away in tatters —Gabriel García Márquez, *The General in his Labyrinth*
    The ancient instrument is a logical choice for an aging hero, Simon Bolivar, to lament the end of his career. There's an implied metaphor of a flag in "ruined glory."

42. But fate had been kind: death had written the full stop in the right place —W. Somerset Maugham, "Home"

43. Down you mongrel! Death! —Edna St. Vincent Millay, "The Poet and His Book"

   The poet builds on the metaphor of death as a nipping puppy with "You shall scratch and you shall whine / Many a night, and you shall worry / Many a bone, before you bury / One sweet bone of mine.

44. Death . . . on his pale horse —John Milton, *Paradise Lost,* Book 10

45. Death was already lurking in the wings by the time Fielding had really prospered —J. H. Plumb, Introduction, *The Life of Mr. Jonathan Wild the Great*

46. No way back through the long arbors of the dead —Theodore Roethke, *Straw for the Fire, Notebooks of Theodore Roethke*

47. Remember me when I am gone away, / Gone far away into the silent land —Christina Rossetti, "Remember"

48. Death snarled at her and she gave it the finger. Death tore at her and she stuck out her tongue —Salman Rushdie, Tribute to Angela Carter, *The New York Times Book Review,* March 8, 1992

   Ms. Carter fought a valiant though losing battle with cancer. "She cut death down to size . . . a grubby little murderous clown," wrote Rushdie.

49. Her hand upon the latch of the door of death, she had no intention of troubling the young with a recital of her own past problems —Vita Sackville-West, *All Passion Spent*

   A woman of eighty-eight is visited by a granddaughter who asks her to support her struggle to become a musician instead of a conventional society wife.

50. The planet's tyrant, dotard Death, had held his gray mirror before them for a moment and shown them the image of things to come —Dorothy L. Sayers, *The Unpleasantness at the Bellona Club*

51. Jesus has turned to Piero, holding out to him / Death's unravelled, pitiful bandages —Gjertrud Schnackenberg, "The Resurrection (Piero Della Francesca)," *The New Yorker,* September 21, 1992

52. The interest we have to pay on the capital which is called in at death; and the higher the rate of interest and the more regularly it is paid, the further the date of redemption is postponed —Arthur Schopenhauer, "Our Relation to Ourselves"

53. Death's a sad bone . . . —Anne Sexton, "Wanting to Die"

54. Antony: I will o'retake thee, Cleopatra . . . since the torch is out —William Shakespeare, *Antony and Cleopatra,* Act 4, scene 10, line 48

   Cleopatra is dead, or so Antony thinks, and he wants to die too. The metaphor of the torch appears elsewhere, as in Plantagenet's speech The First Part of Henry the Sixth: "Here dies the dusky torch of Mortimer, / Chok'd with ambition of the meaner sort" (Act 2, scene 5, line 122).

55. Antony: The next time I do fight / I'll make death love me, for I will contend / Even with his pestilent scythe —William Shakespeare, *Antony and Cleopatra,* Act 3, scene 11, line 192

56. Posthumus: He had rather / Groan so in perpetuity than be cur'd / By the sure physician death —William Shakespeare, *Cymbeline,* Act 5, scene 4, line 6

57. Posthumus: Death / . . . being an ugly monster, / 'Tis strange he hides him in fresh cups, soft beds, / Sweet words; or hath more ministers than we / That draw his knives i' the war —William Shakespeare, *Cymbeline,* Act 5, scene 4, line 69.

58. Mortimer: But now the arbitrator of despairs, / Just death, kind umpire of men's miseries, . . . doth dismiss me hence —William Shakespeare, *The First Part of Henry the Sixth,* Act 2, scene 5, line 28

   Death is here personified.

59. Hamlet: Ay, there's the rub; / For in that sleep of death what dreams may come, / when we have shuffled off this mortal coil / Must give us pause —William Shakespeare, *Hamlet*, Act 3, scene 1, line 67

60. Macbeth: After life's fitful fever he sleeps well —William Shakespeare, *Macbeth*, Act 3, scene 2, line 24

61. Duke: thou art Death's fool, / For him thou labor'st by the flight to shun, / And yet run'st toward him still —William Shakespeare, *Measure for Measure*, Act 3, scene 1, line 11

62. Roderigo: It is silliness to live, when to live is a torment; and then we have a prescription to die, when death is our physician —William Shakespeare, *Othello*, Act 1, scene 3, line 309

63. Margaret: my son, now in the shade of death; / Whose bright out-shining beams thy cloudy wrath / Hath in eternal darkness folded up —William Shakespeare, *The Tragedy of King Richard the Third*, Act 1, scene 3, line 262

64. Clarence: I pass'd, methought, the melancholy flood, / with that sour ferryman / Unto the kingdom of perpetual night — William Shakespeare, *The Tragedy of King Richard the Third*, Act 1, scene 4, line 45
    The metaphor alludes to Charon, the ferryman who escorted the newly-dead over the river Styx to Hades, in Greek mythology.

65. Duchess of York: death hath . . . / pluck'd two crutches from my feeble hands, Clarence and Edward —William Shakespeare, *The Tragedy of King Richard the Third*, Act 2, scene 2, line 57
    The two crutches are the Duchess' sons, whose lives she has been unable to save.

66. Richard: The sons of Edward sleep in Abraham's bosom —William Shakespeare, *The Tragedy of King Richard the Third*, Act 4, scene 3, line 36
    The metaphor is an allusion to the O.T. (Luke, 16), when Lazarus the beggar dies and is carried to "Abraham's bosom." Another Shakespearean twist, in The Tragedy of King Richard the Second, *(Act 4, scene 1), is Bolingbroke's "sweet peace conduct his sweet soul to the bosom / Of good old Abraham!" The phrase is currently used as a metaphoric allusion to paradise.*

67. Friar: In a man as well as herbs, Grace and rude Will, / And where the worser is predominant / Full soon the canker Death eats up that plant —William Shakespeare, *Romeo and Juliet*, Act 2, scene 2, line 24
    A simile lays the groundwork for the metaphor of death as a canker.

68. Capulet: When the sun sets, the air doth drizzle dew; / But for the sunset of my brother's son / It rains downright — William Shakespeare, *Romeo and Juliet*, Act 3, scene 5, line 126
    Capulet compares the setting sun to the death of Tybalt.

69. Capulet: Death is my son-in-law, Death is my heir: / My daughter he hath wedded —William Shakespeare, *Romeo and Juliet*, Act 4, scene 4, line 66
    Capulet's grim metaphor of inheritance continues with: "I will die / And leave him all: life, living—all is Death's."

70. Romeo: shall I believe / That unsubstantial Death is amorous / And that the lean abhorred monster keeps / Thee here in dark to be his paramour —William Shakespeare, *Romeo and Juliet*, Act 5, scene 3, line 102

71. Romeo: Death! / . . . Thou desp'rate pilot, now at once run on / The dashing rocks thy seasick weary bark —William Shakespeare, *Romeo and Juliet*, Act 5, scene 3, line 115

72. Romeo: O true apothecary, / Thy drugs are quick —William Shakespeare, *Romeo and Juliet*, Act 5, scene 3, line 119
    Romeo, personifies death as an apothecary.

73. But be contented; when that fell [cruel] arrest / Without all bail shall carry me away —William Shakespeare, "Sonnet 74," line 1

74. Warwick: These eyes, that now are dimm'd with death's black veil, / Have been as piercing as the mid-day sun, / To search the secret treasons of the world —William Shakespeare, *The Third Part of Henry the Sixth*, Act 5, scene 2, line 16
    The simile lends contrast to the opening metaphor.

75. Death is the mother of beauty; / Hence from her, / Alone, shall come fulfillment to our dreams —Wallace Stevens, "Sunday Morning"

76. Death may be knocking at the door, like the Commander's statue —Robert Louis Stevenson, "Aes Triplex"
    The metaphor is personification translated into stone, since the simile contains an allusion to Don Giovanni, *where the funeral statue of a wronged woman's father casts the salacious Don down into hell.*

77. The eternal dawn, beyond a doubt, / Shall break on hill and plain, / And put all stars and candles out —Robert Louis Stevenson, "To Minnie," *A Child's Garden of Verses*

78. Do not go gentle into that good night. / Rage, rage against the dying of the light — Dylan Thomas, "Do Not Go Gentle Into That Good Night"

79. Death is an old jester, but every man sees him in a fresh guise —Ivan Turgenev, *Fathers and Sons*

80. Tomorrow or the day after, my brain, as you know, will hand in its resignation — Ivan Turgenev, *Fathers and Sons*

81. You see, one of the boys has passed in his checks, and we want to give him a good send-off, and so the thing I'm on now is to roust out somebody to jerk a little chin-music for us and waltz him through handsome —Mark Twain, "Buck Fanshaw's Funeral," *Roughing It*
    The minister, exasperated, asks the petitioner to restrict himself to "categorical statements of fact unencumbered with obstructing accumulations of metaphor and allegory."

82. Dying is the last favor we do the world, the last tax we pay —John Updike, "A Sandstone Farmhouse," *The New Yorker*, 1990
    The narrator's observation is prompted by his mother's death and his inability to grieve because she was "old, in pain, worn-out" and "it was time."

83. Dear, beauteous Death! the jewel of the just —Henry Vaughan, "They Are All Gone into the World of Light"
    The title used here is taken from the first line of Vaughan's poem which is also known as "Departed Friends."

84. Duchess: I know death hath ten thousand several doors / For men to take their exits; and 'tis found / They go on such strange geometrical hinges, / You may ope them both ways —John Webster, *The Duchess of Malfi*, Act 4, scene 2
    The duchess, about to be killed, declares that she's not concerned with the manner of her death.

85. Death had simply closed the book in which he had long ago read the last word — Edith Wharton, *Hudson River Bracketed*

86. Gone from this rotten taxable world to a higher standard of living —Richard Wilbur, "To an American Poet Just Dead"

87. Blanche: The Grim Reaper had put up his tent on our doorstep! . . . Stella, Belle Reve was his headquarters —Tennessee Williams, *A Streetcar Named Desire*, Scene 10
    The metaphor of the "Reaper" dates back to Longfellow's poem, "The Reaper and the Flowers."

88. There is a Reaper whose name is Death, / And, with his sickle keen, / He reaps the

bearded grain at breath, / And the flowers that grow between —Henry Wadsworth Longfellow, "The Reaper and the Flowers"

89. Dead we become the lumber of the world —John Wilmot, "A Satire Against Mankind"

90. Thus Nature spake—The work was done— / How soon my Lucy's race was run! —William Wordsworth, "Lucy"

■ DEATH, DEFINED

1. Death is a fisherman . . . and we the fishes be —Anon., English Epitaph

A variation, pertaining to the world: The world is a fish point . . . and we the fishes.

2. The grave is God's bankrupt court, which clears a man of his property and his debts at the same time —Henry Ward Beecher, Sermon

3. Death . . . that common revenger of all injuries —Aphra Behn, *Oroonoko, The Royal Slave*

4. Death is the cure of all diseases —Sir Thomas Browne, *Religio Medici*

A variation of this, also attributed to Sir Thomas: "The world is the cure of all diseases not an inn, but a hospital and a place not to live, but to die in."

5. Yes, death is the last line of the book — Giacomo Girolamo Casanova, *Memoirs*

6. Death—Life's servitor and friend—the guide / That safely ferries us from shore to shore! —Florence Earle Coates, "Sleep"

7. Death is the door which leads to perdition or to salvation —Alexandre Dumas, *The Three Musketeers*

8. Death is the king of this world: 'tis his park where he breeds life to feed him — George Eliot, *The Spanish Gypsy*

9. Death is an eternal sleep —Joseph Fouché, Signs placed, at Fouché's orders, at all cemetery gates, 1794

In Greek mythology Death and Sleep were brothers. "Death be not proud," wrote John Donne in a sonnet that went on to explain that death need not be feared since it is like sleep, which is pleasurable.

10. To die is landing on some silent shore — Samuel Garth, *The Dispensary*

11. Macheath: for Death is a Debt, / A Debt on demand —John Gay, *The Beggar's Opera*, Act 3, scene 11, song 16

12. Death is not a period but a comma in the story of life —Vern McLellan, Quoted in *The Wheel of Life and Death* by Philip Kapleau

13. Death is a nurse mother with big arms — Carl Sandburg, "Death Snips Proud Men"

14. Hamlet: Death / The undiscovered country from whose bourn [boundary] / No traveller returns —William Shakespeare, *Hamlet*, Act 3, scene 1, line 79

15. Duke: Death's a great disguiser —William Shakespeare, *Measure for Measure*, Act 4, scene 2, line 180

16. [Death:] A gate of dreariness and gloom —Percy Bysshe Shelley, *Queen Mab, IX*

17. Death's a debt; his mandamus binds all alike—no bail, no demurrer —Richard Brinsley Sheridan, *St. Patrick's Day*, Act 1, scene 1

18. Death is a door —Nancy Byrd Turner, Title of poem

19. Death isn't something slimy and catching like life —A. B. Yehoshua, *Mr. Mani*

Hagar does not mind sleeping in the bed of a woman who died.

■ DEBT

See also: ECONOMICS; PROBLEMS AND SOLUTIONS

1. Debt is the new slavery shackling Africa —Anon.

The metaphor is one much bruited about at the United Nations in a plea to the World Bank, the

IMF, and debtor nations to forgive some debt repayment from the underdeveloped world.

2. The borrower is a servant to the lender — The Bible, *O.T., Proverbs 22:7*

3. Borrowing is the canker and death of every man's estate —(Sir)Walter Ralegh (also spelled Raleigh), *Sir Walter Raleigh's Instructions to His Sonne and to Posterity*

4. With such fine-tuning [of legislation to cut the budget deficit], they must have that Mississippi of red ink tamed. Like the river. —George Will, *Washington Post Syndicate,* July 18, 1993
   Will used the tragic Mississippi River floods in the Midwest to poke fun at legislators who think they can anticipate "the consequences of their legislative decisions on hundreds of millions of people."

5. The idea was to recouple his tax proposal to the argument that helped get Mr. Clinton elected: that the Government is bobbing down a raging river of red ink and his plan is the only way to rescue it. —Michael Wines, *The New York Times,* May 16, 1993

■ DECADENCE

See: CORRUPTION

■ DECAY

See: AGE/AGING;   DETERIORATION/ DIMINISHMENT

■ DECENCY

See: GOODNESS

■ DECEPTION

See also: DANGER; GOOD/EVIL; HYPOCRISY; LIES/LIARS; MALICE; NAME CALLING; TREACHERY; TRUSTWORTHINESS/UNTRUSTWORTHINESS; VILLAINY/VILLAINS

1. The knight . . . had knotted the nets of deceit —Anon., *Sir Gawain and the Green Knight*
   The work combines elements of irony and folklore in a romantic tale of King Arthur's court. Its anonymous author was probably a contemporary of Chaucer.

2. With their tongues they have practiced deceit, the poison of asps is under their lips —The Bible, *N.T., Romans 3:13*
   A simile / metaphor variation from O.T., Psalms 140:3 is "They have sharpened their tongues like a serpent; adders' poison is under their lips."

3. Beware of false prophets, which come to you in sheep's clothing, but inwardly they are ravening wolves —The Bible, *N.T., Matthew 7:15*
   The wolf in sheep's clothing metaphor has become a common expression for anyone who seems benign but represents danger.

4. Press reports said that . . . the president's statement was carefully constructed to skirt the truth. If so, that skirt dipped into the mud of an apparent lie —Richard Cohen, *Washington Post Writers Group,* September 1, 1993
   Cohen expressed concern over the appointment of Gen. John Shalikashvili, whose father served with the Waffen SS, to be the new chairman of the Joint Chiefs of Staff.

5. We've seen this before—smoke and mirrors. And here we are once again. Step right up, ladies and gentlemen, because Magical Bill and his band of liberal magicians have a bag of tricks for you —(Senator) Alfonse D'Amato, Quoted in *The New York Times,* August 7, 1993
   There was no smoke hiding the Republican senator's feelings about the Democratic president's budget package.

6. They played the fool, not to appear as fools / in time's long glass —Donald Davie, "Remembering the 'Thirties, I"

7. We know Roy Innis is the stalking horse for Rudolph Giuliani —David N. Dinkins,

Quoted in *The New York Times*, September 10, 1993

> *The Mayor of New York, a tennis player, borrowed from another sport, hunting, to discredit Innis for his association with his opponent, Rudolph W. Giuliani. Hunters used the stalking horse to camouflage their strategy. Neither trotting out this old war horse from the political lexicon or flying in prestigious supporters to give speeches could prevent Mr. Dinkins' defeat.*

8. If malice and vanity wear the coat of philanthropy, shall that pass? —Ralph Waldo Emerson, "Self Reliance"

> *"I ought to go upright and vital, and speak the rude truth in all ways," writes Emerson.*

9. Gov. Bill Clinton . . . [is] fending off criticism from the Bush White House that he is a closet dove masquerading as a hawk —Thomas L. Friedman, *The New York Times*, October 4, 1992

> *". . . and that his experience in world affairs is limited to breakfast at the International House of Pancakes," continued Friedman.*

10. Rameses: I'm to inherit the kingdom / Of desperate measures, to be not a self / But a glove disguising your hand —Christopher Fry, *The Firstborn*, Act 3, scene 2

11. [He] wrote a whitewashing report on the prisoners' condition and strenuously denied that anything off was happening — Robert Hughes, *The Fatal Shore*

> *Another way to "whitewash" the truth would be to paper over it.*

12. They are pigs masquerading as peacocks —Bernard Malamud, "The German Refugee"

> *The character coining this figure is a German refugee with a heavy accent.*

13. Oh what a crocodilian world is this! — Francis Quarles, *Emblems*

> *An everyday use version of this is "false as a crocodile."*

14. [False love:] A poisoned serpent covered all with flowers —Sir Walter Ralegh (also spelled Raleigh), "Farewell, False Love"

15. King: And never yet did insurrection want / Such water-colors to impaint his cause —William Shakespeare, *The First Part of King Henry the Fourth*, Act 5, scene 1, line 79

16. Gloucester: Thee I'll chase hence, thou wolf in sheep's array —William Shakespeare, *The First Part of Henry the Sixth*, Act 1, scene 3, line 55

> *Shakespeare's metaphor is borrowed from the N.T. (Matthew, 7:15), when Jesus warns "Beware of false prophets, which come to you in sheep's clothing, but inwardly they are ravening wolves."*

17. Antonio: A goodly apple rotten at the heart, / O what a goodly outside falsehood hath! —William Shakespeare, *The Merchant of Venice*, Act 1, scene 3, line 103

18. Iago: Thus do I ever make my fool my purse —William Shakespeare, *Othello*, Act 1, scene 3, line 382

> *Iago gulls Roderigo into giving him money, supposedly to gain favor with Desdemona.*

19. Iago: She that so young could give out such a seeming, / To seal her father's eyes up, close as oak —William Shakespeare, *Othello*, Act 3, scene 3, line 213

> *There is some speculation that "seal" should be "seel." This would make it a metaphor from falconry since to seel a hawk's eyes is to sew them up during the bird's training period.*

20. Juliet: O serpent heart, hid with a flow'ring face! Did ever dragon keep so fair a cave? —William Shakespeare, *Romeo and Juliet*, Act 3, scene 2, line 73

> *Juliet has just learned that Romeo killed Tybalt.*

21. Juliet: Was ever book containing such vile matter / So fairly bound? O that deceit should dwell in such a gorgeous palace! —William Shakespeare, *Romeo and Juliet*, Act 3, scene 2, line 83

> *The "palace" is Romeo who is responsible for Tybalt's death.*

22. King: Thou hid'st a thousand daggers in thy thoughts, / Which thou hast whetted on thy stony heart —William Shake-

speare, *The Second Part of King Henry the Fourth*, Act 4, scene 5, line 105.

The king is accusing his son of cold-blooded ill will toward himself.

23. York: O tiger's heart wrapp'd in a woman's hide! —William Shakespeare, *The Third Part of Henry the Sixth*, Act 1, scene 1, line 6

24. Richard: So smooth he daub'd his vice with show of virtue —William Shakespeare, *The Tragedy of King Richard the Third*, Act 3, scene 5, line 29

25. Duke: O thy dissembling cub, what wilt thou be / When time hath sow'd a grizzle on thy case [skin, as of a fox]? / Or will not else thy craft so quickly grow / That thine own trip shall be thine overthrow? —William Shakespeare, *Twelfth Night*, Act 5, scene 1, line 164

■ DECISIVENESS/ INDECISIVENESS

See also: CHOICES AND DECISIONS; WORRY

1. Indecision is the graveyard of good intentions —Anon.

2. Worry grows best in the soil of indecision —Anon., Proverb

3. If I feel impelled to do anything, I seem to be pitchforked into it —Fyodor Mikhailovich Dostoevsky, *Notes from Underground*

    The narrator argues for choice, but allows things to propel him instead of making rational decisions.

4. Clinton stepped up to the plate and grabbed the bull by the horn —Paul Duke, "Washington Week In Review," National Public Broadcasting, January, 1993

    In a February 26 broadcast, the amiable moderator read a viewer's letter taking him to task for thus mixing his metaphors to analyze the new president.

5. Mr. Clinton [Bill] is riding tall in the straddle —Mary Matalin, Republican party's deputy campaign manager

    One might call Ms. Matalin's twist on an Americanism a portmanteau metaphor.

6. Cade: Was ever feather so lightly blown to and fro as this multitude? —William Shakespeare, *The Second Part of Henry the Sixth*, Act 4, scene 8, line 58.

7. King Edward: Wind-changing Warwick now can change no-more —William Shakespeare, *The Third Part of Henry the Sixth*, Act 5, scene 1, line 57

■ DECLINE

See: DISINTEGRATION; OLD AGE

■ DEDICATION

See: COMMITMENT; PERSEVERANCE

■ DEEDS

See: ACTIONS

■ DEFEAT

See also: CAUSE AND EFFECT; ENTRAPMENT; FAILURE; LIFE AND DEATH; MASTERY/SUBORDINATION; POLITICS/POLITICIANS; WINNING/LOSING

1. Others worried that a defeat for the tax bill would, by dooming the rest of his economic program, strangle Mr. Clinton's infant Presidency in its crib —Anon., Editorial, *The New York Times*, May 14, 1993

2. After two years of legal squabbling, Harry and Leona Helmsley appeared close to losing the crown jewel of their real-estate empire —Anon., *The New York Times*, July 29, 1992

    The troubled hotel tycoons were about to lose The Palace Hotel.

3. Astrov: Ten years or so of this life of ours, this miserable life, have sucked us under —Anton Chekhov, *Uncle Vanya,* Act 4

4. Do not keep saying to yourself . . . "But how can it be like that?" because you will get "down the drain," into a blind alley from which nobody has yet escaped — Richard Feynman, Quoted in James Gleick's *Genius: The Life and Science of Richard Feynman.*
   In this classically mixed metaphor, Feynman proves that he is better at quantum mechanics than at figures of speech.

5. Hart was convinced that . . . his fall was "an accident, a car crash in history" — Gary Hart, Quoted in "Gary Hart in Exile," by David Remnick, *The New Yorker,* April 19, 1993

6. Conducting business as usual sank John Tower's nomination four years ago — Gwen Ifill, *The New York Times,* January 24, 1993

7. Indeed, the Roman world is falling . . . . in the year just past, the wolves of the North have been let loose from their remotest fastnesses —Saint Jerome, Letter to a Friend, 410
   Saint Jerome witnessed the sack of Rome in 410. Rome was in headlong decline: the fall would come soon afterward.

8. Every man meets his Waterloo at last — Wendell Phillips, Speech about John Brown, November 1, 1851
   The metaphoric allusion to Napoleon's last and losing battle has become a common metaphor for any situation of complete failure.

9. Mr. Babbitt [Interior Secretary, Bruce Babbitt] who had been shot out of the saddle, rallied to his boss's defense —Keith Schneider, *The New York Times,* April 4, 1993

10. Talbot: And in that sea of blood my boy did drench / His overmounting spirit — William Shakespeare, *The First Part of Henry the Sixth,* Act 4, scene 7, line 14

11. Iago: I'll have our Michael Cassio on the hip —William Shakespeare, *Othello,* Act 2, scene 1, line 300
    This is a wrestling term for a position from which the opponent can be easily thrown.

12. It's all over with me. I'm caught under the wheel —Ivan Turgenev, *Fathers and Sons*
    Eugenie Vassilyvich acknowledges his impending end, adding "Death is an old trick, yet it strikes everyone as something new."

13. We'll make a grovelling bitch of her [of France] —Vercors, *The Silence of the Sea*
    A German expresses his contempt for an idealist compatriot who wants to make friends with France.

■ DEJECTION
See: DESPAIR; EMOTIONS

■ DELAY
See: ACTION/INACTION; PATIENCE

■ DELIGHT
See: JOY

■ DELUSION
See: ILLUSION/REALITY

■ DEMANDS
See: ACCUSATIONS

■ DEMOCRACY
See also: FREEDOM/RESTRAINT; GOVERNMENT; INTERNATIONAL RELATIONS

1. What is democracy?—an aristocracy of blackguards —Lord George Gordon Byron, Diary entry, May, 1821

2. The Ship of Democracy, which has weathered all storms, may sink through the

mutiny of those on board —Grover Cleveland, Letter, February 15, 1894

> In using a ship to portray a government's steadiness or unsteadiness, Cleveland was following in the footsteps of Jefferson and Lincoln, both of whom borrowed from the Greek playwright, Sophocles.

3. It seems to be a law in human nature that where, in any corporate society, the idea of self-government sets foot it refuses to take that foot up again —John Galsworthy, "American and Briton"

> A democracy is then "freed from the danger of pounce by autocracies." Galsworthy's image of the foot in the door as a first step toward advancement has been part of everyday speech since the nineteenth century. Variants include to get a toehold as in "There are many Grisham / Turow wannabes trying to get a toehold in the legal thriller genre" "Behind the Best Sellers," Publishers Weekly, August 16, 1993.

4. Some African specialists contend that much more attention should be paid to what happens before and after elections, including the basic civil liberties that make democracy more than a kind of periodic political Mardi Gras —Bill Keller, The New York Times, January 17, 1973

5. Our concept of democracy in the United States is winner take all —Charles William Maynes, "New Realities: Disarmament, Peacebuilding, and Global Security," NGO Committee on Disarmament Conference at the United Nations, April 20–23, 1993

> The editor of Foreign Policy used a card-game metaphor to contrast the democratic system in the United States with the power-sharing concepts of other nations.

6. Democracy is the art of running the circus from the monkey cage —H. L. Mencken, Quoted in Dreyfuss newsletter, "Letter from the Lion," Fall 1992

7. We must be the great arsenal of democracy —Franklin Delano Roosevelt, Radio address, December 29, 1940

> According to language maven William Safire, the phrase was first used by Jean Monnet, the French ambassador to the United States during a discussion with Supreme Court Justice Felix Frankfurter about the best way for the United States to assist in the struggle against tyranny. Frankfurter, struck by the power of the image, persuaded Monnet to let President Roosevelt give it currency.

8. I am one of the sportsmen of the democratic game. If we didn't want to play the democratic game, we would not have signed the peace agreement —Hun Sen, Quoted in "Cambodia Voting Seems to Lure Hard-Line Rebels," The New York Times, May 25, 1993

> The former Prime Minister was commenting on the voting in Cambodia.

9. The democracies are islands lost in the immense river of history. The water never stops rising —Aleksandr Solzhenitsyn, Quoted by Saul Bellow in To Jerusalem and Back

> An erstwhile resident of a totalitarian society, Solzhenitsyn feels democracies can survive only if Western "liberalism" will recognize the constant danger.

■ DENIAL

See also: PROBLEMS AND SOLUTIONS

1. It's a worthy wish [to get on with current business], but pardons are an unworthy way of sweeping suspected subversion of law under an already lumpy rug —Anon., Editorial, The New York Times, December 29, 1992

> The figurative "lumps" are the facts of the Iran-contra arms-for-hostages sale dogging the Reagan and Bush administration, and once again in the news when George Bush issued pardons to those who might otherwise have been prosecuted. Speakers have been metaphorically sweeping facts under rugs since the 1960s.

2. Mowbray: If ever I were traitor, / My name be blotted from the book of life —William Shakespeare, The Tragedy of King Richard the Second, Act 1, scene 3, line 201

■ DENUNCIATION

See: INSULTS

■ DEPENDENCY

See: CLINGING

■ DESCRIPTIONS, MISC.

See also: CHARACTERIZATIONS

1. Her hull was a cauliflower of shells and lichens —Isabel Allende, *The Stories of Eva Luna*

   The ship in this messy condition has been sailing around the hemisphere trying to find a haven for its human cargo.

2. He eyed that humming hive with a look that foretold its despoliations, as if he already felt on his lips the sweetness of its honey —Honoré de Balzac, *Old Goriot*

3. I've made this awful pilgrimage to one / who cannot visit me, who tore his page / out: I come back for more —John Berryman, "The Dream Songs 384"

   The speaker visits the grave of his dead father.

4. The whole world became to him a mire of excrement —Bruno Bettleheim, "Joey: A 'Mechanical Boy'"

   A disturbed youth draws his fantasies with pencil and paper in the process of becoming toilet-trained.

5. Always the silence, the gesture, the specks of birds / suspended on invisible threads above the Site, / or the smoke rising solemnly, pulled by threads —Elizabeth Bishop, "Over 2,000 Illustrations and a Complete Concordance"

   The poet visits foreign tourist sites.

6. The lines that move apart / . . . dispersing storms, God's spreading fingerprint — Elizabeth Bishop, "Over 2,000 Illustrations and a Complete Concordance"

   Bishop looks for meaning in the sad foreign vignettes engraved in a travel book.

7. The still explosions on the rocks, / the lichens, grow / by spreading, gray, concentric shocks —Elizabeth Bishop, "The Shampoo"

   The lichens "have arranged to meet the rings around the moon."

8. On scaffolds stretch the acres of the dead, / Corroding in their sepulchres of air — Robert Bly, "A Missouri Traveller Writes Home: 1830"

9. A cigarette lying on an ashtray and insidiously releasing a serpent of smoke — Andre Breton, *Nadja*

10. A carp gleams in its steel chain-mail — Joseph Brodsky, "Einem alten Architekten in Rom"

11. Through the snow the ship's numerous fiery eyes were barely visible —Ivan Bunin, "The Gentleman from San Francisco," translated by David Richards

    See entries under "houses" for variations of this metaphor of personification.

12. These people [the executive, the lawyer, the secretary] cannot *use* their traumas as the painter, the writer, or the composer may. Use is the great anodyne for these wounds —Roger Burlingame, "The Analyst's Couch and the Creative Mind"

13. I want this Boston man to know that the drivel he's been hearing here to-night is the only tribute any truly great man could ever have from the lot of sick, side-tracked, burnt-dog, land-poor sharks as the here-present financiers of Sand City—upon which town may God have mercy! — Willa Cather, "The Sculptor's Funeral," *Youth and the Bright Medusa*

14. Beau Brummel's remark applies to every rung of the spiritual ladder —Jean Cocteau, "The Cat That Walks by Itself"

    "I could not be elegant at Ascot," [Beau Brummel] said, "because you had noticed how elegant I was."

15. Once when he jabbed out harpoon-fashion with his fork to pinion a biscuit, the

weapon nearly impaled the hand of the Easterner, which had been stretched quietly out for the same biscuit —Stephen Crane, "The Blue Hotel"

16. He sharpens is to am / he sharpens say to sing / you'd almost cut your thumb / so right he sharpens wrong —e. e. cummings, "Who Sharpens Every Dull"

The itinerant knife sharpener disappeared with changes in technology, except in poems that still keep him alive.

17. His april touch / drove sleeping selves to swarm their fates / woke dreamers to their ghostly roots —e. e. cummings, "My Father Moved Through Dooms of Love"

18. The tallest story really packed a gun — Donald Davie, "Remembering the Thirties, I"

19. Where my right hand, buried beneath me, / Hoveringly tingles, with grasping / The source of all song at the root —James Dickey, "Sleeping Out at Easter"

In this mystical poem of Resurrection, the Word rises out of the darkness where the poet's hand is buried, and the poet's daughter, sleeping, "hears the song in the egg of a bird."

20. I more than once, at morn, / Have passed, I thought, a whip-lash / Unbraiding in the sun —Emily Dickinson, Poem 986

Dickinson ends with one of the most startling images in poetry: when she sees the snake she feels "zero at the bone."

21. *The New York Times Book Review* . . . It puts itself forward, bidding itself up as the venue of masterpieces—the bourse of books —Stanley Elkin, "Some Overrated Masterpieces," *Art & Antiques*, 1991

22. We spread our hair, / Caught it. Under the comb the strands / Whipped into fresh harmonies, untangled / Again — Donald Finkel, "The Sirens"

The poem uses the conceit that the hair of the sirens was the instrument that created the music Odysseus heard—and resisted.

23. If, by allowing no other thought to enter his head, he could preserve this state of emotion unimpaired until he went into that large coffin set on end [the confessional], he would have survived another crisis in his religious life —F. Scott Fitzgerald, "Absolution"

24. I can still see my father looking up from his dissection and telling us [the author and his sister] to go away. He too, was a cadaver —Gustave Flaubert, Letter, d.u.

The is part of a childhood recollection of his father, a doctor with whom he had a complex relationship.

25. The dance of a bee drunken with sunlight —John Gould Fletcher, "Irradiations"

26. Miriam: And the curses . . . / The shout of command kicking at the ribs, / All human words torn to a scream —Christopher Fry, *The Firstborn*, Act 1, scene 1

27. Cymen: Are you still rolling your marbles of thunder? —Christopher Fry, *Thor, With Angels*

Cymen thinks his son is "still breaking wind to make a hurricane."

28. Demokos: Face the great Hector . . . / He is the storm, and you the after-calm — Jean Giraudoux, *Tiger at the Gates*, Act 1

Demokos, the poet, devises a piece of triumphal doggerel so bad that Hector's only response can be, "Get out!" The quotation here is the most innocuous part of that doggerel.

29. In a tempest they thundered by [the circus performer on her horse], in a whirlwind, a *scirocco* of tan; her cheeks bore the kiss of an Eastern sun, and the sand-storms of her native desert were her satellites — Kenneth Grahame, "The Magic Ring"

30. The kind of mystique that surrounds [Gustave] Flaubert inevitably becomes a double-edged sword —Francine Du Plessix Gray, "A Critic At Large," *The New Yorker*, July 26, 1993

The reviewer clarified her use of this common metaphor with "It is bound to incite the writing of considerable rubbish as well as the unearthing of great riches.

31. Deep in the festering hold thy father lies, / of his bones New England pews are made, / those are altar lights that were his eyes —Robert Hayden, "Middle Passage, 1"

   Hayden twists the song from Shakespeare's The Tempest *to indicate the horror of a slave ship in 1800. The sea-change he pictures is a terrifying one.*

32. He is Jehu, and you are goods in transit — O. Henry, "From the Cabby's Seat," *The Four Million*

   The metaphor which alludes to the Israelite king who was noted for his fast chariot driving appears in a story about the hansom drivers in old New York.

33. They say he became deaf—but it isn't true / the demons of his hearing worked tirelessly / and the dead lake never slept in the shells of his ears —Zbigniew Herbert, "Beethoven"

34. The permanent license that arrived weeks later was actually a Temporary Driver's License in sheep's clothing —Philip C. Hochman, "Coming to Terms," unpublished manuscript

   The wolf clothed in the license was disability: by the time it arrived, the writer was too disabled to use it. He would have needed a driver's license for a motorized wheelchair.

35. The thousand footed bridges . . . crusted with green and oozy growths, studded with minute barnacles, and belted with rings of dark mussels —Oliver Wendell Holmes, "Boating"

36. Now the protective glass of distance broke, in an instant, never to be restored — Robert Hughes, *The Fatal Shore*

   The Australian Aborigines had possessed the land "since time immemorial," until the British came to colonize. They were protected by the vast distances of oceans surrounding their continent.

37. The spell of arms and voices: the white arms of roads, their promise of close em-

braces and the black arms of tall ships that stand against the moon, their tale of distant nations —James Joyce, *A Portrait of the Artist As a Young Man*

38. In the gathering winter twilight the forest of tombstones and Jizo figures would soothe his feelings —Kawabata Yasunari, *Beauty and Sadness*

   Oki, the tormented protagonist of this work, looks to a graveyard and the eternity of stone to calm him.

39. Into his revulsion flashed the image of the Inamura girl, a vein of light —Kawabata Yasunari, *A Thousand Cranes*

   Kikuji is contrasting a scarred old woman with the lovely girl of the thousand-crane kerchief who instills a sense of discomfort and desire in him.

40. The movie [*Riff-Raff*]—essentially an episodic crazy quilt patched together with deceptive casualness—is laced with the same passionate political savvy that has informed his [Director Ken Loach] past work —David Kronke, *Los Angeles Daily News,* June 21, 1993

41. If you try to tie *The Piano* down as a costume picture, or as a love story, or as a gothic horror, it slips its moorings and drifts away —Anthony Lane, "Sheet Music," *The New Yorker,* November 29, 1993

   The title of the review about the steamy relationship between a mute woman whose attachment to her piano is transformed into passion for her husband's employee can be interpreted as a double metaphor.

42. He [economist John Kenneth Galbraith] has summed up a lifetime's ballet in a single soft-shoe dance —Christopher Lehmann-Haupt, "Books of The Times," *The New York Times,* April 6, 1992

   Lehmann-Haupt's review of The Culture of Contentment, *summed up Mr. Galbraith's prose with a simile that compared it to the roll of "the thunder of a distant storm."*

43. Earthmovers gripped the chained and stripped trunks, / . . . and the stumps / howled as they turned their black, prized

groins / skyward / for the first times in their lives —Philip Levine, "Innocence"

The tree stumps that are being yanked out of the ground howl as their cleft roots—their "groins"— are exposed. Levine seems to be working with the old legend of the mandrake, with its root shaped like a man's torso, that screamed if it were pulled out of the ground.

44. Behind their cage, / yellow dinosaur steamshovels were grunting —Robert Lowell, "From the Union Dead"

The steamshovels, seen from behind a galvanized fence, were building an underground garage.

45. The port burns with poppies—Turkish flags —Osip Mandelstam, "Feodosia"

46. That dawn he officiated at the daily mass of his ablutions with more frenetic severity than usual, trying to purge his body and spirit of twenty years of fruitless wars and the disillusionments of power —Gabriel García Márquez, *The General in his Labyrinth*

Márquez pictures Simon Bolivar at his morning shaving and scrubbing ritual.

47. Even the swift, gritty breeze that rushed through the slices of open windows seemed at this hour to be losing the freshness of morning—some cool air clung to it, but in patches and tatters —Alice McDermott, *At Weddings and Wakes*

48. Lottie stands there wet and shivery, watching the thick, silver ribbon of water from the shower divide and splash over the tops of her feet —Sue Miller, *For Love*

49. When a ship founders it settles slowly . . . On the ocean floor of death the bleeding hull bedecks itself with jewels; remorselessly the anatomic life begins —Henry Miller, "The Creative Life"

Or, as the Bard would say, it has suffered a sea-change into something rich and strange.

50. The tramcar, / rattling greenish caterpillar —Marianne Moore, "Old Amusement Park"

51. The water drives a wedge / of iron through the iron edge / of the cliff —Marianne Moore, "The Fish"

52. The smokestack's blunt, swift-moving cigar / Blurring the trees in a smudge of smoke —Howard Moss, "Elegy for My Sister. III"

53. A colored snowstorm of confetti left its flakes sticking to her bare back —Vladimir Nabokov, *King, Queen, Knave*

54. There are only two prominent women in this dark tapestry —John J. O'Connor, "Review/Television," *The New York Times,* October 19, 1992

The figures in the tapestry were exiled writers from Nazi Germany in Hollywood during the 1930s, as portrayed in an American Playhouse drama, Tales from Hollywood.

55. Exhausted they would drift to sleep, separately wandering the corridors of an unknown building, opening one door after another in dread and fascination —Joyce Carol Oates, "The Hair," *Partisan Review*

The story is about a husband and wife who have a very intense relationship with another couple.

56. The boy . . . went climbing up to the top of the tree as the scaly fingers of the leaves caressed him . . . to the very summit, up into the gentle trembling, to the fine delicate heights where the branches became a high-pitched melody —Amos Oz, *The Hill of Evil Counsel*

57. I embrace, in supplication, the hallowed knees of Aiakos, bearing / this Lydian veil embroidered with clashing song — Pindar, "Nemea 8," *Odes*

The supplicant comes with a gift for the gods: a veil from the country of Lydia that is decorated, no doubt, with scenes of battle.

58. The engine's five-hundred horse-power bred in its texture a very gentle current, fraying its ice-cold rind into a velvety bloom —Antoine de Saint-Exupery, *Night Flight*

The pilot of this early plane felt "the mystery of metal turned to living flesh."

59. The forty-eight keys of the typewriter / each an eyeball that is never shut —Anne Sexton, "The Room of My Life"

Sexton describes the objects in her room that haunt her, like "the books, each a contestant in a beauty contest" and "the black chair, a dog coffin made of Naugahyde."

60. But if I look past the buzzing machine monotonously unzipping the crusted soil . . . the seemingly stationary fields are always flowing toward one farmer and away from another —Jane Smiley, *A Thousand Acres*

61. Iya Agba: They will take root with their spirit, not with their bodies on some unblessed soil —Wole Soyinka, *Madmen and Specialists*, Part 1

Iya Agba, an old woman and a gatherer of herbs, uses earth imagery.

62. After the first powerful plain manifesto / The black statement of pistons, . . . she leaves the station —Stephen Spender, "The Express"

63. Sight / Hangs heaven with flash drapery. Sight / Is a museum of things seen — Wallace Stevens, "Examination of the Hero in a Time of War"

64. The peach the apricot and soon the pear / Drip in the teasing hand their sugared tear —Trumbull Stickney, "At Sainte-Marguerite"

"Sugared tear" is an oxymoron for the sweetness of nectar that drains the vital juices of the fruit.

65. Your Afghanistan hammock, a man-sized cocoon / slung from wall to wall —May Swenson, "Staying at Ed's Place"

66. Yet were thy silver skies my Beer bowle fine —Edward Taylor, "Sacramental Meditations X"

67. I make the netted sunbeam dance —Lord Alfred Tennyson, "The Brook"

68. He carries . . . a tin of new shaving-lather which . . . covers not only the face but the whole bathroom and, instantly freezing, makes an arctic, icicled cave from which it takes two sneering bellboys to extract him —Dylan Thomas, "A Visit to America"

Thomas reports on the travails of the lionized, poets like himself, who go "spry-eyed with clean white lectures" to a "remunerative doom in the great State University factories" after their misadventures with shaving cream and bellboys.

69. The bough with white blossoms was death— if it reared up its slack —Robert Penn Warren, "Deep-Deeper Down"

The "slack" is the extra length of dark snake.

70. The body, / With the towel now trailing loose from one hand, is / A white stalk from which the face flowers gravely toward the / high sky —Robert Penn Warren, "Birth of Love"

A man watches a woman he loves emerge from the water, as though he were seeing the Birth of Venus.

71. He entered the park . . . and swallowed mouthfuls of the heavy shade that curtained its arch —Nathanael West, *Miss Lonelyhearts*

The metaphor lies in the curtain of shade, but the "mouthfuls" of shade, the transference of a sensation from one sense to another, is synesthesia.

72. Up there, behind that motionless mask of trees, lived the girl with whom he had wandered in another world —Edith Wharton, *Hudson River Bracketed*

73. The blue tractor zippers the field —Nancy Willard, "The Exodus of Peaches," *The New Yorker*, July 27, 1992

74. [He was] putting everything in its proper perspective and then, passionately, by the end of the day, scrambling it all up again, expertly stirring faiths, languages, peoples, and races together and pitilessly baking them in the desert sun until they turned into the special Jerusalem soufflé that was his favorite dish —A. B. Yehoshua, *Mr. Mani*

A guide shows visitors his home city, Jerusalem.

■ DESERTION

See: ABANDONMENT

■ DESIRE

*See also: AFFECTION; LOVERS' DECLARA-
TIONS AND EXCHANGES; MEN AND
WOMEN; PASSION; SEX/SEXUALITY;
YEARNING*

1. Your sweet desire / Breeds flames of ice
   and freeze in fire —Anon., "Through
   Amaryllis Dance in Green"
   *The metaphor is an example of oxymoron, with
   its contradictory images.*

2. I dar wel sayn, if she hadde been a mous, /
   And he a cat, he wolde hire hente anoon
   —Geoffrey Chaucer, "The Miller's Tale"
   *If she had been a mouse and he a cat, he would
   have pounced on her. (And the "if" is a mark of a
   figure that purists might prefer to classify as a
   simile.)*

3. As infants smile and sleep, we are rocked
   in the cradle of our desires, and hushed
   into fancied security by the roar —William Hazlitt, "On the Feeling of Immortality in Youth"
   *The metaphor is dependent upon the introductory
   simile.*

4. [Siddhartha] saw his son . . . eagerly ad-
   vancing along the burning path of life's
   desires —Hermann Hesse, *Siddhartha*

5. The strings of existence and of my soul
   vibrated with a hidden melody —Naguib
   Mahfouz, *Palace of Desire*
   *The Nobel Prize–winning novelist compares a
   young man's desire to a stringed instrument.
   "The pleasure was so intense that it verged on
   pain," thinks the lover.*

6. She felt the strange beast that had slumbered so long within her bosom stir, stretch
   itself, yawn, prick up its ears, and suddenly bound to its feet, and fix its longing,
   hungry stare upon those far away places
   —Katherine Mansfield, "A Dill Pickle"
   *The narrator's desire was not for the man himself,
   but for the faraway places he might help her
   explore.*

7. The slopes are barren / Of all the vegeta-
   tion of desire —William Stanley Merwin,
   "Deception Island (For Arthur Mizener)"

8. The ping of desire . . . first he pocketed it
   . . . then he unboxed it to bring out and
   admire at his leisure —Toni Morrison,
   Jazz
   A man gives in to feeling he initially held back.

9. Chorus: Now old Desire doth in his deathbed lie, / And young Affection gapes to
   be his heir —William Shakespeare, *Romeo and Juliet,* Act 1, scene 4, line 261

10. Thou web of will whose end is never
    wrought —Sir Philip Sidney, "Thou blind
    man's mark, thou fool's self-chosen snare"
    *The unending web stands for desire, which Sidney
    also calls "Fond fancy's scum" and "cradle of
    causeless care."*

11. Music is feeling then, not sound; / And
    thus it is that what I feel, / Here in this
    room, desiring you, / . . . Is music —
    Wallace Stevens, "Peter Quince at the
    Clavier"

12. Desire, / If it wished, could cast its
    rainbow over the coarse porcelain / Of
    the world's skin —Mark Strand, "Our
    Masterpiece is the Private Life," *The New
    Yorker,* November 2, 1992

13. In my frail canoe I struggle to cross the sea
    of desire —Rabindranath Tagore, "Play-
    things," *The Crescent Moon*
    *The narrator contrasts a baby happily playing
    with a broken stick with his own search for
    "lumps of gold and silver."*

14. Desire and longing are the whips of God
    —Anna Wickham, "Sehnsucht," *The Con-
    templative Quarry*

■ DESPAIR

See also: DEATH; EMOTIONS; ENDINGS;
GRIEF; HOPE; ISOLATION; LAMENTS;
SUCCESS/FAILURE; TEARS

1. She set about at once to pull me out of the
    rapids of despond which were loosening
    my grip on rationality —Louis Auchincloss,
    "The Epicurean," *Three Lives*
    > *A mother comes to rescue her son from unexpected*
    > *despondency after the father he hated dies.*

2. I am a brother to dragons and a compan-
    ion to owls —The Bible, *O.T., Job 30:29*

3. She has given up the ghost. Her sun is
    gone down while it was yet day —The
    Bible, *O.T., Jeremiah 15:9*

4. Astrov: Life holds nothing for me; my
    race is run —Anton Chekhov, *Uncle
    Vanya*, Act 2

5. In the real dark night of the soul it is
    always three o'clock in the morning —F.
    Scott Fitzgerald, *The Crack-Up*

6. I am crammed with coffins. That comes
    from the sun in your heart —Gustave
    Flaubert, Letter to George Sand, 1874
    > *Flaubert has lost his father and a dear friend and*
    > *now sees himself as a cemetery.*

7. The whole earth / Had turned in its bed /
    To the wall —Ted Hughes, "In these
    fading moments I wanted to say"
    > *Hughes writes of the despair of feeling too deeply*
    > *those things one cannot change.*

8. Krogstad: I am a shipwrecked man cling-
    ing to a spar —Henrik Ibsen, *A Doll's
    House*, Act 3
    > *Krogstad accuses Mrs. Linden whom he once*
    > *planned to marry of thus leaving him "with no*
    > *firm ground." She suggests that since she too is*
    > *shipwrecked that they join hands since "two on a*
    > *raft have a better chance than if each clings to a*
    > *separate spar."*

9. She was hunched there tasting the bitter-
    ness at the bottom of her life —Ross
    MacDonald, *The Moving Target*

> *The cup of life metaphor continues to inspire*
> *many a twist and turn of phrase.*

10. Aethelwold: From this day out, my life is
    a dingy web, / A threadbare thing —
    Edna St. Vincent Millay, *The King's Hench-
    man*, Act 2

11. I had lived in a house of many rooms, but
    there had been a fire, and it was all charred
    to hell except for a small attic bedroom —
    John O'Hara, *Free Fall In Crimson*
    > *O'Hara's Travis McGee during a period of his life*
    > *when nothing seems worth doing anymore.*

12. Enobarbus: We cannot call her [Cleopatra's]
    winds and waters sighs and tears: they are
    greater storms and tempests than almanacs
    can report. —William Shakespeare, *Antony
    and Cleopatra*, Act 1, scene 2, line 153

13. King: How is it that the clouds still hang
    on you? —William Shakespeare, *Hamlet*,
    Act 1, scene 2, line 66
    > *Hamlet turns the metaphor around with a line*
    > *that veils a play on 'son': "Not so, my lord, I am*
    > *too much i' the' sun."*

14. Queen Elizabeth: Why grow the branches
    now the root is wither'd? / Why wither
    not the leaves the sap being gone? —
    William Shakespeare, *The Tragedy of King
    Richard the Third*, Act 2, scene 2, line 41
    > *Her husband has been murdered and the meta-*
    > *phor expresses her hopelessness and despair.*

15. Troilus: My hopes lie drown'd —William
    Shakespeare, *Troilus and Cressida*, Act 1,
    scene 1, line 51
    > *Troilus's hopes "lie indrench'd" because he is*
    > *"mad / In Cressid's love."*

16. A sea of despair rages —Leo Tolstoy, *The
    Death of Ivan Ilyich*
    > *The sea has become a common metaphor for*
    > *overpowering emotions.*

17. 'Catch my death!' he echoed; and he felt
    like adding: 'But I've caught it already. I
    am dead—I've been dead for months and
    months' —Edith Wharton, *The Age of
    Innocence*

May Archer is referring to the literal danger from catching a chill; Newland Archer feels figuratively dead because he has lost the chance to be with his true love.

■ DESTINY

See: FATE

■ DESTRUCTION/ DESTRUCTIVENESS

See also: DEFEAT; DETERIORATION/DI-MINISHMENT; ENDINGS; EVIL; FAIL-URE; HELL AND DAMNATION; RE-VENGE/VENGEANCE; WARNINGS

1. First Bob Dole, the Senate minority leader, strangled the President's economic stimulus plan. Now the Dark Prince of Gridlock has pledged to give the same killing treatment to Mr. Clinton's long-promised campaign finance reform package —Anon., *The New York Times,* editorial, April 25, 1993

2. Justices O'Connor and Kennedy, who had been part of Chief Justice William Rehnquist's wrecking crew . . . felt compelled to file dissenting opinions —Anon., Editorial, *The New York Times,* May 7, 1992
   The case in question involved state prison inmate rights and the wrecking crew metaphor alludes to the dissenters' previous votes favoring the court's conservative opinions.

3. State Thruway officials were hoping to implement a speedier toll collection system along the superhighway today, but a judge put a nail in their tire —Anon., "Judge Derails Speedy Collection Booths," *The Berkshire Eagle,* August 2, 1993
   The metaphor in the title indicates a different sort of wheel.

4. The capital had changed her superficially, yet the Parisian veneer left her spirit of strongly-tempered metal to rust —Honoré de Balzac, *Cousin Bette*

   Cousin Bette, a peasant woman has become a Parisienne.

5. Norma: You've made a rope of words and strangled this business —Charles Brackett, Billy Wilder, and D. M. Marshman, Jr., *Sunset Boulevard*
   The metaphor is voiced in response to Gillis's protest that he's "just a writer."

6. The old bear, solitary, indomitable . . . widowered, childless, and absolved of mortality—old Priam reft of his old wife and outlived all his sons —William Faulkner, "The Bear"
   The allusion makes a powerful metaphor for the bear, whose death will signal the destruction of the wilderness, and the old king who will be destroyed with the ancient city of Troy.

7. Winter's coffin is already encasing ex-Yugoslavia —Leslie H. Gelb, "Foreign Affairs," *The New York Times,* January 10, 1993
   This followed a statement that time was against U.N. diplomat Cyrus Vance's efforts to negotiate a peace settlement among Muslims, Croatians, and Serbs.

8. [Japan] is the spider's web that destroys the butterfly, leaving only the ugly skeleton —William Johnston, Translator's Preface, to Shusaku Endo's *Silence*
   The translator paraphrases Endo, creating a metaphor.

9. This system contains in itself the seeds of destruction —Stephen Leacock, "Oxford as I See It"

10. The aristocrats [of pre-revolutionary China] would be the kindling for a roaring fire fueled by the fats of social exploitation — Gus Lee, *China Boy*
    The fate of the Mandarins of old China is recounted through the eyes of a young American-born son of such a family.

11. Before entering upon so grave a matter as the destruction of our national fabric, with all its benefits, its memories, and its hopes, would it not be wise to ascertain precisely

why we do it? —Abraham Lincoln, Inaugural Address, March 4, 1861

Fabric has become a common metaphor for a person's strength or weakness.

12. Only man thinning out his kind / sounds through the Sabbath noon, the blind / swipe of the pruner and his knife / busy about the tree of life —Robert Lowell, "Waking Early Sunday Morning"

The tree of life is a venerable and common image here sharpened by the second metaphor of man as the awful pruner of that tree.

13. George Bush made the "deficit reduction deal" with Democrats that helped torpedo his presidency . . . Now we have similar snake oil from Mr. Clinton —William Safire, "Essay," *The New York Times*, February 18, 1993

Safire's fired off his attack on the President's first economic policy speech with a war metaphor and an allusion to the chicanery embodied in the carpetbagger's "spiel."

14. The wheels are coming off the driverless carriage that is the Bush administration — Sydney Schanberg, *Newsday*, October 17, 1992

15. Viktor S. Chernomyrdin may not be the reactionary many had feared . . . This alone offers strong reason to think that the doomsday notion of a fascist dictatorship slouching toward Moscow is overblown —Serge Schemann, *The New York Times*, January 24, 1993

This was a tongue-in-cheek reference to the Beast of the Apocalypse, *and to the poet Yeats's depiction of it: "And what rough beast, its hour come round at last, / Slouches towards Bethlehem to be born?"*

16. Buckingham: her fume needs no spurs, / She'll gallop far enough to her destruction —William Shakespeare, *The Second Part of Henry the Sixth*, Act 1, scene 3, line 153

Buckingham's opinion about the Queen's fate is stated with a horsemanship metaphor.

17. York: Thus are my blossoms blasted in the bud, / And caterpillars eat my leaves away —William Shakespeare, *The Second Part of Henry the Sixth*, Act 3, scene 1, line 89

York likens the defeat reported from France, which has blasted his hopes, to a garden blight.

18. Clarence: But when we saw our sunshine made thy spring, / And that thy summer bred us no increase, / We set the axe to thy usurping root —William Shakespeare, *The Third Part of Henry the Sixth*, Act 2, scene 3, line 163

Once again destruction of an enemy is linked to the destruction of a harmful root.

19. Richard: I'll blast his harvest —William Shakespeare, *The Third Part of Henry the Sixth*, Act 5, scene 7, line 21

In an aside, Richard threatens to destroy the hard-won security of the king's throne.

20. It is odd that one of the keys to abundance should be handed to civilization on a platter of destruction —Adlai Stevenson, "The Nature of Patriotism," speech to American Legion Convention, August 27, 1952

Stevenson referred to the power of the atom, of which he also said "the power of the atom to work evil gives only the merest hint of its power for good."

21. The Other One: Storm and Hail are his names; destruction nestles under his wings, and in his claws he carries punishment — August Strindberg, *Advent*, Act 2

The Judge and the Old Lady are being threatened with death and retribution for their sins by the Mephistophelian, The Other One.

22. [In prison] all but Lust, is turned to dust in Humanity's machine —Oscar Wilde, "The Ballad of Reading Goal"

23. I think they love not Art / Who break the crystal of a poet's heart —Oscar Wilde, "On the Sale by Auction of Keats' Love-Letters"

Crystal, known for its purity and fragility, serves to point out these qualities in a poet.

24. They're [women in operas are] little whirlpools of destruction —Thornton Wilder, *The Eighth Day*

Wilder is really talking about all overly possessive, greedy passion.

■ DETACHMENT

See: COMMUNICATION/NON-COMMUNICATION

■ DETERIORATION/ DIMINISHMENT

See also: DESTRUCTION/DESTRUCTIVENESS; FAILURE

1. Wither have sunk / The Himalayas of character, / The peaks of thought? —Theodore Dreiser, "Where?" *Vanity Fair*, 1926
   These shipwreck and climbing metaphors conclude a poetic lament for past pleasures and strengths.

2. International Business Machines Corporation, the humbled giant of the American computer industry —Steve Lohr, *The New York Times*, January 24, 1993
   "Some fear that IBM may not be able to pull out of its slide," the metaphor continued.

3. Macbeth: My way of life / has fall'n into the sere, the yellow leaf —William Shakespeare, *Macbeth*, Act 4, scene 2, line 4
   Macbeth pictures himself as a tree whose leaves are desiccated (sere) and yellow. In "The Stranger," Thomas Hardy wrote about a woman in the autumn of life: "The grass has long been green on the graves of Shepherd Fennel and his frugal wife; . . . the baby in whose honor they all had met is a matron in the sere and yellow leaf."

4. Suffolk: Thus droops this lofty pine and hangs his sprays —William Shakespeare, *The Second Part of Henry the Sixth*, Act 2, scene 3, line 45
   This is another example of a no longer fruitful person pictured as an tree with drooping flowers or cut limbs. The drooping "tree" in this case is Duke Humphrey.

5. Queen: But soft, but see, or rather do not see, / My fair rose wither —William Shakespeare, *The Tragedy of King Richard the Second*, Act 5, scene 1, line 7
   The metaphoric rose is Richard, who has just passed the lamenting queen on his way to the Tower. She also refers to Richard as "a beauteous inn" and laments that "hard-favor'd grief be lodg'd" in him.

6. The huge doll of my body / refuses to rise —Mark Strand, "My Life"
   The poet calls himself "the toy of women" as he details how his mother, his wife, and his daughter have diminished him.

7. Over them the green mould of the perfunctory was already perceptibly spreading. It made Archer shiver to think that it might be spreading over him too —Edith Wharton, *The Age of Innocence*
   The "mould" is caused by law careers apathetically undertaken and pursued.

8. She was a sinking ship firing upon her rescuers —Alexander Woollcott, "Bernhardt"
   The shooting metaphor refers to the aging actress' refusal to give in to the decline of old age.

■ DETROIT

See: CITIES

■ DEVELOPMENT

See: MATURATION

■ DEVOTION

See also: LOVE; LOVERS' DECLARATIONS AND EXCHANGES; MASTERY/ SUBORDINATION

1. Macheath: My Hand, my Heart, my Dear, is so rivited to thine, that I cannot unloose my Hold —John Gay, *The Beggar's Opera*, Act 1, scene 17
   An early illustration of the effectiveness of the one-word metaphor.

2. Antony: My heart was to thy rudder tied by th' strings, / And thou shouldst tow

me after —William Shakespeare, *Antony and Cleopatra*, Act 3, scene 9, line 58
Antony responds to Cleopatra's declaration that she never expected him to follow her "fearful sail."

3. Helena: I am your spaniel —William Shakespeare, *A Midsummer Night's Dream*, Act 2, scene 1, line 203
Helena thus expresses her subservient love, her willingness even to be beaten, as long as she can follow Demetrius.

4. Claudio: For thee I'll lock up all the gates of love —William Shakespeare, *Much Ado About Nothing*, Act 4, scene 1, line 106

■ DIARIES

See: JOURNAL WRITING

■ DICTIONARIES

See: BOOKS

■ DIFFERENCE/SAMENESS

See also: CONSISTENCY/INCONSISTENCY; MONOTONY

1. Weekdays revolved on a sameness wheel. They turned into themselves so steadily and inevitably that each seemed to be the original of yesterday's rough draft —Maya Angelou, *I Know Why the Caged Bird Sings*
There were always Saturdays, however which "always broke the mold and dared to be different."

2. But for you, I guess, it's another kettle of fish —Louis Auchincloss, "Portrait of the Artist by Another," *Skinny Island*
This is a twist on the familiar expression a fine kettle of fish *as a figurative alternative to* a fine mess. *The meaning here is "but that's a different story."*

3. Since we don't know what kind of soldier we're going to need in the future, we ought not to select future recruits using the same cookie cutter —James Pinkerton, "Today's yuppie military," *The Berkshire Eagle*, August 23, 1993

If Mr. Pinkerton had spent more time in the kitchen, he would have known that cookies are cut out, not selected, with cookie cutters.

■ DIFFICULTIES

See also: ADVERSITY; DANGER; PROBLEMS AND SOLUTIONS

1. Another factor draining wind from the recovery's sails —Anon., Editorial, *The Wall Street Journal*, October 26, 1992
Sailing metaphors, common to journalism and everyday language, tend to reach epidemic proportions during economic downturns.

2. A dilemma is a wolf in front of you and a precipice behind your back —Anon., Latin Proverb
Shakespeare solved that dilemma in King Lear, *when he wrote "Thou'ldst shun a bear; / But if thy flight lay towards the raging sea, / Thou'ldst meet the bear i' the mouth."*

3. Metaphorically speaking what Clinton had to deal with in New York were mere random street muggings. I say "mere" because Republicans don't waste time deploying muggers; they send out death squads —Russell Baker, "The Observer," *The New York Times*, April 11, 1992

4. Difficulty is a nurse of greatness—a harsh nurse who rocks her foster children roughly but rocks them into strength and athletic proportions —William Cullen Bryant

5. Her way was strewn with invisible rocks and lions —John Cheever, "The Angel of the Bridge"

6. In the working conditions of our world and theater the dedicated ones are forced under emotional whips to greater and greater effort —Agnes DeMille, "The Milk of Paradise"

7. Thorns in a rose garden —Agnes DeMille, Headline, *The New York Times*, July 2, 1992
The metaphoric thorns referred to lack of ideas that made President George Bush's televised CBS Morning Show interview from the White House

Rose Garden less than an unqualified success. Other articles during this period referred to the President's "rose garden strategy" as actions designed to surround him with the trappings of the presidency.

8. We have a mountain to climb in the House to achieve an override —Christopher Dodd, Quoted in "What's News," *The Wall Street Journal,* September 25, 1992
   Dodd was quoted after the Senate voted to reject President George Bush's veto of a family leave measure.

9. Mr. Tillinger [John], usually a fine director, has steered the play right into an iceberg —Mel Gussow, "Review/Theatre," *The New York Times,* April 14, 1993
   The ill-fated "ship" was the revival of Three Men on a Horse.

10. Many thousands of young men who are Orthodox Jews studying in yeshivas automatically enjoy virtual exemptions from military service, and the situation has created a monumental fault line that runs clear across Israeli society —Clyde Haberman, *The New York Times,* September 3, 1992
    Elsewhere in the article, another metaphor declares that "The soldier and the yeshiva student are strands in the fabric of Israel that sometimes wear on each other."

11. To the end, he was loyal to George Bush, saying during the campaign that the savings and loan bailout, a nasty thorn in the economic paw, was nearly complete —Herbert B. Herring, "Business Diary," *The New York Times,* November 15, 1992
    Would that Bush had learned extraction from Androcles!

12. The year [1969] was also one in which marital infidelity seemed to become an epidemic . . . and when a generalized bewilderment ran up and down the land in boots —Edward Hoagland, "Americana by the Acre," *Harper's,* October, 1970
    The author might have done better to seesaw a bit before making his choice.

13. He had barely dodged a bullet in nominating Ms. [Janet] Reno . . . before his prolonged search for an Attorney-General completely clouded his economic plan — Gwen Ifill, *The New York Times,* February 15, 1993
    Ifill managed to pack her sentence with a double-barreled metaphor.

14. They know they could lose a job or get very sick and land in the same boat as Maria Weirather . . . who had to sell her car to pay a hospital bill —Peter T. Kilborn, *The New York Times,* May 9, 1993
    Kilborn went on to write that whether President Clinton's health care bill "passes or sinks" will depend upon the responses of ordinary Americans.

15. The next few weeks were thorny with events —David Leavitt, "A Place I've Never Been"

16. Fasten your seat belts. It's going to be a bumpy night —Joseph Mankiewicz, *All About Eve*
    Bette Davis said it in the now-classic movie. The metaphor of buckling up in anticipation of trouble has become common.

17. In the twisted skein that is the post-cold-war world, a big tangle is Cocom, the 17-nation Western trade organization that polices high-technology exports to Russia —Anthony Ramirez, *The New York Times,* January 24, 1993

18. Speed bumps in the road to capitalism — Anthony Ramirez, Blurb, *The New York Times,* October 29, 1991
    The blurb summed up an article on Poland's economic reforms.

19. Mr. Speaker, I smell a rat; I see him floating in the air; but mark me, sir, I will nip him in the bud —Sir Boyle Roche, Speech to Irish Parliament, early 19th century
    Sir Boyle typifies many a politician's inability to nip a tendency to stumble into a mixaphor.

20. The biggest stumbling block, now and probably in the future, is Bosnia —Wil-

liam E. Schmidt, *The New York Times,* January 24, 1993

> *Nations need really big blocks on which to stub their toes.*

21. Rosalind: O, how full of briers is this working-day world —William Shakespeare, *As You Like It,* Act 1, scene 3, line 12

22. Blood on the board-room floor was good news for General Motors stockholders — Randall Smith, —Joseph B. White, *The Wall Street Journal,* April 8, 1992

> *The metaphor was used as a lead in a story about a management shake-up. Another report on this situation by* The New York Times *reporter Steve Lohr described G.M's board as "long a docile rubber-stamp for management . . . "*

23. These [questions] are nuts beyond my ability to crack —Robert Louis Stevenson, Dedication letter, *Kidnapped,* 1886

> *This is a common metaphor, usually expressed as a tough nut to crack.*

24. Life is thick sown with thorns, and I know no other remedy but to pass quickly through them —Voltaire

> *Voltaire also referred to life as "a war."*

25. When Darrow, that night, regained his room, he reflected with a flash of irony that each time he entered it he brought a fresh troop of perplexities to trouble its serene seclusion —Edith Wharton, *The Reef*

■ DIGNITY

See also: *HONOR*

1. Gravity is only the bark of wisdom's trees, but it preserves it —Confucius

2. Paris: A naked queen is dressed in her dignity —Jean Giraudoux, *Tiger at the Gates,* Act 2

> *Paris is trying to preserve the honor of Helen, whom he abducted when she was swimming nude.*

3. Dignity is a mask we wear to hide our ignorance —Elbert Hubbard

■ DIGRESSION

See: *CONCENTRATION/DISTRACTION*

■ DILEMMAS

See: *DIFFICULTIES; PROBLEMS AND SOLUTIONS*

■ DILIGENCE

See: *COMMITMENT*

■ DIMINISHMENT

See: *DETERIORATION/DIMINISHMENT*

■ DIPLOMACY

See also: *INTERNATIONAL RELATIONS; TACT*

1. Mr. Clinton will need to continue repairing his bridges to the moderate and conservative Democrats —R. W. Apple, Jr., *The New York Times,* May 28, 1993

2. The "new thinking" in the region is concerned about preventive medicine and how to build upon positive processes. Asia needs to develop a positive, conflict-prevention approach —Peter Chan, *The Singapore Symposium,* United Nations, 1992

> *The image builds on the disease metaphor for war.*

3. The U.N. will is becoming a more controversial actor on the world stage —Jan Eliasson, Briefing for the U.N. Department of Public Information, January 14, 1993

> *The Under-Secretary-General was talking about the changes in peacekeeping.*

4. The Cambodian peace plan is brilliant . . . because it creates a level playing-field, allows the Cambodian people to decide who they want to govern them, and none can claim to have won or lost as a result — Kishore Mahbubani, *The Singapore Symposium,* United Nations, 1992

> *The art of negotiation is equated with game-playing in this metaphor.*

5. We are thus left with a continuation of the cat-and-mouse game of Iraqi cheat and retreat —Charles William Maynes, *The New York Times,* January 19, 1993
    Has anyone ever heard of a mouse that won this game?

6. International politics is not bean bag and if you're are going to play the game, you had better be prepared to play the game against guys who play rough —George Melloan, "Global View," *The Wall Street Journal,* October 19, 1992

7. Someone had come to complain and argue. The owner was asked for. Fetisova went instead to pour oil on the troubled waters —Boris Pasternak, *Doctor Zhivago*
    Pasternak use a common metaphor to picture an easing of a difficult situation. Its use dates back to 731 A.D. when the Venerable Bede in his Ecclesiastical History depicts St. Aidan giving a priest a bottle of oil, urging him to throw it into the sea so that "the winds will abate, and a calm and smiling sea will accompany you throughout your voyage."

8. Vietnam is a major player [in the Cambodian conflict]. It is a shadow play to shift the focus of attention to the four parties —K. S. Sandhu, *The Singapore Symposium,* United Nations, 1992
    Sandhu, who is from Singapore, draws his image from puppetry, an art that is largely unfamiliar in the West.

9. Policy makers debated how to do this with a combination of diplomatic sticks (and perhaps carrots) that might persuade Mr. Hussein at last to abide by the United Nations resolutions intended to curb his power —Elaine Sciolino, *The New York Times,* January 24, 1993
    This is frequently mistermed a carrot and stick approach. It should be carrot or stick, since only one of the two is offered to a mule that balks.

10. The judge is a great settler. She takes the ramrod out of the back of you, and sticks in something more flexible —Harvey I. Sladkus, Quoted by Bruce Weber, *The New York Times,* August 26, 1992

A lawyer coined a metaphor for mediation.

■ DISAGREEABLENESS
See: CHARACTERIZATIONS

■ DISAGREEMENT
See: AGREEMENT/DISAGREEMENT

■ DISAPPEARANCE
See also: PERMANENCE/IMPERMANENCE

1. Margo [Bette Davis]: I must have frightened her away . . . poor little flower. Just dropped her petals and folded her tent . . . / Bill [Gary Merrill]: Don't mix your metaphors. / Margo: I'll mix whatever I like —Joseph L. Mankiewicz, *All About Eve*
    This exchange is about Eve, the young actress threatening the star's career opens the movie.

2. Phrases die out first, everyone forgets / What doornails are; then after certain decades / As a dead metaphor, *"dead as a doornail"* flickers / And fades away — Robert Pinsky, "Dying"
    The dead metaphor is just the beginning. "every day / Things that were in my memory fade and die," Pinsky writes.

3. Prospero: Our revels now are ended: these our actors— / As I foretold you—were all spirits and / Are melted into air, into thin air —William Shakespeare, *The Tempest,* Act 4, scene 1, line 148
    This metaphor is the prelude to a speech that is usually interpreted as Shakespeare's farewell to the theater. He would never write another play. Prospero is often thought to represent his creator.

4. If this country can't find its way to a human path . . . then all of us, black as well as white, are going down the same drain —Richard Wright, *Black Boy*
    The metaphor depicting irretrievable loss as water down the drain pipe has been in common usage since the 1930s. The advent of television

brought the currently more popular variation,
down the tubes *(originally a surfing expression).*

■ DISAPPOINTMENT

See also: FRUSTRATION

1. From this moment on he must . . . feed on
   gall, drink every morning from the cup of
   bitterness —Honoré de Balzac, "Colonel
   Chabet"

2. Remember now thy Creator in the days of
   thy youth, while the evil days come not
   . . . Or ever the silver cord be loosed, or
   the golden bowl be broken . . . Then shall
   the dust return to the earth as it was; and
   the spirit shall return unto God who gave
   it —The Bible, *O.T., Ecclesiastes 12:6*
   > *In his novel,* The Golden Bowl, *Henry James
   > uses the device of an imperfect golden bowl as a
   > metaphor for the imperfections in his characters
   > lives and relationships*

3. It is a bitter pill—but I shall have to
   swallow it —Ivan Turgenev, *Fathers and
   Sons*
   > *A still common metaphor for disappointment
   > depicts a father's rumination on the generational
   > gulf between himself and his son.*

4. Vance's dream dropped with a crash to
   the floor of the porch and lay there between them in rainbow splinters —Edith
   Wharton, *Hudson River Bracketed*
   > *The "crash" is caused by his grandmother's ina-
   > bility to see beyond her own narrow religion.*

■ DISAPPROVAL

See: APPROVAL/DISAPPROVAL

■ DISASTER

*See: ADVERSITY; DESTRUCTION/DESTRUC-
TIVENESS; FORTUNE/MISFORTUNE*

■ DISCIPLES

See: LEADERS/FOLLOWERS

■ DISCIPLINE

See: SELF-CONTROL

■ DISCOMFORT

See: GRIEF

■ DISCONTENT

See: DISAPPOINTMENT; GLOOM

■ DISCRETION

See: PRUDENCE; TACT

■ DISCRIMINATION

See: FAIRNESS/UNFAIRNESS

■ DISDAIN

See: ARROGANCE/HUMILITY

■ DISEASE

See: ILLNESS

■ DISHONESTY

*See: CORRUPTION; CRAFTINESS; DECEP-
TION; LIES/LIARS*

■ DISILLUSIONMENT

See: DISAPPOINTMENT

■ DISINTEGRATION

See also: DESTRUCTION/DESTRUCTIVENESS

1. [Clark] Clifford's cherished law firm was
   turning to sand —Michael R. Beschloss,
   "The Political Life," *The New Yorker,* September 6, 1993
   > *The article discussed how a trial for commercial
   > bribery destroyed the man once a member of the*

few said to lead "charmed lives." Clifford was cleared of the charges.

2. [France with its royal privileges intact:] What is it but a wilderness of misery and ruin? ... a crumbling tower of waste, mismanagement, extortion, debt, mortgage, oppression, hunger, nakedness, and suffering —Charles Dickens, *A Tale of Two Cities*
   A Marquis expresses this very realistic view of the state of his world.

3. [Mr. Clinton's] promise to focus on the economy like a laser seemed to come unstuck in the Washington centrifuge — Eric Engberg, Quoted in *The New York Times*, January 31, 1993
   The uncommon metaphor follows hard on the heels of the common simile.

4. Much of Mr. Fernandez' [Joseph A.] work on school-based management in Dade is apparently coming unglued —Robert Kuttner, *The New York Times Book Review*, January 17, 1993
   In reviewing the autobiography of the New York City Superintendent of Schools, Kuttner commented on his achievements in his previous post in Dade County, Florida.

5. The ceiling, / which is blue like heaven but is / coming down in long bandages / revealing the wounds of the last rain — Philip Levine, "Rain Downriver"

6. All collapsed, and the great shroud of the sea rolled on as it rolled five thousand years ago —Herman Melville, *Moby Dick*
   This metaphor concludes Melville's epic novel.

7. The world as they had taught it to us broke in pieces —Erich Maria Remarque, *All Quiet on the Western Front*
   An eighteen-year-old soldier reflects on how literal experience of being under fire, figuratively explodes everything he has been taught to believe.

8. Edgar: the strings of life / Began to crack —William Shakespeare, *King Lear*, Act 5, scene 3, line 216

9. Othello: when I have pluck'd thy rose, / I cannot give it vital growth again, / It must needs wither: I'll smell it on the tree —William Shakespeare, *Othello*, Act 5, scene 2, line 13
   Othello, looking at the sleeping Desdemona, expresses his agony ... then kills her.

■ **DISORDER**
See: ORDER/DISORDER

■ **DISPOSITION**
See: TEMPERAMENT

■ **DISPUTE**
See: ARGUMENTS; QUARRELS/QUARREL-SOMENESS

■ **DISSENT/DISSENTERS**
See also: AGREEMENT/DISAGREEMENT; POLITICS/POLITICIANS

1. When my string's tuned tight as Igor's Song, / when I get my breath back, you can hear / in my voice the earth —Osip Mandelstam, "Stanza 8"—translated by W. S. Merwin & Clarence Brown, 1973
   The poet has survived being shunned for his political beliefs, and will continue to write.

2. And still other writers of the silence are those who ... have concealed a call to arms in an elegy, who have hidden a harpoon in the honey and a hook in the paste, writing only to make what is left unsaid more potent than anything they say —M.D., Preface to *The Silence of the Sea* by Vercors
   The author of the preface, identified only as M.D., speaks of the writers of the French Resistance, who "go on writing in the shadow" during the German occupation.

3. Martius: What's the matter, you dissentious rogues, / That, rubbing the poor itch

of your opinion, / Make yourselves scabs?
—William Shakespeare, *Coriolanus,* Act
1, scene 1, line 170

4. The prudent precautions taken by the National Convention to prevent a tumult made me suppose that the dogs of faction would not dare to bark, much less to bite, however true to their scent, and I was not mistaken —Mary Wollstonecraft (Godwin), Letter to her literary adviser, J. Johnson, December 26, 1792

> *Wollstonecraft was pleased to be able to report on a day "not stained with blood."*

■ DISTRUST

See: MISTRUST

■ DISTURBANCES

1. The phone . . . a barbarous intrusion . . . a lesion in the sacred body of her solitude — Rebecca Goldstein, *The Dark Sister*

2. The sound of her broom became the sound of a broom sweeping the contents from his skull, and her cloth polishing the veranda a cloth rubbing at his skull —Kawabata Yasanari, *A Thousand Cranes*

> *Kikuji's tea cottage had been invaded by the woman who insisted on cleaning it for him, a woman he heartily disliked.*

3. Her menstrual period . . . a monthly thunderbolt —John Updike, "His Mother Inside Him," *The New Yorker,* April 20, 1992

■ DIVERSITY

See also: CHARACTERIZATIONS; DESCRIPTIONS, MISC.; MIXTURE; PEOPLE, INTERACTIONS

1. Variety's the very spice of life, that gives it all its flavor —William Cowper, "The Timepiece"

> *Like many catchy metaphors, overuse has dulled the flavor of this one.*

2. Indeed, Mr. Clinton's team of foreign policy advisers is an ideological peacock made up of every wing of the Democratic Party —Thomas L. Friedman, "Clinton's Foreign Policy Agenda Reaches Across Broad Spectrum" *The New York Times,* 1992

3. In a huge, still half-developed country, where every kind of national type and habit comes to run a new thread into the rich tapestry of American life and thought —John Galsworthy, "American and Briton"

4. Our Garrick's a salad; for in him we see / Oil, vinegar, sugar and saltness agree! — Oliver Goldsmith, *Retaliation,* Act 4

> *Goldsmith also eulogized David Garrick as "an abridgement of all that was pleasant in man."*

5. I must cast myself / into work that I love, as the keeper hurls / horsemeat to the lion:—I am meat, lion, and keeper — Donald Hall, "To Build a House"

> *In this mix of simile and metaphor, Hall is engaged by the multiplicity of roles within the self. That is why he takes as an epigraph Pablo Picasso's "Every human being is a colony."*

6. [*Portrait of the Artist as a Young Man*] is a mosaic of jagged fragments that does altogether render with extreme completeness the growth of a rather secretive, imaginative boy in Dublin —H. G. Wells, *The New Republic,* March 10, 1917

■ DIVORCE

See also: MARRIAGE

1. Divorce is the sacrament of adultery — Anon., French Proverb

2. Clay is busy these days ironing out the last wrinkles of a complicated divorce —Andrea Lee, "Full Moon Over Milan," *The New Yorker,* April 5, 1995

> *This domestic image has gained much currency for smoothing out tricky situations.*

3. It was one thing to theorize on the detachability of human beings, another to watch them torn apart by the bleeding roots —Edith Wharton, *Twilight Sleep*
   Divorce has become easy, but far from painless.

■ DOCTORS

See: OCCUPATIONS

■ DOCTRINES

See: BELIEFS

■ DOGMA

See: BELIEFS; OPINION

■ DOGS

See: ANIMALS

■ DOMINANCE

See also: MASTERY/SUBORDINATION

1. For once the rising sun was eclipsed by the setting sun —Thomas Hart Benton
   The senator's remark was prompted by the crowds at Martin Van Buren's inaugural who, upon seeing the outgoing President Jackson, gave him a tremendous ovation.

2. How can such brainy individuals [as Mary McCarthy and Broadwater Bowden] continue to be . . . so eager to ride herd on everyone who's dared to do anything that doesn't meet with their exquisite approval —Truman Capote, Quoted in John Malcolm Brinnon's journal entry, October 6, 1947

3. I hadde hem hoolly in myn hand — Geoffrey Chaucer, "The Wife of Bath's Prologue and Tale"
   The wife had her husband wholly in her hand. (After that, she would do nothing to please him unless he paid her off.)

4. It is very difficult for a sapling to grow up in the shadow of a giant oak —Randolph Churchill
   The "oak" was Churchill's father Winston.

5. In this particular hive she was undoubtedly queen bee —Mary McCarthy, "Cruel and Barbarous Treatment"
   A woman is in an adulterous relationship with a young man and it is she who controls the relationship—at least during the first part of McCarthy's story.

6. "The Blue Streak" is told from the point of view of a young man . . . who has lived in his father's formidable shadow and shivered there from the lack of warmth — Barbara Quick, *The New York Times Book Review*, August 2, 1992

7. Though show-biz lingo plays a role in political discourse, and Big Jawn [Governor Connally] has a need to upstage the rest of the cast of characters, will the ex-actor he's playing opposite find him a tough act to follow? —William Safire, *On Language*
   Hemingway once wrote that all American fiction derived from Huckleberry Finn. *It might be argued that all theater metaphors derive from Shakespeare's "All the world's a stage."*

8. The fiercest of these, a wealthy huntress of small, seedy lions (such as himself) who stalks the middle-western bush with ears and rifle cocked, is his hostess for the evening —Dylan Thomas, "A Visit to America"
   Thomas was prophetic in fearing such literary predation: he was helped to his death by an overdose of lionizing.

9. All the other actors in the show faded into insignificance beside the dominant figure of Mrs. Newell, became mere marionettes pulled hither and thither by the hidden wires of her intention —Edith Wharton, "The Last Asset"
   A similar combination of life as theater and the people as easily manipulated marionettes appears in "The Senior Partner's Ethics" by Louis Auchincloss. Here a lawyer is "the only actor,

and the others marionettes whose strings were pulled by the angel (or demon) who was composing the lines of the comedy (or tragedy) of his life."

■ DOUBT

See also: FEAR; SUSPICION; UNCERTAINTY

1. Jane read this letter . . . with a slowly gathering doubt that seemed to materialize at last into a very dark cloud —Louis Auchincloss, "The Stations of the Cross," *Skinny Island*

2. What profit hath he that hath laboured for the wind? —The Bible, *O.T., Ecclesiastes 5:16*
   > Another familiar metaphor, "He who sows the wind will reap the whirlwind," can be found in O.T., Hosea 8:7. An example of the figure in fiction is "Indiscriminate profusion . . . is sowing the wind to reap the whirlwind" from The Black Dwarf by Sir Walter Scott (1817).

3. Doubt . . . the vestibule which all men pass, before they can enter into the temple of truth —Charles Caleb Colton, *Lacon*

4. Skepticism is the chastity of the intellect, and it is shameful to surrender it too soon or to the first comer; there is nobility in preserving it cooly and proudly through a long youth, until at last, in the ripeness of instinct and discretion, it can be safely exchanged for fidelity and happiness — George Santayana, *Skepticism and Animal Faith*

5. The Duke: Our doubts are traitors — William Shakespeare, *Measure for Measure,* Act 1, scene 4, line 78

6. Chorus: I am stretched on the rack of doubt, and terror and trembling hold / my heart —Sophocles, *Oedipus the King*
   > The chorus comments on the plague that is afflicting Thebes.

7. Skepticism is a good watchdog if you know when to take the leash off —Rex Stout, *Fer-de-Lance*

A Nero Wolfe witticism cited by his sidekick, Archie Goodwin to a skeptical character in the first of the famous Wolfe novels.

8. A doubt shot up its serpent head in his own bosom —Edith Wharton, *The Reef*
   > A young man reflects on a love not fulfilled.

■ DRAMA

See: ARTS AND ENTERTAINMENT; CRITICISM/CRITICS

■ DREAMS

See also: DAYDREAMS; HOPE; ILLUSION/ REALITY; SLEEP

1. As he looked out the [railroad] car window the town of Winesburg had disappeared and his life had become but a background on which to paint the dreams of his manhood —Sherwood Anderson, "Departures," *Winesburg, Ohio*
   > Anderson's young protagonist is headed toward a new life but the Winesburg experience will always be with him.

2. Were it my tendency to analyze, I would suggest that deep in his heart he was displeased with the winds that disperse illicit fantasies —Shmuel Yosef Agnon, *Shira*
   > A character wonders whether old age will overtake him, and begins to dream about the love of young women.

3. The river slides under our dreams / but land flows more silently —John Ashbery, "Chaos"
   > A feeling of barely controlled terror permeates the poem.

4. A landscape glittered behind her voice. There were icicles in it and savage fields of ice, great storms, boiling over a flat countryside striped with white rails—a chessboard underneath a storm —Enid Bagnold, *National Velvet*

5. They had bitten off a piece of dream together —Enid Bagnold, *National Velvet*
   Beyond the dream of winning the race everything "was an uncharted sea" to Velvet and Mi.

6. Slowly the land is rolled /Sleepward under a sea of gentle fire —Charles Baudelaire, "L'Invitation au Voyage"
   The poet invites a woman to accompany him on a voyage, to "dream / How sweet all things would seem" if they could live together in some land of "richness, quietness, and pleasure."

7. Sleep's entanglements would put to shame / whatever depths the analysts might plumb —Joseph Brodsky, "Six Years Later"

8. They [Jim's dreams] had a gorgeous virility, the charm of vagueness, they passed before him with a heroic tread; they carried his soul away with them and made it drunk with the divine philtre of an unbounded confidence in itself —Joseph Conrad, *Lord Jim*
   Jim is taken with the calm joys of sailing at the beginning of a voyage.

9. Meadows: A dream / Has got you prisoner —Christopher Fry, *A Sleep of Prisoners*
   The dreamer is, in reality, already a prisoner; the dream then imprisons the prisoner. The metaphor is like a nested Matrushka doll.

10. Fantasies are more than substitutes for unpleasant reality; they are also dress rehearsals, plans —Barbara Grizzuti Harrison, "Talking Dirty," *Ms.*, October, 1973
    Expanding on the dress rehearsal metaphor, Harrison stated that "all acts performed in the world begin in the imagination."

11. He sleeps / and his sleep is the dance of all the birds / on earth flying north —Jim Harrison, "Dogen's Dream"

12. This was, in truth, a senile, old, toothless wreck of a dream, doddering and wheezing and buckling at the knees, a balding retread of the dreams of '48 and '67 and '73 [Amman, Jordan's dream of destroy-

ing the Jews] —Michael Kelly, *Chronicles of a Small War*

13. Dreams are blind arrows that never leave the bow —Lewis Mumford, "The Little Testament of Bernard Martin, Aet. 30"

14. Luxuriously she floated on innocent visions of days after the morrow —Dorothy Parker, "Glory in the Daytime"

15. My dreams were skim milk and albumin —Marge Piercy, "The Homely War," *Living In the Open*

16. My soul hastens on the wings of a dream —Friedrich Rückert, "Gestille Sehnsucht" [Stilled Longing]
    This verse was set to music by Brahms in the songs of Op. 91.

17. Hamlet: A dream itself is but a shadow —William Shakespeare, *Hamlet*, Act 2, scene 2, line 262

18. Mercutio: Dreams . . . are the children of an idle brain —William Shakespeare, *Romeo and Juliet*, Act 1, scene 4, line 96

19. Prince: Then let us fly upon the wings of sleep —August Strindberg, *Swanwhite*

■ DRINKING/DRUNKENNESS

See: INTOXICATION/INTOXICANTS

■ DUBLIN

See: CITIES

■ DULLNESS

See also: MONOTONY; ORDINARINESS/ EXTRAORDINARINESS

1. Half a century later the goal of rational happiness . . . is rejected contemptuously by the new, romantic generation in continental Europe, for whom pleasure is but *tepid water on the tongue*; the phrase is Holderlin's, but it could just as well have

been uttered by Musset or Lermontov — Isaiah Berlin, "The Apotheosis of the Romantic Will"

2. This was one of those rye-bread days, all dull and damp without —Margaret Fuller, Diary entry, *Life of Margaret Fuller-Ossoll*

   Had she lived today Fuller might have called it a white-bread day since that's become synonymous with dullness.

3. They're bland, Venus, they're skimmed milk —John Hersey, "Fling"

   "They" are the middle aged.

4. It was a dull, screwed-down life she led — Rosamond Lehmann, *The Ballad and the Source*

5. The party instantly sank back into a coma —Sinclair Lewis, *Main Street*

   The comatose party is a typical Gopher Prairie gathering, after an initial flurry of stunts and party games.

6. While the gathering in Munich, Germany, was a snooze—economic summit meetings are convened to reassure, not entertain—some subjects conspicuously not on the agenda are very interesting indeed —Peter Passell, "Economic Scene," *The New York Times*, June 9, 1992

7. Polonius: Therefore since brevity is the soul of wit / And tediousness the limbs and outward flourishes, / I will be brief— William Shakespeare, *Hamlet*, Act 2, scene 2, line 90

   Speakers often quote only the first half of this sentence, and thus miss the anatomical metaphor.

8. Thersites: There's Ulysses and old Nestor, whose wit was moldy ere their grandsires had nails on their toes —William Shakespeare, *Troilus and Cressida*, Act 4, scene 5, line 225

9. He was . . . somehow bleached out, a faded negative of Peter —Anne Rivers Siddons, *Colony*

   Peter is the "bleached out" man's son.

10. The [Republican] platform is, in vast stretches, chloroform in print —George F. Will, *The Washington Post Writers Group*, August 16, 1992.

    What happens in politics is often more soporific than stimulus.

■ DUTY

See: RESPONSIBILITY

E

■ EARTH

1. The earth is a beehive we all enter by the same door, but live in different cells — Anon., African Proverb

2. [He] rushed into the darkness. For the Earth, too, had on her Black Veil —Nathaniel Hawthorne, "The Minister's Black Veil"
   The minister wore a black veil over his face until the day he died, instilling a fear of the unknown, as does the night's darkness.

3. Ecosaints—their karma / to be Earth's latest, maybe terminal fruits— / are slow to ripen —James Merrill, "Self-Portrait in Tyvek(TM) Windbreaker," *The New Yorker,* February 24, 1992
   Merrill does not seem to be very sanguine about the fate of the world when he speaks of "terminal" fruits.

4. This earth is a spot, a grain, an atom — John Milton, *Paradise Lost,* Book 8

5. The whole earth is the monument of great characters —Pericles, Oration during Peloponnesian war, 431–30 B.C.

6. Bolingbroke: here we march / Upon the grassy carpet of this plain —William Shakespeare, *The Tragedy of King Richard the Second,* Act 3, scene 3, line 49

7. The earth, a brittle globe of glass / Lies in the hollow of thy hand —Oscar Wilde, "Eleutheria"

■ ECOLOGY

See also: PROBLEMS AND SOLUTIONS

1. [The environmental summit] gave us a prescription-but the United Nations does not have the money to run to the pharmacy —Noel Brown, speaking at the United Nations NGO Briefing, November 4, 1993
   The cure for environmental degradation was worked out in the document known as Agenda 21; but the financially strapped U.N. was unable to act on the knowledge and "go to the pharmacy" to fill the prescription.

2. In fact the greatness of this book is . . . how the ebb and flow of species works within an ecological community in dynamic equilibrium —Charles E. Little, "Books," *Wilderness,* Winter 1992
   In this review of Edward O. Wilson's The Diversity of Life, *the metaphor of the tides is obvious; the 'equilibrium' would seem to balance items of physical matter. The image is not altogether logical.*

3. Aside from strangling a national park in its cradle, the timber sales would harm the area's anadromous fish —David Rains Wallace, "The Klamath Surprise," *Wilderness,* Winter 1992

■ ECONOMICS

See also: BUSINESS DESCRIPTIONS; INTERNATIONAL RELATIONS; MONEY; POLITICS/POLITICIANS

1. A county caught between the devil of tax increases and the deep blue sea of worker layoffs —Anon., *The New York Times*, May 16, 1992
   This blurb for an article about troubled Nassau county in Long Island reignites the embers of a cliché.

2. The U.S. Government is hemorrhaging red ink at a record pace this year — Anon., "Business Digest," *The New York Times*, May 26, 1992

3. For months, Alan Greenspan, chairman of the Federal Reserve, has been saying the economy is sailing into headwinds — Anon., Editorial, *The New York Times*, August 30, 1992

4. For the past few months buyers, sellers and real estate brokers have had their poles in the water in a search for signs of a bottoming out in the cooperative apartment market —Anon., *The New York Times*, April 5, 1992

5. Alan Greenspan, chairman of the Federal Reserve, can only use interest rates to make the economy's muscles twitch — Anon., *The New York Times*, April 12, 1992

6. Japan's is the classic "bicycle economy": It performs brilliantly at high speeds but has trouble keeping its balance when it slows down —Anon., Quoted in *The Wall Street Journal*, by Clay Chandler, Jacob M. Schlesinger and John Bussey, December 7, 1992

7. The economic recovery, if you want to call it that, is going to be working against the headwind of very slow consumer spending —Gary Ciminero, Quoted by an economist, *The New York Times*, August 26, 1992

8. Now, as China's economy continues to blossom, many of the Chinese-Americans are coming back with their checkbooks and skills —Sheryl Dunn, *The New York Times*, November 15, 1992

9. Because imports cannot be stanched as quickly as those funds can flow back abroad, the current-account deficit would probably rise —Tim Golden, "In Mexico, NAFTA Isn't Just About Trade," *The New York Times*, August 22, 1993
   Golden speaks of the flow of money and goods in waterborne terms.

10. Inflation—the beast supposedly in long hibernation—poked its nose out last week and growled —Herbert H. Herring, "Business Diary," *The New York Times*, May 16, 1993

11. Some of these invisible energies were harnessed at the very dawn of civilization and have been turning the wheels of industry ever since —Aldous Huxley, "Mother"

12. There are too many channels where you must look for funds for economic conversion. We should have one-stop shopping —Anne Markusen, Speech at the United Nations NGO Conference on Disarmament, April 1993

13. In the battle of the budget, [many firms] are choosing trench warfare —Anne Markusen, —Joel Yudkin, *Dismantling the Cold War Economy*
    Since the budget deficit "slapped the lid on military spending," defense contractors have been lobbying to preserve their bailiwicks.

14. An unexpected surge in wholesale prices last month . . . left many economists and investors wondering whether the inflation genie was starting to slip out of the bottle —Sylvia Nasar, *The New York Times*, May 13, 1993

15. [They] conclude that the world's most populous democracy is well along the runway to an economic takeoff —Peter Passell, "Economic Scene," *The New York Times*, August 26, 1993
    The article portrays an India poised to improve its GNP, as many other Asian "miracle economies" have done.

16. And the price exacted by the World Bank and the International Monetary Fund [to provide India with money] was a commitment by India to tighten its fiscal belt — Peter Passell, "Economic Scene," *The New York Times*, August 26, 1993
    Belt-tightening is the dieting down of a fiscal waistline so the resultant figure is leaner-and-meaner.

17. Exports were viewed with malign indifference, a diversion from the noble effort of pulling the nation up by its socks —Peter Passell, "Economic Scene," *The New York Times*, August 26, 1993

18. The global Economy's engines are out of tune and sputtering —Peter Passell, Business article headline, *The New York Times*, April 1992

19. Many Americans . . . have accepted that the economy is an alligator and Mr. Bush [President George] is no alligator wrestler —Anna Quindlen, "Public & Private," *The New York Times*, September 16, 1992
    Quindlen reminded Governor Bill Clinton who "said he can wrestle the alligator" that, if elected, he would be expected to prove his claim.

20. As a result, company officials say, Russia and other former Soviet republics aren't getting technology that could be immediately useful in jump-starting their economy —Anthony Ramirez, *The New York Times*, January 24, 1993
    Anyone who has ever been trapped in a stalled car will recognize that image.

21. With his new anti-deficit budget, Uncle Sam is asking taxpayers to dig deeper into their pockets. Fair enough. But while he's at it, he should also mend the holes in his own —P. Norman Roy, *The New York Times*, August 22, 1993

22. The global marketplace has become the world's new closet dictator —Wolfgang Sachs, Quoted in *Who Will Tell the People* by William Greider
    Greider used this mordant metaphor as a chapter heading in his book about American politics.

23. Then followed the economic equivalent of Dunkirk . . . The value of the pound will float on the rolling sea of supply and demand, and not be moored to the mark —William Safire, "Essay," *The New York Times*, September 21, 1992
    Using two seafaring metaphors, Safire's commentary on the union of European currencies slyly asked: "Who needs Kohl in Newcastle?"

24. If voters are not brought aboard the tax juggernaut now, the pain . . . will be all that matters when the President seeks re-election in 1996 —Michael Wines, *The New York Times*, May 16, 1993
    Those standing in front of the juggernaut will be too dead to feel pain.

■ ECSTASY
See: PASSION

■ EDUCATION AND LEARNING
See also: KNOWLEDGE; WISDOM

1. Learning can become impotent; fed on its regular diet, in the end it loses its potency —Shmuel Yosef Agnon, *Shira*
   The scholar has been taking many notes, with "every additional part seeming to diminish the whole."

2. Learning is rowing upstream —Anon., Chinese Proverb
   The image is commonly applied for anything that's difficult.

3. Those who do not study are cattle dressed in men's clothing —Anon., Chinese Proverb

4. Strepsiades: Teach him, and flog him, and be sure you well / Sharpen his mother wit, grind the one edge / Fit for my little law-suits, and the other / Why make that serve for more important matters — Aristophanes, *The Clouds*
   Wit is here shown as a double-edged weapon.

5. The roots of education are bitter, but the fruit is sweet —Aristotle

6. If . . . I find [a man] enriching his mind with constant drafts upon the treasures of song, or feeding his soul upon the spiritual meat of the great masters of letters, or delving deep into the veins of the mines of philosophy, he seems to me to have become a promising initiate into the goodly company of the immortals —John Kendrick Bangs, "My Silent Servants"

7. Learning sleeps and snores in libraries, but wisdom is everywhere, wide awake, on tiptoes —Josh Billings
   Billings uses two metaphors of personification.

8. Learning will be cast into the mire and trodden down under the hoofs of the swinish multitude —Edmund Burke, "Reflections on the Revolution in France"

9. In planning coursework, modules are islands upon which we have some footing, but we must not just focus on separate bases: let us see the islands as also continents in formation —David Burleson, International Association of University Presidents / United Nations Commission on Arms Control Education, May, 1993
   The spokesperson from UNESCO warns against compartmentalizing education.

10. Medical school was a mountain of facts, a giant granite peak full of outcroppings and hidden crevices —Ethan Canin, "The Carnival Dog, the Buyer of Diamonds"
    The protagonist, though not averse to climbing the mountain, wanted to quit because he hated the idea of his helplessness and did not want to face health problems without the possibility of medical care.

11. The wise Brahmins . . . had already poured the sum total of their knowledge into his waiting vessel; the vessel was not full, his intellect was not satisfied —Hermann Hesse, *Siddhartha*
    Learning is here pictured as passive acceptance, which does not satisfy a seeker of knowledge.

12. The backyard rabbits and squirrels his [a boy's] kindergarten, the wilderness . . . his college and the old male bear itself . . . was his alma mater —William Faulkner, "The Bear"

13. Seek for truth in the groves of Academe —Horace, *Epistles*

14. college . . . where pebbles are polished and diamonds are dimmed —Robert Green Ingersoll, *Prose-Poems and Selections*

15. They [the students] all go humping together over the hurdles, with the professor chasing them with a set of "tests" and "recitations." —Stephen Leacock, "Oxford as I See It"
    This method can be described as "the convoy system of education."

16. There was no link between his beloved and the law or economics, but there were many ties, no matter how slender and concealed, between her and religion, spirituality, morality, philosophy, and other comparable branches of learning that tempted him to drink from their springs —Naguib Mahfouz, *Palace of Desire*
    In a mixed metaphor that combines trees and water, Kamal tries to choose a course of university study that will bring him closer to his beloved.

17. Learning that cobweb of the brain / Performs erroneous and vain —Thomas Middleton, *The Mayor of Quinborough*

18. With us, a / school . . . is both a tree of knowledge / and of liberty —Marianne Moore, "The Student"

19. By day college is tick-tock on a useless metronome —Lewis Mumford, "The Little Testament of Bernard Martin, Aet. 30"
    As for college life generally "This is life! This is Learning! Bernard wants to drain it dry," Mumford writes.

20. No bubble is so iridescent or floats longer than that blown by the successful teacher —Sir William Osler, *Life of Sir William Osler*

21. It would let in some fresh air, or at least different air, to blow away some of the cobwebs which grow in the unventilated ivory towers —I. I. Rabi, "Scientist and Humanist"

Rabi suggests that professors of philosophy and medieval history might benefit from learning about relativity and quantum mechanics.

22. Here [in the universities] are all the strands of the tapestry which is to represent our culture —I. I. Rabi, "Scientist and Humanist"

23. To learn is to suck out the *best* in a fashion —Theodore Roethke, *Straw for the Fire, Notebooks of Theodore Roethke*

Fashion is transient as an orange or an egg to Roethke, but it, too, can provide "straw for the fire."

24. Education . . . It makes a straight-cut ditch of a free, meandering book —Henry David Thoreau, Journal entry, 1850

25. We must cultivate our garden —Voltaire, *Candide*

■ EFFECTIVENESS/ INEFFECTIVENESS

See also: PROBLEMS AND SOLUTIONS; STRENGTH/WEAKNESS

1. He was lashing with wet noodles. It didn't hurt that much —Anon., Public Television broadcast of documentary on Armistead Maupin, author of *Tales of the City*, June 24, 1993

The comment was made by a television minister, one of the many real-life models for Maupin's characters. "He picked large targets who could take the burrs under the saddle," the minister explained with a horsemanship metaphor.

2. Clinton keeps setting off powder kegs and then he dowses the blaze with gasoline — Lewis Black, Political humorist, quoted in *The New York Times*, July 26, 1993

The metaphoric joke was prompted by embarrassing incidents about high-priced haircuts, business

given to hometown travel agents, the latest in a series that made some people think of the Clinton presidency as accident-prone.

3. But many of the professionals who work daily with the mentally ill in shelters and on the streets say the state's action is just one small stitch in a tattered safety net — Celia W. Dugger, *The New York Times*, January 24, 1993

Cuomo's administration sent workers to a shelter to identify the mentally ill among the homeless, after an 80 year old woman was bludgeoned to death on her way to church.

4. Cymen: I curse this kingdom . . . curse the creaking of its boughs / And the slaver on the mouth of its winds! —Christopher Fry, *Thor, With Angels*

Cymen pictures the rough, backward civilization as prey to winds that salivate like predatory beasts.

5. But playing Dr. Frankenstein and pumping new juices into the Saddamite Monster is not the solution —Leslie H. Gelb, "Foreign Affairs," *The New York Times*, January 17, 1973

Gelb suggested that the U.S. stay out of the Gulf affairs by alluding to Mary Shelley's Dr. Frankenstein, and suggesting a similarity between his creation and the monster the U.S. helped to create in Saddam Hussein.

6. William Bradford Reynolds, the Reagan Administration official who removed the teeth from the civil rights division and didn't even bother to replace them with cosmetic dentures —Anna Quindlen, "Public & Private," *The New York Times*, June 6, 1993

7. Why remove a splinter with pliers? — Lynne Sharon Schwartz, "The Two Portraits of Rembrandt"

A young girl whose parents have quarreled bitterly feels certain they will divorce—yet, in reviewing the situation she feels both are at fault and could avoid such a drastic step by moderating their behavior.

8. Orlando: thou prun'st a rotten tree / That cannot so much as a blossom yield —

William Shakespeare, *As You Like It*, Act 2, scene 3, line 63

Orlando tells Adam that his brand of loyal servitude is out of fashion.

9. Isabella: Thou rather with thy sharp and sulphurous bolt / Splits the unwedgeable and gnarled oak than the soft myrtle — William Shakespeare, *Measure for Measure*, Act 2, scene 2, line 116

10. The Council adopted resolution 530, and even then barely nibbled around the edges of the problem —Alvaro de Soto, *The Singapore Symposium*, United Nations, 1992

But the edges were nibbled with great resolution.

11. Suspicion mounts every time another tax touted as a cure-all turns out to be another vial of snake oil —Michael Wines, *The New York Times*, May 16, 1993

■ EFFICIENCY

1. His movements . . . were activated with oiled precision —Maya Angelou, *I Know Why the Caged Bird Sings*

This is the author's brother who "was able to find more hours in the day than I thought existed.

2. She made a quick hash of the customers —Bernard Malamud, "The Loan"

The lady is a baker's wife.

■ EGO/EGOTISM

See also: BOASTERS/BOASTFULNESS; VANITY

1. In the mental attitude seek thy refuge; / Wretched are those whose motive is the fruit —Anon., *The Bhagavad Gita, 2:49*

Action should be entered into for its own sake, not for the desire of reward.

2. A man is a lion in his own cause —Anon., Scottish Proverb

3. Socrates: Don't wrap your mind for ever round yourself —Aristophanes, *The Clouds*

Aristophanes compares the mind's inward turning to a cloak.

4. My first obligation would be to make a happy man of Nathaniel Chisholm . . . that was the only garden that I could hope to cultivate with any real chance of success —Louis Auchincloss, "The Epicurean," *Three Lives*

The novella's protagonist becomes what the title has promised.

5. [One] whose own mind is an abject slave to his own greatness —Henry Fielding, *The Life of Mr. Jonathan Wild the Great*

6. Perhaps her memories of their love affair had been dyed by the color of her love for herself, had even been transformed — Kawabata Yasunari, *Beauty and Sadness*

7. Some saints have called them [fleas, bugs, and lice] "pearls of God," but what these men delighted in was the opportunity of displaying their own sanctity —Bertrand Russell, "The Good Life"

8. Norfolk: Out of his self-drawing web, a' gives us note [he tells us] / The force of his own merit makes his way —William Shakespeare, *The Life of King Henry the Eighth*, Act 1, scene 1, line 62

The web extends the metaphor of the cardinal (the spider) who creates his own greatness just as a spider weaving a web.

9. But thou contracted to thine own bright eyes, / Feed'st thy light's flame with self-substantial fuel —William Shakespeare, "Sonnet 1," line 4

The poet chides the lover for being self-centered.

10. Unthrifty loveliness, why dost thou spend / Upon thyself thy beauty's legacy? — William Shakespeare, "Sonnet 4," line 1

It is sometimes conjectured that Shakespeare had a legal background because he frequently used metaphors of leases, legacies, and jurisprudence.

■ EGO/ID

See also: AWARENESS/UNAWARENESS;
CONSCIOUSNESS; DESIRE; PERSONALI-
TY PROFILES; SELF-IMAGES

1. It is the old game of hammer and anvil: Between them the patient iron is forged into an indestructible whole, an individual —Marcia Sinetar, "Using Our Flaws and Faults"
   The "game" is the contention between conscious and unconscious.

2. Beneath this voice, flowing more sweetly, was the story . . . And beneath this was an animal, a dog living in me, shaking itself, jumping, barking, attacking —Jane Smiley, *A Thousand Acres*
   The narrator separates the animal from the self, presenting a metaphoric picture of an ego and an id that have obviously not learned to coexist.

3. It comes to this: / That the guerilla I should be booked / And bound —Wallace Stevens, "Prelude to Objects"
   "One is always seeing and feeling oneself," one need not "go to the Louvre to behold himself," writes Stevens elsewhere in the poem, knowing that each "I" is the guerrilla of the id.

4. Everyone is a moon and has a dark side which he never shows to anybody — Mark Twain, *Mark Twain's Notebooks and Journals*

5. In herself she discerned for the first time instincts and desires, which, mute and unmarked, had gone to and fro in the dim passages of her mind, and now hailed each other with a cry of mutiny —Edith Wharton, *The Reef*
   Three metaphors—muteness, passageways and mutiny—describe Anna Leath's struggle with her impulses her sense that "her body and soul divided against themselves.

■ ELATION

See: JOY

■ ELOQUENCE

See also: PERSUASIVENESS/PERSUADERS

1. Gov. Mario M. Cuomo is planning to publish a book . . . that will include some highlights of Mr. Cuomo's years as a silver-tongued orator —Jerry Grey, "Political Notes," *The New York Times*, February 14, 1993
   The headline took advantage of the metaphor as follows: "A Collection of Cuomo's Speeches to Mine his Silver Tongue."

2. Eloquence is the painting of thought —Blaise Pascal, *Pensée*, XXIV

3. Prince: His industry is up-stairs and downstairs, his eloquence the parcel of a reckoning —William Shakespeare, *The First Part of King Henry the Fourth*, Act 2, scene 4, line 102
   A "parcel of a reckoning" is an item on a bill.

■ EMBELLISHMENT

See: BEAUTY

■ EMBRACES

See also: AFFECTION; KISSES; PASSION

1. underneath / the bridge of our arms shall go / . . . the river's flow —Guillaume Apollinaire, "Mirabeau Bridge"
   "All love goes by as water to the sea," writes Apollinaire.

2. I had been starved of the coarse, invigorating bread of physical contact [such as a kiss or a hug] —Colette, "Bella Vista"

3. Your arms a garland around my neck entwined —Gabriela Mistral, "Poem of the Son"
   The Chilean poetess was awarded the Nobel Prize for literature in 1945.

4. I am lost in you, wrapped in the folds of your caresses —Rabindranath Tagore, "The Gardener, 47"

5. He thought she had come to be nearer to him, and circled her body with a loving, turning snake of an arm —Dame Rebecca West, *The Thinking Reed*

■ EMINENCE

See: FAME

■ EMOTIONS

See also: DESPAIR; FEELINGS; GRIEF; GUILT; JOY; PASSION; SORROW; WORRY

1. A great block of ice settled in my belly . . . It was a special kind of ice. It kept melting, sending trickles of ice water all up and down my veins —James Baldwin, "Sonny's Blues"

2. The tide that had been sweeping in so strongly had begun to ebb —Dorothy Canfield, "Murder on Jefferson Street"
   The tide, a much-used metaphor, in this case refers to feelings of discontent and hate for a more successful brother.

3. So operatic are the emotions expressed that readers had best limit themselves to a few chapters at a time —Joel Conarroe, *The New York Times Book Review*, May 17, 1992
   The emotion-draining novel was Edna O'Brien's Time and Tide.

4. Melancholy and remorse form the deep laden keel which enables us to sail into the wind of reality —Cyril Connolly, *The Unquiet Grave*
   The metaphor is extended with "we run around sooner than the flat-bottomed pleasure-lovers, but we venture out in weather that would sink them.

5. Your reason and your passion are the rudder and sails of your seafaring soul — Kahlil Gibran, *The Prophet*

6. The crescent of nerves described itself / in the ordinary curve of bliss —Donald Hall, "Shrubs Burnt Away"

7. I view it all with sorrow, of course, but if one is to produce he cannot be a prisoner of his emotions —Nizar Hamdoon, Quoted in *The New York Times*, January 17, 1993
   Iraq's U.N. delegate was commenting on the crisis in the Gulf.

8. Tess Durbeyfield at this time of her life was a mere vessel of emotion untinctured by experience —Thomas Hardy, *Tess of the D'Urbervilles*

9. Clay lies still, but blood's a rover —A. E. Housman, "Reveille," *Shropshire Lad*

10. Mother's mountains and valleys had been stretched by some hand, maybe her own, into one long thin line —Barbara Hudson, *Apalachee Quarterly*, 1990

11. Emotional life in animals is essentially a patchwork —Julian Huxley, "What Do We Know about Love?"
    Animals lack man's capacity to coordinate their emotions, according to Huxley.

12. One way or the other, the emotion was always flowing. There were hardly any intervals of comfortably slack water. The tide was always running —Aldous Huxley, *Point Counter Point*
    The metaphor depicts a character whose moods swing from loving to hostile. To use a common metaphor, "he was an emotional see-sawer."

13. She was an indentured servant of the emotion —Alfred Kazin, *Starting Out in the Thirties*
    The woman thus portrayed is Kazin's mother and the emotion that imprisons her is an ever-present sense of powerlessness.

14. Was that how she was to pour herself out, in a little dribble when she felt herself to be a great wave? —Susan Minot, *Folly*
    The author devotes a whole paragraph to the image of emotions as narrow streams, wide oceans, floods. The young woman who tries to contain the rush of emotion is often "amazed by the amount of feeling sloshing about inside her" thinking that if she let it out "there would be a terrible flood—

eddies in the parlor and waterfalls down the narrow stairs."

15. Worry and doom and guilt are veils / that may as well be vaults the way they don't budge / even for optimism —Thylias Moss, "When I Was 'Bout Ten We Didn't Play Baseball," Op-Ed, *The New York Times,* June 20, 1992
  The poem appeared on a day devoted to the arrival of summer.

16. Without the least warning, a blue sea-wave swelled under my heart —Vladimir Nabokov, *Lolita*
  Humbert Humbert thus reacts to his first encounter with the nymphet Lolita.

17. There are chords in the hearts of the most reckless which cannot be touched without emotion —Edgar Allan Poe, "The Masque of the Red Death"
  A more common version of this metaphor is to pluck on someone's heartstrings.

18. Guiderius: Grief and patience, rooted in him both, / Mingle their spurs [roots] together —William Shakespeare, *Cymbeline,* Act 4, scene 2, line 57
  Arviragus picks up on the metaphor with "Grow, patience! / And let the stinking-elder, grief, untwine / His perishing root with the increasing vine.

19. The pressure of various conflicting emotions . . . had brought her to the brink of an abyss: and as she peered over it, she saw no abyss but only a void . . . a shapeless chaos —Ivan Turgenev, *Fathers and Sons*

20. I adore strong feeling having myself a heart that paints exquisitely but only in water colours —Dame Rebecca West, *There Is No Conversation*

21. She often felt she was nothing but a sponge sopped full of human emotions —Virginia Woolf, *To the Lighthouse*

22. A rain of tears, a cloud of dark disdain —Sir Thomas Wyatt, the Elder, "My Galley"

■ EMPATHY

See: KINDNESS/UNKINDNESS; PITY; SYMPATHY; UNDERSTANDING/MISUNDERSTANDING

■ ENCOURAGEMENT

See also: CRITICISM/CRITICS; PROMISES

1. The generous critic fanned the poet's fire —Alexander Pope, "Essay on Criticism"
  Fanning those poetic fires, according to Pope also "taught the world with reason to admire."

2. Joseph Surface: To smile at the jest which plants a thorn in another's breast is to become a principal in the mischief —Richard Brinsley Sheridan, *The School for Scandal,* Act 1, scene 1

3. The behind-the-sewing-machine "Angels" [of a decade or so ago] . . . were fashion's farmers—seeding, nurturing and cultivating young designers —Stephanie Strom, "Designer Fashion's New Frugality," *The New York Times,* May 3, 1993
  After linking the fashion industry to the theater and farming the writer points out that designers today have no "farmers" to give them the backing enjoyed by designers like Oscar de la Renta and Calvin Klein.

■ ENDINGS

See also: DEATH; ENTRANCES/EXITS

1. The sun of my political life sets in the deepest gloom —John Quincy Adams
  Adams, recently defeated by Andrew Jackson, drew on a popular metaphor for the endings.

2. Plug is pulled on Heathkits —Anon., Headline in *The New York Times,* March 30, 1992
  This medical metaphor referred to the demise of the famous do-it-yourself kits.

3. I have come back / To drink the stale cup of repose —Joseph Auslander, "Ulysses in Autumn"

The title of the poem is itself a metaphor for the "autumn" in the life of Ulysses, when the fabled adventurer still hears the songs of the sirens in his head while he is forced to plough his fields. Compare this with Tennyson's handling of the same subject.

4. In your twilight years, having hung up your gloves (or sheathed your knife), you don't want to keep doing what you did throughout your life —Saul Bellow, *The Bellarosa Connection*

Bellow uses three metaphors to depict a man facing his later years. A more aggressive boxing image often crops up during political campaigns when candidates take off their gloves when a political contest reaches the countdown stage.

5. Was it likely that under the stimulus and joy of his return I would suddenly bank my fires? —Agnes DeMille, "The Milk of Paradise"

DeMille wonders whether she will quit the theater when her husband returns after a long separation.

6. Their death was not meaningless. It was a stone which in time will be the foundation of the Church —Shusaku Endo, *Silence*

A priest muses on the persecution of two peasant converts.

7. It was the closing act of South Africa's lengthy drama of tyranny, fear, bloodshed and death. Mrs. Mandela, the champion of liberation, is headed toward the wings —Emma Gilbey, *The New York Times*, April 14, 1992

The theatrical metaphor introduced an article about the marital separation of Nelson and Winnie Mandela.

8. The sun sets in you [America] —D. H. Lawrence, "The Evening Land"

The image is metaphorically underlined as follows: "Are you the grave of our day?"

9. *Girl Interrupted* . . . is Turtle Bay's swan song [after being discontinued by its parent company, Random House] —Sarah Lyall, "Book Notes," *The New York Times*, June 30, 1993

The blurb writer drew attention to the fact that the book of the discontinued branch of Random House was a surprise success with "A swan song, but still floating."

10. King: My worldly business makes a period —William Shakespeare, *The Second Part of King Henry the Fourth*, Act 4, scene 5, line 229

11. Richard: Now is the winter of our discontent / Made glorious summer by this sun of York —William Shakespeare, *The Tragedy of King Richard the Third*, Act 1, scene 1, line 1

"And all the clouds that lour'd upon our house / In the deep bosom of the ocean buried," continues Richard.

12. Lady Teazle: No more in vice or error to engage / Or play the fool at large on Life's great stage —Richard Brinsley Sheridan, Epilogue *The School for Scandal*

The play concludes with a still common metaphor, based on the idea that all the world's a stage and we are but players on it.

13. After 35 years as king of the art jungle, Leo Castelli may be nearing the end of his reign —Paul Taylor, *The New York Times*, February 16, 1992

The article details the reason Castelli's three art galleries have in recent years been "hemorrhaging artists" and been overshadowed by others.

14. How dull it is to pause, to make an end, / To rust unburnished, not to shine in use, / As though to breathe were life! —Lord Alfred Tennyson, *Ulysses*

15. Your father is a good-natured old boy, but he's a back number. He's sung his swan song —Ivan Turgenev, *Fathers and Sons*

There is a persistent myth that swans are always silent, but that they die singing.

16. It has been said that she died in harness. That expression of a plodder overtaken by death is inadequate for so gallant, so defiantly twinkling an exit. She was a boat that went to the bottom with its orchestra playing gaily —Alexander Woollcott, "Bernhardt"

Woollcott was adept at giving the familiar metaphor a uniquely "Woollcottian" twist.

ENDURANCE

See also: PERMANENCE/IMPERMANENCE

1. I hope my determination will remain firm to endure until it pleases the inexorable Parcae to break the thread —Ludwig Van Beethoven, Letter to his brothers Karl and Johann, 1802

   The notion of life as a thread that would be cut by the Fates dates back to ancient Greek mythology.

2. With a flick of the wrist I fashioned an invisible rope, / And climbed it and it held me —Czeslaw Milosz, "A Magic Mountain"

   "Endurance comes from casting invisible ropes strong enough to hold up the spirit when reality overwhelms and only imagination can save," writes this poet of protest.

3. Neighbor: To be permitted to suffer unjustly, that's a grace and a trial out of which steadfast souls bring home golden fruits —August Strindberg, *Advent,* Act 1

ENEMIES

1. You don't get enemies for nothing. You pay for them. —Anon., Yiddish Proverb

2. Seti: You have at least / Hands less calloused with enemies —Christopher Fry, *The Firstborn,* Act 3, scene 2

   Seti seemingly prepares to abdicate his throne to his son, though he has no intention of yielding the power.

3. King Edward: Brave followers, yonder stands the thorny wood, / Which, by the heavens' assistance and your strength, / Must by the roots be hewn up yet ere night —William Shakespeare, *The Third Part of Henry the Sixth,* Act 5, scene 4, line 66

ENERGY

See also: ANIMATION; POWER

1. He was the spark plug as well as the transmission of the machine —Anon., Quoted in Ralph Martin's dual biography, *Henry and Clare,* 1991

   The "machine" is the magazine Time; *the spark plug, Henry Luce.*

2. My energy [if healthy] would lift the roof off —W. N. P. Barbellion, Diary entry, January 22, 1913

   To lift the roof or to blow the roof off are fairly common metaphors for an explosion of the status quo.

3. Mr.[Bill] Clinton's campaign organization was ... a high-octane 24-hour-a-day war room —Thomas L. Friedman, *The New York Times,* November 11, 1992

4. [Seji] Ozawa was in rare form ... he ran on 12 cylinders —Andrew L. Pincus, "Classical Review," *The Berkshire Eagle,* July 20, 1993

5. *Ain't Broadway Grand* ... recounts the efforts of the piston-driven impresario Mike Todd to rise above his reputation as a purveyor of leggy, low-comedy musicals —David Richards, "Sunday Review," *The New York Times,* May 2, 1993

   The energy of the show's subject unfortunately did not translate to the show which sputtered to a quick closing.

6. I explode with energy ... my mind swarms with the rarest of ideas —Irvin D. Yalom, *When Nietzsche Wept*

   A fictional Nietzsche describes his mental state after one of his migraine attacks with two graphic metaphorical verbs.

ENGLAND

See: COUNTRIES, MISC.

ENJOYMENT

See: PLEASURE

ENNUI

See: DULLNESS

ENTANGLEMENTS

See also: PEOPLE, INTERACTION

1. The snares of the world were its ways of sin —James Joyce, *Portrait of the Artist as a Young Man*

   The soul was the quarry caught in sin's traps.

2. What I secretly longed for was to disentangle myself of all those lives which had woven themselves into the pattern of my own life and were making my destiny a part of theirs —Henry Miller, "The Creative Life"

   "Now and then I lunged and tore at the net, but only to become more enmeshed," Miller continues.

3. Cleopatra: this knot intrinsicate [intricate] / Of life at once untie —William Shakespeare, *Antony and Cleopatra*, Act 5, scene 2, line 311

   In everyday usage a knot that's difficult to untie has become a metaphor for any situation from which we want to be free.

4. Prospero: mine enemies are all knit up in their distraction —William Shakespeare, *The Tempest,* Act 3, scene 3, line 89

5. This *was* business, as he understood it; his father's life was a labyrinth of such underground arrangements —Edith Wharton, *Hudson River Bracketed*

   The reference is to deals, transactions, and compromises in business.

6. Here he was, at the very moment of his betrothal . . . pitchforked into a coil of scandal —Edith Wharton, *The Age of Innocence*

   Archer, a very proper lawyer, has been drawn into the effort to dissuade his fiancee's cousin from a divorce suit. But the real threat to his equilibrium will come from his growing attraction to the lady.

7. Tangled I was in love's snare —Sir Thomas Wyatt the Elder, "Tangled I Was in Love's Snare"

ENTHUSIASM

See: ZEAL

ENTRANCES/EXITS

See also: ENDINGS; POLITICS/POLITICIANS

1. Harrison [President William Henry] comes in upon a hurricane, God grant that he may not go out upon a wreck —John Quincy Adams, 1841.

   More people voted William Henry Harrison into office than ever before. The potential wreck Adams' foresaw came all too quickly since he did not survive the pneumonia contracted during his inaugural address.

2. And two centuries of aesthetic philosophy go sailing out the window —David Lehman, *Signs of the Times*: Deconstruction and the Fall of Paul de Man

   Lehman notes that literature itself may be devalued, and a work of Dickens have no more value to some deconstructionists than an episode of All In The Family, *a concept that Lehman calls "the leveling of literature to the status of soap opera."*

3. The closing of a door is irrevocable. It snaps the packthread of the heart —Christopher Morley, "On Doors"

4. My hat is in the ring —Theodore Roosevelt, Announcement of his presidential candidacy, February 21, 1912

   This phrase has been taken up by many entering any sort of competitive situation. One of the most original twists is attributed to a 1968 New York Times *report that movie moppet-turned politician, Shirley Temple Black, "threw her curls in the ring." [saved for posterity in* Safire's Political Dictionary*].*

ENTRAPMENT

See also: MANIPULATION; MASTERY/SUBORDINATION; PEOPLE, INTERACTION

1. Can I be so ill that you talk to me of wills and confession? . . . How will I ever get out of this labyrinth? —Simon Bolivar, Quoted in Gabriel García Márquez's *The General in his Labyrinth*

   Márquez quotes Simon Bolivar in his chronology of the life of The Liberator, and takes the meta-

phor, spoken just a few days before Bolivar's death, as the title of his book.

2. He was caught in a skin that had gotten too tight —Jan Brenning McNamara, "Most Likely to Succeed," quoted *The New York Times Magazine,* by Alessandra Stanley, November 22, 1992

The emotionally discomfited young man was Frank Aller, President Bill Clinton's roommate at Oxford who committed suicide.

3. Truman [Capote] is seated between Mary [McCarthy] and Bowden [Broadwater] and, I expect, caught in the sort of Nick and Nora crossfire they tend to indulge in when they have an audience —John Malcolm Brinnin, Journal entry, October 6, 1947

The metaphor gains color through the allusion to the popular husband and wife detective team played in the movies by Myrna Loy and William Powell.

4. For too long the young of the Middle East have been caught in a web of hatred not of their own making —Bill Clinton, Statement at the signing of the Middle East Pact, September 13, 1993

5. Lockit: The Bird that hath been trapt, / When he hears his calling Mate, / To her he flies, again he's clapt / Within the wiry Grate. Peachum: But what signifies catching the Bird, if your Daughter Lucy will set open the Door of the Cage? —John Gay, *The Beggar's Opera,* Act 3, scene 5

In this satire of political and social immorality, men are rogues and their daughters are dupes used as bait. The two men are trying to lure Macheath back to Newgate Prison so they can hang him.

6. If it [the Clinton administration] relies on cold war thinking and does not develop a new strategic vision, President Clinton may be mousetrapped by a crisis—say, Japan's withdrawal of advanced technology from our military projects —Chalmers Johnson, *The New York Times,* February 8, 1993

By turning the noun "mousetrap" into a verb, Mr. Johnson added a sense of urgency to his metaphor.

7. She had tripped into the meadow to teach the lambs a pretty educational dance and found the lambs were wolves. There was no way out between their pressing gray shoulders. She was surrounded by fangs and sneering eyes —Sinclair Lewis, *Main Street*

Later in the novel Carol Kennicott reaffirms her resolve to awaken the narrow-minded town, and with a variation of the above metaphor: "What if they were wolves instead of lambs? They'd eat her all the sooner if she was meek to them. Fight them or be eaten."

8. I'm not a humming-bird. I'm a hawk; a tiny leashed hawk, pecked to death by these large, white, flabby, wormy hens — Sinclair Lewis, *Main Street*

Carol tells her only friend in town that she plans to buckle down and be dull, a plan he compares to "blood on the wings of a humming-bird."

9. Aethelwold: a grim and iron God, / . . . Hath set this lime, / Wherein with besmearèd feet and feathers / I flutter and beat —Edna St. Vincent Millay, *The King's Henchman,* Act 2

Birds were snared with lime, which caught their feet in a sticky substance. Although the date of the actual play is 1927, there are deliberate archaisms because the action of the play takes place in the tenth century.

10. The only way to stop German industry from taking over its competitors, the French had long been told, was to enmesh that Gulliver in a web of Lilliputian bureaucracy—a form of unaccountable control in which France is pre-eminent —William Safire, "Essay," *The New York Times,* September, 21, 1992

The metaphor contains an allusion to Jonathan Swift's Gulliver, a giant compared to his opponents who tied him down while he slept.

11. Canterbury: For once the eagle England being in prey, / To her unguarded nest the weasel Scot / Comes sneaking, and so sucks her princely eggs, / Playing the mouse in absence of the cat, / To tame and havoc more than she can eat —William Shakespeare, *The Life of Henry the Fifth*, Act 1, scene 2, line 169

> *An elaborate metaphor built on the proverbially elaborate entrapment of the mouse by the cat—on which Exeter comments "It follows then the cat must stay at home"*

12. Ursula: She's limed, I warrant you. We have caught her, madam —William Shakespeare, *Much Ado About Nothing*, Act 3, scene 1, line 103

> *Ursala compares Beatrice to a bird that has been snared with birdlime, a sticky substance used to trap small birds.*

13. Falstaff: they would whip me with their fine wits till I were as crest-fallen as a dried pear —William Shakespeare, *The Merry Wives of Windsor*, Act 4, scene 5, line 102

> *The metaphor is followed by a simile.*

14. The questions of the driver had the tone of a subtle examination. He seemed to spread nets, to set traps with his questions —John Steinbeck, *The Grapes of Wrath*

> *This cross-examination occurs when Tom Joad hitches a ride to take him home after four years in prison.*

■ ENVIRONMENT

See: ECOLOGY

■ ENVY

See also: JEALOUSY; COMPETITION/ COMPETITORS

1. The poison of the Snake & Newt / Is the sweat of Envy's Foot —William Blake, "Auguries of Innocence"

2. Then, as I watched you, Don Jeronimo, a gap of hunger opened in me —Jose Donoso, *The Obscene Bird of Night*

3. Envy is the tax which all distinction must pay —Ralph Waldo Emerson, *Journals*

4. David Mamet understands that envy is the gasoline on which a competitive society runs —John Lahr, "Dogma Days," *The New Yorker*, November 16, 1992

> *The play that demonstrated Mamet's astuteness was* Oleanna.

5. Larry knows Bob wants to piss up his tree —Jane Smiley, *A Thousand Acres*

> *The reference is to a dog marking his property to warn off intruders. A contender simply has to urinate higher up on the tree.*

6. He is still slipping on the skins of sour grapes —Dorrie Weiss

> *A twist on a common metaphor, this was said in response to a snide speech by a defeated presidential candidate.*

■ EPITAPHS

1. Thus, for our guilt, this jewel have we lost; / The earth his bones, the heaven possess his ghost —Henry Howard (Earl of Surrey), "Epitaph on Sir Thomas Wyatt"

> *Surrey makes Wyatt's death seem like religious expiation for the survivors.*

2. A hand that taught what may be said in rhyme, / That reft [robbed] Chaucer the glory of his wit— —Henry Howard, Earl of Surrey, "Epitaph on Sir Thomas Wyatt"

> *This was high praise indeed for Wyatt, since Chaucer was considered to be the greatest poet in the English language at that time.*

3. Here lies one whose name was writ in water —John Keats, Epitaph

> *The epitaph was dictated by the poet for his own monument. In* The Life of King Henry the Eighth *this reads "Men's evil manners live in brass; their virtues / We writ in water."*

4. His [Abraham Lincoln's] grave a nation's heart shall be, / His monument a people free! —Caroline Mason, "President Lincoln's Grave"

5. The sun that has warmed and brightened our lives has set, and we shiver in the cold and dark. —Jawaharlal Nehru, Eulogy for Indira Priyadorshini Nehru Ghandi, February 2, 1984

> "The light has gone out of our lives and there is darkness everywhere," said Nehru, adding that it was a light that would inspire eternally.

6. This model mother, sister, wife, / believed, through all her joys and woes, / that life is death, and death is life— / And now she knows —Kathleen Norris, Her own epitaph, *Vanity Fair*, 1925

> One might say that Mrs. Norris' used a mirror-metaphor. *for her epitaph.*

■ EPITHETS

See: BOASTERS/BOASTFULNESS

■ EQUALITY

See: BARRIERS

■ EQUANIMITY

See: CALMNESS/VOLATILITY

■ ERRORS

See: MISTAKES

■ ESCAPE

See also: EVASIVENESS; FREEDOM/RESTRAINT

1. I am escaped with the skin of my teeth —The Bible, *O.T., Job 19:20*

> In Thornton Wilder's play The Skin of our Teeth, *George Antrobus and his family endure the travails and temptations of centuries, surviving them all 'by the skin of their teeth.'*

2. As I flee . . . the pursued marionette dancing like a hallucination in the red lights that snap at his calves as he runs —Jose Donoso, *The Obscene Bird of Night*

> Two metaphors sandwich a simile here.

3. I wouldn't have married Stephen Halifax had he been the last exit open to me —Margaret Drabble, *A Summer Bird-Cage*

> The protagonist feels trapped in her unfocused, post-graduate existence. The title, itself a metaphor, comes from seventeenth-century playwright John Webster's line "'tis just like a summer bird cage in a garden, the birds that are without despair to get in, and the birds that are within despair and are in consumption for fear they shall not get out."

4. From that bedlam he had fled . . . But he had jumped out of the frying pan into the fire —Boris Pasternak, *Doctor Zhivago*

> The earliest use of this common metaphor is attributed to Sir Thomas More in 1528: "Lepe they lyke a flounder out of a frying-panne into the fyre."

5. Republicans running for office are increasingly preoccupied with escaping the undertow of the sinking Bush presidency —George Will, *The Washington Post Syndicate*, July 19, 1992

> Wills used a double seafaring metaphor to suggest that the President should not run for office again.

6. I would that we were, my beloved, white birds on the foam of the sea! —William Butler Yeats, "The White Birds"

> The poet longs for escape from sorrow and weariness.

■ ESSENCE

1. The foundation-stone of this work [of the United Nations] is and must remain the State —Boutros Boutros-Ghali, *Report on the Work of the Organization*, United Nations, 1992

> Boutros-Ghali treats the work of the U.N. in architectural terms, and notes the concern of the Charter for the maintenance of national sovereignty.

2. He [Clint Eastwood in *In the Line of Fire*] is the movie's spine —Vincent Canby, "Review/Film," *The New York Times*, July 9, 1993

3. The rafters of my body, bone / Being still with you, the Muscle, Sinew and Veine, / Which tile this house, will come againe — John Donne, "A Valediction: Of My Name in the Window"

    The lover is at one with his beloved, since she keeps the essential framework of his self (the rafters) when he leaves, while he takes only the facade (the tile) away with him.

4. In his address to parliament, he [Dingiri Banda Wijetunga, president of Sri Lanka] pointed to the violence that many people here believe has insinuated itself into the very marrow of this society —Edward A. Gargan, *The New York Times,* May, 9, 1993

    The more frequent metaphor lies at the heart of an issue, so that marrow makes for a less-hackneyed trope.

5. This is the buckle of the Bible Belt —Ann Hamilton, Quoted in "Book Notes," *The New York Times,* February 3, 1993

    The executive director of the Oklahoma Center for the Book explained why she did not approve a lesbian speaker for a workshop.

6. "The vital nerve of the problem of pauperism," Nikolaeivich read from the revised manuscript —Boris Pasternak, *Doctor Zhivago*

    "Essence would be better, I think," said Ivan Ivanovich—and his prosaic correction immediately destroyed the metaphor.

Actually, Burlingame changes a simile and provides us with a new metaphor.

2. Suggestions like this typify a spreading corrosion in college finance and personal ethics —Claire L. Gaudiani, *The New York Times,* August 26, 1992

    The article was headlined "Dirty Tricks for Scholarships."

3. [She] had in her time plunged through countless ethical hedges and ditches, without apparent discomfiture to her muslin —George Meredith, *The Ordeal of Richard Feverel*

4. President-elect Clinton wanted his new ethics rules to shut the revolving door between government service and special-interest lobbying —Asra Q. Nomani, *The Wall Street Journal,* December 23, 1992

5. What am I, a spiritual gigolo? —Theodore Roethke, *Straw for the Fire, Notebooks of Theodore Roethke*

6. And maiden virtue rudely strumpeted — William Shakespeare, "Sonnet 66," line 6

    This is an image of corruption, of virtue prostituted.

7. But where bread is short ideals are bread —Yevgeny Yevtushenko, *A Precocious Autobiography*

    ". . . to those who suffer real deprivation an ideal is a first necessity of life," writes Yevtushenko.

∎ ETERNITY
See: IMMORTALITY

∎ ETHICS
See also: CORRUPTION; VICE/VIRTUE

1. As to the unreasoned dicta about right and wrong, these established a code like the multiplication table . . . Yet it may also, to change the metaphor, be a springboard from which to take off —Roger Burlingame, "The Analyst's Couch and the Creative Mind"

∎ ETIQUETTE
See: MANNERS; TACT

∎ EUPHEMISMS
See: LANGUAGE

∎ EVASIVENESS
See also: ESCAPE

1. The teflon Don is gone and the Don is covered with velcro —Jim Fox, Assistant Director, FBI, quoted April 2, 1992

Crime boss John Gotti, to whom no charge seemed to stick, was finally convicted. The teflon metaphor was often applied to Ronald Reagan, often tagged as "the teflon President."

2. Van Buren rowed to his object with muffled oars —John Randolph, of Roanoke, Virginia, during Van Buren's one-term presidency (1837–41)

   The Virginia governor was not alone in his criticism of President Martin Van Buren's political evasiveness, which briefly added a new adjective to the language—"van-burenish"—to describe a waffler.

3. Agamemnon: But his evasion, wing'd thus swift with scorn, / Cannot outfly our apprehension —William Shakespeare, *Troilus and Cressida*, Act 2, scene 3, line 118

■ EVENING

See also: DAWN; MORNING; NIGHT AND DAY

1. Evening wrapped about me the quickening moisture of its twilight sheets; evening laid a mother's hand upon my burning forehead —Isaac Babel, "My First Goose," *Red Cavalry*

2. Six o'clock. / The burnt-out ends of smoky days —T. S. Eliot, "Two Preludes"

3. Peter: The free and evening air / Swans from hill to hill —Christopher Fry, *A Sleep of Prisoners*

   Fry creates his metaphor by changing a noun to a verb.

4. Day hath put on his jacket, and around / his burning bosom buttoned it with stars —Oliver Wendell Holmes, Sr., "Evening"

   Several lines later, the poet added this metaphor about Nature's changing of the guards: "how lovely is the golden braid, / That binds the skirt of night's descending robe!"

5. Evening soon came with its black veil — Natsume Soseki, *Botchan*

   The black veil is a fairly common image for night or its approach.

6. Lieutenant: The gaudy, blabbing, and remorseful day / Is crept into the bosom of the sea —William Shakespeare, *The Second Part of Henry the Sixth*, Act 4, scene 1, line 1

7. The body dies; the body's beauty lives. / So evenings die, in their green going, / A wave interminably flowing —Wallace Stevens, "Peter Quince at the Clavier"

8. And evening trails her robes of gold / Through the dim halls of the night — Sarah Power Whitman, "Summer's Call"

■ EVIL

See also: CORRUPTION; GOOD/EVIL; GREED; TREACHERY; VILLAINY/VILLAINS

1. Evil is unspectacular and always human, / And shares our bed and eats at our table —W. H. Auden, "Herman Melville"

   This example of personification as metaphor was featured in the Williamstown Playhouse program notes for a new play, 2, by Romulus Linney about the second-in-command Nazi Hermann Goering. A local reviewer used it as his lead.

2. Take us . . . the little foxes, that spoil the vines; for our vines have tender grapes — The Bible, *O.T.*, *Song of Solomon 7:4*

   Lillian Hellman used the metaphor as the title of her play, The Little Foxes, *which depicts a nasty family of spoilers. The title was also used for an 1865 novel by Harriett Beecher Stowe who meant it as a metaphor for "the unsuspected, unwatched, insignificant* little *causes that nibble away domestic happiness."*

3. O generation of vipers, who hath warned you to flee from the wrath to come? — The Bible, *N.T.*, *Matthew 3:7*; *Luke 3:7*

   In 1942, Philip Wylie used this as the title for his scathing commentary on modern society.

4. Miriam: Take evil by the tail / And you find you are holding good head-downwards —Christopher Fry, *The Firstborn*, Act 3, scene 1

5. The sky . . . lost its color of blue when Dr. Mengele painted it weeping gray. The fire leaping toward the heavens was kept aglow with the bodies of our mothers, our children —Isabella Leitner, *Saving the Fragments: From Auschwitz to New York*

6. Well, savagery and greed have been the tongues / We've spoken since the beginning —James Merrill, "Self-Portrait in Tyvek (TM) Windbreaker," *The New Yorker*, February 24, 1992

   The metaphor purports to deal with language: it actually is a condemnation of man's basic nature.

7. Adultery, blackmail and usury are mother's milk to the titled inhabitants of Belgravia [in London] —Herbert Mitgang, "Books of The Times," *The New York Times*, June 12, 1992

   The book being reviewed was Belgrave Square by Anne Perry.

8. Perhaps even now the sirens, / the bells pealing their salute to the monsters in the night / of their hellish Halloween — Eugenio Montale, "Hitler Spring"

   Montale offers a picture of devastation and death in this poem, but also a hope for a "Dawn which will shine tomorrow for us all" after the Nazi terror, after the sound of the sirens ends.

9. Sicinius: [Coriolanus] He's a disease that must be cut away —William Shakespeare, *Coriolanus*, Act 3, scene 1, line 293

   Menenius counters by urging less drastic action, stating that Coriolanus is "a limb that has but a disease; / Mortal to cut it off; to cure it easy."

10. Brutus: Pursue him to his house, and pluck him thence; / Lest his infection, being of catching nature, / Spread further —William Shakespeare, *Coriolanus*, Act 3, scene 1, line 307

    The metaphor of Coriolanus as a spreading disease is designed to incite an already anti-Coriolanus crowd to murder. It reiterates an earlier cry for drastic action: "Where the disease is violent. Lay hands upon him, / And bear him to the rock," (3, 1, 220).

11. Menenius: This Martius has grown from a man to a dragon; he has wings; he's more than a creeping thing —William Shakespeare, *Coriolanus*, Act 5, scene 4, line 14

12. Gardiner: he is a pestilence that does infect the land —William Shakespeare, *The Life of King Henry the Eighth*, Act 5, scene 1, line 44

    The metaphor of infectious disease for evil men appears throughout Shakespeare's plays. Coriolanus is called an infectious disease and, after he becomes disillusioned, declares himself to be "no more infected with my country's love." In Hamlet, the melancholy Dane refers to rank corruption as an unseen infection.

13. King: What rein can hold licentious wickedness / When down the hill he holds his fierce career? —William Shakespeare, *The Life of Henry the Fifth*, Act 3, scene 3, line 22

    The runaway horse is Henry's metaphor for soldiers despoiling their victims.

14. Othello: O thou black weed, why art so lovely fair? —William Shakespeare, *Othello*, Act 4, scene 2, line 68

    The black weed is Desdemona.

15. Queen: His realm a slaughter house . . . / And yonder is the wolf that makes this spoil —William Shakespeare, *The Third Part of Henry the Sixth*, Act 1, scene 4, line 137

16. Titus: Why, there they are both, baked in that pie / Whereof their mother daintily hath fed, / Eating the flesh that she herself hath bred —William Shakespeare, *Titus Andronicus*, Act 5, scene 3, line 60

    With these words Titus stabs the Empress and is in turn killed by Saturnius.

17. Richmond: A base foul stone, made precious by the foil / Of England's chair, where he is falsely set —William Shakespeare, *The Tragedy of King Richard the Third*, Act 5, scene 3, line 251

    The foul stone is Richard.

18. Behind the subdued voice . . . something else, goatish and rank, seemed to prance and toss its swollen neck —Anne Rivers Siddons, *Colony*

19. He poisons life at the well-head —Robert Louis Stevenson, "An Apology for Idlers"
    Poisoning the well *has become a metaphor for any evil intervention at the source. The term is used to designate one form of fallacious reasoning. Here, it is used for anyone who negates life.*

20. This Anderson is a disease —Rex Stout, *Fer-de-Lance*
    Private detective Nero Wolfe's metaphor dates back to Shakespeare who used it in several plays, including Coriolanus and King Lear.

21. Neighbor: The measure of her wickedness has been heaped full and is now overflowing —August Strindberg, *Advent*, Act 1

22. Men . . . must have corrupted nature a little, for they were not born wolves, and they have become wolves —Voltaire, *Candide*

■ EVOLUTION

See: HISTORY

■ EXACTNESS/INEXACTNESS

1. [Wild] told him he had hit the nail on the head —Henry Fielding, *The Life of Mr. Jonathan Wild the Great*
   The metaphoric expression predates the novel by over two hundred years.

2. Many a man strikes with his hammer here and there on the wall, and thinks he hits every time the nail on the head —Johann Wolfgang von Goethe
   Another illustration that a common metaphor such as to hit the nail on the head can always be presented in a writer or speaker's own style.

3. Literalness is the devil's weapon —Theodore Roethke, *Straw for the Fire, Notebooks of Theodore Roethke*

4. The film makers re-create the colonial world with a needlepointer's scrupulosity —Julie Salamon, *The Wall Street Journal*, December 17, 1992
   In her review of the film, Indochine, she also capsulizes a character's more Asian than French sense of identity by referring to them as "a succulent mango, not a crisp apple."

5. He talks about the moon, not about the streets—about the ramparts, not about the houses—about the Germans and the Turks, not about the Jews—about the future, not about the present. He is in love with the recipe, Father, not with the ingredients —A. B. Yehoshua, *Mr. Mani*

■ EXAGGERATION

1. Exaggeration is to paint a snake and add legs —Anon.

2. A tempest in a teapot —Anon.
   This common metaphor for a big to-do over a trifle has evolved from such variants as "storm in a cream bowl!" (17th century) and "storm in a teacup" (19th century).

3. Voynitsky: For twenty-five years he has been reading and writing things that clever men have long known and stupid ones are not interested in; for twenty-five years he has been making his imaginary mountains out of molehills —Anton Chekhov, *Uncle Vanya*, Act 1

4. Millie: Frank—you're making a frightening mountain out of an absurd little molehill. Frank: Of course, but the mountain I'm making in my imagination is so frightening that I'd rather try to forget both it and the repulsive little molehill that gave it birth —Terence Rattigan, *The Browning Version*
   The slang term to make a big deal out of something is a popular variation, as the mountain-molehill metaphor is said to be a variation of to make an elephant out of a fly.

■ EXCELLENCE

See: ACHIEVEMENTS

■ EXCESS

See also: ABUNDANCE; MANY

1. They pumped the magazine full of steroids when they should have been making it leaner —Anon., Former *New Yorker* executive, quoted in *The New York Times*, July 1, 1992

    This appeared in an article about the appointment of Tina Brown as the magazine's new editor. The metaphor referred to the magazine's use of expensive but ineffective promotions to increase circulation.

2. He [Reggie Jackson] was the hot dog that couldn't be covered by all the mustard in the world —Catfish Hunter, Quoted by Roger Angell, *The New Yorker*, August 2, 1993

    The batter said of himself that he was "the straw that stirred the drink."

3. I have made a mountain of debts —Henry James, *Roderick Hudson*

    This is a common metaphor for any tasks or obligations that have exceeded the norm—a mountain of unanswered letters, a mountain of work, etc.

4. In the hailstorm of publicity that surround the film's opening, Ms.[Chambers] Lynch has been trying hard to leap past the lurid to the metaphorical —Janet Maslin, "Review/Film," *The New York Times*, September 3, 1993

    The director of Boxing Helena *wanted audiences to look beyond a doctor's amputation of a lover's limbs to the metaphorical theme of love and obsession.*

5. Drunken Desire must vomit his receipt, / Ere he can see his own abomination — William Shakespeare, *The Rape of Lucrece*, line 703

6. Hostess Quickly: He [Sir John Falstaff] hath eaten me out of house and home — William Shakespeare, *The Second Part of King Henry the Fourth*, Act 2, scene 1, line 82

This common metaphor was popularized but not invented by The Bard. In the play it continues with "he hath put all my substance into that fat belly of his; but I will have some of it out again, or I will ride thee o'nights like the mare."

■ EXCITEMENT

See also: ANIMATION; CALMNESS/VOLATILITY; ENERGY

1. From sly title through breath-stopping climax to funny wrap-up, readers will relish [Elmore] Leonard's latest roller coaster ride [*Pronto*] —Anon., *Publishers Weekly*, August 16, 1993

    The roller coaster is a commonly used metaphor for any very fast-paced and unpredictable action.

2. By this evening, effervescent as an Alka-Seltzer—which will surely be needed in the morning—Washington was a bubbly, carbonated city —Patricia Leigh Brown, *The New York Times*, January 21, 1993

    In linking the image of the city bubbly with presidential inaugural festivities with the effervescence of an Alka-Seltzer, the writer managed to suggest the day-after-reality that inevitably follows the highs of such days.

3. an echo from those days came back to me, / something from the fire of the young life we shared —C. P. Cavafy, "In the Evening"

4. He couldn't sleep; words, ideas, plans, stock quotations kept unrolling in endless tickertape in his head —John Dos Passos, *U.S.A., The 42nd Parallel*

    The big-thinking insomniac is J. Ward Morehouse, Dos Passos' public relations tycoon.

5. Her life was a glittering Christmas tree — Ralph Martin, *Henry & Clare*

    The subject of the metaphor is Clare Boothe Luce.

6. *My Favorite Year* uncorks the intoxicating vintage of 1954 only to send its audience crashing right back into morning-after sobriety of that less-than-favorite year, 1992 —Frank Rich, "Review/Theater," *The New York Times*, December 11, 1992

The much-dreaded critic's closing words were literally and figuratively speaking the "kiss of death" for a just-opened musical at New York's Lincoln Center.

7. Under the flying clouds of her excitement it was no longer a shallow flower cut but a darkening gleaming mirror that might give back strange depth of feeling —Edith Wharton, *The Reef*

    George Dallow seeing a new side of a young lady realizes "The girl had stuff in her."

■ EXCLUSIVITY/NON- EXCLUSIVITY

See: IMPORTANCE/UNIMPORTANCE

■ EXCUSES

See: APOLOGY

■ EXHAUSTION

See: WEARINESS

■ EXISTENCE

See: BEING/BECOMING; FATE; HUMANI- TY/HUMANKIND; LIFE

■ EXITS

See: ENDINGS; ENTRANCES/EXITS

■ EXPECTATIONS

See also: HOPE

1. That talented man just emerging from his chrysalis to breathe in the fragrant air of a rosy future —Jose Donoso, *The Obscene Bird of Night*

2. He had drawn his check on the Bank of Expectation, and it had got to be cashed then and there —Kenneth Grahame, "The Magic Ring"

3. In a sense we have come to our nation's capital to cash a check. When the architects of our republic wrote the magnificent words of the Constitution and the Declaration of Independence, they were signing a promissory note to which every American was to fall heir. This note was a promise that all men would be guaranteed the unalienable rights of life, liberty and the pursuit of happiness —Martin Luther King, Jr., speech to Civil Rights marchers, August 23, 1963

    "America has given the Negro people a bad check; a check which has come back marked 'insufficient funds,'" King continued.

4. Great expectation, wear a train of shame —Sir Philip Sidney, "Sonnet 21," *Astrophel and Stella*

5. Iya Agba: It's my life that's gone into his. I haven't burrowed so deep to cast good earth on worthless seeds —Wole Soyinka, *Madmen and Specialists*, Part 1

    The old women are waiting for Bero to respond to their hopes by returning to his roots, his people.

■ EXPEDIENCY

See: ADVANTAGEOUSNESS

■ EXPERIENCE

See also: BEING/BECOMING; LIFE

1. Experience has already been the prophet of events —Fisher Ames, Speech to the House of Representatives, April 28, 1796

2. Experience is a comb that nature gives to bald men —Anon.

    The image of a comb given to a bald man is also used to describe a useless or futile action.

3. Experience is a good teacher, but she sends in terrific bills —Minna Antrim, *Naked Truth and Veiled Allusions*

    Experience also "has no textbooks or proxies" and "she demands that her pupils answer her roll-call personally."

4. Osmer: I'm not quite a child in this cleft-stick of life —Christopher Fry, *Thor, With Angels*

> *The cleft stick, used to pin down a snake so it can be killed, will fasten on the young speaker. He will be killed by the dark forces of irrationality.*

5. His personal contact with ever-recurrent danger seasons his book with an authentic and inimitable tang —André Gide, "Preface," *Night Flight* by Antoine de Saint-Exupery

6. I have but one lamp by which my feet are guided, and that is the lamp of experience —Patrick Henry, Speech at the Virginia convention, March 23, 1775

> *This is from the fiery orator and statesman famous for "give me liberty or give me death" speech.*

7. It was his own soul going forth to experience, unfolding itself sin by sin, spreading abroad the balefire of its burning stars and folding back upon itself, fading slowly, quenching its own light and fires —James Joyce, *Portrait of the Artist as a Young Man*

> *The image is both confusing and powerful, seeming to picture a flower that enfolds its pistils of burning stars.*

8. Thither he was flying, an Arrow loosened from the bow —George Meredith, *The Ordeal of Richard Feverel*

9. Each venture / Is a new beginning, a raid on the / inarticulate —Frank O'Hara, "East Coker," quoted in "Books," *The New Yorker*, July 19, 1993

10. It is a long baptism into the sea of human-kind, . . . Better immersion than to live untouched —Tillie Olsen, "O Yes"

11. Life, whose sweet and fortifying milk he had not yet completely drained, held out her breast to dissuade him —Marcel Proust, *Pleasures and Regrets*

> *The admonition is against retiring into the desert with a few friends, away from a more active life].*

12. Every day is yesterday's disciple — Publilius Syrus

13. Today is the pupil of yesterday —Publilius Syrus, *Sententiae*

14. Regan: O, sir, to wilful men / The injuries that they themselves procure / Must be their schoolmasters —William Shakespeare, *King Lear*, Act 2, scene 4, line 303

15. All experience is an arch where through / Gleams that untravelled world whose margin fades —Alfred, Lord Tennyson, "Ulysses"

16. I wanted to live deep and suck out all the marrow of life —Henry David Thoreau, *Walden*

17. He had a sense of waste that is the bitterest harvest of experience —Edith Wharton, *The Reef*

> *A young man reflects on a love not fulfilled.*

■ EXPLANATIONS

See: APOLOGY

■ EXPLOITATION

See also: UTILIZATION

1. Roger Clinton [the President's half-brother] . . . is feasting at the buffet of nepotism, grabbing goodies with both hands —Maureen Dowd, *The New York Times*, August 15, 1993

2. He loathed the money sharks who on land, in houses, traded on the courage and endurance and fidelity of ships' masters and crews —Joseph Hergesheimer, "The Token"

> *Exacting excessive interest on money lent is still called "loan sharking."*

3. It is not linen you're wearing out, / But human creature's lives! —Thomas Hood, "The Song of the Shirt" *Punch*, 1843

4. It would seem to me that I was nothing but a pit stop in the middle of a race — Norman Mailer, *Harlot's Ghost*

The "racers" alludes to Frank Sinatra and President Kennedy, who were romantically involved with the protagonist's girl friend.

5. He'd squeezed the lemon dry and there was nothing to do but throw away the rind —W. Somerset Maugham, "Episode"
   The figurative lemon is a woman; the "lemon squeezer" a young man who had wanted her so much that by the time she was ready to marry him he'd "exhausted every emotion she could give him" and was sick to death of her.

6. Then they mean to make a wedge of me, and just put me in for the time being, and then bid me good-bye —Natsume Soseki, *Botchan*
   Botchan exclaims that he knows he is being used, and the teaching position he is being offered is just a temporary one.

7. Hamlet: When he needs what you have gleaned, it is but squeezing you, and, sponge, you shall be dry again —William Shakespeare, *Hamlet*, Act 3, scene 6, line 19
   Hamlet is talking about the fact that Claudius will use Rosencrantz for his own purposes.

8. Without all ornament, itself and true, / Making no summer of another's green — William Shakespeare, "Sonnet 68," line 10
   Fashion allowed the wearing of a dead person's hair to augment one's own; the subject of the poem disdains borrowing such "dead fleece."

9. The rest of mankind is the carving knife and the serving dish, while we are the fish and the meat —Sun Yat-Sen, Lecture on "The Three Principles of the People"

10. I preach the cause of free industry in the United States, for I think they are slowly girding the tree that bears the inestimable fruits of our life, and that if they are permitted to gird it entirely nature will take her revenge and the tree will die — Woodrow Wilson, "The New Freedom"
    Wilson was afraid that the monopolists would stifle competition, and that industry and the economy would suffer.

■ **EXPLORATION**

1. Fra Timoteo: Then comes this devil Ligurio, who made me first dip my finger into mischief, then my arm, and then my whole body —Niccolo Machiavelli, *Mandragola*, Act 4
   Machiavelli seems to mock baptism here. The friar's greed and sophistry will help corrupt a virtuous woman.

2. Delicately they touched their instruments, exploring the magnetic sky, dowsers in quest of hidden gold —Antoine de Saint-Exupery, *Night Flight*
   The operators at an early radio station are trying to contact a 1932 light plane.

■ **EXTRAVAGANCE**

See also: EXCESS; MONEY

1. There was a hole in Mr. Franklin's pocket that nothing would sew up —Wilkie Collins, *The Moonstone*
   We still say of a spendthrift that he has a hole in his pocket.

2. Money . . . flew out of my pocket — Laurie Colwin, "Saint Anthony of the Desert"

3. Let's face it, I have been momentary. / A luxury. A bright red sloop in the harbor — Anne Sexton, "For My Lover, Returning to his Wife"
   After comparing the wife to whom the lover is returning to a monument, the poet concludes "As for me, I am a watercolor. / I wash off."

■ **EXULTATION**

See: JOY

■ **EYEBROWS**

See also: FACES

1. Judge Whinman's eyebrows did a little dance when he saw Samson Honniger come smiling up the aisle again —John Hersey, "Affinities," *Shenandoah*, Vol. 37–2

2. Her long lashes and the two little feathers traced above were most important — Katherine Mansfield, "Je Ne Parle Pas Français"

3. Her eyebrows were black wings made with pencil —Alice Munro, "Wigtime"

    Munro's stories are rich with the landscapes of Ontario's Lake Huron region, and, as illustrated, often mix simile and metaphor.

■ EYE EXPRESSIONS

See also: LOOKS; SCRUTINY

1. She turned, and looking on the bitter view / Her eyes were welded shut by mortal pain —Anna Akhmatova, "Lot's Wife"

    In the Bible, Lot's wife was turned into a pillar of salt. Here the wife, looking back on Sodom, her home, "for a single glance, gave up her life."

2. In your eyes there lives / a green egyptian noise —e. e. cummings, "irreproachable ladies firmly lewd"

3. A storm seemed to break in King Ra's eyes —Eleanor Farjeon, "The King and the Corn"

4. Her green eyes . . . a sea waiting for the storm —Bill Granger, *The Last Good German*

5. Two desolate pools in the small, pale oval of her face stared back at her—two pools with something drowned in their lonely depths —Frances Noyes Hart, "Contact," *Contact and Other Stories*

    A grieving woman bent on shutting out memories of a fiance killed in the war, determines "to drown it deeper."

6. For I have beheld her, the princess, / Firelight and starlight her eyes —Vachel Lindsay, "Aladdin and the Jinn"

7. Maria dos Prazeres stared at him [the Count of Cardona] with the burning eyes of a royal cobra and saw the passionless pupils behind gold-rimmed spectacles, the ravening teeth, the hybrid hands of an animal accustomed to dampness and dark. Saw him just as he was —Gabriel García Márquez, "Maria Dos Prazeres," *The New Yorker,* March 22, 1993

    Franco has just condemned three Basque separatists to death, and Maria will break with her long term patron, Cardona, who approves the sentence. There are two metaphors here. The first pictures Maria's eyes as those of a cobra. The second pictures her patron as a ravening animal—a hyena, perhaps.

8. The eyes of the Gray Man filled with lights —Carl Sandburg, "What Six Girls with Balloons Told the Gray Man on Horseback"

    Later in the story the author expands on this with a simile: "His eyes were lit like a morning sun coming up over harvest fields."

9. Berowne: Behold the window of my heart, mine eye —William Shakespeare, *Love's Labour's Lost,* Act 4, scene 3, line 244

10. That inward sun in thine eyes shineth so —Sir Philip Sidney, "Sonnet 71," *Astrophel and Stella*

11. When she turned full-face . . . you got the impact of her bright, pale, cold, seagull's eye —Josephine Tey, *The Franchise Affair*

    While this woman resembles Whistler's mother in profile, her name—Sharpe—indicates that her front-face image represents her true character.

12. [It] left us saucer-eyed —François Villon, "A Ballade to End With"

13. Mrs. Toy's large shallow eyes floated the question towards him on a sea-blue wave of curiosity —Edith Wharton, *Twilight Sleep*

14. Her dull black eyes glinted with bright knives of fear —Thomas Wolfe, *Look Homeward Angel*

■ EYES

See also: FACES

1. Vi's eyes are hopping hens from one face to the other —Alice Adams, "Overland," *Boulevard*, No. 12–13

2. Lotus-petal-eyed One —Anon., *The Bhagavad Gita, 11:2*
   The epithet is used by Arjuna for Krishna.

3. [Everlasting Spirit] . . . whose eyes are the moon and sun, / I see Thee, whose face is flaming fire —Anon., *The Bhagavad Gita, 11:18*
   The Blessed One's dialogue with Arjuna is meant to convince the warrior to enter the battle (a battle that is the subject of The Mahabarata*). Arjuna here is humble before Krishna.*

4. Ancient fires for eyes, his head full / & his heart full, he's making ready to move on —John Berryman, from "The Dream Songs 77"
   Henry, the persona of "The Dream Songs," is tired of the winter.

5. Her big sheep eyes squinted, as if distrustful of what they saw —Truman Capote, "A Tree of Night"

6. The eyes those silent tongues of Love — Miguel de Cervantes, *Don Quixote*

7. Eyes which are really petals and see / nothing —e. e. cummings, "If There Are Any Heavens"
   Cummings pictures his mother in heaven, and his father watching her lovingly with his petaled eyes.

8. She looked straight up in his boiled blue eyes —John Dos Passos, *U.S.A., The Big Money*
   Boiled eyes were a Dos Passos favorite. In this instance they belong to a major player in the novel, aviation tycoon Charley Anderson.

9. He stared hard . . . with his magpie's eyes —John Dos Passos, *U.S.A., Nineteen Nineteen*
   J. P. Morgan's hungry eyes took in potential additions for his art collection.

10. Martina: . . . his eyes were two pale stones / Dropping in a dark well —Christopher Fry, *Thor, With Angels*

11. His eyes were warm green discs —Dashiell Hammett, *The Maltese Falcon*

12. Alas! how oft in dreams I see / Those eyes that were my food —Henry Howard (Earl of Surrey), "Complaint of the Absence of Her Lover being upon the Sea"

13. Her eyes were great blue windows with timidities inside —Jack Kerouac, "The Mexicana Girl"

14. Pretty eyes—radiant jellies—shooting stars —Charles Lamb, "A Dissertation Upon Roast Pig"
    No, Lamb is not describing the eyes of a woman, but a pig upon a spit.

15. Saphires set in snow —Thomas Lodge, *Rosalynde*

16. The pearl of the face —John Lyly, *Euphues*

17. His eyes were only two gleaming cracks —Thomas Mann, "Tonio Kroger"

18. What are the eyes / A. The wells have fallen in and have / Inhabitants —William Stanley Merwin, "Some Last Questions"
    The poem consists of questions without question marks and answers that often riddle like Buddhist koans. Most of the answers are metaphors, like, "What are the feet / A. Thumbs left after the auction."

19. She had tigers' eyes, greenly chiaroscuro, dappled with unexpected tinsel flecks — Cynthia Ozick, "Alfred Chester's Wig," *The New Yorker*, April 20, 1992
    We're introduced to the young lady of the tigers' eyes as she lies in the middle of a carpet "in a mustard glow" with "mustard-colored hair" flowing out over the floor and a "mustard-colored New Look skirt" flung into folds around her.

20. Her eyes . . . They were dark, yes, and certainly liquid, but they were set in little hammocks of folded flesh —Dorothy Parker, "Glory in the Daytime"
    Parker returns to the hammocks framing the eyes of a dissipated actress when she shows her trying to focus on a memory: "Her shoulders jerked upward . . . her eyes sought to start from their hammocks."

21. The eye is a shrew —John Ray, *Proverbs*

22. At the urging of his advisers, he [Vice-President Dan Quayle] has learned to give the camera his profile instead of his startled, faded-denim eyes —Andrew Rosenthal, "Quayle's Moment," *The New York Times Magazine,* July 5, 1992

23. But from thine eyes my knowledge I derive, / And, constant stars, in them I read such art / As truth and beauty shall together thrive —William Shakespeare, "Sonnet 14," line 9

    Comparing eyes with stars has become a commonplace.

24. Ariel: Those are pearls that were his eyes —William Shakespeare, *The Tempest,* Act 1, scene 2, line 398

    The metaphor comes from a song that begins "Full fadom five."

25. Human double-barreled eyes, / in their narrow blind, —May Swenson, "Teology"

    Swenson adds, in a second metaphor, that they "hope to shoot and hit / —if they can find it / — the backward-speeding hole / in the Cyclops face of the future."

26. Her eyes are candles burning in a shrine —James Thurber, *The Thirteen Clocks*

    At another point Thurber talks of eyes as "candles burning on a tranquil night.

27. Willow-leaf eyes —Wei Chung-hsien, "To the Tune of Nu Kuan-tzu." Five Dynasties

28. Three girls . . . their eyes were long lakes of lustrous substance right across their faces —Dame Rebecca West, *The Abiding Vision*

F

■ FACES

See also: PHYSICAL APPEARANCE

1. Looking at him [Henry Wadsworth Long-
   fellow] you had the feeling that the white
   head of hair and beard were a mask put on
   to conceal a young man's face; and that if
   the poet chose he could throw off the
   disguise and appear as a man in the very
   prime and bloom of youth —Anon.,
   Daily Telegraph, 1868
   > *This article was written at the time Cambridge
   > awarded the poet his LL.D.*

2. Nature had carved him into a human
   monument, and he spent his life trying to
   live up to the importance of his face —
   Anon., "The Talk of the Town," *The New
   Yorker,* July 5, 1993
   > *The column about the former Texas Governor
   > John Connally was prompted by his death and the
   > subsequent petition by Kennedy assassination re-
   > searchers to retrieve bullet fragments from his body.*

3. Faces are but a gallery of pictures —Sir
   Francis Bacon, *Essays*

4. Men whose . . . faces give out at every
   pore . . . the poisons with which their
   brains are pregnant; not faces so much as
   masks —Honoré de Balzac, "The Girl
   With the Golden Eyes"

5. She gazed at the class with a jolly look
   breaking across her marionette face —
   Charles Baxter, "Gryphon"

   > *The lines on a woman's face remind a schoolboy
   > of the "marionette lines" he remembers from
   > Pinocchio.*

6. Now I cannot judge what it [my face] is
   . . . I only know that time has worked with
   its axe over my features —Nina Berberova,
   Quoted in *The New Yorker,* October 25, 1993
   > *The quotation was part of a tribute to the writer,
   > shortly after her death at age ninety-three.*

7. Her countenance was long, vacant, and
   weakly lighted, a passage for the gentle
   transports and miseries of the poor —
   John Cheever, "O City of Broken Dreams"
   > *This follows a simile likening the face to a "tene-
   > ment doorway."*

8. A scarlet serpent of blood crawled from
   under his fallen face —Gilbert Keith
   Chesterton, "The Secret Garden"

9. He had a nut-cracker face—chin and
   nose trying to come together over a sunk-
   en mouth —Joseph Conrad, "Youth"

10. The face is often only / A smooth impos-
    tor —Pierre Corneille, *Le Menteur,* II

11. Firelight shone across the solid slope of
    his cheek, making a shadow up from the
    arrogant hedge of eyebrow —James Gould
    Cozzens, *The Last Adam*
    > *This linkage of facial features to landscape is from
    > the last paragraph of a novel about young doctors.*

12. See the leftward glancing of her color-
    coordinated eyes inside the puffy, hori-

zontal parenthesis of her lashless lids — Stanley Elkin, "Some Overrated Masterpieces," *Art & Antiques,* 1991

13. His eyes were shiny in a wooden Satan's face —Dashiell Hammett, *The Maltese Falcon*

14. Mrs. Jardine turned to the window, so that only her bleached stone profile was visible to us —Rosamond Lehmann, *The Ballad and the Source*

15. Faces are books in which not a line is written, save perhaps a date —Henry Wadsworth Longfellow, *Hyperion*

16. The judge chopped the air with his hatchet face —Ross MacDonald, "Wild Goose Chase," *The Name is Archer*

17. His forehead was furrowed by passing storm clouds —Gabriel García Márquez, *The General in his Labyrinth*
    A farming and weather metaphor depicts Simon Bolivar as an old man "circling the government like a bull round a herd of cows." The Nobel Laureate author, himself no longer young, must also have been looking backward.

18. Her face was painted / Clown-white, white of the moon by daylight, / Lidded with pearl, mouth a poinsettia leaf — James Merrill, "Days of 1964"
    Merrill describes the woman with four swift metaphors.

19. Each face in the street is a slice of bread / wandering on / searching —William Stanley Merwin, "Bread"
    "Somewhere in the light the true hunger / appears to be passing them by," writes Merwin.

20. Drink and dissipation had done their work on the coin-clean profile and now it was no longer the head of a young pagan prince on new-minted gold but a decadent, tired Caesar on copper debased by long usage —Margaret Mitchell, *Gone With the Wind*
    This is Rhett Butler when Mitchell's saga draws to a close.

21. Deep parenthesis around her mouth made her look older than her twenty-seven years —Marcia Muller, Eye of the Storm
    Punctuation marks serve as an interesting metaphor to fill in physical details.

22. She had a pocketmirror of a face —Cynthia Ozick, "The Shawl"

23. The term [stepmother] . . . seemed to have nothing to do with Whitey, with her gay little monkey's face —Dorothy Parker, "I Live On Your Visits"

24. A pleasant face is a silent recommendation —Publilius Syrus, *Sententiae*

25. A profile that could carve a joint —Salman Rushdie, [analysis of] *The Wizard of Oz*
    In his lengthy analysis of this film for the British Film Institute (printed by Indiana University Press and excerpted in The New Yorker,*) Miss Gulch, the lady of the angular face, is depicted as the movie's force of evil.*

26. The face of the old woman is hoof-beaten with intersecting curves of loose skin — Richard Selzer, "Toenails"

27. Demetrius: Thy lips, those kissing cherries, tempting grow —William Shakespeare, *A Midsummer Night's Dream,* Act 3, scene 2, line 140

28. Tyrrell: Their lips were four red roses on a stalk —William Shakespeare, *The Tragedy of King Richard the Third,* Act 4, scene 3, line 12
    "The tyrannous and bloody act is done"—Edward's young sons have been murdered.

29. Under the shiny white globe of his brow, his features huddled together in a dead, gray triangle —Nathanael West, *Miss Lonelyhearts*

30. His nutcracker chin reposing on a spotless stock —Edith Wharton, *Hudson River Bracketed*
    Grant Wood would have loved Grandpa, the possessor of that chin.

31. The Marchesa's little ferret face with sharp impassioned eyes darted conversationally forward —Edith Wharton, *Twilight Sleep*

■ FACIAL COLOR

See also: COMPLEXION

1. They are coffee-with-milk color and the khaki they wear is the same color as their skin, so they look all beige —Julia Alvarez, *How the Garcia Girls Lost Their Accents*
   This describes two men on the side of the dictator who prompted the Garcia family to flee the Dominican Republic.

2. "No, dear," snapped Philomena—red to the summit of her nose —Sean O'Faolain, "Mother Matilda's Book"

3. King: What see you in those papers that you lose / So much complexion? . . . / Their cheeks are paper —William Shakespeare, *The Life of Henry the Fifth*, Act 2, scene 2, line 74
   This metaphor contains a play on the word paper, with the change of complexion caused by cowardice.

4. Macbeth: Go prick thy face, and over-red thy fear, / Thou lily-liver'd boy . . . those linen cheeks of thine / Are counselors to fear —William Shakespeare, *Macbeth*, Act 5, scene 5, line 16
   Pallor is also associated with cowardice in The Life of Henry the Fifth (2, 2, 74).

5. Romeo: Dry sorrow drinks our blood —William Shakespeare, *Romeo and Juliet*, Act 3, scene 5, line 59

6. Friar: The roses in thy lips and cheeks shall fade / To wanny ashes —William Shakespeare, *Romeo and Juliet*, Act 4, scene 1, line 99
   The metaphor foreshadows Juliet's death.

7. O! what a sight . . . / To note the fighting conflict of her hue, / How white and red each other did destroy: But now her cheek was pale, and by and by / It flashed forth fire as lightning from the sky —William Shakespeare, *Venus and Adonis,* line 345
   Shakespeare scholar Caroline Spurgeon surmises that Shakespeare was so sensitive to the shift of facial color induced by emotion because he himself tended to flush easily.

8. The Redde rose medled with the White yfere, / In either cheeke depeincten lively chere —Edmund Spenser, "A Ditty"
   The red rose and the white rose, commingling in each cheek, indicate "lively cheer."

■ FACIAL EXPRESSIONS

See also: EYE EXPRESSIONS; LOOKS

1. When he speaks his white teeth give off white lightning —Frank Conroy, "Midair," *The New Yorker*, 1985
   The lightning-toothed man radiates energy "like an electrical charge."

2. The girl's face . . . The cream-at-the-top-of-the-milkpail face of someone who will never work for anything; someone who picks up things lying on other people's dressers and is not embarrassed when found out —Toni Morrison, *Jazz*
   "It is the face of a sneak who glides over to your sink to rinse the fork you have laid by her plate," Morrison adds.

3. The father's mouth opened in a little zero of shock —Julia Alvarez, *How the Garcia Girls Lost Their Accents*

4. Those cement faces and eyes of hate that burned the clothes off you if they happened to see you lounging on the main street downtown on Saturday —Maya Angelou, *I Know Why the Caged Bird Sings*
   This is how the author remembers the bigoted white men in the small town of her childhood.

5. Hancock's face fell with a sudden thud —Paul F. Boller, Jr., Presidential Anecdotes
   John Hancock, the president of the Continental Congress expected John Adams to nominate him as the first President of the United States. When Adams chose George Washington instead Hancock could not hide his shock.

6. In the midst of this consummate acting, however, the volcano that raged within caused his eyes to glare and his nostrils to dilate, like that of some wild beast that is suddenly prevented from taking the fatal leap —James Fenimore Cooper, *The Deerslayer*

   The Indian pretends to keep his composure despite the raging volcano of alarm.

7. The expert orchestration of a frown — Donald Davie, "The Evangelist"

8. The clouds were dark on many a brow — Oliver Wendell Holmes, Sr., "The Mysterious Visitor"

9. Under the bright September sun I could see . . . the deep small scars of strain around his mouth —Ross MacDonald, "Wild Goose Chase," *The Name is Archer*

10. His face came apart at the seams —Ross MacDonald, *The Barbarous Coast: Archer in Hollywood*

    The figure, a favorite for all types of disintegration, is here rounded out as follows: "He tried to put it together again around the fixed point of the pipe which he jammed into his mouth. But he couldn't control the grimace tugging like hooks at the end of his lips."

11. His face always seemed boiled and angry —Norman Mailer, *The Naked and the Dead*

12. Winter had fled the city streets but Sam Tomashevsky's face, when he stumbled into the back room of his grocery store, was a blizzard —Bernard Malamud, "The Cost of Living"

    This metaphoric opening establishes the time, place and mood of the sad saga of a grocer who can't compete with a large new store.

13. Martha [was] accustomed to the fireworks of his face —Vladimir Nabokov, *King, Queen, Knave*

14. Cyrano: Imagine how it feels to face / The volley of a thousand angry eyes — Edmond Rostand, *Cyrano de Bergerac*, Act 1

    Cyrano explains that he aims to displease as a form of self-defense against the thorns he must bear. He likens the ruff he wears to "a ring of enemies" he bears erectly "At once a fetter and— a halo."

15. He was smooth of face . . . a finely chiseled mask touched with fox wariness — Carl Sandburg, *Abraham Lincoln, The War Years*. Vol. One.

    The subject of this profile is Abraham Lincoln's Secretary of War, Simon Cameron.

16. Menenius: The tartness of his face sours ripe grapes —William Shakespeare, *Coriolanus*, Act 5, scene 4, line 19

    The metaphor is most commonly used as a simile—a face like sour grapes. Menenius combines simile and metaphor to show Coriolanus talking "like a knell with a 'hum!' [of impatience] that is a battery."

17. Worcester: Look how we can, or sad or merrily, / Interpretation will misquote our looks —William Shakespeare, *The First Part of King Henry the Fourth*, Act 5, scene 2, line 13

18. Don Pedro: Why what's the matter, / That you have such a February face, so full of frost, of storm of cloudiness? — William Shakespeare, *Much Ado About Nothing*, Act 5, scene 4, line 40

19. Though men can cover crimes with bold stern looks, / Poor women's faces are their own faults' books —William Shakespeare, *The Rape of Lucrece*, line 1252

    "Women's smoothness, like a goodly champaign plain, / Lays open all the little worms that creep" whereas "In men, as in a rough-grown grove, remains / Cave-keeping evils that obscurely sleep."

20. King: in thy face I see / The map of honor, truth and loyalty —William Shakespeare, *The Second Part of Henry the Sixth*, Act 3, scene 1, line 202

21. Saturninus: Clear up, fair queen, that cloudy countenance —William Shakespeare, *Titus Andronicus*, Act 1, scene 1, line 263

22. Agrippa: He has a cloud in 's face —
   William Shakespeare, *Antony and Cleopatra*,
   Act 3, scene 2, line 52

23. Stella oft sees the very face of woe /
   Painted in my beclouded, stormy face —
   Sir Philip Sidney, "Sonnet 45," *Astrophel
   and Stella*

24. Let clouds bedim my face, break in mine
   eye —Sir Philip Sidney, "Sonnet
   64," *Astrophel and Stella*

25. His honest countenance was a good letter
   of recommendation —Tobias Smollett,
   The Expeditions of Humphrey Clinker

26. Each care-worn face is but a book / To
   tell of houses bought or sold —Jones
   Very, "The Strangers"

27. The grim visage of murder . . . the brow
   knitted by revenge, the face black with
   settled hate and the blood-shot eye emit-
   ting livid fires of malice —Daniel Webster, Summation in the Knapp-White
   Murder Case at Salem, Massachussets,
   April 7, 1830

28. Her look was a wounded bird that flew to
   him for shelter —Edith Wharton, "The
   Confessional"

29. Mr. Paul Goodson, of the Dependable
   Life, closed his dish-face abruptly, and
   ceased talking —Thomas Wolfe, *Look
   Homeward Angel*

■ FACIAL HAIR

1. A ram's horn mustache —Norman Mailer, *Harlot's Ghost*

2. Beneath a baldish head . . . he wears a
   thick cloud of mustache —Stephen Schiff,
   "Edward Gorey and the Tao of Non-
   sense," *The New Yorker*, November 9, 1992

3. He's currently making one of his periodic
   stabs at a beard: it's growing in little red

islands —Stephen Schiff, "Cultural Pursuits," *The New Yorker*, December 20, 1993
   *The beard grower was Fred Schepsis, the Austra-
   lian movie director.*

4. Some [of the aristocratic men of the time]
   had a thick jungle of hair under the chin
   and hiding the throat—the only pattern
   recognized there as being the correct thing
   in whiskers —Mark Twain, *The Gilded
   Age*

■ FACT-FINDING

See: SUSPICION

■ FACTS

1. Facts are high explosives —Hallie Flanagan,
   Quoted in *The New York Times*,
   March 4, 1992

2. The fact is the sweetest dream that labor
   knows —Robert Frost, "Mowing"

3. They [Facts] are the brute beasts of the
   intellectual domain —Oliver Wendell
   Holmes, *The Autocrat of the Breakfast-Table*
   *According to Holmes, all generous minds have a
   horror of these "brute beasts."*

4. Facts are the air of science. Without them
   you can never fly —Ivan Pavlov

■ FAILURE

*See also: DESTRUCTION/DESTRUCTIVE-
NESS; FORTUNE/MISFORTUNE*

1. "Pit Bull" At the White House Falls Victim To His Own Role —Anon., Headline, *The New York Times*, December 4, 1991
   *The metaphor refers to John H. Sununu, the
   abrasive White House chief of staff who had been
   forced to resign his post on this day.*

2. Madrigal: You have not a green thumb,
   Mrs. St. Maugham, with plant or girl —
   Enid Bagnold, *The Chalk Garden*, Act 3, 1953

The remark is literal in relation to a failed garden, and figurative in its indictment of Mrs. St. Maugham as a mother and grandmother.

3. What is a ruin but Time easing itself of endurance? —Djuna Barnes, *Nightwood*

4. Since I soon found that the ideas I presented sank without ripples into the impenetrable lethargy of that boardroom only to resurface on the lists of other publishers, my place there was as redundant as my prospects were bleak —John Malcolm Brinnin, Journal entry, c. 1949

   The site of this "shipwreck" was a publishing house that had hired Brinnin to generate ideas.

5. Quite soberly I am telling you that my ship is going down and that the water is already coming over the bridge —Mikhail Bulgakov, Letter to his brother, quoted in J. A. E. Curtis' 1992 biography of the author of *The Master and His Margarita*

6. We are in front of a cadaver —Fernando Henrique Cardoso, *The New York Times*, August 22, 1992

   Cardoso's reference was to Brazil's President Fernando Collor de Mello and his chances of overcoming a corruption scandal.

7. This is the kind of extreme twist of plot that has unmoored many a story —Ron Carlson, *The New York Times Book Review*, April 11, 1993

   The seafaring metaphor refers to a freak accident which kills a young woman, in Sue Miller's novel For Love.

8. A wind has blown upon the tree, shattering down all its leaves, and showing it to us quite bare, and shaken from its very root —Saint John Chrysostom, Sermon c. 387

   The image refers to the fall of Eutropius, Minister of State.

9. I just fell on my own sword —Governor Bill Clinton, *The New York Times*, July 15, 1992

   The presidential candidate was ruefully reflecting on his unsuccessful nominating speech at the 1988 Democratic convention.

10. Everything around me was bankrupt —Maxim Gorky, One Autumn Night

    The bankruptcy ranges from an overturned canoe to trees stripped of their leaves to the sky flowing with "undryable tears."

11. [*Eating Raoul*] is over its head in a vat of whimsy —Mel Gussow, *The New York Times*, May 16, 1992

    Gussow clearly did not like the movie.

12. She too was cut down by the drastic scythe of taste —Elizabeth Hardwick, "Wind from the Prairie," *The New York Review of Books*, 1991

    The metaphor is apt since it describes a writer from the midwestern farmlands, Sara Teasdale, whose fading popularity was exacerbated by her divorce and its attendant loss of money and social status.

13. The quality of its only product plunged to its lowest level since the business opened in 1960, sending sales into a tailspin —Thomas C. Hayes, *The New York Times*, January 24, 1993

    For anything that goes up and then comes down, an aeronautic image is a natural.

14. [IBM's] stock price, which had already thudded to earth, started digging its way toward China —Herbert B. Herring, "Business Diary," *The New York Times*, January 24, 1993

    Thousands of shareholders are not amused by the imagery.

15. A legendary lion of Congress lies wounded, a victim of a famous Potomac malady—great power gone greatly sour —Marianne Means, *Hearst Newspapers*, July 28, 1993

    The House Ways and Means Chairman Dan Rostenkowski wasn't roaring but in very hot water in connection with an embezzlement charge.

16. [Paul Rudnick's play *I Hate Hamlet* was] capsized by the onstage misbehavior of its star, Nicol Williamson —Frank Rich, "Critic's Notebook," *The New York Times*, February 3, 1993

17. We are frustrated because we seem to be on the down escalator to the bargain basement and we are the cheap goods —Ann W. Richards, Op-Ed, *The New York Times*, June 7, 1992

> *The Texas Governor was one of several political leaders quoted on the Presidential campaign.*

18. The withered leaves of industrial enterprise lie on every side —Franklin Delano Roosevelt, First inaugural address, March 4, 1933

19. Antonio: ebbing men indeed— / Most often—do so near the bottom run / By their own fear or sloth —William Shakespeare, *The Tempest*, Act 2, scene 1, line 230

20. Gardener: He that hath suffer'd this disordered spring / Hath now himself met with the fall of leaf. / The weeds which his broad-spreading leaves did shelter, / . . . / Are plucked up root and all by Bolingbroke —William Shakespeare, *The Tragedy of King Richard the Second*, Act 3, scene 4, line 50

> *The garden represents England. Had the king been a thrifty gardener, the land would have flourished.*

21. George: When it comes to life I have a brown thumb. I mean nothing goes right. Ever —Bernard Slade, *Same Time Next Year*, Act 1, scene 1

22. Poor Arthur—from the first he had been one of her failures. She had a little cemetery of them—a very small one—planted over with quick-growing things, so that you might have walked all through her life and not noticed there were any graves in it —Edith Wharton, *Twilight Sleep*

> *Wharton's sardonic assessment of a society awash with self-deluded people is epitomized in the character of Pauline Manford.*

23. Everywhere about me . . . this shipwreck of a great spirit —Thomas Wolfe, "The Spanish Letter"

> *The "shipwreck" was Germany during the rise of Nazism.*

■ FAIRNESS/UNFAIRNESS

See also: JUSTICE/INJUSTICE

1. The new policy [on Gays in the military] must be instituted as a step towards fairness, not a fig leaf to cover continued discrimination —Anon., Editorial, *The New York Times*, July 20, 1993

> *The influence of conservative Chiefs of Staff on President Clinton's compromised measure on gays in the military made the metaphoric allusion to the fig leaf especially fitting. Long after Adam and Eve covered their nakedness with a fig leaf, museum curators thus covered their Greek statues in deference to Victorian prudery.*

2. The guards took a lion's share of the purse full of money he gave me —Orhan Pamuk, *The White Castle*

> *This common metaphor to depict someone getting an unequal share of what's due originated with one of Asesop's fables in which a lion, a sheep, a heifer and a goat agreed to share their catch equally. However, when they caught a stag, the lion took the best and largest part for himself.*

3. It appears . . . the dice are to be loaded —Charles Stewart Parnell, Speech to the House of Commons, April 18, 1887

> *The Irish member of Parliament had already received a setback to his cause with the passage of the Coercion Act which eventually led to his imprisonment; the publication of a letter to which his signature had been falsely appended added another blow to his cause.*

4. When women began to enter science careers in the 1940's and 1950's, they were expected to renounce any intention of having a family. This is the ultimate unlevel playing field, one that persists to this day —Shirley M. Tilghman, *The New York Times*, January 26, 1993

> *Women are excluded from many playing fields, even those that are supposedly on-the-level.*

■ FAITH

See also: BELIEFS; RELIGION

1. If we look before we leap [take the leap of faith], some of us will be unable to crucify our intellects without impaling our integrity —William Warren Bartley III, "I Call Myself a Protestant"

   But, according to the author, rationalists make mistakes too.

2. My people hath been lost sheep —The Bible, *O.T., Jeremiah 50:6*

   Today the metaphor refers to anyone who is floundering.

3. Let us, who are of the day, be sober, putting on the breastplate of faith and love; and for an helmet, the hope of salvation —The Bible, *N.T. 1 Thessalonians 5:8*

4. Faith needs her daily bread —Dinah Mulock Craik, *Fortune's Marriage*

5. Faith loves to lean on Time's destroying arm —Oliver Wendell Holmes, Sr., "Urania"

   This is followed by a simile: And age, like distance, lends a double charm.

6. His faith had dried up, turned into a mound of dust in the corner —Alice Munro, "Oranges and Apples," *Friend of Youth,*

7. The man without faith is a walking corpse —Pope Nystus I, "The Ring"

8. That's the river you have to lay your pain in, the River of Faith, in the River of Life, in the River of Love, in the rich red river of Jesus' Blood, you people! —Flannery O'Connor, "The River"

   A preacher with a reputation for healing, exhorts his listeners to baptism.

9. I have fought the good fight, I have finished my course, I have kept the faith —Saint Paul

   In this letter written in 57 A.D., Saint Paul pictures himself as a soldier in the battle of faith.

10. Faith builds a bridge across the gulf of death —Edward Young, *Night Thoughts,* IV

■ FAITHLESSNESS

See: TREACHERY

■ FALL

See also: SEASONS

1. The fires of autumn were burning gold and drowsy in the beeches —H. E. Bates, "The Evolution of Saxby"

2. The autumn winds strum on its dry leaves sighing human music, a harp of voices —Truman Capote, "The Grass Harp"

   The metaphor refers to a field of high Indian grass in late September. Capote returns to this image at the novella's closing: "A waterfall of color flowed across the dry and strumming leaves and I wanted then for the Judge to hear what Dolly had told me: that it was a grass harp, gathering, telling, a harp of voices remembering a story."

3. The maple wears a gayer scarf, / The field a scarlet gown —Emily Dickinson, Poem 12

4. The year comes to its death, / In such a glory of burning is consumed, / The bright air trembles . . . / With the spicy smoke of its expiring breath —Elizabeth B. Harrod, "Calvinist Autumnal"

5. The leafless trees are feathery, / A foxed, Victorian lace, / Against a sky of milk-glass blue —Anthony Hecht, "Persistences"

6. This was one of those perfect New England days in late summer, when the spirit of autumn . . . puts her cool cloak of bracing air about leaf and flower and human shoulders —Sarah Orne Jewett, "The Courting of Sister Wisby"

7. Autumn was a bold seductress on that late Monday afternoon —Ed McBain, *The Mugger*

8. The winds of fall— / and the things one looks upon / are *haiku*, all! —Kyoshi Takahama, Haiku

   As a common metaphor this would be, when I look at the Autumn leaves, I see pure poetry!

9. And over us all, in a flood, poured the golden October light —Robert Penn Warren, "October Picnic Long Ago"

10. The field has droned the summer's final mass —Richard Wilbur, "Exuent"

11. The leaves . . . / seem to yield us through a rustled sieve / The very light from which time fell away —Richard Wilbur, "October Maples, Portland"

12. One wading a Fall meadow finds on all sides / The Queen Anne's Lace .. it turns / Dry grass to a lake —Richard Wilbur, "The Beautiful Changes"

13. Rich autumn time, the season's usurer, / Will lend his hoarded gold to all the trees, / And see his treasure scattered by the wild and spendthrift breeze —Oscar Wilde, "The Garden of Eros"
    In another poem, "Humanitad," Wilde writes about "Autumn's gaudy livery."

14. The air is wild with leaves —Humbert Wolfe, "Autumn"

■ FALSE VALUES

See: SUPERFICIALITY

■ FALSENESS

See: DECEPTION

■ FALSIFICATION

See: EXPLOITATION

■ FAME

See also: SUCCESS/FAILURE

1. Public men are bees working in a glass hive —Henry Ward Beecher, *Proverbs from Plymouth Pulpit*
    Poet Emily Dickinson wrote "Fame is a bee / It has a song— / It has a sting—"

2. Fame is the thirst of youth —Lord George Gordon Byron, "Childe Harold's Pilgrimage"

3. Fame is but wind —Thomas Coryate, *Coryate's Crudities*

4. The beauty parlor of the dead —Benjamin De Casseres, "Fantasie Impromptu"

5. Fame is a food that dead men eat —Henry Austin Dobson, "Fame and Friendship"
    "I have no stomach for such meat," continues the poet.

6. Mark Antony: Why was I raised the meteor of the world / Hung in the skies and blazing as I travelled, / Till all my fires were spent —John Dryden, *All For Love*, Act 1, scene 1

7. History did not even brush her [Emily Dickinson] with its wings —Clifton Fadiman, "The Bubble Reputation"
    The title of Fadiman's essay is a metaphor for how literary reputations can burst, only to re-inflate many years after an author is literally dead.

8. Glory . . . a murdering poison, and to bear it is an art —Oriana Fallaci, "Federico Fellini"

9. Fame is a magnifying glass —Thomas Fuller, *Gnomologia*
    "Fame is but the breath of the people and that often unwholesome," Fuller adds.

10. What is fame? An empty bubble —James Grainger, "Solitude"

11. What is fame? / A fitful tongue of leaping flame: / A giddy whirlwind's fickle gust, / That lifts a pinch of mortal dust —Oliver Wendell Holmes, "Bill and Jane"

12. People who live in glass houses should be careful how they fling stones —James I, King of England
    The king's response to a complaint by one of his dukes that a mob had broken the glass windows of his house has evolved into a common metaphor for the vulnerability of people in the limelight.

13. Fame is no plant that grows on mortal soil —John Milton, "Lycidas"

14. Fame is the spur that the clear spirit doth raise / (That last infirmity of noble minds) —John Milton, *Lycidas*

15. Fame is a bugle call / Blown past a crumbling wall —Lizette Reese, "Taps"

16. You seek to nurse at fullest breast of Fame —Sir Philip Sidney, "Sonnet 15," *Astrophel and Stella*

■ FAMILIARITY/UNFAMILIARITY

See also: AWARENESS/UNAWARENESS

1. I walked through the Bridges' door, which for me was the walking into another country —Laurie Colwin, "Saint Anthony of the Desert," *The Lone Pilgrim*

2. Two years ago, I didn't know her name. She occupied another seat on that train of nameless somebodies —Diana Tuite, Op-Ed, *The New York Times,* page, March 6, 1993
    The metaphor appeared in a winning high school essay on the theme of admired women. "No longer in my cellar of consciousness, Hillary Clinton has become a role model," the writer continued.

■ FAMILIES/FAMILY RELATIONSHIPS

See also: ANCESTRY/ANCESTORS; PEOPLE, INTERACTION

1. Mother and Bailey were entangled in the Oedipal skein —Maya Angelou, *I Know Why the Caged Bird Sings*

2. The ungrateful son is a wart on his father's face; to leave it is a blemish, to cut it off a pain —Anon., Afghanistan Proverb

3. How could he have had the folly to encase himself in that black suit of armor and slam the visor shut over eyes and lips that might have smiled at me? —Louis Auchincloss, "The Epicurean"
    The novella's protagonist's father is dead and he reflects angrily on his stunted relationship with a man he has earlier referred to as a "lonely Puritan."

4. Within it [the family structure], all the violent temperaments in our family . . . lay swaddled in a fleece of security — Hortense Calisher, "Time, Gentlemen!"
    The author attributes the uniqueness of a family with strong ties to the Victorian era to an element composed of "all the ways that people had found to carve intaglio from smaller moments of their lives."

5. Milagro and I . . . we're a double helix, right and impervious —Cristina Garcia, *Dreaming in Cuban*
    Celia is a Cuban revolutionary, and Lourdes her antagonistic Americanized daughter.

6. My expectation for my daughters has been that after I polish a few tarnished places, I can put down the cloth and they will continue to shine —Michelle Gillett, "Mothers to Daughters," *The Berkshire Eagle,* July 5, 1993
    "But," added the writer, "there is no guarantee that the world will be stunned by that brightness or that my daughters' happiness no longer will be defined as traditional female success."

7. After so long a lapse of years, the old trunk of the family tree, with so much venerable moss upon it, [has] borne, as its topmost bough, an idler like myself —Nathaniel Hawthorne, *The Scarlet Letter*
    Hawthorne has correctly depicted himself, not as the idler, but as the topmost bough of his family tree. How many other Hawthornes do we know?

8. There is within me a feeling for old Salem . . . The sentiment is probably assignable to the deep and aged roots which my family has struck into the soil —Nathaniel Hawthorne, *The Scarlet Letter*
    The metaphor is explicit in the term "family tree," and the word roots has come to mean originations.

9. When I go home my mother and I play a cannibal game; we eat each other over the years, tender morsel by morsel, and there

is nothing left but dry bone and wig — Maureen Howard, *Bridgeport Bus*

10. In Egypt, for example, Mother sometimes modulates imperceptibly into a hippopotamus —Aldous Huxley, "Mother"
    In ancient cultures, metaphors became flesh.

11. They were a kissing family, and after her mother's death the habit had taken a fresh spring —Henry James, "The Marriages"
    Spring remains an enduring metaphor for renewal. President Bill Clinton's inaugural speech opened with a reference to "forcing the spring"—a welcome change from the Democrats' long political winter of discontent (Shakespeares' The Tragedy of King Richard the Third, 1, 1, 1).

12. For the mother, her daughter seemed to be a mirror reflecting Oki, and for her daughter her mother was another such mirror. And each saw her own reflection in the other's mirror —Kawabata Yasunari, *Beauty and Sadness*

13. She was the glue that held our family together —John F. Kennedy, Quoted in Op-Ed, *The New York Times*, 1993
    Members of the Kennedy family used the Op-Ed page to refute the portrait of their mother in J.F.K, Reckless Youth.

14. Father has been my rock ahead, and Mother tried to hold me back and bury me between moss-tufts —Selma Lagerlöf, *The Girl from the Marsh Croft*
    The writer compares her life to a stream and envisions herself by-passing both the "rock" and the "moss-tufts" to get out into the world.

15. This was not a family that relied on therapists occasionally . . . the fabric of the psychiatrist's couch was knitted into virtually every aspect of their lives —Peter Marks, *The New York Times*, April 4, 1993
    The reference was to Woody Allen and Mia Farrow and their life style which was much in the news during their acrimonious child custody battle

16. The result [of the feminist movement] was a generation of educated young women who heard . . . little about the silken chains of mother love —Anna Quindlen, "Public & Private," *The New York Times*, February 28, 1993
    What they did hear about, according to Quindlen was the glass ceiling, the metaphoric barrier to the top echelons of power.

17. When she is older she sees her grandparents in an incessant game of running bases: they throw the ball back and forth—the ball is truth, how to live—and she, Rita, must run between them, pulled now to the safety of rules and traditions, now back to the thrills of defiance and pride —Lynne Sharon Schwartz, "The Melting Pot"

18. She sees the two sides of the family as opposing teams, opposing stances towards life —Lynne Sharon Schwartz, "The Melting Pot"

19. Conception. It is something . . . wherein a woman becomes a vessel, a harbor, folding her body about a jot of yolk and protein —Richard Selzer, "The Virgin and the Petri Dish"

20. Thou art thy mother's glass, and she in thee / Calls back the lovely April of her prime —William Shakespeare, "Sonnet 3," line 9
    The daughter is the looking-glass, or younger reflection, of her lovely mother.

21. Their intermittently shared life was being lifted to new octaves —John Updike, "A Sandstone Farmhouse," *The New Yorker*, 1990
    The metaphor applies to the relationship of a sick mother and her middle-aged son.

22. Nona [his daughter] was the one warm rich spot in his life: the corner on which the sun always shone —Edith Wharton, *Twilight Sleep*

■ FAMOUS PEOPLE

See: PERSONALITY PROFILES; POLITICS/ POLITICIANS

■ FANTASIES

See: DREAMS

■ FASCINATION

See: ATTRACTION

■ FASHION AND STYLE

1. Deconstructionist designers are the pit bulls of avant-garde fashion —Anon., "On the Street," New York Times, May 16, 1993

   Their clothes, "with seams and darts torn open," seem to be going to the dogs anyway.

2. So weave for us a garment of brightness / May the warp be the white light of morning / May the weft be the red light of evening —Anon., "Song of the Sky Loom," American Indian poem

   "May the fringes be the falling rain / May the border be the standing rainbow," the poem continues.

3. Good clothes are the embroidered trappings of pride, and good cheer the very eryngo-root of gluttony; so that fine backs and fat bellies are coach-horses to two of the seven deadly sins; in the boots of which coach Lechery and Sloth sit like the waiting-maid —Thomas Dekker, The Gull's Hornbook

   Decker serves up three metaphors topped by a simile. Adding several more metaphors he concludes that "fashion then was counted a disease, and horses died of it; but now, thanks to folly, it is held the only rare physic, and the purest golden asses live upon it."

4. Her hat . . . It was romance, it was mystery, it was strange, sweet sorrow —Dorothy Parker, "Glory in the Daytime"

   The hat is a metaphor for it's wearer's former glamour. The fact that the glamour is gone is clear from Parker's description of the hair beneath it which "had the various hues of neglected brass."

5. Clothes upon her ceased to be clothes and became draperies; she had the secret of line. A fluid loveliness ran all over her limbs —Vita Sackville-West, All Passion Spent

6. My whites were . . . a wild canvas depicting the dark side of metropolitan life — Richard Selzer, "A Pint of Blood"

   A surgical resident describes his uniform after a session in a metropolitan emergency ward.

7. Fashions, after all, are only induced epidemics, proving that epidemics can be induced by tradesmen —George Bernard Shaw, Preface, The Doctor's Dilemma

   Shaw elaborates with "You use a glass mirror to see your face; you use works of art to see your soul."

8. Her body jammed excruciatingly into her prison of a dress —Wilfrid Sheed, The New York Times Book Review, October 4, 1992

   Sheed's review of Marlene Dietrich described the movie legend's struggle with age during her nightclub career.

9. It / Is wholly charming, . . . / And may be hung now in the fragrant dark / Of her soft armory —Richard Wilbur, "The Catch"

   The title refers to a dress which, after much twisting and turning before the mirror by its wearer, is found to be perfect.

■ FATE

See also: CHANCE; FORTUNE/MISFORTUNE

1. Who can drain the bitter draught of destiny? —Ibn Al-Arabi, "Ode"

2. Thus the current of destiny carries us along. None but a madman would swim against the stream, and none but a fool would exert himself to swim with it. The best way is to float quietly with the tide — William Cullen Bryant, Letter to his mother, 1821

   Bryant's letter informed his mother of his recent marriage to a young lady "whom I perceived standing by my side" after "certain cabalistical expressions" had been said.

3. Men are the sport of circumstance —
Lord George Gordon Byron, "Don Juan"
In another poem, Byron spoke of man as the "slave of circumstance."

4. To fate that flings the dice, and as she flings / Of kings makes peasants, and of peasants kings —John Dryden, "Jupiter Cannot Alter the Decrees of Fate"

5. David: I am history's wish and must come true —Christopher Fry, *A Sleep of Prisoners*

6. Cassandra: Destiny, the tiger, is getting restive, Andromache! —Jean Giraudoux, *Tiger at the Gates,* Act 1
The tiger at the gates is destiny—which, for Troy, is war with the Greeks.

7. Amid the fluctuating waves of our social life [in America], somebody is always at the drowning-point —Nathaniel Hawthorne, *The House of Seven Gables*
"The tragedy," Hawthorne writes, "is enacted with as continual a repetition as that of a popular drama on a holiday."

8. Life is made up of marble and mud. And without all the deeper trust in a comprehensive sympathy above us, we might be led to suspect . . . an immitigable frown, on the iron countenance of fate —Nathaniel Hawthorne, *The House of Seven Gables*

9. When we were tossed on the ocean of the world we could hear of nothing but your verses, which published everywhere our joys and pleasures —Heloise, Letter to Peter Abelard
The world's ocean had become a confining lake for each of them: she had retired to a convent, he to a monastery.

10. I am the master of my fate; / I am the captain of my soul —William Ernest Henley, "Echoes"

11. We are all sentenced to capital punishment for the crime of living —Oliver Wendell Holmes, Sr., *Once Over the Teacups*
Holmes built on the metaphor with "though the condemned cell of our earthly existence is but a narrow and bare dwelling place, we have . . . made it tolerably comfortable for the little while we are confined in it.

12. Gallimard: We are all prisoners of our time and place —David Henry Hwang, *M. Butterfly,* Act 2, scene 4

13. She gave him from the first . . . an attaching impression of . . . having learned to butter her bread with a certain acceptance of fate —Henry James, "Fordham Castle"

14. The children of the Panhandle [a tough neighborhood in San Francisco] became soldiers, until the Big Card Dealer issued a permanent recall —Gus Lee, *China Boy*

15. There does seem to be a moment when you realize that . . . everything is arranged for you . . . just for once you've beaten the old hag —Katherine Mansfield, "Je Ne Parle Pas Français"
The story's protagonist explains that he keeps coming back to a cafe because it's "where I had the old bitch by the throat for once and did what I pleased with her."

16. Oh busy weaver! Unseen weaver! pause! one word! whither flows the fabric? What palace may it deck? Wherefore all these ceaseless toilings? Speak, weaver! Stay thy hand! —Herman Melville, *Moby Dick*

17. The gods play games with men as balls — Titus Maccius Plautus, *Captivi*

18. The wheels of circumstance that grind / So terribly within the mind —Theodore Roethke, "Silence"

19. This generation of Americans has a rendezvous with destiny —Franklin Delano Roosevelt, Acceptance speech, June 27, 1936
The President probably took his inspiration from "I Have a Rendezvous with Death," by poet Alan Seager.

20. Fate is the helmsman of the ship of life, no matter though the owner rend his clothes —Saadi (also known as Sadi), *Apologue*
The metaphor of government as the ship of state is a common variation.

21. Florizel: But as the unthought-on accident is guilty / To what we wildly do, so we profess / Ourselves to be the slaves of chance and flies / Of every wind that blows —William Shakespeare, *The Winter's Tale*, Act 4, scene 4, line 552

22. Edmund: The wheel is come full circle —William Shakespeare, *King Lear*, Act 5, scene 3, line 145

    In the coventional imagery of Elizabethan England, fortune was pictured as a wheel much like the Ferris wheels in today's amusement parks. Edmund had risen with to the height of fate's wheel, and is now being cast down.

23. I am Fate, / The thrown back noose . . . / The brow of Destiny —Michael Strange, "Fate," *Vanity Fair*, 1919

24. That's one of the few decent cards fate dealt us in the whole hand . . . unfortunately, that's not a card we can play except in the direst circumstances —Donna Tartt, *The Secret History*

    Games of chance are favorite metaphors for life's uncertainties—to play with a stacked deck or from the bottom of a stacked deck being amongst the most common. In Tartt's novel a group of students thus assess their options for dealing with a criminal act.

25. One sees one's possessions—friendships, loves—ground up in the hopper of Fate's garbage truck —Helen Vendler, "Books," *The New Yorker*, August 3, 1992

    Vendler reviewed John Asberry's Flow Chart.

26. [Fortune] makes us blindly play her terrible game, and we never see beneath the cards —Voltaire, *Philosophical Dictionary*

27. There she lay, she felt, in the hand of the Goddess who was the world . . . a little lamb laid on the altar —Virginia Woolf, "The New Dress"

28. The world has raised its whip; where will it descend? —Virginia Woolf, *Mrs. Dalloway*

    As Clarissa Dalloway is walking along a busy street, a momentary apprehension overtakes her.

■ FATHERS

See: CHILDHOOD/CHILDREN; FAMILIES/ FAMILY RELATIONSHIPS

■ FATNESS/THINNESS

See also: BODIES/THE BODY; PHYSICAL APPEARANCE

1. Velvet . . . winced at a sign at regret or weakness in the beloved mountain —Enid Bagnold, *National Velvet*

    The mountain is Velvet's mother, a former channel swimmer who has become fat with domesticity and motherhood.

2. The splendid fat cushion of a wife was there —H. E. Bates, "A Month by the Lake"

3. My flesh is boundless. An Everest of lipoids —Saul Bellow, *The Bellarosa Connection*

    The man to whom this woman thus reveals herself notes that "exquisite singers can make you forget what hillocks of suet their backsides are."

4. Dédé was a broomstick —Mavis Gallant, "Dédé"

5. The fat man was flabbily fat with bulbous pink cheeks and lips . . . with a great soft egg of a belly that was all his torso . . . pendant cones for arms and legs —Dashiell Hammett, *The Maltese Falcon*

6. He was a stringy rooster—stringy but tough —Alice Munro, "Pictures of the Ice"

    The "rooster" has gone through a period of great weight and muscle loss.

7. I'm fat, but I'm thin inside. Has it ever occurred to you that There's a thin man inside every fat man, just as they say there's a statue inside every block of stone? —George Orwell, *Coming Up for Air*

    Five years' after Orwell's novel was published, playwright Cyril Connolly offered this twist on the metaphor in The Unquiet Grave: "Imprisoned in every fat man a thin one is wildly signalling to be let out."

8. Her knees were tumors on sticks, her elbows chicken bones —Cynthia Ozick, "The Shawl"
   This wrenching image appears in a story about a concentration inmate.

9. But how did father account for great-aunt Eliza . . . who when seated, was one solid pyramidal monument from floor to neck? —Katherine Anne Porter, "Old Mortality," *Pale Horse, Pale Rider*
   The protagonist's father claims that the women in the family had always been "thin as a match" and "graceful as sylphs" supported by photos of her mother who "proved to be a candle-wick."

10. She was a puddingy woman, reposing on a big sleepy belly —V. S. Pritchett, "Tea with Mrs. Bittell"

11. His eloquence was . . . in the full-moon expansion of his stomach under his smooth waistcoat —V. S. Pritchett, "The Aristocrat"

12. A flight of smooth double chins, led down to the dizzy depths of a still-snowy bosom —Edith Wharton, *The Age of Innocence*
    Below the bosom on which the lady's stair-step chins rest "wave after wave of black silk surged away over the edges of a capacious armchair . . . "

13. Her soul hides in a dense fog of flesh — James Wolcott, "Roseanne Hits Home," *The New Yorker*, October 26, 1992
    Note the baseball metaphor of the title.

■ FAULT FINDING

See: ACCUSATIONS; CRITICISM/CRITICS

■ FAVORITES

See also: INFLUENCE; POWER

1. Great princes' favorites their fair leaves spread —William Shakespeare, "Sonnet 25," line 5

2. Duchess: Who are the violets now / That strew the green lap of the newcome spring? —William Shakespeare, *The Tragedy of King Richard the Second*, Act 5, scene 2, line 46
   The violets represent the new favorites and the new spring is the new seat of power.

■ FEAR

See also: WORRY

1. Had I been offered my deliverance from that field of horror at the cost of victory . . . I would have nodded my head eagerly to the chorus of my chattering teeth — Louis Auchincloss, "The Epicurean," *Three Lives*
   The novella's protagonist reflects on his loss of all courage when he came face to face with the realities of the battlefield during the first World War.

2. Terror in the house does roar, / But Pity stands before the door —William Blake, "Fragment"
   Terror and pity are the two emotions that bring about catharsis in classical tragedy.

3. Fear . . . the fire that melts Icarian wings —Florence Earle Coates, "The Unconquered Air?"
   The metaphor alludes to Icarus, whose father gave him wings of wax to escape from the Labyrinth of Minus. When Icarus, contrary to his father's warning, flew too close to the sun, the wings melted.

4. Fear . . . is a carrion crow —Ralph Waldo Emerson, "Compensation," *Essays: First Series*

5. Thomas: What, does everyone still knuckle / And suckle at the big breast of irrational fear? —Christopher Fry, *The Lady's Not For Burning*, Act 2

6. For weeks she had lived in a black sea of nausea and fear —Mavis Gallant, "Bernadette," *The New Yorker*, 1950–60

7. You cannot stare that hatred down / or chain the fear that stalks the watches / and breathes on you its fetid scorching

breath. —Robert Hayden, "Middle Passage. III"

8. Now comes the evening of the mind. / Here are the fireflies twitching in the blood —Donald Justice, "The Evening of the Mind"

There is a haunting quality to this poem about vague losses and forebodings—even the peach trees are "nailed to their trellises," and "martyred."

9. Maria dos Prazeres, who had lived through that time of great passions, could not control her uneasiness, and for the first time she was awakened from her sleep by the clawing of fear —Gabriel García Márquez, "Maria Dos Prazeres." *The New Yorker,* March 22, 1993

The aging courtesan sees around her manifestations of death, and responds with sleeplessness.

10. Seeded in childhood, watered every day since, fear had sprouted through her veins all her life —Toni Morrison, *Jazz*

The metaphor continues with "Thinking war thoughts it had gathered, blossomed into another thing."

11. First Fury: Soon his nerves will be throbbing like harp-strings, in exquisite arpeggios of terror —Jean-Paul Sartre, *The Flies,* Act 3

A musical duo of figures, with the simile paving the way for the metaphor.

12. Proteus: Thus have I shunn'd the fire for fear of burning, / And drench'd me in the sea, where I am drown'd —William Shakespeare, *Two Gentlemen of Verona,* Act 1, scene 1, line 78

An even older and still commonly used metaphor for being moved from one difficulty to one that's as bad or worse is to leap out of the frying pan into the fire.

13. Horatio: they, distill'd / Almost to jelly with the act of fear, / Stand dumb and speak not to him —William Shakespeare, *Hamlet,* Act 1, scene 2, line 204

Horatio is describing the reaction of the soldiers on watch duty when they see the Ghost.

14. King: we will fetters put about this fear, / Which now goes too free-footed —William Shakespeare, *Hamlet,* Act 3, scene 3, line 25

15. Thou are a frighted owl / Blind with the light of life thou'ldst not forsake —Trumbull Stickney, "Be Still. The Hanging Gardens Were a Dream"

16. Fear is a slinking cat I find / Beneath the lilacs of my mind —Sophie Tunnell, "Fear"

17. All her pride and tenderness for her brother stiffened into ice about her heart —Edith Wharton, *Twilight Sleep*

Nona is concerned about her brother's pain over his shaky marriage.

■ FEELINGS

See also: ANGER; EMOTIONS; JOY; PAIN AND SUFFERING

1. And let an empty space begin to gape / among your feelings —Joseph Brodsky, "Einem alten Architekten in Rom"

The poet counsels the old architect to be open to new, softer feelings after the fear and anger that had gripped him.

2. The tides of feeling round me rise and sink —Donald Davie, "The Evangelist"

3. Every person's feelings have a front-door and a side-door by which they may be entered. The front door is on the street. Some keep it always open; some keep it latched; some locked; some bolted,—with a chain that will let you peep in, but not get in; and some nail it up so that nothing can pass its threshold. This front-door leads into a passage which opens into an ante-room, and this onto the interior apartments. The side-door opens at once into the sacred chambers —Oliver Wendell Holmes, *The Autocrat of the Breakfast-Table*

Holmes had a penchant for extending his metaphors into essays. The metaphor of the house as a receptacle for the emotions, continued on for several paragraphs, and concluded with a warning to be careful about whom to entrust with a "key" to the side door."

4. Pride and hope and desire . . . sent up vapours of maddening incense before the eyes of his mind —James Joyce, *Portrait of the Artist as a Young Man*

   The metaphor, were it logical rather than poetic, would send the incense to the nose of the mind rather than the eyes.

5. Perhaps it is the great cyclone of feelings unleashed between Dorothy and Miss Gulch that are made actual in the great dark snake of cloud that wriggles across the prairie, eating the world —Salman Rushdie, [analysis of] *The Wizard of Oz*

   Rushdie uses the cyclone as the metaphor for overwhelming emotion, and the snake as the metaphor for the cyclone.

6. On such a whetstone as war all one's feelings get sharpened splendidly —Mikhail Sholokhov, "A Lesson In Hatred"

7. Lust, anger and greed . . . the soul-destroying gates of hell —Archilochus, *The Bhagavad-Gita*

8. It is a thing to have, / A lion, an ox in his breast, / To feel it breathing there —Wallace Stevens, "Poetry is a Destructive Force"

   "The lion sleeps in the sun. / Its nose is on its paws. / It can kill a man," writes Stevens.

9. Please! That is not your mind speaking, it's the foam of churned feelings and has no meaning" —Rex Stout, *Fer-de-Lance*

   Nero Wolfe tries to calm down the daughter of a man who has just been murdered.

10. He feels freedom like oxygen everywhere around him. Tothery is an eddy of air, and the building he is in, the streets of the town, are mere stairways and alleyways in space —John Updike, *Rabbit, Run*

    The metaphor is dependent on the simile that precedes it.

11. Joy fixes us to eternity and pain fixes us to time —Simone Weil, *The New York Notebook*

    Weill also refers to pain as the root of knowledge.

12. He's romantic and extravagant: he can't live on the interest of his feelings —Edith Wharton, *The Reef*

    Anna Leath uses a financial metaphor to express her concern about her stepson's relationship with his fiancee. "Things go deep with him, and last long," she explains. "It took him a long time to recover from his other unlucky love affair."

■ FEMINISTS/FEMINIST BEHAVIOR

See: WOMEN

■ FENCES

See: BARRIERS

■ FERTILITY/INFERTILITY

1. We are two-legged wombs, that's all; sacred vessels, ambulatory chalices —Margaret Atwood, *The Handmaid's Tale*

   The novel's "handmaids" had, the single purpose of bearing children for sterile couples.

2. This country is a swamp . . . a more terrible swamp than you can imagine. Whenever you plant a sapling in this swamp the roots begin to rot; the leaves grow yellow and wither. And we have planted the sapling of Christianity in this swamp —Shusaku Endo, *Silence*

   This was an explanation of the failure of Catholicism, which tried to supplant the native religions but could not gain a foothold in seventeenth century Japan.

3. The baron was a dry branch of the great family Katzenellenbogen, and inherited the relics of the property, and all the pride

of his ancestors —Washington Irving, "The Specter Bridegroom"

> *The baron of the cat's elbow was not so dry, however, that he could not manage a single daughter.*

4. Joan: Murder not then the fruit within my womb —William Shakespeare, *The First Part of Henry the Sixth*, Act 5, scene 4, line 63

5. Who lets so fair a house fall to decay, / Which husbandry in honor might uphold / Against the stormy gusts of winter's day / And barren rage of death's eternal cold? —William Shakespeare, "Sonnet 13," line 9

> *The sonnet ends with "Dear my love, you know, / You had a father; let your son say so," and a major theme of the cycle voice.*

■ FICTION

See: BOOKS; WRITING/WRITERS

■ FIDELITY

See: LOYALTY

■ FIGHTING

See also: CONFLICT

1. The blood of budget battles washed from his hands, President Clinton is finally focused on health-care reform —Natalie Angier, *The New York Times*, August 22, 1993

> *The metaphor, an allusion to Shakespeare's Lady Macbeth, introduced an article about the changing image of doctors in the movies. A front page blurb called attention to the piece with "As movies put the knife to doctors and nurses, the medical profession suffers from a serious image problem."*

2. I fought with tooth and nail to save my niche —Robert Browning, "The Bishop Orders his Tomb at Saint Praxed's Church"

> *This image, dating to the sixteenth century, has become so common that few are aware of the implied animal metaphor.*

3. Shots and salvoes smacked, thudded, and plopped, flattening the distances into a pancake —Boris Pasternak, *Doctor Zhivago*

> *Strikers are causing the Cossacks to react.*

4. Gore's red cape enticed Perot into insulting charges and insolent digs, which Americans recognize as symptoms of blown cool —William Safire, "Essay," *The New York Times*, November 11, 1993

> *This analysis of a televised debate on NAFTA (North American Free Trade Agreement) pictured Vice-President Al Gore as a matador and Ross Perot as a mean-spirited bull. To blow one's cool is a popular variant of to blow one's fuse or to blow one's stack.*

5. Thus you often see a common sharper in Competition with a Gentleman of the first Rank; tho' all Mankind is convinced, that a fighting Gamester is only a Pickpocket, with the Courage of an Highway-Man — Richard Steele

6. Go to the wall on this issue if the events demand it —William Lowndes Yancey, Southern rights speech, 1860

> *The "orator of secession" used a military metaphor from the Middle Ages. The image has been extended to apply to any situation demanding extreme action.*

■ FINGERS

See: BODIES/THE BODY

■ FIRMNESS

See: TOUGHNESS

■ FISH

See also: ANIMALS

1. The fish / whose scales turn aside the sun's sword by their polish —Marianne Moore, "An Egyptian Pulled Glass Bottle in the Shape of a Fish"

2. Goldfish . . . are flowers that move — Han Suyin, *The Crippled Tree*

■ FLATTERY

1. A flatterer carries water in one hand and fire in the other —Anon., German Proverb

2. He was charming to his daughter-in-law and plied her with compliments, a diet to which Célestine's vanity was unaccustomed —Honoré de Balzac, *Cousin Bette*

3. A man that flattereth his neighbors spreadeth a net for his feet —The Bible, *O.T., Proverbs 29:5*
   > *A much quoted variation of this from Sir Walter Scott's* Marmion *(1808) is "Oh, what a tangled web we weave, / When first we practice to deceive."*

4. He set my heart floating on the honey stream of his words —Kshetrayya, "Dancing-Girl's Song"

5. With regard to flatterers, of which courts are full, men . . . can with difficulty guard against this plague —Niccolo Machiavelli, *The Prince*

6. From long experience I knew that a compliment from Fabert was an investment. What dividend was he after now? —André Maurois, "Reality Transposed"

7. Valère: There is no fear of overdoing flattery . . . There is nothing so impertinent or so ridiculous that they [the dupes] cannot be made to swallow, provided it is seasoned with praise —Molière, *The Miser*, Act 1

8. Joan: By fair persuasions mix'd with sugar'd words, / We will entice the Duke of Burgundy —William Shakespeare, *The First Part of Henry the Sixth*, Act 3, scene 3, line 18
   > *The sugar metaphor reappears in* The Second Part of Henry the Sixth, *(3,2, 44), when the*

King *says "Hide not thy poison with such sugar'd words.*

9. Helicanus: flattery is the bellows [that] blows up sin —William Shakespeare, *Pericles, Prince of Tyre*, Act 1, scene 2, line 39
   > *He adds that the object of flattery is "but a spark / To which the blast [of the bellows] gives heat and stronger glowing."*

10. York [responding to Gaunt's "My death's sad tale may yet undeaf his ear:" No, it is stopp'd with other flattering sounds, / . . . Lascivious metres, to whose venom sound / The open ear of youth doth always listen —William Shakespeare, *The Tragedy of King Richard the Second*, Act 2, scene 1, line 17
    > *It is the venom sound that makes Gaunt's sad tale fall on Richard's metaphorically deaf ears. The notion of a snake's poison poured into the ear has concrete reality in* Hamlet. *The elder Hamlet is killed by the literal venom; Richard's death is hastened by the figurative venom.*

■ FLAWS

1. He's [Professor John Shelton Reed is] not really curmudgeonly about the traditional culture of the South, which he defends as "an honorable tradition, if one with a serpent in its belly" —Peter Applebome, *The New York Times*, January 24, 1993

2. Small faults indulged are little thieves that let in greater —Thomas Fuller, *Gnomologia*

3. Among other deformities it [the Constitution] . . . has an awful squinting. It squints towards monarchy —Patrick Henry, From a debate before the Virginia convention, June 5, 1788, on the adoption of the constitution
   > *Henry was arguing against adoption.*

4. A deepening recession made it harder for nations with weaker currencies to keep up with the likes of Germany and France, and fault lines started slicing through Eu-

rope —Herbert H. Herring, "Business Diary," *The New York Times,* May 14, 1993

5. The defects of a mere acquaintance, and even of a friend, are to us real poison, against which we are fortunately "mithridated" —Marcel Proust, *Cities of the Plain*

∎ FLEXIBILITY/INFLEXIBILITY

See also: CHANGEABLENESS/UNCHANGE-ABLENESS; COMPROMISE

1. Thy neck is an iron sinew, and thy brow brass —The Bible, *O.T., Jeremiah 48:4*
   Iron and brass are metaphors for obstinacy.

2. Some foreign diplomats said a staring contest may be shaping up between Israel and Lebanon, with the fate of the exiles perhaps depending on who blinks first — Clyde Haberman, "400 Arabs Ousted by Israel are Mired in Frozen Limbo," *The New York Times,* December 19, 1992

3. The rulers [in Japan] are politicians and large businesses. The ruled are everyone else, the "grass people," so aptly termed because they bow in whatever direction the wind blows —Reiko Hatsumi, "Can Japanese Politics be Purified?" *The New York Times,* September 1992

4. Valere: There are certain natures which can be overcome only by indirect means; . . . restive minds, who rear at truth, who always stiffen against the straight path of reason —Molière, *The Miser,* Act 1
   Valere uses a horsemanship metaphor to persuade his beloved to humor her miserly father so that in the end the lovers may get their own way.

5. Max is liquid. He changes shape. He fills the container whatever the container is — Martin Cruz Smith, *Red Square*
   Smith adds "In a fluid situation, he's king."

6. You must learn to drink the cup of life as it comes, Connie, without stirring it up from

the bottom. That's where the bitter dregs are —Agnes Sligh Turnbull, *The Rolling Year*

∎ FLIES

See: INSECTS

∎ FLOWERS

See also: NATURE; NATURE SCENES; TREES

1. [The rose] Queen of the garden art though, / And I—the Clay at thy feet —Julia Dorr, "The Clay to the Rose"

2. Blossoms are the clocks of the seasons — Kara Ann Marling, *The New York Times Book Review,* March 14, 1993
   The reviewer of a book about the relationship between people and their surroundings, The Power of Place *by Winifred Gallagher, accounted for the pleasure we take in flowers.*

3. The shaggy golden suds of blooming forsythia glow through the smoke that fogs the garden —John Updike, *Rabbit, Run*

4. Each flower wears on the roof of its mouth two fans of freckles where the anthers tap —John Updike, *Rabbit, Run*
   Rabbit is working as a gardener. His floral observations include "Those ugly purple tatters the iris."

∎ FOG

See also: NATURE SCENES

1. The fog . . . was so dense without, that although the court was of the narrowest, the houses opposite were mere phantoms —Charles Dickens, *A Christmas Carol*
   In an afterword Clifton Fadiman remarks on the weather as an important "character" that dominates the pages "like a jolly giant, wreathed in fog and myth." Dickens himself refers to its importance with "One might have thought that Nature lived hard by, and was brewing on a large scale."

2. The yellow fog that rubs its back upon the window-panes, / The yellow smoke that rubs its muzzle on the window-panes, / Licked its tongue into the corners of the evening —T. S. Eliot, "The Love Song of J. Alfred Prufrock"

> The fog-as-cat image that appears in this long poem, is the single image in Carl Sandburg's six-line poem "Fog," which begins "The fog comes / on little cat feet."

3. [Baghdad on the eve of the Persian Gulf war:] The fog is so dirty that it has a texture . . . and, worst of all, teeth — Michael Kelly, *Chronicles of a Small War*

> He tops this with another metaphor: "with each breath you are an involuntary Hoover."

4. Beyond them [waves rising at the surf-line] a padded wall of fog was sliding shoreward —Ross MacDonald, *The Barbarous Coast*

5. He kept them so breathlessly eager for the fog to lift . . . Thus they were quick to profit by the least rift in the armor of the skies —Antoine de Saint-Exupery, *Night Flight*

■ FOLLY

See: FOOLHARDINESS

■ FOOD AND DRINK

1. The food here is plain poison. And such small portions! —Anon., Quoted in Bennett Cerf's *Try And Stop Me*

> The purported source of this oft-quoted remark is not a youngster at Boy Scout camp, as most of us have supposed, but the mother of the author Arthur Kober.

2. Gastronomy, the seducer of virtuous monks, opened its arms to him —Honoré de Balzac, *Cousin Pons*

> At one point Balzac's gourmet, who is also passionate about the acquisition of fine art objects, expresses the thought that "within him heart and stomach were enemies; that the stomach demanded what the heart feared."

3. To a man with an empty stomach food is God —Mohandes Karamchand Gandhi

4. There's a tasty bit here we call the pope's nose —James Joyce, *Portrait of the Artist as a Young Man*

> During a Christmas dinner full of religious and political contention, Mr. Dedalus uses a coarse metaphor for the turkey's tailpiece to heighten the strife.

5. In every grain and legume, history's thumb print is present —Molly O'Neill, *The New York Times*, July 18, 1993

> The Arabs, according to O'Neill, felt that it was the berry of a giant wheat plant, not an apple, that corrupted Eve.

6. Professor Cassidy reports that, on occasion, strength and viscosity [of coffee] go too far, and in rural Wisconsin farmers complain: "It's too thick to drink, and too wet to plow" —William Safire, *On Language*.

■ FOOLHARDINESS

See also: DANGER; MISTAKES; STUPIDITY

1. Men will ride you when you make an ass of yourself —Anon., Proverb

2. The energy, intelligence, and enterprise the Baron employed in order to dive head first into a hornet's nest might have made an honest fortune —Honoré de Balzac, *Cousin Bette*

> The hornet's nest is the salon of Madame Marneffe and the intrigues to which the love-struck Baron is blind.

3. Folly is the cloke of knavery —William Blake, "Proverbs of Hell"

> In another proverb, Blake uses the same image of the cloak, and says "Shame is Pride's cloke."

4. They talk of Feavours that infect the Brains, / But Non-sense is the new Disease that reigns —John Dryden, "Prologue," Nahum Tate's *The Loyal General*

5. My manhood, long misled by wandring fires, / Follow'd false lights —John Dryden, "The Hind and the Panther"
   "Good life be now my task," writes the poet.

6. He [Woody Allen] flew too near the sun of license, and melted the wax right out of his wings—the Icarus of the Arts & Leisure section —Adam Gopnik, *The New Yorker,* October 25, 1993
   Gopnik's profile linked Allen's personal troubles with Oscar Wilde's trial as well as with the mythical Icarus.

7. Antony: My very hairs do mutiny, for the white / Reprove the brown for rashness, and they them —William Shakespeare, *Antony and Cleopatra,* Act 3, scene 9, line 12
   Antony is contemplating an act of cowardice. His nature is turning against itself just as his hair is turning gray.

8. Kent: Kill thy physician, and thy fee bestow / Upon the foul disease —William Shakespeare, *King Lear,* Act 1, scene 1, line 166
   Lear will not take good counsel from Kent, who upbraids him.

9. Gloucester: Ah! thus King Henry throws away his crutch / Before his legs be firm to bear his body —William Shakespeare, *The Second Part of Henry the Sixth,* Act 3, scene 1, line 189
   "Thus is the shepherd beaten from thy side," warns Gloucester, "And wolves are gnarling who shall gnaw thee first."

10. Suffolk: were'it not madness then, / To make the fox surveyor of the fold? —William Shakespeare, *The Second Part of Henry the Sixth,* Act 3, scene 1, line 252
    The fox has been a symbol for slyness since the thirteenth century. In this case, the fox is Humphrey. Common variants include to be a sly fox or to be foxy.

11. King Richard: and must I ravel out / My weav'd-up folly? —William Shakespeare, *The Tragedy of King Richard the Second,* Act 4, scene 1, line 228

12. When the past is de-fogged / And old foot tracks of folly show fleetingly clear before / rationalization again descends —Robert Penn Warren, "Vision"

13. Blanche: But I have been foolish—casting my pearls before swine! —Tennessee Williams, *A Streetcar Named Desire,* scene 10
    The metaphor comes from the Sermon on the Mount (Matthew, 7:6). When Dorothy Parker and Clare Boothe Luce approached a door, Luce stepped aside with "Age before Beauty" to which Parker replied "Pearls before swine!"

∎ FOOTBALL
See: SPORTS

∎ FORBEARS
See: ANCESTRY/ANCESTORS

∎ FORCE
See: AGGRESSION; POWER; STRENGTH/ WEAKNESS

∎ FOREBODING
See also: FATE; FEAR; WORRY

1. The vacant terraces / Wet, chill and glistening / Towards the sunset / beyond the broken doors of to-day —John Gould Fletcher, "Irradiations"

2. Anath: He has stood all day under my brain's stairway —Christopher Fry, *The Firstborn,* Act 1, scene 1

3. Martina: The house was crowned with crows this morning —Christopher Fry, *Thor, With Angels*

4. A red flag at once began to flutter in her stomach —Sean O'Faolain, "The Faithless Wife"

5. Ever afterward, when we embraced, and I boarded the train or plane that would take

me away from her, a heavy, prickly blanket woven with mixed stripes of apprehension and gloom enveloped me —Eileen Simpson, *Orphans*

The narrator's separation anxiety evidenced itself in her friendships as well as during partings from her sister.

FOREIGN RELATIONS

See: INTERNATIONAL RELATIONS

FORESIGHT

See: ALERTNESS

FORGETFULNESS

See: MEMORY/MEMORIES

FORGETTING

See: MEMORY/MEMORIES

FORGIVENESS

See also: SIN/REDEMPTION

1. When with the scourge of penance man doth him (himself) bind / The oil of forgiveness then shall he find —Anon., *Everyman*

2. Forgiving the unrepentant is drawing pictures on water —Anon., Japanese Proverb

   To draw a picture on water or on sand is also used as a metaphor for any type of futile action.

3. Christ has thrown the door of mercy wide open —Jonathan Edwards, "Sinners in the Hands of an Angry God"

4. His days and works and thoughts could make no atonement for him, the fountains of sanctifying grace having ceased to refresh his soul —James Joyce, *Portrait of the Artist as a Young Man*

   Joyce includes an allusion to Hesiod's Works and Days *before the metaphor.*

5. The forgiving state of mind is a magnetic power for attracting good —Catherine Ponder, Epigraph

6. Prince: I do beseech your majesty may salve / The long-grown wounds of my intemperance —William Shakespeare, *The First Part of King Henry the Fourth,* Act 2, scene 4, line 433

7. King: The gates of mercy shall be all shut up —William Shakespeare, *The Life of Henry the Fifth,* Act 3, scene 3, line 10

8. In distance, lynx-scream or direful owl-stammer / Freezes the blood in a metaphysical shudder—which / Might be the first, feather-fine brush of Grace —Robert Penn Warren, "Vision"

   There are two metaphors. The first—freezing the blood-is made fresh by the use to which it is put; the second by the fact that it is antithetical to the first metaphor.

FORTUNE/MISFORTUNE

See also: FAILURE; FATE; SUCCESS/FAILURE

1. Fortune is a god and rules men's life —Aeschylus, "Agamemnon"

2. Fortune is of glass; she glitters just at the moment of breaking —Anon.

   Chance was often personified as the Goddess of luck or fortune, in this example (attributed to Napoleon III), not lasting even a moment beyond its initial glitter.

3. Every man is the architect of his own fortune —Anon., Greek Expression

4. Industry is fortune's right hand and frugality her left —Anon., Proverb

5. I have fallen into the abyss of misfortune —Anon., "The Story of the Negro Dorerame"

6. Strepsiades: My goods are seized, I'm robbed, and mobbed, and plundered / . . . A galloping consumption seized my money —Aristophanes, *The Clouds*

7. Every man was not born with a silver spoon in his mouth —Miguel Cervantes, *Don Quixote*

   Texas Democrat Ann Richards made this popular metaphor one of her key phrases to picture President George Bush as a rich man unable to respond to the needs of the less fortunate.

8. Well, there I was in clover, you will say — Wilkie Collins, *The Moonstone*

   The expression indicating good-fortune is still current.

9. The protagonist . . . is a veritable magnet for fortune's slings and arrows —Joel Conarroe, *The New York Times Book Review*, May 17, 1992

   The reviewer of Edna O'Brien's Time and Tide, links his metaphor to Hamlet's "to be or not to be" speech.

10. Anath: The face of all this land is turned to the wall —Christopher Fry, *The Firstborn*, Act 2, scene 2

    A plague is visited on Egypt. "The terrace crackles with dying locusts," says Anath.

11. Fortune is so blind that in a crowd in which there is perhaps but one wise and brave man, it is not be expected that she should single him out —Heloise, Letter to Peter Abelard

    Personification is used as a metaphor. The letters between Heloise and Abelard were translated anonymously and first published in London in 1722.

12. Men's fortunes are on a wheel, which in its turning suffers not the same man to prosper forever —Herodotus

13. Conrad: My ship of fortune furl'd her silken sails,— / Let her glide on! —John Keats, *Otho the Great*, Act 1, scene 1

14. Fortune, [a river] which shows her power where no measures have been taken to resist her, and directs her fury where she knows that no dykes or barriers have been made to hold her —Niccolo Machiavelli, *The Prince*

    "I think that fortune is the ruler of half our actions, but that she allows the other half or

    thereabouts to be governed by us," writes the author.

15. Fortune is a woman, and it is necessary, if you wish to master her, to conquer her by force; and it can be seen that she lets herself be overcome by the bold rather than by those who proceed coldly — Niccolo Machiavelli, *The Prince*

    Maybe women were different in the sixteenth century, or men in that century never outgrew their adolescent fantasies.

16. Ill news . . . swallow-winged, but what's good walks on crutches —Philip Massinger, *The Picture*, II

17. His [Alexander's] high fortune, so liable to be tossed by stormy winds, required ample ballast and a master hand at the helm —Plutarch, *Plutarch's Lives*

    Plutarch reports on the meeting between Alexander the Great and Diogenes, the philosopher who Alexander professed to envy.

18. And why could not Mr. Budd also have burst out into marble and electricity and swum to fortune on the rising tide? — Dorothy L. Sayers, "The Inspiration of Mr. Budd"

    A crooked brother caused Budd to abandon a successful hairdressing business and "run to vast London, the refuge of all who shrink from the eyes of their neighbors." Having paid off the brother's debts, Budd can't afford to compete with a competitor's sleek shop.

19. Leicester: and now amid / This shipwreck of my fortunes I am seeking / A spar to which I can cling fast —Johann Christoph Friedrich von Schiller, *Mary Stuart*, Act 2

    Leicester has wooed the queen for ten years, submitted to her whims, "the toy of petty, whimsical caprices," only to rejected for a more royal suitor.

20. Talbot: Misfortune was a rigorous school to you —Johann Christoph Friedrich von Schiller, *Mary Stuart*, Act 2

21. Parolles: I am a man whom Fortune hath cruelly scratched —William Shakespeare,

All's Well That Ends Well, Act 5, scene 2, line 28

> *Lavache, the clown to whom this remark is addressed, answers: "And what would you have me do? 'tis too late to pare her nails down."*

22. Pisanio: Fortune brings in some boats that are not steered —William Shakespeare, *Cymbeline,* Act 4, scene 3, line 46

23. Worcester: It rain'd down fortune show'ring on your head, / And such a flood of greatness fell on you —William Shakespeare, *The First Part of King Henry the Fourth,* Act 5, scene 1, line 47

24. Hamlet: To be, or not to be, that is the question: / Whether 'tis nobler in the mind to suffer / the slings and arrows of outrageous fortune, or to take arms against a sea of troubles / And by opposing end them —William Shakespeare, *Hamlet,* Act 3, scene 1, line 57

> *Hamlet's quandary illustrates that Shakespeare was not immune to mixing his metaphors. The first metaphor is frequently quoted and adapted; for example, during the 1993 Tanglewood Music festival a negative review of an Israeli Philharmonic concert prompted a* Berkshire Eagle *reader to write "evidently the security at the concert could not shield the musicians from the slings and arrows of an outrageous critic."*

25. Kent: Fortune, good night: smile once more; turn thy wheel! —William Shakespeare, *King Lear,* Act 2, scene 2, line 179

> *In the last act, Edmund, who has played falsely and lost all, brings the houses of Lear and Gloucester down with his own and says, "The wheel has come full circle." (5, 3, 176).*

26. Fool: Fortune, that arrant whore, / Ne'er turns the key to th' poor —William Shakespeare, *King Lear,* Act 2, scene 4, line 52

27. Fluellen: Fortune is painted blind, with a muffler afore his eyes to signify to you, that Fortune is blind. And she is painted also with a wheel, to signify to you, which is the moral of it, that she is turning and inconstant —William Shakespeare, *The Life of Henry the Fifth,* Act 3, scene 6, line 30

Fluellen interrupts Pistol's "And giddy fortune's furious fickle wheel, / That goddess blind, / That stands upon the rolling restless stone" The image of fortune's giddy wheel can also be found in The Rape of Lucrece, *line 952.*

28. King: Will Fortune never come with both hands full / But write her fair words still in foulest letters? —William Shakespeare, *The Second Part of King Henry the Fourth,* Act 4, scene 4, line 103

> *The king elaborates with "She either gives a stomach and no food; / Such are the poor, in health; or else a feast / And takes away the stomach; such are the rich, / That have abundance and enjoy it not.*

29. Timon: Thou art a slave, whom Fortune's tender arm / With favor never clasp'd, but bred a dog. / . . . But myself / Who had the world as my confectionary — William Shakespeare, *Timon of Athens,* Act 4, scene 3, line 251

> *Timon is addressing Apemantus, the churlish philosopher who has come to see him, in the cave where he retreated after the friends who once "stuck as leaves / Do on the oak, have with one winter's brush / Fell from their boughs, and left me open, bare / For every storm that blows."*

30. Oedipus: I hold myself son of Fortune . . . She is the mother from whom I spring — Sophocles, *Oedipus the King*

> *Oedipus boasts that he is worthy no matter what his lineage may prove.*

31. O fortune, fortune thou art / A bitch — John Vanbrugh, *The Relapse, I*

> *In a 1906 letter to H. G. Wells, Henry James wrote "The moral flabbiness born of the exclusive worship of the bitch-goddess SUCCESS . . . is our national disease.*

32. [In this best of all possible worlds] these [misfortunes] are only the shadows in a fair picture —Voltaire, *Candide*

33. And my father said, "My ship will come in yet, / And you'll see all the beautiful world there is to see" —Robert Penn Warren, "October Picnic Long Ago"

> *This common metaphor is mercantile rather than nautical, since most trading was done by ship.*

34. The loss of her insignificant fortune . . . had represented only the means of holding her in bondage and its disappearance was the occasion of her immediate plunge into the wide bright sea of life surrounding the island of her captivity —Edith Wharton, *The Reef*

35. Life went on through Lily's teens: a zig-zag broken course down which the family craft glided on a rapid current of amusement, tugged at by the undertow of a perpetual need . . . of more money — Edith Wharton, *The House of Mirth*

Lily has been struggling with money problems since her coming-out party, which was "fringed by a heavy thunder-cloud of bills."

36. This is the cause that I could never yet / Hang on their sleeves, that weigh, as thou mayst see, / A chip of chance more than a pound of wit —Sir Thomas Wyatt, the Elder, "Mine Own John Poins"

A small bit of good fortune is worth more than a large sum of intelligence, in the eyes of some.

■ FRAGILITY

See also: HELPLESSNESS

1. Our house is made of glass . . . and our lives are made of glass; and there's nothing we can do to protect ourselves — Joyce Carol Oates, *American Appetites*

2. Electra: The repose of cities and men's souls hang on a thread —Jean-Paul Sartre, *The Flies*, Act 1

To hang by a thread has been a popular metaphor for any precarious situation since the sixteenth century. The flies of the playwright's title are a more complicated metaphor, symbolizing the French people's guilt for their action during the German occupation during the Second World War.

3. Desdemona: If I be left behind, / A moth of peace, and he go to the war, / The rites for which I love him are bereft me — William Shakespeare, *Othello*, Act 1, scene 3, line 255

"Moth of peace" would seem to indicate fragility.

4. More than 25 songs hang from the fragile reed of the radio program —Lawrence Van Gelder, "Review/Theater," *The New York Times*, November 23, 1992

The show being reviewed, The Sheik of Avenue B, *recreated a 1930s radio program . . . though not for long. It was a failure.*

■ FRAGMENTATION

See: CONCENTRATION/DISTRACTION

■ FRANKNESS

See: CANDOR

■ FRAUD

See: DECEPTION

■ FRECKLES

See also: FACES

1. There was a saddle of freckles across her small nose —John Cheever, "The Hartleys"

2. The kid was a boy with bas-relief freckles —O. Henry, "The Ransom of Red Chief"

3. Across her skin a galaxy of freckles glowed with health —Joyce Carol Oates, "Accomplished Desires"

■ FREE WILL

See: SELF-RELIANCE

■ FREEDOM OF EXPRESSION

See also: JOURNALISM/JOURNALISTS

1. The Republican war on interviewers has another swift sword that may be even more effective in the strategy to force reporters to sit down and shut up —Phil Donahue, *New York Times*, August 26, 1992

The resonance of the quotation emanates from the "terrible, swift sword" of the Lord, in Julia Ward Howe's "The Battle Hymn of the Republic."

2. If I am [still around after Hong Kong once again becomes part of China in 1997], they will be allowing a few cats to meow —Christine Loh, Quoted in "At Home Abroad," *New York Times*, July 19, 1993

   The outspoken businesswoman and member of the Hong Kong Legislative Council was quoted by Anthony Lewis in his survey of the economic changes in East Asia.

3. No man and no force can put thought in a concentration camp forever —Franklin Delano Roosevelt, Speech to American Booksellers Association, April 23, 1942

   The metaphor referred to the Nazis' burning of books and was extended as follows: "Books are weapons . . . make them weapons for man's freedom."

4. Coriolanus: At once pluck out / that multitudinous tongue; let them not lick / The sweet which is their poison —William Shakespeare, *Coriolanus*, Act 3, scene 1, line 155

   Coriolanus does not believe in freedom of expression for the masses and urges the senators not to permit it.

5. Mowbray: Within my mouth you have enjail'd my tongue —William Shakespeare, *The Tragedy of King Richard the Second*, Act 1, scene 3, line 166

   Mowbray's banishment condemns him to silence.

■ FREEDOM/RESTRAINT

See also: CONTROL; ENTRAPMENT; LIBERTY; MASTERY/SUBORDINATION

1. He will not be chained. He tears her little cords to bits with a single toss of his head —Louis Auchincloss, "Afterword"

   Auchincloss seems to allude to Samson when writing about the refusal of the novel's hero, to be tied down by his wife.

2. Slavery . . . a weed that grows in every soil —Edmund Burke, Speech, March 22, 1775

3. My very chains and I grew friends, / So much a long communion tends —Lord George Gordon Byron, "The Prisoner of Chillon"

   This confession of "friendship" is a surprising stanza in a poem about a political prisoner literally shackled and incarcerated.

4. Let blood and flesh be mud and mire; / . . . freedom a drug that's bought and sold —e. e. cummings, "My Father Moved Through Dooms of Love"

   Though wars may turn people to "mud and mire," and cruelty abound, Cummings's father surmounts all that is worst in the world in this poem of love.

5. The freedom she had glimpsed as an ambitious girl of twenty had turned into a narrow tunnel, and nobody would let her out —Margaret Drabble, *The Middle Ground*

6. Now pay her no attention, you. / Your gears do not engage. / By and large it's meet you should / Keep to your gelded cage —W. S. Graham, "Baldy Bane"

   This drinking song has many puns; its humor comes from the substitution of a single vowel in the more common bird in a gilded cage.

7. First Young Weaver: We want to *live* that's all. An' so we've cut the rope we were hung up with —Gerhart Hauptmann, *The Weavers*, Act 5

   The rope represents the factory owner's hold on the factory workers who, in Hauptman's dramatization of an 1848 uprising, finally free themselves.

8. Freedom is the open window through which pours the sunlight of the human spirit and of human dignity —Herbert Hoover, on his ninetieth birthday, August 10, 1967

9. The general spread of the light of science has already laid open to every view the palpable truth, that the mass of mankind has not been born with saddles on their backs, nor a favored few booted and spurred, ready to ride them legitimately by the grace of God —Thomas Jefferson

This was probably Jefferson's last metaphor, since it was part of his response to an invitation to the fiftieth anniversary of the Declaration of Independence, just a few days before his death.

10. The strongest power in Europe, Germany, is no longer a shackled Gulliver — Josef Joffe, Op-Ed, "After the Geldkrieg," *The New York Times*, September 20, 1992
    This allusion-as-metaphor was used in an analysis of the explosion of the European Monetary System and Germany's shedding of its old dependencies. A day later William Safire commented on the "slim as a mannequin's waist" vote by which France okayed a union of European currencies, even though they'd been told that the only way to stop German industry from taking over its competitors "was to enmesh that Gulliver in a web of Lilliputiana bureaucracy."

11. She had done her best to clip his wings — Katherine Mansfield, "Mr. Reginald Peacock's Day"
    A vain man feels everyone except his wife appreciates his charm and talent. The common metaphor of the title slyly hints at the truth.

12. Jacques: If I don't give you as sumptuous a dinner as I'd like to, it's your steward's fault, who clipped my wings with the scissors of his economy —Molière, *The Miser*, Act 4
    High fliers are still likely to have their wings clipped and, while this has become a trite metaphor, the scissors image is fresh and startling.

13. Heaven knows how to put a proper price upon its goods; and it would be strange indeed, if so celestial an article as FREEDOM should not be highly rated — Thomas Paine, "The Crisis, Number 1," *Common Sense*
    The metaphor of the power in heaven as a merchant savvy in the art of proper pricing is part of the paragraph that begins with Paine's much-quoted "These are the times that try men's souls."

14. I did not let them nail my soul —Rita Boumy Pappas, "Roxanne M."

15. Once the mind is free it will be destroyed rather than be put back in chains —I. I. Rabi, "Scientist and Humanist"

16. Joan: to change bonds of iron to thin spiderwebs / Is a slight thing to Your omnipotence —Johann Christoph Friedrich von Schiller, *Maid of Orleans*, Act 5, scene 3
    Joan's prayer invokes God's ability to turn weak bonds [spiderwebs] to iron and vice-versa.

17. Iago: he will divorce you, / Or put upon you what restraint, and grievance, / That law . . . Will give him cable —William Shakespeare, *Othello*, Act 1, scene 2, line 114
    This is a nautical metaphor for letting out a line to give a ship some leeway.

18. Then, by command, she [St. Joan] followed the King and his frivolous court and endured a gilded captivity for a time, as well as her free spirit could —Mark Twain, "Saint Joan of Arc"
    The metaphor survives in the bird in the gilded cage as an image of lack of freedom no matter how comfortable the "cage."

19. He has points of contact outside the great gilt cage in which we are all huddled for the world to gape at —Edith Wharton, *The House of Mirth*
    Lawrence Selden's movement out of the figurative cage door Lily Barth cannot push open, is essentially a false freedom.

■ FRESHNESS/STALENESS

See also: ORIGINALITY/UNORIGINALITY

1. It's a little saddle worn. It's been ridden hard —Tom Brokaw, Charley Rose Public Television interview, December 11, 1992
   Brokaw thus responded to a question couched in a rather "saddle-worn" metaphor: "Is prime time news a dinosaur?"

2. Fish and visitors smell in three days — Benjamin Franklin, *Poor Richard's Almanack*
   Franklin compares a guest who overstays his welcome, to a dead fish kept too long without cooking.

3. There was one daring new ingredient in the newly minted [*Reader's*] *Digest* formula—sex—and it too would become a

staple —Richard Lingemann, *The New York Times Book Review*, August 22, 1993

A case of the metaphor going into the whole editorial mix.

4. They take issues that have been chewed over for centuries and finally succeed in reducing them to cud —Frank Rich, "Movies in Brief," *The New York Times*, January 19, 1993

This capsule review of the film A Few Good Men *continued "its pseudo-profundity is a piece of glorified banality."*

5. I feel that *Angels in America* . . . the most thrilling new American play of my adult lifetime . . . lets in gusts of fresh air — Frank Rich, "Stage View," *The New York Times*, June 6, 1993

6. I go to my study, to the still-virginal word processor —D. M. Thomas, *Memories and Hallucinations*

■ FRIENDSHIP/FRIENDS

See also: CONNECTIONS; PEOPLE, INTER-ACTION

1. Friendship is a furrow in the sand — Anon., Tongan Proverb

2. Friendship . . . maketh daylight in the understanding —Sir Francis Bacon, *Advancement of Learning*, Book 1

3. A faithful friend is a secure shelter —The Bible, *Apocrypha, Ecclesiasticus 6*

4. Friendship—a ship big enough to carry two in fair weather, but only one in foul — Ambrose Bierce, *The Devil's Dictionary*

5. Friends are the thermometers by which we may judge the temperature of our fortunes —Lady Marguerite Blessington

6. Friendship is Love without wings —Lord George Gordon Byron, "L'Amitié est l'Amour san Ailes"

7. Friendship is a flowering tree —Samuel Taylor Coleridge, "The Reproof and Reply"

8. Fan the sinking flame of hilarity with the wing of friendship —Charles Dickens, *The Old Curiosity Shop*

9. Best friend, my well-spring in the wilderness! —George Eliot, *The Spanish Gypsy*

10. [Friendship:] It must plant itself on the ground before it vaults over the moon — Ralph Waldo Emerson, "Friendship," *Essays: First Series*

11. A friend may well be reckoned the masterpiece of Nature —Ralph Waldo Emerson, "Friendship," *Essays: First Series*

In another essay ["Eloquence," Society and Solitude] Emerson wrote "The ornament of a house is the friends who frequent it."

12. She had exclusive friendships for each of them [the many women who had declared her their "only friend"]. She played simultaneous chess games, ten at a time — Mavis Gallant, "Careless Talk"

13. Your friend is . . . your field which you sow with love and reap with thanksgiving. And he is your board and your fireside. For you come to him with your hunger and you seek him for peace —Kahlil Gibran, *The Prophet*

14. Nicholas Denery: I think as one grows older it is more and more necessary to reach out your hand for the sturdy old vines you knew when you were young and let them lead you back to the roots of things that matter —Lillian Hellman, *The Autumn Garden*, Act 1

15. Life without a friend is death without a witness —George Herbert, *Outlandish Proverbs*

16. The best mirror is an old friend —George Herbert, *Jacula Prudentum*

17. Through life's desert . . . the flower of friendship grows —Oliver Wendell Holmes, Sr., "A Song of Other Days"

18. Friendship is precious, not only in the shade, but in the sunshine of life; and

thanks to a benevolent arrangement of things, the greater part of life is sunshine —Thomas Jefferson, Letter to Maria Cosway, October 12, 1786

19. Arsinoé: The flame of friendship ought to burn brightest in matters of the most concern —Molière, *The Misanthrope*, Act 3, scene 5

20. Constant use had not worn ragged the fabric of their friendship —Dorothy Parker, "The Standard of Living"

21. My old friend . . . / We are each other's film archive and museum / packed in the crumbling arch of the skull —Marge Piercy, "The homely war," *Living In the Open*

22. For us to be friends / is a mating of eagle and ostrich, from both sides —Marge Piercy, "The bumpity road to mutual devotion," *Living In the Open*

23. Aubrey: Let us make up our minds to have no slow bleeding-to-death of our friendship —Arthur Wing Pinero, *The Second Mrs. Tanqueray*, Act 1
    Aubrey has just told his friends that he is marrying a woman quite outside their social circle and is suggesting a clean break as preferable to the metaphorical hemorrhage.

24. Polonius: Grapple them to thy soul with hoops of steel —William Shakespeare, *Hamlet*, Act 1, scene 3, line 115
    Polonious' advice to hold firmly to one's tried and true friends draws on the metaphor of a barrel encircled with strong metal bands. The same image is used by Julius Caesar: "if I knew what hoop should hold us stanch . . ."

25. Before the flowers of friendship faded friendship faded —Gertrude Stein, *Before the Flowers of Friendship Faded Friendship Faded*

26. Company keeps our rind from growing too coarse and rough —Horace Walpole, Letter, 1765

27. I reached out and attempted to build a footbridge to others —Irvin D. Yalom, *When Nietzsche Wept*
    A fictional Nietzsche refers to people who have betrayed his efforts to build a meaningful relationship. The footbridge metaphor comes from one of Nietzsche's books, The Gay Science *in which he refers to the footbridge as the crossover to friendship and brotherhood.*

28. Friendship's the wine of life —Edward Young, *Night Thoughts*, II

■ FROWNS
See: FACIAL EXPRESSIONS

■ FRUSTRATION
See also: ENTRAPMENT

1. The lash of frustration was laid on and the pain stunned Ralph —John Cheever, "The Pot of Gold"
    Success has eluded Ralph and his wife repeatedly. Here, Ralph experiences the story's concluding defeat.

2. Men, like myself, still ambitious enough to know rage that their careers were in irons —Norman Mailer, *Harlot's Ghost*
    "yet old enough to suffer the knowledge that their best years were committed and gone," Mailer continues.

3. Juliet: I have bought the mansion of a love / But not possess'd it, and though I am sold / Not yet enjoy'd —William Shakespeare, *Romeo and Juliet*, Act 3, scene 2, line 26
    Juliet looks forward to love's fulfillment.

4. For the rest of my life, I shall be . . . Pegasus yoked to the plow! —Irvin D. Yalom, *When Nietzsche Wept*
    A fictional Sigmund Freud alludes to the winged horse to explain why he should do research instead of pursuing the role of physician for which he feels he has no gift.

■ FULFILLMENT

See: SELF-ACTUALIZATION

■ FURNITURE/FURNISHINGS

See also: ROOMS

1. Each treasure sparkled in its own place, and uttered its own note to the soul in this concert of masterpieces arranged by two musicians, the one as true a poet as the other —Honoré de Balzac, *Cousin Pons*
   This metaphor describes the protagonist's apartment which he and his friend treat as if it were a museum, since it houses many carefully collected art objects.

2. A polychromatic rug . . . lay surrounded by a billowy sea of soiled matting —O. Henry, "The Furnished Room," *The Four Million*
   The sea metaphor is preceded by a simile which likens the rug to "some brilliant flowered, rectangular tropical islet."

3. The furniture was chipped and bruised; the couch, distorted by bursting springs, seemed a horrible monster that had been slain during the stress of some grotesque convulsion —O. Henry, "The Furnished Room"

4. She saw the furniture as a circle of elderly judges, condemning her to death by smothering —Sinclair Lewis, *Main Street*
   The furnishings in her new husband's house were clearly a far cry from Carol Kennicott's tastes.

5. Stick incense / cold / in bronze lion boat / Bedcover rumpled / in crimson seas — Ch'ing-Chao Li, "To the Air of Fenghuang," Sung Dynasty
   The crimson counterpane forms a sea of waves.

6. Daylight shines in or lamplight down / Upon the tense oasis of green felt — James Merrill, "Lost in Translation"
   Merrill describes a card table.

7. All the ashtrays in sight were in full blossom with crumpled facial tissues and lipsticked cigarette ends —J. D. Salinger, "Raise High The Roof Beam, Carpenters," *The New Yorker*, 1950–60

8. [The chairs were] fearfully shabby. Their entrails . . . were all over the floor — Virginia Woolf, *To the Lighthouse*

■ FURTIVENESS

See: SECRECY

■ FUTILITY

See also: DEFEAT; EFFECTIVENESS/INEFFECTIVENESS; USELESSNESS

1. But what is to be done if the direct and sole vocation of every intelligent man is babble, that is, the intentional pouring of water through a sieve? —Fyodor Mikhailovich Dostoevsky, *Notes from Underground*

2. Pity those men who . . . marched through continents or tried / to till the desert of the heart —Michael Hamburger, "A Song About Great Men"

3. The Bush people stubbornly continued, in the immortal words of Gib Lewis, speaker of the Texas State House of Representative, "beating their heads against a dead horse" —Gib Lewis, Quoted in Op-Ed, *The New York Times*, December 4, 1992
   James Carville and Paul Begala gave a mixaphoric twist to the common no use beating a dead horse in their post-mortem piece on the election campaign.

4. Thy mourning cannot availe me, I am but dust —Sir Walter Raleigh (also spelled Ralegh), Letter to his wife, 1603
   Raleigh, scheduled to be executed the following morning, thought himself to be as good as dead.

5. Mercutio: Nay, if our wits run the wild goose chase, I am done. For thou hast more of the wild goose in one of thy wits than (I am sure) I have in my whole five — William Shakespeare, *Romeo and Juliet*, Act 2, scene 3, line 76

Certain races required all the horses to follow the course of the leader, in the V formation of wild geese. A wild goose chase remains a popular metaphor for any senseless plan.

■ FUTURE

See also: HISTORY; PAST

1. The future is a faded song, a Royal Rose or a lavender spray / Of wistful regret . . . / Pressed between yellow leaves of a book that has never been opened —T. S. Eliot, "The Dry Salvages"

2. Rameses: It's you who invite the future but it's I / Who have to entertain it — Christopher Fry, *The Firstborn,* Act 2, scene 2
   Rameses is afraid to inherit a throne that his father has besmirched.

3. The house of the future is always dark — John Galsworthy, "American and Briton"
   The dark is a common symbol for the unknown.

4. Violence and pessimism. They are the finest kind of hope. They arm me against a thousand tomorrows. The future is an enemy, marching —Ben Hecht, *A Guide for the Bedevilled*
   This is Hecht's adieu, summing up his attitude for handling prejudice.

5. The future is . . . a big tangle of black thread —D. H. Lawrence, *The Captain's Doll*
   The metaphor expands as follows: Every morning you begin to untangle one loose end—and that's your day. And every evening you break off and throw away what you've untangled, and the heap is much less: just one thread less, one day less.

6. No more they sought to gaze with feverish fear, or still more feverish hope, beyond the present's horizon line; but into the furthest future their own silent spirits sailed —Herman Melville, "Norfolk Isle and the Chola Widow"
   There are two metaphors here. One indicates time as an ocean, with the horizon the division between past and future. The second, building on the first, has the human spirit sailing on the metaphoric sea.

7. Pinero spoke nonsense when he made Paula Tanqueray say, "The future is only the past entered through another gate." Alas, there is no other gate —Christopher Morley, "On Doors"
   Morley's reference is to Arthur Wing Pinero's play The Second Mrs. Tanqueray.

8. The Twentieth Century looms before us big with the fate of many nations —Theodore Roosevelt, "The Strenuous Life"
   The century was pregnant with possibilities in 1900 but delivery has since proved difficult.

9. Circles open and circles close, losses gather, and already the future is dust under their wheels —Sharon Sheehe Stark, "Overland," *Boulevard,* No.12–13
   A young girl ponders on the instability of "the arrangement of things" after her father dies.

10. The future was a desert, except for music —Dame Rebecca West, *This Real Night*
    The emptiness marks life without a much loved mother for daughters trained to follow in her footsteps as musicians.

11. You who stand here, chisel in hand, about to hew out the future, have something in you . . . the eternal resilience, the everlasting bounce in man —William Allen White, Commencement address, 1936
    The new graduates were going out into a troubled world but White assured them that "the tide will turn" and that they did indeed possess the sculptor's creative power and strength.

GAIETY

See: LAUGHTER

GALAXY

See: STARS

GARDENING

See: FLOWERS

GASTRONOMY

See: FOOD AND DRINK

GENEALOGY

See: ANCESTRY/ANCESTORS

GENERALITIES

See: EXACTNESS/INEXACTNESS

GENEROSITY

See also: ABUNDANCE; MONEY; REWARDS

1. Elephants don't catch mice —Anon., French Proverb

   An even older variant of this proverbial metaphor for being wise and generous enough to stand above pettiness is eagles don't hawk flies.

2. I opened my vault, my doors, my cupboards, my windows. I flung every gold piece and copper piece that I had at your feet. —Louis Auchincloss, "The 'Fulfillment' of Grace Eliot," *Skinny Island*

   An excerpt from a love letter by a woman who discovers sexual passion and pursues it freely, with no holds barred.

3. Cast thy bread upon the waters: for thou shalt find it after many days —The Bible, *O.T., Ecclesiastes 11:15*

   In its most commonly used sense this is a metaphor for generosity without expectation of immediate or specific rewards. It is also used to imply that generosity will be repaid, as with humorist Elbert Hubbard's twist, "Cast your bread upon the waters and it will come back to you—buttered."

4. Valere: Has our master invited people here to murder them by overeating? . . . You must learn, Jacques, you and your kind, that an overladen table is a cutthroat —Molière, *The Miser*, Act 3

   Valere realizes that his master, the miser Harpagon, does not want to spend money on a wedding feast.

5. Cleopatra: His bounty, / There was no winter in't; an autumn it was / That grew the more by reaping —William Shakespeare, *Antony and Cleopatra*, Act 5, scene 2, line 86

6. My father . . . emptied himself / Into the pockets round my mother's table —Hy Sobiloff, "My Mother's Table"

■ GENIUS

See also: PERSONALITY PROFILES

1. A Frankenstein of test tubes; a "refugee"— / A shaman full of secrets who could touch / Physics with a wand and body forth / The universe's baby wrapped in stars —Howard Moss, "Einstein's Bathrobe"

   Einstein managed all that with the simple formula that solved for "E" and changed the world.

2. Knock at thine heart, 'tis there that genius dwells —Luc de Clapiers (Marquis de) Vauvenargues, Maxim

3. Genius is the fire that lights itself —Anon., quoted by James Gleick in "Part Showman, All Genius," *The New York Times Magazine,* September 20, 1992

4. Natural genius is but the soil, which, let alone, runs to weeds. If it is to bear fruit and harvests worth reaping, it must be ploughed and tilled with incessant care —Henry Ward Beecher, Sermon

5. Why does the stream of genius so seldom break out as a torrent, with roaring high waves . . . ? —Johann Wolfgang von Goethe, *The Sorrows of Young Werther*

6. A work of genius is but the newspaper of a century, or perchance of a hundred centuries —Nathaniel Hawthorne, *Mosses From an Old Manse*

7. Men of genius are the real chemicals operating on the mass of neutral intellect —John Keats, Letter, November 22, 1817

8. Height deterred / from his verdure, any / polecat or snake that / might have burdened his vine —Marianne Moore, "An Expedient—Leonardo da Vinci's—and a Query"

   Leonardo is compared to a vine because "problems that seemed to perplex him bore fruit."

■ GENTLENESS

See: KINDNESS/UNKINDNESS

■ GLOOM

See also: DESPAIR; EMOTIONS; FACIAL EXPRESSIONS; OPTIMISM/PESSIMISM

1. Gloom the black sun of melancholy. —Gerard De Nerval

2. An insinuating heaviness slowly penetrates Mr. Andesmas, it . . . now rules over his whole life, settled there, for the time being, a prowler asleep on its victory —Marguerite Duras, *The Afternoon of Mr. Andesmas*

3. King: There's something in his soul / O'er which his melancholy sits on brood. —William Shakespeare, *Hamlet,* Act 3, scene 1, line 168

   After equating Hamlet's depression with a chicken's hatching, the King expresses his plan to send Hamlet away to prevent any trouble he "hatches."

4. Through its giant loom the web of gloom / Crept till each thread was spun —Oscar Wilde, "The Ballad of Reading Goal"

   Images of gloom and despair pervade Wilde's poem, including "the cave of black Despair."

■ GLORY

See: FAME

■ GLUTTONY

See: EXCESS

■ GOALS

See: ACTION/INACTION; SUCCESS/FAILURE

■ GO-BETWEENS

See also: MEN AND WOMEN

1. Emotionally, he was a foreigner. Elinor was his interpreter, his dragoman —Aldous Huxley, *Point Counter Point*

2. Juliet: He made you for a highway to my bed —William Shakespeare, *Romeo and Juliet*, Act 3, scene 2, line 134
   Juliet's words are directed at her nurse, the go-between for the lovers' meetings.

■ GOD

See also: AUTHORITY; FAITH; GUIDANCE/ GUIDES; LEADERS/FOLLOWERS; RELIGION

1. We are the clay, and Thou our potter —The Bible, *O.T., Isaiah 64:8*
   Bible scholars have suggested that God literally made man of clay. Common usage has turned the expression "to be clay in a potter's hands" into a metaphor for being easily influenced.

2. The Lord is my Shepherd —The Bible, *O.T., Psalms 23:1*
   References to God as a shepherd appear throughout the Bible.

3. God my rock, Why hast Thou forgotten me? —The Bible, *O.T., Psalms, 42:9*
   The image of God as a rock appears several times, as in "He is not only my rock and salvation: He is my defense; I shall not be moved." (Psalms 62:6).

4. My fortress; my high tower —The Bible, *O.T., Psalms, 144:2*

5. Thou art my lamp, O Lord —The Bible, *O.T., 2, Samuel, 22:29*

6. Maybe the Almighty Himself has turned a bit bourgeois / and uses a credit card —Joseph Brodsky, "Transatlantic," *The New Yorker*, August 3, 1992
   "For otherwise," Brodsky writes, "time's passage makes no sense."

7. God, whose puppets, best and worst, / Are we —Robert Browning, "Pippa Passes"

8. He [God] paints the wayside flower, / He lights the evening star —Jane Montgomery Campbell, "We Plough the Fields"

9. In that same vessel which our Savior bore / Himself the Pilot, let us leave the shoar, / And with a better guide a better world explore —John Dryden, "The Hind and the Panther"

10. There is a crack in everything that God has made —Ralph Waldo Emerson, "Compensation," *Essays: First Series*
    The implied metaphor pictures God as a potter.

11. The dice of God are always loaded —Ralph Waldo Emerson, "Compensation," *Essays: First Series*

12. God is not a comic bell-boy for whom we can press a button to get things —Harry Emerson Fosdick, Quoted in *The Home Book of American Quotations*

13. Mine eyes have seen the glory of the coming of the Lord; / He is trampling out the vintage where the grapes of wrath are stored —Julia Ward Howe, "The Battle Hymn of the Republic"
    John Steinbeck used this as the title for a novel considered by many to be his best, The Grapes of Wrath.

14. Often God shuts a door in our face, and then subsequently opens the door through which we need to go —Catherine Marshall, *A Man Called Peter*

15. I must endeaver to walke closer with God or I cannot keepe cart on wheels —Rev. Henry Newcombe, Diary entry

16. King: God shall be my hope / . . . and lantern to my feet —William Shakespeare, *The Second Part of Henry the Sixth*, Act 2, scene 3, line 24

17. God comes to me in the dusk of my evening with the flowers from my past

kept fresh in his basket —Rabindranath Tagore, "Stray Birds, 313"

Tagore uses two metaphors to depict God as a gardener and the past as a garden.

18. A circle whose center is everywhere and circumference nowhere —Timaeus of Locris, Quotation in Voltaire's *Philosophical Dictionary*

19. But Vance did not want to hear about her [grandmother's] God, who, once you stripped Him of her Biblical verbiage, was merely the Supreme Moralist of a great educational system in which Mrs. Scrimser held an important job —Edith Wharton, *Hudson River Bracketed*

■ GODS

See: GUIDANCE/GUIDES; FATE

■ GOLF

See: SPORTS

■ GOOD/EVIL

See also: CORRUPTION; EVIL; SIN/ REDEMPTION

1. Evil and good are God's right hand and left —Philip James Bailey, "Fetus"

2. Leopold / Fulfilled the treachery four years before / Begun—or was he well-intentioned, more / Roadmaker to hell than king —John Berryman, "The Moon and the Night and the Men"

   Berryman ponders the origins of war.

3. That is the true and eternal wonder of it, anyway; that it [goodness] can come even from the dung heap like this —Willa Cather, "The Sculptor's Funeral," *Youth and the Bright Medusa*

4. Sin writes histories, goodness is silent — Johann Wolfgang von Goethe, *Table-Talk*

5. But I am old; and good and bad / Are woven in a crazy plaid —Dorothy Parker, "The Veteran," *Enough Rope*

6. A man is born into this world with only a tiny spark of goodness in him. The spark is God, it is the soul: the rest is ugliness and evil, a shell —Chaim Potok, *The Chosen*

7. Then—churls—their thoughts, although their eyes were kind, / To thy fair flower add the rank smell of weeds; / But why thy odour matcheth not thy show, / The soil is this, that thou dost common grow —William Shakespeare, "Sonnet 69," line 11

   The sonnets, for the most part, immortalize lovers. In this sonnet an angry Shakespeare excoriates his subject.

8. Hotspur: To put down Richard, that sweet lovely rose, / And plant this thorn, this canker Bolingbroke? —William Shakespeare, *The First Part of King Henry the Fourth*, Act 1, scene 3, line 170

   Two of the Bard's favorite metaphors, gardening and bodily ills, express Hotspur's love for Richard and disgust for Bolingbroke.

■ GOODNESS

See also: CHARACTER; KINDNESS

1. He [a mutual friend] says you are just a feast of the most human qualities —Saul Bellow, *Herzog*

2. I was eyes to the blind, and feet to the lame —The Bible, *Job 29:15*

3. You are the salt of the earth —The Bible, *N.T., Matthew 5:13*

   Salt, long a symbol of goodness, is here used by Jesus to praise his disciples. The metaphor has become common for anyone of praiseworthy character.

4. This brave and tender man in every storm of life was oak and rock, but in the sun-

shine he was love and flowers —Robert Green Ingersoll, eulogy for his brother

5. Turn his soul wrong side outwards and there is not a speck on it —Thomas Jefferson, Letter, January 30, 1787

   Various versions of this quote about President James Monroe have been circulated, but the metaphor of the coat turned inside out appears in all.

6. King: goodness, growing to a plurisy, / Dies in his own too-much —William Shakespeare, *Hamlet*, Act 4, scene 7, line 116

   In trying to persuade Laertes to fall in with his scheme for a fencing match, the king uses a variation of one of Shakespeare's favorite metaphors, the diseased body.

■ GOSSIP

See also: INSULTS; NAME CALLING; SLANDER

1. Woman / has a long tongue— / ladder / to perdition swung —Anon., "Ancient Poem," Chou Dynasty

2. The world rests on the tip of her tongue — Anon., Yiddish Proverb

3. Listening at closed doors, to the Wives, over their tea and wine, spinning their webs —Margaret Atwood, *The Handmaid's Tale*

   The respectable women in the novel are denied gainful occupation and distract themselves with spiderlike intrigue.

4. Eadgar: I would be wed again. / Nor have the world run clucking to its window, / "Come quick! 'Tis the King's leman!" —Edna St. Vincent Millay, *The King's Henchman*

   The use of hens for gossips is very common. The world, here, seems to be a female gossip.

5. Sir Peter Teazle: Fiends! Vipers! Furies! Oh, that their own venom would choke them! —Richard Brinsley Sheridan, *The School for Scandal*, Act 5, scene 2

   Throughout the play, gossips are pictured as vipers. Indeed, one character is named Snake.

■ GOVERNMENT

See also: POLITICS / POLITICIANS

1. States are great engines moving slowly — Sir Francis Bacon, *On the Advancement of Learning*

2. Accountancy—that is government —Louis D. Brandeis, January 30, 1914

3. Congress is a swamp that must be cleared —Pat Buchanan, Speech during campaign for presidential nomination, March 30, 1992

4. Keeping the ship [of State] on an even keel, or dying once for all —Marcus Tullius Cicero, *Ad Quintum Fratrem*

   Four hundred years later, in Seven Against Thebes, Aeschylus wrote "It is for you to judge how you must steer the ship of State." It's been a popular political metaphor ever since.

5. The state does not consist of lath and plaster, but of hearths and altars. —Marcus Tullius Cicero, *Ad Atticum*

6. The state is bodies of armed men —Nikolai Lenin, s.u.

7. Sail on, O Ship of State! / Sail on, O Union, strong and great! / Humanity with all its fears, / With all the hopes of future years, / Is hanging Breathless on thy Fate! —Henry Wadsworth Longfellow, "The Building of the Ship"

   Longfellow's poetic variant of the ship of state metaphor was borrowed by Franklin D. Roosevelt in a wartime message to Winston Churchill.

8. Moreover, states quickly founded . . . cannot have deep roots and wide ramifications, so that the first storm destroys them —Niccolo Machiavelli, *The Prince*

9. There are small fish, and there are big fish. And then there is the whale, and the whale is the government. For support to continue for the President and for Congress too . . . the blubber must go —Anna Quindlen, "Public & Private," *The New York Times*, February 21, 1993

The whale metaphor concluded Quindlen's column on the economic policies of the new Clinton administration.

10. Creon: The vessel of our state after being tossed on wild waves has once more been safely steadied —Sophocles, *Antigone*

    Creon returned to the metaphor with a warning about his enemies: "Our country is the ship that bears us safe, and only while she prospers in our voyage can we make true friends." His metaphor has been borrowed by politicians ever since. Some of these have been mixaphors and metabloopers: "The president will put the ship of state on its feet," and "There will always be powerful men with minute minds trying to kick over the ship of state . . . " (the last attributed to Ralph Nader).

11. If monopoly persists, monopoly will always sit at the helm of the government — Woodrow Wilson, "The New Freedom"

12. The House is lightning, unpredictable and borne along by political squall lines that trigger sudden ruckuses and then die. The Senate is the lightning bug —Michael Wines, *The New York Times*, August 7, 1993

■ GRACE

See: FORGIVENESS

■ GRACEFULNESS

See: MOVEMENTS

■ GRAMMAR AND STYLE

See also: LANGUAGE; WRITING/WRITERS

1. [Gordon] Lish does love his sentences. Chewing them up, spitting them out, sucking them back, he sends them tumbling over one another in a sort of waterfall of consciousness —Anon., "Fiction," *Publishers Weekly*, June 28, 1993

   The reviewer of Lish's novel, Zimzum, proved himself to be fond of spitting out his own colorful images.

2. Ruthlessly I would slash away at two flowery weeds only to find them popping up again on the next page —Edna Ferber, *A Kind of Magic*

   Ferber comments on her early tendency to load up her writing with adjectives.

3. Nouns and verbs are almost pure metal; adjectives are cheaper ore —Marie Gilchrist

4. [Gustave] Flaubert . . . worked slowly and laboriously . . . chiselling his clauses so meticulously that he seldom finished more than a paragraph or two a day —Francine Du Plessix Gray, "A Critic At Large," *The New Yorker*, July 26, 1993

   The critic was reviewing Flaubert—Sand: The Correspondence.

5. Prose is architecture, not interior decoration, and the Baroque is over —Ernest Hemingway, *Death in the Afternoon*

   Hemingway's lean style confirmed this.

6. Her style [Mme. de Sévigné] . . . is that of a nursery rhyme . . . the stringing together of large bright beads of fact —Lyn Irvine, quoted in introduction to a letter written in the seventeenth century by Mme. de Sévigné to her daughter

7. Even the tiniest sampling of their niggling, insinuating prose is enough to make you scream for release from the straitjackets of their syntax —Christopher Lehmann-Haupt, "Books of the Times," *The New York Times*, November 23, 1992

   The psychological metaphor pertained to David O. Selznick's memos, samples of which were included in Showman, The Life of David O. Selznick *by David Thomson.*

8. What I really do [when I write fiction] is take real plums and put them in an imaginary cake. If you're interested in the cake, you get rather annoyed with people saying what species the real plum was — Mary McCarthy, Interview, *Paris Review*, 1962

9. I am familiar with the shrapnel of footnotes. The Ibids and the Op. Cits. have

not only ruined the flow of the writing I have read, they have also made my eyes function very much like the pump-shaft of the old windmill we had on the farm in Pleasant Prairie —Howard Teichmann, Introduction, *George S. Kaufman*

Teichmann, who learned about footnotes as a graduate history student, thus explains why details about his biographical sources will be found at the back of the book.

10. It is a hot-weather sign, the asterisk. The cicada of the typewriter, telling the long steaming noons —E. B. White, *Harper's Magazine*, 1939

The typewriter may have metamorphosed into a computer keyboard, but the asterisk retains its hot-weather signature.

GRANDCHILDREN

See: CHILDHOOD/CHILDREN; FAMILIES/ FAMILY RELATIONSHIPS

GRATITUDE/INGRATITUDE

See also: KINDNESS/UNKINDNESS

1. Ye have stabbed me with ingratitude — Robert Browning, "The Bishop Orders his Tomb at Saint Praxed's Church"

2. He was shaking . . . perhaps from the cold bath of ingratitude he was taking —John Hersey, "Fling," *Grand Street*

3. If a small kindness is not forgotten it becomes a gnawing worm —Friedrich Wilhelm Nietzsche, *Thus Spake Zarathustra*

4. Lear: Ingratitude, thou marble-hearted fiend —William Shakespeare, *King Lear*, Act 1, scene 4, line 266

5. Bolingbroke: All my treasury / Is yet but unfelt thanks —William Shakespeare, *The Tragedy of King Richard the Second*, Act 2, scene 3, line 60

6. Bolingbroke: thanks, the exchequer of the poor, / Which, till my infant fortune comes to years, / Stands for my bounty —William Shakespeare, *The Tragedy of King Richard the Second*, Act 2, scene 3, line 65

Since Bolingbroke has no wealth as yet, he can offer no reward to his followers except his words of appreciation.

GRAVITY

See: DIGNITY

GREATNESS

See: GENIUS

GREED

See also: MONEY

1. A young child is a pig and a grown one is a wolf —Anon., Yiddish Proverb

The pig image is often used to define the difference between simile and metaphor. It might also be noted that people who ask for clarification between similes and metaphors are most frequently given a pig illustration: "A child who's a little pig" is a metaphor and "eats like a pig," is a simile.

2. All he does is shove / Succulent lumps of revenue down his maw —Catullus, Poem 29

3. There's a lot of yield piggishness out there —Jay Diamond, Publisher of *Grant's Interest Rate Observer*, quoted in "Market Place," *The New York Times*, August 20, 1993

This was headlined "Yield pigs" are feeding on ever-more-risky investments."

4. Avarice is a wild beast, monstrous and irresistible —Sallust, *Ad Caesarem Epistula*

GRIEF

See also: DEATH; DESPAIR; EMOTIONS; SORROW; TEARS

1. Why did that image . . . grab at my grief-lapels? —Nicholson Baker, "Reading Aloud," *The New Yorker,* March 1, 1993

2. But when she doth of mourning speak, / Ev'n with her sights the strings do break —Thomas Campion, "When to her Lute Corinna Sings"

3. Who can say which sadness when it takes over, / becomes rudder? —Deborah Digges, "Nursing the Hamster," *The New Yorker,* March 1, 1993

4. Griefe brought to numbers cannot be so fierce, / For, he tames it, that fetters it in verse —John Donne, "The Triple Foole Rising"

   The lover tries to allay his pains by drawing them "through Rimes vexation."

5. By childrens' births, and death, I am become / So dry, that I am now mine owne sad tombe —John Donne, "Epigrams: Niobe"

   The title refers to the mythological mother whose hubris caused her downfall. Her children were slain and she was turned to stone, but she continued to weep for her loss even after she was ossified.

6. But it is just in that cold, abominable half despair, half belief, in that conscious burying oneself alive for grief in the underworld for forty years —Fyodor Mikhailovich Dostoevsky, *Notes from Underground*

   The narrator has "buried" himself in the underworld of degradation.

7. Moses: . . . to see grief grow big / With what has died, and in some spirit differently / Bear it back to life —Christopher Fry, *The Firstborn,* Act 3, scene 2

   The image of pregnancy to illustrate death is powerful because it is antithetical.

8. My heart is turned into a wailing child —Nahabed Kouchak, 15th-century poem

9. The news of Hearn's death . . . wrenched his heart with a cruel fist —Norman Mailer, *The Naked and the Dead*

10. His clouded heart was oddly dissonant with the sunny, candid autumn day —Carson McCullers, *The Ballad of the Sad Cafe*

11. Such grief is . . . an endless motive asserting itself with all possible variations of rhythm and tonal coloring and melodic structure —Carson McCullers, "The Aliens," *The Collected Stories of Carson McCullers*

    The musical image pertains to the missing daughter of a refugee from Hitler's Germany who happens to be a musician. McCullers elaborates on it in considerable detail, explaining how it comes and goes without "fixed summons, such as the signal from the conductor's hand, that activates a dormant sorrow."

12. Maccus: My heart has a stone in its shoe —Edna St. Vincent Millay, *The King's Henchman,* Act 2

13. Grief is a tree that has tears for its fruit —Philemon

14. Grief falls a dead weight / as goods wax in strength —Pindar, "Olympia 2," *Odes*
    Grief is solidified, and falls down as a "thing" when people accumulate wealth.

15. Fountain of tears, river of grief / torrent of pain, sea brimful with bitterness / I am submerged, I drown in deep misery —Christine de Pisan, Untitled poem
    This might be described as a rushing stream of metaphors.

16. Her back / is a tiny but bitter hill, carrying the dead —Yannis Ritsos, "Women"

17. Gratiano: Poor Desdemona, I am glad thy father's dead; / Thy match was mortal to him, and pure grief / Shore his old thread a-twain. —William Shakespeare, *Othello,* Act 5, scene 2, line 205.
    The cutting of the thread of life comes from Greek mythology. Atropos, one of the three Fates, cut the thread with her shears.

18. King: My heart is drown'd with grief. —William Shakespeare, *The Second Part of Henry the Sixth,* Act 3, scene 1, line 198.

In The Third Part of Henry the Sixth *(2, 1, 103), Warwick declares "Ten days ago I drown'd these news in tears."*

19. Edward: Now my soul's palace is become a prison. —William Shakespeare, *The Third Part of Henry the Sixth*, Act 2, scene 1, line 75.
    Without the slain Duke of York, Edward feels all joy has been locked away forever.

20. Duchess: Grief boundeth where it falls, / Not with empty hollowness, but weight —William Shakespeare, *The Tragedy of King Richard the Second*, Act 1, scene 2, line 57
    Grief is a ball that falls and bounces back but with more weight than a ball.

21. Queen: Yet I know no cause / Why I should welcome such a guest as grief —William Shakespeare, *The Tragedy of King Richard the Second*, Act 2, scene 2, line 7

22. Queen: So, Green, thou art the midwife to my woe —William Shakespeare, *The Tragedy of King Richard the Second*, Act 2, scene 2, line 61

23. York: What a tide of woes / Comes rushing on this woeful land at once —William Shakespeare, *The Tragedy of King Richard the Second*, Act 2, scene 2, line 98

24. King Richard: Two buckets, filling one another, / . . . That bucket down and full of tears am I, / Drinking my griefs whilst you mount up on high —William Shakespeare, *The Tragedy of King Richard the Second*, Act 4, scene 1, line 185

25. Queen: Thou most beauteous inn, / Why should hard-favor'd grief be lodg'd in thee. —William Shakespeare, *The Tragedy of King Richard the Second*, Act 5, scene 1, line 13
    Richard is the inn who has housed the lodger, grief.

26. As I was letting myself in the empty apartment, grief sprang out of the dark hall and clubbed me —Eileen Simpson, *Orphans*
    The narrator is recently widowed.

27. I am sure now grief is a ghost—only a ghost in Hades where ungrateful Odysseus is going—waiting on him —Eudora Welty, "Circe"
    This metaphor concludes Welty's story.

■ GROUP SCENES

See also: CHARACTERIZATIONS; DESCRIPTIONS, MISC.

1. From the dimly-lighted passages of the court, the last sediment of the human stew that had been boiling there all day was straining off —Charles Dickens, *A Tale of Two Cities*
   This passage introduces the chapter following the court trial that saved Charles Darnay's life.

2. Couples sitting huddled together in the strangleholds of l'amour —John Dos Passos, *U.S.A., Nineteen Nineteen*
   The scene is Paris; the time, the first World War.

3. The bar and the tables and the sticky, salty, half-naked tourists were covered alike with zebra stripes of light and shade —Mavis Gallant, "By the Sea"

4. A Knot of Dreamers —Nathaniel Hawthorne, *The Blithedale Romance*
   This is the title of Chapter 3 in Hawthorne's novel about his own experiences as a member of a utopian community.

5. A jungle of innumerable trees and dangling creepers—it was in this form that parties always presented themselves to Walter Bidlake's imagination —Aldous Huxley, *Point Counter Point*

6. In company with Lynch followed a sizable hospital nurse. Two lean hungry greyhounds walking after a heifer —James Joyce, *Portrait of the Artist as a Young Man*
   The quick imagery portrays Joyce and his friends as greyhounds (with a brief nod to Shakespeare's characterization of Cassius), while the nurse becomes a heifer.

7. They were all scarecrows [old people in Florida] blown about under the murder-

ing sunball with empty ribcages —Cynthia Ozick, "Rosa"

8. The brassy-bossy men-women, with corrugated-iron perms, and hippo hides. —Dylan Thomas, "A Visit to America"

9. There they go, every spring, from New York to Los Angeles . . . men with elephantiasis of the reputation (huge trunks and teeny minds) . . . potboiling philosophers, professional Irishmen (very lepricorny) and, I am afraid, fat poets with slim volumes —Dylan Thomas, "A Visit to America"

10. An earnest crew-cut platoon of giant collegiates, all chasing the butterfly culture with net, notebook, poison-bottle, pin and label —Dylan Thomas, "A Visit to America"

11. On pedestals / Of mounting shade / Stood all our friends —Richard Wilbur, "Leaving"
    A group of people at a garden party are compared to statues, their pedestals indicating that the party's over.

12. They looked like something out a Greek movie, all these quiet little early birds all bundled up and dressed in black —A. B. Yehoshua, *Mr. Mani*
    The widows were up early for the funeral of one of their cronies. Perhaps the metaphor implies the connection between death and worms, which are the proverbial treat for early birds.

■ GUIDANCE/GUIDES

See also: LEADERS/FOLLOWERS; RELIGION

1. Socrates: These, these alone, for true Deities own, / the rest are all God-ships of straw —Aristophanes, *The Clouds*
    "Let Zeus be left out: He's a God beyond doubt," pleads Strepsiades.

2. Catullus, a beacon flashing across black water. —Louis Begley, *Wartime Lies*

3. Our Lord Jesus, that great shepherd of the sheep —The Bible, *N.T., Hebrews 13:20*

4. Jesus: I am the living bread —The Bible, *N.T., John 6:51*

5. Jesus: I am the door —The Bible, *N.T., John 14:6*

6. That if gold rust, what shal iren do? / For if a preest be foul, on who we trust, no wonder is a lewed man to rust —Geoffrey Chaucer, "The Prologue," *The Canterbury Tales*
    A priest must serve as an example to men, for if gold rusts, what shall iron do? It is no wonder that a lewd man will rust if a priest is foul.

7. Wel oughte a preest ensample for to yive / By his clennesse how that he sheep sholde live —Geoffrey Chaucer, "The Prologue," *The Canterbury Tales*
    A priest, by his uprightness, should set the example for his sheep. The metaphor of a flock of sheep and the pastor or priest as the shepherd is built into the history of ecclesiastical writing.

8. Mr. Taruskin is especially skilled at leading one through the thickets of various performing versions —Donal Henahan, *The New York Times Book Review,* January 31, 1993
    The book being reviewed was Musorgsky, *by Richard Taruskin.*

9. The best physicians are Dr. Diet, Dr. Quiet, and Dr. Merryman —Sydney Smith
    Smith's metaphoric doctors remain good guides for well-being.

10. It is even difficult to become his [Maeterlinck's] pupil, for there are no free passes that give entrance to his world of beauty —August Strindberg, Introduction, *Plays.* Third Series

■ GUILT

1. Repent of all the moments of your life which you have wasted in the world and on pleasure; demand them of me, 'tis a

robbery of which I am guilty —Peter (Pierre) Abelard, Letter to Heloise

Abelard takes the blame for his relationship with Heloise, and exhorts her to sublimate her love.

2. Otoko asked herself if women were more stubborn toward each other than toward men, and felt the needle prick of the same old guilty thought —Kawabata Yasunari, *Beauty and Sadness*

In this tale of passion and revenge, Kawabata often used the image of the needle or knife of guilt. "He felt a stab of guilt at having robbed her of the possibility of marriage and motherhood," he writes elsewhere.

3. Ghost: Leave her to heaven, / And to those thorns that in her bosom lodge, / To prick and sting her —William Shakespeare, *Hamlet,* Act 1, scene 5, line 86

The implied metaphor equates thorns with guilt.

4. Queen: So full of artless jealousy is guilt, / It spills itself in fearing to be spilt — William Shakespeare, *Hamlet,* Act 4, scene 5, line 19

5. Macbeth: O, full of scorpions is my mind, dear wife! —William Shakespeare, *Macbeth,* Act 3, scene 2, line 37

6. Doctor: Infected minds / To their deaf pillows will discharge their secrets —William Shakespeare, *Macbeth,* Act 5, scene 1, line 74.

That's why, according to the doctor, Lady Macbeth can only unburden her trouble to an unresponsive object like the "deaf" pillow.

7. Bolingbroke: Lords, I protest my soul is full of woe / That blood should sprinkle me to make me grow —William Shakespeare, *The Tragedy of King Richard the Second,* Act 5, scene 6, line 45

Bolingbroke, who has earnestly wished for Richard's death, is trapped in the guilt of the fulfillment of that wish.

■ HABIT

See also: *CHANGEABLENESS/ UNCHANGEABLENESS; CONFORMITY/ NONCONFORMITY*

1. Habits are cobwebs at first and cables at last —Anon., Chinese Proverb

2. Habit . . . a shirt made of iron —Anon., Czechoslovakian Proverb

3. Habit is the chloroform of love . . . the cement that unites married couples — Geneviève Antoine-Dariaux, "The Men in Your Life"
   > *The metaphor is extended to also depict habit as "the fog that masks the most beautiful scenery" and, finally, as "the end of everything."*

4. Habit is the enormous fly-wheel of society, its most precious conservative agent — William James, "Habit," *The Principles of Psychology*

5. Powerful indeed is the empire of habit — Publilius Syrus

6. Habit is habit, and not to be flung out the window, but coaxed downstairs a step at a time —Mark Twain, *Pudd'nhead Wilson*
   > *This metaphor of personification comes from one of the "Pudd'nhead Wilson's Calendar" entries that introduce each chapter of the book.*

7. Inwardly he was recalling the warm cocoon of habit in which his own nursery and school years had been enveloped — Edith Wharton, *The Children*

8. Rigid, the skeleton of habit alone upholds the human frame —Virginia Woolf, *Mrs. Dalloway.*

■ HAIR

See also: PHYSICAL APPEARANCE

1. The fair hair rippled in a shower of curls —Honoré de Balzac, "The Firm of Nucingen"

2. She [actress Natasha Richardson] is a beauty, with a waterfall of hair —Peter Conrad, "Natasha Richardson and the Redgrave Dynasty," *The New York Times Magazine*, June 6, 1993

3. Her arms and upper lip were furred with black —Ross MacDonald, *The Moving Target*

4. Hair gathered around her face in droopy rolls and curtains —Alice Munro, "Meneseteung," *Friend of Youth*

5. And the hair on top of their heads was a dark wild grass —Carl Sandburg, "How They Broke Away to Go to the Rootabaga Country"

6. Bassanio: In her hairs, / The painter plays the spider, and hath woven / A golden mesh to entrap the hearts of men —Wil-

liam Shakespeare, *The Merchant of Venice,*
Act 3, scene 2, line 120

7. She brushed a cloud of hair out of her eyes
—John Steinbeck, "The Chrysanthemums"

8. On this horrible and grotesque mask of
nothingness, the hair, that beautiful hair,
retaining its sun-like fire, fell in a stream
of gold —Émile Zola, *Nana*
   *With this grim metaphoric portrait, Zola draws
   the curtain on the life of the disease-ravaged
   central character of his novel.*

■ HAIR COLOR

*See also: AGE/AGING; PHYSICAL APPEAR-
ANCE*

1. Gray hairs are death's blossoms —Anon.,
English Proverb

2. Gray hairs are leaves from the grave —
Anon., Yiddish Proverb

3. Mi . . . with his red hair boiling up in curls
on his skull —Enid Bagnold, *National
Velvet*
   *Mi is the character played by Mickey Rooney in
   the movie version of this popular children's novel.*

4. The hoary head is a crown of glory —The
Bible, *O.T. Psalms,* 88:3
   *The hoary head, however, does not automatically
   metamorphose into a crown. According to O.T.,
   Song of Solomon, 7:4, (which is full of imagery,
   though predominantly similes,) the hoary head
   must "be found in the way of righteousness."*

5. His [Truman Capote's] butterscotch hair
was cut in bangs —John Malcolm Brinnin,
Journal entry, 1940s

6. His head was silver'd o'er with age —
John Gay, "The Shepherd and the Philospher," *Fables*

7. She had . . . rosettes of white in her curly
black hair —John D. MacDonald, *Slam
the Big Door*
   *In one of his other novels, Barrier Island,
   MacDonald described a man's chest hair as a
   "mat of wiry grey."*

8. Murray Kempton . . . he had this amazing
red hair that just *launched* out of his head
—David Remnick, "Prince of the City,"
The New Yorker, March 1, 1993

9. His shoeblack hair is now cracked white
paint —James Wolcott, "They Talk By
Night," *The New Yorker,* April 12, 1993
   *The grizzly-headed talk show host being "roast-
   ed" was Tom Snyder.*

■ HANDS

*See: BODIES/THE BODY; PHYSICAL AP-
PEARANCE*

■ HAPPINESS/UNHAPPINESS

See also: CONTENTMENT; DESPAIR; JOY

1. Bliss is happiness boiling over and running down both sides of the pot —Josh
Billings

2. Happiness is a rare plant, that seldom
takes root on earth —Lady Marguerite
Blessington, *The Victims of Society*

3. That dancing dust mote, happiness, should
forever flee before her —Rebecca Goldstein,
The Dark Sister
   *The character's unhappiness is attributed to an
   "engorged" sense of personal grievance.*

4. Youth had seemed to teach that happiness
was but the occasional episode in a general drama of pain —Thomas Hardy, *The
Mayor of Casterbridge*
   *A character, currently enjoying a state of "unbro-
   ken tranquility" looks back on a youth beset by
   "the persistence of the unforeseen."*

5. Gallimard: Happiness is so rare that our
mind can turn somersaults to protect it —
David Henry Hwang, *M. Butterfly,* Act
2, scene 4
   *The speaker should know, since he deluded him-
   self for twenty years that the mistress with whom
   he'd found happiness was a woman and not a man.*

6. He believed that happiness was . . . the only torch —Robert Green Ingersoll, *Eulogy for his brother*

7. What's gone / is common happiness, / plain bread we could eat / with the old apple of knowledge —Denise Levertov, "Prisoners"

   The apple has served as a metaphor for forbidden knowledge ever since Eve bit into a piece of fruit; here bread joins it as an image for everyday happiness.

8. So we stood there face to face—you a torch of dazzling happiness and I ashes of despondent dejection —Naguib Mahfouz, *Palace of Desire*

   Kamal feels that he will be "compelled by an overwhelming force to revolve in orbit" around his beloved, who seems totally inaccessible.

9. Happiness . . . is a flower that must not be picked —Andre Maurois, "The Kingdom of God," *I Remember, I Remember*

10. Happiness is simple / a box of sunshine —Marge Piercy, "The Homely War," *Living In the Open*

11. He laid bare all his wretchedness. A moral eczema. His prison —Antoine de Saint-Exupery, *Night Flight*

    A lonely man bares his needs to a friend.

12. Happiness is a wine of the rarest vintage, and seems insipid to the vulgar taste-station between too little and too much —Logan Pearsall Smith, *Afterthoughts*

13. I'm a little drunk with the spring—and finding you. —Edith Wharton, *Hudson River Bracketed*

■ HARD-HEARTEDNESS

See also: CHARACTERIZATIONS

1. She is most fair, though she be marble-hearted —Anon., "How can the Heart forget her?"

2. Madame Marneffes are to be seen at every level in society . . . sweetly smiling angels with . . . a strong-box for a heart —Honoré de Balzac, *Cousin Bette*

   Balzac returns to the figure of a strong-box of a heart a few pages later to describe the lady's tendency to "pull the wool thoroughly over the eyes" of a man she "saw as a perennially available cash-box." The common metaphor to pull the wool over someone's eyes has its origins in the nineteenth-century fashion for men's wool wigs, which when pulled over the wearer's eyes obscured vision.

3. His heart's a rock, / a metronome, a clock, / a foghorn drone of murder —Jim Harrison, "Malediction"

   "Man's not a singing animal," writes Harrison, asking God to curse "this self-maimed beast."

4. Dromio S.: A devil in an everlasting garment hath him [Dromio's master], / One whose hard heart is buttoned up with steel —William Shakespeare, *The Comedy of Errors*, Act 4, scene 2, line 66

5. King: Bow, stubborn knees; and heart with strings of steel / Be soft as sinews of the new-born babe —William Shakespeare, *Hamlet*, Act 3, scene 3, line 70

   The "steely" heart metaphor paves the way for a simile.

6. Young Clifford: Even at this sight / My heart is turn'd to stone —William Shakespeare, *The Second Part of Henry the Sixth*, Act 5, scene 2, line 50

7. Richard: Not contented that he lopp'd the branch / In hewing Rutland when his leaves put forth, / But set his murdering knife unto the root / From whence that tender spray did sweetly spring. —William Shakespeare, *The Third Part of Henry the Sixth*, Act 2, scene 6, line 47

   Richard pictures the extent of Clifford's ruthlessness.

8. Launce: He is a stone, a very pebble stone, and has no more pity in him than a dog —William Shakespeare, *Two Gentlemen of Verona*, Act 2, scene 4, line 10

■ HARMONY/DISHARMONY

See also: *AGREEMENT/DISAGREEMENT;*
ARGUMENTS; CONTENTMENT; DIS-
SENT/DISSENTERS

1. Shall we begin to wrangle? / No, no, no,
   my heart is fast, and cannot disentangle
   —Anon., "Since First I saw your Face"

2. Harmony exists in difference no less than
   in likeness, if only the same key-note
   govern both parts —Margaret Fuller,
   Epigraph

3. Iago: You are well tun'd now, / But I'll
   set down the pegs that make this music —
   William Shakespeare, *Othello,* Act 2, scene
   1, line 200
   > *Iago, in an aside, threatens to destroy the exqui-*
   > *sitely tuned music of Othello's joy.*

4. Mark how one string, sweet husband to
   another, / Strikes each in each by mutual
   ordering —William Shakespeare, "Sonnet 8," line 8

5. When all the strings of my life will be
   tuned, my Master, then at every touch of
   thine will come out the music of love —
   Rabindranath Tagore, "Stray Birds, 314"

■ HASTE

See: *SLOWNESS; SPEED*

■ HATE

See also: *EMOTIONS; LOVE*

1. Arrows of hate have been shot at me too;
   but they never hit me, because somehow
   they belonged to another world, with which
   I have no connection whatsoever —Albert Einstein, *Out of My Later Years*
   > *The author, who found solitude painful in youth,*
   > *has learned to appreciate it in maturity, so that he*
   > *can exist with or without the admiration he has*
   > *generally enjoyed.*

2. Seeing Woody's [Allen] films now one is
   struck by the cold breeze of misanthrophy
   that blows through them —Adam Gopnik,
   The New Yorker, October 25, 1993
   > *Gopnik explains this as follows: "The realism of*
   > *Annie Hall and Manhattan unleashed Woody*
   > *Allen's honesty. That meant that it also released*
   > *his ill will."*

3. Hatreds are the cinders of affection —Sir
   Walter Raleigh, (also spelled Ralegh), Letter, 1593

4. The winds of hatred blow / Cold, cold
   across the flesh —Theodore Roethke,
   "Lull"

5. Joan: One drop of hate left in the cup of
   joy renders the blissful drink a poison —
   Johann Christoph Friedrich von Schiller,
   Maid of Orleans, Act 3, scene 1
   > *Joan foresees the danger of a reconciliation tainted*
   > *with vestiges of ill feeling.*

6. It rasped her, though, to have stirring
   about in her this brutal monster! . . . to
   hear twigs cracking and feel hooves planted down in the depths of that leaf-encum-
   bered forest, the soul. —Virginia Woolf,
   Mrs. Dalloway.
   > *There are two metaphors here: hate as a monster*
   > *and the soul as a thick forest.*

■ HEART

See also: *EMOTIONS; FEELINGS; LOVE*

1. When you consider / the radiance, that it
   will look into the guiltiest / swervings of
   the weaving heart —A. R. Ammons,
   "The City Limits"
   > *The radiance "does not withhold / itself but*
   > *pours its abundance without selection / into every*
   > *nook and cranny," writes Ammons.*

2. The heart is the best preacher —Anon.,
   Proverb

3. Perhaps a heart in love becomes a deep
   ravine? —Anon., Untitled poem

4. A family portrait that is also a near-epic
   investigation into the broad landscape,

the thousand dark acres of the human heart —Anon.

The metaphor is from an unattributed review of Jane Smiley's Pulitzer Prize–winning 1992 novel, A Thousand Acres, *quoted in an ad for the paperback edition.*

5. The heart is half a prophet —Anon., Yiddish Proverb

6. If you in your bush indeed know her / Where shall my heart's vagrant tides place her? —John Ashbery, "Eclogue"

   Colin addresses his father Cuddie in this sly imitation of an old form of pastoral poetry.

7. Her heart rolled slowly over, a wheel on which something is written —Enid Bagnold, *National Velvet*

8. He had learned . . . to make his heart a sanctuary, into whose solitude he withdrew —Honoré de Balzac, *Cousin Pons*

9. The fickle climates of the heart —William Bell, "Elegy IX"

10. Her fingers on her breasts felt the soft hoofs of her own heart beating —Kay Boyle, "Uncle Anne," *Wedding Day and Other Stories*

11. For the human heart is the mirror / Of the things that are near and far —Alice Cary, "The Time to Be"

    The metaphor is followed by this simile: "Like the wave that reflects in its bosom / The flower and the distant star."

12. My heart is wax moulded as she pleases, but enduring as marble to retain —Miguel de Cervantes, *The Little Gypsy*

    A variation—"Wax to receive, and marble to retain"—appeared in Byron's "Beppo."

13. A vast crack had appeared magically in Ellen's heart the night Father died — John Cheever, "The Summer Farmer"

14. Secret Gardens of the Heart —Judy Collins, Song title, 1972

    The title and first line are followed by "where the old stay young forever

15. There are no wrinkles in the heart, and you will see my face only in the reflection of your attachment —Juliette Drouet, Letter to Victor Hugo, November 19, 1841

    The image was used a century earlier by Madame de Sévigné as "The heart has no wrinkles."

16. Adams: He has / A foiling heart: the sharp world glances off —Christopher Fry, *A Sleep of Prisoners*

    The fencing image recalls another image of imperviousness: a U.S. president was called "the Teflon president" because he survived criticism the way events glanced off the "foiling heart."

17. [I] step into the corridor and start, / Directed by the compass of my heart — Thom Gunn, "The Nature of an Action"

18. I groped to feel a handle in my heart — Thom Gunn, "The Nature of an Action"

19. The great conservative is the heart — Nathaniel Hawthorne, Journal entry, January 6, 1834

20. My heart is a kicking horse / Shod with Kentucky steel! —Vachel Lindsay, "My Fathers Came from Kentucky"

21. His heart was a fist that rose up into his mouth and pushed him into a leap — Gabriel García Márquez, "Innocent Eréndira and Her Heartless Grandmother"

22. The world is in the heart / And the heart is clogged in the sea lanes out of port — Josephine Miles, "Merchant Marine"

23. My heart is what it was before, / A house where people come and go —Edna St. Vincent Millay, "Alms," *Second April*

24. The heart is a triumphant and mighty emperor that ends as the breakfast of a silly little worm —Michel Equem de Montaigne, *Essays, II*

25. The heart is a free and fetterless thing— / A wave of the ocean, a bird on the wing— Julia Pardoe, "The Captive Greek Girl"

26. Her heart was a stone lying upon her breast outside of her —Katherine Anne

Porter, "Noon Wine." *Pale Horse, Pale Rider*

27. There is a little watchman in my heart / Who is always telling me what time it is —Edward Arlington Robinson, "Tristram"

28. Your true image pictured lies, / Which in my bosom's shop is hanging still —William Shakespeare, "Sonnet 24," line 6

    In this conceit, the poet is a painter who has "steeled / Thy beauty's form in table of my heart," so that his heart becomes the shop, or art gallery, in which the lover's picture is on display.

29. Always the heart / Clumps in the breast with heavy stride —Karl Shapiro, "Nostalgia"

30. Juno: Do you think a man's heart is a potato? or a turnip? or a ball of knitting wool? that you can throw it away like this? —George Bernard Shaw, *Overruled* 1912.

31. Where no sea runs, the waters of the heart / Push in their tides —Dylan Thomas, "Light Breaks Where No Sun Shines"

32. With heart more old than the horn / That is brimmed from the pale fire of time — William Butler Yeats, "A Poet To His Beloved"

    The poet, with reverent hands and old heart, brings to his beloved his "passionate rhyme."

■ HEAT

See also: SEASONS; SUMMER; SUN

1. Cut the heat: / Plow through it, / Turning it on either side / Of your path — H.D., "The Garden"

    The poet Hilda Doolittle chose to publish using only the initials H.D., which eventually became known to the reading public. She is still credited only with her initials, although later collections sometimes add her full name in parentheses.

2. I walk without flinching through the burning cathedral of the summer —Violette Leduc, *Mad in Pursuit*

3. The whole world's a blazing pyre, especially the oven room —Naguib Mahfouz, *Palace of Desire*

    The homely metaphor comes from a simple Egyptian woman.

4. I never appreciated before what a cruel giant the heat is —Lady (Mary) Monkswell (Mrs. Robert Collier), Diary entry, October 16, 1881

    The entry was made after the Englishwoman's summer tour of the American West.

5. The streets were a furnace, the sun an executioner —Cynthia Ozick, "Rosa"

6. A promise, late on a broiling day in late September, of the cold kiss / Of marble sheets —James Schuyler, "The Crystal Lithium"

7. The sun was a hammer in late afternoon —Robert James Waller, *The Bridges of Madison County*

■ HEAVEN

See also: GOD

1. Thy walls are made of precious stones, / Thy bulwarks diamonds square —Anon., "The New Jerusalem"

    In this song of Mary, the Mother of Jesus, the poet describes the heavenly Jerusalem in very earthly terms.

2. Strepsiades: There dwell the men who teach—aye, who persuade us, / That Heaven is one vast fire-extinguisher / Placed round about us, and that we're the cinders —Aristophanes, *The Clouds*

    Socrates, perhaps the greatest teacher of all, is one of the teachers being derided.

3. Thou hast an house on high erect, / Framed by that mighty Architect, / With glory richly furnished —Anne Bradstreet, "Upon the Burning of Our House July 10, 1666"

    Bradstreet comes to terms with losing her house and possessions to fire by remembering the tran-

sience of this life, and the house and furnishings that await her in heaven.

4. You'll find your happy hunting grounds, if you've been a just Injin; if an onjust, you'll meet your desarts in another way —James Fenimore Cooper, *The Deerslayer*
   "Happy hunting grounds" was the white man's idea of the Indian's idea of paradise.

5. Heaven is our heritage, / Earth but a player's stage —Thomas Nashe, "A Litany in Time of Plague"

6. Bolinbroke: Me thinks King Richard and myself should meet / With no less terror than the elements / Of fire and water when their thund'ring shock / At meeting tears the cloudy cheeks of heaven —William Shakespeare, *The Tragedy of King Richard the Second*, Act 3, scene 3, line 54
   The metaphor rests on the foundation of the introductory simile.

■ HELL AND DAMNATION

1. Now of penance I will wade the water clear / To save me from purgatory, that sharp fire —Anon.

2. Jesus: It is better for thee to enter life maimed, than to have two hands to go . . . into the fire that never shall be quenched —The Bible, *N.T., Mark 9:43*

3. Hell is paved with granite blocks hewn from the hearts of those who said, "I can do no other" —Heywood Broun, Syndicated column, January 1934
   The proverbial metaphor which seeded this variant appears later in this section.

4. But best, dead, damned, to rock forever / Beside Hell's fireside —Randall Jarrell, "Cinderella"
   Cinderella has become a "sullen wife and a reluctant mother" who joins all those who distrust men.

5. He wished that purgatory for [Andrew] Greeley would be a typewriter with no ribbon —Nancy Q. Keefe, "Letter Home"
   Ms. Keefe quoted an anonymous priest who dislikes the writing of one of his colleagues.

6. Hell is paved with good intentions — John Ray, *English Proverbs*

7. Porter: I had thought to have let in some of all professions, that go the primrose way to everlasting bonfire. —William Shakespeare, *Macbeth*, Act 2, scene 3, line 18
   The primrose path remains a popular metaphor for the road to Hell; an example, from William Safire's March 29, 1992 "Essay" (New York Times): "The new President has already started down the primrose path of dallying with Saddam Hussein."

8. Hells Spider gets / His intrails spin to whip Cords thus, / And wove to nets, / and sets. / To tangle Adams race — Edward Taylor, "Upon a Spider Catching a Fly"

■ HELP

See: ASSISTANCE

■ HELPLESSNESS

See also: SIGNIFICANCE/INSIGNIFICANCE; SUCCESS/FAILURE

1. Why did I, a poor worm, have to twist in the flame of their repulsive ardor? —Louis Auchincloss, "The 'Fulfillment' of Grace Eliot," *Skinny Island*
   A literary agent and executor is caught up in his client's extramarital affair.

2. What was really immoral [about the Vietnam war] was to send a soldier there and tie his hands behind his back by not winning —President George Bush, NBC *Today*, October 1992
   On October 19, 1992, The New York Times columnist Anthony Lewis derided this as "a

familiar right-wing metaphor for the way the United States fought the Vietnam War.

3. Thou art slave to Fate, Chance, kings, and desperate men —John Donne, "Holy Sonnets: X"

   Death is personified in this sonnet, and Donne writes that Death does not decide to end a person's life: it can be ended accidently, or by a king's order, or at the hands of a rogue.

4. So we beat on, boats against the current, borne back ceaselessly into the past —F. Scott Fitzgerald, *The Great Gatsby*

   The metaphor sums up what Jay Gatsby finds so hard to accept—that the dream he'd struggled so hard to attain might forever remain beyond his reach.

5. Aethelwold [in response to Aelfrida's "Art thou a-cold, my dear?"]: I know not . . . I am a tree in a storm —Edna St. Vincent Millay, *The King's Henchman*, Act 2

6. Even a *bungakushi* [a graduate of the Imperial University] turns out to be a mere puppet when placed in the post of dean. —Natsume Soseki, *Botchan*

   Botchan considers the flatterer Noda, who is an incompetent.

7. Men—motes in the sunshine—perished . . . in the very noon of life —Frank Norris, *The Octopus*

   The ruthless Westerners who populate the novel are eventually crushed by the inexorable forces of nature and capital they sought to control. With a combination of metaphor and simile, the author concludes that "in that isolated group of human insects, misery, death and anguish spun like a wheel of fire."

8. Leontes: I am a feather for each wind that blows. —William Shakespeare, *The Winter's Tale*, Act 2, scene 3, line 153.

9. Hector: We of this house are only moths flying into the candle —George Bernard Shaw, *Heartbreak House*, Act 3

   Hector, in a final moment of self-awareness is telling Ellie to head for safety instead of trying to help those who cannot be helped.

10. Life is difficult . . . our frail barks founder in darkness —Virginia Woolf, *To the Lighthouse*

11. He had, by his flight, abandoned himself to be tossed and buffeted by the tyranny of daily minutia —Richard Wright, *The Outsider*

    The sentence contains two popular metaphors: Man as a storm-tossed wave and routine as a tyrant.

■ HISTORY

See also: PAST

1. History is a tangled skein that one may take up at any point, and break when one has unravelled enough —Henry Adams, *The Education of Henry Adams*

2. History is a tired old man with a long beard —Anon., s.u.

3. The distance that man has traveled in the intervening centuries [between Dante's *Divine Comedy* and Faulkner's *The Sound and the Fury*] is revealed to us . . . And the road that has been traveled is irreversible — William Barrett, "Modern Art"

   The substitution of distance for time is predicated on the image of history as a road.

4. History was a drama with many acts — Isaiah Berlin, "The Pursuit of the Ideal," *The Crooked Timber of Humanity*

5. This existence . . . had stayed as it was while elsewhere, history jerked itself painfully off the spool —Elizabeth Bowen, "Ivy Grips the Steps," *The Demon Lover and Other Stories*

6. History is the torch that is meant to illuminate the past —Claude G. Bowers, Introduction to *The U.S. and the Spanish Civil War* by F. Jay Taylor

7. History, the evidence of time, the light of truth, the life of memory, the directress of

the herald of antiquity, committed to immortality —Marcus Tullius Cicero, *De Oratore*

8. Lacking that sort of historic anchor, most of his [Truman's] successors' images seem less firmly fixed —Adam Clymer, *The New York Times,* January 24, 1993

    The author commented on the changing evaluation of past presidents.

9. And the lonely psyche goes up thru the boy to the king / that in the caves of history dreams —Robert Duncan, "A Poem Beginning with a Line by Pindar"

10. Moses: Do you think / If we swung the rattle of conversation / Those centuries would fly off like so many crows?. — Christopher Fry, *The Firstborn,* Act 1, scene 2

    Moses knows that the weight of Egyptian history precludes the possibility of swift change for the Hebrews. The rattle metaphor refers to an instrument used by farmers to scare crows off the fields.

11. Moses: Egypt is only / One golden eruption of time, one flying spark / Attempting the ultimate fire —Christopher Fry, *The Firstborn,* Act 1, scene 3

12. Shuttles in the rocking loom of history, / the dark ships move, the dark ships move —Robert Hayden, "Middle Passage. III"

    The long poem deals with a mutiny aboard a slave ship.

13. History is but the merest outline of the exceptional . . . A few mountain peaks are touched, while all the valleys of human life . . . are left in the eternal shadow — Robert Green Ingersoll, Decoration Day address, 1870

14. Chronology is the eye of history —Samuel Johnson, Quoted, *Short Saying of Great Men*

15. History . . . a nightmare from which I am trying to awake —James Joyce, *Ulysses*

16. My time, my monster, who will be able / to with his own blood glue together / the vertebrae of these two centuries? —Osip Mandelstam, "The Age (135)"

17. When you were a tadpole and I was a fish / In the Paleozoic time —Langdon Smith, "Evolution"

    If this were a lesson, it might be titled "Darwinism made Easy."

18. The twentieth century . . . is a citadel guarded by thick walls of ignorance and of mistrust which do not fall before the trumpets' blast or the politicians' imprecations or even a general's baton —Adlai Stevenson, Acceptance speech for nomination for the Presidency at the Democratic National Convention, July 26, 1952

    Turning his metaphoric statement into action, Stevenson continued "They are, my friends, walls that must be directly stormed by the hosts of courage, of mortality and of vision, standing shoulder to shoulder, unafraid of ugly truth, contemptuous of lies, half-truths, circuses and demagoguery."

19. History is little else than a picture of crimes and misfortunes —Voltaire, *L'Ingenu*

    In a similar vein Edward Gibbon in The Decline and Fall of the Roman Empire *(1784), called history "little more than the register of the crimes, follies and misfortunes of mankind.*

20. For the sake of Germany and the Germans, to see if one couldn't return to the starting point and become *simply human again,* a new man who can cancel the scab of history that sticks to us like ugly dandruff —A. B. Yehoshua, *Mr. Mani*

    A German soldier looks at Hitler's disastrous policies and wants to cancel that part of German history.

21. He was the first to call for casting the rusty anchor of German history back into that sea you see down there, because there, he used to say, was the warm, true, blue womb of the German genius —A. B. Yehoshua, *Mr. Mani*

    "He" is the old classicist Gustav Koch, who told stories about Greece and Rome. There are two metaphors: the anchor of history, and the womb of genius.

■ HONESTY

See: *CANDOR; TRUTH/FALSEHOOD*

■ HONOR

See also: *REPUTATION; TRUSTWORTHI-NESS/UNTRUSTWORTHINESS*

1. However, it would never do for me to be beaten. My honor would be trodden down in the dust, if I should let things go on as they stood —Natsume Soseki, *Botchan*
   Honor is here treated as tangible, like a fallen escutcheon.

2. Julia: His words are bonds, his oaths oracles —William Shakespeare, *Two Gentlemen of Verona*, Act 2, scene 7, line 74

3. Honor wears different coats to different eyes —Barbara Tuchman, *The Guns of August*

■ HOPE

See also: *DESPAIR; DREAMS; OPTIMISM/PESSIMISM; YEARNING*

1. Hope is a waking dream —Anon., s. u.
   This has been variously ascribed to Aristotle, Plato and other Greeks.

2. I have seen her fern-colored eyes *open* mornings on a world where the beating of hope's great wings is scarcely distinct from the other sounds —André Breton, *Nadja*

3. Mellfont: Thy presence is a view of land, appearing to my shipwracked hopes —William Congreve, *The Double Dealer*, Act 2, scene 1

4. Comforting hope, how you have kept me warm! —Catherine Davis, "Insights: 9"

5. Mind a beehive of hopes buzzing and stinging —John Dos Passos, *U.S.A., The 42nd Parallel*
   The phrase is from the prologue to the author's groundbreaking trilogy.

6. David: The world's back / Is bent and heavily burdened, and yet he thinks / He can leapfrog over —Christopher Fry, *A Sleep of Prisoners*
   The personification of the world as an old person is augmented by the further image of a young man's leaping over that world.

7. Cymen: . . . hope, with her ambitious shovel, sweats / To dig the pit which swallows us at last —Christopher Fry, *Thor, With Angels*

8. Hope is a great falsifier —Baltasar Gracian, *The Art of Worldly Wisdom*

9. Shall we gather strength by . . . hugging the delusive phantom of hope? —Patrick Henry, Speech in the Virginia convention, March 23, 1775
   The fiery orator and statesman urged an immediate posture of strong defense.

10. I have a dream that one day . . . the glory of the Lord shall be revealed, and all flesh shall see it together . . . With this faith we will be able to hew out of the mountain of despair a stone of hope. With this faith we will be able to transform the jangling discords of our nation into a beautiful symphony of brotherhood —Martin Luther King, Jr., speech to civil rights marchers, August 23, 1963

11. And Hope, that fouls my brightness with its grace, / Will anchor in the narrows of your face —Robert Lowell, "Her Dead Brother"

12. On the wings of hope, of love, of joy, Miss Meadows sped back to the music hall —Katherine Mansfield, "The Singing Lesson,"
    A young woman is transformed when she learns that the man she loves has not rejected her.

13. Was I deceiv'd, or did a sable cloud / Turn forth her silver lining on the night? —John Milton, "Comus"
    The cloud with the silver lining is an enduring metaphor for finding a bright side to a less-than-bright situation. In Bleak House Dickens ac-

knowledged the source as follows: I turn my silver lining outward like Milton's cloud.

14. This flickering at night / in the casing of my thoughts, / mother-of-pearl tracing of snail —Eugenio Montale, "Little Testament"

The flickering was "a hope that burned more slowly / than a tough log on the grate."

15. The time is coming when man will no more shoot the arrow of his longing out over mankind, and the string of his bow will have forgotten how to twang! —Friedrich Wilhelm Nietzsche, *Thus Spake Zarathustra*

16. Our limbs are shackled to shameless / hope, and the streams of forethought lie afar —Pindar, "Nemea 8," *Odes*

Optimists are shackled to hope; pessimists would be shackled to despair—which is consistent with forethought. When we know what lies ahead, it is hard to be optimistic.

17. All the birds she'd woven / flying low on the level sky of her final enduring — Yannis Ritsos, "Penelope's Despair"

Penelope, after Odysseus returns and slaughters the suitors, recognizes the futility of her dreams during the years she had woven and unraveled her cloth at the loom.

18. The white bird of hope flew out the window —Richard Selzer, "A Pint of Blood," *Letters to a Young Doctor*

19. A flame of hope blazes up. It leaps out of her blue eyes and singes him [a doctor] — Richard Selzer, "Semiprivate, Female," *Letters to a Young Doctor*

20. Claudio: The miserable have no other medicine. But only hope —William Shakespeare, *Measure or Measure*, Act 3 scene 1 line 2

"I have hope to live, and am prepar'd to die," Claudio adds.

21. Provost: It is a bitter deputy —William Shakespeare, *Measure for Measure*, Act 4, scene 2, line 79

Provost, seeking comfort for the imprisoned Claudio, cannot accept the duke's opinion that "There's some in hope."

22. Pistol: Hope is a curtal dog in some affairs —William Shakespeare, *The Merry Wives of Windsor,* Act 2, scene 1, line 112

A curtal dog is one whose tail has been cut off.

23. Cassio: Therefore my hopes, not surfeited to death, / Stand in bold cure —William Shakespeare, *Othello,* Act 2, scene 1, line 50

This is a puzzling metaphor, and one that has been variously interpreted, the most simple explanation being that Iago's hopes are strong.

24. Richmond: True hope is swift, and flies with swallow's wings —William Shakespeare, *The Tragedy of King Richard the Third,* Act 5, scene 3, line 23

25. Proteous: Hope is a lover's staff —William Shakespeare, *Two Gentlemen of Verona,* Act 3, scene 1, line 247

26. Hope is a fawning traitor of the mind, while under color of friendship, it robs it of its chief force of resolution —Sir Phillip Sidney, *Arcadia*

27. You never can stand it [privation] unless you have within you some imperishable food . . . the food of those visions of the spirit where a table is set before us laden with . . . the fruits of hope, the fruits of the imagination —Woodrow Wilson, "The New Freedom"

28. Hopes . . . beads of morning strung on slender blades of grass —William Wordsworth, "Inscriptions Supposed to be Found In and Near a Hermit's Cell."

■ HOPELESSNESS

See: DESPAIR

■ HORSES

See: ANIMALS

■ HOUSES

1. That house . . . / Which is my realm and crown, and more beside —Joachim du Bellay, "Happy the Man"

2. Home was . . . a frail eggshell house, set off on the edge of the prairie where people of no consequence lived —Willa Cather, *A Lost Lady*

3. Sherebyakov: I hate this house. It is a regular labyrinth —Anton Chekhov, *Uncle Vanya*, Act 3
   It is boredom and a sense of futility that lead to cross-purposes and make the house a labyrinth.

4. A man's house is his castle —Sir Edward Coke, Part of legal doctrine by the English jurist
   This has become an enduring cliche.

5. What a good shield a house is, emblazoned everywhere with the message that shared daily life was lived within —Laurie Colwin, "Intimacy," *The Lone Pilgrim*
   Like many of Colwin's characters, the protagonist in this story reflects on the "domestic artifacts" that differentiate a marriage from an affair.

6. A big white birthday cake of a house — Robert Cormier, "President Cleveland, Where Are You?" *Eight Plus One*

7. But garages and cotton gins had encroached and obliterated even the august names of that neighborhood; only Miss Emily's house was left, lifting its stubborn and coquettish decay above the cotton wagons and gasoline pumps—an eyesore among eyesores —William Faulkner, "A Rose for Emily"
   The house is compared to a faded, once-beautiful woman.

8. The old house creaks again, and makes a vociferous but somewhat unintelligible bellowing in its sooty throat, (the big flue, we mean, of its wide chimney) —Nathaniel Hawthorne, *The House of Seven Gables*

9. The rows of elegantly proportioned windows were empty eyes —P. D. James, *An Unsuitable Job for a Woman*
   The "empty-eyed" windows are found in an eerily silent family home where the victim's father, and murderer, still lives.

10. The summer house was a museum of golden childhoods. —John LeCarré, *The Russia House*

11. It was a wonderful old house . . . all its empty windows gazing wide-eyed down the river valley —Sean O'Faolain, "Midsummer Night Madness"

12. A crumbling, gloomy Victorian house; its owner a crumbling, tiny, stooped old woman —D. M. Thomas, *Memories and Hallucinations*

■ HUMANITY/HUMANKIND

See also: DIVERSITY; LIFE AND DEATH; SIGNIFICANCE/INSIGNIFICANCE

1. Man is an imperceptible atom always trying to become one with God —Henry Brooks Adams, *Mont-Saint Michel and Chartres*

2. The masses are asses —Anon., Yiddish Proverb

3. Dust thou art, and unto dust shalt thou return —The Bible, *O.T. Genesis 3:19*
   A variation from Ecclesiastes 3:20: *All are of the dust, and all turn to dust again.*

4. The Human Dress is forged Iron, / The Human Form a fiery Forge, / The Human Face a Furnace seal'd, / The Human Heart is hungry Gorge —William Blake, "A Divine Image"

5. What shadows we are, and what shadows we pursue —Edmund Burke, Speech, 1780
   Wordsworth's twist on this metaphor is, "We all laugh at pursuing a shadow, though the lives of the multitude are devoted to the chase."

6. Man is but a perambulating tool-box and workshop, or office fashioned for itself by

a piece of very clever slime, as the result of long experience —Samuel Butler

7. A man is the history of his breaths and thoughts, acts, atoms and wounds, love, indifference and dislike —A. S. Byatt, *Possession*

> The metaphor continues with a list of other historic markers such as race and nation and finally "a single flame . . . lit and put out from one moment to the next."

8. The people is a beast of muddy brain that knows not its own strength —Tommaso Campanella

> While the Italian philosopher probably said it first, it was made famous by American statesman Alexander Hamilton.

9. The Vagrant: What's a man anyway . . . a butterfly, or a beetle, or an ant? —Joseph Capek and Karel Capek, *The World We Live In*, Prologue, adapted by Owen Davis

10. Man . . . a two-legged animal without feathers —Thomas Carlyle, *Past and Present, I* 1843.

11. We are all pilgrims and wayfarers in this life —Catherine of Siena, Undated letter

12. Mr. President, what is an individual man? An atom, almost invisible without a magnifying glass—a mere speck upon the surface of the immense universe —Henry Clay, Speech, 1850

13. One viewed the existence of man then as a marvel, and conceded a glamor of wonder to these lice which were caused to cling to a whirling, fire-smote, ice-locked, disease-stricken, space-lost bulb —Stephen Crane, "The Blue Hotel"

14. Pity the busy monster, manunkind —e. e. cummings, "Pity the busy monster, manunkind"

15. Every live thing is a survivor on a kind of extended emergency bivouac —Annie Dillard, *Pilgrim at Tinker Creek*

> The author returned to this metaphor with "I am a frayed and nibbled survivor in a fallen world and I am getting along."

16. Man's a poor deluded bubble, wandering in a midst of lies —Robert Dodsley, Song, 1745

17. The mighty tide of being flows / Through countless channels —Elizabeth Doten, "Reconciliation"

18. All the ties which attach him to life break in the hand of man, particularly the golden ties —Alexandre Dumas, *The Three Musketeers*

19. A man is a bundle of relations, a knot of roots, whose flowers and fruitage is the world —Ralph Waldo Emerson, "History," *Essays: First Series*

20. The great majority of men are bundles of beginnings —Ralph Waldo Emerson, *Journals*

21. Man is a weaver on the earth . . . / his own days are the thread, / And when the length allotted he hath spun, / All life is over, and all hope is dead —Abraham Ibn Ezra, "Songs"

22. Dr. Macguire: We can't turn back the days that have gone . . . We are a flash of fire—a brain, a heart, a spirit. We are three cents' worth of lime and iron—which we cannot get back —Ketti Frings, *Look Homeward*, Angel, Act 2, scene 2

> The doctor's melancholy statement is prompted by Ben Gant's death. The play was an adaptation of Thomas Wolfe's novel by the same name.

23. Meadows: Each man is the world —Christopher Fry, *A Sleep of Prisoners*

24. You are bows from which your children as living arrows are sent forth —Kahlil Gibran, *The Prophet*

> The archer as life-giving power "bends you with His might that His arrows may go swift and far." Therefore, Gibran advises "let your bending in the archer's hand be for gladness."

25. We're all beautiful golden sunflowers inside, we're blessed by our own seed & golden hairy naked accomplishment-bodies growing into mad black formal sunflowers in the sunset —Allen Ginsberg, "Sunflower Sutra"

26. Mankind are earthen jugs with spirits in them —Nathaniel Hawthorne, *American Note-Books*

27. Man is a watch, wound up at first, but never wound up again; once down, he's down forever —Robert Herrick, *Hesperides*

28. Man is an onion consisting of a hundred skins, a fabric of many threads —Hermann Hesse, *Uncollected Prose*
    The onion is a favorite metaphor to show that there's more than meets the eye to someone or something.

29. Out of the crooked timber of humanity no straight thing was ever made —Immanuel Kant, Quoted in "The Pursuit of the Ideal," *The Crooked Timber of Humanity*, by Isaiah Berlin

30. Nature has many tricks . . . but the most tremendous, the most stupefying of all is the passive phase of the White Silence. All movement ceases . . . and man becomes timid . . . realizes that his is a maggot's life, nothing more —Jack London, "The White Silence," *The Son of the Wolf*

31. Humanity is a pigsty where liars, hypocrites, and the obscene in spirit congregate —George Moore, *Confessions of a Young Man*

32. Man is a rope stretched between the animal and the Superman—a rope over an abyss —Friedrich Wilhelm Nietzsche, *Thus Spake Zarathustra*
    What is great in man, according to Nietzsche, is that he "is a bridge and not a goal."

33. Man is a sun and the senses are his planets —Novalis

34. Brown: Man is born broken. He lives by mending. The grace of God is glue! —Eugene O'Neill, *The Great God Brown*, Act 4, scene 1

35. Man is but a reed, the most feeble thing in nature, but he is a thinking reed —Blaise Pascal, *Pensée*
    In 1936 Dame Rebecca West chose this metaphor as the title for a novel, The Thinking Reed.

36. I think that if the beast who sleeps in man could be held down by threats . . . then the highest emblem of humanity would be the lion tamer in the circus with his whip, not the prophet who sacrificed himself —Boris Pasternak, *Doctor Zhivago*
    President Ronald Reagan quoted the metaphor in a 1988 speech at Moscow State University.

37. What has for centuries raised man above the beast is . . . an inward music: the irresistible power of unarmed truth —Boris Pasternak, *Doctor Zhivago*

38. Every human being is a colony —Pablo Picasso, Epigraph

39. Man is a two-footed animal, wingless —Plato
    Diogenes filled this out by adding " and flat-nailed." Aristotle changed it to "Man is by nature a political animal."

40. Man is heaven's masterpiece —Francis Quarles

41. Man is essentially a beast, only he butters it over like a slice of bread with a little decorum —Erich Maria Remarque, *All Quiet on the Western Front*

42. Jaques: from hour to hour we ripe and ripe, / And then from hour to hour we rot and rot —William Shakespeare, *As You Like It*, Act 2, scene 7, line 26

43. Mowbray: Men are but gilded loam or painted clay —William Shakespeare, *The Tragedy of King Richard the Second*, Act 1, scene 1, line 179

44. We are but dust / And die we must —
John Skelton, "Upon a Dead Man's Head"

45. Man is a prisoner who has no right to
open the door of his prison and run away
—Socrates, "Apology"

   *To "run away" would be to end one's life before
   "God summons."*

46. Every human being has some handle by
which he may be lifted, some groove in
which he was meant to run; and the great
work of life, as far as our relations with
each other are concerned, is to lift each
one by his own proper handle, and run
each one in his own proper groove —
Harriet Beecher Stowe, *Little Foxes*

   *The author explained her use of the title from
   Song of Solomon (7:4), as a metaphor for
   "those unsuspected, unwatched, insignificant little causes that nibble away domestic happiness."
   Lillian Hellman reactivated the title for her play
   about a nasty family of spoilers.*

47. I do not agree with this century's fashion
of running down the human species as a
failed try, a doomed sport . . . At our
worst, we may be going through the early
stages of a species' adolescence —Lewis
Thomas, *The Fragile Species*

48. Man the machine—man the impersonal
engine —Mark Twain, "What is Man?"

49. We're all imprisoned . . . all of us mid-
dling people, who don't carry our freedom
in our brains —Edith Wharton, "Autre
Temps"

   *"We've accommodated ourselves to our different
   cells, and if we're moved suddenly into new ones
   we're likely to find a stone wall where we thought
   there was thin air, and to knock ourselves senseless
   against it," Wharton continues.*

50. The still sad music of humanity —William Wordsworth, "Lines Composed a
Few Miles Above Tintern Abbey"

∎ HUMILIATION

See: DEFEAT; RIDICULE

∎ HUMILITY

See: ARROGANCE/HUMILITY

∎ HUMOR

See also: CHARACTERISTICS; WIT

1. [False Humor:] The impostor of whom
I'm speaking descends originally from
Falsehood, who was the mother of Non-
sense, who was brought to bed of a son
called Frenzy, who married one of the
daughters of Folly, commonly known by
the name of Laughter, on whom he begot
the monstrous infant of which I have been
speaking —Joseph Addison, "False Wit
and Humor," *The Spectator*, April 10, 1711

2. A sense of humor is the pole that adds
balance to our steps as we walk the tightrope of life —Anon.

3. A humorless man is a wagon without
springs —Anon.

4. Humor is wit with a rooster's tail feather
stuck in its cap, and wit is wisdom in tight
harness —Josh Billings

5. Jonson . . . Winnowing with his flail of
comedy —Thom Gunn, "A Mirror for
Poets"

6. The frozen witticisms of past generations
were thawed out, and came bubbling with
laughter from their lips —Nathaniel Hawthorne, *The Scarlet Letter*

7. Humor usually does not travel well, and
"Far Side" images would seem a particularly unlikely cargo—at least for a national advertising campaign —Steve Lohr,
The New York Times, November 27, 1992

   *Yet Lohr could see why the British who, after all,
   were "known for nurturing eccentrics would choose
   an American cartoonist who once gave his girl
   friend a tarantula"*

8. Wisecracking is simply calisthenics with
words —Dorothy Parker, Quotation, *Paris
Review*

Parker contrasted this to genuine wit, which she said "has truth in it."

9. Southern humor is the macramé of literature—hokey, fuzzy around the edges, resolutely middle class and much too cute for its own good —Robert Plunket, *The New York Times Book Review*, August 22, 1993
   The reviewer of Crazy in Alabama *by Mark Childress ended up figuratively eating his words, admitting that thanks to the author's skill "he soon had me eating out of his hand. I don't know how he did it but he managed to confront . . . every convention of the genre head on and pound it into submission."*

10. Her humor was a continual bubble of joy —William Allen White, "Mary White"
    The essay is a tribute to White's daughter, who was thrown from a horse.

■ HUNGER

1. Hunger makes a thief of man —Pearl S. Buck, *The Good Earth*

2. Hunger is the best sauce in the world —Miguel de Cervantes, *Don Quixote*

3. Hunger is the best pickle —Benjamin Franklin, *Poor Richard's Almanack*

4. Cleon: So sharp are hunger's teeth, that man and wife / Draw lots who first shall die to lengthen life —William Shakespeare, *Pericles, Prince of Tyre*, Act 1, scene 4, line 45

■ HUSBANDS AND WIVES

See also: MARRIAGE; SEX/SEXUALITY

1. He yaf me al the bridel in myn hand, / To han the governance of hous and land —Geoffrey Chaucer, "The Wife of Bath's Prologue," *The Canterbury Tales*
   The implied metaphor of horse and rider shows the dominance of the wife, whose husband puts the bridle into her hand and allows her to take care of both house and land.

2. For winning wolde I al his lust endure, / And make me a feined appetit— / And yit in bacon hadde I never delit —Geoffrey Chaucer, "The Wife of Bath's Prologue and Tale," *The Canterbury Tales*
   The Wife of Bath was willing to feign desire if her elderly husband were willing to bribe her, but she never delighted in 'bacon'—in old meat.

3. And did he mean to suggest that he himself had been well pickled . . . And herself, was she the brine and the vale of tears? —D. H. Lawrence, "Two Blue Birds"
   Husband and wife spar enigmatically when they are together, which occurs as infrequently as possible.

■ HYPOCRISY

See also: CRAFTINESS; DECEPTION; TREACHERY

1. Out of the same mouth you blow hot and cold —Aesop, *Fables:The Man and the Satyr*
   A man explained to a Satyr that he blew on his hands to warm them. When he blew on his soup to cool it, the Satyr refused to be his friend because "he blew hot and cold out of the same mouth." The phrase has been a metaphor for two-sided, deceitful behavior ever since.

2. To these crocodile tears, they will add sobs, fiery sighs, and sorrowful countenance —Robert Burton, English clergyman and writer
   This enduring image of falseness served as the title of a collection of similes gathered by the editor of this volume (False Than a Weeping Crocodile, Visible Ink Press).

3. Why this dirty foul trick, this devilish, serpent's game? —Anton Chekhov, "Enemies"
   The serpent as an evil influence dates back to the story of Adam and Eve. The "serpent's game" player here is a doctor's wife.

4. Hector: Listen to this solid wall of negation which says Yes! —Jean Giraudoux, *Tiger at the Gates*, Act 1

Hector speaks about Helen of Troy, who says whatever people want to hear, without any thought to carrying through on her words.

5. That insidious smile with which our petition has been lately received . . . it will prove a snare to your feet. Suffer not yourselves to be betrayed with a kiss — Patrick Henry, "Give Me Liberty or Give Me Death" speech, March 23, 1775
   Henry likened the King of England's response to Congress's petition to the betrayal of Jesus, when Judas identified him to his enemies with a kiss.

6. When it comes to this, I shall prefer emigrating to some country where they make no pretense of loving liberty,—to Russia, for instance, where despotism can be taken pure, and without the base alloy of hypocrisy —Abraham Lincoln, Letter to Joshua F. Speed, August 24, 1855
   If the Know-Nothings gained control, said Lincoln, the declaration would resolve to "all men are created equal, except negroes and foreigners and Catholics."

7. He was a river of bullshit —Scott Turow, *The Burden of Proof*
   A lawyer thus describes another lawyer.

8. Clive Champion-Cheney: Her soul is as thickly rouged as her face. She hasn't an emotion that's sincere. She's tinsel —W. Somerset Maugham, *The Circle*, Act 2

9. Eadgar: Yea, for if thy tongue be forkèd, Aethelwold, / Then from sea to sea my kingdom hisses! —Edna St. Vincent Millay, *The King's Henchman*, Act 3

10. Hotspur: what a candy deal of courtesy / This fawning greyhound then did proffer me —William Shakespeare, *The First Part of King Henry the Fourth* Act 1, scene 3, line 251

11. King: Thy wish was father, Harry, to that thought —William Shakespeare, *The Second Part of King Henry the Fourth*, Act 4, scene 5, line 91
    The King feels his son Harry wishes him dead.

12. The season of falsity had formed a scab, soon to fall away altogether. There is no health, she thought, for me, outside of honesty —Muriel Spark, "Bang-bang You're Dead"

13. Ferdinand: Hypocrisy is woven of a fine small thread / Subtler than Vulcan's engine [the net in which he caught Mars and Venus]; yet, believ't / Your darkest actions . . . / Will come to light —John Webster, *The Duchess of Malfi*, Act 1, scene 2

∎ HYSTERIA

See: MADNESS

■ IDEALISM

See: REFORM

■ IDEALS

See: ETHICS

■ IDEAS

See also: CREATIVITY; IMAGINATION; MIND; THINKING/THOUGHT

1. To possess ideas is to gather flowers; to think, is to weave them into garlands —Anon.

2. No idea is more than an imaginary potency, a mushroom cloud (destroying nothing, making nothing) rising from blinding consciousness —Saul Bellow, *The Bellarosa Connection*

3. The Sentimentalist . . . will not see that one must pay for an idea . . . he will have them all at once in one wild intellectual harem, no matter how much they quarrel and contradict each other —Gilbert Keith Chesterton, "Alarms and Discussions"

4. Hang ideas! They are tramps, vagabonds, knocking at the back-door of your mind, each taking a little of your substance, each carrying away some crumb of that belief in a few simple notions you must cling to if you want to live decently and would like to die easy! —Joseph Conrad, *Lord Jim*
   Jim admires the ability to face temptation backed by faith alone, without the contagion of ideas.

5. In the mind-world ideas are the indestructible elements which form the jewelled constellations of the interior life —Henry Miller, "The Creative Life"

6. When Mr. Kunitz talks, he doesn't throw out his ideas helter-skelter. Rather, he places them carefully into the air, creating a sort of quality-thinking zone, where small-mindedness had best find somewhere else to park —Bob Morris, *The New York Times*, August 29, 1993
   Morris's interview with Provincetown gardener and Pulitzer Prize–winning poet Stanley Kunitz was aptly headlined "growing metaphors."

7. You cannot put a rope around the neck of an idea; you cannot put an idea up against the barrack-square wall and riddle it with bullets —Sean O'Casey, 1918
   The Irish dramatist thus commented on the death of Thomas Ashe.

8. Ideas come fast and low across the net —John Russell, "Thoroughly Modern Maestro," *The New York Times Magazine*, April 12, 1992
   The profile of Simon Rattle, conductor of the Birmingham Symphony, shows him to be a man "on a conversational boil" with ideas on every subject imaginable.

9. In 1948 one of the most successful radio producers of the Columbia Broadcasting System came up with a sunburst of ideas —Howard Teichmann, *George S. Kaufman*

   One of these ideas turned out to be a show called This Is Broadway; another was to get George S. Kaufman to be on it.

■ IDENTITY

See also: SELF-KNOWLEDGE

1. The Department of Energy, conceived during World War II and nurtured in the bosom of the cold war, is also undergoing an identity crisis —Thomas L. Friedman, "Cold War Without End," *The New York Times Magazine,* August 22, 1993

2. He was a well-built man, wide-shouldered, but he felt within himself the presence of his own femininity, sometimes contained in a chickadee's egg, the size of a pale blue or pink sugared almond, but sometimes brimming over to flood his entire body with its milk —Jean Genet, *Querelle*

   "He himself believed in this quality of weakness, this frailty of an enormous, unripe nut, whose pale white interior consisted of the stuff children call milk."

3. The watery blister of personal identity can be lanced through by imagination —Rebecca Goldstein, *The Dark Sister*

4. I am undefined, weeds are growing between my ribs —Joyce Carol Oates, "I Was in Love"

5. Identity is a bag and a gag —Judith Rossner, *Nine Months in the Life of an Old Maid*

   "It exists for me with all the force of a fatal disease," the author continues.

6. A Chinaman of the T'ang Dynasty—and, by which definition, a philosopher— dreamed he was a butterfly, and from that moment he was never quite sure that he was not a butterfly dreaming it was a Chinese philosopher —Tom Stoppard, *Rosencrantz & Guildenstern are Dead*

7. Are you quite certain, Colonel, that you wish me to expound on such questions of identity? It's a dreadful bog, you know — A. B. Yehoshua, *Mr. Mani*

   ". . . The Jews themselves start out across it with the greatest confidence and end up floundering madly," says the speaker, noting how hard it is to define a Jew.

■ IDLENESS

See also: ACTIVENESS/INACTIVENESS

1. Sonia: We have not eaten the bread of idleness —Anton Chekhov, *Uncle Vanya,* Act 3

2. Astrov: You and he have infected us with your idleness. —Anton Chekhov, *Uncle Vanya,* Act 4

   The disease metaphor is a common one, particularly in relation to negative character traits.

3. Idleness . . . the refuge of weak minds, and the holiday of fools —Earl of Chesterfield (Philip Dormer Stanhope), *Letters to His Son*

4. Doomed to be idle, / . . . They grow into a vegetable peace —Jorge Guillén, "The Horses"

5. The swamp of spiritual and bodily sloth in which his whole being had sunk —James Joyce, *Portrait of the Artist as a Young Man*

6. Antony: Ten thousand harms, . . . / My idleness doth hatch. —William Shakespeare, *Antony and Cleopatra,* Act 4, scene 10, line 103

   Eros has killed himself rather than Antony, as the latter requested. Now, Antony knows he must die by his own hand and vows to rush into death bravely and happily "as to a lover's bed."

7. Indolence is the sleep of the mind —Luc de Clapiers de (Marquis) Vauvenargues, *Reflexions*

■ IGNORANCE

See also: STUPIDITY

1. He has earned his wage of ignorance, and is entitled to its increment of dross — John Kendrick Bangs, "My Silent Servants"
   Bangs here derides nonreaders.

2. Ignorance is a blank sheet, on which we may write —Caleb Colton, *Lacon*

3. Ignorance is a delicate fruit: touch it and the fruit is gone —Oscar Wilde, s.u.
   A much–quoted metaphor can often serve as a skeleton on which to hang one's own. To illustrate, an essay by Harold Nicolson about the differences between the people of the United States and Great Britain (Vanity Fair, 1933): "I agree with Oscar Wilde—" he writes by way of repeating Wilde's metaphoric bon mot. "I therefore write upon this invidious topic while the bloom is still as dust upon the damask of my ignorance."

■ ILLNESS

See also: LIFE AND DEATH; MORTALITY

1. I live in a bigger, dirtier city [than London]—ill-health —W. N. P. Barbellion, January 22, 1913, diary entry
   The writer explains why his diary does not reflect his living in "mighty London."

2. [Lyme] disease is a great masquerader; its early symptoms mimic those of many other ailments —Jane E. Brody, "Personal Health," *The New York Times,* August 26, 1992

3. Physical ills . . . the taxes laid upon this wretched life; some are taxed higher, and some lower, but all pay something —Earl of Chesterfield (Philip Dormer Stanhope), *Letters to His Son*

4. These burning fits but meteors bee, / Whose matter in thee is soone spent — John Donne, "A Feaver"
   The poet worries that his love might die of her illness, and then consoles himself by thinking her fever a meteor that will burn swiftly away.

5. Cancer was running races through her mother's remaining bones —Elizabeth Graver, "The Body Shop,"
   The almost playful comparison of a rapidly spreading illness to a race, underscores the emotional trauma of the situation.

6. In November a cold, unseen stranger, whom the doctors called Pneumonia, stalked about the colony, touching one here and there with its icy fingers —O. Henry, "The Last Leaf," *The Trimmed Lamp*
   The colony referred to in this metaphoric personification was Manhattan's Greenwich Village section. O. Henry himself was felled by another equally deadly "unseen stranger"—tuberculosis.

7. The infection begins with a brushfire in the immune system. —Gina Kilata, *The New York Times,* March 17, 1992
   The infection described is AIDS.

8. But if 20% of those ruddy faces and hearty appetites were concealing the suffering caused by a traffic jam in the *transit intestinal,* what else could they be concealing? —Peter Mayle, *Toujours Provence*
   The author reflects on a leaflet's claim that 20% of the French population suffers from constipation.

9. King: Health . . . with youthful wings is flown / From this bare wither'd trunk — William Shakespeare, *The Second Part of King Henry the Fourth,* Act 4, scene 5, line 227

10. Everyone who is born holds dual citizenship, in the kingdom of the well and in the kingdom of the sick —Susan Sontag, *Illness As Metaphor*

11. My whole life has become a journey, and . . . the only familiar place to which I

always return, is my illness —Irvin D. Yalom, *When Nietzsche Wept*

> *A fictional Nietzsche in consultation with the famous Viennese doctor, Joseph Breuer.*

ILLUSION/REALITY

See also: DECEPTION; TRUTH

1. Led astray by many fancies, / Enveloped by the snares of delusion —Anon., *The Bhagavad Gita, 16:16*

2. Illusion is the dust the devil throws in the eyes of the foolish —Minna Antrim, *Naked Truth and Veiled Allusions*

3. She knew very well that for the past twenty years Baron Hulot had been habitually unfaithful to her; but she had sealed her eyes with lead —Honoré de Balzac, *Cousin Bette*

4. Galileo: This age of ours turned out to be a whore, splattered with blood —Bertolt Brecht, *Galileo*, scene 12

   > *This is Galileo's response to Andrea's question as to whether he now thinks that the "new age" was an illusion.*

5. In age, when the flowers are so few, it's a great unkindness to destroy any that are left in a man's heart —Willa Cather, *My Mortal Enemy*

   > *The speaker is a sick, embittered woman and the flowers refer to the beliefs in past love and happiness that some, like her husband, manage to keep alive.*

6. Reality is a lightning flash that quivers imprisoned in every stone. If you do not awaken it, the stone remains a stone —Hermann Hesse, *Uncollected Prose*

7. To use a political term: almost everybody gerrymanders, carving an idealized self-portrait from the Gospels and much less attractive straw men from the literatures of other faiths —Walter Kaufmann, "The Faith of a Heretic"

   > *Kaufman combines the image of man as a sculptor with the familiar weakling, the man of straw. Safire's Political Dictionary traces this to a highly sexist seventeenth-century proverb, "A man of straw is worth a woman of gold."*

8. Men moved like shadows in this cave of noise, while outside them, outside the glare, stirring the black leaves, hung the great hungry silence of the jungle —Peter Matthiessen, *At Play in the Fields of The Lord*

   > *The beginning simile evokes Plato's parable of the cave; the metaphor that follows introduces a novel that explores the differences between what is, and what merely seems.*

9. They think their shaman is a jaguar—I mean, that he can become a jaguar at night —Peter Matthiessen, *At Play in the Fields of The Lord*

   > *Modern thinking relegates metaphor to language and intellect. Metaphor in more ancient cultures is tangible, the thing itself and not the name of the thing. In this tribe of Amazon Indians, the shaman and the jaguar were interchangeable.*

10. A seductive promise of a quick and easy peace is a potent anesthetic to dull the senses of an embattled people —Benjamin Netanyahu, Op-Ed, *The New York Times*, September 5, 1993

    > *The chairman of Israel's Likud Party felt that the latest efforts for peace in the region were "gambling with Israel's survival."*

11. King: Thy son is banish'd upon good advice / . . . Why at our justice seem'st thou then to low'r? / Gaunt: Things sweet to taste prove in digestion sour —William Shakespeare, *The Tragedy of King Richard the Second*, Act 1, scene 3, line 233

    > *Gaunt has agreed to the decision not as a father, but as a judge. The same conflict of loyalties will trouble York later in the play.*

12. Let us settle ourselves, and work and wedge our feet downward through the mud and slush of opinion and prejudice . . . till we come to a hard bottom and rocks in place, which we can call reality —Henry David Thoreau, *Walden*, 1854.

■ ILLUSTRIOUSNESS

See: *FAME; REPUTATION*

■ IMAGINATION

See also: *CREATIVITY; SELF-EXPRESSION; THINKING/THOUGHT*

1. The conversation with the café owner rescued Herbst from a whirlpool of imagination —Shmuel Yosef Agnon, *Shira*

2. Imagination took the reins, and Reason slow-paced, though sure-footed, was unequal to a race with so eccentric and flighty a companion —Fanny Burney (also known as Madame D'Arblay), *Diary and Letters of Madame D'Arblay*

3. The story drained / The wells of fancy dry —Lewis Carroll, *Alice's Adventures in Wonderland*
   Many contend that the wells of fancy have been considerably drier since Carroll's death, though Alice stays alive and well and living in the hearts of children.

4. The canvas of my imagination, when it came to limning the Man About Town, was blank —O. Henry, "The Man About Town," *The Four Million*

5. The vast cycle of starry life bore his weary mind outward to its verge and inward to its centre, a distant music accompanying him outward and inward —James Joyce, *Portrait of the Artist as a Young Man*
   The mind of the artist is released from its earthly moorings.

6. In the virgin womb of the imagination the word was made flesh —James Joyce, *Portrait of the Artist as a Young Man*

7. My imagination is a monastery, and I am its monk —John Keats, Letter to Percy Bysshe Shelly, 1820

8. Open wide the mind's cage-door, / She'll dart forth, and cloudward soar —John Keats, "Fancy"

9. Imagination is a happy enchantress: she will put up a fine castle in the air — Natsume Soseki, *Botchan*
   The old woman-servant, Kiyo, hopes that Botchan will be successful and will take her to live in a luxurious mansion.

10. Edgar: I know not how conceit may rob / The treasury of life, when life itself / Yields to the theft —William Shakespeare, *King Lear,* Act 4, scene 6, line 42
    Edgar wonders how imagination has taken hold of his father, making him desire death.

11. Great with child to speak —Sir Philip Sidney, "Sonnet 1," *Astrophel and Stella*
    The poet compares himself, "undelivered" as yet of his thoughts, to a pregnant woman who has almost come to term.

12. The music is playing in his mind —George Stephanopoulos, Quoted in "Clinton Hopes to Curb Tongue in Inaugural Address," *The New York Times,* January 19, 1993
    Mr. Clinton's "music" led to a fully orchestrated inaugural speech.

13. It is pitiful to witness the tiny gnat of Ms. Ripley's imagination beating against the impenetrable glass of fiction —Patricia Storace, "Look Away Dixie Land," *The New York Review of Books*
    The critic's caustic eye was fixed on Alexandra Ripley's written-to-order sequel to Gone With the Wind.

14. [Shelley] danced in and out the gates of Heaven: its floor was littered with his broken fancies —Francis Thompson, quoted in *The World's Great Letters.*

■ IMMATURITY

See: *EMOTIONS*

■ IMMIGRATION

See: *BIGOTRY; TRAVEL*

■ IMMODESTY

See: *BOASTERS/BOASTFULNESS*

■ IMMORALITY/MORALITY

See also: *EVIL; SEX/SEXUALITY; SIN*

1. The Winner's Shout, the Loser's Curse, / Dance before dead England's Hearse — William Blake, "Auguries of Innocence"
   Blake feels that gambling will hasten the death of English morality.

2. The Harlot's cry from Street to Street / Shall weave Old England's winding sheet —William Blake, "Auguries of Innocence"
   Immorality will cause the death of England.

3. He was, I trowe, twenty winter old, / And I was fourty, if I shal saye sooth- / But yit I hadde alway a coltes tooth —Geoffrey Chaucer, "The Wife of Bath's Prologue and Tale," *The Canterbury Tales*
   The Wife of Bath had lickerish (lecherous) tastes and a "colt's tooth" that made her crave the love of a twenty-year-old when she was twice his age.

4. "Give them half a chance and they'll foul up the whole world and we'll all be wading knee-deep in shit." [snorted the driver] —Yevgeny Yevtushenko, *A Precocious Autobiography*
   An insinuating man has taunted the driver until the latter responds with "Every time you open your mouth, toads come hopping out."

■ IMMORTALITY

See also: *LIFE AND DEATH; SOUL*

1. Dear, be the tree your sleep awaits; / Worms be your words, you are not safe from ours —John Ashbery, "Sonnet"
   Ashbery here inverts the standard Elizabethan conceit that ends so many sonnets, that though the beloved dies, she will live on in the poet's words.

2. Eternity's a Five Year Plan: / if Joy with Pain shall hang in hock / who dares to call himself a man? —e. e. cummings, "I & selfdiscovery"

Two metaphors are linked to very practical images.

3. So much the deathless plant the dying fruit surpasse'd —John Dryden, "The Hind and the Panther"
   A mother keeps breeding though her offspring die. "Their corps to perish, but their kind to last," writes Dryden.

4. Oh may I join the choir invisible / Of those immortal dead who live again — George Eliot, "Oh May I Join the Choir Invisible"

5. Death does not extinguish the flame of life: it merely changes its form and direction —Philip Kapleau, *The Wheel of Life and Death*

6. Thou hast but taken thy lamp and gone to bed; / I stay a little longer, as one stays / To cover up the embers that still burn — Henry Wadsworth Longfellow, "Three Friends of Mine
   The poet expresses his faith in man's continued existence after death.

7. So, till the judgment that yourself arise, / You live in this, and dwell in lover's eyes —William Shakespeare, "Sonnet 55," line 13
   This is the conceit that a poet confers immortality upon his subject. "You live in this" means that the sonnet itself will keep the subject deathless.

8. Gaunt: the grave . . . / Whose hollow tomb inherits naught but bones —William Shakespeare, *The Tragedy of King Richard the Second*, Act 2, scene 1, line 69
   The tomb is the "inheritor" of the body, but the implied will leaves the soul to heaven.

■ IMPATIENCE

See also: *CALMNESS/VOLATILITY*

1. I did [passed a requested pad and pencil]—without looking over at the Matron of Honor, from whom great waves of impatience were rising —J. D. Salinger, "Raise High the Roof Beam, Carpenters"

2. Cleopatra: Impatience does / Become a dog that's mad —William Shakespeare, *Antony and Cleopatra*, Act 4, scene 11, line 80

■ IMPERMANENCE

See: PERMANENCE/IMPERMANENCE

■ IMPORTANCE/ UNIMPORTANCE

See also: SELF-EFFACEMENT; SIGNIFI-CANCE/INSIGNIFICANCE

1. The well-kept old women in chauffeured cars and blond girls in buckskin shoes and cashmere sweaters . . . were at most gilt on the frame of my portrait of the city — Maya Angelou, *I Know Why the Caged Bird Sings*

2. You're not the only pebble on the beach —Harry Braisted, Title and first line of 19th-century poem
   As used here, this is a variant of there's plenty of other fish in the sea. The pebble metaphor is also used to picture a person's insignificance in the larger scheme of things, since he or she is just one more pebble on the beach.

3. This poor gambler isn't even a noun. He is kind of an adverb —Stephen Crane, "The Blue Hotel"
   "Every sin is the result of collaboration," says the Easterner, knowing that the gambler alone will be punished for a murder, although several men were actually responsible.

4. I was a mere fly in the eyes of all this world, a nasty disgusting fly—more intelligent, more highly developed, more refined in feeling than any of them, of course, but a fly that was continually making way for every one, insulted and injured by every one —Fyodor Mikhailovich Dostoevsky, *Notes from Underground*

5. *And* is less a play than an ampersand — Mel Gussow, "Review/Theater," *The New York Times*, April 5, 1992
   Playwrights beware: Titles can be magnets for barbed pens.

6. Poets and kings are but the clerks of Time —Edwin Arlington Robinson, "The Clerks"
   The rejection of this early poem by a newspaper editor prompted the poet to publish his own work.

7. Euro-skepticism, previously on the back benches, is now in the saddle —William Safire, "Essay," *The New York Times*, September 21, 1992
   "Back benches" may be a sports metaphor, or a reference to the upstarts in the House of Commons—but however you take the term, you don't take it on horseback.

8. You have just come from being rather large frogs in a very small puddle. You are now very small frogs in a rather large puddle . . . . Don't try to fill the puddle; try to fill yourselves instead —Henry Morse Stevens, Address to University of California freshman, 1908, quoted by Percy Marks in "Advice to Freshmen"
   Marks said that the college puddle was small and calm enough for a weak swimmer to swim across or around "if he battles hard enough or has the right kind of water-wings." He warned that winning "races in the still waters of the college puddle" was not proof the swimmer could survive "beyond the breakers in the great ocean."

9. Let us not be upset and overwhelmed in that terrible rapid and whirlpool called a dinner, situated in the meridian shallows —Henry David Thoreau, "Where I Lived, and What I Lived For"
   Thoreau invites his readers to relax, and not exert themselves over petty affairs.

10. We're all weevils in a captain's biscuit! — Virginia Woolf, "The New Dress"
    Mabel is worried about her dependence on other people's opinions, so that she blows her own feelings out of proportion.

■ IMPOSSIBILITY

See also: EFFECTIVENESS/INEFFECTIVE-NESS; FUTILITY

1. We've been trying to make snowballs in the Mohave Desert —Anon.

    Ross Perot, the third party would-be candidate, was getting so much attention that the Clinton people were unable to get their message out.

2. The task of shaping the senseless and dizzying stuff of dreams is . . . harder than weaving a rope of sand or coining the faceless wind —Jorge Luis Borges, "The Circular Ruins"

3. Unlike Mr. Bush, who began his Presidency with the politics of minimalism . . . Mr. Clinton is trying to lasso the moon — Thomas L. Friedman and Maureen Dowd, "White House Memo," *The New York Times,* April 25, 1993

    The cowboy metaphor appeared in an article assessing President Clinton's first 100 days in office.

4. Whoso list to hunt, I know where is an hind / But as for me, alas, I may no more: / . . . I leave off therefore, / Since in a net I seek to hold the wind —Francis Petrarch, Sonnet 157, In Vita Di Madonna Laura

    The image of trying to catch the wind, as an attempt to capture the impossible, is popular in everyday language.

5. Green: Alas, poor Duke! The task he undertakes / is numb'ring sands and drinking oceans dry —William Shakespeare, *The Tragedy of King Richard the Second,* Act 2, scene 2, line 142

    This is hyperbole as well as metaphor.

6. Captain: This is a knot that cannot be untied, you see —August Strindberg, *The Father,* Act 1

    The knot in a rope or skein of yarn is a common metaphor for problems that defy solution, a knotty problem being the most concise usage.

7. One might as well have tried to bring down one of the Pyramids by poking it with a parasol as attempt to disarrange the close mosaic of Mrs. Manford's engagement-list —Edith Wharton, *Twilight Sleep*

    This metaphor begins Wharton's caustic portrait of a woman who is preoccupied with social busi-ness and vague self-actualization "exercises." The novel's title is a metaphor for a society that avoids not just the pain of childbirth, but the pain that might accompany being fully awake to the emotional undercurrents of human relationships.

■ IMPOTENCE

See: FRUSTRATION; HELPLESSNESS

■ IMPRECISION

See: CLARITY/AMBIGUITY

■ IMPRISONMENT

See also: CONFINEMENT; ISOLATION

1. So long as they seemed doomed to be a chain gang, they must have chosen to glory in their shackles —Louis Auchincloss, "The Senior Partner's Ethics"

    The prison metaphor is used in relation to lawyers "constantly droning about the number of billable hours they clocked per week."

2. When Blake says "A Robin Red breast in a Cage / Puts all Heaven in a Rage," the cage is the Newtonian system. Locke and Newton are devils; reasoning is "secret murder"; art is the "Tree of Life" . . . science is the "Tree of Death" —Isaiah Berlin, "The Apotheosis of the Romantic Will"

    Berlin uses five metaphors to turn Blake's lines to his own uses.

3. And each man trembled as he crept / Into his numbered tomb —Oscar Wilde, "The Ballad of Reading Goal"

    The numbered tomb is the jail cell in which Wilde and his fellow prisoners at Reading Goal were locked each night.

■ INACTION

See: ACTION/INACTION

■ INCAUTIOUSNESS

See: FOOLHARDINESS

■ INCOMPETENCE

See: STUPIDITY; USELESSNESS

■ INCORRECTNESS

See: MISTAKES

■ INDECISION

See: DECISIVENESS/INDECISIVENESS

■ INDEPENDENCE

See: FREEDOM/RESTRAINT; LIBERTY

■ INDIFFERENCE

See: APATHY

■ INDIGNATION

See: ANGER

■ INDIVIDUALITY

See also: CONFORMITY/NONCONFORMITY;
HUMANITY/HUMANKIND; ORIGINALI-
TY/UNORIGINALITY; PERSONALITY
PROFILES

1. Nature made him—then broke the mold
   —Ludovico Ariosto, *Orlando Furioso*
   People with less outstanding qualities are often
   described as stamped out with the same cookie
   cutter or Xerox copies of one another.

2. He [Alexander Woollcott] sported the Joseph coat of personality. On him it became a blazer —John Mason Brown,
   Introduction, *The Portable Woollcott*

3. Lucy was of another clay [than the rest of
   her family] —E. M. Forster, *A Room With
   a View*

4. I had a lover's quarrel with the world —
   Robert Frost, "The Lesson for Today"
   In an October 27, 1963, tribute to the poet,
   President John F. Kennedy used this line to
   champion the artist's difficult and solitary role in
   which he "must often sail against the currents of
   his time."

5. Though all men be made of one metal, yet
   they be not cast in one mold —John Lyly,
   The Anatomy of Wit

6. Neither in environment nor in heredity
   can I find the exact instrument that fashioned me, the anonymous roller that
   pressed upon my life a certain intricate
   watermark whose unique design becomes
   visible when the lamp of art is made to
   shine through life's foolscap —Vladimir
   Nabokov, *Speak Memory*

7. Aafaa: Oh, look at him, Monsieur l'homme
   sapiens, look at the lone usurper of the
   ancient rights and privileges of the priesthood—look at the dog in dogma raising
   his hindquarters to cast the scent of his
   individuality on the lamppost of Destiny!
   —Wole Soyinka, *Madmen and Specialists,* Part 1
   When the wrong-headed homo sapiens make a
   mess of things, the earth-mothers will inherit.

8. If a man does not keep pace with his
   companions, perhaps it is because he hears
   a different drummer. Let him step to the
   music which he hears —Henry David
   Thoreau, *Walden*
   In a September 5, 1993, New York Times
   article about Sir Michael Tippett, Cori Ellison
   put a fresh spin on this now common metaphor:
   "Many early hearers were sure that Sir Michael's
   different drummer had led him round the bend."

9. I'd like to be a useful citizen, a specialized
   cell in the body politic —Kurt Vonnegut,
   Jr., Interview, *Playboy*, 1973
   Asked if his books were a type of therapy, Vonnegut
   responded with this larger view of himself, which
   he hoped went beyond such a narrow scope.

10. The "we" that drummed and thundered
    from the printed page drowning out the

music, subtle and unique, of the individual personality —Yevgeny Yevtushenko, *A Precocious Autobiography*
> Under the Soviet regime, all was inescapably communal: "even the simple words 'I love' were sometimes spoken in so abstract, so oratorical a voice that they might have been 'we love,'" writes the poet.

■ INDOLENCE
See: ACTION/INACTION

INDUSTRIOUSNESS
See: WORK/WORKERS

INDUSTRY
See: ECONOMICS

■ INEQUALITY
See: BIGOTRY; FAIRNESS/UNFAIRNESS

■ INERTIA
See: ACTIVENESS/INACTIVENESS

■ INEXPERIENCE
See: YOUTH

INFIDELITY
See: MARRIAGE; TREACHERY

INFLATION
See: ECONOMICS

■ INFLUENCE
See also: CHARACTERIZATIONS; FAVORITES; MANIPULATION; PERSONALITY PROFILES; POWER

1. She was the split-second experience that changes everything; the car smash; the letter we shouldn't have opened; the lump in the breast or groin; the blinding flash — Josephine Hart, *Damage*

2. Elwood in his cynicism believes that "every man has a key." He continues, "Once you have another man's key, you can hold him in the palm of your hand" —Robert O'Connor, Quoted, *The New York Times Book Review* of *Buffalo Soldiers,* January 24, 1993

3. Know you not that kings have long arms —Ovid, *Heroides*
> The far-reaching powers of kings probably account for the expression the long reach of the law.

4. Now and then an author comes along who rewires a part of our brains —Gahan Wilson, *The New York Times Book Review,* May 30, 1993
> Wilson felt that Rachel Carson, author of Silent Spring *was one such author and that Jan Harold Brunvald, author of* The Baby Train, *is another—but "only around the edges."*

■ INFORMATION
See also: BOOKS; COMMUNICATION/NON-COMMUNICATION; EDUCATION AND LEARNING; KNOWLEDGE

1. We are trying to make our organization [UNICEF] a central switchboard for disseminating information, and not disintegrate into a series of conference calls as we hop from one conference to another — Djibril Diallo, United Nations Department of Public Information briefing, May 6, 1993
> The image of the switchboard as an information link is often used about individuals in a family who keep other members of the family informed and connected.

2. An ocean of data is sloshing around out there, and most of us are trying to sip it through a very narrow straw —James

Gleick, *The New York Times Magazine,* May 16, 1993

> *Gleick's article was headlined "The Telephone Transformed—Into Almost Everything." An alternative would have read "Water, water, everywhere and ne'er a drop to drink."*

3. This book [*What Jane Austen Ate and Charles Dickens Knew*] is a delightful reader's companion that lights up the literary dark — Florence King, *The New York Times Book Review,* July 25, 1993

> *The metaphor, a twist on the common to shed new light on, summed up a review of a book about references that have often puzzled American readers of Jane Austen and Charles Dickens.*

4. [David] Durk's regular conversants [those who use his information about police corruption] . . . profess to find in the whitewater stream of his consciousness useful clues to an understanding of current events —James Lardner, "The Whistle-Blower—Part I," *The New Yorker,* July 5, 1993

■ INGRATITUDE

See: GRATITUDE/INGRATITUDE

■ INHERITANCE/INHERITORS

See also: ANCESTRY/ANCESTORS; FAMILIES/FAMILY RELATIONSHIPS

1. The tears of an heir are laughter under a mask —Anon., Latin Proverb

2. Thy father all from thee, by his last Will, / Gave to the poore; Thou hast good title still —John Donne, "Epigram: Disinherited"

3. Well had I been Depos'd, if you had reign'd! / The Father had descended for the Son; / For only you are lineal to the Throne —John Dryden, "To My Dear Friend Mr. Congreve, On His Comedy, Call'd, The Double-Dealer"

> *In this 1693 mium to Congreve, Dryden speaks of himself in god-like terms, almost in a religious parable. Do you detect some arrogance here?*

4. Ross: No good at all that I can do for him; / . . . bereft and gelded of his patrimony —William Shakespeare, *The Tragedy of King Richard the Second,* Act 2, scene 1, line 235

> *The disinheriting of Bolingbroke is compared to his being stripped of his manhood.*

5. Teiresias: The double lash of your mother's and your father's curse shall one day drive you from this land —Sophocles, *Oedipus the King*

6. Bridget Fonda isn't so much a chip off the old block as a wary inheritor —Jeffrey Wells, *The New York Times,* August 30, 1992

> *The tree-cutting metaphor has become so trite that it must be altered to freshen it, as in the phrase added here.*

■ INHIBITION

See: SELF-CONTROL

■ INJURY

See also: PAIN AND SUFFERING

1. But the untreated masses will hold his [Clinton's] feet to the fire on one point: Two-thirds of them expect the President to "make significant progress in getting health insurance for all Americans." — Herbert B. Herring, "Business Diary," *The New York Times,* January 24, 1993

2. For injuries should be done all together, so that being less tasted, they will give less offence —Niccolo Machiavelli, *The Prince*

> *The same advice is given to all who must swallow bitter pills.*

■ INJUSTICE

See: JUSTICE/INJUSTICE

■ INNOCENCE/INEXPERIENCE

See also: AWARENESS/UNAWARENESS; VULNERABILITY

1. To be left alone on the tightrope of youthful unknowing is to experience the excruciating beauty of full freedom and the threat of eternal indecision —Maya Angelou, *I Know Why the Caged Bird Sings*

2. Jesus: I send you forth as sheep in the midst of wolves —The Bible, *N.T.*, *Matthew 10:16*
   > To arm his metaphorically defenseless followers against their enemies, Jesus said: be ye therefore wise as serpents and harmless as doves.

3. Edward's family was more prosperous, and the cold winds of insecurity hadn't shredded the dreamy chrysalis of his childhood. He was still immersed in the dim, wet wonder of the folded wings that might open if someone loved him; he still hoped, probably, in a butterfly's unthinking way —Harold Brodkey, "The State of Grace," *The New Yorker*, d.u.

4. In its two seasons on Broadway, the National Actors Theatre has often seemed like the greenest of expansion teams —Mel Gussow, "Review/Theatre," *The New York Times*, April 14, 1993
   > The sports metaphor introduces another unsuccessful venture [Three Men on a Horse] by a company with good intentions but bad luck.

5. Needles of light impale / The shadowed innocence —Robert Layzer, "Saint's Parade"

6. My sex life . . . was still an empty ledger —Norman Mailer, *Harlot's Ghost*

7. Hermione: innocence shall make / False accusation blush —William Shakespeare, *The Winter's Tale*, Act 3, scene 2, line 31

8. The minister, a fragile, gentle, spiritual new fledgling from an Eastern theological seminary —Mark Twain, "Buck Fanshaw's Funeral," *Roughing It*
   > The minister was so newly hatched that he had trouble understanding his rough-and-tumble charges.

9. Miss Prism: Ripeness can be trusted. Young women are green. I spoke metaphorically. My metaphor was drawn from fruits —Oscar Wilde, *The Importance of Being Earnest*, Act 2

10. The waves were more gay, / When I was a boy with never a crack in my heart —William Butler Yeats, "The Meditation of the Old Fisherman"
    > This is an implied metaphor, where the heart is treated like a piece of porcelain, a plate or a cup that can crack when it is mistreated.

■ INNOVATION

See: CHANGE; FRESHNESS/STALENESS

■ INSANITY

See: MADNESS

■ INSECTS

See also: ANIMALS; DESCRIPTIONS, MISC.

1. Flies assemble / In whirling swarms, making a drunken hum —Francis Jammes, "A Prayer to Go to Paradise with the Donkeys"

2. Slim dragonfly / too rapid for the eye / to cage —Marianne Moore, "Arthur Mitchell"

3. Their [stinging insects'] death-pegs stud your gloves —Sylvia Plath, "Stings"
   > Afterward, "they crawl / despatched, into trenches of grass."

■ INSENSITIVITY

See: MISTAKES; SENSITIVITY

■ INSIGHT

See: *AWARENESS/UNAWARENESS; SELF-
KNOWLEDGE; UNDERSTANDING*

■ INSIGNIFICANCE

See: *SIGNIFICANCE/INSIGNIFICANCE*

■ INSINCERITY

See: *HYPOCRISY*

■ INSOLENCE

See: *PRIDE*

■ INSPIRATION

See also: *AROUSAL/ROUSERS; IMAGINA-
TION; POETRY/POETS; SPEECHES;
WRITING/WRITERS*

1. [James] Otis' oration against the writs of
   assistance breathed into this nation the
   breath of life . . . Otis was a flame of fire!
   —John Adams
   *The comment was prompted by James Otis's
   powerful argument against illegal search and
   seizure.*

2. Inspiration . . . is not even balanced on a
   razor's edge, but instantly in the air and
   flying with the quick alarm of crows. Inspiration has no scarf by which the poet
   may grasp it —Honoré de Balzac, *Cousin
   Bette*

3. There was a time . . . when folk music lit a
   match in our soul —Theodore Bikel,
   Quoted in "Classical View," *The New
   York Times,* May 30, 1993

4. Sweet fire the sire of muse —Gerard
   Manley Hopkins, "To R.B."
   *Hopkins is appealing for "the one rapture of an
   inspiration."*

5. The energy, the faith, the devotion which
   we bring to this endeavor will light our
   country and all who serve it, and the glow
   of that fire can truly light the world —
   John F. Kennedy, Inaugural address, January 20, 1961
   *Kennedy's uses the "glow of that fire" in reference
   to ending tyranny, poverty, disease, and war.*

6. Nothing warms like a good dose of burning prose —Harry Middleton, "Portraits
   in Winter Light," *Wilderness,* Winter 1992
   *It is a far, far better dose than the castor oil the
   narrator has been offering the animals in his barn.*

7. [General Ibrahim Babangida] raised hopes
   that Nigeria was at last about to become
   . . . a powerful beacon for the rest of the
   continent —Kenneth B.Noble, "The
   World," *The New York Times,* August
   22, 1993
   *The hopes were dashed, however: the beacon led
   only to rocks and as Noble wrote in a later
   metaphor, the economy was "in tatters."*

8. Iago: My muse labours, / and thus she is
   delivered. —William Shakespeare, *Othello,* Act 2, scene 1, line 127
   Iago's muse delivers him of many jibes against women.

9. Lady Percy: He was the mark and glass,
   copy and book, / That fashioned others.
   —William Shakespeare, *The Second Part
   of King Henry the Fourth,* Act 2, scene
   3, line 31
   *Lady Percy notes that the youths aped Harry's
   fashion; "he was indeed the glass[mirror] /
   Wherein the noble youth did dress themselves."*

10. I sought fit words . . . / Oft turning
    others' leaves, to see if thence would flow
    / Some fresh and fruitful showers upon
    my sunburnt brain —Sir Philip Sidney,
    "Sonnet 1," *Astrophel and Stella*
    *There are two metaphors here. The first has
    become the common to turn over a new leaf,
    though many of us have forgotten that a leaf is a
    page in a book. The other is the search for the
    "showers" of inspiration in the works of others.*

11. O helpe thou my weake wit, and sharpen
    my dull tong [tongue] —Edmund Spenser,
    The Faerie Queene
    *Spenser's plea comes in the traditional invocation
    to the Muse that precedes the work itself.*

12. I was simmering, simmering. Emerson brought me to a boil —Walt Whitman, Quoted, "Ralph Waldo Emerson Greets Walt Whitman at the Beginning of a Great Career"

■ INSTABILITY

See: TRANSIENCE

■ INSTITUTIONS

1. Great libraries are temples of hope for the future —Stewart Brand, "Immigration," educational video, broadcast, Public Television, April 9, 1990

2. Public schools have become spiritual fly-traps —Stanley Crouch, Quoted, *The New York Times*, August 29, 1993

3. An institution is the lengthened shadow of one man . . . and all history resolves itself very easily into the biography of a few stout and earnest persons —Ralph Waldo Emerson, "Self Reliance"
   This much-quoted metaphor appears in the introductions to many history books.

4. Every year thousands of British boys enter these mills which grind exceeding small —John Galsworthy, "American and Briton"
   "Though the mills of God grind slowly, yet they grind exceeding small," wrote Longfellow. Galsworthy is paraphrasing here.

5. Museums, the cemeteries of the arts — Alphonse de Lamartine, "Voyage en Orient"

6. [The British royal family is] the gold filling in a mouthful of rot —John Osborne, Quoted, *The Berkshire Eagle*, August 30, 1992
   The royal family live in a beautifully appointed fishbowl, and are expected to behave as though they wore their corsets even to bed.

■ INSULTS

See also: NAME CALLING

1. Goodbye, good riddance, hacks! / Limp back on lame / Feet to the stable out of which you came— / Terrible poets — Catullus, Poem 14

2. What, amble or trotte or pisse or go sitte down! —Geoffrey Chaucer, "The Wife of Bath's Prologue," *The Canterbury Tales*
   The implied metaphor of the horse is highly uncomplimentary here.

3. You were made on the tracks, you jelly-fish, under your father's very nose — Boris Pasternak, *Doctor Zhivago*

4. To this day, I have no idea at all how my guests reacted to my outbreak, the polluted little stream of invective I'd loosed on them —J. D. Salinger, *Raise High The Roof Beam, Carpenters*

5. Iago: this poor trash of Venice, whom I trash for his quick hunting —William Shakespeare, *Othello*, Act 2, scene 1, line 298
   The pun combines the refererence to Roderigo as "trash" with the hunting term for putting weights on a hound that hunts too fast.

■ INTEGRITY

See: CHARACTER; LOYALTY

■ INTELLIGENCE

See also: EDUCATION AND LEARNING; KNOWLEDGE; MIND

1. If a man empties his purse into his head, no one can take it from him —Benjamin Franklin
   A proverbial metaphor to draw a picture of knowledge as having value that's not likely to be lost, spent or stolen.

2. If his notice was sought, an expression of courtesy and interest gleamed out upon his features; proving that there was light within him, and that it was only the outward medium of the intellectual lamp that obstructed the rays in their passage — Nathaniel Hawthorne, *The Scarlet Letter*

3. One-story intellects, two-story intellects, three-story intellects with skylights — Oliver Wendell Holmes, *The Poet at the Breakfast Table*

> Holmes was fond of house metaphors. In this instance he described one-story men as fact-collectors, two-story men as reasoners and generalizers, and the three-story men as those with ideals and imaginations whose "best illumination comes from above, through the skylight."

■ INTENSITY

1. The fever pitch of *The Baltimore Waltz*, almost an oxygen rush at times, is always enlivened by the playwright's antic literacy —Frank Rich, "Reviews / Theater," *The New York Times*, May 1992

2. The publicity campaign now reaching gale force cannot drown out some long sighs of disappointment —Calvin Tomkins, "Madonna's Anticlimax," *The New Yorker*, October 26, 1992

> The subject was the superstar's book, Sex.

■ INTERNATIONAL RELATIONS

See also: DIPLOMACY; PEACE

1. Obviously we all support elections, but we were wrong to make support for elections the central pillar of our policy —Michael Clough, Quoted in "What the U.S. Can Learn from Angola's Loser," *The New York Times*, January 17, 1973

> The Africa expert criticized how U.S. aid money was being distributed.

2. When we look at the post-cold-war policies of Russia and the U.S., we realize that the players change, but the game remains the same —Randall Forsberg, "New Realities: Disarmament, Peace-building, and Global Security," April 20–23, 1993. NGO Committee on Disarmament Conference at the United Nations

3. We wish to open a new chapter in the sad book of our lives together—a chapter of mutual recognition, of good neighborliness, of mutual respect, of understanding —Yitzhak Rabin, Statement at the signing of the Middle East Pact, September 13, 1993

4. The tensions of the modern world have overtaken U.N. security procedures. The organization cannot afford the risk of having a security net with so coarse a mesh that potential threats might slip through —Dorrie Weiss, NGO / DPI Reporter (United Nations), Vol. 2 No. 5., July 1993

5. National security provides the bricks to make a wall. International security means using those bricks to build a house. If nations seek basic security rather than insular privacy, they must invite their neighbors to join them and come in out of the rain —Dorrie Weiss

6. The CTB [Comprehensive Test Ban] was viewed as the cornerstone of the disarmament edifice on which depended nuclear disarmament in general and the Non-Proliferation Treaty in particular. —Jim Wurst, "General Assembly Highlights Linkage of CTB and NPT"

> In these paired metaphors a specific treaty was regarded as the cornerstone and disarmament as the building itself.

7. [Disarmament, economic and social development, and environmental protection are] the three pillars of global security . . . Are they achievable in sufficient measure to launch a new world order? —Douglas Roche, Former Ambassador for Disarmament of Canada, quoted in "Closing Remarks," *Disarmament Times*, May 1993

> A new world order launched by three pillars might be a real cause for despair.

■ INTOLERANCE

See: BIGOTRY

■ INTOXICATION/INTOXICANTS

See also: COMFORT/COMFORT-GIVERS; FOOD AND DRINK; FOOLHARDINESS

1. Brandy is an untrustworthy messenger. When you send it to the stomach, it goes to the head —Anon., Middle European Proverb

2. D.T.'s of the worst kind . . . . Four bottles of that kind of brandy in a day, I am told. Sheeted with boiler-iron inside, I should think —Joseph Conrad, *Lord Jim*
   We say now of someone who can eat or drink to excess that he has a cast-iron stomach.

3. If I couldn't put down a little bit of the hair / Of the dog each day, I'd be as good as dead —Anthony Hecht, "The Thoughtful Roisterer Declines the Gambit"
   The Falstaffian persona prefers to drink rather than fight for his king. If he is to die by the mouth, he says, it won't be by the cannon's mouth. The metaphor is drawn from old folk medicine, which claims rabies can be cured by swallowing a little of the hair of the dog that bit you.

4. You mean a couple of quarts will make anybody a tiger? —Kume Masao, "The Tiger"
   A tiger is Japanese slang for a drunken person. The metaphor is built into the language.

5. Iago: He'll watch the horologe a double set, / If drink rock not his cradle — William Shakespeare, *Othello*, Act 2, scene 3, line 78
   Iago pretends that Cassio cannot get to sleep without drinking himself into a stupor.

6. Cassio: O God, that men should put an enemy in their mouths, to steal away their brains —William Shakespeare, *Othello*, Act 2, scene 3, line 281
   Cassio upbraids himself for drinking too much.

■ INTRIGUE

See: MYSTERY/MYSTERIOUSNESS

■ INTROSPECTION

See: SELF-KNOWLEDGE

■ IRONY

1. We're conceived in irony. We float in it from the womb. It's the amniotic fluid — Alan Bennett, Line from 1977 play, *The Old Country*, quoted in review of *The Madness of George III, The New Yorker*, October 11, 1993

2. When they cry . . . "Jerusalem, the eternal city," surely every stone of Jerusalem bursts out laughing —Amos Oz, *The Hill of Evil Counsel*
   Personification is used as a metaphor for the bitterness of a people that escaped from the Holocaust to a city grinding under the yoke of British rule.

■ IRREVOCABILITY

See: ENTRANCES/EXITS

■ IRRITANTS

See also: AROUSAL/ROUSERS; TROUBLE/ TROUBLEMAKERS

1. There were those who had been a thorn in the flesh of their Christian colleagues — Shmuel Yosef Agnon, *Shira*
   Many learned men emigrated from Germany during the persecution of the Jews.

2. Mr. Clinton now not only had Mr. [Paul] Tsongas, but a newly inspired Mr. [Jerry] Brown yapping at his heels —Anon., Editorial, *The New York Times*, August 18, 1992
   Bill Clinton's presidential primary campaign was beset by attacks from competitors and, as the editorial headline writer put it, he had to "tighten the vise" that was needed to hold his position.

3. Ross Perot is back on the hustings, trying to hold President Clinton's feet to the fires of fiscal responsibility but mainly stoking

a few political fires of his own —B. Drummond Ayres, Jr., *The New York Times,* February 21, 1993

Two well-known metaphors introduced an article about two well-known political figures.

4. Sherebyakov: The ways of it [this country life] stick in my throat —Anton Chekhov, *Uncle Vanya,* Act 3

This is a variant of to stick in one's craw which literally refers to the place in the bird's digestive track where the food is ground up but is used figuratively for anything repugnant or unacceptable.

5. Ross Perot is the squirrel in the attic of American politics. You know he's up there because his pattering feet won't let you have a night's sleep —Daniel Henninger, "Leisure & Arts," *The Wall Street Journal,* June 22, 1992.

The third-party presidential effort of Ross Perot didn't continue for long, but it was much in the news while it lasted.

6. But perhaps there lurked always this hair in her soup! Won't they be glad to be rid of me again! —D. H. Lawrence, "Two Blue Birds"

When a wife infrequently returns to her marital home, her husband's staff treats her like a visiting sovereign.

7. For many people here [in Battle Creek, Michigan], Mr. Boyle's fiction is a fungus around the roots of the town's claim to glory —Molly O'Neill, *The New York Times,* June 2, 1993

T. Coraghessan Boyle was being interviewed at the birthplace of Dr. John Harvey Kellogg, who inspired his critically acclaimed novel The Road to Wellville.

8. Now that . . . the first installment of the income tax fades into a discolored bruise, that annual bugbear, the vegetable garden, arises to plague me —Sidney Joseph Perelman, *Acres and Pains*

9. Hamlet: There is much music, excellent voice, in this little organ, . . . call me what instrument you will, though you can fret me, yet you cannot play upon me —

William Shakespeare, *Hamlet,* Act 3, scene 2, line 371

This contains a play on the word "fret" meaning both to irritate and the frets of an instrument.

10. Buckingham: No man's pie is freed / From his ambitious finger —William Shakespeare, *The Life of King Henry the Eighth,* Act 1, scene 1, line 52

The commonly used variant of this to have a finger in every pie applies not just to meddlers but to people of many interests and activities.

11. Judge Shoob . . . is unapologetic about being a thorn in the side of the Justice Department —Martin Tolchin, "Disillusioned with Government, Judge is Thorn in Side of U.S. Prosecutors," *The New York Times,* October 9, 1992

12. Ah, I shall be a thorn between two roses —Katharine Weber, "Friend of the Family," *The New Yorker,* January 25, 1993

The speaker does prove to be a thorn in the openness between the woman who's his lover and her friend.

13. Professor Emerson Sillerton was a thorn in the side of Newport society; and a thorn that could not be plucked out, for it grew on a venerable and venerated family tree —Edith Wharton, *The Age of Innocence*

■ ISOLATION

See also: LONELINESS

1. *She* would have the enjoyment of such oases [New York, Newport, Paris], for as many months of the year as she desired, while he remained perched, a lonely puritan, on his Trojan rock —Louis Auchincloss, "The Epicurean," *Three Lives*

The metaphoric allusion to ancient Troy is aptly used to picture the protagonist's father clinging to a doomed business in Troy, New York, while his mother escapes to a social life more suited to her needs. The mixaphor of the puritan on his "Trojan rock" leaves no doubt that he is doomed.

2. At her first appearance . . . at Lincoln Center, she was relegated to the back

dressing room, the soloist's Siberia — Linda, Blandford, "Baby Diva," *The New York Times Magazine*, March 14, 1993

The metaphor is cloaked in allusion.

3. Everything that has existed around me has disappeared, and I find myself in a desert —Gustave Flaubert, Letter to George Sand, c. 1874

Flaubert has come to the realization that his singleminded pursuit of writing at the expense of family relationships, has led to a state of extreme loneliness.

4. Oh, bars of my own body, open, open! / The world goes by my cage and never sees me —Randall Jarrell, "The Woman at the Washington Zoo."

The animals in the zoo are trapped, as the poet is trapped inside the body of the self.

5. The hard piece of pipe [of a hypodermic] stuck in him . . . was a constant reminder of how wide and unswimmable the gulf was becoming between him and the ever-receding shoreline of the well —David Leavitt, "Gravity," *A Place I've Never Been*

6. Each one of us is a prisoner in a solitary tower and he communicates with the other prisoners, who form mankind, by con-

ventional signs that have not quite the same meaning for them as for himself — W. Somerset Maugham, "The Happy Man"

7. We are all prisoners in solitary confinement: . . . there remains for us only the wall alphabet in which we tap our hopes and thoughts. Nobody should learn this alphabet who can abuse it, . . . who wastes the time of his fellow prisoners by tapping out stale rhetoric, false news, or untranslatable messages, and so brings a perfect achievement of civilization into confusion. —Michael Sheldon, *Friends of Promise: Cyril Connolly and the World of Horizon*

Sheldon's existential message is a cautionary one that mingles hope with despair. Communication between people is difficult, but not impossible, and it implies a responsibility to use it well.

8. The White House—The finest prison in the world —Harry S Truman, April 12, 1945

In recent years, the image of the President's insulation from the outside world has given way to "living in a bubble," generally attributed to the Texas boy whose immune system was so fragile that he lived his brief life in an actual room or bubble.

J

JARGON

See: ARTICULATENESS/INARTICULATE-NESS; WORDS

JEALOUSY

See also: ENVY

1. The jealous man poisons his own dinner and then eats it —Anon., Proverb

2. Lisbeth instantly took him up, in a tone behind which could be heard the roar of a tigerish jealousy —Honoré de Balzac, *Cousin Bette*

3. Jealousy . . . the coals whereof are coals of fire —The Bible, *O.T., Song of Solomon 8:6*
   The most quoted figures of speech from these passages are both similes: "Jealousy is cruel as the grave" and "love is strong as death."

4. Jealousy is a bitter root that we keep to gnaw on secretly —Josh Billings

5. The poison of the Honey Bee / Is the Artist's jealousy —William Blake, "Auguries of Innocence"

6. Jealousy is a kind of civil war in the soul, where judgment and imagination are at perpetual jars —William Penn, *Some Fruits of Solitude*
   Penn's title is also a metaphor.

7. Iago: O, beware jealousy; / It is the green-ey'd monster, which doth mock / That meat it feeds on —William Shakespeare, *Othello*, Act 3, scene 3, line 170
   The association of jealousy with green-eyed animals who toy with their victims before devouring remains a much-used, and twisted, common metaphor. In Naked Truth and Veiled Allusions *(1902), American author Minna Antrim wrote "The 'Green-Eyed Monster' causes much woe, but the absence of this ugly serpent argues the presence of a corpse whose name is Eros."*

8. This canker that eats up Love's tender spring, / . . . dissentious Jealousy. —William Shakespeare, *Venus and Adonis*, line 656

9. Oedipus: Great store of jealousy fill your treasury chests, / if my friend Creon, friend from the first and loyal, / thus secretly attacks me —Sophocles, *Oedipus the King*
   Oedipus threatens Teiresias, thinking Creon has suborned him.

10. Pride and reticence went down in a hurricane of jealousy —Edith Wharton, *The Reef*

JERUSALEM

See: CITIES

JESUS

See: GUIDANCE/GUIDES; RESCUE/RESCUERS

■ JOBS

See: OCCUPATIONS

■ JOURNALISM/JOURNALISTS

See also: WRITING/WRITERS

1. Journalism's a shrew and a scold / . . . She's love and hate and death and life — Franklin Pierce Adams, *The New York World,* February 27, 1931

    At the end of his verse Adams explains that the "shrew" is his wife and that he "likes her"—a fitting end to his "marriage" with the newspaper which printed its last issue on this day.

2. Some of America's best sports columnists never wrote autobiographies . . . Perhaps they thought of themselves as sprinters, not marathoners. Accustomed to writing 800 words . . . maybe they considered 80,000 words too much distance —Dave Anderson, *The New York Times Book Review,* July 25, 1993

    But sports writer Jim Murray, according to the reviewer, has not only "run a marathon, but won it."

3. The press has since [the 1948 campaign] diversified into an octopus called "media" —Russell Baker, *"Observer," The New York Times,* October 20, 1992

4. He was a nasty little muckraker, was Terry Pardick—a terrier with a nose for rotting meat —Robert Barnard, *A Scandal in Belgravia*

5. The press is a mill that grinds all that is put into its hopper. Fill the hopper with poisoned grain and it will grind it to meal, but there is death in the bread —William Cullen Bryant, Prose Writings II

6. Thou God of idolatry, the Press / . . . thou fountain, at which drink the good and wise; / Thou ever-bubbling spring of endless lies —William Cowper, "The Progress of Error"

7. Although the early morning set [of television interviewers] are not performing peacocks . . . they are not exactly foxes either. Call them attack pussycats —Walter Goodman, "Critic's Notebook," *The New York Times,* October 26, 1992

    Television critic Goodman, thus concluded a column that expanded on Isaiah Berlin's metaphoric division of writers as hedgehogs who pursue a single issue, or foxes who pursue a variety of related and unrelated topics.

8. I aimed at the public's heart and by accident I hit it in the stomach. And here is the head of that arrow I shot,—the account of the pigs and their sad fate —Upton Sinclair, Introduction to excerpt from *The Jungle* selected for inclusion in Will Burnett's anthology, *This is My Best*

9. In the eye of an extraordinary media storm, Woody Allen and Mia Farrow met in court by proxy yesterday —Bruce Weber, *New York Times,* August 26, 1992

10. A raw boy whose experience was bounded by a rooming house and a library would find it even harder to weave a tale out of the millions of strands of a great city's activities than to evolve copy for a newspaper —Edith Wharton, *Hudson River Bracketed*

■ JOURNAL WRITING

See also: WRITERS/WRITING

1. My Journal keeps open house to every kind of happening in my soul —W. N. P. Barbellion, Diary entry, January 22, 1913

    The writer also viewed his diary as a married or engaged man's metaphorical other woman "a secret super-confidante who knows things which are concealed from his lady" and thus a form of "deliberate infidelity."

2. This Book is my Savings Bank. I grow richer because I have somewhere to deposit my earnings; and fractions are worth more to me because corresponding frac-

tions are waiting here that shall be made integers by their addition —Ralph Waldo Emerson, Journal entry, January 1, 1834

Emerson's "Bank" is his journal.

3. When people come to tea I can't say to them, "Now wait a minute while I write an account of you" . . . and thus, at the very time I'm brewing thoughts & descriptions meant for this page I have the heartbreaking sensation that the page isn't there; they've spilt on the floor. Indeed it's difficult to mop them up again —Virginia Woolf, Diary entry, April 18, 1918

■ JOY

See also: EMOTIONS; HAPPINESS/UNHAPPINESS; PASSION; PLEASURE; SEX/ SEXUALITY

1. I left the presence on the wings of elation —Louis Auchincloss, "Portrait of the Artist by Another," *Skinny Island*

   The "presence" is that of a kindly headmaster.

2. There are evenings . . . after rain (and triumph) when mist curls out of the mind, when reason is asleep, stretched out on a low beach at the bottom of the heart — Enid Bagnold, *National Velvet*

   On such evenings "something sings like a cock at dawn, a long-drawn, wild note."

3. Joy is . . . the falling / or fallen pride of summer's lark / calling the leaves to hide him —William Bell, "To a Lady on Her Marriage"

4. Come, on wings of joy we'll fly / To where my Bower hands on high —William Blake, "The Birds

   "On wings of joy" has become a common metaphor, appearing frequently in songs.

5. Joy is the sweet voice, Joy the luminous cloud —Samuel Taylor Coleridge, "Dejection: An Ode"

6. The very honey of all earthly joy / Does of all meats the soonest cloy —Abraham Cowley, "The Wish"

7. What was there in the touch of that cool arm that could fan . . . the fire of bliss that Bertha did not know what to do with? — Katherine Mansfield, "Bliss"

8. The magical bluebird of joy and human satisfaction that may be seen flitting distantly through the branches of life —Christopher Morley, "What Men Live By"

9. Parolles: make the coming hour o'erflow with joy, / And pleasure drown the brim —William Shakespeare, *All's Well That Ends Well,* Act 2, scene 4, line 48

10. Anna was intoxicated with the wine of admiration she had aroused —Leo Tolstoy, *Anna Karenina*

11. But he feels joy now . . . the water of his heart has been poured into a thin vase of joy that Eccles' voice jars and breaks — John Updike, *Rabbit, Run*

    Harry is in the hospital where his baby son was just born.

12. He was in the state of lucid ecstasy when no material detail seems too insignificant to be woven into the pattern of one's bliss —Edith Wharton, *Hudson River Bracketed*

13. Anna . . . was floating in the mid-current of felicity, on a tide so bright and buoyant that she seemed to be one with its warm waves —Edith Wharton, *The Reef*

    "The first rush of bliss had stunned and dazzled her," Wharton explains, "but now that, each morning, she woke to the calm certainty of its recurrence, she was growing used to the sense of security it gave."

14. Evidently she was always going to understand . . . the discovery made his cup of bliss overflow —Edith Wharton, *The Age of Innocence*

    Wharton's cup of bliss is borrowed from the Old Testament *(Psalms, 23:5).*

15. She . . . unpacks her singing heart in the sight of everyone —Alexander Woollcott, "A Plot for Mr. Dreiser"

 > *Woollcott uses a travel and a musical metaphor to draw a portrait of a young woman quite open in displaying her love for an aviator.*

16. A baptism of clean joy swept over Taylor —Richard Wright, "Fire and Cloud,"

 > *The metaphor concludes Wright's story of a man's gradual redemption.*

■ JOY/SORROW

See also: EMOTIONS; GRIEF; HAPPINESS/ UNHAPPINESS; PAIN AND SUFFER- ING; SORROW

1. Joy and sorrow often wear the same clothing —Anon., Proverb

2. Joy & Woe are woven fine; / A Clothing for the Soul divine —William Blake, "Auguries of Innocence"

3. Sorrow and joy two sisters coy —Robert Bridges, "Sorrow and Joy"

4. Now no joy but lacks salt / That is not dashed with pain —Robert Frost, "To Earthward"

5. Your joy is your sorrow unmasked — Kahlil Gibran, *The Prophet*

 > *"And the selfsame well from which your laughter rises was often filled with your tears," Gibran continues.*

6. She would have none the less to reckon with his continued existence as the drop of bitterness in her cup that seasoned, undisguisably, each draught —Henry James, "Fordham Castle"

7. Rivers: Drown desperate sorrow in dead Edward's grave, / And plant your joys in living Edward's throne —William Shakespeare, *The Tragedy of King Richard the Third*, Act 5, scene 2, line 23

■ JUSTICE/INJUSTICE

See also: BIGOTRY; FAIRNESS/UNFAIR- NESS; GOD; LAW/LAWYERS

1. I know that the lust for empire often corrupts the laws of nature; that justice has no sword to punish those who offend in this way —Agrippina, Letter to her son, the emperor Nero, 59 A.D.

 > *Agrippina pleads for her life to the infamous Nero.*

2. Esdras: justice / this blind snake that strikes men down in the dark, / . . . keep your hand back from it —Maxwell Anderson, *Winterset*, Act 1, scene 2

3. What will become of the sheep if a wolf is the judge? —Anon., Proverb

 > *This proverb goes back at least to the time of Chaucer, who used a version of it in* The Canterbury Tales *when a good priest explains why he must be upright himself in order to care for his flock.*

4. He . . . cut off in his State the tree of panderism at the root, and burnt the trunk —Anon., "The Story of the Negro Dorerame"

 > *The king orders the execution of the old woman who debauches younger women.*

5. It is across great scars of wrong / I reach toward the song of kindred men —Robert Duncan, "A Poem Beginning with a Line by Pindar. II"

 > *The poet speaks of the songs that Whitman sang.*

6. Wild is hanged / For thatten he a pocket fanged, / While safe old Hubert and his gang, / Doth pocket o' the nation fang. — Henry Fielding, *The Life of Mr. Jonathan Wild the Great*

 > *The ditty protests that petty pickpockets are hanged while politicians pick the nation's pockets with impunity. The jibe is directed at Sir Robert Walpole.*

7. Hector: What is the use of justice if it doesn't hammer out a shield for innocent people? —Jean Giraudoux, *Tiger at the Gates*, Act 2

 > *"Forge us a truth," he adds, in a second metaphor.*

8. God's mill grinds slow, but sure —George Herbert, *Jacula Prudentum*

    A variant published in the Reader's Digest *in 1941 and attributed to Charles A. Beard: "The mills of God grind slowly, but they grind exceeding small."*

9. *Now* is the time to lift our nation from the quicksands of racial injustice to the solid rock of brotherhood —Martin Luther King, Jr., Speech to civil rights marchers, August 23, 1963

10. But we refuse to believe that the bank of justice is bankrupt. We refuse to believe that there are insufficient funds in the great vaults of opportunity of this nation —Martin Luther King, Jr., Speech to civil rights marchers, August 23, 1963.

    King extended his image of the freedom marchers as collectors of an unpaid promissory note with "We have come to cash this check . . . that will give us upon demand the riches of freedom and the security of justice."

11. But over the next year and a half, the case known as Bowers v. Hardwick became a high-stakes poker game among the Justices, as conservatives and liberals on the Court struggled behind the scenes to make it a definitive constitutional statement on homosexual rights —Neil A. Lewis, *The New York Times,* May 23, 1993

    Lewis was writing about the insights into the workings of the Supreme court yielded by the publication of Thurgood Marshall's private papers.

12. Cleopatra: Some innocents 'scape not the thunderbolt —William Shakespeare, *Antony and Cleopatra,* Act 2, scene 5, line 47

    Among the ancients the messenger of untimely tidings was often killed. This is Cleopatra's response to Charmian's plea to control her anger toward the messenger who brought news of Antony's marriage.

13. Angelo: We must not make a scarecrow of the law, / Setting it up to fear the birds of prey / And let it keep one shape, till custom make it / Their perch and not their terror —William Shakespeare, *Measure for Measure,* Act 2, scene 1, line 1

    Escalus responds to this with "Ay, but yet Let us be keen and rather cut a little, / Than fall and bruise to death."

14. Duke: the bloody book of law / You shall yourself read, in the bitter letter —William Shakespeare, *Othello,* Act 1, scene 3, line 67

    The Duke assures Brabantio he shall have redress for his wrongs.

15. Bolingbroke: Had you first died, and he been thus trod down, / He should have found his uncle Gaunt a father / To rouse his wrongs and chase them to the bay —William Shakespeare, *The Tragedy of King Richard the Second,* Act 2, scene 3, line 135

    Bolingbroke appeals to his uncle York, using a metaphor from hunting.

KINDNESS/UNKINDNESS

See also: CHARACTERIZATIONS; GOODNESS;
HARD-HEARTEDNESS; SYMPATHY

1. Lyndon [President Lyndon B. Johnson]
   has a clock inside him with an alarm that
   tells him at least once an hour to chew
   somebody out —Anon.

   The remark was made by a friend of President
   Lyndon Johnson's who knew that he could be a
   cruel taskmaster. Wordsmiths trace the origins of
   the now common to chew someone out *to the*
   U.S. Army during World War II. The body clock
   image has also gained currency as a metaphor for
   regularity.

2. The humble virtue of simple kindness . . .
   is the one essential vitamin of the soul —
   Joshua Loth Liebman, *Peace of Mind*

   "Too few of us," according to the author "pour
   this anointing oil on the relationships of our
   daily lives.

3. King Henry: A good heart, Kate, is the
   sun and the moon, or rather the sun and
   not the moon, for it shines bright and
   never changes, but keeps its course truly
   —William Shakespeare, *The Life of Henry*
   the Fifth, Act 5, scene 2, line 164

4. Richard: I am not made of stone, / But
   penetrable to your kind entreaties. —William Shakespeare, *The Tragedy of King*
   Richard the Third, Act 3, scene 7, line 222

   The ruthless murderer's statement that the image
   of the stone does not apply to him is more sham
   than substance—and illustrates Shakespeare's
   use of negaphor.

5. Kindness is very indigestible. It disagrees
   with very proud stomachs —William
   Makepeace Thackeray, *The Adventures of*
   Philip

6. There is a tide which pierces the pores of
   the air. These aerial rivers, let us not
   pollute their current. —Henry David Thoreau, Letter to Ralph Waldo Emerson, 1843

   The kindness that is unsaid is longest remem-
   bered, according to Thoreau.

KISSES

See also: MEN AND WOMEN; PASSION; SEX/
SEXUALITY

1. He covers me with kisses of fire —Anon.,
   "The Story of the Negro Dorerame"

2. His kisses were a vengeance . . . And
   suddenly sharp fingers seemed to pluck,
   pizzicato, at the fiddle strings of her nerves
   —Aldous Huxley, *Point Counter Point*

3. I had the mad idea that they were kissing
   in that quiet room—a long comfortable
   kiss. One of those kisses that not only puts
   one's grief to bed, but nurses it and warms
   it and tucks it up and keeps it fast enfolded
   until it is sleeping sound —Katherine
   Mansfield, "Je Ne Parle Pas Français

4. Cyrano: When all is said, what is a kiss? An oath of allegiance taken in closer proximity . . . a fashion of inhaling each other's heart —Edmond Rostand, *Cyrano de Bergerac*, Act 3

Cyrano expands on this with a list of similes with a final likening of the kiss as a way of two people tasting each other's soul.

5. Cyrano: a kiss, / . . . a rosy dot / Over the i of Loving —Edmond Rostand, *Cyrano de Bergerac*, Act 3

6. Celia: He hath bought a pair of cast lips of Diana . . . the very ice of chastity is in them —William Shakespeare, *As You Like It*, Act 3, scene 4, line 16

According to Celia, "A nun of Winter's sisterhood couldn't kiss more religiously."

7. Hermione: you may ride's / With one soft kiss a thousand furlongs ere / With spur we heat an acre —William Shakespeare, *The Winter's Tale*, Act 1, scene 2, line 94

The horsemanship metaphor incorporates a bawdy pun on the sexual act.

8. The small moist cushion of slack willingness with which her lips had greeted his dries up and turns hard —John Updike, *Rabbit, Run*

9. He kissed her, and she kissed back, longtime soft kissing, a river of it —Robert James Waller, *The Bridges of Madison County*

These romantic metaphors contributed to the rivers of money earned by this surprise best-seller.

■ KNOWLEDGE

See also: EDUCATION AND LEARNING; IGNORANCE; REVELATION

1. All whose undertakings / Are free from desire and purpose, / His actions burnt up in the fire of knowledge, / Him the wise call the man of learning —Anon., *The Bhagavad Gita*, 4:19

2. Merely by the boat of knowledge all / evil shalt thou cross over —Anon., *The Bhagavad Gita*, 4:36

Evil is compared to the sea here, in a second metaphor that is implied from the metaphor of the boat.

3. The fox knows many things but the hedgehog knows one big thing —Archilochus, "Fragment"

Professor Isaiah Berlin used this metaphor to tag writers who relate everything to one central issue as hedgehogs and those who pursue a multitude of topics as foxes. On October 26, 1992, New York Times *television critic Walter Goodman devoted an entire column to classifying television interviewers as animal types. George Will seemed closest to Berlin's image of the hedgehog, though Goodman thought him to be "closer to an American setter sniffing somewhat disdainfully at the lesser pedigrees." Sam Donaldson was portrayed as "the terrier" who "enjoys burrowing into the morning's headlines." David Brinkley was the trusty St. Bernard . . . he may have lost some teeth in a long career" but "now and then the all-knowing old fellow barks to life with a crack that glints like a still sharp incisor." Bob Schieffer was tagged as "a cuddly pooch who can turn aggressive if crossed . . . like Jim Lehrer who sometimes seems to want to lick his guests, sometimes to nip them."*

4. It's an event, a small defiance of rule . . . Such moments are possibilities, tiny peepholes —Margaret Atwood, *The Handmaid's Tale*

In the guarded, Orwellian world of the narrator, a smile or a wink represents an opening into a world of potential knowledge.

5. If we do not plant it [knowledge] when young, it will give us no shade when we are old —Earl of Chesterfield (Philip Dormer Stanhope), *Letters to His Son*, December 11, 1748

6. All ignorance toboggans into know / and trudges up to ignorance again. —e. e. cummings, "All ignorance toboggans into know"

The second stanza follows up on the image of the toboggan with "all history's a winter sport or three."

7. Twice two makes four is a pert coxcomb who stands with arms akimbo barring your path and spitting —Fyodor Mikhailovich Dostoevsky, *Notes from Underground*
   "Once you have mathematical certainty there is nothing left to do or to understand," says the writer.

8. And she [the librarian] sweetly takes all knowledge for her province, as did Bacon, / All the fruit that's dropped and mellowed since the Knowledge tree was shaken —Sam Walter Foss, "Song of the Library Staff"
   Foss's tribute to the library's staff, first read at an American Library Association annual meeting, featured a stanza for each specialist, including the children's librarian who guides youngsters seeking wisdom through "thought's misty morning light."

9. Clinton has a CD-ROM in his head. — Thomas L. Friedman and Maureen Dowd, "White House Memo," *The New York Times*, April 25, 1993
   The metaphor was used to demonstrate why President Reagan, who came to power with knowledge that fit a few "three-by-five cards" had an easier time delivering on his campaign themes than the much more knowledgeable President Clinton.

10. My sister pitied my eyes / That were burning / With insatiable thirst for knowledge —Ishikawa Takuboku, "Song of My Youth"

11. He contained within him a reservoir of learning of such depth as to be practically bottomless —Stephen Leacock, "Oxford as I See It"

12. What he really wanted was to learn what 'they' thought, those like me, the 'others'

who had taught me all that science, placed those compartments, those drawers full of learning inside my head —Orhan Pamuk, *The White Castle*

13. The ladder's privilege is the hammer's knowledge —Theodore Roethke, *Straw for the Fire, Notebooks of Theodore Roethke*
    This is a poetic twist to a proverbial metaphor: "Truth is an anvil that wears out countless hammers."

14. It is supposed that all knowledge is at the bottom of a well, or the far end of a telescope —Robert Louis Stevenson, "An Apology for Idlers"

15. Never again will Europe be lit up by that flame —Vercors, *The Silence of the Sea*
    The "flame" is the flame of knowledge lit by French writers and thinkers.

16. In addition to this forest of family trees, Mr. Sillerton Jackson carried between his narrow hollow temples . . . a register of most of the scandals and mysteries that had smouldered under the unruffled surface of New York society within the last fifty years —Edith Wharton, *The Age of Innocence*

17. How she [Mrs. Dalloway] had got through life on the few twigs of knowledge Fräulein Daniels gave them she could not think. — Virginia Woolf, *Mrs. Dalloway*

18. Barlas was, for me, a living encyclopedia —Yevgeny Yevtushenko, *A Precocious Autobiography*
    A new friend teaches Yevtushenko new interests.

L

■ LAMENTS

1. What have I said, / That you should hurl this plague upon my head, / This shower of poets? —Catullus, Poem 14

2. I stumble in the crowd; . . . Time's cheat, and living's shroud —Ellen de Young Kay, "Tiresias' Lament"

   The poet is drawing on mythological material. Tiresias was cursed with blindness and, in recompense, was given the gift of prophesy.

3. Cleopatra: this dull world, which in thy absence is / No better than a sty — William Shakespeare, *Antony and Cleopatra*, Act 4, scene 11, line 63

4. Lear: O, you are men of stones: / Had I your tongues and eyes, I'ld use them so / That heaven's vault should crack —William Shakespeare, *King Lear*, Act 5, scene 3, line 256

   "Howl, howl, howl, howl!" cries Lear after Cordelia has been hanged.

5. Kent: O, let him pass! he hates him much / That would upon the rack of this tough world / Stretch him out longer —William Shakespeare, *King Lear*, Act 5, scene 3, line 312

6. Oedipus: Were there still a way to choke the fount of hearing, I would not have hesitated to make a fast prison of this wretched frame —Sophocles, *Oedipus the King*

   The king has blinded himself. Only his hearing now connects him to his fellow man and allows him to respond.

7. Duchess of York: O my accursed womb, the bed of death! —William Shakespeare, *The Tragedy of King Richard the Third*, Act 4, scene 1, line 53

   This is the cry of a mother whose sons have been murdered.

8. King Richard: O that I were a mockery king of snow, / Standing before the sun of Bolingbroke / To melt myself away in water drops! —William Shakespeare, *The Tragedy of King Richard the Second*, Act 4, scene 1, line 260

   Earlier in the play, Richard pictured himself as the sun.

9. Queen Elizabeth: Ah! my poor princes! . . . / My sunblown flowers —William Shakespeare, *The Tragedy of King Richard the Third*, Act 4, scene 4, line 9

■ LANDSCAPES

See also: DESCRIPTIONS, MISC.; NATURE SCENES; PLACES, MISC.; SEASONS

1. In that field, the sun lay hot on sheets of buttercups —H. E. Bates, "The Cowslip Field"

2. It is a dear little lullaby of a place sleeping between two small mountains —Josh Billings

The place is Billings' home town—New Ashford, Massachusetts.

3. Below them, in the midst of that wavy ocean of sand, was a green thread of verdure —Willa Cather, *Death Comes for the Archbishop*

    This is Cather's metaphoric view of New Mexico.

4. They had come up on the grassy scalp of the hill, one of the few bald spots that stood clear of the crashing and roaring pine forest —Gilbert Keith Chesterton, "The Honour of Israel Gow"

5. An unintended dandelion breaks the hasp / of the adjoining plot's neglected ivy — Amy Clampitt, "Burial in Cypress Hills"

6. This lawn graced with the candle-flames of crocus —C(ecil). Day-Lewis, "Overtures to Death"

7. On the hill before the wind came / the grass moved toward the one sea, / blade after blade dancing in waves —Robert Duncan, "A Poem Beginning with a Line by Pindar IV"

    The meadow becomes, with the help of the wind, a sea.

8. Pioneer families . . . must have felt much as the Ferber family did as it arrived in Appleton, Wisconsin, and looked about at the smiling valley in whose arms the town so contentedly nestled —Edna Ferber, *A Peculiar Treasure*

    The metaphor of Ferber's childhood home pictured as if it were a child nestling in its mother's arms, underscores her affection for the place.

9. I was afraid the waking arm would break / From the loose earth and rub against his eyes / A fist of trees —Donald Hall, "The Sleeping Giant"

    A four-year-old looks at a hill in Connecticut called "The Sleeping Giant," and turns the metaphoric description into reality.

10. The plantation was very quiet. Then all those rounded, rolling waves of fresh green began to stir —Kawabata Yasunari, *Beauty and Sadness*

The Nobelist compares the terraces of tea bushes to the sea that is never very far away in Japan.

11. Nature lay frozen dead,—and still and slow / A winding sheet fell o'er her body fair, / Flakey and soft, from his wide wings of snow —Fanny Kemble, "Winter"

12. The pasture lands . . . embroidered, according to the season, with iris, columbine, Indian paintbrush, tiger lilies or cardinal flowers —Oliver La Farge, "Wedding at Rociada," *The New Yorker,* 1950–60

13. But the wheat and grass were sleek velvet under the sunset —Sinclair Lewis, *Main Street*

14. The countryside once more unfolded its quilt of green —Lorrie Moore, "Which Is More Than I Can Say About Some People," *The New Yorker,* November 8, 1993

15. At my feet lay the Great Central Valley of California, level and flowery . . . a lake of pure sunshine —John Muir, *The Mountains of California*

16. Stand on Mesa Verda and look out and each mesa is an acropolis, each canyon a cathedral —John Muir, "The Custer Syndrome," *Newsweek,* 1992

17. Tilled fields had long been unfolding their patchwork past the railway car window —Vladimir Nabokov, *King, Queen, Knave*

18. Farther on there was an enchanting mist where another picture postcard turned on its stand showing a translucent tower against a black background —Vladimir Nabokov, *King, Queen, Knave*

    Franz, the Knave of the title, is traveling by train through a countryside of impeccable views.

19. The unruly colors of the universe were confined once more to their official compartments and cells —Vladimir Nabokov, *King, Queen, Knave*

    The wild countryside has changed, in the course of travel, to a domesticated one.

20. He gazed out of the [train] window . . . Then, resolving an iron chord, a bridge banged overhead and instantly the green slope vanished and open country unfurled —Vladimir Nabokov, *King, Queen, Knave*
    The implied metaphor is of the countryside as a green flag, or green scroll, unfurling.

21. The lough was vacant under the midday sun, its vast expanse of stillness broken only . . . by its eyelash fringe of reeds — Sean O'Faolain, "Lovers of the Lake"

22. The hills are webs of shadow, slowly spun —Dorothy Parker, "Midnight," *Death and Taxes*

23. Gold flowers to flame / on land in the glory of trees —Pindar, *Odes*

24. Gradually, the sharp snaggled edge of the ridge stood out above them, rotten granite tortured and eaten by the winds of time — John Steinbeck, "Flight," *The Long Valley*
    Pepe, the protagonist, is fleeing on horseback for his life. The descriptions of nature provide a background of doom for the thoughts of the desperate man.

25. At the bottom of the slope, there was a dark crease . . . A scar of green grass cut across the flat —John Steinbeck, "Flight," *The Long Valley*
    Words like "scar" in the descriptions of nature provide a foreshadowing of the doom that stalks the protagonist of this story.

26. Five-fingered ferns hung over the water and dripped spray from their finger tips — John Steinbeck, "Flight," *The Long Valley*
    The alliteration leads, finally, to a form of personification.

27. Bowl-hollow of woodland —Robert Penn Warren, "No Bird Does Call"
    The metaphor that opens the poem is expanded and enriched by allusion, as the poet notes, "The hollow is Danae's lap lavished with gold by the god."

28. That patched land of Mississippi winter, trees in their rusty wrappers —Eudora Welty, "Old Mr. Marblehead"

29. The last gleam of sunset could be seen going on behind the threadbare curtain of wisteria —Eudora Welty, "Kin," *The New Yorker, 1950–60*

30. The turf was hemmed with an edge of scarlet geraniums and coleus —Edith Wharton, *The Age of Innocence*

■ LANGUAGE

See also: GRAMMAR AND STYLE; POETRY/ POETS; SPEECH; WORDS; WORDS AS WEAPONS; WRITING/WRITERS

1. Language is a steed that carries one into a far country —Anon., Arab Proverb

2. And new-found urns as fresh as day, / And marble's language —Robert Browning, "The Bishop Orders his Tomb at Saint Praxed's Church"
    The marble funeral-urns had a language of death.

3. The phrase "that doesn't say a thing to me" is an outworn metaphor; but the saying I am referring to is real speech. In the house of speech are many mansions, and this is one of the inner —Martin Buber, "Dialogue"

4. Sex often makes language a mine field — Anthony Burgess, *A Mouthful of Air*
    To illustrate his point, Burgess gave several examples of words which while ordinary in the United States may be charged with sexual implications in Great Britain. He stepped on a mine field of his own making when he suggested that Leo Rosten's term Yinglish *might sound better as* Yidlish—*a coinage that would probably offend Yiddish-speaking and non-Yiddish-speaking Jews everywhere.*

5. It's an end to the word-smith now, / an end to the Skald, / an end to the erudite, elated rover / threading a fiord of words —Donald Davie, Quoted, "Election and Reprobation," by Helen Vendler, *The New Yorker, January 18, 1993*

6. Colgrin: There's not a devil / In the length of the land could pick such a posy

of words / And not swoon smelling it — Christopher Fry, *Thor, With Angels*

7. Mr. Paz especially likes to end his essays with a verbal Roman candle that leaves the reader saying "Ahhh!" —Hayden Herrara, *New York Times Book Review*, May 30, 1993

    The headline of this review of Paz's Essays on Mexican Art, *"Surrounding Art with Language," seemed to imply that Paz's words are a frame for the art he writes about.*

8. Banks of light bulbs float onto the stage and flare and dim with the changes in the language's emotional temperature —Stephen Holden, *The New York Times* theater review, June 9, 1992

    The book reviewed was Dr. Faustus Lights the Lights *by Gertrude Stein, whose could indeed get feverish.*

9. Latin, Queen of Tongues, / Is not yet free from rime's wrongs —Ben Jonson, "A fit of rime against rime"

    Poetry, or rhyme (rime), is a great adulterator of language, according to Jonson.

10. Somewhere on a continuum between tactfulness at one end and downright hypocrisy at the other, there lies the euphemism, that rose-tinted, foot-shuffling linguistic artifice which we use to airbrush out imperfections in the human condition — Louise Kehoe, "Airbrushing our language," *The Berkshire Eagle*, August 29, 1993

    Once again we see that if there's a single good metaphor in an essay, it's a sure bet that the staff headline writer will pounce on it.

11. Hebrew forms a canopy over the mundane world of Yiddish —Shirley Kumove, *Words Like Arrows*

    Readers of a book rich with metaphors are likely to look for a few in the editor's introduction, and Ms. Kumove does not disappoint.

12. His words are a show in themselves; language that is constantly dancing out to change its wardrobe from motley to funeral, clownish to sober citizen, wordy bore to snarling villain, all masking in the end

your heart-wrenching reporter —Robert MacNeil, *Wordstruck*

    MacNeil, describing Dickens shows himself quite adept at reaching out to grab his readers with a colorful wardrobe of language.

13. The fluted nouns / Made taller, lonelier than life / By leaf-carved capitals in the afterglow. / The owlet umlaut peeps and hoots / Above the open vowel —James Merrill, "Lost in Translation"

    Merrill writes that "all is translation / And every bit of us is lost in it (or found—)."

14. Language is the only homeland — Czeslaw Milosz

    The emigre Polish writer and Nobel laureate was quoted in Mothers: Memories, Dreams and Reflections by Literary Daughters, *edited by Susan Cahill (Mentor, 1992).*

15. Free frank / impartial sunlight, / moonlight, / starlight, lighthouse light, / are language —Marianne Moore, "Light is Speech"

16. Her vocabulary was a thin soup —Cynthia Ozick, "Envy, or, Yiddish in America," *The Pagan Rabbi and Other Stories*

17. Language is a map of our failures — Adrienne Rich, "The Burning of Paper Instead of Children"

18. But this linguistic prairie fire will be fun to watch —William Safire, "On Language," *The New York Times*, May 24, 1992

    The brushfire metaphor appeared in an article on the increasing use of "Enjoy!" His concluding "but, sorry, you're not my table," slyly illustrated how the phrase could lead to more "dropped subjects."

19. English is a stretch language: one size fits all —William Safire, *On Language*

20. [Horace] Greeley, scolded, argued, set off bombs of language —Carl Sandburg, *Abraham Lincoln, The War Years.* Vol. One

    Sandburg used the metaphor to contrast Horace Greeley's scolding and argumentative style to that of the more persuasive Benjamin Franklin's.

21. Benedick: He was wont to speak plain . . . and now he is turned orthography; his words are a very fantastical banquet, just so many strange dishes —William Shakespeare, *Much Ado About Nothing,* Act 2, scene 3, line 19

    Claudio, who once spoke in the straightforward manner of a man who loves military things, is now given to effusive language.

22. Language is but a poor bull's-eye lantern wherewith to show off the vast cathedral of the world —Robert Louis Stevenson, *Familiar Studies of Men and Books*

23. The prism of language —Stephen Ullman, "The Prism of Language"

    Ullman decries "linguistic claustrophobia" and feels that language is a prism that "refracts and analyzes our experiences in its own particular way."

24. He adds piquancy to his offered dish with the condiments of the past: archaisms, the dated language of flappers . . . nursery rhymes —Helen Vendler, "Books," *The New Yorker,* August 3, 1992

    Vendler reviewed John Asberry's Flow Chart.

25. [Ashbery uses] a hatful of colored scarves of language —Helen Vendler, "Books," *The New Yorker,* August 3, 1992.

    The metaphor appeared in a review of John Ashbery's Flow Chart.

■ LANGUAGE EXPERTS

See also: WORDS AS WEAPONS

1. He [Winston Churchill] mobilized the English language and sent it into battle — John F. Kennedy, Speech when Churchill was granted honorary citizenship by a one-time act of Congress, April 9, 1963

2. For nearly four years he rode herd on 132,000 entries for the 1,472-page volume —Wolfgang Saxon, from obituary for dictionary editor Clarence Lewis Barnhart, *The New York Times,* October 26, 1993

    After his stint as linguistic cowboy for Random House, Mr. Barnhart formed his own dictionary

    publishing enterprise and continued to ride herd on words until shortly before his death at the age of 92.

3. As a weekday political columnist and the Sunday constable of the word police, he has the awesome power to insinuate into the language the very words and phrases he now seeks to immortalize in his chewy dictionary —Martin Walker, *The New York Times Book Review,* October 31, 1993

    The review of Safire's New Political Dictionary, *ended with this refrain of the second metaphor: "Still, wild horses would not drag this chewy tome from my reference shelf."*

■ LAUGHTER

1. Genuine laughing is the vent of the soul, the nostrils of the heart —Josh Billings

2. Laughter is the cipher key wherewith we decipher the whole man —Thomas Carlyle, *Sartor Resartus*

3. Unextinguished laughter shakes the skies —Homer, *The Iliad*

4. The ghost of a laugh came out of his throat —Rosamond Lehmann, *The Ballad and the Source*

5. Laughter is the mind sneezing —Wyndham Lewis, "Inferior Religions"

6. Laughter . . . the joyous, beautiful, universal evergreen of life —Abraham Lincoln, As a young man, Quoted in Carl Sandburg's *Prairie Years*

7. Laughter shakes the universe, places it outside itself, reveals its entrails —Octavio Paz, Quoted in *New York Times Book Review,* of Paz's *Essays on Mexican Art,* May 30, 1993

8. Nona was still in the whirlpool of her laugh. She struggled to its edge only to be caught back, with retrospective sobs and gasps, into its central coil —Edith Wharton, *Twilight Sleep*

9. His laugh was a ticking bomb —James Wolcott, *The New Yorker,* April 12, 1993
   Wolcott's metaphor depicted the rather manic laugh of talk show host, Tom Snyder.

■ LAW/LAWYERS

See also: JUSTICE/INJUSTICE; OCCUPATIONS

1. Law is a bottomless pit —John Arbuthnot, Title of a pamphlet, 1712

2. Judge: Judges don't age. Time decorates them —Enid Bagnold, *The Chalk Garden,* Act 1

3. Good laws execute themselves; bad laws are their own executioners —Josh Billings

4. Law is the safest helmet —Sir Edward Coke, Motto the English jurist had inscribed on rings in Latin, c. 1592

5. The law is an ass, a idiot —Charles Dickens, *Oliver Twist*

6. Foolish legislation is a rope of sand, which perishes in the twisting —Ralph Waldo Emerson, "Politics," *Essays: Second Series*

7. Jenny: The Gamesters and Lawyers are Jugglers alike / If they meddle your All is in danger —John Gay, *The Beggar's Opera,* Act 2, scene 4
   Lawyer-bashing is clearly not a twentieth century phenomenon.

8. His gluttony / Is a strange one—his leavings are guilt and sentence —Ted Hughes, "The Judge"
   A bird, depicted as a metaphor for the law, is squatting and obscene.

9. Her feathers are leaves, the leaves tongues, / The mouths wounds, the tongues flames / The feet / Roots / Buried in your chest —Ted Hughes, "The Plaintiff"
   Hughes' vision of the law evokes an image of a frightening bird.

10. In the secret world, when I duly entered it, the law was the ghost at every clandestine feast —John Le Carré, Speech to the Boston Bar Association, May 3, 1993
    Le Carré returned to this metaphor of the law as an unseen presence with the conclusion that "the rule of law is a far safer haven for our questing political morality than the abracadabra fantasies of secret government.

11. The law . . . the great stone column of authority which has been dragged by an adulterous, careless, negligent and half criminal humanity down the ages —John Mortimer, *A Voyage Round My Father*
    The play's narrator feels that his father, by suggesting that he "learn a little law," hands him this "stone column" as if it were a small mechanical toy which might occupy an occasional rainy afternoon.

■ LEADERS/FOLLOWERS

See also: ALLIANCES; GUIDANCE/ GUIDES; POWER

1. Bill Clinton has assembled a band of talented instrumentalists to confront the New World Order. The score remains to be composed —Anon., Editorial, *The New York Times,* January 1, 1993
   The editorial about President-elect Bill Clinton's cabinet choices began with another musical metaphor: "caution and competence stir no souls, if there's to be music, all now depends on the conductor."

2. Jesus: I am the true vine —The Bible, *N.T., John 15:2*
   In 15:3, Jesus repeats the vine metaphor with this addition: ye are the branches.

3. Jesus: My sheep hear my voice, and I know them, and they will follow me — The Bible, *N.T., John 10:27*

4. It is better to have a lion at the head of an army of sheep, than a sheep at the head of an army of lions —Daniel Defoe

5. Louis XIV absorbed all the smaller stars of his court in his own vast radiance — Alexandre Dumas, *The Three Musketeers*

6. Only the amoeba is immortal; the rest of us little mayfly bugs attach ourselves to bigger bugs with greater survival value — Clifton Fadiman, "I Shook Hands with Shakespeare"

7. The high priest of frivolity —George Konrad

    This is the title of a story by a Hungarian writer translated by Imre Goldstein for The New Yorker, *March 9, 1992.*

8. Yet he [Robert McNamara] was sometimes openly emotional when toughness was considered the proper public face for the Kennedys and their spear carriers — Herbert Mitgang, "Books of the Times," *The New York Times,* February 3, 1993

    The book being reviewed: Promise and Power, *by Deborah Shapley.*

9. The European leaders have taken as their symbol a herd of sheep huddling under the wing of a superpower eagle —William Safire, "Essay," *The New York Times,* May 3, 1993

    The sheep / eagle metaphor was prompted by the delayed action on the Serbian aggression against Bosnia.

10. Gaunt: Landlord of England are thou now, not King. / Thy state of law is bondslave to the law —William Shakespeare, *The Tragedy of King Richard the Second,* Act 2, scene 1, line 113

11. I need such louts. It is not for the gods to glaze pottery! —Ivan Turgenev, *Fathers and Sons*

    Bazarov, the anarchist, explains his need for followers so that he does not have to do the dull, routine work himself.

■ LEADERSHIP

See also: BUSINESS DESCRIPTIONS; COMPETITION/COMPETITORS; GUIDANCE/ GUIDES; REFORM

1. Jesus: I am the light of the world —The Bible, *N.T., John 8:12*

2. People will think differently of him the moment he assumes the mantle of leadership. People shift gears when a person becomes President —Phillip C. Brooks, The inaugural committee's historian, Quoted in "An Inauguration Designed to Play to the Cameras," *The New York Times,* January 18, 1993

    "Assuming the mantle" of leadership can be a physical act, as when conductor Leonard Bernstein wore the long dark cape of his mentor before concerts. For drivers of automatic transmission cars, "shifting gears" is indeed strictly a metaphor.

3. Shanghai will be the dragon's head, leading the way for the entire Yangtze River Valley as the dragon's body —Jiguang Chen, "Shanghai Journal," *New York Times,* September 1, 1992

    Mr. Chen, a novelist, expressed the belief that Shanghai will lead the country in economic reform.

4. You promise to become one of the lights of the Church. Heaven grant that this light prove not a devouring fire! —Alexandre Dumas, *The Three Musketeers*

    The Jesuit feels that Aramis can become a leader in the church if he is ordained.

5. Sam Walton was a Napoleon of merchandising, keeping his troops lean and competitive —Richard Lingeman, *The New York Times Book Review,* July 8, 1992

    This appeared in a review about the merchandising magnate's biography, Sam Walton.

6. All honor must be paid to the architects of our material prosperity; to the great captains of industry who have built our factories and our railroads —Theodore Roosevelt, "The Strenuous Life"

    Prosperity is here equated with a building, and industry with an army.

7. Chorus: . . . you who steered the country I love safely when she was crazed in troubles —Sophocles, *Oedipus the King*

    Oedipus arrived when the country was foundering.

8. A leader who has not his people's love is a very miserable little puppet —Vercors, *The Silence of the Sea*

The government set up by the French collabora-tors was actually called a "puppet government."

9. Frequently the insurrections [within States] are nearly rudderless, led by temporary inciters to violence, so that there is no accountable leader or organization with whom to negotiate —Dorrie Weiss, "U.N. Considers Regional Conflict," *ECAAR News Network*: The Newsletter of Economists Allied for Arms Reduction, Fall 1992
   "The preferred way is by preventive diplomacy in order to head off the conflagrations," the article notes later. Insurrections are compared first to foundering ships and later to fires.

■ LETTERS

See also: WRITERS/WRITING

1. My letter has unsealed volcanoes in Oldham —Winston Churchill, October 9, 1903
   Oldham was Churchill's district.

2. A few days later . . . we mobilize pen and paper and literary shock troops and pre-pare to hurl several battalions at Bill — Christopher Morley, "On Unanswering Letters"
   Morley, the reluctant correspondent, writes, "To use O. Henry's immortal joke, we have days of Damon and Knights of Pythias writing those uninked letters to Bill."

3. Letters, like wines, accumulate bright fumes and bubblings if kept under cork . . . We find in the lees of the heap two or three that have gone for six months and can safely be destroyed —Christopher Morley, "On Unanswering Letters"
   The opening simile provides the context for the metaphor.

4. Letters provide a high-fidelity tap into the stream of history —Roger Shattuck, *The New York Times Book Review*, February 21, 1993
   This introduced Shattuck's review of Flaubert-Sand, *a book of the famous author's long correspondence.*

■ LIBERTY

See also: FREEDOM/RESTRAINT; FREE-DOM OF EXPRESSION

1. Liberty's a glorious feast! —Robert Burns, "The Jolly Beggars"

2. Liberty is the bread of man's spirit — Salvador de Madariaga, *Anarchy or Hierarchy*

3. You whose wealth, whose tree of liberty / are rooted in the labor of your slaves — Robert Hayden, "Middle Passage III"
   There are two metaphors here: liberty as a tree, and slave labor as the earth

4. Liberty . . . the spark and flame in every noble breast . . . the many-colored dream in every honest brain —Robert Green Ingersoll, Decoration Day Address, 1870s
   The speaker went on to say that liberty was a word that has "filled the dungeon with its holy light" and has "put a halo round the martyr's head."

5. The tree of liberty must be refreshed from time to time with the blood of patriots and tyrants —Thomas Jefferson, Letter, November 13, 1787
   In another letter, Jefferson likened good govern-ment to good health and dissent to medicine.

6. Liberty does not always have clean hands —André Malraux, *Man's Hope*

7. Duke: Our decrees, / Dead to infliction, to themselves are dead, / And Liberty plucks justice by the nose. —William Shakespeare, *Measure for Measure*, Act 1, scene 3, line 29
   Because laws have gone unenforced for years "The baby beats the nurse, and quite athwart / Goes all decorum."

8. Liberty, when it begins to take root, is a plant of rapid growth —George Wash-ington, Letter to James Madison, March 2, 1788

9. The preservation of the sacred fire of liber-ty . . . as finally staked on the experiment entrusted to the hands of the American people —George Washington, First In-augural Address, April 30, 1789

10. Instead of dwelling in those caverns of darkness . . . let us enjoy the fresh air of Liberty and Union —Daniel Webster, Senate speech on the problem of a slave policy with respect to new Western territories, March 7, 1850

    Webster used the dark caverns as a metaphor for the breakdown of the nation's major institutions.

■ LIES/LIARS

See also: TRUTH/FALSEHOOD

1. A fib is a lie painted in watercolors —Josh Billings

2. [A lie:] 'Tis but / The truth in masquerade —Lord George Gordon Byron, "Don Juan"

3. Falsehood . . . is a beautiful twilight that enhances every object —Albert Camus, *The Fall*

    The author contrasts this with truth, "a blinding light."

4. Falsehood is often rocked by truth, but soon outgrows her cradle and her nurse — Charles Caleb Colton, *Lacon*

5. Sin has many tools, but a lie is the handle which fits them all —Oliver Wendell Holmes, *The Autocrat of the Breakfast-Table*

6. Mr. Sims: Your lips are blistering with lies —Sidney Kingsley, *Detective Story*, Act 2

7. Polonius: Your bait of falsehood takes this carp of truth —William Shakespeare, *Hamlet*, Act 2, scene 1, line 63

    Shakespeare links falseness to the fisherman's bait.

8. They were . . . so faultlessly orchestrated in the variations and counterpoint of falsehood . . . that I usually found myself believing them —Donna Tartt, *The Secret History*

9. Perhaps a case can be made during wartime for a doctor surrounding a Presidential patient with a "body-guard of lies" to keep a Commander in Chief's condition from the enemy —Dr. Janet Travel, Quot-

ed in "Essay" by William Safire, *The New York Times,* April 23, 1992

10. The gauze of lies that the Soviet regime wraps around reality has never been thick enough to muffle this question: Where is Raoul Wallenberg? —George Will, "Raoul Wallenberg: Lost in a Gauze of Lies," *Washington Post Syndicate,* January 8, 1983

    The Wallenberg story remained a mystery even after the dissolution of the U.S.S.R.

11. The more time I let pass, the more tightly he would weave the tissue of lies he had cocooned himself in —A. B. Yehoshua, *Mr. Mani*

    The narrator despairs of ever getting a confession out of the cocooned man, his prisoner.

■ LIFE

See also: ACHIEVEMENT; COURAGE; EXISTENCE; FRAGILITY; HAPPINESS; HUMANITY/HUMANKIND; PERMANENCE/IMPERMANENCE; SELF-ACTUALIZATION; TRANSIENCE; VULNERABILITY

1. My life has been one great big joke, / A dance that's walked / A song that's spoke —Maya Angelou, "When I Think About myself," *Just Give Me a Cool Drink of Water 'fore I Diie*

2. The wheel thus set in motion / Who does not keep turning in this world —Anon., *The Bhagavad Gita, 3:16*

3. Life was a labyrinth of petty turns —Ruth Benedict, Quotation from *An Anthropologist at Work* by Margaret Mead

4. Our days upon earth are a shadow —The Bible, *O.T., Job 8:9*

5. For what is your life? It is even a vapour, that appeareth for a little time and then vanishes away —The Bible, N.T., *James 4:14*

6. Life is a copycat and can be bullied into following the master artist who bids it

come to heel —Heywood Broun, *It Seems to Me*

7. Climb the rounds / Of life's long ladder, one by slippery one —Robert Browning, "Jochanan Hakkadosh"

8. Is all our Life but a dream / Seen faintly in the golden gleam / Athwart Time's dark resistless stream? —Lewis Carroll, Untitled poem
    This metaphoric picture of life as a dream and its movement as a sort of uncontrolled drift through a powerful stream marks the beginning of the verse.

9. Sadie Thompson: Life's a quaint present from somebody, there's no doubt about that —John Colton and Clemence Randolph, *Rain*, Act 3, scene 2
    Movie goers will recall Joan Crawford as Sadie Thompson.

10. She could see now that an individual life is, in the end, nothing more than a stirring of air, a shifting of light —Harriet Doerr, *Consider This, Señora*

11. Every day a wilderness—no / shade in sight —Rita Dove, "Dusting," *Thomas and Beulah*

12. We live amid surfaces, and the true art of life is to skate well on them —Ralph Waldo Emerson, "Experience," *Essays: First Series*
    In "Prudence," Emerson wrote "In skating over thin ice our safety is in our speed."

13. David: Life is a hypocrite if I can't live / The way it moves me! —Christopher Fry, *A Sleep of Prisoners*

14. All your hours are wings that beat through space from self to self —Kahlil Gibran, *The Prophet*

15. Hector: I am happy I gave them one final swig of life . . . they died drinking it — Jean Giraudoux, *Tiger at the Gates*, Act 2
    Hector tried to comfort his dying soldiers by joking with them.

16. A useless life is an untimely death — Johann Wolfgang von Goethe, *Iphigenia*, Act 1, scene 2
    Some sources quote this as "an unused life is an early death."

17. Life lies at their feet, a party-colored India-rubber ball —Kenneth Grahame, "The Magic Ring"
    Through the eyes of a child, grown-ups have all the fun.

18. Life was a comedy . . . and it seemed to me that we were all . . . driven by an authoritative practical joker towards the extreme point of comedy —Graham Greene, *The Comedians*

19. We quaff the cup of life with eager thirst without draining it, and joy and hope seem ever mantling to the brim —William Hazlitt, "On the Feeling of Immortality in Youth"

20. And every life . . . will, at its close, become a tragedy as deep and dark as can be woven of the warp and woof of mystery and death —Robert Green Ingersoll, Eulogy for his brother, 1879

21. Life is but a day; / a fragile dew-drop on its perilous way from a tree's summit — John Keats, "Sleep and Poetry"

22. Life . . . is full of steep stairs to go puffing up, and, later, of shaky stairs to totter down —Louis Kronenberger, *The Cart and the Horse*

23. I warm'd both hands before the fire of life —Walter Savage Landor, "Dying Speech of an Old Philospher"

24. My world is a painted fresco . . . / An endless tapestry —D. H. Lawrence, "Dreams Old and Nascent"
    Lawrence extends the metaphor of the tapestry with "the past has woven drapes."

25. Life, / The painted dragon, . . . with flat glass eyes pushed at him on a stick — Robert Lowell, "Mother and Son," *Between the Porch and the Altar I*

26. You walk through all your days . . . And you go from room to room, opening one door, closing the other behind you — John D. MacDonald, "The Reference Room"

The author builds on his metaphor with a simile: Now all the doors of all the rooms were open, and it was like a great roaring freight train running through all the rooms, through all the days of my life.

27. In matters of life, three acts is the whole play. Now to set a certain time to every man's acting, belongs unto him only, who as first he was of the composition, so is now the cause of the dissolution —Marcus Aurelius, *Meditations of Marcus Aurelius*

28. What a strange pattern the shuttle of life can weave —Frances Marion, *Westward the Dream*

29. Not that I don't value my life . . . but sometimes I wish I could spread it all out on a piece of paper and take some White-out to it —Jill McCorkle, "First Union Blues"

30. This life is a fleeting breath —Louisa Moulton, "When I Wander Away With Death"

31. If life is a tree, let us smell the flower and dig at the roots —Lewis Mumford, "The Little Testament of Bernard Martin, Aet. 30"

32. The cradle rocks above an abyss, and common sense tells us that our existence is but a brief crack of light between two eternities of darkness —Vladimir Nabokov, *Speak Memory*

This marks the beginning of Nabokov's autobiography.

33. Hickey: Life is a crazy monkey face! — Eugene O'Neill, *The Iceman Cometh*

34. It is a long baptism into the seas of human-kind, my daughter. Better immersion than to live untouched —Tillie Olsen, "O Yes"

35. Life was . . . a lake offering its even surface to many reflections, gilded by the sun, silvered by the moon, darkened by a cloud, roughened by a ripple; but level always, a plane, keeping its bounds, not to be rolled up into a tight, hard ball, small enough to be held in the hand —Vita Sackville-West, *All Passion Spent*

36. To live is intoxication —George Sand, Letter to Charles Duvernet, July 19, 1831

37. We cannot tear out a single page of our life, but we can throw the whole book in the fire —George Sand, *Mauprat*

38. First Lord: The web of our life is of a mingled yarn, good and ill together — William Shakespeare, *All's Well That Ends Well* Act 4, scene 3, line 83

39. Gloucester: His thread of life hath not so soon decayed —William Shakespeare, *The First Part of Henry the Sixth* Act 1, scene 1, line 35

40. Falstaff: I know also life is a shuttle — William Shakespeare, *The Merry Wives of Windsor* Act 5, scene 1, line 26

The metaphor alludes to Job's lament that "my days are swifter than a weaver's shuttle," (O.T., Job 7:6).

41. Pericles: Life's but breath, to trust it error —William Shakespeare, *Pericles, Prince of Tyre*, Act 1, scene 1, line 46

In Love's Labour's Lost, *Act 4, scene 3, Berowne uses the same metaphor in relation to honor: Vows are but breath, and breath a vapor is.*

42. Timon: In life's uncertain voyage I will some kindness do them —William Shakespeare, *Timon of Athens* Act 5, scene 1, line 207

43. Bolingbroke: Must I not serve a long apprenticehood / To foreign passages, and, in the end, / Having my freedom, boast of nothing else / But that I was a journeyman to grief? —William Shakespeare, *The Tragedy of King Richard the Second*, Act 1, scene 3, line 271

44. The game of life is a game of boomerangs. Our thoughts, deeds and words, return to

us sooner or later, with astounding accuracy —Florence Scovel Shin, Epigraph

45. The rope of my life, coiling into this knot, then out of it, seemed again more like a thread, easily broken —Jane Smiley, *A Thousand Acres*

"Away from the farm it was easier to see a life as a sturdy rope with occasional knots in it," Smiley writes.

46. My life's a pool which can only hold / One star and a glimpse of blue —Mary Riley Smith, "My Life's a Bowl"

47. The lessons of life amount not to wisdom but to scar tissue —Wallace Stegner, *The Spectator Bird*

48. Whether we regard life as a lane leading to a dead wall . . . or as a vestibule or gymnasium, where we wait our turn and prepare our faculties for some more noble destiny . . . a man should stop his ears against paralyzing terror, and run the race that is set before him with a single mind — Robert Louis Stevenson, "Aes Triplex"

49. Only, what a checkered picnic we have of it, even while it lasts? And into what great waters, not to be crossed by any swimmer, God's pale Pretorian throws us over in the end! —Robert Louis Stevenson, "Aes Triplex"

"We live the time that a match flickers," writes Stevenson.

50. Many of the wisest, most virtuous, and most beneficient parts that are to be played upon the Theater of Life are filled by gratuitous performers, and pass, among the world at large, as phases of idleness — Robert Louis Stevenson, "An Apology for Idlers"

51. I still loved life . . . is there anything sillier than to desire to bear continually a burden one always wishes to throw to the ground . . . to caress the serpent which devours us until he has eaten our heart? —Voltaire, *Candide*

52. My life is a combat —Voltaire, *Mahomet,* II

53. Life does not need to mutilate itself in order to be pure —Simone Weil, *First and Last Notebooks*

54. What a hideous mystery life was! And yet Pauline and her friends persisted in regarding it as a Sunday school picnic, with lemonade and sponge cake as its supreme rewards —Edith Wharton, *Twilight Sleep*

55. From the prison of her flesh have we come into the unspeakable and incommunicable prison of this earth —Thomas Wolfe, *Look Homeward Angel*

The metaphor from a flyleaf passage sets the mood for Wolfe's best-known novel.

56. Life has become to most of us one swift headlong race—a continuous fight in which there is so much to do that the half of it has to be left undone —[Mrs. Henry] Ellen Wood, *Our Children*

■ LIFE AND DEATH

See also: DEATH; ENDINGS; ESCAPE; JOY

1. Birth is the messenger of death —Anon., Arab Proverb

2. When ye to your journey's end shall come —Anon., *Everyman*

3. Jim Marble: It seems to me life's nothing but a sleeper-jump to death —Philip Barry, *Here Come the Clowns,* Act 3

4. These struggling tides of life / . . . Are eddies of the mighty stream / That rolls to its appointed end —William Cullen Bryant, "The Crowded Street"

5. I think of death as a fast approaching end of a journey —George Eliot, Letter, November 22, 1861

6. The wine of life keeps coming drop by drop. The leaves of life keep falling one by one —Edward Fitzgerald, *The Rubáiyát of Omar Khayám*

7. Faust: Birth and the grave, / An infinite sea, / A web ever growing, / A life ever glowing —Johann Wolfgang von Goethe, *Faust*

8. People like Lerice and me . . . regard life as something to be spent extravagantly and, if we think about death at all, regard it as the final bankruptcy —Nadine Gordimer, "Six Feet of the Country"
   An African farmer watches a funeral, irritated at the sacrifice of these and other poor people everywhere—people who "stint themselves the decencies of life in order to ensure themselves the decencies of death"

9. I thought she was destined to go on forever, from one graceful, ageless accommodation to the next. Unlike that unsightly genius Maud, who left the party early — Doris Grumbach, *The Magician's Girl*
   The guests dominating Grumbach's party of life are three talented women who meet as college students. Maude is a Sylvia Plath-like poet who commits suicide.

10. Do they hint . . . / That my garden of life . . . / Is frozen and dying, or fallen and dead? —Sarah Josepha Hale, "Beautiful Rainbow"

11. In the first enjoyment of the state of life we discard the fear of debts and duns, and never think of the final payment of our great debt to Nature —William Hazlitt, "On the Feeling of Immortality in Youth"

12. Life's a piece in bloom / Death goes dogging everywhere, she's the tenant of the room, / he's the ruffian on the stair — William Ernest Henley, *Book of Verses*

13. The human body is a furnace which keeps in blast three score years and ten, more or less . . . when the fire slackens, life declines; when it goes out, we are dead — Oliver Wendell Holmes, *The Autocrat of the Breakfast-Table*
    A few pages later Holmes writes "when that fire of life we spoke of has burned so low that where its flames reverberated there is only the somber stain of regret, and where the coals glowed, only the

white ashes that cover the embers of memory,— don't let your heart grow cold, and you may carry cheerfulness and love with you into the teens of your second century."

14. Yes, death is at the bottom of the cup, / And every one that lives must drink it up —William Dean Howells, "Pordenone"

15. And that was life . . . a succession of street corners. You met with something . . . and the next moment you were at another corner; it had turned and was gone — Aldous Huxley, *Time Must Have a Stop*

16. Yet, after all, it may be best, just in the happiest, sunniest hour of all the voyage, while eager winds are kissing every sail, to dash against the unseen rock, and in an instant hear the billows roar above a sunken ship —Robert Green Ingersoll, Eulogy for his brother, 1879
    Ingersoll thus gives his view of death in the prime of life.

17. My own race is nearly run —Andrew Jackson, Farewell Address, 1837

18. You just hope that when the ship comes to dock, you can say, "Damn, we had a good time" —James Jordan, Editorial, *The Berkshire Eagle*, June 6, 1993
    The ship came to dock more suddenly than the father of basketball great Michael Jordan could have anticipated. The quotation was occasioned by his murder.

19. The life of an animate / Is a procession of deaths / With but a secret sorrowing candle, /Guttering lower and lower, / On the path to the grave —Alfred Kreymborg, "Manikin and Minikin: A Bisque Play"
    Macbeth's image—"out, out, brief candle"— preceded that of the bisque figurine in Kreymborg's play by over three hundred years.

20. What is our life but a succession of preludes to that unknown song whose first solemn note is sounded by Death? — Alphonse de Lamartine, "Méditations Poétiques"

21. She knew she submitted to life, which was her immediate master. But from death, her ultimate master, she winced with fear and shame —D. H. Lawrence, "Odour of Chrysanthemums"

22. All the long road / in chains, even if, after all, / we come to death's ordinary door, with time / smiling its ordinary / long-ago smile —Denise Levertov, "Prisoners"

    There is a string of metaphors here, one being built on the other: Life is a road, people traveling that road are prisoners, death and time are personified, and dying means going through death's door.

23. It is good to have an end to journey towards; but it is the journey that matters in the end —Ursula K. LeGuin, *The Left Hand of Darkness*

24. Life is but a suburb of the life elysian, whose portal we call death —Henry Wadsworth Longfellow, "Resignation

25. All men live enveloped in whale-lines. All are born with halters round their necks; but it is only when caught in the swift, sudden turn of death, that mortals realize the silent, subtle, ever-present perils of life —Herman Melville, *Moby Dick*

26. Thank Heaven! . . . / the fever called 'Living' / Is conquered at last —Edgar Allan Poe, "For Annie"

27. Cleopatra: Our lamp is spent, it's out — William Shakespeare, *Antony and Cleopatra*, Act 4, scene 2, line 86

28. Cardinal Wolsey: This is the state of man: today he puts forth / the tender leaves of hopes; tomorrow blossoms, / And bears his blushing honours thick upon him; / The third day a comes a frost, a killing frost —William Shakespeare, *The Life of King Henry the Eighth*, Act 3, scene 2, line 353

    In As You Like It, *(2, 7, 139), Jaques divides the ages of man into seven acts covering the life of the infant, the schoolboy, the lover, the soldier, the justice, the aging man and finally the very old man in his second childhood.*

29. Macbeth: Out, out, brief candle! Life's but a walking shadow, a poor player that struts and frets his hour upon the stage and then is heard no more —William Shakespeare, *Macbeth* Act 5, scene 5, line 23

    This famous quotation incorporates two recurring Shakespearian metaphors: life as a candle and life as a drama.

30. Duke: If thou art rich, thour't poor; / For, like an ass whose back with ingot bows, / Thou bear'st thy heavy riches but a journey, / And Death unloads thee —William Shakespeare, *Measure for Measure*, Act 3, scene 1, line 25

    The simile supports the metaphor of riches as baggage unloaded at the end of life's journey.

31. Othello: Here is my journey's end, here is my butt / And very sea-mark of my utmost sail —William Shakespeare, *Othello*, Act 5, scene 2, line 268

32. Bevis: their thread of life is spun —William Shakespeare, *The Second Part of Henry the Sixth*, Act 4, scene 2, Line 33

    The metaphor implicitly alludes to the Three Fates of Greek mythology, who spun, and then cut, the thread of life.

33. Clifford: Here burns my candle out; ay here it dies —William Shakespeare, *The Third Part of Henry the Sixth*, Act 2, scene 6, line 1

34. Gaunt: My inch of taper will be burnt and done —William Shakespeare, *The Tragedy of King Richard the Second*, Act 1, scene 3, line 223

    The candle as a metaphor for the brevity of life is used elsewhere by Shakespeare. When Macbeth begins to long for death, he cries, "Out, Out, brief candle!"

35. Our days be dated / To be checkmated / With draughts of death —John Skelton, "Upon a Dead Man's Head"

36. [Life:] Whose flowering pride, so fading and so fickle / Short Time shall soon cut down with his consuming sickle —Edmund Spenser, *The Faerie Queene*, Canto 8

37. Looking back over the ecstacies of a lifetime, the gentle tides of death lapping at his feet, he makes the second half of this piece ["Death in Venice"] a single nocturne of adoration —George Steiner, "Books," *The New Yorker*, July 5, 1993
   From a review of Humphrey Carpenter's biography of Benjamin Britten.

38. This luscious and impeccable fruit of life / Falls, it appears, of its own weight to earth —Wallace Stevens, "Le Monocle de Mon Oncle"
   On the heels of the metaphor, this simile: ". . . like skulls, comes rotting back to ground."

39. The whole way [toward death] is one wilderness of snares; and the end of it, for those who fear the last pinch, is irrevocable ruin —Robert Louis Stevenson, "Aes Triplex"

40. Old and young, we are all on our last cruise —Robert Louis Stevenson, *Virginibus Puerisque*
   Stevenson returns to the image with "Into what great waters, not to be crossed by any swimmer, God's pale Praetorian throws us over in the end!"

41. I cling to this living raft, my body, in the narrow stream of my earthly years —Rabindranath Tagore, "Fruit-Gathering, 42"

42. Death's stamp gives value to the coin of life; making it possible to buy with life what is truly previous —Rabindranath Tagore, "Stray Birds, 49"

43. This life is the crossing of a sea, where we meet in the same narrow ship. / In death we reach the shore and go to our different worlds —Rabindranath Tagore, "Stray Birds, 242"

44. There is a land of the living and a land of the dead and the bridge is love, the only survival, the only meaning —Thornton Wilder, *The Bridge of San Luis Rey*
   This concludes Wilder's novel.

45. Mrs. Venable: Most people's lives—what are they but trails of debris, each day more debris . . . with nothing to clean it all up but, finally, death —Tennessee Williams, *Suddenly Last Summer*, Act 1, scene 1

46. Joy woke him, and exultation. They had escaped from the dark prison of death, they were joined to the bright engine of life again. Life, ruddered life, that would not fail, began its myriad embarkations— Thomas Wolfe, *Look Homeward Angel*
   Wolfe's protagonist welcomes the day with a metaphor of sleep as death and life firmly steered like a ship.

■ LIFE, DEFINED

1. Life is a jigsaw puzzle with most of the pieces missing —Anon., s.u.

2. Life is a one-way street —Anon., s.u.

3. Life is a dance. If you're smart, you learn the steps —Anon., Yiddish Proverb

4. This life is a hospital in which every patient is possessed with a desire to change his bed —Charles Baudelaire, "Le Spleen de Paris"

5. Life is patchwork—here and there, / Scraps of pleasure and despair —Anne Bronaugh, "Patchwork"
   Patchwork quilts are a popular metaphor for the variedness of life. In this case the poet must have had a crazy quilt in mind when she concluded with "Join together, hit or miss."

6. Life is just a bowl of cherries —Lew Brown and Ray Henderson, Song title and opening line
   This line from a song written for George White's Scandals *served as a title for one of humorist Erma Brombeck's best-selling books.*

7. Life is a dream —Pedro Calderon, *La Vida es Sueno*
   The Spanish author was Shakespeare's contemporary; the metaphor served as the title for his best-known work.

8. Life is a disease from which sleep gives us relief every sixteen hours —Sèbestian Roch Nicolas Chamfort, *Maximes et Pensèes*
   The French man of letters extended this with "Sleep is a palliative, death is a remedy." More than a hundred years later, George Bernard Shaw, gave his own twist to the "disease" metaphor.

9. Life is a battle —Lydia M. Child, *Letters From New York*

10. Life is an incurable disease —Abraham Cowley, "To Dr. Scarborough"

11. Human life is an anthology of states — Lawrence Durrell, *Tunc*

12. Life is our dictionary —Ralph Waldo Emerson, Speech, "The American Scholar," Harvard College, August 31, 1837
    The speaker elaborated on this with "Life lies behind us as the quarry from whence we get the ties and cornerstones for the masonry of today."

13. This life is but a bridge —Abraham Ibn Ezra, "In the Night"

14. Life is a run-on sentence. The object is to punctuate it with experience —William Finegan, "The Sporting Scene—Playing Doc's Games, Part 2," *The New Yorker*, August 31, 1992
    The metaphor continues as follows: "You stick in a comma here, a comma there. You try to figure out where to put a semicolon. It takes balls to put in a period. If you want to get profound, you stick in a few question marks . . . And, if you're the impatient type . . . just throw exclamation points all over the place."

15. Life is itself exile . . . It is a blow from which only death will recover us —William H. Gass, "Exile," *Salmagundi*

16. Life's a last year's Nightingale —William Ernest Henley, "Echoes,"
    "Love's last year's rose" adds the poet.

17. Life is a fatal complaint, and an eminently contagious one —Oliver Wendell Holmes, *The Poet at the Breakfast Table*

18. Human life is a state of probation, and adversity is the post of honour in it —

John Hughes, *The Spectator*, December 1, 1711

19. Life is an abyss —Victor Hugo, *The History of a Crime*

20. Life is a narrow vale between the cold and barren peaks of two eternities —Robert Green Ingersoll, Eulogy for his brother, 1879
    "We strive in vain to look beyond the heights," said Ingersoll.

21. Life is a highway and its milestones are the years —Joyce Kilmer, "Love's Lantern"

22. Life is a loom, weaving illusion —Vachel Lindsay, "The Chinese Nightingale"

23. Life is a mirror. If you smile, it smiles back at you; if you frown, it frowns back — William P. Magee, United Nations NGO Briefing, June 10, 1993
    To the plastic surgeons volunteering for Operation Smile, the task is to brighten the mirror by removing the deformities of third-world children.

24. Our life is a warfare, and a mere pilgrimage —Marcus Aurelius, *Meditations of Marcus Aurelius*
    "Fame after life is no better than oblivion," wrote the philosopher.

25. Life is a game from which no one can withdraw with his winnings at any time —André Maurois, "The Kingdom of God"

26. Life in itself / Is nothing,— / An empty cup, a flight of uncarpeted stairs —Edna St. Vincent Millay, "Spring," *Vanity Fair*, 1921

27. On life's vast ocean diversely we sail / Reason the card, but passion is the gale — Alexander Pope, "Essay on Man"

28. Our life is nothing but a winter's day — Francis Quarles, "Emblems"

29. What is our life? a play of passion: / Our mirth the music of division —Sir Walter Ralegh (also spelled Raleigh), "On the Life of Man,"

30. And life is itself but a game of football —
Sir Walter Scott, "Song"

31. Life is a bank in which emotional currency gets put in and drawn out —Merle Shain, *When Lovers are Friends*

32. Macbeth: [Life] It is a tale / Told by an idiot, full of sound and fury, / Signifying nothing —William Shakespeare, *Macbeth*, Act 5, scene 5, line 27
    In the shorthand of metaphor, which communicates by association, Faulkner's book, The Sound and the Fury, *is literally a tale told by an idiot.*

33. Life is a disease; and the only difference between one man and another is the stage of the disease at which he lives —George Bernard Shaw, *Back to Methuselah*, Act 1

34. Life is a tragedy wherein we sit as spectators for a while, and then act out parts in it —Jonathan Swift, "Thoughts on Various Subjects"

35. Life is a dream in the night, a fear among fears —Arthur Symons, "In the Wood of Finvara"
    Symons was a member of the so-called "Celtic Twilight," along with better known poets like Yeats.

36. Life . . . A naked runner lost in a storm of spears —Arthur Symons, "In the Wood of Finvara"

37. Life, a fury slinging flame —Lord Alfred Tennyson, *In Memoriam*, I 1850

38. Life is a game of chance —Voltaire, Letter, 1755

39. Life's just a perpetual piecing together of broken bits —Edith Wharton, *The Reef*
    "We're struck blind sometimes, and mad sometimes," explains George Dallow, but eventually sanity returns and we "build up, little by little, bit by bit, the precious things we've smashed to atoms without knowing it."

40. Lady Windermere: Nowadays people seem to look on life as a speculation. It is not a speculation. It is a sacrament —Oscar Wilde, *Lady Windermere's Fan*, Act 1

■ LONELINESS

See also: FRIENDSHIP/FRIENDS; ISOLATION; LOVE

1. So lonely am I, / My body is a floating weed severed at the roots —Anon., Japanese poem, "Kokinshu"

2. He faced the blind wall of human loneliness —Zona Gale, "The Biography of Blade"

3. These are the wilds / of loneliness, huge, vacant, sour and plain —Anthony Hecht, "Auspices"
    In this desolate field, "baneberry lofts its little poisoned pledges."

4. A woman alone, or alone with small children, becomes a monologist, often not really talking to the children but using their presence to unbutton her feelings —Robert MacNeil, *Wordstruck*
    MacNeil's mother's regaled him with stories about her courtship and early marriage.

5. When friendships decay, / And from Love's shining circle / The gems drop away —Thomas Moore, "The Last Rose of Summer"

6. My son . . . there are but desert sands for me between your comings . . . I live on your visits —Dorothy Parker, "I Live On Your Visits," *Stories from The New Yorker, 1950–60*
    The metaphor concludes the story.

7. Every day alone whittles me —Marge Piercy, "Going in," *The Twelve-Spoked Wheel Flashing*

8. Val Xavier: We're all of us sentenced to solitary confinement inside our own skins, for life! —Tennessee Williams, *Orpheus Descending*, Act 2, scene 1

The sentence leading into this is "Nobody ever gets to know no body!"

■ LOOKS

See also: FACIAL EXPRESSIONS; PEOPLE, INTERACTION

1. Marsha's look wraps fingers around his throat and he can't go on —T. Coraghessan Boyle, "Filthy With Things," *The New Yorker,* February 15, 1993
   The man in this figurative stranglehold has just introduced his wife to the organizer he's hired to unclutter their compulsively over-furnished and over-decorated home.

2. I am awaiting the moment when the thong of Irina's gaze would be loosened —Italo Calvino, *If on a winter's night a traveler*
   Irina has fixed the narrator "with diamond eyes."

3. That look [of pain and tenderness] was the beam of the headlights on a car that was about to run her over —Laurie Colwin, "The Smile Beneath the Smile"
   Colwin likens this man's seductive power to the beauty appeal in product advertising, an appeal which "had never come across so receptive a public as Rachel Manheim"

4. A glacial look that turned blue eyes into ice fields —Bill Granger, *The Last Good German*

5. He gave her a look that you could have poured on a waffle —Ring Lardner, s.u.

■ LOVE

See also: DEVOTION; EMOTIONS; ENDINGS; HATE; LUST; MEN AND WOMEN; PASSION; PERMANENCE/IMPERMANENCE; SORROW; REVENGE/VENGEANCE; VULNERABILITY

1. This tyrant of the mind [love] triumphed over all my wisdom; his darts were of greater force than all my reasoning —Peter (Pierre) Abelard, Letter to Philintus

2. Love wing'd my Hopes and taught me how to fly / Far from base earth, but not to mount too high —Anon., "Icarus," first published in Robert Jone's *Second Book of Songs and Airs*

3. She's still caught up in the breathlessness, the airlessness of love —Margaret Atwood, "Wilderness Tips"
   The metaphor implicitly alludes to a room so close that it seemed like a vacuum.

4. Don't worry, my dear little demon . . . love and vengeance, hunting together, will always strike down their prey —Honoré de Balzac, *Cousin Bette*

5. Love is the gold, but hate is the iron of that mine of emotions that lies within us —Honoré de Balzac, *Cousin Bette*
   Balzac thus explains the enduring hold of hatred on Cousin Bette

6. Love with a farewell smile may gild the sky —Maurice Baring, "As Leaden as the Aftermath of Wine"

7. I tend to believe that it [love] will make you unhappy, either immediately unhappy, as you are impaled by incompatibility; or unhappy later when the woodworm has quietly been gnawing away for years and the bishop's throne collapses —Julian Barnes, Quoted "Chameleon Novelist," by Mira Stout, *The New York Times Magazine,* November 22, 1992
   His triple metaphor notwithstanding, Barnes added his feeling that "love is our only hope."

8. Love is the crocodile in the river of desire —Barthriari, *The Vairaguya Sataka*

9. Your words are my food, your breath my wine —Sarah Bernhardt, Love letter to Victorian Sardou
   Sarah also told her lover that his words had a positive effect on her work: "My art has been suckled by them and softly rocked in their tender cradle."

10. Many waters cannot quench love, neither can the floods drown it —The Bible, *O.T., Song of Solomon 8:7*

The implied metaphor is a common one, the comparison of love to fire.

11. They stood before the altar and supplied / The fire themselves in which their fat was fried —Ambrose Bierce, *The Devil's Dictionary*

12. You shall lick the dust for Meat; / And tho'you cannot Love, but Hate, / Shall be beggars at Love's Gate —William Blake, "The Everlasting Gospel"

13. Till the wide desert planted o'er / With Labyrinths of wayward Love, / Where roam the Lion, Wolf & Boar —William Blake, "The Mental Traveller"

    In the beginning of this visionary poem, a Babe is nailed to a rock while an old woman "catches his shrieks in cups of gold." After roaming the labyrinth, the man becomes the Babe again.

14. Not till the knife of love gained sufficient edge could he cut her figure from its surroundings —Elizabeth Bowen, "Ivy Grips the Steps," *The Demon Lover and Other Stories*

    A young man has been strongly influenced by a wealthy friend of his mother's.

15. Love is no oracle —Charlotte Brontë, *Villette*

    Brontë offers an example of a metaphor—or, negaphor—since it describes what something is not.

16. Love is a pardonable insanity —Sébastien R.M. Chamfort, *Maxims and Thoughts*

17. Love hath my name ystrike out of his sclat —Geoffrey Chaucer, "Merciless Beauty"

    Love has struck Chaucer's name off the slate. It becomes evident from the rest of the poem that he is congratulating himself on his narrow escape from love.

18. Sin I fro Love escaped am so fat / I nevere thenke to been in his prison lene: / Sin I am free, I counte him not a bene — Geoffrey Chaucer, "Merciless Beauty"

    The poet congratulates himself on having escaped from love's prison, and no longer gives a bean for his would-be jailer.

19. A spring of love gushed from my heart — Samuel Taylor Coleridge, "The Ancient Mariner"

20. Theirs was a / music sinuous globular — e. e. cummings, "Cleopatra built"

    Cummings pictures Cleopatra and Antony together.

21. Whilst thus to ballast love . . . With wares which would sinke admiration, / I saw, I had loves pinnace overfraught —John Donne, "Aire and Angells"

22. Alas, alas, who's injur'd by my love? / What merchants ships have my sighs drown'd? —John Donne, "The Canonization"

    "For Godsake hold your tongue and let me love," writes Donne.

23. Call us what you will, wee are made such by love; / Call her one, mee another flye, / We'are Tapers too, and at our owne cost die —John Donne, "The Canonization"

    The two metaphors for love, flies and candles, have transience in common.

24. But if this medicine, love, which cures all sorrow / With more, not onely bee no quintessence, / But mixt of all stuffes — John Donne, "Loves Growth"

25. Some that have deeper digged love's mine than I, / Say where his centric happiness doth lie —John Donne, "Love's Alchemy"

26. Love, all alike, no season knowes, nor clyme, / Nor houres, dayes, moneths, which are the rags of time —John Donne, "The Sunne Rising"

    Love transcends the seasons and time itself, according to Donne.

27. Thence write our Annals, and in them will bee / To all whom loves subliming fire invades, / Rule and example found — John Donne, "A Valediction: Of the Booke"

    The lover suggests that the manuscript detailing their love could serve as a paradigm for other lovers. The metaphor of fire for love or passion is as common today as it was in the seventeenth century.

28. Wee for loves clergie only'are instruments —John Donne, "A Valediction: Of the Booke"

    The line suggests love as a religion.

29. Do I venture away too far / from the hot coast of your love / whose southern virtues charmed me? —Keith Douglas, "Song"

30. Love . . . had sunk into some cold wintry hibernating part of herself —Margaret Drabble, *The Middle Ground*

    Yet, the novel's protagonist tells herself it can't be dead but is "just waiting for some kind of spring" when "it would wake up and blossom again."

31. Gentle Murmurs, sweet Complaining, / Sighs that blow the Fire of Love —John Dryden, "Song" (from *King Arthur*, or *The British Worthy*)

32. The pain of love is the pain of being alive. It's a perpetual wound —Maureen Duffy, "Wounds"

33. Love . . . the bright foreigner, the foreign self —Ralph Waldo Emerson, *Journals*

34. Adams: When I was young, the trees of love forgave me —Christopher Fry, *A Sleep of Prisoners*

35. Our hours in love have wings; in absence, crutches —Colley Cibber, "Xerxes IV"

36. A life without love . . . is nothing but a mere magic-lantern show —Johann Wolfgang von Goethe, *Elective Affinities*

37. Love . . . / An impermanent treaty waiting to be signed / By the two enemies? — Thom Gunn, "To His Cynical Mistress," *Fighting Terms*

    The title of the poet's first book serves notice that this is not the only military metaphor in his armory of words.

38. Love is a dunghill . . . and I'm the cock that gets on it to crow —Ernest Hemingway, "The Snows of Kilimanjaro"

In response to this bitter remark by her dying husband, a wife asks "If you have to go away . . . do you have to kill your horse, and your wife and burn your saddle and your armor?"

39. Love's vast sea cannot be emptied / And springs of grace flow everywhere —Ho Xuan Hong, "Spring Watching Pavilion"

40. And so love becomes the chief plank in their platform —Julian Huxley, "What Do We Know about Love?"

    A presidential candidate discovers that "love" is the thing that interests people most.

41. Love has a tide! —Helen Fiske Hunt Jackson, "Tides"

42. In the religion of love, to pray is to pass, / by a shining word, into the inner chamber / of the other —Galway Kinnell, "The Man on the Hotel Room Bed"

43. Love never dies of starvation, but often of indigestion —Ninon de L'Enclos

    The French courtesan who coined this metaphoric bon mot also called beauty without grace "a hook without bait."

44. There is a harvest for the heart alone; / The seed of love must be / Eternally / Resown —Anne Morrow Lindbergh, "Second Sowing," *The Unicorn and Other Poems*

45. Love is a game—yes? / I think it is a drowning —Amy Lowell, "Twenty-four Hokku on a Modern Theme," *What's O'Clock*

46. Love can be the most dreadful disguise that hate assumes —William March, "The Dog and Her Rival"

47. Her husky voice still suited the penumbra of love —Gabriel García Márquez, *The General in his Labyrinth*

    The aging Bolivar's mistress was herself shadowed by age.

48. They say love is a two-way street. But I don't believe it, because the one I've been

on for the last two years was a dirt road — Terry McMillan, *Waiting to Exhale*

McMillan manages to find a new twist out of the familiar metaphor of the one-way or two-way street.

49. Love is the mind's strong physic, and the pill that leaves the heart sick and overturns the will —Thomas Middleton, *Blurt, Master Constable, III*

50. I know I am but summer to your heart, / And not the full four seasons of the year —Edna St. Vincent Millay, "I Know I am But Summer"

51. In the great seesaw of love, she's up now and you're down —Sue Miller, *For Love*

The couple thus teetering on the metaphoric seesaw is the wife of an unfaithful husband, now in an affair of her own.

52. Cléante: They say that love is often the fruit of marriage —Molière, *The Miser*, Act 4

Cléante is trying to hoodwink his father. If Cléante marries Mariane, perhaps he may love her after the marriage. Actually, he already loves her and is trying to keep Harpagon from discovering this fact.

53. Eel, torchlight, lash, / arrow of love on earth —Eugenio Montale, "The Eel"

Montale sees a symbol of hope in this "coldwater siren," this "green soul seeking life" in a world of desolation.

54. An obsession with love's fierce geometry has given unity to Elizabeth Tallent's work —Jay Parini, *The New York Times Book Review*, November 7, 1993

Parini's review of Ms. Tallent's latest short story collection, Honey, also praised her ability to "loop deftly through the layered fabric" of a character's mind.

55. Cover with ashes our love's cold crater — Dorothy Parker, "Nocturne," *Enough Rope*

Love's bitter endings were a favorite theme of Parker's poems.

56. But love is a durable fire / in the mind ever burning —Sir Walter Ralegh (also spelled Raleigh), "Walsinghame"

57. Love must have wings to fly away from love / And to fly back again —Edward Arlington Robinson, "Tristram"

58. Second Marquis: Our hearts, grown all warm with loving her, / May catch their death of cold! —Edmond Rostand, *Cyrano de Bergerac*, Act 1

59. Love as an emotion . . . moves between two poles: on one side, pure delight in contemplation; on the other, pure benevolence —Bertrand Russell, "The Good Life"

With opposite poles so apposite, why are the divorce courts so busy?

60. Love's a nervous, awkward, overmastering brute; if you can't rein him, it's best to have no truck with him —Dorothy L. Sayers, *Gaudy Night*

61. King: Our own love waking cries to see what's done, / While shameful hate sleeps out the afternoon —William Shakespeare, *All's Well That Ends Well*, Act 5, scene 3, line 65

The metaphor of sleep and wakefulness describes the effect of love delayed.

62. Caesar: Let not the piece of virtue, which is set / Betwixt us as the cyment [cement] of our love / . . . be the ram to batter / The fortress of it. —William Shakespeare, *Antony and Cleopatra*, Act 3, scene 2, line 23

The marriage of Caesar's sister, "the piece of virtue," to Antony is intended in the metaphor to cement the fortress of the men's soldierly love for each other, rather than being the battering ram that would breach its walls.

63. Rosalind: Love is merely a madness. And deserves as well a dark house and a whip as madmen —William Shakespeare, *As You Like It*, Act 3, scene 2, line 400

According to Shakespeare scholar Caroline Spurgeon, Shakespeare's psychological comprehension may have been well ahead of its time. To make her point she cites this underlying suggestion in the second part of the above image: If madmen should be treated in darkness and with whips, so should lovers, since both are irresponsible and thus to be held blameless.

64. Silvius: You meet in some fresh cheek the power of fancy, / Then shall you know the wounds invisible / That Love's keen arrows make —William Shakespeare, *As You Like It,* Act 5, scene 2, line 18

    The more common metaphor for such open display of one's feelings is expressed by Iago in Othello: "But I will wear my heart on my sleeve."

65. Imogen: I draw the sword myself; take it, and hit / The innocent mansion of my love, my heart —William Shakespeare, *Cymbeline,* Act 3, scene 4, line 64

66. Queen: Wing'd with fervour of her love, she's flown / To her desired Posthumus —William Shakespeare, *Cymbeline,* Act 3, scene 5, line 61

    The queen compares Imogen's going to Posthumus to the speed of a bird in flight.

67. King: There lives within the very flame of love / A kind of wick or snuff that will abate it —William Shakespeare, *Hamlet,* Act 4, scene 7, line 113

68. Princess: If frosts and fasts, hard lodgings and thin weeds, / Nip not the gaudy blossoms of your love . . . / I will be thine —William Shakespeare, *Love's Labour's Lost,* Act 5, scene 2, line 809

    The Princess is testing the declaration of love made "in heat of blood."

69. Jessica: Love is blind, and lovers cannot see / The pretty follies that themselves commit —William Shakespeare, *The Merchant of Venice,* Act 2, scene 6, line 36

    The metaphor is also used by Speed in Two Gentlemen of Verona, *Act 2, scene 1, line 78.*

70. Mrs. Page: Ask me no reason why I love you; for though / Love use Reason for his physician, he admits him / not for his counsellor —William Shakespeare, *The Merry Wives of Windsor,* Act 2, scene 1, line 4
    Mrs. Page is reading from a love letter.

71. Against love's fire fear's frost hath dissolution —William Shakespeare, *The Rape of Lucrece,* line 355

72. Chorus: And she steal love's sweet bait from fearful hooks —William Shakespeare, *Romeo and Juliet,* Act 1, scene 4, line 269

73. York: I fear me you, but warm the starved snake, / Who, cherish'd in your breasts, will sting your hearts —William Shakespeare, *The Second Part of Henry the Sixth,* Act 3, scene 1, line 342

74. My heart doth plead that thou in him dost lie— / A closet never pierced with crystal eyes —William Shakespeare, "Sonnet 46," line 5

    There is a double meaning to 'crystal eyes'—one, as the lack of windows in the darkness of the closet, and the second as the eyes of the poet, which contend with his heart for possession of the beloved in this sonnet.

75. When that mine eye is famished for a look / . . . With my love's picture then my eye doth feast, / And to the painted banquet bids my heart —William Shakespeare, "Sonnet 47," line 3

76. Where, alack, / Shall Time's best jewel from Time's chest lie hid? —William Shakespeare, "Sonnet 65," line 9

    The conceit is that the beloved is a jewel that Time will try to hide away in his strongbox.

77. It [love] is the star to every wandering bark / Whose worth's unknown, although his height be taken —William Shakespeare, "Sonnet 116," line 7

    Navigation was done by fixing the instruments on the stars.

78. Love's not Time's fool —William Shakespeare, "Sonnet 116," line 9

    The metaphor alludes to the fool kept by every monarch to help pass idle time and, sometimes, to serve as the butt of his annoyance.

79. King Richard: Love . . . / Is a strange brooch in this all-hating world. —William Shakespeare, *The Tragedy of King Richard the Second,* Act 5, scene 5, line 66
    Richard, in prison, muses on the anomaly of love when the world is full of hatred.

80. Troilus: Sweet love is food for Fortune's tooth —William Shakespeare, *Troilus and Cressida*, Act 4, scene 5, line 293

81. Viola [responding to Olivia's "How does he love me?"]: With groans that thunder love, with sighs of fire —William Shakespeare, *Twelfth Night*, Act 1, scene 5, line 255

82. Proteus: O! how this spring of love resembleth / The uncertain glory of an April day —William Shakespeare, *Two Gentlemen of Verona*, Act 2, scene 1, line 84

83. Valentine: Love's a mighty Lord —William Shakespeare, *Two Gentlemen of Verona*, Act 2, scene 4, line 137

84. Free vent of words love's fire doth assuage; / But when the heart's attorney once is mute, / The client breaks, as desperate in his suit —William Shakespeare, *Venus and Adonis*, line 333

85. Love surfeits not, Lust like a glutton dies —William Shakespeare, *Venus and Adonis*, line 803
    There are two food figures here, one a metaphor and one a simile.

86. Charles Surface: Oh, damn the surname! Tis too formal to be registered in love's calendar —Richard Brinsley Sheridan, *The School for Scandal*, Act 3, scene 3
    The lover proposes a toast, but does not want the full name of his beloved to be known.

87. What we call Cupid's dart / An image is, which for ourselves we carve, / And, fools, adore in temple of our heart —Sir Philip Sidney, "Sonnet 5," *Astrophel and Stella*

88. The couple might doze in each other's arms for a few moments, drawing a veil between what had been and the approaching everyday dawn —Frans Eemil Sillanpää, *The Maid Silja*
    The Finnish Nobel Prize winner is describing a night of first love during a harvest festival.

89. Love is full of showers —Robert Southwell, "Love's Servile Lot"
    That's why, according to the poem, April is the month of love.

90. [Love] comes, it blooms, it bears its fruit and dies —Wallace Stevens, "Le Monocle de Mon Oncle"

91. Love was the pearl of his oyster —Algernon Charles Swinburne, "Our Lady of Pain"

92. Let Love clasp Grief lest both be drowned —Lord Alfred Tennyson, *In Memoriam, II*

93. Wordsworth complained in a charming piece of unreasonableness that his wife's love, which had been a fountain, was now only a well —Francis Thompson, Quoted in *The World's Great Letters*

94. But within a month it was all over: the fire had kindled for the last time and then had died for ever —Ivan Turgenev, *Fathers and Sons*

95. He had loved her too long to want to pity her; it endangered the investment of worship on which he had not yet realized any return —John Updike, "The Sense of Shelter"

96. I add a touch of malice, some spicy scenes / and stirring, and screw the lid on love's breathless jar —Mona Van Duyn, "Homework"
    The poet, in her domestic mode, calls herself "a sweating Proust of the pantry shelves" as she pickles her peaches.

97. Does each cell have a soul within it? / . . . all your souls shall flutter like the linnet / In the cages of my pores —Andrei Voznesensky, "Dead Still"
    The metaphor depends upon the simile that precedes it.

98. Real loving was not the delicate distraction, the food for dreams . . . it was this breaking on the rack of every bone, and tearing apart of every fibre. And his ap-

prenticeship to it was just beginning — Edith Wharton, *The Children*

99. She was the vessel from which he had drunk this divine reassurance, this moment of union with the universe —Edith Wharton, *Hudson River Bracketed*

Woman as a vessel is an old metaphor that is used in many ways, including a sexual one. Feminists have happily brought this usage closer to extinction.

100. Their love arched over them open and ample as the day; in all its sunlit spaces there was no cranny for a fear to lurk — Edith Wharton, *The Reef*

"The first rush of bliss had stunned and dazzled her," Wharton explains, "but now that, each morning, she woke to the calm certainty of its recurrence, she was growing used to the sense of security it gave"

101. The rose of our love and the clean / horse of our courage —Richard Wilbur, "Advice to a Prophet"

Wilbur follows the two metaphors with a third: "The singing locust of the soul."

102. Love lights more fires than hate extinguishes —Ella Wheeler Wilcox, "Optimism"

103. Love lodged in a woman's breast / Is but a guest —Sir Henry Wotton, "A Woman's Heart"

104. Weary of the heat of hell, / The perfumed palace of thy love —Theodore Wratislaw, "Satiety"

105. Tangled was I in love's snare —Sir Thomas Wyatt, the Elder, "Tangled was I in Love's Snare"

106. The love tales wrought with silken thread / By dreaming ladies upon cloth / That has made fat the murderous moth —William Butler Yeats, "He Remembers Forgotten Beauty"

■ **LOVE, DEFINED**

See also: PASSION

1. Love is a fiend, a fire, a heaven, a hell — Richard Banfield, "The Affectionate Shepherd"

2. Love is a mask, with death behind — William Bell, "To a Lady on Her Marriage"

3. Love—a temporary insanity curable by marriage —Ambrose Bierce, *The Devil's Dictionary*

4. Love is Nature's second sun —George Chapman, *All Fools*, Act 1, scene 1

5. Love is a spaniel that prefers even punishment from one hand to caresses from another —Charles Caleb Colton, *Lacon*

In Shakespeare's A Midsummer Night's Dream *Helena tells Demetrius "I am your spaniel" to show him she is willing even to be beaten, as long as she can follow him (2, 1, 208).*

6. Love is a tyrant sparing none —Pierre Corneille, *The Cid*, Act 1, scene 2

In The Lover's Melancholy, *Corneille's contemporary, John Ford added this twist: "Love is a tyrant. / Resisted."*

7. Love is a sickness full of woes, / All remedies refusing —Samuel Daniel, "Hymen's Triumph"

8. Love is . . . A tempest everlasting —Samuel Daniel, "Love is a Sickness"

9. Love is a rope, for it ties and holds us in its yoke —Hadewijch, Dutch poetess

10. Love is the master key that opens the gates of happiness, of hatred, of jealousy, and, most easily of all, the gate of fear —Oliver Wendell Holmes, *The Autocrat of the Breakfast-Table*

11. Love unbridled is a volcano that burns down and lays waste all around —Baron Richard von Kraft-Ebing, *Psychopathia Sexualis*

12. Love is a jewel that wins the world — Moira O'Neill, "Beauty's a Flower"

The poet's title is an old metaphor. Shakespeare used it in Twelfth Night, *Act 1, scene 5; his contemporary, Thomas Nash extended it as "Beauty is but a flower / Which wrinkles will devour."*

13. Dion: Love is a word—a shameless ragged ghost of a word—begging at all doors for life at any price! —Eugene O'Neill, *Prologue, The Great God Brown* Prologue

14. Love is woman's moon and sun —Dorothy Parker, "General Review of the Sex Situation," *Enough Rope*

    Parker here perpetuates the myth espoused by Byron in Don Juan *that a man can separate his love from his life, but "'Tis woman's whole existence."*

15. Romeo: Love is a smoke made with the fume of sighs —William Shakespeare, *Romeo and Juliet,* Act 1, scene 1, line 193

16. Love is a sour delight, a sugar'd grief, / A living death, an ever-dying life; / A breach of Reason's law, a secret thief, / a sea of tears, an everlasting strife; / A bait for fools, a scourge of noble wits, / A deadly wound, a shot which ever hits — Thomas Watson

    And love often inspires a surfeit of metaphors!

■ LOVERS' DECLARATIONS AND EXCHANGES

See also: MEN AND WOMEN; PRAISE; SUCCESS/FAILURE

1. Come, if you think fit, and in your holy habit thrust yourself between my God and me, and be a wall of separation —Peter (Pierre) Abelard, Letter to Heloise

    Heloise has already become a nun; Abelard is in a monastery, trying to subdue his love for her and devote himself to God.

2. Elizabeth: Without you . . . the sun will be empty and circle around an empty earth . . . and I will be queen of emptiness and death —Maxwell Anderson, *Elizabeth The Queen,* Act 3

    This is Elizabeth's farewell to the Earl of Essex, the lover she has condemned to death as a traitor.

3. You sobbed and sighed / burning in flames beyond measure / —Three days endured your love to me, And it was lost in other three —Anon., "The Faithless" originally collected in Will Byrd's *Songs of Sundry Nature*

    The image of love as a consuming flame is one of the earliest metaphors, and its use continues unabated.

4. Lover! / I can only / burn for you — Anon, Folk Song. Ming Dynasty

5. We'll cross / the Bridge to the Land of Death together —Anon., Folk song. Ming Dynasty

    The singer threatens to commit suicide if the lover leaves, but if their spirits return after five hundred years, "O! but I'll still / want to make up with you!"

6. What do ye, hony-comb, sweete Alisoun, / My faire brid, my sweete cinamome? — Geoffrey Chaucer, "The Miller's Tale," *The Canterbury Tales*

    There are three metaphors here: the lover compares his mistress to a honeycomb, to a bird, to cinnamon. He continues by assuring her that he moons after her "as doth a lamb after the tete."

7. And all my treasure, which should purchase thee, / Sighs, teares, and oathes, and letters I have spent —John Donne, "Lovers Infinitenesse"

    The metaphor extends to the next stanza, in which the lover protests against other men, "which have their stocks intire and can in teares, / In sighs, in oathes, and letters outbid mee."

8. Macheath: As soon as the Search begins to be a little cool, I will send to thee—'Till then my Heart is thy Prisoner —John Gay, *The Beggar's Opera,* Act 2, scene 15

    Macheath's deceptive words are the undoing of weak women—he is prisoner to none and master of many.

9. Olpides: And then she said: 'You are my darling oak-tree'— / Topman: And he called her his birch-tree: 'My trembling silver birch tree!' —Jean Giraudoux, *Tiger at the Gates,* Act 2

Two sailors have watched Paris and Helen making love.

10. I walk the dead water / Burning language towards / You where you lie in the dark / Ascension of all words —W. S. Graham, "Letter II"

   Love transcends any words that aspire to express it.

11. But if you will fully love me, though there may be some fire 'twill not be more than we can bear when moistened and bedewed with Pleasures —John Keats, Letter to Fanny Brawne

12. When we try to kiss, / Our eyes are slits and cringing, and we hiss; / Scales glitter on our bodies as we fall —Robert Lowell," Adam and Eve," *Between the Porch and the Altar II*

   "Man tasted Eve with death," writes the poet, and compares this with his own love and his own serpent-like Fall.

13. But you were everywhere beside me, masked, / As who was not, in laughter, pain, and love —James Merrill, "Days of 1964"

14. I want you to be / the air in the house / the footfall inside me —William Stanley Merwin, "Green Island"

   "I want to be the dream / you feel / and the light you wake to," writes the lover.

15. Aethelwold: Nay, be not wroth with me; / Nor chide mine eyes. / Two children are mine eyes before thy shining wonder — Edna St. Vincent Millay, *The King's Henchman,* Act 2

16. Aethelwold: —and canst thou with thy summer-mouth / Utter these dry leaves? —Edna St. Vincent Millay, *The King's Henchman,* Act 2

   Aethelwold's beloved tries to bid him goodbye, her words foreshadowing leafless winter.

17. Aethelwold: Unfretted there, / Shall I watch thee preen thy rainbow feathers, / Bright bird of my heart —Edna St. Vincent Millay, *The King's Henchman,* Act 3

18. Lolita, light of my life, fire of my loins. My sin, my soul —Vladimir Nabokov, *Lolita*

19. Helena: 'twere all one / That I should love a bright particular star —William Shakespeare, *All's Well That Ends Well* Act 1, scene 1, line 97

   The star is Bertram.

20. Helena: Yet, in this captious and intenible sieve / I still pour in the waters of my love —William Shakespeare, *All's Well That Ends Well* Act 1, scene 3, line 210

   The metaphor of the sieve represents Helena's acknowledgement that she loves in vain.

21. Romeo: Arise fair Sun —William Shakespeare, *Romeo and Juliet,* Act 2, scene 1, line 46

   Romeo compares Juliet to the rising sun.

22. Juliet: This bud of love / by summer's ripening breath, / May prove a beauteous flower when next we meet —William Shakespeare, *Romeo and Juliet,* Act 2, scene 2, line 121

23. Take all my loves, my love, yea take them all; / What has thou then more than thou hadst before? / . . . I do forgive thy robb'ry, gentle thief, / Although thou steal thee all my poverty —William Shakespeare, "Sonnet 40," line 1

24. When I shall see thee frown on my defects, / Whenas thy love hath cast his utmost sum, / Called to that audit by advised respects —William Shakespeare, "Sonnet 49," line 2

   The poet sees his beloved as an auditor who will make a reckoning of his flaws.

25. 'Tis thee, myself, that for myself I praise, / Painting my age with beauty of thy days —William Shakespeare, "Sonnet 62," line 13

   The poet regards himself in the glass, admires himself, and then protests that what he admires is the beauty that his love confers upon him.

26. Nature bankrout [bankrupt] is . . . For she hath no exchequer now but his —William Shakespeare, "Sonnet 67," line 9

   The perfection of the loved one is such that Nature has no more 'money in the bank' because all has been spent on the design of this one person.

27. Troilus: Th' imaginary relish is so sweet / That it enchants my sense. What will it be / When the wat'ry palates taste indeed / Love's thrice reputed nectar? —William Shakespeare, *Troilus and Cressida,* Act 3, scene 3, line 119

   Troilus is a man given to food images.

28. I'll be a park, and thou shalt be my deer; / . . . Graze on my lips, and if those hills be dry, / Stray lower, where the pleasant fountains lie —William Shakespeare, *Venus and Adonis,* line 231

   Though Venus's invitation to Adonis seems bucolic, the couple is actually lingering at the edge of lasciviousness.

29. Come into the garden, Maud, / For the black bat, Night, has flown —Lord Alfred Tennyson, "Maud"

30. Farewell love . . . / Thy baited hooks shall tangle me no more —Sir Thomas Wyatt, Sonnet

■ LOYALTY

See also: DEVOTION; FIDELITY; MARRIAGE

1. Her loyalty [to her husband] . . . something that could never become worn or shabby; steel of Damascus —Willa Cather, *A Lost Lady*

2. Voynitsky: . . . such fidelity is false and unnatural, root and branch —Anton Chekhov, *Uncle Vanya,* Act 1

3. Boon was a mastiff, absolutely faithful, dividing his fidelity equally between Major de Spain and the boy's cousin McCaslin —William Faulkner, "The Old People"

4. The summer soldiers and the sunshine patriot will, in this crisis, shrink from the service of their country —Thomas Paine, *The Crisis,* paper no. 1, December 23, 1776

   President Franklin Delano Roosevelt wound up his morale-boosting Fireside Chat by quoting the image that began Paine's paper, concluding: "So spoke Americans in the year 1776. So speak Americans today!"

5. The sun is my father, and the earth is my mother, and on her bosom will I recline — Tecumseh

   The Shawnee chief thus replied to an aide to the Governor of Indiana Territory, William Henry Harrison who had told him "Warrior, your father, General Harrison offers you a seat." Tecumseh underscored his reply by stretching himself out on the ground. The battle of Tippecanoe soon followed.

■ LUST

See also: DESIRE; PASSION; SEX/SEXUALITY

1. You even could assuage / the ever-changing fever of man's lust —William Bell, "To a Lady on Her Marriage"

2. And his hard life-lust—the blind / Swan of insemination —Ted Hughes, "The Accused"

   The metaphor contains an allusion to Zeus, who impregnated Leda in the form of a swan. Blindness is not a part of the allusion, but a description of lust.

3. The wasting fires of lust sprang up again —James Joyce, *Portrait of the Artist as a Young Man*

   "His blood was in revolt," Joyce continues.

4. Lust is the oldest lion of them all — Marjorie Allen Seiffert, "An Italian Chest"

MADNESS

See also: CHARACTERIZATIONS

1. He was a runaway train on a track of madness, picking up steam all the time, on and on and on —Gerald Boyle, Closing argument by the defense lawyer for mass murderer Jeffrey Dahmer, February 15, 1992

2. For [madmen] never cease to dream that they are dreaming. They stood before the mirror with eyes open and fell sound asleep; they sealed their shadow in the tomb of memory —Henry Miller, "The Creative Life"

3. The insane hold up the cardboard pieces / Of a world they can no longer fit together —Howard Moss, "Elegy for My Sister. IV"

   "How stupid the endings of life can be," writes Moss, trying to make sense of the senseless roads to death. His sister, who died of cancer, was in a hospital where others suffered different endings.

4. The wing-tip of madness for Baudelaire: me, I live in the aviary —Theodore Roethke, *Straw for the Fire, Notebooks of Theodore Roethke*

5. Ophelia: O What a noble mind is here o'erthrown! . . . / Th' expectancy and rose of the fair state —William Shakespeare, *Hamlet,* Act 3, scene 1, line 154

   Hamlet has ranted and raved at Ophelia, telling her to "get thee to a nunnery," and she, in turn mourns the loss of the prince to madness.

6. The shrill in Celine's ear somehow brought with it the new grammars of hysteria, of mass propaganda, of self-deafening —George Steiner, "Books," *The New Yorker,* August 24, 1992

   The book reviewed was Frederic Vitoux's biography of Celine. The new grammars of hysteria incorporated repressive and abusive regimes and ushered in their mass murders.

7. The man's [Hitler's] mind . . . was a swamp of seething, demented ambition —George Will, *Washington Post Syndicate,* March 18, 1985

MALICE

See also: ENTRAPMENT

1. There is no one even for you to feel vindictive against, that you have not, and perhaps never will have, an object for your spite, that it is a sleight-of-hand, a bit of juggling, a card-sharper's trick, that it is simply a mess —Fyodor Mikhailovich Dostoevsky, *Notes from Underground*

   The narrator knows that his actions have no "objective correlative."

2. Until now New York—media and public—has seemed less an audience than a giant bowl of malevolent jelly quivering to

swallow him [candidate Bill Clinton] up
—A. M. Rosenthal, "On My Mind," *The
New York Times*, April 3, 1992
> "Now" referred to the time just before the state's
> Democratic primary.

3. Iago: So will I turn her virtue into pitch, /
And out of her own goodness make the
net / That shall enmesh 'em all —William Shakespeare, *Othello*, Act 2, scene 3,
line 352
> Iago, in his "motiveless malignity" prepares to
> sacrifice Desdemona to his own free-floating
> hatred.

4. King Richard: Deep malice makes too
deep an incision —William Shakespeare,
The Tragedy of King Richard the Second, Act
1, scene 1, line 153
> The wounds inflicted by anger and hate are
> pictured as surgical incisions.

■ MANHATTAN

See: CITIES; CITYSCAPES

■ MANIPULATION

*See also: CRAFTINESS; DECEPTION; EN-
TRAPMENT; EXPLOITATION; MASTERY
/ SUBORDINATION; MEN AND WOM-
EN; PEOPLE, INTERACTION*

1. Men are sex machines, said Aunt Lydia
. . . You must learn to manipulate them,
for your own good. Lead them around by
the nose; that is a metaphor —Margaret
Atwood, *The Handmaid's Tale*

2. I used to twit her about his silent canine
adoration —Louis Auchincloss, "The
Epicurean," *Three Lives*
> The protagonist's wife snipes slyly at his own
> inattention with "If I keep Tommy as a pet, it's to
> remind myself that I'm still a woman."

3. They have to be always twitching the
curtains and straightening the rug to keep
the clumsy boobs from making a complete

mess of the whole stage set —Louis
Auchincloss, "The Epicurean," *Three Lives*
> The protagonist's sister thus sums up how women
> like their mother and his future wife view the
> male-female relationships. When he angrily asks
> her "what stage set?" she explains "That's what
> they think life is. It's certainly what they make of
> it, anyway. A pretty parlor comedy, with a lot of
> witty lines and a sweet clinch at the final curtain."

4. I wolde no lenger in the bed abide / . . .
Til he hadde maad his raunson unto me /
. . . With empty hand men may no hawkes
lure —Geoffrey Chaucer, "The Wife of
Bath's Prologue and Tale," *The Canter-
bury Tales*
> The lady refused to sleep with her husband until
> he had paid her off. He had to offer ransom, bait.
> The poet's conclusion? Men can't lure hawks with
> an empty hand.

5. For him, a man was a mere lump of wax
to be kneaded into shape —Antoine de
Saint-Exupery, *Night Flight*
> The chief who sent the aviators out on dangerous
> assignments felt that he was bringing out the best
> in them.

6. Determined as he was to make his three
friends the instruments of his fortune,
D'Artagnan was not sorry at getting into
his grasp beforehand the invisible strings
by which he reckoned upon moving them
—Alexandre Dumas, *The Three Musketeers*

7. Peachum: I love to let Women scape. A
good Sportsman always lets the Partridges
fly, because the breed of the Game depends upon them —John Gay, *The Beggar's Opera*, Act 1, scene 2
> The image of man as the hunter and women the
> prey pre-dates Gay's play.

8. Peachum: My Daughter to me should be,
like a Court Lady to a Minister of State, a
Key to the whole Gang —John Gay, *The
Beggar's Opera*, Act 1, scene 4
> Gay's contemporaries would have recognized
> Peachum as Robert Walpole, the prime minister.
> The simile impeaches Walpole; the metaphor
> condemns the court itself.

9. I hate the man who builds his name / On ruins of another's fame —John Gay, *Fables,* "The Poet and the Rose"

10. She had quarreled with him often, perhaps to starch up a certain rumpled softness in him —John Hersey, "The Announcement," *The Atlantic,* October 1989

11. [Husbands' tempers] . . . rendered pliant and malleable in the fiery furnace of domestic tribulation —Washington Irving, "Rip Van Winkle"

    Homes ruled by termagant wives drive many a village man to the local pub in Irving's story of the town's most hen-pecked husband, Rip Van Winkle. The most famous of all was Socrates' wife Xantippe.

12. Asleep is Bertram, that bronze boy, / Who, having wound her around a spool, / Sends her spinning like a toy —Donald Justice, "In Bertram's Garden"

    The metaphor of a top is obvious, but in using "toy" Justice makes it equally obvious that Bertram has toyed with the girl's affections.

13. I *will* resent my heart having been made a football —John Keats, Letter to Fanny Brawne, 1820

14. And let no one oppose my opinion in this by quoting the trite proverb, "He who builds on the people, builds on mud" —Niccolo Machiavelli, *The Prince*

    The proverb may have been trite in the sixteenth century, but fashions in triteness change, and the metaphor seems newly-minted in the twentieth century.

15. [She felt the young man was] warm, healthy young wax that one can manipulate and mold till its shape suits your pleasure —Vladimir Nabokov, *King, Queen, Knave*

16. Hamlet: You would play upon me; you would seem to know my stops; you would pluck out the heart of my mystery; you would sound me from my lowest note to the top of my compass —William Shakespeare, *Hamlet,* Act 3, scene 2, line 367

Hamlet is not about to relinquish the mystery of his inner self.

17. To succeed in chaining the multitude, you must seem to wear the same fetters —Voltaire, *Philosophical Dictionary*

18. Women who adore their husbands throw a thousand little ropes around them. They rob them of their freedom. They lull them to sleep —Thornton Wilder, *The Eighth Day*

    Many modern women making it argue that many a husband has been known to use such ropes, as much a male as a female trait.

■ **MANKIND**

See: HUMANITY/HUMANKIND; LIFE

■ **MANNERS**

1. Politeness is a guilt-edged investment that seldom misses a dividend —Minna Antrim, *Naked Truth and Veiled Allusions*

2. He has rough corners, craggy edges —Louis Auchincloss, "A Diary of New York," *Three Lives*

    Such types are atypical of the well-bred, socialites who inhabit Auchincloss' fiction.

3. Politeness, that cementer of friendship and soother of enmities —Lady Marguerite Blessington, *The Repealers*

4. They write that you are . . . tolerably well-bred; and that the English crust of awkward bashfulness, shyness, and roughness . . . is pretty well rubbed off —Earl of Chesterfield (Phillip Dormer Stanhope), Letter to his natural son, March 6, 1747

5. It [good form] has grown up like callous shell round two fine ideals—suppression of the ego lest it trample on the corns of other people, and exaltation of the maxim: "Deeds before words" —John Galsworthy, "American and Briton"

    A simile serves as a stepstool for the metaphor of the stepped-on toe.

6. Without a doubt good form had become a kind of disease in England —John Galsworthy, "American and Briton"

"The English hardly ever say just what comes into their heads," writes Galsworthy.

7. Beatrice: Courtesy itself must convert to disdain, if you come in her presence. / Benedick: Then is courtesy a turncoat —William Shakespeare, *Much Ado About Nothing,* Act 1, scene 1, line 128

8. Cecily: This is no time for wearing the shallow mask of manners —Oscar Wilde, *The Importance of Being Earnest,* Act 2

■ MANY

See also: ABUNDANCE

1. An abundant shower of curates has fallen upon the north of England —Charlotte Brontë, *Shirley*

2. [Alexander Woollcott:] His anecdotes came not singly but in dynasties. He approached his main story through a labyrinth of lesser ones —John Mason Brown, Introduction, *The Portable Woollcott*

3. [*The New Grove Dictionary of Opera:*] Its ocean of inclusions will mean so much and so little to so many different people — Bernard Holland, "Critic's Notebook," *The New York Times,* January 2, 1993

4. The Croisette [in Cannes, France] was planted with a forest of posters —Peter Mayle, *Toujours Provence*

5. In a dream I returned to the river of bees —William Stanley Merwin, "The River of Bees"

Merwin's poem is a reflection on mortality. He thinks back to his childhood and remembers a blind singer who had long since died.

6. Every morning a snowy avalanche of manuscripts swelled the dust-gray piles in the office of the Fiction Editor —Sylvia Plath, *The Bell Jar*

7. I have not read every word in the hurricane of statements made by President Bush and Governor Bill Clinton —Herbert Stein, Op-Ed, *The New York Times,* September 21, 1992

■ MARRIAGE

See also: CHARACTERIZATIONS; COMMITMENT; DIVORCE; HUSBANDS AND WIVES; LOVE; LUST; MEN AND WOMEN; PERMANENCE/IMPERMANENCE; TREACHERY

1. Marriage . . . the hospital of love —Anon., German Proverb

2. Marriage . . . a fever in reverse: it starts with heat and ends with cold —Anon., German Proverb

3. A wife and a floor mat are good when fresh and new —Anon., Japanese Proverb

This sexist Japanese proverb is counterbalanced by another Japanese proverbial metaphor that says "A wife and a kettle get better as they grow older."

4. Marriage is the scud missile of relationships —Anon. proverb, quoted on *Murphy Brown,* aired April 13, 1992

5. A pretty wife is half a livelihood —Anon., Yiddish Proverb

6. Libbie had married a comfortable, wise old dog, the kind who always turned out to have large reserves of understanding and humanity —Saul Bellow, *Herzog*

7. Marriage is a trap that men set for themselves, then bait, and then deliberately get into, and then—GROWL —Josh Billings

8. Love-matches are made by people who are content, for a month of honey, to condemn themselves to a life of vinegar — Lady Marguerite Blessington, *The Victims of Society*

9. Belinda: Courtship . . . a very witty Prologue to a very dull Play. —William

Congreve, Belinda, *The Old Bachelor*, Act 5, scene 1

> *This is a retort to Bellmour's image of courtship as "the music in the play-house till the curtain's drawn; but that once up, then opens the scene of pleasure."*

10. Wedlock's a lane where there is no turning —Dinah Mulock Craik, *Magnus and Morna*

11. Marriage . . . a lottery in which men stake their liberty and women their happiness —Renée de Chateauneuf Rieux

12. Rilke had begun to slip out of the knot of his marriage in the moment that he tied it —William H. Gass

13. [Air] Polly: No Power on Earth can e'er divide, / The Knot that Sacred Love hath ty'd —John Gay, *The Beggar's Opera*, Act 2, scene 14

> *Getting married is still often described as* tying the knot.

14. A husband who stands by his wife while she climbs the corporate ladder is dutifully dubbed "supportive." But when she jumps out of the marriage she remembers him as the ball and chain rather than the helium of her ascent —Ellen Goodman, "In sickness and in wealth," *The Boston Globe*, August 14, 1992

> *The crux of Goodman's article is that "from the front lines of divorce" we are learning that working couples were always "keeping books on each other."*

15. He would marry and go into harness . . . he would be a subject animal now —D. H. Lawrence, "The Horse Dealer's Daughter"

> *A young man reflects on his family's waning fortune and the prospect of now having to rely on his fiancée's family for his livelihood.*

16. He had the good fortune even to sail safely through those perilous, unquiet straits of marriage in which so many wise and good men have made shipwreck —W. Somerset Maugham, "The Treasure,"

17. They had . . . endured the misery of . . . the fiber by fiber . . . destruction of the fabric of married love —Carson McCullers, *The Ballad of the Sad Cafe*

18. Mariane: Can you not imagine the fears of a girl about to see the rack on which she is to be bound? —Molière, *The Miser*, Act 3

> *The "rack" is Mariane's impending marriage to the father of the man she loves.*

19. A marriage aged one / . . . A green horse, / A stiff course, / And miles to be run — Ogden Nash, "The Anniversary"

> *Nash takes his readers from the first to the twenty-first anniversary.*

20. Marriage: a souvenir of love —Helen Rowland, *Reflections of a Bachelor Girl*

> *Rowland, known for her many one-liners, preceded this with: "Love the quest. Marriage the conquest. Divorce the inquest."*

21. Marriage the wastepaper basket of the emotions —Bertrand Russell, *Portraits from Memory*

22. In their youth divorce had been a germ confined to movie stars and misfits — Lynne Sharon Schwartz, "The Subversive Divorce," *The Melting Pot*

23. Portia: Dwell I but in the suburbs / Of your good pleasure? If it be no more, / 'Portia is Brutus' harlot, not his wife — William Shakespeare, *Julius Caesar*, Act 2, scene 1, line 285

> *Brutus is the strong, silent type who does not want to confide in his wife, but Portia insists upon sharing his burdens.*

24. Benedick: Go to i'faith, an thou wilt needs thrust thy neck into a yoke, wear the print of it, and sigh away Sundays —William Shakespeare, *Much Ado About Nothing*, Act 1, scene 1, line 210

> *Benedick may mock marriage, but "In time the savage bull doth bear the yoke," says Don Pedro, predicting Benedick's fall.*

25. Iago: I do suspect the lustful Moor / Hath leaped into my seat —William Shakespeare, *Othello*, Act 2, scene 1, line 290

Iago, in his casting about for reasons to justify his hatred of Othello, accuses him of adultery. "For I fear Cassio with my night-cap too," he continues. Except when it is impugned by Iago, Emilia's honesty is never called into question.

26. Capulet: I'll have this knot knit up tomorrow morning —William Shakespeare, *Romeo and Juliet*, Act 4, scene 2, line 24
    Capulet, determined that Juliet will marry as he wishes, is using a variation of to tie the knot, a metaphor that gained currency in the thirteenth century. In another Elizabethean drama, The Maid's Tragedy by Francis Beaumont and John Fletcher, a character named Melantius says "may the holy knot / That thou hast tied to-day, last till the hand / Of age undo it!"

27. Sir Peter Teazle: 'Tis now six months since Lady Teazle made me the happiest of men,—and I have been the most miserable dog ever since! —Richard Brinsley Sheridan, *The School for Scandal*, Act 1, scene 2

28. Sir Oliver Surface [commenting on a man who had been married only seven months]: Then he has been just half a year on the stool of repentance! —Richard Brinsley Sheridan, *The School for Scandal*, Act 2, scene 3

29. It seems to me that marriage is a small container . . . barely large enough to hold some children. Two inner lives, two life-long meditations of whatever complexity, burst out of it and out of it, cracking it, deforming it —Jane Smiley, *The Age of Grief* in *The Quarterly*, Vol 1, Spring 1987
    A man thus reflecting on his reconciliation with his unfaithful wife.

30. [After marriage] . . . no more by-path meadows, where you may innocently linger, but the road lies long and straight and dusty to the grave —Robert Louis Stevenson, *Virginibus Puerisque*

31. All around them, as he and his wife stood hip-deep in children, marriages blew up —John Updike, "Playing With Dynamite," *The New Yorker*, October 5, 1992

32. Once more it was borne in on him that marriage was not the safe anchorage he had been taught to think, but a voyage on uncharted seas —Edith Wharton, *The Age of Innocence*
    And so it still is!

33. In all probability she had moved off across the matrimonial chess-board at the same rate of progression as her first husband —Edith Wharton, *The Children*

34. Pauline herself could conceive of nothing more shocking than a social organization which did not recognize divorce, and let all kinds of domestic evils fester undisturbed instead of having people's lives disinfected and whitewashed at regular intervals, like the cellar —Edith Wharton, *Twilight Sleep*
    Wharton tacks a simile to the end of her metaphor. Pauline's belief is a sham for, though she divorced her first husband, she's blind to the emotional dust stirring around the corners of her second marriage.

35. The pair [a couple married for two years] were beginning to be regarded as one of the 'old couples' of their set, one of the settled landmarks in the matrimonial quicksands of New York —Edith Wharton, *Twilight Sleep*
    Unlike the indissoluble marriages of the author's youth, marriages in the late twenties were founded on much less durable foundations.

36. Lady Bracknell: You could hardly imagine that I and Lord Bracknell would dream of allowing our only daughter . . . to marry into a cloakroom, and form an alliance with a parcel —Oscar Wilde, *The Importance of Being Earnest*, Act 1
    The "parcel" was a gentleman who had been misplaced, in a handbag, in Victoria Station by a careless nursemaid.

■ MARTYRDOM

See: ENDINGS

■ MASCULINITY/FEMININITY

See: MEN AND WOMEN

■ MASOCHISM

See: PAIN AND SUFFERING; SELF-DESTRUCTIVENESS

■ MASTERY/SUBORDINATION

See also: CONTROL; EXPLOITATION; FAMILIES/FAMILY RELATIONSHIPS; MARRIAGE; MEN AND WOMEN; PEOPLE, INTERACTION; POLITICS/POLITICIANS; POWER

1. A poor man who takes a rich wife has a ruler, not a wife —Anon., Greek Proverb

2. Are you a cow? Then eat straw —Anon., Yiddish Proverb

3. And oh ye high flown quills that soar the Skies, / . . . This mean and unrefined ore of mine / Will make your glistring gold but more to shine —Anne Bradstreet, "The Prologue"

    Bradstreet is deferring, not just to better poets, but to men. In a line that will not endear her to feminists she writes "Men have precedency and still excel."

4. If I crushed her . . . conqueror I might be of the house; but the inmate would escape to heaven before I could call myself possessor of its clay dwelling-place —Charlotte Brontë, *Jane Eyre*

    Rochester has come to realize that it is Jane's indomitable spirit that he loves and not "her brittle frame" which feels in his hands like "a mere reed."

5. Dictators ride to and fro upon tigers which they dare not dismount. And the tigers are getting hungry —Winston Churchill, *While England Slept*

    *Churchill's metaphor is a twist on an old proverb, He who rouses a sleeping tiger exposes him-*self to danger. *In his 1961 inaugural address, President John F. Kennedy gave new life to the metaphor with "We shall . . . remember that, in the past, those who foolishly sought power by riding the back of the tiger ended up inside."*

6. Women have bent to the yoke, and the scars of their endurance are upon their children —Agnes DeMille, "The Milk of Paradise"

7. Rameses: Then get / Yourself another heir, and make him eat / Your black bread of policy —Christopher Fry, *The Firstborn*, Act 2, scene 2

    "Black bread" may indicate bad or moldy bread—or perhaps simply the coarse bread of poverty. In this context, obviously it is associated with something foreboding.

8. You seeled me with your love, / . . . The habit of your words / Has hooded me —Thom Gunn, "Tamer and Hawk"

    The persona is a hawk who, literally, loves his master blindly: the hawk's eyes have been seeled, sewn up with thread, as was the practice in falconry.

9. Here is love's true anatomy: / His rib is gone; he'll have her heart —John Hollander, "The Lady's-Maid Song"

    Because of the loss of Adam's rib, man is constantly trying for mastery over woman. "So women bear the debt alone," writes Hollander, ". . . For though we throw the dog his bone, He wants it back with interest."

10. Firmly seated now, all reins in his hand, Macquarie begins the inchmeal conversion of a jail into a colony —Robert Hughes, *The Fatal Shore*

    The British proconsul sent to run New South Wales tries to clean up the mess his predecessors had allowed.

11. My father once cruelly and accurately referred to Fred and his mother as monkey and organ-grinder, saying Fred would dance to her tune —Calvin Kentfield, "The Bell of Charity," *The New Yorker*

12. He dictated to her, she slaved for him and adored him, and the whole thing went on

wheels —D. H. Lawrence, "Two Blue Birds"

13. Though he labored to extricate his fate from hers, he was already a plucked bird, greased, and ready for frying —Bernard Malamud, "Still Life"

14. Little by little, I felt the leash pulling on my neck, and I wanted to be free —André Maurois, "For Pianao Alone"

   The dog on a leash metaphor is popular for picturing relationships of mastery and subservience. In "The Letters" Maurois uses a variant for a woman who says her lover "kept me on a very tight leash, for no reason except to prove his own power."

15. You fell right into the blueprint of *his* life and gave up your own —Terry McMillan, *Waiting to Exhale*

16. Basically, they're housebroken Southerners —John Shelton Reed, *The New York Times*, January 24, 1993

   The Southern scholar was referring to Clinton and Gore.

17. The southern Democrats are in the saddle and the northern Democrats must tag along as best they may —Representative John Jacob Rodgers, Speech in the House, May 2, 1913

18. For 30 years I have submitted to the social dictatorship of silence that women always had to submit to or be put through shame —Mary Lee Settle, Op-Ed, *The New York Times*, October 17, 1992

   Ms. Settle revealed a long-ago rape and also a date rape experience. She wrote about the latter in a novel with the metaphorically apt title: The Clam Shell.

19. Cleopatra: Not being Fortune, he's but Fortune's knave, / a minister of her will —William Shakespeare, *Antony and Cleopatra*, Act 5, scene 1, line 3

20. Luciana: He is the bridle of your will —William Shakespeare, *The Comedy of Errors*, Act 2, scene 1, line 13

   To which Adriana replies "There's none but asses will be bridled so."

21. Coriolanus: Thus we debase / The nature of our seats, and make the rabble / Call our cares fears; which will in time break ope / The locks o' the senate, and bring in the crows / To peck the eagles —William Shakespeare, *Coriolanus*, Act 3, scene 1, line 134

   Coriolanus warns the senators, the eagles, to guard against being overtaken by the common people, the crows.

22. Don John: I had rather be a canker in a hedge than a rose in his grace —William Shakespeare, *Much Ado About Nothing*, Act 1, scene 3, line 28

   "If I had my mouth, I would bite," adds the evil Don.

23. Being your slave, what should I do but tend / Upon the hours and times of your desire? —William Shakespeare, "Sonnet 57," line 1

24. Edward: You are the fount that makes small brooks to flow; / Now stops thy spring, my sea shall suck them dry, / And swell so much the higher by their ebb —William Shakespeare, *The Third Part of Henry the Sixth*, Act 4, scene 8, line 54

   "Hence with him [Henry] to the Tower! let him not speak," continues Edward.

25. Olivia: If one should be a prey, how much the better / To fall before the lion than the wolf —William Shakespeare, *Twelfth Night*, Act 3, scene 1, line 132

   The lion is the noble Duke Orino; the wolf, the cruel Cesario.

26. Florizel: What I was, I am: / More straining on for plucking back; not following / My leash unwillingly —William Shakespeare, *The Winter's Tale*, Act 4, scene 4, line 477

   Florizel is ready to die.

27. I will not play the horse to your Lady Godiva —George Bernard Shaw, Quoted in Bennett Cerf's *Try And Stop Me*

Shaw supposedly said this to actress Ellen Terry
when she asked permission to publish the letters
Shaw had written to her.

28. Mickey [Burgess Meredith]: I coulda
starched any lightweight husky on the
East Coast —Sylvester Stallone, *Rocky*
*An ex-fighter describing his ability to knock out
an opponent when he "had the tools."*

■ **MATERIALISM**

See: PRUDENCE; RELIGION

■ **MATURATION**

*See also: BEING/BECOMING; TRANSFOR-
MATION*

1. A maize plant coming into flower —
Anon., Mayan expression
*This Mayan metaphor for a girl or boy approach-
ing marriage age represented one of the joys of
learning another language for archeologist J. Eric
Thompson (quoted in "Lost Cities of the Maya,"
by Claude Baudez and Sydney Picasso).*

2. Later on you get coated over. S'a good
thing to be coated over. You don't change
nothin' underneath —Enid Bagnold, *National Velvet*
*Velvet Brown's mother contemplates the inno-
cence of youth and the process of growing up.*

3. Oxford liberated him, uncorked the bot-
tled-up desires of his chaste adolescence
—Ronald Bryden, *The New York Times
Book Review*, November 7, 1993
*The man likened champagne bubbling forth from
an uncorked bottle to Tony Richardson, the theater and film luminary whose posthumous autobiography Bryden was reviewing. His impact on his
contemporaries was likened to that of a hurricane.*

4. Miriam: . . . he's ripping up the bare boards
/ His boyhood lay on, to make himself a
fire / Which will warm his manhood —
Christopher Fry, *The Firstborn*, Act 3, scene 1
*Miriam's son has suffered deprivation as a child,
and now his overweening ambition causes him to*

do things that his mother understands, but does
not approve.

5. The children are sleeping through fourth
grade / so as to be ready for what is
ahead, / the monumental boredom of
junior high / and the rush forward /
tearing their wings / loose and turning
their eyes forever inward —Philip Levine,
"Among Children"

6. This was a new bird taking wing. Jeannie
was leaving the nest, testing her feathers
—Ed McBain, *The Mugger*

7. [He] led his old chrysalis life from which
he was some day to emerge a resplendent
butterfly —George Meredith, *The Ordeal
of Richard Feverel*

8. We are not youth any longer. We don't
want to take the world by storm —Erich
Maria Remarque, *All Quiet on the Western
Front*
*The soldiers of Remarque's story are not only too
weary to literally take any enemy strongholds by
storm, but have lost their appetite for life after the
war. As a common metaphor to take by storm
refers to any sudden success or change. Charlotte
Brontë's Jane Eyre, for example, is shaken by
new ideas: "How I looked when these ideas were
taking my spirit by storm, I cannot tell."*

9. In the end, ceasing to be children, we all
become magicians without magic [like the
Wizard of Oz], exposed conjurers, with
only our simple humanity to get us through.
We are the humbugs now —Salman
Rushdie, [analysis of] *The Wizard of Oz*
*This passage ends Rushdie's essay on how the
movie classic, The Wizard of Oz, affected him.*

10. Viola: when wit and youth is come to
harvest, / Your wife is like to reap a
proper man —William Shakespeare,
Twelfth Night, Act 3, scene 1, line 135

11. She was laughing, she was all in a whirl—
a once neatly closed little pocket knife that
had suddenly sprung open with all its
blades —A. B. Yehoshua, *Mr. Mani*

A young girl attends a dance and instantly acquires poise.

rant —Oscar Wilde, *The Picture of Dorian Gray*

■ MEDIA

See: ARTS AND ENTERTAINMENT; JOURNALISM/JOURNALISTS

■ MEDIOCRITY

1. The slam-bang playoffs and the World Series, while falling somewhat short of last year's gaunt, Aeschylean dramas, were engrossing entertainment —Roger Angell, "The Sporting Scene: Shades of Blue," *The New Yorker,* December 7, 1992
   The theater metaphor alludes to the great Greek playwright of tragedies.

2. Thomas Hampson [a star of the operatic world] was replaced by Robert Frontali, a competent foot soldier and not much more —Bernard Holland, "Review/Music," *The New York Times,* November 24, 1992
   According to Holland, the 1992 Richard Tucker music gala had more vocal foot soldiers than generals.

3. What a dry meal of clichés without cream or sugar —Christopher Lehmann-Haupt, "Books of The Times," *The New York Times,* January 31, 1992
   Mr. Lehmann-Haupt's review was hardly the stuff to make the author's day.

4. She felt herself being ironed into glossy mediocrity —Sinclair Lewis, *Main Street*

5. Has America become a nation of short-hitters, of corporate managers who issue dividend checks at the expense of quality and innovation —Peter Passell, *The New York Times,* February 9, 1992
   Passell's article, metaphorically titled "Economic Myopia" questioned whether Japan has a better economic vision.

6. My dear fellow, she tried to open a *salon* and only succeeded in opening a restau-

■ MEDITATION

See: THINKING/THOUGHT

■ MELANCHOLY

See: DESPAIR; EMOTIONS; GLOOM

■ MEMORY/MEMORIES

See also: ILLUSION/REALITY; PAST

1. And Memory . . . / With noiseless hand unwinds her lengthy scroll —Maurice Baring, "Remembrance"

2. All the pictures that hung in my memory before I knew you have faded and given place to our radiant moments together —Sarah Bernhardt, Love letter to Victorian Sardou

3. He [Alexander Woollcott] had a ruminative mind. It was a samovar of memories —John Mason Brown, Introduction, *The Portable Woollcott*

4. In our minds we've . . . watered the ever-green images of happiness . . . crisply lopped off the more gnarled, ill-shaped moments —Ken Chowdern, "Aegean Idyll: Was It *Really* That Good?" *The New York Times,* June 20, 1993
   The writer reflected on the way travellers tend to edit their experiences.

5. In plucking the fruit of memory one runs the risk of spoiling its bloom —Joseph Conrad, *The Arrow of Gold*

6. His memory lifted its skirt over this bad patch and hurried convulsively —Noel Coward, "Traveller's Joy"

7. Along the brittle treacherous bright streets / of memory comes my heart, . . . / whispering like a drunken man / who (at a certain corner, suddenly) meets / the

tall policeman of my mind —e. e. cummings, "along the brittle treacherous bright streets"

8. Their memories: a heap of tumbling stones, / Once builded stronger than a city wall —Babette Deutsch, "Old Women"

9. In the summer of 1963 . . . [Martin Luther King] forever etched into public memory the eloquent words of his Washington "I have a dream" oration —Michael Eric Dyson, "King's Light, Malcolms's Shadow," *The New York Times,* January 18, 1993

10. Most [of what I remember] is probably filtered through the blown circuits of confusion and madness and is, I suppose, artful forgery, rigged document, a knocked-off passport of the soul —Stanley Elkin, "Out of One's Tree," *Harper's,* January 1933

11. Why drag about this corpse of your memory, lest you contradict somewhat you have stated in this or that public place? —Ralph Waldo Emerson, "Self Reliance"
    Emerson says that consistency is a "terror that scares us from self-trust," and is not important to truth.

12. Doctor Diver . . . sometimes looked back with awe at the carnivals of affection he had given, as a general might gaze upon a massacre he had ordered to satisfy an impersonal blood lust —F. Scott Fitzgerald, *Tender Is the Night*
    The interlocked metaphor and simile picture a man who undercuts his serious aspirations by expending excess effort to charm women into loving him.

13. Hoel: She has caught / An echo that booms in the deepest cave of my race —Christopher Fry, *Thor, With Angels*
    A Christian prisoner in the land of the pagan Jutes has just heard the name of Merlin spoken.

14. She had raised the drawbridge between her heart and memory, leaving the lonely thoughts to shiver desolately on the other side of the moat —Frances Noyes Hart, "Contact," *Contact and Other Stories*
    The drawbridge is drawn to shut out painful memories of a fiance killed in the war.

15. Belle: I'm not going to bathe his memory in sunshine —Ronald Harwood, *Another Time,* Act 1, scene 4
    The just-widowed Belle is not going to pretend that her marriage was not fraught with problems and that her husband was a constant source of disappointment to her.

16. For the mind to adventure on its half-hidden path / . . . Journeying backwards on a winter trip —Anthony Hecht, *The Venetian Vespers*

17. Memory is a net; one finds it full of fish when he takes it from the brook; but a dozen miles of water have run through it without sticking —Oliver Wendell Holmes, *The Autocrat of the Breakfast-Table*

18. She rarely took the recollection out of its pushed-back corner in her mind —Norah Hoult, "Mrs. Johnson," *Poor Women*

19. Perhaps people were progressively harder to paint in the mind as they were near one, loved by one —Kawabata Yasunari, *A Thousand Cranes*

20. Memory is a storm I can't repel —Dilys Laing, "The Double Ghost"

21. Now, buried under tons of years, / my eye of sense still sees / that mound coiled full of bright shining new ears —Richmond Lattimore, "The Korean Mound at Peitaiho"
    When the speaker was five years old, someone told him a mound was full of Korean ears cut off in a battle with the Chinese.

22. The mystic chords of memory, stretching from every battlefield, and patriotic grave . . . will yet swell the chorus of the Union, when again touched, as surely they will be, by the better angels of our nature. —

Abraham Lincoln, Inaugural Address, March 4, 1861

This powerful double metaphor marked the closing of Lincoln's speech. It was actually a rewrite of a passage submitted to him by William H. Seward who considered Lincoln's original was too war-like.

23. My brother, / I've saved you in the ice-house of my mind —Robert Lowell, "Her Dead Brother"

24. Old age begins when you open the trap-doors of memory —Artur Lundkvist, *Journeys in Dream and Imagination*

25. Behind the eyes was a card-index brain that contained the vital statistics of Los Angeles —Ross MacDonald, *The Moving Target*

26. She felt mugged by memory, suddenly — Sue Miller, *For Love*

27. On the switchboard of my memory two pairs of gloves crossed wires—those leather gloves of Omi's and a pair of white ceremonial gloves —Mishima Yukio, "Omi"

The gloves represent an older boy for whom the narrator has a schoolboy crush.

28. No good-luck charm / to stand against the hurricanes / battering the spiderweb of memory —Eugenio Montale, "Little Testament"

29. His memory opened its gallery of wax-works, and he knew, he knew that there, at its far end somewhere a chamber of horrors awaited him —Vladimir Nabokov, *King, Queen, Knave*

30. Franz would appear gesticulating wildly at the wrong telescope end of his mind — Vladimir Nabokov, *King, Queen, Knave*

Memory comes back to Franz unbidden and only at inconvenient times.

31. Pictures pass me in long review— / Marching columns of dead events —Dorothy Parker, "Ballade at Thirty-Five," *Enough Rope*

32. My galley charged with forgetfulness / Through sharp seas in winter nights doth pass / . . . and every oar, a thought in readiness —Francis Petrarch, "Sonnet 156, In Vita Di Madonna Laura"

Petrarch wrote 227 sonnets to Laura in this sequence.

33. All that she had, and all that she had missed, were lost together, and were twice lost in this landslide of remembered losses —Katherine Anne Porter, "Theft"

In the process of forcing the man who stole her purse to return it, a woman also comes to realize "I was right not to be afraid of any thief but myself, who will end up leaving me nothing."

34. [When one is old] the map in one's head . . . empties and loses its contours —V. S. Pritchett, "On the Edge of the Cliff"

"The protective faces of friends vanish and one is suddenly alone, naked and exposed," Pritchett continues.

35. A society dependent on oral traditions and oral communications is, by our standard, a slow-paced one: there is time enough, for grownups as well as children, to roll back the carpet of memories — David Riesman, "Books: Gunpowder of the Mind"

Note the title of the essay for another metaphor.

36. My memory, my prison —Theodore Roethke, *Straw for the Fire*

37. I have a little handkerchief bundle of re-members —Carl Sandburg, "New Hampshire Again," *Vanity Fair*

38. Her fierce mind works on the fabric of the past, ripping stitches, patching —Lynne Sharon Schwartz, "The Melting Pot"

39. "It don't hurt," he said, and gave me a smile that I shall keep in my safety-deposit box at the bank until the day I die — Richard Selzer, "Toenails," *Letters to a Young Doctor*

40. Iachimo: Why should I write this down that's riveted, / Screw'd to my memory?

—William Shakespeare, *Coriolanus*, Act 2, scene 2, line 43

41. Hamlet: From the table of my memory / I'll wipe away all trivial fond records, / All saws of books, all forms, all presures past, / That youth and observation copied there —William Shakespeare, *Hamlet*, Act 1, scene 5, line 98

42. Lady Macbeth: Memory, the warder of the brain, / Shall be a fume, and the receipt of reason —William Shakespeare, *Macbeth*, Act 1, scene 7, line 65

43. When to the sessions of sweet silent thought / I summon up remembrance of things past —William Shakespeare, "Sonnet 30," line 1

 The image concerns a court of justice, where remembrance is "summoned" to the "sessions." Marcel Proust later added luster to the phrase "remembrance of things past" by using it as the title of his great work.

44. How could a man who was the lodestar of all my impulses for five years have been so thoroughly drowned in the black lakes of forgetting? —Kate Simon, *Etchings in an Hourglass*

45. I can imagine what he probably chose never to remember . . . This is the gleaming obsidian shard I safeguard above all the others —Jane Smiley, *A Thousand Acres*

46. Duke: Far, far away where sleeps the heron of forgetfulness, with head beneath his wing —August Strindberg, *Swanwhite*

47. I stared at the texture wondering why it spoke to me so strongly, in the smoky cave of lost time —John Updike, "First Things First," *Art & Antiques*

 The author comes across an old fur-trimmed coat as he sifts through his recently deceased mother's possessions.

48. Archer hung a moment on a thin thread of memory, but it snapped and floated off with the disappearing face —Edith Wharton, *The Age of Innocence*

 Archer has the common experience of seeing someone he feels he has met before, but unable to connect the sense of recognition with a concrete memory

49. The visible world is a daily miracle for those who have eyes and ears; and I still warm my hands thankfully at the old fire, though every year it is fed with the dry wood of more old memories —Edith Wharton, *A Backward Glance*

 The image concludes Wharton's autobiography.

50. Young as she is, the stuff / Of her life is a great cargo —Richard Wilbur, "The Writer"

 The poet is listening to the sound of his daughter's typing as she writes a story. He wishes her "a lucky passage."

51. Miss Prism: Memory, my dear Cecily, is the diary that we all carry about with us —Oscar Wilde, *The Importance of Being Earnest*, Act 2

52. She unwound her ball of memories —Virginia Woolf, *To the Lighthouse*

53. My Galley Charged with forgetfulness / Thorough (through) sharp seas, in winter nights, doth pass. —Sir Thomas Wyatt, the Elder, "My Galley"

 Wyatt continues metaphorically, "And every oar a thought in readiness."

∎ MEN AND WOMEN

See also: CONFLICT; DOMINANCE; ENTRAPMENT; LOVERS' DECLARATIONS AND EXCHANGES; MARRIAGE; MASTERY/ SUBORDINATION; PEOPLE, INTERACTION; PERSONALITY PROFILES; CONFLICT

1. Man is fire; woman is firewood; the devil comes along and blows on them —Anon., Spanish Proverb

2. Woman is the chain by which man is attached to the chariot of folly —Bhartrihari, "The Sringa Satak"

3. That at a revel whan that I see you daunce / It is an oinement unto my wounde —Geoffrey Chaucer, "To Rosamond,"

   When the beloved dances at a party, it is an ointment to the wound of love that has been inflicted on the poet.

4. He had lifted some cloud from around her —Laurie Colwin, "Intimacy" *The Lone Pilgrim*

   Even though it did not culminate in the perennial happy ending, the story's protagonist's affair resulted in her ability to enter another, more satisfactory relationship.

5. I don't know what was between Edna and me, just beached by the same tides when you get down to it —Richard Ford, "Rock Springs," *Esquire*, 1985

   It may not be much of a foundation for a relationship, but as the author observes "love has been built on frailer ground than that."

6. I conjure you by the chains I bear here to ease the weight of them —Heloise, Letter to Peter Abelard

   Heloise asks Abelard to write and reassure her of his love. The "chains" are those of her confinement in a convent.

7. To forgive or to be forgiven was for Kikuji a matter of being rocked in that wave, the dreaminess of the woman's body — Kawabata Yasunari, *A Thousand Cranes*

   In an expression of Oedipal longing, Kikuji cohabits with the woman who had been his dead father's mistress. The wave evokes the womb.

8. And he had that air of easy *aplomb* and good humour which is so becoming to a man, and which he only acquires when he is cock of his own little walk, made much of by his own hens —D. H. Lawrence, "Two Blue Birds"

   According to The Dictionary of Cliches, *one of the earliest uses of this common metaphor was in Randle Holme's* The Academy of Armoury *(1688): The Cock's Walk is the place where he is bred.*

9. Their meeting was an arabesque, orchestrated by a USO function . . . for veterans and widows —Gus Lee, *China Boy*

   The "dancers" are the protagonist's father, an aristocratic Chinese immigrant, and a Philadelphia socialite widow.

10. My tongue / . . . stroked and restroked your cheek / roughly until you said, "Cat" —Philip Levine, "My Grave"

11. We'll never understand each other, never; and it's madness for us . . . to lie together in a hot bed in a creepy room—enemies yoked —Sinclair Lewis, *Main Street*

   Carol Kennicott laments the state of her marriage.

12. She floats upon the river of his thoughts —Henry Wadsworth Longfellow, *The Spanish Student*, Act 1, scene 3

13. *She* was that glove that he held in his fingers —Katherine Mansfield, "A Dill Pickle"

   The glove is being stroked by the man she had dismissed.

14. His wife . . . was the order and arithmetic of this house of commerce, while he was the life of it through his joyous activity — Guy de Maupassant, "Ball-of-Fat"

   This was the author's first published story and regarded by many as one of his masterpieces.

15. On the wall of our life together hung a gun waiting to be fired in the final act —Mary McCarthy, *Intellectual Memoirs*

   McCarthy talks about the breakup of her relationship with Phillp Rahv.

16. These two were rapid falcons in a snare, / Condemned to do the flitting of the bat — George Meredith, "Thus Piteously Love Closed What He Begat"

   The title, which is also the first line, sums up the poem's theme, the failure of a relationship—specifically, Meredith's own marriage.

17. I come / From the deep bourn of your hand, / A stranger up from the sunned /

Sea of your eyes —William Stanley Merwin, "When I Came from Colchis"

The poet is "amazed" at the encounter with the woman who is never, in the poem, named Medea, though the title proclaims her.

18. She thought . . . of his reeling the girl in with his story. —Sue Miller, *For Love*

The protagonist overheard her twenty-year-old son use his life story as a means of seduction.

19. His buttonless shirt open to a knot at the waist exposed a chest she claimed as her own smooth pillow —Toni Morrison, *Jazz*

20. Wendi was slow-growth. Emilou was strictly Chapter Eleven —Bharati Murkherjee, "Fighting for the Rebound"

Compared with two women in his past, a mid-level financial adviser's current girlfriend, a Manila-born aristocrat, is "a hothouse orchid you worship but don't dare touch."

21. [A relationship:] It's all done, it is quiet and still, / a piece of old cheese too hard to chew —Marge Piercy, "Letter to be disguised as a gas bill," *4-Telling*

22. The last thing I wanted was infinite security and to be the place an arrow shoots off from —Sylvia Plath, *The Bell Jar*

This is how Plath's alter-ego explains why she never wanted to get married.

23. The struggle of the sexes is the motor of history —Alain Robbe-Grillet, *Djinn*

24. Roxanne: I ask for cream— / You give me milk and water —Edmond Rostand, *Cyrano de Bergerac*, Act 3

Roxanne, accustomed to Cyrano's powerful poetry, expresses her disappointment in Christian's words.

25. The man-to-woman mainspring . . . came as an unexpected revival . . . awaking some echo whose melody she could not quite recapture —Vita Sackville-West, *All Passion Spent*

The lady trying to recapture the "melody" is an 88-year-old woman.

26. Rosalind: Men are April when they woo, December when wed; maids are May when they are maids, but the sky changes when they are wives —William Shakespeare, *As You Like It*, Act 4, scene 1, line 147

27. Bassanio: ornament is but the guiled [guileful] shore / To a most dangerous sea . . . therefore, thou gaudy gold / Hard food for Midas, I will none of thee —William Shakespeare, *The Merchant of Venice*, Act 3, scene 2, line 97

Bassanio, rejecting false show, assures Portia "Thy plainness moves me more than eloquence."

28. Benedick: O God sir, here's a dish I love not. I cannot endure my Lady Tongue — William Shakespeare, *Much Ado About Nothing*, Act 2, scene 1, line 284

Benedick will soon be starved for Beatrice, the "dish" he now rejects.

29. Iago: Faith, he to-night hath boarded a land carrack: / If it prove lawful prize, he's made for ever —William Shakespeare, *Othello*, Act 1, scene 2

Winning Desdemona is compared to capturing a treasure ship.

30. Bianca: Am I your bird [target]? I mean to shift my bush —William Shakespeare, *The Taming of the Shrew* Act 5, scene 1, line 46

In this hunting metaphor, Bianca means to shift her cover.

31. The Sergeant: When men and women pick one another up just for a bit of fun, they find they've picked up more than they bargained for, because men and women have a top story as well as a ground floor, and you can't get to one without the other —George Bernard Shaw, *Too Good to Be True*, Act 3

32. Mark my words, the first woman who fishes for him, hooks him —William Makepeace Thackeray, *Vanity Fair*

The "fish" is Joseph Sedley, and the young lady who tries to "hook" him, Thackeray's heroine, Becky Sharp.

33. They never met again; she had been a false dawn —John Updike, "Baby's First Step," *The New Yorker*, July 27, 1992

34. Geoffrey: Love is love—gender is merely spare parts —Wendy Wasserstein, *The Sisters Rosensweig*
> *The observation is made by a bi-sexual character in Wasserstein's 1992 hit comedy drama.*

35. He held so many shares in his wife's personality, and his predecessors were his partners in the business —Edith Wharton, "The Other Two"
> *This wife's current husband, who happens to be an investment banker, continues "She was as easy as an old shoe—a shoe that too many feet had worn. Her elasticity was the result of tension in too many directions.*

36. The load of her accumulated impressions of him tilted up, and down poured in a ponderous avalanche all she felt about him —Virginia Woolf, *To the Lighthouse*

37. His immense self-pity, his demand for sympathy poured and spread itself in pools at her feet, and all she did . . . was to draw her skirts a little closer round her ankles, lest she should get wet —Virginia Woolf, *To the Lighthouse*

■ MERCY

See: FORGIVENESS

■ METAPHORS

See also: LANGUAGE

1. This wide garden of metaphors, of figures of speech, of elegances, is inhospitable to the least detail not strictly upholding of truth —Jorge Luis Borges, "The Aleph"

2. Embroidering a few metaphors on his pale convictions —Theodore Roethke, *Straw for the Fire, Notebooks of Theodore Roethke*

3. Masturbatory metaphors. Many people in Hollywood liberally sprinkle their speech with such expressions as, "The studio is jerking me off," or "It's down to the short strokes" —William Safire, *On Language*
> *The quotation is from a letter sent to Safire by Robert Bookman of Los Angeles, California.*

4. At this point—sometime in the 60s— plumbing metaphors merged with the surfing metaphor. "Down the drain" and the more recent "down the pipe" combined with the surfer slang to become "down the tube" —William Safire, *On Language*

5. We may assume with confidence that the metaphor will be turned around one day to apply to its opposite: "Sitting pretty" or "in the catbird seat" will have as a jocular synonym "between a marshmallow and a soft place" —William Safire, *On Language*

■ METAPHYSICS

See: PHILOSOPHY

■ MIAMI

See: CITYSCAPES

■ MICROCOSM/MACROCOSM

See: HUMANITY/HUMANKIND; THINKING/THOUGHT

■ MIDDLE AGE

See also: AGE/AGING; CHARACTERIZATIONS; PERSONALITY PROFILES

1. And what is middle age if not the home office of tired blood? —Russell Baker, "The Observer," *The New York Times*, January 23, 1993

Baker slyly reminds readers that the young generation who came into power with President Clinton is not so young, that real youth is closer to age seventeen, than the mid-forties.

2. And, indeed, at past forty-seven, the Baroness might have been preferred to her daughter by those who admire the setting sun —Honoré de Balzac, *Cousin Bette*

3. Perhaps middle-age is, or should be, a period of shedding shells, the shell of ambition, the shell of material accumulations and possessions, the shell of the ego —Anne Morrow Lindbergh, *Gift From the Sea*
   The shell is the metaphor that drives the book. Instead of simply telling readers "don't try to do too much" she writes "one cannot collect all the beautiful shells on the beach."

4. Let us, then, love the perfect day, / The twelve o'clock of life —Joaquin Miller, "The Sea of Fire"

5. Her fire [a woman at age 40] may be covered with ashes, but it is not extinguished —Mary Wortley Montagu, Letter, January 13, 1716

6. At the unsatisfying age of fifty-plus, Ruth Puttermesser . . . had bled out a wide tract of her life in the corridors of the Municipal Building —Cynthia Ozick, "Puttermeyser Paired," *The New Yorker*, 1990
   After Ozick's tragi-comedic protagonist decides to take a leave from her work as a lawyer / government official to contemplate her fate she becomes embroiled in her own version of George Eliot's romance with the poet George Lewes.

7. So thou, thyself outgoing in thy noon, / Unlooked on diest unless thou get a son —William Shakespeare, "Sonnet 7," line 13
   "Noon" is shorthand here for approaching middle age. There is a pun on the word "son" for sun, as the poet exhorts the beloved to have a child before she gets too old.

8. Middle age was not approaching on stealthy little cat feet this summer —Tennessee Williams, "Happy August 10th," *Anateus*, 1970

■ MIGRATION
See: MOVEMENTS

■ MIND
See also: BRAIN; FEELINGS; IMAGINATION; INTELLIGENCE; THINKING/THOUGHT

1. A little kingdom I possess, / Where thought and feeling dwell —Louisa May Alcott, "My Kingdom"
   According to the poet, this kingdom is no easy street but one she has difficulty "governing well."

2. My mind to me a kingdom is; / Such perfect joy therein I find —Anon., "In Praise of a Contented Mind"
   This poem was set to music by the Elizabethan composer William Byrd, and may have been written by either Sir Edward Dyer or by Edward de Vere, seventeenth Earl of Oxford.

3. Rich soils are often to be weeded —Sir Francis Bacon, Letter, c. 1607–17
   The letter urged a lawyer friend to spend less time laboring of what to say and concentrate on what to leave unspoken.

4. In the magazine we run many useful and sensible pieces of this kind, portages through the whirlpool country of the mind —Donald Barthelme, "Florence Green is 81"

5. Gird up the loins of your mind —The Bible, *N.T., 1 Peter 1:13*

6. In every voice, in every ban, / The mind-forg'd manacles I hear —William Blake, "The Tiger," *Songs of Experience*
   In an op-ed piece about the religious sect leader David Koresh, Jan Jarboe quoted Blake's metaphor to explain the "internal prison" which she saw as his real enemy. The piece was headlined "Manacles of the Mind."

7. Measure your mind's height by the shade it casts! —Robert Browning, "Paracelsus"

8. [His] mind was an exhaustless gallery of beautiful impressions —Willa Cather, "The Sculptor's Funeral," *Youth and the Bright Medusa*

9. A man should keep his little brain attic stocked with all the furniture that he is likely to use, and the rest he can put away in the lumber-room of his library, when he can get it if he wants it —Sir Arthur Conan Doyle, "Five Orange Pips," *The Adventures of Sherlock Holmes*

10. The mind has an idler switch, an automatic pilot. That is where the pretty inventions come from —Lawrence Durrell, *Monsieur or The Prince of Darkness*

11. So that was the set of tracks along which one's mind trundled —Nadine Gordimer, *Burger's Daughter*
    The novel's main character ponders how South African Blacks feel toward the whites who risk imprisonment on their behalf

12. My brain is blanketstitched —W. S. Graham, "Baldy Bane"
    This is a drinking song and it's a drink that has stitched up the brain.

13. I was also feeling the presence of many men whose names had been legends . . . already installed in an amphitheater of my mind —Norman Mailer, *Harlot's Ghost*

14. Your mind is made of crumbs —Edna St. Vincent Millay, "Aria Da Capo"

15. Aethelwold: The doors of my mind burst open from within, / And out throng the wild words —Edna St. Vincent Millay, *The King's Henchman*, Act 2
    "Thou fillest the still house of my mind / With a shrill din," Aethelwold says.

16. The mind, intractable thing / even with its own ax to grind, sometimes / helps others —Marianne Moore, "The mind, intractable thing"
    The common metaphor is used in a chatty poem, helping to set the informal tone.

17. The mind is but a barren soil—a soil which is soon exhausted, and will produce no crop, or only one, unless it be continually fertilized and enriched with foreign matter —Joshua Reynolds, *Discourses*

18. Your mind now, moldering like a wedding-cake, / . . . crumbling to pieces under the knife-edge / of mere fact. In the prime of your life —Adrienne Rich, "Snapshots of a Daughter-in-Law," *The Fact of a Doorframe: Poems Selected and New*
    The metaphor is dependent on the simile about the wedding cake.

19. Antony: We bring forth weeds / When our quick minds lie still —William Shakespeare, *Antony and Cleopatra* Act 1, scene 2, line 113

20. March: Yield not thy neck / To fortune's yoke, but let thy dauntless mind / Still ride in triumph over all mischance —William Shakespeare, *The Third Part of Henry the Sixth* Act 3, scene 3, line 15

21. Thersites: Would the fountain of your mind were clear again, that I might water an ass at it —William Shakespeare, *Troilus and Cressida* Act 3, scene 3, line 312

22. And thou, my mind, aspire to higher things; / Grow rich in that which never taketh rust —Sir Philip Sidney, "Leave Me, O Love"
    Sidney seeks only universal knowledge, not time-bound facts that will change when the times change.

23. Alas, like Dorian Gray, the true picture is hidden in the attic of the mind, locked and kept from view to all except wife, family, a few close friends and a plethora of medical men who daily struggle to keep the deadly radiation of neurosis from melting down and destroying this Proliflicity Plant —Neil Simon, Introduction to *The Collected Plays of Neil Simon*, Volume 2
    Simon's metaphor for the creative mind as power plant rests on a simile that alludes to Oscar Wilde's famous character. When Simon's ulcer acted up "The plant was immediately shut down and six hundred and twelve spicy foods and alcoholic beverages were laid off."

24. Uncultivated minds . . . villainous weeds grow in them and they are the haunt of toads —Logan Pearsall Smith, *Afterthoughts*

25. I went and sat in the roadster and let my mind out for a stroll to see if it would run across an idea for passing the time [until a person he wants to question is available — Rex Stout, *Fer-de-Lance*
    The mind personified as a stroller belongs to Archie Goodwin, the wise-cracking sidekick of private detective Nero Wolfe.

26. The intellect is a cleaver; it discerns and rifts its way into the secret of things — Henry David Thoreau, "Where I Lived, and What I Lived For"

27. The mind's a musical instrument with a certain range of tones, beyond which in both directions we have an infinitude of silence —John Tyndall, *Fragments of Science for Unscientific People, II*

28. A young mind . . . that remained a kind of cold storage from which anything which had been put there could be taken out at a moment's notice, intact but congealed — Edith Wharton, "The Mission of Jane," *Crucial Instances*

29. Waken to the myriad cinquefoil / In the waving grass of your minds! —William Carlos Williams, "Abroad"

30. The statue stood / Of [Isaac] Newton . . . / The marble index of a mind forever voyaging through strange seas of thought, alone —William Wordsworth, "The Prelude"

31. The balloon of the mind . . . / bellies and drags in the wind —William Butler Yeats, "The Balloon of the Mind"

32. What tumbling cloud did you cleave, / Yellow-eyed hawk of the mind / Last evening? —William Butler Yeats, "The Hawk"
    The seeking, predatory mind can cleave the upper reaches of the imagination, of knowledge, like a hawk stooping at incredible speed.

■ MIRACLES

See: RELIGION

■ MISANTHROPY

See: HATE

■ MISERY

See: PAIN AND SUFFERING

■ MISFORTUNE

See: FORTUNE/MISFORTUNE

■ MISOGYNY

See: NAME CALLING

■ MISTAKES

See also: EVIL; FORGIVENESS; SENSITIVITY; SIN/REDEMPTION

1. The mistakes of a learned man are a shipwreck which wrecks many others as it goes down —Anon., Arabian Proverb

2. Sending forces here [to Sarajevo] would be to plunge into a cesspool of atavism and vengeance —John F. Burns, "The World," *The New York Times*, January 17, 1973

3. Perhaps we had put our finger on an open wound which should not have been touched —Shusaku Endo, *Silence*
   The missionaries had questioned a man who was suppressing visions of the torture of his colleagues.

■ MISTRUST

See also: DOUBT

1. Bassanio: None but that ugly treason of mistrust, / Which makes me fear th' enjoying of my love —William Shake-

speare, *The Merchant of Venice*, Act 3, scene 2, line 28

> *Bassanio thus replies to Portia's demand to confess what treason is mingled with his love.*

2. All of us when we are starting out in life have our special demons ... who try to lure us forever into dark labyrinths of cynical distrust —Yevgeny Yevtushenko, *A Precocious Autobiography*

■ MISUNDERSTANDINGS

See: QUARRELS/QUARRELSOMENESS

■ MIXTURE

See also: DIVERSITY

1. [Under federal program reform:] A clear division of labor would replace today's haphazard "marble cake" approach —Michael Horowitz, Op-Ed, *The New York Times*, November 24, 1992

2. The play [*Wonderful Tennessee* by Brian Friel] is a brilliantly notated fugue of laughter and lament —John Lahr, "The Theatre," *The New Yorker*, July 19, 1993

> *The critic's praise, notwithstanding, the play wasn't wonderful enough to make a successful run.*

3. My father was ... a salad of racial genes —Vladimir Nabokov, *Lolita*

> *The concept of the mixed salad has become a popular metaphor for America's multiracial society.*

4. When Mr. Wolfe [George C.] gets both of the play's couples on stage simultaneously to enact their parallel, overlapping domestic crackups, *Angels in America* becomes a wounding fugue of misunderstanding and recrimination committed in the name of love —Frank Rich, "Review/Theater," *The New York Times*, May 5, 1993

5. Every American is a bouquet of special interests. Some just smell better to particular noses —A. M. Rosenthal, "On My Mind," *The New York Times*, December 15, 1992

> *Rosenthal commented on President-elect Clinton's appointment of many people representing powerful special interests, adding a list of his own.*

■ MOBILITY/IMMOBILITY

See also: ACTION/INACTION; GUIDANCE/GUIDES

1. Her legs seem suddenly to have been hammered into the ground beneath her —Julia Alvarez, *How the Garcia Girls Lost Their Accents*

2. When in effect told by Waltham, [a voter participant in the Presidential Debate], that his attacks on Clinton's character were hardly germane, he simply stopped in his tracks —Richard Cohen, *Washington Post Writers Group*, October 17, 1992

> *A sailing metaphor pointed out that George Bush had "had the wind taken out of his sails" when another debate participant put down his attacks on Bill Clinton.*

3. My limbs are glued to the earth —Erich Maria Remarque, *All Quiet on the Western Front*

4. Only by building a floating majority can he build the momentum—in any direction—to overcome his bete noir, gridlock; hence, "Forward *Together*" —William Safire, "Essay," *The New York Times*, September 6, 1993

> *Safire's column analyzed a Presidential speech that presented three policies for forward movement on a single "tripod" despite warnings of "legislative indigestion." The term gridlock, which entered the lexicon somewhere in the mid–1970s, has zoomed into the fast lane as a political metaphor for inaction.*

5. Sebastian: Well, I am standing water. / Antonio: I'll teach you how to flow —William Shakespeare, *The Tempest* Act 2, scene 1, line 225

> *Sebastian is poised to become a conspirator against the life of Prospero. Though unwilling to make the*

first move, he is ready to be taught to "flow" by Antonio.

■ **MODERATION**

See: CAUTION; PRUDENCE

■ **MODESTY**

See: CHARACTERISTICS

■ **MONEY**

See also: CHARACTERIZATIONS; ECONOMICS; RICHES

1. Money should be your servant, not your master —Anon., Proverb

2. Money is an eel in the hand —Anon., Welsh Proverb
   This is a variation of the simile slippery as an eel *for an elusive or* hard-to-pin-down *person.*

3. Money is great soap—it removes almost any stain —Anon., Yiddish Proverb

4. His faith in money as the circulating blood to sustain an otherwise presumably purposeless humanity seemed his only creed —Louis Auchincloss, "The Stoic"

5. Five thousand pounds stewing gently in its interest, making old age safe —Marjorie Barnard, "The Lottery"
   A husband reflects on how he will invest his wife's unexpected lottery win—only to discover that she has plans of her own.

6. Ready money is Aladdin's lamp —George Gordon Byron, "Advice to Young Man"

7. To you, my purs, and to noon other wight / Complaine I, for ye be my lady dere — Geoffrey Chaucer, "Complaint to His Purse"
   Chaucer makes his complaint to his purse. She is his dear lady, but she is "light" and he threatens

that she will be the death of him if she doesn't get heavy again.

8. The sinews of war, unlimited money — Marcus Tullius Cicero

9. Man's the elm / and Wealth the vine; / Stanch and strong the tendrils twine — Ralph Waldo Emerson, "Compensation," *Essays: First Series*

10. Money is another kind of blood —Ralph Waldo Emerson, "Wealth," *Conduct of Life*

11. A vast reversal of values has taken place . . . money is our country now. We go where it goes —William H. Gass, "Exile," *Salmagundi*

12. Peachum: But Money, Wife, is the true Fuller's Earth for Reputations, there is not a Spot or a Stain but what it can take out —John Gay, *The Beggar's Opera*, Act 1, scene 9
    "A rich Rogue now-a-days is fit Company for any Gentleman," says Peachum, in a bit of cynicism as true now as it was then. Rubbing a spot with fuller's earth was the eighteenth century equivalent to dry-cleaning.

13. La Flèche: In a word, he loves money more than reputation, than honor, than virtue, and the mere sight of anyone asking for money sends him into convulsions. It's a mortal wound. It pierces his heart. It rips out his entrails —Molière, *The Miser*, Act 2
    La Flèche is talking about Harpagon, the miser.

14. While waiting around my doctor's anteroom to have a swelling excised from my checkbook, I ran across an extremely informative article in a medical journal — Sidney Joseph Perelman, *Acres and Pains*
    Perelman here suits his metaphor to the setting that inspires it.

15. You can have the best Rolls Royce, but if you don't have gas the machine won't go —Benon Vahe Sevan, commenting on

the monetary crisis, at the United Nations NGO Briefing, September 25, 1993
> *What the United Nations needs to fill up the tank is the payment of back dues from delinquent member states. Right now it is running on empty.*

16. Falstaff: Money is a good soldier, sir, and will on —William Shakespeare, *The Merry Wives of Windsor* Act 2, scene 2, line 177

17. Iago: Who steals my purse, steals trash, 'tis something, nothing, / 'Twas mine, 'tis his, and has been slave to thousands— William Shakespeare, *Othello,* Act 3, scene 3, line 161
> *According to Iago, money is amoral and belongs to anyone who holds it.*

18. The view from those who sell investment products is that the Internal Revenue Service will reap a rich harvest next year — Calvin Sims, *The New York Times,* August 11, 1993
> *The popular farming metaphor was headlined with an equally familiar cowboy image: "Rich Aren't Stampeding to Avoid Higher Taxes."*

19. Money is the mother's milk of politics— and we've got plenty of mothers —Paul Tsongas, Quoted during radio broadcast, February 17, 1992
> *At the time Tsongas was on the presidential campaign trail.*

20. This happened all the time down here, money hopscotching across the planet — Scott Turow, *Pleading Guilty*
> *The story's intrigue is set on a fictional island where secret bank accounts are rampant.*

■ MONOTONY

See also: DULLNESS; ENTRAPMENT; LIFE; WORK/WORKERS

1. Her life was a chain of routines that varied only with the seasons —Isabel Allende, *Of Love and Shadows*

2. As shaken Post Office officials gathered information on the latest shootings in Michigan and California, some psychologists described much of postal work today as a treadmill of angry monotony, with labor-management hostility making many post offices mine fields of carefully nurtured grievances —Felicity Barringer, "Postal Officials Examine System After 2 Killings." *New York Times,* February, 8, 1993
> *To be perfectly logical, the setting that followed the treadmill metaphor should have been a gym rather than a war zone.*

3. My life was one long yawn —Mary Elizabeth Braddon, *Dead Sea Fruit*
> *The only reason this bored-by-life woman carries on is she did not know whether "perpetual ennui" might not be waiting for her on "Acheron's further shore."*

4. There were twenty-six of us [workers laboring away in the basement of a biscuit factory]—twenty-six living machines shut up in a damp cellar —Maxim Gorky, "Twenty-Six and One"
> *This picture of people reduced to automatons opens Gorky's powerful story. The workers' grim lives, writes Gorky, were "as grievous to us as if all the three upper stories of this house had been built right upon our very shoulders."*

5. The University of Winnemac [near Lewis' fictional city of Zenith] . . . is a mill . . . a Ford Motor Factory, and if its products rattle a little, they are beautifully standardized, with perfectly interchangeable parts —Sinclair Lewis, *Arrowsmith*

6. What one gapes at, hour after weary hour, is simply a performance of marionettes— worse, a performance of marionettes without heads—mere inanimate sticks —H. L. Mencken, *The Impossible H. L. Mencken*
> *This is Mencken's jaundiced view of the Republican convention.*

7. They were caught in the wheel from birth and they kept at it till death—and this treadmill they tried to dignify by calling it "life" —Henry Miller, "The Creative Life"

8. When One upon the dial looms / They hurry to their office tombs, / There to

hide in dust till five, / When they come again alive —Ogden Nash, "Dance Unmacabre"

The metaphor of the office as a tomb will hit home for anyone who's ever worked in a strictly controlled, routine job.

■ MOOD SWINGS

See: DARKNESS/LIGHT; OPTIMISM/ PESSIMISM

■ MOODS

See: EMOTIONS; FEELINGS

■ MOON

See also: DESCRIPTIONS, MISC.; NATURE SCENES; NIGHT AND DAY; SKY/ SKYSCAPES; SUN

1. Chorus: And the Moon in haste eclipsed her, and the Sun in anger swore / He would curl his wick within him and give light to you no more —Aristophanes, *The Clouds*

2. The thin gold shaving of the moon floating slowly downwards had lost itself on the darkened surface of the waters — Joseph Conrad, *Lord Jim*

3. Slowly, silently, now the moon / Walks the night in her silver shoon —Walter de la Mare, "Silver"

4. The moon . . . a circumambulating aphrodisiac divinely subsidized to provoke the world into a rising birthrate —Christopher Fry, *The Lady's Not For Burning*, Act 3

5. The moon beyond glass, / in a net of branches —Jim Harrison, "Three Night Songs"

6. We lie by towering hollyhocks / And watch the moon drip down the stalks / To spill on us from every leaf —Elizabeth B. Harrod, "August Night"

7. Moonlight is sculpture —Nathaniel Hawthorne, *American Notebooks*

8. A lean moon rode the lake in a silver boat —Zora Neale Hurston, "The Gilded Six-Bits"

9. The pale / thin cuticle of the mid-day moon —Philip Levine, "Snails"

10. The moon is but an emery-wheel — Vachel Lindsay, "The Scissors Grinder"

    The moon was a favorite object of comparison for Lindsay. In the poem "Yet Gentle will the Griffin Be" he writes, "The moon? It is a griffin's egg."

11. The moon's a steaming chalice / Of honey and venom-wine —Vachel Lindsay, "What Semiramis Said"

12. The moon comes, parting the curtain of a million misty pearls —Ryūhoku Narushima, "Niagara Falls"

13. The moon was a ghostly galleon tossed upon cloudy seas —Alfred Noyes, "The Highwayman"

14. The moon had left my window and crossed the lane . . . stopped over our roof and was feeling the sheets and vests on the clothesline —Amos Oz, *The Hill of Evil Counsel*

    Personification very aptly serves as metaphor since the scene is envisioned through the eyes of a child.

15. I stared, and a garden stone / Slowly became the moon —Theodore Roethke, "Words for the Wind I"

16. The only light in the sky is a moon so thinly carved as to have been a skin graft taken by a plastic surgeon —Richard Selzer, "Rounds"

    Here's a case of the shoemaker—in this case, the surgeon—sticking to his metaphoric last!

17. Lorenzo: How sweet the moonlight sleeps upon this bank! —William Shakespeare, *The Merchant of Venice* Act 5, scene 1, line 54

18. Timon: the moon's an arrant thief, / And her pale fire she matches from the sun — William Shakespeare, *Timon of Athens*, Act 4, scene 3, line 443

Nabokov used "pale fire" as a title for one of his novels.

19. Whether the Turkish new-moon minded be / To fill his horns this year on Christian coast —Sir Philip Sidney, "Sonnet 30," *Astrophel and Stella*

    Other poets have used 'horned' as a metaphor for the new moon. Sidney goes a step further and treats the horns as though they were a cornucopia.

20. With how sad steps, Oh Moon, thou climb'st the skies! —Sir Philip Sidney, "Sonnet 31," *Astrophel and Stella*

21. The moon is a sickle for pruning the stars —Jane Yolen, "The Old Woman Who Never Dies"

    The title of Yolen's poem for children is the Sioux name for the moon. In another line she pictures the moon as a "coin hung in the sky."

■ MORALITY/IMMORALITY

See also: GOOD/EVIL; POETRY/POETS; SIN/REDEMPTION

1. Prisons are built with stones of Law, Brothels with bricks of Religion —William Blake, "Proverbs of Hell"

    "The Proverbs of Hell," said Blake, "show the nature of Infernal wisdom;"—as this cynical equation demonstrates.

2. So you dare conclude / Because my verse is wanton that I'm lewd? . . . / Indeed, it will taste dry and dull unless / It's sauced and salted with licentiousness — Catullus, Poem 16

    The poet combines metaphor with synaesthesia, the use of terms to describe one sense that would be more appropriate to another. Here, taste replaces sight.

3. Voynitsky: It is thought immoral for a woman to deceive an old husband whom she hates, but quite moral for her to strangle her poor youth in her breast —Anton Chekhov, *Uncle Vanya*, Act 1

4. Anath: You had stirred up the muck / Which the sweet gods thought fit to make us of / When they first formed man, the primal putrescence / We keep hidden under our thin dress of health —Christopher Fry, *The Firstborn*, Act 2, scene 2

    Anath accuses Pharaoh, her brother, of giving vent to evil when he tricked Moses and brought misfortune upon the land.

5. He who wears his morality as his best garment were better naked —Kahlil Gibran, *The Prophet*

6. The curates . . . know the best black sheep of the flock —Sir Walter Scott, *Old Morality*

    Scott's use marked the shift from the ancient shepherd's literal dislike of black sheep because they were worth less than white ones, to the figurative picture of the rebel or misbehaved person who stands outside the family or social group. In Edith Wharton's The Age of Innocence, the Mingott family earned Newland Archer's admiration for "their resolute championship of the few black sheep that their blameless stock had produced."

■ MORNING

See also: DAWN; EVENING; NATURE SCENES; NIGHT AND DAY

1. The bright morning doth arise / Out of her bed of roses —Anon., "Sister, Awake!"

2. The flute of morning stilled in noon— / noon the implacable bassoon —e. e. cummings, "Always before your voice my soul"

3. The morning is bleaching the edges of the sky —Cristina Garcia, *Dreaming in Cuban*

4. Morn, / Wak'd by the circling hours, with rosy / hand / Unbarrd the gates of light. —John Milton, *Paradise Lost*, Book 6

    In Comus, Milton again used a metaphor of personification for the morning: "Under the opening eyelids of the morn, / We drove afield . . . "

5. I saw [the pond] throwing off its nightly clothing of mist —Henry David Thoreau, "Where I Lived, and What I Lived For"

■ MORTALITY

See also: DEATH

1. Mortality is a cancer, a running sore —T. Coraghessan Boyle, *Water Music*

2. Mortality is a game of musical chairs —Anna Quindlen, "Public & Private," *The New York Times,* February 14, 1993
   Quindlen's reflections on mortality were prompted by a memorial reading of the works of Laurie Colwin, whose death at age 48 prematurely ended a thriving literary career.

■ MOSCOW

See: CITIES

■ MOTHERS AND DAUGHTERS

See: FAMILIES/FAMILY RELATIONSHIPS

■ MOTION

See: MOBILITY/IMMOBILITY

■ MOUNTAINS

See also: CITYSCAPES; LANDSCAPES; NATURE

1. Mountains are earth's undecaying monuments —Nathaniel Hawthorne, "The Notch of the White Mountains," *Sketches from Memory*

2. The whole city was surrounded by mountains, and as night fell they tightened their grip on us —Amos Oz, *The Hill of Evil Counsel*
   The metaphor of the vise is implicit rather than explicit, and serves to instill a claustrophobic sense of the city.

3. Indeed, by standing on tiptoe I could catch a glimpse of some of the peaks of the still bluer and more distant mountain ranges in the northwest, those true-blue coins from heaven's own mint, and also of some portion of the village —Henry David Thoreau, "Where I Lived, and What I Lived For"

4. They [the Klamath Mountains] form a biodiversity keystone in the woodland arch of the Sierras and the Cascades —David Rains Wallace, "The Klamath Surprise," *Wilderness,* Winter 1992

■ MOURNFULNESS

See: DESPAIR

■ MOUTHS

See also: FACES; FACIAL EXPRESSIONS

1. His [Jesse Jackson's] Zapata mustache curling over a small pouch of a mouth —Marshall Fraidy, *The New Yorker,* April 15, 1992
   The metaphor alludes to the Mexican revolutionary.

2. A hog jaw —Dashiell Hammett, *Red Harvest*

3. That small mouth pursed forward by the Giaconda expression into a little snout with a round hole in the middle —Aldous Huxley, "The Giaconda Smile"
   The allusion to the Mona Lisa's mysterious smile combined with the writer's animal-like Giaconda, seems to hint at mysterious happenings to come.

4. Watch her mouth . . . a mouth that clearly expects a spoonful of honey from life and gets a shot of vinegar every time —David Richards, "Sunday View," *The New York Times,* April 26, 1992
   The lady of the metaphoric mouth was actress Faith Prince as Miss Adelaide in Guys and Dolls. *The sour doses of life notwithstanding she always resumed her optimistic pose "eagerly anticipating the next spoonful of honey."*

5. When he spoke, spittle cobwebbed the corners of his mouth —Philip Roth, *Goodbye, Columbus*

"His breath smelled of hair oil and his hair of breath," writes Roth. No wonder the narrator was not fond of this man.

6. A woman's unheard laugh exposing / Glitter of gold in the mouth's dark ghetto —Robert Penn Warren, "Cocktail Party"
   The narrator wonders if perhaps he is a bit drunk, after he reviews his perceptions at the party.

■ MOVEMENTS

See also: ADMIRATION; BODIES/THE BODY; DESCRIPTIONS, MISC.; GROUP SCENES; PHYSICAL APPEARANCE

1. For Asians, the newest immigrants, migration streams were more like droplets splashed around the country —Felicity Barringer, *The New York Times*, June 6, 1993
   In the changing demography of the country, Asians were scattering.

2. The Swede, tightly gripping his valise, tacked across the face of the storm — Stephen Crane, "The Blue Hotel"

3. Her tall black-suited body seemed to carve its way through the crowded room —Josephine Hart, *Damage*

4. When she moved, it was a swan moving —Rosamond Lehmann, *The Ballad and the Source*

5. Magda flopped onward with her little pencil legs scribbling this way and that — Cynthia Ozick, "The Shawl"
   The image is of a child in a concentration camp.

6. Ah, when she moved, she moved more ways than one: / The shapes a bright container can contain! —Theodore Roethke, "I Knew A Woman"

7. One hand . . . went to the other hand and they folded quite still, holding nothing until they lost their force by lying on her breast and made a funny little house with

peaks and gables —Eudora Welty, "June Recital"

■ MURDER

See also: ACCUSATIONS; DESTRUCTION/ DESTRUCTIVENESS; EVIL; FAMILIES/ FAMILY RELATIONSHIPS; GUILT; VILLAINY/VILLAINS

1. Orestes: Another murderer showed himself to you, his arms . . . gloved in blood —Jean-Paul Sartre, *The Flies*, Act 3
   The flies of the playwright's title are a metaphor representing the French people's guilt for their complicity with the Germans during the second World War.

2. Ghost: The serpent that did sting thy father's life / Now wears his crown — William Shakespeare, *Hamlet*, Act 1, scene 5, line 39
   The king was supposedly killed by a serpent that stung him while he was asleep but figuratively the serpent is Claudius, who usurps his brother's crown.

3. Macbeth: I am in blood / Stepp'd in so far that, should I wade no more, / Returning were as tedious as go o'er —William Shakespeare, *Macbeth* Act 3, scene 4, line 136

4. Edward: Thou hast slain / The flower of Europe —William Shakespeare, *The Third Part of Henry the Sixth*, Act 2, scene 1, line 70
   The figurative flower is the Duke of York.

5. Queen: How sweet a plant have you untimely cropp'd! —William Shakespeare, *The Third Part of Henry the Sixth*, Act 5, scene 5, line 62
   The metaphoric plant is Prince Edward, who has just been stabbed by his cousins.

6. Duchess: One vial full of Edward's sacred blood, / One flourishing branch of his most royal root, / Is crack'd . . . hack'd down, and his summer leaves all faded — William Shakespeare, *The Tragedy of King Richard the Second*, Act 1, scene 2, line 17

Edward the Black Prince (1330–1376) had seven sons, one of whom was husband to the Duchess of York.

■ MUSEUMS

See: INSTITUTIONS

■ MUSIC/MUSICIANS

See also: FAME; PLEASURE; SINGING/ SONGS/SINGERS; SUCCESS/FAILURE

1. Music is but a fart that's sent / From the guts of an instrument —Anon.

    It's clear that wind metaphors have been blowing around for a long time.

2. The music lingered, a palimpsest of unheard sound —Margaret Atwood, *The Handmaid's Tale*

3. I want someone to build me music I can live in, like a house. Music is not all the time a gondola, or a racehorse, or a tightrope. It is sometimes a chair as well — Jean Cocteau, "The Public and the Artist," *Vanity Fair*, 1922

4. Nothing is so enervating as to lie and soak for a long time in a warm bath. Enough of music in which one lies and soaks —Jean Cocteau, "The Public and the Artist," *Vanity Fair*, 1922

5. The two superstars [Bobby McFerrin and Yo Yo Ma] have prepared a warm bath and scented the waters appropriately — Peter G. Davis, *New York Magazine*, February 24, 1992

    Davis wrote about the musical mix of pop star and classical cellist on an album called "Hush."

6. The work [*Child of Our Time*] first performed in 1944, landed Sir Michael [Tippett] squarely on the musical map —Cori Ellison, "Classical Music," *The New York Times,* September 5, 1993

7. Sir Michael was viewed by many as a sort of musical Shirley MacLaine, casting about in the supermarket of classical and popular culture to find the right words and music to clothe his sprawling mystical vision —Cori Ellison, "Classical Music," *The New York Times*, September 5, 1993

    The 88-year-old Tippett, long recognized as a national treasure, was to be guest-of-honor at the first New York performance of his first opera The Midsummer Marriage.

8. Sometimes the front door stands ajar, and from it issue the airs of a player piano, blue strains, serpentines of music unrolling in the dark shadows, curling round the wrists and necks of the workmen who just happen to be walking past —Jean Genet, *Querelle*

    The music curls around them to entice them into a brothel.

9. [The Shostakovich Fourth Symphony:] A triumph of excess, a paean to sarcasm, a drunken extravaganza, a military band run amok, a marche grotesque that jeers a subtlety and tenderness and manages a loudness using acoustical instruments that U2, with all its electrical resources, might envy —Bernard Holland, "Review/Music," *The New York Times*, March 15, 1992

10. Mr. Rouse's work was a Trojan horse. It was wheeled through the gates of a festival that was once a staid outpost of the most formal brand of contemporary music, and unleashed an assault that included rhythmic quotations from a handful of rock and blues songs —Allan Kozinn, "Critic's Notebook," *The New York Times*, August 10, 1992

    The reviewer wrote about Christopher Rouse's departure from the usual fare of the annual Tanglewood Music Festival of Contemporary Music.

11. Music my rampart, and my only one — Edna St. Vincent Millay, "On Hearing a Symphony of Beethoven," *The Buck in the Snow*

12. Men playing out their maple-sugar hearts, tapping it from four-hundred-year-old trees and letting it run down the trunk,

wasting it because they didn't have a bucket to hold it and didn't want one either. They just wanted to let it run that day, slow if it wished, or fast, but a free run down trees bursting to give it up —Toni Morrison, *Jazz*

The players are jazz musicians in 1927.

13. The American pianist [John Browning] loosed Niagaras of notes in the splashy solo part, yet found his way surely to the passionate vein beneath the virtuosic displays and musings on death —Andrew Pincus, "Classical Review," *The Berkshire Eagle*, July 18, 1993

The review of Rachmaninoff's "Rhapsody on a Theme of Paganini" neatly connected a water image with that of the vein beneath the skin's surface

14. In the Rachmaninoff Second [Symphony] . . . he went for the roller coaster —Andrew Pincus, "Classical Review," *The Berkshire Eagle*, July 18, 1993

The roller coaster rider was pianist John Browning.

15. The mounting excitement of the ball scene [during a performance of Berlioz's "Romeo et Juliette"] was capped by the rifle-shot final chords —Andrew Pincus, "Classical Review," *The Berkshire Eagle*, July 25, 1993

16. Music . . . the moonlight in the gloomy night of life —Jean Paul Richter, *Titan*

17. Played . . . at the electronic keyboards, the interlocking phrases were hypnotic, a demonstration of moire patterns created by overlapping musical wheels —Edward Rothstein, "Review/Music," *The New York Times*, November 16, 1992

Rothstein was writing about the music of Phillip Glass.

18. Music has been my playmate, my lover, my crying towel —Buffy Sainte-Marie

Ms. Sainte-Marie knows whereof she speaks; she's a songwriter.

19. His playing [pianist Shura Cherkassky] wraps 20th century listeners in a warm 19th century blanket —Harold C. Schonberg, "Classical Music," *The New York Times*, December 1, 1991

The metaphor was used as a caption for a photo of the artist.

20. Cleopatra: Give me some music . . . moody food / Of us that trade in love —William Shakespeare, *Antony and Cleopatra*, Act 2, scene 4, line 1

A frequently quoted variant is the opening line of Twelfth Night: *"If music be the food of love, play on!"*

21. Duke: If music be the food of love, play on! —William Shakespeare, *Twelfth Night*, Act 5, scene 1, line 1

The duke expands on the metaphor with "Give me excess of it, that surfeiting, / The appetite may sicken and so die."

22. I had long had in mind skimming the cream of our most beautiful folk-ballads in order to turn them into a picture for the stage —August Strindberg, Introduction, *Plays*. Third Series

Further along, Strindberg writes that he examined a number of folk tales, "poured it all into my separator . . . and in a short while the cream began to flow. In common usage "to skim off" generally refers less to selecting the best of something than to a type of theft.

23. I think that we're now riding the dinosaur, and concerts will be different, just as they were different in the 18th century and the 19th century —David Zinman, Interview, *The Berkshire Eagle*, August 2, 1992

The dinosaur has become a favorite metaphor for anything obsolete, or on the verge of so being.

■ MUSTACHES

See: FACIAL HAIR

■ MYSTERY/MYSTERIOUSNESS

See also: ALLIANCES; CHARACTERIZATIONS

1. Laurel: Look how she came to us—with nothing! A lady from a shipwreck! — Enid Bagnold, *The Chalk Garden*, Act 2, 1953

   A mysterious governess arrived with everything she owned new, as if all else had been lost at sea.

2. The devil's dance of the Indian Diamond has threaded its way to London; and to London you must go after it —Wilkie Collins, *The Moonstone*

   The two metaphors appear in what may be the first real detective story in English literature. It centers on a gem stolen from the head of an idol, and the mysterious complications attending its recovery.

3. The more committed relationship in the book is Mr. Lord's affair with Dora Maar . . . a sphinx of a woman —James R. Mellow, *New York Times Book Review*, July 19, 1993

   The book being reviewed was James Lord's personal memoir, Picasso and Dora.

4. Mr. Clinton, who repeatedly criticized President Bush for missing signs of Iraq's military buildup . . . may face a parallel problem with Iran, the Bermuda Triangle of foreign policy for the Carter and Reagan Administrations —Elaine Sciolino, "C.I.A. Says Iran Makes Progress on Atom Arms," *The New York Times*, November 30, 1992

   The writer metaphorically linked Iran to the area where various crafts have mysteriously disappeared.

5. Lady Sneer: Then at once to unravel this mystery, I must inform you that love has no share whatever in the intercourse between Mr. Surface and me —Richard Brinsley Sheridan, *The School for Scandal*, Act 1, scene 1

   A clew of thread, another version of the ball-of-yarn metaphor, is provided to Theseus to find his way out of the famous maze of the Minotaur. Mysteries or mazes are often associated with yarn.

6. It was a nut to crack for many, what these two could see in each other, what subject they could find in common —Robert Louis Stevenson, *Dr. Jeckyll and Mr. Hyde*

   As Stevenson writes, the meetings between the two men who explore the strange story of Dr. Jekyll and Mr. Hyde, were counted by each as "the chief jewel of each week."

7. She was shrouded in some somber secret —Ramón del Valle-Inclán, "My Sister Antonia"

8. You have this great mass of collective wisdom behind you, . . . but you're so painfully spooked by the least hint of mystery, which is why you have to root it out so ruthlessly with the iron logic of broad daylight —A. B. Yehoshua, *Mr. Mani*

   Hagar suggests that the dead grandmother has left in her room an aura that haunts her son.

NAME CALLING

See also: EVIL; INSULTS

1. Strepsiades: Aha! poor dupes, why sit ye mooning there, Game for us Artful Dodgers, you dull stones, / You ciphers, lambkins, butts piled up together! — Aristophanes, *The Clouds*

2. Why make this shark the object of your love? / What is he good for? — Catullus, Poem 29

   The shark is commonly associated with predation. One of the warring gangs in Lenoard Bernstein's Westside Story *called themselves "The Sharks."*

3. You're a fool!'' cried the Easterner, viciously. ''You're a bigger jackass than the Swede by a million majority'' —Stephen Crane, ''The Blue Hotel''

4. In the *National Review*'s many anti-Hillary [Clinton] broadsides, the magazine's contributors were in highest dudgeon . . . calling her ''that smiling barracuda.'' —Susan Faludi, *The New York Times,* December 20, 1993

5. Hecuba: I was saying that you're a cuckoo, Demokos. If cuckoos had the absurdity, the affectation, the ugliness and the stench of vultures, you would be a cuckoo —Jean Giraudoux, *Tiger at the Gates,* Act 1

6. Mathemetician: You third cousin of a toad, they yell! You son of a sow! —Jean Giraudoux, *Tiger at the Gates,* Act 2

Ancient armies faced off and hurled invectives before they hurled spears. The mathemetician feels that the Trojans "suffer from a grave shortage of insults."

7. Paris: You old parasite! You filthy-footed iambic pentameter! —Jean Giraudoux, *Tiger at the Gates,* Act 2

   The insult is addressed to a poet, with a pun on the "foot" in pentameter, which has five beats, or "feet" to the line.

8. Paris: Demokos! Bloodshot bullock's eye! You fungus-ridden plum-tree! —Jean Giraudoux, *Tiger at the Gates,* Act 2

   Demokos thinks the insult is "grammatically reasonable, but very naive."

9. Old Hilse: What is it you want in my house, you limbs of Satan? —Gerhart Hauptmann, *The Weavers,* Act 5

   This is a case of "the kettle calling the pot" since Old Hilse addresses the workers he has been exploiting.

10. When a newspaper hires a snake like [Murray] Kempton they can expect the worst . . . I am surprised that Scripps-Howard are taking on this rat —J. Edgar Hoover, Note in 1964 document

    The note was quoted in David Remnick's profile of Kempton in The New Yorker, *"Prince of the City," March 1, 1993.*

11. What are you, you pale citizens? You subdued beast in sheep's clothing —D. H. Lawrence, *The Rainbow*

Ursula, a college student, has become increasingly outraged with the pretense of people and their "mechanization." The title, a metaphor for the freedom from earth's corruption, is summed up in the closing scene which finds Ursula studying a rainbow.

12. He should thank his lucky stars he's still alive, the slit-eyed devil—all I did was tweak his ears and pull his hair a bit —Boris Pasternak, *Doctor Zhivago*

    The metaphor implies a feline nature to the devil.

13. I know your mother, the slut, the mangy cat, the crumpled skirt! —Boris Pasternak, *Doctor Zhivago*

14. You've got him to the life. Buzz, buzz, buzz—a real bumblebee —Boris Pasternak, *Doctor Zhivago*

15. My brother is a gentleman. You are vultures —Gaetano Rina, Quoted *The New York Times*, January 17, 1993

    The insult was hurled at reporters, who have been called worse. The "gentleman" referred to by his brother was the man known as "Salvatore (Toto) Rina, boss of all bosses of the Sicilian Mafia."

16. Kent: Thou whoreson zed! thou unnecessary letter! —William Shakespeare, *King Lear*, Act 2, scene 2, line 66

    The letter Z (zed) was sometimes omitted in Elizabethan dictionaries.

17. Lear: thou art my flesh . . . / Or rather a disease that's in my flesh . . . / thou art a boil, / . . . an embossed carbuncle, / In my corrupted blood —William Shakespeare, *King Lear*, Act 2, scene 4, line 222

    Lear's terrible condemnation of Goneril reflects his agony and rage.

18. Iago: You are pictures out o'doors, / Bells in your parlours; wild-cats in your kitchens —William Shakespeare, *Othello* Act 3, scene 1, line 109

    Iago's wife Emilia is the butt of his misogyny.

19. Othello: This is a subtle whore, / A closet, lock and key, of villainous secrets —William Shakespeare, *Othello*, Act 4, scene 2, line 21

    Othello's mistrust of his wife brooks no denial.

20. Juliet: Dove-feathered raven, wolvish-rav'ning lamb! / Despised substance of divinest show! —William Shakespeare, *Romeo and Juliet*, Act 3, scene 2, line 75

    Juliet has just learned about the fight that has led to Romeo's killing Tybalt.

21. Lucullus: Thou disease of a friend — William Shakespeare, *Timon of Athens*, Act 3, scene 1, line 57

22. Because you are an ill-bred Puppy, I will meet you in Hide-Park an Hour hence; and because you want both Breeding and Humanity, I desire you would come with a Pistol in your Hand . . . to teach you more Manners. —Richard Steele, in an essay, 1709

23. Jack: Never met such a Gorgon . . . I don't really know what a Gorgon is like, but I am quite sure Lady Bracknell is one. In any case, she is a monster, without being a myth —Oscar Wilde, *The Importance of Being Earnest*, Act 1

24. Blanche: His poker night!—you call it— this party of apes! —Tennessee Williams, *A Streetcar Named Desire*, scene 4

    This culminates Blanche's scathing attack on her brother-in-law as a "survivor of the stone age bearing the raw meat home from the kill in the jungle."

■ NATIONAL TRAITS

See: CHARACTERIZATIONS

■ NATIONALISM

See: INTERNATIONAL RELATIONS; PATRIOTISM

■ NATURE

See also: DESCRIPTIONS, MISC.; EARTH; HUMANITY/HUMANKIND; SEA; SEASONS; SKY/SKYSCAPES; SOUND; WIND

1. Ice is the silent language of the peak; / and fire the silent language of the stars — Conrad Aiken, "Sonnet 10,"*And In the Human Heart*

2. There is a need to recover nature, now buried under successive layers of ideological ash —Allan Bloom, "The Death of Eros," *New York Times Magazine,* May 23, 1993
   "Legalism takes the place of sentiment," Mr. Bloom wrote.

3. Sonia: Forests are the ornaments of the earth —Anton Chekhov, *Uncle Vanya,* Act 1

4. I nearly fell into a very narrow ravine, almost no more than a scar in the hillside —Joseph Conrad, *The Heart of Darkness*

5. Nature never writes a bad hand. Her writing, as it may be read in the human countenance, is invariably legible, if we come at all trained to the reading of it —Charles Dickens, "Palmer, the Rugely Poisoner"

6. To my quick ear the leaves conferred / The bushes they were bells —Emily Dickinson, Poem 1732

7. Nature is no spendthrift, but takes the shortest way to her ends —Ralph Waldo Emerson, "Fate," *Essays: First Series*
   Emerson's metaphor personifies nature as a shrewd manager.

8. The book of Nature is the book of Fate. She turns the gigantic pages,—leaf by leaf,—never returning one —Ralph Waldo Emerson, "Fate," *Essays: First Series*

9. Nature is a mutable cloud, which is always and never the same —Ralph Waldo Emerson, "History," *Essays: First Series*

10. Nature uses only the longest threads to weave her patterns, so each small piece of her fabric reveals the organization of the entire tapestry —Richard Feynman, *The Character of Physical Law*
    The Nobel Prize winning physicist's metaphoric nuggets were not random remarks, but carefully crafted for later inclusion in his lectures.

11. Nature seldom produces anyone who is afterwards to act a notable part on the stage of life but she gives some warning of her intention —Henry Fielding, *The Life of Mr. Jonathan Wild the Great*

12. The thin leaves, quivering on their silken threads, / Do make a music —Oliver Wendell Holmes, Sr., "Evening"

13. The poetry of earth is never dead —John Keats, "The Grasshopper and the Cricket"

14. The daisy stands, a bastard flower, / Like flowers that bear an honest name. —Edna St. Vincent Millay, "Weeds," *Vanity Fair, 1920*
    The simile builds on the metaphor.

15. Pity the poor houseplants in custody of neglectful owners . . . stuffed into undersized pots. Kept in the dark . . . soil-bound hostages yearning to be free—or at least moved to better light —Griffin Miller, "Totally Self-Sufficient Plants?" *The New York Times,* July 1, 1993
    The metaphor introduced advice on minimal care requirements for even the sturdiest indoor plants.

16. My footstool earth, my canopy the skies —Alexander Pope, "Essay on Man"

17. The green chickweed has not sprouted, / The grass has not yet laid its carpet — Shimazaki Tōson, "Song on Traveling the Chikuma River"

18. The force that through the green fuse drives the flower / Drives my green age —Dylan Thomas, "The Force That Through the Green Fuse Drives the Flower"

19. All nature is your congratulation —Henry David Thoreau, *Walden*

20. My "best" room . . . always ready for company, on whose carpet the sun rarely fell, was the pine wood behind my house —Henry David Thoreau, *Walden*
    Otherwise, according to Thoreau, "it may plow out again through the side of his head.

21. Nature is no temple but merely a workshop, and man is the craftsman —Ivan Turgenev, *Fathers and Sons*

22. I believe a leaf of grass is no less than the journey-work of the stars —Walt Whitman, "Song of Myself"

23. *What is the grass?* . . . / it must be the flag of my disposition, out of hopeful green stuff woven. / Or I guess it is the handkerchief of the lord —Walt Whitman, "Grass"

24. A weed is but an unloved flower —Ella Wheeler Wilcox, "The Weed"

25. This sea that bares her bosom to the moon, / The winds that will be howling at all hours, / . . . For this, for everything we are out of tune —William Wordsworth, "The World Is Too Much With Us"

> Wordsworth uses three metaphors in quick succession: personification, an animal metaphor, and a metaphor from music. Two of the three are implied metaphors.

■ NATURE SCENES

See also: DESCRIPTIONS, MISC.; EARTH; LANDSCAPES; NIGHT AND DAY; SEASCAPES; SEASONS; SKY/SKYSCAPES; TREES

1. The constellated sounds / ran sprinkling on earth's floor / As the dark vault above / with stars was spangled o'er —Robert Bridges, "Noel, Christmas Eve, 1913"

> This first appeared in The London Times on December 24, 1913, after Bridges became Poet Laureate.

2. The leaves of grass are trembling timidly —Joseph Brodsky, "Einem alten Architekten in Rom"

> Leaves of Grass is the title of a book of poems by Walt Whitman, and is obviously being quoted in this metaphor of personification.

3. The stood staring at the water, a wavering mirror of sunset —Gilbert Keith Chesterton, "The Sins of Prince Saradine"

> Chesterton scholar Owen Edwards offers some fascinating conjectures on Chesterton's names. He thought the Prince of the above story's title was named to tie in with the word sardine since he and his brother were as hard to tell apart as the sardines in a can. He also thought the name Brown for the author's sleuth was a metaphor to underscore his "plain as a brown paper bag" appearance in contrast to the "white brilliance of his mind."

4. [The dandelion spends] its single / fringed medallion, alms for the sun —Amy Clampitt, "Burial in Cypress Hills"

5. The vault of trees opened out above them, showing a river of sky in which stars twinkled —Colette, "Bella Vista"

> An example of Colette's talents as a metaphoric landscape artist.

6. I set my broad sole upon silver, / On the skin of the sky —James Dickey, "The Lifeguard"

7. Leaves got up in a coil and hissed / Blindly struck at my knee and missed —Robert Frost, "Bereft"

8. By June our brook's run out of song and speed / . . . Its bed is left a faded paper sheet / Of dead leaves stuck together by the heat —Robert Frost, "Hyla Brook"

> There are two metaphors here—the brook as a singer, and the river bed as a sheet of paper.

9. In the gullies, where streams of water slid from pool to pool leaving beards of rusty algae on their sandstone lips . . . —Robert Hughes, *The Fatal Shore*

10. June falls asleep upon her bier of flowers —Lucy Larcom, "Death of June"

11. Our river wore the green sleeves of the forest / that spelled on her slow depth the mirrored problem / of dark green trees reversed upon the river —Richmond Lattimore, "Sestina For a Far-Off Summer"

12. Twice a week, at least, she drove into the country with Kennicott, to hunt ducks in lakes enameled with sunset —Sinclair Lewis, *Main Street*

The novel's heroine seemed much more content in the countryside than the town with all its social narrowness.

13. Ghost among ghosts, maniacal flowering, among the spun-glass / Architecture of jellyfish —John Lindgren, "Octopus," *The New Yorker,* July 27, 1992
    The first two metaphors describe the octopus and the third its bubble of a companion. Lindgren describes starfish as "five-pointed meat-stars atop their black steeples of hunger."

14. It was the early afternoon of a sunshiny day with little winds playing hide-and-seek in it —Katherine Mansfield, "How Pearl Button Was Kidnapped"

15. Hedges steam, / I ride through a damp tunnel of sweetness —John Montague, "Dowager"
    Montague pictures a scene after the rain. The dowager rides in her Rolls through the countryside, self-satisfied, "An old bitch, with a warm mouthful of game."

16. Someone was saying / how the wind dies down but comes back / how shells are the coffins of wind —Mark Strand, "My Life," *Selected Poems*
    Mark Strand served as Poet Laureate of the United States when this volume of poetry was reissued in 1990.

17. A sea of lead, a sky of slate; / Already autumn in the air, alas! —Arthur Symons, "Dieppe: Grey and Green"

18. I chatter over stony ways, / In little sharps and trebles —Lord Alfred Tennyson, "The Brook"

19. When summer came, we locked up our lives and fled / to the woods in Maine, and pulled up over our heads / a comforter filled with batts of piney dark tied with crickets' chirreting and the *bork* of frogs —Mona Van Duyn, "The Gentle Snorer"

20. Later, / If there is no moon, you can see the red eyes of fire / Wink at you from / The blass mass that is the mountain —Robert Penn Warren, "Rattlesnake Country"

21. The great snake . . . the Mississippi River —Thomas Wolfe, "The Promise of America"
    Most of Wolfe's short stories were taken from novels-in-progress, this one from, You Can't Go Home Again, *1940.*

■ NECESSITY

1. The most accursed / Of Want's fell scorpions, is thirst —Eliza Cook, "Metala"

2. Necessity starves on the stoop of invention —Theodore Roethke, "The Gentle"

■ NECK
See: BODIES/THE BODY

■ NEED
See: DESIRE

■ NEGLECTFULNESS
See: ACTION/INACTION

■ NERVOUSNESS
See: WORRY

■ NEW YORK
See: CITIES

■ NICKNAMES
See: PERSONALITY PROFILES

■ NIGHT AND DAY
See also: DAWN; EVENING; MORNING; NATURE SCENES; SKY/SKYSCAPES; WINTER

1. They journeyed, / When the darkness of night / Had let down her curtain —Ibn Al-Arabi, "Ode"

2. Pillars of smoke . . . turned the metal of the night to rust —Jorge Luis Borges, "The Aleph"

3. As dusk drew in on cultivated cries, / Faces hung pearls upon a cedar-bough — Donald Davie, "The Garden Party"
   The line sets up echoes of Pound's apparition of faces in a crowd as "petals on a wet, black bough." Davie's garden party with its charming conversation sets up a far gentler image.

4. All is silent under the steep cone of afternoon —John Gould Fletcher, "Irradiations"

5. Will night already spread her wings and weave / Her dusky robe about the day's bright form —Solomon Ibn Gabirol, "Night"

6. The night is stenciled with stars —Cristina Garcia, *Dreaming in Cuban*

7. And the tent of night in tatters / Straws the sky-pavilioned land —A. E. Housman, "Reveille," *Shropshire Lad*

8. Twilight is also the mind's grazing time — Alfred Kazin, *A Walker in the City*

9. Our Night / Is a blue balcony— / And therewith close your inquisition! —Alfred Kreymborg, "Nun Snow—A Pantomime of Beads"

10. The night-black raven . . . weaves a net of slumber over the snow-capped homes — Joseph Langland, "Hunters in the Snow: Brueghel"

11. The day is done and the darkness / Falls from the wings of Night —Henry Wadsworth Longfellow, "The Day is Done"

12. I heard the trailing garments of the Night / Sweep through her marble halls! — Henry Wadsworth Longfellow, "Hymn to the Night"

13. Night has a thousand eyes and the day just one —John Lyly, *The Maydes Metamorphosis,* Act 3, scene 1

14. Now came still evening on, and twilight gray / Had in her sober livery all things clad —John Milton, *Paradise Lost,* Book 4

15. When I saw him, he was at the door, but it did not matter, / he was already sliding along the wall of the night —Charles Olson, "The Kingfishers"

16. The womb of night was carrying life, and over it Riviere kept his watch —Antoine de Saint-Exupery, *Night Flight*
    The "life" was the plane with its freight of pilot and wireless operator.

17. This is how / I want to die: / into that rushing beast of the night, / sucked up by that great dragon —Anne Sexton, "The Starry Night"

18. Hubert: Why here walk I in the black brow of night, / To find you out — William Shakespeare, *The Life and Death of King John,* Act 5, scene 6, line 17

19. Romeo: The grey-ey'd Morn smiles on the frowning Night —William Shakespeare, *Romeo and Juliet,* Act 2 scene 1, line 163

20. Juliet: Come civil Night, / Thou sober-suited matron all in black —William Shakespeare, *Romeo and Juliet* Act 3, scene 2, line 10

21. Juliet: Night's candles are burnt out and jocund Day / Stands tiptoe on the misty mountain tops —William Shakespeare, *Romeo and Juliet,* Act 3, scene 5, line 11
    Juliet uses two metaphors; the second is a personification.

22. This closing night / Will be the dome of a vast sepulchre —Percy Bysshe Shelley, "Ode to the West Wind"

23. Night has closed all in her cloak —Sir Philip Sidney, "Only Joy! now here you are," *Astrophel and Stella*

This metaphor appears in one of the songs sprinkled among the sonnets in the cycle.

24. That sweet black which veils the heav'nly eye —Sir Philip Sidney, "Sonnet 20," *Astrophel and Stella*

25. Night was at one time almost non-existent, a mere holding of the breath, as it were, by the heavens while evening gave way to morning —Frans Eemil Sillanpää, *The Maid Silja*

    This is the opening of a chapter entitled "The Night of the Harvest Festival" from a novel by the Finnish Nobel Prize winner.

26. Night's darkness is a bag that bursts with the gold of dawn. —Rabindranath Tagore, "Stray Birds, 208"

■ NIGHTMARES

See also: DREAMS

1. In the loft / the hot straw suffocates / the rafters become snakes —Jim Harrison, "Nightmare"

    The nightmare pictures a hayloft. Snakes inhabit many nightmares, twinning the Biblical perception of them as evil creatures, and perhaps invoking sexual reactions.

2. His nightmare was a great success, while mine / Plays on the ceiling of my rented room / Or on the bone concavity of my skull —Anthony Hecht, *The Venetian Vespers*

    Some people can't even have successful nightmares.

3. At the edge of knowledge, overhanging / The canyons of nightmare —John Hollander, "The Night Mirror"

4. Spectres and fears, the nightmare and her foal, / Drown in the golden deluge of the morn —A. E. Housman, "Revolution"

    Nightmares usually just fade away when morning comes. Houseman drowns them in the sun.

5. Aethelwold: Thinkest thou a man hath a nightmare pawing his chest / . . . And knoweth not if she be iron-gray or dun? —

Edna St. Vincent Millay, *The King's Henchman*

6. Those giggling muckers who / Saddled my nightmares thirty years ago —James Wright, "At the Executed Murderer's Grave 3"

    The image of the nightmare as a horse that rode through sleep is a common one. Wright freshens the image by shifting the emphasis to the saddle.

■ NONCONFORMITY

See: INDIVIDUALITY

■ NOSES

See also: FACES; PHYSICAL APPEARANCE

1. Dédé had a button of a nose that looked ridiculous in someone so tall —Mavis Gallant, "Dédé"

2. The eyes might blaze, the eyebrows bristle, the forehead soar ever more lofty, but the nose was of chapel and sin. Around the bridge, it had a pinched look of virtue and condemnation —Penelope Mortimer, "The Parson," *Stories from The New Yorker, 1950–60*

    Mortimer leads into this "churchly" nose with a pungent simile: "this nose was like the prow of Methodism rising out of a receding sea."

3. Custard the dragon . . . chimney for a nose —Ogden Nash, "The Tale of Custard the Dragon"

    Nash's popular dragon also had "a mouth like a fireplace."

4. Old Phillips would sniff through his great red beak of a nose —Sean O'Faolàin, "A Born Genius"

5. His nose is Harry's, a neat smooth button —John Updike, *Rabbit, Run*

    The button-nose belongs to Harry's infant son.

■ NOVELS

See: BOOKS

OBESITY

See: *FATNESS/THINNESS*

OBJECTIVES

See: *ACTION/INACTION*

OBLIVION

See also: *HISTORY; MEMORY/MEMORIES*

1. Somebody has pushed the fast-forward button on history —Anon., Annual Report of Control Data Corporation, quoted *The New York Times,* 1992

2. The dark trumpets of oblivion were less loud at the patter of his child's feet —F. Scott Fitzgerald, "The Baby Party," *All the Sad Young Men*

   The life of the man thus freed from fear "had been a series of struggles up a series of rugged hills."

3. He had buried her at the bottom of a water-tight oblivion as a brutal means of living without her. —Gabriel García Márquez, *The General in his Labyrinth*

OBSCURITY

See also: *HUMANITY/HUMANKIND; ISOLATION; ORDINARINESS/EXTRAORDINARINESS*

1. All men lead their lives behind a wall of misunderstanding they themselves have built, and most men die in silence and unnoticed behind the walls —Sherwood Anderson, *Poor White*

   Occasionally a man "becomes absorbed in doing something that is impersonal, useful, and beautiful. Word of his activities is carried over the walls," Anderson continues.

2. Voynitsky: He's totally obscure . . . a soap bubble! —Anton P. Chekhov, *Uncle Vanya,* Act 2

3. A quiet old couple . . . so usual as to merge unrecorded into the general sea of lives —Vita Sackville-West, *All Passion Spent*

OBSESSION

See: *PASSION*

OBSOLESCENCE

See also: *FAILURE*

1. [The world of President George Bush:] It is an old crumbling chessboard where kings play with each other and are indifferent to their subjects —Leslie H. Gelb, "Foreign Affairs," *The New York Times,* April 4, 1992

   This assessment of Governor Bill Clinton's potential as a presidential candidate also attacked Jerry

Brown's bid for the office: "He has returned from his latest deep space probe as Jack D. Ripper, full of anger and nastiness," Gelb wrote.

2. To opponents, ... the station is another cold-war dinosaur —Joel Greenberg, "Hatzeva Journal," *The New York Times*, November 27, 1992

   The Voice of America relay station, to the local farmers, would produce "a forest of radio antennas looming over the silent wilderness."

3. I am comparatively a dead cult with my statues cut down and the grass growing over them in the moonlight —William Dean Howells, Letter to Henry James, 1915

   Howell, aware that changing tastes were eroding his popularity, identified with fallen, overgrown statues.

4. Some unreconstructed old Cold Warriors strap on their rusty armor and come over here on the floor and tell us, "oh no, you can't reduce this military spending" —Jim Sasser, Quoted in "A Program for Conversion," *ECAAR News Network*: The Newsletter of Economists Allied for Arms Reduction, Fall 1992

   The Senator from Tennessee, Chairman of the Senate Budget Committee, felt that many representatives did not yet understand the global changes that should result in reduced military expenditures.

5. Should the European monetary union some day become a reality, ... the Bundesbank will be consigned to the dustbin of history —Craig R. Whitney, *The New York Times*, October 22, 1992

   Ashbin is often used as a variation of this common metaphor for something that's been discarded. The modern vacuum cleaner has pretty much sucked the air out of both types of bins.

■ **OBSTACLES**

See: DIFFICULTIES

■ **OBSTINACY**

See: FLEXIBILITY/INFLEXIBILITY

■ **OBSTRUCTIONS**

See: BARRIERS

■ **OCCUPATIONS**

See also: CHARACTERIZATIONS; MUSIC/ MUSICIANS; POLITICS/POLITICIANS; SCIENCE; WARRIORS AND PEACE-MAKERS

1. Given the extraordinary and retarded infancy of psychiatry, we simply cannot speak of cures effected under such conditions —André Breton, *Nadja*

2. Teaching . . . It's a cul-de-sac. I don't like that —Willa Cather, *My Mortal Enemy*

   This metaphor is sometimes used to represent something isolated from the mainstream; for example, in a May 16, 1993, New York Times column, Anna Quindlen referred to the airline industry's attitude toward flight attendants' weight as a "small cul-de-sac of institutional stupidity."

3. Many a young dancer has drowned in the mirrors before which she spends her life —Agnes DeMille, "The Milk of Paradise"

   Dancing, says DeMille, is "a sort of automarriage," a "narcissistic union" that carries with it a melancholy, and the promise of death.

4. Psychology . . . a consummate knowledge of human nature in general, of its secret springs, various windings, and perplexed mazes —Henry Fielding

5. One of the great satisfactions of the garden is that you're the priest and attendant through this annual ritual of birth and departure —Stanley Kunitz, Quoted, *The New York Times*, August 29, 1993

   The Pulitzer Prize winning poet tends to his Provincetown garden by day and "grows metaphors" at night.

6. She regretted her appearance even more when she opened the door and saw that he was not a mournful notary, as she supposed all death's merchants must be, but a timid young man wearing a checked jacket and a tie with birds in different colors —

Gabriel García Márquez, "Maria Dos Prazeres," *The New Yorker*, March 22, 1993
Maria greets the "funeral salesman" in her bathrobe, because he has come on time—an unusual occurrence in Catalonia.

7. He [the Nantucketer] alone, in Bible language, goes down to it in ships; to and fro ploughing it as his own special plantation —Herman Melville, *Moby Dick*
Melville is probably referring to "They that go down to the sea in ships, that do business in great waters; These see the works of the Lord, and His wonders in the deep." (Psalms 107:23–24)

8. Soldiers are citizens of death's grey land —Siegfried Sassoon, "Dreamers"

9. Surgery . . . is not the privet hedge that is uprooted in a hurricane; it is the royal palm —Richard Selzer, "Letter to a Young Surgeon, 1"

10. The surgeon is burly, brawling Friar Tuck, out in the world, taking up his full share of space, and always at some risk of exposing rather too much of his free-swinging beef from beneath his habit —Richard Selzer, "Letter to a Young Surgeon, 1"
The metaphor makes use of literary allusion.

11. Deep down, I keep the vanity that surgery is the red flower that blooms among the leaves and thorns that are the rest of medicine —Richard Selzer, "Letter to a Young Surgeon, 2"

12. The surgeon is an explorer in the tropical forest of the body —Richard Selzer, "Letter to a Young Surgeon, 3"
"Now and then he reaches up to bring closer one of the wondrous fruits he sees there. Before he departs this place, he knows that he must pluck one of them," Selzer writes.

13. Am I a machine with observations going in one end and scientific papers coming out the other; an automatically recording angel in a white coat? —John H. Steele, "The Fiction of Science"

14. A psychologist, an unriddler of souls, needs hardness more than anyone. Else he will bloat with pity. And his students drown in shallow water —Irvin D. Yalom, *When Nietzsche Wept*
The multiple metaphor is from the fictional notebook of the philosopher Friedrich Nietzsche.

■ OCEAN

See: SEA

■ OLD AGE

See also: AGE/AGING; YOUTH AND AGE

1. An old man is a bed full of bones — Anon., Yiddish Proverb

2. [In old age] the pegs fall out, the tone is gone, the harmony becomes dissonance —Aristophanes, *The Knights*
In another work, The Clouds, *old age is described as a second childhood.*

3. It is time that you were thinking of providing a crutch for old age —Honoré de Balzac, *Cousin Bette*
A young cousin advises the forty-three-year-old Bette to marry her secret sweetheart. Bette, alluding to the young man's poverty, replies "That would be hunger marrying thirst"

4. Soon the chill of old age began to creep about him, that keen north wind which penetrates and lowers the moral temperature —Honoré de Balzac, *Cousin Pons*

5. Old age is life's parody —Simone de Beauvoir, *The Coming of Age*

6. [An aged person:] One who is left alone at a banquet, the lights dead, the flowers faded —E. G. Bulwer-Lytton, *The Last Days of Pompeii*, V

7. Old age, a second child, by Nature curst —Charles Churchill, *Gotham*, I
"With more and greater evils than the first" the poet concludes.

8. Old men are only walking hospitals — Wentworth Dillon, *Art of Poetry*
A variation is "old age is an incurable disease."

9. It's time to be old, / To take in sail — Ralph Waldo Emerson, "Terminus"

   This is linked to the common image of life as a voyage.

10. Old age . . . is gentle and gradual in its approaches . . . but the iron hand is not less irresistible because it wears the velvet glove —Oliver Wendell Holmes, *The Autocrat of the Breakfast-Table*

11. Perhaps being old is having lighted rooms inside your head, and people in them, acting —Philip Larkin, "The Old Fools"

12. The thing is that when one's old, in the sunset of one's life . . . one acquires a new approach to everything, and especially to affection —George Sand, Letter to Gustave Flaubert, c. 1870

    Sand here expresses her uplifted attitude toward the twilight of life, a sharp contrast to her friend Flaubert's pessimism.

13. There's no doubt that old age is a journey into a foreign country, so that one is constantly being astonished by what is not possible —May Sarton, *Endgame, A Journal of the Seventy-Ninth Year*

14. King Henry: My comfort is that old age, that ill layer-up of beauty, can do no more spoil upon my face —William Shakespeare, *The Life of Henry the Fifth*, Act 5, scene 2, line 244

■ OMNIPRESENCE

See: CHARACTERIZATIONS; POWER

■ OPEN-MINDEDNESS

See: CHANGEABLENESS/UNCHANGEABLENESS; FLEXIBILITY/INFLEXIBILITY

■ OPENNESS/PRIVACY

See also: CANDOR; LIFE; SECRECY

1. What is this compulsion of your to leave the bathroom door open? —Louis Auchincloss, "The Epicureans" *Three Lives*

   A wife is irritated at her husband's constant discussions of their private life.

2. Forever curious about what's going to happen next in the open book that is her life, [Martina] Navratilova thinks she will probably quit competitive tennis after next year —Robin Finn, *The New York Times*, November 17, 1992

3. Mama . . . wore herself on the outside. Everything about her hung in view — Fannie Hurst, *Anatomy of Me*

4. She but showed us her soul's lid, and the strange ciphers thereon engraved; all within, with pride's timidity, was withheld — Herman Melville, "Norfolk Isle and the Chola Widow"

   Hunilla, the Chola, or half-breed, widow, withheld from view her sorrow at having seen her husband and brother perish in the sea. The soul is depicted as a seagoer's chest.

5. As is her right, she [Hillary Rodham Clinton] has kept her private personality private. Yet her very blankness has made her the country's Rorschach test —Frank Rich, "End Paper," *The New York Times Magazine*, June 13, 1993

6. Yet the idea that it is somehow more egalitarian, thus more American, to dry every life on the line undermines individualism —Roger Rosenblatt, "Who Killed Privacy?" *The New York Times Magazine*, January 31, 1993

7. Walls have ears —James Shirley, *A Bird in a Cage* I

   The image of a wall as a surreptitious listener continues to be in use as a metaphoric warning to speak discreetly. The most common variant is if walls could hear!

8. All the map of my state I display —Sir Philip Sidney, "Sonnet 6," *Astrophel and Stella*

The poet opens himself to inspection as though he were a map.

■ OPINION

1. They were always on tap; kept in a state of constant cross-ventilation —John Mason Brown, Introduction, *The Portable Woollcott*
   Woollcott's opinions are likened to beer ready to pour at the pull of the tap on a keg.

2. Opinion . . . the temple of human nature; and if it be polluted, there is no longer anything sacred or venerable in sublunary existence —William Godwin, *An Inquiry Concerning Political Justice, and Its Influence on General Virtue and Happiness*, Volume 2, Book 5

3. Let me warn you, you who are thirsty for knowledge, against the thicket of opinions and the conflict of words —Hermann Hesse, *Siddhartha.*
   There are two metaphors in the Buddha's words: seeking as a thirst, and conflicting opinions as a thicket.

4. Dogmatism is puppyism come to its full growth —Douglas Jerrold, *Wit and Opinions of Douglas Jerrold*

5. King: Opinion's but a fool, that makes us scan / The outward habit by the inward man —William Shakespeare, *Pericles, Prince of Tyre*, Act 2, scene 3, line 56
   Compare this with a speech by Polonius (Hamlet, 1, 3, 68): "Take each man's censure, but reserve thy judgment. / Costly thy habit as thy purse can buy, / But not express'd in fancy; rich not gaudy; / For the apparel oft proclaims the man."

6. It is true that dogmatism can be unselfishly fanatical, but much more often—as I have realized ever since my childhood—it serves as a cloak for selfish vested interests —Yevgeny Yevtushenko, *A Precocious Autobiography*

■ OPPORTUNITY

See also: ACTION/INACTION; FAIRNESS/ UNFAIRNESS; FEAR; CHANCE; INSPIRATION

1. They [the protagonist's students] were growing up with a rush and their heads bumped abruptly against the low ceiling of their actual possibilities —James Baldwin, "Sonny's Blues," *Going to Meet the Man*

2. Ours is a business of windows of opportunity . . . you've got to make hay while the sun shines —Ed Bernard, Vice-president of retail marketing, T. Rowe Price, Baltimore—quoted by Stuart Elliott in "The Media Business," *The New York Times*, September 7, 1993
   "Those windows must be in a barn," quipped Mr. Elliott about the metaphor that has become a common description for opportunities with distinct time restrictions.

3. Nothing had been wanting to Treville but opportunity; but he was ever on the watch for it, and he faithfully promised himself that he would not fail to seize it by its three hairs whenever it came within reach of his hand —Alexandre Dumas, *The Three Musketeers*

4. I hope the inaugural will . . . give them a firebreak and a new beginning —Hamilton Jordan, quoted in "Generations in Transition," *The New York Times*, January 19, 1993
   The metaphor of the path cleared to prevent the spread of forest fires refers to the many "fires" needing the attention of Bill Clinton even before his inaugural.

5. One goes forward instead [of being able to live one's life over again], dragging a cart piled high with lost opportunities —William Maxwell, "What He Was Like," *The New Yorker*, December 7, 1992

6. Harpagon: This is an opportunity that must be grasped by the forelock —Molière, *The Miser*, Act 1

The implication is that, unless grasped, the moment will buck away like an untamed horse. Compare this with the seventeenth century Spanish metaphor to seize the bull by the horns.

7. Bailey's sits right on the margin between the edge of the world and infinite possibility —Gloria Naylor, *Bailey's Cafe*
Some people step across this "margin" and back "into the midst of nothing" but some find an unexpected sort of salvation.

8. [David] Gergen is in an enviable position; he has been given options to buy Clinton stock at the all-time low —William Safire, "Essay," *The New York Times*, May 31, 1993
Gergen had just been appointed Counsellor of Communications to the troubled Clinton administration.

9. Pistol: Why then the world's mine oyster, / Which I with sword shall open — William Shakespeare, *The Merry Wives of Windsor*, Act 2, scene 2, line 2
Pistol's response to Falstaff's refusal to lend him money has become a common metaphor to indicate that life's going well with plenty of opportunities.

10. Why hath thy servant, Opportunity, / Betray'd the hours thou gav'st me to repose? —William Shakespeare, *The Rape of Lucrece*, line 932

11. Fabian: The double gilt of this opportunity you let time wash off—William Shakespeare, *Twelfth Night*, Act 3, scene 2, line 24
The goldsmith's method of double plating an object is used figuratively for a doubly golden opportunity to prove one's superiority as a lover or fighter—in this case, unsuccessfully.

12. In a country where only six people out of a thousand have any voice in the government, what the 994 dupes need is a new deal —Mark Twain, *A Connecticut Yankee In King Arthur's Court*
Of the many card playing metaphors that entered the language of politics during the nineteenth century, this is probably most famous because of its association with President Franklin D. Roosevelt's era of reform.

13. We have got to cheer and inspirit our people ... with the vision of the open gates of opportunity for all —Woodrow Wilson, "The New Freedom"

■ OPPOSITION

See: AGREEMENT/DISAGREEMENT

■ OPTIMISM/PESSIMISM

See also: GLOOM; HOPE; JOY; LIFE

1. A lot of journalists like to indulge in worst-case scenarios of civil war —Yasushi Akashi, Quoted in article headlined "Chinese Support for Khmer Rouge Grows Cooler," *New York Times*, May 9, 1993
The head of the U.N. peacekeeping operation in Cambodia compared political events to a script.

2. Is't not fine to dance and sing / When the bells of death do ring? / Is't not fine to swim in wine —Anon., "Hey nonny no!"

3. To the artist, morbid thought is a pigment —Roger Burlingame, "The Analyst's Couch and the Creative Mind"
"It must be squeezed early on the palette of the child's mind," writes Burlingame.

4. You have seen the world through a golden haze. That comes from the sun in your heart —Gustave Flaubert, Letter to George Sand, 1871
Flaubert, though he admired Sand, felt she was too optimistic and in this letter urged her to be more realistic and to "Shout! Thunder!"

5. In any organization, you can't sell short the need that things are going to get better. It's a big need —Jerry Jones, Quoted, *The New York Times*, January 24, 1993
The owner of the Dallas Cowboys used an image from the stockmarket as an equation for hope.

6. I don't believe that man will turn this earth into a bed of roses either with the aid of God or without it —Walter Kaufmann, "The Faith of a Heretic"

7. Earthling, the dark is true; the sun's an accident —Theodore Roethke, *Straw for the Fire, Notebook of Theodore Roethke*

8. King: Thou mayst see sunshine and a hail / In me at once; but to the brightest beams / Distracted clouds give way —William Shakespeare, *All's Well That Ends Well*, Act 5, scene 3, line 33

9. Romeo: You have dancing shoes / With nimble soles, / I have a soul of lead — William Shakespeare, *Romeo and Juliet* Act 1, scene 4, line 15
   There's a pun on soles / souls in this metaphor.

10. Life is all Turner sunsets and Ibsen dramas to her —Margaret Widdemer, "Black Magic"
    Widdemer, a popular writer during the early part of the century, had a knack for quick metaphoric character brush strokes.

■ ORATORY

See: ELOQUENCE; SPEECHES

■ ORDER/DISORDER

See also: CONFUSION; CROWDS; GOVERNMENT; LIBERTY

1. Voynitsky: Ever since the professor and his wife have come, our daily life seems to have jumped the track —Anton Chekhov, *Uncle Vanya*, Act 1

2. We are the ballast of the new order — John Galsworthy, "American and Briton"
   Galsworthy uses a seafaring metaphor to plead for unity between Americans and Britons.

3. It was the clutter of a sunken ship, where every cloud of sea dust drifts away to reveal some new treasure —Laurence Gonzales, "Deep in with David Carradine"
   The clutter was found in the Malibu home of the essay's subject.

4. [She] began to dig down in a rat's nest of paper bags for the potatoes and onions — O. Henry, "The Third Ingredient"

5. He had tried to build a breakwater of order and elegance against the sordid tide of life —James Joyce, *Portrait of the Artist as a Young Man*

6. A book reviewer striving to convey the spirit of Thomas Pynchon's latest novel, *Vineland*, tells us that the book "is an intentional subversion of orderliness. You'd deconstruct it by pulling its pin and heaving it" —David Lehman, *Signs of the Times: Deconstruction and the Fall of Paul de Man*

7. The shock of getting so immediate a retort would surely unhinge the well-fitted panels of his intellect —Christopher Morley, "On Unanswering Letters"

8. Hamlet: The time is out of joint, Oh cursed spite / That ever I was born to set it right! —William Shakespeare, *Hamlet*, Act 1, scene 5, line 186
   The bard popularized but did not coin the figurative use of a twisted or dislocated bone for confusion. The common metaphor, to have one's nose out of joint, implies disgruntlement rather than confusion.

9. Cathness: He cannot buckle his distemper'd cause / Within the belts of rule. — William Shakespeare, *Macbeth*, Act 5, scene 2, line 15
   Cathness pictures Macbeth as someone unsuccessfully trying to hold together a loose garment with too small a belt. Five lines later, Angus voices a variation of the same image with a combination of metaphor and simile: "he feels his title / Hang loose about him, like a giant's robe / Upon a dwarfish thief.

10. Ulysses: Take but degree away, untune that string, / And, hark, what discord follows! —William Shakespeare, *Troilus and Cressida*, Act 1, scene 3, line 109

11. The nation itself . . . is just such an unwieldy and overgrown establishment, clut-

tered with furniture and tripped up by its own traps . . . as the million households in the land —Henry David Thoreau, "Where I Lived, and What I Lived For"

"Simplify, simplify, simplify," implores Thoreau—a motto applied to writing in E.B. White's famous The Elements of Style.

12. Her desk was completely clean, windswept but for one file she was examining —Scott Turow, *Pleading Guilt*

13. Our supreme governors: the mob —Horace Walpole, Letter, September 7, 1743

■ ORDINARINESS/ EXTRAORDINARINESS

See also: DULLNESS; EXCITEMENT; ILLUSION/REALITY; MEDIOCRITY; SELF IMAGES

1. Liked? *Liked* is so margarine —Margaret Atwood, "Isis in Darkness," *Wilderness Tips*
   The character who uses margarine as a metaphor for weakness then suggests: "How about adored?"

2. She was sucked back into the whirlwind of ordinary life continuing around her and eager to force her, among other concessions, to eat, to sleep —André Breton, *Nadja.*
   The use of the word 'whirlwind' startles because it turns on its head our notion of ordinariness.

3. [Alexander] Woollcott's dish was trivia. Dish? More precisely, his caldron. He could ladle it out endlessly, enchantingly —John Mason Brown, Introduction, *The Portable Woollcott*

4. Women and men (both little and small) / cared for anyone not at all / they sowed their isn't they reaped their same —e. e. cummings, "Anyone Lived in a Pretty How Town"
   Cummings takes ordinariness and gilds it with charm. "Women" is the only word capitalized in the entire poem—all nine stanzas of it.

5. To friends and workmates, I'm just another suburban warrior looking for that perfect parking place in the strip mall of life, but thanks to a telephone call from the Bureau of Census, I am a secret agent, a 007 in the war of indexes —Robert Goldman, Op-Ed, *The New York Times*, July 17, 1993
   The author humorously reflected on the effects of his replies to a Census survey on the Consumer Price Index.

6. What a girl called "the dailiness of life" . . . is well water / Pumped from an old well at the bottom of the world —Randall Jarrell, "Well Water"
   And after the water is pumped, "you cup your hands / And gulp from them the dailiness of life."

7. I am not concerned with the moron, the ordinary hairless ape who takes everything in his stride —Vladimir Nabokov, "Lance," *The New Yorker*, 1950–60
   Unlike this "hairless ape," Nabokov's hero is a man of imagination and science "surmounting the panic the ape might not experience at all."

8. On this warm afternoon, the musical temperature never rose out of the comfort zone and into the steamy tropics of excitement —Andrew Pincus, *The Berkshire Eagle*, July 19, 1993
   Pincus credited violinist Izhak Perlman for giving a flawless performance, but noted that such perfection tends to be too pleasing to arouse great emotion—a reminder of the common expression, to damn with faint praise.

■ ORIGINALITY/ UNORIGINALITY

See also: CHANGE; CREATIVITY; INDIVIDUALITY; MUSIC/MUSICIANS; PEOPLE, INTERACTION; PRAISE; WRITING/ WRITERS

1. For fifty years to come, musical composers will do little more than pour water on his leaves —Anon., Quotation, *The London Morning Chronicle*, May 4, 1795

The quote is attributed to a music aficionado after he had attended a concert featuring mostly compositions by Franz Joseph Haydn. It appeared in the program notes of a performance of Haydn's "Symphony No. 104 in D major" by the Philadelphia Orchestra at Avery Fisher Hall, March 1, 1993.

2. I would not say that Bates opened up new territory, but he achieved such sovereignty of what literary land he inherited that he deserves the homage of our uncomplicated enjoyment —Anthony Burgess, Introduction, *H. E. Bates. A Month by the Lake & Other Stories*

3. She offered him increasingly his own ideas, sometimes the reverse side of the knitting, but essentially his —A. S. Byatt, *Possession*

   This describes the relationship of two graduate students.

4. The ruse consists of never repeating ourselves; of taking care, when once a work has fallen from the tree, not to shake the tree to bring down others of the same kind —Jean Cocteau, "The Cat That Walks by Itself"

5. They sun themselves in the great man's light, and feel it to be their own element —Ralph Waldo Emerson, Speech, "The American Scholar," Harvard College, August 31, 1837

   "They" is a reference to the people known as "the mass" and "the herd."

6. Living as we did the herd-life of boys . . . we were debarred from any real interest in philosophy, history, art, literature, and music. I speak of the generality, not of the few black swans among us —John Galsworthy, "American and Briton"

7. You might suppose Ms. Glendinning would be a bit abashed to find herself so far back in line, telling us the barn is on fire long after the arsonist has been tried and hanged —James R. Kincaid, *The New York Times Book Review*, January 31, 1993

   Kincaid noted that since every year brings forth a new Trollope biography, Glendinning was dealing with yet another version of the same story. The author herself was apparently jolted "as news of the threefold wave of new Trollope biographies broke over me."

8. And this I swear by blackest brook of hell, / I am no pick-purse of another's wit —Sir Philip Sidney, "Sonnet 74," *Astrophel and Stella*

   When you swear by the Styx, can you be taken seriously? Sidney probably pilfered ideas as many other writers have done.

9. With his compelling new book *A Violent Act* . . . Alec Wilkinson takes the true-crime form and pilots it into new territory —Amanda Smith, *Publishers Weekly*, February 1, 1992

■ ORIGINS
See: DESCRIPTIONS, MISC.

■ OUT OF PLACE
See: BELONGING/OUTCAST

■ OUTSPOKENNESS
See: CANDOR

■ OVERREACHING
See: SUCCESS/FAILURE

■ PAIN AND SUFFERING

See also: DIFFICULTIES; FAMILIES/FAMILY RELATIONSHIPS; GRIEF; ILLNESS; SENSITIVITY; MEN AND WOMEN; SORROW

1. If growing up is painful for the Southern Black girl, being aware of her displacement is the rust on the razor that threatens the throat —Maya Angelou, *I Know Why the Caged Bird Sings*

2. Life is a bitter sea of suffering —Anon., Chinese Proverb

3. No matter what I do, it's as if my heart is wrapped around with barbed wire —Sheila Bosworth, *Slow Poison*

4. His old inner wound opened slowly, gaping here and there, and began to bleed —Dorothy Canfield, "Murder on Jefferson Street"

5. Pain [like iron left in the rain] . . . rusts into beauty too —Mary Carolyn Davies, "A Prayer for Every Day"

6. Hoover, Coolidge, Harding, Wilson / hear the factories of human misery turning out commodities —Robert Duncan, "A Poem Beginning with a Line by Pindar. II"

7. The desertion [by his wife] had cut a deep ravine in his mind which he was careful not to show —Winston Graham, *Stephanie*

8. Venerable Mother Toothache / . . . Stop twisting in your yellow fingers / The fourfold rope of nerves —John Heath-Stubbs, "A Charm Against the Toothache"

9. Though length of time ought to have closed up my wounds, yet the seeing them described by your hand was sufficient to make them all open and bleed afresh —Heloise, Letter to Peter Abelard
   In a letter to a friend, Abelard writes of his love for Heloise. Heloise opens this letter after she has gone to a convent.

10. Pain is a watchdog medically, telling us when to consult a doctor, and then it's the true-blue dog at the bedside who rivals the relatives for fidelity —Edward Hoagland, "The Threshold and the Jolt of Pain," *The Village Voice*, April 17, 1969

11. Looking at him, Mrs. Ockham felt a sword in her heart —Aldous Huxley, *Time Must Have a Stop*
    A few pages later, a handsome schoolboy who arouses memories of a dead son gives "the sword in Mrs. Ockham's heart . . . another agonizing twist."

12. *Dukkha* is "a wheel not running true on its axle, or a bone slipped out of its socket. Because life is out of joint, there is friction and pain —Philip Kapleau, *The Wheel of Life and Death*
    Dukkha is a Sanscrit word that implies grief and frustration as well as suffering. The anatomical metaphor became part of our everyday language

after Shakespeare popularized it with Hamlet's statement: "The time is out of joint" (Hamlet, 1, 5, 186).

13. How many swords had Lady Beveridge in her pierced heart! —D. H. Lawrence, *The Ladybird*

    The metaphor opens Lawrence's short World War I novel; the wounds inflicted with the metaphoric sword are the deaths of her sons and brother.

14. Great tides of pain go ebbing and flowing among the piers of the teeth —Henry Wadsworth Longfellow, Journal, 1855

    Longfellow who suffered from assorted ailments, also remarked that "pain never kills any one, but it is a most uncomfortable bedfellow.

15. I was more afraid of him than five oceans of pain —Norman Mailer, *Harlot's Ghost*

    The man pushing the narrator beyond his capacities is his father.

16. Her gray-green eyes were bright, her mouth was big . . . he glimpsed a savage animal, mad with the suffering twisted and crammed into her big racked body —Peter Matthiessen, *At Play in the Fields of The Lord*

17. My natural sensitiveness gradually increased . . . and my mind was one open wound —Guy de Maupassant, "Looking Back"

    The story's super-sensitive protagonist envies those "to whom nature has given a thick skin and the armour of stoicism!" He goes on to explain how he eventually shrank from all contacts since he had "no defence against the blows of chance or fate."

18. The anguish of the world is on my tongue; / My bowl is filled to the brim with it; there is more than I can eat —Edna St. Vincent Millay, "The Anguish"

    The poet writes that toothless babies and old people are happy because they "cannot rend this meat."

19. Pain. I seem to have an affection, a kind of sweet tooth for it —Toni Morrison, *Jazz*

20. A pain, of another musical tone than intercostal neuralgia . . . entered into excruciating concords with the orchestra — Vladimir Nabokov, *King, Queen, Knave*

21. Suddenly a sunbeam, a gleam of glass, would stab him painfully in the pupil — Vladimir Nabokov, *King, Queen, Knave*

    Nabokov makes the reflection of sunlight an actual shard that inflicts physical pain.

22. He is buckled fast in torment —Pindar, "Olympia 1," *Odes*

23. I live in a cocoon of pain most of the day —May Sarton, February 1, 1991, *Endgame, A Journal of the Seventy-Ninth Year*

24. Othello: Avaunt, be gone, thou has set me on the rack —William Shakespeare, *Othello,* Act 3, scene 1, line 341

    Othello is tortured by Iago's assertions of Desdemona's infidelity.

25. I fall upon the thorns of life! I bleed! — Percy Bysshe Shelley, "Ode to the West Wind"

26. He [Keats] was first half chewed in London and finally spit dying into Italy — Francis Thompson, Quoted in *The World's Great Letters*

27. Old woman cried / Enough to twist your bowels! —Tu Fu, "Recruiting Officer at Shih-hao Village," T'ang Dynasty

    The old woman's sons have been killed in battle, and she tells the recruiting officer, "There are no more men in this house."

28. A bright rapids of sorrow. / . . . pain's clean piercing arrow —Andrei Voznesensky, "An Arrow in the Wall"

29. I woke up with a freight train in my head —Scott Wentworth, *Gunmetal Blues*

    The speaker is the unnamed hero (and author) of a 1992 Off-Broadway musical mystery spoof of 1940s hard-boiled detective thrillers.

30. We wanted to drain the bitter draft to the dregs —Elie Wiesel, *Night*

The Jews in Wiesel's childhood community were determined to know everything about the Nazi atrocities facing them.

31. One instinct told him to ignore her, but she had cut too deeply into his bleeding feelings for him to leave off —Richard Wright, *The Outsider*

The release of the protagonist's inner self is prompted by his relationship with a woman.

■ PALLOR

See: FACIAL COLOR

■ PARENTS/CHILDREN

See: CHILDHOOD/CHILDREN; FAMILIES/ FAMILY RELATIONSHIPS

■ PARIS

See: CITIES

■ PARTICIPATION

See: ENTRANCES/EXITS

■ PASSION

See also: CALMNESS/VOLATILITY; CHARACTERIZATIONS; DESIRE; DESPAIR; EMOTIONS; ENDINGS; FEELINGS; HEART; LOVE; LOVER'S DECLARATIONS AND EXCHANGES; MEN AND WOMEN; SEX/SEXUALITY; TEMPTATION; ZEAL

1. Weep rather for me now and extinguish the fire which burns me —Peter Abelard, Letter to Heloise

The fire was his great love for Heloise, which he wanted to subsume into his love of God.

2. My heart, drunk with voluptuousness — Peter Abelard, Letter to Heloise

3. Violent passions . . . will eat up your leaves, destroy your fruit and leave you a withered tree —The Bible, *Apocrypha, Ecclesiasticus*

4. It is better to marry than to burn —The Bible, *N.T., 1 Corinthians, 7:9*

The use of fire for passion is a metaphor that no doubt antedates The Bible.

5. Her whole life was spent riding at breakneck speed along the wilder shores of love —Lesly Blanch, "The Wilder Shores of Love"

6. I've been covered by the pimples of ecstasy and have rooted in the mud of despair —Ethan Canin, "We Are Nighttime Travelers"

An aging man reminisces about times when he was not as emotionally dead as he now seems to be.

7. His old passion . . . shivered and broke into pieces —Charles Dickens, *Little Dorrit*

Dickens, like the fictional Arthur Clenam, had the experience of a reunion which sent his passion crashing like a dropped dish.

8. Passion and her reverence for rarest goodness rushed together in an undivided current —George Eliot, *Felix Holt, The Radical*

The protagonist's love also makes her realize that her previous passion was a "silken bondage" and "nothing better than a well-cushioned despair."

9. A man in a passion rides a mad horse — Benjamin Franklin, *Poor Richard's Almanack*

10. The passions are the gates of the soul — Baltasar Gracian, *The Art of Worldly Wisdom*

11. The passion that Blue feels for Luna . . . is supposed to be the motor that drives this novel, the event that triggers the avalanche of losses and confusions —Michiko Kakutani, "Books of The Times," *The New York Times*, May 8, 1992

The novel being reviewed was Blue Calhoun *by Reynolds Price.*

12. Even to sit here together created a current of feeling that flowed back and forth between them —Kawabata Yasunari, *Beauty and Sadness*

13. Trudi: I meet 10 billion other men a day but I see you, my heart has a little heart attack —Wendy MacLeod, *Apocalyptic Butterflies*

14. " . . . I'm afraid I'll light up the darkness with the intense fire flaming inside my body" —Naguib Mahfouz, *Palace of Desire*
    To the common metaphor of love as fire, Mahfouz adds the metaphor of fire as light.

15. Overnight her body became a torch —Bernard Malamud, "The Cost of Living"

16. Her heart—her fleshly heart—was curled around itself, like a spiralled loaf of hot, new bread. Inside the cavity that rocked it, this good bread was swelling —Cynthia Ozick, "Puttermeyser Paired," *The New Yorker*, 1990
    The interlocked simile and metaphor pictures a middle-aged woman's first and sadly comic encounter with passion. The author builds on the metaphor with "Puttermesser waited for Rupert's head to come into her arms, against her heart's loaf.

17. They sicken of the calm, who knew the storm —Dorothy Parker, "Fair Weather"

18. What is this fire devouring me? A volcano roars within me —George Sand, Journal entry, November, 1834
    Sand extended the volcano image with a simile: "and I am about to explode like a crater."

19. Hamlet: Give me that man / That is not passion's slave, and I will wear him / In my heart's core, ay, in my heart of heart, / As I do thee —William Shakespeare, *Hamlet*, Act 3, scene 2, line 71

20. Passions . . . the winds which fill the sails of the vessels; sometimes they sink it; but without them it would be impossible to make way —Voltaire, *Zadig*

21. She felt again that silver hammer strike her nerves and shatter them into a thousand slivers of ecstacy —Dame Rebecca West, *Sunflower*
    The writer returns to and expands on the hammer metaphor a few pages later: "Again the silver hammer struck her nerves, again she drowned in a deep sea, again she slowly rose into the sunshine of her garden."

22. This obsession with Bertha—it's a whirlpool in my mind. It sucks up my every clean thought! —Irvin D. Yalom, *When Nietzsche Wept*

∎ PAST

See also: FUTURE; HISTORY; ILLUSION/REALITY; MEMORY/MEMORIES

1. The past is another country —Lois Battle, title of popular novel, 1990

2. The present enshrines the past —Simone de Beauvoir, *The Second Sex*

3. I don't want even to remember those bits and broken pieces [of the past]. Let me build with everybody else something new. Broken crockery is not for me —Nina Berberova, *The Italics Are Mine*
    Berberova's past goes back to her birth in Russia in 1901. She died in 1993, a year after Knopf reissued the memoir from which this is taken.

4. The best of prophets of the future is the past —Lord George Gordon Byron, Letter, January 28, 1821

5. Come, come, my girl, your past life is all sponged out —Wilkie Collins, *The Moonstone*
    The metaphor recalls the tabula rasa, *the blank slate on which an infant's personality will be written.*

6. The past was a tunnel—a long, dark tunnel you strolled down on your own —Laurie Colwin, "Intimacy"
    A woman reflecting on an affair she thought was finished realizes "whatever had been between them was not past."

7. Life was full of small opportunities of enjoyment; the sudden meeting of an old friend . . . hashing over the past lightly enough not to rumple the dust of illusion, which more and more as the years advanced, was settling deeper upon it —Noel Coward, "Traveller's Joy"

8. The past is a foreign country; they do things differently there —L. P. Hartley, *The Go-Between*

9. In ship, freight with rememberance / Of thoughts and pleasures past —Henry Howard (Earl of Surrey), "Complaint of the Absence of Her Lover being upon the Sea"

   The ship that is loaded with remembrances of things past is also reminiscent of Petrarch's "galley charged with forgetfulness."

10. All the soil is thick with shells, the tide-rock feasts of a dead people —Robinson Jeffers, "Apology for Bad Dreams, III"

11. Jane Campion peels back the past and finds it shockingly alive, in no need of resuscitation —Anthony Lane, "Sheet Music," *The New Yorker,* November 29, 1993

    The title for this review of The Piano *links the instrument that dominates the film and its underlying theme of repressed passions that are unleashed as the story "worms" its way "into the guts of Victorian experience."*

12. There's something / in a bony hill town sucking on the blood of its past / that holds the inwards of you like a cold hand —Richmond Lattimore, "Andritsaina Revisited"

    A returning visitor sees the hill town in the light of its history: "Nazis were bad: who else good, who bad, my God, who knows now?" The town is made a vampire, the blood that of the Nazi victims.

13. The past / is cities from a train —Robert Lowell, "At the Altar," *Between the Porch and the Altar IV*

    Trains are common metaphors for the swift passage of time, since views rush past before you can digest their meaning.

14. The grandmother floated through the swamps of the past —Gabriel García Márquez, "Innocent Eréndira and Her Heartless Grandmother"

15. The Strange Lady: There are all the colors of the rainbow in my past —Luigi Pirandello, *As You Desire Me,* Act 1

16. O, there are Voices of the Past, / Links of a broken chain / Wings that can bear me back to Times / Which cannot come again —Adelaide Proctor, "Voices of the Past"

17. The past is the only dead thing that smells sweet —Edward Thomas, "Early One Morning"

18. The days on the Mississippi . . . life has swallowed them up . . . they were days when the tide of life was high and when the heart was full of the sparkling wine of romance —Mark Twain, Quoted by Helen Keller in "Our Mark Twain"

    In her reminiscences of Twain, Keller remarked that the Mississippi seemed to be "forever flowing through his speech, through the shadowless white sands of thought.

■ PATIENCE

1. Patience is bitter, but its fruit is sweet — Anon., French Proverb

2. Patience is a flatterer . . . and an ass — Aphra Behn, *The Feigned Curtezans,* Act 3, scene 1

3. Patience is a plaster for all sores —Miguel de Cervantes, *Don Quixote*

4. Patience is sorrow's salve —Charles Churchill, "The Prophecy of Famine"

5. Rosalind: One inch of delay more is a South Sea of discovery —William Shakespeare, *As You Like It,* Act 4, scene 2, line 199

6. Lear: I will be the pattern of all patience; I will say nothing —William Shakespeare, *King Lear,* Act 3, scene 2, line 37

7. Nym: Though patience be a tired mare, yet she will plod —William Shakespeare, *The Life of Henry the Fifth* Act 2, scene 1, line 24

   The image of the endurance of the weary, probably spur-driven horse bears out Caroline Spurgeon's analysis of Shakespeare's metaphors as reflecting his sympathy for the plight of the animal.

8. I am to wait, though waiting so be hell —
William Shakespeare, "Sonnet 58," line 13

9. Patience is the best seasoning for trouble
—Titus Maccius Plautus
   In other words, if you can't cure it, learn to endure it.

10. Patience is the heart of hoping —Marquis
Luc de Clapiers de [Marquis] Vauvenargues

■ PATRIOTISM

See also: BIGOTRY

1. Nationalism is an infantile disease . . . the measles of mankind —Albert Einstein, Letter, 1921

2. Coriolanus: I am return'd your soldier; /
No more infected with my country's love / Than when I parted hence —William Shakespeare, *Coriolanus*, Act 5, scene 5, line 71
   Coriolanus, who has been called an infectious disease, now applies a variation of the metaphor to himself.

3. To strike freedom of the mind with the fist of patriotism is an old and ugly subtlety —Adlai Stevenson, "The Nature of Patriotism," speech to American Legion Convention, August 27, 1952
   Stevenson's metaphor is a clear strike at the ugliness of Senator Joseph McCarthy's communist "witch hunts."

4. The anatomy of patriotism is complex. But surely intolerance and public irresponsibility cannot be cloaked in the shining armor of rectitude and righteousness —Adlai Stevenson, "The Nature of Patriotism," Speech to American Legion Convention, August 27, 1952
   Stevenson's metaphor alluded to the corrosive influence of the McCarthy communist hunting craze.

5. There are no points of the compass on the chart of true patriotism —Robert C.

Winthrop, Letter to the Boston Commercial Club, June 12, 1879

■ PEACE

See also: AGREEMENT/DISAGREEMENT; ENTANGLEMENTS; FRIENDSHIP/ FRIENDS; INTERNATIONAL RELATIONS; WAR; WARRIORS AND PEACEMAKERS

1. This treaty, like a rainbow on the edge of the cloud . . . afforded the sure prognostic of fair weather. If we reject it the vivid colors will grow pale—it will be a baleful meteor portending tempest and war — Fisher Ames, Speech to the House of Representatives, April 28, 1796
   In this speech supporting a treaty with Great Britain the metaphor is dependent on the rainbow simile.

2. This time I am coming with two olive branches —Yasir Arafat, Quoted day of signing of Middle East Peace Pact, September 14, 1993
   When the dove sent out of the ark returned carrying an olive leaf, Noah took it as a sign that the flood—and God's wrath—were abating (Genesis 8:10-11). The PLO leader chose the familiar metaphor to show the world he was no longer the man who in 1974 addressed the United Nations with a gun at his side.

3. Thinkers from Bacon to the present have been inspired by the certainty that there must exist a total solution . . . that this springtime in human affairs will come once the obstacles, natural and human, are overcome, and then at last men will cease to fight each other —Isaiah Berlin, "The Apotheosis of the Romantic Will"

4. The wolf and the lamb shall feed together and the lion shall eat straw —The Bible, *O.T., Isaiah 65:25*
   The Peaceable Kingdom, where there is no predation and the animals take their rest together, is a favorite image in art, most notably in a well-known painting by Rousseau.

5. The noisy banquet of the bombing planes / is over now —Joseph Brodsky, "Einem alten Architekten in Rom"

6. It is true that the last few years have seen the United Nations build up its efforts to untie the knots of regional peacekeeping —Yuri Fedotov, *The Singapore Symposium*, United Nations

    Since he uttered these words, the Department Chief from the Soviet Union's Ministry of Foreign Affairs has seen more knotted tie-ups in that former Union.

7. Hector: Do let us get our feet on to a few inches of peace, touch it, if only with the tips of our toes —Jean Giraudoux, *Tiger at the Gates*, Act 2

    Hector who has just returned from one war to be faced by a second says peace is "like solid ground to someone who was drowning or sinking in the quicksands."

8. Priam: The soldiers will rush to buy the bread of peace, to drink the wine of peace, to hold in their arms the woman of peace, and in an hour you will put them back to face a war —Jean Giraudoux, *Tiger at the Gates*, Act 2

9. The species called peace-keeping is evolving into a genus, also called peace-keeping. The genus will include a number of different species—already includes a number of species —Marrack Goulding, *The Singapore Symposium*, United Nations

    As though keeping the peace were not already complicated enough!

10. Servant 1: Peace is a / very apoplexy, lethargy; mulled, deaf, sleepy, / insensible; a getter of more bastard children than war's a destroyer of men —William Shakespeare, *Coriolanus*, Act 4, scene 6, line 239

11. Talbot: Renounce your soil, give sheep in lions' stead —William Shakespeare, *The First Part of Henry the Sixth*, Act 1, scene 5, line 29

    Sheep and lions as metaphors for the meek and the strong comes from The Bible. Since lions were

embroidered into the armour of the English kings of the day, they have added meaning as used here.

12. Hamlet: Peace should . . . / stand a comma 'tween their amities —William Shakespeare, *Hamlet*, Act 5, scene 2, line 41

13. Peace comes dropping slow, / Dropping from the veils of the morning —William Butler Yeats, "The Lake Isle of Innisfree"

■ PEACEFULNESS
See: STILLNESS

■ PEAK
See: ZENITH

■ PEDANTRY
See also: KNOWLEDGE

1. Pedantry is a little knowledge on parade —Josh Billings

■ PEOPLE
See: HUMANITY/HUMANKIND

■ PEOPLE, INTERACTION
See also: ALLIANCES; CONVERSATION; FRIENDSHIP/FRIENDS; GROUP SCENES; MANIPULATION; MEN AND WOMEN; POLITICS/POLITICIANS; SEX/SEXUALITY

1. A committee is a cul-de-sac into which ideas are lured to be quietly strangled — Anon., Quoted by George F. Will, *Washington Post Writers Group*, August 16, 1992

2. [A party:] A close-knit, if temporary whole, a world whipped out of conversation and sherry —Marjorie Barnard, "The Party"

3. Still, she would give him one bottle if he bought two. That made the other peasants laugh and clap Kula on the back saying

that the scythe had struck a hard stone — Louis Begley, *Wartime Lies*

4. Two people may be talking to each other . . . and inside each of the two there runs a kind of dark river of unconnected thought . . . which keeps pace with the flow of talk —A. S. Byatt, "The Chinese Lobster," *The New Yorker*, October 26, 1992

5. In their contact with the Tuttles, the Warders uneasily felt the need to make an effort towards more ease, pleasantness, reticence and quietness that was natural to them. It was fatiguing. And they were never sure they had quite caught the new tune —Dorothy Canfield, "Murder on Jefferson Street"

     The story illustrates the tragic consequences suffered by people who never manage to tune in on each others' sensitivities.

6. Your hand full of hours, you came to me —Paul Celan, "Memory of France"

7. By God, he smoot me ones on the list / For that I rente out of his book a leef — Geoffrey Chaucer, "The Wife of Bath's Prologue and Tale," *The Canterbury Tales*

     The wife was boxed on the ear for "taking a leaf out of her husband's book." This remains a common metaphor for all who want others to do as they say, not as they do.

8. Jim was caught in the cross fire of his mother-in-law's soliloquy and her gardener's rage —John Cheever, "The Common Day"

9. A moist and Fahrenheit handshake. You know the type —Lawrence Durrell, "La Valise"

10. But this coolness with which he treated the other's flame had rather the effect of oil than of water —Henry Fielding, *The Life of Mr. Jonathan Wild the Great*

11. I do not want a honeymoon with you. I want a good marriage —President Gerald R. Ford, Speech to a joint session of Congress, August 12, 1974

12. They were dispatched in a soup of good feeling —John Fowles, *Daniel Martin*

13. He was gazing at Gil and Roger, who were united by the almost visible thread of their glances —Jean Genet, *Querelle*

     When Querelle keeps watching the young men, they become nervous, "as if the entire ball of string had been unrolled."

14. She'd fired at random and hit the target by accident —Ross MacDonald, *The Moving Target*

     The "shooter" is a woman who's come uncomfortably close to guessing that the man she's having a drink with is a private detective.

15. Her powers of detection sliced my intelligence into microscopic wavers —Norman Mailer, *Harlot's Ghost*

16. What a spectacle I've cut wagging my tail and leaping round you, only to be left like this while the boat sails off —Katherine Mansfield, "Je Ne Parle Pas Français"

     The protagonist, who has referred to himself as a "little fox terrier" here expresses irritation with a friend because "after all, it was you who whistled to me." When the young man contacts him again, the protagonist's pique is forgotten: "Away the little fox-terrier flew."

17. Again, he would tease me by fluttering his gloved fingers at me. To my eyes those fingers were the sharp points of some dangerous weapon about to run me through —Mishima Yukio, "Omi"

18. He served for me as an abrasive stone on which I could sharpen my own ideas — Lewis Mumford, Autobiographical fragment, 1963

     Mumford thus writes about a friend.

19. Don't stare me in the face; there is no parade there —Natsume Soseki, *Botchan*

     Botchan, newly independent, tries to face down a servant girl at the hotel.

20. I failed utterly to kindle a spark of affection in her eyes, a flush of colour in her cheeks —Marcel Proust, *Cities of the Plain*

21. Iago: I have rubb'd this young quat almost to the sense, / And he grows angry now —William Shakespeare, *Othello*, Act 5, scene 1, line 11
   Iago speaks of Roderigo as though he were a boil that had been itching and had been rubbed raw.

22. They were two tectonic plates moving in different directions —Martin Cruz Smith, *Red Square*

23. All this goodness and honeymoon sweetness ... I'm bound to put my muddy boots on the vast soft carpet of her character —Muriel Spark, *Symposium*
   This "treacherous cloud of thought" comes suddenly to the man of the muddy boots.

24. Glynora confronted me in silence, a beautiful totem —Scott Turow, *Pleading Guilty*

25. He seized the straw of her suggestion — Thomas Wolfe, *Look Homeward Angel*
   Wolfe uses the proverbial metaphor of grabbing hold of a straw to find a solution or escape.

26. He turned abruptly, slammed his private door on them —Virginia Woolf, *To the Lighthouse*

27. The eyes of others our prisons, their thoughts our cages —Virginia Woolf, "An Unwritten Novel"

28. This woman ... invaded my mind and set up housekeeping there. I still cannot dislodge her —Irvin D. Yalom, *When Nietzsche Wept*

29. The interview [between Joseph Breuer and Friedrich Nietzsche] resembled more a chess contest than a professional consultation. He [Breuer] had made a move ... which Nietzsche immediately countered —Irvin D. Yalom, *When Nietzsche Wept*
   Yalom returns to the chess metaphor when Nietzsche eludes a "move" by Breuer who refers to this as "another file on the chessboard closed off," A page later he rounds it out with "But there was no turning back now. Breuer went for checkmate."

30. Am I destined to be merely a stage on which memories of Bertha eternally play out their drama? —Irvin D. Yalom, *When Nietzsche Wept*
   A fictionalized Dr. Joseph Breuer referring to his obsession with a patient.

31. Finally, an outing worthy of us. Deep water, quick dips in and out —Irvin D. Yalom, *When Nietzsche Wept*
   A fictional Friedrich Nietzsche comments on his sessions with Joseph Breuer aimed at gaining emotional understanding. He concludes his notes by asking himself "Will a quick dip in and out of "understanding" be sufficient? Or must it be a prolonged submersion?

■ PERCEPTIVENESS

See: ALERTNESS; AWARENESS/UNAWARENESS

■ PERFECTION

See also: ADMIRATION; CHARACTERIZATIONS; PRAISE; SEX/SEXUALITY

1. She was ... sexually, a natural masterpiece —Saul Bellow, *Herzog*
   This "masterpiece" was also understanding, educated and rich.

2. Down with the view of perfection which can be purchased only at the price of putting chains on the free, independent will, the unbridled imagination, the wild wind of inspiration which goeth where it listeth —Isaiah Berlin, "The Apotheosis of the Romantic Will"
   Perfection's impossibly high price is illustrated with three metaphors.

3. The search for perfection does seem to me a recipe for bloodshed, no better even if it is demanded by the sincerest of idealists, the purest of heart —Isaiah Berlin, "The Pursuit of the Ideal,"
   Berlin advocates an "uneasy equilibrium" which will have to be kept in constant repair.

4. I never promised you a rose garden — Hanna Green, *I Never Promised You a Rose Garden*

The title, has become a common metaphor for anyone who wants to forestall unrealistic expectations. In the novel, the phrase appeared as follows: "Look here," Furji said. "I never promised you a rose garden. I never promised you perfect justice."

5. I could rehearse, if that I wold, [would] / The whole effect of Nature's plaint, / When she had lost the perfect mold — Henry Howard (Earl of Surrey), "Give Place, Ye Lovers, Here Before"

   This metaphor has become a common sort of praise, as in "When God made you, He broke the mold."

6. In the paradise of commercialized maternity no Freudian reptile, it is evident, has ever reared its ugly head —Aldous Huxley, "Mother"

   Huxley is scornful about Mother's Day cards, in which all the mothers inhabit a "delicious Disneyland."

7. King: We lost a jewel of her —William Shakespeare, *All's Well That Ends Well* Act 5, scene 3, line 1

   The jewel is Helen.

8. Othello: had she been true, / If heaven would make me such another world, / Of one entire and perfect chrysolite, / I'd not have sold her for it —William Shakespeare, *Othello* Act 5, scene 2, line 144

■ PERMANENCE/ IMPERMANENCE

See also: BELIEFS; PROMISES; TRANSIENCE

1. Don't be such a rolling stone, Prof. Start leading a normal life —Saul Bellow, *Herzog*

   This is a take-off on the proverbial a rolling stone gathers no moss *which has been in common usage for over 500 years.*

2. On occasion he is transported by a transient beauty that can't be pickled in time —Vincent Canby, "Reviews / Film," *The New York Times*, June 17, 1992

   Canby thus described the narrator of a travel film.

3. Call us what you will, we are made such by love; / Call her one, me another fly, / We're tapers too, and at our own cost die —John Donne, "The Canonization"

   Donne is concerned with transience, both in the image of the fly and in the candle which consumes itself.

4. Dunstan: The Church of God is not a candle. Blow on —Edna St. Vincent Millay, *The King's Henchman*, Act 1

5. Wolsey: That sun, I pray may never set! —William Shakespeare, *The Life of King Henry the Eighth* Act 1, scene 1, line 6

   Shakespeare regularly pictured kings as suns.

6. Pistol: oaths are straws, men's faiths are waver cakes / and hold-fast is the only dog —William Shakespeare, *The Life of Henry the Fifth* Act 2, scene 3, line 49

   The metaphor elaborates on Pistol's advice to "trust noone."

7. Griffith: Men's evil manners live in brass; their virtues / We write in water — William Shakespeare, *The Life of King Henry the Eighth* Act 4, scene 2, line 45

   In Julius Caesar, (3, 2, 81), Antony declares "The evil that men do lives after them, / The good is oft interred with their bones." A variation, dictated by John Keats for his epitah, reads "Here lies one whose name was writ in water."

8. It's been . . . one of those things that come up out of the sea, on a full-moon night, playing the harp —Edith Wharton, *The Children*

   The protagonist reflects on his passion for a young girl.

■ PERSEVERANCE

See also: JOURNALISM/JOURNALISTS; LIFE AND DEATH; PEOPLE, INTERACTION

1. But now the threefold happiness / Hear from Me, bull of Bharatas / That in which he comes to delight thru long practice — Anon., *The Bhagavad Gita, 18:36*

   Just as the Blessed One is praised by Arjuna, He in turn praises the warrior with epithets that compare his courage and tenacity to that of strong animals.

2. Hold on with a bulldog grip, and chew and choke as much as possible —Abraham Lincoln, Telegram to General Grant, August 17, 1964

3. Once more she ambushed official after official —Sean O'Faolain, "Teresa"
   A nun demands information from a railroad attendant.

4. A rat-trap sensibility: slams down on subject, maims and kills it but retains it —Theodore Roethke, *Straw for the Fire*

5. Don Hewitt, the producer of *60 Minutes* . . . whose journalistic jaw never bit an ankle it would let go of, pursued him [Ross Perot] for months —A. M. Rosenthal, "On My Mind," *The New York Times*, October 27, 1992

6. King: But to the quick o' the' ulcer: / Hamlet comes back —William Shakespeare, *Hamlet* Act 4, scene 7, line 123
   To describe Hamlet's persistence with a common metaphor, he's a thorn in the king's side.

7. I must keep on rowing, not until I reach port but until I reach my grave —Germaine de Staël, Letter to her daughter, July, 1814

8. To keep a lamp burning we have to keep putting oil in it —Mother Teresa, Quoted, *Time Magazine*, December 29, 1975
   To translate energy into action needs the "fuel" of inspiration.

■ PERSONAL TRAITS

See: CHARACTERISTICS

■ PERSONALITY PROFILES

See also: CHARACTERIZATIONS; INSULTS; POLITICS/POLITICIANS; VOICES

1. A Mausoleum 100 feet square at the base, and 200 feet high —John Adams

The reference is to George Washington as portrayed in a biography by Chief Justice John Marshall.

2. When God had finished creating Madame Necker, he stiffened her with starch inside and out —Anon.
   In his biography of Madame Necker's daughter, Germaine de Staël, Christopher J. Herold picked up on the above metaphor to describe his subject: "Germaine resembled her mother . . . she was, in fact, Madame Necker without the starch."

3. Lincoln is a cross between a sand-hill crane and an Andalusian jackass —Anon., Letter that appeared on the front page of *The Louisville Daily Courier*, March 1, 1861
   The letter was attributed to a prominent member of Congress.

4. I couldn't help wondering: How would the sober Poetry Center audience receive this childlike packet of a man [Truman Capote] with . . . his baby seal's voice, his tendency to illustrate his points with little arabesques of emphasis —John Malcolm Brinnin, Journal entry, 1950
   Brinnin's portrait is quite a packet of metaphors.

5. His spleen could be merciless, his sweetness diabetic; his behavior unhousebroken —John Mason Brown, Introduction, *The Portable Woollcott*
   Brown uses two health metaphors and an animal metaphor to paint his portrait of Alexander Woollcott.

6. She filled the room; the men were obliterated, seemed tossed about like twigs in an angry water, and even Steavens felt himself being drawn into the whirlpool —Willa Cather, "The Sculptor's Funeral," *Youth and the Bright Medusa*
   The simile sets the stage for the metaphor: the angry water becomes a whirlpool of evil influence.

7. Who is this rare bird, perched at the eerie dead center of the world's hurricane, whom all men delight to praise? —Alistair Cooke, *Manchester Guardian*
   The man profiled by Cooke was Dag Hammarskkjöld the second Secretary General of the United Nations.

8. Taft is an amiable island, entirely surrounded by men who know exactly what they want —Jonathan Prentiss Dolliver

9. Success was his keynote, adroitness his panoply, and the mellow music of laughter his instant reward —Kenneth Grahame, "The Magic Ring"

10. This poet [Walt Whitman] with the private soul leaking out of him all the time. All his privacy leaking out in a sort of dribble, oozing into the universe —D. H. Lawrence, *Studies in Classic American Literature*

11. He [Abraham Lincoln] stands six feet two in his stockings—a colossus holding his burning heart in his hand to light up the sea of life —Henry Wadsworth Longfellow, Quoted in Carl Sandburg's *Abraham Lincoln, The War Years*. Vol. One.

12. Charley: A salesman . . . he's a man way out there in the blue, riding on a smile and a shoeshine. And when they start not smiling back that's an earthquake —Arthur Miller, *Death of a Salesman*, Requiem
    This sums up the life of Willy Loman, the salesman Miller immortalized.

13. Assign Yogi Berra to Cape Canaveral; / he could handle any missile. / He is no feather —Marianne Moore, "Baseball and Writing"

14. This wasn't some oily pol . . . going up in flames—Judge Sol] Wachtler had always seemed greaseless, fireproof —Eric Poley, "Crazy for You," *New York Magazine*, December 14, 1992
    Wachtler was the New York State Judge whose "Jekyll and Hyde" pursuit of a former lover sent shock waves through the legal community.

15. He is one of those survivors, of post-war American intellectual firestorms, no less than Old Europe's bloodbaths, who run Manhattan with an iron tongue —Frank Rich, "Theater," *The New York Times*, March 18, 1991

    This is actually a double metaphor: the embodiment of intellectual upheavals as fires and acerbic, outspokenness as a tongue made of iron; the last a twist on the more commonly used iron fist.

16. [Secretary of State James Baker:] The iceman of Foggy Bottom —William Safire, "Essay," *The New York Times*, March 2, 1992

17. Her [Marlene Dietrich's] manner . . . a serpentine lasso whereby her voice casually winds itself around our most vulnerable fantasies —Kenneth Tynan, Quoted in Dietrich obituary, *The New York Times*, May 7, 1992

18. There she sat . . . a ruin, if you will, but one with a bit of gay bunting fluttering jaunty and defiant from the topmost battlement —Alexander Woollcott, "Bernhardt"

■ PERSPIRATION

See: SWEAT

■ PERSUASIVENESS/ PERSUADERS

See also: GUIDANCE/GUIDES; PEOPLE, INTERACTION; POLITICS/POLITICIANS

1. The debate followed days of arm twisting by the President and his allies —Richard L. Berk, *The New York Times*, May 28, 1993
   Metaphoric arm twisting is a favorite form of persuasion, and in this case helped President Clinton's economic plan squeak through the approval process in the House of Representatives.

2. Jesus: Come with me and I will make you fishers of men —The Bible, *N.T., Matthew 4:18; Mark 1:17.*
   Jesus here offers to turn Peter and his brother Andrew's real fishermen's nets into figurative nets for winning souls. In "The Queer Feet," G.K. Chesterton has his detective priest, Father Brown, recall this passage as follows: "Yes . . . I caught him with an unseen hook and an invisible line which is long enough to let him wander to the ends

of the world, and still to bring him back with a twitch upon the thread."

3. Allow me to congratulate you on the masterly manner in which you have opened the full fire of your batteries on me at the moment when I least expected it —Wilkie Collins, *The Moonstone*

    Mr. Bruff, the loyal solicitor, has been confounded for a moment by the cantankerous Miss Clack.

4. Hotspur: And by this face, / This seeming brow of justice, did he win / The hearts of all that he did angle for —William Shakespeare, *The First Part of King Henry the Fourth*, Act 4, scene 3, line 82

    The use of the word angle evokes an image of fishing for loyalty and love.

5. The Colonel's tongue was a magician's wand that turned dried apples into figs and water into wine as easily as it could change a hovel into a palace and present poverty into imminent future riches — Mark Twain, *The Gilded Age*

    To illustrate the Colonel's persuasiveness, Twain shows Washington Hawkins still under the influence of the Colonel's talk, waking to a sense of being in a palace instead of the barren room he in fact occupies.

■ PETS

See: ANIMALS

■ PHILOSOPHY

See also: THINKING/THOUGHT

1. Philosophy . . . a filter turned upside down, where what goes in clear comes out cloudy —Anon.

2. Philosophy's the best medicine for the mind —Marcus Tullius Cicero

3. Content is the Philosophy's Stone, that turns all it touches into gold —Benjamin Franklin, *Poor Richard's Almanack*

Franklin's reference is to the alchemist's quest for a "philosophers stone," a substance that would transmute base metal into gold.

4. The pensive man . . . He sees that eagle float / For which the intricate Alps are a single nest —Wallace Stevens, "Connoisseur of Chaos"

    "A great disorder is an order," says Stevens elsewhere in the poem, approaching a poetic definition of chaos theory

5. Light / Is the lion that comes down to drink. There / And in that state, the glass is a pool —Wallace Stevens, "The Glass of Water"

    Stevens makes of a glass of water a metaphysical concept.

6. Philosophy is language idling —Ludwig Wittgenstein, *Tractatus Logico-Philosophicus*

■ PHYSICAL APPEARANCE

See also: AGE/AGING; BEAUTY; BODIES/ BODY; BREASTS/BOSOMS; DISINTEGRATION; EYES; HAIR COLOR; MOUTHS

1. He was a gentleman of sixty who seemed to be made out of highly durable leather —Louis Auchincloss, "The Wedding Guest," *Skinny Island*

2. She's looking a crime —Enid Bagnold, *National Velvet*

3. By degrees the Baron . . . got rid of all his harness. His stomach sagged; obesity was obvious. The oak tree became a tower — Honoré de Balzac, *Cousin Bette*

    The Baron, no longer bothers with his appearance.

4. Her bosom gleamed dazzlingly white, framed in lace whose russet tint set off the matt satin of her beautiful shoulders — Honoré de Balzac, *Cousin Bette*

5. Seeing ourselves every day, we come, like the Baron, to think of ourselves little changed . . . while other people see on our heads hair turning to chinchilla . . . great

pumpkins in our bellies —Honoré de Balzac, *Cousin Bette*

This unrealistic self-image has exacerbated the Baron's penchant for womanizing

6. This other different diamond, a black diamond, the most rare of all . . . was appreciated at its full value by several ambitious clerks —Honoré de Balzac, *Cousin Bette*

The black diamond is a metaphor for the plain Cousin Bette's transformation into a handsome woman.

7. The Baroness . . . that so well-preserved flower began to look like the last solitary frost-touched rose on a November bush —Honoré de Balzac, ''The Firm of Nucingen''

Balzac combines smoothly combines metaphor and simile.

8. She came in looking flushed and fine, with diamonds of sleet in her hair — Laurie Colwin, ''A Mythological Subject''

9. Sarah Pocket . . . a little dry brown corrugated old woman. —Charles Dickens, *Great Expectations*

Sarah face is a ''walnut shell countenance.''

10. This gruff man with thick strings of veins rising against his collar had nothing to do with the father who would put his cheek next to hers, and ask humbly for a kiss — Nadine Gordimer, ''Charmed Lives''

11. Pale dowagers hiding their liver-spots / In a fine chalk, confectionery dust — Anthony Hecht, *The Venetian Vespers*

12. Imagine, the inborn courtesy, calling a ruined fortress like me ''Miss'' —John Hersey, ''Fling,'' *Grand Street*

A woman of seventy recalls her lively past during a ''last fling'' trip.

13. She was a dried-up apricot of the fuzzy variety —John Hersey, ''Peggety's Parcel of Shortcomings,'' *The Atlantic*, June, 1950

14. A smooth pear of a skull —Robert Hughes, *The Fatal Shore*

The man being described was Capt. Arthur Phillip, appointed to govern the Australian ''penal colony'' in 1786.

15. She would have loved to conform to the national obsession with reddening, blistering, getting bronzed, this Celt from the headwaters of her gene pool —Tom Keneally, *The New York Times*, May 24, 1992

The author described the Australian actress, Nicole Kidman.

16. Ed Downe . . . a paunchy fireplug —N. R. Kleinfeld, *The New York Times*, June 16, 1992

The publishing executive was profiled in an article on his involvement with insider trading. Gets Suspicious.''

17. I tuck her several chins into her neck, / smooth the fan of wrinkles from her cheek —Dannye Romine Powell, ''In the Periodical Room''

The poem's narrator imagines a younger version of a woman sitting near him in the library.

18. She was a beautiful bird with a crushed beak —Richard Selzer, ''Imelda''

A young Indian girl with a disfiguring cleft palate.

19. A thin dark Indian girl about fourteen years old. A figurine, orange-brown, terracotta, and still attached to the unshaped clay from which she had been carved — Richard Selzer, ''Imelda''

20. So tall, he seems an unlikely rabbit, but the breadth of white face, the pallor of his blue irises, and a nervous flutter under his brief nose as he stabs a cigarette into his mouth partially explain the nickname, which was given to him when he too was a boy —John Updike, *Rabbit, Run*

This introduces readers to the metaphorically nicknamed hero of the first of Updike's most famous novels.

21. The carved lids of the unimaginable / ebony mask unwrapped from its cotton-wool cloud —Derek Walcott, ''Helen at the Beach''

A beautiful woman of proud bearing looks for work in a restaurant.

22. She had been for a row on the river, and the sun that netted the little waves with gold seemed to have caught her in its meshes —Edith Wharton, *The Age of Innocence*

23. Yet here in the sunshine, her hat thrown off her rumpled hair, and all the children scrambling over her, her mouth became a flame, her eyes fountains of laughter, her thin frail body a quiver of light —Edith Wharton, *The Children*

24. Though Nona was as tall and nearly as slim, she seemed to herself to be built, while Lita was spun of spray and sunlight —Edith Wharton, *Twilight Sleep*

■ PHYSICIANS

See: OCCUPATIONS

■ PIGS

See: ANIMALS

■ PITY

See also: EMOTIONS; ENVY; SYMPATHY

1. Helen: I am sure people pity others to the same extent that they would pity themselves. Unhappiness and ugliness are mirrors they can't bear to look into —Jean Giraudoux, *Tiger at the Gates*, Act 2
   Helen admits that she's not very good at pity, when Andromache asks her to return to Greece and prevent the war.

2. Pity made him a knight errant —Aldous Huxley, *Point Counter Point*
   This "knight errant" has not so much fallen in love with a woman as with her unhappiness.

3. The gilded sheath of pity conceals the dagger of envy —Friedrich Wilhelm Nietzsche

4. York: Forget to pity him, lest thy pity prove / A serpent that will sting thee to the heart —William Shakespeare, *The Tragedy of King Richard the Second* Act 5, scene 3, line 56
   York, caught between two duties, chooses to protect his king rather than his own son.

5. Pity thereof got in her breast such place / That, from that sea derived, tears' springs did flow —Sir Philip Sidney, "Sonnet 45," *Astrophel and Stella*

■ PLACES, MISC.

See also: ARTS AND ENTERTAINMENT; CITIES; EDUCATION AND LEARNING; WORK/WORKERS

1. A place where the gods strode the earth —Sarah Caldwell, Quoted 1991 Tanglewood program notes
   The place which embodied the magic of the gods to the conductor, was Tanglewood, site of the original summer music festival and summer home of the Boston Symphony.

2. His diocese lay within the icy arms of the Great Lakes —Willa Cather, *Death Comes for the Archbishop*
   This comes from the Prologue of Cather's story of the first bishop of New Mexico.

3. Nile, the seven-tongued river —Catullus, Poem 11

4. Room 315 [the main reading room of the New York Public Library] . . . it seemed silly to call it a room; it was more a *place, an acreage* —William Cole, "The Heart of the Heart of the Library." *The New York Times*, 1972
   Cole also uses two common metaphors to describe the front desk librarians and the readers they serve: "They are the ones on the firing line" as their "customers come in waves."

5. My patriotic Flensborg or Stettin Australian. I really don't recollect now what decent little port of the shores of the Baltic

was defiled by being the nest of that precious bird —Joseph Conrad, *Lord Jim*

> *Jim thinks the man he desribes has "made himself so warm that the top of his bullet head positively smoked."*

6. Vulgaria . . . an unspeakable place full of unspeakable people. It was the usual Iron Curtain post to which the F.O. had exposed its soft white underbelly in the person of Smith-Cromwell —Lawrence Durrell, "La Valise"

> *It was the kind of place where always "some dastardly Frenchman (always French) reaches for the safety-catch on his revolver and starts to introduce culture into our lives invariably."*

7. The Great American Desert, as settlers called the arid basin, is a sponge —Timothy Egan, *The New York Times*, January 18, 1993

> *Yuma, Arizona, one of the driest cities in the nation . . . has received 840 percent of its normal precipitation since Dec. 1," the article explained.*

8. But most any place is Baghdad if you don't know what will happen in it — Edna Ferber, *So Big*

> *Here is a metaphor of allusion.*

9. Parks . . . pavement disguised with a growth of grass —George Gissing, "Spring"

10. This is elbow-grease country —Edward Hoagland, "In Hazelton and Flying North"

> *In describing Hazelton, California, Hoagland alludes to an image associated with hard work since the seventeenth century, at which time it was a negative definition for sweat.*

11. Texas is one great windy lunatic —Socrates Hyacinth, *Overland Monthly*

12. 315 was my intellectual armory —Alfred Kazin, *New York Jew*

> *That's Room 315, the main reading room of the New York Public library, a source of fond memories for many writers.*

13. The homes, shopping strips, farms, offices and all the other places where people live and work are today nothing more than gruel for a front-end loader —Peter T. Kilborn, *New York Times*, September 3, 1992

> *Hurricane Andrew reduced the Florida area near Homestead to rubble.*

14. It's the old park in a nutshell —Marianne Moore, "Old Amusement Park"

> *The common metaphor is consistent with the tone of the poem, which has a childlike quality. It harks back to Hamlet's musing "I could be bounded in a nutshell and count myself a king of infinite space . . . " (2,2, 256).*

15. A town has a nervous system and a head and shoulders and feet —John Steinbeck, *The Pearl*

■ PLAGIARISTS

See also: EXPLOITATION; WRITING/ WRITERS

1. They lard their lean books with the fat of others' works —Robert Burton, *The Anatomy of Melancholy*

2. He liked those literary cooks / Who skim the cream of others' books —Hannah More, "Florio, the Bas Blue"

■ PLANNING

See: STRATEGIES

■ PLEAS AND PRAYERS

See also: JOY; LOVERS' DECLARATIONS AND EXCHANGES; MASTERY/SUBORDINATION; MEN AND WOMEN; RELIGION

1. By this ye shall procreate yourselves— / Let this be your Cow-of-Wishes —Anon., *The Bhagavad Gita, 3:10*

> *Giving to the gods in return for their gifts is good; enjoyment without worship makes a man "a thief."*

2. Do I have the smallest chance? . . . Of marrying you. Of living with you. Of having an affair with you. Of kissing you. Oh, I'm a starving beggar. I'll take any crumbs —Louis Auchincloss, "The Epicurean," *Three Lives*

A middle-aged man is ready to settle for less if he can't have all of a young woman's love.

3. Be merciful to a broken reed —Sir Francis Bacon

   Part of his plea for mercy upon being impeached for corruption

4. The Bleat, the Bark, Bellow & Roar / Are Waves that Beat on Heaven's Shore —William Blake, "Auguries of Innocence"

   Blake makes a plea for kindness to animals.

5. And but your word wol helen hastily / Myn hertes wounde, whil that it is greene —Geoffrey Chaucer, "Merciless Beauty"

   The plea to the merciless beloved is that she heal the wound in his heart while it is still fresh.

6. Adams: God, have mercy / On our sick shoals, darting and dying. / We're strange fish to you —Christopher Fry, *A Sleep of Prisoners*

   Man's early life was often dependent on fishing, indicating that Fry's "fish" symbolize religious mysticism. Since the words are addressed to a character named Peter, (known as "a fisher of men") / the playwright is also calling on New Testament imagery. "Shoals" is a pun on "souls."

7. Mark Antony: Friends, Romans, Countrymen, lend me your ears —William Shakespeare, *Julius Caesar* Act 3, scene 2, line 80

   William Safire used this figure as a title to catch the reader's attention to the speeches in his 1992 anthology of the great speeches in history.

8. Where the clear stream of reason has not lost its way / into the dreary desert sand of dead habits . . . let my country awake —Rabindranath Tagore, "Prayer, 1013"

9. Make me, O Lord, thy Spinning Wheele compleat; / The Holy Worde my Distaffe make for mee —Edward Taylor, "Huswifery"

   The housewife asks that God regard her as His tool, on which He weaves His will.

10. Lord, make my Soule thy Plate . . . Then I shall be thy Money, thou my Hord —Edward Taylor, "Sacramental Meditations VI

Orthography had not yet been subjected to standardized rules during this period, so that 'hord' for 'hoard' was common (even, some would argue, more sensible.)

11. Am I thy gold? Or Purse, Lord, for thy Wealth; / Whether in mine or mint refinde for thee? —Edward Taylor, "Sacramental Meditations VI"

    It is interesting to note that rules for capitalization had not been codified, and "thee" is left in lower case.

12. May she become a flourishing hidden tree / That all her thoughts may like the linnet be —William Butler Yeats, "A Prayer for my Daughter"

    Yeats uses the simile in the second line to reinforce the metaphor in the first.

■ PLEASURE

See also: JOY; LIFE; PEOPLE, INTERACTION

1. His visits . . . have given a silver tip to leaden days —Henry James, *Roderick Hudson*

   The young lady's days are about to turn to lead again since the sculptor whose visits she so enjoyed is about to embark for Europe.

2. The dancing girls brought sunshine with them into the room —Natsume Soseki, *Botchan*

   At the farewell party [all male] the young women brought their instruments, their shamisen, to play on, and they encouraged the tipsy men to dance.

3. Pleasure . . . the bait of sin —Plato, *Timaeus*

4. I hear my being dance from ear to ear —Theodore Roethke, "The Waking"

   "I wake to sleep, and take my waking slow" writes Roethke in this villanelle that is one of his most anthologized poems.

5. Elizabeth: she [Mary Stuart] drank / The brimming cup of pleasure to the lees —Johann Christoph Friedrich von Schiller, *Mary Stuart*, Act 2

"And now she drinks the bitter cup of sorrow,"
Leicester replies.

6. Let us gather up the sunbeams / Lying all around our path —Mary Riley Smith, "If We Knew"

7. In the past he would have . . . basked sunnily in this warm atmosphere of devotion —William Styron, *Lie Down in Darkness*

8. Why was I not letting my pleasure open its windows wide? —Derek Walcott, Nobel Prize acceptance speech, December 8, 1992

9. No successful artist ever drank a deeper draft of satisfaction than she took from the little fame her work was getting among her schoolfellows —William Allen White, "Mary White"
   Mary had become a promising cartoonist before she was killed by a fall from a horse.

10. I believe in human liberty as I believe in the wine of life —Woodrow Wilson, "The New Freedom"

■ POETRY/POETS

See also: ABILITY; CREATIVITY; CRITICISM/ CRITICS; INSPIRATION; WRITING/ WRITERS

1. Pray observe the Gliding of that Verse; there is scarce a Consonant in it; I took Care to make it run upon Liquids — Joseph Addison, from an essay, 1710

2. Should poets bicycle-pump the human heart / Or squash it flat? —Kingsley Amis, "A Bookshop Idyll"

3. His head / Locked into mine. We were a seesaw —John Ashbery, "And Ut Pictura Poesis Is Her Name"
   Ashbery ruminates about the ways to write poetry. "Bothered about beauty you have to / Come out into the open, into a clearing, / And rest" and put into a poem some important words, and a lot of dull-sounding ones.

4. He is merely / An ornament, a kind of lewd / Cloud placed on the horizon — John Ashbery, "The Mythological Poet. II"
   The mythological poet "has eloped with all music."

5. The poem streaked by, its tail afire, a bad / Comet screaming hate and disaster, but so turned inward / That the meaning, good or other, can never / Become known —John Ashbery, "Syringa"

6. He lashed out unsparingly at bad poets . . . accusing them of dressing their poems in the warlike armor of erudition, and of flapping in vain their unavailing wings — Jorge Luis Borges, "The Aleph"
   Borges couples the weapons metaphor with the implied metaphor of the poet as a bird to make sly fun of ineptitude. The character who speaks this line is himself a bad poet who revels in overblown metaphor.

7. I stretched thy joints to make thee even feet, / Yet still thou run'st more hobling than is meet —Anne Bradstreet, "The Author to her Book"
   Bradstreet puns on the word "feet" so that the meaning is both metrical and anatomical.

8. —So into me has it gone, and part of me has it become, this great living poetry of yours, not a flower of which but took root and grew —Robert Browning, Letter to Elizabeth Barrett, 1845

9. Either give my linen back / or massed hendecasyllables will attack — Catullus, Poem 12
   The common conceit that poetry will immortalize a lover is here turned on its head. Catullus threatens to vilify in poetry a visitor who has "pinched" his "napkins."

10. Poetry is a religion without hope, but its martyrs guarantee the eternal truth of its dogma —Jean Cocteau, "The Cat That Walks by Itself"

11. A poet ought not to pick nature's pocket; let him borrow, and so borrow as to repay

by the very act of borrowing —Samuel Taylor Coleridge

12. What I want is this poem to be small, / a ghost town / on the map of wills —Rita Dove, "Ars Poetica"

The 1993 American Poet Laureate adds, "Then you can pencil me in as a hawk."

13. He would not match his Verse with those who live: / . . . A losing Gamester, let him sneak away; / He bears no ready Money from the Play —John Dryden, Prologue to *Aureng-Zebe, or, The Great Mogul*

14. Our Author by experience finds it true, / 'Tis much more hard to please himself than you: / . . . And to confess a truth, (though out of time) / Grows weary of his long-lov'd Mistris, Rhyme —John Dryden, Prologue to *Aureng-Zebe, or, The Great Mogul*

15. Poetry the common carrier / for the transportation of the public / to higher places —Lawrence Ferlinghetti, "Populist Manifesto"

Urging his fellow poets to reach out to a wider audience than that addressed from their stuffy "closed world" Ferlinghetti writes "come out of your closets."

16. Hecuba: Rhyme is still the most effective drum —Jean Giraudoux, *Tiger at the Gates,* Act 2

"As soon as war is declared it will be impossible to hold the poets back," says Hecuba.

17. Then in a welding flash / He found his poetry arm / And turned the coat of his trade —W. S. Graham, "Letter II"

18. Everything here is intended by not being crossed out . . . This form of composition grows a poem cell by cell —Donald Hall, "A Note on This Poem"

19. The green felt seems / an evil playground, . . . and he a fool caught in the water weeds of dreams —Michael Hamburger, "A Poet's Progress"

The simile continues a comparison of the chancy game of poetry to snookers pool. The metaphor abruptly shifts the imagery.

20. If people need to exercise the spirit as well as the body, then poetry is gymnastics for the soul —Dorothy L. Hatch, Quoted in *The New York Times,* April 19, 1992

The quotation marked the opening of an article about her essay "The Curious Act of Poetry."

21. Twenty years may have passed since your ears last caught the thunder of that mighty ode of hexameters which the sea has always sung and will sing forever, since your eyes sought the far line where the vaulted blue of heaven touches the level immensity of rolling water,—since you breathed the breath of the ocean, and felt its clear ozone living in your veins like an elixir —Lafcadio Hearn, "New Orleans"

The "mighty ode of hexameters" sung by the sea is no doubt Homer's Odyssey. *The second metaphor is the breath of the ocean in the veins.*

22. Poets are the leaven in the lump of civilization —Elizabeth Janeway, Quoted in *The Writer's Book* by Helen R. Hull

23. Rime, the rack of finest wits —Ben Jonson, "A fit of rime against rime"

Jonson ends the stanza with another metaphor, indicating that poetry is "cozening judgement with a measure, / But false weight."

24. I began with a little [poetry], but habit has made me a Leviathan —John Keats, Letter to John Hamilton Reynolds, 1819

25. He [a poet] could chew over the same words for hours on end till he had succeeded in beating them into verse —Halldòr Laxness, *Independent People*

26. Poets die adolescents, their beat embalms them —Robert Lowell, "Fishnet"

"The line must terminate," writes Lowell, "implying three meanings for the word 'line': death, a line of poetry, and a fishline."

27. Poetry is preparation for death —Nadezhda Mandelstam, Epigraph

28. Nor till the poets among us can . . . present / for inspection, imaginary gardens with real toads in / them, shall we have . . . poetry —Marianne Moore, "Poetry"
   Moore is a poet who always surprises. Had she given us the line, "Poetry is an imaginary garden with real toads in it" she would have presented a compelling image but a more conventional one. Any poet who begins a description of poetry with the words, "I, too, dislike it:" is bound to get your attention.

29. Poetry is the Mogul's dream: to be intensively toiling at what is a pleasure —Marianne Moore, "Subject, Predicate Object"

30. The objective is architecture, not demolition; grudges flower less well than gratitudes —Marianne Moore, "Subject, Predicate, Object"
   To shape, to shear, compress, and delineate— these are the necessaries of poetry.

31. Poetry is uncouth, unshaven, boisterous prose afflicted with a crying drunk — George Jean Nathan, *Materia Critica*

32. Twentieth century poetry has become garrulous. We are drowning not in a sea but in a swamp of words —Octavio Paz, Quoted by Roger Rosenblatt, *The New York Times,* January 31, 1993

33. And I, lighting a city beloved / with blaze of whirling song, / . . . will carry the message —Pindar, "Olympia 9," *Odes*

34. Many famous poems are simply landmarks of bad taste —Theodore Roethke, *Straw for the Fire, Notebooks of Theodore Roethke*

35. A Sonnet is a moment's monument — Dante Gabriel Rossetti, "The House of Life"

36. Poetry is devil's wine —Saint Augustine, *Confessions*

37. Poems . . . / they are the tongue's wrangle, / the world's pottage, the rat's star — Anne Sexton, "With Mercy for the Greedy

38. Sir Benjamin Backbite: I think you will like them [poems] when you shall see them on a beautiful quarto page, where a neat rivulet of text shall meander through a meadow of margin —Richard Brinsley Sheridan, *The School for Scandal,* Act 1, scene 1
   Sheridan's use of a name that encapsulates a character may have helped to popularize this term that originated in the twelfth century.

39. For though my rhyme be ragged, / tattered and jagged / . . . It hath in it some pith —John Skelton, "Colin Clout"

40. And when the stubborne stroke of stronger stounds [efforts] / Has somewhat slackt the tenor of thy string: / Of love and lustihead tho mayst sing —Edmund Spenser, "October" The Shepheardes Calendar
   The poet is compared to a stringed instrument.

41. Unhappy Verse, the witnesse of my unhappie state, / Make thy selfe fluttring wings of thy fast flying / Thought —Edmund Spenser, "Iambicum Trimetrum"

42. But the Poets are a Nest of Hornets, and I'll drive these Thoughts no farther, but must mention some hard Treatment I am like to meet with from my Brother Writers —Richard Steele, from an essay, 1709

43. But words came halting forth . . . / Thus, great with child to speak, / And helpless in my throes, / Biting my truant pen, beating myself for spite, / Fool! said my Muse to me, look in thy heart and write — Sir Phillip Sydney, "Astrophel and Stella"
   Sydney compares the poet to a pregnant woman. The metaphor is commonly used today, as in a pregnant pause *and* the words were pregnant with meaning.

44. A poet has put his farm in rhyme, the most admirable kind of invisible fence, has fairly impounded it, milked it, skimmed it, and got all the cream, and left the farmer only skimmed milk —Henry David Thoreau, "Where I Lived, and What I Lived For"

The farmer, says Thoreau, thought the poet "had got a few wild apples only."

45. Poetry, which is perfection's sweat but which must seem as fresh as the raindrops on a statue's brow, combines the natural and the marmoreal; it conjugates both tenses simultaneously: the past and the present, if the past is the sculpture and the present the beads of dew or rain on the forehead of the past —Derek Walcott, Nobel Prize acceptance speech, December 8, 1992

46. He [the poet] unzips the veil from beauty, but does not remove it —E. B. White, *One Man's Meat*

47. I was simply developing my poetic muscles —Yevgeny Yevtushenko, *A Precocious Autobiography*

    "I swung alliterations, rhymes, and metaphors like Indian clubs," writes the poet, swinging a simile.

48. Poetry is a vindictive woman who never forgives a lie —Yevgeny Yevtushenko, *A Precocious Autobiography*

■ POLITENESS

See: MANNERS

■ POLITICS/POLITICIANS

See also: CHANGE; CHARACTERIZATIONS; DESCRIPTIONS, MISC.; ENCOURAGEMENT; FAILURE; RISK-TAKING; SELF-DESTRUCTIVENESS

1. The parachute candidacy —Anon.

    This metaphoric description of a situation where an outside candidate would descend upon a convention and become the choice of the Party came up several times before the 1992 Democratic convention.

2. The President isn't going to demand he get off the ticket, but a lot of us wish he would fall on his sword —Anon., *The New York Times*, August, 1992

    This wish for Vice-President Quayle's political death was expressed by a leading Midwestern Senator during the 1992 Presidential primary.

3. A political landslide buries nearly everything but the hatchet —Anon., Proverb

    Here's a twist on a metaphor which, according to William Safire's Political Dictionary, *made its first headline appearance in 1838.*

4. Members of Congress in the modern era . . . tend to see themselves as soloists. Like prima donnas everywhere, they demand pampering —R. W. Apple, Jr., *The New York Times*, August 8, 1993

    Apple topped his musical metaphor and follows it up with a simile to explain why President Clinton had to work so hard to get his budget plan passed.

5. One switched vote . . . and Bill Clinton would have lost his economic package and perhaps his Presidency. So all the bargaining in the great souk on Capital Hill over the last three months, all the searching for backbone by legislators terrified of the editorial guillotine, clearly was worth it —R. W. Apple, Jr., *The New York Times*, August 8, 1993

    Apple filled his market basket with three metaphors—the Congress as an Arabian market place and the senators and congressman, spineless jellyfish subject to a public with the power of an executioner.

6. Ross Perot shook the scaffolding of American politics by re-entering the Presidential race today —R. W. Apple, Jr., *The New York Times*, October 2, 1992

7. The tongue is a very fast member of the body politic—it does all the talking and two thirds of the thinking —Josh Billings

8. Old Hickory [Andrew Jackson] was seen by the first Roosevelt as the exemplar of a strong Presidency, and by the second as a great upper and lower case Democrat, and the histories have reflected these shifts — Adam Clymer, "Presidents Ask a Place in Posterity," *The New York Times*, January 24, 1993

The author cleverly used "shifts" to reflect both the obvious meaning, and a continuation of the keyboarding image. "Old Hickory" exemplifies metaphors used as colorful nicknames.

9. If you don't interrupt politicians . . . they'll seize the bit and ride with it into the sunset —Sam Donaldson, "Prime Time," ABC Broadcasting, March 12, 1993

    Donaldson thus replied to viewers who felt he too frequently interrupted candidates.

10. Three weeks before the [1992 presidential] election, the long knives were not only being used among Republicans but were being used openly —Elizabeth Drew, "End Game," *The New Yorker,* November 2, 1992

11. The Presidency . . . a bleak mountain —James A. Garfield, 1881

    According to The Garfield Orbit *by Margaret Leech and Harry J. Brown, President Garfield's bleak view of his presidency stemmed from a bitter political campaign fraught with accusations and bribery. His time on "the bleak mountain" was cut short by an assassin's bullet.*

12. Politics . . . the fly in the amber, the worm in the bud, the rift in the loot —Katherine Gerould, *Conquistador*

13. Gov. Mario M. Cuomo's tantalizing hems and haws about his Presidential plans have set off an acapella chorus of Congressman calling on him to run —Lindsey Gruson, *The New York Times,* October 31, 1991

    The headline writer picked up on Gruson's metaphor with "Cuomo courted by Washington chorus." In a previous article about Cuomo's unpredictable plans, another reporter, Robin Toner, called the press "a Greek chorus" for the guessing game surrounding the Governor's plans.

14. The independent position of the Collector had kept the Salem Custom House out of the whirlpool of political vicissitude —Nathaniel Hawthorne, "The Custom House"

15. The new Surveyor was not a politician . . . hardly a man of the old corps would have drawn the breath of official life, within a month after the exterminating angel had come up the Custom House steps. It would have been nothing short of duty, in a politician, to bring every one of those white heads under the axe of the guillotine —Nathaniel Hawthorne, *The Scarlet Letter*

    The metaphor has survived in the phrase to be axed *as synonymous with being fired, and every modern incumbent of an ousted party in an election year has known the fear of the* exterminating angel.

16. Perhaps Mr. Clinton was following the wrong score. He was listening for the sounds of organized opposition, not the absence of organized support —Gwen Ifill, *The New York Times,* January 24, 1993

    This "clashed with the chord Mr. Clinton struck in his campaign book, "Putting People First," the metaphor continued.

17. It took about 18 hours for President Clinton's tentatively declared second honeymoon with the White House press corps to collapse in a heap —Gwen Ifill, *The New York Times,* June 15, 1993

18. This insider so dedicated to the insider's art of leaking that old colleagues call him the Sieve —Michael Kelly, "David Gergen, Master of the Game," *The New York Times Book Magazine,* October 31, 1993

    Gerken earned his metaphoric nickname for his "leaks" to Woodward and Bernstein when they wrote their Watergate exposé and as "the chief leaker" in the Reagan administration.

19. [President-elect] Clinton received from [vice-president-elect] Gore a dowry, not of geographical balance or political supporters, but of image —Michael Kelly and Maureen Dowd, "The Company He Keeps," *The New York Times Magazine,* January 17, 1993

20. Politics . . . a dog's life without dog's decencies —Rudyard Kipling

21. He [Governor William F. Weld] has put liberal Massachusetts politics under arrest

—Christopher Lydon, *The New York Times Magazine*, August 2, 1992

The conservative governor's campaign speeches explained his positions with nautical images such as "You need somebody who has a deep keel . . . who can steer by his wake."

22. Yet we must give Mr. Carter credit for staging a supreme piece of inaugural choreography: his pas de deux on Pennsylvania Avenue, hand in hand with Rosalynn, out among the applauding crowd, in open air and sunshine —Edmund Morris, "Auguries, Pieties, and Scraps of Memory," *The New York Times*, January 17, 1973

23. After months of quiet campaigning . . . the race for the Democratic Senate nomination from New York has at last moved squarely onto the real battleground: your television set —Todd S. Purdum, *New York Times*, August 26, 1992

24. Moving from the hermetically sealed high-security bubble of President Bush's entourage to Gov. Bill Clinton's campaign is a journey through the political looking glass —Andrew Rosenthal, *The New York Times*, March 24, 1992

There are two metaphors here, the second incorporating literary allusion.

25. Presidents have a kind of political bank account in American minds. When a President takes an important step, or ducks one, each of us makes a mental deposit or withdrawal according to our political tastes —A. M. Rosenthal, "On My Mind," *The New York Times*, April 2, 1993

This opening metaphor was extended for two paragraphs with the columnist stating that in his bank President Clinton's cancellation of the Reagan-Bush ban on U.S. aid to any birth control group "fattens his balance against some early withdrawals."

26. Those of us who have undertaken to practice the ancient but imperfect art of government will always make enough mistakes to keep our critics well supplied with standard ammunition. There is no need

for poison gas —Adlai Stevenson, "The Nature of Patriotism," Speech to American Legion Convention, August 27, 1952

The poison gas user alluded to was Joseph McCarthy, the senator who investigated anyone even remotely suspected of sympathy with communism.

27. The spirit of party . . . a fire not to be quenched, it demands a uniform vigilance to prevent its bursting into flame, lest, instead of warming, it should consume — George Washington, Farewell Address, September 19, 1796

28. He [Alberto Fujimori, president of Peru] can't argue 'I'm against the ropes.' If he plays the democratic card, he can put everyone in his pocket . . . If he uses this to consolidate authoritarian rule, he risks throwing it all down the drain" —Enrique Zileri, Editor of the weekly magazine *Caretas* quoted by Thomas Kamm, *The Wall Street Journal*, September 25, 1992

In this mixed metaphor the boxer, the card, the pocket, and the Peruvian economy all risk going down the drain.

■ POPULARITY/UNPOPULARITY

See also: FAME; POLITICS/POLITICIANS

1. Count Wenceslas went to sleep in the purple sheets that Popular Acclaim spreads for us, without one crumpled rose leaf — Honoré de Balzac, *Cousin Bette*

2. Ulysses: All I have tried to do is to read the world's hand —Jean Giraudoux, *Tiger at the Gates*, Act 2

Ulysses, known for his cunning, has tried "to see which way the wind was blowing," to use a more common metaphor for interpreting the public will.

3. Although thus buried at a crossroads with a stake through its heart, the word [depression] has risen, Draculalike, again — William Safire, *On Language*

The improbable simile, Draculalike, was provided for those readers who might not know that witches and werewolves were thus interred.

4. The Republican Party remains in danger of being regarded as political castor oil, to be taken occasionally for medicinal purposes —George Will, "The Splendid Legacy of FDR," *Washington Post Syndicate,* January 1, 1982

■ POVERTY/PROSPERITY

See also: MONEY; RICHES

1. When it rains oatmeal, the poor man has no spoon to catch it with —Anon., Swedish Proverb

2. Sir Timothy: Come away! Poverty's catching —Aphra Behn, *The Rover,* Act 1, scene 1
   The metaphor of contagion is commonly employed to picture anything unpleasant.

3. Poverty is infertile soil for democracy — Boutros Boutros-Ghali, *Report on the Work of the Organization,* United Nations, 1992

4. Ye purs, that been to me my lives light / And saviour —Geoffrey Chaucer, "Complaint to His Purse"
   Chaucer appeals to the mercy of his purse, who is the light of his life, his savior, for he is "shave as neigh as any frere" (as closely shaven as a friar.)

5. Every wind that blew over France shook the rags of the scarecrows in vain, for the birds fine of song and feather, took no warning —Charles Dickens, *A Tale of Two Cities*
   In Dickens's novel of the French Revolution the scarecrows are the poor and the birds are the nobility who ignored their needs.

6. How different is virtue, clothed in purple and enthroned in state, from virtue, naked and destitute, and perishing obscurely in a wilderness! —Washington Irving, "Traits of Indian Character"

7. Luxury spreads its ample board before their eyes, but they are excluded from the banquet —Washington Irving, "Traits of Indian Character"

8. Poverty, repining and hopeless poverty, a canker of the mind unknown in savage life, corrodes their spirits and blights every free and noble quality of their natures — Washington Irving, "Traits of Indian Character"

9. His shirt—a shirt incidentally which only existed in a abstract form since all its visible parts, judging by a treacherous gloss, were pieces of starched armor of rather low quality —Vladimir Nabokov, *King, Queen, Knave*

10. The poor have been the slop-pails of capitalism —Kenneth Patchen, "The Journal of Albion Moonlight"

11. The poor . . . all broken, humble ruins of nations —Carl Sandburg, "Masses"

12. Lucullus: 'tis deepest winter in lord timon's purse —William Shakespeare, *Timon of Athens* Act 3, scene 4, line 15
    No matter how deep one reaches, one is likely to find little.

13. Poverty . . . is a life near the bone where it is sweetest —Henry David Thoreau, *Walden*
    Thoreau explains that the person who can't afford to buy books or newspapers is "compelled to deal with the material which yields the most sugar and the most starch."

■ POWER

See also: ALLIANCES; CONFLICT; DETERIORATION/DIMINISHMENT; DOMINANCE; INFLUENCE; INTERNATIONAL RELATIONS; MASTERY/SUBORDINATION; PERSONALITY PROFILES; POLITICS/ POLITICIANS; STRENGTH/WEAKNESS; SUCCESS/FAILURE

1. Power is poison —Henry Adams, *The Education of Henry Adams*

2. To describe my mother would be to write about a hurricane in its perfect power. Or the climbing, falling colors of a rainbow

—Maya Angelou, *I Know Why the Caged Bird Sings*

3. I am taste in water, son of Kunti, / I am light in the moon and sun, / The sacred syllable in all the Vedas, / Sound in ether, manliness in men —Anon., *The Bhagavad Gita, 8:8*

    The Blessed One explains his nature to Arjuna in a series of metaphors. The sacred syllable is Om.

4. I am the ritual act, I am the act of worship, / I am the offering to the dead, I am the medicinal herb, / I am the sacred formula, I alone am the sacrificial butter, / I am the fire of offering, I am the poured oblation —Anon., *The Bhagavad Gita, 9:19*

    The Blessed One, by using metaphor instead of simile, shows that he is not represented by the acts of worship; he is the worship itself. In other metaphors The Blessed One depicts himself as "the dwelling-place, refuge, friend, / . . . treasure-house, the imperishable seed."

5. Of syllables I am the letter A —Anon., *The Bhagavad Gita, 10:33*

    The meaning here is the same as "I am Alpha and Omega" (N.T., Revelation 1:8, 1:11, 21:6, 22:13)

6. I am Alpha and Omega —The Bible, *N.T., Revelation 1:8, 1:11, 21:6, 22:13*

    The first and last letters of the Greek alphabet were Christ's metaphor for the be all and end all of power.

7. If they have a weakness as a group, it is their lack of pre-cooked clout —Leslie Gelb, *The New York Times,* December 20, 1992

8. Three old pals—[National Security Adviser Anthony Lake, Under Secretary of State Peter Tarnoff, and Under Secretary of Defense Frank Wisner]—bureaucratic black belts all, will control interdepartmental deliberations and tamp down internal conflicts [in the new Clinton administration] —Leslie Gelb, "Foreign Affairs," *The New York Times,* January 24, 1993

The sports metaphor was used to depict how these men earned their power through a long period of service, starting with the time they were all junior Foreign Service officers in Saigon.

9. He has practically written the book on how to seize power and use it in an impoverished neighborhood, how to pull the interlocking levers of social services, politics and personal gain —David Gonzalez and Martin Gottlieb, "Power Built on Poverty: One Man's Odyssey," *The New York Times,* May 14, 1993

    Ramon Velez, for twenty-five years "reigned as the political baron of the South Bronx," using social services for mechanical advantage.

10. The 4865X–25 chip is not going to leave scorch marks on your desk, but it is far more powerful than the anemic 3865X chips used in many home computers — Peter H. Lewis, "Personal Computers," *The New York Times,* August 31, 1993

    The image of the burnt tire marks left by a speeding car is well suited to a product often called the 90's "hot rod" or "muscle car." The second metaphor plays on the linkage between a burn and illness

11. In the struggle between nations, one country is the hammer and another is the anvil —Charles William Maynes, "New Realities: Disarmament, Peacebuilding, and Global Security," NGO Committee on Disarmament Conference at the United Nations, April 20–23, 1993

    This common metaphor was attributed to an unnamed German chancellor.

12. Thanks to Mr. Clinton's demarche, Saddam Hussein almost succeeded in splitting the seam of our transfer of power —William Safire, "Essay," *The New York Times,* January 18, 1993

    The usual metaphor for power is a mantle. Mr. Safire evokes the image of a pair of pants.

13. Power was ebbing from the center — Serge Schmemann, *The New York Times,* March 30, 1993

    In reporting on the power clash between Boris N. Yeltsin and the Congress of People's Deputies,

Schmemann drew on the common metaphor of a receding tide.

14. In the Persian Gulf war, in Bosnia, and, most recently, in the renewed conflict with Iraq, the United States and Britain have become the axis around which at least part of the new world order spins — William E. Schmidt, *The New York Times*, January 24, 1993

15. Power breeds resentment and withers the slow-growing plant that is trust —Merle Shain, *When Lovers are Friends*

16. Antony: Authority melts from me —William Shakespeare, *Antony and Cleopatra* Act 4, scene 7, line 26

17. Antonio: His word is more than the miraculous harp —William Shakespeare, *The Tempest* Act 2, scene 1, line 88
    Sebastion builds on the allusion to Zeus' son, who raised the walls of Thebes with his playing with "He hath rais'd the wall, and houses too."

18. The corridors of power —C. P. Snow, *Homecoming*

19. University faculties are extraordinarily hierarchical, and the graduate students and assistant professors at the bottom of the totem pole are very vulnerable —Shirley M. Tilghman, "Science vs. Women—A Radical Solution," *The New York Times*, January 26, 1993

20. The New York Governor's name recognition, fund-raising ability, political skills and organizational base make him the 800-pound gorilla in Democratic circles —Robin Toner, "Washington Talk," *The New York Times*, October 16, 1992
    People were still speculating that Mario Cuomo might throw his hat into the presidential ring at the time this was written.

21. Political power grows out of the barrel of a gun —Mao Tse-tung

22. He [Lew R. Wasserman, chairman of MCA] was a behind-the-scenes kingmaker whose Beverly Hills home served as a virtual station of the cross for national political candidates —Bernard Weintraub, *The New York Times Magazine*, May 2, 1993
    The subject of the article, David Geffen, was "considered the Clinton Administration's Lew Wasserman."

■ PRACTICALITY

See: PRUDENCE

■ PRAISE

See also: ADMIRATION; LOVERS' DECLARATIONS AND EXCHANGES

1. She is the full moon of the full moons, afore God! —Anon., "The Story of the Negro Dorerame"

2. Up until now / I've polished you bright / to give light to others —Anon., Folk Song. Ming Dynasty
   "I've treated you like a bronze mirror," writes the poet, claiming his praise is responsible for her gleam.

3. When angling for praise, modesty is the best bait —Anon., Proverb

4. Thou art my star, shin'st in my skies — Thomas Carew, "Ingrateful beauty threatened"

5. France: She is herself a dowry —William Shakespeare, *King Lear* Act 1, scene 1, line 243
   When Lear disinherits Cordelia, most of her suitors withdraw their suit, but the King of France knows that Cordelia herself is worth more than any dowry.

6. Duncan: in his commendations I am fed: / It is a banquet to me —William Shakespeare, *Macbeth* Act 1, scene 4, line 57

7. Benedick: Would you buy her, that you enquire after her? / Claudio: Can the world buy such a jewel? / Benedick: Yea, and a case to put it into —William Shakespeare, *Much Ado About Nothing* Act 1, scene 1, line 188

8. Hermione: one good deed, dying tongueless; / Slaughters a thousand waiting upon that —William Shakespeare, *The Winter's Tale* Act 1, scene 2, line 91

> *Hermione wants Leontes to praise. In* The Merchant of Venice, *Portia reflects on a candle throwing light on her garden at dawn with this simile: "How far that little candle throws his beams! / So shines a good deed in a naughty world."*

9. Troilus: Why, she is a pearl / Whose price hath launch'd above a thousand ships, / And turn'd crown'd kings to merchants —William Shakespeare, *Troilus and Cressida* Act 2, scene 2, line 81

> *There is an echo in Marlowe's* Dr. Faustus, *where the face of Helen of Troy was the face "that launch'd a thousand ships, / And burnt the topless towers of Ilium?" In an October 11, 1993 article in* The New Yorker *about British playwright Allan Bennett, John Lahr gave the metaphor this twist: "his owlish presence . . . has been the face of enduring disenchantment which has launched a thousand quips."*

10. Troilus: She is a theme of honor and renown, / A spur to valiant and magnanimous deeds —William Shakespeare, *Troilus and Cressida* Act 2, scene 2, line 198

11. Hermione: Our praises are our wages — William Shakespeare, *The Winter's Tale* Act 1, scene 2, line 94

12. Sike prayse is smoke, that sheddeth in the skye / Sike words bene wynd, and wasten soon in vayne —Edmund Spenser, "October," *The Shepheardes Calendar*

> *The speaker compares such praise to smoke and wind that dissipate quickly.*

13. O Mademoiselle Cunegonde! The pearl of women! —Voltaire, *Candide*

> *The humor of the praise lies in the fact that there was more sand than nacre in the lady.*

■ PRECISION

See: EXACTNESS/INEXACTNESS

■ PREDATORS

See: AGGRESSION

■ PREDICAMENTS

See: DIFFICULTIES

■ PREGNANCY

See: PROCREATION

■ PREJUDICE

See: BIGOTRY; ILLUSION/REALITY; JUSTICE/INJUSTICE

■ PREPAREDNESS/ UNPREPAREDNESS

See also: STRATEGIES

1. Bush braces for a political hurricane — Anon., Headline, *The New York Times* White House report, June 19, 1992

> *The headline was pulled from a report on President Bush's admission that the voter discontent with the nation and his campaign was "a hurricane blowing out there," and his vow "to ride it out."*

2. How sad a spectacle . . . to see a young man . . . ready for his voyage of life—and to see that the entire ship is made of rotten timber —Ralph Waldo Emerson, *Journal, 1839*

3. My parents were digging emotional fallout shelters for fear of what was to come —Philip C. Hochman, "Coming to Terms"

> *The writer looks with dispassion on the toll that his downward-spiraling illness takes on his family.*

4. Cesare Borgia acquired the state by the influence of his father and lost it when that influence failed. He who does not lay his foundations beforehand may by great abilities do so afterwards, although with great trouble to the architect and danger to the building —Niccolo Machiavelli, *The Prince*

To Machiavelli, the building of an empire was like the building of any man-made structure.

■ PRESS

See: JOURNALISM/JOURNALISTS

■ PRESUMPTUOUSNESS

See: PRIDE

■ PRETTINESS

See: BEAUTY

■ PREVENTION

See: RESTRICTION

■ PRIDE

See also: AMBITION; ARROGANCE/HUMILITY

1. Circumcise therefore the foreskin of your heart, and be no more stiffnecked —The Bible, *O.T., Deuteronomy 10:16*
   This startling image also appears in Jeremiah *4:4 as "Take away the foreskin of your heart."*

2. The Lord: Though thou set thy nest among the stars, thence will I bring thee down — The Bible, *O.T., Obadiah 4*
   Man may aspire to raise himself up like an eagle, but God controls his lofty ambitions. The Greeks gave us the word hubris *for overweening pride, a character flaw punished by the gods.*

3. One coat of pride, perhaps a bit thread-bare; / Illusion's trinkets, splendid for the young —Theodore Roethke, "The Auction"
   The poet pictures himself at an auction of his life's baggage, and he leaves with a lighter heart after he has seen "all the rubbish of confusion sold."

4. Talbot: and there died / My Icarus, my blossom, in his pride —William Shakespeare, *The First Part of Henry the Sixth* Act 4, scene 7, line 16

The first metaphor alludes to the son whose father gave him wings but warned him not to fly too near the sun. Because he ignored the warning, Icarus died.

5. Othello: my demerits / May speak unbonneted to as proud a fortune / As this that I have reached —William Shakespeare, *Othello* Act 1, scene 2, line 23
   Othello says that he does not need to apologize for his background, or doff his cap to anyone.

6. Ulysses: The seeded pride / That hath to this maturity blown up / In rank Achilles must or now be cropp'd / Or, shedding, breed a nursery of like evil / To overbulk us all —William Shakespeare, *Troilus and Cressida* Act 1 scene 3, line 316
   Achilles' pride is compared to a seed that, having grown too large a tree, must now be cut down.

7. Chorus: Insolence breeds the tyrant — Sophocles, *Oedipus the King*
   Insolence (pride or hubris*) was the flaw that most concerned early Greek writers of tragedy, since it was a flaw consistent with greatness.*

8. Pride, the lone pennant, ravelled by the storm-wind / Stands in the sunset fires — Sara Teasdale, "Truce"

9. For arrogance and hatred are the wares / Peddled in the thoroughfares —William Butler Yeats, "A Prayer for my Daughter"

■ PRINCIPLES

See: BELIEFS; ETHICS

■ PROBLEMS AND SOLUTIONS

See also: ACTION/INACTION; DESCRIPTIONS, MISC.; DIFFICULTIES; ECONOMICS; GRIEF; INTERNATIONAL RELATIONS; REFORM

1. You can't stop the birds of sorrow from flying overhead, but you can stop them from building nests in your hair —Anon., Chinese Proverb

2. Occasionally, indeed, I was stung by the wasp of family trouble; but I knew a heal-

ing ointment—my faith in America — Mary Antin, *The Promised Land*

> *Except for this metaphoric wasp, Antin views her early life as an immigrant as that of a "child let loose in a garden to play and dig and chase the butterflies."*

3. In Florida, repair crews began trying to unscramble the ganglia of power lines and telephone wires —James Barron, *New York Times,* August 26, 1992

4. Since I know the only true path to the ultimate solution of the problems of society, I know which way to drive the human caravan —Isaiah Berlin, "The Pursuit of the Ideal," *The Crooked Timber of Humanity*

> *The belief in a final solution that would solve the problems of society was one held by many leaders, who each tried to make an omelette and didn't care how many eggs were broken in the process.*

5. At times, the fabric of her world has even more threads per inch than John Updike's —Ron Carlson, *The New York Times Book Review,* April 11, 1993

> *The image appeared in a review of Sue Miller's novel For Love.*

6. His plane is on fire, he's miles from the target, he's hurtling down with a ton of bombs underneath . . . and there's no one in the air or on the ground who thinks he can get out of this one —Richard Ben Cramer, "Bush Is Down. Now Watch Out," *The New York Times,* August 18, 1992

> *"Can James A. Baker, on his way back to the bridge make the White House and campaign churn the water together?" asked the writer during the Republican National convention. Another fighting metaphor suggested that "Bush, so immaculately polite, could come at Michael Dukakis with a broken bottle in each fist."*

7. If you are going to go in, you have to go in with enough force to deter other countries from moving up the escalation ladder — Donald C. F. Daniel, "New Realities: Disarmament, Peacebuilding, and Global Security," NGO Committee on Disarmament Conference at the United Nations, April 20–23, 1993

> *Mr. Daniel, from the U.S. Naval War College, expressed his belief that peace enforcement in war-torn countries requires enough initial force to knock out all opposition, before warring factions are given time to arm more heavily.*

8. We're going to finally wrestle to the ground this gigantic orgasm that is just out of control —Dennis DeConcini, *The Berkshire Eagle,* May 19, 1992

> *The senator from Arizona managed a mixaphor that would delight any financial Freudian.*

9. I'm not saying that public-works investment is a silver bullet, but it is helping to reduce unemployment —Thomas M. Downs, Quoted in "Finding What Works," *The New York Times,* November 24, 1992

> *The image of a silver bullet as a magical solution goes back to the Lone Ranger's silver bullet. Those recognizing the fallacy of "mallets" tend to use another much-used phrase* to bite the bullet, *a war metaphor traced to the times when wounded soldiers were given a lead bullet to bite on during surgery. Credit for the broader, figurative meaning usually goes to Rudyard Kipling who in* The Light That Failed *(1890) had one character tell another: "Bite on the bullet, old man, and don't let them think you're afraid."*

10. We have the wolf by the ears, and we can neither hold him, nor safely let him go — Thomas Jefferson, Quoted in *The Wall Street Journal,* December 2 1992

> *The article on ethnic identity clashes referred to Jefferson's desire to abolish slavery [the wolf], and his fear that a simple biracial America, with white and black as equals, would not long endure.*

11. Now the trumpet summons us again . . . to bear the burden of a long twilight struggle . . . a struggle against the common enemies of man: tyranny, poverty, disease and war itself —John F. Kennedy, Inaugural address, January 20, 1961

12. President Harry S Truman . . . was handed the task of steering the country out of the storm of World War II and into the straits of the cold war, and that surpassed most people's expectations of his skills as a captain —Christopher Lehmann-Haupt,

"Books of The Times," *The New York Times*, June 15, 1992

The review was for Truman, *by David McCullough whom the reviewer referred to as "a sorcerer at commanding seeming incidental details to serve him."*

13. We are like whalers who have been on a long chase. We have at last got the harpoon into the monster but we must now look how we steer, or with one flop of his tail he will send us all into eternity — Abraham Lincoln, Speech after the Proclamation to free the slaves, 1863

The metaphor of slavery as a monster whale, rests on the foundation of the simile comparing the slave-owning nation to whalers. Biographer Carl Sandburg referred to this imagery as "the metaphor of the hour."

14. Other ways to help stanch the hemorrhaging, in Wilson's view: promote sustainable development, do what we can to save what remains through debt-for-nature swaps and other means, and "restore" the wildlands —Charles E. Little, "Books," *Wilderness*, Winter 1992

Edward O. Wilson, author of The Diversity of Life, *worries about the loss of species.*

15. She [Italy] awaits one who may heal her wounds . . . and cure her of those sores which have long been festering —Niccolo Machiavelli, *The Prince*

The book was directed to Lorenzo the Magnificent, who was being invited by the author to seize the reins [metaphor!] of government.

16. Yesterday . . . Bonn loosened its interest rate tourniquet —Allen R. Meyerson, *The New York Times*, September 15, 1992

With the metaphoric tourniquet thus relaxed, stock prices in the United States took their biggest leap of the year.

17. Health care is the 900-pound gorilla of deficit finance. And unless Washington curbs the animal's appetite or sharply raises taxes to keep it supplied with bananas—or both—the deficit will break records by the end of the century —Peter Passell, "Economic Scene," *The New York Times*, February 25, 1993

18. We're buying a front row box seat, and we're not even getting to see a bad show from the bleachers —Ross Perot, June 1992

The man who almost ran as a third party Presidential candidate was filled with metaphoric sound bites and fury, in this instance about the nation's high medical costs.

19. Everybody's nibbling around the edges; let's go to the center of the bull's-eye, the core problem —Ross Perot, 1992 Presidential Debate, October 19, 1992

20. Our challenge is to stop the financial bleeding —Ross Perot, 1992 Presidential Debate, October 19, 1992

The independent candidate extended the image with "If you take a patient into the hospital that's bleeding arterially, step one is to stop the bleeding. And we are bleeding arterially."

21. The Angel [arriving at the deathbed of an AIDS victim] . . . is addressing a character who is spent and confused, just as she is addressing a checkmated nation —David Richards, "Sunday View," *The New York Times*, May 16, 1993

With AIDS, the metaphor for a more general malaise that has swept the country, Richards wondered whether the playwright of Angels in America, *having identified the illness in this first part of his epic play will "envision the cure" in the second."*

22. Yes, Russia is in a perilous state . . . But not so long ago, many pundits were similarly arguing that only Mikhail S. Gorbachev's finger in the dike was keeping a new cold war at bay —Serge Schemann, *The New York Times*, January 24, 1993

This is a classic mixaphor, *combining a water image and a hunting image. The "finger in the dike" is also allusory. Everyone remembers the little Dutch boy with his finger in the hole in the dike.*

23. Menenius: this must be patch'd / With cloth of any colour —William Shakespeare, *Coriolanus* Act 3, scene 1, line 251

The homely metaphor of the patchwork refers to the need to take some action to save what Cominius has called the "falling fabric" of the Roman power structure.

24. Queen: Now 'tis the spring, and weeds are shallow-rooted; / Suffer them now, and they'll o'ergrow the garden, / And choke the herbs for want of husbandry —William Shakespeare, *The Second Part of Henry the Sixth* Act 3, scene 1, line 31

The queen compares Gloucester to a weed that will ruin the garden if not removed in timely fashion.

25. Northumberland: If then we shall shake off our slavish yoke, / Imp out our drooping country's broken wing, / Redeem from broking pawn the blemish'd crown, / . . . And make high majesty look like itself —William Shakespeare, *The Tragedy of King Richard the Second* Act 2, scene 1, line 292

There are three metaphors in dizzying array. The first pictures the lords as beasts of burden to the king, the second—an image from falconry—pictures England as a wounded hawk whose wing must be mended, and the third suggests that the king's crown has been left with a pawnbroker.

26. Viola: O time! thou must untangle this, not I; / It is too hard a knot for me to untie! —William Shakespeare, *Twelfth Night* Act 2, scene 2, line 40

Viola hopes somehow, some time, the tangled love relationships all around her will sort themselves out.

27. Now she unweaves the web she hath wrought —William Shakespeare, *Venus and Adonis,* line 991

28. The imprisoned winds are let loose. The east, the North, and the stormy South combine to throw the whole sea into commotion, to toss its billows to the skies, and disclose its profoundest depths —Daniel Webster, Senate speech on the problem of a slave policy with respect to new Western territories, March 7, 1850

29. It was Darrow's instinct, in difficult moments, to go straight to the bottom of the difficulty; but he had never before had to take so dark a dive as this —Edith Wharton, *The Reef*

Anna Summer's passionate feelings for George Dallow are kept in check by her inhibitions.

30. A number of Somali civilians were killed and wounded, and an enraged Somali mob killed four journalists . . . as our "nationbuilding" progresses, political levees presumably will be built to control the flow of such passions —George Will, *Washington Post Syndicate,* July 18, 1993

Will used the tragic Mississippi River floods in the Midwest as a jumping-off point to discuss several out-of-control political situations.

31. The way to stop financial *joy-riding* is to arrest the chauffeur, not the automobile —Woodrow Wilson

■ PROCREATION

1. And many maiden gardens, yet unset, / With virtuous wish would bear your living flowers, / Much liker than your painted counterfeit —William Shakespeare, "Sonnet 16" line 6

A forerunner of the photograph, the "painted counterfeit" or "portrait in little" provided a livelihood for many Elizabethan painters.

2. Teiresias: He shall be proved father and brother both / . . . a fellow sower in his father's bed —Sophocles, *Oedipus the King*

3. I can feel it encoded inside me —A. B. Yehoshua, *Mr. Mani*

Elsewhere, in another metaphor, Hagar refers to the embryo she imagines she is carrying as "the little tadpole that's swimming inside me."

■ PROFESSIONS
See: OCCUPATIONS

■ PROFICIENCY
See: ABILITY

■ PROFILES

See: FACES

■ PROFUSION

See: ABUNDANCE

■ PROGRESS

See also: CIVILIZATION; FREEDOM/RE-STRAINT; HUMANITY/HUMANKIND; LIFE

1. Human horizons altered with each new step in the evolutionary ladder —Isaiah Berlin, "The Pursuit of the Ideal," *The Crooked Timber of Humanity*

   Hegel and Marx, according to Berlin, thought there were no timeless truths.

2. In the industrial or post-industrial societies the protest is that of individuals or groups whose members do not wish to be dragged along by the chariot-wheels of scientific progress, interpreted as the accumulation of material goods and services and of utilitarian arrangements to dispose of them —Isaiah Berlin, "The Bent Twig," *The Crooked Timber of Humanity*

   There is a strong new movement toward individual and nationalist self-assertion.

3. We can build upon foundations anywhere if they are well and firmly laid —Dame Ivy Compton-Burnett, *Two Worlds and Their Ways*

4. Progress is a comfortable disease; / your victim (death and life safely beyond) / plays with the bigness of his littleness —e. e. cummings, "Pity this busy monster, manunkind"

5. Beyond th'old Pillers many have travailed / Towards the Sun's cradle, and his throne, and bed —John Donne, "Epigrams: Sir John Wingefield"

   The normal progression would be the cradle to the grave, but, since the sun never dies and rises again every morning, the Western sun is pictured in his bed for the night. The "Pillers" are the Pillars of Hercules, or Gibraltar. [The epigram continues beyond the metaphor].

6. Most [of her classmates] have sailed into classes from which they will sail out again and into college, then marriage and careers —Deborah Eisenberg, "The Custodian"

   This is how the protagonist of Eisenberg's short story, a young girl who does not do well in school, views others' ability to move through life.

7. Democracy is the rising tide; it may be dammed or delayed, but cannot be stopped —John Galsworthy, "American and Briton"

8. If I could only put one drop into the long river of human progress, then my purpose would be fulfilled —Sidney Rittenberg, *The Man Who Stayed Behind*

   Rittenberg, twice imprisoned by the Chinese Communists, managed to keep his sanity and his ideals (some would say his illusions) intact.

9. The result is a wonderful forward fumble —William Safire, "Essay," *The New York Times,* June 10, 1993

   The Polish Prime Minister had fired her Minister of Justice. Prior to this the parliament had been a "wrangle of 29 splinter parties, many nibbling at the Ms. Suchocka's market reforms, deficit reduction and privatization of industry" with little expectation of more than "the usual reshuffling of the old deck."

10. For is it not true that human progress is but a mighty growing pattern woven together by the tenuous single threads united in a common effort? —Mei-Ling Soong (Madame Chiang Kai-shek), Speech, March 7, 1943

■ PROMINENCE/PERIPHERY

See also: VISIBILITY/INVISIBILITY

1. Mr. [Ben] Vereen lurks splendidly on the margins of the jazzman's life story — Anon., "The Theatre," *The New Yorker,* July 12, 1993

Vereen replaced Gregory Hines, who created the role of "the concierge of the Roll's soul," in the musical Jelly's Last Jam.

2. In 1954 Baudelaire would not be left in the wings, but dragged on to the stage on the pretence that he approved of the fashions of the day —Jean Cocteau, "The Cat That Walks by Itself"
   Dragged on in drag, no doubt.

3. [Sir Michael] Tippett was in on many of Britten's triumphs—a bridesmaid in the festive background —George Steiner, "Books," *The New Yorker,* July 5, 1993
   This appeared in a review of Humphrey Carpenter's biography of Benjamin Britten.

4. He was a society lion in his day —Ivan Turgenev, *Fathers and Sons*
   To lionize a person means to make him an object of special interest and even, perhaps, of veneration.

■ PROMISES

1. Nor should I now swell to halloo the names / Of feelings that no one needs to remember, / Nor caper with my spray of wilted avowals —Kingsley Amis, "Departure"

2. White House officials said that Mr. Clinton was also planning to name a working group on welfare to begin putting meat on the bones of the campaign pledge to "end welfare as we know it" —Gwen Ifill, *The New York Times,* January 31, 1993

3. *Till then* we say, / Watching from a bluff the tiny, clear / Sparkling armada of promises draw near —Philip Larkin, "Next, Please"

4. The stranger had given a blithesome promise, and anchored it with oaths; but oaths and anchors equally will drag; naught else abides on fickle earth but unkept promises of joy —Herman Melville, "Norfolk Isle and the Chola Widow"

The stranger was a ship's captain who promised to pick up the small band of people he had set ashore, but left them marooned.

■ PROPHECY
See: DEATH

■ PROS AND CONS
See: AGREEMENT/DISAGREEMENT

■ PROSE
See: WRITING/WRITERS

■ PROTECTION/PROTECTORS
See also: FAMILIES/FAMILY RELATIONSHIPS; MARRIAGE; MEN AND WOMEN

1. I have a large umbrella. A lot of people stand under it —Maya Angelou, quoted *The New York Times,* January 20, 1993
   The author was interviewed on the eve of reading a poem written for President Bill Clinton's inauguration. Those under the figurative umbrella include "young blacks and whites and students" and "some plain, some tall some very smart and some slow."

2. Yet someone had loved him . . . But for her the race of the world would have trampled him under foot, a squashed boneless snail —James Joyce, *Ulysses*
   Joyce reflects on the death of his mother.

3. To this day, there is a widespread impression that Mr. Mu has a powerful "kaoshan"—a "mountain to lean on" — Nicholas D. Kristof, *New York Times,* August 30, 1992
   The article translated the meaning of the mountain to "a leader behind him."

4. It was nice to feel him at the back of her days, solid and firm, her rock of ages — Frieda Lawrence, Letter, c. 1938

His virtues notwithstanding "He bored her a bit occasionally."

5. Whenever he and his last boyfriend, Ralph had something difficult to face . . . they would say to each other, "Don't worry, I'll be there with you. I'll be in your pocket." —David Leavitt, "When You Grow to Adultery"

    The narrator related this to his next boyfriend who "in turn appropriated the metaphor." In every day use being in each others' pockets has also come to mean interdependency.

6. Her vigilant love was a child-size suit of armor, to which he has added buckles and breastplates over the years —Arthur Lubow, *The New Yorker,* September 20, 1993

    Lubow's thus describes how director George Wolfe was influenced by his grandmother's love.

7. "What I really wanted then," he said softly, "was to be a sort of carpet—to make myself into a sort of carpet for you to walk on so that you need not be hurt by the sharp stones and the mud that you hated so" —Katherine Mansfield, "A Dill Pickle"

8. The *bubble* is what surrounds the traveling road show of any Presidential campaign. It includes the candidate, the staff, the press, the plane, the bus and all the electronic gear of the 20th-century bustle . . . it is where you find both the real story and yet an utterly false one, a speed-blurred picture of a very large country —David Maraniss, *Washington Post,* November 2, 1992-quoted in William Safire's "On Language" column, November 29, 1992

    The Safire column devoted considerable space the term's use as a metaphoric protective shield, which replaced the cocoon as a favorite image. According to Safire, the current meaning probably has its roots in the name for the see-through shield used to protect presidents riding in open motorcades.

9. Tiverzin had taken the boy under his wing, and this added fuel to Khudoleiev's hostility —Boris Pasternak, *Doctor Zhivago*

Both metaphors are common ones, the first dating back to a simile in the New Testament, Matthew, 23:37: *"I have gathered thy children together, even as a hen gathereth her chickens under her wings."*

10. Hektor, Troy's unassailable / tall column of strength —Pindar, "Olympia 2," *Odes*

11. I'm going to be as publicly engaged in the Clinton crusade [for economic reform] as I can. I'm not the quarterback. I'm more the downfield blocker —Dan Rostenkowski, Spring, 1993, quoted in *The New York Times,* July 20, 2993

    The July quote appeared in an article on the effect of a looming indictment for embezzlement.

12. She had always been surrounded by servants, secretaries, and aides-de-camp, fulfilling the functions of those little fenders which prevent a ship from bumping too roughly against the quay —Vita Sackville-West, *All Passion Spent*

13. If the United States fails to shore him [Yeltsin] up, goes the argument, Russia could fall to communists —Serge Schemann, *The New York Times,* January 24, 1993

    The metaphor suggests that supporting a shaky politician is like buttressing a wall.

14. Bolingbroke: That sun that warms you here shall shine on me, / And those his golden beams to you here lent / Shall point on me and gild my banishment — William Shakespeare, *The Tragedy of King Richard the Second* Act 1, scene 3, line 145

15. Candida: I build a castle of comfort and indulgence and love for him and stand sentinel always to keep little vulgar cares out —George Bernard Shaw, *Candida,* Act 3

16. I have always considered the Federal judiciary to be a thin black line between the awesome powers of the United States Government and the citizens and the citizens rights —Judge Marvin H. Shoob, quoted by Martin Tolchin, *The New York Times,* October 9, 1992

■ PROTEST

See: DISSENT/DISSENTERS

■ PROTESTS

See: REVOLT

■ PROVOCATION

See: AROUSAL/ROUSERS

■ PRUDENCE

See also: CAUTION; CHARACTERISTICS; REASON; STINGINESS

1. Deluded by the Strands of material nature, / Men are attached to the actions of the Strands —Anon., *The Bhagavad Gita*, 3:29

   The material world is outside the Self; only by truth and by knowing can man free himself to attain the highest good.

2. "Oh, she's got her wheels in line," I said —Stephen Vincent Benet, "Famous"

   A young man reassures his father who has just expressed concern about his younger sister.

3. Prudence is a rich, ugly old maid courted by Incapacity —William Blake, "Proverbs of Hell"

4. Cléante: We would rather trust the light of their prudence than the blindness of our passion, for the eagerness of youth leads us most often toward troublesome precipices —Molière, *The Miser*, Act 1

   The brother of Élise uses three metaphors to instruct her to respect her elders, which he, himself, does not plan to do.

5. Harpagon: Invest at good interest the money that you win, so that you'll have it on a rainy day —Molière, *The Miser*, Act 1

   The implied metaphor is that straitened circumstances are akin to rainy days—a common comparison.

6. He knew which side his bread was buttered on and enough to come in out of a Monsoon —Ogden Nash, "The Strange Case of the Wise Child"

   Nash gives a fresh twist to the proverbial I know which side my bread is buttered on.

7. His [the idler's] way takes him along a by-road, not much frequented, which is called Commonplace Lane and leads to the Belvedere of Commonsense —Robert Louis Stevenson, "An Apology for Idlers"

8. I won't quarrel with my bread and butter —Jonathan Swift, *Polite Conversation*

   The bread and butter metaphor is widely used for anything pertaining to life's essentials. A popular variant: to know which side one's bread is buttered on.

■ PSYCHOLOGY

See: OCCUPATIONS

■ PUBLIC OPINION

See also: OPINION

1. Public opinion is a giant which has frightened stouter-hearted Jacks on bigger beanstalks than hers —Louisa May Alcott, "Life in the Iron Mills," *The Atlantic Monthly*, April, 1861

2. The public only takes up yesterday as a weapon with which to castigate today —Jean Cocteau, "The Public and the Artist," *Vanity Fair*, 1922

■ PUNISHMENT

See: RETRIBUTION

■ PURPOSE

See: RESOLVE

■ PURSUIT
See: MEN AND WOMEN

■ PUTDOWNS
See: ACTING/ACTORS

QUARRELS/ QUARRELSOMENESS

See also: AGREEMENT/DISAGREEMENT

1. Chorus: O most sapient wise spectators, hither turn attention due, / We complain of sad ill-treatment, we've a bone to pick with you —Aristophanes, *The Clouds*
   > *If the expression is indeed that of Aristophanes and not the translator's, then the expression* I've got a bone to pick with you *has been around for a couple of thousand years.*

2. Quarreling is / A cave where the spirit sits deafened and dumbfounded —John Hollander, "Disagreements"

3. His crackers don't sit well in my bowl of soup —Bo Jackson, s.u.

4. A damned seam, a foolishness, / came between us —Osip Mandelstam, "Stanza 3"

5. She had fanned each faint spark of disagreement into glowing coals of hostility and distrust that needed only a faint breeze to burst into flames —Ann Rule, *Everything She Ever Wanted*
   > *A psychopath almost annihilates her husband and his family.*

QUICKNESS

See: SPEED

QUIET

See: STILLNESS

QUOTATIONS

See also: LANGUAGE; WIT

1. A fine quotation is a diamond on the finger of a man of wit, and a pebble in the hand of a fool —Anon., French Proverb

2. All mankind is but a carrier, and part of our precious burden consists of things that have been said perfectly. To repeat them, appositely and not too frequently . . . is a kind of good citizenship, for we are all citizens of History, a country whose continually threatened borders we must at any time be prepared to defend. To still in ourselves the golden voices of the past is to regress toward the voiceless condition of the fishes —Clifton Fadiman, "In Praise of Quotation"
   > *When you've finished counting the metaphors in the above, consider this additional reason for quoting the wisdom of the ages: "Just because we no longer talk like the Elizabethans is no reason for rejecting an occasional loan from the treasury of their wits and the vaults of their vigor."*

3. Benedick: Shall quips and sentences and these paper bullets of the brain awe a man from the career of his humour? —William Shakespeare, *Much Ado About Nothing*, Act 3, scene 1, line 103

Beatrice's words may be fired off like bullets from a gun, but since they come from books, Benedick sees no reason to let them affect his humor and willingness to relinquish his confirmed bachelor status.

4. Henry James [was quoted] in one of [John] Ashbery's raisin-quotations elaborating the pudding —Helen Vendler, "Books," *The New Yorker,* August 3, 1992

The more common expression for a goodie embedded in a whole is "nuggets"—here we have raisin-quotations rather than the more familiar nuggets of wisdom.

R

■ RACISM
See: BIGOTRY

■ RAGE
See: ANGER

■ RAIN
See also: SKY/SKYSCAPES; STORMS

1. The spring rain / is a / thread of pearls —Anon., 9th-century poetess

2. The rain came down in long knitting needles —Enid Bagnold, *National Velvet*

3. A crushing curtain of rain . . . dropped suddenly from the sky —Colette, "Bella Vista"

4. [Rain] pulled the spigot from the hills / And let the floods abroad —Emily Dickinson, Poem 1235

5. Everything's doused and diamonded with wet / . . . Each drop a paperweight of Steuben glass —Anthony Hecht, "Still Life"

6. Pathway's a bog, and the road's a torrent —William Wymark Jacobs, "The Monkey's Paw"

7. The slender threads of rain vanished into the river without a ripple —Kawabata Yasunari, *Beauty and Sadness*

8. Fool: Prithee, uncle, be contented; 'tis a naughty night to swim in —William Shakespeare, *King Lear*, Act 3, scene 4, line 108
   The "naughty night" was the occasion of a drenching storm. It is here pictured as a body of water.

9. Rain dimples the still canal —Wallace Stegner, *The Spectator Bird*

10. The sky seems to ride fast upon the madly rushing rain —Rabindranath Tagore, "The Rainy Day," *The Crescent Moon*

11. It was one of those steady business-like rains . . . not so much a caprice of the weather as the drop-curtain punctually let down by Nature between one season and the next —Edith Wharton, *The Children*
    "Behind its closely woven screen one had the sense of some tremendous annual scene-shifting, the upheaval and overturning of everything in sight," Wharton writes.

■ RAINBOWS
See: SKY/SKYSCAPES

■ READING/READERS
See also: POETRY/POETS

1. All his life he dunked himself each day in a sea of printer's ink —John Mason Brown, Introduction, *The Portable Woollcott*

Alexander Woollcott viewed himself as "an ink-stained wretch," but according to Brown "the ink which stained him was not limited to his own."

2. From this thin gruel they make a culture by which their minds apprehend the Mysteries —E. L. Doctorow, "Standards," *Harper's Magazine*, 1991
   Doctorow thus describes the type of subjects favored by songwriters.

3. What is reading but silent conversation? —Walter Savage Landor, *Imaginary Conversations*

4. I wolfed down what I could but found a good deal of it indigestible —Phyllis McGinley, "The Consolations of Illiteracy," *The Saturday Review*
   The avidly consumed but often unsatisfactory books in her father's limited and specialized library were all that was available during the author's childhood on a Colorado ranch.

5. I pick my own way among the landmarks. No Baedaker distracts me from the scenery . . . peak upon peak unfolds. But there are also delightful little fenced fields and flowery culverts where I can rest when I do not wish to climb —Phyllis McGinley, "The Consolations of Illiteracy," *The Saturday Review*
   The author, raised without access to a library or solid cultural training, uses the metaphor of a journey to describe her independent reading as an adult. She explains that because she came to the journey late she's not "on fire to see everything at once" and that she wanders "as far afield as I care to, one range of hills opens into another which I shall explore in due time."

6. Reading poetry is seeing a room lit by lightning—the details are jagged and sparse, but the illumination is stunning —Dorrie Weiss

7. By the time I was eight, I was devouring indiscriminately Dumas, Flaubert, Schiller, Balzac, Dante . . . . It all made an indescribable salad in my head —Yevgeny Yevtushenko, *A Precocious Autobiography*

■ REALITY/UNREALITY

See also: DREAMS

1. Form here is only emptiness, / emptiness is only form —Anon., The Heart Sutra
   This chant transmits the teachings of Buddha and deals with the nature of ultimate reality.

2. The skull of life suddenly showed through its smile —Dorothy Canfield Fisher, *The Deepening Stream*

3. Such is my bewilderment: lasting / to the point where it resists the wasting / consumption of the day —Eugenio Montale, "Two in Twilight"
   The speaker of the poem questions his own reality, which has been threatened by a changed relationship.

4. Reality may have been flat . . . But now everything is three-dimensional, reality has shadows, don't you see; even the most ordinary ant patiently carries his shadow around on his back —Orhan Pamuk, *The White Castle*
   An abstraction has here been treated as a bulky reality.

5. To and fro in the seven chambers there stalked, in fact, a multitude of dreams. And these—the dreams—writhed in and about, taking hue from the rooms, and causing the wild music of the orchestra to seem as the echo of their steps —Edgar Allan Poe, "The Masque of the Red Death"
   The costumed and masked courtiers who inhabited the castle seemed like the phantasmagorical inhabitants of a fevered sleep.

6. On the surface, life is much the same as before . . . But it is a through-the-looking glass-world —Jeffrey Schmaltz, *The New York Times*, December 20, 1992
   The writer uses allusion as a metaphor to show how his world became submerged in his battle with the AIDS virus.

7. Wipe the dew off your spectacles, and see that the world is moving —Elizabeth Cady Stanton, *The Woman's Bible*
   An admonition to a conservative.

REASON

See also: PRUDENCE

1. Socrates conquers you by stratagem, Aristotle by force: the one takes the town by sap, the other sword in hand —Joseph Addison, "Various Ways of Managing a Debate," *The Spectator*, December 4, 1711

   Addison comments on the Socratic method of constant questioning with a boxing metaphor: "This way of debating drives an enemy up into a corner, seizes all the passes through which he can make an escape, and forces him to surrender at discretion."

2. Nature has given man reason and showed him how to use it, but man loves to open the throttle and let reason hum. This accounts for his running off from the track so often and getting bust up —Josh Billings

3. Each individual must foment a private conspiracy . . . by thrusting one's head, then an arm, out of the jail—thus shattered—of logic, that is, out of the most hateful of prisons —André Breton, *Nadja*

4. Reason your viceroy in mee, mee should defend, / But is captiv'd, and proves weak or untrue —John Donne, "Holy Sonnets: XIV"

   The sonnet is addressed to the "three person'd God" whom the poet tries to worship. He feels he is deficient in adoration.

5. Cymen: I've still got rags of reason / To make our stark apprehension decent — Christopher Fry, *Thor, With Angels*

6. Teddie: I think we ought to be sensible. Elizabeth: You owl! —W. Somerset Maugham, *The Circle*, Act 2

7. Enobarbus: I'll yet follow the wounded chance [fortune] of Antony, though my reason / Sits in the wind against me — William Shakespeare, *Antony and Cleopatra*, Act 3, scene 8, line 48.

   Enarbus will stick with Antony despite his deteriorated fortunes.

8. King: poor Ophelia / Divided from herself and her fair judgment / Without the which we are pictures, or mere beasts — William Shakespeare, *Hamlet*, Act 4, scene 5, line 84

   The king is in despair that Ophelia has lost her wits.

9. Toby: [judgment and reason] And they have been grand-jurymen since before Noah was a sailor —William Shakespeare, *Twelfth Night*, Act 3, scene 2, line 15

10. My reason, the physician to my love, / Angry that his prescriptions are not kept, / Hath left me —William Shakespeare, "Sonnet 147," line 5

11. With what sharp checks I in myself am shent [reproved], / When into Reason's audit I do go, / And by just counts myself a banckrout [bankrupt] know —Sir Philip Sidney, "Sonnet 18," *Astrophel and Stella*

    In this bookkeeping metaphor, Sidney chides himself for his lacks.

12. I wish I could travel by the road that crosses baby's mind . . . Where Reason makes kites of her laws and flies them — Rabindranath Tagore, "Baby's World," *The Crescent Moon*

13. Colonel Tadeusz Boleslav Stjerbinsky: What is reason? A dried-up little bureaucrat with a green eye-shade —Franz Werfel, *Jacobowsky and the Colonel*, Act 2, scene 1

    The colonel underscores his metaphor with "reason always rebels against life."

RECOLLECTION

See: MEMORY/MEMORIES

RECRIMINATION

See: CALMNESS/VOLATILITY; INSULTS; NAME CALLING

■ REFORM

See also: CHANGE; GOVERNMENT; POLITICS/POLITICIANS

1. In a war then, in a *good* war, I might unite pleasure with the satisfaction of being a straw in the broom that cleansed the world —Louis Auchincloss, "The Epicurean," *Three Lives*

    The middle-aged anti-hero refreshes his long-dead idealism by resurrecting and revitalizing a metaphor so old it has become a cliché.

2. I'll turn over a new leaf —Miguel de Cervantes, *Don Quixote*

    This still common metaphor was already known when Cervantes used it, having appeared in John Heywood's Proverbs *as "Nae she will tourne the leafe."*

3. We must demonstrate to all the American people that change for the better is at hand . . . Because the ship of state is headed for the rocks. The crew know it. The passengers know it. Only the captain of the ship, President Bush, appears not to know it. He seems to think that the ship will be saved by imperceptible undercurrents, directed by the invisible hand of some cyclical economic god, that will gradually move the ship so that at the last moment it will miraculously glide past the rocks to safer shores —Mario Cuomo, Nominating speech, for Bill Clinton, 1992

    Governor Cuomo's speech offers one of the best and longest variations of the ship of state metaphor first used by Cicero in 59 B.C. and borrowed and adapted many times since.

4. The besom of reform has swept him out of office; and a worthier successor wears his dignity, and pockets his emoluments — Nathaniel Hawthorne, *The Scarlet Letter*

    Or, to give an old twist to a modern metaphor, A new besom sweeps clean.

5. [Beijing] last week moved to slap some fresh paint on its human-rights image — Herbert B. Herring, "Business Diary," *The New York Times*, January 24, 1993

6. A new broom sweeps clean. —John Heywood, *Proverbs, Part 2*

    An Irish addition to this proverbial metaphor, is "but the old one finds the corner." Political applications abound; for example, when Israel's Labor Party swept the Likud Party out of office in 1992 The New York Times *headlined the story "Israel's New Broom: How Much of a Sweep?"*

7. This is the year American voters were going to blow the dome off the Capitol and sweep out the House and the Senate —Kwame Holman, *The MacNeill / Lehrer News Hour,* National Public Television, November 4, 1992

8. He went on to urge the slashing of Government bureaucracies and a retooling of welfare and entitlement programs benefiting retirees that Democrats have worked to expand since the New Deal —Clifford Krauss, *The New York Times*, January 31, 1993

    In this machinist's metaphor, the programs are compared to factories in need of overhaul.

9. Russia's shock therapy is the most daunting test yet of a prescription for rejuvenating state-dominated, inflation-prone economies —Peter Passell, "Economic Scene," *The New York Times*, November 19, 1992

10. We'll be down in the trenches, under the hood working on fixing the old car to get it back on the road —Ross Perot, Presidential debate, October 19, 1992

    Perot's metaphoric "sound bites" became instant clichés through his frequent re-use of them.

11. The money changers have fled from their high seats in the temple of our civilization. We may now restore that temple to the ancient truths —Franklin Delano Roosevelt, First inaugural address, March 4, 1933

12. Suffolk: we'll weed them all at last, / And you yourself shall steer the happy helm — William Shakespeare, *The Second Part of Henry the Sixth*, Act 1, scene 3, line 102

Suffolk combines a gardening and a seafaring metaphor to assure the queen that they'll get rid of all her enemies.

13. Cade: I am the besom [broom] that must sweep the court clean of such filth as thou are —William Shakespeare, *The Second Part of Henry the Sixth*, Act 4, scene 7, line 34

14. Gardener: Give some supportance to the bending twigs / . . . Cut off the heads of too fast growing sprays —William Shakespeare, *The Tragedy of King Richard the Second*, Act 3, scene 4, line 30
    The weeding process is a metaphor for creating a more equitable government.

15. For eleven long years we have been in the middle of the stream. We are not amphibious. We want to get across. We want to feel dry and solid ground under our feet again —Earl Warren, Keynote speech at the Republican National Convention, June 1944
    During the 1992 campaign being stuck was likened to gridlock and moving forward to being an agent of change.

16. The world must examine its blemishes in the mirror of Hiroshima and turn from the reflected image of its own brutality —Dorrie Weiss, Letter to Mayor Takashi Hiraoka of Hiroshima, November 6, 1992

17. You're the kind of man the country wants, Archer. If the stable's ever to be cleaned out, men like you have got to lend a hand in the cleaning —Edith Wharton, *The Age of Innocence*
    In the days of Wharton's New York, men like Archer looked on politics as something dirty.

■ REGENERATION
See: DEATH; RENEWAL

■ REGRETS
See: APOLOGY

■ REJECTION
See: ABANDONMENT; PEOPLE/INTERACTIONS

■ RELATIONSHIPS
See: FAMILIES/FAMILY RELATIONSHIPS; FRIENDSHIP/FRIENDS; MEN AND WOMEN; PEOPLE, INTERACTION

■ RELIEF
See: COMFORT/COMFORT-GIVERS

■ RELIGION
See also: BELIEFS; FAITH

1. Would you have me forsake my piety in its infant state? —Peter Abelard, Letter to Heloise
   A letter from Heloise has thrown Abelard into a quagmire of doubt, and he is afraid he will forsake his newfound religious haven.

2. A man without religion is a horse without a bridle —Anon., Latin Proverb

3. Religion is a journey, not a destination —Anon., Proverb

4. Religion is a collective insanity —Mikhail A. Bakunin
   The author of this expression was a Russian writer and anarchist, an opponent of Karl Marx.

5. As (Karl) Barth "threw the Revelation at men," Reinhold Niebuhr, in America, began to try to fit them with catcher's mitts —William Warren Bartley III, "I Call Myself a Protestant"
   The neo-orthodox theologian from Switzerland is the pitcher; the American theologian will coach the catchers.

6. Far from "healing" the Christian concepts, his [Paul Tillich's] cure seems more damaging than the disease —William Warren Bartley III, "I Call Myself a Protestant"

The author argues that Tillich does not reinterpret Christianity: he presents a new religion.

7. Man shall not live by bread alone but by every word that proceedeth out of the mouth of God —The Bible, *N.T., Matthew 4:4, Luke 4:4*

   The metaphor is implied and still commonly used as a criticism of materialistic values. In Deuteronomy (O.T., 8:3), "only" is used instead of the more cadenced "alone."

8. Mystics . . . fall back on symbols: to signify the godhead, one Persian speaks of a bird that somehow is all birds; Alanus de Insulis, of a sphere whose center is everywhere and circumference is nowhere; Ezekiel, of a four-faced angel who at one and the same time moves east and west, north and south. Perhaps the gods might grant me a similar metaphor —Jorge Luis Borges, "The Aleph"

   In giving up idolatry, with its tangible representations of deity, people were forced to substitute metaphor to do intellectually what formerly had been done visually.

9. The hidden Manna I doe eat, / The word of life it is my meat —Anne Bradstreet, "The Flesh and the Spirit"

10. He retraced the path backwards through Christianity to Judaism, revealing the groundwork of Jewish thought and experience which supported . . . the scaffolding of Christian "unreason" —Arthur A. Cohen, "Why I Choose to Be a Jew"

11. We must sow the good seed somehow. I waited till the door was shut on me, and slipped the tract into the letter-box — Wilkie Collins, *The Moonstone*

    To the onerous Miss Clack "sowing the good seed" meant persuading someone to accept her own restrictive view of religion.

12. Among the timorous kind the *Quaking Hare* . . . The bristl'd *Baptist Boar* —John Dryden, "The Hind and the Panther"

    The quaking hare is a Quaker, the boar a self-explanatory Baptist. The Unitarians are put down with the appellation "Reynard," the Freethinkers

as Buffoon Ape. *This is not a poem noted for its tolerance.*

13. You touch that famous point of free-will which is a mortal rock —Alexandre Dumas, *The Three Musketeers*

    The Jesuit proposes a dilemma: God is God, and the world is the Devil. To regret the world is to regret the Devil, he tells a wavering Aramis.

14. As for the tree of Christianity, in a foreign country its leaves may grow thick and the buds may be rich, while in Japan the leaves wither and no bud appears — Shusaku Endo, *Silence*

    "A tree which flourishes in one kind of soil may wither if the soil is changed," was the metaphorical explanation of why Japan, in the seventeenth century, did not offer the proper nutrients for the transfer of Catholicism.

15. Miracles . . . the swaddling clothes of infant churches —Thomas Fuller, *The Church History of Britain*

16. Somewhere within the great symphony of Catholicism is a strain that fits the Japanese tradition and touches the Japanese heart —William Johnston, Translator's Preface, to Shusaku Endo's *Silence*

17. You may say that Ikhnaton was wrong and that it is the essence of religion to pour new wine into old skins, reading one's current insights into ancient beliefs — Walter Kaufmann, "The Faith of a Heretic"

18. Marx may have regarded religion as an opiate of the people, but Beijing regards it as an amphetamine —Nicholas D. Kristof, "Christianity is Booming in China Despite Rifts," *The New York Times*, February 7, 1993

    Kristof took Karl Marx's famous metaphor and turned it on its head, with amusing effect.

19. Religion . . . is the opium of the people — Karl Marx, *Critique of the Hegelian Philosophy of Right*

    This has also been translated as "Religion is the opiate of the masses."

20. Prayer constructs a velvet bridge / And walking it we are aloft —Czeslaw Milosz, "On Prayer"

21. Religion put claws on Aunt Sally and gave her a post to whet them on —Katherine Anne Porter, "Old Mortality," *Pale Horse, Pale Rider*

    "She had out-argued, out-fought, and out-lived her entire generation . . . she bedeviled the second generation without ceasing, and was beginning hungrily on the third," the author continues.

22. So I am still stuck with the Roman Catholic Church, the Sacred Cow of Gerard Manley Hopkins —Phillip Scharper, "What a Modern Catholic Believes"

    The author explains why, in spite of all his doubts, he remains faithful to Catholicism.

23. These are the impassioned words of a Christ-intoxicated man —M. Lincoln Schuster, Foreword, *The World's Great Letters*

24. Thou makest Glory's chiefest Grape to bleed / into my cup: And this is Drink-Indeed —Edward Taylor, "Sacramental Meditations X"

    Taylor seems to refer to the wine of the sacraments, which is the blood of Jesus.

25. For in Christs Coach they sweetly sing, / As they to Glory ride therein —Edward Taylor, "The Joy of Church Fellowship rightly attended"

26. Who blew the Bellows of his Furnace Vast? / Or held the Mould wherein the world was Cast? —Edward Taylor, "The Preface"

    Blake, in "Songs of Experience," questioned the creation of the tiger, asking, "What immortal hand or eye / Could frame thy fearful symmetry?" For both of these poets, some things are so difficult to comprehend that God is the only answer to the question.

27. Nobody had managed . . . to evolve a new religion, and they were all still trying to catch a new generation with the old bait —Edith Wharton, *Hudson River Bracketed*

Though the metaphor is flippant, Wharton might have been thinking of the attribute of Jesus as a "fisher of men."

■ REMEMBRANCE

See: PAST; REGRETS

■ REMORSE

See: EMOTIONS

■ RENEWAL

See also: CHANGE; REFORM; SEASONS

1. The process of adjustment will be painful and costly, yet we have an opportunity to breathe new life into our vocabulary and institutions —Boutros Boutros-Ghali, *Report on the Work of the Organization*, United Nations, 1992

2. This ceremony is held in the depth of winter, but by the words we speak and the faces we show the world, we force the spring —(President) Bill Clinton, Inaugural speech, January 21, 1993

    The familiar metaphor of Spring as a renewal is invigorated by "forcing the spring" which columnist William Safire linked to the practice of forcing roses into an early bloom.

3. The utmost any generation can do is to rebaptize each spiritual or emotional rebirth in its own tongue —Rudyard Kipling, "Independence"

    "Nothing in life changes," writes Kipling.

4. And everything the lascivious earth raised up / From a cold slumber, threw off sheets of clay / To fold the sunlight in an amorous grip —Robert Layzer, The Lawn Roller

5. To deliver life out of captivity, The gnarled knees of the days / Must be bound to a flute —Osip Mandelstam, "The Age"

    Mandelstam proposes to build a new world, delivering the old through music

6. Let us pick up again these lost strands and weave them again into the fabric of America —Eugene McCarthy, Speech to Conference of Concerned Democrats, December 2, 1967

> *McCarthy, a poet as well as a senator, was in the forefront of the anti-Vietnam war movement. His weaving metaphor was meant to evoke the memory of President Kennedy and the unsuccessful presidential candidate, Adlai Stevenson. He followed it with a musical metaphor: "Let us sort out the music from the sounds and again respond to the trumpet and the steady drum."*

7. [The eel] spark that says / everything begins when everything seems / ashes — Eugenio Montale, "The Eel"

8. There can be no purpose more enspiriting than to begin the age of restoration, reweaving the wondrous diversity of life that still surrounds us —Edward O. Wilson, *The Diversity of Life*

■ RENUNCIATIONS

See: LOVERS' DECLARATIONS AND EXCHANGES

■ REPENTANCE

See: SIN/REDEMPTION

■ REPETITION

See: TALKATIVENESS

■ REPOSE

See: STILLNESS

■ REPRESSION

See: ANGER; SELF; SOUL

■ REPROACH

See: ACCUSATIONS

■ REPUTATION

See also: CHARACTER; SLANDER

1. Reputation is a bubble which a man bursts when he tries to blow it for himself — Emma Carleton, *The Philistine*

2. Glass, china and reputations, are easily crack'd and never well mended —Benjamin Franklin, *Poor Richard's Almanack*

3. Along with Mr. [Kirk] Douglas, figures like Darryl F. Zanuck, Juliette Greco, Dino De Laurentis, Laurence Olivier, Terence Rattigan, Neil Diamond and Charles Bronson have arrows of various lengths and lethality shot in their reputations —Christopher Lehmann-Haupt, "Books of the Times," *The New York Times*, July 5, 1993

> *The metaphoric sharpshooter was Richard Fleischer, author of* Just Tell Me When to Cry.

4. Cyrano: I go caparisoned [finely dressed] in gems unseen, / Trailing white plumes of freedom, garlanded / With my good name —Edmond Rostand, *Cyrano de Bergerac*, Act 1

5. Lear: When she was dear to us, we did hold her so; But now her price is fall'n — William Shakespeare, *King Lear*, Act 1, scene 1, line 199

> *Lear repudiates Cordelia.*

6. Edgar: my name is lost, / By treason's tooth bare-gnawn and canker-bit —William Shakespeare, *King Lear*, Act 5, scene 3, line 122

7. Othello: what's the matter, / That you unlace your reputation thus —William Shakespeare, *Othello*, Act 2, scene 3, line 184

> *The metaphor depends not just on the simple act of untying something (like a shoe), but on dressing killed meat after a hunt.*

8. Iago: Good name in man and woman's dear, my lord; / Is the immediate jewel of our souls —William Shakespeare, *Othello*, Act 3, scene 3, line 159

Some of the most moral sounding platitudes that originated with Shakespeare have issued from the mouths of his basest villains.

9. Mowbray: A jewel in a ten-times-barr'd-up chest / Is a bold spirit in a loyal breast —William Shakespeare, *The Tragedy of King Richard the Second*, Act 1, scene 1, line 180

   Mowbray assures the king that a spotless reputation is the best of all treasures.

10. Fabian: you are now sail'd into the north of my lady's opinion where you will hang like an icicle on a Dutchman's beard — William Shakespeare, *Twelfth Night*, Act 3, scene 2, line 24

    The icicle simile depends on the seafaring metaphor.

11. Our names are labels, plainly printed on the bottled essence of our past behavior — Logan Piersall Smith

12. It was sad to see his name . . . shorn of its aforetime gaudy gear of compliments and clothed on with rhetorical tar and feathers —Mark Twain, *The Gilded Age*

    The man thus shorn of renown and respect is the colorful Colonel Sellers who dominates the novel.

■ RESCUE/RESCUERS

See also: VILLAINY/VILLAINS; ESCAPE

1. The decision to grant the Haitians "humanitarian parole" is the first breach in a wall of rule, policies and court decisions —Barbara Crossette, *The New York Times*, September 3, 1992

2. Gaunt: the world's ransom, blessed Mary's son —William Shakespeare, *The Tragedy of King Richard the Second*, Act 2, scene 1, line 56

   Gaunt refers to Jesus, son of Mary, as the redeemer of the world.

3. Antonio: This youth that you see here / I snatch'd one half out of the jaws of death —William Shakespeare, *Twelfth Night*, Act 3, scene 4, line 367

4. Kate: Get the Board to authorize the search for a "white knight" . . . you know, someone to rescue the damsel in distress — Jerry Sterner, *Other People's Money*, Act 1

   When Kate's suggestion for finding a protector is rejected, she suggests this metaphoric alternative: "We can formulate a shark repellent. The strategy here is for the company to make itself so unattractive that no one will want to buy it."

5. He was so thrilled by the rope I had thrown him —A. B. Yehoshua, *Mr. Mani*

   To throw someone a rope—to save him—is a common metaphor for getting someone out of an unpleasant situation. In this case the rope is being thrown to a "catcher" who is thrilled with it "because he's not especially good-looking or anything . . . ."

■ RESENTMENTS

See: AROUSAL/ROUSERS

■ RESERVE

See: SELF-ACTUALIZATION

■ RESIGNATION

See: DESPAIR

■ RESOLVE

1. The good resolution, taken when it is sure to be broken, becomes macadamized into pavement for the abyss —James Clerk-Maxwell, Quoted in *The Practical Cogitator*

2. Player King: Purpose is but the slave to memory, / Of violent birth, but poor validity —William Shakespeare, *Hamlet*, Act 3, scene 2, line 191

■ RESPONSIBILITY

1. Duty's a slave that keeps the keys / But Love the master goes in and out . . . Just

as he pleases—just as he pleases —Dinah Mulock Craik, "Plighted"

2. Moses: But hell is old; / And you yourself sitting in sunlight / Embroidered on it with your needle —Christopher Fry, *The Firstborn*, Act 2, scene 2
Even complicity by silence can implicate the bystander in a disaster.

3. " . . . I'm with my little millstone." He pointed with his chin at the child —Kume Masao, "The Tiger"
The actor is using his child as an excuse to get away from a critic. In common usage, someone who turns into an unwelcome responsibility is referred to as a millstone around my neck.

4. Responsibilities roost on our fingers and toes / clucking and blinking —Marge Piercy, "Letter to be disguised as a gas bill," *4-Telling*

5. And at his prow the pilot held within his hands his freight of lives, eyes wide open, full of moonlight —Antoine de Saint-Exupery, *Night Flight*
The plane is compared to a ship sailing the sky.

6. King: And thou shalt prove a shelter to thy friends, / A hoop of gold to bind thy brothers in, / That the united vessel of their blood, / . . . Shall never leak — William Shakespeare, *The Second Part of King Henry the Fourth*, Act 4, scene 4, line 41
With these three metaphors the king tells Clarence he must learn to be responsible for the actions of Prince Hal and his brothers.

■ RESTLESSNESS

1. Siddartha had begun to feel the seeds of discontent within him —Hermann Hesse, *Siddhartha*
Seeds are a popular metaphor to picture something in its beginning or fertilization stage. In an essay titled "Oxford as I See It," humorist Stephen Leacock wrote "This system contains in itself the seeds of destruction." The noun has also been fertilized as a single verb metaphor, as in the success of Scott Turow's novels has seeded a large crop of legal thrillers.

2. I am fevered with the sunset, / . . . For the wander-thirst is on me —Richard Hovey, "The Sea Gypsy"

3. She is . . . on a sort of indefinite sabbatical, an extension of her role as family grasshopper —Andrea Lee, "Full Moon Over Milan," *The New Yorker*, April 5, 1995
The metaphor sets the scene for a story about a young American woman working and living in Italy.

4. What am I, Life? A thing of watery salt / Held in cohesion by unresting cells — John Masefield, "Sonnets 14,"

5. A wind's in the heart of me, a fire's in my heels —John Masefield, "A Wanderer's Song"

■ RESTRICTION

See also: CONTROL; MASTERY/ SUBORDINATION

1. Lassoing the Nuclear Renegades —Anon., Editorial, *The New York Times*, July 22, 1993
The cowboy metaphor for this headline was inspired by the opening paragraph: "The Clinton Administration . . . has sensibly decided that stripping two dangerous outlaws [North Korea and Iraq] of the capacity to blow up the rest of the world is far more important than satisfying each and every technical doubt along the way."

2. In the course of humanitarian relief, we must do more preventive action: on a street where there are many accidents there must be more red lights —Jan Eliasson, "New Realities: Disarmament, Peacebuilding, and Global Security," NGO Committee on Disarmament Conference at the United Nations, April 20–23, 1993
Jan Eliasson, the UN Undersecretary-General for Humanitarian Affairs, expressed concern that most relief comes too late for countries like Somalia.

3. It is not the labor [of being a college teacher], but the being bound hand and

foot, the going round and round in a tread-mill that depresses me —Henry Wadsworth Longfellow, Journal

4. [George] Bush . . . had always been held on someone's short leash —John Newhouse, "Shunning the Losers," *The New Yorker*, October 26, 1992

5. Duke: We have strict statutes and most biting laws— / The needful bits and curbs to headstrong steeds— / Which for this fourteen years we have let slip — William Shakespeare, *Measure for Measure*, Act 1, scene 3, line 19

■ RETIREMENT

See: ACTIVENESS/INACTIVENESS; ENDINGS

■ RETRIBUTION

See also: GOD; REVENGE/VENGEANCE

1. God waits long and pays with interest — Anon., Yiddish Proverb

2. They say that Heaven's net, however big the meshes may be, is sure to catch the wicked —Natsume Soseki, *Botchan*
   Botchan and his friend spy at a peephole to catch the perfidious Dean as he leaves a brothel.

3. Duchess of York: I am your sorrow's nurse, / And I will pamper it with lamentation —William Shakespeare, *The Tragedy of King Richard the Third*, Act 2, scene 2, line 87
   The duchess will keep Richard's murderers from being forgotten with her lamentations.

4. If she finds out, she'll eat me alive —Isaac Bashevis Singer, "Under the Knife,"
   "She" is a madam and the speaker a prostitute who has given her favors away without payment.

5. Oedipus: Yet he was paid with interest, by one swift blow —Sophocles, *Oedipus the King*

Oedipus, angered by the arrogant Laius, responds with his own arrogant violence.

6. Oedipus: redeem the debt of our pollution / that lies on us because of this dead man —Sophocles, *Oedipus the King*
   Oedipus is speaking to Teiresias, the blind prophet who, he hopes, will free Thebes from plague.

■ REVELATION

See also: CANDOR; COMMUNICATION/NON-COMMUNICATION; OPENNESS/PRIVACY; SECRECY

1. Now go we together lovingly / to Confession, that cleansing river —Anon., *Everyman*

2. What I have withheld has given me more joy that what I have expressed because it has helped build a storehouse, a potential of great pregnancy. Secret after secret, I can now give birth to it in sublime pain — Roger Burlingame, "The Analyst's Couch and the Creative Mind"
   The author argues that psychoanalysis relieves and neutralizes the internal tension that drives an artist to creativity, and so must be avoided by the artist.

3. Cap [Caspar Weinberger] takes notes but never referred to them so never had to cough them up —M. Charles Hill, *The New York Times*, August 26, 1992
   The metaphor to cough up always connotes something unpleasant that has been retained—in this case, information about the Iran-Contra affair.

4. The Central Intelligence Agency . . . is letting the public see some bleached bones from the skeletons in its closet —Tim Weiner, "Files and Whispers: The C.I.A. Opens Its Safe," *The New York Times*, August 29, 1993
   The attention-getting blurb asked "But will candor from the tomb of secrets be believed?" The use of the skeleton in the closet as a metaphor for family secrets has been traced back to the first half of the nineteenth century.

■ REVENGE/VENGEANCE

See also: RETRIBUTION

1. I made him of the same wode a croce— / . . . in his owene grece I made him frye — Geoffrey Chaucer, "The Wife of Bath's Prologue and Tale," *The Canterbury Tales*
    The fourth husband of the Wife of Bath took a mistress, but she had her revenge: she made him a cross of the same wood, she fried him in the same grease. In other words, she out-cuckolded the cuckold.

2. Armand . . . thought that God had dealt cruelly and unjustly with him; and felt somehow that he was paying him back in kind when he stabbed thus into his wife's soul —Kate Chopin, "Désirée's Baby"
    The stabbing is a metaphor for Armand's rejection of the wife he loves when he discovers his infant son has "negroid features."

3. Italy may at length find her liberator . . . with what thirst for vengeance, with what steadfast faith, with what love —Niccolo Machiavelli, *The Prince*
    The metaphor persists today, usually as to thirst for revenge.

4. Norfolk: and I know his sword / Hath a sharp edge: it's long, and't may be said, / It reaches far; and where 'twill not extend, / Thither he darts it —William Shakespeare, *The Life of King Henry the Eighth*, Act 1, scene 1, line 109
    Norfolk is talking about Richard and his vengeful nature.

5. King Philip: our hands . . . / they were besmear'd and overstain'd / With slaughter's pencil, where revenge did paint / The fearful difference of incensed kings — William Shakespeare, *The Life and Death of King John*, Act 3, scene 1, line 234

6. Malcolm: Let's make us med'cines of our great revenge, / To cure this deadly grief —William Shakespeare, *Macbeth*, Act 4, scene 3, line 251

7. Gaunt: Put we our quarrel to the will of heaven, / Who, when they see the hours ripe on earth, / Will rain hot vengeance on offenders' heads —William Shakespeare, *The Tragedy of King Richard the Second*, Act 1, scene 2, line 6

8. Biskra: I'll water the sand, so that revenge may grow out of it, and I'll dry up my heart —August Strindberg, *Simoom*

■ REVOLT

See also: ARGUMENTS; CONFRONTATION; DISINTEGRATION; DISSENT/ DISSENTERS

1. The last puffs of the ozone of revolt went stale in the whispers of speakeasy arguments —John Dos Passos, *U.S.A., The Big Money*
    The revolt compared to the transience of cigar smoke was directed against the conservative bankers and rich "Coupon clippers" who people a profile of Thorstein Veblein.

2. The man who serves a revolution plows the sea —Gabriel García Márquez, *The General in his Labyrinth*

3. Revolution was the religion of our family —Yevgeny Yevtushenko, *A Precocious Autobiography*
    The poet came from a long line of Russian revolutionists.

■ REWARDS

See also: GRATITUDE/INGRATITUDE

1. Of action well done, they say / The fruit is spotless and of the nature of goodness; / But the fruit of passion is pain; / The fruit of darkness is ignorance —Anon., *The Bhagavad Gita, 14:16*

2. Ligurio: He might be more attractive than you; in which case the fruits of our labours would be picked by someone else — Niccolo Machiavelli, *Mandragola*, Act 1
    Machiavelli may not have coined the hoary metaphor, but he proves that it has been around since the sixteenth century.

3. She crowns him with her gratitude —
Edwin Arlington Robinson, "The Gift
of God"

■ RHETORIC

See: SPEECHES

■ RICHES

*See also: ABUNDANCE; FORTUNE/MISFOR-
TUNE; MONEY; POVERTY/PROSPERITY*

1. Insignificant thieves are hanged by the
neck and important thieves are hanged by
the purse —Anon., Proverb

2. Our wells are gushing —Jane Danowitz,
Head of the bipartisan Women's Campaign Fund, *The New York Times*, May
24, 1992
   *The wells were the funds raised to get more women
   into elected positions.*

3. Property, possessions and riches . . . were
no longer a game and a toy: they had
become a chain and a burden —Hermann
Hesse, *Siddhartha*

4. Ostharu: Dear Lady, he dare not stand too
nigh the fire, / Lest he melt in his hose /
And come out candlesticks —Edna St.
Vincent Millay, *The King's Henchman*, Act 1
   *The response is occasioned by the question, "Is he
   so rich in silver?"*

5. Thus we have seen that a small State may
lay up a great wealth in necessary provisions, which are Princes Jewels, no less
precious than their Treasure, for in time of
need they are ready —Thomas Mun,
England's Treasure by Forraign Trade, 1664
   *The metaphor, which equates the value of the food
   and provisions stored up by the inhabitants of a
   state with the prince's jewels. Indeed, in times of
   siege, food was much more valuable than inedible
   gemstones.*

6. Florizel: Prosperity's the very bond of
love, / Whose fresh complexion and
whose heart together / Affliction alters —

William Shakespeare, *The Winter's Tale*,
Act 4, scene 4, line 586

7. Blanche: How strange that I should be
called a destitute woman! When I have all
these treasures locked in my heart —
Tennessee Williams, *A Streetcar Named
Desire*, Scene 10
   *The treasures she alludes to are intelligence and
   breeding.*

■ RIDICULE

*See also: INSULTS; NAME CALLING; MEN
AND WOMEN*

1. He ne hadde for his labour but a scorn. /
And thus she maketh Absolon hir ape —
Geoffrey Chaucer, "The Miller's Tale,"
The Canterbury Tales
   *The woman made an ape of her suitor, and that
   was all he got for his pains.*

2. Mr. Clemens [Mark Twain] poured out a
volcano of ridicule —Helen Keller, "Our
Mark Twain"
   *Twain's verbal volcano is directed at a dinner
   party discussion of the situation in the Philip-
   pines. One of the dinner party guests was Woodrow
   Wilson.*

3. What she'd done, you see, she'd caught
'im a slap clean across the face in front of
the 'ole world —Rosamond Lehmann,
The Ballad and the Source
   *A family servant explains the effect of a wife's
   desertion on her husband.*

■ RISK-TAKING

See also: CAUTION; COURAGE; TIMIDITY

1. The data isn't unequivocal, but . . . I'm
not prepared to be a guinea pig —A
farmer quoted by Joel Greenberg, "Hatzeva
Journal," *The New York Times*, November
27, 1992
   *The speaker did not want "a giant monster
   spewing radiation near my house," he said, in
   protesting the building of a Voice of America relay
   station.*

2. Madrogal: You try your foot upon the ice, don't you? —Enid Bagnold, *The Chalk Garden,* Act 1

3. This act of resolution was . . . a straight and possibly dangerous dive into the very depth of truth —Henry James, "Fordham Castle"

4. By pledging that workers' compensation and automobile insurance will be part of an overhaul of the nation's health-care system, the Clinton Administration appears ready to plunge into quagmires that have never been the territory of the Federal Government —Peter Kerr, *The New York Times,* May 9, 1993

   Here we see how the choice of metaphor can influence thinking. A bias against the plan is indicated by the word "quagmire." Think of how the meaning would change had the author used "lake" or "river" instead.

5. This is a crap game we're playing . . . only nobody wants to roll the dice —Terry McMillan, *Waiting to Exhale*

6. He felt ready to cast dice with death and glory —Orhan Pamuk, *The White Castle*

7. Talbot: O! too much folly is it, . . . / To hazard all our lives in one small boat — William Shakespeare, *The First Part of Henry the Sixth,* Act 4, scene 6, line 32

   A common variation of this is to put or not put all your eggs in one basket.

■ RIVALRY

See: COMPETITION/COMPETITORS

■ ROAD SCENES

See also: STREET SCENES

1. The road out of town is a frosty tunnel — John Malcolm Brinnin, Journal entry, January 9, 1948

2. Six years ago the Hazelton-Smithers Highway [in California] was a corkscrew dirt road —Edward Hoagland, "In Hazelton and Flying North"

3. The Cadillac was a space ship skimming just above the ground —Ross MacDonald, *The Moving Target*

4. The neons along the Strip glared with insomnia —Ross MacDonald, *The Moving Target*

   MacDonald's Archer novels are filled with colorful images of Los Angeles and its environs.

5. The highway [as I doubled speed limit] was no more than a long white arrow launched against the horizon —Norman Mailer, *Harlot's Ghost*

   Mailer continues with a simile: "then clouds would appear like hooded strangers."

6. The road was a ribbon of moonlight — Alfred Noyes, "The Highwayman"

■ ROLE MODELS

See: GUIDANCE/GUIDES; INSPIRATION

■ ROMANCE

See: LOVE; MEN AND WOMEN

■ ROME

See: CITIES

■ ROOMS

See also: FURNITURE/FURNISHINGS

1. The lazy autumn sunlight dazzled its way through ribbons of clouds past the windows on the east side of the classroom, and crept across the linoleum floor — Charles Baxter, "Gryphon"

2. They're standing in the living room—or, rather, on the narrow footpath between the canyons of furniture that obscure the walls —T. Coraghessan Boyle, "Filthy

RUDENESS

With Things," *The New Yorker,* February 15, 1993

> *The image sets the scene for Boyle's story about a couple of obsessive accumulators who call in an organizer to unclutter their home.*

3. Motes of dust danced in sunlight —A. S. Byatt, *Possession*

4. The kitchen floor-squares make a chessboard —Gjertrud Schnackenberg, "Paper Cities"

5. The walls were padded with standing policemen —Nadine Gordimer, *Burger's Daughter*

6. The room filled with the kettle's breath — Geoffrey Hill, "In Memory of Jane Frazer"

7. The bookcases were always crammed full . . . and the bedrooms and hallways were turned into narrow passes between steep cliffs of books and mountains of errant documents that proliferated as he passed and pursued him without mercy in their quest for archival peace —Gabriel García Márquez, *The General in his Labyrinth*

> *This figurative phrase teeters precariously at the edge of* mixaphor *territory.*

8. The furniture had been herded into the middle of the room —J. D. Salinger, *Franny and Zooey*

■ RUDENESS
See: CHARACTERISTICS

■ RUIN
See: FAILURE

■ RUMOR
See also: GOSSIP

1. Rameses: I tell you I've been out walking / Under the burning windows of the people's eyes —Christopher Fry, *The Firstborn,* Act 2, scene 2

2. You, doubtless, hear wings, / . . . And nests of rumour clustered in the world — Geoffrey Hill, "Asmodai"

3. Rumour, the profane vagabond, who will not take service in any respectable household —George Meredith, *The Ordeal of Richard Feverel*

4. Rumour: Rumour is a pipe / blown by surmises, jealousies, conjectures, / And of so easy and so plain a stop / that the still-discordant wavering multitude, / Can play upon it —William Shakespeare, *The Second Part of King Henry the Fourth,* Introduction, line 15

> *The play opens with Rumour entering the stage painted full of tongues.*

■ RUTHLESSNESS
See: VILLAINS / VILLAINY

S

■ SACRIFICE

See also: DEATH; SORROW; SUFFERING

1. Death and sorrows will be the companions of our journey; hardship our garment —Winston Churchill, Speech, House of Commons, October 8, 1940

2. This world in arms is not spending money alone. It is spending the sweat of its laborers, the genius of its scientists, the houses of its children . . . Under the cloud of war . . . it is humanity hanging itself on a cross of iron —Dwight David Eisenhower, Speech, April 16, 1953

   These eloquent images, like many presidential utterances, were produced by a ghost writer—an apt metaphor for writers hired to make presidents sound good.

3. The 150 Representatives who attended the conference here heard one senior member of the Administration after another plead with them to swallow the bitter medicine of austerity —Clifford Krauss, *The New York Times,* January 31, 1993

   The headline writer apparently felt one common metaphor deserved another. "Democrats Live It Up (a Bit) Before Biting Bullet (Maybe)."

4. I pray that our Heavenly Father may assuage the anguish of your bereavement . . . to have laid so costly a sacrifice upon the altar of freedom —Abraham Lincoln, Letter to Mrs. Bixby, November 21, 1864

   Mrs. Bixby had purportedly lost five sons in the Civil War. According to Carl Sandburg, two of her sons had indeed died. One returned home. Two were deserters.

5. We have given so many hostages to fortune —Lucian, *Mortuorum Dialogi*

   This metaphor by a little-known Greek satirist owes its fame to the seventeenth-century essayist and philosopher Sir Francis Bacon, who used it in relation to marriage: "He that hath wife and children hath given hostages to fortune; for they are impediments to great enterprise.

6. Harpagon: Have you told her that she ought to help a little, if only slightly; that she should bleed herself for an occasion such as this? —Molière, *The Miser,* Act 2

   Even though he is very wealthy, Harpagon wants the mother of the poor girl he plans to marry to give him dowry money. A less miserly person would heed the common metaphor for futility, there's no getting blood from a stone.

■ SADNESS

See: DARKNESS / LIGHT; DESPAIR; GRIEF

■ SAFETY

See also: CAUTION; ECONOMICS; PROBLEMS AND SOLUTIONS; SURVIVAL

1. The highest-flying economy in the world is searching for a soft landing —Robert Benjamin, *Baltimore Sun,* June 21, 1993

While flying has become a common mode of transportation, flying metaphors still lag far behind those tied to automobiles and sailing (the most popular). Another transportation metaphor headlined the above story: "Booming Chinese economy showing signs of overheating."

2. It may well be that we shall, by a process of sublime irony, have reached a stage where safety will be the sturdy shield of terror, and survival the twin brother of annihilation —Winston Churchill
   Churchill was commenting on the hydrogen bomb.

3. Fabian: Still you keep o' the windy side of the law —William Shakespeare, *Twelfth Night,* Act 3, scene 4, line 171
   In this seafaring metaphor, "windy" means windward or safe.

4. Ensconced in the fortress of his consulting room . . . he felt strong and safe —Irvin D. Yalom, *When Nietzsche Wept*
   A fictionalized Dr. Joseph Breuer referring to his obsession with a patient.

■ SANCTIMONIOUSNESS

See: EGO / EGOTISM

■ SARCASM

See also: ACCUSATIONS; HUMOR; WORDS AS WEAPONS

1. For a man who hasn't a taste for artillery . . . you are keeping up a pretty lively fire on my inner works. But go on. Cynicism is a small brass field-piece that eventually bursts and kills the artilleryman —Thomas Bailey Aldrich, "Marjorie Daw"
   The metaphoric artilleryman is a friend engaged in a correspondence designed to enliven a friend's enforced inactivity due to a broken leg.

2. True sarcasm is in the point, not in the shaft, of the arrow —Josh Billings
   At another time, Billings called sarcasm "an undertaker in tears."

3. A gift for the unfrocking phrase is a dangerous talent [since neither friends or foes

like it] —John Mason Brown, Introduction, *The Portable Woollcott.*
   According to Brown, Alexander Woollcott, though often sentimental, was as frequently sarcastic.

4. Jests which slap the face are not good jests —Miguel Cervantes, *Don Quixote*

■ SATIRE

See also: REVELATION

1. Satire is a cruel weapon, but in malicious hands the handle is more dangerous than the blade —Josh Billings

2. Only a few of the nearly 30 songs are tinged with satire. Ms. Richards [Mae Richards, lyricist], prefers a soft brush to a stiff bristle —Mel Gussow, "Review/ Theater," *The New York Times,* September 21, 1992
   The show being reviewed was Cut the Ribbons.

3. Haynes and Roberts [set designers for the film of Edith Wharton's novel] dressed the French doors all in white inscribed, for a piquant twist, with lines from *The Age of Innocence,* an acid valentine penned to the pretentious world of her youth —Julie V. Iovine, "The Wharton School of Design," *The New York Times Magazine,* August 22, 1993
   Wharton would undoubtedly have liked this fabric since she was quoted as saying that she "felt hemmed in by the lead-heavy draperies of the day."

4. What was revolutionary about *Dulcy* [George S. Kaufman's first play] was that it blew up a balloon labelled Business, held it up for the audience to laugh at, and then stuck the sharp pin of satire into the balloon—and when it burst the audience laughed even harder —Howard Teichmann, *George S. Kaufman*
   And what Teichman has done is to give a fresh twist to a familiar metaphor—to burst someone's bubble to illustrate the fragility of people's illusions. In a profile in The New Yorker, *(August 16, 1993), Joan Acocelia used the image of the burst balloon to explain Dorothy Parker's*

technique for letting her poems express a consistent message of hope's broken promises: "she inflates the balloon, then pops it."

5. At a stroke she had pricked the van der Luydens and they collapsed —Edith Wharton, *The Age of Innocence*
   Using the familiar image of the easily-burst balloon, Wharton has Ellen Olenska awaken Newland Archer to the pretentiousness and fragility of an Old New York society family.

■ SCAPEGOATING

See: ACCUSATIONS; BIGOTRY

■ SCHOOLS

See: EDUCATION AND LEARNING

■ SCIENCE

See also: CREATIVITY; EXPLOITATION; IMAGINATION; MANIPULATION; RELIGION

1. Food analysis is a veritable toddler among scientific fields —Anon., Editorial, *The New York Times*, April 14, 1993
   The metaphor was prompted by a report that diets rich in vegetables may prevent budding tumors from getting the blood needed to grow.

2. Science without religion is lame, religion without science is blind —Albert Einstein, *The World as I See It*

3. It took him [Freeman Dyson] awhile to realize how obsessively his new friend was tunneling into the very bedrock of modern science —James Gleick, *Genius: The Life and Science of Richard Feynman*
   Two metaphors—bedrock and tunneling—depict Feynman (the "new friend") when he helped to develop the atomic bomb.

4. Scientific creativity is imagination in a straitjacket —James Gleick, "Part Showman, All Genius," *The New York Times Magazine*, September 20, 1992

5. Astrology is a disease, not a science . . . It is a tree under the shadow of which all sorts of superstitions thrive —Moses ben Maimon, Letter, 1195

6. Science! . . . / whose wings are dull realities —Edgar Allan Poe, "Sonnet-To Science"

7. Genetic engineering techniques that manipulate the bodies of animals to produce biological products have made real the possibility that the animal kingdom will become nothing more than spare parts supply houses and drug-producing factories for humankind —Suzanne E. Roy, Letter by the Public Affairs Director in Defense of Animals, *The New York Times*, July 7, 1992

8. If an operation be thought of as a painting in progress, and blood red the color on the brush, it must be suitably restrained and attract no undue attention; yet any insufficiency of it will increase the perishability of the canvas —Richard Selzer, "Letter to a Young Surgeon, 2," *Letters to a Young Doctor*

9. [Science is] a black hole, prepared to suck up whatever proportion of your life that you allow it —Shirley M. Tilghman, *The New York Times*, January 26, 1993

10. Science is a match that man has just got alight —H. G. Wells, s.u., 1891.

■ SCRUTINY

See also: APPROVAL/DISAPPROVAL; AWARENESS/UNAWARENESS; CRAFTINESS; CRITICISM/CRITICS; EYE EXPRESSIONS; EXACTNESS/INEXACTNESS; LOOKS; MISTAKES; PEOPLE, INTERACTION

1. He's warily sniffing the cultural aromas as the Clinton-Gore era unfolds. —Peter Applebome, *The New York Times*, January 24, 1993.

The author described the Southern scholar, John Shelton Reed, as if he were a houn' dog.

2. Unfortunately, Ms. Baumgold is so busy burning holes in her subjects' hides with a magnifying glass that she never steps back to gain any larger perspective —Christopher Lehmann-Haupt, "Books of the Times," *The New York Times*, June 28, 1993
   Mr. Lehmann-Haupt was "burning holes" into Ms. Baumgold's first novel, Creature of Habit.

3. He stood on the podium and pinned us with his eyes —Norman Mailer , *Harlot's Ghost*
   The eyes, Mailer continues, are "a hole impinging on you."

4. We have to cut out the business of pulling Bill Clinton up by the roots every week to see how he's doing —William Safire, "Essay," *The New York Times*, June 21, 1993
   Leave it to the master "word maven" to create a sandwich filled with metaphors, beginning with the above and concluding with "details . . . do not power the roller coaster of trend addicts demanding their weekly fix of fresh angles." A mixed sports and a horseback riding metaphor were layered in the middle: 1. The broken-field runner in the Oval Office (mixed metaphors are allowed when the stately pendulum turns into a propeller) encourages this man-to-media coverage. 2. Centrism is in the saddle.

5. He whispered constantly . . . his small eyes drilling into Markham's face —William Trevor, "A School Story"

■ SEA

See also: COLOR; NATURE; NATURE SCENES; SOUND

1. John Claggart: The sea's a taskmaster . . . It salts the sweetness out of boyish faces —Robert Chapman and Louis O. Coxe, *Billy Budd*, Act 1, scene 1
   The play was adapted from Herman Melville's novel of the same name.

2. The voice of the sea speaks to the soul. The touch of the sea is sensuous, enfolding the body in its soft, close embrace — Kate Chopin, *The Awakening*
   The sea is a metaphor for the only embrace and comfort left to the protagonist after she has become disillusioned with her idealized love for a man. It sums up her aloneness.

3. He has offered his bit of sacrifice to the sea . . . he shall be fit to live or die as the sea may decree; and the man who had taken a hand in this fool game, in which the sea wins every toss, will be pleased to have his back slapped —Joseph Conrad, *Lord Jim*
   Jim has been "slapped" in this game of horseshoes and has "winced, for the slap was heavy."

4. [The Sea] . . . this great wink of eternity — Hart Crane, "Voyages 2"

5. Whirl up, sea— / Whirl up your pointed pines —Hilda Doolittle (H. D.), "Oread"
   Sarah Orne Jewett, a contemporary of H.D., used a greatly extended form of the metaphor in The Country of the Pointed Firs.

6. The sea remembers nothing. It is feline. It licks your feet,—its huge flanks purr very pleasantly for you; but it will crack your bones and eat you, for all that, and wipe the crimsoned foam from its jaws as if nothing had happened —Oliver Wendell Holmes, *The Autocrat of the Breakfast-Table*
   The image of the sea as a sly cat is followed by "The sea smooths its silver scales until you cannot see their joints,—but their shining is that of a snake's belly, after all."

7. The snotgreen sea —James Joyce, *Ulysses*

8. Let the sea-gulls wail / For water, for the deep where the high tide / Mutters to its hurt self, mutters and ebbs —Robert Lowell, "The Quaker Graveyard in Nantucket"

9. Chris: It's better Anna live on farm, den she don't know dat ole devil, sea —Eugene O'Neill, *Anna Christie*, Act 1
   The devil as metaphoric personification is by no means limited to the sea.

10. The waves on the shore stammered quietly, spreading softly on the sand —Jean Baptiste Racine, *Andromaque*

11. Agamemnon: The sea being smooth, / How many shallow bauble boats dare sail / Upon her patient breast, making their way / With those of nobler bulk! — William Shakespeare, *Troilus and Cressida* Act 1 scene 3, line 35

12. The sea's white claws / Still flung their eight fathoms to have my blood —Robert Penn Warren, "The Cross"

∎ SEASCAPES

See also: FOG; NATURE SCENES; SKY/SKYSCAPES; STORMS

1. The sprinkled isles, / Lily on lily, that o'erlace the sea —Robert Browning, *Men and Women.* Cleon 18

2. The rested waters, the cold wet breath of the fog, are of a world in which man is an uneasy trespasser —Rachel Carson, *The Edge of the Sea*
   The metaphoric trespasser "punctures the night with the complaining groan and grunt of a foghorn, sensing the power and menace of the sea.

3. The mist lifted . . . vanished into thin flying wreaths; and the unveiled lagoon lay, polished and black, in the heavy shadows at the foot of the wall of trees — Joseph Conrad, "The Lagoon"

4. The *Patna*, with a slight hiss, passed over that plain luminous and smooth, unrolled a black ribbon of smoke across the sky, left behind her on the water a white ribbon of foam that vanished at once, like the phantom of a track drawn upon the lifeless sea by the phantom of a steamer —Joseph Conrad, *Lord Jim*
   The two ribbon metaphors pave the way for the poetic concluding simile.

5. The ship flies in a heaven of blue waters — Henri Coulette, "Antony and Cleopatra"
   The metaphor is a reflection of sky as it is mirrored in the sea—the ship becomes a bird or plane, and the sea the heavens.

6. When it came night, the white waves paced to and fro in the moonlight — Stephen Crane, *The Open Boat*
   This is the book's concluding image, an example of personification as metaphor.

7. Under the leaden weight of sky the golden music of the waves was tarnished — Antoine de Saint-Exupery, *Night Flight*

8. The cold sea where the teeth of the waves flashed like white buds —Shusaku Endo, *Silence*

9. This sea, holding in its embrace a number of small islands, flashed like a needle in the faint sunlight, while the waves biting at the shore foamed white with froth — Shusaku Endo, *Silence*
   A simile is framed by two metaphors.

10. The mirror of water whitened . . . White breast of the dim sea . . . . Wavewhite wedded words shimmering on the dim tide —James Joyce, *Ulysses*

11. There was light only in the waves curling the river . . . all its empty windows gazing wide-eyed down the river valley —Sean O'Faolain, "Midsummer Night Madness"

12. The sea was mountains rolling —William Pitt, "The Sailor's Consolation"
    The image is of the sea during a hurricane

13. The Gulf of Mexico is . . . flogged by the landing of a storm —James Robison, "Between Seasons," *The New Yorker*, June 14, 1993

14. The waves clamber the loudening shores —Paul Ambroise Valéry, "Helen"

15. The surf, insatiably promiscuous, / groans through the walls —Derek Walcott, "Europa," *Collected Poems*

16. The parching stones along the shore / hastily sip the listless waves, / In doubt the sea will pour them more —Richard Wilbur, "From the Lookout Rock"

■ SEASONS

*See also: FALL; NATURE SCENES; PERMA-
NENCE/IMPERMANENCE; SPRING;
SUMMER; SUN; TRANSIENCE; WIND*

1. Spring is a virgin, Summer a mother,
   Autumn a widow, and Winter a stepmother —Anon., Polish Proverb
   > *For the sake of kind stepmothers everywhere, the
   > last of these four metaphors of personification
   > should probably be relegated to its own win-
   > try grave.*

2. Here then was April . . . scalping them
   with a flexible blade of wind —Kay
   Boyle, "Wedding Day"

3. The Indian Summer, the dead Summer's
   soul —Mary Clemmer, "Presence"

4. The small clumsy feet of April came /
   into the ragged meadow of my soul —e.
   e. cummings, "If I Have Made, My Lady"

5. He says that leaves are old and that for
   flowers / Mid-summer is to spring as one
   to ten —Robert Frost, "The Oven Bird"

6. In March the ice unloosed the brook /
   And water ruffled the sun's hair —Geoffrey
   Hill, "In Memory of Jane Frazer"

7. "The sun weaves the seasons," thought
   Many Swans, "I have been under and
   over the warp of the world" —Amy
   Lowell, "Many Swans"

8. Overhead the seasons rock / They are
   paper bells / Calling to nothing living —
   William Stanley Merwin
   > *The transience of the seasons is likened to the
   > paper bells, and, by inference, to the brief lives of
   > Asian soldiers killed in battle.*

9. January, laid out on a bed of ice, disgorg-
   ing / February, shaped like a flounder,
   and March with her steel / bead pocket-
   book —James Schuyler, "The Crystal
   Lithium"
   > *The metaphor's sense of January as a cold fish,
   > comes from the follow-up simile of February as a
   > flounder.*

10. Rough winds do shake the darling buds of
    May, / And summer's lease hath all too
    short a date —William Shakespeare, "Son-
    net 18," line 3
    > *Many of Shakespeare's metaphors are landlord's
    > images.*

11. Titania: The spring, the summer, / The
    childing [fruitful] autumn, angry winter,
    change / Their wonted liveries —Wil-
    liam Shakespeare, *A Midsummer Night's
    Dream*, Act 2, scene 1, line 111

12. Doubtless it is dangerous to love / This
    somersault of seasons —Richard Wilbur,
    "Winter Spring"

■ SECRECY

*See also: CANDOR; INTERNATIONAL
RELATIONS*

1. An iron curtain is drawn down upon their
   front [the Russians] —Winston Churchill, telegram to President Harry S Truman, May 12, 1945
   > *Churchill used this metaphor several times in a
   > 1946 speech which he named with an anatomical
   > metaphor, "The Sinews of War." According to
   > William Safire, the metaphor was also used by the
   > German general staff and even earlier by H. G.
   > Wells. Its literal use as a description for a fireproof
   > theater curtain goes back to the early nineteenth
   > century.*

2. Nowadays, we've upped the ante on secret subjects —Letty Cottin Progrebin,
   "Hers," *The New York Times Magazine*,
   November 29, 1992
   > *Progrebin's essay about family secrets also alludes
   > to the metaphor of the closet for hidden homosexu-
   > ality and ends with another metaphor: "the wag-
   > ons of denial are still pulled in close around the
   > incest perpetrator."*

3. Iya Agba: That was two lives we poured
   into her hands. Two long lives spent peck-
   ing at secrets grain by grain —Wole
   Soyinka, *Madmen and Specialists*, Part 1

The conversation between Iya Agba and Iya Mate is held in metaphor, and is enigmatic. The two old women are earth-mothers.

4. When Britten . . . accepted a peerage, he did so in the proud name of a long sufferance of a twilight he had helped to disperse —George Steiner, "Books," *The New Yorker*, July 5, 1993
   Steiner referred to Benjamin Britten's acknowledgement of his homosexuality at a time when this still entailed opprobrium and even legal measures. .

■ SEDUCTION

See: MEN AND WOMEN

■ SEGREGATION

See: BIGOTRY

■ SELF

See also: EGO/ID; EMOTIONS; SELF-ACTU-ALIZATION; SELF-CONTROL; SELF-KNOWLEDGE;THINKING/THOUGHT; YEARNING

1. Maggie's life-struggles had lain almost entirely within her own soul, one shadowy army fighting another, and the slain shadows forever rising again —George Eliot, *The Mill on the Floss*
   Maggie's inner struggles mark a sharp contrast to her brother's "dustier, noisier warfare."

2. There is only the one self; my day is to carve it —Donald Hall, "To Build a House"

3. Sir: There are dangers in covering the cracks [of one's emotional veneer] —Ronald Harwood, *The Dresser*, Act 1

4. He had never really found his Self, because he had wanted to trap it in the net of thoughts —Hermann Hesse, *Siddhartha*
   Siddhartha tries to substitute thinking for experience.

5. Do you know I sometimes think that I'm a man of genius half-finished? The genius has been left out, the faculty of expression is wanting; but the need for expression remains, and I spend my days groping for the latch of a closed door —Henry James, *Roderick Hudson*

6. I too am a world —Theodore Roethke, *Straw for the Fire, Notebooks of Theodore Roethke*

7. Many people are living in an emotional jail without recognizing it —Virginia Satir, Epigraph

8. The self is a cloister full of remembered sounds —Wallace Stevens, "The Woman That Had More Babies Than That"

9. His real life had always lain in the universe of thought, in that enchanted region which . . . comes to have so much more color and substance than the painted curtain hanging before it —Edith Wharton, "The Descent of Man"
   A professor for whom marriage merely provided "a comfortable lining" reflects on his inner life.

10. She looked back with melancholy derision on her old conception of life as a kind of well-lit and well-policed suburb to dark places one need never know about —Edith Wharton, *The Reef*
    But now, as the novel draws to a close, Anna Leath knows that "Here they were, these dark places, in her own bosom, and henceforth she would always have to traverse them to reach the being she loved best!"

■ SELF-ABSORPTION

See: EGO/EGOTISM

■ SELF-ACTUALIZATION

See also: ACHIEVEMENT; ADVICE; EMOTIONS; HAPPINESS/UNHAPPINESS; HUMANITY/HUMANKIND;OPPORTUNITY; SELF IMAGES

1. The outer crust of her life [her reserve] . . . was torn away and she gave herself to the

emotion of love —Sherwood Anderson, "Adventure," *Winesburg, Ohio*

> *The young woman who lets love into her life is one of the many lonely, disappointed characters who people* Winesburg, Ohio.

2. Schiller too struggles to reconcile the will, man's inborn freedom, his vocation to be his own master, with the laws of nature and history; he ends by believing man's only salvation is in the realm of art, where he can achieve independence of the causal treadmill where, in Kant's words, man is a mere turnspit, acted upon by external forces —Isaiah Berlin, "The Apotheosis of the Romantic Will"

> *Here we have three philosophers involved in two metaphors: Kant is cited for the turnspit metaphor; and Schiller's ideas are ransacked for Berlin's treadmill metaphor.*

3. Hone and spread your spirit, till you yourself are a sail, whetted, translucent, broadside to the merest puff —Annie Dillard, *Pilgrim at Tinker Creek*

> *Dillard introduces this with "The secret of seeing is to sail on solar wind."*

4. One day . . . the water-tight compartments in her will break down, and music and life will mingle —E. M. Forster, *A Room With a View*

> *A talented young woman has yet to break out of the shell of a quiet, unadventurous life.*

5. Sir: You have to learn to wait . . . and the moment comes when you launch your own barque and take the rudder —Ronald Harwood, *The Dresser*, Act 1

6. Everyone knows on any given day that . . . that compared with what we ought to be, we are only half awake. Our fires are damped, our drafts are checked —William James, "The Energies of Man," *The Will to Believe and Other Essays*

7. I do not want to die . . . until I have cultivated the seed that was placed in me until the last small twig has grown —

Käthe Kollwitz, *Diaries and Letters*, February 15, 1915

8. Stumbling up the breathless stair / To burst into fulfillment's desolate attic —Philip Larkin, "Deceptions"

9. If you would be armed well [in the battle for happiness] . . . the armor must be an alloy of your own soul and all wisdom; it must be welded with your brain, your strength, your dreams —Percy Marks, "Advice to Freshmen"

10. All the strings of her nature were, at last, vibrant —Mary McCarthy, "Cruel and Barbarous Treatment"

> *The protagonist's exhilaration is due to an extramarital affair.*

11. You are your own magician. / . . . stretch out your hand and look: / each finger is a snake of energy —Marge Piercy, "The butt of winter," *Hard Loving*

■ SELF-CONFIDENCE

See also: ADVICE; AGE/AGING; CHARACTERISTICS; FATE; PRIDE

1. Nothing could dent his cast-iron assurance —Stanley Elkin, "The Moment of Decision"

2. Trust thyself: every heart vibrates to that iron string —Ralph Waldo Emerson, "Self Reliance"

> *Or, as the old courtier advised, "To thine own heart be true."*

3. Seti: Fate has taken a hammer / To chip and chip at our confidence —Christopher Fry, *The Firstborn*, Act 2, scene 2

4. I look at a bird and I see myself: a native South African, soaring above the injustices of arpatheid on wings of pride —Miriam Makeba (with James Hall), Prologue, *Makeba, My Story*, 1987.

5. Confidence is a plant of slow growth in an aged bosom —William Pitt, Speech in House of Commons, January 14, 1766

 On the other hand, "Youth is the season of credulity."

6. How subtle a thing is this confidence! . . . A new behavior springs; the ship carries a new ballast in her hold —Henry David Thoreau, Letter to Ralph Waldo Emerson, 1843

■ SELF-CONSCIOUSNESS

See also: DESCRIPTIONS, MISC.

1. As he walked back to his pew the sharp taps of his cloven hoofs were loud upon the floor —F. Scott Fitzgerald, "Absolution"

 The boy has not told the complete truth in the confessional, and feels he has taken on the attributes of the devil.

2. A rich compost of negative images applied over three centuries has given rise to one of the state's hardiest crops, the collective inferiority complex —Elisabeth Ginsburg, *The New York Times,* May 24, 1992

3. She had spent her life trying to escape from the parlorlike jaws of self-consciousness —Eudora Welty, "June Recital"

4. She was a fly, but the others were dragonflies, butterflies, beautiful insects, dancing, fluttering, skimming, while she alone dragged herself up out of the saucer —Virginia Woolf, "The New Dress"

 Mabel is worried about the cut of her new dress, which causes her to feel insecure in a fashionable world.

■ SELF-CONTROL

See also: CAUTION; CHARACTERIZATIONS; CONCENTRATION/DISTRACTION; CONTROL; EMOTIONS; FEELINGS; PERSONALITY PROFILES; PASSION; REASON

1. An action so diametrically opposed to my newfound philosophy of discriminating pleasure-seeking I can only attribute to the explosion of the natural emotions that I had supposed were under lock and key in the comely mansion of my aestheticism —Louis Auchincloss, "The Epicurean," *Three Lives*

2. The passions may rage furiously . . . but judgment shall still have the last word in every argument, and the casting vote in every decision —Charlotte Brontë, *Jane Eyre*

 The two images depicting passion as a raging storm and judgment as a more considered, political action are preceded by a third metaphor: Feeling without judgment is a washy draught indeed.

3. Reason sits firm and holds the reins, and she will not let the feelings burst away and hurry her to wild chasms —Charlotte Brontë, *Jane Eyre*

 And yet when Jane mistakenly believes that Rochester is going to marry Miss Ingram, she asks him with great passion "Do you think I am an automaton?—a machine without feelings? and can bear to have my morsel of bread snatched from my lips, and my drop of living water dashed from my cup?"

4. It was up to me to bring my nerves to heel —Albert Camus, *The Stranger*

5. After more than six months of near silence about the baseball team that he owns, rules and cherishes, George Steinbrenner shed his muzzle today and challenged the Yankees to produce a pennant —Jack Curry, *The New York Times,* September 14, 1993

 "Steinbrenner Transforms His Muzzle Into a Prod," wrote the headline writer, mounting the horse metaphor with one of his own.

6. Mother: Always in my breast there's a shriek standing tiptoe that I have to beat down and hold under my shawls —Frederico Garcia Lorca, *Blood Wedding,* Act 2, scene 2

7. To-day . . . I am walking all round my heart and building up the defenses. I do not mean to leave a loophole even for a tuft of violets to grow in —Katherine Mansfield, Journal entry, December, 1914

8. Her mind lives tidily, apart / From cold and noise and pain, / And bolts the door against her heart, / Out wailing in the rain —Dorothy Parker, "Interior," *Sunset Gun*

9. He is an empty suit longing to breathe free —Frank Rich, "Review/Theater,"
    Rich drew on an increasingly common metaphor to sum up the leading character in A. R. Gurney's latest play about an emotionally repressed "Wasp."

10. I'd had him wrong in every way: in reality he'd been living under an ice cap . . . with his wonderful manners and his refined virility not only masking the pain of dispossession and exile but concealing even from himself how scorched he was by shame —Philip Roth, *Operation Shylock*

11. King: Therefore, brave conquerors, . . . / That war against your own affections / And the huge army of the world's desires —William Shakespeare, *Love's Labour's Lost*, Act 1, scene 1, line 25
    The King pledges Browne, Dumaine, and Longaville to three years dedicated to scholarship.

12. Bolingbroke: First, the fair reverence of your Highness curbs me / From giving reins and spurs to my free speech —William Shakespeare, *The Tragedy of King Richard the Second*, Act 1, scene 1, line 55
    He will ride to the kingship, and a horse will be the symbol of Richard's overthow by Bolingbroke.

13. For a man who . . . permitted so little of himself to be seen above water, and ultimately, for a man with so caustic a tongue, one might think it curious that George Kaufman had not only enemies but friends as well —Howard Teichmann, *George S. Kaufman*

14. For years now she had barricaded her heart against her daughter's presence — Edith Wharton, *The Mother's Recompense*

15. As soon as he reappeared her head straightened itself on her slim neck and she sped little shafts of irony, or flew her little kites of erudition, while hot and cold waves swept over her —Edith Wharton, *The Reef*
    Anna Summer's passionate feelings for George Dallow are kept in check by her inhibitions.

16. Tears came hard to her, and the storms of her heart spent themselves inwardly — Edith Wharton, *Summer*
    The self-contained young woman is the protagonist of Wharton's short, powerful novel about the constrained opportunities of small town life.

17. Goddam! He reined in his feelings — Richard Wright, *The Outsider*

■ SELF-DEFENSE
See: FUTURE

■ SELF-DELUSION
See: ILLUSION/REALITY

■ SELF-DESTRUCTIVENESS
See also: CHARACTERIZATIONS; HUMANITY/HUMANKIND; PLACES, MISC.

1. Do not keep saying to yourself, if you can possibly avoid it, "But how can it be like that?" because you will get "down the drain," into a blind alley from which nobody has yet escaped. Nobody knows how it can be like that —Richard Feynman, *The Character of Physical Law*
    This is a much-quoted mixed metaphor from the Nobel Prize winning physicist's published lectures.

2. Ireland is the old sow that eats her farrow —James Joyce, *Portrait of the Artist as a Young Man*

3. The bridge underneath is ever so slightly /
Tearing a suture of itself in secret —
Howard Moss, "Elegy for My Sister. III"

4. That man [Ross Perot] has stamped himself canceled as a choice, hope or a trolley
car —A. M. Rosenthal, "On My Mind,"
The New York Times, November 3, 1992
> *The trolley car reference followed Rosenthal's
> scornful view of the things Perot could have done
> to legitimize his candidacy: "Yes, and if my aunt
> had wheels she would be a trolley car."*

5. Duke: I'll sacrifice the lamb that I do love,
/ To spite a raven's heart within a dove —
William Shakespeare, *Twelfth Night,* Act
5, scene 1, line 129
> *A slang version of this would be* to cut off your
> nose to spite your face.

6. I still loved life . . . is there anything sillier
than to desire to bear continually a burden
one always wishes to throw to the ground
. . . to caress the serpent which devours us
until he has eaten our heart? —Voltaire,
Candide

7. Each man kills the thing he loves / . . .
Some strangle with hands of Lust, / Some
with hands of Gold —Oscar Wilde, "The
Ballad of Reading Goal"

■ SELF-DETERMINATION

See: SELF-RELIANCE

■ SELF-EFFACEMENT

*See also: MASTERY/SUBORDINATION;
SACRIFICE*

1. The person who makes a worm of himself
will be stepped on —Anon., Proverb

2. I'll obliterate myself . . . I'll empty myself,
truly, become a chalice —Margaret Atwood,
The Handmaid's Tale
> *The narrator tries to bargain with God, assuming
> that total self-abnegation will save her.*

3. I tell you solemnly that I have many times
tried to become an insect —Fyodor
Mikhailovich Dostoevsky, *Notes from
Underground*
> *"But I was not equal even to that," the narrator
> continues. Kafka's Gregor Samsa will succeed
> where the narrator failed.*

■ SELF-EXPRESSION

See also: WORDS

1. Formerly silent words unfolded themselves
like lawn chairs in my mouth and emerged
one by one wearing large Siberian hats of
consonants and long erminous vowels —
Nicholson Baker, "Reading Aloud," *The
New Yorker,* March 1, 1993
> *The startling simile seems totally alienated from
> the following metaphor, and the result is complete-
> ly disorienting.*

2. It was a prodigious, towering, immense,
enormous scream. A speeding subway car
whose wheels need oiling. A large opera
singer stepping on a tack in the middle of a
mad scene. The space shuttle taking off —
Ellen Weiss and Mel Friedman, *The Poof
Point*
> *Spare us if she should scream twice.*

3. For the first time in his life he found
himself talking freely, emptying out of his
soul the dammed up waters of reflection
—Richard Wright, *The Outsider*
> *The release of the protagonist's inner self is prompted
> by his relationship with a woman.*

■ SELF IMAGES

*See also: ALERTNESS; CALMNESS/VOLA-
TILITY; DESCRIPTIONS, MISC.;
LONELINESS*

1. I was Typhoid Mary. I carried the disease,
you, everywhere —Ray Bradbury, *Death
is a Lonely Business*
> *A budding mystery writer realizes that he has
> inadvertently led a killer to his prey, "a death
> goat."*

2. I am the thought on the bath in the room without mirrors —André Breton, *Nadja*

   When she bathes, writes Breton, "her body withdraws while she stares at the surface of the bath water."

3. Cousin Bette called herself the family confessional —Honoré de Balzac, *Cousin Bette*

   The family that entrusts her with its problems would have been better served elsewhere.

4. I was inwardly conscious with shame that I was not only not a spiteful but not even an embittered man, that I was simply scaring sparrows at random and amusing myself by it —Fyodor Mikhailovich Dostoevsky, *Notes from Underground*

   The narrator will finally catch a "sparrow"—a vulnerable woman—and will try to ruin her self-image completely.

5. I am a wheeling swallow, / Blue all over is my delight —John Gould Fletcher, "Irradiations"

   The poet says he belongs to the sunlight, and follows the preceding metaphor with another one for emphasis: I am a drowsy grass-blade / In the greenest shadow.

6. And he was apprehensive that some light, emanating from within his body, or from his true consciousness, might not be illuminating him, might not, in some way from inside the scaly carapace, give off a reflection of that true form and make him visible to men, who would then have to hunt him down —Jean Genet, *Querelle*

   "Querelle was not used to the idea . . . that he was a monster." His deeds confuse him, as though he had metamorphosed into an alligator, though his soul was intact.

7. I am a camera with its shutter open, quite passive, recording, not thinking —Christopher Isherwood, *Goodbye to Berlin*

   This marks the opening of the author's diary of Berlin during the 1930s.

8. I reached my North and it had meaning. / Here at the actual pole of my existence / . . . I am still alone —Randall Jarrell, "90 North"

   Jarrell is using the chill as Emily Dickinson does when she speaks of "zero at the bone."

9. I stood still and was a tree amid the wood —Ezra Pound, "The Tree"

10. I was a slow-burning fuse . . . who could not fail to blow up the little gathering around the table —Jane Smiley, *Ordinary Love*

    A woman's marriage to a dominating, egomaniacal husband becomes increasingly unbearable.

11. Bech . . . felt precariously tall; a sky-high prodigy about to topple, or crumple —John Updike, *Bech: A Book*

12. From the depths of the mirror, a corpse gazed back at me —Elie Wiesel, *Night*

    This is the image of the newly released concentration camp victim. "The look in his eyes, as they stared into mine, has never left me," Wiesel writes.

13. She knew (she kept on looking into the glass, dipping into that dreadfully showing-up blue pool) that she was condemned, despised, left like this in a backwater —Virginia Woolf, "The New Dress"

    A second metaphor—the backwater—is built on the first, the mirror as a pool. Because Mabel sees herself as dowdy, she will be out of the swim of things, to use another common metaphor.

■ SELF-IMPROVEMENT

1. Our own rough edges become smooth as we help a friend smooth her edges —Sue Atchley Ebaugh, Epigraph

2. Lady Rosaline: weed this wormwood from your fruitful brain —William Shakespeare, *Love's Labour's Lost*, Act 5, scene 2, line 855

   Lady Rosaline tells Berowne he must curb his often mocking tongue if he wants to win her.

3. Oedipus: If you will . . . minister to your own disease—you may hope to find succor and relief from woes —Sophocles, *Oedipus the King*

Ignorance is the disease that Oedipus bemoans,
yet he himself is most in the dark about the true
nature of things.

∎ SELFISHNESS

See: EGO/EGOTISM

∎ SELF-KNOWLEDGE

See also: AWARENESS/UNAWARENESS;
EGO/ID; HUMANITY/HUMANKIND;
ILLUSION/REALITY; PEOPLE, IN-
TERACTION; SELF-CONTROL; UN-
DERSTANDING

1. We hate to face our real natures, so we drop over the scene of our theatricals a thick scrim of sentimentality —Louis Auchincloss, "The Epicurean," *Three Lives*

2. There's a period of life when we swallow a knowledge of ourselves and it becomes either good or sour inside —Pearl Bailey, *The Raw Pearl*

3. It's ironic, but until you can free those final monsters within yourself, your life, your soul, is up for grabs —Rona Barrett, Prologue, *Miss Rona, An Autobiography*

4. He [the ordinary man] has already limited "understanding" to the habitual pigeon-holes into which he slips every experience —William Barrett, "Modern Art"

5. Each of us is encased in an armour whose task it is to ward off signs. Signs happen to us without respite. —Martin Buber, "Dialogue"
   Buber continues that the risk is too dangerous for us (in having to make connections with others) and "from generation to generation we perfect the defence apparatus."

6. He thinks a whole world of which my thought is but a twopenny mirror. And his feelings, too, his whole experience—what a lake compared with my little pool!" —George Eliot, *Middlemarch*

It is this kind of self-analysis in relation to her future husband, that traps the idealistic Dorothea Brooke into a loveless marriage.

7. [Richard] Feynman seemed to hoard shadow pools of ignorance, seemed to protect himself from the light, like a waking man who closes his eyes to preserve a fleeting image from a dream —James Gleick, "Part Showman, All Genius," *The New York Times Magazine*, September 20, 1992
   The simile at the end both enhances and defines the earlier metaphor, which would have seemed puzzling in the absence of a context.

8. The stories we tell ourselves, particularly the silent or barely audible ones . . . become invisible enclosures. Rooms with no air. One must open the window to see further, the door to possibility —Susan Griffin, *A Chorus of Stones*; entrances / exits: doors

9. Mrs. Alving: We are all of us ghosts . . . Whenever I take up a newspaper, I seem to see ghosts gliding between the lines —Henrik Ibsen, *Ghosts*, Act 2
   "It is not only what we have inherited from our father and mother that 'walks' in us," Mrs. Alvin explains. "It is all sorts of dead ideas and lifeless old beliefs, and so forth."

10. With all her love of knowledge, Isabel has a natural shrinking from raising curtains and looking into unlighted corners —Henry James, *Portrait of a Lady*

11. What am I, Life? A thing of watery salt / Held in cohesion by unresting cells —John Masefield, "What Am I, Life?"

12. I feel my slippery self eluding me, gliding into deeper and darker waters than I care to probe —Vladimir Nabokov, *Lolita*

13. You land . . . on the shore of your own being in total innocence . . . and it takes decades to penetrate inland, and map the mountain passes, and trace the rivers to their sources. Even then there are large blanks, where monsters roam —John

Updike, "Baby's First Step," *The New Yorker*, July 27, 1992

14. I had remembered a remark Etienne had made . . . which had sent a searchlight into the uncomprehended parts of his soul and shown them a desert —Dame Rebecca West, *There Is No Conversation*

■ SELF-PITY

1. The hem of self-pity is showing —Louis Begley, *Wartime Lies*

2. He drapes himself in victimhood —Jamie James, responding to complaint about a critical review, *The New York Times*, March 15, 1992

■ SELF-PRAISE

See: BOASTERS/BOASTFULNESS

■ SELF-PROTECTIVENESS

See: DECEPTION

■ SELF-RELIANCE

See also: COURAGE; HUMANITY/HUMANKIND; INDIVIDUALITY; SELF-KNOWLEDGE

1. I'm not afraid of storms for I'm learning to sail my ship —Louisa May Alcott, "Life in the Iron Mills," *The Atlantic Monthly*, April, 1861

2. I am my own Universe, I my own Professor —Sylvia Ashton-Warner, *Myself*

3. If you want to break your chains afterwards, you won't be able to: you will be more and more fast in the snares. It is an accursed bondage —Fyodor Mikhailovich Dostoevsky, *Notes from Underground*

The narrator lectures Liza, the young prostitute.

4. But who would want to choose by rule? Besides, he will at once be transformed from a human being into an organ-stop . . . for what is a man without desires, without free will and without choice, if not a stop in an organ? —Fyodor Mikhailovich Dostoevsky, *Notes from Underground*
The narrator wants to satisfy all his capacities for life, and not simply his "capacity for reasoning." Later, he will make of Liza just such an organ-stop.

5. There is a time in every man's education when he arrives at the conviction that envy is ignorance; that imitation is suicide —Ralph Waldo Emerson, "Self-Reliance," *Essays: First Series*

6. She would have the reins of her own life between her own hands —D. H. Lawrence, *The Fox*

7. Man is his own star —John Fletcher and Philip Massinger, Epilogue, *Honest Men's Fortune*

8. Man did not weave the web of life, he is merely a strand in it. Whatever he does to the web, he does to himself —Chief Seattle, Quoted in an undated bulletin from The Association on American Indian Affairs

9. For Virtue hath this better lesson taught, / Within myself to seek my only hire —Sir Philip Sidney, "Thou blind man's mark, thou fool's self-chosen snare"
One can look only to one's self for answers—in this case, the poet wants to discover how to quench desire.

10. You have to start so fast, with empty bookcases and no user's manual —Gerald L. Warren, Assistant press secretary in the Nixon White House, quoted *The New York Times*, January 19, 1993
Warren commented on the lack of guidelines available to a new administration which nevertheless has to move forward at full speed.

11. My idea of success is personal freedom
. . . to keep a kind of republic of the spirit
—Edith Wharton, *The House of Mirth*
> "It's a country one has to find the way to one's self," writes Wharton.

■ SELF-RIGHTEOUSNESS

See: COMMUNICATION/NON-COMMUNICATION

■ SENSES

See also: FEELINGS; MIND; SEX/SEXUALITY

1. In all the gates in this body / An illumination appears, / Which is knowledge —Anon., *The Bhagavad Gita*, 14:11
> The gates of the body are probably the senses. Some versions footnote them as "openings" though this does not make strict sense.

2. Our eyes and ears refused obedience / the princes of our senses proudly chose exile —Zbigniew Herbert, "The Power of Taste"
> The poet speaks of "taste / in which there are fibers of soul and cartilage of conscience." If the dictators had wooed with good taste, they would not have offended the senses of those they tried to subjugate.

3. All my warning devices, the nameless things that ring bells in the back of your head, that touch your spine gingerly with ice, they were working —John D. Mac-Donald, "The Reference Room"
> This verbal alarm bell sets the scene for a mystery story with a library background.

4. As your senses awaken, all the inlets to the mind are set open —Cathleen Schine, *Rameau's Niece*

5. Angelo: I give my sensual race [nature] the rein —William Shakespeare, *Measure for Measure*, Act 2, scene 4, line 160

6. Pericles: You're a fair viol, and your sense the strings / Who finger'd to make man his lawful music, / Would draw heaven down and all the gods to hearken. —William Shakespeare, *Pericles, Prince of Tyre* Act 1, scene 1, line 81
> "But being play'd upon before your time, / Hell only danceth at so harsh a chime. Good sooth, I care not for you," Pericles continues.

7. The senses paint / By metaphor. The juice was fragranter / than wettest cinnamon —Wallace Stevens, "Poem Written at Morning"

8. My taste buds experienced a violent ecstacy. A whole opera of sensations rolled off my tongue —Henri Troyat, quoted in *The New York Times* by Dorie Greenspan, July 22, 1992
> This description of Troyat's first taste of a coffee ice cream sundae appeared in an article on the longstanding popularity of ice cream.

9. Eugene was loose now in the limitless meadows of sensation —Thomas Wolfe, *Look Homeward Angel*

10. Any turn in the wheel of sensation has the power to crystallize and transfix the moment upon which its gloom or radiance rests —Virginia Woolf, *To the Lighthouse*

■ SENSITIVITY

See also: CALMNESS/VOLATILITY; FEELINGS; FRAGILITY; HUMANITY/HUMANKIND

1. Drunk first with shame and then with anger . . . he had a drunken man's glowering readiness to take offense at nothing —Dorothy Canfield, "Murder on Jefferson Street"

2. Porcupine was the nickname I gave this chestnut burr, and thought it very appropriate —Natsume Soseki, *Botchan*
> Mr. Hotta's nickname indicates his prickly nature. Natsume uses the animal and the tree-burr as metaphors for the man, and for each other.

3. Aubrey: After a cruel life one's perceptions grow a thick skin —Arthur Wing Pinero, *The Second Mrs. Tanqueray*, Act 3

Aubrey is accusing his wife of having become sharp-tongued and insensitive to his young daughter's feelings.

4. Antigonus: Weep I cannot, / But my heart bleeds —William Shakespeare, *The Winter's Tale*, Act 3, scene 3, line 51

    The metaphor of the bleeding heart stems from its long association with the most deep-seated of emotions, extreme grief. Current usage has given this an ironic twist, as in you're making my heart bleed or my heart bleeds for you. Actually, Elizabethans considered the liver as the seat of the emotions.

5. It was well to remember that authors . . . were nervous, irritable, self-conscious; the slightest unfavourable criticism flayed them alive —Edith Wharton, *Hudson River Bracketed*

    As criticism equals flaying, this is a metaphor; as it greatly exaggerates, it is hyperbole.

6. Blanche: Some tender feelings . . . we have got to . . . cling to, and hold as our flag! — Tennessee Williams, *A Streetcar Named Desire*, Scene 10

7. Matt Friedman: People are eggs —Lanford Wilson, *Talley's Folley*

    This metaphor recurs throughout the play. It poses a "Humpty Dumpty complex" which makes it difficult to choose between two courses of action. On one hand, people should avoid banging against each other to keep the self-protective shells they've built around themselves intact; on the other, they should risk having "their yolks broken."

■ SENTIMENTALITY

See: WRITING/WRITERS

■ SEPARATION

See also: ACCUSATIONS; DEATH; PEOPLE, INTERACTION; POETRY/POETS

1. The senses know that absence blots people out —Elizabeth Bowen, *The Death of the Heart*

2. Two graves must hide thine and my coarse, / If one might, death were no divorce — John Donne, "The Anniversarie"

    The comparison between death and divorce for a married pair depends upon physical togetherness. If the poet's corpse—"coarse"—could be interred with his wife's, then the marriage would persist even after death.

3. But a gulf of many years lay between them —Kawabata Yasunari, *Beauty and Sadness*

4. Albany: She that herself will sliver and disbranch / From her material sap, perforce must wither / And come to deadly use —William Shakespeare, *King Lear*, Act 4, scene 2, line 34

    Albany accuses his wife of having cut herself off from the fatherly tree.

5. Speed: he is shipp'd already, / And I have play'd the sheep in losing him —William Shakespeare, *Two Gentlemen of Verona*, Act 1, scene 1, line 73.

    Speed's metaphor is prompted by his master's departure from Verona for Milan. It's been speculated that Shakespeare chose of "shipp'd" because it sounded enough like "sheep" for a pun, and not for any specific geographical reference to a waterway between the two cities.

■ SEX/SEXUALITY

See also: ATTRACTION; MASTERY/SUBORDINATION; MEN AND WOMEN; PASSION; SENSES; WOMEN

1. Their first dip in sensual waters left them non-plussed —Harold Brodkey, "Sentimental Education," *The New Yorker*

2. Sex is a black tarantula —Luis Buñuel, *New York Times*, 1973

    The Spanish moviemaker extended the metaphor with this simile: And sex without religion is like an egg without salt.

3. She was a primerole, a piggesnye. / For any lord to leggen in his bedde —Geoffrey

Chaucer, "The Miller's Tale," *The Canterbury Tales*

> *She was a cowslip, a pig's eye for any lord to lay in his bed. (If there were lords around who wanted to get a woman into bed these days, not many of them would choose a pig's eye, I trowe.)*

4. Sharper: A delicious melon, pure and consenting ripe, and only waits the cutting up —William Congreve, Belinda, *The Old Bachelor*, Act 1, scene 1

> *This portrayal of a woman would not go over too well with feminists.*

5. The world is a bed ... only adultery proves / devotion by risk; only the pulse of betrayal / makes blood pelt in the chest as if with joy —Donald Hall, "Shrubs Burnt Away"

6. He was in another world: he had awakened from the slumber of centuries — James Joyce, *Portrait of the Artist as a Young Man*

> *The sixteen-year-old Joyce recognizes the call of his hormones.*

7. Sex with Sally was a football mêlée with bites and bruises and chocolate squashed in your crotch —Norman Mailer, *Harlot's Ghost*

8. In the room he rents to fuck in ... his private candy box opens for him —Toni Morrison, *Jazz*

> *Joe compares his sweetheart to a box of candy only he can enjoy.*

9. Sex ... the ersatz or substitute religion of the 20th century —Malcolm Muggeridge, *The New York Times Magazine*, March 24, 1968

10. Electric flesh arrows ... traversing the body. A rainbow of color strikes the eyelids. A foam of music falls over the ears. It is the gong of orgasm —Anaïs Nin, *The Diaries of Anaïs Nin*, Vol. 2, October, 1937

11. Once more I will shyly let you undress me and gently unlock my sealed jewel —

Hung O, "A Farewell to a Southern Melody"

12. Suddenly he's touched you ... with a rush you find yourself blazing into a living torch of joy —Luigi Pirandello, "All Passion Spent"

13. Not since I had last read Strindberg could I remember having run across such a tantalizing layer cake of female excitement —Philip Roth, *Operation Shylock*

> *The food metaphor is used to portray a woman in whom "everything existed in generous proportions."*

14. Iago: you'll have your daughter cover'd with a Barbary horse; you'll have your nephew neigh to you; you'll have coursers for cousins and gennets for germans — William Shakespeare, *Othello*, Act 1, scene 1, line 111

> *Iago pictures the sexual act in animal terms to arouse the worst fears of Desdemona's father.*

15. He set off fireworks, a great multicolored explosion of sexual fullness —Kate Simon, *Etchings in an Hourglass*

> *"My adolescent experiences had been collages of curiosity, ineptitude, and hopefulness," Simon continues, making this a case of metaphor upon metaphor.*

16. What was it like for her, those many years with drunken old Mack, whose sails on rare occasions would blow full of lust and fall upon her, riding her waves, mast in her harbor? —Scott Turow, *Pleading Guilty*

> *The author displays a bent for seafaring metaphors in this novel.*

17. She subscribes to feminism of her own vision, which seems to be inspired by piracy on the high seas, regarding it as an achievement to board every passing male ship —Scott Turow, *Pleading Guilty*

> *Turow's novel is laced with seafaring metaphors.*

18. Sex is the tabasco sauce which an adolescent national palate sprinkles on every course in the menu —Mary Day Winn, *Adam's Rib*

■ SHALLOWNESS

See: SUPERFICIALITY

■ SHAME

See also: GUILT

1. Shame is pride's cloak —William Blake, *Proverbs of Hell*

2. Kent: A sovereign shame so elbows him: his own unkindness, / . . . [stings] His mind so venomously that burning shame; / Detains him from Cordelia —William Shakespeare, *King Lear*, Act 4, scene 3, line 44

3. For no man well of such a salve can speak, / That heals the wound, and cures not the disgrace, / Nor can thy shame give physic to my grief —William Shakespeare, "Sonnet 34," line 7
    Disgrace causes a grief that defies healing with any medicine.

4. The latest entry in my account book of humiliations was to have a woman paying for every droshky —Isaac Bashevis Singer, *The Certificate*

5. Every prison that men build / Is built with bricks of shame —Oscar Wilde, "The Ballad of Reading Goal"

■ SHELTER

See also: ASSISTANCE; COMFORT/COMFORT-GIVERS; PROTECTION/PROTECTORS

1. Thence to Bethlehem, where was builded / Dens of despair in the house of bread — William Blake, "Jerusalem," Chapter 2

2. The four-and-a-half mat room during those three years was my castle . . . but now I had to part with the dear old nest which had given me shelter and protection so long —Natsume Soseki, *Botchan*

Japanese rooms are often described by the number of tatami mats they will hold. There is an irony implied in the switch from "castle" to "nest" in this obviously tiny room.

3. Iago: And I . . . must be lee'd, and calm'd —William Shakespeare, *Othello*, Act 1, scene 1, line 29
    The metaphor is nautical. Although Iago was a soldier, much of the fighting required the use of ships.

■ SHOCK

See also: FEAR; WORDS AS WEAPONS

1. Malkovich keeps detonating these little vocal bombs in Eastwood's ear —Terrence Rafferty, "Current Cinema," *The New Yorker*, July 12, 1993
    Actor John Malkovich playing a would-be assassin detonated his metaphoric bombs during the telephone exchanges with Clint Eastwood in the movie In the Line of Fire.

2. *The Destiny of Me* is polemical when it wants to be . . . sending forth a seismic jolt of visceral theatricality —Frank Rich, "Review/Theater," *The New York Times*, October 21, 1992
    Rich was reviewing a play by AIDS activist Larry Kramer.

3. Buckingham: My hair doth stand on end to hear her curses —William Shakespeare, *The Tragedy of King Richard the Third*, Act 1, scene 3, line 304
    This remains an everyday metaphor to express fear or shock, probably derived from the physical responde to danger by animals.

■ SHREWDNESS

See: CRAFTINESS

■ SHYNESS

See: TIMIDITY

■ SIGHS

See also: GRIEF; TEARS

1. What merchant's ships have my sighs drowned? / Who says my tears have overflowed his ground? —John Donne, "The Canonization"

   "Alas, alas, who's injured by my love?" asks Donne.

2. Isobel breathes—just a feather of a sigh —Deborah Eisenberg, "The Custodian"

■ SIGHT

See: DESCRIPTIONS, MISC.

■ SIGNIFICANCE/ INSIGNIFICANCE

See also: IIUMANITY/IIUMANKIND; IM-PORTANCE/UNIMPORTANCE

1. I allow myself eddies of meaning — Archibald Randolph Ammons, "Corson's Inlet"

   Significance runs "like a stream through the geography of my work," writes Ammons.

2. Men in history, men in the world of today are bugs . . . and are called "the mass" and "the herd" —Ralph Waldo Emerson, Lecture, "The American Scholar," at Harvard College, August 31, 1837

3. His four-fifteen patient . . . came and went without making a bubble on the afternoon's surface —Patricia Highsmith, "Mrs. Afton, among Thy Green Braes"

4. We are little better than straws upon the water —Mary Wortley Montagu, Letter to James Stewart, July 19, 1759

5. Sometimes I get the feeling that's all we are—ants —Chaim Potok, *The Chosen*

6. My profession may have become a tail on a big kite—the media industry. But at seventy-five I still see journalism as a noble and ennobling profession —Daniel

Schorr, Speech at party in honor of his birthday, October 3, 1991

7. Menenius: what do you think, / You, the great toe of this assembly? —William Shakespeare, *Coriolanus*, Act 1, scene 1, line 100

   Menenius explains that the toe represents the "lowest, basest, poorest" members of the assembled dissenters."

8. Men [seeking praise or fame] are . . . but bubbles on the rapid stream of time — Edward Young, "Love of Fame"

■ SILENCE

See also: CHARACTERIZATIONS; COMMU-NICATION/NON-COMMUNICATION; FAITH; PEOPLE, INTERACTIONS; PLEAS AND PRAYERS; SPEECHLESSNESS; TRANQUILITY

1. Silence . . . the fence around wisdom — Anon., Greek expression

   A Spanish proverb calls it "the fool's wisdom."

2. By thunders of white silence overthrown —Elizabeth Barrett Browning, "Hiram Powers' Greek Slave"

3. No use your painting hearts on the window: / the duke of silence / is down in the castleyard, recruiting —Paul Celan, "Your Hair Over the Sea"

4. She had answered only with a nod. You might call her a miser with words — Colette, "Bella Vista"

5. Silence . . . a friend who will never betray —Confucius, *Analects*

6. The silence slowly petrified —Bernard Malamud, "Angel Levine"

7. President Calvin Coolidge is . . . Wrapped in magnificent silence —H. L. Mencken

   Rarely satisfied a single image, Mencken continued "He was no fiddler like Nero; he simply yawned and while he yawned and stretched, the United States went slam-bang down the hill."

8. The air of those rooms was saturated with the fine bouquet of a silence so nourishing, so succulent that I could not enter them without a sort of greedy enjoyment —Marcel Proust, *Remembrance of Things Past. Swann's Way*
   This is Proust's concluding sentence.

9. Give me my scallop—shell of quiet, / My staff of faith to walk upon —Sir Walter Raleigh (also spelled Ralegh), "His Pilgrimage"
   The first metaphor has metamorphosed into the more common simile, as quiet as a clam. The Elizabethan spelling of the author's name is Ralegh.

10. Enobarbus: Go to, then; you considerate stone —William Shakespeare, *Antony and Cleopatra*, Act 2, scene 2, line 114
    While Enobarbus will remain silent, as Antony has requested, he will not stop thinking.

11. I automatically did believe in the unbroken surface of the unsaid —Jane Smiley, *A Thousand Acres*
    What is not spoken cannot disturb the surface of tranquillity. Modern psychology believes in free expression of inner conflict, but it does cause ripples.

12. The immobility of my niece, and for that matter my own, made it [the silence] even heavier, turned it to lead —Vercors, *The Silence of the Sea*
    Silence is sometimes spoken of as leaden silence.

13. At dinner that evening Madame de Chantelle's slender monologue was thrown out over gulfs of silence —Edith Wharton, *The Reef*

14. But if silence is golden, the gold is not pure —Yevgeny Yevtushenko, *A Precocious Autobiography*
    The poet builds on a common metaphor to make a new statement.

■ SILLINESS
See: *FOOLHARDINESS*

■ SIMILARITY/DISSIMILARITY
See also: *HUMANITY/HUMANKIND; INDIVIDUALITY*

1. Everyone is kneaded out of the same dough, but not baked in the same oven —Anon., Proverb

2. If the mother is a cow, the daughter is a calf —Anon., Yiddish Proverb
   As everybody knows, the apple doesn't fall far from the tree.

3. Whereas security and disarmament were rather antagonistic concepts at one time, today they are two sides of the same coin—the coin of cooperative security —Prvoslav Davinic, Closing statement at UN conference, "Disarmament and National Security in the Interdependent World," Kyoto, April, 1993
   The director of the United Nations Office for Disarmament Affairs stated that the new political realities, since the end of the metaphorically named Cold War, demand changing notions of disarmament.

4. On most days he received more than thirty letters, all of them alike, stamped from the dough of suffering with a heart-shaped cookie knife —Nathanael West, *Miss Lonelyhearts*

■ SIMPLICITY/SIMPLIFICATION
See also: *FURNITURE/FURNISHINGS*

1. Mrs. St. Maugham: In a village one is down to the bones of things —Enid Bagnold, *The Chalk Garden*, Act 1

2. She's a simple girl, toast and butter —Ethan Canin, "We Are Nighttime Travelers"

3. She had very nearly obliged him, when he moved into his new office, to have concave surfaces, as in a hospital ward or a hygienic nursery . . . People's lives ought to be like that: with no corners in them. She wanted to de-microbe life —Edith Wharton, *Twilight Sleep*

The simile comparing an office designed with surgically clean architectural details, paves the way for the metaphor depicting Mrs. Manford's vision of life as something to be disinfected.

■ SINGING/SONGS/SINGERS

See also: ARTS AND ENTERTAINMENT; CHARACTERIZATIONS; DIVERSITY; MUSIC/MUSICIANS; VOICES

1. They were singers who had vibratos that you could skip rope with. —Whitney Balliett, "Profiles," *The New Yorker,* April 6, 1992.

2. I would rather sing one day as a lion than a hundred years as a sheep —Cecilia, Bartoli, quoted *The New York Times Magazine,* March 14, 1993
   The diva thus summed up her feeling that her musical life will probably be short-lived.

3. She turns out her entire musical wardrobe for them [the cheering audience] —Linda Blandford, "Baby Diva," *The New York Times Magazine,* March 14, 1993
   The diva being interviewed was Cecilia Bartoli.

4. Songs . . . they are such short and linear things. Little sale tags on life —E. L. Doctorow, "Standards," *Harper's Magazine*

5. A mezzo-soprano never gives in, old boy. She dies standing up, with swelling port curved to the stars —Lawrence Durrell, "La Valise"
   "When she hit a top note I could hear the studs vibrating in my dinner-shirt," the narrator shudders.

6. If there is anything worse than a soprano . . . it is a mezzo-soprano. One shriek lower in the scale, perhaps, but with higher candle-power —Lawrence Durrell, "La Valise"

7. Death is that remedy all singers dream of —Allen Ginsberg, "Kaddish"

8. Mr. [John] Astin . . . tiptoes around upper notes by means of little shouts —Bernard Holland, "Review/Music," *The New York Times,* January 11, 1993
   The singer is tiptoeing around the score of H.M.S. Pinafore.

9. Breaking off the song of the refrain, putting the brakes / On the way that the ever-returning chorus tends / To run away with the whole song —John Hollander, "Refrains"
   Hollander feels that poets must stop the "frightening joyride" of the old refrains and venture into the new, the unexpected, before poetry wraps itself around a tree.

10. And sing what is wholly true, . . . Songs which scoop up courage from the pit of shame —Nakano Shigeharu, "Song"
    Songs and shame are depicted with two industrial metaphors, the miner's scoop and the pit.

11. Marian Anderson . . . wore the glorious crown of her voice with the grace of an empress —Jessye Norman, *The New York Times,* April 18, 1993
    The great coloratura's death garnered many words of praise.

12. Marietta Alboni . . . an elephant who swallowed a nightingale —Gioacchino Rossini, quoted, "The Last Italian Tenor," by David Remnick, *The New Yorker,* June 21, 1993
    The nineteenth-century opera composer's remark about a well-known contralto of his era was quoted in Remnick's profile of Luciano Pavarotti.

■ SIN/REDEMPTION

See also: BODIES/BODY; EVIL; FORGIVENESS; GOOD/EVIL

1. There are many people who think that Sunday is a sponge to wipe out all the sins of the week —Henry Ward Beecher, *Life Thoughts*
   Beecher, a minister, knew what he was talking about.

2. Therefore, the attention of Tania now became focused on my circumcised penis; in the new life stretching before us, it was

for grandfather and me the mark of Cain oddly place on the body of Abel —Louis Begley, *Wartime Lies*

> *The mark of Cain is a metaphor for ultimate sin. The Polish Jews who were trying to escape deportation to the ovens of Auschwitz were not the sinners, but those sinned against.*

3. This halfbrother of the clergy . . . [who] pleaded at the bar of God's justice for the souls of the lax and the lukewarm and the prudent —James Joyce, *Portrait of the Artist as a Young Man*

4. To leave church by backdoor of sin and reenter through the skylight of repentance —James Joyce, *Portrait of the Artist as a Young Man*

5. It is easy to imagine what numbers might be reclaimed from . . . error, if the door is left open to repentance —Pliny the Younger, Letter to the Emperor Trajan

6. Leonato: Why she, o she is fallen / Into a pit of ink, that the wide sea / Hath drops too few to wash her clean again, / And salt too little, which may season give / To her foul tainted flesh —William Shakespeare, *Much Ado About Nothing*, Act 4, scene 1, line 141

> *The image of a sea not wide enough to wash away sins is also used in* Macbeth.

7. King Richard: And water cannot wash away your sin. —William Shakespeare, *The Tragedy of King Richard the Second*, Act 4, scene 1, line 242

> *Shakespeare's most famous use of this metaphor appears in* MacBeth *when Lady MacBeth repeatedly attempts the impossible.*

■ SKEPTICISM

See: DOUBT

■ SKILL

See: ABILITY

■ SKY/SKYSCAPES

See also: CITIES; CLOUDS; DAWN; HEAVEN; MOON; NATURE SCENES; NIGHT AND DAY; SNOW; STORMS; SUNSET

1. Drowned suns that glimmer there / Through cloud-disheveled air —Charles Baudelaire, "L'Invitation au Voyage,"

2. Hare-skin sky A distinct / wing is still writing —Paul Celan, "By Day"

3. A sharp moon was fighting with the flying rags and tatters of a storm —Gilbert Keith Chesterton, "The Secret Garden"

4. The hours rise up putting off stars and it is / dawn / into the street of the sky light walks scattering poems —e. e. cummings, "Impressions: IV"

5. The sky turns into a white, billowing cloth that hides the trees and farmhouses. —Deborah Eisenberg, "The Custodian"

6. That inverted bowl they call the Sky —Edward Fitzgerald, *The Rubáiyát of Omar Khayám*

> *And under this metaphoric bowl "crawling co-op'd we live and die."*

7. There was no sky—only a dark, ominous tent that draped in the tops of the streets and was in reality a vast army of snowflakes —F. Scott Fitzgerald, "The Ice Palace," *Flappers and Philosphers*

8. The iridescent vibrations of midsummer light . . . / The palpitant mosaic of the midday light —John Gould Fletcher, "Irradiations"

> *This is followed by another metaphor describing the same scene, "the mad ballet of the midsummer sky."*

9. O that the white scroll of heaven might be rolled up, / And the naked red lightning thrust at the smouldering earth! —John Gould Fletcher, "White Symphony"

10. O, beautiful rainbow, all woven of light! —Sarah Josepha Hale, "Beautiful Rainbow"

11. And yet the sky was cloven / By flame that left the air cold and engraven — Geoffrey Hill, "God's Little Mountain"

12. It is a titanic mineral display . . . a diamond, incalculable diamonds —Le Corbusier, "The Fairy Catastrophe"

    Le Corbusier views New York from the top of a skyscraper. He continues with a metaphor linked to a simile: "New York standing up above Manhattan is like a rose-colored stone in the blue of a maritime sky . . . a limitless cluster of jewels.

13. Sunset / molten bronze / evening clouds / marbled white jade —Ch'ing-Chao Li, "To the Air of Yung Yu Lo," Sung Dynasty

14. He now observed the round white moon moving high in the sky through a cloud menagerie, and watched . . . as it penetrated a huge hen and dropped out of her like an egg laying itself—Bernard Malamud, "The Magic Barrel"

    The simile at the end of this sentence adds color to the metaphor.

15. The winter sun, poor ghost of itself, hung milky and wan behind layers of clouds — Thomas Mann, "Tonio Kröger"

16. Between rafts of silver-edged clouds were channels of ocean-blue sky —Christopher Morley, *Where the Blue Begins*

17. The Iroquois sky passes the windows . . . it crayon-colors their love —Toni Morrison, *Jazz*

18. The rain stops and there is a white grease pat of sun cooking up there in its sky — Toni Morrison, *Jazz*

19. The city sky was hidden . . . otherwise it could show me stars cut from the lame gowns of chorus girls, or mirrored in the eyes of sweethearts furry and happy under the pressure of a deep, touchable sky — Toni Morrison, *Jazz*

20. The day was secretly bright behind a gray fisherman's net about to dissolve into a full autumn rain —Cynthia Ozick, "Puttermeyser Paired," *The New Yorker,* 1990.

21. Smoke rose in endless ladders to the sky —Boris Pasternak, *Doctor Zhivago*

    The smoke comes from locomotives in the train station.

22. The sky is a snotty handkerchief —Marge Piercy, "The butt of winter," *Hard Loving*

23. Lorenzo: look how the floor of heaven / Is thick inlaid with the patines of bright gold —William Shakespeare, *The Merchant of Venice,* Act 5, scene 1, line 58

24. A ray of sunset hidden in the west struck through the tops of the topmost trees, far and small up there, a thin, bright hem — Wilbur Daniel Steele, "How Beautiful with Shoes," *Harper's Magazine*

25. The sky was velvet —John Steinbeck, *The Grapes of Wrath*

    Steinbeck led into this with "The dusk passed into dark . . . stars stabbing and sharp."

26. The sky was brushed clean by the wind — John Steinbeck, *The Pearl*

27. The sky is no longer a junk-shop, / Full of javelins and old fire-balls —Wallace Stevens, "Dezembrum"

    "Tonight there are only the winter stars," the poem begins.

28. The springlike transparent sky shed a rain of silver sunshine on the roofs of the village —Edith Wharton, *Summer*

    From this idyllic opening description, Wharton moves to a relentlessly bleak picture of small town life.

29. Upon the little tent of blue / Which prisoners call the sky, / And at every drifting cloud that went / With sails of silver by —Oscar Wilde, "The Ballad of Reading Goal"

    The image stems from Wilde's own imprisonment. Later in the poem the prisoner's wistful eyes are again cast to the "tent of blue" and "every wandering cloud that trailed / Its ravelled fleeces by."

30. He lies beneath God's seamless veil of blue —Oscar Wilde, "Ravenna"

31. Light broke against the east, in a murky rim. The far dark was eaten cleanly away. The horizon sky was barred with hard fierce strips of light —Thomas Wolfe, *Look Homeward Angel*

32. I loved watching the searchlights fingering the Moscow sky at night —Yevgeny Yevtushenko, *A Precocious Autobiography*
    At the beginning, the boy found war "decorative."

■ SLANDER

See also: GOSSIP; MALICE

1. Pisanio: slander / . . . whose tongue / Outvenoms all the worms [serpents] of Nile, whose breath / Rides on the posting winds and doth belie / All corners of the world —William Shakespeare, *Cymbeline*, Act 3, scene 4, line 35

2. Mowbray: Pierc'd to the soul with slander's venom'd spear, / The which no balm can cure but his heart-blood / Which breathed this poison —William Shakespeare, *The Tragedy of King Richard the Second* Act 1, scene 1, line 170
   Mowbray takes up Bolingbroke's challenge and hopes to kill him in the joust.

3. Joseph Surface: The malice of a good thing is the barb that makes it stick — Richard Brinsley Sheridan, *The School for Scandal*, Act 1, scene 1

4. Lady Sneer: Wounded myself . . . by the envenomed tongue of slander, I confess that I have since known no pleasure equal to the reducing others to the level of my own injured reputation —Richard Brinsley Sheridan, *The School for Scandal*, Act 1, scene 1
   The lady who protests her wound indeed has the sharpest serpent's tooth of all.

5. Sir Peter Teazle: Many a wretch has rid on a hurdle who has done less mischief than these utterers of forged tales, coiners of scandal, and clippers of reputation —Richard Brinsley Sheridan, *The School for Scandal*, Act 2, scene 1
   The underlying metaphor deals with coinage, which could be 'forged' or 'clipped.' Clipping coins was paring the gold edges, which devalued them and enriched the clipper. Knurling the edges put an end to this practice. "To coin a phrase," remains a common metaphor.

6. Sir Oliver Surface: I know there are a set of . . . gossips, both male and female, who murder characters to kill time and will rob a young fellow of his good name before he has years to know the value of it —Richard Brinsley Sheridan, *The School for Scandal*, Act 2, scene 3

7. Self-buzzing slander: silly moths that eat an honest name —James Thomson, *Liberty*, IV

■ SLAVERY

See: FREEDOM/RESTRAINT

■ SLEEP

See also: DEATH; NIGHT AND DAY; PLEAS AND PRAYERS; SLEEPLESSNESS

1. Sleep's but a short death; death's but a longer sleep —Phineas Fletcher, "The Locusts"

2. Clodesuida: Dip him / In sleep, that blue well where shadows walk / In water over their heads, and he'll be washed / Into reason —Christopher Fry, *Thor, With Angels*
   Clodesuida is sure that a good night's sleep will cure her husband of compassion for his prisoner.

3. Hoel: I sit / On the kerb of sleep — Christopher Fry, *Thor, With Angels*

4. Sleep the twin of death —Homer, *The Iliad*, Book 14

5. Sleep and Death, two twins of winged race, / Of matchless swiftness, but of silent pace —Homer, *The Iliad.* Book 16

6. O magic sleep! O comfortable bird, / That broodest o'er the troubled sea of the mind / Till it is hush'd and smooth! —John Keats, "Endymion"

7. Most people want to crash into sleep. Get knocked into it with a fist of fatigue —Toni Morrison, *Jazz*

8. Sleep, with a bow, handed him the key of its city: he understood the meaning of all the lights, sounds, and perfumes as everything blended into a single, blissful image —Vladimir Nabokov, *King, Queen, Knave*

9. There were nights when she had a hummingbird sleep as she hovered above the bloom of oblivion, dipping a moment to suck its sweetness, then hover again. But there were the nights, black holes of Calcutta, from which she emerged with a weight on her chest, her limbs in chains —Helen Norris, "Raisin Faces," *The Virginia Quarterly Review,* 1990

10. Immediately she lay down she spiralled to the bottom of a deep lake of sleep —Sean O'Faolain, "Lovers of the Lake"

11. Immoderate sleep is rust to the soul —Sir Thomas Overbury, *Characters*

12. The best nurse of troubles, Night —Ovid

13. Iachimo: O sleep! Thou ape of death —William Shakespeare, *Coriolanus,* Act 2, scene 3, line 31

14. Brutus: Enjoy the honey-heavy dew of slumber —William Shakespeare, *Julius Caesar,* Act 2, scene 1, line 230

15. Macbeth: Sleep that knits up the ravel'd sleave of care, / The death of each day's life, sore labor's bath, / Balm of hurt minds, great nature's second course, / Chief nourisher in life's feast, —William Shakespeare, *Macbeth,* Act 2, scene 2, line 34

16. King: O gentle sleep! / Nature's soft nurse —William Shakespeare, *The Second Part of King Henry the Fourth,* Act 3, scene 1, line 5

17. How wonderful is Death, / Death and his brother Sleep! —Percy Bysshe Shelley, "Queen Mab"

18. Oh make in me those civil wars to cease; / I will good tribute pay, if thou do so —Sir Philip Sidney, "Sonnet 39," *Astrophel and Stella*
   Picturing the day's cares as filled with strife and stress, Sidney appeals to sleep, the conqueror, to give him surcease.

19. Come sleep! Oh sleep, the certain knot of peace —Sir Philip Sidney, "Sonnet 39," *Astrophel and Stella*

20. [Sleep:] The poor man's wealth, the prisoner's release —Sir Philip Sidney, "Sonnet 39," *Astrophel and Stella*
   Sidney also calls sleep "The indifferent judge between the high and low."

21. Sleep was my voluptuous sanctuary —Mona Simpson, *The Lost Father*
   The young woman who loves sleep is a medical student.

22. Turn back the sheets—I'm heading for the arms of Morpheus —Mae West, *Klondike Annie*
   This famous movie line has become a popular every day metaphoric allusion.

23. The soul shrinks / From all that it is about to remember, / From the punctual rape of every blessed day —Richard Wilbur, "Love Calls us to the Things of This World"
   In the same poem, about an epiphany experienced upon awakening from sleep, the poet says "The morning air is all awash with angels."

24. We hibernated the whole first winter, and I'm still withdrawing sleep from that account —A. B. Yehoshua, *Mr. Mani*
   Egon explains that he can afford to miss a night's sleep.

■ SLEEPLESSNESS

1. To go to bed not tired was from habit unsatisfactory. Without a weight against it the door of sleep kept flying open — Marjorie Barnard, "The New Dress"

2. I lay awake at night flipping the channels of my attention —Stanley Elkin, "Out of One's Tree," *Harper's,* January 1933

3. But often at night something asks / the brain to ride, run riderless; / plumed night swirling, brain riding itself / through blackness —Jim Harrison, "The Sign"

4. He goes over / the mathematics of lying awake all night alone / in a strange room: still the equations require / multiplication, by fear, of what is, / to the power of desire —Galway Kinnell, "The Man on the Hotel Room Bed"
   A sleepless man lies in a hotel room, thinking of love.

5. When day's oppression is not eased by night, / But day and night by day oppressed, / And each, though enemies to either's reign, / Do in consent shake hands to torture me —William Shakespeare, "Sonnet 28," line 3

6. Sleep, the foreshadow of death, the dab of poison we daily take to forestall convulsion, became impossible —John Updike, *Bech: A Book*
   When he did manage to sleep his dreams were "light as feathers, and blew this way and that," writes Updike.

■ SLOWNESS

See also: ARTS AND ENTERTAINMENT; TIME

1. Pamela Berlin has directed the work as an adagio movement —Mel Gussow, "Review/Theater," *The New York Times,* November 16, 1992
   The play described was Joined at the Head.

2. The hours went past on their rusty ankles —Zora Neale Hurston, "The Gilded Six-Bits"
   Time moves slowly for a woman whose beloved husband caught her committing adultery.

■ SLYNESS

See: CRAFTINESS; SMILES

■ SMALLNESS

See also: CHILDREN/CHILDHOOD; PHYSICAL APPEARANCE

1. For a small slice of society something has gone terribly, unprecedentedly wrong — Julian Barnes, "Letter from London," *The New Yorker,* September 20, 1993
   The "slice" refers to the upper-middle class for whom the ailing Lloyd's of London investment membership has become a "fool's dupe" now that "one of the pillars of British society has turned out to be made of Styrofoam."

2. Mr. [Ross] Perot is no showboat. He is not built to Texas proportions —Larry King, CNN broadcast, April 1992
   King's program served as a launching pad for Perot's short-lived but much publicized third party candidacy.

3. I was small once, hardly bigger / than the laughter of a lemon —Philip Levine, "Burned"

4. Well, then: why don't I sketch his biography on a thumbnail —A. B. Yehoshua, *Mr. Mani*
   The more common form of this metaphor is a thumbnail sketch.

■ SMELLS

See also: CHARACTERIZATIONS; INSULTS; SENSES

1. Smells detonate softly in our memory . . . poignant land mines, hidden under the weedy mass of many years of experience.

Hit a tripwire of smell, and memories explode all at once. A complex vision leaps out of the undergrowth —Diane Ackerman, *A Natural History of the Senses*

2. Smell is a potent wizard that transports us across thousands of miles and all the years we have lived —Helen Keller, quoted, "Smell"

3. An enchanting woman *but,* my dear, a breath you could trot a mouse on —Edith Sitwell, quoted in John Malcolm Brinnon's journal October, 1950

   The subject of this acerbic metaphor was actress Ethel Barrymore.

■ SMILES

See also: DECEPTION; FACIAL EXPRESSIONS; LOOKS

1. Smiles are the soul's kisses —Minna Antrim, *Naked Truth and Veiled Allusions*

2. He gives her a hyena grin —Margaret Atwood, "The Bog Man," *Wilderness Tips*

3. He [Truman Capote] smiles a pussycat smile —John Malcolm Brinnin, Journal entry, February 21, 1949

4. He smiled, in half-coma, / A stone temple smile —Ted Hughes, "The Scream"

5. The brothers turn up the wattage of their smiles —Toni Morrison, *Jazz*

   The smiling brothers are two young men flirting with two young women in Harlem during the late 1920s.

6. Donalbain: Where we are, / There's daggers in men's smiles —William Shakespeare, *Macbeth*, Act 2, scene 3, line 141

   Donaldbain fears he and Malcolm together will cause the metaphoric daggers to become real because "the near in blood, / The nearer bloody."

7. His grin was suddenly made of crumbling plaster —Wilfrid Sheed, *Office Politics*

8. She gave him a rainbow smile —Edith Wharton, *Hudson River Bracketed*

■ SMUGNESS

See: COMMUNICATION/NON-COMMUNICATION

■ SNOW

See also: DESCRIPTIONS, MISC.; LANDSCAPES; NATURE SCENES; SEASONS; SKY/ SKYSCAPES; STORMS; WINTER

1. Chorus: ... the snow peppered down —Aristophanes, *The Clouds*

2. [The boys] gathered up the crystal manna to freeze / their tongues with tasting —Robert Bridges, "London Snow"

3. Announced by all the trumpets of the sky, / arrives the snow —Ralph Waldo Emerson, "The Snow-Storm"

4. The frolic architecture of snow —Ralph Waldo Emerson, "The Snow-Storm"

5. Home was a rambling frame house set in a white lap of snow —F. Scott Fitzgerald, "The Ice Palace," *Flappers and Philosphers*

6. Each snowflake is a lacey white hieroglyphic, a messenger detailing the story of its birth and its journey to the ground ... some are intricate white fronds, some are icy hexagons, some are frosted flowerheads —Harry Middleton, "Portraits in Winter Light," *Wilderness*, Winter 1992

7. The Snow-drop, Winter's timid child —Mary Robinson, "The Snow-Drop"

8. Snow was falling in earnest now-big silent petals drifting through the springtime woods, white bouquets segueing into snowy dark —Donna Tartt, *The Secret History*

   The metaphor is introduced with a startling simile: A November stillness was settling like a deadly oxymoron on the April landscape.

9. The snow ... / Covered the town with simple cloths —Richard Wilbur, "First Snow in Alsace"

10. From an invisible February sky a shimmering curtain of snowflakes fluttered down upon Chicago —Richard Wright, *The Outsider*
    The metaphor opens Wright's novel.

11. We shall step upon the white down, / Upon silver fleece, / Upon softer than these —Elinor Wylie, "Velvet Shoes"
    Wylie uses contiguous metaphors for snow.

■ SOCIETY/SOCIAL SITUATIONS

See also: CHANGE; CHANGEABLENESS/ UNCHANGEABLENESS; GROUP SCENES; HUMANITY/HUMANKIND; ISOLATION; MIXTURE; PEOPLE, INTERACTION; SEPARATION

1. Society is a cage of idiots —Marie de Jars, "A Lenten"

2. Traddles and I were separated at table, being billeted in two remote corners — Charles Dickens, *David Copperfield*

3. Society is a masked ball, where every man hides his real character, and reveals it in hiding —Ralph Waldo Emerson, "Worship," *Conduct of Life*

4. Society is a joint-stock company, in which the members agree, for the better securing of his bread to each shareholder, to surrender the liberty and culture of the eater —Ralph Waldo Emerson, "Self-Reliance"

5. Society is a wave. The wave moves onward, but the water of which it is composed does not —Ralph Waldo Emerson, "Self-Reliance"

6. The state of society is one in which the members have suffered amputation from the trunk, and strut about so many walking monsters—a good finger, a neck, a stomach, an elbow, but never a man — Ralph Waldo Emerson, Speech, "The American Scholar," Harvard College, August 31, 1837

7. The room was going to be packed . . . writers, politicians, musicians, business types . . . A queer gazpacho —John Hersey, "Requiescat," *Paris Review,* No. 197, Summer 1988

8. Unlike his friend Paul he preferred the ragged edges of gatherings, not their quicksilver centers —Joyce Carol Oates, "The Hair"

9. The Law of Raspberry Jam: The wider any culture is spread, the thinner it gets — Alvin Toffler, *The Culture Consumers*

10. She was able . . . to trace each new crack in its [society's] surface, and all the strange weeds pushing up between the ordered rows of social vegetables —Edith Wharton, *The Age of Innocence*
    Mrs. Archer, while not a participant in New York's social scene, is a keen observer, particularly of the outsiders who try to become insiders.

11. The New York of Newland Archer's day was a small and slippery pyramid in which, as yet, hardly a fissure had been made or a foothold gained —Edith Wharton, *The Age of Innocence*

12. The Marchesa . . . was still, in Pauline's set, a pretext for dinners, a means of paying off social scores, a small but steady luminary in the uncertain New York heavens —Edith Wharton, *Twilight Sleep*

■ SOLITUDE

See: ISOLATION; LONELINESS

■ SONS

See: FAMILIES/FAMILY RELATIONSHIPS

■ SORROW

See also: DESPAIR; GRIEF; JOY/SORROW; PAIN AND SUFFERING

1. Alone / in my inner chamber / every inch / of intestine / bound / in a thousand turns of woe —Ch'ing-Chao Li, "To the Air of Tien Chiang Ch'un," Sung Dynasty

2. I too / would like to go rowing in a light boat / but I'm afraid / that little boat on Twin Stream / would not carry / so much sorrow! —Ch'ing-Chao Li, "Late Spring," Sung Dynasty

3. I hear / my ill-spirit sob in each blood cell, / as if my hand were at its throat —Robert Lowell, "Skunk Hour"

   The speaker is watching lovers in the distance. No one is there for him: only skunks.

4. Sorrow is a trail of dreams —Madeline Mason-Manheim, "Compensation," *Hill Fragments*

5. Aethelwold [in response to Maccus's "In God's name, what hath worn thee down?"]: The teeth of Sorrow. I am Sorrow's bone —Edna St. Vincent Millay, *The King's Henchman*, Act 2

6. Sorrow . . . came in gusts, shaking the woman —Marjorie Kinnan Rawlings, *South Moon Under*

7. They went about their tasks as usual and to her it was as if they were trampling on a corpse; in their ledgers no human sorrow but dwindled to dross of brittle figures. — Antoine de Saint-Exupery, *Night Flight*

   The wife of a doomed pilot waits in the office for news of him.

8. King: When sorrows come, they come not single spies, / But in batallions. —William Shakespeare, *Hamlet*, Act 4, scene 5, line 78.

9. Macduff: Each new morn / New widows howl, new orphans cry, new sorrows / Strike heaven on the face —William Shakespeare, *Macbeth*, Act 4, scene 3, line 4

   In this metaphor, both sorrow and heaven are personified as combatants.

10. Macbeth: Canst thou not minister to a mind diseas'd, / Pluck from the memory a rooted sorrow? —William Shakespeare, *Macbeth*, Act 5, scene 3, line 40

    Macbeth likens the grief that has unhinged his wife's mind to a deep root.

11. Cleon: One sorrow never comes but brings an heir / That may succeed as his inheritor —William Shakespeare, *Pericles, Prince of Tyre*, Act 1, scene 4, line 63

    The most famous variant of this is "When sorrows come, they come not single spies, / But in battalions," (Hamlet, 4, 5, 78).

12. Bolingbroke: Fell sorrow's tooth doth never rankle more / Than when he bites, but lanceth not the sore —William Shakespeare, *The Tragedy of King Richard the Second*, Act 1, scene 3, line 302

13. Don't let the dogs of sorrow out —Sharon Sheehe Stark, "Overland" *Boulevard*, No.12–13

    The silent plea accompanies a simple "Please don't" and the thinker's clamping her hand across her mother's mouth.

■ SOUL

See also: CONTINUITY; DEATH; IMMORTALITY; HUMANITY/HUMANKIND; LAMENTS

1. The sea of the round of deaths —Anon., *The Bhagavad Gita*, 12:7

   The "round of deaths" is the transmigration of souls from one body or thing to another, in everlasting continuation.

2. The soul, fortunately, has an interpreter—often an unconscious, but still truthful interpreter—in the eye —Charlotte Brontë, *Jane Eyre*

3. We suffer from a sleeping sickness of the soul —Hillary Rodham Clinton, Speech, Spring 1991, quoted by Anna Quindlen in "Public & Private," *The New York Times*, October 17, 1993

"America's Sleeping Sickness" read the attention-grabbing headline. To explain the metaphor, Mrs. Clinton said, "we lack at some core level meaning in our individual lives, and meaning collectively, that sense that our lives are part of some greater effort, that we are connected to one another."

4. The Soul unto itself / Is an imperial friend —Emily Dickinson, Poem 683
   The metaphor is extended by also depicting the soul as "the most agonizing Spy" that an enemy could possibly send.

5. Your soul is oftentimes a battlefield, upon which your reason and your judgment wage war against your passion and your appetite —Kahlil Gibran, *The Prophet*

6. There is an internal landscape, a geography of the soul; we search for its outlines all our lives —Josephine Hart, *Damage*
   The image appears at the beginning and several times throughout this best-selling first novel.

7. It is written [in the Upanishads]: "Your soul is the whole world" —Hermann Hesse, *Siddhartha*
   The holy books of the Brahmins, the Vedic literature, contained wisdom "pure as honey collected by bees."

8. Flushed with wrath, I raised my fist, / When in a chink of my mad soul, / I found a soul that was not mad / Crouching, blinking, meek, and guilty —Ishikawa Takuboku, "A Fist"

9. When the soul of a man is born in this country there are nets flung at it to hold it back from flight —James Joyce, *Portrait of the Artist as a Young Man*

10. Inaccessible solitudes of being, / The rushing of the sea-tides of the soul — Henry Wadsworth Longfellow, "The Sound of the Sea"

11. I don't want to pay down the last penny of my soul / among hothouse adolescents —Osip Mandelstam, "Stanza 1"

12. The soul is the captain and the ruler of the life of mortals —Sallust, *Jugurtha*

13. Poor soul . . . Why dost thou pine within and suffer dearth, / Painting thy outward walls so costly gay? —William Shakespeare, "Sonnet 146," line 1
    "Painting the outward walls" of the soul meant ornamenting the body with clothes and cosmetics and, sometimes, wigs.

14. Magda: My soul . . . used to be an Aeolian harp which was left mouldering because my father could not bear it. Such a silent harp was my soul; and through you it was given storm. And it sounded almost to breaking—the whole scale of passions — Hermann Sudermann, *Magda*, Act 3
    The "storm of passion" is for the child Magda raised after the pious former lover she now confronts deserted her.

15. My soul is a broken field / Ploughed by pain —Sara Teasdale, "The Broken Field"

■ SOUND

See also: ANIMALS

1. Merlin: . . . the wall of sky / Breached by larksong —Christopher Fry, *Thor, With Angels*

2. When there was a momentary calm in that tempestuous sea of sound, the leader gave the sign —Nathaniel Hawthorne, "My Kinsman, Major Molineux"

3. It [the sound of the crickets] never changes. Just the same monotonous thrumming that saws the silence into dry little chips — A. B. Yehoshua, *Mr. Mani*

■ SPECIALISTS

See: WORDPLAY/WORD-WATCHING

■ SPEECH

See also: ARTICULATENESS/INARTICULATENESS; LANGUAGE; PERSUASIVENESS/PERSUADERS; TALKATIVENESS; WORDS

1. The polished pearls of impeccable speech
   —Anon., *Sir Gawain and the Green Knight*

2. The tongue is the pen of the heart. —
   Anon., *Yiddish Proverb*

3. Honey and milk are under your tongue —
   The Bible, *O.T., Song of Solomon 4:11*

4. Verily their rhetoric was made of cheap
   sacking —Zbigniew Herbert, "The Power of Taste"
   *The rhetoric of dictatorship is full of "chains of
   tautologies a couple of concepts like flails."*

5. Being in these vocal handcuffs made me a
   desperate, devoted writer at twenty —
   Edward Hoagland, "The Threshold and
   the Jolt of Pain," *The Village Voice*, April
   17, 1969
   *The author also describes his stutter "as a sort of
   miasma behind the Ivy League-looking exterior."*

6. Spoken language is so plastic,—you can
   pat and coax, and spread and shave, and
   rub out, and fill up, and stick on so easily,
   when you work that soft material, that
   there is nothing like it for modelling —
   Oliver Wendell Holmes, *The Autocrat of
   the Breakfast-Table*
   *For writers this is the source out of which "come
   the shapes which you turn into marble or bronze
   in your immortal books."*

7. The first "Uncle" came out unconvincingly,
   and he resolved not to repeat it for a while
   so as to let the word ripen on its twig —
   Vladimir Nabokov, *King, Queen, Knave*
   *Franz, the Knave of the title, has just found his
   uncle, the King of the title, who is trying out the
   new avuncular relationship.*

8. Speech is the mirror of the soul —Publilius
   Syrus, *Sententiae*
   *According to an English Proverb speech is also the
   picture of the mind.*

■ SPEECHES

*See also: ARTICULATENESS/INARTICU-
LATENESS; GRAMMAR AND STYLE;
POLITICS/POLITICIANS*

1. Every speech, written or otherwise, has to
   have punctuation. Tonight I am the punctuation—the period —Dwight D.
   Eisenhower
   *The above was Eisenhower's complete address at
   a dinner where he followed a number of long
   speeches.*

2. And with his Roman rhetoric weave a
   hero's / garland for Cinquez —Robert
   Hayden, "Middle Passage. III"
   *The pilot of a slave ship whose cargo has muti-
   nied, excoriates John Quincy Adams who passionately defends Cinquez, the slave leader of the
   mutiny.*

3. He's [Pat Buchanan] a man with a golden
   tongue —Frank Luntz, Buchanan's campaign manager, *The New York Times*, February 18, 1992
   *Buchanan, who launched a short-lived campaign
   in an effort to become president, was pictured as
   often expressing views with "the subtlety of a tidal
   wave." The headline used a seafaring metaphor:
   "Mutineer Rocking the GOP Boat."*

4. His speeches were beautiful songs, but all
   of them were sung *pianissimo* —H. L.
   Mencken, in *The Impossible H. L. Mencken*
   *Mencken explains why Governor Thomas E.
   Dewey lost to the more feisty Harry S Truman.*

5. For all its apparent gibberish—Mr. Prescott
   [of the British Labor Party] went twelve
   rounds with the English language, and
   "left it slumped and bleeding over the
   ropes" —Matthew Parris, quoted "London Journal," by William E. Schmidt,
   The New York Times, October 29, 1993
   *According to Schmidt, Prescott's speech "inspired
   thunderous applause because of its fire, but by
   many accounts, left the English Language tattered
   and torn."*

6. First, take the three foreign affairs' speeches
   made in the past week by President Clinton, his national security adviser and his
   U.N. Delegate. Then squeeze them good
   and hard to get rid of the inevitable pulp of
   jargon, pieties and diplomatic roundabouts.
   What's left is the juice of some important
   policies —A. M. Rosenthal, "On My

Mind," *The New York Times,* September 28, 1993

> *Rosenthal followed up his opening food metaphor with a discussion of the policies.*

7. This is a Beethoven Symphony of a speech —William Safire, *Lend Me Your Ears: Great Speeches in History*

> *Safire follows up his introduction to Winston Churchill's "Sinews of War" speech by describing its development in symphonic terms; for example: "It begins with the sounds of an orchestra tuning up."*

8. And now to the mother's milk of this anthologist, the political speech —William Safire, Introduction, *Lend Me Your Ears:*

9. Hamlet: A knavish speech sleeps in a foolish ear —William Shakespeare, *Hamlet,* Act 3, scene 6, line 23

■ SPEECHLESSNESS

See also: ARTICULATENESS/INARTICU-LATENESS; EFFECTIVENESS/INEF-FECTIVENESS; SILENCE; VOICES

1. How could my throat have been retrofitted with this massive service elevator? —Nicholson Baker, "Reading Aloud," *The New Yorker,* March 1, 1993

> *Baker wrote of the "narcissus bulb in the throat" that "very nearly blossomed" as he was brought to the point of tears—inappropriately—when reading from his own work.*

2. There was a silence. Potter's mouth seemed to be merely a grave for his tongue — Stephen Crane, "The Bride Comes to Yellow Sky"

3. His lips were stones. His voice dry, dusty —Richard Selzer, "Imelda," *Letters to a Young Doctor*

> *A surgeon faced with the mother of a young girl who has just died on the operating table.*

4. King: He has strangled / His language in his tears —William Shakespeare, *The Life*

of King Henry the Eighth, Act 5, scene 1, line 158

> *Here is a classic* mixaphor *since logic would have drowned language, not strangled it in tears.*

5. Mowbray: my tongue's use is to me no more / Than an unstringed viol or a harp —William Shakespeare, *The Tragedy of King Richard the Second,* Act 1, scene 2, line 161

> *In act 2, scene 1, line 149, Northumberland says of Richard "His tongue is now a stringless instrument.*

6. She tried again and again to say something important, but she had a draught blowing through her head, and it blew all her thoughts away —Mikhail Sholokhov, "A Lesson In Hatred"

7. One of the pirates, who knew me from my shop in Salonika, said to me, "Your rabbi's lute has popped a string" —A. B. Yehoshua, *Mr. Mani*

> *The rabbi has had a stroke which has left him mute.*

■ SPEED

1. The president has charged out of the box [to effect change] —Roger Altman, MacNeill Lehrer broadcast, April 30, 1993

> *The deputy treasury secretary thus defended critics of President Bill Clinton as a change agent during his first 100 days of office.*

2. Yesternight the Sunne went hence, / . . . But beleeve that I shall make / Speedier journeys, since I take / More wings and spurres than hee —John Donne, "Lovers Infinitenesse"

> *It was love that caused the poet to exceed the speed of the sun. The combination of wings and spurs suggests that Pegasus is the lover's steed.*

3. I wrote as rapidly as I could. The meteor shower continued for several weeks — Donald Hall, "A Note on This Poem"

4. I should like to put a little wind in her sails —Henry James, *Portrait of a Lady*

The metaphor appears several times in this novel and, quite often, in everyday speech.

5. They shall . . . steer chariots with storm in their feet —Pindar, "Pythia 4," *Odes*; weather: storms

6. The greatest assassin of life is haste — Theodore Roethke, *Straw for the Fire, Notebooks of Theodore Roethke*

■ SPIRIT

1. The spirit stirs, chafes at its bonds, exults, burns, and rises again from its ashes — Jean Cocteau, "The Cat That Walks by Itself"
   The metaphor of the phoenix is implicit here.

2. —There's a crack of the whip left in me yet, said Mr. Dedalus —James Joyce, *Portrait of the Artist as a Young Man*

■ SPITE

See: CRIME AND PUNISHMENT; MALICE; SELF-DESTRUCTIVENESS

■ SPORTS

See also: COMPETITION/COMPETITORS; FAILURE; MISTAKES; POWER

1. The spectre of debacle attends every [baseball] game, waiting ghoulishly to climb up on this or that player's back and hitch a ride —Roger Angell, "The Sporting Scene," *The New Yorker*, May 3, 1993

2. On a course built for big games, two fireplugs who wear approximately the same abbreviated jacket size took the lead today after 36 holes of the 56th Masters —Jaime Diaz, *The New York Times*, April 11, 1992
   The fireplugs were Ian Woosnan of Wales and Craig Parry of Australia, measuring 5 feet 4½ inches and 5 feet 6 inches respectively.

3. Dogging [Nick] Faldo's even-par 70 all the way was a ravenous pack, led by the terrier-like Corey Pavin —Jaime Diaz, *The New York Times*, July 18, 1993
   The image of a pack of predatory hunting dogs headlined Diaz's report of the final round of the 122nd British Open golf tournament: "Pavin Ties Faldo at 8 Under as Pack Closes In."

4. That hit may have been the respirator for this team —Tim McCarvor, Broadcast of Mets vs. Phillies game, April 13, 1992

5. Studded with stars in belt and crown, / the Stadium is an adastrium —Marianne Moore, "Baseball and Writing"
   Moore was an avid baseball fan so most of her stars were to be found on the diamond.

6. Michael Jordan, 'Air' to his compatriots, played a game 10 feet off the ground. You needed the R.A.F. [Royal Air Force] to stop him. He only came down periodically to refuel —Jim Murray, *Jim Murray, An Autobiography*

7. That particular ninth inning gives me a slight nausea even now; yet it is one of the imperishable stars in Princeton's crown. —William Lyon Phelps, "The Great American Game"
   All the people who left early, thinking the game was over and Yale had won, did not know until the Sunday papers reported the outcome that they had been jubilant too soon.

8. "Stop giving it to them on a silver platter and they won't hit like that."—"Who's giving it to them on a silver platter? That was a great pitch" —Chaim Potok, *The Chosen*
   Potok puts a common metaphor into the mouths of boys playing sandlot baseball. An alternative would have been stop spoonfeeding them.

9. The first wave he caught . . . spun him around like a top, drilled him into the sand and then pinned him there —Jonathan Rabinovitz, *The New York Times*, August 30, 1993
   A description of a surfer is made vivid with a toy simile and an industrial metaphor.

10. Sports figures are cardboard figures cut out in color —Joan Ryan, Essay, National Public Radio, February 2, 1993

11. Could boxing—a violent, passionate pas de deux where blood, from noses, mouths and tender eyelids, stains the other, and where it is sometimes difficult to tell who has actually been cut—be a dance of death? —Arlene Schulman, *New York Times,* May, 9, 1993

    Ms. Schulman contrasted two dance metaphors in this warning about AIDS in the ring: one, the lovely ballet figure executed by two dancers, and the other, the Medieval allegory of Death leading his troupe in a winding dance to the grave.

12. His ball is hung way out . . . Rabbit thinks it will die, but he's fooled, for the ball makes this hesitation the ground of a final leap: with a kind of visible sob takes a last bite of space before vanishing in falling —John Updike, *Rabbit, Run*

13. They may have 100 feet apiece . . . but sooner or later these baseball owners are going to shoot enough of their own feet to bring their game to an ugly halt —George Vecsey, "Sports of the Times," *The New York Times,* December 9, 1992

    Vecsey's reference to the baseball owners' latest contract dealing was metaphorically headlined "Club Owners: Centipedes With Pistols."

■ SPRING

See also: CHANGE; LANDSCAPES; NATURE SCENES; SEASONS; TREES

1. Spring comes laughing down the valley / All in white, from the snow —Amelia Burr, "New Life"

    A metaphor of personification pictures Spring as a young girl.

2. Spring slattern of seasons —e. e. cummings, "Spring omnipotent goddess thou dost"

    "Spring omnipotent goddess" is also the slattern with a "muddy petticoat . . . a sloppy body from being brought to bed of crocuses."

3. The year has cast its cloak away / That was of driving rains and snows, / And now in flowered arras goes —Charles D'Orléans, "Rondeau"

4. The soote (sweet) season, that bud and bloom forth brings, / With green hath clad the hill and eke (also) the vale — Henry Howard (Earl of Surrey), "Description of Spring"

5. Spring, the sweet spring, is the year's pleasant king —Thomas Nashe, "Spring, the Sweet Spring"

6. Spring—that corn-fed, husky milkmaid —Boris Pasternak, *Doctor Zhivago*

    The line is from "The Poems of Yurii Zhivago" which concludes Pasternak's novel.

7. The leafy mind, that long was tightly furled, / Will turn its private substance into green —Theodore Roethke, "The Light Comes Brighter"

8. Fresh Spring, the herald of loves mighty king, / In whose cote-armour richly are displayd. / All sorts of flowers —Edmund Spenser, "Whilst it is prime"; weapons / armaments: armour

9. The hounds of spring are on winter's traces —Algernon Charles Swinburne, "Chorus from 'Atalanta'"

    "The faint fresh flame of the young year flushes / From leaf to flower and flower to fruits" Swinburne writes later in the poem, picturing the encroachment of lovely spring on the winter's "snows and sins."

10. What a time of year it was—the freed earth suddenly breaking into life from every frozen seam! —Edith Wharton, *Twilight Sleep*

11. She had never seen the Cedarledge dogwood in bud, the woods trembling into green —Edith Wharton, *Twilight Sleep*

    Personification paints a metaphor for Springtime.

12. The green girl, spring, has found her voice, / My heart is pierced through —E. B. White, "Pigeon, Sing Cuccu!"

STARS

See also: NATURE SCENES; SKY/SKYSCAPES

1. The stars are golden fruit upon a tree all out of reach —George Eliot, *Spanish Gypsy*

2. The twinkling steel above me is a star; / I am a fallen Christmas tree —Robert Lowell, "At the Altar"

3. The galaxy, that milky way / Which nightly as a circling zone thou seest / Powdere'd with stars —John Milton, *Paradise Lost*, Book 7

4. The stars leak drop by drop on the tin plates / of the sea almonds —Derek Walcott, "Europa"
   The poet tops his image with a simile: "the jeering clouds are luminously rumpled as the sheets."

STEALTH

See: CRAFTINESS

STILLNESS

See also: NATURE SCENES; ROOMS; SILENCE

1. Repose is a snaffle / In exuberance's mouth —John Hollander, "Disagreements"
   Two partners disagree on everything. One uses this horsemanship metaphor to contend that equanimity curbs exuberance, thus justifying the need to quarrel.

2. The thickly carpeted, softly lighted basement was a funeral parlor where the evening we had killed was laid out —Ross MacDonald, *The Moving Target*

3. The air was so quiet he could hear the broken pieces of the sun knocking in the water. —Flannery O'Connor, "The River"

4. Here is no peace, although the air has fainted —Elinor Wylie, "Innocent Landscape"

This first line sets the mood for several other single word metaphors: footfalls that "die" and are "buried" in the deep grass and trees that are "painted."

STINGINESS

See also: MONEY

1. O little foplings of the pride of mind, / Who wrap the phrase in lavender, and keep it / In order to display it —Conrad Aiken, "One Star Fell and Another"
   The speaker derides those who hoard words. If stars fall, and heaven be the same, why should we not be as prodigal? What will we lose of ourselves by giving of ourselves?

2. The husband is doing the death grip on his wallet —Anon., "Talk of the Town," *The New Yorker*, May 15, 1992
   The wife's eye has been gripped by designer Judith Leiber's high-priced handbags.

STOPPING AND STARTING

See: ADVICE

STORMS

See also: NATURE SCENES; NIGHT AND DAY; RAIN; SOUND; STREET SCENES; THUNDER AND LIGHTNING; WIND; WINTER

1. Hurricane Betsy swirled her billowing skirts along the Florida coast —Edna Buchanan, *Never Let Them See You Cry*
   Like many newcomers to Florida, the author ignored warnings to get out of the storm's path. Once was enough!

2. With the bugles of the tempest pealing, it was hard to imagine a peopled earth — Stephen Crane, "The Blue Hotel"

3. The Doom's electric Moccasin / That very instant passed— / On a strange mob

of panting trees —Emily Dickinson, Poem 1593

> *The poem tells about a wind that comes "like a bugle" and concludes that much can come and go, "And yet abide the World."*

4. Meadows: There's a howling wind outside plays ducks and drakes / With a flat moon —Christopher Fry, *A Sleep of Prisoners*

5. Pine wind / blowing hard / quick rain / Torn windpaper / talking to itself —Hsin Ch'i-Chi, "Ch'ing P'ing Yueh: Passing a Night Alone in Wang's Temple on Po Shan," Sung Dynasty

6. Swirling, merciless blizzards have the Dakotas and Montana by the neck and there is no relief in sight —Harry Middleton, "Portraits in Winter Light," *Wilderness*, Winter 1992

> *Having a mountain 'by the neck' is a strange image if examined closely, but it seems to work here.*

7. Fuflygina sat admiring the silver beads of sleet glittering in the light of the office lamps —Boris Pasternak, *Doctor Zhivago*

8. The wind spat hard raindrops against the window —Allan Seager, "The Street," *Vanity Fair*

9. Alonso: The winds did sing to me, and the thunder— / That deep and dreadful organ pipe—pronounc'd / The name of Prosper! —William Shakespeare, *The Tempest* Act 3, scene 3, line 97

10. The storm redefined itself, gained muscle and speed and became so tightly wound a band of energy that its sustained winds of 150 miles per hour approached the most powerful a hurricane can produce —William K. Stevens, *New York Times*, August 26, 1992

> *Hurricane Andrew was so intense that it overcame metaphorical logic.*

11. Suddenly the black night showed its teeth, in a flash of lightning —Rabindranath Tagore, *Fruit-Gathering*, 37

■ STRATEGIES

See also: CRAFTINESS; MANIPULATION; POLITICS/POLITICIANS; PREPAREDNESS/UNPREPAREDNESS; REFORM; THINKING/THOUGHT

1. Madame Marneffe had placed her guns in position —Honoré de Balzac, *Cousin Bette*

> *The lady, a quintessential schemer, schemes to obtain a higher government post for her husband.*

2. Do you imagine my green infant Machiavelli, that I would send Henri away? Does France disarm her feet? . . . Henri is a dagger hanging in its sheath suspended from a nail —Honoré de Balzac, *Cousin Bette*

> *Henri is but one pawn in Madame Marneffe's own Machiavellian schemes.*

3. The Iraqi Air force is planning a cat-and-mouse game along the 32nd parallel, sending its planes south of the line and then quickly turning back north —Michael R. Gordon McMillan, *New York Times*, August 26, 1992

> *A cat-and-mouse maneuver is often regarded as canny, but who ever heard of a mouse that actually won the game?*

4. Like everything else he did, you could tell that he'd been creating the software for this program for some time —Terry McMillan, *Waiting to Exhale*

> *A wife reflects on her failed marriage in the idiom of her husband's profession as a software entrepreneur. She wants to remind him that she too knows how "to exit DOS, how to search and replace, how to merge" but decides she no longer has to prove anything but to simply "move her cursor."*

5. Every day must have a plan, a track upon which to guide the restless colt of one's ambition —Meg Pei, *Salaryman*

6. In his post-election campaign, Clinton has selected no fewer than four villains to be the anvil on which he hammers counter-revolution —William Safire, "Essay," *The New York Times*, February 18, 1993

> *This morning-after attack on the President's first economic policy speech, identified the villains as*

the rich, special interests, the pharmaceutical industry and the deficit.

7. Within Russia's leadership, after all, the power struggle being played out so far is less a mortal contest between democrats and reactionaries than a tactical tug-of-war between shock therapists and gradualists —Serge Schemann, *The New York Times,* January 24, 1993

8. York: My brain, more busy than the labouring spider, / Weaves tedious snares to trap mine enemies —William Shakespeare, *The Second Part of Henry the Sixth* Act 3, scene 1, line 339
   To borrow from Shakespeare's image, metaphor is woven onto simile.

■ STREET SCENES

See also: CITIES; DESCRIPTIONS, MISC.; GROUP SCENES; HEAT; PLACES, MISC.; SNOW; SUMMER; WINTER

1. The street . . . presented itself in one of its winter aspects, creased and with thin sidelocks of snow —Saul Bellow, *Dangling Man*

2. What a glorious garden of wonders the lights of Broadway would be to anyone lucky enough to be unable to read —Gilbert Keith Chesterton
   Here's an Englishman's view of all the neon advertisements of New York's theater district.

3. They threaded the steep side streets already powdered with silver —Gilbert Keith Chesterton, "The Invisible Man"

4. Glass was the street —Emily Dickinson, "Poem 1498"

5. Jefferson Street . . . its roofs sheltered complex and unstable beings, perilously feeling their way, step by step, along the knife-edge-narrow path of equilibrium that winds across the morasses and clings to the precipitous cliffs of life —Dorothy Canfield Fisher, "Murder on Jefferson Street"
   This image of life in a typical, uneventful American setting as a perilous journey sets the scene for the author's chilling portrait of people beset by their secret demons.

6. Rosa, moving away out of the small crowd, entered the strands of pedestrians crossing the street, intersecting with the strands coming across from the other side —Nadine Gordimer, *Burger's Daughter*

7. The pavements of New York are filled with people escaping the prison sentence of personal history into the promise of an open destiny —Vivian Gornick, *The New Yorker,* October 17, 1993

8. The high road into the village of Wydon Priors was again carpeted with dust —Thomas Hardy, *The Mayor of Casterbridge*

9. A clear fretwork of shadows / From huge umbrellas littered the pavement and made / A sort of lucent shallows in which was moored / A small navy of carts —Anthony Hecht, "A Hill"
   Hecht describes an Italian piazza.

10. The fiesta was solid and unbroken, but the motor-cars and tourist-cars made little islands of onlookers —Ernest Hemingway, *The Sun Also Rises*

11. It was one insufferable evening when the overplus of the day's heat was being hurled quiveringly back to the heavens by every surcharged brick and stone and inch of iron in the panting town —O. Henry, "The Dog and the Playlet"
    The metaphor personifies the city as a panting beast and continues with a description of a cool restaurant as "an oasis where the hoofs of Apollo's steed had not been allowed to strike."

12. For Dr. Felix Bauer, staring out the window of his ground-floor office on Lexington Avenue, the afternoon was a sluggish stream that had lost its current —Patricia

Highsmith, "Mrs. Afton, among Thy Green Braes"

13. Cambridge Street with its iron river of the horse-railroad —Oliver Wendell Holmes, "Boating"

14. Sunset Boulevard was a bouillabaisse of rage and squalor mixed with immigrant hope and livened by the spice of easy felony —Jonathan Kellerman, *Devil's Waltz*

15. These hell-fire streets / Of Boston, where the sunlight is a sword —Robert Lowell, "As a Plane Tree By the Water"

16. The long dusty ribbon of a long city street —John Masefield, "All Ye That Pass By"

17. The Great White Way —Albert Bigelow Paine, 1901.
   The phrase was coined as a title for a novel but has become a universally known metaphor for the neon-lit Broadway theater district.

18. The streets are but the drains for the discharge of a tormented mob, in which the only object in reaching any spot is to be transferred to another —John Ruskin
   Ruskin not only reviles the modern city, but its inhabitants as well by picturing the "tormented" mob as the effluence that flows into the city sewers.

19. We all got out of the car——abandoned ship, as it were, in the middle of Madison Avenue, in a sea of hot, gummy macadam —J. D. Salinger, "Raise High The Roof Beam, Carpenters," *The New Yorker,* 1950–60

20. Piero, blind, and following a child guide along / The chessboard of his native city's streets —Gjertrud Schnackenberg, "The Resurrection. (Piero Della Francesca)," *The New Yorker,* September 21, 1992

21. The wind rises and bowls / The day's litter of news in the alleys —Richard Wilbur, "After the Last Bulletins"
   The poem pictures the cycle from the end of one day to the start of another.

■ STRENGTH/WEAKNESS

See also: ABILITY; BUSINESS DESCRIPTIONS; EFFECTIVENESS/INEFFECTIVENESS; ENDURANCE; FRAGILITY; LEADERSHIP; POLITICS/POLITICIANS; POWER; SELF-RELIANCE; SMALLNESS

1. I am a lioness and will never allow my body to be anyone's resting place —Aisha bint Ahmad al-Qurtubiyya, Untitled poem

2. We weighed President Bush's sensible stewardship of foreign affairs against domestic leadership so limp it has prompted the title President Noodle —Anon., *The New York Times,* Editorial, November 1, 1992
   The editorial illustrates an implied simile, limp as a noodle, metamorphosing into a metaphoric nickname.

3. Even worse for Mr. Bush, there was only one question on foreign policy, his strong suit —Anon., Editorial, *The New York Times,* October 17, 1992, two days after a debate between the presidential candidates.
   The bridge game metaphor continued with "It is a devastating irony that the end of the cold war, for which the President can claim some credit, has robbed him of his trump card."

4. Not all of you will make it through . . . Some of you are shallow-rooted —Margaret Atwood, *The Handmaid's Tale*
   The young women being groomed as "handmaids" are schooled by an Aunt.

5. The Endangered Species Act is the pit bull of environmental laws—it's short, compact and has a hell of a set of teeth — Donald Barry, *The New York Times,* May 26, 1992
   These metaphoric words of praise come from a vice president of the World Wildlife Fund, an environmental organization.

6. Germany, long a handcuffed giant, is shaking its frame and testing its muscles — Anon., Editorial, *Danube Courier,* quoted in *The New York Times,* December 27, 1991
   The quote appeared in an article on Germany's emerging strength in Post-Soviet Europe.

7. What end have I to expect, that I should be patient? Is my strength the strength of stones? or is my flesh of brass? —The Bible, *O.T., Job 6:12*

8. Strength came up in waves that had their source in a sea of calm and unconquerable devotion —Maeve Brennan, "The Eldest Child," *The New Yorker*, June 23, 1968

9. Thurlow was a sturdy oak at Westminster, and a willow at St. James's —Edmund Burke

    Thurlow, an English lawyer and politician, was known for servility in court and severity in the House of Lords. During the 1992 presidential campaign CBS newsman Bill Krulwich updated the metaphor, saying "Both candidates bend to the wind—you have two willows!"

10. And having put it [strength of character] away, how could she recover herself, and give one . . . the sense of tempered steel, a blade that could fence with anyone and never break —Willa Cather, *A Lost Lady*

    A woman of great moral strength has displayed a less "steely" side of herself.

11. In terms of political capital . . . Mr. Clinton approached his first Supreme Court choice as a pauper. Partly because of his stumbles in recent weeks, and partly because he has taken on more tough challenges than any other President in years —Thomas L. Friedman, *The New York Times,* June 15, 1993; types: paupers

12. Plants of great vigor will always struggle into blossom, despite impediments —Margaret Fuller, "The Great Lawsuit. Man Versus Men. Woman Versus Women," *The Dial,* July, 1843

    Fuller added that for more timid people, encouragement and a genial atmosphere was needed.

13. She was the rock on which weaker natures broke —Mavis Gallant, "Careless Talk"

14. Carl Sandburg lived to be eighty-nine years old, and spent those years going here and yon, a hardy tumbleweed of a populist, blown by the wind across the plains —Elizabeth. Hardwick, "Wind from the Prairie," *The New York Review of Books*

    Sandburg, wrote Hardwick "can be said to have sucked up all the nutrients in the soil."

15. In an era when the average movie budget is $24 million, Goldwyn is a mouse among elephants. But mice are adept at stealing crumbs —Aljean Harmetz, "Sam Goldwyn's Little Studio That Could," *The New York Times,* October 19, 1992

    The editorial "blurb" writer quickly picked the image to catch the readers' attention.

16. You're not seaworthy. You are cut away too much through the middle: you would go over in a good blow —Joseph Hergesheimer, "The Token"

    A sturdy younger sister thus derides her beautiful older sister with whom she competes for the attentions of a sailor.

17. Mr. Hussein, of course, is playing without much of a hand —Youssef M. Ibrahim, "Iraq's Gamble: Sharp Words, Dull Claws," *The New York Times,* January 18, 1993

    "He is playing poker again," said an Iraqi dissident who has watched Mr. Hussein closely for years.

18. That proud independence, which formed the main pillar of savage virtue, has been shaken down, and the whole moral fabric lies in ruins —Washington Irving, "Traits of Indian Character"

    Irving's metaphor relies on an allusion to the destruction of the temple where Samson was chained. The second term of the metaphor is illogical, so that it becomes a mixed metaphor.

19. The vengeful God is a stallion; in Graham's hands he is a gelding —Murray Kempton, quoted in "Prince of the City," *The New Yorker,* by David Remnick, March 1, 1993

    This quote from a Kempton profile on the Reverend Billy Graham illustrated the journalist's ability to concisely deflate unctuous piety or any other character flaw. In paragraphs to come, Remnick wrote "Kempton brings the pastor to his knees."

20. The Republican leader found himself in the unfortunate position of being a general with too few troops, and he quickly backed off . . . and watered down his proposal —Clifford Krauss, "Dole Tries To Rein In President But Slips," *The New York Times,* October 22, 1993

Krauss used a military and a drinking metaphor to describe Senator Dole's misstep on American involvement in the latest Haitian crisis. The headline writer chose a common horsemanship metaphor to sum it all up.

21. If we are to have a jellyfish economy, we can at least take away some of the sting —Robert Kuttner, *Washington Post Writer's Group,* May 30, 1993

The author commented on an invertebrate economy with none of the reliable factors, such as regulated industries, of an erstwhile "vertebrate" economy.

22. All reactionaries are paper tigers —Mao Tse-tung

During a 1957 visit to Moscow the Chinese leader incorporated this into a speech as "Was not Hitler a paper tiger?" The metaphor has joined the linguistic mainstream as a term for any person of deceptive power and strength.

23. The problem is . . . how to remain strong, no matter what shocks come in at the periphery and tend to crack the hub of the wheel —Anne Morrow Lindbergh, Epigraph

24. His own life seemed . . . a fragile column supporting nothing amidst the wreckage of the years —Carson McCullers, *The Ballad of the Sad Cafe*

25. In this business we are the sheep and you the wolves —Joseph Priestly, Letter to the Citizens of Birmingham

Priestley's house had been burned and his library destroyed by a town that decried his views on the French Revolution.

26. Servant: Some o' their / plants are ill-rooted already; the least wind i' the' world will blow them down —William Shakespeare, *Antony and Cleopatra,* Act 2, scene 7, line 1.

This is one of Shakespeare's many scenes where the characters clown around, in this case about the effect of drinking.

27. Cleopatra: When he meant to quail and shake the orb, / He was a rattling thunder —William Shakespeare, *Antony and Cleopatra,* Act 5, scene 2, line 85

Antony is dead and Cleopatra recalls his strengths.

28. York: how quickly should this arm of mine, / Now prisoner to the palsy chastise thee —William Shakespeare, *The Tragedy of King Richard the Second,* Act 2, scene 3, line 102

29. Stepmother: Lord—how you have rendered soft this lion heart! Where is my strength? —August Strindberg, *Swanwhite*

The wicked stepmother, in this fantasy, will prove to have been herself bewitched.

30. This mighty empire has but feet of clay —Oscar Wilde, "Theoretikos"

This metaphor actually dates back to The Book of Daniel *(2:31–40) when Daniel interprets a dream of King Nebuchadnezzar about a king with "feet part of iron and part of clay" whose kingdoms would finally break up and become the kingdom of God.*

■ STUBBORNNESS

See: AGREEMENT/DISAGREEMENT; FLEXIBILITY/INFLEXIBILITY

■ STUDENTS AND TEACHERS

See: EDUCATION AND LEARNING

■ STUPIDITY

See also: IGNORANCE; INSULTS; INTELLIGENCE; MIND

1. An unmistakable fog of political incompetence is beginning to form around the White House. The Bush and Carter Presidencies showed the danger of letting small droplets of error condense into an enveloping miasma —Anon., Editorial, *New York Times*, February, 8, 1993

> *The metaphor shows a logical consistency, with the second part enlarging and strengthening the basic metaphor.*

2. Some Beams of Wit on other souls may fall, / Strike through and make a lucid interval; / But Sh—'s genuine night admits no ray, / His risings Fogs prevail upon the Day —John Dryden, "MacFlecknoe, or a Satyr Upon the True-Blew Protestant Poet, T.S"

3. A Tun of Man in thy large Bulk is writ, / But sure thou'rt but a Kilderkin of wit — John Dryden, "MacFlecknoe, or a Satyr Upon the True-Blew Protestant Poet, T.S"

> *This is like saying,* You're a wine keg in girth and a thimble in wit. *"The comparison is in the holding capacity of each vessel.*

4. Half-wits are fleas; so little and so light, / We scarce could know they live, but that they bite —John Dryden, Prologue, *All For Love*

5. Hector: By what peculiar vagary did the world choose to place its mirror in this obtuse head? —Jean Giraudoux, *Tiger at the Gates*, Act 1

> *Hector is speaking to Helen, who is pictured in this play as a* bubble head *or* air head *or* feather brain, *to use three contemporary metaphors for one whose intellect is not great. She reflects in her mirror the current thinking of mediocrity.*

6. How could learning have any intrinsic value for two happy oxen?" —Naguib Mahfouz, *Palace of Desire*

> *The question is Kamal's ironic response to the pretentious Ibraham's assurance that he "sat for the primary certificate."*

7. To such charges, even from the Autocrat of all Asses—a man is *compelled* to answer —Edgar Allan Poe, Letter to George Eveleth, January 4, 1848

> *Poe was satirically commenting on a man named English, a "blatherskite."*

8. Guiderius: This Cloten was a fool, an empty purse, / There was no money in it —William Shakespeare, *Cymbeline*, Act 4, scene 2, line 113

> *The metaphor of an empty purse as an empty brain is underscored with "Not Hercules / Could have knocke'd out his brains, for he had none."*

9. Chorus: I would have been . . . bankrupt in sane council if I should put you away — Sophocles, *Oedipus the King*

> *"Bankrupt in sane council" would now be called loss of mind. The subjects of Oedipus assure him that they want him to stay as King.*

10. Either she knows something, or the inside of her head is so unfurnished that she can't remember what she ate for breakfast — Rex Stout, *Fer-de-Lance*

> *Private detective, Nero Wolfe's comment to this comment by a police investigator is "she's not perfectly equipped."*

11. He [President Warren Harding] has a bungalow mind —Woodrow Wilson

> *Wilson's quip may have been inspired by Oliver Wendell Holmes Senior's essay about the "one-two-three-story intellect" which is included under the heading, Intelligence.*

∎ SUBSERVIENCE

See: MASTERY/SUBORDINATION

∎ SUBSTANTIALITY/ INSUBSTANTIALITY

1. Some Scenes in Sippets wou'd by worth our time, / Those wou'd go down: some Love that's poach'd in Rime —John Dryden, Prologue (for Nahum Tate's *The Loyal General*)

> *'Sippets' are snippets of toast dunked in liquid. Dryden suggests that plays dealing with weighty subjects are too hard to swallow.*

2. Banana Yoshimoto's *Kitchen* is a tangy, imperfect little snack —Deborah Garrison, "Books," *The New Yorker*, January 25, 1993

With an author and title like this, a reviewer is unlikely to resist the temptation of using a food metaphor at some point, in this case in the opening statement.

3. In 193 pages, Joyce Carol Oates's *Where is Here?* serves up a dazzling assortment of fictional hors d'oeuvres. But it's not my intent to be misleading—many of these 35 stories are quite a meal in themselves —Randall Kenan, *The New York Times Book Review,* November 1, 1992

4. Your Constitution is all sail and no anchor —Thomas Babbington Macaulay, Letter to Henry S. Randall, May 23, 1857
   In 1937, President Franklin Delano Roosevelt alluded to this in relation to detractors of his New Deal: "Their anchor for the salvation of the ship of state is Macaulay's anchor."

5. This [question] brought down a whole shower bath of information, but let us say that the Webbs' shower baths are made of soda water. They never sink one, or satiate —Virginia Woolf, Diary Entry, September 18, 1918

■ SUBTLETY

See: TACT

■ SUCCESS, DEFINED

See also: ACHIEVEMENT; FAME; INDIVIDUALITY; SELF-RELIANCE; WINNING/ LOSING

1. Success is a ladder you can't climb with your hands in your pockets. —Anon., American Proverb

2. If Mr. Clinton and his associates . . . can keep up the momentum, they may even have a chance of hitting big casino: carrying out an effective reform of the nation's faltering health-care system —R. W. Apple, Jr., *The New York Times,* May 28, 1993
   The gambling metaphor referred to the President's just approved economic plan.

3. So glorious was the glittering gold at the apex of the corporate mountain that its mere reflection had to be reward enough for the toilers on the rocky slopes below, most of whom . . . were themselves mere handmaidens in the procession marching round and round that refulgent peak — Louis Auchincloss, "The Senior Partner's Ethics"

4. When I first came to New York, [Alexander] Woollcott was in the flood tide of his career as a dramatic critic —John Mason Brown, Introduction, *The Portable Woollcott*

5. After his moonshot of a year in 1992, Fred Couples would prefer to maintain a steady orbit of excellence in 1993 —Jaime Diaz, "Golf," *The New York Times,* February 11, 1993
   The metaphor is used as the opening sentence or what journalists refer to as the "grabber."

6. Yes, I have climbed to the top of the greasy pole —Benjamin Disraeli
   The metaphoric pole he climbed was to the post of Prime Minister of Great Britain.

7. He had flown up very high . . . beating his wings tenaciously . . . he had stayed up there longer than most of us —F. Scott Fitzgerald, *The Last Tycoon*
   The lofty flier is the movie tycoon and central character of Fitzgerald's last, unfinished novel.

8. Moses: The golden bear Success / Hugs a man close to its heart; and breaks his bones —Christopher Fry, *The Firstborn,* Act 2, scene 1
   Moses warns his nephew not to be dazzled by Egyptian bribes.

9. Success can only be measured in terms of distance traveled —Mavis Gallant, *Green Water, Green Sky*

10. The Persian Gulf War took Mr. Sawyer [ABC-TV correspondent Forrest Sawyer] from pinch-hitter to power slugger —Jill Gerston, *The New York Times,* April 12, 1992

The sports metaphor tied in with Sawyer's description of himself as a "utility infielder" and his executive producer, Richard Kaplan's statement that "he hit home run after home run."

11. Drew: How do you measure your success—by the amount of pain you cause? Well, in that case, I'm your masterpiece —Richard Greenberg, *Eastern Standard*, Act 2, scene 1

The image comes naturally to Drew since he's a painter.

12. Your self-made man, whittled into shape with his own jack-knife deserves more credit . . . than the regular engine-turned article shaped by the most approved pattern, and French-polished by society and travel —Oliver Wendell Holmes, *The Autocrat of the Breakfast-Table*

13. The moral flabbiness born of the exclusive worship of the bitch-goddess Success — William James, Letter to H.G. Wells, September 11, 1906

James's metaphor was born of his belief that worshipping success gave rise to moral decay.

14. At one step she has reached the top of the stair-case up which the rest of us climb on our knees year after year —Henry Wadsworth Longfellow, Journal entry, 1853

Longfellow expressed his amazement at the skyrocketing fame of Harriet Beecher Stowe after publication of Uncle Tom's Cabin.

15. Oh, the pathology of the American obsession with success —John Pauker, quoted, 1979 Public Broadcasting program about poet Howard Nemerov

Pauker was reacting to his friend's plaintive "Daddy never praised me until I made money in Hollywood."

16. To stand on the edge of achievement: that is one of the more horrible of all states: an uncertain egg about to roll off the wall — Theodore Roethke, *Straw for the Fire, Notebooks of Theodore Roethke*

17. Iago: If consequence do but approve my dream, / My boat sails freely, both with wind and stream —William Shakespeare, *Othello*, Act 2, scene 3, line 58

Iago's plans are working out exactly as anticipated.

18. Success is a rare paint, hides all the ugliness —Sir John Suckling, "A Ballad upon a Wedding"

19. Lena was my touchdown for the year — Scott Turow, *Pleading Guilty*

Lena is a desirable law student the protagonist has recruited as an intern for his firm.

20. The family curve had been continually upward —Edith Wharton, *Hudson River Bracketed*

Wharton quickly graphs the family's economic success.

■ SUCCESS/FAILURE

See also: *ARTS AND ENTERTAINMENT; FORTUNE/MISFORTUNE; MISTAKES; WINNING/LOSING*

1. Standing on the burning deck, President Clinton sailed his ship to victory in the House of Representatives tonight —R. W. Apple, Jr., *The New York Times*, May 28, 1993

The much-used ship of state metaphor launched Mr. Apple's report on the passage of the President's economic plan, after weeks of setbacks.

2. Bialystock [Zero Mostel]: I'm drowning. Other men sail through life. Bialystock has struck a reef . . . I'm going under. I am being sunk by a society that demands success, when all I can offer is failure — Mel Brooks, *The Producers*

Bialystock is begging an accountant to help him cheat his way off the metaphoric reef.

3. With clouds all around him, Yitzhak Shamir plucked the thread of a silver lining out of the morning headlines —Clyde Haberman, *The New York Times*, April 3, 1992

Contrary to the headline's claim that the Israeli Prime Minister though "in rough water, still swims confidently," Shamir's stroke was not strong enough to survive the election.

4. When I was so far away from the target that my arrows never hit . . . I had the pleasure of using all my strength to pull a long bow, and even the misses did not lower my self-esteem —Lewis Mumford

This metaphor began with the author's reflection that "All my essays and miscellanies count for no better than a bull's eye when one is on top of the target."

5. The trustees of the City University of New York last night appointed a black anthropologist . . . as the next president of City College, long the jewel but now one of the most troubled of the university system's 21 campuses —Maria Newman, *New York Times,* May 25, 1993

6. It's all very well for you . . . you caught the tide —Sean O'Faolain, "A Born Genius"

A man who aspired to a professional singing career addresses a woman who succeeded and in so doing got to go to places like Paris and Milan.

7. Success played hide-and-seek with Fielding —J. H. Plumb, *The Life of Mr. Jonathan Wild the Great*

8. Though only 34 years old, he [Playwright Paul Rudnick] might be a household-name by now . . . had *I Hate Hamlet,* his Broadway debut, not been capsized by the onstage misbehavior of its star, Nicol Williamson —Frank Rich, "Review/ Theater," *The New York Times,* February 3, 1993

The playwright's Off-Broadway play, Jeffrey enjoyed a successful run.

9. Brutus: There is a tide in the affairs of men, / Which, taken at the flood, leads on to fortune. / Omitted, all the voyage of their life / Is bound in shallows and in miseries —William Shakespeare, *Julius Caesar,* Act 4, scene 3, line 217.

"On such a full sea are we now afloat; / And we must take the current when it serves / Or lose our venture," Brutus continues.

10. In the midst of this chopping sea of civilized life, such are the clouds and storms and quicksands and thousand-and-one items to be allowed for, that a man has to live, if he would not founder and go to the bottom and not make his port at all, by dead reckoning, and he must be a great calculator indeed who succeeds —Henry David Thoreau, "Where I Lived, and What I Lived For"

"Keep your accounts on a thumbnail," says Thoreau, since life itself is so precarious.

11. The materialism you preach has gained currency more than once and has invariably proved bankrupt —Ivan Turgenev, *Fathers and Sons*

12. Right now Masson is ahead on points. But it is the eighth inning —Richard N. Wingfield, quoted *The New York Times,* June 4, 1993

The baseball metaphor was prompted by the jury's finding for psychiatrist Jeffrey M. Masson in his libel suit against journalist Janet Malcolm . . . but without awarding the damages he asked for.

■ SUFFERING

See: ADVERSITY; PAIN AND SUFFERING

■ SUMMER

See also: NATURE SCENES; NIGHT AND DAY; SEASONS; TIME

1. The beautiful day had within it the seeds of its own fragility: it was the last day of summer —Anita Brookner, *Hotel du Lac*

2. When in the festival of August heat / the air stops throbbing over balustrades — John Hollander, "Horas Tempestatis Quoque Enumero," [The Sundial]

3. The summer days moved with the pace of a caged lion —Claire McAllister, "July In the Jardin Des Plantes"

4. Summer's distillation left / A liquid prisoner pent in walls of glass —William Shakespeare, "Sonnet 5," line 9

The water of summer has become the icy "glass" of winter.; houses / interiors: walls

5. O, how shall summer's honey breath hold out / Against the wrackful siege of batt'ring days —William Shakespeare, "Sonnet 65," line 5

   There are two metaphors here—summer personified with its "honey breath," and time as an enemy besieger battering the ramparts of youth.

6. Steep thyself in a bowl of summer — Virgil, "Syrica, a Dancing Girl"

■ SUN

See also: NATURE SCENES; ROOMS; SKY/ SKYSCAPES; STREET SCENES

1. The sun . . . that punctual servant of all work —Charles Dickens, *Pickwick Papers*

2. Busie old foole, unruly Sunne, / Why dost thou thus, / Through windowes, and through curtains call on us? —John Donne, "The Sunne Rising"

   Donne also describes the sun as a "sawcy pedantique wretch" because it intrudes on lovers.

3. Andromache: Look at the sunshine. It's finding more mother-of-pearl on the rooftops of Troy than was ever dragged up from the bed of the sea —Jean Giraudoux, *Tiger at the Gates*, Act 1

4. Daily the prowling sunlight whets its knife / Along the sidewalk —Anthony Hecht, "Third Avenue in Sunlight"

   Knives were often sharpened on stones or pavement or the edges of plates.

5. The sun—my almighty physician —Thomas Jefferson, Letter to James Monroe, 1785

6. Captain Littlepage moved his chair out of the wake of the sunshine, and still sat looking at me —Sarah Orne Jewett, *The Country of the Pointed Firs*

   Sea imagery describes the things around Littlepage, a man more accustomed to boats than to furniture.

7. The late-afternoon sun is a bronze fruit / that glazes the pond with its bronze juice —Julia Kasdorf, "Prospect Park, Holy Week," *The New Yorker*, April 2, 1992

8. The sun is a huntress young, / . . . The sun is an Indian girl, / of the tribe of Illinois —Vachel Lindsay, "An Indian Summer Day on the Prairie"

   Lindsay continues to ply his metaphoric descriptions with "The sun is a smoldering fire . . . The sun is a wounded deer . . . The sun is an eagle old . . . ," elaborating on each of the comparisons.

9. From the thin slats of the Venetian blinds / The sun has plucked a sudden metaphor: / A harp of light, reflected on the floor —Howard Moss, "Underwood"

10. Sunlight is the ultimate charlatan, nature's preeminent trickster —David Muench, quoted in "Portraits in Winter Light," *Wilderness*, Winter 1992

11. The sun was high in the sky and poured down a blazing fire —Isaac Bashevis Singer, "Old Love"

12. The closing Sun? / At noon a pomegranate / At dusk a red whole-note —Robert L. Smith, "Last Days," *Riverrun*, Fall 1992

13. The sun is a corbeil of flowers the moon Blanche / Places there, a bouquet — Wallace Stevens, "The Man on the Dump"

14. A dash in a window shade throws a long knife of sun on a side wall, above an unmade army cot —John Updike, *Rabbit, Run*

    The metaphor reappears in somewhat different form a few pages later when "The slash of sun on the wall above him slowly knifes down, cuts across his chest, becomes a coin on the floor, and vanishes.

15. Sunshine, the old clown, rims the room — John Updike, *Rabbit, Run*

16. Sunshine . . . its golden finger-tips pressed her lids open —Edith Wharton, *The Mother's Recompense*

    The sun personified as a lover sets the mood for the protagonist's sense of optimism about the day ahead.

17. He feels the warm sun sculpt his cheek —
Richard Wilbur, "A Finished Man"

18. With open mouth he drank the sun / As
though it had been wine! —Oscar Wilde,
"The Ballad of Reading Goal"

■ SUNRISE

*See also: DAWN; NATURE SCENES;
NIGHT AND DAY*

1. I'll tell you how the sun rose,— / A
ribbon at a time —Emily Dickinson,
Poem 318

> *Dickinson continues, "The steeples swam in ame-
> thyst, / The news like squirrels ran," capping two
> metaphors with a simile.*

2. At dawn, where the ocean has netted its
catch of lights, / The sun plants one lithe
foot / On that spill of mirrors —Anthony
Hecht, "A Letter"

> *"A Letter" offers a tip of the hat to Ezra Pound,
> who himself drew inspiration from an old Chi-
> nese poem.*

3. Dying dawn saw him hustling home around
the lake where the challenging sun flung a
flaming sword from east to west across the
trembling water —Zora Neale Hurston,
"The Gilded Six-Bits"

4. How the sun burst up early in the morning
behind Mount Scopus to torment the whole
city and suddenly turn the gold and silver
domes to dazzling flames —Amos Oz,
The Hill of Evil Counsel

5. Full many a glorious morning have I seen
/ Flatter the mountain-tops with sovereign eye, / Kissing with golden face the
meadows green, / Gilding pale streams
with heavenly alchemy —William Shakespeare, "Sonnet 33," line 1

> *There are two metaphors here. One is the personi-
> fication of the sun as a king, the second pictures
> the sun as an alchemist.*

6. Still buried in night, they looked across at
the sun-impinging sheet of day. They
looked under the lifted curtain at brightness —Thomas Wolfe, *Look Homeward
Angel*

■ SUNSET

*See also: LANDSCAPES; NATURE SCENES;
NIGHT AND DAY; SKY/SKYSCAPES*

1. The sun breaks on the hilltops, spilling its
crimson yolk —Julia Alvarez, *How the
Garcia Girls Lost Their Accents*

2. The splendor of the sunsets over New
Jersey . . . fill our western sky with tongues
of fire —Brooks Atkinson, "The Fabu-
lous Port of New York," *The New York
Times*, 1949

3. As the sun set its light slowly melted the
landscape, till everything was made of fire
and glass —Elizabeth Bowen, "Summer
Night"

4. The sun . . . flung wide its cloak and
stepped down over the edge of the fields at
evening —Willa Cather, *One of Ours*

5. The sun is spent, and now his flasks /
Send forth light squibs —John Donne,
"A Nocturnal upon Saint Lucy's Day"

> *The flasks are powder flasks; the squibs gunshot.*

6. Only a thread of light was left between the
horizon and the sea —Marguerite Duras,
The Afternoon of Mr. Andesmas

7. The sun, / closing his benediction, /
sinks —William Ernest Henley, "Marga-
ritae Sorori"

> *The title means "sister Margaret."*

8. The low sun dropped a spendthrift flood
of gold upon the fortunate fields of wheat
—O. Henry, "The Defeat of the City"

> *The author uses the double metaphor of excessive
> spending and a flood to picture the opulence, the
> abundance of the sunset.*

9. The sun stepped down from his golden
throne —Oliver Wendell Holmes, Sr.,
"The Star and the Water-Lily"

10. The lower half of the sky was daubed with a streak of blood —Cynthia Ozick, "Puttermeyser Paired," *The New Yorker*, 1990

11. The golden lightning / of the sunken sun —Percy Bysshe Shelley, "To a Skylark"

12. The setting sun had left behind the redness of a heavenly slaughter —Isaac Bashevis Singer, "Brother Beetle"

13. The sun was down and all the west was paved with sullen fire —Alexander Smith, "A Life Drama"

14. The sun fell in graceful surrender to the night, throwing out its last miracles —Melanie Sumner, "The Guide," *The New Yorker*, April 26, 1993

15. A broad expanse of the river was turned to blood —Mark Twain, *Life on the Mississippi*

∎ SUPERFICIALITY

See also: *CHARACTERISTICS; HUMANITY/ HUMANKIND*

1. Roland has the inner life of a tree, or possibly a stump —Margaret Atwood, "Wilderness Tips"

2. Jesus: Ye blind guides, which strain at a gnat and swallow a camel —The Bible, *N.T., Matthew 23:24*
   > *The metaphor is directed to those who fail to pay attention to the weightier demands of the Law, justice, mercy, and good faith.*

3. You would rather black the boots of / success than enquire whose soul dangles from his / watch chain —e. e. cummings, "La Guerre I"
   > *"Humanity i love you" writes Cummings, and lists forthwith the stupidities of mankind.*

4. The majority . . . is composed . . . skaters upon the surface of life —Honoré de Balzac, *Cousin Bette*

∎ SUPERSTITION

1. Superstition . . . the religion of feeble minds —Edmund Burke, *Letters on a Regicide Peace*

2. Seti: These plagues were not my doing / . . . Only a woman with her mind hung / With a curtain of superstition would say so —Christopher Fry, *The Firstborn*, Act 2, scene 2

3. Tear away / The blinds of superstition —Ella Wheeler Wilcox, "Progress"
   > *The same poem urged readers to "Sweep down the cobwebs of worn-out beliefs" and to open themselves up to "the light of Reason and Knowledge."*

∎ SURFING

See: *SPORTS*

∎ SURVIVAL

See also: *CHARACTERIZATIONS; ENDURANCE; INHERITANCE/INHERITORS*

1. He was always between wind and water, keeping himself afloat by his bold, sudden strokes and the nervous energy of his play —Honoré de Balzac, "The Firm of Nucingen"
   > *The swimming image continues: "Hither and thither he would swim over a vast sea of interests in Paris, in quest of some little isle that should be so far a debatable land that he might abide upon it.*

2. Andromache: The soldiers who march back under the triumphal arches are death's deserters —Jean Giraudoux, *Tiger at the Gates*, Act 2
   > *It takes luck or judgment to survive, not just bravery, Andromache says.*

3. We can't glance ahead with pleasure to the world our children will inhabit—they will have to swim for dear life —Edward

Hoagland, "Home is Two Places," *Commentary*, April 1968

■ SUSPICION

See also: DOUBT; LOVERS' DECLARATIONS AND EXCHANGES; MISTRUST

1. Smells fishy, they used to say; or, I smell a rat. Misfit as odour —Margaret Atwood, *The Handmaid's Tale*

    The ultimate misfit, Shakespeare's Caliban, had "a very ancient and fish-like smell."

2. I begin to smell a rat —Miguel de Cervantes, *Don Quixote*

3. Valere: Do not kill me, I beg of you, with the sharp blows of outrageous suspicion —Molière, *The Miser*, Act 1

    The lover asks Élise's grace in order to prove that his affections are sincere.

4. I became an inveterate doubter, always peeling the onion trying to get at the truth beneath the "facts" —Letty Cottin Pogrebin, "Hers," *The New York Times Magazine*, November 29, 1992

    Pogrebin's need to look beneath the surface stemmed from her discovery that her parents' wedding date post-dated the one they claimed and that her older sister was actually a half-sister.

5. Worcester: Suspicion all our lives shall be stuck full of eyes —William Shakespeare, *The First Part of King Henry the Fourth*, Act 5, scene 2, line 8

    Edmund Spenser's The Fairie Queen *pictures envy as a canvas that's "painted full of eyes."*

6. Northumberland: See, what a ready tongue suspicion hath! —William Shakespeare, *The Second Part of King Henry the Fourth*, Act 1, scene 1, line 84

■ SWEAT

See also: FACES; PHYSICAL APPEARANCE

1. Two little rivers [of perspiration] were running down his throat —Roald Dahl, "Edward the Conqueror"

2. His [Jesse Jackson's] face is shellacked with sweat —Marshall Fraidy, *The New Yorker*, April 15, 1992

3. She wiped a dew of sweat from her forehead —Rosamond Lehmann, *The Ballad and the Source*

■ SYMBOLS

See also: CHARACTERIZATIONS; RELIGION

1. He [Al Hirschfield] is the logo of the American theatre —Anon., quoted, by Mel Gussow in "Celebrating Hirschfield," *The New Yorker*, June 21, 1943

2. That graven image, word made wood — Edgar Bowers, "The Virgin Mary"

    In conventional religious terms, God's word is made flesh. Bowers turns the image around, and in the carving the word is made wood.

■ SYMPATHY

See also: FEELINGS; PITY; SENSITIVITY; UNDERSTANDING

1. It takes a little time for minds to turn face to face —Christopher Morley, "What Men Live By"

2. Magda: Oh, I could tell you everything. Your heart has tendrils which twine about other hearts and draw them out —Hermann Sudermann, *Magda*, Act 3

3. Because of his grief she felt a bodily pain, a bruise over the heart —Dame Rebecca West, *Sunflower*

■ TACITURNITY

See: SILENCE

■ TACT

See also: DIPLOMACY

1. As she watched her cousin . . . that complaint long repressed, was on the point of breaking the frail envelope of discretion —Honoré de Balzac, *Cousin Bette*

   Balzac thus explains the enduring hold of hatred on Cousin Bette.

2. Sophie Tuckerman: Sometimes it is wise to let things grow more roots before one blows them away with many words —Lillian Hellman, *The Autumn Garden*, Act 3

3. In his discretion he [a hairdresser] occupies his unruly tongue with the weather and the political situation, lest, restless with inaction, it plunge unbridled into a mad career of inconvenient candor —Dorothy L. Sayers, "The Inspiration of Mr. Budd"

   The horsemanship metaphor sets the scene for Sayers' hero to trap a murderer with his professional discretion as well as skill.

4. It was a "show" tact, a huge unique, disbudded tact grown under glass, and destined to be labelled, exhibited and given a prize and a name, and a page to itself in the florists' catalogues —Edith Wharton, *The Children*

■ TACTICS

See: STRATEGIES

■ TACTLESSNESS

See: CHARACTERISTICS

■ TALKATIVENESS

See also: ANIMATION; EFFECTIVENESS/IN-EFFECTIVENESS; EXCITEMENT; FOOL-HARDINESS; GOSSIP; INSULTS

1. To talk much and get nowhere is to climb a tree to catch a fish —Anon., Chinese Proverb

2. Socrates: you'll be the flower of talkers, prattlers, gossips: / only keep quiet —Aristophanes, *The Clouds*

   To which Strepsiades puns, "I shall be flour indeed with all this peppering."

3. On this string he would harp by the hour; it was a lofty subject on which he had pondered much in his solitary life —William Henry Hudson, *Green Mansions*

   In this variation of the common metaphor, he has only one string to his harp, the old man wants to discuss politics, while the young man wants to discuss Rima, the bird-girl.

4. Volpone: Such a hail of words / She has let fall —Ben Johnson, *Volpone,* or *The Fox,* Act 3, scene 2

5. Sir, we are a nest of singing birds — Samuel Johnson, *Boswell's Life of Johnson*

6. The difficulty is compounded vastly by Derrida's notorious word-drunkenness —David Lehman, *Signs of the Times: Deconstruction and the Fall of Paul de Man*
    Understanding Derrida'a Glas *is made more difficult by the fact that the work is printed in two columns: "the one on the left deals with Hegel and the one on the right with Jean Genet."*

7. He fairly darkened the air around us with a cloud of empty, rambling talk —André Maurois, "The Fault of M. Balzac"

8. Chester's talk sped, the toe of the next sentence stumbling over the heel of the last —Cynthia Ozick, "Alfred Chester's Wig," *The New Yorker*, April 20, 1992
    Ozick sums up this fast talker with "He was an engine of eagerness."

9. Holofernes: He draweth out the thread of his verbosity finer than the staple of his argument —William Shakespeare, *Love's Labour's Lost*, Act 5, scene 1, line 18

10. There are always lots of clubs in farm towns, where the wives are ostensibly doing good works, but the good works are afloat in a river of talk —Jane Smiley, *A Thousand Acres*

■ TASTE

1. Good taste is the flower of good sense — Anon., Proverb

2. Both as a critic and reader [Alexander] Woollcott dodged the peaks. He chose instead the green pastures at his own level. Off the sweet clover and sour sorrel of these he nibbled quite happily, and cajoled thousands of others to find joy by following his example. His tastes were safely below the timberline. If he seldom lifted his eyes to the hills, it was because he was too engrossed in what was happen-ing next door. —John Mason Brown, Introduction, *The Portable Woollcott*.
    If Woollcott's taste ran to easily accessible drama and literature, John Mason Brown's was for extended metaphors.

■ TEACHERS/TEACHING

See: EDUCATION AND LEARNING; OCCUPATIONS

■ TEARS

See also: ACTING/ACTORS; DECEPTION; GRIEF; LAMENTS; LOVERS' DECLARATIONS AND EXCHANGES; SELF-CONTROL; SORROW

1. I think of him / and the tears / come down in floods / filling up / the Eastern Sea. —Anon., Folk Song, Ming Dynasty

2. Between condolence and consolation there flows an ocean of tears —Minna Antrim, *Naked Truth and Veiled Allusions*

3. Tears are summer showers to the soul — Alfred Austin, *Savonarola*, IV

4. Oh that my head were waters, and mine eyes a fountain of tears, that I might weep day and night —The Bible, *O.T., Jeremiah 9:1*

5. Rivers of waters run down mine eyes — The Bible, *O.T., Psalms 119:136*
    In The Traged;   , Richard the Third (1, 3, 176), Richard says, "And with thy scorns drew'st rivers from his eyes."

6. I can love both faire and browne, / . . . Her who still weepes with spungie eyes, / And her who is dry corke, and never cries —John Donne, "The Indifferent, The Sunne Rising"
    "I can love her, and her, and you and you," writes the poet, who enjoys variety.

7. Oft a flood / Have we two wept, and so / Drowned the whole world —John Donne, "A Nocturnal upon Saint Lucy's Day"

8. Hither with christall vyals, lovers come, / And take my teares, which are loves wine —John Donne, "Twicknam Garden"

   "For all [tears] are false, that taste not just like mine," writes the poet.

9. Lockit: And so, after all this Mischief, I must stay here to be entertain'd with your catterwauling, Mistress Puss! —John Gay, *The Beggar's Opera*, Act 3, scene 1

   Lucy has lost her lover after helping him escape from Newgate Prison, and her father Lockit, the jailer, is angry at her catlike wailing.

10. Tears . . . the ultimate toy weapon —Lois Gould, *Final Analysis*

11. Enobarbus: The tears live in an onion that should water this sorrow —William Shakespeare, *Antony and Cleopatra*, Act 1, scene 2, line 174

12. Antony: The April's in her eyes: it is love's spring, / And these the showers to bring it on —William Shakespeare, *Antony and Cleopatra*, Act 3, scene 2, line 43

    The showers are the tears Octavia sheds over her brother's departure.

13. Hamlet: What would he do / Had he the motive and the cue for passion / That I have? He would drown the stage with tears —William Shakespeare, *Hamlet*, Act 2, scene 2, line 564

14. Leonato: Did he break out into tears? / Messenger: In great measure. Leonato: A kind overflow of kindness; there are no faces truer than those that are so washed —William Shakespeare, *Much Ado About Nothing*, Act 1, scene 1, line 26

    According to the messenger Claudio's uncle was joyful to learn of his nephew's achievements, but because "much that joy could not show itself modest enough without a badge of bitterness" he cried "in great measure."

15. Othello: If that the earth could teem with women's tears, / Each drop she falls would prove a crocodile —William Shakespeare, *Othello*, Act 4, scene 1, line 240

    Opinions vary about the origins of "crocodile tears" as a metaphor, but everyone agrees such tears are false, and intended to defraud the person who is moved by them. A "similistic" twist, served as a title for a collection of similes, Falser than a Weeping Crocodile (Visible Ink Press. Elyse Sommer, Ed.).

16. Capulet: Evermore showering? In one little body / Thou counterfeits a bark, a sea, a wind —William Shakespeare, *Romeo and Juliet*, Act 3, scene 5, line 130

    Capulet elaborates on this with a virtual flood of metaphors: "Thy eyes, which I may call the sea, / Do ebb and flow with tears; the bark thy body is / Sailing in this salt flood; the winds, thy sighs, / Who raging with thy tears and they with them, / Without a a sudden calm will overset / Thy tempest-tossed body."

17. Ah, but those tears are pearl which thy love sheeds [sheds] —William Shakespeare, "Sonnet 34," line 13

18. But that so much of earth and water wrought, / I must attend time's leisure with my moan, / Receiving naught by elements so slow / But heavy tears, badges of either's woe. —William Shakespeare, "Sonnet 44," line 11

    The lover complains that he is made of the dull elements, earth and water, so that he cannot "leap large lengths of miles when thou art gone."

19. Henry: Her tears will pierce into a marble heart —William Shakespeare, *The Third Part of Henry the Sixth*, Act 3, scene 1, line 37

    The appeal of tears or anything arousing strong sympathy are commonly said to melt a heart of stone.

20. Titus: Let me say, that never wept before, / My tears are now prevailing orators — William Shakespeare, *Titus Andronicus*, Act 3, scene 1, line 25

21. Marcus: But floods of tears will drown my oratory —William Shakespeare, *Titus Andronicus*, Act 5, scene 3, line 90

22. King Richard: With rainy eyes / Write sorrow on the bosom of the earth —William Shakespeare, *The Tragedy of King Richard the Second,* Act 3, scene 2, line 146

23. King: Aumerle, thou weep'st, my tender-hearted cousin! / We'll make foul weather with despised tears —William Shakespeare, *The Tragedy of King Richard the Second,* Act 3, scene 3, line 160

24. Richard: And with thy scorns drew'st rivers from his eyes —William Shakespeare, *The Tragedy of King Richard the Third,* Act 1, scene 3, line 176

25. Julia: an ocean of tears, / And instances of infinite of love / Warrant me welcome to my Proteus —William Shakespeare, *Two Gentlemen of Verona,* Act 2, scene 7, line 69.

26. Julia: His tears [are] pure messengers sent from his heart —William Shakespeare, *Two Gentlemen of Verona,* Act 2, scene 7, line 77

27. Her tears began to turn their tide —William Shakespeare, *Venus and Adonis,* line 979

28. Antigonus: Her eyes became two spouts —William Shakespeare, *The Winter's Tale,* Act 3, scene 3, line 24.
    Current slang has twisted this into "turn on the waterworks."

29. Tears, those springs that water love —Mrs. Taylor, Untitled poem

30. A few [German prisoners] . . . cried quietly the whole time, letting the tears cut white channels down their grimed cheeks . . . —Keith Vaughan, October 11, 1944 diary entry

■ TECHNOLOGY

See also: PROGRESS

1. Prometheus: Technology's resources cannot withstand / Necessity's remorseless iron hand —Aeschylus, Prometheus Bound, Episode 7

2. Technology is in the saddle and rides mankind —Noel Brown, United Nations NGO Briefing, November 4, 1993
   Dr. Brown, of the United Nations Development Programme voiced concern that the advances of modern science are threatening to engulf mankind in the lethal byproducts of effluence and hazardous waste.

3. Mr. Gore argues that the private sector won't gamble on such a risky investment [as a new electronic data system.] Even if it did, he says, it would build not a super-highway available to all but rather a kind of private toll road open only to a business and scientific elite —John Markoff, "Building the Electronic Superhighway," *The New York Times,* January 24, 1993

■ TELEVISION

See: ARTS AND ENTERTAINMENT

■ TEMPERAMENT

1. The world has long realized he enjoys the central heating of temper —John Mason Brown, "The Trumans Leave the White House," *The Saturday Review*
   According to the article, those close to President Harry S Truman said he showed his temper but rarely while others said his moments of irritation sometimes "got out of hand."

2. I told Bobby Kennedy that I was not district judge material because my fuse was too short —Thurgood Marshall, Editorial, *The New York Times,* January 31, 1993
   Marshall's words were remembered at the time of his death.

3. Portia: The brain may devise laws for the blood but temper leaps o'r a cold decree: such a hare is madness the youth, to skip o'er the meshes of good counsel the crip-

ple —William Shakespeare, *The Merchant of Venice,* Act 1, scene 2, line 20

4. Their temper is a cross to all who come about them, as though Pharaoh should set the Israelites to make a pin instead of a pyramid —Robert Louis Stevenson, "An Apology for Idlers"

   Bearing a cross is a common metaphor for any troublesome burden. The metaphor depends upon the Biblical allusion.

5. The spectacle of paltriness can often prove a useful lesson in life: it may loosen strings that have been pitched too high —Ivan Turgenev, *Fathers and Sons*

   This gives us an implied comparison of the play of temperament to the loosening or tightening of the strings of a musical instrument.

6. The Doctor: A temper? My dear, I can only tell you—he's not a man, he's a mountain of dough —Ivan Turgenev, *A Month in the County,* Act 2, scene 3

   To doctor underscores his humorous assessment of another man's pliable disposition with "You just dump him on to the kitchen table, roll up your sleeves. . . ."

■ TEMPTATION

See also: LUST; SIN/REDEMPTION

1. If you sup with the devil, use a long spoon —Anon., Yiddish Proverb

   The proverb predates Chaucer, who, in The Canterbury Tales, *writes "Therfore bihoveth hire a ful long spoon / That shal ete with a feend."*

2. The cup of sinners overflows with so enchanting a sweetness, and we are naturally so much inclined to taste it, that it needs only to be offered to us —Peter Abelard, Letter to Heloise

   Abelard says that, on the other hand, "the chalice of saints is filled with a bitter draught."

3. The man who has tasted pleasure once will go to the well again —Honoré de Balzac, *Cousin Bette*

4. Can a man take fire in his bosom and his clothes not be burned. —The Bible, *O.T., Proverbs 6:27*

   In the Bible the metaphoric fire related to adultery. The proverb that follows asks "Can one go upon hot coals, and his feet not be burned?"

5. This does not mean, however, that Americans have been lulled by the dangerous siren song of the new isolationists —David Boren, *New York Times,* August 26, 1992

   The metaphor alluded to the sirens who tried to lure the ships of Ulysses to their destruction. Ulysses made his mariners stuff their ears with wax to protect them from temptation.

6. The natural inheritance of everyone who is capable of spiritual life is an unsubdued forest where the wolf howls and the obscene bird of night chatters —Henry James, Sr., quoted in Jose Donoso's *The Obscene Bird of Night*

   The metaphor, which provided the title for Donoso's book, is taken from a letter written by Henry James, Sr., to his sons Henry and William. Though man aspires to spirituality, he must first brave the elemental forest of sin.

7. Plagued by the nightingale / . . . he says of it: / "It clothes me with a shirt of fire" —Marianne Moore, "Marriage"

   Adam is "Unnerved by the nightingale and dazzled by the apple."

■ TENACITY

See: PERSEVERANCE

■ TENDERNESS

See: SENSITIVITY

■ TENSION/TENSION RELIEF

See also: AGREEMENT/DISAGREEMENT; ARTS AND ENTERTAINMENT; MEN AND WOMEN; POLITICS/POLITICIANS

1. *Fool Moon* . . . is a far more effective safety valve for urban pressures than drinking

two martinis or yelling at a runaway taxi driver —Ben Brantley, "Theater," *The New York Times*, September 3, 1993

> *Brantley, in urging readers to see the popular mime show before its closing, assured them that when they left the show they might "feel slightly better steeled to face the anarchy of city streets."*

2. When there's nothing in view, he's mute, unapproachable, hummingbird tense — John Malcolm Brinnin, Journal entry, April 23, 1947

> *Brinnin was travelling around the country on a book collaboration with the famous photographer Henri Cartier-Bresson.*

3. Behind their expressions of good intentions . . . President Bush and President François Mitterand of France danced a tense minuet today —Andrew Rosenthal, *The New York Times*, July 8, 1992

> *The headline picked up on the reporter's opening metaphor with a circus image: "Bush on a tightrope."*

4. Horne cried out wildly . . . releasing in her outcry an arsenal of tensions —Tennessee Williams, "Happy August 10th," *Anateus*

5. It must appear as though Henry and I live on very whimsical terms, gilding the pill of our daily disagreements with a lot of private jokes —Angus Wilson, "More Friend Than Lodger," *Stories from The New Yorker: 1950–60*

> *The "gilding" also encompasses generally "ghastly arch behavior."*

■ TENTATIVENESS

See: UNCERTAINTY

■ TERROR

See: FEAR

■ THANKFULNESS

See: GRATITUDE/INGRATITUDE

■ THEATER

See: ACTORS/ACTING

■ THINKING/THOUGHT

See also: COMMUNICATION/NON-COMMUNICATION; EMOTIONS; IDEAS; IMAGINATION; MIND; SOCIETY; TALKING

1. [The intellect] widens the horizon of the heart —W. H. Auden, *The Prolific and the Devourer*

2. Things are, in truth, the leeches / of thought —Joseph Brodsky, "New Life," *The New Yorker*, April 26, 1993

3. Stung by the splendour of a sudden thought —Robert Browning, "A Death In the Desert," *Dramatis Personae*

4. One's thoughts fly so fast that one must shoot them; it is no use trying to put salt on their tails —Samuel Butler, Quoted on the value of keeping a notebook

> *As for editing one's notes, Butler commented on his: My notes always grow longer if I shorten them. I mean the process of compression makes them more pregnant, and they breed new notes.*

5. "Good evening," muttered John, summoning his brains from the wild places — F. Scott Fitzgerald, "The Diamond As Big As the Ritz," *Tales of the Jazz Age*

6. Thought is a bird of space, that in a cage of words may indeed unfold its wings but cannot fly —Kahlil Gibran, *The Prophet*

> *The image appeared under the heading of talking which, according to the prophet / narrator, is something you do when you cease to be at peace with your thoughts.*

7. Alas! for him who dwells / In frigid air of thought —Sir Edmund Gosse, "Revelation"

8. My thoughts went wildly into battle with each other —Josephine Hart, *Damage*

9. "Om is the bow, the arrow is the soul, / Brahman is the arrow's goal / At which

one aims unflinchingly" —Hermann Hesse, *Siddhartha*

> *The sacred syllable Om is the way to reach the godhead through meditation.*

10. Thoughts are duty-free —Martin Luther

11. What steadiness and sympathy are needed if the thread of thought is to be unwound without tangles of snapping! —Christopher Morley, "What Men Live By"

12. The merry-go-round in Franz's head never stopped —Vladimir Nabokov, *King, Queen, Knave*

13. Thoughts that come with doves' footsteps guide the world —Friedrich Wilhelm Nietzsche, *Thus Spake Zarathustra*

14. We're becoming a short-take society . . . Our food for thought is junk food —William Safire, *On Language*

15. King Richard: My brain I'll prove the female to my soul, / My soul the father; and these two beget / A generation of still-breeding thoughts; / And these thoughts people this little world —William Shakespeare, *The Tragedy of King Richard the Second*, Act 5, scene 5, line 6.

> *The microcosm of the prison is compared with the macrocosm of the world. To make the comparison, Richard must first populate his little world.*

16. I would think until I found / Something I can never find, / Something lying on the ground, / In the bottom of my mind —James Stephens, "The Goat Paths"

> *The image concludes the poem.*

17. The bullet of your thought must have overcome its lateral and ricochet motion and fallen into its last and steady course before it reaches the ear of the hearer —Henry David Thoreau, *Walden*

> *Otherwise, according to Thoreau, "it may plow out again through the side of his head.*

18. You want room for your thoughts to get into sailing trim and run a course or two before they make their port —Henry David Thoreau, *Walden*

> *Thoreau thus explains his preference for communicating with people across the pond rather than within the confines of his house.*

19. Life trills along the alcoved hall, / The lords of thought await our call —John Greenleaf Whittier, "The Library"

> *These lines concluded a verse sung at the opening of the Haverhill Library.*

20. Thoughts may be bandits. Thoughts may be raiders. Thoughts may be invaders. Thoughts may be disturbers of the international peace —Woodrow Wilson, Speech, May 1916

21. How did she put it? *To keep the pus of repressed thoughts from festering,* ha ha —A. B. Yehoshua, *Mr. Mani*

> *A psychologist wants Hagar to talk about her dead father.*

22. [Pasternak] seemed to me too complicated and I lost the thread of his thought in the chaos of his imagery —Yevgeny Yevtushenko, *A Precocious Autobiography*

23. Thoughts shut up want air, / And spoil, like bales unopen'd to the sun —Edward Young, "Night Thoughts"

> *The metaphor and simile are interdependent.*

■ THOUGHTLESSNESS

See: SELF-IMAGES

■ THREATS

See: WARNINGS

■ THRIFT

See: STINGINESS

■ THUNDER AND LIGHTNING

See also: SKY/SKYSCAPES; STORMS

1. The bright branches of sheer lightning / broke in flame —Pindar, "Pythia 4," *Odes*

2. Thunder crumples the sky, / Lightning tears at it —Leonora Speyer, "The Squall"

3. The fierce lightning is scratching the sky with its nails —Rabindranath Tagore, "The Land of the Exile," *The Crescent Moon*

■ TIME

See also: AGE/AGING; ANCESTRY/ANCES-TORS; DEATH; FOREBODING; FRAGILI-TY; INHERITANCE/INHERITORS; LIFE AND DEATH; MASTERY/SUBORDINA-TION; MATURATION; MEMORY/MEMO-RIES; PAST; PEOPLE, INTERACTION; TRANSIENCE

1. The eighteen years he has lived seem but a moment, a breathing space in the long march of humanity —Sherwood Anderson, "Sophistication," *Winesburg, Ohio*
   The "sadness of sophistication" has come to George Willard, the young man who sees himself as "merely a leaf blown by the wind through the streets of his village."

2. Time is the best teacher. —Anon., Proverb

3. None of us ever graduates from college, / For time is an emulsion —John Ashbery, "Soonest Mended"
   ". . . and probably thing not to grow up / Is the brightest kind of maturity for us, right now at an rate," writes Ashbery.

4. Now those years were a canyon between us —Margaret Atwood, "Betty," *Dancing Girls and Other Stories*
   Using a simile, Atwood continues "an empty stretch like a beach along which I could see her disappearing ahead of me on the empty beach."

5. Time's a trap, I'm caught in it —Margaret Atwood, *The Handmaid's Tale*
   The heroine does not want to live in the moment, but her past has been wrenched from her and her future is tremulous.

6. Time is a tease —André Breton, *Nadja*
   "Time is a tease—because everything has to happen in its own time."

7. Time the avenger —Lord George Gordon Byron, "Childe Harold"

8. We are all together with him . . . rocking in the upholstered moment, in the fur-lined teacup of Time —Hortense Calisher, "Time, Gentlemen!" *Tale of the Mirror*
   "We" refers to the family of a father with strong links to the Victorian era.

9. And these my days their sounds and flowers / Fall in a pride of petaled hours —e. e. cummings, "Always before your voice my soul"

10. And Time the ruined bridge has swept / Down the dark stream which seaward creeps —Ralph Waldo Emerson, "Concord Hymn"
    This hymn also portrayed the embattled farmers who "fired the shot heard around the world"—a metaphor for the American Revolution's world-wide influence and now associated with any action with wide-ranging effect.

11. Illusion, Temperament, Succession, Surface, Surprise, Reality, Subjectiveness,—these are threads on the loom of time, these are the lords of life —Ralph Waldo Emerson, "Experience," *Essays: First Series*

12. Confusing time with its mathematical progression, as the old do, to whom all the past is not a diminishing road but, instead, a huge meadow which no winter ever quite touches, divided from them now by the narrow bottle-neck of the most recent decade of years —William Faulkner, "A Rose for Emily"

13. The Leaves of Life keep falling one by one —Edward Fitzgerald, *The Rubáiyát of Omar Khayám*

14. The bird of time has but a little way to flutter—and the bird is on the wing —Edward Fitzgerald, *The Rubáiyát of Omar Khayám*

15. A long single file of minutes went by —F. Scott Fitzgerald, "The Ice Palace," *Flappers and Philosphers*

16. Remember, that time is money —Benjamin Franklin

> *Like many metaphors and phrases that have slipped into our everyday language, this may have been coined or popularized by Franklin.*

17. White-haired sea-troughs / That ride the foam / Of time's bare back —W. S. Graham, "The Hill of Intrusion"

18. Time rode through my life—a victor. I barely even clung to the reins —Josephine Hart, *Damage*

19. Time flies over us but leaves its shadow behind —Nathaniel Hawthorne, *The Marble Faun*

20. A giant clock on a brick tower / rattles its scissors —Anthony Hecht, "Cape Cod Lullaby," version of a poem by Joseph Brodsky

> *The shears of time are usually wielded by one of the Fates; here, the hands themselves become shears.*

21. The next two hours tripped by on rosy wings —O. Henry, "The Gift of the Magi," *The Four Million*

> *O. Henry stumbled into a* mixaphor *here, since to go on wings the hours should have flown, not tripped. The anthology's title offers a bit of metaphoric arithmetic, four million being the total population of New York as opposed to the four hundred people that constituted the city's "high society."*

22. Time, you old gypsy man —Ralph Hodgson, first line and title of poem

23. Time, you thief —Leigh Hunt, "Rondeau"

24. The great belt on the wheel of Time slipped and eternity stood still —Zora Neale Hurston, "The Gilded Six-Bits"

> *The man caught up in this frozen moment in time has just discovered his wife in bed with another man.*

25. These privileged moments of memory . . . remind him of the yawning chasm between time past and time present and of the inexorable march we must all make toward old age and extinction —Michiko Kakutani, "Books of the Times," *The New York Times*, October 9, 1992

> *The protagonist of* The Orient Express *by Gregor von Rezzori thus reflects on time.*

26. Time passed. But time flows in many streams —Kawabata Yasunari, *Beauty and Sadness*

> *"Cosmic time is the same for everyone," writes Kawabata, "but human time differs with each person."*

27. How time gallops! —Rosamond Lehmann, *The Ballad and the Source*

28. Time is an irreversible arrow . . . The man trying to wear youth's carefree clothing, the woman costuming her emotions in doll's dresses—these are pathetic figures who want to reverse time's arrow —Joshua Loth Liebman, *Peace of Mind*

29. Time what an empty vapor 'tis! —Abraham Lincoln, Untitled poem

30. Time . . . robber of the best / Which earth can give —Amy Lowell, "New York at Night," *A Dome of Many-Coloured Glass*

31. The scythers, Time and Death, / Helmed locusts, move upon the tree of breath —Robert Lowell, "Where the Rainbow Ends"

> *This is a compound metaphor. Time and Death are scythers; Time and Death are locusts; therefore, locusts are scythers.*

32. It was all that the rust of time had left intact —Gabriel García Márquez, "Maria Dos Prazeres," *The New Yorker*, March 22, 1993

> *A man leaves the same amount of money to an old prostitute that he left her when they were both still young.*

33. But at my back I always hear / Time's winged chariot hurrying near —Andrew Marvell, "To His Coy Mistress"

34. Time, the healer, did not assuage his grief —Guy de Maupassant, "The False Gems"

Death as a metaphoric healer can be traced back to Aeschylus' sixth century B.C. "Fragments."

35. Ferris glimpsed the disorder of his life . . . and time, the sinister glissando of the years, time always —Carson McCullers, *The Ballad of the Sad Cafe*

36. She was aware of . . . time draining itself from the scene in a slow leak —Alice McDermott, *At Weddings and Wakes*

37. Time is the thief you cannot banish — Phyllis McGinley, "Ballads of Lost Objects"
    Amongst "lost objects" the poet laments are her daughters, once "girls in pinafores" and "two tall strangers."

38. Time was her labyrinth, in which Hunilla was entirely lost —Herman Melville, "Norfolk Isle and the Chola Widow"
    Borges, too, returns again and again to the metaphor of time as a labyrinth.

39. Full of unfulfillment, life goes on, / Mirage arisen from time's trickling sands — James Merrill, "Lost in Translation"
    Merrill extracts two meanings from "sands"— the trickle in the hourglass, and the desert sands that cause distortion in the perception of time.

40. Aethelwold: Time, drawn by the snail and the hare, / Asleep in his rattling wain — Edna St. Vincent Millay, *The King's Henchman*, Act 2
    The wain, or wagon, would be bound to rattle when drawn by such unequal partners. It is a wonder that Time can sleep at all.

41. Time does strange things. It's high tide before you know it —Jason Miller, *That Championship Season*

42. Time is a flowing river. Happy those who allow themselves to be carried, unresisting with the current —Christopher Morley, *Where the Blue Begins*

43. The sheets of time have a common wrinkle / For youngsters will take their flaking chalk / And write of love on wall and sidewalk —Howard Moss, "Chalk From Eden"

44. The days of my youth . . . seem to fly away from me in a flurry of pale repetitive scraps —Vladimir Nabokov, *Lolita*
    Nabokov pictures time flying by as swiftly and transiently as bits of tissue paper.

45. Initially, I was unaware that time, so boundless at first blush, was a prison — Vladimir Nabokov, *Speak Memory*

46. Time, that enemy of labels —Ann Petry, "The Novel as Social Criticsm"

47. This subtle Thief of Life, this paltry Time —Alexander Pope, "The Second Epistle"

48. Time seemed to proceed with more than usual eccentricity, leaving twilight gaps in her mind —Katherine Anne Porter, "Pale Horse, Pale Rider," *Pale Horse, Pale Rider*

49. One by one the sands are flowing — Adelaide Proctor, "One by One," *The Poems of Adelaide Proctor*
    Another Proctor metaphor about the passing of time: See how time makes all grief decay (from "Life in Death").

50. Time . . . His hands do neither wash, nor dry, / But being made of steele and rust, / Turnes snow, and silke, and milke to dust —Sir Walter Raleigh, (also spelled Ralegh), *The History of the World*

51. I dropped my watch into the stream of time —Theodore Roethke, *Straw for the Fire, Notebooks of Theodore Roethke*

52. Time seemed to have made a little jump forward, now that the figure of old Slane was no longer there with outstretched arms to dam it back —Vita Sackville-West, *All Passion Spent*

53. Time is the school in which we learn, / Time is the fire in which we burn — Delmore Schwartz, "For Rhoda"

54. King: on our quick'st decrees / Th' inaudible and noiseless foot of time / Steals ere we can effect them —William Shakespeare, *All's Well That Ends Well*, Act 5, scene 3, line 41

55. Rosalind: Time is the old justice that examines all such offenders [the unfaithful] —William Shakespeare, *As You Like It*, Act 4, scene 1, line 198

56. King Philip: This little abstract does contain that large / Which died in Geoffrey, and the hand of time / Shall draw this brief into as huge a volume —William Shakespeare, *The Life and Death of King John*, Act 2, scene 1, line 101

> *King Philip compares Geoffrey, who Young Arthur resembles, to a book and Arthur to an abstract of it. Time, the book's author, will gradually expand the "little abstract" into a volume as large as the original.*

57. Claudio: Time goes on crutches till love have all his rites —William Shakespeare, *Much Ado About Nothing*, Act 2, scene 1, line 374

58. Iago: There are many events in the womb of time / which will be delivered —William Shakespeare, *Othello*, Act 1, scene 3, line 370

59. Pericles: Time's the king of men; / He's both their parent, and he is their grave —William Shakespeare, *Pericles, Prince of Tyre*, Act 2, scene 3, line 45

60. Hastings: We are time's subjects, and time bids be gone —William Shakespeare, *The Second Part of King Henry the Fourth*, Act 1, scene 3, line 110

61. Archbishop: We see which way the stream of time doth run, / And are enforced from out most quiet there / By the rough current of occasion —William Shakespeare, *The Second Part of King Henry the Fourth*, Act 4, scene 1, line70

> *The second metaphor, "the rough current of occasion," refers to chance as a factor in man's fortune.*

62. And nothing 'gainst Time's scythe can make defense —William Shakespeare, "Sonnet 12," line 13

> *Time, the servant of death, is commonly pictured as the scyther of people.*

63. But wherefore do not you a mightier way / Make war upon this bloody tyrant Time? —William Shakespeare, "Sonnet 16," line 1

64. Time . . . delves the parallels in beauty's brow, / Feeds on the rarities of nature's truth, / And nothing stands but for his scythe to mow —William Shakespeare, "Sonnet 60," line 9

65. Gaunt: Thou canst help time to furrow me with age, / But stop no wrinkle in his pilgrimage —William Shakespeare, *The Tragedy of King Richard the Second*, Act 1, scene 3, line 229

> *Time is pictured as a ploughman.*

66. King Richard: I wasted time, and now doth time waste me; / For now hath time made me his numb'ring clock: / My thoughts are minutes —William Shakespeare, *The Tragedy of King Richard the Second*, Act 5, scene 5, line 49

67. Ulysses: Time hath, my lord, a wallet at his back, / Wherein he puts alms for oblivion —William Shakespeare, *Troilus and Cressida*, Act 3, scene 3, line 144

> *Ulysses also compares time to "a fashionable host."*

68. Hector: the end crowns all, / And that old common arbitrator, Time, / Will one day end it —William Shakespeare, *Troilus and Cressida*, Act 4, scene 5, line 225

69. Proteus: Time is the nurse and breeder of all good —William Shakespeare, *Two Gentlemen of Verona*, Act 3, scene 1, line 243

> *A metaphor of personifaction pictures time's life-giving powers.*

70. Time's poison fruits . . . will still fall in your lap, of course, but beside the sea they do not taste bitter —Anne Rivers Siddons, *Colony*

> *The novel is set in a Maine seaside resort.*

71. Niggard Time threats, if we miss / This large offer of our bliss —Sir Philip Sidney, "Only Joy! now here you are," *Astrophel and Stella*

> *The poet urges his love to accept him quickly, since time is a miser, and man's span is short.*

72. For me, the firefly's quick, electric stroke / Ticks tediously the time of one more year —Wallace Stevens, "Le Monocle de Mon Oncle"

73. And the high gods took in hand / . . . a measure of sliding sand / From under the feet of the years —Algernon Charles Swinburne, "Chorus from Atalanta"

74. And Time [is], a maniac scattering dust — Lord Alfred Tennyson, "In Memoriam"

75. Time is but a stream I go a-fishing in — Henry David Thoreau, *Walden*

> *"I drink at it," writes Thoreau, "but while I drink I see the sandy bottom and detect how shallow it is."*

76. Time, as we all know, is sometimes a bird on the wing, and sometimes a crawling worm —Ivan Turgenev, *Fathers and Sons*

77. Through the night the rats of time and silence gnaw the timbers of the old house of life —Thomas Wolfe, "The Return of the Prodigal"

> *The story became part of* The Hills Beyond.

78. Time flaps on the mast —Virginia Woolf, *Mrs. Dalloway*

> *The sailing metaphor is used to convey the sense of everything having come to a momentary standstill.*

79. Was there no escape from the prison of time? —Irvin D. Yalom, *When Nietzsche Wept*

> *A fictional Dr. Joseph Breuer sees the decline of age as a sentence to be served, and wishes desperately that he could begin again.*

■ TIMELINESS/UNTIMELINESS

See also: ACTION/INACTION; DEATH; FATE; INSULTS; OBSOLESCENCE; OPPORTUNITY

1. Whoever hesitates for a second perhaps allows the bait to escape which during that exact second fortune held out to him —Alexandre Dumas, *The Three Musketeers*

2. He is a clock that always goes too slow — Honoré Gabriel de Riquetti, Marquis de Mirabeau

> *The metaphoric insult was directed at Mirabeau's foe, the financier Monsieur Necker.*

3. Here is a play bursting over the finish line, and way back there, panting in the dust, is the cast —David Richards, "Sunday View," *The New York Times*, April 12, 1992

> *Mr. Richards' disapproval was aimed at a revival of* 'Tis Pity She's a Whore.

4. Mr. [Leon] Botstein's concept has potential to convince younger listeners that classical music is not some cobwebbed ghost ship lost in time —Alex Rose, "Classical View," *The New York Times*, January 10, 1993

> *This summed up Rose's appraisal of the conductor / educator's first three concerts as the leader of the American Symphony.*

5. The Destinies . . . / They bid thee crop a weed, thou pluck'st a flower —William Shakespeare, *Venus and Adonis*, line 945

■ TIMIDITY

See also: CAUTION; COURAGE; COWARDICE

1. The only person before whom Marcus would dare raise the timid flag of his spirit was a man who couldn't trust himself to interpret the challenge clearly —Nadine Gordimer, "Charmed Lives"

2. The play's main character . . . a man with the spine of a sapling —David Richards, "Theater," *The New York Times*, March 8, 1992

> *The play reviewed was* Hidden Laughter *by Simon Gray. One of the most famous and malicious metaphors about someone's backbone was Theodore Roosevelt's putdown of President McKinley*

as someone with "no more backbone than a chocolate eclair."

3. Maurice: You timid man! . . . Who robbed you of your self-assurance and turned you into a dwarf? —August Strindberg, *There Are Crimes and Crimes,* Act 2, scene 1
   "A dwarf? Yes, you are right," Maurice responds. "I am not working up in the clouds, like a giant, with crashing and roaring, but I forge my weapons deep down in the silent heart of the mountain."

4. Let us not be pygmies in a case that calls for men —Daniel Webster, Senate speech on the problem of a slave policy with respect to new Western territories, March 7, 1850

■ TOLERANCE/INTOLERANCE

See: BIGOTRY

■ TORONTO

See: CITIES

■ TOUGHNESS

See also: CHARACTERISTICS; CHARACTERIZATIONS; COURAGE; ENDURANCE; MASTERY/SUBORDINATION; STRENGTH/WEAKNESS

1. Here, root yourselves beside me. / I am that Tree planted by the River, / Which will not be moved. / I, the Rock, I, the River, I, the Tree —Maya Angelou, "On the Pulse of Morning," January 21, 1993
   Angelou read her poem of hope for the future of the U.S. on the occasion of Bill Clinton's inaugural.

2. His leaf also shall not wither —The Bible, *O.T., Psalms 1:3*
   Man is pictured as a sturdy and fruitful tree.

3. I ruled over the tribes of the desert with a rod of iron —Jorge Luis Borges, "Ibn Hakkan al-Bokhari, Dead in his Labyrinth"

4. An iron hand in a velvet glove —Charles V

King Charles was credited with this now common metaphor by essayist Thomas Carlyle.

5. What a blade of steel! —Philip Larkin, quoted, "Letter from London," *The New Yorker,* November 15, 1993
   The poet's description of former British Prime Minister Margaret Thatcher was quoted in a review of her recently published memoirs. Mrs. Thatcher was also known as The Iron Lady.

6. There is a natural firmness in some minds which cannot be unlocked by trifles, but which, when unlocked, discovers a cabinet of fortitude —Thomas Paine, "The Crisis, Number 1," *Common Sense*

7. Guard 2: [The general] he's the rock, the oak, not to be wind-shaken —William Shakespeare, *Coriolanus,* Act 5, scene 2, line 116

8. King: For he is gracious, . . . Yet, notwithstanding, being incens'd, he's flint. —William Shakespeare, *The Second Part of King Henry the Fourth,* Act 4, scene 4, line 33

9. That iniquity . . . had made her turn to steel and adamant —Virginia Woolf, *To the Lighthouse*

■ TRADITION

See also: CHANGE; REFORM

1. A sacred cow is being prepared for slaughter—free medicine for the poor and elderly to pay for Britain's budget deficit —Stephen Beard, National Public Radio, May 20, 1993

2. Tradition wears a snowy beard —John Greenleaf Whittier, "Mary Garvin"
   Romance, on the other hand, "is always young."

■ TRAFFIC

See: ROAD SCENES

■ TRANQUILITY

See also: CALMNESS/VOLATILITY; NATURE SCENES; SINGERS/SINGING/SONGS

1. Mrs. St. Maugham: It has upset her nerves. We are waiting as it were for calmer weather —Enid Bagnold, *The Chalk Garden,* Act 1

2. Nature seemed prim and staid that day, and the globe gave no hint that it was flying round in a circus ring of its own — Kenneth Grahame, "The Magic Ring"

3. Drenched in the delicate dew / of hymns outpoured —Pindar, "Pythia 5," *Odes*

4. Pauline sat bolt upright, the torn garment of her serenity fluttering away like a wisp of vapour —Edith Wharton, *Twilight Sleep*
   The simile depends on the clothing metaphor.

5. The people's lives in Boston / Are flowers blown in glass —E. B. White, "Boston is Like No Other Place in the World Only More so!"

■ TRANSFORMATION

See also: CHANGE; CHARACTERIZATIONS; STRENGTH/WEAKNESS

1. The apprentice had the feeling that the dim oil lamp was the vague light of the moon, and the room a valley shut in the ill-omened air of some remote mountain —Ryūnosuke Akutagawa, "Hell Screen"

2. Moses: I am the Hebrew / . . . the cry / whipped off the sanded tongue of that prince of Egypt —Christopher Fry, *The Firstborn,* Act 1, scene 1
   "The prince of Egypt died. I am the Hebrew / Smitten out of the shadow of that prince," says Moses, who will exchange his cushioned existence in the royal household for a hunted existence as the leader of his oppressed people.

3. He was a figure in a canvas, over which another had been painted —Josephine Hart, *Damage*
   The "figure" is a young man transformed by love.

4. Siddartha . . . became a heron, ate fishes, suffered heron hunger, used heron language, died a heron's death —Hermann Hesse, *Siddhartha*
   The ascetics Siddartha had joined did not think of spiritual understanding as empathy: they strove to become the creatures they saw. This is metaphor-made-flesh.

5. Visitors [are taken] to the coffeehouse where Bobby Zimmerman alchemized into Bob Dylan —Neal Karlen, "The Mall that Ate Minnesota" *New York Times,* August 30, 1992
   The alchemist transmuted base metal into gold, turning dross into something precious. Poor Bobby Zimmerman!

6. In Penny Marshall's *Big* . . . he [movie actor Tom Hanks] took the central conceit—a child's soul padlocked in an adult body—and turned it into a rhapsody — Anthony Lane, "The Current Cinema," *The New Yorker,* July 19, 1993

7. Ms. Schnackenberg [Gjertrud] can spin straw into gold —William Logan, *The New York Times Book Review,* November 15, 1992
   The reviewer added a parenthetical wish that the poet would sometimes start with gold.

8. You have put me in here a cub, but I will go out a roaring lion, and I will make all hell howl —Carrie Nation
   This was the anti-alcohol crusader's statement when she was arrested for her lion-like activities in the saloons of Kansas.

9. His fame, once merely a novelist's fame, is now the fame of terror. A writer has been transmuted into a pharaoh, wrapped in hiddenness, mummified in life —Cynthia Ozick, "Life and Letters, *The New Yorker,* December 13, 1993

Ozick's subject was Salman Rushdie, who became a fugitive after publication of his Satanic Verses *was condemned.*

■ TRANSIENCE

See also: CHANGE; DEATH; LAMENTS; LIFE; PERMANENCE/IMPERMANENCE

1. It's [this world is] all shifting sands . . . and changing winds —Zoë Atkins, *Daddy's Gone A-Hunting,* Act 3

2. Fortune, honor, beauty, youth / Are but blossoms dying —Thomas Campion, "What if a Day"
   Campion continues with another metaphor: Wanton pleasure, doting love / Are but shadows flying.

3. She has begun to measure her future with an hourglass —Robin Finn, *The New York Times,* November 17, 1992
   The 36-year-old tennis champ, Martina Navratilova, was under the spotlight during the 1992 Virginia Slims playoffs.

4. [Ross Perot's unofficial campaign:] That summertime tent is not a political home and will fold —William Safire, "Essay," *The New York Times,* July 16, 1992
   The column was printed on the very day that Mr. Perot withdrew as a possible presidential candidate.

5. Our sages . . . say that it [life] is a vapor, or a show, or made out of the same stuff with dreams —Robert Louis Stevenson, "Aes Triplex"
   "We are such stuff as dreams are made on," wrote Shakespeare.

6. But where are the snows of yesteryear? —François Villon, "Ballade of the Ladies of Time Past"
   This oft-quoted line has become a classic metaphor for the ephemeral nature of life.

7. Within a month his name would be a blown dust on the desert of centuries — Morris L. West, *The Devil's Advocate*
   A priest reflects on the grim prognosis his doctor has just handed him.

■ TRAVEL

1. Travelling is a fool's paradise —Ralph Waldo Emerson, "Self-Reliance," *Essays: First Series*
   He elaborated on this with "My giant goes with me wherever I go"—the "giant" being the unrelenting, inner self.

2. My tourist hands, / Who traveled on their own / Without a helping brain — Donald Hall, "Abroad Thoughts from Home"
   The poet, now settled, thinks back on past, mindless travel.

■ TREACHERY

See also: ACCUSATIONS; DANGER; DECEPTION; GOOD/EVIL; NAME CALLING

1. If you dig a pit for someone, you may fall into it yourself. —Anon., Proverb
   The proverb changes its metaphor, but not its meaning, when it is rendered, If you set a trap for someone, you may be caught in it yourself.

2. Where the canal comes out / pacing / back and forth —Wen-Chun Cho, "'Till White Hair We'll Stay Together," Han Dynasty
   For the metaphor to work, the Imperial Canal must be subject to tides. The poet's beloved has taken another lover, and a change of direction must be indicated.

3. After Wally and Lila died in the early 1990's, the *Digest,* always a hotbed of intrigue, became a veritable court of the Borgias —Richard Lingemann, *The New York Times Book Review,* August 22, 1993
   The title being reviewed was Theirs Was the Kingdom.

4. Richard: And that I love the tree from whence thou sprang'st, / Witness the loving kiss I give the fruit —William Shakespeare, *The Third Part of Henry the Sixth,* Act 5, scene 7, line 31
   This brings to mind the popular expression the kiss of death. Richard's professed love for the

figurative fruit, the king, is strictly lip service to cover up his evil thoughts.

5. Albany: I arrest thee / On capital treason; and, in thy arrest, / This gilded serpent — William Shakespeare, *King Lear*, Act 5, scene 3, line 83

    The gilded serpent was Goneril, wife to Albany and perfidious daughter to Lear.

6. Troilus: The fractions of her faith, orts of her love, / The fragments, scraps, the bits and greasy relics / Of her o'er-eaten faith are bound to Diomed. —William Shakespeare, *Troilus and Cressida*, Act 5, scene 2, line 166

    The image of indigestible food fits Troilus' mood of disgust at Cressida's treachery in becoming Diomed's mistress.

7. And yet, so he says, the thought of treachery had yet to sprout in him, for the cold, bare kernel that had worked its way into the dark, dry earth still lacked the stimulation of moisture. —A. B. Yehoshua, *Mr. Mani*

■ TREES

See also: ANCESTORS/ANCESTRY; DESCRIPTIONS, MISC.; FALL; LANDSCAPES; NATURE SCENES; SEASONS; SNOW; STREET SCENES; WINTER

1. The cedar's gothic-clustered / spires could make / green religion in winter bones —Archibald Randolph Ammons, "Gravelly Run"

    In addition to the metaphor of trees as churches, there are the implied metaphors of the color green for spring-like youth, and winter for age.

2. The eternal peepal-tree . . . Whose leaves are the hymns —Anon., *The Bhagavad Gita*, 14:

    "Who knows it, he knows the Veda," says the poet of the sacred tree.

3. It was the toothless murmuring / of ancient willows, who kept their trouble /

In a stage of music —John Ashbery, "The Mythological Poet. I"

    Music "innocent and monstrous / As the ocean's bright display of teeth" fell on the willows.

4. The trees lie tangled in each other's arms —Robert Bly, "The Puritan on His Honeymoon"

    Personification here becomes extended into a metaphor of love.

5. Now in October they [trees] had thinned into ghosts —Phyllis Bottome, "Found"

6. The shadow of the ashtree is / a fish-net —Joseph Brodsky, "Spring Season of Muddy Roads"

7. The night express . . . wound along the river shore under the long lines of shivering poplars that sentinelled the meadows —Willa Cather, "The Sculptor's Funeral," *Youth and the Bright Medusa*

    By making a verb of the noun sentinel, *Cather coins a swift metaphor.*

8. High arching boughs made a chapel — Stephen Crane, *The Red Badge of Courage*

    The tranquility of the secluded forest turns out to be an illusion when upon pushing aside "the green doors" the protagonist discovers a corpse.

9. Those sweet chestnuts . . . clothed the contours of the hills and valleys in a most pleasing way, their veil being only broken by two clearings, in one of which we were sitting —E. M. Forster, "The Story of a Panic"

10. Oaks are the true conservatives; / They hold old leaves till summer gives / A green exchange —Roy Helton, "Come Back to Earth"

11. The many dogwoods were stretching out their pretty paper hands to the sun —John Hersey, "Requiescat," *Paris Review*, No. 197, Summer 1988

12. Through the years the trees had woven a brownish-green carpet —John Hersey, "God's Typhoon," *The Atlantic*, January 1988

13. Astonished poplars hide / Their faces in leafy hands / Pale green with feigned horror —John Hollander, "Paysage Moralise"

14. We were standing where there was a fine view of the harbor and its long stretches of shore all covered by the great army of the pointed firs, darkly cloaked and standing as if they waited to embark —Sarah Orne Jewett, *The Country of the Pointed Firs*
    Although an army is usually landbound, Jewett describes a place where land and sea meet, and speaks of their "embarking." When she looks back, "the trees seemed to march seaward still."

15. [Willows] toss their palaces of tangled heads / In green felicities of trailing rooms —Joseph Langland, "Willows"

16. Bloodred and wrinkled, the new elm unleaved / in public, shuddering with the ache of its growing —Philip Levine, "Agnus Dei"

17. The trees have turned inward to become so many pages unmarked by mistakes — Philip Levine, "Burned," *What Work Is*
    What Work Is, won the 1991 National Book Award.

18. The maples of Hill Street were golden clouds —Maud Hart Lovelace , *Betsy and Tacy Go Down Town*

19. Cynric: A hemlock put out its braided foot / And trapped him —Edna St. Vincent Millay, *The King's Henchman*
    In this odd metaphor the tree is first personified, then qualified with an adjective more suited to hair than feet.

20. The trees in truth are our parents, / We sprang from the oak —Czeslaw Milosz, "Into the Tree"

21. The firs stand in a procession, each with an emerald turkey— / foot at the top — Marianne Moore, "A Grave"

22. The wind shook the heavy leaves of the chestnuts and . . . they scattered benedic-

tion on us —Sean O'Faolain, "Midsummer Night Madness"

23. The great dark cypresses in the wet failing light were plumes of billowy smoke against the sky —Sean O'Faolain, "Midsummer Night Madness"

24. The willow was winding the moon in her tresses —Dorothy Parker, "The Willow," *Death and Taxes*

25. The white flowers of the *yatsude* have vanished / And the ginko trees have turned into brooms —Kōtarō Takamura, "Winter Has Come"

26. [A couple in a canoe:] Above us was a green sky of willow trees —Arturo Vivante, "The Stream," *Stories from The New Yorker: 1950–60*

27. Their [the trees'] icy cerements . . . began to slip / . . . and made / on every twig a bauble at the tip —Richard Wilbur, "A Courtyard Thaw"

28. Gold ranks of temples flank the dazzled street —Richard Wilbur, "October Maples, Portland"

■ TRITENESS

See also: ORIGINALITY/UNORIGINALITY

1. I've heard it before. That joke has a long beard —Anon., Yiddish Proverb

2. Mr. Clinton spiced his boilerplate remarks about working closely with Congress with some pointed jabs at the Bush Administration —Thomas L. Friedman, *The New York Times,* November 17, 1992
    Friedman used a newspaper and a bosing image to spice his report on the President Elect's meeting with top legislators. Boilerplate type, while no longer used, remains a common metaphor for repetition—along with to be cut from the same cookie cutter or a Xerox copy.

3. Now we have come to the bone of contention that has been gnawed by everyone

who works in the world of words: Do we "go with the flow," as the laid-back set advises, or do we try to direct the flow? —William Safire, *On Language*

> *There are three metaphors in the single sentence. Safire gnaws at the metaphoric bone and tickles our funny bone. He encloses "go with the flow" to disassociate himself from its triteness, and breezes past laid-back.*

4. [Catching our words on the wing:] This metaphor has tired wings —William Safire, *On Language*

> *Many metaphors have become exhausted through overuse. Safire's wit expresses itself in forming a new metaphor to chide the old.*

■ TRIVIA

See: ORDINARINESS/EXTRAORDINARINESS

■ TROUBLE/TROUBLEMAKERS

See also: CAUSE AND EFFECT; CHARAC-TERIZATIONS; PERSONALITY PROFILES

1. They looked at him and saw a hand grenade with a bad hair cut —Peggy Noonan, *Forbes Magazine*, September 14, 1992

> *The former Reagan-Bush speech writer thus summed up her impression of the voters' reaction to Ross Perot's presidential aspirations.*

2. Paul's presence has thrown a monkey wrench into the works, jamming the gears and conveyors that keep New York on the go —Stephen Schiff, "Cultural Pursuits," *The New Yorker*, December 20, 1993

> *Schiff is writing about the movie version of John Guare's* Six Degrees of Separation *and Paul the impostor who upsets the lives of several New York families. The monkey wrench metaphor has been in common usage for more than fifty years.*

■ TRUSTWORTHINESS/ UNTRUSTWORTHINESS

See also: ADVICE; CHARACTER; FEAR; PER-SONALITY PROFILES

1. If Johnson were a snake, he would hide himself in the grass and bite the heels of the children of rich people —Anon.

> *This grumbling comment from a secessionist leader was typical of the feelings aroused by President Andrew Johnson's bitter denunciation of the Southern aristocrats he felt misled the masses of people. It also illustrates how a fresh context can always pump new life—or in this case, venom—into an old metaphor.*

2. If his word were a bridge, we'd be afraid to cross —Anon., Yiddish Proverb

3. Build a little fence of trust / Around today —Mary Frances Butts, "Trust"

4. I think the rest of the world will assume that you are a black sheep until you prove you are a white sheep —Ken Hughes, United Nations Conference on Regional Security. Kyoto, Japan, April 13–16, 1993

> *The Honorable Mr. Hughes addressed his remark to a delegate from the Ukraine in a working group on non-proliferation, suggesting that no one would believe in the good intentions of the Ukrainians until they began to dispose of their nuclear arsenal.*

5. The waters of trust run as deep as the river of fear / through the dark caverns in the bone —Marge Piercy, "The homely war," *Living In the Open*

6. Martius: He that depends / Upon your favours swims with fins of lead / And hews down oaks with rushes —William Shakespeare, *Coriolanus*, Act 1, scene 1, line 185

7. King: Thou that art like enough through vassal fear, / Base inclinations, and the start of spleen, / To fight against me under Percy's pay, / To dog his heels, and curtsy at his frowns —William Shakespeare, *The First Part of King Henry the Fourth*, Act 3, scene 2, line 124

> *The prince vows his loyalty, saying that he'd "die a hundred thousand deaths / Ere break the smallest parcel of this vow."*

8. When one confides greatly in you, he will feel the roots of an equal trust fastening

themselves in him —Henry David Thoreau, Letter to Ralph Waldo Emerson

9. I cannot be what before I was [if someone reposes his trust in me.] Other chains may be broken, but in the darkest night, in the remotest place, I trail this thread. —Henry David Thoreau, Letter to Ralph Waldo Emerson

   "What if God were to confide in us for a moment? Should we not then be gods?" asks Thoreau.

■ TRUTH/FALSEHOOD

See also: DESTRUCTION/DESTRUCTIVENESS; EVASIVENESS; FACTS; LIES/LIARS; MARRIAGE; PEOPLE, INTERACTION; PERSONALITY PROFILES

1. Honesty's an icicle: if it begins to melt, that's that! —Anon., American Proverb

2. Truth is a lion —Anon., Moroccan Proverb

3. Truth is an anvil that wears out countless hammers —Anon., Proverb

4. Alice [Walker] weaves her whole cloth from pieces of the truth —Elaine Brown, Op-Ed, *The New York Times*, May 5, 1993

   The former Black Panther leader felt Walker's assessment of another former Panther's book was unjust and failed to assess the whole picture. The Op-Ed exchange between Walker and Brown was headlined with an automotive metaphor: "They Ran On Empty."

5. Nor has there been agreement about the right road to truth —Isaiah Berlin, "The Apotheosis of the Romantic Will," *The Crooked Timber of Humanity*

6. This kind of omniscience was the solution of the cosmic jigsaw puzzle —Isaiah Berlin, "The Pursuit of the Ideal," *The Crooked Timber of Humanity*

   In older philosophies truth formed a single whole, and one truth was always compatible with another, according to Berlin. There was not the multiplicity of truths that exists today.

7. A lie is quick of tongue and nimble of foot, and gets a long start of the truth, but at the finish truth comes jogging in always the winner of the race —Josh Billings

8. Truth is a citizen of the world; it has no pedigree, and is the same in all languages —Josh Billings

   And while truth "can speak for itself . . . a lie must have an interpreter."

9. [Laurence Tisch as portrayed by Ken Auletta] . . . a man who shaves the truth with a meat cleaver —Bill Carter, "Books of The Times," *The New York Times*, September 24, 1991

   From a review of Three Blind Mice.

10. Truth is a good dog; but beware of barking too close to the heels of an error, let you get your brains kicked out —Samuel Taylor Coleridge, *Table Talk*

11. The greatest friend of truth is Time, her greatest enemy is Prejudice, and her constant companion is Humility —Charles Caleb Colton, *The Lacon*

12. Truth is a river that is always splitting up into arms that reunite. Islanded between the arms the inhabitants argue for a lifetime as to which is the main river —Cyril Connolly, *The Unquiet Grave*, 1945

13. Truth has rough flavors if we bite it through —George Eliot, *Armgart*, Scene 2

14. Truth is such a fly-away, such a sly-boots . . . that it's as bad to catch as light —Ralph Waldo Emerson, *Literary Ethics*

15. Sir Charles Freeman: Truth, sir, is a profound sea, and few there be that dare wade deep enough to find out the bottom on't —George Farquhar, *The Beaux' Stratagem*, Act 5, scene 1

16. For every alchemist who spent in vain his years / seeking the stone of truth, a motor-horn / Shall scare the sheep that

wander among the corn —John Gould Fletcher, "Song of the Moderns"

17. Truths are fruits which should only be plucked when quite ripe —Bernard le Bavier Fontenelle, Letter, December 24, 1761

18. Truth is a torch, but a terrific one, therefore we all try to grasp it with closed eyes, fearing to be blinded —Johann Wolfgang von Goethe, *Conversations with Eckemann*

19. Know how to play the card of truth —Baltasar Gracian, *Orácula Manual*

20. We were both crucified by the truth. —Barry Hannah, "Water Liars," *Airships*
    "We" refers to a couple who reveal their pasts to each other in a truth-telling session. The affect on the husband is illustrated with another metaphor: "I was driven wild by the bodies that had tres passed her twelve and thirteen years ago."

21. Truth is a cow which will yield such people [skeptics] no more milk, and so they are gone to milk the bull —Samuel Johnson, *Boswell's Life of Johnson*

22. Superstition, idolatry and hypocrisy, have ample wages, but truth goes a-begging —Martin Luther
    Personification serves as a metaphor.

23. The mind, like a splintered diamond, was pulverized by the hammer-blows of truth —Henry Miller, "The Creative Life"
    The metaphor encapsulates a simile.

24. We are all afraid of truth: we keep a battalion of our pet prejudices and precautions ready to throw into the argument as shock troops, rather than let our fortress of Truth be stormed —Christopher Morley, "What Men Live By"

25. Truth is a mobile army of metaphors —Friedrich Wilhelm Nietzsche

26. King: Truth shall nurse her. —William Shakespeare, *The Life of King Henry the Eighth,* Act 5, scene 5, line 24

27. Timon: for each true word, a blister! and each false / Be as a cauterizing to the root o' the tongue —William Shakespeare, *Timon of Athens,* Act 5, scene 1, line 137

28. Mowbray: Truth hath a quiet breast. —William Shakespeare, *The Tragedy of King Richard the Second,* Act 1, scene 3, line 97

29. The stream of truth flows through its channels of mistakes —Rabindranath Tagore, "Stray Birds, 243"
    Water and boat stream through Tagore's work.

30. For my part, I would like to compose music which is on the scale of man; that also is a road by which one can reach the truth —Vercors, *The Silence of the Sea*

31. When one is adult one must raise to one's lips the wine of the truth, heedless that it is not sweet like milk but draws the mouth with its strength —Dame Rebecca West, *The Return of the Soldier*

32. I started speaking quickly and gently right into his dreams, casting a fine net to trap the fish of truth in its muddy swamp —A. B. Yehoshua, *Mr. Mani*

■ TWILIGHT

See: NIGHT AND DAY

UNATTRACTIVENESS

See: CHARACTERIZATIONS

UNAWARENESS

See: AWARENESS/UNAWARENESS

UNCERTAINTY

See also: DANGER; ENDINGS; PAST; UNI-TY/DISUNITY

1. They had entered the thorny wilderness, and the golden gates of their childhood had forever closed behind them —George Eliot, *The Mill on the Floss*
   The wilderness is what we today refer to as "the real world."

2. Peter: Stand: move: as though we were living, / In this narrow shaking street / Under the eaves of seven-storeyed flames —Christopher Fry, *A Sleep of Prisoners*

3. People have come unsoldered; nothing's intact —Andrei Voznesensky, "Foggy Street"
   In the fog, the poet will plod on "stumbling, or flounder in cotton wool."

4. Duchess: Wish me good speed; / For I am going into a wilderness / Where I shall find nor path nor friendly clue / To be my guide —John Webster, *The Duchess of Malfi*, Act 1, scene 2

The Duchess, anxious about embarking on a new relationship, asks her woman attendant, Cariola, to hide herself behind a curtain.

UNCLEANLINESS

See: FASHION AND STYLE

UNDERSTANDING

See also: CHARACTERIZATIONS; COMMU-NICATION/NON-COMMUNICATION; EDUCATION AND LEARNING; GUID-ANCE/GUIDES; HUMANITY/HUMAN-KIND; KNOWLEDGE; PEOPLE, INTER-ACTION; SELF-KNOWLEDGE; SYMPATHY; THINKING/THOUGHT

1. The goals and motives that guide human action must be looked at in the light of all that we know and understand; their roots and growth, their essence, and above all their validity, must be critically examined —Isaiah Berlin, "The Pursuit of the Ideal," *The Crooked Timber of Humanity*

2. I shall light a lamp of understanding in thine heart —The Bible, *Apocrypha, 2 Esdras 14:2*

3. We have advanced to the point where we can put our hand on the hem of the curtain that separates us from an understanding of the nature of our minds —Percy W. Bridgman, The proceedings of the Ameri-

can Academy of Arts and Sciences, *Daedalus*, Winter

4. I remember distinctly the suddenness with which a key turned in a lock and I found I could read —Graham Greene, "The Lost Childhood," *Collected Essays*

5. But I, who wished to read the book of the world and the book of my own nature, did presume to despise the letters and signs. —Hermann Hesse, *Siddhartha*
   "I called the world of appearances, illusion. I called my eyes and tongue, chance," says Siddhartha of the letters and signs.

6. Gallimard: I can talk . . . and to anyone listening, it's only air—too rich a diet to be swallowed by a mundane world — David Henry Hwang, *M. Butterfly*, Act 2, scene 4

7. It's no surprise that he should play off so neatly against the children in this movie; they seem tuned in to his channels of thought —Anthony Lane, "The Current Cinema," *The New Yorker*, July 19, 1993
   Lane was writing about actor Tom Hanks in Sleepless in Seattle.

8. But if there's a key that unlocks the mystery of this strange public personality, it would probably have to be found in the autobiography that Mr. McNamara promises never to write —Herbert Mitgang, "Books of the Times," *The New York Times*, February 3, 1993
   The book being reviewed: Promise and Power *by Deborah Shapley.*

9. David Crampton: When [you] can say, 'I am eight miles north of water; I am three thoughts under love; I am ten beats past despair,' then you'll know where you are —Paul Osborne, *Morning's At Seven*, Act 3

10. Then think, my dear, that you in me do read / Of lover's ruin some sad tragedy. / I am not I; pity the tale of me —Sir Philip Sidney, "Sonnet 45," *Astrophel and Stella*

One is reminded here of Othello, who claimed that Desdemona first loved him because he told her ravishing stories of his life.

11. Queen Elizabeth: Pitchers have ears. — William Shakespeare, *The Tragedy of King Richard the Third*, Act 2, scene 4, line 37
    This still popular proverbial metaphor—usually little pitchers have big ears—*means that children understand more of what they hear than one might think. The metaphor derives from the actual resemblance of the human ear to the handle of a pitcher.*

■ UNDERSTANDING/ MISUNDERSTANDING

See also: COMMUNICATIONS/NON-COM-MUNICATION; MEN AND WOMEN; PEO-PLE, INTERACTION; STUPIDITY

1. She seemed particularly anxious that I should appreciate the man behind the tycoon in her husband, perhaps suspecting me of being one of those for whom the pedestal obscures the statue —Louis Auchincloss, "The Stoic," *Three Lives*
   The tycoon's wife bases her suspicion on the admiration many people have for a man's status rather than his true essence.

2. A window in Merton's mind let in that strange light of surprise in which we see for the first time things we have known all along —Gilbert Keith Chesterton, "The Three Tools of Death"

3. [A wall between two friends:] The stones of it are laid in scorn / And plastered high with pride —Elizabeth Reeve Morrow, "The Wall"

4. None of you knows where the shoe pinches —Lucius Aemilius Paulus, Quoted in Plutarch's *Lives*
   During the fourth century, a Roman aristocrat, criticized for having divorced his wife, held out his shoe to show that while it was indeed new and handsome only the wearer could know how it fit.

5. He had suffered the thousand irritations inseparable from a hard-working life: . . .

the endless labour of rolling human stupidity up the steep hill of understanding —Edith Wharton, *Twilight Sleep*

> Wharton alludes to the myth of Sisyphus, who was condemned to roll a stone to the top of a steep hill only to have it roll back just as it reached the summit.

6. Manford's lips narrowed in a smile; again she [his wife] had a confused sense of new deserts widening between them —Edith Wharton, *Twilight Sleep*

■ UNFAIRNESS

See: *FAIRNESS/UNFAIRNESS*

■ UNHAPPINESS

See: *DESPAIR; GLOOM; HAPPINESS/ UNHAPPINESS*

■ UNIMPORTANCE

See: *IMPORTANCE/UNIMPORTANCE*

■ UNITY/DISUNITY

See also: *CONFLICT; FATE; GOVERNMENT*

1. The nation's hoop is scattered —Black Elk, Quoted in an exhibit of American history under the great silver arches of the museum in Saint Louis.

2. We're all in the same boat —Clement I

> This now common metaphor was coined by the Bishop of Rome at a period of dissension.

3. If we do not make common cause to save the good old ship of the Union on this voyage, nobody will have a chance to pilot her on another voyage —Abraham Lincoln, Farewell Speech to the Springfield, Illinois legislature, February 15, 1861

> A contemporary politician, Governor Mario Cuomo of New York, took the metaphor for a long ride in his 1992 nominating speech for Bill Clinton: "We must demonstrate to all the American people that change for the better is at hand . . . Because the ship of state is headed for the rocks. The crew know it. The passengers know it. Only the captain of the ship, President Bush, appears not to know it. He seems to think that the ship will be saved by imperceptible undercurrents, directed by the invisible hand of some cyclical economic god, that will gradually move the ship so that at the last moment it will miraculously glide past the rocks to safer shores."

4. A house divided against itself cannot stand —Abraham Lincoln, Speech at Republican State Convention, June 16, 1858

> Lincoln underscored this with "I do not expect the house to fall—but I do expect it will cease to be divided. It will become all one thing or all the other." The metaphor has been much borrowed and paraphrased. President Lyndon B. Johnson referred to it in his resignation speech: "And in these times as in times before, it is true that a house divided against itself by the spirit of faction, of party, of region, of religion, of race, is a house that cannot stand." In a 1988 speech commemorating the 125th anniversary of the Battle of Gettysburg, astrologer Carl Sagan said "A planet divided against itself cannot stand." And in a 1991 essay on Lincoln for The New York Review of Books, Gore Vidal wrote "for better or worse, we still live in the divided house that Lincoln cobbled together for us . . . "

■ UNIVERSE

See: *WORLD*

■ UNPREDICTABILITY

See: *TROUBLE/TROUBLEMAKERS*

■ UNREALITY

See: *ILLUSION/REALITY*

■ UNREST

See: *AGITATION*

■ UNTRUSTWORTHINESS

See: *TRUSTWORTHINESS/*
UNTRUSTWORTHINESS

■ UNWIELDINESS

See: ORDER/DISORDER

■ USELESSNESS

See also: ABILITY; OPPORTUNITY; SIGNIFI-
CANCE/INSIGNIFICANCE

1. Luck without brains is a perforated sack
   —Anon., Yiddish Proverb

2. I tell you, I'm utterly incompetent. I'm the
   parasite on the British oak, like the mistle-
   toe —D. H. Lawrence, "Two Blue Birds"
   The metaphor is capped with a simile.

3. The phrase "politics of meaning" is an
   empty vessel . . . there for politicians, good
   and bad, to try to fill with content —
   James Pinkerton, *Newsday*, June 28, 1993
   This phrase attributed to Tikkun *editor Michael*
   Lerner gained currency when used by Hillary
   Rodham Clinton. To make his point that a phrase
   is just words unless and until it's backed up with
   action, the writer states that Lincoln's famous
   "mystic chords of memory" would be remembered
   as "19th-century psychobabble if the President
   had not backed up his determination to save the
   Union with the Army of the Potomac."

■ UTILIZATION

See also: BUSINESS DESCRIPTIONS

1. This is all about slicing and dicing what
   you have, packaging it and getting it into
   different forms —John Beni, Senior vice-
   president and general manager of con-
   sumer-entertainment at Cahner Publica-
   tions, quoted "Technology Opens Doors
   for Cahners Magazines, *New York Times,*
   July 19, 1993
   The slicing and dicing referred to using a maga-
   zine's editorial content for special editions, books, etc.

2. Voynitsky: Sonia and I have squeezed this
   estate dry for his sake —Anton Chekhov,
   Uncle Vanya, Act 2
   The estate is portrayed as an orange from which
   every drop of juice possible has been extracted.

3. I shall try to get the honey from each
   moment —Lucy Stone

VAGUENESS
See: CLARITY/AMBIGUITY

VALOR
See: COURAGE

VANITY
See also: PEOPLE, INTERACTION; PRIDE

1. The Baroness had poured balm on his vanity's bleeding wounds —Honoré de Balzac, *Cousin Bette*
    The balm consists of words to assuage her husband's rejection by his mistress. Even in nineteenth century Paris where many women overlooked their husbands' infidelity, this was a rare wife.

2. Vanity has a ravenous appetite and a remorseless digestion —Josh Billings
    Billings here uses a metaphor of personification.

3. The greatest magnifying glasses in the world are a man's own eyes when they look upon his own person —Alexander Pope, Letter, 1705

4. Romeo: A lover may bestride the gossamer / That idles in the wanton summer air / And yet not fall; so light is vanity —William Shakespeare, *Romeo and Juliet*, Act 2, scene 5, line 18

5. Joan: Let frantic Talbot triumph for a while, / And like a peacock sweep along his tail; / We'll pull his plumes and take away his train —William Shakespeare, *The First Part of Henry the Sixth*, Act 3, scene 3, line 7
    Talbot stripped of his vanity illustrates a metaphor built on a simile.

6. Ulysses: Among ourselves / Give him allowance as the worthier man, / For that will physic [cure] the great Myrmidon [Achilles] / Who broils in loud applause, and make him fall —William Shakespeare, *Troilus and Cressida*, Act 1, scene 3, line 376

VARIETY
See: DISSENT/DISSENTERS; MIXTURE

VERBOSITY
See: TALKATIVENESS

VICE/VIRTUE
See also: CHASTITY; GOOD/EVIL; GOODNESS; HARD-HEARTEDNESS

1. Those souls which vice's moody mists doth blind; / Blind fortune, blindly, most their friend doth prove —William Drummond, "Doth Then the World Go Thus"

The poet decries the miscarriages of justice. Those who most indulge in vice are fortunate, while those who follow virtue are distressed.

2. There seems but little soil in his heart for the support of the kindly virtues —Washington Irving, "Traits of Indian Character"
   Irving treats the heart of the Indian as a garden and virtues as plants. He then expands on the word "seems," and ascribes kindness and nobility to the "North American savage."

3. Purity is the new-fallen snow which can be melted or sullied; chastity is steel tempered in the fire by white heat. —Ellen Key, "The Morality of Women," *The Morality of Women and Other Essays*

4. One man's virtue is another man's poison —Friedrich Wilhelm Nietzsche, *Thus Spake Zarathustra*
   A more commonly used variant is one man's meat is another's poison.

5. Iago: Do but see his vice, / 'Tis to his virtue a just equinox, / The one as long as th' other. —William Shakespeare, *Othello,* Act 2, scene 3, line 116
   Iago has plied Cassio with drink and then undermines his reputation by pretending that the ancient is frequently drunk.

6. Antonio: Virtue is beauty but the beauteous evil / Are empty trunks o'erflourished by the devil. —William Shakespeare, *Twelfth Night,* Act 3, scene 4, line 377

7. With margerain (marjoram) gentle, / The flower of goodlihead, / Embroidered the mantle / Is of your maidenhead —John Skelton, "To Mistress Margery Wentworth"

8. We are double-edged blades, and every time we whet our virtue the return stroke straps our vice —Henry David Thoreau, *Walden*

■ VICTIMS

See also: ENTRAPMENT; FEAR; HELPLESSNESS

1. The boy seemed to have fallen / From shelf to shelf of someone's rage —John Ashbery, "A Boy"
   The boy struggles to understand war, and the "thunder" in man's heart.

2. I was born under a glass heel and have always lived there —Theodore Roethke, *Straw for the Fire, Notebooks of Theodore Roethke*

3. People starving and dying, caught between the jaws of opposing clans and opposing philosophies, must have a voice to demand for them the justice they cannot demand for themselves —Dorrie Weiss, Comment at The American Economics Association, January 6, 1993

4. I myself had no idea then, Grandmother, that this was but my first taste of the sweet-and-sour dish known as Fear-of the Conqueror that we've been eating ever since then until it's coming out of our ears —A. B. Yehoshua, *Mr. Mani*
   Egon, a German who has parachuted into Crete, has just taken his first prisoner.

■ VIENNA

See: CITIES

■ VIGOR

See: STRENGTH/WEAKNESS

■ VILLAINY/VILLAINS

See also: EVIL; GOOD/EVIL; HARD-HEARTEDNESS; NAME CALLING

1. Demagogues are the mobs' lackeys —Diogenes

2. Salisbury: They will guard you, whe'r you will or no, / From such fell serpents as false Suffolk is, / With whose envenomed and fatal sting, / Your loving uncle, twenty times his worth, / They say is shamefully bereft of life —William Shake-

speare, *The Second Part of Henry the Sixth,* Act 3, scene 2, line 265

3. Warwick: Pernicious blood-sucker of sleeping men! —William Shakespeare, *The Second Part of Henry the Sixth,* Act 3, scene 2, line 226

   Warwick thus bears out Salisbury's metaphoric comparison of Suffolk to a serpent with forked tongue.

4. Richard: Not contented that he lopp'd the branch / In hewing Rutland when his leaves put forth, / But set his murdering knife unto the root / From whence that tender spray did sweetly spring —William Shakespeare, *The Third Part of Henry the Sixth,* Act 2, scene 6, line 47

   Richard pictures the extent of Clifford's ruthlessness.

5. Bolingbroke: Bushy, Bagot, and their complices, / The caterpillars of the commonwealth, / Which I have sworn to weed and pluck away —William Shakespeare, *The Tragedy of King Richard the Second,* Act 2, scene 4, line 165

6. King: O villains, vipers, damn'd without redemption! / Dogs easily won to fawn an any man! —William Shakespeare, *The Tragedy of King Richard the Second,* Act 3, scene 2, line 128

   This vilification in triple metaphor later proved unjustified.

7. [Christopher] Marlowe's Jew of Malta is, by contrast to [Shakespeare's] Shylock . . . an etude in villainy —Wilfrid Sheed, "Books," *The New Yorker,* July 12, 1993

8. Shakespeare, by making Shylock a Jew, gave him, as it were, an extra coat of villainy, a coat of fresh poison —Wilfrid Sheed, "Books," *The New Yorker,* July 12, 1993

   Sheed's review of Shylock *by John Gross discussed the author's theory that most Elizabethans, including The Bard, knew few Jews, that usury was an old English craft, and that Shylock was probably originally played for laughs.*

■ VIOLENCE

See also: WAR

1. We must choose where to intervene [between warring states], and there are several factors in the choice. The CNN factor is one; another is that, if my ox is being gored, I would argue that it is more likely that I would make a move —Donald C. F. Daniel, "New Realities: Disarmament, Peacebuilding, and Global Security," NGO Committee on Disarmament Conference at the United Nations, April 20–23, 1993

   Mr. Daniel, from the U.S. Naval War College, used a common metaphor to indicate that a protective interest in one's property is a strong motivating force.

2. The blow he would strike me with his fist, right in the mouth, would make my ears ring with this oboe murmur: "My vulgarity is regal, and it accords me every right" —Jean Genet, *Querelle*

   The violence of the musing is in strong contrast to the musicality of the metaphor.

■ VISIBILITY/INVISIBILITY

See also: BELONGING/OUTCAST; DISAPPEARANCE; ILLUSION/REALITY; PHYSICAL APPEARANCE; PROMINENCE/PERIPHERY; REVELATION; SELF IMAGES

1. I am not revealed to every one, / Being veiled by My magic trick-of-illusion — Anon., *The Bhagavad Gita,* 8:25

   Krishna has revealed himself to Arjuna in the god's human form.

2. Senator Orrin G. Hatch worked on behalf of B.C.C.I. behind the scenes —Anon., "Business Digest," *New York Times,* August 26, 1992

   Stage metaphors extend to comedy, tragedy, and sometimes farce, or politics-as-theater.

3. I myself shall continue living in my glass house . . . where I sleep nights in a glass bed, under glass sheets, where *who I am*

will sooner or later appear etched by a diamond —André Breton, *Nadja*

4. I have often viewed . . . your shining qualities confined to a sphere where they can never reach the eyes of those who would introduce them properly into the world, and raise you to an eminence where you may blaze out to the admiration of all men —Henry Fielding, *The Life of Mr. Jonathan Wild the Great,* 1743

    The modern form of this metaphor describes someone as a rising star.

5. He had managed to paint himself out of the picture —John LeCarré, *The Russia House*

6. Her face was drowned in the shadow of an ugly rolled-brim brown felt hat —Paule Marshall, "To Da-Duh, In Memorium"

7. Though we have long been concerned about the dangers of proliferation, we now live in an environment in which rivalries which had been suppressed, contained or in some cases merely masked by the frozen surface of the Cold War landscape, are now re-appearing around the globe —Peggy Mason, "Non-Proliferation Through Effective International Control: Prospects for a CTB." United Nations Conference on Regional Security. Kyoto, Japan, April 13-16, 1993

    The Canadian Ambassador for Disarmament is concerned about the effect that regional conflict will have on nuclear proliferation.

8. Imogen: I would have broke mine eye-strings, crack'd them, but / To look upon him . . . till he had melted from / The smallness of a gnat to air. —William Shakespeare, *Cymbeline,* Act 1, scene 3, line 20

    Imogen tells Pisanio she would have strained her eyesight to the limits to catch a final glimpse of Posthumus's ship fading from sight.

■ VISION

1. Bernadette / Who saw Our Lady standing in the cave / At Massabielle, saw her so squarely that / Her vision put out reason's eyes —Robert Lowell, "As a Plane Tree By the Water"

2. Stern men with empires in their brains —Theodore Roosevelt, "The Strenuous Life"

    These are the men who do not fear the strenuous life, and who will see the nation "undertake its new duties."

■ VIVACIOUSNESS

See: ANIMATION

■ VOICES

1. Voices thinning to the sound of a thumb drawn across a wet window; an insect squeak —Margaret Atwood, "Betty," *Dancing Girls and Other Stories*

2. Blessed be the fruit, Janine, Aunt Lydia would have said . . . May the Lord open, Janine would have replied, tonelessly, in her transparent voice, her voice of raw egg white —Margaret Atwood, *The Handmaid's Tale*

3. His [Alexander Woollcott's] voice was now pure caramel where on occasion it had been a caramel dipped in vinegar —John Mason Brown, Introduction, *The Portable Woollcott*

4. The voice was full of honey —Raymond Chandler, "Red Wind," *The Simple Art of Murder*

5. Our voices, the endless ball of yarn that is our talk, crack with age —Jose Donoso, *The Obscene Bird of Night*

6. These grumblings are only the thread their voices are rolling into a ball that never grows, because it's only another version of silence —Jose Donoso, *The Obscene Bird of Night*

7. Her voice is full of money —F. Scott Fitzgerald, *The Great Gatsby*

8. Merlin: A British voice. / It breaks a fast of years; I roll you / Wonderfully on my tongue —Christopher Fry, *Thor, With Angels*

9. What largely makes up for the death of entertainment values in Ms. Houston's [Whitney] shows is a voice made of steel and smoke that can send chills through an audience —Stephen Holden, "Review/Pop," *The New York Times*, July 22, 1993
   Later in the review, the writer spoke about the "shivery melismas" and "twirling embellishments" that infused her interpretations with flashes of "emotional lightning."

10. His voice is a modulated honk —Arthur Lubow, *The New Yorker*, September 20, 1993
    Lubow's subject was the director George Wolfe.

11. She had a voice silky with deceit. —Alice Munro, "Differently," *Friend of Youth*
    The voice evokes the memory of betrayal.

12. In the streets there was noise: / The voices of children tangling. —Chuya Nakahara, "The Hour of Death"

13. Baker's [Oregon's Senator Edward Dickinson] silver-bell voice rang out —Carl Sandburg, *Abraham Lincoln, The War Years, Vol. One*
    At another point in his biography, Sandburg describes a Civil War Generals as having a "trumpet voice."

14. The human voice is nothing but flogged air —Seneca

15. In the wind, the voices / Have shapes that are not yet fully themselves, / Are sounds blown by a blower into shapes, / The blower squeezed to the thinnest *mi* of falsetto —Wallace Stevens, "Parochial Theme"

16. "Whoa there, my beauties!" cried grandpa. His voice sounded very young and loud, and his tongue had powerful hooves, and he made his bedroom into a great meadow —Dylan Thomas, "A Visit to Grandpa's"
    Grandpa is mad about horses, and at night the boy hears the old man shouting horsey commands and "trotting his tongue on the roof of his mouth."

17. Her voice was faraway music —James Thurber, *The Thirteen Clocks*

■ VULNERABILITY

See also: HEART; INSULTS

1. There are strings . . . in the human heart that had better not be vibrated —Charles Dickens, *Barnaby Rudge*

2. The missile carrying submarine . . . is a vulnerable Goliath carrying far too many eggs in one fragile basket —Freeman Dyson, *Weapons and Hope*

3. His smile was probably assumed in order to hide the weak spot in his armor which my understanding had chanced upon —Mishima Yukio, "Omi"
   Undermining someone's defenses is sometimes called "finding the chink in his armor."

4. Stick a fork in him and he's done —Governor Ann Richards, Quoted on television news broadcast, the day after the first televised Presidential debates, October 12, 1992
   The Texas governor who ridiculed President George Bush for being "born with a silver spoon in his mouth" during the 1988 Democratic Convention, once again made the President the foil for her incisive wit.

5. Apostrophes has always been my Achilles' heel —William Safire, *On Language*
   The mythologically inclined will remember that the nymph who was the mother of Achilles dipped the baby into the river Styx to make him invulnerable, but held him by the heel, which was the only place Achilles could be attacked.

6. Malcolm: Macbeth / Is ripe for shaking —William Shakespeare, *Macbeth,* Act 4, scene 3, line 237

7. Iago: But I will wear my heart upon my sleeve, / For doves to peck at: I am not what I am —William Shakespeare, *Othello,* Act 1, scene 1, line 29

Many texts render this as "for daws to peck at."

8. Senator: for, I do fear, / When every feather sticks in his own wing, / Lord Timon will be left a naked gull, / Which flashes now a phoenix —William Shakespeare, *Timon of Athens,* Act 2, scene 1, line 30

■ WANDERLUST

See: RESTLESSNESS

■ WAR

*See also: BELIEFS; HONOR; PROBLEMS AND
SOLUTIONS; REVENGE/VENGEANCE;
VICTIMS*

1. Let us not be deceived—we are today in
   the midst of a cold war —Bernard M.
   Baruch, Speech, April 16, 1947
   *According to William Safire, credit for this much-
   quoted metaphor really belongs to Baruch's ghost
   writer, Herbert Bayard Swope, a newspaper editor.*

2. Meanwhile, the Luftwaffe, flying very low,
   was bombing and burning Warsaw in a
   wheel of fire; we, in the Old Town, were
   the hub of that wheel —Louis Begley,
   Wartime Lies

3. For a Tear is an Intellectual Thing, / And
   a Sigh is the Sword of an Angel King, /
   And the Bitter Groan of the Martyr's woe
   / Is an Arrow from the Almightie's Bow
   —William Blake, "The Grey Monk"
   *The monk says that arms can never work War's
   overthrow: only a hermit's prayer and a widow's
   tear can free the world from fear.*

4. O war is a casual mistress / And the
   world is her double bed —Charles Causley,
   "A Ballad for Katherine of Aragon"

5. In wartime, truth is so precious that she
   should always be attended by a body-
   guard of lies —Winston Churchill
   *The editors came across the metaphor as the title
   of a book by Anthony Cave Brown:* Bodyguard
   of Lies *(Quill / Morrow, 1975).*

6. War, he sung, is Toil and Trouble; /
   Honour but an empty Bubble —John
   Dryden, "Alexander's Feast; or, the Pow-
   er of Musique. An Ode, In Honour of St.
   Cecilia's Day"
   *The lines echo the chant of the three witches, the
   Weird Sisters in Shakespeare's* Macbeth, *which
   appeared in the First Folio in 1623.*

7. For him the war was a disgusting disease
   which the people's body must overcome
   —Ilya Ehrenburg, *The Storm*

8. Demokos: War must be tired of the mask
   we always give it, of Medusa's venomous
   hair and a Gorgon's lips —Jean Giraudoux,
   Tiger at the Gates, Act 2
   *The Gorgon Medusa, with her hair made of
   writhing snakes, turned to stone whoever looked
   at her. That was the mask given to war.*

9. War . . . death's feast —George Herbert,
   Outlandish Proverbs

10. Military glory—that attractive rainbow
    that rises in showers of blood —Abraham
    Lincoln, Speech against the war with Mexi-
    co to the House of Representatives, Janu-
    ary 12, 1848

11. Wars / flicker, earth licks its open sores, / fresh breakage, fresh promotions, chance / assassinations, no advance —Robert Lowell, "Waking Early Sunday Morning"

 There has been little progress in the history of morality.

12. Global war has become a Frankenstein's monster, threatening to destroy both sides —Douglas MacArthur, Speech, July 5, 1961

 The General moved from a metaphor of allusion to a science metaphor: "It contains now only the germs of a double suicide."

13. The tanks . . . stabbed the gray desert sky with their antennas —Amos Oz, *The Hill of Evil Counsel*

14. Cutting the unnerving wall of fog into waves of color more than ten Turkish galleys were upon us at once —Orhan Pamuk, *The White Castle*

15. The war in ex-Yugoslavia is without exaggeration a throbbing wound on the CSCE body —Bo Petersson, Paper: "Expansion of Political Dialogue and Building Confidence Through Regional Organization: The CSCE Experience," April 13–16, 1993. United Nations Conference on Regional Security. Kyoto, Japan

 CSCE is The Conference of Security and Cooperation in Europe.

16. When war is declared, Truth is the first casualty —Arthur Ponsonby, *Falsehood in Wartime*

17. To me the front is a mysterious whirlpool —Erich Maria Remarque, *All Quiet on the Western Front*

 The image is from a famous World War I novel. "Though I am in still water far away from its centre, I feel the whirl of the vortex sucking me slowly, irresistibly, inescapably into itself," the author writes.

18. War is a contagion —Franklin Delano Roosevelt, Speech, October 5, 1937

19. Whether all five had died on the field of battle, or only two, four of her sons had been poured away into the river of war — Carl Sandburg, Quoted in afterword to Abraham Lincoln's letter to a bereaved mother.

 Sandburg's comment pointed out that though Lincoln's compassionate letter was based on the misapprehension that a woman had lost all five of her sons, it was valid in its intent.

20. Aufidius: We must muster all / From twelve to seventy, and pouring war / Into the bowels of ungrateful Rome, / Like a bold flood o'er-bear —William Shakespeare, *Coriolanus*, Act 4, scene 5, line 134

21. King: Will you again unknit / This churlish knot of all-abhorred war —William Shakespeare, *The First Part of King Henry the Fourth*, Act 5, scene 1, line 15

22. Othello: The tyrant custom . . . / Hath made the flinty and steel couch of war / My thrice-driven bed of down —William Shakespeare, *Othello*, Act 1, scene 3, line 229

 The down was "thrice driven" because the softest and lightest down was blown away to separate it from the coarser material.

23. Young Clifford: O war! thou son of hell, / Whom angry heavens do make their minister, / Throw in the frozen bosoms of our part / Hot coals of vengeance! —William Shakespeare, *The Second Part of Henry the Sixth*, Act 5, scene 2, line 33

24. Aubrey: The iron lightning of war has burnt great rents in these angelic veils [of idealism] . . . our souls go in rags now; and the young are spying through the holes and getting glimpses of the reality that was hidden —George Bernard Shaw, *Too Good to Be True*, Act 3

 Shaw extends the sewing image with "when we their elders desperately try to patch our torn clothes with scraps of old material, the young lay violent hands on us and tear from us even the rags that were left to us.

25. She [St. Joan] won the memorable victory of Patay against Talbot, "the English lion," and broke the back of the Hundred Year's War —Mark Twain, "Saint Joan of Arc"

The second metaphor continues the beast imagery of the first.

26. I, Private Egon Bruner, had arrived all by myself, the first German arrow to be shot from that great bow [the bow of the Führer], a one-man conqueror in the night —A. B. Yehoshua, *Mr. Mani*

■ WARNINGS

1. The official press asserted today that the region would be "a graveyard for the fleeing invaders" —Anon., *New York Times,* August 26, 1992

2. Life is shrunk, / dead and interred; yet all these seem to laugh / Compared to me, who am their epitaph —John Donne, "A Nocturnal upon Saint Lucy's Day"

> *On the shortest day of the year, when the world seems dead, the poet feels that he, himself, is dead. He warns all lovers to take advantage of their "summer."*

3. Woe to him who seeks to pour oil upon the waters when God has brewed them into a gale! —Herman Melville, *Moby Dick*

4. Lear: The bow is bent and drawn, make from the shaft —William Shakespeare, *King Lear,* Act 1, scene 1, line 1440

> *Lear warns the saddened Kent, who replies, "Let it fall rather, though the fork invade the region of my heart . . . "*

■ WARRIORS AND PEACEMAKERS

See also: CHARACTERISTICS; PEACE

1. And we in us find the eagle and the dove —John Donne, "The Canonization"

2. Bill Clinton . . . is trying to replace the old hawk-dove divide by exploring new standards for U.S. military intervention — Leslie H. Gelb, "Foreign Affairs," *The New York Times,* October 8, 199.

Hawk-dove metaphors crop up in political reportage as regularly as street vendors in July. Just five months after the above metaphor appeared, a The New York Times *article on the Israeli elections was headlined "An Israeli Hawk [Ezer Weizman] Turned Dove is Elected President."*

3. Napoleon was the red and fiery comet, shooting wildly through the realms of space and scattering pestilence and terror . . . Lafayette was the pure and brilliant planet, beneath whose grateful beams the mariner directs his bark and the shepherd tends his flocks —Sargent S. Prentiss, Speech on the death of Lafayette, August 1835

4. Bolingbroke: Be he the fire, I'll be the yielding water; / The rage be his, whilst on the earth I rain / My waters—on the earth, and not on him —William Shakespeare, *The Tragedy of King Richard the Second,* Act 3, scene 3, line 58

> *If you read the line ending with "rain" as though it were end-stopped rather than run-on, it foreshadows Bolingbroke's "reign."*

■ WASHINGTON, D.C.

See: CITIES

■ WASTEFULNESS

See also: FOOLHARDINESS

1. Give not that which is holy unto the dogs, neither cast your pearls before swine, lest haply they trample them under their feet, and turn and rend you —The Bible, *N.T.,* Matthew 10:16

> *This may be a warning against giving gifts to unappreciative people who may turn those gifts against you. In* A Streetcar Named Desire, *for example, the hapless Blanche bewails the fact that she has wasted her personal assets on boorish men: "But I have been foolish—casting my pearls before swine!" Dorothy Parker, known for her acerbic wit, cast it as a* bon mot *as she swept past Clare Booth Luce who had sarcastically offered to let her precede her into a room with "Age before beauty!"*

2. Spill not the morning —Thomas Fuller, *The Holy State: Of Recreations*
   > *The metaphor is implied, as if the morning were a bottle of wine to be drunk or wasted.*

3. My candle burns at both its ends; / It will not last the night —Edna St. Vincent Millay, "Figs"
   > *As an everyday expression for the dissipation of one's energies,* to burn one's candle at both ends *has been in general use since the seventeenth century.*

■ WATCHFULNESS

See also: CHARACTERIZATIONS

1. I had seen Jeff York a thousand times or near, standing like that on the street corner in town while people flowed past him, under the distant and wary and dispassionate eyes in ambush —Robert Penn Warren, "The Patented Gate and the Mean Hamburger," 1947

2. She sat with her back to the books and facing the stairs, her dragon eye on the front door —Eudora Welty, *One Writer's Beginnings*
   > *"I never knew anyone who's grown up in Jackson without being afraid of Mrs. Calloway, our librarian" writes Welty.*

■ WATER

See: SEA; SEASCAPES

■ WEAKNESS

See: STRENGTH/WEAKNESS

■ WEALTH

See: RICHES

■ WEARINESS

1. A little sunburnt by the glare of life —Elizabeth Barrett Browning, "Aurora Leigh"

2. I'm feeling wrung out hard and hung up wet —Katie Couric, Interview, *The New York Times*, April 9, 1992
   > *The co-anchor of the NBC's* Today *show thus referred to her hectic schedule.*

3. You behold a range of exhausted volcanoes. Not a flame flickers on a single pallid crest —Benjamin Disraeli, Speech, April 3, 1872

4. By the time I got to him . . . the treads were worn off his tires. —John Hersey, "Requiescat," *Paris Review*, No. 197, Summer 1988
   > *A widow reflects on her marriage to a man who had been through many relationships and career upheavals.*

5. My head is a squeezed rag, so don't expect *le mot juste* in this letter —Ezra Pound, Letter to James Joyce, 1915

6. I have wooden hinges around my eyelids —Irwin Shaw, "Main Currents of American Thought"
   > *Faced with a morning meeting this sleepy character exclaims "Dig me out of the arms of sleep."*

■ WEATHER

See: CLOUDS; FOG; HEAT; RAIN; SEASONS; SNOW; STORMS; SUMMER; THUNDER AND LIGHTNING; WINTER

■ WHISKERS

See: FACIAL HAIR

■ THE WHITE HOUSE

See: ISOLATION; POLITICS/POLITICIANS

■ WICKEDNESS

See: EVIL

WILINESS

See: CRAFTINESS

WIND

See also: EVENING; FALL; LANDSCAPES; NATURE SCENES; NIGHT AND DAY; STORMS; WINTER

1. The galloping / Wind balks at its shadow —John Ashbery, "Pyrography"

2. The river breeze— / Out in a thin russet kimono / On a summer evening —Basho, Quoted in Yasunari Kawabata's *Beauty and Sadness*
    Personification cloaks itself in a butterfly kimono in this seventeenth-century haiku.

3. What if a keen of a lean wind flays / screaming hills with sleet and snow: / and strangles valleys by ropes of thing —e. e. cummings, "What if a Much of a Which of a Wind"

4. Come see the north wind's masonry — Ralph Waldo Emerson, "The Snow-Storm"

5. I was now standing up and watching a catspaw of wind that was running down one of the ridges, turning the light green to dark as it travelled —E. M. Forster, "The Story of a Panic"
    The more common metaphor would have been a finger of wind. The metaphor has been frozen into the language as a nautical term for a vagrant wind.

6. The North Wind, footman of the mansion of All Outdoors —O. Henry, "The Cop and the Anthem"

7. The wind was snarling in from the northeast with its teeth bared, chewing the tops off eight-foot seas —John Hersey, "The Captain," *The Yacht*

8. The wind [in autumn] has a rough manliness in its voice,—not the tone of a lover, but of a husband —Henry Wadsworth Longfellow, Journal entry
    This use of personification as metaphor is one of many journal entries reflecting Longfellow's love of seasonal changes

9. The snake-tailed sea-winds coughed and howled / For alms outside the church whose double locks / Wait for St. Peter —Robert Lowell, "New Year's Day"

10. The wind's wings beat upon the stones, / Cousin, and scream for you and the claws rush / At the sea's throat and wring it — Robert Lowell, "The Quaker Graveyard in Nantucket"

11. An outlaw wind frightened the gulls and made away with the last leaves —Gabriel García Márquez, "Bon Voyage, Mr. President," *The New Yorker,* September 13, 1993

12. A wintry knife thrust caught them unprotected in the middle of the street —Gabriel García Márquez, "Bon Voyage, Mr. President," *The New Yorker,* September 13, 1993

13. Aethelwold: Would I could put an arrow in the heart of the wind, / And bring his beating feathers down! —Edna St. Vincent Millay, *The King's Henchman,* Act 3
    The wind is often described as "beating" at something. Here, Millay makes the wind a bird to be hunted and quelled.

14. Winds are the spirit of the sky's ocean — Guy Murchie, *Song of the Sky*

15. The wind's still there that I remember afire / In the manes of the racing horses —Salvatore Quasimodo, "The Agrigentum Road"
    The wind "erodes the hearts / Of downed columnar statues in the grass."

16. Where were the greenhouses going, / Lunging into the lashing / Wind — Theodore Roethke, "Big Win"
    "That old rose-house, she hove into the teeth of it . . . carrying her full cargo of roses," concludes the poem which is an extended metaphor of the greenhouse as a ship in heavy seas.

17. Then the chilly chills came whistling with icy mittens —Carl Sandburg, "How The Animals Lost Their Tails and Got Them Back Traveling from Philadelphia to Medicine Hat," *Rootabaga Stories*

18. In the old apple orchard / where the wind swept by counting its money and throwing it away —Carl Sandburg, "Wind Song"

    The leaves of the trees—fingered, then scattered and blown away by the wind—are the wind's "money."

19. In my garden goes a fiend / Dark and wild, whose name is Wind —Geoffrey Scott, Speech, House of Commons, October 8, 1940

20. Lorenzo: The moon shines bright in such a night as this, / When the sweet wind did gently kiss the trees —William Shakespeare, *The Merchant of Venice*, Act 5, scene 1, line 1

    The metaphor personifies the wind as a lover.

21. O wild West Wind, thou breath of Autumn's being —Percy Bysshe Shelley, "Ode to the West Wind"

22. As night closed in the wind bore down on the [war prisoner] camp and fastened its million claws into every crevice . . . hollowing out all secret places, overturning the little tables of incomplete justice —Keith Vaughan, October 11, 1944 Diary entry

23. A word sticks in the wind's throat —Richard Wilbur, "Apology"

■ WINNING/LOSING

See also: DEFEAT; FIGHTING; LIFE AND DEATH; POLITICS/POLITICIANS; STRATEGIES; WARRIORS AND PEACE-MAKERS

1. I send you a kaffis of mustard seed, that you may taste and acknowledge the bitterness of my victory —Alexander the Great, Letter to King Darius III

2. I don't want to sell the bearskin before I kill the bear . . . but, put it this way, we can take a deposit on the bearskin —Anon., used by former Vietnamese-installed Prime Minister Hun Sen in "Cambodia Voting Seems to Lure Hard-Line Rebels," *New York Times*, May 25, 1993

    Sen drew on this aphorism to predict a large victory for the ruling party to win in UN supervised, democratic elections

3. Victory finds a hundred fathers but defeat is an orphan —Count Galeazzo Ciano

4. [Treasury Secretary Richard] Darman was . . . seriously disloyal to a President on the rope —Elizabeth Drew, "End Game," *The New Yorker,* November 2, 1992

    Drew, after citing the abundance of sports metaphors surrounding the 1992 Presidential campaign's final debate, herself pulled out a long-standing favorite. When Franklin D. Roosevelt mounted his challenge against the incumbent President, H. L. Mencken wrote "He has Hoover on the ropes, and is still punching hard." (The Baltimore Evening Sun, October 26, 1932).

5. Everything in the way of office goes west. We shall hardly get the parings of a toenail —William Fessendon, Letter, 1861

    The Senator from Maine was unhappy about job appointments during the early part of the Lincoln administration.

6. But the Republicans do not plan to cede the stage to Mr. Clinton so easily —Gwen Ifill, *The New York Times*, January 31, 1993

    Ms. Ifill later continued the theater imagery with "It is important to Mr. Clinton that he snatch the spotlight back."

7. Warwick: And by my fall, the conquest to my foe, / Thus yields the cedar to the axe's edge —William Shakespeare, *The Third Part of Henry the Sixth*, Act 5, scene 1, line 11

    Warwick likens his dying to that of a cut-down tree.

8. Win or lose, George Bush finished on his feet today, throwing roundhouses —source unknown

    This is a boxing metaphor for a fighter throwing wild punches.

9. But I do not want to see the Republican party ride to political victory on the Four Horsemen of Calumny—fear, ignorance, bigotry, and smear —Margaret Chase Smith, "Declaration of Conscience" Speech, June 1, 1950

> *The Republican senator from Maine thus disassociated herself and a group of others from the extreme anti-communist tactics of Senator Joseph McCarthy. Her metaphor alluded to the biblical Horsemen of the Apocalypse representing death, bloodshed and Hell (Revelations, 6:2–8).*

10. If this is a dream, then the Pittsfield players aren't interested in waking up —Brian Sullivan, *The Berkshire Eagle*, June 6, 1993

> *The ball team was having a winning streak.*

■ WINTER

See also: NATURE SCENES; SEASONS; STORMS; TREES; WEATHER

1. Often you must have seen them / [birch trees] loaded with ice . . . shattering . . . / Such heaps of broken glass to sweep away / You'd think the inner dome of heaven had fallen —Robert Frost, "Birches"

2. Merlin: This wide harp of winter / Reverberates —Christopher Fry, *Thor, With Angels*

> *"I bless you from the bottom of my slowly budding grave," says Merlin to the Briton who has just made winter more bearable by speaking to Merlin in his native tongue.*

3. Bent into grotesque shapes and statuary by their burden of ice, the trees have become a gallery of crystaline sculptures . . . Rocks are encased in smooth helmets of ice, leaving them translucent crystal balls, sooth-sayers of the icy future — Harry Middleton, "Portraits in Winter Light," *Wilderness*, Winter 1992

4. Our vernal wisdom moves from ripe to sere —Theodore Roethke, "Slow Season,"

> *"The blood flows trance-like in the altered vein," writes Roethke as he pictures the slowing and thickening that accompanies winter's approach.*

5. Icicles filled the window / With barbaric glass —Wallace Stevens, "Thirteen Ways of Looking at a Blackbird"

6. When the storms of February had pitched their white tents about the devoted village, and the wild cavalry of March winds had charged down to their support; I began to understand why Starkfield emerged from its six months' siege like a starved garrison capitulating without quarter —Edith Wharton, *Ethan Frome*

7. The fierce frost / Interns poor fish, ranks trees in an armed host, / hangs daggers from house eaves —Andrew Young, "Hard Frost"

> *There are three metaphors here: the frozen pond as a prison, the trees as an armed force, and the icicles as daggers.*

■ WISDOM

See also: ADVICE; CHARACTERIZATIONS; EDUCATION AND LEARNING; GUIDANCE/GUIDES; KNOWLEDGE

1. Expound further; for satiety / Comes not to me as I listen to Thy nectar —Anon., *The Bhagavad Gita*, 10:18

> *In Greek mythology, nectar is the drink of the gods. Here, Arjuna uses it to denote the wisdom that comes from the Blessed One's mouth. He is drinking that wisdom.*

2. Wisdom travels by oxcart —Anon., Yiddish Proverb

3. The road of excess leads to the palace of wisdom —William Blake, "Proverbs of Hell"

> *This is the route of every Prodigal Son.*

4. Wilson apparently had now climbed a peak of wisdom from which he could perceive himself as a wee thing —Stephen Crane, *The Red Badge of Courage*

> *In climbing this "peak" a loud young braggart becomes aware of his humble place in the larger scheme of things and yields himself to the larger*

purpose of leading his regiment in a charge against the enemy.''

5. The doors of wisdom are never shut — Benjamin Franklin, *Poor Richard's Almanack*

6. Wisdom is the oil of love, and love is the oil of the lamp —Count Maurice Maeterlinck, *Wisdom and Destiny,* c. 1903

7. Count La Ruse: To be wise . . . when you come to the shade, as you will, do not disparage it because you have seen the sun: there may be wonders in the darkness —Edwin Justus Mayer, *Children of Darkness,* Act 3

8. Wisdom never kicks at the iron walls it can't bring down —Olive Schreiner, *The Story of an African Farm*

9. Ulysses: The amity that wisdom knits not, folly may easily untie —William Shakespeare, *Troilus and Cressida,* Act 2, scene 3, line 102

10. Your wisdom's golden mine / Dig deep with learning's spade —Sir Philip Sidney, "Sonnet 21," *Astrophel and Stella*

■ WISHES

See: DESIRE; YEARNING

■ WIT

See also: CONVERSATION; INTELLIGENCE; WORDS

1. Wit is educated insolence —Aristotle, *Rhetoric,* II

2. She threw away wicked lines before I could catch them —John Malcolm Brinnin, Journal entry, September, 1950

   The sharp-witted lady was the woman thought to be Gertrude Stein's supernumerary, Alice B. Toklas. Brinnin discovered that she was not only witty but that her judgments "sizzled like acid on a grill."

3. Bon mots, persiflage, and repartee fly upon the air—the jewels of thought and conversation —O. Henry, "Tracked to Doom"

4. Wit's an unruly engine, wildly striking, sometimes a friend, sometimes the engineer —George Herbert, "The Temple"

5. When Bruce M. Selya became a judge . . . he vowed that he would forge at his judicial smithy a gleaming alloy of wit and erudition rather than the leaded dross pounded out on lesser legal anvils —David Margolick, "At the Bar," *The New York Times,* March 27, 1992

   Margolick's column profiled a judge known for his penchant for word play.

6. Rosalind: Make the doors upon a woman's wit, and it will out at the casement; shut that, and 'twill out at the keyhole; stop that, 'twill fly with the smoke out at the chimney —William Shakespeare, *As You Like It,* Act 4, scene 1, line 159

   Shakespeare's witty women often run metaphoric circles around the men.

7. Mercutio: Thy wit . . . it is a most sharp sauce —William Shakespeare, *Romeo and Juliet,* Act 2, scene 3, line 85

8. Sebastian: He's winding up the watch of his wit —William Shakespeare, *The Tempest,* Act 2, scene 1, line 12

9. Silvia: A fine volley of words, gentlemen, and quickly shot off —William Shakespeare, *Two Gentlemen of Verona,* Act 2, scene 4, line 33

10. Valentine: you have an exchequer of words and, I think, no other treasures to give your followers; for it appears by their bare liveries that they live by your bare words —William Shakespeare, *Two Gentlemen of Verona,* Act 2, scene 4, line 44

    Valentine thus responds to Thurio's "If you spend word for word with me, I shall make your wit bankrupt."

■ WOE

See: GRIEF

■ WOMEN

See also: FAMILIES/FAMILY RELATION-SHIPS; MEN AND WOMEN

1. A woman is a bountiful table that one sees with different eyes before and after the meal —Anon., French Proverb

   The more common way of saying this is the way to a man's heart is through his stomach. Today's woman, however, is apt to spend more time at the computer than the stove.

2. The daughter came for her father's birthday, and in the way of women, soothed and stitched and patched over the hurt feelings —Julia Alvarez, *How the Garcia Girls Lost Their Accents*

3. Astrov: Beautiful, sleek tigress, you must have your victims —Anton Chekhov, *Uncle Vanya,* Act 3

   The man is the wooer here, but he acts as though the predator is the woman who attracts him.

4. Granger: But what is a woman?—Only one of Nature's agreeable blunders — Hannah Cowley, *Who's the Dupe,* Act 2, scene 1

5. To prove our femininity and avoid the slings and arrows of antifeminism, we have learned to assure the world that while we may have more mastery of our lives, we've balanced it with more misery — Susan Faludi, *The New York Times,* December 20, 1993

   It was outrageous fortune whose slings and arrows Hamlet suffered (and Ms. Faludi Danes to borrow).

6. Our contemporary literature is drowning in women's menses —Gustave Flaubert, Letter to Louise Colet

   Flaubert often seemed to be drowning in a sea of confusing attitudes toward women.

7. You ought to remember that the woman is the weaker vessel.—Hang her, let her carry less sail, then! —Sarah Orne Jewett, ''The Courting of Sister Wisby''

   An old metaphor is given a neat twist!

8. Woman would leaven the male mass by her presence —George Meredith, *The Ordeal of Richard Feverel*

   Woman, to Meredith, was yeast to the heavy dough of masculinity.

9. The fact of woman / is ''not the sound of the flute / but very poison'' —Marianne Moore, ''Marriage''

   Adam feels that ''a wife is a coffin'' as he fearfully contemplates the first liaison with the first woman.

10. A woman is not a pear tree / thrusting her fruit in mindless fecundity into the world —Marge Piercy, ''Right to life,'' *The Moon Is Always Female*

    The poet makes her point with many other striking metaphors; for example: ''A woman is . . . / Not a bank where your genes gather interest'' and ''You may not use me as your factory.''

11. Women and God . . . the two rocks on which a man must either anchor or be wrecked. —Frederick William Robertson, Sermon

12. Le Bret: Who and what is this woman? Cyrano: Nature's own snare to allure manhood. A white rose wherein / Love lies in ambush for his natural prey —Edmond Rostand, *Cyrano de Bergerac,* Act 1

13. You can't have scholars and saints so long as your mothers are ground to powder between the upper and nether millstone of tyranny and lust —Elizabeth Cady Stanton, Keynote address, First Woman's Rights Convention, July 19, 1848

■ WORDINESS

See: LANGUAGE; TALKATIVENESS

■ WORDPLAY/WORD-WATCHING

1. To increase your enjoyment of this book I've cooked up a dessert to top off the main menu, a rhymed review. While hardly a Michelin guide of prosody, it should nourish your powers of precision. And so, *bon appétit . . .* or, to be more precise, *bon mot* —Elyse Sommer, Introduction, *The Words You Confuse*

    The "main course" defined often confused groups of words. The "dessert" featured several metaphors, including this metaphoric fill-in rhyme: (kudos) butters your ego, / Not your bread. It's (lucre) you need to stay out of debt.

2. As a weekday political columnist and the Sunday constable of the word police, he has the awesome power to insinuate into the language the very words and phrases he now seeks to immortalize in his chewy dictionary —Martin Walker, *The New York Times Book Review*, October 31, 1993

    The review of Safire's New Political Dictionary, *ended with this refrain of the second metaphor: "Still, wild horses would not drag this chewy tome from my reference shelf."*

■ WORDS

1. Words corral ideas . . . they paint watercolors of perception —Diane Ackerman, *A Natural History of the Senses*

    You might say that the author has corralled two metaphors.

2. Words are the physicians of the mind diseased —Aeschylus, "Suppliants"

3. I am amazed that even the most skillful sorcery of words could make you pay the least attention to such barbarous inhumanity —Agrippina, Letter to her son, the Emperor Nero

    Nero's mistress influenced the emperor to bring false charges against his mother. The letter did not help. He had his mother strangled.

4. Words are a ruin / no animal's heed, so kiss / me to silence —Phillip Booth, "The Wilding"

    Mute love is more akin to nature's ways than spoken love.

5. The epidemic sickening of the word in our time, by which every word is at once covered with the leprosy of routine and changed into a slogan —Martin Buber, "The Question to the Single One"

    Buber is concerned that words, meant to unite us, in fact distance us.

6. Our words have wings, but fly not where we would —George Eliot, *Spanish Gypsy*

7. Marjorie waited until the shower of broken words collapsed into little sniffles —F. Scott Fitzgerald, "Bernice Bobs Her Hair," *Flappers and Philosphers*, 1920

    The person of the broken words is Marjorie's cousin Bernice whose visit has put a crimp into Marjorie's busy social life.

8. Signora Scafetti screamed, and let loose a flood of Italian, most of which, I am glad to say, I could not follow —E. M. Forster, "The Story of a Panic"

    The Italian landlady asks her servant to fetch a young man who is acting strangely, and the flood of words is in answer to his refusal. The metaphor is a common one for overabundance of any sort. Forster himself uses it again in the same story: "As soon as we entered the house he stopped shrieking; but floods of tears silently burst forth, and spread over his upturned face."

9. Tart words make no friends; a spoonful of honey will catch more flies than a gallon of vinegar —Benjamin Franklin, *Poor Richard's Almanack*, 1742.

10. [Querelle's words] . . . pile up inside him, to settle and to form a thick mud deposit, out of which, at times, a transparent bubble rises, exploding delicately on his lips —Jean Genet, *Querelle*

    Querelle has adopted a raunchy thieves' argot, and his "mental makeup and very feelings depend upon, and assume the form of, a certain syntax, a particular murky orthography."

11. Words are the shadows of deeds —Baltasar Gracian, *The Art of Worldly Wisdom*

12. Once sent out a word takes wing irrevocably —Horace, *Epistles*

13. Words . . . are the assault of thoughts on the unthinking —Lord John Maynard Keynes, *The New Statesman*, July 15, 1933

14. Words . . . the most powerful drug used by mankind —Rudyard Kipling, Speech, February 14, 1923

15. But soon she was veering downstream on the flow of his words —D. H. Lawrence, "Two Blue Birds"

    The little secretary, taking dictation from the novelist she adores, is too busy to have any feelings of her own.

16. My words are little jars / For you to take and put upon a shelf —Amy Lowell, "Gift," *Sword Blades and Poppy Seeds*

17. Words are . . . a mirror which reflects the beauty of all that surrounds it —Count Maurice Maeterlinck, "Preface to the Modern Drama," *Wisdom and Dignity*

18. The through-train of words with white-hot whistle / Shrills past the heart's mean halts, the mind's full stops, / With all the signals down —W. R. Rogers, Express

    The poet continues the metaphor as the train slides into "Age, the last of all stations."

19. Aufidius: Each word thou hast spoke hath weeded from my heart / a root of ancient envy —William Shakespeare, *Coriolanus*, Act 4, scene 5, line 108

20. Clown: words are very rascals since bonds disgrac'd them. —William Shakespeare, *Twelfth Night*, Act 3, scene 1, line 22

    Once a man's word was as good as his bond, but with the need to have bonds or pledges enforced by law, man's honor has been disgraced.

21. How can words ease, which are / The glasses of thy daily vexing care? —Sir Philip Sidney, "Sonnet 34," *Astrophel and Stella*

    The poet claims that it hardly pays to write down his troubles since he simply mirrors them in his writing, in the looking glasses of his words.

22. One must be chary of words because they turn into cages. —Viola Spolin, *Improvisations for the Theatre*

23. Words are but wind. —Jonathan Swift, *A Tale of a Tub*, VIII, 1704.

24. —What is his name?— . . . whose words, he says, were full of pus, and another person whose words were all vinegar —Voltaire, *Candide*

■ WORDS AS WEAPONS

See also: ABILITY; INSULTS; INTENSITY; SATIRE; SLANDER; SPEECHES; WOMEN; WRITING/WRITERS

1. Auntie Bye had a tongue that could take the paint off a barn —Joseph W. Alsop, *I've Seen the Best of It*

    The sharp-tongued lady was the Alsop's great-aunt and Theodore Roosevelt's sister.

2. Sir Timothy: The Devil's in her tongue and so 'tis in most women of her age —Aphra Behn, *The Town Fop*

    Take note that this negative view of the female of the species from the pen of one of our first female playwrights is expressed by a male character.

3. I thought it hard . . . that he should have written to me so with a sword . . . to use his love for me to half break my heart with such a letter —Elizabeth Barrett Browning, Letter to her sisters, October 2, 1846

    Browning was hurt by her brother's disapproval of her marriage. In Macbeth *Macduff says: "My voice is my sword."*

4. Bert let fly his arrow with all his might. His words were but trivial . . . but his panic tipped them well with the poison of the wish to hurt, and he put his back into the bending of his bow —Dorothy Canfield, "Murder on Jefferson Street"

    The story delineates the tragic consequences of misunderstanding of one's own and other people's true emotions.

5. He wrote . . . a speech so full of poison and pure pus / It gave me a vile cough-

and-cold that jolted / my lungs to smith-
ereens —Catullus, Poem 44, *The Poems of
Catullus*

> *Compare Voltaire's comment on language, which
> uses 'pus and vinegar' rather than pus and poison.*

6. Lady Wish: Oh, he carries poison in his
tongue that would corrupt integrity itself!
—William Congreve, *The Way of the
World*, Act 3, scene 1

7. She . . . fired her words. Bang! the charge
in her soul was ignited, the words whizzed
forth at the narrow barrel of her mouth.
She was a machine gun riddling her hostess with sympathy —Aldous Huxley,
"The Giaconda Smile"

> *And you might call this a triple-barreled meta-
> phor; that's without counting the story's title
> which illustrates allusion as metaphor.*

8. A sharp tongue is the only edged tool that
grows keener with constant use —Washington Irving, "Rip Van Winkle"

> *Rip Van Winkle's wife had one of the sharpest
> tongues in literary history.*

9. You can cut, or you can drug, with words
—Amy Lowell, "Sword Blades and Poppy Seeds," *Sword Blades and Poppy Seeds*

10. "Uncle Joe's" [convention chairman Joe
Cannon] weapon was the meat cleaver of
burlesque. Governor Black's was the keen-
edged razor-tipped arrow of satire and
sarcasm —H. L. Mencken in *The Impossible
H. L. Mencken*

> *These were Mencken's perception of the oratorical
> styles displayed at the Democratic convention.*

11. Hamlet: I will speak daggers to her but use
none, / My tongue and soul in this be
hypocrites —William Shakespeare, *Hamlet*, Act 3, scene 2, line 399

> *In scene 4, the metaphor of the dagger becomes a
> simile when the Queen begs Hamlet to stop speak-
> ing because "these words like daggers enter in my
> ears." The power of words to stab is also made
> clear in The Second Part of Henry the Sixth,
> (4, 1, 64), when a lieutenant instead of having a
> boatswain literally stabbed says "First let my
> words stab him."*

12. Lear: She hath . . . struck me with her
tongue —William Shakespeare, *King Lear*,
Act 2, scene 4, line 159

13. Macduff: I have no words; / My voice is
in my sword. —William Shakespeare,
Macbeth, Act 5, scene 7, line 35

> *The sword continues as a popular metaphor for
> incisive language. Elizabeth Barrett Browning
> was pained by her brother George's disapproval of
> her marriage—"that he should have written to
> me so with a sword," she wrote to her sister,
> [October 2, 1846).*

14. Benedick: She speaks poniards, and every
word stabs —William Shakespeare, *Much
Ado About Nothing*, Act 2, scene 1, line 257

15. Titus: These words are razors to my
wounded heart —William Shakespeare,
Titus Andronicus, Act 1, scene 1, line 314

16. They twisted the knife within an hour of
her arrival —Muriel Spark, "Bang-bang
You're Dead"

> *The knife-twisting couple have snared the pro-
> tagonist into a neurotic relationship which ends
> only after she refuses to go along with the lies they
> tell each other.*

17. There is not nothing, no, no, never nothing, / Like the clashed edges of two words
that kill —Wallace Stevens, "Le Monocle de Mon Oncle"

> *The implied metaphor is of angry words as swords.*

18. A self-admitted physical coward . . . he
was learning to jab with words —Howard
Teichmann, *George S. Kaufman*

> *The biographer returns to the metaphor when he
> writes "As he grew older, words not only earned
> his livelihood, they were also the weapons with
> which he fought his way to the championship."*

19. Words, words, words, words. They were
the chisels with which George S. Kaufman
carved his reputation into the granite of
Manhattan and whatever makes up the
rest of the world . . . he was learning to jab
with words —Howard Teichmann, *George
S. Kaufman*.

20. I have no sceptre, but I have a pen —
Voltaire, Letter

A famous variant (not a metaphor) is the pen is
mightier than the sword *(Richlieu,* Bulwer-
Lytton, *1838).*

■ WORK/WORKERS

*See also: BUSINESS DESCRIPTIONS; EXCESS;
MONOTONY*

1. Living without working is entering a jew-
el-mine and coming out empty-handed
—Anon., Japanese Proverb

2. Work is the grand cure for all the maladies
and miseries that ever beset mankind —
Thomas Carlyle, Speech as Lord Rector
of Edinburgh University, April 2, 1866

3. Work is love made visible —Kahlil
Gibran, *The Prophet*

4. When you work you are flute through
whose heart the whispering of the hours
turns to music —Kahlil Gibran, *The
Prophet*

    *"Which of you would be a reed, dumb and silent,
    when all else sings together in unison?" Gibran asks.*

5. —Ironic, uxorious, the five / children
grown and gone; he waters his lawn with
irony; / he works forty hours of irony a
week and lives / to retire —Donald Hall,
"Shrubs Burnt Away," *The One Day*

6. Matisse said, "Work / is paradise"; Rodin,
"To work is to live without dying"; /
Flaubert, "It passes the time" —Donald
Hall, "To Build a House" *The One Day*

    *The last, while not a metaphor is included here
    since, to use a common metaphor, it's the third leg
    of the poet's stool.*

7. Labor is life —Victor Hugo, Speech to
meeting of workingmen

    He followed this with "thought is light."

8. Why should I let the toad *work* / Squat on
my life? —Philip Larkin, "Toads"

    "Ah, were I courageous enough / To shout Stuff
    your pension!" *the poet mourns.*

9. The question now is how Mr. Spindler's
nuts-and-bolts management style will
mesh with his employees' nuts-and-
granola work style —John Markoff, "It's
Batten-Down, Button-Down Time at
Apple," *New York Times,* July 9, 1993

    *The hard-driving style of Apple Computer chief
    executive, Michael Spindler also earned him the
    metaphoric nickname, "the Diesel."*

10. Those in the thick of life, "the plugs in
harness," had no time for such idle questions. [questions about the nature of life]
—Henry Miller, "The Creative Life"

    *A hard worker is often called a work horse. Here,
    the slang term* plug *is substituted as a pejorative
    for horse.*

11. The necessity of holding a job: what an
iron filing that is on the compass card of a
man's brain! —Christopher Morley, "What
Men Live By"

12. Put in your oar, and share the sweat of the
brow with which you must both start up
the stream —Elizabeth Phelps, *What Sent
One Husband to California*

13. How did we manage to put our house and
our life in order / with a hand made of
stone? —Yannis Ritsos, "Our Land"

    *Ritsos pictures a life of subsistence farming, with
    hands made hard by labor and loss*

14. One shouldn't burn the candle at both
ends; the thing is to light each end about.
—George Sand, Letter to Gustave Flaubert

    *Sand urges Flaubert, who's going through a
    period of depression, not to burn himself out by
    concentrating only on literature instead of enjoy-
    ing some of life's pleasures.*

■ WORLD

*See also: HISTORY; HUMANITY/HUMAN-
KIND; ORDER/DISORDER; PAST*

1. The world is a dream and death is the
interpreter. —Anon., Yiddish Proverb

2. The world's a bubble —Sir Francis Bacon, "Life"

3. He has no need to erect a labyrinth when the whole world already is one —Jorge Luis Borges, "Ibn Hakkan al-Bokhari, Dead in his Labyrinth"

   The world is a maze, and all who are born must learn to thread it.

4. The universe; / whoever through its endless mazes wanders / hears door on door click shut behind his stride. —Jorge Luis Borges, "Everness"

   Borges was fascinated by labyrinths, puzzles, and mazes. In his short stories as well as his poems he used the figure of a man in a maze to portray the human condition.

5. We are living in a closed-circuit world where it is always Prime Time —Noel Brown, United Nations NGO Briefing

   Dr. Brown, of the United Nations Development Programme, noted that information travels so quickly that everything is always known everywhere.

6. The world is a bundle of hay, / Mankind are the asses that pull —Lord George Gordon Byron, Letter to Thomas Moore, June 22, 1821

   These human asses, according to Byron "each tugs in a different way."

7. This world is but a thoroughfare full of woes —Geoffrey Chaucer, "The Knight's Tale," *The Canterbury Tales*

8. They [the best historians] are able to people the reader's mind with ghosts of a vanished world—a world that is indeed a "foreign" country where they do things differently —Carlo M. Cipolla, *Between Two Cultures: An Introduction to Economic History*

   In the implied metaphor the mind itself becomes the world of imagination, peopled with the ghosts of history.

9. I take the world to be but a stage / Where net-maskt men do play their personage — Guillaume de Salluste, Seigneur Du Bartas, *Dialogues Between Heraclitus and Democritus*

   Regardless of its origins, the credit for this stage metaphor usually goes to Shakespeare who used variations of it in several of his plays.

10. The world,—this shadow of the soul, or other me—lies wide around —Ralph Waldo Emerson, Speech, "The American Scholar," Harvard College, August 31, 1837

11. Adams: He steals your good, he steals your strength, / He riddles your world until it sinks —Christopher Fry, *A Sleep of Prisoners*

    The world is here compared to a ship.

12. The world has been shut up in a heated stifling room . . . I wish I knew where the door was so I could open it wide. But I don't know yet and I don't want to open the wrong door, one that might lead only into another suffocating room. The door I want to open leads to the fresh air, to the natural freedom of things —Eduardo Mallea, "Pillars of Society," *Fiesta in November*

    The Chilean poet was awarded the Nobel Prize for literature in 1945.

13. It was really the world that was your brutal mother, the one that nursed and neglected you and your own mother was only your sibling in that world —Lorrie Moore, "Which Is More Than I Can Say About Some People, *The New Yorker*, November 8, 1993

    A young woman makes this observation after travelling through Ireland with her mother.

14. With the end of the cold war, the international community breathes easier . . . But if we look beneath this global umbrella, the picture is quite different —Olara A. Otunnu, *The Singapore Symposium*, United Nations

    The president of the International Peace Academy commented on peacekeeping.

15. Jaques: All the world's a stage. And all the men and women merely players —William Shakespeare, *As You Like It*, Act 2, scene 7, line 139

    In a poem called "Prologue," Oliver Wendell Holmes, Sr., alluded to this as follows: "The world's a stage,—as Shakespeare said one day; / The stage a world—was what he meant to say."

16. Hamlet: this world / 'tis an unweeded garden, / That grows to seed —William Shakespeare, *Hamlet*, Act 1, scene 2, line 134
    Another famous garden metaphor appears in The Tragedy of King Richard the Second, *Act 3, scene 4, line 44.*

17. Antonio: I hold the world but as a world, Gratiano; / A stage where every man must play a part, / And mine a sad one — William Shakespeare, *The Merchant of Venice*, Act 1, scene 1, line 77
    The stage metaphor shows up in other Shakespeare plays, including As You Like It, Hamlet *and* Macbeth.

18. Northumberland: And let this world no longer be a stage / To feed contention in a lingering act. —William Shakespeare, *The Second Part of King Henry the Fourth*, Act 1, scene 1, line 155
    Variations of this theater metaphor appear in several Shakespeare plays.

19. Messiers, / It is an artificial world. The rose / Of paper is of the nature of its world. / The sea is so many written words —Wallace Stevens, "Extracts from Addresses to the Academy of Fine Ideas"

20. This world is better than an ode / And evening more than elegy —Trumbull Stickney, "In Ampezzo, II"

21. The world is an old coquette who conceals her age —Voltaire

22. [The world:] A comedy to those that think, a tragedy to those that feel —Horace Walpole

23. The beauty of the world has two edges, one of laughter, one of anguish, cutting the heart asunder —Virginia Woolf, *A Room of One's Own*

24. The world that was visible was a grey, translucent screen that had begun to shimmer and waver —Richard Wright, *The Outsider*
    The protagonist's doomed attempts to lead a free life have come to an end and his vision of the world is thus blurred just before his death.

25. The world is a wheel always turning. Those who are high go down low, and those who've been low go up higher — Anzia Yezierska, "The Fat of the Land"

■ WORRY

See also: FEAR; PERSONALITY PROFILES

1. If you go on painting the devil on the walls, it ends up by his appearing in person. —Anon., French Proverb
   Worrying or talking about calamities is one way to make them come true.

2. Heavy, galloping hoofbeats seem to have taken the place of her heart —Mary Ward Brown, "A New Life," *The Atlantic Monthly*

3. Every nerve in my body was a steel spring —Albert Camus, *The Stranger*

4. Sweet sleep has been but ill exchanged for the broken slumbers which haunt the uneasy pillow of care —Wilkie Collins, *The Moonstone*

5. Anxiety is the rust of life, destroying its brightness and wakening its power — Tryon Edwards

6. At the rider's back sits dark anxiety — Horace, *Epistles*

7. The last moments [before a trip] are earthquake and convulsion, and the feeling that you are a snail being pulled off your rock —Anne Morrow Lindbergh, Letter, September 7, 1929

8. Will his breath scorch the red dragon of my nerves to death? —Robert Lowell, "Adam and Eve," *Between the Porch and the Altar* II

9. Care is beauty's thief —Shakerly Marmion

10. Orestes: A dreadful band of gloomy cares surround me, / And lay strong siege to my distracted soul! —Jean Baptiste Racine, *Andromaque*

11. The black ink of anxiety spilled and spread, saturating the fabric of my life —Eileen Simpson, *Orphans*

     The woman being mugged has been recently widowed.

12. A spider of anxiety crawled up the back of my neck —Donna Tartt, *The Secret History*

13. His insides are a clenched mass of dread, a tough bubble that can't be pricked —John Updike, *Rabbit, Run*

14. I felt knifed by anxiety —A. B. Yehoshua, *Mr. Mani*

■ WRINKLES

See also: FACES; PHYSICAL APPEARANCE

1. He was a sunburned reckless-eyed fellow, with a network of lines and wrinkles all over his mahogany features —Sir Arthur Conan Doyle, "The Sign of the Four"

2. Faint lines . . . beginning to make nets around her eyes —Dashiell Hammett, *Red Harvest*

3. [David] Durk . . . droopily handsome features, and spider tracks that radiate out from the corners of his eyes —James Lardner, "The Whistle-Blower—Part I," *The New Yorker*, July 5, 1993

4. Behind her eyeglasses there was a fan of delicate lines, fine as paper cuts —Sue Miller, *For Love*

     Metaphor and simile combine to picture a woman's aging skin.

5. The skin of her face is . . . netted with spidery red lines from years of drinking —Sue Miller, *For Love*

6. Camped there was a plump man with a seamed face —James Robison, "Between Seasons," *The New Yorker*, June 14, 1993

7. A fine tapestry of wrinkles had traced itself across the ghostly face —William Styron, *Lie Down in Darkness*

■ WRITING ADVICE

See also: POETRY/POETS; WRITING/ WRITERS

1. In the first place a comic essay must have a short back, be sharp on the withers, not too long-legged, kind in all harness, hard to scare, and able to show its heels to a road wagon. —Josh Billings

     He also advises would-be humor columnists that such writing is "no place to hide among the debris of abstracted thoughts or skulk behind a flame-colored paragraph, or doze in recital upon an ebb tide." He concludes with several similes: "It must be short as a newsboy's prayers, as sudden as the end of a rope, as quick as a sneeze."

2. All good writing is swimming under water and holding your breath. —F. Scott Fitzgerald, Letter

3. Wheels, racks, and fires / in every writer's mouth, and not mere rant —Thom Gunn, "A Mirror for Poets"

     Dylan Thomas spoke of someone whose words "had forked no lightning." Gunn is suggesting, as Thomas did, that the poet must avoid blandness.

4. The five winnowed volumes on her shelf . . . are so potent a distillation of nectar and wormwood, of ambrosia and deadly nightshade, as might suggest to the rest of us that we write too much —Alexander Woollcott, "Some Neighbors," *While Rome Burns*

     Woollcott's words of praise are for Dorothy Parker's poems and stories.

■ WRITING/WRITERS

See also: ABILITY; BOOKS; CHARACTERIZATIONS; IMAGINATION; JOURNALISM/ JOURNALISTS; MISTAKES; POETRY/ POETS

1. Should I commit an error here my words would blush —Peter Abelard, Letter to Heloise

2. His book is still but an embryo in the womb of scholarship; at full term, a book will emerge —Shmuel Yosef Agnon, *Shira*

3. Among the virtues his prose [Alexander Woollcott's] can claim is the uncommon one that it functioned as the perfect thermos bottle for his likes and dislikes — John Mason Brown, Introduction, *The Portable Woollcott*

4. [Alexander Woollcott as reader and writer]: Words sang for him, and he could make them sing —John Mason Brown, Introduction, *The Portable Woollcott*

5. Literary men . . . are a perpetual priesthood —Thomas Carlyle, Essay, *Edinburgh Review*, 1827

6. The pen is the tongue of the mind — Miguel de Cervantes, *Don Quixote*

7. Writing a book is an adventure. To begin with, it is a toy and an amusement; then it becomes a mistress, and then it becomes a master, and then a tyrant. The last phase is that just as you are about to be reconciled to your servitude, you kill the monster, and fling him out to the public —Winston Churchill, November 2, 1949

    This multiple metaphor was quoted in Martin Gilbert's biography of Sir Winston Churchill.

8. Leave writing plays, and choose for thy command / Some peaceful province in Acrostic Land. / There thou mayest wings display and altars raise, / And torture one poor word ten thousand ways. —John Dryden, "Second Prologue to Secret Love; or The Maiden Queen"

9. The American short story of a passing generation was the hot pancake of literature. The same deft pouring of the batter, the same expert jerk, the same neat flip of the wrist at the end —Edna Ferber, Preface, *They Brought Their Women*

    Ferber prefaces this image of the short story writer with a long paragraph about the once widely visible apron-clad, white-capped pancake chef.

10. I think of a writer as a river: you reflect what passes before you —Natalia Ginsburg, Quoted in her obituary *The New York Times*, October 7, 1991.

    The quoted metaphor was pulled out of the obituary as a blurb of the novelist, essayist, translator who died at age 75.

11. And I can't fix my eyes on the page / Where Flaubert writes that prose / Is a permanent rage —Gjertrud Schnackenberg, "Paper Cities"

    According to Flaubert, notes Schnackenberg, "Books grow huge / Like pyramids, and in the end / They almost frighten you."

12. No sooner does he take a pen in his hand, than it becomes a torpedo to him, and benumbs all his faculties —Samuel Johnson, *Boswell's Life of Johnson*

    As a conversationalist this same man was "brisk as a bee."

13. Many authors remain dark houses to me, houses I pass in ignorance —Robert MacNeil, *Wordstruck*.

    MacNeil's memoir is full of observations about "houses" he discovers and gets to know well.

14. Year after year perfecting your art, / Choosing bookish wisdom for your mistress, / Only to discover you wander in the dark —Czeslaw Milosz, "Poet at Seventy"

15. It was Howard Dietz . . . who on reading one curiously lace-edged bit of prose, referred to its author as Louisa M. Woolcott —Dorothy Parker, "A Valentine for Mr. Woollcott," *Vanity Fair*, 1934

    Parker slyly uses someone else's putdown instead of directly criticizing Alexander Woollcott's sometimes overly sentimental prose.

16. True ease in writing comes from art, / not chance, / As those move easiest who have learn'd / to dance —Alexander Pope, "Essay on Criticism"

17. It is harder to put your foot in your mouth when you have your pen in your hand — William Safire, *On Language*

Safire urges a return to letter writing as an escape from "the tyranny of the telephone."

18. Before I began dictating the cover memo, I actually thought I would do . . . something anesthetized and lawyerly, prose in a straitjacket —Scott Turow, *Pleading Guilty*

    Instead, the protagonist's memo is the first of a series of journal-like revelations of his and other characters' secret lives and plot background developments.

19. Writers create Houses of the Imagination, from whose doors the generations greet each other —Fay Weldon, *Letters to Alice*

    The house metaphor grows out of a larger metaphor Weldon calls the City of Invention which "today, stretches far and wide" with "all kinds of people" choosing to build and "not just those born to it." Some of these newer writers choose a safe course of "Pre-Fabs" which are "neatly swept" free from the grander emotions tapped into by authors like Hardy and Austen.

YEARNING

See also: DESIRE; HOPES; MEN AND WOMEN; SELF; SELF-ACTUALIZATION

1. Bound by hundreds of bonds of longing —Anon., *The Bhagavad Gita*, 16:12
   Desire results in ignorance of a higher good.

2. But rustling within her was another person who wanted to . . . be carried away, and peeled back by a force that she could sense —Robert James Waller, *The Bridges of Madison County*
   If the immense popular success of Waller's book is any indication, millions of women share his heroine's yearning for romantic passion.

3. Since then there had been no further communication between them, and he had built up within himself a kind of sanctuary in which she throned among his secret thoughts and longings —Edith Wharton, *The Age of Innocence*
   Newland Archer is married to the woman he so wanted at the novel's beginning, his love for Ellen Olenska unconsummated—but never forgotten.

4. Vance walked on in a fog of formless yearnings —Edith Wharton, *Hudson River Bracketed*

YOUTH

See also: AGE/AGING; EXPERIENCE/INEXPERIENCE; INNOCENCE/INEXPERIENCE; TRANSIENCE

1. But spontaneity is beyond them at present. They're simply calves, after all, rather sophisticated calves —Elizabeth Bowen, "Daffodils"
   A high school teacher tries to make her students more observant, less imitative. After a brief period of closeness with a small group of girls, she observes that "tomorrow they will be again impersonal; three pink moons in a firmament of faces."

2. Yours is . . . the seed-time of life —Thomas Carlyle, Speech as Lord Rector of Edinburgh University, April 2, 1866

3. Youth is . . . a provision of Nature; a decoy to secure mothers for the race —Kate Chopin, *The Awakening*
   This expresses one of the major themes of the novel.

4. In youth we clothe ourselves with rainbows, and go as brave as the zodiac —Ralph Waldo Emerson, "Fate," *Conduct of Life*

5. Filch: Really, Madam, I fear I shall be cut off in the Flower of my Youth —John Gay, *The Beggar's Opera*, Act 1, scene 5
   Filch, a young lad being schooled in the fine art of picking pockets, has nearly been caught, and is worried about his prospects.

6. From the morning hills of existence he beheld a clear horizon —George Meredith, *The Ordeal of Richard Feverel*

7. Frosine: [Young men] What are they but worthless trash! They are mere puppies,

show-offs that make you envy their complexions —Molière, *The Miser*, Act 2
The matchmaker tries to cozen old Harpagon into a May-December marriage.

8. Youth is fair, a graceful stag, / Leaping, playing in a park —Isaac Peretz, *Sewing The Wedding Gown*

9. Youth is a perpetual intoxication . . . the fever of reason —François, Duc de la Rochefoucauld, *Maxims*

10. Youth is a very brief illness, one quickly gets over it —Nathalie Sarraute, *The Planetarium*

11. Life's May blossoms once and not again —Johann Christoph Friedrich von Schiller, *Resignation*

12. Cleopatra: My salad days, when I was green in judgment —William Shakespeare, *Antony and Cleopatra*, Act 1, scene 5, line 75
In The Life of Henry the Fifth, *Act 2, scene 4, Exeter says "you'll find a difference . . . Between the promise of his greener days and these he masters now."*

13. Antony: He wears the rose of youth upon him —William Shakespeare, *Antony and Cleopatra*, Act 3, scene 11, line 21

14. York: Deal mildly with his youth: / For young hot colts, being rag'd, do rage the more —William Shakespeare, *The Tragedy of King Richard the Second*, Act 2, scene 1, line 69
Richard's uncle York still hopes that the young king will be tamed.

15. Thy youth's proud livery, so gazed on now, / Will be a tottered weed of small worth held —William Shakespeare, "Sonnet 2," line 3
This is a forerunner to the "Gather ye rosebuds while ye may" theme expressed by the Cavalier poets, who threaten that women must lose their beauty, so they had better make haste to make love.

16. But thy eternal summer shall not fade — William Shakespeare, "Sonnet 18," line 9

17. Really, the fellow's not housebroken — Edith Wharton, *Hudson River Bracketed*
Elsewhere, the speaker refers to the subject as "a young puppy."

■ YOUTH AND AGE

See also: AGE/AGING; HUMANITY/HU-MANKIND; LAMENTS; MIDDLE AGE; OLD AGE

1. What the old chew, the young spit — Anon., Yiddish Proverb

2. The Child's Toys & the Old Man's Reasons / Are the Fruits of the Two Seasons —William Blake, "Auguries of Innocence"

3. Anath: . . . what a girl of fire I was before I made these embers —Christopher Fry, *The Firstborn*, Act 1, scene 1
Anath comments on her aging.

4. At 20 a man is a peacock, at 30 a lion, at 40 a camel, at 50 a serpent, at 60 a dog, at 70 an ape —Baltasar Gracian, *The Age of Worldly Wisdom*
"And at 80 nothing" concludes the writer.

5. Autumn can be golden, milder and warmer than summer, and is the most productive season of the year —Germaine Greer, *The Change: Women Aging and Menopause*
The autumn season is Greer's metaphor for a woman's post menopausal years.

6. We cannot at once enjoy the flowers of the Spring of life and the fruits of its Autumn —Thomas Babbington Macaulay, *John Dryden*

7. Frosine: Well, what is sixty? A mere trifle! It's the flower of one's age —Molière, *The Miser*, Act 2
The matchmaker is trying to arrange a marriage between the miser and a young girl.

8. Not perhaps in their first youth but by no means blighted by the frosts of age — Alice Munro, "Meneseteung," *Friend of Youth*

9. On the day I decided to put youth behind me I immediately felt twenty years younger. You'll say the bark of the tree still has to bear the ravages of time. I don't mind that—the core is sound and the sap goes on doing its work —George Sand, Letter to Gustave Flaubert

Sand expressed her very positive attitude toward aging.

10. King: Let me not live, / After my flame lacks oil, to be the snuff / Of younger spirits. —William Shakespeare, *All's Well That Ends Well*, Act 1, scene 2, line 58

The king does not want his diminishment to adversely affect the younger generation.

11. King: For youth no less becomes / the light and careless livery that it wears / Then settled age his sables and his weeds, / Importing health and graveness — William Shakespeare, *Hamlet*, Act 4, scene 3, line 77

12. Capulet: For you and I are past our dancing days —William Shakespeare, *Romeo and Juliet*, Act 1, scene 4, line 147

In common usage this is My dancing days are over.

13. Where wasteful Time debateth with Decay / To change your day of youth to sullied night —William Shakespeare, "Sonnet 15," line 10

14. When his youthful morn / Hath traveled on to Age's steepy night —William Shakespeare, "Sonnet 63," line 4

The hours of the day are frequent metaphors for the passage of time in life. Age is "steepy" because it descends so precipitously into death.

15. And thou present'st a pure unstained prime. / Thou hast passed by the ambush of young days —William Shakespeare, "Sonnet 70," line 8

16. That time of year thou mayst in me behold / When yellow leaves, or none, or few, do hang / upon those boughs which shake against the cold —William Shakespeare, "Sonnet 73," line 1

The turning of the seasons is the metaphoric equivalent to the ages of man.

17. In me thou see'st the glowing of such fire, / That on the ashes of his youth doth lie —William Shakespeare, "Sonnet 73," line 9, 1609.

The fire is dying down because it is being smothered by its own ashes.

18. If now the May of my years much decline, / What can be hoped my harvest time will be? —Sir Philip Sidney, "Sonnet 21," *Astrophel and Stella*

19. Judge: Life's eve has at last brought the sunshine which its morning promised us —August Strindberg, *Advent*, Act 1

The opening line of the play is ironic, since the judge's sunshine is based on the misery of others.

20. [Paul] was just crossing the threshold of that troubled, twilight period, when regrets come to resemble hopes, and hopes are beginning to resemble regrets, when youth is fled and old age is fast approaching —Ivan Turgenev, *Fathers and Sons*

Turgenev uses the threshold as a metaphor, as though passing from one age to the next were a matter of stepping from one room into another.

21. How swift are the feet of the days of the years of youth —Mark Twain, Quoted by Helen Keller in "Our Mark Twain"

The metaphor of personification pictures time as a runner.

22. Man is a Summer's day, whose youth and fire to a glorious evening and expire — Henry Vaughan, *Silex Scintillans*, Part 1

23. Teach my twilight to recover / (if it but could) the flush of dawn —Voltaire, "To Madame du Chatelet"

24. Lord Illingworth: The middle-aged are mortgaged to Life. The old are in Life's lumber room. But youth is the Lord of Life —Oscar Wilde, *A Woman of No Importance*, Act 3

25. Blanche: My youth was suddenly gone up the water-spout. —Tennessee Williams, *A Streetcar Named Desire*, Scene 10

> *The more common metaphor for sudden disappearance is* gone up in smoke.

Z

■ ZEAL

See also: *AMBITION; ANIMATION; CHARAC-TERIZATIONS; ENERGY; PASSION*

1. That restless fever . . . zeal. —Aphra Behn, Prologue, *The Rover*

2. Zeal is the faculty igniting the other mind powers into the full flame of activity —Sylvia Stitt Edwards, Epigraph

3. Merlin: I lost my trumpet of zeal when Arthur died / And now I only wind a grey note / of memory —Christopher Fry, *Thor, With Angels*
   > The sophisticated Merlin, used to the majesty of King Arthur's court, feels exiled and abandoned among the cruel rustics of a pagan land.

4. Her enthusiasm was always on the boil —Aldous Huxley, *Point Counter Point*

5. Years may wrinkle the skin, but to give up interest wrinkles the soul —General Douglas MacArthur, Speech.

6. He was alive, he was full of passion—a barrel waiting to be tapped —John Updike, "Baby's First Step," *The New Yorker,* July 27, 1992

■ ZENITH

See also: *SUCCESS*

1. His insolent bravery . . . had borne him to the top of that difficult ladder called Court Favor, which he had climbed four steps at a time —Alexandre Dumas, *The Three Musketeers*

2. The Matterhorn of Robert Walmsley's success was not scaled until he married Alicia Van Der Pool —O. Henry, "The Defeat of the City"
   > A farm boy's down-to-earth values become obscured as he reaches for social success in the city—until, O. Henry's usual surprise twist at the end.

3. Her life was at its highest tide . . . —Margaret Widdemer, "Changeling"
   > The story is about a teenager who stood out in people's minds "like an electric light among candles" but whose insensitive father breaks her spirit.

Common Metaphors

A listing of metaphors from everyday speech, alphabetized by key word(s). Background information and variants of most of these phrases can be found under their appropriate thematic headings.

A

abandon: to a. ship

abyss: to fall into an a., as of despair

aim: to a. high

air head: to be an a.

altitude: to gain or not gain a.

apple: the a. doesn't fall far from the tree

apple: to be the a. of someone's eye

apron strings: to be tied to someone's a.

arm: to twist someone's a.

armor: to penetrate (or try to) someone's a.

auto-pilot: to be on a.

ax: to have an s. to grind

B

back burner: to put/be on the b.

ball: to keep/start the b. rolling

ballpark: a b. figure

ballpark: to be in the b.

bandwagon: climb on someone's b.

bark: to b. up the wrong tree

base: to be way off b.

base: not get to first b.

bases: cover/touch all b.

bat: to go to b. for

bat: to move like a b. out of hell

bear: to be a b. for work

beat: to b. a dead horse

beaver: to be an eager b.

bed: a situation that is or isn't a b. of roses

bedfellows: to make strange b.

bee line: to make a b. for

bird-brain: to have a b.

birds: b. of a feather

bite: to b. the bullet

471

bite: to b. the dust

bite: to b. off more than one can chew

bite: to b. someone's head off

blanket: to be a wet b.

blaze: to b. new ground/a fresh trail

blind alley: to lead up a b.

blow: to b. a fuse

blow: to b. hot and cold

blow: to b. one's stack

blow: to b. up

boat: all in the same b.

bone: to have a b. to pick

book: to go by the b.

bread: to know on which side one's b. is buttered

bridges: burn one's b.

broom: to sweep with a new b.

bubble head: to be a b.

bubble: to burst someone's b.

bull: to grab/seize the b. by the horn

bulldoze: to b. one's way in

bullseye: to hit the b.

bush: to beat around the b.

bushel: not one to hide one's light under a b.

bushy-tailed: to be bright-eyed and b.

butterflies: to have b. in the stomach

button: to b. one's lip

C

candle: to burn one's c. at both ends

cannon: a loose c.

cards: lay/put one's c. on the table

cards: to live in a house of c.

cast-iron: a c. stomach/constitution

castles: built c. in the air

cat-and-mouse: to play a c. game

catbird seat: in the c.

chain: to have a c. reaction

champ: to c. at the bit

chart: to c. one's own course

checkered: have a c. past/career

cheek: c. by jowl

chew: to c. somebody out

chicken: to c. out or be c.-hearted

chip: to be a c. off the old block

claim: to c. one's pound of flesh

clam: to c. up

cloud: to be off on a c./up in the clouds

cloud: to be under a c.

clover: to be in c.

cock: to be the c. of the walk

cold: to be left out in the c.

cold water: to throw c. on

cookie cutter: to be cut from the same c.

cool: to blow one's c.

crocodile: to weep c. tears

crow: to eat c.

current: go against/with the c.

curtain: ring down the c.

curve: throw someone a c.

cut: to c. the ground from under someone

cutting edge: to be on the c., as of technology

D

daggers: look d. at someone

dancing: to be past one's d. days

deck: to play or not play with a full d.

deck: a stacked d. or play with a stacked d.

depth: to be out of one's d.

dice: let the d. fall where they may

dig: to d. in one's heels

dinosaur: to be/ride a d.

dip: to d. one's pen in venom

dip: to d. one's toes in the water

dish: to d. out, as gossip or punishment

dog: To d. at someone's heels

dog-eat-dog: live a d. world.

domino: to have a d. effect

double-edged: a d. sword

drain: go down the d.

drum: to beat your own drum

drummer: to hear/listen to a different d.

duck: a lame d.

duck: a sitting d.

dust: to d. off

dust: wait for the d. to settle

dustbin: consigned to the d.

E

ear: keep one's e. to the ground

eat: to e. one's words

egg: to lay an e.

eggs: to put (or not put) all one's e. to one basket

eggs: to walk on eggs

elbow-grease: to apply e.

empty suit: to be an e.

envelope: to push the e.

F

fan: to f. the flames

fast lane: to be/live in the f.

feather: to f. one's nest

feather brain: to be a f.

feet: to get one's f. wet

feet of clay: to have f. of c.

fences: to mend one's f.

fifth wheel: to be a f.

finger: to have a f. in every pie

fire: have f. in the belly

fire: to be a ball of f.

fire: to be on f.

firing line: to be on the f.

fish to fry: to have other f.

fishy: to smell f.

floodgates: open the f.

fold: take back into the f.

food: to provide f. for thought

foot: to get one's f. in the door

foot: to put one's f. in one's mouth

fox: a sly f.

frog: to be a big f. in a small pond

frying pan: out of the f. into the fire

fuel: add f. to someone's fire

fur: make the f. fly

fuse: to blow one's f.

fuse: to have a short f.

G

ghost: to give up the g.

ghost: to have/not have a g. of a chance

Gibraltar: to be a rock of G.

gilded cage: a bird in a g.

glutton: to be a g. for work

goose: a wild g. chase

grain: to accept with a g. of salt

grain: to go against one's g.

grapes: sour g.

green-eyed: the g. monster

ground floor: to get in on the g.

H

hackles: raise someone's h.

hair: to get in each other's h.

hands: to have one's h. tied

hang: to h. five

hang: to h. by a thread/thin thread

harp: to h. on the same string

harp: to have only one string to one's h.

hat: to throw one's h. in the ring

hatchet: to bury the h.

hay: to make h. while the sun shines

haywire: to go h.

head: to be in over one's h

head: to have/not have one's h. screwed on tight

heart: wear one's h. on one's sleeve

heels: to cool one's h.

high horse: to get on one's h.

hitch: h. your wagon to a star

hoe: a hard/long row to h.

hole: to have a h. in one's pocket

horn: to blow one's own h.

hornet's: to stir up a h. nest

horns: to be on the h. of a dilemma

hot water: to be in h.

I, J, K

ice: to break the i.

ice: to put on i.

iron hand: to rule with an i.

irons: to have many i. in the fire

ivory tower: to live in an i.

jackpot: to hit the j.

jaws: out of the j. of death

jell: to j. or not j.

jump: on the bandwagon

jump: to j. down someone's throat

kettle: a fine k. of fish

knot: to tie the k.

knotty: a k. problem

L

ladle: to l. out praise

lap: in the l. of luxury

lead: to l. someone by the nose

lead: to l. someone on a wild goose chase

leaf: to take/borrow a l. out of someone's book

leaf: to turn over a new l.

lease: to get/take a new l. on life

leash: to keep on a tight l.

left field: to be out in l.

legs: an enterprise (such as a book or movie with l.)

light: to l. a fire/fuse under

light: to see l. at the end of the tunnel

limb: out on a l.

limelight: hog (or stay out of) the l.

lion's share: to take the l.

loaf: to take half a loaf

lock: to l. horns

loop: to be out of the l.

lunch: to be out to l.

M

mark: to be an easy m.

melt: to m. a heart of stone

milk: the m. of human kindness

mill: to be put through or put someone through the m.

millstone: to be or hang like a m. around one's neck

monkey wrench: to throw a m. into something, usually the works

mountain: to make a m. out of a molehill

mountain: a m. of, as of problems or work

musical chairs: play m.

N

nail: to hit the n. on the head

nest-egg: to accumulate a n.

Niagara: a N. of discontent or other feelings

noose: to put one's head in a n.

nose: cut off one's n. to spite one's face

nose: to have one's n. out of joint

nose: right on the n.

nut: a tough n. to crack

nutshell: in a n.

O, P

oil: to pour o. on the troubled waters

ostrich: be an o.

paddle: to p. one's own canoe

paint: to p. a rosy picture

Pandora's box: to open a P.

paper: to create/leave a p. trail

paper: to p. over

pearls: to cast p. before swine

pebble: to not be the only p. on the beach

pig: to buy a p. in a poke

pill: a bitter p. to swallow

pinch: to p. pennies

pinch hit: to p. for someone, as a scheduled speaker

play: to p. by ear

play: to p. fast and loose

play: to p. the field

pluck: to p. on someone's heartstrings

poison: to p. someone's mind

pot: to keep the p. boiling

pregnant: to be p. with ideas/meaning

pull: to p. out all the stops

putty: to be p. in someone's hands

Q, R

queen-bee: to be the q.

quick: to be q. on the trigger

rabbit: to pull a r. out of a hat

rack: to r. one's brains

rainmaker: to be a r.

rainy day: to save for a r.

rat: smell a r.

razor-sharp: to have a r. mind/wit

reap: to r. a rich harvest

red carpet: to roll out the r./give the r. treatment

red flag: to raise a r.

rein: to give free r.

reins: to take the r.

reshuffle: to r. the deck

ring: to r. a bell

rising star: to be a r.

rock: to r. the boat

roll: to r. with the punches

roof: to lift/blow the r. off

roost: to rule the r.

roots: to pluck/pull up by the r.

rope: to be at the end of one's r.

rope: to give a man enough r.

rope: to throw someone a r.

ropes: to know/learn the r.

row: to r. upstream

rubberstamp: to be r. of someone/have r. opinions

run-of-the-mill: to be r.

S

saddle: to be in the s.

sail: to s. close to the wind

sailing: to be smooth s.

sails: To take in or trim one's s.

salt: to be the s. of the earth

scenes: to work behind the s.

screw: to have a s. loose

screw: to s. up one's courage

sea: to be all at s.

sea: a s. change

seeds: to contain the s. of, as destruction

shave: to have a close s.

shed: to s. new light on

ship: to run a tight s.

ship: to wait for one's s. to come in

shipshape: everything is s.

shoe: to know where the s. pinches

shoot: to s. oneself in the foot

shoulder: to put one's s. to the wheel

sitting: s. pretty

skate: to s. on thin ice

skeleton: to have a s. in one's closet/background

skim: to s. off

sleeping dogs: to let s. lie

smoke: to go up in s.

smoking gun: a s.

snake: a s. in the grass

sow: to s. one's wild oats

split: to s. hairs

spoonfeed: to s.

stack: to blow one's s.

stacked deck: to play with (or from the bottom of) a s.

stage: all the world's a s.

stakes: to pull up s.

stars: to reach for the s.

steam: to run out of s.

stew: s. in her own gravy/juice

stick: to be a s. in the mud

stone: to leave no s. unturned

storm: to take by s.

straight arrow: to be a s.

straitjacket: to be in an (emotional/philosophical) s.

straw: to grab/take hold of a s.

straw: s. or cardboard person

strike: to s. out

string: to have just one or more than one s. to one's bow

strong suit: to play one's s.

stumbling block: to be a s.

swallow: to s. hook, line and sinker

swan song: sing one's s.

sweep: to make a clean s. of

sweep: to s. under the rug

swim: to be out of the s. of things

swim: to s. with/against the current

sword: a two-edged s.

swords: to cross s. with

T

tail: to have one's t. between one's legs

tail: to turn t.

target: to be on t.

tatters: to be in t. (as a business or policy)

teeth: to escape by the skin of one's t.

tempest: a t. in a teapot

thickets: cut through the t., as of the argument

thorn: to be a t. in someone's side

thorny: a t. problem

thread: to hang by a t.

throat: to stick in one's t.

throw: to t. in the sponge/towel

thumbs: to be all t.

tide: a t. of feelings

tie: to t. someone's hands behind his or her back

tightrope: to walk a t. (or a fine line)

toehold: to get a t.

toot: to t. one's own horn

tooth and nail: to fight t.

track: to be on t.

trample: to t. all over, as someone's ideas

tree: the t. of knowledge

tree: t. of life

trump card: to play one's t.

tubes: down the t.

tune: to be in/out of t. with

two-way street: a situation or relationship that's a t.

U, V

umbrella: to be under the u. of

unglued: to come u. (or unstuck)

unravel: to try to u., as a problem

upbeat: to be in an u. mood

vanish: to v. into thin air

velvet glove: someone with an iron had in a v.

W, X

wagon: to be on the w.

wall: have one's b. to the/up against a wall

wallflower: to be/not be a w.

wash: to w. one's hands of something it

Waterloo: to meet one's W.

wave length: on the right/same w.

waves: to make w.

weasel: to w. one's way out of something

weasel: w. words

web: to be caught in a w.

wet: to be all w.

wheels: to spin one's w.

whip: to crack the w.

whistleblower: to be a w.

whitewash: to w. the truth

wind: to see which way the w. was blowing

wind: take the w. out of someone's sail

window: a w. of opportunity

wings: to clip someone's w.

wipe: to w. the floor with someone

wires: to get one's w. crossed

wolf: to w. one's food

wolf: w. in sheep's clothing

wolves: to throw to the w.

woods: not yet out of the w.

wool: to pull the w. over someone's eyes

words: to eat one's w.

world: have the w. on a string

X-ray vision: to have X.

Xerox copy: to be a X.

Metaphors from Shakespeare

Arranged alphabetically by key word(s) (and then alphabetically by title of work), this is a partial list of the metaphors culled from Shakespeare's works. The complete selection will be found under thematic headings throughout the book, where all include the speaker and many are annotated with comments, and can be found by searching for "Shakespeare" in the Author/Speaker Index. Key words that do not appear next to each other in the entry are separated by a slash (i.e.: bits/curbs). If a metaphor begins in lower case, the line has been picked up in the middle. For plays, the first known performance date is provided in parentheses after the source; for poems and sonnets, the first published folio date is provided.

A

Abraham's bosom: The sons of Edward sleep in A. —*The Tragedy of King Richard the Third,* (c. 1591–92) Act 4, scene 3, line 36

abstract: This little a. does contain that large / Which died in Geoffrey, and the hand of time / Shall draw this brief into as huge a volume —*The Life and Death of King John,* (c. 1594–6) Act 2, scene 1, line 101

actors: Our revels now are ended: these our a.— / As I foretold you—were all spirits and / Are melted into air, into thin air . . . —*The Tempest,* (1611) Act 4, scene 1, line 148

advantage: a. [caution] is a better soldier than rashness —*The Life of Henry the Fifth,* (1599) Act 3, scene 6, line 125

affection: The itch of his a. should not then / Have nick'd his captainship —*Antony and Cleopatra,* (c. 1606–7) Act 3, scene 2, line 7

affection: If I could temporize with my a. / Or brew it to a weak and colder palate, / The like allayment could I give my grief —*Troilus and Cressida,* (c. 1601–2) Act 4, scene 4, line 5

affection: A. is a coal that must be cool'd / Else, suffered, it will set the heart on fire —*Venus and Adonis,* (1611) line 231

affections: Your a. / Are a sick man's appetite —*Coriolanus,* (1607–8) Act 1, scene 1, line 183

affections/desires: Therefore, brave conquerors, . . . / That war against your own a. / And the huge army of the world's d. —*Love's Labour's Lost,* (c. 1594–95) Act 1, scene 1, line 25

age: But on us both did haggish a. steal on —*All's Well That Ends Well,* (1623) Act 1, scene 2, line 29

age: My a. is a lusty Winter, / Frosty, but kindly —*As You Like It,* (c. 1599–1600) Act 2, scene 3, line 52

age: a. with his stealing steps, / Hath claw'd me in his clutch —*Hamlet*, (c. 1600–1) Act 5, scene 1, line 73

age: My comfort is that old a., that ill layer-up of beauty, can do no more spoil upon my face —*The Life of Henry the Fifth*, (1599) Act 5, scene 2, line 244

age: Wast thou ordain'd, dear father, / . . . to achieve / The silver livery of advised a. —*The Second Part of Henry the Sixth*, (c. 1590–2) Act 5, scene 2, line 45

age: 'Tis thee, myself, that for myself I praise, / Painting my a. with beauty of thy days — "Sonnet 62," (1609) line 13

age's cruel knife: I now fortify / Against confounding A., / That he shall never cut from memory / My sweet love's beauty — "Sonnet 63," (1609) line 9

Age's steepy night: when his youthful morn / Hath traveled on to A. —"Sonnet 63," (1609) line 4

ambition: Ill-weav'd a. how much art though shrunk! —*The First Part of King Henry the Fourth*, (c. 1596–7) Act 5, scene 3, line 88

ambition: I have no spur / To prick the sides of my intent, but only / Vaulting a., which o'er-leaps itself / And falls on the'other — *Macbeth*, (1606) Act 1, scene 7, line 25

ambition: Thoughts tending to a., . . . / how these vain weak nails / May tear a passage through the flinty ribs / Of this hard world —*The Tragedy of King Richard the Second*, (c. 1595) Act 5, scene 5, line 18

ambition's: A. debt is paid —*Julius Caesar*, (1599) Act 3, scene 1, line 82

ambitious thoughts: the eagle-winged pride / Of sky-aspiring and a. / With rival-hating envy set on you / To wake our peace, which in our country's cradle / Draws the sweet infant breath of gentle sleep —*The Tragedy of*

King Richard the Second, (c. 1595) Act 1, scene 3, line 130

anger's: A. my meat; I sup upon myself / And so shall starve with feeding —*Coriolanus*, (1607–8) Act 4, scene 2, line 50

apothecary: O true a., / Thy drugs are quick —*Romeo and Juliet*, (1595–96) Act 5, scene 3, line 119

applause: Give him allowance as the worthier man, / For that will physic [cure] the great Myrmidon [Achilles] / Who broils in loud a., and make him fall —*Troilus and Cressida*, (c. 1601–2) Act 1, scene 3, line 375

apple: A goodly a. rotten at the heart, / O what a goodly outside falsehood hath! —*The Merchant of Venice*, (c. 1596–7) Act 1, scene 3, line 103.

April's: The A. in her eyes: it is love's spring, / And these the showers to bring it on — *Antony and Cleopatra*, (c. 1606–7) Act 3, scene 2, line 43

Arise: A. fair Sun —*Romeo and Juliet*, (1595–96) Act 2, scene 1, line 46

arrest: I a. thee / On capital treason; and, in thy a., / This gilded serpent —*King Lear*, (c. 1605–6) Act 5, scene 3, line 83

arrest: But be contented; when that fell [cruel] a. / Without all bail shall carry me away — "Sonnet 74," (1609) line 1

arrogance: Shall the proud lord / That bastes his a. with his own seam [lard] / . . . shall he be worshipp'd / Of what we hold an idol more than he? —*Troilus and Cressida*, (c. 1601–2) Act 2, scene 3, line 188

art: and a. made tongue-tied by authority — "Sonnet 66," (1609) line 9

Authority: a. melts from me —*Antony and Cleopatra*, (c. 1606–7) Act 4, scene 7, line 26

authority: A., though it err like others, / Hath yet a kind of medicine in itself, / That skins the vice o'the'top —*Measure for Measure,* (1604) Act 2, scene 2, line 135

Authority: though a. be a stubborn bear, yet he is oft led by the nose with gold —*The Winter's Tale,* (1611) Act 4, scene 4, line 835

B

baked in that pie: Why, there they are both, b. / Whereof their mother daintily hath fed, / Eating the flesh that she herself hath bred —*Titus Andronicus,* (1594) Act 5, scene 3, line 60

Barbary horse: you'll have your daughter cover'd with a B.; you'll have your nephew neigh to you; you'll have coursers for cousins and gennets for germans —*Othello,* (1604) Act 1, scene 1, line 111

beauty: B. doth varnish age, as if new-born, / And gives the crutch the cradle's infancy —*Love's Labour's Lost,* (c. 1594–95) Act 4, scene 3, line 244

beauty: B. . . . O 'tis the sun that maketh all things shine! —*Love's Labour's Lost,* (c. 1594–95) Act 4, scene 3, line 244

beauty: b. is a witch / Against whose charms faith melteth into blood —*Much Ado About Nothing,* (c. 1598–9) Act 2, scene 1, line 188

beauty: B. . . . / A brittle glass that's broken presently. —*The Passionate Pilgrim,* (1607–8) section 12, line 4

beauty: What doth her b. serve but as a note / Where I may read who pass'd that passing fair? —*Romeo and Juliet,* (1595–96) Act 1, scene 1, line 238

beauty: that b. which you hold in lease —"Sonnet 13," (1609) line 5

beauty: For all the b. that doth cover thee / Is but the seemly raiment of my heart —"Sonnet 22," (1609) line 5

beauty: The ornament of b. is suspect / A crow that flies in heaven's sweetest air —"Sonnet 70," (1609) line 3

beauty: B. within itself should not be wasted: / Fair flowers that are not gather'd in their prime / Rot and consume themselves in little time —*Venus and Adonis,* (1611) line 131

beauty's: B. a flower —*Twelfth Night,* (c. 1601) Act 1, scene 5, line 52

beauty's field: When forty winters shall beseige thy brow, / And dig deep trenches in thy b. —"Sonnet 2," (1609) line 1

beauty's legacy: Unthrifty loveliness, why dost thou spend / Upon thyself thy b.? —"Sonnet 4," (1609) line 1

bee: 'Tis seldom when the b. doth leave her comb / In the dead carrion —*The Second Part of King Henry the Fourth,* (c. 1597) Act 4, scene 4, line 79

bells: you are . . . / B. in your parlours; / wild-cats in your kitchens —*Othello,* (1604) Act 3, scene 1, line 110

besom [broom]: I am the b. that must sweep the court clean of such filth as thou are —*The Second Part of Henry the Sixth,* (c. 1590–2) Act 4, scene 7, line 34

bird: Am I your b. [target]? I mean to shift my bush —*The Taming of the Shrew,* (1594) Act 5, scene 1, line 46

birds: For both of you are b. of the self-same feather —*The Third Part of Henry the Sixth,* (c. 1590–2) Act 3, scene 3, line 161

bits/curbs: We have strict statutes and most biting laws— / The needful b. and c. to headstrong steeds— / Which for this fourteen years we have let slip —*Measure for Measure,* (1604) Act 1, scene 3, line 19

black weed: O thou b., why art so lovely fair? —*Othello,* (1604) Act 4, scene 2, line 68

bleeding rings: My father with his b., / Their precious stones new lost. —*King Lear,* (c. 1605–6) Act 5, scene 3, line 189

blood-sucker: Pernicious b. of sleeping men! —*The Second Part of Henry the Sixth,* (c. 1590–2) Act 3, scene 2, line 226

blossoms: Thus are my b. blasted in the bud, / And caterpillars eat my leaves away —*The Second Part of Henry the Sixth,* (c. 1590–2) Act 3, scene 1, line 89

blushes: Come quench your b. —*The Winter's Tale,* (1611) Act 4, scene 4, line 67

boat: My b. sails freely, both with wind and stream —*Othello,* (1604) Act 2, scene 3, line 63

bodies: Our b. are gardens, to which our wills the gardeners; so that if we will plant nettles or some lettuce . . . either to have it sterile with idleness or manured with industry, why, the power and corrigible authority of this lies in our will —*Othello,* (1604) Act 1, scene 3, line 323

bounded: O God, I could be b. in a nutshell, and count myself a king of infinite space, were it not that I have bad dreams —*Hamlet,* (c. 1600–1) Act 2, scene 2, line 256

bounty: his b., / There was no winter in't; an autumn it was / That grew the more by reaping —*Antony and Cleopatra,* (c. 1606–7) Act 5, scene 2, line 86

bounty: thanks, the exchequer of the poor, / Which, till my infant fortune comes to years, / Stands for my b. —*The Tragedy of King Richard the Second,* (c. 1595) Act 2, scene 3, line 65

bow: The b. is bent and drawn, make from the shaft —*King Lear,* (c. 1605–6) Act 1, scene 1, line 144

brain/soul: My b. I'll prove the female to my s., / My soul the father; and these two beget / A generation of still-breeding thoughts; / And these thoughts people this little world —*The Tragedy of King Richard the Second,* (c. 1595) Act 5, scene 5, line 6

brains: O God, that men should put an enemy in their mouths, to steal away their b. —*Othello,* (1604) Act 2, scene 3, line 281

braving arms: But in this kind to come, in b., / Be his own carver and cut out his way / To find out right with wrong—it may not be —*The Tragedy of King Richard the Second,* (c. 1595) Act 2, scene 3, line 142

brevity: Therefore since b. is the soul of wit / And tediousness the limbs and outward flourishes, / I will be brief —*Hamlet,* (c. 1600–1) Act 2, scene 2, line 90

C

calamity: there is no true cuckold but c. —*Twelfth Night,* (c. 1601) Act 1, scene 5

candle: Out, out, brief c.! Life's but a walking shadow, a poor player that struts and frets his hour upon the stage and then is heard no more —*Macbeth,* (1606) Act 5, scene 5, line 23

candle: Here burns my c. out; ay here it dies —*The Third Part of Henry the Sixth,* (c. 1590–2) Act 2, scene 6, line 1

canker / rose: I had rather be a c. in a hedge than a r. in his grace —*Much Ado About Nothing,* (c. 1598–9) Act 1, scene 3, line 28

caterpillars: Bushy, Bagot, and their complices, / The c. of the commonwealth, / Which I have sworn to weed and pluck away —*The Tragedy of King Richard the Second,* (c. 1595) Act 2, scene 4, line 165

chance: But as the unthought-on accident is guilty / To what we wildly do, so we profess / Ourselves to be the slaves of c. and flies / Of every wind that blows —*The Winter's Tale,* (1611) Act 4, scene 4, line 552

cheek: Why is your c. so pale? / How chance the roses there do fade so fast? —*A Midsummer Night's Dream*, (c. 1595–96) Act 3, scene 2, line 129

cheek: Thus is his c. the map of days outworn, / When beauty lived and died as flowers do now —"Sonnet 68," (1609) line 1

cheeks: Their c. are paper —*The Life of Henry the Fifth*, (1599) Act 2, scene 2, line 75

choler: Let's purge this c. without letting blood —*The Tragedy of King Richard the Second*, (c. 1595) Act 1, scene 1, line 153

cloud: He has a c. in 's face —*Antony and Cleopatra*, (c. 1606–7) Act 3, scene 2, line 52

clouds: How is it that the c. still hang on you? —*Hamlet*, (c. 1600–1) Act 1, scene 2, line 66

cock: The c., that is the trumpet to the morn, / Doth with his lofty and shrill-sounding throat / Awake the god of day —*Hamlet*, (c. 1600–1) Act 1, scene 1, line 148

commendations: in his c. I am fed: / It is a banquet to me —*Macbeth*, (1606) Act 1, scene 4, line 57.

complexion: Mislike me not for my c., / The shadow'd livery of the burnish'd sun —*The Merchant of Venice*, (c. 1596–7) Act 2, scene 1, line 1

conceit: I know not how c. may rob / The treasury of life, when life itself / Yields to the theft —*King Lear*, (c. 1605–6) Act 4, scene 6, line 42

conscience: The worm of c. shall begnaw thy soul —*The Tragedy of King Richard Richard the Third*, (c. 1591–92) Act 1, scene 3, line 221

conscience: My c. hath a thousand several tongues —*The Tragedy of King Richard the Third*, (c. 1591–92) Act 5, scene 3, line 192

content: My crown is in my heart, not in my head . . . / My crown is called c. —*The*

Third Part of Henry the Sixth, (c. 1590–2) Act 3, scene 1, line 62

corruption: rank c., mining all within, / Infects unseen —*Hamlet*, (c. 1600–1) Act 3, scene 4, line 148

corruption: My business in this state / Made me a looker-on here in Vienna, / Where I have seen c. boil and bubble / 'Till it o'errun the stew —*Measure for Measure*, (1604) Act 5, scene 1, line 320

countenance: Clear up, fair queen, that cloudy c. —*Titus Andronicus*, (1594) Act 1, scene 1, line 263

courage: We fail? But screw your c. to the sticking-place, / And we'll not fail —*Macbeth*, (1606) Act 1, scene 7, line 60

courtesy: what a candy deal of c. / This fawning greyhound then did proffer me —*The First Part of King Henry the Fourth*, (c. 1596–7) Act 1, scene 3, line 251

courtesy: Beatrice: C. itself must convert to disdain, if you come / in her presence. / Benedick: Then is c. a turncoat. —*Much Ado About Nothing*, (c. 1598–9) Act 1, scene 1, line 128

coward: Foul-spoken c., that thunder'st with thy tongue —*Titus Andronicus*, (1594) Act 2, scene 2, line 58

crows/eagles: fears; which will in time break ope / The locks o' the senate, and bring in the c. / To peck the e. —*Coriolanus*, (1607) Act 3, scene 1, line 134

curses: My hair doth stand on end to hear her c. *The Tragedy of King Richard Richard the Third*, (c. 1591–92) Act 1, scene 3, line 304

custom: The tyrant c. . . . . / Hath made the flinty and steel couch of war / My thrice-driven bed of down —*Othello*, (1604) Act I, scene 3, line 229

D

daggers: Thou hid'st a thousand d. in thy thoughts, / Which thou hast whetted on thy stony heart —*The Second Part of King Henry the Fourth,* (c. 1597) Act 4, scene 5, line 105

dalliance: silken d. in the wardrobe lies —*The Life of Henry the Fifth,* (1599) Act 2, Introductory Chorus, line 2

dancing days: For you and I are past our d. —*Romeo and Juliet,* (1595–96) Act 1, scene 4, line 147

danger/safety: Out of this nettle, d., we pluck this flower, s. —*The First Part of King Henry the Fourth,* (c. 1596–7) Act 2, scene 3, line 10

day: The gaudy, blabbing, and remorseful d. / Is crept into the bosom of the sea —*The Second Part of Henry the Sixth,* (c. 1590–2) Act 4, scene 1, line 1

death: the next time I do fight / I'll make d. love me, for I will contend / Even with his pestilent scythe —*Antony and Cleopatra,* (c. 1606–7) Act 3, scene 11, line 192

death: he had rather / Groan so in perpetuity than be cur'd / By the sure physician d. —*Cymbeline,* (1609) Act 5, scene 4, line 6

death: d. / . . . being an ugly monster, / 'Tis strange he hides him in fresh cups, soft beds, / Sweet words; or hath more ministers than we / That draw his knives i' the war —*Cymbeline,* (1609) Act 5, scene 4, line 69

death: But now the arbitrator of despairs, / Just d., kind umpire of men's miseries, . . . doth dismiss me hence —*The First Part of Henry the Sixth,* (c. 1592) Act 2, scene 5, line 28

death: Ay, there's the rub; / For in that sleep of d. what dreams may come, / when we have shuffled off this mortal coil / Must give us pause —*Hamlet,* (c. 1600–1) Act 3, scene 1, line 67

death: d. / The undiscovered country from whose bourn [boundary] / No traveller returns —*Hamlet,* (c. 1600–1) Act 3, scene 1, line 79

death: It is silliness to live, when to live is a torment; and then we have a prescription to die, when d. is our physician —*Othello,* (1604) Act I, scene 3, line 309

death: In a man as well as herbs, Grace and rude Will, / And where the worser is predominant / Full soon the canker D. eats up that plant —*Romeo and Juliet,* (1595–96) Act 2, scene 2, line 24

death: D. is my son-in-law, D. is my heir: / My daughter he hath wedded —*Romeo and Juliet,* (1595–96) Act 4, scene 4, line 66

death: shall I believe / That unsubstantial D. is amorous / And that the lean abhorred monster keeps / Thee here in dark to be his paramour —*Romeo and Juliet,* (1595–96) Act 5, scene 3, line 102

death: D.! / . . . Thou desp'rate pilot, now at once run on / The dashing rocks thy seasick weary bark —*Romeo and Juliet,* (1595–96) Act 5, scene 3, line 115

death: my son, now in the shade of d.; / Whose bright out-shining beams thy cloudy wrath / Hath in eternal darkness folded up —*The Tragedy of King Richard the Third,* (c. 1591–92) Act 1, scene 3, line 262

death: d. hath . . . / pluck'd two crutches from my feeble hands, Clarence and Edward —*The Tragedy of King Richard the Third,* (c. 1591–92) Act 2, scene 2, line 57

death: This youth that you see here / I snatch'd one half out of the jaws of d. —*Twelfth Night,* (c. 1601) Act 3, scene 4, line 367

death's: thou art d. fool, / For him thou labor'st by the flight to shun, / And yet run'st toward him still —*Measure for Measure,* (1604) Act 3, scene 1, line 11

death's: D. a great disguiser —*Measure for Measure,* (1604) Act 4, scene 2, line 180

decay: Who lets so fair a house fall to d., / Which husbandry in honor might uphold / Against the stormy gusts of winter's day / And barren rage of death's eternal cold? — "Sonnet 13," (1609) line 9

deceit: O that d. should dwell in such a gorgeous palace! —*Romeo and Juliet,* (1595–96) Act 3, scene 2, line 83

declined: I am d. into a vale of years —*Othello,* (1604) Act 3, scene 3, line 265

deed: one good d., dying tongueless; / Slaughters a thousand waiting upon that —*The Winter's Tale,* (1611) Act 1, scene 2, line 91.

deeds: She is a theme of honor and renown, / A spur to valiant and magnanimous d. —*Troilus and Cressida,* (c. 1601–2) Act 2, scene 2, line 198

delay: One inch of d. more is a South Sea of discovery —*As You Like It,* (c. 1599–1600) Act 4, scene 2, line 199

demerits: my d. / May speak unbonneted to as proud a fortune / As this that I have reached —*Othello,* (1604) Act 1, scene 2, line 23

desire: Now old D. doth in his deathbed lie, / And young Affection gapes to be his heir —*Romeo and Juliet,* (1595–96) Act 1, scene 4, line 261

Destinies: The D. . . . / They bid thee crop a weed, thou pluck'st a flower —*Venus and Adonis,* (1611) line 945

destruction: her fume needs no spurs, / She'll gallop far enough to her d. —*The Second Part of Henry the Sixth,* (c. 1590–2) Act 1, scene 3, line 153

Destruction: D. straight shall dog them at the heels —*The Tragedy of King Richard the Second,* (c. 1595) Act 5, scene 4, line 140

digestion: Things sweet to taste prove in d. sour —*The Tragedy of King Richard the Second,* (c. 1595) Act 1, scene 3, line 233

discontent: Now is the winter of our d. / Made glorious summer by this sun of York —*The Tragedy of King Richard the Third,* (c. 1591–92) Act 1, scene 1, line 1

discord: Take but degree away, untune that string, / And, hark, what d. follows! —*Troilus and Cressida,* (c. 1601–2) Act 1, scene 3, line 109

discourse: The body of your d. is sometimes guarded [decorated] with fragments, and the guards [decorative additions] are but slightly basted on neither; ere you flout old ends any further, examine your conscience —*Much Ado About Nothing,* (c. 1598–9) Act 1, scene 1, line 204

disease: He's a d. that must be cut away —*Coriolanus,* (1607) Act 3, scene 1, line 293

disgrace: For no man well of such a salve can speak, / That heals the wound, and cures not the d., / Nor can thy shame give physic to my grief —"Sonnet 34," (1609) line 7

disordered spring: He that hath suffer'd this d. / Hath now himself met with the fall of leaf. / The weeds which his broad-spreading leaves did shelter, / . . . / Are plucked up root and all by Bolingbroke —*The Tragedy of King Richard the Second,* (c. 1595) Act 3, scene 4, line 50

distraction: mine enemies are all knit up in their d. —*The Tempest,* (1611) Act 3, scene 3, line 89

doubts: Our d. are traitors. —*Measure for Measure,* (1604) Act 1, scene 4, line 78

dove: Seems he a d.? His feathers are but borrowed, / For he's disposed as the hateful raven —*The Second Part of Henry the Sixth,* (c. 1590–2) Act 3, scene 1, line 75

Dove-feathered raven: D., wolvish-rav'ning lamb! / Despised substance of divinest show! —*Romeo and Juliet,* (1595–96) Act 3, scene 2, line 75

dowry: She is herself a d. —*King Lear,* (c. 1605–6) Act 1, scene 1, line 243

dream: A d. itself is but a shadow —*Hamlet,* (c. 1600–1) Act 2, scene 2, line 262

dreams: D. . . . are the children of an idle brain —*Romeo and Juliet,* (1595–96) Act 1, scene 4, line 96

drink: He'll watch the horologe a double set, / If d. rock not his cradle —*Othello,* (1604) Act 2, scene 3, line 78

Drunken desire: D. must vomit his receipt, / Ere he can see his own abomination —*The Rape of Lucrece,* (1595) line 703

E

eagle / weasel: For once the e. England being in prey, — / To her unguarded nest the w. Scot / Comes sneaking, and so sucks her princely eggs, / Playing the mouse in absence of the cat, / To tame and havoc more than she can eat —*The Life of Henry the Fifth,* (1599) Act 1, scene 2, line 169

ears: Friends, Romans, countrymen, lend me your e.; —*Julius Caesar,* (1599) Act 3, scene 2, line 80

ears: Aged e. play truant at his tales —*Love's Labour's Lost,* (c. 1594–95) Act 2, scene 1, line 74

eaten: He hath e. me out of house and home. —*The Second Part of King Henry the Fourth,* (c. 1597) Act 2, scene 1, line 82

ebbing men: e. indeed— / Most often—do so near the bottom run / By their own fear or sloth —*The Tempest,* (1611) Act 2, scene 1, line 230

envy: Each word thou hast spoke hath weeded from my heart / A root of ancient e. —*Coriolanus,* (1607) Act 4, scene 5, line 108

evasion: But his e., wing'd thus swift with scorn, / Cannot outfly our apprehension —*Troilus and Cressida,* (c. 1601–2) Act 2, scene 3, line 118

evil / virtues: Men's e. manners live in brass; their v. / We write in water —*The Life of King Henry the Eighth,* (1613) Act 4, scene 2, line 45

eyes: thy e., which I may call the sea, / Do ebb and flow with tears; the bark thy body is / Sailing in this salt flood; the winds, thy sighs, / Who raging with thy tears and they with them, Without a a sudden calm will overset / Thy tempest-tossed body —*Romeo and Juliet,* (1595–96) Act 3, scene 5, line 132

eyes: But thou contracted to thine own bright e., / Feed'st thy light's flame with self-substantial fuel —"Sonnet 1," (1609) line 4

eyes: But from thine e. my knowledge I derive, / And, constant stars, in them I read such art / As truth and beauty shall together thrive —"Sonnet 14," (1609) line 9

eyes: Those are pearls that were his e. —*The Tempest,* (1611) Act 1, scene 2, line 398

eyes: These e., that now are dimm'd with death's black veil, / Have been as piercing as the mid-day sun, / To search the secret treasons of the world —*The Third Part of Henry the Sixth,* (c. 1590–2) Act 5, scene 2, line 16

eyes: Her e. / became two spouts —*The Winter's Tale,* (1611) Act 3, scene 3, line 24

F

face: The tartness of his f. sours ripe grapes —*Coriolanus,* (1607) Act 5, scene 4, line 19

face: in thy f. I see / The map of honor, truth and loyalty —*The Second Part of Henry the Sixth,* (c. 1590–2) Act 3, scene 1, line 202

faith: The fractions of her f., orts of her love, / The fragments, scraps, the bits and greasy relics / Of her o'er-eaten faith are bound to Diomed —*Troilus and Cressida,* (c. 1601–2) Act 5, scene 2, line 166

faiths: men's f. are waver cakes —*The Life of Henry the Fifth,* (1599) Act 2, scene 3, line 49

falsehood: Your bait of f. takes this carp of truth —*Hamlet,* (c. 1600–1) Act 2, scene 1, line 63

favours: He that depends / Upon your f. swims with fins of lead / And hews down oaks with rushes —*Coriolanus,* (1607) Act 1, scene 1, line 185

fear: they, distill'd / Almost to jelly with the act of f., / Stand dumb and speak not to him —*Hamlet,* (c. 1600–1) Act 1, scene 2, line 204

fear: we will fetters put about this f., / Which now goes too free-footed —*Hamlet,* (c. 1600–1) Act 3, scene 3, line 25

fear: those linen cheeks of thine / Are counselors to f. —*Macbeth,* (1623) Act 5, scene 5, line 16

fear: Thus have I shunn'd the fire for f. of burning, / And drench'd me in the sea, where I am drown'd —*Two Gentlemen of Verona,* (c. 1594) Act 1, scene 1, line 78

feather: Was ever f. so lightly blown to and fro as this multitude? —*The Second Part of Henry the Sixth,* (c. 1590–2) Act 4, scene 8, line 58

feather: I am a f. / for each wind that blows —*The Winter's Tale,* (1611) Act 2, scene 3, line 153

February face: Why what's the matter, / That you have such a F., so full of frost, of storm of cloudiness? —*Much Ado About Nothing,* (c. 1598–9) Act 5, scene 4, line 40

ferryman: I pass'd, methought, the melancholy flood, / with that sour f. / Unto the kingdom of perpetual night —*The Tragedy of King Richard the Third,* (c. 1591–92) Act 1, scene 4, line 45

fever: After life's fitful f. he sleeps well —*Macbeth,* (1606) Act 3, scene 2, line 24

fire/water: Be he the f., I'll be the yielding w.; / The rage be his, whilst on the earth I rain / My waters—on the earth, and not on him —*The Tragedy of King Richard the Second,* (c. 1595) Act 3, scene 3, line 58

flame: Let me not live, / After my f. lacks oil, to be the snuff / Of younger spirits —*All's Well That Ends Well,* (c. 1602–3) Act 1, scene 2, line 58

flattery: f. is the bellows [that] blows up sin —*Pericles, Prince of Tyre,* (1607–8) Act 1, scene 2, line 39

flint: For he is gracious . . . / Yet, notwithstanding, being incens'd, he's f. —*The Second Part of King Henry the Fourth,* (c. 1597) Act 4, scene 4, line 33

flow: I'll teach you how to f. —*The Tempest,* (1611) Act 2, scene 1, line 226

flower of Europe: thou hast slain / The f. —*The Third Part of Henry the Sixth,* (c. 1590–2) Act 2, scene 1, line 70

flowers: Ah! my poor princes! . . . / My sunblown f. —*The Tragedy of King Richard the Third,* (c. 1591–92) Act 4, scene 4, line 9

folly: and must I ravel out / My weav'd-up f.? —*The Tragedy of King Richard the Second,* (c. 1595) Act 4, scene 1, line 228

fortune: I am a man whom F. hath cruelly scratched —*All's Well That Ends Well,* (c. 1602–3) Act 5, scene 2, line 28

Fortune: Not being F., he's but fortune's knave, / a minister of her will —*Antony and Cleopatra,* (c. 1606–7) Act 5, scene 1, line 3

fortune: F. brings in some boats that are not steered —*Cymbeline,* (1609) Act 4, scene 3, line 46

fortune: It rain'd down f. show'ring on your head, / And such a flood of greatness fell on you —*The First Part of King Henry the Fourth,* (c. 1596–7) Act 5, scene 1, line 47

fortune: To be, or not to be, that is the question: / Whether 'tis nobler in the mind to suffer / the slings and arrows of outrageous f., or to take arms against a sea of troubles / And by opposing end them —*Hamlet,* (c. 1600–1) Act 3, scene 1, line 57

fortune: F., good night: smile once more; turn thy wheel! —*King Lear,* (c. 1605–6) Act 2, scene 2, line 179

fortune: F., that arrant whore, / Ne'er turns the key to th' poor —*King Lear,* (c. 1605–6) Act 2, scene 4, line 52

fortune: F. is painted blind, with a muffler afore his eyes to signify to you, that Fortune is blind. And she is painted also with a wheel, to signify to you, which is the moral of it, that she is turning and inconstant —*The Life of Henry the Fifth,* (1599) Act 3, scene 6, line 30

Fortune: Will F. never come with both hands full / But write her fair words still in foulest letters? —*The Second Part of King Henry the Fourth,* (c. 1597) Act 4, scene 4, line 103

Fortune's: Thou art a slave, whom F. tender arm / With favor never clasp'd, but bred a dog —*Timon of Athens,* (c. 1608) Act 4, scene 3, line 251

fortune's yoke: Yield not thy neck / To f., but let thy dauntless mind / Still ride in triumph over all mischance —*The Third Part of Henry the Sixth,* (c. 1590–2) Act 3, scene 3, line 15

fount: You are the f. that makes small brooks to flow; / Now stops thy spring, my sea shall suck them dry, / And swell so much the higher by their ebb —*The Third Part of Henry the Sixth,* (c. 1590–2) Act 4, scene 8, line 54

fountain: Thou sheer, immaculate, and silver f., / From whence this stream through muddy passages / Hath held his current and defil'd himself! —*The Tragedy of King Richard the Second,* (c. 1595) Act 5, scene 3, line 61

fox: were'it not madness then, / To make the f. surveyor of the fold? —*The Second Part of Henry the Sixth,* (c. 1590–2) Act 3, scene 1, line 252

fox/lamb: The f. barks not when he would steal the l. —*The Second Part of Henry the Sixth,* (c. 1590–2) Act 3, scene 1, line 54

fox/wolf: Attend. This holy f., / Or w., or both—for he is equal ravenous as he is subtle, and as prone to mischief —*The Life of King Henry the Eighth* (1613) Act 1, scene 1, line 159

free speech: First, the fair reverence of your Highness curbs me / From giving reins and spurs to my f. —*The Tragedy of King Richard the Second,* (c. 1595) Act 1, scene 1, line 55

friend: I profess me thy f., and I confess me knit to thy deserving, with cables of perdurable toughness —*Othello,* (1604) Act I, scene 3, line 338

friend: Thou disease of a f. —*Timon of Athens,* (c. 1608) Act 3, scene 1, line 57

fuel: I need not add more f. to your fire —*The Third Part of Henry the Sixth,* (c. 1590–2) Act 5, scene 4, line 70

G

gem: Never so rich a g. / Was set in worse than gold —*The Merchant of Venice,* (c. 1596–7) Act 2, scene 7, line 54

girdle: within the g. of these walls / Are now confin'd two mighty monarchies —*The Life of Henry the Fifth,* (1599) Prologue, line 19

God: G. shall be my hope / . . . and lantern to my feet —*The Second Part of Henry the Sixth,* (c. 1590–2) Act 2, scene 3, line 24

gold: I'll set thee in a shower of g., and hail rich pearls upon thee —*Antony and Cleopatra,* (c. 1606–7) Act 2, scene 5, line 47

Good name: G. in man and woman's dear, my lord; / Is the immediate jewel of our souls —*Othello,* (1604) Act 3, scene 3, line 159

goodness: g., growing to a plurisy, / Dies in his own too-much —*Hamlet,* (c. 1600–1) Act 4, scene 7, line 116

Grapple: G. them to thy soul with hoops of steel —*Hamlet,* (c. 1600–1) Act 1, scene 3, line 115

grassy carpet: here we march / Upon the g. of this plain —*The Tragedy of King Richard the Second,* (c. 1595) Act 3, scene 3, line 49

grave: the g. . . . . / Whose hollow tomb inherits naught but bones —*The Tragedy of King Richard the Second,* (c. 1595) Act 2, scene 1, line 69

grief: Thy match was mortal to him, and pure g. / Shore his old thread a-twain —*Othello,* (1604) Act 5, scene 2, line 206

grief: my heart is drown'd with g. —*The Second Part of Henry the Sixth,* (c. 1590–2) Act 3, scene 1, line 198

grief: G. boundeth where it falls, / Not with empty hollowness, but weight —*The Tragedy of King Richard the Second,* (c. 1595) Act 1, scene 2, line 57

grief: Must I not serve a long apprenticehood / To foreign passages, and, in the end, / having my freedom, boast of nothing else / But that I was a journeyman to g.? —*The Tragedy of King Richard the Second,* (c. 1595) Act 1, scene 3, line 271

grief: Yet I know no cause / Why I should welcome such a guest as g —*The Tragedy of* *King Richard the Second,* (c. 1595) Act 2, scene 2, line 7

grief: Thou most beauteous inn, / Why should hard-favor'd g. be lodg'd in thee —*The Tragedy of King Richard the Second,* (c. 1595) Act 5, scene 1, line 13

grief/patience: G. and p., rooted in him both, / Mingle their spurs together —*Cymbeline,* (1609) Act 4, scene 2, line 57

griefs: two buckets, filling one another, / . . . That bucket down and full of tears am I, / Drinking my g. whilst you mount up on high —*The Tragedy of King Richard the Second,* (c. 1595) Act 4, scene 1, line 185

guilt: So full of artless jealousy is g., / It spills itself in fearing to be spilt —*Hamlet,* (c. 1600–1) Act 4, scene 5, line 19

H

hairs: in her h., / The painter plays the spider, and hath woven / A golden mesh to entrap the hearts of men —*The Merchant of Venice,* (c. 1596–7) Act 3, scene 2, line 120

hare: You are the h. of whom the proverb goes, / Whose valour plucks dead lions by the beard —*The Life and Death of King John,* (c. 1594–6) Act 2, scene 1, line 137

harvest: I'll blast his h. —*The Third Part of Henry the Sixth,* (c. 1590–2) Act 5, scene 7, line 21

hate: For thou art so possessed with murd'rous h., / That 'gainst thyself thou stick'st not to conspire, / Seeking that beauteous roof to ruinate, / Which to repair should be thy chief desire —"Sonnet 10," (1609) line 5

health: h. . . . . with youthful wings is flown / From this bare wither'd trunk —*The Second Part of King Henry the Fourth,* (c. 1597) Act 4, scene 5, line 227

heart: My h. was to thy rudder tied by th' strings, / And thou shouldst tow me after —*Antony and Cleopatra,* (c. 1606–7) Act 3, scene 9, line 58

heart: A devil in an everlasting garment hath him, / One whose hard h. is buttoned up with steel —*The Comedy of Errors,* (c. 1592–4) Act 4, scene 2, line 66

heart: Bow, stubborn knees; and h. with strings of steel / Be soft as sinews of the new-born babe —*Hamlet,* (c. 1600–1) Act 3, scene 3, line 70

heart: A good h., Kate, is the sun and the moon, or rather the sun and not the moon, for it shines bright and never changes, but keeps its course truly —*The Life of Henry the Fifth,* (1599) Act 5, scene 2, line 164

heart: But I will wear my h. upon my sleeve, / For doves to —peck at: I am not what I am —*Othello,* (1604) Act 1, scene 1, line 29

heart: Even at this sight / My h. is turn'd to stone —*The Second Part of Henry the Sixth,* (c. 1590–2) Act 5, scene 2, line 50

heart: My h. doth plead that thou in him dost lie— / A closet never pierced with crystal eyes —"Sonnet 46," (1609) line 5

heart: my h., all mad with misery, / Beats in this hollow prison of my flesh —*Titus Andronicus,* (1594) Act 3, scene 2, line 9

heart: Weep I cannot, / But my h. / bleeds —*The Winter's Tale,* (1611) Act 3, scene 3, line 51

heart's: his h. his mouth —*Coriolanus,* (1607) Act 3, scene 1, line 255

heaven: look how the floor of h. / Is thick inlaid with the patines of bright gold —*The Merchant of Venice,* (c. 1596–7) Act 5, scene 1, line 58

heaven: Me thinks King Richard and myself should meet / With no less terror than the elements / Of fire and water when their thund'ring shock / At meeting tears the cloudy cheeks of h. —*The Tragedy of King Richard the Second,* (c. 1595) Act 3, scene 3, line 54

heavenly pay: For every man that Bolingbroke hath press'd / . . . God for his Richard hath in h. / A glorious angel —*The Tragedy of King Richard the Second,* (c. 1595) Act 3, scene 2, line 58

highway: He made you for a h. to my bed —*Romeo and Juliet,* (1595–96) Act 3, scene 2, line 134

hope: The miserable have no other medicine. But only h. —*Measure or Measure,* (1604) Act 3, scene 1, line 2

hope: h. is a curtal dog in some affairs —*The Merry Wives of Windsor,* (1597) Act 2, scene 1, line 112

hope: H. is a lover's staff —*Two Gentlemen of Verona,* (c. 1594) Act 3, scene 1 line 247

hope: True h. is swift, and flies with swallow's wings —*The Tragedy of King Richard the Third,* (c. 1591–92) Act 5, scene 3, line 23

hopes: This is the state of man: today he puts forth / the tender leaves of h.; to-morrow blossoms, / And bears his blushing honours-thick upon him; / The third day a comes a frost, a killing frost —*The Life of King Henry the Eighth,* (1613) Act 3, scene 2, line 353

hopes: Therefore my h, , not surfeited to death, / Stand in bold cure. —*Othello,* (1604) Act 2, scene 1, line 50

hopes: My h. lie drown'd —*Troilus and Cressida,* (c. 1601–2) Act 1, scene 1, line 51

hue: O! what a sight . . . / To note the fighting conflict of —her h., / How white and red each other did destroy: But now her cheek was pale, and by and by / It flashed forth fire as lightning from the sky —*Venus and Adonis,* (1611) line 345

humour: Shall quips and sentences and these paper bullets of the brain awe a man from the career of his h.? —*Much Ado About Nothing,* (c. 1598–9) Act 3, scene 1, line 103

hunger's teeth: So sharp are h., that man and wife / Draw lots who first shall die to lengthen life —*Pericles, Prince of Tyre,* (1607–8) Act 1, scene 4, line 45

I

idleness: Ten thousand harms, . . . / My i. doth hatch —*Antony and Cleopatra,* (c. 1606–7) Act 4, scene 11, line 63

image: your true i. pictured lies, / Which in my bosom's shop is hanging still —"Sonnet 24," line 6

impatience: i. does / Become a dog that's mad —*Antony and Cleopatra,* (c. 1606–7) Act 4, scene 11, line 80

indigested and deformed: Thy mother felt more than a mother's pain, / And yet brought forth less than a mother's hope; / To wit an i. and d. lump / Not like the fruit of such a goodly tree —*The Third Part of Henry the Sixth,* (c. 1590–2) Act 5, scene 6, line 49

industry/eloquence: His i. is up-stairs and down-stairs, his e. the parcel of a reckoning —*The First Part of King Henry the Fourth,* (c. 1596–7) Act 2, scene 4, line 102

ingratitude: I., thou marble-hearted fiend —*King Lear,* (c. 1605–6) Act 1, scene 4 line 266

injuries: O, sir, to wilful men / The i. that they themselves procure / Must be their schoolmasters —*King Lear,* (c. 1605–6) Act 2, scene 4, line 303

innocence: i. shall make / False accusation blush —*The Winter's Tale,* (1611) Act 3, scene 2, line 31

instrument: call me what i. you will, though you can fret me, yet you cannot play upon

me —*Hamlet,* (c. 1600–1) Act 3, scene 2, line 371

insurrection: And never yet did i. want / Such water-colors to impaint his cause . . . —*The First Part of King Henry the Fourth,* (c. 1596–7) Act 5, scene 1, line 79

intemperance: I do beseech your majesty may salve / The long-grown wounds of my i. —*The First Part of King Henry the Fourth,* (c. 1596–7) Act 2, scene 4, line 433

interpretation: Look how we can, or sad or merrily, / I. will misquote out looks —*The First Part of King Henry the Fourth,* (c. 1596–7) Act 5, scene 2, line 13

invention: If there be nothing new, but that which is / Hath been before, how are our brains beguiled, / Which, laboring for i., bear amiss / The second burden of a former child! —"Sonnet 59," (1609) line 1

J

jealousy: O, beware j.; / It is the green-ey'd monster, which doth mock / That meat it feeds on —*Othello,* (1604) Act 3, scene 3, line 170

Jealousy: This canker that eats up Love's tender spring, / . . . dissentious J. —*Venus and Adonis,* (1611) line 656

jewel: Can the world buy such a j.? / Yea, and a case to put it into —*Much Ado About Nothing,* (c. 1598–9) Act 1, scene 1, line 188

journey's end: Here is my j., here is my butt / And very sea-mark of my utmost sail —*Othello,* (1604) Act 5, scene 2, line 268

joy: make the coming hour o'erflow with joy, / And pleasure drown the brim —*All's Well That Ends Well,* (c. 1602–3) Act 2, scene 4, line 48

judgment: poor Ophelia / Divided from herself and her fair j. / Without the which we are pictures, or mere beasts —*Hamlet,* (c. 1600–1) Act 4, scene 5, line 84

K

kindle/quench: This is the way to k., not to q. —*Coriolanus,* (1607) Act 3, scene 1, line 196

kindness: Yet do I fear thy nature; / It is too full o'the' milk of human kindness —*Macbeth,* (1606) Act 1, scene 5, line 16

kindness: A kind overflow of k.; there are no faces truer than those that are so washed —*Much Ado About Nothing,* (c. 1598–9) Act 1, scene 1, line 26

kiss: you may ride's / With one soft k. a thousand furlongs ere / With spur we heat an acre —*The Winter's Tale,* (1611) Act 1, scene 2, line 94

kisses: k. . . . the very ice of chastity is in them —*As You Like It,* (c. 1599–1600) Act 3, scene 4, line 16

knit your hearts: To k. / With an unslipping knot, take Antony / Octavia to his wife —*Antony and Cleopatra,* (c. 1606–7) Act 1, scene 5, line 130

knot: I'll have this k. knit up tomorrow morning —*Romeo and Juliet,* (1595–96) Act 4, scene 2, line 24

L

ladder: Northumberland, thou l. wherewithal / The mounting Bolingbroke ascends my throne —*The Tragedy of King Richard the Second,* (c. 1595) Act 5, scene 1, line 55

Lady Tongue.: O God sir, here's a dish I love not. I cannot endure my L. —*Much Ado About Nothing,* (c. 1598–9) Act 2, scene 1, line 284

lamb/lion: He hath borne himself beyond the promise of his age, doing in the figure of a l., the feats of a l. —*Much Ado About Nothing,* (c. 1598–9) Act 1, scene 1, line 12

lamp: Our l. is spent, it's out —*Antony and Cleopatra,* (c. 1606–7) Act 4, scene 2, line 86

lamp: My oil-dried l. and time-bewasted light / Shall be extinct with age and endless night —*The Tragedy of King Richard the Second,* (c. 1595) Act 1, scene 3, line 221

Landlord: L. of England are thou now, not King. / Thy state of law is bondslave to the law —*The Tragedy of King Richard the Second,* (c. 1595) Act 2, scene 1, line 113

law: We must not make a scarecrow of the l., / Setting it up to fear the birds of prey / And let it keep one shape, till custom make it / Their perch and not their terror —*Measure for Measure,* (1604) Act 2, scene 1, line 1

law: the bloody book of l. / You shall yourself read, in the bitter letter —*Othello,* (1604) Act I, scene 3, line 67

law: Still you keep o' the windy side of the l. —*Twelfth Night,* (c. 1601) Act 3, scene 4, line 171

lee'd: And I. . . . must be l., and calm'd —*Othello,* (1604) Act 1, scene 1, line 29

Liberty: L. plucks justice by the nose —*Measure for Measure,* (1604) Act 1, scene 3, line 30

life: this knot intrinsicate / Of l. at once untie —*Antony and Cleopatra,* (c. 1606–7) Act 5, scene 2, line 311

life: His thread of l. hath not so soon decayed —*The First Part of Henry the Sixth,* (c. 1592) Act 1, scene 1, line 35

life: the strings of l. / Began to crack —*King Lear,* (c. 1605–6) Act 5, scene 3, line 216

life: I know also l. is a shuttle —*The Merry Wives of Windsor,* (1597) Act 5, scene 1, line 26. 1699–1

life: their thread of l. is spun —*The Second Part of Henry the Sixth,* (c. 1590–2) Act 4, scene 2, Line 33

life: If ever I were traitor, / My name be blotted from the book of l. —*The Tragedy of King Richard the Second,* (c. 1595) Act 1, scene 3, line 201

life: I have set my l. upon a cast, / And I will stand the hazard of the die —*The Tragedy of King Richard the Third,* (c. 1591–92) Act 5, scene 4, line 9

life's: L. but a walking shadow, a poor player that struts and frets his hour upon the stage and then is heard no more —*Macbeth,* (1606) Act 5, scene 5, line 23

life's: l. but breath, to trust it error —*Pericles, Prince of Tyre,* (1607–8) Act 1, scene 1, line 46

limed: She's l., I warrant you. We have caught her, madam —*Much Ado About Nothing,* (c. 1598–9) Act 3, scene 1, line 103

Lions/lambs: O bloody times! / While l. war and battle for their dens, / Poor harmless l. abide their enmity —*The Third Part of Henry the Sixth,* 1590–2) Act 2, scene 5, line 73

lip: Their l. were four red roses on a stalk — *The Tragedy of King Richard the Third,* (c. 1591–92) Act 4, scene 3, line 12

lips: Thy lips, those kissing cherries, tempting grow; —*A Midsummer Night's Dream,* (c. 1595–96) Act 3, scene 2, line 140

London: How L. doth pour out her citizens! — *The Second Part of King Henry the Fourth,* (c. 1597) Act 5, line 24

love: 'twere all one / That I should l. a bright particular star —*All's Well That Ends Well,* (1623) Act 1, scene 1, line 97

love: Yet, in this captious and intenible sieve / I still pour in the waters of my l. —*All's Well That Ends Well,* (c. 1602–3) Act 1, scene 3, line 210

love: L. is merely a madness. And deserves as well a dark house and a whip as madmen — *As You Like It,* (c. 1599–1600) Act 3, scene 2, line 400

love: I draw the sword myself; take it, and hit / The innocent mansion of my l., my heart — *Cymbeline,* (1609) Act 3, scene 4, line 64

love: wing'd with fervour of her l., she's flown / To her desired Posthumus —*Cymbeline,* (1609) Act 3, scene 5, line 61

love: There lives within the very flame of l. / A kind of wick or snuff that will abate it — *Hamlet,* (c. 1600–1) Act 4, scene 7, line 113

love: If frosts and fasts, hard lodgings and thin weeds, / Nip not the gaudy blossoms of your l. . . . / I will be thine —*Love's Labour's Lost,* (c. 1594–95) Act 5, scene 2, line 809

love: l. is blind, and lovers cannot see / The pretty follies that themselves commit —*The Merchant of Venice,* (c. 1596–7) Act 2, scene 6, line 36

love: "Ask me no reason why I l. you; for though / L. use Reason for his physician, he admits him / not for his counsellor . . ." — *The Merry Wives of Windsor,* (1597) Act 2, scene 1, line 4

love: For thee I'll lock up all the gates of l. — *Much Ado About Nothing,* (c. 1598–9) Act 4, scene 1, line 106

love: L. is a smoke made with the fume of sighs —*Romeo and Juliet,* (1595–96) Act 1, scene 1, line 193

love: This bud of l. by Summer's rip'ning breath / May prove a beauteous flow'r when next we meet —*Romeo and Juliet,* (1595–96) Act 2, scene 1, line 163

love: This bud of l. / by summer's ripening breath, / May prove a beauteous flower when next we meet —*Romeo and Juliet,* (1595–96) Act 2, scene 2, line 121

love: I have bought the mansion of a l. / But not possess'd it, and though I am sold / Not yet enjoy'd —*Romeo and Juliet,* (1595–96) Act 3, scene 2, line 26

love: When I shall see thee frown on my defects, / Whenas thy l. hath cast his utmost sum, / Called to that audit by advised respects —"Sonnet 49," (1609) line 2

love: L. . . . . / Is a strange brooch in this all-hating world —*The Tragedy of King Richard the Second,* (c. 1595) Act 5, scene 5, line 66

love: sweet l. is food for Fortune's tooth — *Troilus and Cressida,* (c. 1601–2) Act 4, scene 5, line 293

love: L. is blind —*Two Gentlemen of Verona,* (c. 1594) Act 2, scene 1, line 78

love: O! how this spring of l. resembleth / The uncertain glory of an April day —*Two Gentlemen of Verona,* (c. 1594) Act 2, scene 1, line 84

love: L. surfeits not, Lust like a glutton dies — *Venus and Adonis,* (1611) line 803

love/hate: Our own l. waking cries to see what's done, / While shameful h. sleeps out the afternoon —*All's Well That Ends Well,* (c. 1602–3) Act 5, scene 3, line 65

love's: You meet in some fresh cheek the power of fancy, / Then shall you know the wounds invisible / That L. keen arrows make —*As You Like It,* (c. 1599–1600) Act 5, scene 2, line 18

loves: Take all my l., my love, yea take them all; / What has thou then more than thou hadst before? / . . . I do forgive thy robb'ry, gentle thief, / Although thou steal thee all my poverty —"Sonnet 40," (1609) line 1

Love's: L. not Time's fool —"Sonnet 116," (1609) line 9

love's: L. a mighty Lord —*Two Gentlemen of Verona,* (c. 1594) Act 2, scene 4, line 137

love's fire: Against l. fear's frost hath dissolution —*The Rape of Lucrece,* (1595) line 355

love's fire: Free vent of words l. doth assuage; / But when the heart's attorney once is mute, / The client breaks, as desperate in his suit —*Venus and Adonis,* (1611) line 333

love's picture: When that mine eye is famished for a look / . . . With my l. then my eye doth feast, / And to the painted banquet bids my heart —"Sonnet 47," (1609) line 3

love's sweet bait: And she steal l. from fearful hooks —*Romeo and Juliet,* (1595–96) Act 1, scene 4, line 269

lover's eyes: So, till the judgment that yourself arise, / You live in this, and dwell in l. — "Sonnet 55," (1609) line 13

lowliness: l. is young ambition's ladder, / Whereto the climber-upward turns his face; / But when he once attains the upmost round, / He then unto the ladder turns his back —*Julius Caesar,* (1599) Act 2, scene 1, line 23

lustful Moor: I do suspect the l. / Hath leaped into my seat —*Othello,* (1604) Act 2, scene 1, line 290

M

maiden gardens: And many m., yet unset, / With virtuous wish would bear your living flowers, / Much liker than your painted counterfeit —"Sonnet 16," (1609) line 6

malice: Deep m. makes too deep an incision —*The Tragedy of King Richard the Second,* (c. 1595) Act 1, scene 1, line 153

melancholy: There's something in his soul / O'er which his m. sits on brood —*Hamlet,* (c. 1600–1) Act 3, scene 1, line 168

memory: Why should I write this down that's riveted, / Screw'd to my m.? —*Coriolanus,* (1607) Act 2, scene 2, line 43

memory: From the table of my m. / I'll wipe away all trivial fond records, / All saws of books, all forms, all presures past, / That youth and observation copied there; —*Hamlet,* (c. 1600–1) Act 1, scene 5, line 98

memory: m., the warder of the brain, / Shall be a fume, and the receipt of reason —*Macbeth,* (1606) Act 1, scene 7, line 65

Men: m. are but gilded loam or painted clay —*The Tragedy of King Richard the Second,* (c. 1595) Act 1, scene 1, line 179

Men/maids: M. are April when they woo, December when wed —m. are May when they are maids, but the sky changes when they are wives —*As You Like It,* (c. 1599–1600) Act 4, scene 1, line 147

mercy: The gates of m. shall be all shut up —*The Life of Henry the Fifth,* (1599) Act 3, scene 3, line 10

mind: O What a noble m. is here o'erthrown! . . . / Th' expectancy and rose of the fair state —*Hamlet,* (c. 1600–1) Act 3, scene 1, line 154

mind: The m. shall banquet, though the body pine: Fat paunches have lean pates, and dainty bits / Make rich the ribs but bankrupt quite the wits —*Love's Labour's Lost,* (c. 1594–95) Act 1, scene 1, line 25

mind: O, full of scorpions is my m., dear wife! —*Macbeth,* (1606) Act 3, scene 2, line 37

mind: Would the fountain of your m. were clear again, that I might water an ass at it —*Troilus and Cressida,* (c. 1601–2) Act 3, scene 3, line 312

minds: we bring forth weeds / When our quick m. lie still —*Antony and Cleopatra,* (c. 1606–7) Act 1, scene 2, line 113

mistrust: None but that ugly treason of m., / Which makes me fear th' enjoying of my love —*The Merchant of Venice,* (c. 1596–7) Act 3, scene 2, line 28

modesty: I should make very forges of my cheeks, / That would to cinders burn up m., / Did I but speak thy deeds —*Othello,* (1604) Act 4, scene 2, line 76

money: M. is a good soldier, sir, and will on —*The Merry Wives of Windsor,* (1597) Act 2, scene 2, line 177

moon's: the an arrant thief, / And her pale fire she matches from the sun —*Timon of Athens,* (c. 1608) Act 4, scene 3, line 443

moonlight: How sweet the m. sleeps upon this bank! —*The Merchant of Venice,* (c. 1596–7) Act 5, scene 1, line 54

morn/night: The grey-ey'd M. smiles on the frowning N. —*Romeo and Juliet,* (1595–96) Act 2, scene 1, line 163

morning/night: the m. steals upon the n., / Melting the darkness —*The Tempest,* (1611) Act 5, scene 1, line 65

moth of peace: if I be left behind, / A m., and he go to the war, / The rites for which I love him are bereft me —*Othello,* (1604) Act 1, scene 3, line 255

murder: M. not then the fruit within my womb —*The First Part of Henry the Sixth,* (c. 1592) Act 5, scene 4, line 63

murder: Thou showest the naked pathway to thy life, / Teaching stern m. how to butcher thee —*The Tragedy of King Richard the Second,* (c. 1595) Act 1, scene 2, line 30

Muse: my M. labours, / And thus she is delivered —*Othello,* (1604) Act 2, scene 1, line 127

music: Give me some m. . . . . moody food / Of us that trade in love —*Antony and Cleopatra,* (c. 1606–7) Act 2, scene 4, line 1

music: you are well tun'd now, / But I'll set down the pegs that make this m. —*Othello*, (1604) Act 2, scene 1, line 200

music: If m. be the food of love, play on! —*Twelfth Night*, (c. 1601) Act 5, scene 1, line 1

N

Nature: N. bankrout [bankrupt] is / . . . For she hath no exchequer now but his —"Sonnet 67," (1609) line 9

naughty night: Prithee, nuncle, be contented; 'tis a n. to swim in —*King Lear*, (c. 1605–6) Act 3, scene 4, line 108

newcome spring: Who are the violets now / That strew the green lap of the n.? —*The Tragedy of King Richard the Second*, (c. 1595) Act 5, scene 2, line 46

night: Why here walk I in the black brow of n., / To find you out —*The Life and Death of King John*, (c. 1594–6) Act 5, scene 6, line 17

night: Come civil N., / Thou sober-suited matron all in black —*Romeo and Juliet*, (1595–96) Act 3, scene 2, line 10

night's candles: N. are burnt out and jocund Day / Stands tiptoe on the misty mountain tops —*Romeo and Juliet*, (1595–96) Act 3, scene 5, line 11

nurse: This n., this teeming womb of royal kings —*The Tragedy of King Richard the Second*, (c. 1595) Act 2, scene 1, line 51

O

oak: he's the . . . o., not to be wind-shaken —*Coriolanus*, (1607) Act 5, scene 2, line 116

oaths: o. are straws, men's faiths are wafer cakes / and hold-fast is the only dog —*The*

Life of Henry the Fifth, (1599) Act 2, scene 3, line 49

opinion: What's the matter, you dissentious rogues, / That, rubbing the poor itch of your o., / Make yourselves scabs? —*Coriolanus*, (1607) Act 1, scene 1, line 170

opinion: you are now sail'd into the north of my lady's o. where you will hang like an icicle on a Dutchman's beard —*Twelfth Night*, (c. 1601) Act 3, scene 2, line 24

opinion's: O. but a fool, that makes us scan / The outward habit by the inward man —*Pericles, Prince of Tyre*, (1607–8) Act 2, scene 3, line 56

opportunity: Why hath thy servant, O., / Betray'd the hours thou gav'st me to repose? —*The Rape of Lucrece*, (1595) line 932

opportunity: The double gilt of this o. you let time wash off —*Twelfth Night*, (c. 1601) Act 3, scene 2, line 24

ornament: o. is but the guiled [guileful] shore / To a most dangerous sea . . . therefore, thou gaudy gold / Hard food for Midas, I will none of thee —*The Merchant of Venice*, (c. 1596–7) Act 3, scene 2, line 97

ornament: Thou that art now the world's fresh o., / And only herald to the gaudy spring —"Sonnet 1," (1609) line 9

ornament: Without all o., itself and true, / Making no summer of another's green —"Sonnet 68," (1609) line 10

oyster: Why then the world's mine o., / Which I with sword shall open —*The Merry Wives of Windsor*, (1597) Act 2, scene 2, line 2

P

park'd and bounded: How are we p. in a pale, / A little herd of England's timorous deer, / Mazed with a yelping kennel of French curs!

—*The First Part of Henry the Sixth,* (c. 1592) Act 4, scene 2, line 46

passion: in the very torrent, tempest, and (as I may say) whirlwind of your p., you must acquire and beget a temperance that may give it smoothness —*Hamlet,* (c. 1600–1) Act 3, scene 2, line 6

passion: O it offends me to the soul to hear a robustious periwig-pated fellow tear a p. to tatters, to very rags —*Hamlet,* (c. 1600–1) Act 3, scene 2, line 9

passion's slave: Give me that man / That is not p., and I will wear him / In my heart's core, ay, in my heart of heart, / As I do thee —*Hamlet,* (c. 1600–1) Act 3, scene 2, line 71

patch'd: this must be p. / With cloth of any colour —*Coriolanus,* (1607) Act 3, scene 1, line 251

patience: I will be the pattern of all p.; I will say nothing —*King Lear,* (c. 1605–6) Act 3, scene 2, line 37

patience: Though p. be a tired mare, yet she will plod —*The Life of Henry the Fifth,* (1599) Act 2, scene 1, line 24

patrimony: No good at all that I can do for him; / . . . bereft and gelded of his p. —*The Tragedy of King Richard the Second,* (c. 1595) Act 2, scene 1, line 235

peace: P. is a / very apoplexy, lethargy; mulled, deaf, sleepy, / insensible; a getter of more bastard children than war's a destroyer of men —*Coriolanus,* (1607) Act 4, scene 6, line 239

peace: p. should . . . / stand a comma 'tween their amities —*Hamlet,* (c. 1600–1) Act 5, scene 2, line 41

pearl: Why, she is a p. / Whose price hath launch'd above a thousand ships, / And turn'd crown'd kings to merchants —*Troilus and Cressida,* (c. 1601–2) Act 2, scene 2, line 81

pearls: I'll . . . hail rich p. upon thee —*Antony and Cleopatra,* (c. 1606–7) Act 2, scene 5, line 47

persuasions: By fair p. mix'd with sugar'd words., / We will entice the Duke of Burgundy —*The First Part of Henry the Sixth,* (c. 1592) Act 3, scene 3, line 18

pestilence: he is a p. that does infect the land —*The Life of King Henry the Eighth,* (1613) Act 5, scene 1, line 44

philosophy: I'll give thee armor to keep off that word, / Adversity's sweet milk, p. / To comfort thee though thou art banished —*Romeo and Juliet,* (1595–96) Act 3, scene 3, line 54

pictures: you are p. out o'doors, / Bells in your parlours; wild-cats in your kitchens —*Othello,* (1604) Act 3, scene 1, line 109

pie: no man's p. is freed / From his ambitious finger —*The Life of King Henry the Eighth,* (1613) Act 1, scene 1, line 52

pine: Thus droops this lofty p. and hangs his sprays —*The Second Part of Henry the Sixth,* (c. 1590–2) Act 2, scene 3, line 45

Pitchers: P. have ears —*The Tragedy of King Richard the Third,* (c. 1591–92) Act 2, scene 4, line 37

pity: Forget to p. him, lest thy p. prove / A serpent that will sting thee to the heart —*The Tragedy of King Richard the Second,* (c. 1595) Act 5, scene 3, line 56

pity: He is a stone . . . and has no more p. in him than a dog —*Two Gentlemen of Verona,* (c. 1594) Act 2, scene 4, line 10

plague: A p. a [on] both your houses. / They have made worms' meat of me —*Romeo and Juliet,* (1595–96) Act 3, scene 1, line 110

plants: Some o' their / p. are ill-rooted — already; the least wind i' the' world will blow them down —*Antony and Cleopatra,* (c. 1606–7) Act 2, scene 7, line 1

poison: Hide not thy p. with such sugar'd words —*The Second Part of Henry the Sixth,* (c. 1590–2) Act 3, scene 2, line 44

Poison/treason: p. and t. are the hands of sin, / Ay, and the targets, to put off the shame — *Pericles, Prince of Tyre,* (1607–8) Act 1, scene 1, line 139

praises: Our p. are our wages —*The Winter's Tale,* (1611) Act 1, scene 2, line 94.

precious stone: This p. [England] set in a silver sea —*The Tragedy of King Richard the Second,* (c. 1595) Act 2, scene 1, line 46

prey: If one should be a p., how much the better / To fall before the lion than the wolf —*Twelfth Night,* (c. 1601) Act 3, scene 1 line 132

pride: and there died / My Icarus, my blossom, in his p. —*The First Part of Henry the Sixth,* (c. 1592) Act 4, scene 7, line 16

pride: the seeded p. / That hath to this maturity blown up / In rank Achilles must or now be cropp'd / Or, shedding, breed a nursery of like evil / To overbulk us all — *Troilus and Cressida,* (c. 1601–2) Act 1, scene 3, line 316

primrose: Himself the p. path of dalliance treads / And recks [heeds] not his own rede —*Hamlet,* (c. 1600–1) Act 1, scene 3, line 50

primrose way: I had thought to have let in some of all professions, that go the p. to everlasting bonfire —*Macbeth,* (1606) Act 2, scene 3, line 18

prosperity's: P. the very bond of love, / Whose fresh complexion and whose heart together / Affliction alters —*The Winter's Tale,* (1611) Act 4, scene 4, line 586

purpose: P. is but the slave to memory, / Of violent birth, but poor validity; —*Hamlet,* (c. 1600–1) Act 3, scene 2, line 191

purse: Who steals my p., steals trash, 'tis something, nothing, / 'Twas mine, 'tis his,

and has been slave to thousands —*Othello,* (1604) Act 3, scene 3, line 161

purse: 'Tis deepest winter in Lord Timon's p. —*Timon of Athens,* (c. 1608) Act 3, scene 4, line 15

Q, R

quicksand : what is . . . Clarence but a q. of deceit? —*The Third Part of Henry the Sixth,* (c. 1590–2) Act 5, scene 4, line 25

ransom: the world's r., blessed Mary's son — *The Tragedy of King Richard the Second,* (c. 1595) Act 2, scene 1, line 56

reason: I'll yet follow the wounded chance [fortune] of Antony, though my r. / Sits in the wind against me —*Antony and Cleopatra,* (c. 1606–7) Act 3, scene 8, line 48

reason: My r., the physician to my love, / Angry that his prescriptions are not kept, / Hath left me —"Sonnet 147," (1609) line 5

rebellion: In soothing them we nourish . . . The cockles of r. . . . / Which we ourselves have plough'd for, sow'd and scatter'd — *Coriolanus,* (1607) Act 3, scene 1, line 68

remembrance: When to the sessions of sweet silent thought / I summon up r. of things past —"Sonnet 30," (1609) line 1

reputation: what's the matter, / That you unlace your r. thus —*Othello,* (1604) Act 2, scene 3, line 184

reputation: Thy deathbed is no lesser than thy land, / Wherein thou liest in r.; / And thou, too careless patient as thou art, / Committ'st thy anointed body to the cure / Of those physicians that first wounded thee —*The Tragedy of King Richard the Second,* (c. 1595) Act 2, scene 1, line 95

revenge: our hands . . . / they were besmear'd and overstain'd / With slaughter's pencils, where r. did paint / The fearful difference of incensed kings —*The Life and Death of King John,* (c. 1594–6) Act 3, scene 1, line 234

revenge: Let's make us med'cines of our great r., / To cure this deadly grief —*Macbeth,* (1606) Act 4, scene 3, line 215

riches: If thou art rich, thour't poor; / For, like an ass whose back with ingot bows, / Thou bear'st thy heavy r. but a journey, / And Death unloads thee —*Measure for Measure,* (1604) Act 3, scene 1, line 25

ripe for: Macbeth / Is r. shaking —*Macbeth,* (1606) Act 4, scene 3, line 237.

ripe/rot: from hour to hour we r. and r., / And then from hour to hour we rot and rot — *As You Like It,* (c. 1599–1600) Act 2, scene 7, line 26

rock: he's the r., the oak, not to be wind-shaken —*Coriolanus,* (1607) Act 5, scene 2, line 116

rock: And what is . . . Richard but a ragged fatal r.? —*The Third Part of Henry the Sixth,* (c. 1590–2) Act 5, scene 4, line 25

rose: when I have pluck'd thy r., / I cannot give it vital —growth again, / It must needs wither: I'll smell it on the tree —*Othello,* (1604) Act 5, scene 2, line 13

roses: The r. in thy lips and cheeks shall fade / To wanny ashes —*Romeo and Juliet,* (1595–96) Act 4, scene 1, line 99

royal root: One vial full of Edward's sacred blood, / One flourishing branch of his most r., / Is crack'd . . . hack'd down, and his summer leaves all faded —*The Tragedy of King Richard the Second,* (c. 1595) Act 1, scene 2, line 17

royal tree: The r. has left us royal fruit, / Which, mellow'd by the stealing hours of time, / Will well become the seat of majesty —*The Tragedy of King Richard the Third,* (c. 1591–92) Act 3, scene 7, line 166

rudeness: This r. is a sauce to his good wit, / Which gives men stomach to digest his words / With better appetite —*Julius Caesar,* (1599) Act 1, scene 2, line 305

rule: He cannot buckle his distemper'd cause / Within the belts of r. —*Macbeth,* (1606) Act 5, scene 2, line 15

rumour: R. is a pipe / blown by surmises, jealousies, conjectures, / And of so easy and so plain a stop / that the still-discordant wavering multitude, / Can play upon it — *The Second Part of King Henry the Fourth,* (c. 1597) Introduction, line 15

S

salad: My s. days, when I was green in judgment —*Antony and Cleopatra,* (c. 1606–7) Act 1, scene 5, line 75

sea: And what is Edward, but a ruthless s.? What Clarence but a quicksand of deceit? And Richard but a ragged fatal rock? —*The Third Part of Henry the Sixth,* (c. 1590–2) Act 5, scene 4, line 25

sea: The s. being smooth, / How many shallow bauble boats dare sail / Upon her patient breast, making their way / With those of nobler bulk! —*Troilus and Cressida,* (c. 1601–2) Act 1, scene 3, line 35

sea-walled garden: our s., the whole land / Is full of weeds; her fairest flowers choked up, / Her fruit-trees all unpruned, her hedges ruin'd, / Her knots disorder'd, and her wholesome herbs / Swarming with caterpillars —*The Tragedy of King Richard the Second,* (c. 1595) Act 3, scene 4, line 44

secrets: Infected minds / To their deaf pillows will discharge their s. —*Macbeth,* (1606) Act 5, scene 1, line 74

secrets: this is a subtle whore, / A closet, lock and key, of villainous s. —*Othello,* (1604) Act 4, scene 2, line 21

self-drawing web: Out of his self-drawing web, a' gives us note [he tells us] / The force of his own merit makes his way —*The Life of King Henry the Eighth,* (1613) Act 1, scene 1, line 62

sensual race: I give my s. the rein —*Measure for Measure,* (1604) Act 2, scene 4, line 160

sere: My way of life / has fall'n into the s., the yellow leaf —*Macbeth,* (1606) Act 4, scene 2, line 4

serpent: Where's my s. of old Nile? —*Antony and Cleopatra,* (c. 1606–7) Act 1, scene 5, line 24

serpent: The s. that did sting thy father's life / Now wears his crown —*Hamlet,* (c. 1600–1) Act 1, scene 5, line 39

serpent heart: O s., hid with a flow'ring face! Did ever dragon keep so fair a cave? —*Romeo and Juliet,* (1595–96) Act 3, scene 2, line 73

serpents: they will guard you, whe'r you will or no, / From such fell s. as false Suffolk is, / With whose envenomed and fatal sting, / Your loving uncle . . .·/ is shamefully bereft of life —*The Second Part of Henry the Sixth,* (c. 1590–2) Act 3, scene 2, line 226

serpents: they will guard you, whe'r you will or no, / From such fell s. as false Suffolk is, / With whose envenomed and fatal sting, / Your loving uncle, twenty times his worth, / They say is shamefully bereft of life —*The Second Part of Henry the Sixth,* (c. 1590–2) Act 3, scene 2, line 265

shame: A sovereign s. so elbows him: his own unkindness, / . . . [stings] His mind so venomously that burning shame; / Detains him from Cordelia —*King Lear,* (c. 1605–6) Act 4, scene 3, line 44

sheep: Renounce your soil, give s. in lions' stead —*The First Part of Henry the Sixth,* (c. 1592) Act 1, scene 5, line 29

sheep: he is shipp'd already, / And I have play'd the s. in losing him —*Two Gentlemen of Verona,* (c. 1594) Act 1, scene 1, line 73

shelter: And thou shalt prove a s. to thy friends, / A hoop of gold to bind thy brothers in, / That the united vessel of their blood, / . . . Shall never leak —*The Second Part of King Henry the Fourth,* (c. 1597) Act 4, scene 4, line 41

shower/thunder: the commons made / A s. and t. with their caps and shouts —*Coriolanus,* (1607) Act 2, scene 1, line 284

siege: O, how shall summer's honey breath hold out / Against the wrackful s. of batt'ring days —"Sonnet 65," (1609) line 5

sin: Thus was I . . . / Cut off even in the blossom of my s —*Hamlet,* (c. 1600–1) Act 1, scene 5, line 74

sin: My sable ground of s. I will not paint, / To hide the truth —*The Rape of Lucrece,* (1595) line 1074

sin: And water cannot wash away your s. —*The Tragedy of King Richard the Second,* (c. 1595) Act 4, scene 1, line 242

slander: s. / . . . whose tongue / Outvenoms all the worms of Nile, whose breath / Rides on the posting winds and doth belie / All corners of the world —*Cymbeline,* (1609) Act 3, scene 4, line 35

slander's: Pierc'd to the soul with s. venom'd spear, / The which no balm can cure but his heart-blood / Which breathed this poison —*The Tragedy of King Richard the Second,* (c. 1595) Act 1, scene 1, line 170

slaughter house: His realm a s. . . . / And yonder is the wolf that makes this spoil —*The Third Part of Henry the Sixth,* (1590–2) Act 1, scene 4, line 137

slave: Being your s., what should I do but tend / Upon the hours and times of your desire? —"Sonnet 57," (1609) line 1

sleep: O s.! Thou ape of death —*Coriolanus,* (1607) Act 2, scene 3, line 31

sleep: o gentle s.! / Nature's soft nurse —*The Second Part of King Henry the Fourth,* (c. 1597) Act 3, scene 1, line 5

sleep: S. that knits up the ravel'd sleave of care, / The death of each day's life, sore labor's bath, / Balm of hurt minds, great nature's second course, / Chief nourisher in life's feast, —*Macbeth,* (1606) Act 2, scene 2, line 34

slumber: Enjoy the honey-heavy dew of s. —*Julius Caesar,* (1599) Act 2, scene 1, line 230

smiles: Where we are, / There's daggers in men's s. —*Macbeth,* (1606) Act 2, scene 3, line 141

sorrow: Canst thou not minister to a mind diseas'd, / Pluck from the memory a rooted s.? —*Macbeth,* (1606) Act 5, scene 3, line 40

sorrow: Dry s. drinks our blood —*Romeo and Juliet,* (1595–96) Act 3, scene 5, line 59

sorrow's nurse: I am your s., / And I will pamper it with lamentation —*The Tragedy of King Richard the Third,* (c. 1591–92) Act 2, scene 2, line 87

sorrow's tooth: Fell s. doth never rankle more / Than when he bites, but lanceth not the sore —*The Tragedy of King Richard the Second,* (c. 1595) Act 1, scene 3, line 302

sorrows: When s. come, they come not single spies, / But in batallions —*Hamlet,* (c. 1600–1) Act 4, scene 5, line 78

sorrows: Each new morn / . . . new s. / Strike heaven on the face —*Macbeth,* (1606) Act 4, scene 3, line 4

sorrows: One s. never comes but brings an heir / That may succeed as his inheritor —*Pericles, Prince of Tyre,* (1607–8) Act 1, scene 4, line 63

soul: You have dancing shoes / With nimble soles, / I have a s. of lead —*Romeo and Juliet,* (1595–96) Act 1, scene 4, line 15

soul: Poor s. . . . . Why dost thou pine within and suffer dearth, / Painting thy outward walls so costly gay? —"Sonnet 146," (1609) line 1

soul's palace: Now my s. is become a prison —*The Third Part of Henry the Sixth,* (c. 1590–2) Act 2, scene 1, line 75

sovereign eye: Full many a glorious morning have I seen / Flatter the mountain-tops with s., / Kissing with golden face the meadows green, / Gilding pale streams with heavenly alchemy —"Sonnet 33," line 1

spaniel: I am your s. —*A Midsummer Night's Dream,* c. 1595–96) Act 2, scene 1, line 203

speak daggers: I will s. to her but use none, / My tongue and soul in this be hypocrites —*Hamlet,* (c. 1600–1) Act 3, scene 2, line 399

speech: A knavish s. sleeps in a foolish ear —*Hamlet,* (c. 1600–1) Act 3, scene 6, line 23

spider: Why strew'st thou sugar on that bottled s., / Whose deadly web ensnareth thee about? —*The Tragedy of King Richard Richard the Third,* (c. 1591–92) Act 1, scene 3, line 242

spite: I'll sacrifice the lamb that I do love, / To s. a raven's heart within a dove —*Twelfth Night,* (c. 1601) Act 5, scene 1 line 129

stage of fools: When we are born, we cry that we are come / To this great s. —*King Lear,* (c. 1605–6) Act 4, scene 6, line 178

starved snake: I fear me you, but warm the s., / Who, cherish'd in your breasts, will sting your hearts —*The Second Part of Henry the Sixth,* (c. 1590–2) Act 3, scene 1, Line 342

stone: Go to, then; you considerate s. —*Antony and Cleopatra,* (c. 1606–7) Act 2, scene 2, line 114

stone: I am not made of s., / But penetrable to your kind entreaties —*The Tragedy of King Richard the Third,* (c. 1591–92) Act 3, scene 7, line 222

stones: O, you are men of s.: / Had I your tongues and eyes, I'd use them so / That heaven's vault should crack —*King Lear,* (c. 1605–6) Act 5, scene 3, line 256

summer: But thy eternal s. shall not fade —"Sonnet 18," (1609) line 9

summer bird: O Westmoreland! thou art a s., / Which ever in the haunch of winter sings / The lifting up of day —*The Second Part of King Henry the Fourth,* (c. 1597) Act 4, scene 4, line 91

summer's distillation: s. left / A liquid prisoner pent in walls of glass —"Sonnet 5," (1609) line 9

summer's lease: Rough winds do shake the darling buds of May, / And s. hath all too short a date —"Sonnet 18," (1609) line 3

sun: That s., I pray may never set! —*The Life of King Henry the Eighth,* (1613) Act 1, scene 1, line 6

sunshine/hail: thou mayst see s. and a h. / In me at once; but to the brightest beams / Distracted clouds give way —*All's Well That Ends Well,* (c. 1602–3) Act 5, scene 3, line 33

sunset: for the s. of my brother's son / It rains downright —*Romeo and Juliet,* (1595–96) Act 3, scene 5, line 127

supportance: Give some s. to the bending twigs / . . . Cut off the heads of too fast growing sprays —*The Tragedy of King Richard the Second,* (c. 1595) Act 3, scene 4, line 30

suspicion: S. all our lives shall be stuck full of eyes —*The First Part of King Henry the Fourth,* (c. 1596–7) Act 5, scene 2, line 8

suspicion: See, what a ready tongue s. hath! —*The Second Part of King Henry the Fourth,* (c. 1597) Act 1, scene 1, line 84

sweet: let them not lick / The s. which is their poison —*Coriolanus,* (1607) Act 3, scene 1, line 155

sword: and I know his s. / Hath a sharp edge: it's long, and't may be said, / It reaches far; and where 'twill not extend, / Thither he darts it —*The Life of King Henry the Eighth,* (1613) Act 1, scene 1, line 109

T

tale: [Life] It is a t. / Told by an idiot, full of sound and fury, / Signifying nothing —*Macbeth,* (1606) Act 5, scene 5, line 27

taper: My inch of t. will be burnt and done —*The Tragedy of King Richard the Second,* (c. 1595) Act 1, scene 3, line 223

task: Alas, poor Duke! The t. he undertakes / is numb'ring sands and drinking oceans dry —*The Tragedy of King Richard the Second,* (c. 1595) Act 2, scene 2, line 142

tears: the t. live in an onion that should water this sorrow —*Antony and Cleopatra,* (c. 1606–7) Act 1, scene 2, line 174

tears: Had he the motive and the cue for passion / That I have? He would drown the stage with t. —*Hamlet,* (c. 1600–1) Act 2, scene 2, line 565

tears: He has strangled / His language in his t. —*The Life of King Henry the Eighth,* (1613) Act 5, scene 1, line 158

tears: Ah, but those t. are pearl which thy love sheeds [sheds] —"Sonnet 34," (1609) line 13

tears: Let me say, that never wept before, / My t. are now prevailing orators —*Titus Andronicus,* (1594) Act 3, scene 1, line 25

tears: But floods of t. will drown my oratory —*Titus Andronicus,* (1594) Act 5, scene 3, line 90

tears: Her t. will pierce into a marble heart —*The Third Part of Henry the Sixth,* (c. 1590–2) Act 3, scene 1, line 37

tears: We'll make foul weather with despised t. —*The Tragedy of King Richard the Second,* (c. 1595) Act 3, scene 3, line 160

tears: an ocean of t., / And instances of infinite of love / Warrant me welcome to my Proteus —*Two Gentlemen of Verona,* (c. 1594) Act 2, scene 7, line 69

tears: His t. [are] pure messengers sent from his heart —*Two Gentlemen of Verona,* (c. 1594) Act 2, scene 7, line 77

tears: her t. began to turn their tide —*Venus and Adonis,* (1611) line 979

tears/crocodile: If that the earth could teem with women's t., / Each drop she falls would prove a c. —*Othello,* (1604) Act 4, scene 1, line 240

temper: The brain may devise laws for the blood but t. leaps —o'r a cold decree: such a hare is madness the youth, to skip o'er the meshes of good counsel the cripple —*The Merchant of Venice,* (c. 1596–7) Act 1, scene 2, line 20

tempest: But, lords, we hear this fearful t. / sing, / Yet seek no shelter to avoid the storm. / We see the wind sit sore upon our sails, / And yet we strike not —*The Tragedy of King Richard the Second,* (c. 1595) Act 2, scene 1, line 263

thinking: She puts her tongue a little in her heart, / And chides with t. —*Othello,* (1604) Act 2, scene 1, line 106

thorns: Leave her to heaven, / And to those t. that in her bosom lodge, / To prick and sting her —*Hamlet,* (c. 1600–1) Act 1, scene 5, line 86

thorns: O! the t. we stand upon —*The Winter's Tale,* (1611) Act 4, scene 4, line 599

thorny wood: Brave followers, yonder stands the t., / Which, by the heavens' assistance and your strength, / Must by the roots be hewn up yet ere night —*The Third Part of Henry the Sixth,* (c. 1590–2) Act 5, scene 4, line 66

thoughts: Then—churls—their t., although their eyes were kind, / To thy fair flower add the rank smell of weeds; / But why thy odour matcheth not thy show, / The soil is this, that thou dost common grow —"Sonnet 69," (1609) line 11

thoughts: For now hath time made me his numb'ring clock: / My t. are minutes —*The Tragedy of King Richard the Second,* (c. 1595) Act 5, scene 5, line 49

thunder: when he meant to quail and shake the orb, / He was a rattling t. —*Antony and Cleopatra,* (c. 1606–7) Act 5, scene 2, line 85

thunder: The winds did sing to me, and the t.— / That deep and dreadful organ pipe— pronounc'd / The name of Prosper! —*The Tempest,* (1611) Act 3, scene 3, line 97

tide: There is a t. in the affairs of men, / Which, taken at the flood, leads on to fortune. / Omitted, all the voyage of their life / Is bound in shallows and in miseries —*Julius Caesar,* (1599) Act 4, scene 3, line 217

tiger's heart: O t. wrapp'd in a woman's hide! —*The Third Part of Henry the Sixth,* (c. 1590–2) Act 1, scene 1, line 6

time: Th' inaudible and noiseless foot of t. / Steals ere we can effect them —*All's Well That Ends Well,* (c. 1602–3) Act 5, scene 3, line 41

time: T. is the old justice that examines all such offenders [the unfaithful —*As You Like It,* (c. 1599–1600) Act 4, scene 1, line 198

time: The t. is out of joint, Oh cursed spite / That ever I was born to set it right! —*Hamlet,* (c. 1600–1) Act 1, scene 5, line 186

time: There's the respect / That makes calamity of so long a life; / For who would bear the whips and scorns of t.? —*Hamlet,* (c. 1600–1) Act 3, scene 1, line 70

time: Now he weighs t. / Even to the utmost grain —*The Life of Henry the Fifth,* (1599) Act 2, scene 4, line 137

time: T. goes on crutches till love have all his rites —*Much Ado About Nothing,* (c. 1598–9) Act 2, scene 1, line 374

time: There are many events in the womb of t. / which will be delivered —*Othello,* (1604) Act 1, scene 3, line 370

time: We see which way the stream of t. doth run, / And are enforced from out most quiet there / By the rough current of occasion — *The Second Part of King Henry the Fourth,* (c. 1597) Act 4, scene 1, line 70

Time: But wherefore do not you a mightier way / Make war upon this bloody tyrant T.? —"Sonnet 16," (1609) line 1

time: T. . . . delves the parallels in beauty's brow, / Feeds on the rarities of nature's truth, / And nothing stands but for his scythe to mow —"Sonnet 60," (1609) line 9

time: Thou canst help t. to furrow me with age, / But stop no wrinkle in his pilgrimage —*The Tragedy of King Richard the Second,* (c. 1595) Act 1, scene 3, line 229

time: For now hath t. made me his numb'ring clock: / My thoughts are minutes —*The Tragedy of King Richard the Second,* (c. 1595) Act 5, scene 5, line 49

time: T. hath, my lord, a wallet at his back, / Wherein he puts alms for oblivion —*Troilus and Cressida,* (c. 1601–2) Act 3, scene 3, line 144

time: the end crowns all, / And that old common arbitrator, T., / Will one day end it —*Troilus and Cressida,* (c. 1601–2) Act 4, scene 5, line 225

time: T. is the nurse and breeder of all good — *Two Gentlemen of Verona,* (c. 1594) Act 3, scene 1, line 243

time: O t.! thou must untangle this, not I; / It is too hard a knot for me to untie! —*Twelfth Night,* (c. 1601) Act 2, scene 2, line 40

time's: T. the king of men; / He's both their parent, and he is their grave —*Pericles, Prince of Tyre,* (1607–8) Act 2, scene 3, line 45

Time's: where, alack, / Shall T. best jewel from T. chest lie hid? —"Sonnet 65," (1609) line 9

time's scythe: And nothing 'gainst T. can make defense —Sonnet 12, line 13

time's subjects: We are t., and time bids be gone —*The Second Part of King Henry the Fourth,* (c. 1597) Act 1, scene 3, line 110

toe: what do you think, / You, the great t. of this assembly? —*Coriolanus,* (1607–8) Act 1, scene 1, line 100

tongue: She hath . . . struck me with her t. — *King Lear,* (c. 1605–6) Act 2, scene 4, line 159

tongue: Within my mouth you have enjail'd my t. —*The Tragedy of King Richard the Second,* (c. 1595) Act 1, scene 3, line 166

tongue's: my t. use is to me no more / Than an unstringed viol or a harp —*The Tragedy of King Richard the Second,* (c. 1595) Act 1, scene 2, line 161

torch: I will o'retake thee, Cleopatra . . . since the t. is out —*Antony and Cleopatra,* (c. 1606–7) Act 4, scene 10, line 48

trash: this poor t. of Venice, whom I trash for his quick hunting —*Othello,* (1604) Act 2, scene 1, line 298

tree: And that I love the t. from whence thou sprang'st, / Witness the loving kiss I give the fruit —*The Third Part of Henry the Sixth,* (c. 1590-2) Act 5, scene 7, line 31

Truth: T. shall nurse her —*The Life of King Henry the Eighth,* (1613) Act 5, scene 5, line 24

truth: T. hath a quiet breast —*The Tragedy of King Richard the Second,* (c. 1595) Act 1, scene 3, line 97

U

unfelt thanks: All my treasury / Is yet but u. —*The Tragedy of King Richard the Second,* (c. 1595) Act 2, scene 3, line 60

unnecessary letter: Thou whoreson zed! thou u.! —*King Lear,* (c. 1605-6) Act 2, scene 2, line 66

untimely cropp'd: How sweet a plant have you u.! —*The Third Part of Henry the Sixth,* (c. 1590-2) Act 5, scene 5, line 62

upraidings: Thou say'st his meat was sauc'd with thy —u.: / Unquiet meals make ill digestions —*The Comedy of Errors,* (c. 1592-4) Act 5, scene 1, line 73

V

vanity: A lover may bestride the gossamer / That idles in the wanton summer air / And yet not fall; so light is v. —*Romeo and Juliet,* (1595-96) Act 2, scene 5, line 18

vengeance: Put we our quarrel to the will of heaven, / Who, when they see the hours ripe on earth, / Will rain hot v. on offenders' heads —*The Tragedy of King Richard the Second,* (c. 1595) Act 1, scene 2, line 6

verbosity: He draweth out the thread of his v. finer than the staple of his argument —*Love's Labour's Lost,* (c. 1594-95) Act 5, scene 1, line 18

vice: do but see his v., / 'Tis to his virtue a just equinox, / The one as long as th' other —*Othello,* (1604) Act 2, scene 3, line 116

vice: V. repeated is like the wandering wind / Blows dust in others' eyes, to spread itself— *Pericles, Prince of Tyre,* (1607-8) Act 1, scene 1, line 96

vice: So smooth he daub'd his v. with show of virtue —*The Tragedy of King Richard the Third,* (c. 1591-92) Act 3, scene 5, line 29

viol: You're a fair v., and your sense the strings / Who finger'd to make man his lawful music, / Would draw heaven down and all the gods to hearken —*Pericles, Prince of Tyre,* (1607-8) Act 1, scene 1, line 81

vipers: O villains, v., damn'd without redemption! / Dogs easily won to fawn an any man! —*The Tragedy of King Richard the Second,* (c. 1595) Act 3, scene 2, line 128

virtue: Let not the piece of v., which is set / Betwixt us as the cyment [cement] of our love / . . . be the ram to batter / The fortress of it —*Antony and Cleopatra,* (c. 1606-7) Act 3, scene 2, line 23

virtue: If then the tree may be known by the fruit, as the fruit by the tree . . . there is v. in that Falstaff —*The First Part of King Henry the Fourth,* (c. 1596-7) Act 2, scene 4, line 433

virtue: And maiden v. rudely strumpeted — "Sonnet 66," (1609) line 6

virtue: V. is beauty but the beauteous evil / Are empty trunks o'erflourished by the devil —*Twelfth Night,* (c. 1601) Act 3, scene 4, line 377

voyage: In life's uncertain v. I will some kindness do them —*Timon of Athens,* (c. 1608) Act 5, scene 1, line 207

W

waiting: I am to wait, though w. so be hell — "Sonnet 58," (1609) line 13

war: Will you again unknit / This churlish knot of all-abhorred war —*The First Part of King Henry the Fourth,* (c. 1596–7) Act 5, scene 1, line 15

war/vengeance: O w.! thou son of hell, / Whom angry heavens do make their minister, / Throw in the frozen bosoms of our part / Hot coals of v.! —*The Second Part of Henry the Sixth,* (c. 1590–2) Act 5, scene 2, line 33

water: Smooth runs the w. where the brook is deep —*The Second Part of Henry the Sixth,* (c. 1590–2) Act 3, scene 1, line 53

water: I am standing w. —*The Tempest,* (1611) Act 2, scene 1, line 225

weapon's edge: This news, I think, has turned your w. —*The Second Part of Henry the Sixth,* (c. 1590–2) Act 2, scene 1, line 178

web: The w. of our life is of a mingled yarn, good and ill together —*All's Well That Ends Well,* (c. 1602–3) Act 4, scene 3, line 83

weed: we'll w. them all at last, / And you yourself shall steer the happy helm —*The Second Part of Henry the Sixth,* (c. 1590–2) Act 1, scene 3, line 102

weeds: Now 'tis the spring, and w. are shallow-rooted; / Suffer them now, and they'll o'ergrow the garden, / And choke the herbs for want of husbandry —*The Second Part of Henry the Sixth,* (c. 1590–2) Act 3, scene 1, line 31

weeds: Most subject is the fattest soil to w.; / And he, the noblest image of my youth, / Is overspread with them —*The Second Part of King Henry the Fourth,* (c. 1597) Act 4, scene 4, line 54

wheel: The w. is come full circle —*King Lear,* (c. 1605–6) Act 5, scene 3, line 145

whistling: I have been worth the w. —*King Lear,* (c. 1605–6) Act 4, scene 2, line 28

wickedness: What rein can hold licentious w. / When down the hill he holds his fierce career? —*The Life of Henry the Fifth,* (1599) Act 3, scene 3, line 22

wild-cats: you are . . . w. in your kitchens — *Othello,* (1604) Act 3, scene 1, line 110

will: He is the bridle of your w. —*The Comedy of Errors,* (c. 1592–4) Act 2, scene 1, line 13

wind: the sweet w. did gently kiss the trees — *The Merchant of Venice,* (c. 1596–7) Act 5, scene 1, line 1

Wind-changing: W. Warwick now can change no-more —*The Third Part of Henry the Sixth,* (c. 1590–2) Act 5, scene 1, line 57

winds: the w., thy sighs, / Who raging with thy tears and they with them, Without a a sudden calm will overset / Thy tempest-tossed body —*Romeo and Juliet,* (1595–96) Act 3, scene 5, line 134

winter lion: Of Salisbury, who can report of him, / That w., who in rage forgets, / Aged contusions and all brush of time —*The Second Part of Henry the Sixth,* (c. 1590–2) Act 5, scene 3, line 1

winter: Now is the w. of our discontent / Made glorious summer by this sun of York —*The Tragedy of King Richard Richard the Third,* (c. 1591–92) Act 1, scene 1, line 1

wisdom: The amity that w. knits not, folly may easily untie —*Troilus and Cressida,* (c. 1601–2) Act 2, scene 3, line 102

wish: Thy w. was father, Harry, to that thought —*The Second Part of King Henry the Fourth,* (c. 1597) Act 4, scene 5, line 91

wit and youth: when w. is come to harvest, / Your wife is like to reap a proper man — *Twelfth Night,* (c. 1601) Act 3, scene 1, line 135

wit: Make the doors upon a woman's w., and it will out at the casement; shut that, and 'twill out at the keyhole; stop that, 'twill fly with the smoke out at the chimney —*As You Like It*, (c. 1599–1600) Act 4, scene 1, line 159

wit: Thy w. . . . it is a most sharp sauce —*Romeo and Juliet*, (1595–96) Act 2, scene 3, line 85

wit: he's winding up the watch of his w. —*The Tempest*, (1611) Act 2, scene 1, line 12

wit: There's Ulysses and old Nestor, whose w. was moldy ere their grandsires had nails on their toes —*Troilus and Cressida*, (c. 1601–2) Act 4, scene 5, line 225

wits: Fat paunches have lean pates, and dainty bits / Make rich the ribs but bankrupt quite the w. —*Love's Labour's Lost*, (c. 1594–95) Act 1, scene 1, line 26

wits: they would whip me with their fine w. till I were as crest-fallen as a dried pear —*The Merry Wives of Windsor*, (1597) Act 4, scene 5, line 102

wits: Nay, if our w. run the wild goose chase, I am done. For thou hast more of the wild goose in one of thy w. than (I am sure) I have in my whole five —*Romeo and Juliet*, (1595–96) Act 2, scene 3, line 76

woe: So, Green, thou art the midwife to my w. —*The Tragedy of King Richard the Second*, (c. 1595) Act 2, scene 2, line 61

woes: What a tide of w. / Comes rushing on this woeful land at once —*The Tragedy of King Richard the Second*, (c. 1595) Act 2, scene 2, line 98

wolf: Thee I'll chase hence, thou w. in sheep's array —*The First Part of Henry the Sixth*, (c. 1592) Act 1, scene 3, line 55

wolves: Thus is the shepherd beaten from thy side, / And w. are gnarling who shall gnaw thee first —*The Second Part of Henry the Sixth*, (c. 1590–2) Act 3, scene 1, line 190

womb: O my accursed w., the bed of death! —*The Tragedy of King Richard the Third*, (c. 1591–92) Act 4, scene 1, line 53

women's faces: Poor w. are their own faults' books —*The Rape of Lucrece*, (1595) line 1252

word: She speaks poniards, and every w. stabs —*Much Ado About Nothing*, (c. 1598–9) Act 2, scene 1, line 257

word: Will you not eat your w.? —*Much Ado About Nothing*, (c. 1598–9) Act 4, scene 1, line 284

word: for each true w., a blister! and each false / Be as a cauterizing to the root o' the tongue —*Timon of Athens*, (c. 1608) Act 5, scene 1, line 137

words: So tender of rebukes that w. are strokes, / And strokes death to her —*Cymbeline*, (1609) Act 3, scene 5, line 40

words: I . . . unpack my heart with w. —*Hamlet*, (c. 1600–1) Act 2, scene 2, line 590

words: I have no w.; / My voice is in my sword —*Macbeth*, (1606) Act 5, scene 7, line 35

words: his w. are a very fantastical banquet, just so many strange dishes —*Much Ado About Nothing*, (c. 1598–9) Act 2, scene 3, line 19

words: These w. are razors to my wounded heart —*Titus Andronicus*, (1594) Act 1, scene 1, line 314

words: w. are very rascals since bonds disgrac'd them —*Twelfth Night*, (c. 1601) Act 3, scene 1, line 22

words: A fine volley of w., gentlemen, and quickly shot off —*Two Gentlemen of Verona*, (c. 1594) Act 2, scene 4, line 33

words: you have an exchequer of w. and, I think, no other treasures to give your followers; for it appears by their bare liveries that they live by your bare words —*Two Gentlemen of Verona*, (c. 1594) Act 2, scene 4, line 44

words/oaths: His w. are bonds, his o. oracles —*Two Gentlemen of Verona,* (c. 1594) Act 2, scene 7, line 74

working-day world: O, how full of briers is this w. —*As You Like It,* (c. 1599–1600)

world: this dull w., which in thy absence is / No better than a sty —*Antony and Cleopatra, (c. 1606–7) Act 4, scene 11, line 63*

world: this w. / 'tis an unweeded garden, / That grows to seed —*Hamlet,* (c. 1600–1) Act 1, scene 2, line 134

world: the w. . . . . / A stage where every man must play a part, / And mine a sad one —*The Merchant of Venice,* (c. 1596–7) Act 1, scene 1, line 77

world: And let this w. no longer be a stage / To feed contention in a lingering act —*The Second Part of King Henry the Fourth,* (c. 1597) Act 1, scene 1, line 155

world's: All the w. a stage. And all the men and women merely players —*As You Like It,* (c. 1599–1600) Act 2, scene 7, line 139

worldly business: My w. makes a period — *The Second Part of King Henry the Fourth,* (c. 1597) Act 4, scene 5, line 229

wormwood: weed this w. from your fruitful brain —*Love's Labour's Lost,* (c. 1594–95) Act 5, scene 2, line 855

wren: Look where the youngest w. of mine comes —*Twelfth Night,* (c. 1601) Act 3, scene 2, line 66

X, Y, Z

yields the cedar: And by my fall, the conquest to my foe, / Thus y. to the axe's edge —*The*

Third Part of Henry the Sixth, (c. 1590–2) Act 5, scene 1, line 11

young days: And thou present'st a pure un-stained prime. / Thou hast passed by the ambush of y. —"Sonnet 70," (1609) line 8

youth: he wears the rose of y. upon him —*Antony and Cleopatra,* (c. 1606–7) Act 3, scene 11, line 21

youth: Where wasteful Time debateth with Decay / To change your day of y. to sullied night —"Sonnet 15," (1609) line 10

youth: In me thou see'st the glowing of such fire, / That on the ashes of his y. doth lie — "Sonnet 73," (1609) line 9

youth: Deal mildly with his y.: / For young hot colts, being rag'd, do rage the more — *The Tragedy of King Richard the Second,* (c. 1595) Act 2, scene 1, line 69

youth: No, it is stopp'd with other flattering sounds, / . . . Lascivious metres, to whose venom sound / The open ear of y. doth always listen —*The Tragedy of King Richard the Second,* (c. 1595) Act 2, scene 1, line 17

youth/age: for y. no less becomes / the light and careless livery that it wears / Then settled a. his sables and his weeds, / Importing health and graveness —*Hamlet,* (c. 1600–1) Act 4, scene 3, line 77

Youth of England: Now all the Y. are on fire, / And silken dalliance in the wardrobe lies — *The Life of Henry the Fifth,* (1599) Act 2, Introductory Chorus, line 1

youth's proud livery: Thy y., so gazed on now, / Will be a tottered weed of small worth held —"Sonnet 2," (1609) line 3

Bibliography

A

Ackerman, Diane. *A Natural History of the Senses.* Vintage/Random House, 1990.

Addison, Joseph, and Sir Richard Steele. *Selections from The Tatler and The Spectator.* Edited by Robert J. Allen. Holt, Rinehart & Winston, 1961.

Adventures in American Literature. Harcourt Brace Jovanovich, 1980.

Agnon, Shmuel Yosef. *Shira.* Translated by Zeva Shapiro. Schocken Books, 1989.

Aiken, Conrad. *The Best Short Stories of Conrad Aiken.* Duell Sloan Pierce, 1930.

Allende, Isabel. *Of Love and Shadows.* Knopf, 1987.

Allende, Isabel. *The Stories of Eva Luna.* Atheneum, 1989.

Alsop, Joseph W., with Adam Platt. *I've Seen the Best of It: Memoirs.* W. W. Norton, 1992.

Alvarez, Julia. *How the Garcia Girls Lost Their Accents.* New American Library, 1992.

The American Poetry Review: The Pushcart Prize, XVI. Edited by Bill Henderson. Simon & Schuster/Touchstone, 1991.

The American Treasury, 1455–1955. Edited by Clifton Fadiman and Charles Van Doren. Harper, 1955.

Amis, Kingsley. *Kingsley Amis: Poems.* Oxford: Fantasy Press, 1954.

An Anthology of World Poetry. Edited by Mark Van Doren. Harcourt, Brace, 1928.

Anderson, Sherwood. *Winesburg, Ohio.* Edited by Horace Gregory. Viking, 1949.

Anderson, Sherwood. *The Portable Sherwood Anderson.* Viking Press, 1960.

Angelou, Maya. *I Know Why the Caged Bird Sings.* Random House, 1970.

Angelou, Maya. *Just Give Me a Cool Drink of Water 'fore I Diiie.* Random House, 1971.

The Antaeus Anthology. Edited by Daniel Halpern. Bantam, 1986.

Antin, Mary. *The Promised Land.* Houghton Mifflin, 1912.

Ashbery, John. *Some Trees.* The Ecco Press. 1978.

Multi-author works (collections) are listed alphabetically by title of the collection.

Ashton-Warner, Sylvia. *Myself.* Simon & Schuster, 1967.

Atkins, Zoë. *Daddy's Gone A-Hunting.* Liveright, 1923.

Atwood, Margaret. *Dancing Girls and Other Stories.* Simon & Schuster, 1979.

Atwood, Margaret. *The Handmaid's Tale.* McClelland and Stewart, 1985.

Atwood, Margaret. *Wilderness Tips.* Doubleday, 1991.

Auchincloss, Louis. *Skinny Island.* Houghton Mifflin, 1987.

Auchincloss, Louis. *Three Lives.* Houghton Mifflin, 1993.

Auden, W. H. *The Prolific and the Devourer.* Antaeus, 1981.

B

Babel, Isaac. *Red Cavalry: The Collected Stories of Isaac Babel.* S. G. Phillips, 1955.

Babitz, Eve. *Eve's Hollywood.* Delacorte, 1972.

Bagnold, Enid. *National Velvet.* William Morrow, 1949.

Bagnold, Enid. *The Chalk Garden.* Samuel French, 1956.

Bailey, Pearl. *The Raw Pearl.* Harcourt, Brace & World, 1968.

Baldwin, James. *Going to Meet the Man.* Doubleday, 1948.

Balzac, Honoré de. *Cousin Pons.* Roberts Brothers: Boston, 1892.

Balzac, Honoré de. *Old Goriot.* Modern Library/Random House, 1950.

Balzac, Honoré de. *The Girl with the Golden Eyes.* In *Balzac.* Dell, 1960.

Balzac, Honoré de. *Cousin Bette.* Viking, Penguin, 1965.

Baring, Maurice. *Last Letters.* Knopf, 1932.

Barnard, Robert. *A Scandal in Belgravia.* Scribner's, 1991.

Barthelme, Donald. *Come Back Dr. Caligari.* Little, Brown, 1971.

Bates, H. E. *A Month by the Lake & Other Stories.* New Directions, 1987.

Beauvoir, Simone de. *The Second Sex.* Knopf, 1953.

Beauvoir, Simone de. *The Coming of Age.* Putnam, 1972.

Beecher, Henry Ward. *Beecher As a Humorist.* Edited by Eleanor Kirk. Fords, Howard, and Hulbert, 1887.

Begley, Louis. *Wartime Lies.* Knopf, 1991.

Bellow, Saul. *Dangling Man.* New American Library/Signet, 1944.

Bellow, Saul. *Herzog.* Viking, 1961.

Bellow, Saul. *The Bellarosa Connection.* Viking Penguin, 1989.

Benet, Stephen Vincent. *The Last Circle.* Farrar Straus & Giroux, 1941.

Bent, Samuel Arthur. *Short Saying of Great Men.* James R. Osgood, 1882.

Berberova, Nina. *The Italics Are Mine.* Knopf, 1992.

Berlin, Isaiah. *The Crooked Timber of Humanity.* Edited by Henry Hardy. Knopf, 1990.

The Best American Essays of 1992. Edited by Susan Sontag. Ticknor & Fields, 1992.

Best American Plays 1945–1951. Edited by John Gassner. Crown, 1952.

Best American Plays 1918–1958. Edited by John Gassner. Crown, 1961.

Best American Plays 1958–1963. Edited by John Gassner. Crown, 1961.

Best American Plays 1974–1982. Edited by Clive Barnes. Crown, 1983.

The Best American Short Stories of the Eighties. Edited by Shannon Ravenel. Houghton Mifflin, 1990.

Best American Short Stories of 1973. Edited by Martha Foley. Houghton Mifflin, 1973.

The Best American Short Stories 1991. Edited by Alice Adams and Katrina Kenison. Houghton Mifflin, 1991.

The Best Women's Stage Monologues. Smith and Kraus, 1990.

The Bhagavad Gita. Translated by Franklin Edgerton. Harvard University Press, 1972.

Bierce, Ambrose. *The Collected Works of Ambrose Bierce.* Vol. 7. Neale, 1911.

Billings, Josh. *Uncle Sam's Uncle Josh.* Edited by Donald Day. Little, Brown, 1953.

Blake, William. In *The Complete Poetry and Selected Prose of John Donne & The Complete Poetry of William Blake.* Random House, 1941.

Bly, Robert. In *Meeting the Shadow.* Edited by Connie Zweig and Jeremiah Abrahams. Jeremy P. Tarcher, 1990.

A Book of English Literature. Vol. 1. Edited by Franklyn Bliss Snyder and Robert Grant Martin. Macmillan, 1947.

Borges, Jorge Luis. *The Aleph and Other Stories.* Dutton, 1978.

Bosworth, Sheila. *Slow Poison.* Knopf, 1992.

Bottome, Phyllis. *The Best Stories of Phyllis Bottome.* Edited by Daphne du Maurier. Faber and Faber, 1963.

Bowen, Elizabeth. *The Demon Lover and Other Stories.* Johnathan Cape, 1946.

Bowen, Elizabeth. *The Collected Stories of Elizabeth Bowen.* Knopf, 1981.

Boyle, Kay. *Wedding Day and Other Stories.* Jonathan Cape, 1930.

Boyle, T. Coraghessan. *Water Music.* Little, Brown, 1980–1.

Bradbury, Ray. *Death is a Lonely Business.* Knopf, 1985.

Breton, Andre. *Nadja.* Translated by Richard Howard. Grove Press, 1960.

Brinnin, John Malcom. *Sextet: T. S. Eliot & Truman Capote & Others.* Delacorte/Seymour Lawrence, 1981.

Brontë, Charlotte. *Villette.* John Grant, 1915.

Brontë, Charlotte. *Jane Eyre.* Dutton, 1963.

Brontë, Charlotte. *Shirley.* Dutton, 1963.

Brookner, Anita. *Hotel du Lac.* Pantheon, 1984.

Browning, Elizabeth Barrett. *The Complete Poetical Works of Elizabeth Barrett Browning.* Edited by Harriet Waters Preston. Scholarly Press, 1971.

Browning, Robert. *Dramatis Personae: The Poetical Works of Robert Browning.* Edited by Jack and Margaret Smith. Oxford: Clarendon, 1991.

Broyard, Anatole. *Intoxicated by My Illness.* Clarkson Potter, 1992.

Buber, Martin. "Dialogue" from *Four Existentialist Theologians.* Doubleday, 1958.

Buchanan, Edna. *Never Let Them See You Cry.* Random House, 1992.

Buck, Pearl S. *The Good Earth.* John Day, 1931.

Burgess, Anthony. *A Mouthful of Air.* Morrow, 1993.

Burns, Robert. *The Poems and Songs of Robert Burns.* Edited by James Kinsley. Oxford/Clarendon, 1968.

Byatt, A. S. *Possession.* Random House, 1990.

Byron, Lord George Gordon. *The Complete Poetical Works/Lord Byron.* Edited by Jerome J. McGann. Oxford/Clarendon, 1980.

C

Calisher, Hortense. *Tale of the Mirror.* Little, Brown, 1956.

Calisher, Hortense. *Queenie.* Arbor House, 1971.

Calisher, Hortense. *Herself.* Arbor House, 1972.

Calvino, Italo. *If on a winter's night a traveler.* Harcourt Brace Jovanovich, 1979.

Camus, Albert. *The Stranger.* Knopf, 1946.

Camus, Albert. *The Fall.* Random House, 1957.

Canfield, Dorothy. *A Harvest of Stories.* Harcourt, Brace, 1957.

Canin, Ethan. *Emperor of the Air.* Houghton Mifflin, 1985.

Capote, Truman. *A Capote Reader.* Random House, 1987.

Carew, Thomas. *The Poems of Thomas Carew.* Edited by Dunlap Rhodes. Oxford/Clarendon, 1949.

Carroll, Lewis. *Alice's Adventures in Wonderland.* Random House, 1946.

Carson, Rachel. *The Edge of the Sea.* Houghton Mifflin, 1955.

Carter, Angela. *The War of Dreams.* Harcourt Brace Jovanovich, 1972.

Cather, Willa. *One of Ours.* Knopf, 1922.

Cather, Willa. *Youth and the Bright Medusa.* Knopf, 1922.

Cather, Willa. *My Mortal Enemy.* Knopf, 1926.

Cather, Willa. *Cather, Later Novels.* The Library of America, 1990.

Catullus. *The Poems of Catullus.* Translated by James Michie. Random House, 1969.

Cerf, Bennett. *Try and Stop Me.* Simon & Schuster, 1944.

Cervantes, Miguel de. *Don Quixote.* Viking, 1949.

Chandler, Raymond. *The Simple Art of Murder.* Houghton Mifflin, 1950.

Chaucer, Geoffrey. *The Canterbury Tales.* Random House, 1965.

Chaucer, Geoffrey. *The Complete Poetry and Prose of Geoffrey Chaucer.* Edited by John H. Fisher. Holt, Rinehart & Winston, 1977.

Cheever, John. *The Enormous Radio and Other Stories.* Funk and Wagnalls, 1953.

Cheever, John. *The Stories of John Cheever.* Knopf, 1978.

Chekhov, Anton. *The Short Stories of Anton Chekhov.* Random House, 1932.

Chesterton, Gilbert Keith. *The Annotated Innocence of Father Brown.* Edited by Martin Gardner. Oxford University Press, 1988.

Chopin, Kate. *The Complete Works of Kate Chopin.* 2 vols. Edited by Peter Seyerstadt. Louisiana State University Press, 1969.

Churchill, Winston. Quoted in *Churchill* by Martin Gilbert. Henry Holt, 1992.

Cipolla, Carlo M. *Between Two Cultures: An Introduction to Economic History.* W. W. Norton, 1992.

Classical and Foreign Quotation. Edited by W. Francis H. King. Frederick Ungar, n. d.

Classic Tales from Modern Spain. Edited by William E. Colford. Barron, 1964.

Colette. *The Tender Shoot & Other Stories.* Farrar Straus and Cudahy, 1961.

Collins, Wilkie. *The Moonstone.* Doubleday, 1946.

Colwin, Laurie. *The Lone Pilgrim.* Knopf, 1981.

Complete Speaker's and Toastmaster's Library. Edited by Jacob M. Braude. Prentice-Hall, 1965.

Concise Dictionary of British Literary Biography. Vol. 5. Bruccoli Clark Layman/Gale, 1991.

The Concise Oxford Dictionary of Quotations. Oxford University Press, 1982.

Congreve, William. *Love for Love.* In *Twelve Famous Plays of the Restoration and Eighteenth Century.* Edited by Bennet A. Cerf and Donald S. Klopfer. The Modern Library/Random House, 1933.

Congreve, William. *The Comedies of William Congreve.* Edited by Eric S. Rump. Viking Penguin, 1985.

Connolly, Cyril (and Patrick Le Femor, Evelyn Waugh, Christopher Sykes, W. H. Auden). *The Seven Deadly Sins.* Morrow, 1962.

Conrad, Joseph. *Youth: A Narrative and Two Other Stories.* Blackwood, 1902.

Conrad, Joseph. *Tales of Unrest.* Doubleday, Page, 1908.

Conrad, Joseph. *Lord Jim.* Bantam, 1958.

Conrad, Joseph. *The Heart of Darkness.* Bantam, 1969.

The Contemporary American Poets. Edited by Mark Strand. NAL/World, 1969.

Contemporary American Poetry. Vintage Books, 1990.

Cooke, Alistair. *Talk about America.* Knopf, 1968.

Cormier, Robert. *Eight Plus One.* Pantheon, 1980.

Cowan, Paul. *An Orphan in History: Retrieving a Jewish Legacy.* Doubleday/Dell, 1982.

Coward, Noel. *To Step Aside.* Avon Books, n. d.

Cozzens, James Gould. *The Last Adam.* Harcourt Brace, World, 1958.

Crane, Stephen. *The Red Badge of Courage and Related Readings.* Prentice-Hall, 1966.

D

Dahl, Roald. In *The Company of Cats.* Edited by Michael J. Rosen. Doubleday, 1992.

Day-Lewis, C. *The Complete Poems of C. Day Lewis.* Stanford University Press, 1992.

Deutsch, Babette. *The Collected Poems of Babette Deutsch.* Doubleday, 1969.

Dickens, Charles. *Great Expectations.* Dodd Mead, 1942.

Dickens, Charles. *A Tale of Two Cities.* Oxford University Press, 1949.

Dickens, Charles. *David Copperfield.* Dutton, 1953.

Dickens, Charles. *A Christmas Carol.* Macmillan, 1963.

Dickens, Charles. *Oliver Twist.* Oxford University Press, 1966.

Dickens, Charles. *Little Dorrit.* Penguin, 1967.

Dickens, Charles. *Barnaby Rudge.* Dutton, 1972.

Dickens, Charles. *The Old Curiosity Shop.* Penguin, 1972.

Dickens, Charles. *Pickwick Papers.* Penguin, 1975.

Dickinson, Emily. *The Complete Poems of Emily Dickinson.* Edited by Thomas H. Johnson. Little Brown, 1957.

Didion, Joan. *Run River.* Obolensky, 1963.

Dillard, Annie. *Pilgrim at Tinker Creek.* Bantam, 1974.

Dillard, Annie. *An American Childhood.* Harper, 1987.

The Dimensions of the Short Story. Edited by James E. Miller, Jr., and Bernice Slote. Dodd, Mead, 1965.

Doerr, Harriet. *Consider This, Señora.* Harcourt Brace, 1993.

Donne, John. In *The Complete Poetry and Selected Prose of John Donne & The Complete Poetry of William Blake.* Random House, 1941.

Donne, John. In *The Norton Reader.* Edited by Arthur M. Eastman. W. W. Norton, 1965.

Donoso, José. *The Obscene Bird of Night.* Knopf, 1973.

Doolittle, Hilda (H. D.). *Collected Poems of H. D.* Boni and Liveright, 1925.

Dos Passos, John. *U. S. A., The 42nd Parallel.* Houghton Mifflin, 1930.

Dos Passos, John. *U. S. A., Nineteen Nineteen.* Houghton Mifflin, 1931.

Dos Passos, John. *U. S. A., The Big Money.* Houghton Mifflin, 1936.

Dostoevsky, Fyodor Mikhailovich. *The Short Novels of Dostoevsky.* Translated by Constance Garnett. Dial Press, 1945.

Dove, Rita. *Thomas and Beulah.* Carnegie Mellon University Press, 1986.

Dove, Rita. *Grace Notes.* W. W. Norton, 1989.

Doyle, Sir Arthur Conan. *The Adventures of Sherlock Holmes.* In *The Complete Sherlock Holmes.* Vol. 1. Doubleday, 1922.

Drabble, Margaret. *A Summer Bird-Cage.* William Morrow, 1964.

Drabble, Margaret. *The Middle Ground.* Knopf, 1980.

Dryden, John. *Absalom and Achitophel.* I. Oxford University Press, 1961.

Dumas, Alexandre. *The Three Musketeers.* Hart, 1975.

Duras, Marguerite. *The Afternoon of Mr. Andesmas.* In *Four Novels.* Grove Press, 1965.

Durrell, Lawrence. *Tunc.* Dutton, 1968.

Durrell, Lawrence. *Monsieur or The Prince of Darkness.* Viking/Penguin, 1975.

Dyson, Freeman. *Weapons and Hope.* Harper, 1984.

E

Each Day a New Beginning. Hazelden. Center City, 1982.

Edelman, Gerald M. *Bright Air, Brilliant Fire.* Basic Books, 1991.

Eight Famous Elizabethan Plays. Edited by Esther Cloudman Dunn. Modern Library/Random House, Random House, 1950.

Eight Great Comedies. New American Library, 1958.

Einstein, Albert. *Out of My Later Years.* Philosophical Library, 1950.

Eliot, George. *Felix Holt, The Radical.* Harper, 1866.

Eliot, George. *Spanish Gypsy.* Ticknor and Fields, 1868.

Eliot, George. *Middlemarch.* The New American Library, 1964.

Eliot, George. *George Eliot's Life as Related in Her Letters and Journals.* Henry Regenery, 1969.

Eliot, George. *Silas Marner.* In *The Best-Known Novels of George Eliot.* The Modern Library, Random House, n. d.

Eliot, T. S. *T. S. Eliot Collected Poems 1909–1962.* Harcourt, Brace & World, 1963.

Emerson, Ralph Waldo. *Ralph Waldo Emerson. Selected Prose and Poetry.* Edited by Reginald I. Cook. Holt, Rinehart & Winston, 1950.

Emerson, Ralph Waldo. *Society and Solitude/Ralph Waldo Emerson.* The Library of America, 1983.

Essays of Our Time. Edited by Leo Hamalian and Edmond L. Volpe. McGraw-Hill, 1960.

Essays Old and New. Edited by Essie Chamberlain. Harcourt, Brace & World, 1926.

The Experience of Literature. Edited by Lionel Trilling. Doubleday, 1967.

F

Fadiman, Clifton. *Any Number Can Play.* World, 1957.

Fallaci, Oriana. *The Egotists.* Henry Regenery, 1969.

Familiar Quotations. Edited by John Bartlett. Thirteenth and Centennial Edition. Little, Brown, 1882–1937, 1948, 1955.

Farjeon, Eleanor. *The Little Bookroom.* Henry Z. Walck, 1955.

Faulkner, William. *Selected Stories of William Faulkner.* Random House, 1930, 1932.

Faulkner, William. *Collected Stories of William Faulkner.* Random House, 1950.

Ferber, Edna. *Roast Beef, Medium: The Business Adventures of*

Emma McChesney. Books for Libraries, 1953.

Ferber, Edna. *They Brought Their Women.* Doubleday, Doran, 1933.

Ferber, Edna. *So Big.* Limited Editions, 1953.

Ferber, Edna. *A Peculiar Treasure.* Doubleday, 1960.

Ferber, Edna. *A Kind of Magic.* Doubleday, 1963.

Ferlinghetti, Lawrence. *Who Are We Now.* New Directions, 1976.

Fielding, Henry. *The Life of Mr. Jonathan Wild the Great.* The New American Library, 1961.

Film Scenes for Actors. Edited by Joshua Karton. Bantam, 1983.

Fisher, Dorothy Canfield. *The Deepening Stream.* Harcourt Brace Jovanovich, 1930.

Fisher, Dorothy Canfield. *A Harvest of Stories.* Harcourt, Brace, 1957.

Fitzgerald, Edward. *The Rubáiyát of Omar Khayám.* Heritage Books, 1946.

Fitzgerald, F. Scott. *The Great Gatsby.* Scribner's, 1925.

Fitzgerald, F. Scott. *Tender Is the Night.* Scribner's, 1934.

Fitzgerald, F. Scott. *The Last Tycoon.* Scribner's, 1941.

Fitzgerald, F. Scott. *The Crack-Up.* New Directions, 1945.

Fitzgerald, F. Scott. *The Stories of F. Scott Fitzgerald.* Scribner's, 1951.

Fitzgerald, Zelda. *Save Me the Waltz.* Southern Illinois University Press, 1967.

Five Modern American Poets. Edited by David Lougee. Holt, Rinehart & Winston, 1968.

Flaubert, Gustave. *Flaubert—Sand: The Correspondence.* Translated by Francis Steegmuler and Barbara Bray. Knopf, 1993.

Forster, E. M. *A Room with a View.* Knopf, 1923.

Fowles, John. *Daniel Martin.* Little, Brown, 1977.

Franklin, Benjamin. *The Complete Poor Richard Almanacs.* Imprint Society, 1970.

Friday, Nancy. *My Mother, My Self.* Delacorte, 1977.

Frost, Robert. *Complete Poems of Robert Frost.* Henry Holt, 1949.

Frost, Robert. *Lend Me Your Ears.* W. W. Norton, 1992.

Fry, Christopher. *The Lady's Not for Burning.* Oxford University Press, 1950.

Fry, Christopher. *Three Plays.* Oxford University Press, 1965.

Fuentes, Carlos. *The Old Gringo.* Farrar, Straus & Giroux, 1985.

G

Gallant, Mavis. *In Transit.* Random House, 1988.

Garcia, Cristina. *Dreaming in Cuban.* Knopf, 1992.

Gardner, Erle Stanley. *Dead Men's Letters and Other Short Novels.* Caroll & Graf, 1990.

Gass, William H. Introduction to *The Notebooks of Malte Laurids Brigge* by Rainer Maria Rilke. Random House/Vintage, 1985.

Genet, Jean. *Querelle.* Translated by Anselm Hollo. Grove Press, 1974.

Gibran, Kahlil. *The Prophet.* Knopf, 1976.

Gide, André. Preface to *Night Flight* by Antoine de Saint-Exupery. Grosset & Dunlap, 1932.

Giraudoux, Jean. *Tiger at the Gate.* In *The Jean Giraudoux Bible.* Translated by Christopher Fry. Oxford University Press, 1955.

Gleick, James. *The Character of Physical Law. Chaos: Making a New Science.* Viking, 1987.

Gleick, James. *Genius: The Life and Science of Richard Feynman.* Pantheon, 1992.

Goethe, Johann Wolfgang von. *The Sorrows of Young Werther.* Translated by W. H. Auden. Random House, 1987.

Goldstein, Rebecca. *The Dark Sister.* Viking Penguin, 1992.

Gonzales, Laurence. *The Still Point.* The University of Arkansas Press, 1989.

Gordimer, Nadine. *An Uncommon Reader.* Avon, 1965.

Gordimer, Nadine. *Burger's Daughter.* Viking, 1979.

Gorky, Maxim. *A Book of Short Stories by Maxim Gorki.* Edited by Avrahm Yarmolinsky and Baroness Moura Budberg. Octagon Books, 1939.

Gould, Lois. *Final Analysis.* Farrar, Straus & Giroux, 1974.

Graham, Winston. *Stephanie.* Carroll & Graf, 1992.

Granger, Bill. *The Last Good German.* Warner Books, 1991.

The Great Thoughts. Edited by George Seldes. Random House, 1985.

Green, Hanna. *I Never Promised You a Rose Garden.* Harper, 1964.

Greene, Graham. *The Comedians.* Viking, 1966.

Greene, Graham. *Collected Essays/ The Portable Graham Greene.* Viking, 1972, 1973.

Greer, Germaine. *The Change: Women Aging and Menopause.* Knopf, 1992.

Griffin, Susan. *A Chorus of Stones.* Doubleday, 1992.

Grumbach, Doris. *The Magician's Girl.* Macmillan, 1987.

H

Hacker, Andrew. *Two Nations.* Scribner's, 1992.

Hall, Donald. *The One Day.* Ticknor & Fields, 1988.

Hammett, Dashiell. *The Maltese Falcon.* Knopf, 1929.

Hammett, Dashiell. *Red Harvest.* Knopf, 1929.

Hannah, Barry. *Airships.* Knopf, 1978.

Hardy, Thomas. *Tess of the D'Urbervilles.* Harper, 1891.

Hardy, Thomas. *Jude the Obscure.* The Modern Library, 1967.

Hardy, Thomas. *The Mayor of Casterbridge.* W. W. Norton, 1977.

Hart, Josephine. *Damage.* Ballantine, 1992.

Hartley, L. P. *The Go-Between.* Stein and Day, 1967.

The Harvard Book of Contemporary Poetry. Edited by Helen Vendler. Belknap Press/Harvard University, 1985.

Harwood, Ronald. *The Dresser.* Grove, 1988.

Hawthorne, Nathaniel. *The Scarlet Letter.* The Heritage Press, 1935.

Hawthorne, Nathaniel. *The Blithedale Romance* and *The House of Seven Gables.* In *Nathaniel Hawthorne.* The Library of America, 1983.

Hazlitt, William. *Essays by William Hazlitt.* Edited by Percy Van Dyke Shelly. Scribner's, 1924.

Hecht, Anthony. *The Venetian Vespers.* Atheneum, 1979.

Hecht, Anthony. *Collected Earlier Poems.* Knopf, 1990.

Hecht, Ben. *A Guide for the Bedevilled.* Scribner's, 1944.

Hemingway, Ernest. *The Short Stories of Ernest Hemingway.* Scribner's, 1953.

Hemingway, Ernest. *Death in the Afternoon.* Scribner's, 1932.

Hemingway, Ernest. *The Sun also Rises.* Scribner's, 1949.

Hemingway, Ernest. *The Complete Short Stories of Ernest Hemingway.* Scribner's, 1987.

Henry, O. *The Four Million: Collected Stories of O. Henry.* Edited by Paul J. Horowitz. Avenel/ Crown, 1986.

Hersey, John. *Fling and Other Stories.* Vintage/Random House, 1991.

Hesse, Hermann. *Siddhartha.* Translated by Hilda Rosner. New Directions, 1951.

Hesse, Hermann. *Reflections.* Farrar, Straus & Giroux, 1974.

Highsmith, Patricia. *Eleven.* Atlantic Monthly Press, 1989.

A History of Modern Poetry. Edited by David Perkins. Belknap Press/ Harvard University, 1976.

Hoagland, Edward. *The Edward Hoagland Reader.* Random House/Vintage, 1979.

Holmes, Sr., Oliver Wendell. *The Professor at the Breakfast Table.* Houghton Mifflin, c. 1859.

Holmes, Sr., Oliver Wendell. *The Autocrat of the Breakfast-Table.* Sagamore Press, 1957.

Holmes, Sr., Oliver Wendell. *The Poet at the Breakfast Table.* Sagamore Press, 1957.

Holmes, Sr., Oliver Wendell. *Poems by Oliver Wendell Holmes.* W. B. Conkey, n. d.

The Home Book of American Quotations. Edited by Bruce Bohle. Dodd Mead, 1967.

Hopkins, Gerard Manley. *The Poems of Gerald Manley Hopkins.* Oxford University Press, 1961.

Hoult, Norah. *Poor Women.* In *The Portable Irish Reader.* Edited by Diarmuid Russell. Viking Press, 1946.

Housman, A. E. *The Collected Poems of A. E. Housman.* Holt, Rinehart & Winston, 1967.

Howard, Maureen. *Bridgeport Bus.* Penguin, 1980.

Hoyt's New Cyclopedia of Practical Quotations. Edited by Kate Louise Roberts. Funk & Wagnalls, 1927.

Hudson, W. H. *Green Mansions.* The Heritage Press, 1936.

Hughes, Robert. *The Fatal Shore*. Knopf, 1987.

Hughes, Robert. *Culture of Complaint*. New York Public Library/Oxford University Press, 1992.

Hughes, Ted. *Cave Birds*. Viking, 1978.

Huxley, Aldous. *Point Counter Point*. Doubleday, Doran, 1928.

Huxley, Aldous. *Time Must Have a Stop*. Harper, 1944.

Huxley, Aldous. *Antic Hay & The Giaconda Smile*. Harper, 1964.

Hwang, David Henry. *M. Butterfly*. Plume/New American Library, 1988.

I

Ibsen, Henrik. *A Doll's House*. Dutton, 1954.

Ingpen, Ada M. *Women as Letter-Writers*. Baker and Taylor, 1909.

The International Thesaurus of Quotations. Edited by Rhoda Thomas Tripp. Harper/Perennial, 1987.

International Treasury of Mystery and Suspense. Doubleday, 1983.

Irving, Washington. *The Complete Tales of Washington Irving*. Doubleday, 1975.

Isherwood, Christopher. *The Berlin Stories*. New Directions, 1945.

J

James, Henry. *The Marriages and Other Stories*. New American Library/Signet, 1961.

James, Henry. *Portrait of a Lady* and *Roderick Hudson*. In *Henry James*. The Library of America, 1985.

James, P. D. *An Unsuitable Job for a Woman*. Faber & Faber, 1973.

James, William. *The Principles of Psychology*. Dover, 1950.

Jewett, Sarah Orne. *The Country of the Pointed Firs*. Doubleday, 1956.

Johnson, Samuel. *Boswell's Life of Johnson*. Oxford University Press, 1933.

Johnson, Samuel. *The Life of Mr. Richard Savage*. Oxford/Clarendon Press, 1971.

Joyce, James. *Ulysses*. Random House, 1924.

Joyce, James. *Finnegans Wake*. Viking, 1939.

Joyce, James. *A Portrait of the Artist as a Young Man*. Viking/Penguin, 1977.

K

Kapleau, Philip. *The Wheel of Life and Death*. Doubleday, 1989.

Kawabata Yusanari. *A Thousand Cranes*. Charles E. Tuttle, 1967.

Kawabata Yasunari. *Beauty and Sadness*. Charles E. Tuttle, 1975.

Kazin, Alfred. *A Walker in the City*. Harcourt Brace Jovanovich, 1951.

Kazin, Alfred. *New York Jew*. Knopf, 1978.

Keats, John. In *The Complete Poems of John Keats and Percy Bysshe Shelley*. The Modern Library/Random House, n. d.

Kellerman, Jonathan. *Devil's Waltz*. Bantam Books, 1993.

Kelly, Michael. *Chronicles of a Small War*. Random House, 1993.

Kerr, Jean. *Mary, Mary*. Doubleday, 1963.

Kesey, Ken. *One Flew over the Cuckoo's Nest*. Viking, 1962.

Knowles, John. *A Separate Peace*. Macmillan, 1960.

Kunstler, James Howard. *The Geography of Nowhere*. Simon & Schuster, 1993.

L

Larkin, Phillip. *All That Jazz*. St. Martin's Press, 1972.

Lawrence, D. H. *The Rainbow*. Methuen, 1915.

Lawrence, D. H. *England My England*. Viking, 1950.

Lawrence, D. H. *The Captain's Doll*. In *4 Short Novels of D. H. Lawrence*. Viking, 1965.

Lawrence, Frieda. *Frieda Lawrence: The Memoirs and Correspondence*. Edited by E. W. Tedlock. Knopf, 1964.

Laxness, Halldòr. *Independent People*. Knopf, 1946.

Le Corbusier. *When the Cathedrals Were White*. Harcourt Brace, 1947.

Leavitt, David. *A Place I've Never Been*. Viking Penguin, 1990.

LeCarré, John. *The Russia House*. Knopf, 1989.

Lee, Gus. *China Boy*. Viking Penguin, 1991.

Lehman, David. *Signs of the Times: Deconstruction and the Fall of Paul de Man*. Poseidon Press, 1991.

Lehmann, Rosamond. *The Ballad and the Source*. Virago Press, 1978.

Leitner, Isabella. *Saving the Fragments: From Auschwitz to New York*. New American Library/Penguin, 1985.

Lend Me Your Ears, Great Speeches in History. Edited by William Safire. W. W. Norton, 1992.

Lessing, Doris. *Doris Lessing Reader*. Knopf, 1988.

Levine, Philip. *What Work Is*. Knopf, 1991.

Lewis, Sinclair. *Lewis at Zenith*. Harcourt, Brace & World, 1961.

Lewis, Sinclair. *Arrowsmith*. Harcourt, Brace, 1925.

Lewisohn, Ludwig. *Up Stream: An American Chronicle*. Boni & Liveright, 1922.

Liebman, Joshua Loth. *Peace of Mind*. Simon & Schuster, 1948.

Lightman, Alan. *Einstein's Dreams*. Pantheon, 1992.

Lindbergh, Anne Morrow. *Gift from the Sea*. Watts, 1955.

Lindsay, Vachel. *Collected Poems of Vachel Lindsay*. Macmillan, 1925.

Lindsay, Vachel. *Poetry of Vachel Lindsay*. Edited by Dennis Camp. Spoon River Poetry Press, 1984–6.

London, Jack. *The Son of the Wolf*. Houghton Mifflin, 1900.

Longfellow, Henry Wadsworth. *Longfellow: A Full-Length Portrait*. Longmans, Green, 1955.

Longfellow, Henry Wadsworth. *The Poems of Henry Wadsworth Longfellow*. Random House, n. d.

Lovelace, Maud Hart. *Betsy and Tacy Go Down Town*. Harper, 1943.

Lowell, Amy. *The Complete Poetical Works of Amy Lowell*. Houghton Mifflin, 1955.

Lowell, Robert. *Between the Porch and the Altar I: Collected Poems*. Edited by Anthony Twaite. Farrar, Straus & Giroux, 1989.

Lundkvist, Artur. *Journeys in Dream and Imagination*. Translated by Ann B. Weissmann and Annika Planck. Four Walls Eight Windows, c. 1991.

M

MacDonald, John D. *Slam the Big Door*. The Mysterious Press, 1987.

MacDonald, Ross. *The Moving Target* and *The Barbarous Coast*. In *Archer in Hollywood*. Knopf, 1967.

MacDonald, Ross. *The Name is Archer*. In *International Treasury of Mystery and Suspense*. Doubleday, 1983.

Machiavelli, Niccolo. *The Prince*. Translated by Luigi Ricci. The New American Library, 1952.

The Macmillan Book of Proverbs, Maxims and Famous Phrases. Edited by Burton Stevenson. Macmillan, 1948.

MacNeil, Robert. *Wordstruck*. Viking Penguin, 1989.

Mahfouz, Naguib. *Palace of Desire*. Translated by William Maynard Hutchins, Lorne M. Kenny, and Olive E. Kenny. Doubleday, 1991.

Mailer, Norman. *The Armies of the Night: History as a Novel, The Novel as History*. New American Library, 1968.

Mailer, Norman. *Harlot's Ghost*. Random House, 1991.

Mailer, Norman. *The Naked and the Dead*. Random House, 1991.

Malamud, Bernard. *The Stories of Bernard Malamud*, Farrar, Straus & Giroux, 1983.

Mansfield, Katherine. *Journal of Katherine Mansfield*. Knopf, 1927.

Mansfield, Katherine. *The Short Stories of Katherine Mansfield*. Knopf, 1981.

Marcus Aurelius. *Meditations of Marcus Aurelius*. Heritage Press, 1956.

Markinson, Ann and Yudkin, Joel. *Dismantling the Cold War Economy*. BasicBooks/HarperCollins, 1992.

Marks, Percy. *Which Way Parnasus?* Harcourt Brace, 1926.

Márquez, Gabriel García. *Innocent Eréndira and Other Stories*. Harper/Perennial, 1978.

Márquez, Gabriel García. *The General in His Labyrinth*. Knopf, 1990.

Marshall, Paule. *Reena and Other Stories*. Feminist Press, 1983.

Martin, Ralph. *Henry & Clare*. G. P. Putnam's, 1991.

Masefield, John. *Poems*. Macmillan. 1925.

Matthiessen, Peter. *At Play in the Fields of the Lord*. Random House, 1965.

Maugham, W. Somerset. *The Complete Short Stories of W. Somerset Maugham*. Vols. 1-2. Doubleday, 1921, 1934.

Maugham, W. Somerset. *Cakes and Ale*. Doubleday, 1930.

Maugham, W. Somerset. *The Circle*. In *A Treasury of the Theatre*. Edited by John Gassner. Simon & Schuster, 1950.

Maupassant, Guy de. *Selected Tales of Guy de Maupassant*. Edited by Saxe Commins. Random House, 1950.

Maupassant, Guy de. *Miss Harriet and Other Stories*. Penguin Books, 1951.

Maurois, André. *The Collected Stories of André Maurois*. Washington Square Press, 1967.

Maurois, André. *I Remember, I Remember*. Harper, 1942.

Mayer, Martin. *Nightmare on Wall Street*. Simon & Schuster, 1993.

Mayle, Peter. *Toujours Provence*. Knopf, 1991.

McBain, Ed. *The Mugger*. In *McBain's Ladies*. The Mysterious Press, 1988.

McCarthy, Mary. *The Company She Keeps*. Dell, 1955.

McCarthy, Mary. *Intellectual Memoirs*. Harcourt Brace, 1992.

McCullers, Carson. *The Ballad of the Sad Cafe*. Houghton Mifflin, 1951.

McCullers, Carson. *The Collected Stories of Carson McCullers*. Houghton Mifflin, 1987.

McDermott, Alice. *At Weddings and Wakes*. Farrar, Straus & Giroux, 1992.

McGinley, Phyllis. *The Love Letters of Phyllis McGinley*. Viking, 1953.

McMillan, Terry. *Waiting to Exhale*. Viking Penguin, 1992.

Melville, Herman. *Moby Dick*. Penguin, 1975.

Mencken, H. L. *Here Is New York*. Harper, 1949.

Mencken, H. L. *The Impossible H. L. Mencken*. Edited by Marion Elizabeth Rodgers. Anchor/Doubleday, 1991.

Meredith, George. *The Ordeal of Richard Feverel*. The Modern Library/Random House, 1927.

Merwin, W. S. *Finding the Islands*. North Point Press, 1982.

Millay, Edna St. Vincent. *The King's Henchman*. Harper, 1927.

Millay, Edna St. Vincent. *The Buck in the Snow and Other Poems*. Harper, 1929.

Millay, Edna St. Vincent. *The Ballad of the Harp-Weaver and Other Poems*. Harper, d. u.

Miller, Arthur. *Death of a Salesman*, Requiem. In *A Treasury of the Theatre*. Edited by John Gassner. Simon & Schuster, 1950.

Miller, Jason. *That Championship Season*. Atheneum, 1972.

Miller, Sue. *For Love*. HarperCollins, 1993.

Minot, Susan. *Folly*. Houghton Mifflin/Seymour Lawrence, 1992.

Mitchell, Margaret. *Gone with the Wind*. Macmillan, 1936.

Modern Japanese Literature. Edited by Donald Keene. Grove Press, 1989.

Molière. *The Misanthrope*. Translated by Bernard D. Grebanier. Barron's, 1959.

Montaigne, Michel Equem de. *The Essays of Montaigne*. Heritage Press, 1947.

Moore, Marianne. *The Complete Poems of Marianne Moore*. Viking, 1981.

Moore, Thomas. *The Poetical Works of Thomas Moore*. Edited by A. D. Godley. AMS Press, 1979.

Morley, Christopher. *Where the Blue Begins*. In *The Week-End Library*. Doubleday, 1903 through 1930.

Morrison, Toni. *Jazz*. Knopf, 1992.

Muller, Marcia. *Eye of the Storm*. The Mysterious Press, 1988.

Mumford, Lewis. *Findings and Keepings*. Harcourt Brace Jovanovich, 1975.

Munro, Alice. *Friend of Youth*, Knopf, 1990.

Murchie, Guy. In *The Practical Cogitator*. Edited by Charles P. Curtis, Jr., and Ferris Greenslet. Houghton Mifflin, 1962.

Murdoch, Iris. *The Black Prince*. Viking, 1973.

Murray, Jim. *Jim Murray, An Autobiography*. Macmillan, 1993.

Murray, William. *The Last Italian*. Simon & Schuster/Touchstone, 1991.

N

Nabokov, Vladimir. *Speak Memory*. Putnam's, 1947.

Nabokov, Vladimir. *Lolita*. Random House, 1955.

Nabokov, Vladimir. *King, Queen, Knave*. McGraw-Hill, 1968.

Nabokov, Vladimir. In *The Nabokov-Wilson Letters: Correspondence between Vladimir Nabokov and Edmond Wilson, 1940–1971*. Edited by Simon Karlinsky. Harper, 1979.

Nash, Ogden. *Verses from 1929 On.* Little Brown, 1959.

Natsume Soseki. *Botchan.* Translated by Umeji Sasaki. Charles E. Tuttle, 1968.

Naylor, Gloria. *Bailey's Cafe.* Harcourt Brace Jovanovich, 1992.

Nefzawi, Shaykh. *The Perfumed Garden.* Translated by Sir Richard F. Burton. Castle Books, 1964.

A New Dictionary of Quotations. Edited by H. L. Mencken. Knopf, 1942.

The New Dictionary of Thoughts. Standard Book Co., 1966.

The New Oxford Book of English Verse. Edited by Sir Arthur Quiller-Couch. Oxford University Press, 1955.

The New Pocket Anthology of American Verse. Edited by Oscar Williams. Washington Square Press, 1955

New Poets of England and America. New American Library, 1957.

The New Quotable Woman, 1800–On. Edited by Elaine Partnow. Facts on File, 1992.

New Stories from the South. Edited by Shannon Ravenel. Algonquin Books, 1992.

Nietzsche, Friedrich Wilhelm. *Thus Spake Zarathustra.* In *The Portable Nietzsche.* Viking, 1954.

Nin, Anaïs. *The Diaries of Anaïs Nin.* Vol. 2. Harcourt Brace Jovanovich, 1967.

Nobody Said it Better! Edited by Miriam Ringo. Rand McNally, 1980.

Norris, Frank. *The Octopus.* In *Frank Norris.* The Library of America, 1986.

The Norton Anthology of English Literature. Edited by M. H. Abrams. W. W. Norton, 1962.

The Norton Anthology of Modern Poetry. Edited by Richard Ellman and Robert O'Clair. W. W. Norton, 1973.

The Norton Reader. Edited by Arthur M. Eastman. W. W. Norton, 1965.

O

Oates, Joyce Carol. *The Wheel of Love.* Fawcett, 1972.

Oates, Joyce Carol. *American Appetites.* Dutton, 1989.

Oates, Joyce Carol. *Heat and Other Stories.* William Abrahams/Dutton, 1991.

O'Connor, Flannery. *The Complete Short Stories of Flannery O'Connor.* Farrar, Straus & Giroux, 1972.

Odets, Clifford. *Waiting for Lefty,* Part 1. In *Six Plays of Clifford Odets.* Modern Library/Random House, 1939.

O'Faolain, Sean. *The Finest Stories of Sean O'Faolain.* Little, Brown, 1957.

O'Hara, John. *Free Fall in Crimson.* Harper, 1981.

Olsen, Tillie. *Tell Me a Riddle.* Dell, 1960.

O'Neill, Eugene. *Anna Christie.* In *Eugene O'Neill.* The Library of America, 1988.

O'Neill, Moira. *Songs of the Glens of Antrim.* Macmillan, 1922.

Orwell, George. *Coming up for Air.* Harcourt Brace, 1950.

The Oxford Book of American Verse. Edited by F. O. Matthiessen. Oxford University Press, 1950.

Oz, Amos. *The Hill of Evil Counsel.* Translated by Nicholas De Lange. Fontana/Collins, 1980.

Ozick, Cynthia. *Levitation, Five Fictions.* Knopf, 1982.

Ozick, Cynthia. *The Pagan Rabbi and Other Stories.* Dutton, 1983.

P

Pamuk, Orhan. *The White Castle.* George Braziller, 1991.

Parker, Dorothy. *The Viking Portable Library Dorothy Parker.* Viking, 1944.

Pasternak, Boris. *Doctor Zhivago.* Translated by Max Hayward and Manya Harari. Pantheon Books, 1958.

Pearson, Ridley. *Hard Fall.* Delacorte, 1992.

Pei, Meg. *Salaryman.* Viking Press, 1992.

Perelman, S. J. *The Most of S. J. Perelman.* Simon & Schuster/Fireside, 1980.

Peretz, I. L. *I. L. Peretz Reader.* Edited by Ruth R. Wisse. Schocken, 1990.

The Perfumed Garden of the Shaykh Nefzawi ("The Story of the Negro Dorerame"). Translated by Sir Richard F. Burton. Castle Books, 1964.

Pindar. *Odes.* University of Chicago Press, 1947.

Pinero, Arthur Wing. *The Second Mrs. Tanqueray.* In *Three Plays.* Methuen, 1985.

Pirandello, Luigi. In *Nobel Crimes.* Translated by Marie Smith. Edited by Frederick May. Carroll & Graf, 1992.

Plath, Sylvia. *The Bell Jar.* Harper, 1971.

The Pleasures of Diaries. Edited by Ronald Blythe. Pantheon, 1989.

Plumb, J. H. Introduction to *The Life of Mr. Jonathan Wild the Great* by Henry Fielding. The New American Library, 1961.

Plutarch. *Plutarch's Lives.* Edited by Edmund Fuller. Dell, 1968.

A Pocket Book of Modern Verse. Edited by Oscar Williams. Washington Square Press, 1968.

The Pocket Book of Quotations. Edited by Henry Davidoff. Pocket Books/Simon & Schuster, 1942.

The Portable Irish Reader. Edited by Diarmuid Russell. Viking, 1946.

The Portable Voltaire. Edited by Ben R. Redman. Viking, 1949.

Potok, Chaim. *The Chosen.* Simon & Schuster, 1967.

Pound, Ezra. *Pound/Joyce.* New Directions, 1966.

Presidential Anecdotes. Edited by Paul F. Boller, Jr. Oxford University Press, 1981.

Pritchett, V. S. *The Collected Stories of V. S. Pritchett.* Random House, 1956.

Prize Stories 1991: The O. Henry Awards. Edited by William Abrahams. Doubleday, 1991.

Proust, Marcel. *Cities of the Plain.* In *The Marcel Proust Bible.* Translated by C. K. Scott Moncrieff. The Modern Library/Random House, 1927.

Proust, Marcel. *Remembrance of Things Past.* Part I: *Swann's Way.* The Modern Library, 1928.

Proust, Marcel. *Pleasures and Regrets.* Translated by Louise Varise. Crown, 1948.

Q

The Quotable Woman, from Eve to 1799. Edited by Elaine Partnow. Facts on File, 1982.

R

Raleigh, Sir Walter. *The History of the World.* Macmillan, 1971.

Rattigan, Terence. *The Browning Version.* Samuel French, 1950.

Rawlings, Marjorie Kinnan. *South Moon Under.* Scribner's, 1933.

Reading Rooms. Edited by Susan Allen Toth and Jouhn Coughlan. Doubleday, 1991.

Remarque, Erich Maria. *All Quiet on the Western Front.* Little, Brown, 1929.

Respectfully Quoted: A Dictionary of Quotations Requested from the Congressional Research Service. Edited by Suzy Platt. Library of Congress, 1989.

Rich, Adrienne. *The Fact of a Doorframe: Poems Selected and New.* W. W. Norton, 1985.

Richardson, Samuel. *Clarissa.* Modern Library, 1950.

Richardson, Samuel. *Pamela.* Norton, 1958.

Rilke, Rainer Maria. *The Notebooks of Malte Laurids Brigge.* Random House/Vintage, 1985.

Rittenberg, Sidney. *The Man Who Stayed Behind.* Simon & Schuster, 1993.

Robbe-Grillet, Alain. *Djinn.* Translated by Yvone Lenard and Walter Wells. Grove Press, 1981.

Roberts, Jordan. *The Best Women's Stage Monologues.* Smith and Kraus, 1990.

Robinson, Edward Arlington. *Collected Poems by Edward Arlington Robinson.* Macmillan, 1937.

Roethke, Theodore. *Straw for the Fire, Notebooks of Theodore Roethke.* Edited by David Wagoner. Doubleday, 1972.

Roethke, Theodore. *The Collected Poems of Theodore Roethke.* Doubleday/Anchor, 1975.

Roosevelt, Franklin Delano. *FDR's Fireside Chats.* Edited by Russell D. Buhite and David W. Levy. University of Oklahoma Press, 1992.

Rossner, Judith. *Nine Months in the Life of an Old Maid.* Dial, 1969.

Rostand, Edmond. *Cyrano de Bergerac.* In *A Treasury of the Theatre.* Edited by John Gassner. Simon & Schuster, 1950.

Roth, Philip. *Goodbye, Columbus.* Houghton Mifflin, 1959.

Roth, Philip. *Portnoy's Complaint.* Random House, 1969.

Roth, Philip. *Operation Shylock.* Simon & Schuster, 1993.

Rule, Ann. *Everything She Ever Wanted.* Simon & Schuster, 1992.

Rushdie, Salman. *[Analysis of] The Wizard of Oz.* British Film Institute/Indiana University Press, 1992.

Ruskin, John. *The Works of John Ruskin.* Longmans Green, 1903–12.

Ruskin, John. *John Ruskin: Selected Writings.* Edited by Kenneth Clark. Penguin, n. d.

S

Sackville-West, Vita. *All Passion Spent.* Carroll & Graf, 1991.

Safire, William. *On Language.* Times Books, 1981.

Saint-Exupery, Antoine de. *Night Flight.* Grosset & Dunlap, 1932.

Salinger, J. D. *Franny and Zooey.* Little, Brown, 1961.

Sand, George. *George Sand in Her Own Words.* Edited by Joseph Barry. Anchor Press/Doubleday, 1979.

Sandburg, Carl. *Chicago Poems.* Holt, 1916.

Sandburg, Carl. *Smoke and Steel.* Harcourt, Brace, 1920.

Sandburg, Carl. *Abraham Lincoln, the War Years.* Vol. 1. Harcourt, Brace, 1939.

Sandburg, Carl. *The Complete Poems of Carl Sandburg.* Harcourt Brace Jovanovich, 1969, 1970.

Sandburg, Carl. *Rootabaga Stories,* Part One. Harcourt Brace Jovanovich, 1988.

Santayana, George. *Skepticism and Animal Faith.* Scribner's, 1923.

Sarraute, Nathalie. *The Planetarium.* In *The Nouveau Roman Reader.* Edited by John Fletcher and John Calder. John Calder, 1986.

Sarton, May. *Endgame, A Journal of the Seventy-Ninth Year.* W. W. Norton, 1992.

Sartre, Jean-Paul. *The Flies.* In *A Treasury of the Theatre.* Edited by John Gassner. Simon & Schuster, 1950.

The Saturday Review Reader, No. 3. Bantam, 1954.

Saul, John Ralston. *Voltaire's Bastards.* The Free Press, 1992.

Sayers, Dorothy L. *In the Teeth of the Evidence.* Harper, 1939.

Sayers, Dorothy L. *The Unpleasantness at the Bellona Club.* Harper, 1956.

Sayers, Dorothy L. *Gaudy Night.* Harper, 1960.

Schiller, Johann Christoph Friedrich von. *Mary Stuart/The Maid of Orleans.* Frederick Ungar, 1961.

Schine, Cathleen. *Rameau's Niece.* Ticknor & Fields, 1993.

Schwartz, Lynne Sharon. *The Melting Pot.* Harper & Row, 1987.

Selections from The Spectator. Macmillan, 1908.

Selzer, Richard. *Letters to a Young Doctor.* Simon & Schuster/Touchstone, 1983.

Seventeenth Century Verse and Prose. Vol. 2. Macmillan, 1952.

Shain, Merle. *When Lovers are Friends.* J. B. Lippincott, 1978.

Shakespeare, William. *The Yale Shakespeare.* Yale University Press, 1917–58.

Shakespeare, William. *Shakespeare's Sonnets.* Edited by Edward Bliss Reed. Yale University Press, 1923.

Shakespeare, William. *The Tragedy of King Richard the Second.* Edited by George Lyman Kittredge. Ginn, 1941.

Shakespeare, William. *The Laurel Shakespeare.* Edited by Francis Fergusson. Dell, 1960.

Shakespeare, William. *Othello.* Methuen, 1969.

Shaw, George Bernard. *Candida.* In *Seven Plays by Bernard Shaw.* Dodd, Mead, 1951.

Shaw, George Bernard. *Overruled.* In *Seven One-Act Plays.* Penguin, 1958.

Shaw, George Bernard. *Too Good to Be True* and *Heartbreak House.* In *Bernard Shaw's Plays.* Edited by Warren Sylvester Smith. W. W. Norton, 1970.

Shaw, George Bernard. *Back to Methusala* and *Getting Married.* In *The Quintessence of G. B. S.* Hutchinson, n. d.

Shaw, Irwin. *Mixed Company.* Random House, 1939.

Sheed, Wilfrid. *Office Politics.* Farrar, Straus & Giroux, 1966.

Sheldon, Michael. *Friends of Promise: Cyril Connolly and the World of Horizon.* Harper Perennial, 1992.

Shelley, Percy Bysshe. *The Complete Poetical Works of Percy Bysshe Shelley.* Edited by Thomas Hutchinson. Oxford University Press, 1905.

Shelley, Percy Bysshe. In *The Complete Poems of John Keats and Percy Bysshe Shelley.* The Modern Library/Random House, n. d.

Sholokhov, Mikhail. *One Man's Destiny and Other Stories, Articles and Sketches 1923–1963.* Knopf, 1967.

Short Saying of Great Men. Edited by Samuel Arthur Bent. James R. Osgood, 1882.

Short Stories. Edited by C. Schweikert. Harcourt, Brace, 1934.

Short Story Masterpieces. Edited by Robert Penn Warren and Albert Erskine. Dell/Laurel, 1954.

Siddons, Anne Rivers. *Colony.* HarperCollins, 1992.

Sidney, Philip. *The Poems of Sir Philip Sidney.* Edited by William A. Ringler, Jr. Oxford/Clarendon, 1962.

Sillanpää, Frans Eemil. *The Maid Silja.* Macmillan, 1933.

Simon, Kate. *Bronx Primitive.* In *The Kate Simon Bible.* Viking, 1982.

Simon, Kate. *Etchings in an Hourglass.* Harper, 1990.

Simon, Neil. *The Collected Plays of Neil Simon.* Vol. 2. New American Library, 1979.

Simpson, Eileen. *Orphans.* Weidenfield & Nicholson, 1987.

Simpson, Mona. *The Lost Father.* Knopf, 1992.

Sinetar, Marcia. In *Meeting the Shadow.* Edited by Connie Zweig and Jeremiah Abrahams. Jeremy P. Tarcher, 1990.

Singer, Isaac Bashevis. *The Collected Stories of Isaac Bashevis Singer.* Farrar, Straus & Giroux, 1990.

Singer, Isaac Bashevis. *The Certificate.* Farrar, Straus & Giroux, 1992.

Six Centuries of Great Poetry. Edited by Robert Penn Warren and Albert Erskine. Dell, 1955.

Six Italian Plays. Vols. 1–2. Edited by Eric Bentley. Classic Theatre, n. d.

Skelton, John. *John Skelton, The Complete English Poems.* Edited by Jon Scattergood. Yale University Press, 1983.

Smiley, Jane. *Ordinary Love & Good Will.* Knopf, 1989.

Smiley, Jane. *A Thousand Acres.* Knopf, 1991.

Smith, Martin Cruz. *Red Square.* Random House, 1992.

Smollett, Tobias. *The Expeditions of Humphrey Clinker.* Edited by Lewis M. Knapp. Oxford University Press. 1966.

Snow, C. P. *Homecoming.* Scribner's, 1964.

Sommer, Elyse. *The Words You Confuse.* Bob Adams, 1992.

Sontag, Susan. *Illness as Metaphor.* Farrar, Straus & Giroux, 1978.

Sophocles. *Sophocles: The Complete Greek Tragedies.* Translated by David Grene. The University of Chicago Press, 1942.

Soyinka, Wole. *Madmen and Specialists.* Hill and Wang, 1987.

Spark, Muriel. *The Collected Stories of Muriel Spark.* Knopf, 1967.

Spark, Muriel. *The Hothouse of the East River.* Viking, 1973.

Spark, Muriel. *Symposium.* Houghton Mifflin, 1990.

Spenser, Edmund. *The Faerie Queene.* Edited by Thomas P. Roche, Jr. Penguin, 1978.

Spolin, Viola. *Improvisations for the Theatre.* Northwestern University, 1963.

Stallone, Sylvester. *Rocky.* In *Film Scenes for Actors.* Edited by Joshua Karton. Bantam, 1983.

Steele, Sir Richard, and Joseph Addison. *Selections from The Tatler and The Spectator.* Edited by Robert J. Allen. Holt, Rinehart & Winston, 1961.

Stegner, Wallace. *Angle of Repose.* Doubleday, 1971.

Stegner, Wallace. *The Spectator Bird.* Doubleday, 1976.

Steinbeck, John. *The Long Valley.* Viking, 1938.

Steinbeck, John. *The Grapes of Wrath.* Viking, 1939.

Steinbeck, John. *The Portable John Steinbeck.* Viking, 1943.

Steinbeck, John. *The Pearl.* Viking, 1945.

Steinbeck, John. *The Red Pony.* Viking, 1945.

Stendhal, Marie-Henri Beyle de. *The Red and the Black.* Modern Library/Random House, 1926.

Stevens, Wallace. *Parts of a World.* Knopf, 1951.

Stevens, Wallace. *The Collected Poems of Wallace Stevens.* Knopf, 1961.

Stevenson, Robert Louis. *Dr. Jeckyll and Mr. Hyde.* Signet/New American Library, 1986.

Stevenson, Robert Louis. *Kidnapped,* 1886. New American Library, 1959.

Stevenson, Robert Louis. *Underwoods.* Scribner's, 1887.

Stickney, Trumbull. *The Poems of Trumbull Stickney.* Houghton Mifflin, 1905.

Stoppard, Tom. *Rosencrantz & Guildenstern are Dead.* Grove Press, 1967.

Stories from The New Yorker, 1950–60. Simon & Schuster, 1960.

Stout, Rex. *Fer-de-Lance.* Bantam, 1983.

Strand, Mark. *Selected Poems.* Knopf, 1990.

Strindberg, August. *Advent.* In *Plays, Third Series.* Scribner's, 1927.

Styron, William. *Lie Down in Darkness.* Random House, 1951.

Sudermann, Hermann. *Magda: A Play in Four Acts*. Samuel French, 1923.

T

Tagore, Rabindranath. *The Collected Poems and Plays of Rabindranath Tagore*. Macmillan, 1961.

Tartt, Donna. *The Secret History*. Knopf, 1992.

Teasdale, Sara. *Mirrors of the Heart*. Edited by William Drake. Macmillan, 1984.

Teichmann, Howard. *George S. Kaufman*. Dell, 1973.

Ten Best European Plays on the American Stage. Edited by John Gassner. Crown, n. d.

Tennyson, Alfred, Lord. *In Memorium*, I. In *The Poetical Works of Tennyson*. Houghton Mifflin, 1974.

Tey, Josephine. *The Franchise Affair*. Macmillan, 1948.

Thackeray, William Makepeace. *Vanity Fair*. Random House, 1940.

Thomas, D. M. *Memories and Hallucinations*. Viking, 1988.

Thomas, Dylan. *In Country Sleep and Other Poems*. New Directions, 1952.

Thomas, Lewis. *The Fragile Species*. Scribner's, 1992.

Thoreau, Henry David. *Walden*. Signet/New American Library, 1942.

Thurber, James. *The Thirteen Clocks*. Simon & Schuster, 1950.

Tolstoy, Leo. *Anna Karenina*. Bantam Books, 1977.

The Top 500 Poems. Edited by William Harmon. Columbia University Press, 1992.

Treasure of World Literature. Edited by Dagobert D. Runes. Philosophical Library, 1956.

A Treasury of the World's Great Speeches. Edited by Houston Peterson. Simon & Schuster, 1954.

A Treasury of the Theatre. Edited by John Gassner. Simon & Schuster, 1950.

Trevor, William. *The Day We Got Drunk on Cake and Other Stories*. Penguin, 1969.

Trollope, Anthony. *The Duke's Children*. Dodd, Mead, 1893.

Tuchman, Barbara. *The Guns of August*. Macmillan, 1962.

Turgenev, Ivan. *A Month in the Country*. Viking Press, 1956.

Turgenev, Ivan. *Fathers and Sons*. In *The Ivan Turgenev Bible*. Penguin, 1975.

Turow, Scott. *The Burden of Proof*. Farrar, Straus & Giroux, 1990.

Turow, Scott. *Pleading Guilt*. Farrar, Straus & Giroux, 1993.

Twain, Mark. *Roughing It*. Routledge, 1872.

Twain, Mark. *A Connecticut Yankee in King Arthur's Court*. In *The Family Mark Twain*, Harper, 1934.

Twelve Famous Plays of the Restoration and Eighteenth Century. Edited by Bennet A. Cerf and Donald S. Klopfer. The Modern Library/Random House, 1933.

Twentieth Century American Poetry. Edited by Conrad Aiken. The Modern Library/Random House, 1944.

20 Best European Plays on the American Stage. Edited by John Gassner. Crown, n. d.

200 Years of Great American Short Stories. Edited by Martha Foley. Houghton Mifflin, 1975.

U

Understanding Drama. Holt, Rhinehart & Winston, 1948.

Undset, Sigrid. *The Longest Years*. Knopf, 1935.

Updike, John. *Rabbit, Run*. Knopf, 1960.

Updike, John. *Pigeon Feathers and Other Stories*. Knopf, 1962.

Updike, John. *Bech: A Book*. Knopf, 1970.

V

Vanity Fair, A Cavalcade of the 1920s and 1930s. Edited by Cleveland Amory and Frederic Bradlee. Viking, 1960.

Vercors. *The Silence of the Sea*. Macmillan, 1944.

The Viking Book of Aphorisms. Edited by W. H. Auden and Louis Kronenberger. Viking, 1966.

Voltaire. *Candide*. In *The Portable Voltaire*. Edited by Ben R. Redman. Viking, 1949.

W

Walcott, Derek. *Omeros*. Farrar, Straus & Giroux, 1990.

Waller, Robert James. *The Bridges of Madison County*. Warner Books, 1992.

Walters, Barbara. *How to Talk with Practically Anybody about Practically Anything.* Doubleday, 1970.

Warren, Robert Penn. *The Circus in the Attic and Other Stories.* Harcourt Brace Jovanovich, 1975.

Warren, Robert Penn. *Being Here.* Random House, 1980.

The Washington Post Book World. Knopf, 1991.

The Week-End Library, Doubleday, 1903–1930.

Weil, Simone. *First and Last Notebooks.* Edited by Richard Rees. Oxford University Press, 1970.

Weiss, Ellen and Friedman, Mel. *The Poof Point.* Knopf, 1992.

Weldon, Fay. *Letters to Alice.* Taplinger, 1985.

Wells, H. G. *The Time Machine: An Invention.* Holt, 1895.

Welty, Eudora. *The Collected Stories of Eudora Welty.* Harcourt Brace Jovanovich, 1980.

Welty, Eudora. *One Writer's Beginnings.* Harvard University Press, 1984.

West, Dame Rebecca. *The Harsh Voice: Four Short Novels.* Jonathan Cape, 1935.

West, Dame Rebecca. *The Thinking Reed.* Viking, 1936.

West, Dame Rebecca. *The Return of the Soldier.* Dial Press, 1980.

West, Dame Rebecca. *This Real Night.* Viking, 1985.

West, Dame Rebecca. *Sunflower.* Viking, 1987.

West, Morris L. *The Devil's Advocate.* William Morrow, 1959.

West, Nathanael. *Miss Lonelyhearts.* In *The Complete Works of Nathanael West.* Farrar, Straus & Giroux, 1957.

Wharton, Edith. *The Descent of Man.* Scribner's, 1904.

Wharton, Edith. *The House of Mirth.* Scribner's, 1905.

Wharton, Edith. *Roman Fever and Other Stories.* Scribner's, 1911.

Wharton, Edith. *Twilight Sleep.* D. Appleton, 1927.

Wharton, Edith. *The Children.* D. Appleton, 1928.

Wharton, Edith. *Hudson River Bracketed.* In *The Edith Wharton Bible.* Signet Classics, 1962.

Wharton, Edith. *The Collected Short Stories of Edith Wharton.* Vol. 1. Scribner's, 1968.

Wharton, Edith. *Ethan Frome* and *A Backward Glance.* In *Edith Wharton.* The Library of America, 1990.

Wharton, Edith. *The Descent of Man.* In *The Selected Short Stories of Edith Wharton.* Edited by R. W. B. Lewis. Scribner's, 1991.

White, E. B. *One Man's Meat.* Harper Brothers, 1942.

White, E. B. *Here Is New York.* Harper, 1949.

White, E. B. *Poems & Sketches of E. B. White 1925–1970.* Harper, d. u.

Whitman, Walt. *Leaves of Grass.* W. W. Norton, 1968.

Widdemer, Margaret. *The Boardwalk.* Harcourt, Brace and Howe, 1920.

Wiesel, Elie. *Night.* Avon Books, 1969.

Wilbur, Richard. *New and Collected Poems.* Harvest/Harcourt Brace Joanovich, 1989.

Wilde, Oscar. *The Picture of Dorian Gray.* Bantam, 1982.

Wilde, Oscar. *A Woman of No Importance.* In *The Plays of Oscar Wilde.* Vintage/Random House, 1988.

Wilde, Oscar. *The Poems and Fairy Tales of Oscar Wilde.* The Modern Library/Random House, n. d.

Wilder, Thornton. *The Bridge of San Luis Rey.* Harper, 1967.

Wilder, Thornton. *The Eighth Day.* In *The Thornton Wilder Bible.* Harper, 1967.

Williams, Tennessee. *A Streetcar Named Desire.* New Directions, 1947.

Williams, Tennessee. *Suddenly Last Summer.* In *The Theatre of Tennessee Williams.* New Directions, 1971.

Williams, William Carlos. *Collected Poems.* New Directions, 1949.

Wolfe, Thomas. *Look Homeward Angel.* Scribner's, 1929.

Wolfe, Thomas. *The Complete Short Stories of Thomas Wolfe.* Scribner's, 1987.

Woolf, Virginia. *Mrs. Dalloway.* Harcourt Brace, 1925.

Woolf, Virginia. *To the Lighthouse.* Harcourt Brace Jovanovich, 1927.

Woolf, Virginia. *A Room of One's Own.* Harcourt Brace Jovanovich, 1929.

Woollcott, Alexander. *The Portable Woollcott.* Viking, 1946.

Words Like Arrows. Edited by Shirley S. Kumove. Warner Books, 1986.

Wordsworth, William. *The Complete Poetical Works of Wordsworth.* Edited by Andrew J. George. Houghton Mifflin, n. d.

The World of Poetry. Edited by Murray Rockowitz and Milton Kaplan. Globe Book Co., 1965.

The World's Best. Edited by Whit Burnett. Dial Press, 1950.

The World's Famous Orations. Vol. 8. Edited by William Jennings Bryan. Funk and Wagnalls, 1906.

The World's Great Letters. Edited by M. Lincoln Schuster. Simon & Schuster, 1940.

Wright, Richard. *Black Boy.* In *Richard Wright.* The Library of America, 1991.

The Writer's Book. Edited by Helen R. Hull. Harper, 1950.

Y

Yalom, Irvin D. *When Nietzsche Wept.* In *The Irvin D. Yalom Bible.* Basic Books/Harper Collins, 1992.

Yeats, William Butler. *The Collected Poems of W. B. Yeats.* Macmillan, 1962.

Yehoshua, A. B. *Mr. Mani.* Translated by Hillel Halkin. Doubleday, 1992.

Yevtushenko, Yevgeny. *A Precocious Autobiography.* Translated by Andrew R. MacAndrew. Dutton, 1963.

Yolen, Jane. *What Rhymes with Moon.* Philomel, 1993.

Z

Zola, Émile. *Nana.* Pocket Books, 1941.

NEWSPAPERS AND OTHER PERIODICALS (current and back-dated editions)

The American Poetry Review

The Atlantic Monthly

The Berkshire Eagle

The Boston Globe

China Daily

DAEDALUS

Daily Telegraph

Danube Courier

Disarmament Times

Eastern Standard

Emporia Gazette

Esquire

Forbes Magazine

Good Housekeeping

Harper's

The London Morning Chronicle

Los Angeles Daily News

The Louisville Daily Courier

Manchester Guardian

Ms.

News Digest

Newsday

The New Republic

The New Statesman

Newsweek

The New Yorker

New York Magazine

The New York Review of Books

The New York Times

The New York Times Book Review

The New York World

Overland Monthly

Paris Review

Partisan Review

Publishers Weekly

The Quarterly

The Saturday Review

The Southern Review

The Spectator

Streetfare Journal

Tales of the City

Time Magazine

Vanity Fair

The Village Voice

The Virginia Quarterly Review

The Wall Street Journal

Washington Post

Wilderness

The Yale Review

Author/Speaker Index

4, 5; Time 3; Trees 3; Victims
1; Wind 1

ASHDOWN, PADDY
Arousal/Rousers 2

**ASHTON-WARNER,
SYLVIA**
(1908–1984)
Self-Reliance 2

ASIMOV, ERIC
Cityscapes 1

ASIMOV, ISAAC
(1920–1992)
Chance 2

ATKINS, ZOË
Transience 1

ATKINSON, BROOKS
(1894–1984)
Sunset 2

ATWOOD, MARGARET
Characterizations 2; Cities 2;
Completeness/Incompleteness
2; Fertility/Infertility 1; Gossip 3; Knowledge 4; Love 3;
Manipulation 1; Music/Musi-
cians 2; Ordinariness/ Extraordinariness 1; Self- Effacement
2; Smiles 2; Strength/Weak-
ness 4; Superficiality 1; Suspicion 1; Time 4, 5; Voices 1, 2

AUCHINCLOSS, LOUIS
Age/Aging 2; Ambition 2;
Calmness/Volatility 2; Dark-
ness/Light 1; Despair 1; Dif-
ference/Sameness 2; Domi-
nance 9-c; Doubt 1; Ego/Egotism
4; Families/Family Relationships
3; Fear 1; Freedom/Restraint 1;
Generosity 2; Helplessness 1; Imprisonment 1; Isolation 1; Joy 1;
Manipulation 2, 3; Manners 2;
Money 4; Openness/Privacy 1;
Physical Appearance 1; Pleas and
Prayers 2; Reform 1; Self-Control 1; Self-Knowledge 1; Success, Defined 3; Understanding/
Misunderstanding 1

**AUDEN, W[YSTAN]
H[UGH]**
(1907–1973)
Buildings and Bridges 2; Evil 1;
Thinking/Thought 1

AUGUSTINE, SAINT
(354–430)
Poetry/Poets 36

AUSLANDER, JOSEPH
(1897–1965)
Endings 3

AUSTIN, ALFRED
(1835–1913)
Tears 3

**AYRES, JR., B.
DRUMMOND**
Irritants 3

B

BABEL, ISAAC
(1894–1941)
Evening 1

BABITZ, EVE
Cities 3

BACON, SIR FRANCIS
(1561–1626)
Bodies/The Body 2; Books 4;
Custom 2; Faces 3; Friendship/
Friends 2; Government 1; Mind
3; Pleas and Prayers 3; Sacrifice
5-c; World 2

BAGNOLD, ENID
(1889–1981)
Arousal/Rousers 3; Dreams 4;
Dreams 5; Failure 2; Fatness/
Thinness 1; Hair Color 3; Heart
7; Joy 2; Law/Lawyers 2;
Maturation 2; Mystery/Mys-
teriousness 1; Physical Appear-
ance 2; Rain 2; Risk-Taking 2;
Simplicity/Simplification 1;
Tranquility 1

BAILEY, PEARL
(1918–1990)
Self-Knowledge 2

BAILEY, PHILIP JAMES
(1816–1902)
America/Americans   1;
Good/Evil 1

BAKER, NICHOLSON
Grief 1; Self-Expression 1;
Speechlessness 1

BAKER, RUSSELL
Difficulties 3; Journalism/Jour-
nalists 3; Middle Age 1; Ameri-
ca/Americans 8-c

BAKUNIN, MIKHAIL A.
(1814–1876)
Religion 4

BALDRIDGE, LETITIA
Approval/Disapproval 1

BALDWIN, JAMES
(1924–1987)
Emotions 1; Opportunity 1

BALLIETT, WHITNEY
Singing/Songs/Singers 1

BALZAC, HONORÉ DE
(1799–1850)
Admiration 1; Art/Artists 2;
Changeableness/ Unchange-
ableness 1; Choices and Decisions 2; Cities 4, 5; Competi-
tion/Competitors 2; Creativity
1; Death 6; Descriptions, Misc.
2; Destruction/Destructiveness
4; Disappointment 1; Faces 4;
Flattery 2; Food and Drink 2;
Foolhardiness 2; Furniture/Fur-
nishings 1; Hair 1; Hard-
Heartedness 2; Heart 8; Illu-
sion/Reality 3; Inspiration 2;
Jealousy 2; Love 4, 5; Middle
Age 2; Old Age 3, 4; Physical
Appearance 3, 4, 5, 6, 7; Popu-
larity/Unpopularity 1; Self-Images 3; Strategies 1, 2; Superficiality 4; Survival 1; Tact 1;
Temptation 3; Vanity 1

manence/Impermanence 1;
Street Scenes 1

BENEDICT, RUTH
(1887–1948)
Life 3

BENET, STEPHEN VINCENT
(1898–1943)
Prudence 2

BENI, JOHN
Utilization 1

BENJAMIN, ROBERT
Safety 1

BENNETT, ALAN
Irony 1

BENNETT, JESSE LEE
Books 7

BENTON, THOMAS HART
(1782–1858)
Dominance 1

BERBEROVA, NINA
(1901–1993)
Communication/Non-Communication 1; Faces 6; Past 3

BERK, RICHARD L.
Persuasiveness/Persuaders 1

BERLIN, ISAIAH
Art/Artists 5; Beliefs 2, 3; Civilization 2, 3, 4; Consciousness 1; Culture 2; Dullness 1; History 4; Imprisonment 2; Knowledge 3-c; Peace 3; Perfection 2, 3; Problems and Solutions 4; Progress 1, 2; Self-Actualization 2; Truth/Falsehood 5, 6; Understanding 1

BERNARD, ED
Opportunity 2

BERNHARDT, SARAH
(1844–1923)
Memory/Memories 2; Love 9

BERRYMAN, JOHN
(1914–1972)
Descriptions, Misc. 3; Eyes 4;
Good/Evil 2

BESCHLOSS, MICHAEL R.
Disintegration 1

BETTLEHEIM, BRUNO
(1903–1990)
Descriptions, Misc. 4

BHARTRIHARI
(c. 570–c. 651)
Men and Women 2

THE BIBLE
See THE HOLY BIBLE

BIERCE, AMBROSE
(1842–c. 1914)
Bigotry 1; Friendship/Friends 4; Love 11; Love, Defined 3

BIKEL, THEODORE
Inspiration 3

BILLINGS, JOSH [HENRY WHEELER SHAW]
(1818–1885)
Beauty 4; Books 8; Education and Learning 7; Happiness/Unhappiness 1; Humor 4; Jealousy 4; Landscapes 2; Laughter 1; Law/Lawyers 3; Lies/Liars 1; Marriage 7; Pedantry 1; Politics/Politicians 7; Reason 2; Sarcasm 2; Satire 1; Truth/Falsehood 7, 8; Vanity 2; Writing Advice 1

BINGEN, HILDEGARDE VON
(12th century)
Bodies/The Body 4

BISHOP, ELIZABETH
(1911–1979)
Automotive Descriptions 1; Descriptions, Misc. 5, 6, 7

BISMARCK, OTTO VON
(1815–1898)
Cause and Effect 3

BLACK ELK
(1863–1950)
Unity/Disunity 1

BLACK HAWK
(1767–1838)
Death 11

BLACK, LEWIS
Effectiveness/Ineffectiveness 2

BLAKE, WILLIAM
(1757–1827)
Advice 3-c; Animation 1; Beauty 5; Change 3; Cities 6; Envy 1; Fear 2; Foolhardiness 3; Humanity/Humankind 4; Immorality/Morality 1, 2; Jealousy 5; Joy 4; Joy/Sorrow 2; Love 12, 13; Mind 6; Morality/Immorality 1; Pleas and Prayers 4; Prudence 3; Shame 1; Shelter 1; War 3; Wisdom 3; Youth and Age 2

BLANCH, LESLY
Passion 5

BLANDFORD, LINDA
Isolation 2; Singing/Songs/Singers 3

BLESSINGTON, LADY MARGUERITE
(1789–1849)
Friendship/Friends 5; Happiness/Unhappiness 2; Manners 3; Marriage 8

BLOOM, ALLAN
(1930–1992)
Nature 2

BLOUNT, ROY
Books 9

BLY, ROBERT
Characteristics 2; Childhood/Children 4; Descriptions, Misc. 8; Trees 4

BOLIVAR, SIMON
(1783–1830)
Entrapment 1

BRONTË, CHARLOTTE
(1816–1855)
Communication/Non-Communication 2; Custom 3; Love 15; Many 1; Mastery/Subordination 4; Maturation 9-c; Self-Control 2, 3; Soul 2

BROOKNER, ANITA
Summer 1

BROOKS, MEL
Cowardice 1; Success/Failure 2

BROOKS, PHILLIP C.
Leadership 2

BROTHERS, JOYCE
Anger 4

BROUN, HEYWOOD
(1888–1939)
Hell and Damnation 3; Life 6

BROWN, ELAINE
Truth/Falsehood 4

BROWN, JOHN MASON
(1900–1969)
Animation 2; Chance 3; Characterizations 5; Consistency/Inconsistency 1; Individuality 2; Many 2; Memory/Memories 3; Opinion 1; Ordinariness/Extraordinariness 3; Personality Profiles 5; Reading/Readers 1; Sarcasm 3; Success, Defined 4; Taste 2; Temperament 1; Voices 3; Writing/Writers 3, 4

BROWN, JR., EDMUND G. [JERRY]
Competition/Competitors 3

BROWN, LEW
(1893–1958)
Life, Defined 6

BROWN, MARY WARD
Worry 2

BROWN, NOEL
Ecology 1; Technology 2; World 5

BROWN, PATRICIA LEIGH
Excitement 2

BROWN, RONALD H.
Arousal/Rousers 4

BROWNE, SIR THOMAS
(12th century)
Death, Defined 4

BROWNING, ELIZABETH BARRETT
(1806–1861)
Clinging 1; Silence 2; Weariness 1; Words As Weapons 3

BROWNING, ROBERT
(1812–1889)
Aggression 1; Art/Artists 7; Death 14; Fighting 2; God 7; Gratitude/Ingratitude 1; Language 2; Life 7; Mind 7; Poetry/Poets 8; Seascapes 1; Thinking/Thought 3

BROYARD, ANATOLE
(1920–1990)
Arousal/Rousers 5

BRULLER, JEAN MARCEL
See VERCORS

BRYANT, WILLIAM CULLEN
(1794–1878)
Difficulties 4; Fate 2; Journalism/Journalists 5; Life and Death 4

BRYDEN, RONALD
Maturation 3

BUBER, MARTIN
(1878–1965)
Action/Inaction 7; Being/Becoming 1; Language 3; Self-Knowledge 5; Words 5

BUCHANAN, EDNA
Cityscapes 3; Storms 1

BUCHANAN, PAT
Government 3

BUCHMAN, SIDNEY
(1902–1975)
Completeness/Incompleteness 4

BUCK, PEARL
(1892–1973)
Hunger 1

BUDDHA
(c. 563–c. 483 B.C.)
Being/Becoming 2

BULGAKOV, MIKHAIL
(1891–1940)
Failure 5

BULWER-LYTTON, EDWARD GEORGE
(1803–1873)
Old Age 6

BUNIN, IVAN
(1870–1953)
Descriptions, Misc. 11

BUÑUEL, LUIS
(1900–1983)
Sex/Sexuality 2

BURGESS, ANTHONY
Language 4; Originality/Unoriginality 2

BURKE, EDMUND
(1729–1797)
Education and Learning 8; Freedom/Restraint 2; Humanity/Humankind 5; Strength/Weakness 9; Superstition 1

BURLESON, DAVID
Education and Learning 9

BURLINGAME, ROGER
(1889–1967)
Childhood/Children 5; Death 15; Descriptions, Misc. 12; Ethics 1; Optimism/Pessimism 3; Revelation 2

BURNEY, FANNY
See MADAME D'ARBLAY

BURNS, JOHN F.
Arousal/Rousers 6; Mistakes 2

CARY, ALICE
(1820–1871)
Heart 11

CASANOVA, GIACOMO GIROLAMO
(1727–1805)
Death, Defined 5

CATHER, WILLA
(1873–1947)
Bodies/The Body 5; Communication/Non-Communication 3; Connections 4; Descriptions, Misc. 13; Good/Evil 3; Houses 2; Illusion/Reality 5; Landscapes 3; Loyalty 1; Mind 8; Occupations 2; Personality Profiles 6; Places, Misc. 2; Strength/Weakness 10; Sunset 4; Trees 7

CATHERINE OF SIENA
(1347–1380)
Humanity/Humankind 11

CATULLUS
(c. 84–c. 54 B.C.)
Accusations 3; Greed 2; Insults 1; Laments 1; Morality/Immorality 2; Name Calling 2; Places, Misc. 3; Poetry/Poets 9; Words As Weapons 5

CAUSLEY, CHARLES
Birthdays 1; Death 17; War 4

CAVAFY, C. P.
(1863–1933)
Excitement 3

CELAN, PAUL
(1920–1970)
People, Interaction 6; Silence 3; Sky/Skyscapes 2

CERF, BENNETT
(1898–1971)
Craftiness 1

CERVANTES, MIGUEL DE
(1547–1616)
Absence 3; Caution 4; Eyes 6; Fortune/Misfortune 7; Heart 12; Hunger 2; Patience 3; Re-

form 2; Sarcasm 4; Suspicion 2; Writing/Writers 6

CHAMFORT, SÉBASTIAN ROCH NICHOLAS
(1741–1794)
Life, Defined 8; Love 16

CHAN, PETER
Diplomacy 2

CHANDLER, RAYMOND
(1888–1959)
Voices 4

CHAO, YI
(Ch'in Dynasty)
Criticism/Critics 3

CHAPMAN, GEORGE
(c. 1559–1634)
Love, Defined 4

CHAPMAN, ROBERT
Sea 1

CHARLES V
(1500–1558)
Toughness 4

CHAUCER, GEOFFREY
(c. 1342–1400)
Arousal/Rousers 7; Desire 2; Dominance 3; Guidance/Guides 6, 7; Husbands and Wives 1, 2; Immorality/Morality 3; Insults 2; Love 17, 18; Lovers' Declarations and Exchanges 6; Manipulation 4; Men and Women 3; Money 7; People, Interaction 7; Pleas and Prayers 5; Poverty/Prosperity 4; Revenge/Vengeance 1; Ridicule 1; Sex/Sexuality 3; World 7

CHEEVER, JOHN
(1912–1982)
Difficulties 5; Faces 7; Freckles 1; Frustration 1; Heart 13; People, Interaction 8

CHEKHOV, ANTON
(1860–1904)
Age/Aging 5; Awareness/Unawareness 2; Courage 4; Defeat

3; Despair 4; Exaggeration 3; Houses 3; Hypocrisy 3; Idleness 1, 2; Irritants 4; Loyalty 2; Morality/Immorality 3; Nature 3; Obscurity 2; Order/Disorder 1; Utilization 2; Women 3

CHEN, JIGUANG
Leadership 3

CHESTERFIELD, LORD
See PHILIP DORMER STANHOPE

CHESTERTON, GILBERT KEITH
(1874–1936)
America/Americans 2; Darkness/Light 2; Death 18; Faces 8; Ideas 3; Landscapes 4; Nature Scenes 3; Sky/Skyscapes 3; Street Scenes 2, 3; Understanding/Misunderstanding 2

CHILD, LYDIA M.
(1802–1880)
Childhood/Children 7; Life, Defined 9

CHO, WEN-CHUN
(Han Dynasty)
Treachery 2

CHOPIN, KATE
(1851–1904)
Revenge/Vengeance 2; Sea 2; Youth 3

CHOWDERN, KEN
Memory/Memories 4

CHRYSOSTOM, JOHN
(c. 347–407)
Advice 2; Failure 8

CHU, TUN-YU
(Sung Dynasty)
Adversity 2

CHURCHILL, CHARLES
(1731–1764)
Old Age 7; Patience 4

CHURCHILL, RANDOLPH
(1911–1968)
Dominance 4

CONFUCIUS
(551–479 B.C.)
Dignity 1; Silence 5

CONGER, JOHN P.
Bodies/The Body 7

CONGREVE, WILLIAM
(1670–1729)
Anger 5; Boasters/Boastfulness 3; Hope 3; Marriage 9; Sex/Sexuality 4; Words As Weapons 6

CONNOLLY, CYRIL
(1903–1974)
Age/Aging 6; Emotions 4; Fatness/Thinness 7-c; Truth/Falsehood 12

CONRAD, JOSEPH [TEODOR JOZEF KONRAD KORZENIOWSKI]
(1857–1924)
Buildings and Bridges 4; Dreams 8; Faces 9; Ideas 4; Intoxication/Intoxicants 2; Memory/Memories 5; Moon 2; Nature 4; Places, Misc. 5; Sea 3; Seascapes 3, 4

CONRAD, PETER
Hair 2

CONROY, FRANK
Facial Expressions 1

COOK, ELIZA (1818–1889)
Necessity 1

COOKE, ALISTAIR
Arousal/Rousers 8; Personality Profiles 7

COOPER, JAMES FENIMORE
(1789–1851)
Boats/Boating 1; Facial Expressions 6; Heaven 4

CORMIER, ROBERT
Houses 6

CORNEILLE, PIERRE
(1606–1684)
Faces 10; Love, Defined 6

CORYATE, THOMAS
(c. 1577–1617)
Fame 3

COULETTE, HENRI
(1927–1988)
Seascapes 5

COURIC, KATIE
Weariness 2

COWAN, PAUL
(1940–1988)
Ancestry/Ancestors 3

COWARD, NOEL
(1899–1973)
Memory/Memories 6; Past 7

COWLEY, ABRAHAM
(1618–1667)
Cities 11; Joy 6; Life, Defined 10

COWLEY, HANNAH
(1743–1809)
Beauty 6; Women 4

COWPER, WILLIAM
(1731–1800)
Diversity 1; Journalism/Journalists 6

COXE, LOUIS O.
Sea 1

COZZENS, JAMES GOULD
(1903–1978)
Faces 11

CRAIK, DINAH MULOCK
(1826–1887)
Faith 4; Marriage 10; Responsibility 1

CRAMER, RICHARD BEN
Problems and Solutions 6

CRANE, HART
(1899–1932)
Sea 4

CRANE, STEPHEN
(1871–1900)
Conformity/Nonconformity 3; Courage 6; Descriptions, Misc. 15; Humanity/Humankind 13; Importance/Unimportance 3; Movements 2; Name Calling 3; Seascapes 6; Speechlessness 2; Storms 2; Trees 8; Wisdom 4

CROSS, MARY ANN EVANS
See
GEORGE ELIOT

CROSSETTE, BARBARA
Rescue/Rescuers 1

CROUCH, STANLEY
Institutions 2

CUMMINGS, COUNTEE
(1903–1946)
Death 1-c

CUMMINGS, BRUCE FREDERICK
See W. N. P. BARBELLION

CUMMINGS, E[DWARD] E[STLIN]
(1894–1962)
Actions 6; Dawn 2; Descriptions, Misc. 16, 17; Eye Expressions 2; Eyes 7; Freedom/Restraint 4; Humanity/Humankind 14; Immortality 2; Knowledge 6; Love 20; Memory/Memories 7; Morning 2; Ordinariness/Extraordinariness 4; Progress 4; Seasons 4; Sky/Skyscapes 4; Spring 2; Superficiality 3; Time 9; Wind 3

CUOMO, MARIO
Reform 3; Unity/Disunity 3-c

CURRY, JACK
Action/Inaction 9; Self-Control 5

D

DAENZER, RICHARD
Caution 5

DAHL, ROALD
(1916–1990)
Sweat 1

D'AMATO, ALFONSE M.
Deception 5

DANIEL, DONALD C. F.
Problems and Solutions 7;
Violence 1

DANIEL, SAMUEL
(c. 1562–1619)
Love, Defined 7, 8

DANIEL, W. B.
Criticism/Critics 5

DANOWITZ, JANE
Riches 2

**D'ARBLAY, MADAME
[FANNY BURNEY]**
(1752–1840)
Imagination 2; Danger 2

DAVENANT, SIR WILLIAM
(1606–1668)
Ambition 5; Books 11

DAVIE, DONALD
Courage 7; Deception 6; Descriptions, Misc. 18; Facial Expressions 7; Feelings 2; Language 5; Night and Day 3

DAVIES, MARY CAROLYN
(d.u.)
Pain and Suffering 5

DAVINIC, PRVOSLAV
Arousal/Rousers 9; Similari-
ty/Dissimilarity 3

DAVIS, ANGELA
Connections 5

DAVIS, CATHERINE
Articulateness/Inarticulateness
1; Hope 4

DAVIS, JEFFERSON
(1808–1889)
Applause 1

DAVIS, PETER G.
Music/Musicians 5

DAY-LEWIS, C[ECIL]
(1904–1972)
Childhood/Children 8; Landscapes 6

DE CASSERES, BENJAMIN
(1873–1945)
Fame 4

**DE CHATEAUNEUF
RIEUX, RENEE**
(1550–1587)
Marriage 11

DECONCINI, DENNIS
Problems and Solutions 8

DEFOE, DANIEL
(1660–1731)
Leaders/Followers 4

DEGLER, CARL N.
America/Americans 8-c

DE JARS, MARIE
(17th century)
Society/Social Situations 1

DEKKER, THOMAS
(c. 1572–c. 1632)
Fashion and Style 3

DE LA MARE, WALTER
(1873–1936)
Moon 3

DEMILLE, AGNES
(1905–1993)
Difficulties 6, 7; Endings 5; Mas-
tery/Subordination 6; Occupations 3

DEUTSCH, BABETTE
(1895–1982)
Memory/Memories 8

DE YOUNG KAY, ELLEN
Laments 2

DIALLO, DJIBRIL
Information 1

DIAMOND, JAY
Greed 3

DIAZ, JAIME
Sports 2, 3; Success, Defined 5

DICKENS, CHARLES
(1812–1870)
Characterizations 8; Connections 6; Disintegration 2; Fog 1;
Friendship/Friends 8; Group
Scenes 1; Law/Lawyers 5; Nature 5; Passion 7; Physical Appearance 9; Poverty/Prosperi-
ty 5; Sun 1; Vulnerability 1

DICKEY, JAMES
Descriptions, Misc. 19; Nature
Scenes 6

DICKINSON, EMILY
(1830–1886)
Birds 4; Daydreams 2; Death
19; Descriptions, Misc. 20; Fall
3; Nature 6; Rain 4; Soul 4;
Storms 3; Street Scenes 4;
Sunrise 1

DIDION, JOAN
Anger 6

DIGGES, DEBORAH
Grief 3

DILLARD, ANNIE
Awareness/Unawareness 3;
Books 12; Humanity/Human-
kind 15; Self-Actualization 3

DILLON, WENTWORTH
(c. 1633–1685)
Old Age 8

DINKINS, DAVID N.
Deception 7

DIODOROUS
(4th century)
Books 10-c

DIOGENES
(c. 300 B.C.)
Villainy/Villains 1

DIONNE, E. J.
Changeableness/
Unchangeableness 3

**DISRAELI, BENJAMIN
[EARL OF
BEACONSFIELD]**
(1804–1881)
Beliefs 4; Success, Defined 6;
Weariness 3

**DOBSON, HENRY
AUSTIN**
(1840–1921)
Death 20; Fame 5

DOCTOROW, E. L.
Culture 3; Reading/Readers 2;
Singing/Songs/Singers 4

DODD, CHRISTOPHER
Difficulties 8

**DODGSON, CHARLES
LUTWIDGE**
See LEWIS CARROLL

DODSLEY, ROBERT
(1703–1764)
Humanity/Humankind 16

DOERR, HARRIET
Life 10

DOLE, ROBERT
Characterizations 9

**DOLLIVER, JONATHAN
PRENTISS**
(d.u.)
Personality Profiles 8

DONAHUE, PHIL
Confrontation 1; Freedom Of
Expression 1

DONALDSON, SAM
Politics/Politicians 9

DONNE, JOHN
(1572–1631)
Age/Aging 7, 8; Birth 1; Civili-
zation 5; Darkness/Light 3;
Death 21; Essence 3; Grief 4, 5;
Helplessness 3; Illness 4; Inher-

itance/Inheritors 2; Love 21,
22, 23, 24, 25, 26, 27, 28; Lovers' Declarations and Exchanges
7; Permanence/Impermanence
3; Progress 5; Reason 4; Separation 2; Sighs 1; Speed 2; Sun
2; Sunset 5; Tears 6, 7, 8; Warnings 2; Warriors and Peacemakers 1

DONOSO, JOSE
Bodies/The Body 8; Envy 2;
Escape 2; Expectations 1;
Voices 5, 6

**DOOLITTLE, HILDA [H.
D.]**
(1886–1961)
Heat 1; Sea 5

D'ORLÉANS, CHARLES
(1391–1465)
Spring 3

DORR, JULIA
(1825–1913)
Flowers 1

DOS PASSOS, JOHN
(1896–1970)
Excitement 4; Eyes 8, 9; Group
Scenes 2; Hope 5; Revolt 1

**DOSTOEVSKY, FYODOR
MIKHAILOVICH**
(1821–1881)
Abundance 4; Consciousness 2;
Decisiveness/Indecisiveness 3;
Futility 1; Grief 6; Importance/
Unimportance 4; Knowledge 7;
Malice 1; Self-Effacement 3;
Self-Images 4; Self-Reliance 3, 4

DOTEN, ELIZABETH
(1829–?)
Humanity/Humankind 17

DOUGLAS, KEITH
(1920–1944)
Love 29

DOVE, RITA
Life 11; Poetry/Poets 12

DOWD, MAUREEN
Exploitation 1; Impossibility 3;
Knowledge 9; Politics/Politi-
cians 19

DOWNS, THOMAS M.
Problems and Solutions 9

**DOYLE, SIR ARTHUR
CONAN**
(1859–1930)
Cities 12; Curiosity 1; Mind 9;
Wrinkles 1

DRABBLE, MARGARET
Ambition 6; Escape 3; Free-
dom/Restraint 5; Love 30

DREISER, THEODORE
(1871–1945)
Art/Artists 14; Bodies/The
Body 9; Characterizations 10;
Deterioration/Diminishment 1

DREW, ELIZABETH
Abandonment 1; Politics/Poli-
ticians 10; Winning/Losing 4

DROUET, JULIETTE
(1806–1883)
Heart 15

DRUMMOND, WILLIAM
(1585–1649)
Vice/Virtue 1

DRYDEN, JOHN
(1631–1700)
Abandonment 2; Approval/Dis-
approval 2; Bodies/The Body
10; Conversation 3; Cowardice
2; Criticism/Critics 6, 7, 8;
Fame 6; Fate 4; Foolhardiness
4, 5; God 9; Immortality 3; In-
heritance/Inheritors 3; Love
31; Poetry/Poets 13, 14; Religion 12; Stupidity 2, 3, 4;
Substantiality/Insubstantiality
1; War 6; Writing/Writers 8

DU BARTAS
See GUILLAUME DE
SALLUSTE

ENDO, SHUSAKU
Endings 6; Fertility/Infertility 2; Mistakes 3; Religion 14; Seascapes 8, 9

ENGBERG, ERIC
Disintegration 3

ERSKINE, THOMAS
(18th century)
Authority 2

EZRA, ABRAHAM IBN
(1092–1167)
Humanity/Humankind 21; Life, Defined 13

F

FADIMAN, CLIFTON
Childhood/Children 9; Compromise 2; Conversation 4; Fame 7; Leaders/Followers 6; Quotations 2

FALLACI, ORIANA
Fame 8

FALUDI, SUSAN
Name Calling 4; Women 5

FARJEON, ELEANOR
(1881–1965)
Eye Expressions 3

FARQUHAR, GEORGE
(1678–1707)
Charity 1; Truth/Falsehood 15

FAULKNER, WILLIAM
(1897–1962)
Characterizations 11; Conflict 3; Death 23; Destruction/Destructiveness 6; Education and Learning 12; Houses 7; Loyalty 3; Time 12

FEDOTOV, YURI
Peace 6

FERBER, EDNA
(1887–1968)
Character 4; Choices and Decisions 1; Cities 14; Complexion 5; Grammar and Style 2; Landscapes 8; Places, Misc. 8; Writing/Writers 9

FERLINGHETTI, LAWRENCE
Poetry/Poets 15

FERRARO, SUSAN
Barriers 3

FESSENDON, WILLIAM
(1806–1869)
Winning/Losing 5

FEYNMAN, RICHARD
(1918–1988)
Defeat 4; Nature 10; Self-Destructiveness 1

FICKE, ARTHUR DAVISON
(1883–1945)
Beauty 7

FIELDING, HENRY
(1707–1754)
Alliances 2; Ancestry/Ancestors 4; Character 5; Craftiness 2; Ego/Egotism 5; Exactness/Inexactness 1; Justice/Injustice 6; Nature 11; Occupations 4; People, Interaction 10; Visibility/Invisibility 4

FINEGAN, WILLIAM
Life, Defined 14

FINKEL, DONALD
Crowds 2; Descriptions, Misc. 22

FINN, ROBIN
Openness/Privacy 2; Transience 3

FISHER, DOROTHY CANFIELD
(1879–1958)
Reality/Unreality 2; Street Scenes 5

FITZGERALD, EDWARD
(1809–1883)
Life and Death 6; Sky/Skyscapes 6; Time 13, 14

FITZGERALD, F. SCOTT
(1896–1940)
Affection 2; Buildings and Bridges 5; Characterizations 12; Descriptions, Misc. 23; Despair 5; Helplessness 4; Memory/Memories 12; Oblivion 2; Self-Consciousness 1; Sky/Skyscapes 7; Snow 5; Success, Defined 7; Thinking/Thought 5; Time 15; Voices 7; Words 7; Writing Advice 2

FITZGERALD, ZELDA
(1900–1948)
Compromise 3

FLANAGAN, HALLIE
(1890–1969)
Facts 1

FLAUBERT, GUSTAVE
(1821–1880)
Descriptions, Misc. 24; Despair 6; Isolation 3; Optimism/Pessimism 4; Women 6

FLETCHER, JOHN
(1579–1625)
Marriage 26-C; Self-Reliance 7

FLETCHER, JOHN GOULD
(1886–1950)
Descriptions, Misc. 25; Foreboding 1; Night and Day 4; Self-Images 5; Sky/Skyscapes 8, 9; Truth/Falsehood 16

FLETCHER, PHINEAS
(1582–1650)
Sleep 1

FLORIO, STEVEN T.
Alertness 1

FONTENELLE, BERNARD LE BAVIER
(1657–1757)
Truth/Falsehood 17

GARDNER, ERLE STANLEY
(1889–1970)
Bodies/The Body 14; Brain 3

GARFIELD, JAMES A.
(1831–1881)
Politics/Politicians 11

GARGAN, EDWARD A.
Essence 4

GARRISON, DEBORAH
Substantiality/Insubstantiality 2

GARTH, SAMUEL
(1661–1719)
Death, Defined 10

GASS, WILLIAM H.
Life, Defined 15; Marriage 12;
Money 11

GATES, JR., HENRY LOUIS
Bigotry 2

GAUDIANI, CLAIRE L.
Ethics 2

GAUTIER, THÈOPHILE
(1811–1872)
Chance 4

GAY, JOHN
(1685–1732)
Beauty 8; Characterizations 14;
Death 29; Death, Defined 11;
Devotion 1; Entrapment 5; Hair
Color 6; Law/Lawyers 7; Lovers' Declarations and Exchanges
8; Manipulation 7, 8, 9; Marriage 13; Money 12; Tears
9; Youth 5

GELB, LESLIE H.
Danger 4, 5; Destruction/De-
structiveness 7, 5; Obsolescence
1; Power 7, 8; Warriors and
Peacemakers 2

GENET, JEAN
(1910–1986)
Cities 15; Identity 2; Music/
Musicians 8; People, Interaction 13; Self-Images 6; Violence 2; Words 10

GERBER, MERRILL JOAN
Concentration/Distraction 1

GEROULD, KATHERINE
(1879–1944)
Politics/Politicians 12

GERSTON, JILL
Success, Defined 10

GIBRAN, KAHLIL
(1883–1931)
Beauty 9; Charity 2; Comfort/
Comfort-Givers 3; Emotions
5; Friendship/Friends 13; Hu-
manity/Humankind 24; Joy/
Sorrow 5; Life 14; Morality/
Immorality 5; Soul 5; Think-
ing/Thought 6; Work/
Workers 3, 4

GIDE, ANDRÉ
(1869–1951)
Experience 5

GILBEY, EMMA
Endings 7

GILCHRIST, MARIE
(1893–?)
Grammar and Style 3

GILLETT, MICHELLE
Advice 4; Ambivalence 1; Fami-
lies/Family Relationships 6

GINSBERG, ALLEN
Cityscapes 4; Humanity/Hu-
mankind 25; Singing/Songs/
Singers 7

GINSBURG, ELISABETH
Self-Consciousness 2

GINSBURG, NATALIA
(1916–1991)
Writing/Writers 10

GIRAUDOUX, JEAN
(1882–1944)
Civilization 7; Confrontation 2;
Corruption 4; Descriptions, Misc.
28; Dignity 2; Fate 6; Hypocrisy 4; Justice/Injustice 7; Life
15; Lovers' Declarations and
Exchanges 9; Name Calling 5,

6, 7, 8; Peace 8; Pity 1; Poetry/
Poets 16; Popularity/Unpopu-
larity 2; Stupidity 5; Sun 3; Survival 2; War 8

GISSING, GEORGE
(1857–1903)
Places, Misc. 9

GLEICK, JAMES
Communication/Non-Com-
munication 4; Connections 7;
Information 2; Science 3, 4; Self-
Knowledge 7

GODWIN, MARY
See MARY GODWIN
WOLLSTONECRAFT

GODWIN, WILLIAM
(1756–1836)
Opinion 2

**GOETHE, JOHANN
WOLFGANG VON**
(1749–1832)
Actions 7; Ambition 7; Archi-
tecture 1, 2; Exactness/
Inexactness 2; Genius 5; Good/
Evil 4; Life 16; Life and Death
7; Love 36; Truth/Falsehood 18

GOLDEN, TIM
Economics 9

GOLDMAN, ROBERT
Ordinariness/
Extraordinariness 5

GOLDSMITH, OLIVER
(1730–1774)
Diversity 4

GOLDSTEIN, REBECCA
Disturbances 1; Happiness/Un-
happiness 3; Identity 3

GONZALES, LAURENCE
Order/Disorder 3

GONZALEZ, DAVID
Power 9

GOODBY, JAMES
Action/Inaction 10

GOODMAN, ELLEN
Danger 6; Marriage 14

GOODMAN, WALTER
Journalism/Journalists 7; Knowledge 3-c

GOPNIK, ADAM
Art/Artists 18; Foolhardiness 6; Hate 2

GORDIMER, NADINE
Life and Death 8; Mind 11; Physical Appearance 10; Rooms 5; Street Scenes 6; Timidity 1

GOREN, RABBI SHLOMO
Completeness/Incompleteness 5

GORKY, MAXIM
(1868–1936)
Failure 10; Monotony 4

GORNICK, VIVIAN
Street Scenes 7

GOSSE, SIR EDMUND
(1849–1928)
Thinking/Thought 7

GOTTLIEB, MARTIN
Power 9

GOULD, LOIS
Tears 10

GOULDING, MARRACK
Peace 9

GRACCHUS, CORNELIA
(19th century)
Childhood/Children 10

GRACIAN, BALTASAR
(1601–1658)
Birthdays 2; Hope 8; Passion 10; Truth/Falsehood 19; Words 11; Youth and Age 4

GRAHAM, W. S.
(1918–1986)
Freedom/Restraint 6; Lovers' Declarations and Exchanges 10; Mind 12; Poetry/Poets 17; Time 17

GRAHAM, WINSTON
Pain and Suffering 7

GRAHAME, KENNETH
(1859–1932)
Descriptions, Misc. 29; Expectations 2; Life 17; Personality Profiles 9; Tranquility 2

GRAINGER, JAMES
Fame 10

GRANGER, BILL
Eye Expressions 4; Looks 4

GRAVER, ELIZABETH
Illness 5

GRAY, FRANCINE DU PLESSIX
Busyness 1; Descriptions, Misc. 30; Grammar and Style 4

GREEN, HANNA
Perfection 4

GREENBERG, JOEL
Obsolescence 2

GREENBERG, RICHARD
Success, Defined 11

GREENE, GRAHAM
(1904–1991)
Books 14; Life 18; Understanding 4

GREENE, ROBERT
(c. 1558–1592)
Contentment 1

GREENHOUSE, STEVEN
Danger 7

GREER, GERMAINE
Youth and Age 5

GREY, JERRY
Eloquence 1

GRIFFIN, SUSAN
Self-Knowledge 8

GRIMES, JOE
Competition/Competitors 5

GRIMES, WILLIAM
Anger 8

GRUMBACH, DORIS
Life and Death 9

GRUSON, LINDSEY
Politics/Politicians 13

GUEREWITSCH, MATTHEW
Death 30

GUILLEN, JORGE
(1893–1984)
Death 31; Idleness 4

GUNN, THOM
Heart 17, 18; Humor 5; Love 37; Mastery/Subordination 8; Writing Advice 3

GUSSOW, MEL
Difficulties 9; Failure 11; Importance/Unimportance 5; Innocence/Inexperience 4; Satire 2; Slowness 1

H

HABERMAN, CLYDE
Candor 1; Difficulties 10; Flexibility/Inflexibility 2; Success/Failure 3

HACKER, ANDREW
Bigotry 3

HADEWIJCH
(1235–1265)
Love, Defined 9

HAIER, RICHARD
Brain 4

HALE, SARAH JOSEPHA
(1788–1879)
Life and Death 10; Sky/Skyscapes 10

HALL, DONALD
Awareness/Unawareness 4; Diversity 5; Emotions 6; Land-

scapes 9; Poetry/Poets 18; Self 2; Sex/Sexuality 5; Speed 3; Travel 2; Work/Workers 5, 6

HAMBURGER, MICHAEL
Achievement 2; Futility 2; Poetry/Poets 19

HAMDOON, NIZAR
Emotions 7

HAMILTON, ANN
Essence 5

HAMMERSTEIN II, OSCAR
(1895–1960)
Arts and Entertainment 3

HAMMETT, DASHIELL
(1894–1961)
Aggression 3; Agitation 1; Eyes 11; Faces 13; Fatness/Thinness 5; Mouths 2; Wrinkles 2

HANNAH, BARRY
Truth/Falsehood 20

HAN SUYIN
Fish 2

HARDENBERG, BARON FRIEDRICH VON
See NOVALIS

HARDWICK, ELIZABETH
Strength/Weakness 14; Failure 12

HARDY, THOMAS
(1840–1928)
Age/Aging 9; Birds 6; Confusion 1; Connections 8; Emotions 8; Happiness/Unhappiness 4; Street Scenes 8

HARMETZ, ALJEAN
Strength/Weakness 15

HARRISON, BARBARA GRIZZUTI
Dreams 10

HARRISON, JIM
Connections 9; Creativity 3; Dreams 11; Hard-Heartedness

3; Moon 5; Nightmares 1; Sleeplessness 3

HARROD, ELIZABETH B.
Fall 4; Moon 6

HART, FRANCES NOYES
(1890–1943)
Eye Expressions 5; Memory/Memories 14

HART, GARY
Defeat 5

HART, JOSEPHINE
Arts and Entertainment 4; Influence 1; Movements 3; Soul 6; Thinking/Thought 8; Time 18; Transformation 3

HARTLEY, L. P.
(1895–1972)
Abandonment 3; Past 8

HARWOOD, RONALD
Memory/Memories 15; Self 3; Self-Actualization 5

HATCH, DOROTHY L.
Poetry/Poets 20

HATSUMI, REIKO
Flexibility/Inflexibility 3

HAUPTMANN, GERHART
(1862–1946)
Freedom/Restraint 7; Name Calling 9

HAWTHORNE, NATHANIEL
(1804–1864)
Advantageousness 1; Age/Aging 10; Art/Artists 19; Characterizations 15; Death 32; Earth 2; Families/Family Relationships 7, 8; Fate 7, 8; Genius 6; Group Scenes 4; Heart 19; Houses 8; Humanity/Humankind 26; Humor 6; Intelligence 2; Moon 7; Mountains 1; Politics/Politicians 14, 15; Reform 4; Sound 2; Time 19

HAYDEN, ROBERT
(1913–1980)
Descriptions, Misc. 31; Fear 7; History 12; Liberty 3; Speeches 2

HAYES, THOMAS C.
Business Descriptions 4; Failure 13

HAZLITT, WILLIAM
(1778–1830)
Desire 3; Life 19; Life and Death 11

HEARN, LAFCADIO
(1850–1904)
Poetry/Poets 21

HEATH-STUBBS, JOHN
Pain and Suffering 8

HECHT, ANTHONY
Arts and Entertainment 5; Birth 2; Color 1; Death 33; Fall 5; Intoxication/Intoxicants 3; Loneliness 3; Memory/Memories 16; Nightmares 2; Physical Appearance 11; Rain 5; Street Scenes 9; Sun 4; Sunrise 2; Time 20

HECHT, BEN
(1894–1964)
Bigotry 4, 5; Future 4

HEINE, HEINRICH
(1797–1856)
Books 15

HELLMAN, LILLIAN
(1905–1984)
Friendship/Friends 14; Tact 2

HELOISE
(c. 1098–1164)
Fate 9; Fortune/Misfortune 11; Men and Women 6; Pain and Suffering 9

HELTON, ROY
(d.u.)
Trees 10

HEMINGWAY, ERNEST
(1899–1961)
Aggression 4; Grammar and Style 5; Love 38; Street Scenes 10

HENAHAN, DONAL
Change 7; Guidance/Guides 8

HENDERSON, RAY
(d.u.)
Life, Defined 6

HENLEY, WILLIAM ERNEST
(1849–1903)
Chance 5; Fate 10; Life and Death 12; Life, Defined 16; Sunset 7

HENNINGER, DANIEL
Irritants 5

HENRY, O.
(1862–1910)
Cities 16; Cityscapes 5, 6; Comfort/Comfort-Givers 4; Conformity/Nonconformity 8, 9; Conversation 6; Courage 11; Craftiness 3; Crowds 3; Descriptions, Misc. 32; Freckles 2; Furniture/Furnishings 2, 3; Illness 6; Imagination 4; Order/Disorder 4; Street Scenes 11; Sunset 8; Time 21; Wind 6; Wit 3; Zenith 2

HENRY, PATRICK
(1736–1799)
Experience 6; Flaws 3; Hope 9; Hypocrisy 5

HERBERT, GEORGE
(1593–1633)
Ability 3; Friendship/Friends 15, 16; Justice/Injustice 8; War 9; Wit 4

HERBERT, ZBIGNIEW
Apathy 3; Death 34; Descriptions, Misc. 33; Senses 2; Speech 4

HERGESHEIMER, JOSEPH
(1880–1954)
Abundance 7; Exploitation 2; Strength/Weakness 16

HERODOTUS
(c. 484–c. 425 B.C.)
Fortune/Misfortune 12

HERRARA, HAYDEN
Language 7

HERRICK, ROBERT
(1591–1674)
Humanity/Humankind 27

HERRING, HERBERT B.
Business Descriptions 5, 6, 7; Competition/Competitors 6; Difficulties 11; Economics 10; Failure 14; Flaws 4; Injury 1; Reform 5

HERSEY, JOHN
(1914–1993)
Anger 9; Candor 2; Dullness 3; Eyebrows 1; Gratitude/Ingratitude 2; Manipulation 10; Physical Appearance 13, 12; Society/Social Situations 7; Trees 11, 12; Weariness 4; Wind 7

HESSE, HERMANN
(1867–1962)
Clarity/Ambiguity 8-c; Desire 4; Education and Learning 11; Humanity/Humankind 28; Illusion/Reality 6; Opinion 3; Restlessness 1; Riches 3; Self 4; Soul 7; Thinking/Thought 9; Transformation 4; Understanding 5

HEYWOOD, JOHN
(c. 1497–c. 1580)
Reform 6

HEYWOOD, THOMAS
(c. 1574–1641)
Contentment 2

HIGHSMITH, PATRICIA
Confusion 2; Significance/Insignificance 3; Street Scenes 12

HILL, GEOFFREY
Creation 2; Rooms 6; Rumor 2; Seasons 6; Sky/Skyscapes 11

HILL, M. CHARLES
Revelation 3

HOAGLAND, EDWARD
Clergy 1; Crowds 4; Death 35; Difficulties 12; Pain and Suffering 10; Places, Misc. 10; Road Scenes 2; Speech 5; Survival 3

HOCHMAN, PHILIP C.
Descriptions, Misc. 34; Preparedness/Unpreparedness 3

HODGSON, RALPH
(1871–1962)
Time 22

HOLDEN, STEPHEN
Language 8; Voices 9

HOLLAND, BERNARD
Books 16, 17; Connections 10; Control 5; Many 3; Mediocrity 2; Music/Musicians 9; Singing/Songs/Singers 8

HOLLANDER, JOHN
Agreement/Disagreement 3; Darkness/Light 4; Mastery/Subordination 9; Nightmares 3; Quarrels/Quarrelsomeness 2; Singing/Songs/Singers 9; Stillness 1; Summer 2; Trees 13

HOLMAN, KWAME
Reform 7

HOLMES, SR., OLIVER WENDELL
(1809–1894)
Action/Inaction 11; Age/Aging 11; Apology 1; Appearance 1; Beliefs 5; Birthdays 3; Boats/Boating 3; Brain 5; Descriptions, Misc. 35; Evening 4; Facial Expressions 8; Facts 3; Faith 5; Fame 11; Fate 11; Feelings 3; Friendship/Friends 17; Intelligence 3; Lies/Liars 5; Life and Death 13; Life, Defined 17; Memory/Memories 17; Nature 12; Old Age 10; Sea 6; Speech 6; Street Scenes 13; Success, Defined 12; Sunset 9

THE HOLY BIBLE
Abundance 1, 2; Affliction 1, 2; Ambition 3; Ancestry/Ancestors 2; Anger, Divine 1, 2; Arguments 2; Beauty 3; Belonging/Outcast 1; Bodies/The Body 3; Change 2; Changeableness/Unchangeableness 2; Childhood/Children 3; Clarity/Ambiguity 1; Comfort/Comfort-Givers 1, 2; Conflict 1; Conformity/Nonconformity 2; Corruption 1, 2; Crime and Punishment 1; Death 7, 8, 9, 10; Debt 2; Deception 2, 3; Despair 2, 3; Disappointment 2; Doubt 2; Evil 2, 3; Escape 1; Faith 2, 3; Flattery 3; Flexibility/Inflexibility 1; Friendship/Friends 3; Generosity 3; God 1, 2, 3, 4, 5; Goodness 2, 3; Guidance/ Guides 3, 4, 5; Hair Color 4; Hell and Damnation 2; Humanity/Humankind 3; Innocence/Inexperience 2; Jealousy 3; Leaders/Followers 2, 3; Leadership 1; Life 4, 5; Love 10; Mind 5; Passion 3, 4; Peace 4; Persuasiveness/Persuaders 2; Power 6; Pride 1, 2; Religion 7; Speech 3; Strength/Weakness 7; Superficiality 2; Tears 4, 5; Temptation 4; Toughness 2; Understanding 2; Wastefulness 1

HOMER
(8th century B.C.)
Danger 8; Laughter 3; Sleep 4, 5

HONG, HO XUAN
(19th century)
Love 39

HOOD, THOMAS
(1799–1845)
Exploitation 3

HOOVER, HERBERT
(1874–1964)
Freedom/Restraint 8

HOOVER, J. EDGAR
(1895–1972)
Name Calling 10

HOPKINS, GERARD MANLEY
(1844–1889)
Inspiration 4

HOPPS, WALTER
Art/Artists 20

HORACE
(65–8 B.C.)
Anger 10; Death 36; Education and Learning 13; Words 12; Worry 6

HOROWITZ, MICHAEL
Mixture 1

HOULT, NORAH
(1898–1894)
Memory/Memories 18

HOUSMAN, A[LFRED] E[DWARD]
(1859–1936)
Breath 2; Emotions 9; Night and Day 7; Nightmares 4

HOVEY, RICHARD
(1864–1900)
Restlessness 2

HOWARD, HENRY [EARL OF SURREY]
(c. 1517–1547)
Blushes 2; Epitaphs 1, 2; Eyes 12; Past 9; Perfection 5; Spring 4

HOWARD, MAUREEN
Families/Family Relationships 9

HOWARD, RICHARD
Art/Artists 21

HOWE, JULIA WARD
(1819–1910)
God 13

HOWELLS, WILLIAM DEAN
(1837–1920)
Life and Death 14; Obsolescence 3

HSIN CH'I-CHI
(1140–1207)
Storms 5

HUBBARD, ELBERT
(1856–1915)
Beliefs 6; Dignity 3

HUDSON, BARBARA
Emotions 10

HUDSON, W[ILLIAM] H[ENRY]
(1841–1922)
Birds 7; Talkativeness 3

HUGHES, JOHN
(1677–1720)
Life, Defined 18

HUGHES, KEN
Trustworthiness/Untrustworthiness 4

HUGHES, ROBERT
Alliances 3; Boats/Boating 2; Countries, Misc. 3, 4; Crime and Punishment 5; Deception 11; Descriptions, Misc. 36; Mastery/Subordination 10; Nature Scenes 9; Physical Appearance 14

HUGHES, TED
Birds 8; Death 37; Despair 7; Law/Lawyers 8, 9; Lust 2; Smiles 4

HUGO, VICTOR
(1802–1885)
Life, Defined 19; Work/Workers 7

HUNT, LEIGH
(1784–1859)
Color 2; Time 23

HUNTER, CATFISH
Excess 2

HURST, FANNIE
(1889–1968)
Openness/Privacy 3

HURSTON, ZORA NEALE
(1903–1960)
Moon 8; Slowness 2; Time 24

JERROLD, DOUGLAS
(1803–1857)
Opinion 4

JEWETT, SARAH ORNE
(1849–1909)
Action/Inaction 12; Characterizations 17; Fall 6; Sun 6; Trees 14; Women 7

JOFFE, JOSEF
Craftiness 4; Freedom/Restraint 10

JOHNSON, CHALMERS
Entrapment 6

JOHNSON, JOSEPHINE W.
(1910–1990)
Death 39

JOHNSON, LYNDON B.
(1908–1973)
America/Americans 3; Unity/Disunity 4-c

JOHNSON, SAMUEL
(1709–1784)
Action/Inaction 13; Assistance 2; Creativity 4; History 14; Talkativeness 5; Truth/Falsehood 21; Writing/Writers 12

JOHNSTON, WILLIAM
Destruction/Destructiveness 8; Religion 16

JONES, JERRY
Optimism/Pessimism 5

JONES, LELAND T.
Accusations 5

JONSON, BEN
(1572–1637)
Applause 2; Language 9; Poetry/Poets 23; Talkativeness 4

JORDAN, HAMILTON
Opportunity 4

JORDAN, JAMES
Life and Death 18

JOYCE, JAMES
(1882–1941)
Agitation 2; Characterizations 18; Clergy 2; Clouds 1; Creativity 5; Descriptions, Misc. 37; Entanglements 1; Experience 7; Feelings 4; Food and Drink 4; Forgiveness 4; Group Scenes 6; History 15; Idleness 5; Imagination 5, 6; Lust 3; Order/Disorder 5; Protection/Protectors 2; Sea 7; Seascapes 10; Self-Destructiveness 2; Sex/Sexuality 6; Sin/Redemption 3, 4; Soul 9; Spirit 2

JUSTICE, DONALD
Fear 8; Manipulation 12

K

KAEL, PAULINE
Acting/Actors 2

KAKUTANI, MICHIKO
Passion 1; Time 25

KANT, IMMANUEL
(1724–1804)
Humanity/Humankind 29

KAPLEAU, PHILIP
Being/Becoming 3; Cause and Effect 6; Immortality 5; Pain and Suffering 12

KARLEN, NEAL
Business Descriptions 8, 9; Transformation 5

KARP, JACK
Competition/Competitors 7

KASDORF, JULIA
Sun 7

KAUFMANN, WALTER
(1921–1980)
Bigotry 6; Communication/Non-Communication 5; Illusion/Reality 7; Optimism/Pessimism 6; Religion 17

KAWABATA YASUNARI
(1899–1972)
Arousal/Rousers 10; Descriptions, Misc. 38, 39; Disturbances 2; Ego/Egotism 6; Families/Family Relationships 12; Guilt 2; Landscapes 10; Memory/Memories 19; Men and Women 7; Passion 12; Rain 7; Separation 3; Time 26

KAZIN, ALFRED
Emotions 13; Night and Day 8; Places, Misc. 12

KEATS, JOHN
(1795–1821)
Aerial Views 2; Beauty 11; Business Descriptions 10; Concentration/Distraction 2, 3; Danger 10; Epitaphs 3; Fortune/Misfortune 13; Genius 7; Imagination 7, 8; Life 21; Lovers' Declarations and Exchanges 11; Manipulation 13; Nature 13; Poetry/Poets 24; Sleep 6

KEEFE, NANCY Q.
Hell and Damnation 5

KEHOE, LOUISE
Language 10

KELLER, BILL
Advantageousness 3; Danger 12; Democracy 4

KELLER, HÄFIZ
(14th century)
Danger 11

KELLER, HELEN
(1880–1968)
Anger 11; Past 18-c; Ridicule 2; Smells 2

KELLERMAN, JONATHAN
Street Scenes 14

KELLY, MICHAEL
Anger 12; Characterizations 19; Dreams 12; Fog 3; Politics/Politicians 18, 19

KRONKE, DAVID
Descriptions, Misc. 40

KRULWICH, BILL
Strength/Weakness 9-c

KSHETRAYYA
(17th century)
Flattery 4

KUME MASAO
(1891–1952)
Criticism/Critics 10; Intoxication/Intoxicants 4; Responsibility 3

KUMOVE, SHIRLEY
Language 11

KUNITZ, STANLEY
Occupations 5

KUNSTLER, JAMES HOWARD
Business Descriptions 11

KUTTNER, ROBERT
Disintegration 4; Strength/Weakness 21

L

LABRUNIE, GÉRARD
See
GÉRARD DE NERVAL

LA FARGE, OLIVER
(1901–1963)
Landscapes 12

LA FOLLETTE, MELVIN WALKER
Animals 2; Breath 3

LAGERLÖF, SELMA
(1858–1940)
Families/Family Relationships 14

LAHR, JOHN
Envy 4; Mixture 2

LAING, DILYS
Memory/Memories 20

LAMARTINE, ALPHONSE DE
(1790–1869)
Institutions 5; Life and Death 20

LAMB, CHARLES
(1775–1834)
Animals 3, 4; Eyes 14

LA METTRIE, J[ULIEN] O[FFROY] DE
(1709–1751)
Bodies/The Body 16

LANDOR, WALTER SAVAGE
(1775–1864)
Ambition 9; Life 23; Reading/Readers 3

LANE, ANTHONY
Arts and Entertainment 6; Descriptions, Misc. 41; Past 11; Transformation 6; Understanding 7

LANGLAND, JOSEPH
Darkness/Light 5; Night and Day 10; Trees 15

LAPOINTE, JOE
Confrontation 3

LARCOM, LUCY
(1820–1893)
Nature Scenes 10

LARDNER, JAMES
Connections 11; Information 4; Wrinkles 3

LARDNER, RING
(1885–1933)
Looks 5

LARKIN, PHILIP
(1922–1985)
Toughness 5; Death 40; Old Age 11; Promises 3; Self-Actualization 8; Work/Workers 8

LATTIMORE, RICHMOND
(1906–1984)
Memory/Memories 21; Nature Scenes 11; Past 12

LAWRENCE, D[AVID] H[ERBERT]
(1885–1930)
Endings 8; Attraction 2; Change 14; Commitment 1; Danger 14; Future 5; Husbands and Wives 3; Irritants 6; Life 24; Life and Death 21; Marriage 15; Mastery/Subordination 12; Men and Women 8; Name Calling 11; Pain and Suffering 13; Personality Profiles 10; Self-Reliance 6; Uselessness 2; Words 15

LAWRENCE, FRIEDA
(1879–1956)
Protection/Protectors 4

LAXNESS, HALLDÒR
Poetry/Poets 25

LAYZER, ROBERT
Innocence/Inexperience 5; Renewal 4

LE CARRÉ, JOHN
Courage 12; Houses 10; Law/Lawyers 10; Visibility/Invisibility 5

LEACOCK, STEPHEN
(1869–1944)
Arousal/Rousers 13; Destruction/Destructiveness 9; Education and Learning 15; Knowledge 11

LEAR, MARTHA WEINMAN
Candor 3

LEAVITT, DAVID
Bodies/The Body 17; Difficulties 15; Isolation 5; Protection/Protectors 5

LE CORBUSIER [CHARLES-ÉDOUARD JEANNERET]
(1887–1965)
Buildings and Bridges 6; Sky/Skyscapes 12

LEDUC, VIOLETTE
(1907–1972)
Heat 2

LEE, ANDREA
Divorce 2; Restlessness 3

LEE, GERALD STANLEY
(1862–1944)
America/Americans 4

LEE, GUS
Destruction/Destructiveness
10; Fate 14; Men and Women 9

LEGUIN, URSULA K.
Life and Death 23

LEHMAN, DAVID
Entrances/Exits 2; Order/Dis-
order 6; Talkativeness 6

LEHMANN, ROSAMOND
(1901–1990)
Beauty 12; Dullness 4; Faces
14; Laughter 4; Movements 4;
Ridicule 3; Sweat 3; Time 27

**LEHMANN-HAUPT,
CHRISTOPHER**
America/Americans 5; Cities
17; Descriptions, Misc. 42; Gram-
mar and Style 7; Mediocrity 3;
Problems and Solutions 12;
Reputation 3; Scrutiny 2

LEITNER, ISABELLA
Evil 5

L'ENCLOS, NINON DE
(1620–1705)
Love 43

LENIN, NIKOLAI
(1870–1924)
Government 6

LERMONTOV, MIKHAIL
(1814–1841)
Awareness/Unawareness 5;
Clouds 2

LESSING, DORIS
Beauty 13; Buildings and
Bridges 7

LEVERTOV, DENISE
Happiness/Unhappiness 7; Life
and Death 22

LEVINE, PHILIP
Descriptions, Misc. 43; Disintegration 5; Maturation 5; Men
and Women 10; Moon 9; Smallness 3; Trees 16; Trees 17

LEWIS, ANTHONY
Accusations 6; Concentration/
Distraction 4

LEWIS, GIB
Futility 3

LEWIS, NEIL A.
Justice/Injustice 11

LEWIS, PETER H.
Business Descriptions 12; Com-
petition/Competitors   8;
Power 10

LEWIS, SINCLAIR
(1885–1951)
Busyness 2; Danger 15; Dullness 5; Entrapment 7; Furni-
ture/Furnishings 4; Landscapes
13; Mediocrity 4; Men and Wom-
en 11; Monotony 5; Nature
Scenes 12

LEWIS, WYNDHAM
(1884–1957)
Laughter 5

LEWISOHN, LUDWIG
(1883–1955)
Character 7

LI, CH'ING-CHAO
(Sung Dynasty)
Furniture/Furnishing 5; Sky/
Skyscapes 13; Sorrow 1, 2

LIEBMAN, JOSHUA LOTH
Kindness/Unkindness   2;
Time 28

LIEHTER, LINDA
Abandonment 4

LIGHTMAN, ALAN
Actions 8

LINCOLN, ABRAHAM
(1809–1865)
Destruction/Destructiveness
11; Hypocrisy 6; Laughter 6;
Memory/Memories 22; Perseverance 2; Problems and Solutions 13; Sacrifice 4; Time 29;
Unity/Disunity 3; Unity/Disu-
nity 4; War 10

**LINDBERGH, ANNE
MORROW**
Love 44; Middle Age 3; Strength/
Weakness 23; Worry 7

LINDGREN, JOHN
Nature Scenes 13

LINDSAY, VACHEL
(1879–1931)
Eye Expressions 6; Heart 20;
Life, Defined 22; Moon 10,
11; Sun 8

LINGEMAN, RICHARD
Leadership 5; Business Descriptions 13; Freshness/Staleness
3; Treachery 3

LI PO
(701–762)
Clouds 3

LITTLE, CHARLES E.
Ecology 2; Problems and Solutions 14

LI YU
(837–978)
Animals 5

LODGE, THOMAS
(1558–1625)
Conscience 4; Eyes 15

LOEWE, FREDERICK
(1904–1988)
Ambition 10

LOGAN, WILLIAM
Transformation 7

LOH, CHRISTINE
Freedom Of Expression 2

LOHR, STEVE
Business Descriptions 14; Deterioration/Diminishment 2; Difficulties 22-c; Humor 7

LONDON, JACK
(1876–1916)
Humanity/Humankind 30

LONGFELLOW, ERNEST
(d.u.)
Calmness/Volatility 3

LONGFELLOW, HENRY WADSWORTH
(1807–1882)
Achievement 3; Books 18; Completeness/Incompleteness 6; Courage 13; Criticism/Critics 11; Curiosity 4; Death 88; Faces 15; Government 7; Immortality 6; Life and Death 24; Men and Women 12; Night and Day 11, 12; Pain and Suffering 14; Personality Profiles 11; Restriction 3; Soul 10; Success, Defined 14; Wind 8

LORCA, FREDERICO GARCIA
(1898–1936)
Self-Control 6

LOVELACE, MAUD HART
(1892–1980)
Trees 18

LOWE, ROB
Acting/Actors 3

LOWELL, AMY
(1874–1925)
Advice 5; Books 19; Love 45; Seasons 7; Time 30; Words 16; Words As Weapons 9

LOWELL, JAMES RUSSELL
(1819–1891)
Compromise 5

LOWELL, ROBERT
(1917–1977)
Activeness/Inactiveness 1; Descriptions, Misc. 44; Destruction/Destructiveness 12; Hope 11; Life 25; Lovers' Declarations and Exchanges 12; Memory/Memories 23; Past 13; Poetry/Poets 26; Sea 8; Sorrow 3; Stars 2; Street Scenes 15; Time 31; Vision 1; War 11; Wind 9, 10; Worry 8

LUBOW, ARTHUR
Protection/Protectors 6; Voices 10

LU, CHIANG
(Sung Dynasty)
Age/Aging 12

LUCIAN
(c. 120–c. 181)
Sacrifice 5

LUNDKVIST, ARTUR
Memory/Memories 24

LUNTZ, FRANK
Speeches 3

LUTHER, MARTIN
(1483–1546)
Thinking/Thought 10; Truth/Falsehood 22

LYALL, SARAH
Competition/Competitors 9; Endings 9

LYDON, CHRISTOPHER
Politics/Politicians 21

LYLY, JOHN
(c. 1554–1606)
Eyes 16; Individuality 5; Night and Day 13

M

MACARTHUR, DOUGLAS
(1880–1964)
Cause and Effect 7; War 12; Zeal 5

MACAULAY, THOMAS BABBINGTON
(1800–1859)
Substantiality/Insubstantiality 4; Youth and Age 6

MACDONALD, JOHN D.
(1916–1986)
Hair Color 7; Life 26; Senses 3

MACDONALD, ROSS
(1915–1983)
Aerial Views 3, 4; Business Descriptions 15; Despair 9; Faces 16; Facial Expressions 9, 10; Fog 4; Hair 3; Memory/Memories 25; People, Interaction 14; Road Scenes 3, 4; Stillness 2

MACHIAVELLI, NICCOLO
(1469–1527)
Action/Inaction 16, 17; Assistance 3; Cause and Effect 8; Change 15; Conflict 5; Exploration 1; Flattery 5; Fortune/Misfortune 14, 15; Government 8; Injury 2; Manipulation 14; Preparedness/Unpreparedness 4; Problems and Solutions 15; Revenge/Vengeance 3; Rewards 2

MACLEOD, WENDY
Passion 13

MACNEIL, ROBERT
Language 12; Loneliness 4; Writing/Writers 13

MADARIAGA Y ROJO, SALVADOR DE
(1886–1978)
Liberty 2

MADRICK, JEFF
Conformity/Nonconformity 11

MAETERLINCK, COUNT MAURICE
(1862–1949)
Wisdom 6; Words 17

MAGEE, WILLIAM P.
Life, Defined 23

MAHBUBANI, KISHORE
Diplomacy 4

MAHFOUZ, NAGUIB
Agreement/Disagreement 6;
Desire 5; Education and Learning 16; Happiness/Unhappiness 8; Heat 3; Passion 14; Stupidity 6

MAILER, NORMAN
America/Americans 6; Arrogance/Humility 4; Beliefs 7; Communication/Non-Communication 7; Craftiness 5; Exploitation 4; Facial Expressions 11; Facial Hair 1; Frustration 2; Grief 9; Innocence/Inexperience 6; Mind 13; Pain and Suffering 15; People, Interaction 15; Road Scenes 5; Scrutiny 3; Sex/Sexuality 7

MAJOR, JOHN
Anger 13

MAKEBA, MIRIAM
Self-Confidence 4

MALAMUD, BERNARD
(1914–1986)
Compassion 2; Deception 12; Efficiency 2; Facial Expressions 12; Mastery/Subordination 13; Passion 15; Silence 6; Sky/Skyscapes 14

MALLEA, EDUARDO
(1903–c. 1982)
World 12

MALRAUX, ANDRE
(1901–1976)
Liberty 6

MANDELSTAM, NADEZHDA
(1899–1980)
Poetry/Poets 27

MANDELSTAM, OSIP
(1891–1938)
Cities 18; Comparisons 2; Descriptions, Misc. 45; Dissent/Dissenters 1; History 16; Quarrels/Quarrelsomeness 4; Renewal 5; Soul 11

MANEGOLD, CATHARINE S.
Alliances 4; Crowds 5

MANKIEWICZ, JOSEPH L.
(1909–1993)
Disappearance 1; Difficulties 16

MANN, THOMAS
(1875–1955)
Childhood/Children 11; Eyes 17; Sky/Skyscapes 15

MANSFIELD, KATHERINE
(1888–1923)
Achievement 4; Desire 6; Eyebrows 2; Fate 15; Freedom/Restraint 11; Hope 12; Joy 7; Kisses 3; Men and Women 13; Nature Scenes 14; People, Interaction 16; Protection/Protectors 7; Self-Control 7

MAO TSE-TUNG
(1893–1976)
Power 21; Strength/Weakness 22

MARANISS, DAVID
Protection/Protectors 8

MARCH, WILLIAM
(1893–1954)
Love 46

MARCUS AURELIUS
(121–180)
Life 27; Life, Defined 24

MARGOLICK, DAVID
Wit 5

MARION, FRANCES
(c. 1732–1795)
Life 28

MARKHAM, EDWIN
(1852–1940)
Books 20

MARKOFF, JOHN
Technology 3; Work/Workers 9

MARKS, PERCY
(1891–1956)
Self-Actualization 9

MARKS, PETER
Families/Family Relationships 15

MARKUSEN, ANNE
Economics 12, 13

MARLING, KARA ANN
Flowers 2

MARMION, SHAKERLY
(1603–1639)
Worry 9

MÁRQUEZ, GABRIEL GARCÍA
Anger 14; Being/Becoming 4; Death 41; Descriptions, Misc. 46; Eye Expressions 7; Faces 17; Fear 9; Heart 21; Love 47; Oblivion 3; Occupations 6; Past 14; Revolt 2; Rooms 7; Time 32; Wind 11, 12

MARSHALL, CATHERINE
(1914–1983)
God 14

MARSHALL, PAULE
Visibility/Invisibility 6

MARSHALL, THURGOOD
(1908–1993)
Temperament 2

MARSHMAN, JR., D. M.
Destruction/Destructiveness 5

MARTIN, RALPH
Beauty 14; Excitement 5

MARVELL, ANDREW
(1621–1678)
Time 33

MARX, KARL
(1818–1883)
Religion 19

MASEFIELD, JOHN
(1878–1967)
Age/Aging 13; Restlessness 4, 5; Self-Knowledge 11; Street Scenes 16

MASLIN, JANET
Abundance 8; Excess 4

MASON, CAROLINE
Epitaphs 4

MASON, PEGGY
Visibility/Invisibility 7

MASON-MANHEIM, MADELINE
Sorrow 4

MASSINGER, PHILIP
(1583–1640)
Fortune/Misfortune 16; Self-Reliance 7

MATALIN, MARY
Decisiveness/Indecisiveness 5

MATTHIESSEN, PETER
Aimlessness 2; Illusion/Reality 8, 9; Pain and Suffering 16

MAUGHAM, W. SOMERSET
(1874–1965)
Beauty 15; Caution 9; Culture 5; Death 42; Exploitation 5; Hypocrisy 8; Isolation 6; Marriage 16; Reason 6

MAUPASSANT, GUY DE
(1850–1893)
Men and Women 14; Pain and Suffering 17; Time 34

MAUROIS, ANDRÉ
(1885–1967)
Changeableness/Unchangeableness 4; Flattery 6; Happiness/Unhappiness 9; Life, Defined 25; Mastery/Subordination 14; Talkativeness 7

MAXWELL, WILLIAM
Opportunity 5

MAY, SAMUEL J.
(19th century)
Agitation 3

MAYER, EDWIN JUSTUS
(d.u.)
Wisdom 7

MAYER, MARTIN
Business Descriptions 16

MAYLE, PETER
Illness 8; Many 4

MAYNES, CHARLES WILLIAM
Democracy 5; Diplomacy 5; Power 11

MCALLISTER, CLAIRE
Summer 3

MCBAIN, ED
Fall 7; Maturation 6

MCCARTHY, EUGENE
Renewal 6

MCCARTHY, MARY
(1912–1989)
Aggression 5; Characterizations 20; Dominance 5; Grammar and Style 8; Men and Women 15; Self-Actualization 10

MCCARVOR, TIM
Sports 4

MCCORKLE, JILL
Life 29

MCCULLERS, CARSON
(1917–1967)
Grief 10, 11; Marriage 17; Strength/Weakness 24; Time 35

MCDERMOTT, ALICE
Buildings and Bridges 8; Descriptions, Misc. 47; Time 36

MCGINLEY, PHYLLIS
(1905–1978)
Reading/Readers 5, 4; Time 37

MCGOLDRICK, JOHN
Connections 12

MCLELLAN, VERN
Death, Defined 12

MCMILLAN, MICHAEL R. GORDON
Strategies 3

MCMILLAN, TERRY
Breasts/Bosoms 1; Love 48; Mastery/Subordination 15; Risk-Taking 5; Strategies 4

MEANS, MARIANNE
Failure 15

MELLOAN, GEORGE
Diplomacy 6

MELLOW, JAMES R.
Mystery/Mysteriousness 3

MELVILLE, HERMAN
(1819–1891)
Disintegration 6; Fate 16; Future 6; Life and Death 25; Occupations 7; Openness/Privacy 4; Promises 4; Time 38; Warnings 3

MENCKEN, H. L.
(1880–1956)
Arguments 4; Cities 19; Clarity/Ambiguity 3; Democracy 6; Monotony 6; Silence 7; Speeches 4; Words As Weapons 10

MEREDITH, GEORGE
(1828–1909)
Arguments 5; Ethics 3; Experience 8; Maturation 7; Men and Women 16; Rumor 3; Women 8; Youth 6

MERRILL, JAMES
Earth 3; Evil 6; Faces 18; Furniture/Furnishings 6; Language 13; Lovers' Declarations and Exchanges 13; Time 39

MERWIN, W[ILLIAM] S[TANLEY]
Desire 7; Eyes 18; Faces 19; Lovers' Declarations and Exchanges 14; Many 5; Men and Women 17; Seasons 8

MOORE, THOMAS
(1779–1852)
Loneliness 5

MORE, HANNAH
(1745–1833)
Books 21; Plagiarists 2

MORLEY, CHRISTOPHER
(1890–1957)
Abundance 9; Articulateness/
Inarticulateness 3; Conformity/
Nonconformity 12; Conversa-
tion 8, 9; Entrances/Exits 3;
Future 7; Joy 8; Letters 2, 3;
Order/Disorder 7; Sky/
Skyscapes 16; Sympathy 1;
Thinking/Thought 11; Time
42; Truth/Falsehood 24; Work/
Workers 11

MORRIS, BOB
Ideas 6

MORRIS, EDMUND
Politics/Politicians 22

MORRISON, TONI
Completeness/Incompleteness
7; Desire 8; Facial Expressions
2; Fear 10; Men and Women
19; Music/Musicians 12; Pain
and Suffering 19; Sex/Sexuali-
ty 8; Sky/Skyscapes 17, 18, 19;
Sleep 7; Smiles 5

**MORROW, ELIZABETH
REEVE**
(1873–1955)
Understanding/
Misunderstanding 3

MORSHEN, NIKOLAI
Creation 3

MORTIMER, JOHN
Law/Lawyers 11

MORTIMER, PENELOPE
Noses 2

MOSES BEN MAIMON
(1135–1204)
Science 5

MOSS, HOWARD
(1922–1987)
Birds 10; Descriptions, Misc.
52; Genius 1; Madness 3; Self-
Destruction 3; Sun 9; Time 43

MOSS, THYLIAS
Emotions 15

MOTHER TERESA
Perseverance 8

MOULTON, LOUISA
(1883–1908)
Life 30

**MOYNIHAN, DANIEL
PATRICK**
Conflict 6-c

MUENCH, DAVID
Sun 10

**MUGGERIDGE,
MALCOLM**
(1903–1990)
Sex/Sexuality 9

MUIR, JOHN
(1838–1914)
Landscapes 15, 16

MULLER, MARCIA
Faces 21

MUMFORD, LEWIS
(1895–1990)
Biographies/Autobiographies
3; Continuity 2; Dreams 13;
Education and Learning 19; Life
31; People, Interaction 18; Suc-
cess/Failure 4

MUN, THOMAS
(1571–1641)
Riches 5

MUNRO, ALICE
Admiration 2; Beauty 17; Com-
plexion 6; Eyebrows 3; Faith 6;
Fatness/Thinness 6; Hair 4;
Voices 11; Youth and Age 8

MURCHIE, GUY
(1920–1945)
Clouds 4, 5; Wind 14

MURDOCH, IRIS
Art/Artists 22

MURKHERJEE, BHARATI
Men and Women 20

MURRAY, JIM
Sports 6

MURRAY, WILLIAM
Cities 20

N

NABOKOV, VLADIMIR
(1899–1977)
Actions 9; Affliction 4; Change-
ableness/Unchangeableness 6;
Criticism/Critics 12; Descriptions, Misc. 53; Emotions 16;
Facial Expressions 13; Individuality 6; Landscapes 17, 18, 19,
20; Life 32; Lovers' Declarations and Exchanges 18; Manipulation 15; Memory/Memo-
ries 29, 30; Mixture 3;
Ordinariness/Extraordinari-
ness 7; Pain and Suffering 20,
21; Poverty/Prosperity 9; Self-
Knowledge 12; Sleep 8; Speech
7; Thinking/Thought 12; Time
44, 45

NADER, RALPH
Government 10-c

NAKAHARA, CHUYA
(1907–1937)
Voices 12

NAKANO SHIGEHARU
Singing/Songs/Singers 10

NARUSHIMA, RYUHOKU
(1837–1884)
Moon 12

NASAR, SYLVIA
Clarity/Ambiguity   6;
Economics 14

kind 37, 36; Insults 3; Name Calling 12, 13, 14; Protection/ Protectors 9; Sky/Skyscapes 21; Spring 6; Storms 7

PATCHEN, KENNETH
(1911–1972)
Poverty/Prosperity 10

PAUKER, JOHN
(1920–1991)
Success, Defined 15

PAUL, SAINT
(1st century)
Faith 9

PAULUS, LUCIUS AEMILIUS
(4th century B.C.)
Understanding/ Misunderstanding 4

PAVLOV, IVAN
(1849–1936)
Facts 4

PAZ, OCTAVIO
Laughter 7; Poetry/Poets 32

PEARSON, RIDLEY
Craftiness 6

PEELE, GEORGE
(1556–1596)
Characteristics 4

PEI, MEG
Strategies 5

PEIRCE, CHARLES S.
(1839–1914)
Beliefs 8

PENN, WILLIAM
(1644–1718)
Jealousy 6

PERELMAN, S[IDNEY] J[OSEPH]
(1904–1979)
Irritants 8; Money 14

PERES, SHIMON
Change 16

PERETZ, I. L. [ISAAC]
(1852–1915)
Age/Aging 14; Youth 8

PERICLES
(c. 495–429 B.C.)
Earth 5

PEROT, ROSS
Arousal/Rousers 17; Problems and Solutions 18, 19, 20; Reform 10

PETERSSON, BO
War 15

PETRARCH, FRANCIS
(1304–1374)
Impossibility 4; Memory/ Memories 32

PETROVSKY, VLADIMIR
Confrontation 4

PETRY, ANN
Time 46

PHELPS, ELIZABETH
(1844–1911)
Work/Workers 12

PHELPS, WILLIAM LYON
(1865–1943)
Sports 7

PHILEMON
(c. 368–c. 264 B.C.)
Grief 13

PHILLIPS, WENDELL
(1811–1884)
Courage 14; Defeat 8

PICASSO, PABLO
(1881–1973)
Diversity 5-C; Humanity/Humankind 38

PIERCY, MARGE
Anger 17; Commitment 2; Dreams 15; Friendship/Friends

22; Friendship/Friends 21; Happiness/Unhappiness 10; Loneliness 7; Men and Women 21; Responsibility 4; Self-Actualization 11; Sky/Skyscapes 22; Trustworthiness/Untrustworthiness 5; Women 10

PINCUS, ANDREW L.
Arts and Entertainment 7; Energy 4; Music/Musicians 13, 14, 15; Ordinariness/Extraordinariness 8

PINDAR
(c. 522–c. 438 B.C.)
Descriptions, Misc. 57; Grief 14; Hope 16; Landscapes 23; Pain and Suffering 22; Poetry/ Poets 33; Protection/Protectors 10; Speed 5; Thunder and Lightning 1; Tranquility 3

PINERO, ARTHUR WING
(1855–1934)
Coldness 1; Friendship/Friends 23; Sensitivity 3

PINKERTON, JAMES
Cause and Effect 9; Characterizations 22; Difference/Sameness 3; Uselessness 3

PINSKY, ROBERT
Disappearance 2

PIRANDELLO, LUIGI
(1867–1936)
Past 15; Sex/Sexuality 12

PISAN, CHRISTINE DE
(c. 1363–1430)
Grief 15

PITT, WILLIAM [EARL OF CHATHAM
(1707–1778)
Seascapes 12; Self-Confidence 5

PLATH, SYLVIA
(1932–1963)
Insects 3; Many 6; Men and Women 22

PLATO
(c. 428–c. 348 B.C.)
Bodies/The Body 19; Humanity/Humankind 39; Pleasure 3

PLAUTUS, TITUS MACCIUS
(c. 254–184 B.C.)
Fate 17; Patience 9

PLINY THE YOUNGER
(c. 61–c. 113)
Sin/Redemption 5

PLUMB, J. H.
Death 45; Success/Failure 7

PLUNKET, ROBERT
Humor 9

PLUTARCH
(c. 46–c. y120)
Fortune/Misfortune 17

POE, EDGAR ALLAN
(1809–1849)
Ancestry/Ancestors 6; Emotions 17; Life and Death 26; Reality/Unreality 5; Science 6; Stupidity 7

POGREBIN, LETTY COTTIN
Secrecy 2, Suspicion 4

POLEY, ERIC
Characterizations 23; Personality Profiles 14

POLLACK, ANDREW
Business Descriptions 18

POLLITT, KATE
Confrontation 5

PONDER, CATHERINE
Forgiveness 5

PONSONBY, ARTHUR
(1871–1946)
War 16

POPE, ALEXANDER
(1688–1744)
Art/Artists 23; Encouragement 1; Life, Defined 27; Nature 16; Time 47; Vanity 3; Writing/Writers 16

POQUELIN, JEAN BAPTISTE
See
MOLIÈRE

PORTER, KATHERINE ANNE
(1890–1980)
Anger 18; Fatness/Thinness 9; Heart 26; Memory/Memories 33; Religion 21; Time 48

PORTER, WILLIAM SIDNEY
See O. HENRY

POTOK, CHAIM
Cityscapes 7; Good/Evil 6; Significance/Insignificance 5; Sports 8

POULSSON, EMILIE
(1853–1939)
Books 23

POUND, EZRA
(1885–1972)
Self-Images 9; Weariness 5

POWELL, DANNYE ROMINE
Physical Appearance 17

PRENTISS, SARGENT S.
(1825–1864)
Warriors and Peacemakers 3

PRIESTLEY, J. B.
(1894–1984)
Cities 25

PRIESTLY, JOSEPH
(1733–1804)
Strength/Weakness 25

PRITCHETT, V[ICTOR] S[AWDON]
Bodies/The Body 20; Fatness/Thinness 10, 11; Memory/Memories 34

PROCTOR, ADELAIDE
Past 16; Time 49

PROUST, MARCEL
(1871–1922)
Being/Becoming 5; Cowardice 4; Experience 11; Flaws 5; People, Interaction 20; Silence 8

PROVERBS
Absence 3-*c*; Action/Inaction 1, 26-*c*; Adversity 1; Advice 1; Agreement/Disagreement 1; Ambition 1; Ancestry/Ancestors 1; Anger 2; Beauty 2; Blindness 1; Boasters/Boastfulness 5-*c*; Books 1; Business Descriptions 6-*c*; Cause and Effect 1, 2; Caution 4; Chance 1; Character 1; Confinement 1; Connections 2; Conscience 1; Control 1; Cowardice 5-*c*; Decisiveness/Indecisiveness 2; Difficulties 2; Divorce 1; Earth 1; Education and Learning 2, 3; Ego/Egotism 2; Enemies 1; Entrapment 12-*c*; Families/Family relationships 2; Flattery 1; Foolhardiness 1; Forgiveness 1; Fortune/Misfortune 4; Friendship/Friends 1; Generosity 1; Gossip 2; Greed 1; Group scenes 12; Habit 1, 2; Hair Color 1, 2; Heart 2, 5; Humanity/Humankind 2; Illusion/Reality 7-*c*; Inheritance/Inheritors 1; Intoxication/Intoxicants 1; Jealousy 1; Joy/Sorrow 1; Justice/Injustice 4; Knowledge 13-*c*; Language 1; Life and Death 1; Life, defined 3; Marriage 1, 2, 3, 4, 5; Mastery/Subordination 1, 2, 5-*c*; Men and Women 1; Mistakes 1; Money 1, 2, 3; Morality/Immorality 1; Old Age 1; Pain and Suffering 2; Patience 5; People, Interaction 25-*c*; Permanence/Impermanence 1-*c*;

Politics/Politicians 3; Poverty/ Prosperity 1; Praise 3; Problems and Solutions 1; Prudence 3, 6-c; Quotations 1; Religion 2, 3; Retribution 1; Riches 1; Seasons 1; Self-Effacement 1; Silence 1; Similarity/Dissimilarity 1, 2; Speech 2, 8-c; Success, Defined 1; Talkativeness 1; Taste 1; Temptation 1; Time 2; Treachery 1; Triteness 1; Trustworthiness/ Untrustworthiness 2; Truth/Falsehood 1, 2, 3; Understanding 11-c; Uselessness 1; Wisdom 2; Women 1; Work/Workers 1; World 1; Worry 1; Youth and Age 1

PUBLILIUS SYRUS
Beauty 20; Caution 10; Experience 12, 13; Faces 24; Habit 5; Speech 8

PURDUM, TODD S.
Politics/Politicians 23

Q

QUARLES, FRANCIS
(1592–1644)
Deception 13; Humanity/Humankind 40; Life, Defined 28

QUASIMODO, SALVATORE
(1901–1968)
Wind 15

QUICK, BARBARA
Dominance 6

QUINDLEN, ANNA
Apology 3; Arts and Entertainment 8; Economics 19; Effectiveness/Ineffectiveness 6; Families/Family Relationships 16; Government 9; Mortality 2; Occupations 2-c

QURTUBIYYA, AISHA BINT AHMAD AL-
(10th century)
Strength/Weakness 1

R

RABELAIS, FRANÇOIS
(c. 1483–1553)
Busyness 3; Comfort/Comfort-Givers 8

RABI, I. I.
(1898–1988)
Change 17; Education and Learning 21; Education and Learning 22; Freedom/Restraint 15

RABIN, YITZHAK
International Relations 3

RABINOVITZ, JONATHAN
Sports 9

RACINE, JEAN BAPTISTE
(1639–1699)
Sea 10; Worry 10

RAFFERTY, TERRENCE
Control 6; Shock 1

RAINES, HOWELL
Danger 19

RALEGH, SIR WALTER (also spelled RALEIGH)
(1554–1618)
Birth 3; Debt 3; Deception 14; Life, Defined 29; Love 56; Futility 4; Hate 3; Silence 9; Time 50

RAMIREZ, ANTHONY
Agreement/Disagreement 7; Difficulties 17, 18; Economics 20

RANDOLPH, CLEMENCE
(d.u.)
Conversation 2; Life 9

RANDOLPH, JOHN
(1773–1833)
Evasiveness 2

RATTIGAN, TERENCE
(1911–1977)
Coldness 2; Exaggeration 4

RAWLINGS, MARJORIE KINNAN
(1896–1953)
Sorrow 6

RAY, JOHN
(c. 1627–1705)
Eyes 21; Hell and Damnation 6

REED, JOHN SHELTON
(1887–1920)
Mastery/Subordination 16

REED, JR., RALPH
Belonging/Outcast 4

REED, THOMAS B.
(1839–1902)
Characterizations 24

REESE, LIZETTE
(1856–1935)
Fame 15

REMARQUE, ERICH MARIA
(1898–1970)
Disintegration 7; Humanity/ Humankind 41; Maturation 8; Mobility/Immobility 3; War 17

REMNICK, DAVID
Hair Color 8; Strength/Weakness 19-c; Connections 13

REYNOLDS, JOSHUA
(1723–1792)
Mind 17

RHODEN, WILLIAM C.
Busyness 4

RICH, ADRIENNE
Language 17; Mind 18

RICH, FRANK
Aimlessness 3; Arts and Entertainment 9; Commitment 3; Excitement 6; Failure 16; Freshness/Staleness 4; Freshness/ Staleness 5; Intensity 1; Mixture 4; Openness/Privacy 5; Personality Profiles 15; Self-Control 9; Shock 2; Success/ Failure 8

RICHARDS, ANN W.
Failure 17; Vulnerability 4

RICHARDS, DAVID
Acting/Actors 4; Energy 5; Mouths 4; Problems and Solutions 21; Timeliness/Untimeliness 3; Timidity 2

RICHARDSON, SAMUEL
(1689–1761)
Anger 19; Arousal/Rousers 18

RICHTER, JEAN PAUL
(1763–1825)
Music/Musicians 16

RIESMAN, DAVID
Memory/Memories 35

RILKE, RAINER MARIA
(1875–1926)
Characterizations 25

RINA, GAETANO
Name Calling 15

RITSOS, YANNIS
(1909–1990)
Age/Aging 15; Grief 16; Hope 17; Work/Workers 13

RITTENBERG, SIDNEY
Progress 8

ROBBE-GRILLET, ALAIN
Men and Women 23

ROBERTS, JORDAN
Breasts/Bosoms 2

ROBERTS, SAM
Competition/Competitors 11

ROBERTSON, FREDERICK WILLIAM
(1816–1853)
Women 11

ROBINSON, EDWARD ARLINGTON
(1869–1935)
Heart 27; Importance/Unimportance 6; Love 57; Rewards 3

ROBINSON, MARY
Snow 7

ROBISON, JAMES
Buildings and Bridges 9; Seascapes 13; Wrinkles 6

ROCHE, SIR BOYLE
(1748–1807)
Difficulties 19

ROCHE, DOUGLAS
International Relations 7

ROCHEFOUCAULD, FRANÇOIS, DUC DE LA
(1613–1680)
Youth 9

ROCKEFELLER, JAY
Conflict 6

RODGERS, JOHN JACOB
(d.u.)
Mastery/Subordination 17

ROETHKE, THEODORE
(1908–1963)
Attraction 3; Bodies/Body the 22; Bodies/The Body 21; Cityscapes 8; Death 46; Education and Learning 23; Ethics 5; Exactness/Inexactness 3; Fate 18; Hate 4; Knowledge 13; Madness 4; Memory/Memories 36; Metaphors 2; Moon 15; Movements 6; Necessity 2; Optimism/Pessimism 7; Perseverance 4; Pleasure 4; Poetry/Poets 34; Pride 3; Self 6; Speed 6; Spring 7; Success, Defined 16; Time 51; Victims 2; Wind 16; Winter 4

ROGERS, W. R.
Words 18

ROGERS, WILL
(1879–1935)
Action/Inaction 19

ROOSEVELT, FRANKLIN DELANO
(1882–1945)
Action/Inaction 20, 21; Appeasement 1; Democracy 7;

Failure 18; Fate 19; Freedom Of Expression 3; Reform 11; War 18

ROOSEVELT, THEODORE
(1858–1919)
Action/Inaction 22; Aggression 6; Entrances/Exits 4; Future 8; Leadership 6; Timidity 2-c; Vision 2

ROSE, ALEX
Timeliness/Untimeliness 4

ROSENBLATT, ROGER
Openness/Privacy 6

ROSENTHAL, A. M.
Countries, Misc. 5; Danger 20; Malice 2; Mixture 5; Perseverance 5; Politics/Politicians 25; Self-Destructiveness 4; Speeches 6

ROSENTHAL, ANDREW
(c. 1918–1979)
Eyes 22; Politics/Politicians 24; Tension/Tension Relief 3

ROSSETTI, CHRISTINA
(1830–1894)
Death 47

ROSSETTI, DANTE GABRIEL
(1828–1882)
Poetry/Poets 35

ROSSINI, GIOACCHINO
(1792–1868)
Singing/Songs/Singers 12

ROSSNER, JUDITH
Identity 5

ROSTAND, EDMOND
(1868–1918)
Facial Expressions 14; Kisses 4, 5; Love 58; Men and Women 24; Reputation 4; Women 12

ROSTENKOWSKI, DAN
Protection/Protectors 11

SARTRE, JEAN-PAUL
(1905–1980)
Cities 27; Fear 11; Fragility 2;
Murder 1

SASSER, JIM
Obsolescence 4

SASSOON, SIEGFRIED
(1886–1967)
Occupations 8

SATIR, VIRGINIA
(1916–1988)
Self 7

SAUL, JOHN RALSTON
Changeableness/
Unchangeableness 7

SAXON, WOLFGANG
Language Experts 2

SAYERS, DOROTHY L.
(1893–1957)
Death 50; Fortune/Misfortune
18; Love 60; Tact 3

SCHANBERG, SYDNEY
Destruction/Destructiveness 14

SCHARPER, PHILLIP
(1919–1985)
Religion 22

SCHEMANN, SERGE
Destruction/Destructiveness
15; Problems and Solutions 22;
Protection/Protectors   13;
Strategies 7

SCHIFF, STEPHEN
Concentration/Distraction 6;
Facial Hair 2, 3; Trouble/Trou-
blemakers 2

**SCHILLER, JOHANN
CHRISTOPH FRIEDRICH
VON**
(1759–1805)
Conscience 6; Fortune/Mis-
fortune 19, 20; Freedom/Re-
straint 16; Hate 5; Pleasure 5;
Youth 11

SCHINE, CATHLEEN
Senses 4

SCHMALTZ, JEFFREY
Change 18; Reality/Unreality 6

SCHMEMANN, SERGE
Compromise 6; Power 13

SCHMIDT, WILLIAM E.
Difficulties 20; Power 14; Speeches 5-*c*

**SCHNACKENBERG,
GJERTRUD**
Books 13; Death 51; Rooms 4;
Street Scenes 20; Writing/
Writers 11

SCHNEIDER, KEITH
Defeat 9

**SCHONBERG, HAROLD
C.**
Music/Musicians 19

**SCHOPENHAUER,
ARTHUR**
(1788–1860)
Death 52

SCHORR, DANIEL
Significance/Insignificance 6

SCHREINER, OLIVE
(1855–1920)
Wisdom 8

SCHULMAN, ARLENE
Sports 11

SCHUSTER, M. LINCOLN
(1897–1970)
Religion 23

SCHUYLER, JAMES
(1923–1991)
Heat 6; Seasons 9

SCHWARTZ, DELMORE
(1913–1966)
Time 53

**SCHWARTZ, LYNNE
SHARON**
Bodies/The Body 23; Effec-
tiveness/Ineffectiveness 7; Fami-
lies/Family Relationships 17,
18; Marriage 22; Memory/
Memories 38

SCIOLINO, ELAINE
Diplomacy 9; Mystery/Myste-
riousness 4

SCOTT, GEOFFREY
Wind 19

SCOTT, SIR WALTER
(1771–1832)
Morality/Immorality 6; Doubt
2-*c*; Flattery 3-*c*; Life, Defined 30

SEAGER, ALLAN
(1906–1968)
Storms 8

SEATTLE, CHIEF
(c. 1786–1866)
Self-Reliance 8

SEGAL, LORE
Conversation 10

**SEIFFERT, MARJORIE
ALLEN**
(1885–1968)
Beauty 21; Lust 4

SELZER, RICHARD
Caution 11; Conversation 11;
Faces 26; Families/Family Relationships 19; Fashion and Style
6; Hope 18; Hope 19; Memo-
ry/Memories 39; Moon 16;
Occupations 10; Occupations
11; Occupations 12; Occupations 9; Physical Appearance
18; Physical Appearance 19; Science 8; Speechlessness 3

SEN, HUN
Democracy 8

SENECA
(c. 4 B.C.–65 A.D.)
Bodies/The Body 24; Chance
7; Voices 14

SHAPIRO, JANE

SHAPIRO, KARL

SHATTUCK, ROGER

SHAW, FIONA

SHAW, GEORGE BERNARD
(1856–1950)

SHAW, HENRY WHEELER
See JOSH BILLINGS

SHAW, IRWIN
(1913–1984)

SHEED, WILFRID

SHELDON, MICHAEL

SHELLEY, PERCY BYSSHE
(1792–1822)

SHERIDAN, RICHARD BRINSLEY
(1751–1816)

SHIMAZAKI TOSON
(1872–1943)

SHIN, FLORENCE SCOVEL

SHIRLEY, JAMES
(1596–1666)

SHOLOKHOV, MIKHAIL
(1905–1984)

SHOOB, JUDGE MARVIN H.

SIDDONS, ANNE RIVERS

SIDNEY, SIR PHILIP
(1554–1586)

STORACE, PATRICIA
Imagination 13

STORY, JUSTICE JOSEPH
Crowds 9

STOUT, REX
(1886–1975)
Agreement/Disagreement 9;
Doubt 7; Evil 20; Feelings 9;
Mind 25; Stupidity 10

**STOWE, HARRIET
BEECHER**
(1811–1896)
Evil 2-c; Humanity/Human-
kind 46

STRAND, MARK
Abandonment 5; Desire 12; De-
terioration/Diminishment 6;
Nature Scenes 16

STRANGE, MICHAEL
(d.u.)
Fate 23

STRINDBERG, AUGUST
(1849–1912)
Age/Aging 31; Alliances 7;
Destruction/Destructiveness
21; Dreams 19; Endurance 3;
Evil 21; Guidance/Guides 10;
Impossibility 6; Memory/
Memories 46; Music/Musi-
cians 22; Revenge/Vengeance
8; Strength/Weakness 29; Timidity 3; Youth and Age 19

STROM, STEPHANIE
Encouragement 3

STYRON, WILLIAM
Pleasure 7; Wrinkles 7

SUCKLING, SIR JOHN
(1609–1642)
Success, Defined 18

SUDERMANN, HERMANN
(1857–1928)
Soul 14; Sympathy 2

SULLIVAN, BRIAN
Winning/Losing 10

SUMNER, MELANIE
Sunset 14

SUN YAT-SEN
(1866–1925)
Exploitation 9

SWENSON, MAY
(1919–1989)
Descriptions, Misc. 65; Eyes 25

SWIFT, AL
Action/Inaction 27

SWIFT, JONATHAN
(1667–1745)
Books 25; Criticism/Critics 15;
Life, Defined 34; Prudence 8;
Words 23

**SWINBURNE, ALGERNON
CHARLES**
(1837–1909)
Love 91; Spring 9; Time 73

SYMONS, ARTHUR
(1865–1945)
Life, Defined 35, 36; Nature
Scenes 17

T

**TAGORE,
RABINDRANATH**
(1861–1941)
Desire 13; Embraces 4; God
17; Harmony/Disharmony 5;
Life and Death 43; Life and
Death 41; Life and Death 42;
Night and Day 26; Pleas and
Prayers 8; Rain 10; Reason 12;
Storms 11; Thunder and Light-
ning 3; Truth/Falsehood 29

TAKAHAMA KYOSHI
(1874–1959)
Fall 8; Trees 25

TARTT, DONNA
Clouds 6; Fate 24; Lies/Liars
8; Snow 8; Worry 12

TAYLOR, EDWARD
(c. 1645–1729)
Descriptions, Misc. 66; Hell and
Damnation 8; Pleas and Prayers
9, 10, 11; Religion 24, 25, 26;
Tears 29

TAYLOR, PAUL
Endings 13

TEASDALE, SARA
(1884–1933)
Pride 8; Soul 15

TECUMSEH
(1768–1813)
Loyalty 5

TEICHMANN, HOWARD
(1916–1987)
Abundance 11; Arousal/Rousers
22; Change 23; Grammar and
Style 9; Ideas 9; Satire 4; Self-
Control 13; Words As Weapons 18, 19

**TENNYSON, LORD
ALFRED**
(1809–1892)
Descriptions, Misc. 67; Endings
14; Experience 15; Life, Defined 37; Love 92; Lovers' Declarations and Exchanges 29; Nature Scenes 18; Time 74

TEY, JOSEPHINE
(1897–1952)
Eye Expressions 11

**THACKERAY, WILLIAM
MAKEPEACE**
(1811–1863)
Books 26; Kindness/Unkind-
ness 5; Men and Women 32

THEOPHRASTUS
(c. 372–c. 287 B.C.)
Beauty 40

THOMAS, D. M.
Conversation 14; Freshness/
Staleness 6; Houses 12

THOMAS, DYLAN
(1914–1953)
Death 78; Descriptions, Misc.
68; Dominance 8; Group Scenes
8, 9, 10; Heart 31; Nature 18;
Voices 16

THOMAS, EDWARD
(1878–1917)
Past 17

THOMAS, LEWIS
Humanity/Humankind 47

THOMPSON, FRANCIS
(1859–1907)
Imagination 14; Love 93; Pain
and Suffering 26

THOMSON, JAMES
(1700–1748)
Slander 7

THOREAU, HENRY DAVID
(1817–1862)
Chance 9; Criticism/Critics 16;
Education and Learning 24; Experience 16; Illusion/Reality
12; Importance/Unimportance
9; Individuality 8; Kindness/
Unkindness 6; Mind 26; Morning 5; Mountains 3; Nature 19,
20; Order/Disorder 11; Poet-
ry/Poets 44; Poverty/Pros-
perity 13; Self-Confidence 6;
Success/Failure 10; Thinking/
Thought 17, 18; Time 75; Trust-
worthiness/Untrustworthiness 8,
9; Vice/Virtue 8

THURBER, JAMES
(1894–1961)
Eyes 26; Voices 17

TILGHMAN, SHIRLEY M.
Fairness/Unfairness 4; Power
19; Science 9

TILLMAN, GERARD
Competition/Competitors 13

TIMAEUS OF LOCRIS
(c. 400 B.C.)
God 18

**TOCQUEVILLE, ALEXIS-
CHARLES-HENRI DE
[COUNT ALEXIS]**
(1805–1859)
America/Americans 7

TOFFLER, ALVIN
Society/Social Situations 9

TOLCHIN, MARTIN
Irritants 11

TOLSTOY, LEO
(1828–1910)
Despair 16; Joy 10

TOMKINS, CALVIN
Intensity 2

TONER, ROBIN
Power 20

TRAVEL, JANET
Lies/Liars 9

TREVOR, WILLIAM
Clarity/Ambiguity 8; Comfort/
Comfort-Givers 7; Craftiness
8; Scrutiny 5

TROLLOPE, ANTHONY
(1815–1882)
Action/Inaction 28

TROYAT, HENRI
Senses 8

TRUMAN, HARRY S
(1884–1972)
Courage 21; Isolation 8

TSONGAS, PAUL
Money 19

TUCHMAN, BARBARA
(1912–1989)
Honor 3

TU FU
(712–770)
Pain and Suffering 27

TUITE, DIANA
Familiarity/Unfamiliarity 2

TUNNELL, SOPHIE
(1884–?)
Fear 16

**TUPPER, M[ARTIN]
F[ARQUHAR]**
(1810–1889)
Cities 29

TURGENEV, IVAN
(1818–1883)
Belonging/Outcast 6; Birds 13;
Change 24; Concentration/Dis-
traction 7; Death 79, 80; Defeat
12; Disappointment 3; Emotions 19; Endings 15; Leaders/
Followers 11; Love 94; Nature
21; Prominence/Periphery 4;
Success/Failure 11; Temperament 5, 6; Time 76; Youth
and Age 20

TURNBULL, AGNES SLIGH
(1888–1982)
Flexibility/Inflexibility 6

TURNER, NANCY BYRD
(1880–1957)
Death, Defined 18

TUROW, SCOTT
Abandonment 6; Agreement/
Disagreement 10; Apathy 5;
Competition/Competitors 14;
Courage 22; Hypocrisy 7; Money 20; Order/Disorder 12; People, Interaction 24; Sex/Sexu-
ality 16, 17; Success, Defined
19; Writing/Writers 18

**TWAIN, MARK [SAMUEL
LANGHORNE CLEMENS]**
(1835–1910)
Animation 4; Biographies/Au-
tobiographies 4; Characterizations 31; Clergy 3; Coldness 4;
Death 81; Ego/Id 4; Facial
Hair 4; Freedom/Restraint 18;
Habit 6; Humanity/Human-
kind 48; Innocence/Inexperi-
ence 8; Opportunity 12; Past
18; Persuasiveness/Persuaders
5; Reputation 12; Sunset 15;
War 25; Youth and Age 21

WALLER, ROBERT JAMES
Heat 7; Kisses 9; Yearning 2

WALPOLE, HORACE
(1717–1797)
Friendship/Friends 26; Order/
Disorder 13; World 22

WALTERS, BARBARA
Conversation 15

WARREN, EARL
(1891–1974)
Reform 15

WARREN, GERALD L.
Self-Reliance 10

WARREN, ROBERT PENN
(1905–1989)
Birds 14; Birds 15; Darkness/
Light 6; Descriptions, Misc. 69,
70; Fall 9; Foolhardiness 12;
Forgiveness 8; Fortune/Mis-
fortune 33; Landscapes 27;
Mouths 6; Nature Scenes 20;
Sea 12; Watchfulness 1

WASHINGTON, GEORGE
(1732–1799)
Liberty 8, 9; Politics/Politi-
cians 27

WASSERSTEIN, WENDY
Men and Women 34

WATSON, THOMAS
(c. 1557–1592)
Love, Defined 16

WATTENBERG, BEN
America/Americans 8-*c*

WEBER, BRUCE
Criticism/Critics 18; Journal-
ism/Journalists 9

WEBER, KATHARINE
Irritants 12

WEBSTER, DANIEL
(1782–1852)
Concentration/Distraction 8;
Facial Expressions 27; Liberty

10; Problems and Solutions 28;
Timidity 4

WEBSTER, JOHN
(c. 1580–c. 1625)
Action/Inaction 29; Ambition
21; Bodies/The Body 32; Death
84; Hypocrisy 13; Uncertainty 4

WEI CHUNG-HSIEN
(1568–1627)
Eyes 27

WEIL, SIMONE
(1909–1943)
Feelings 11; Life 53

WEINER, TIM
Characterizations 33; Revelation 4

WEINRAUB, BERNARD
Aggression 10; Power 22

WEINSTEIN, NATHAN
See WEST, NATHANAEL

WEISS, DORRIE
Envy 6; International Relations
4, 5; Leadership 9; Praise 13-*c*;
Reading/Readers 6; Reform 16;
Victims 3

WEISS, ELLEN
Self-Expression 2

WELD, WILLIAM F.
Politics/Politicians 21-*c*

WELDON, FAY
Criticism/Critics 19; Writing/
Writers 19

WELLS, H. G.
(1866–1946)
Craftiness 9; Criticism/Critics
20; Diversity 6; Science 10

WELLS, JEFFREY
Inheritance/Inheritors 6

WELTY, EUDORA
Complexion 10; Grief 27; Landscapes 28, 29; Movements 7;

Self-Consciousness   3;
Watchfulness 2

WENTWORTH, SCOTT
Agitation 5; Pain and Suffering 29

WERFEL, FRANZ
(1890–1945)
Reason 13

WEST, CORNEL
Bigotry 13

WEST, DAME REBECCA
(1892–1983)
Embraces 5; Emotions 20; Eyes
28; Future 10; Passion 21; Self-
Knowledge 14; Sympathy 3;
Truth/Falsehood 31

WEST, MAE
(c. 1893–1980)
Sleep 22

WEST, MORRIS L.
Transience 7

WEST, NATHANAEL
Descriptions, Misc. 71; Faces
29; Similarity/Dissimilarity 4

WHARTON, EDITH
(1862–1937)
Adversity 7; Ancestry/Ances-
tors 10; Apathy 6; Attentive-
ness/Inattentiveness 2; Aware-
ness/Unawareness 8, 9; Beauty
42, 43; Beliefs 9; Blushes 5;
Change 25; Change 26; Characterizations 34, 35; Comfort/
Comfort-Givers 9; Communi-
cation/Non-Communication
8; Compromise 7; Conformi-
ty/Nonconformity 15; Death
85; Descriptions, Misc. 72; Despair 17; Deterioration/Dimin-
ishment 7; Difficulties 25; Disappointment 4; Divorce 3;
Dominance 9; Doubt 8; Ego/
Id 5; Entanglements 5, 6; Excitement 7; Experience 17; Eye
Expressions 13; Faces 30, 31;

WILMOT, JOHN [EARL OF ROCHESTER]
(1647–1680)
Death 89

WILSON, ANGUS
(1913–1991)
Tension/Tension Relief 5

WILSON, EDWARD O.
Renewal 8

WILSON, GAHAN
Influence 4

WILSON, LANFORD
Sensitivity 7

WILSON, WOODROW
(1856–1924)
Awareness/Unawareness 10; Exploitation 10; Government 11; Hope 27; Opportunity 13; Pleasure 10; Problems and Solutions 31; Stupidity 11; Thinking/Thought 20

WINES, MICHAEL
Activeness/Inactiveness 6; Change 27; Debt 5; Economics 24; Effectiveness/Ineffectiveness 11; Government 12

WINGFIELD, RICHARD N.
Success/Failure 12

WINN, MARY DAY
Sex/Sexuality 18

WINTHROP, ROBERT C.
(1809–1894)
Patriotism 5

WITTGENSTEIN, LUDWIG
(1889–1951)
Philosophy 6

WOLCOTT, JAMES
Belonging/Outcast 7; Fatness/Thinness 13; Hair Color 9; Laughter 9

WOLFE, HUMBERT
(1886–1940)
Fall 14

WOLFE, THOMAS
(1900–1938)
Breasts/Bosoms 5; Cities 31, 32; Clouds 7; Eye Expressions 14; Facial Expressions 29; Failure 23; Life 55; Life and Death 46; Nature Scenes 21; People, Interaction 25; Senses 9; Sky/Skyscapes 31; Sunrise 6; Time 77

WOLLSTONECRAFT, MARY [GODWIN]
(1759–1797)
Dissent/Dissenters 4

WOOD, ELLEN [MRS. HENRY]
(1814–1887)
Life 56

WOOLF, VIRGINIA
(1882–1941)
Animation 5; Articulateness/Inarticulateness 5; Birds 17; Characterizations 36, 37; Confusion 3; Emotions 21; Fate 27, 28; Furniture/Furnishings 8; Habit 8; Hate 6; Helplessness 10; Importance/Unimportance 10; Journal Writing 3; Knowledge 17; Memory/Memories 52; Men and Women 36, 37; People, Interaction 26, 27; Self-Consciousness 4; Self-Images 13; Senses 10; Substantiality/Insubstantiality 5; Time 78; Toughness 9; World 23

WOOLLCOTT, ALEXANDER
(1887–1943)
Characterizations 38; Completeness/Incompleteness 10; Deterioration/Diminishment 8; Endings Profiles 16; Joy 15; Personality Profiles 18; Writing Advice 4

WORDSWORTH, WILLIAM
(1770–1850)
Beauty 44; Birds 18; Birth 5; Death 90; Hope 28; Humanity/Humankind 50; Mind 30; Nature 25

WOTTON, SIR HENRY
(1568–1639)
Love 103

WRATISLAW, THEODORE
(1871–1933)
Love 104

WRIGHT, JAMES
(1927–1980)
Creativity 7; Nightmares 6

WRIGHT, RICHARD
(1908–1960)
Disappearance 4; Helplessness 11; Joy 16; Pain and Suffering 31; Self-Control 17; Self-Expression 3; Snow 10; World 24

WURST, JIM
International Relations 6

WYATT, SIR THOMAS THE ELDER,
(1503–1542)
Emotions 22; Entanglements 7; Fortune/Misfortune 36; Love 105; Memory/Memories 53

WYATT, SIR THOMAS
(c. 1521–1554)
Lovers' Declarations and Exchanges 30

WYLIE, ELINOR
(1885–1928)
Bodies/The Body 34; Snow 11; Stillness 4

Y

YALOM, IRVIN D.
Age/Aging 35, 36; Creativity 8; Energy 6; Friendship/Friends 27; Frustration 4; Illness 11; Occupations 14; Passion 22; People, Interaction 29, 28, 30, 31; Safety 4; Time 79

YANCEY, WILLIAM LOWNDES
(1814–1863)
Danger 25; Fighting 6

YEATS, W[ILLIAM] B[UTLER]
(1865–1939)
Age/Aging 37; Control 7; Escape 6; Heart 32; Innocence/Inexperience 10; Love 106; Mind 31; Mind 32; Peace 13; Pleas and Prayers 12; Pride 9

YEHOSHUA, A. B.
Aggression 11; Belonging/Outcast 8; Bigotry 14; Cities 33, 34; Cityscapes 12, 13; Death, Defined 19; Descriptions, Misc. 74; Exactness/Inexactness 5; Group Scenes 12; History 20, 21; Identity 7; Lies/Liars 11; Maturation 11; Mysteries/Mysteriousness 8; Procreation 3; Rescue/Rescuers 5; Sleep 24; Smallness 4; Sound 3; Speechlessness 7; Thinking/Thought 21; Treachery 7; Truth/Falsehood 32; Victims 4; War 26; Worry 14

YEVTUSHENKO, YEVGENY
Actions 10; Agreement/Disagreement 12; Alliances 8; Ethics 7; Immorality/Morality 4; Individuality 10; Knowledge 18; Mistrust 2; Opinion 6; Poetry/Poets 47; Poetry/Poets 48; Reading/Readers 7; Revolt 3; Silence 14; Sky/Skyscapes 32; Thinking/Thought 22

YEZIERSKA, ANZIA
(1885–1970)
World 25

YOLEN, JANE
Moon 21

YOUNG, ANDREW
(1885–1971)
Winter 7

YOUNG, EDWARD
(1683–1765)
Faith 10; Friendship/Friends 28; Significance/Insignificance 8; Thinking/Thought 23

YUDKIN, JOEL
Economics 13

Z

ZANGWILL, ISRAEL
(1864–1926)
America/Americans 8

ZILERI, ENRIQUE
Politics/Politicians 28

ZINGLE, REV. E. B.
(19th century)
Cities 35

ZINMAN, DAVID
Music/Musicians 23

ZOLA, ÉMILE
(1840–1902)
Arousal/Rousers 23; Bigotry 15; Hair 8

Subject Index

The following index lists the subjects or objects that are used in the metaphors. For example, the text of the entry Devotion 3 refers to a spaniel, and so has been indexed under ANIMAL/MARINE LIFE, under the sub-category DOGS.

A

BEARS: Age/Aging 2; Authority 5; Destruction/Destructiveness 6; Education and Learning 12; Success, Defined 8

BEASTS: Crime and Punishment 5; Crowds 8; Hard-Heartedness 3; Humanity/Humankind 8, 36, 37, 41; Name Calling 11; Problems and Solutions 25; Reason 8; Wind 7

BOARS: Religion 12

BULLS: Business Descriptions 17; Decisiveness/Indecisiveness 4; Opportunity 6; Perseverance 1; Pleas and Prayers 4

CALVES: Similarity/Dissimilarity 2; Youth 1

CAMELS: Age/Aging 4; Superficiality 2; Youth and Age 4

CATS: Art/Artists 10; Confinement 1; Craftiness 4; Diplomacy 5; Fear 16; Fog 2; Freedom of Expression 2; Middle Age 8; Name Calling 12, 13; Religion 21; Sea 6; Smiles 3; Strategies 3; Tears 9; Truth/Falsehood 14

CATTLE: Business Descriptions 8; Education and Learning 3; Originality/Unoriginality 6; Significance/Insignificance 2

CHINCHILLA: Physical Appearance 5

COWS: Arousal/Rousers 8; Mastery/Subordination 2; Religion 22; Similarity/Dissimilarity 2; Truth/Falsehood 21

CROCODILES: Characterizations 3; Deception 13; Hypocrisy 2; Love 8; Tears 15

CUBS: Transformation 8

DEER: Courage 15; Lovers' Declarations and Exchanges 28; Sun 8; Youth 8

DINOSAURS: Descriptions, Misc. 44; Music/Musicians 23; Obsolescence 2

DOGS: Aggression 9; Characteristics 1; Characterizations 6; Competition/Competitors 11; Death 43; Devotion 3; Dissent/Dissenters 4; Doubt 7; Ego/Id 2; Failure 1; Fashion and Style 1; Fortune/Misfortune 29; Group Scenes 6; Hard-Heartedness 8; Hope 22; Hypocrisy 10; Impatience 2; Individuality 7; Intoxication/Intoxicants 3; Journalism/Journalists 4; Love, Defined 5; Loyalty 3; Manipulation 2; Marriage 6, 27; Mastery/Subordination 14; Opinion 4; Name Calling 22; Pain and Suffering 10; People, Interaction 16; Permanence/Impermanence 6; Perseverance 2; Pleas and Prayers 4; Politics/Politicians 20; Scrutiny 1; Self-Control 4; Sorrow 13; Sports Descriptions 3; Spring 9; Strength/Weakness 5; Triteness 3; Trustworthiness/Untrustworthiness 7; Truth/Falsehood 10; Villainy/Villains 6; Youth 7, 17; Youth and Age 4

DONKEYS: Personality Profiles 3

DRAGONS: Watchfulness 2

EELS: Money 2; Renewal 7

ELEPHANTS: Conflict 7; Generosity 1; Singing/Songs/Singers 12; Strength/Weakness 15

FERRETS: Faces 31

FOXES: Craftiness 7; Evil 2; Facial Expressions 15; Foolhardiness 10; Journalism/Journalists 7

FROGS: Communication/Non-Communication 1; Importance/Unimportance 8

GORILLAS: Power 20; Problems and Solutions 17

GROUNDHOGS: Business Descriptions 5

GUINEA PIGS: Risk-Taking 1

HARES: Cowardice 5; Religion 12; Temperament 3; Time 40

HIPPOPOTAMUSES: Families/Family Relationships 10; Group Scenes 8

HYENAS: Smiles 2

JACKASSES: Humanity/Humankind 2; Name Calling 3; Patience 2; Stupidity 7; World 6

JAGUARS: Illusion/Reality 9

JELLYFISH: Insults 3

KITTENS: Appeasement 1

LAMBS: Achievement 8; Aggression 3, 8; Beliefs 5, 9; Caution 3; Entrapment 7; Fate 27; Name Calling 1; Peace 4; Self-Destructiveness 5

LEOPARDS: Changeableness/Unchangeableness 2, 5

LIONS: Achievement 8; Age/Aging 23; Aggression 8; Ambition 3; Arousal/Rousers 16; Beliefs 9; Caution 3; Confinement 1; Courage 5; Cowardice 5; Deception 25; Difficulties 5; Dominance 8; Ego/Egotism 2; Failure 15; Fairness/Unfairness 2; Fear 2; Feelings 8; Leaders/Followers 4; Lust 4; Mastery/Subordination 25; Peace 4, 11; Philosophy 5; Pleas and Prayers 4; Singing/Songs/Singers 2; Strength/Weakness 1, 28; Summer 3; Transformation 8; Truth/Falsehood 2; War 25

LIZARDS: Awareness/Unawareness 2; Characterizations 23

MOSAICS: Diversity 6; Impossibility 7; Sky/Skyscapes 8;
PAINTING(S): Characterizations 19; Comparisons 2; Deception 24; Dreams 1; Eloquence 2; Emotions 20; Evil 5; Exaggeration 1; Facial Expressions 23; Fortune/Misfortune 32; God 8; Importance/Unimportance 1; Lies/Liars 1
Lovers' Declarations and Exchanges 25; Memory/Memories 19; Revenge/Vengeance 5; Science 8; Senses 7; Transformation 3; Visibility/Invisibility 5
PHOTOGRAPHY: Absence 1; Changeableness/Unchangeableness 4; Dullness 9
POTTERY: Leaders/Followers 11
SCULPTURE: Age/Aging 26; Biographies/Autobiographies 3; Freckles 2; God 1; Grammar and Style 4; Group Scenes 11; Illusion/Reality 7; Individuality 3; Manipulation 5; Moon 7; Physical Appearance 19; Self 2; Sun 17; Winter 3

ART MATERIALS:
Ancestry/Ancestors 10; Art/Artists 24; Individuality 6
CANVAS: Imagination 4
CLAY: Bodies/Body 6; Childhood/Children 8; Creativity 2; Connections 4; Speech 6; Strength/Weakness 30
CRAYONS: Sky/Skyscapes 17
DYES: Blushes 4; Ego/Egotism 6
PAINT: Optimism/Pessimism 3; Success, Defined 18
PAINTBRUSHES: Satire 2

PAINTING CANVASES: Creation 3; Fashion and Style 6; Suspicion 5
PAINTING FRAMES: Completeness/Incompleteness 6
SCULPTOR'S CHISELS: Future 11, Words as Weapons 19
SCULPTOR'S MOLDS: Individuality 1
SCULPTOR'S WAX: Heart 12; Manipulation 15
WATERCOLORS: Deception 15; Extravagance 3

AUTOMOTIVE:
Action/Inaction 4; Activeness/Inactiveness 6; Apathy 6; Business Descriptions 7; Characterizations 9; Difficulties 18; Economics 20; Energy 1, 3, 4, 5; Looks 3; Money 15; Philosophy 6; Power 10; Problems and Solutions 31; Safety 1; Truth/Falsehood 4; War 2; Weariness 4
GASOLINE: Envy 4
GEARSHIFTS: Change 23

B

BARRIERS/TRAPS:
Entanglements 1; Illusion/Reality 1; Institutions 2; Time 5
BORDERS: Quotations 2
FISHERMEN'S NETS: International Relations 4
FORTRESSES: Love 62
RAT TRAPS: Perseverance 4
SNARES: Entanglements 7
WALLS: Awareness/Unawareness 6; Hypocrisy 4; Loneliness 2; Lovers' Declarations and Exchanges 1; Obscurity 1; Rescue/Rescuers 1

BEASTS:
See ANIMAL/MARINE LIFE

BIRDS:
(*See also* ANIMAL ANATOMY; ANIMAL HABITATS)
Alliances 1, 6; Ancestry/Ancestors 9; Animation 5; Articulateness/Inarticulateness 5; Bodies/Body 8; Characterizations 13, 27; Comfort/Comfort-Givers 8; Conscience 6; Destruction/Destructiveness 21; Dreams 11; Entrapment 9, 12; Escape 6; Evening 3; Eye Expressions 11; Facial Expressions 28; Foreboding 3; Group Scenes 12; Heart 25; Hope 18; Humanity/Humankind 10; Innocence/Inexperience 8; Law/Lawyers 8, 9; Life, Defined 16; Love 66; Lovers' Declarations and Exchanges 17, 29; Mastery/Subordination 3; Maturation 6; Noses 4; Personality Profiles 7; Physical Appearance 18; Poverty/Prosperity 5; Problems and Solutions 1; Responsibility 4; Self-Confidence 4; Sleep 6, 9; Spirit 1; Talkativeness 5; Temptation 6; Tension/Tension Relief 2; Thinking/Thought 6; Time 14, 76; Wind 13
BLUEBIRDS: Joy 8
CRANES: Personality Profiles 3
CROWS: Beauty 33; Fear 4; Inspiration 2; Mastery/Subordination 21
CUCKOOS: Name Calling 5
DOVES: Aggression 7; Deception 9; Self-Destructiveness 5; Thinking/Thought 13; Warriors and Peacemakers 1, 2
EAGLES: Action/Inaction 20; Ambition 18; Character

PLANETS: Humanity/Humankind 33; Warriors and Peacemakers 3
SATELLITES: Descriptions, Misc. 29
STARS: Aerial Views 5, 7; America/Americans 3; Animation 1; Awareness/Unawareness 1; Childhood/Children 2; Commitment 5; Eye Expressions 6; Eyes 14, 23; God 8; Imagination 5; Language 15; Love 77; Nature 1; Praise 4; Self-Reliance 7; Sports Descriptions 5, 7; Visibility/Invisibility 4
SUN: Age/Aging 5; Awareness/Unawareness 1; Beauty 23; Being/Becoming 1; Brightness 1; Commitment 5; Dominance 1; Endings 1, 11; Eye Expressions 10; Eyes 3; Gloom 1; Hair 8; Happiness/Unhappiness 10; Humanity/Humankind 33; Ideas 9; Kindness/Unkindness 3; Laments 8; Love, Defined 4, 14; Lovers' Declarations and Exchanges 2, 21; Optimism/Pessimism 4; Permanence/Impermanence 5; Protection/Protectors 14

CHILDREN:
See FAMILIES/FAMILY MEMBERS

CLOTHING/ACCESSORIES:
Aerial Views 6; Age/Aging 22, 37; Animals 2, 9, 13, 15; Apology 1; Authority 3; Beauty 19, 31; Biographies/Autobiographies 4; Bodies/Body 4, 20, 21; Buildings and Bridges 5; Character 7; Characterizations 38; Change 2, 12; Character 6; Cities 6; Clouds 5; Conformity/Nonconformity 1; Contentment 4; Creativity 1; Deception 4, 8, 10; Dignity

2; Earth 2; Entrapment 2; Essence 5; Evening 4; Expectations 4; Extravagance 1; Fall 3, 5, 6; Foolhardiness 3; Fortune/Misfortune 36; Grief 1, 12; Habit 2; Hard-Heartedness 4; Joy/Sorrow 1; Language 12; Leadership 2; Morality/Immorality 5; Morning 5; Murder 1; Nature Scenes 11; Night and Day 5, 12, 23; Old Age 10; Opinion 6; Poetry/Poets 46; Poverty/Prosperity 6; Pride 3; Protection/Protectors 5; Reputation 4; Sacrifice 1; Self-Control 9; Self-Expression 1; Self-Pity 1, 2; Shame 1; Singing/Songs/Singers 3; Sky/Skyscapes 19; 30; Spring 1, 4; Storms 1; Sunset 4; Temptation 7; Time 28; Toughness 4; Tranquility 4; Understanding/Misunderstanding 4; Victims 2; Vulnerability 7; War 24; Wind 2; Writing/Writers 15; Youth 4; Youth and Age 11
BAGS: Seasons 9
BELTS: Economics 16; Order/Disorder 9
BLAZERS: Individuality 2
BOOTS: Difficulties 12; People, Interaction 23
BUTTONS: Noses 1, 5
COATS: Goodness 5, Honor 3
CORSETS: Institutions 6
FANS: Wrinkles 4
FURS: Hair 3
GIRDLES: Confinement 6
GLOVES: Insects 3; Men and Women 13
HANDKERCHIEFS: Memory/Memories 37; Nature 23; Sky/Skyscapes 22
HATS: Pride 5
HEMS: Clouds 2
MITTENS: Wind 17
PARASOLS: Impossibility 7
ROBES: Evening 8

SCARVES: Fortune/Misfortune 27; Inspiration 2; Language 25
SHAWLS: Ego/Egotism 3
SHOES: Optimism/Pessimism 9
SOCKS: Economics 17
SWADDLING CLOTHES: Religion 15
UMBRELLAS: Bodies/Body 9; Compromise 5; Protection/Protectors 1; World 14
UNIFORMS: Complexion 8; Seasons 11; Youth 15
VEILS: Death 74; Evening 5; Night and Day 24; Peace 13; Trees 9
WALLETS: Control 1; Time 67
WATCHES: Activeness/Inactiveness 6; Destruction/Destructiveness 23; Humanity/Humankind 27; Wit 8

COMMUNICATIONS:
Isolation 7
CONFERENCE CALLS: Information 1
ELECTRONICS: World 5
SWITCHBOARDS: Information 1; Memory/Memories 27
TELEPHONE LINES: Communication/Non-Communication 6
TELEVISION DEVICES: Oblivion 1

CONTAINERS, MISC.:
Belonging/Outcast 7; Change 6
Characteristics 2; Confinement 7; Disappointment 2; Fertility/Infertility 1; Joy 9; Marriage 29; Movements 6; Responsibility 6; Words 16
BARRELS: Friendship/Friends 24; Zeal 6
BOTTLES: Reputation 11
BOXES: Conflict 2

15; Music/Musicians 4, 5;
Substantiality/
Insubstantiality 5
DRESSING/
UNDRESSING: Spring 3
URINATION: Envy 5
WASHING: Fighting 1; Op-
portunity 11; Sin/
Redemption 7

DANCE:

Action/Inaction 12, 18;
Apology 3; Cityscapes 3;
Civilization 7; Competition/
Competitors 13; Death 20,
81; Descriptions, Misc. 6,
25, 42; Eyebrows 1; Happi-
ness/Unhappiness 3; Imagination 14; Life 1; Life,
Defined 3; Mastery/Subor-
dination 11; Men and
Women 9; Mystery/Myste-
riousness 2; Personality Profiles 4; Rooms 3; Sky/
Skyscapes 8; Sports Descriptions 11; Tension/Tension
Relief 3; Writing/Writers
16; Youth and Age 12

DISABILITIES:

Guilt 6; Hell and Damnation
2; Society/Social Situations
6; Temperament 3
BLINDNESS: Awareness/
Unawareness 5; Bigotry 7;
Fortune/Misfortune 11, 27;
Love 69; Prudence 4;
Science 2
INCAPACITATION:
Change 8
LAMENESS: Conflict 6;
Conversation 14; Fortune/
Misfortune 16; Insults 1;
Science 2
MUTENESS: Ego/Id 5
STAMMERING: Sea 10
VISION IMPAIRMENT:
Beliefs 2

DISASTERS:

Despair 8; Entrances/Exits 1
AIRPLANE CRASHES:
Failure 14

CAPSIZED BOATS: Failure
16; Success/Failure 8
CAR CRASHES: Defeat 5
COLLAPSING
BUILDINGS:
Disintegration 2
COLLISIONS: Difficulties 9
DROWNING: Abundance 4;
Action/Inaction 22;
Articulateness/
Inarticulateness 2;
Assistance 2; Characteriza-
tions 35; Clinging 2; Com-
passion 2; Consciousness 2;
Despair 15; Deterioration/
Diminishment 1; Fate 7;
Fear 12; Grief 15, 18; Joy/
Sorrow 7; Love 45, 92;
Occupations 3, 14; Passion
21; Poetry/Poets 32; Sighs
1; Sky/Skyscapes 1; Suc-
cess/Failure 2; Tears 13,
21; Visibility/Invisibility
6; Women 6
EARTHQUAKES: Change 9;
Shock 2; Worry 7
FALLING OVERBOARD:
Strength/Weakness 16
FIRES: Agreement/
Disagreement 4;
Aimlessness 2; Language 18
FLOODS: Anger, Divine 4;
Blushes 1; Breasts/Bosoms
5; Crowds 3; Death 64;
Debt 4; Fall 9; Fortune/
Misfortune 14, 23; Love 10;
Sunset 8; Tears 1, 7, 16,
21; Words 8
HURRICANES: Animals 12
LANDSLIDES: Politics/
Politicians 3
RAILROAD ACCIDENTS:
Destruction/
Destructiveness 3; Order/
Disorder 1
SHIPWRECKS: Agreement/
Disagreement 8;
Appearance 2; Bigotry 4;
Conversation 8; Defeat 6;
Deterioration/
Diminishment 8; Endings;
Escape 5; Failure 4, 5, 23;
Fortune/Misfortune 19;

Hope 3; Marriage 16; Mis-
takes 1; Mystery/Mysteri-
ousness 1; Order/
Disorder 3
TRAGEDY: Rescue/
Rescuers 3
TRAIN WRECKS:
Change 18

DOMESTIC ACTIVITIES:

HOUSEKEEPING: Beauty
4; Change 27; Disturbances
2; Families/Family Rela-
tionships 6; Marriage 34;
Money 12; People, Interac-
tion 28; Self-Knowledge 10
HOUSE PAINTING:
Deception 11
IRONING: Divorce 2; Per-
sonality Profiles 2
LAUNDRY: Flowers 3;
Openness/Privacy 6; Per-
sonality Profiles 10; Wea-
riness 2
SHOPPING: Economics 12;
Failure 17
SWEEPING: Denial 1; Sky/
Skyscapes 26; Superstition 3
WALLPAPERING:
Deception 11

DOMESTIC CONCERNS:

(See also COOKING
EQUIPMENT)
BROKEN DISHES: Disap-
pointment 4; Disintegration
7; Life, Defined 39; Passion
7; Reputation 2
CLUTTER: Imagination 14
COBWEBS: Education and
Learning 17, 21; Habit 1
DRAINAGE SYSTEMS:
Cities 12
DUST: Cause and Effect 5;
Faith 6; Happiness/Unhap-
piness 3; Illusion/Reality 2;
Past 7; Speechlessness 3;
Street Scenes 8
FIREWOOD: Memory/
Memories 49; Men and
Women 1
FUEL: Arguments 2; Ego/
Egotism 9

boding 1; Forgiveness 3;
Life 26; Life and Death 22;
Mind 15; People, Interaction 26; Self 5; Self-Control
8; Sin/Redemption 4, 5;
Sleeplessness 1; Wisdom
5; Wit 6
THRESHOLDS: Beginnings
3; Death 15; Youth
and Age 20
TRAP DOORS: Memory/
Memories 24

EQUIPMENT/TOOLS:
(*See also* OBJECTS, MISC.)
Apathy 8; Humanity/Humankind 6; Passion 21;
Power 9; Words as Weapons 8; Wit 5
ANVILS: Action/Inaction 1;
Ego/Id 1; Power 11;
Truth/Falsehood 3
AXES: Faces 6
CABLES: Habit 1
CLEAVERS: Mind 26
COMPASSES: Books 7;
Heart 17
CORKSCREWS: Road
Scenes 2
DRILL: Scrutiny 5
FIRE-FIGHTING EQUIP-
MENT: Sports
Descriptions 2
FISHING NETS: Retribution
2; Sky/Skyscapes 20
FUSES: Temperament 2
GRINDSTONES: Concentration/Distractedness 7
HAMMERS: Action/Inaction 1; Characterizations 32;
Ego/Id 1; Exactness/
Inexactness 1; Heat 7; Justice/Injustice 7; Knowledge
13; Passion 21; Power 11;
Self-Confidence 3; Strategies 6; Truth/Falsehood 3
HANDLES: Lies/Liars 5;
Humanity/Humankind 46
HARDWARE: Work/
Workers 9
HATCHETS: Faces 16
HORNS: Voices 10

KEYS: Books 23; Influence
2; Love, Defined 10; Responsibility 1;
Understanding 4, 8
KNIVES: Characterizations
8; Descriptions, Misc. 16;
Exploitation 9; Heart 18;
Sun 4, 14
LADDERS: Ambition 14;
Ambition 19; Darkness/
Light 4; Descriptions, Misc.
14, Misc. 62; Gossip 1;
Knowledge 13; Life 7; Problems and Solutions 7; Progress 1; Sky/Skyscapes 21;
Success, Defined 1, 14;
Zenith 1
LOCKS: Landscapes 5; Understanding 4
MILLSTONES: Comfort/
Comfort-Givers 9
MINING SCOOPS: Singing/
Songs/Singers 10
NAILS: Exactness/
Inexactness 1
RHEOSTATS: Arts and Entertainment 5
SCAFFOLDING: Religion
10
SCALES: Changeableness/
Unchangeableness 1
SCISSORS: Freedom/
Restraint 12; Time 20
TELESCOPES: Books 7;
Knowledge 14; Memory/
Memories 30
THERMOMETERS: Friendship/Friends 5
VISES: Mountains 2

EXPLOSIVES:
Abundance 11; Arousal/
Rousers 2; Books 12; Bodies/Body 28; Conflict 4;
Caution 11; Calmness/
Volatility 1; Danger 5, 6,
20; Effectiveness/Ineffectiveness 2; Energy 2, 6;
Facts 1; Monotony 2; Marriage 31; Reform 7; Self-
Images 10; Shock 1
BOMBS: Danger 15;
Laughter 9

FIREWORKS: Bodies/Body
The 22; Facial Expressions
13; Language 7; Sex/Sexuality 15
GUNPOWDER: Memory/
Memories 35
HAND GRENADES: Trouble/Troublemakers 1
MINE FIELDS: Language 4;
Smells 1;
TORPEDOES: Arguments 4;
Destruction/
Destructiveness 13;
Writing/Writers 12

F

FAMILIES/FAMILY
MEMBERS:
(*See also* HUMAN
RELATIONSHIPS)
Death 66, 69, 75; Dominance
6; Fortune/Misfortune 30;
Heart 4; Humor 1; Snow 7;
Wind 8; World 13
BROTHERS: Responsibility
6; Safety 2
CHILDREN: Books 25; Bigotry 10; Dreams 18;
Grief 8
FATHERS AND
CHILDREN: Grief 17; Hypocrisy 11; Winning/
Losing 3
HEIRS: Sorrow 11
HUSBANDS AND WIVES:
Hunger 4
MOTHERS AND CHILDREN: Grief 5
ORPHANS: Winning/
Losing 3
PARENTS: Generosity 6;
Grief 17; Trees 20
SIBLINGS: America/Americans 1; Sleep 4; Sleep 17
SISTERS: Joy/Sorrow 3
STEP-SISTERS: Concentration/Distractedness 5
STEP-MOTHERS:
Seasons 1
TWINS: Sleep 5

FOOD/DRINK:

(*See also* EATING/
DRINKING)

Abundance 2; Activeness/
Inactiveness 3; Adversity 4;
Aerial Views 3; Affliction 2;
Age/Aging 2; Ambition 4,
13; Ambivalence 1; Anger
20; Appearance 1; Appease-
ment 2; Applause 2; Art/
Artists 14; Arts and Enter-
tainment 8, 10; Beauty 5;
Bigotry 15; Birthdays 1;
Blindness 2; Bodies/Body
18, 32; Books 2, 5, 20, 21,
22, 26; Breasts/Bosoms 1;
Business Descriptions 6, 8,
9; Calmness/Volatility 4;
Caution 4; Characteristics 7;
Characterizations 21, 29;
Choices and Decisions 1, 2;
Cities 2, 18, 19; Clarity/
Ambiguity 2; Clergy 2;
Competition/Competitors
7; Completeness/
Incompleteness 5; Complex-
ion 3, 6; Compromise 1;
Confusion 1; Conversation
7, 13; Corruption 1; Cow-
ardice 3; Criticism/Critics
6; Crowds 4, 7; Danger 21;
Deception 17; Descriptions,
Misc. 1, 7, 64; Difference/
Sameness 2; Difficulties 23;
Diplomacy 9; Diversity 1, 4;
Dreams 15; Dullness 2, 3;
Earth 3, 4; Education and
Learning 1, 6; Effective-
ness/Ineffectiveness 1; Effi-
ciency 2; Ego/Egotism 1;
Embraces 2; Endurance 3;
Entrapment 13; Envy 6;
Ethics 7; Evil 16;
Exactness/Inexactness 4;
Excess 2; Experience 5, 11;
Exploitation 5; Eyes 12, 14;
Faces 19; Facial Color 1;
Facial Expressions 2, 16;
Faith 4; Fame 5; Families/
Family Relationships 19;
Fate 13; Fatness/Thinness
5, 10; Fear 13; Fertility/
Infertility 4; Fighting 3;

Flattery 4, 7, 8; Freedom of
Expression 4; Generosity 3,
4; Grammar and Style 8;
Group Scenes 1; Guidance/
Guides 4; Hair Color 5;
Happiness/Unhappiness 7;
Heart 30; Ideas 4; Jealousy
1; Joy/Sorrow 6; Language
16, 24; Life, Defined 6;
Looks 5; Love 9, 75, 80;
Love, Defined 16; Lovers'
Declarations and Exchanges
27; Malice 2; Manners 4;
Marriage 8; Mediocrity 3;
Men and Women 21, 24,
28; Mind 14; Mixture 1, 3;
Moon 11; Morality/Immo-
rality 2; Mouths 4; Music/
Musicians 20, 21, 22; Mys-
teries/Mysteriousness 6;
Ordinariness/
Extraordinariness 1, 3; Pas-
sion 16; Patience 9; Peace
8; People, Interaction 12;
Permanence/
Impermanence 6; Physical,
Appearance 13; Places,
Misc. 13, 14; Poetry/Poets
44; Poverty/Prosperity 7,
13; Prudence 6, 8; Reading/
Readers 2; Self-Actualiza-
tion 1; Self-Control 3;
Sensitivity 7; Sex/Sexuality
4, 8, 13, 18; Shelter 1;
Simplicity/Simplification 2;
Sleep 15; Smallness 1, 3;
Snow 1, 2; Society/Social
Situations 9, 10; Speech 3;
Speeches 6; Street Scenes
14; Strength/Weakness 2;
Substantiality/
Insubstantiality 1, 3; Suc-
cess, Defined 16; Sun 7, 12;
Sunset 1; Suspicion 4; Tears
11; Thinking/Thought 14;
Timidity 2; Treachery 6;
Truth/Falsehood 17; Utili-
zation 2, 3; Victims 4;
Voices 2, 3, 4; Wisdom 1;
Wit 7; Wordplay/
Wordwatching 1; Words 9,
24; Work/Workers 9; Writ-
ing Advice 4; Youth 12

BACON: Husbands and
Wives 2
BISCUIT: Importance/
Unimportance 10
BREAD: Humanity/Human-
kind 41; Idleness 1; Journal-
ism/Journalists 5; Mas-
tery/Subordination 7;
Religion 7
CAKE: Houses 6
EGGS: Risk-Taking 7
FRUIT: Faces 27; Hope 27;
Knowledge 8; Innocence/
Inexperience 9; Ignorance 3;
Rewards 1, 2
GRAPES: God 13
HONEY: Joy 6
MEAT: Religion 9
MILK: Identity ; Humanity/
Humankind 28
PICKLES: Hunger 3
PIE: Irritants 10
RAISINS: Quotations 4
SALAD: Reading/Readers 7
SALT: Goodness 3; Joy/
Sorrow 4; Sea 1
SOUP: Irritants 6; Quarrels/
Quarrelsomeness 3; Socie-
ty/Social Situations 7
TEA: Journal Writing 3

FUNERALS/BURIALS:

Compromise 4; Group Scenes
12; Hair Color 2; Separation
2; Trees 27
CEMETERIES: Failure 22;
Institutions 5
COFFINS: Bodies/Body 34;
Descriptions, Misc. 23, 59;
Despair 6; Destruction/De-
structiveness 7
CRYPTS: Cities 33
EMBALMING: Beliefs 4, 6;
Books 10; Poetry/Poets 26
FUNERAL PARLORS:
Stillness 2
GRAVES: Endings 8;
Speechlessness 2
GRAVESTONES: Books 16
GRAVEYARDS:
Decisiveness/Indecisiveness
1; Warnings 1

HUMAN ANATOMY:

SUNSETS: Age/Aging 5;
Death 11, 68; Despair 3;
Endings 1, 8; Epitaphs 5;
Middle Age 2; Old Age 12;
Optimism/Pessimism 10
SUNSHINE: Families/Fami-
ly Relationships 22; Friend-
ship/Friends 18;
Pleasure 2, 6
SWAMPS: Past 14
THICKETS: Clarity/Ambi-
guity 5; Opinion 3
THORNS: Cause and
Effect 4
VINES: Affection 2; Age/
Aging 34; Friendship/
Friends 14; Genius 8;
Group Scenes 5; Leaders/
Followers 2
WEEDS: Loneliness 1;
Strength/Weakness 14
WILDERNESS: Life and
Death 39; Uncertainty 1

O

OBJECTS, MISC.:
(*See also* EQUIPMENT/
TOOLS)
Beauty 6, 9; Culture 5; Tran-
sience 3
BALLOONS: Mind 31;
Satire 4, 5
BATTERIES: Activeness/
Inactiveness 3
CAMERAS: Persuasiveness/
Persuaders 3; Flattery 9;
Name Calling 18; Voices
13; Self-Images 7
CANDLES: Control 4;
Riches 4
CANES: Hope 25
CHAINS: Men and
Women 2
CLOCKS: Brain 5; Flowers
2; Hard-Heartedness 3;
Kindness/Unkindness 1;
Time 66, 72; Timeliness/
Untimeliness 2

CRYSTALS: Books 14
DECOYS: Youth 3
DIARIES: Memory/
Memories 51
DOORSTOPS: Barriers 7
FANS: Physical
Appearance 17
FILTERS: Philosophy 1
FIREPLUGS: Physical Ap-
pearance 16
FLAGS: Complexion 10;
Death 41; Foreboding 4;
Pride 8; Sensitivity 6; Ti-
midity 1
FOGHORNS: Hard-
Heartedness 3
HAIR COMBS: Experience 2
LIGHTNING RODS: Arous-
al/Rousers 9
MAGNETS: Forgiveness 5
MAGNIFYING GLASSES:
Fame 9; Humanity/Hu-
mankind 12; Scrutiny 2;
Vanity 3
MATCHES: Science 10
MIRRORS: Actions 7; Art/
Artists 5, 26; Beauty 9, 37;
Death 50; Deception 6; Fac-
es 22; Families/Family Re-
lationships 12, 20; Friend-
ship/Friends 16; Heart 11;
Inspiration 9; Life, Defined
23; Pity 1; Politics/Politi-
cians 24; Reform 16; Sea-
scapes 10; Self-Knowledge
6; Speech 8; Stupidity 5;
Sunrise 2; Words 17, 21
PAPERWEIGHTS: Rain 5
PENDULUMS: Change 7
PICTURES: Reason 8
POLES: Success, Defined 6
PURSES: Stupidity 8
RAZORS: Danger 8; Words
as Weapons 15
RODS: Diplomacy 10;
Toughness 3
SCARECROWS: Age/Ag-
ing 37; Group Scenes 7;
Justice/Injustice 13; Pover-
ty/Prosperity 5
SHIELDS: Houses 5
STICKS: Bodies/Body 15
STILTS: Ambition 9

TOOTHPICKS: Birds 3
TOTEMS: People,
Interaction 24; Power 19
TREASURE CHESTS:
Riches 7
TRUNKS: Vice/Virtue 6
WALKING STICKS:
Silence 9
WEATHERVANES: Being/
Becoming 6

OBJECTS, NATURAL:
(*See also* NATURE)
CORKS: Animation 4;
Tears 6
FEATHERS: Boats/Boating
1; Decisiveness/Indecisive-
ness 6; Eyebrows 2; Help-
lessness 8; Sighs 2
PEBBLES: Education and
Learning 14
REEDS: Pleas and Prayers 3
ROCKS: Characterizations
28; Difficulties 5; God 3;
Goodness 4; Hard-
Heartedness 3; Illusion/Re-
ality 12; Justice/Injustice 9;
Reform 3; Strength/Weak-
ness 13; Toughness 1, 7
SHARDS: Art/Artists 27;
Memory/Memories 45
SPONGES: Tears 6
STONES: Characterizations
10; Endings 6; Eyes 10;
Faces 14; Grief 12; Hard-
Heartedness 6, 8; Heart 26;
Illusion/Reality 6; Impor-
tance/Unimportance 2; Iro-
ny 2; Laments 4; Memory/
Memories 8; Name Calling
1; Silence 10; Speechless-
ness 3; Strength/Weakness
7; Truth/Falsehood 16
STRAWS: People,
Interaction 25

OCCUPATIONS/
TRADES:
ACCOUNTANTS:
Government 2
ACTORS: Disappearance 3
APOTHECARIES: Death 72

SOLDIERS: Fate 14; Government 6; Group Scenes 10; Helplessness 2; Money 16; Ordinariness/ Extraordinariness 5
SPIES: Ordinariness/ Extraordinariness 5; Soul 4
STUNT PILOTS: Ability 4
SURGEONS: Occupations 10
SURVEYORS: Cities 13
TEACHERS: Cities 8; Experience 3, 14; Restriction 3; Self-Reliance 2; Time 2
TIGHTROPE WALKERS: Danger 7; Humor 2; Innocence/Inexperience 1
TRAVEL GUIDES: Death, Defined 6
UNDERTAKERS: Sarcasm 2
WATCHMEN: Criticism/ Critics 11; Heart 27
WEAVERS: Humanity/Humankind 21
WELDING: Eye Expressions 1; Self-Actualization 9; Uncertainty 3
WHALING: Life and Death 25; Problems and Solutions 13
WRITERS: Chance 4

ORNAMENTS:
Beauty 44; Nature 3
BEADS: Aerial Views 5; Grammar and Style 6; Hope 28; Storms 7
DIAMONDS: Character 4; Education and Learning 14; Heaven 1; Physical Appearance 6, 8; Rain 5; Sky/ Skyscapes 12
EARRINGS: Admiration 4
GEMS: Beauty 24; Birds 7; Reputation 4
JEWELRY: Aerial Views 4; Beauty 28; Blindness 3; Childhood/Children 10; Cities 31; Consistency/Inconsistency 3; Countries, Misc. 2; Death 83; Epitaphs 1; Eyes 15; Ideas 5; Loneliness 5; Love, Defined 12; Love 76; Mysteries/Myste-

riousness 6; Perfection 7; Praise 7; Quotations 1; Reputation 8, 9; Riches 5; Sex/Sexuality 11; Sky/ Skyscapes 13; Success/Failure 5; Sunrise 1; Trees 27; Wit 3
PAPER ORNAMENTS: Seasons 8
PEARLS: Caution 8; Ego/ Egotism 7; Eyes 16, 24; Faces 18; Foolhardiness 13; Love 91; Moon 12; Praise 9, 13; Rain 1; Speech 1; Sun 3; Tears 17
PRECIOUS STONES: Evil 17; Countries, Misc. 6

P

PHYSICAL DISCOMFORT:
(See also HEALTH/ SICKNESS)
CHILLS: Old Age 4
CONSTIPATION: Cities 2
ITCHES: Affection 3; Dissent/Dissenters 3
SQUINTING: Flaws 3
SUNBURN: Weariness 1

PHYSICAL IMPERFECTIONS:
(See also HUMAN ANATOMY)
CALLOUSES: Enemies 2
HANGNAILS: Danger 19
PIMPLES: Passion 6
WARTS: Families/Family Relationships 2
WRINKLES: Heart 15; Zeal 5

PLACES:
(See also GEOGRAPHY/ LANDSCAPES)
Death 31; Isolation 2; Language 14; Past 8
ABYSS: Humanity/ Humankind 32

BOGS: Identity 7
CITIES.: Automotive Descriptions 2; Books 13; Illness 1
DUNGHILLS: Love 38
GHOST TOWNS: Poetry/ Poets 12
JUNGLES: Agreement/ Disagreement 3; Cities 3; Competition/Competitors 6; Facial Hair 4
OASES: Isolation 1
PARKS: Bodies/Body 29; Death, Defined 8; Lovers' Declarations and Exchanges 28
PITS: Law/Lawyers 1
PLAYGROUNDS: Aggression 11
REST ROOMS: Exploitation 4
SHOPPING MALLS: Ordinariness/ Extraordinariness 5
SUBURBS: Marriage 23; Self 10

PROBLEMS:
CORROSION: Ethics 2, 6
DECAY: Time 49
FLAT TIRES: Destruction/ Destructiveness 3
MOLD: Deterioration/Diminishment 7; Dullness 8
RUST: Action/Inaction 29; Destruction/ Destructiveness 4; Endings 14; Pain and Suffering 1; Sleep 11; Slowness 2; Worry 5

PUNISHMENT:
BEATING: Activeness/ Inactiveness 4; Seascapes 13; Voices 14
BLOWS: Life, Defined 15; Suspicion 3
CHAINS: Perfection 2
EXECUTION: Creativity 7; Fate 11
FACE SLAPPING: Sarcasm 4
FLOGGING: Control 1

GUILLOTINES: Politics/
Politicians 15
HANGING: Childhood/
Children 6; Destruction/
Destructiveness 5; Fate 23;
Freedom/Restraint 7
PROBATION: Life,
Defined 18
STICKS: Diplomacy 9
TORTURE: Doubt 6; La-
ments 5; Love 98; Marriage
18; Pain and Suffering 24;
Poetry/Poets 23; Writing
Advice 3; Writing/
Writers 8
WHIPPING: Birds 5; Con-
formity/Nonconformity 5;
Entrapment 13; Fate 28;
Frustration 1; Wind 3
WHIPS: Achievement 4;
Age/Aging 19; Desire 14;
Difficulties 6; Inheritance/
Inheritors 5; Spirit 2

R

RELIGION/RELIGIOUS
RITES:

Beauty 42; Business Descrip-
tions 14; Crime and Punish-
ment 2; Descriptions, Misc.
46; Food and Drink 3;
Journalism/Journalists 6;
Joy 16; Life, Defined 40;
Poetry/Poets 10; Power 22;
Religion 24; Renewal 3;
Revelation 1; Revolt 3; Sex/
Sexuality 9; Truth/
Falsehood 20
BENEDICTIONS: Trees 22
CONFESSION: Self-
Images 3
DISCIPLES: Experience 12
HEAVEN/HELL: Patience
8; Street Scenes 15
ICONS: Fertility/Infertility 1
MASS: Fall 10
PRAYERS: Sunset 7
SACRAMENTS: Divorce 1

SACRIFICIAL
OFFERINGS: Sacrifice 4;
Tradition 1
SANCTUARIES: Heart 8;
Yearning 3
SHRINES: Cities 20;
Cities 25
SYMBOLS: Temperament 4

ROADS/PATHS:

(See also
TRANSPORTATION)
Art/Artists 11; Characteriza-
tions 17; Control 6; Conver-
sation 9; Danger 18, 24;
Defeat 4; Descriptions,
Misc. 37; Desire 4; Flexibili-
ty/Inflexibility 4, 5; Go-
Betweens 2; Heat 1; Heart
17; Hell and Damnation 7;
History 3; Humanity/Hu-
mankind 46; Life 48; Life
and Death 22; Life, Defined
2; Love 48; Marriage 10,
30; Memory/Memories 7;
Occupations 2; People, In-
teraction 1; Prudence 7;
Rain 6; Sorrow 4; Street
Scenes 17; Truth/False-
hood 5, 30; Wisdom
3; World 7
ALLEYS: Beauty 15; Self-
Destructiveness 1
CURBS: Sleep 3
HIGHWAYS: Life, Defined
21; Technology 3
LABYRINTHS:
Characterizations 30; Cities
7; Entanglements 5; Entrap-
ment 1; Houses 3; Life 3;
Love 13; Many 2; Mistrust
2; Occupations 4; Time 38;
World 3, 4
STREET CORNERS: Life
and Death 15

ROYALTY/ROYAL
TRAPPINGS:

Crowds 9; Endings 13;
Good/Evil 2; Importance/
Unimportance 6; Influence
3; Singing/Songs/Singers
11; Democracy

COURT INTRIGUE:
Treachery 3
CROWN JEWELS:
Defeat 2
CROWNS: Beauty 39; Child-
hood/Children 3;
Conscience 9; Contentment
1, 5; Hair Color 4; Houses
1; Rewards 3; Sports De-
scriptions 7
DUKES: Silence 3
EMPERORS: Heart 24
KINGS: Animals 8; Death,
Defined 8; History 9; Spring
5; Time 59
LORDS: Thinking/Thought
19; Time 11
PRINCES: Senses 2
THRONES: Conformity/
Nonconformity 1; Sunset 9
TRAFFIC: Apathy 9

S

SCIENCE:

(See also MATHEMATICS)
BIOLOGY: Peace 9
BOTANY: Culture 1
COMPUTERS: Bodies/
Body 23; Connections 1;
Strategies 4
ELECTRIC
WAVELENGTHS:
Animals 14
PATHOLOGY: Success, De-
fined 15; Simplicity/Simpli-
fication 3
RADAR: Alertness 2
TECHNOLOGY: Art/Art-
ists 9; Families/Family
Relationships 5;
Knowledge 9
VIVISECTION: Cities 28

SEA:

(See also ANIMAL AND
MARINE LIFE; WATER)
Abundance 4, 7; Anger 12;
Books 28; Characterizations
28, 35; Charity 2; Choices

SEAFARING:

3; Storms 4; Sun 8; Thinking/Thought 4; Treachery 1; Winning/Losing 2
ICE SKATING: Age/Aging 30; Risk-Taking 2
KARATE: Power 8
MOUNTAIN CLIMBING: Achievement 4; Arts and Entertainment 9; Difficulties 8; Wisdom 4; Zenith 2
PLAYING FIELDS: Diplomacy 4; Fairness/ Unfairness 4
RACING: Competition/ Competitors 1; Death 90; Despair 4; Life 56; Life and Death 17; Speed 1; Timeliness/Untimeliness 3
ROWING: Actions 1; Birds 4; Education and Learning 2; Evasiveness 2; Perseverance 7; Sorrow 2; Work/ Workers 12
RUNNING: Education and Learning 15; Journalism/ Journalists 2; Mobility/Immobility 2; Truth/ Falsehood 7
SAILING: Emotions 5; Old Age 9; Sex/Sexuality 16
SKATING: Life 12; Superficiality 4
SURFING: Metaphors 4
SWIMMING: Action/Inaction 14; Caution 1; Commitment 2; Conformity/ Nonconformity 2; Corruption 3; Courage 4; Fortune/ Misfortune 18; Importance/ Unimportance 8; Isolation 5; Optimism/Pessimism 2; People, Interaction 31; Self-Images 13; Sex/Sexuality 1; Success/Failure 3; Survival 1, 3; Trustworthiness/ Untrustworthiness 6; Writing Advice 2
TARGET SHOOTING: Bigotry 14
TEAMS: Innocence/Inexperience 4
TENNIS: Ideas 8

TOBOGGANING: Knowledge 6
WEIGHT LIFTING: Conflict 6
WRESTLING: Defeat 11; Persuasiveness/Persuaders 1; Problems and Solutions 8; Success, Defined 8

SUPERNATURAL:
ANGELS/ELVES: Art/Artists 13; Brightness 2; Death 13; Fame 7; Hard-Heartedness 2; Politics/ Politicians 15; Sleep 23
GHOSTS: Beauty 44; Fog 1; Hope 9; Grief 27; Love, Defined 13; Self-Knowledge 9; Sky/Skyscapes 15; Trees 5; World 8
GOBLINS: Consistency/Inconsistency 2
SATAN: Faces 13

T

TEXTILE CRAFTS:
(*See also* CRAFTS)
Death 39; Fashion and Style 3
EMBROIDERY: Clergy 1; Compromise 6; Conversation 12; Landscapes 12; Love 106; Metaphors 2; Responsibility 2
KNITTING: Danger 13; Entanglements 4; Families/ Family Relationships 15; Heart 30; Originality/ Unoriginality 3; Rain 2; Sleep 15; Wisdom 9
MACRAMÉ: Humor 9
MENDING: Renewal 8
NEEDLEPOINT: Exactness/ Inexactness 4
NEEDLEWORK: Diversity 3
PATCHWORK: Conversation 12; Emotions 11; Landscapes 17
QUILTING: Landscapes 14; Life, Defined 5

SEWING: Art/Artists 22; Boats/Boating 3; Bodies/ Body 21; Economics 21; Facial Expressions 10; Guilt 2; Landscapes 30; Memory/ Memories 38; Problems and Solutions 23; Quarrels/ Quarrelsomeness 4; Scrutiny 3; Sky/Skyscapes 24; Spring 10; Women 2; Wrinkles 6
SPINNING: Conversation 11; Humanity/Humankind 21; Landscapes 22; Life and Death 32; Physical Appearance 24; Pleas and Prayers 9; Transformation 7
THREAD: Life 39; Rain 7
WEAVING: Ambition 12; Fashion and Style 2; Fate 16; Foolhardiness 11; Gloom 4; Good/Evil 5; Hair 6; History 12; Hope 17; Impossibility 2; Journalism/Journalists 10; Joy 12; Joy/Sorrow 2; Life 20, 28; Life, Defined 22; Nature 10, 23; Night and Day 10; Problems and Solutions 27; Progress 10; Renewal 6; Seasons 7; Self-Reliance 8; Sky/Skyscapes 10; Speeches 2; Time 11
YARN: Difficulties 17

TEXTILES:
Completeness/ Incompleteness 8; Dawn 6; Descriptions, Misc. 47; Difficulties 10; Entanglements 2; Fog 3; Lies/Liars 10; Life 24; Sky/Skyscapes 5; Truth/Falsehood 4; Wrinkles 1
BANNERS: Blushes 2
BLANKETS: Foreboding 5
FABRICS: Clouds 6; Descriptions, Misc. 26; Despair 10; Destruction/Destructiveness 11; Embraces 4; Exploitation 3; Eyes 22; Families/Family Relationships 15; Friendship/

W

tion 4; Progress 8; Revelation 1; Self-Knowledge 13; Street Scenes 13; Sweat 1; Talkativeness 10; Tears 5, 24; Time 42; Toughness 1; Trustworthiness/ Untrustworthiness 5; Truth/ Falsehood 12; War 19; Writing/Writers 10

RIVULETS: Birds 13

SHALLOWS: Importance/ Unimportance 9

SPOUTS: Tears 28

SPRINGS: Journalism/Journalists 6; Love 19; Occupations 4; Pity 5; Tears 29

STREAMS: Birds 11; Calmness/Volatility 3; Charity 2; Choices and Decisions 3; Communication/Non-Communication 2, 4; Fate 2; Flattery 4; Hope 16; Information 4; Insults 4; Life 8; Pleas and Prayers 8; Reform 15; Significance/ Insignificance 8; Street Scenes 12; Time 10, 26, 51, 61, 75; Truth/Falsehood 29; Words 15

WATERFALLS: Hair 2; Music/Musicians

WELLS: Compassion 1; Education and Learning 16; Evil 19; Eyes 18; Friendship/Friends 9; Imagination 3; Knowledge 14; Love 93; Ordinariness/ Extraordinariness 6; Sleep 2; Temptation 3

WHIRLPOOLS: Laughter 8; War 17

WEAPONS/ ARMAMENTS:

(*See also* WAR/FIGHTING)
Biographies/Autobiographies 2; Change 21; Characterizations 20; Future 4; Love, Defined 16; Order/Disorder 6; Sunset 5; Tears 10, 19; War 3

AMMUNITION: Wit 9

ARMAMENTS: Activeness/ Inactiveness 2

ARMOR: Descriptions, Misc. 10; Faith 3; Families/ Family Relationships 3; Fog 5; Obsolescence 4; Patriotism 4; Poetry/Poets 6; Poverty/Prosperity 9; Protection/Protectors 6; Self-Actualization 9; Self-Knowledge 5; Vulnerability 3

ARMORIES: Fashion and Style 9; Places, Misc. 12

ARROWS: Anger, Divine 1; Danger 16; Hate 1; Love 53, 64, 87; Journalism/ Journalists 8; Reputation 3; Road Scenes 5; Sarcasm 2; Sex/Sexuality 10; War 26; Warnings 4

ARSENALS: Democracy 7; Tension/Tension Relief 4

ARTILLERY: Anger 11; Sarcasm 1

AXES: Destruction/Destructiveness 18

BOWS AND ARROWS: Alliances 7; Thinking/ Thought 9

BULLETS: Action/Inaction 27; Difficulties 13; Problems and Solutions 9; Quotations 3; Sacrifice 3; Thinking/ Thought 17

CANNONS: Danger 12

CROSSBOWS: Courage 16

DAGGERS: Deception 22; People, Interaction 17; Pity 3; Smiles 6; Strategies 2; Winter 7; Words as Weapons 11, Weapons 14

DARTS: Conflict 6

FORTIFICATIONS: Comfort/Comfort-Givers 7

GUNS: Action/Inaction 6; Anger 6; Assistance 1; Descriptions, Misc. 18; Eyes 25; Men and Women 15; Power 21; Strategies 1; Words as Weapons 7

GUN SHOTS: Facial Expressions 14

JAVELINS: Sky/ Skyscapes 27

KNIVES: Action/Inaction 16; Age/Aging 27; Anger 15; Bigotry 3; Criticism/ Critics 1; Education and Learning 4; Endings 4; Fighting 1; Politics/Politicians 10; Revenge/Vengeance 2; Satire 1; Wind 12; Words as Weapons 16; World 23; Worry 14

LANCES: Death 12

MISSILES: Marriage 4

PELLETS: Changeableness/ Unchangeableness 8

POISON GAS: Politics/Politicians 26

POISONED ARROWS: Words as Weapons 4

RAMRODS: Conformity/ Nonconformity 8

RIFLES: People, Interaction 14; Music/Musicians 15

SHIELDS: Justice/Injustice 7; Safety 2

SHRAPNEL: Grammar and Style 9

SLINGSHOTS: Competition/Competitors 3

SPEARS: Leaders/Followers 8; Slander 2

SWORDS: Beauty 41; Books 6, 19; Confrontation 5; Criticism/Critics 18; Descriptions, Misc. 30; Failure 9; Fish 1; Freedom of Expression 1; Justice/Injustice 1; Pain and Suffering 11, 13; Politics/Politicians 2; Revenge/Vengeance 4; Street Scenes 15; Sunrise 3; Words as Weapons 3, 13, 17

WEATHER:

(*See also* NATURE; TIME OF DAY)
Anger 5; Calmness/Volatility 5; Coldness 1; Freshness/ Staleness 5; Genius 5; Government 8; Grammar and Style 10; Heaven 6; Joy 2;